ENCYCLOPEDIA of GERONTOLOGY

Age, Aging, and the Aged

Volume 2

L–Z
Index

ENCYCLOPEDIA of GERONTOLOGY

Age, Aging, and the Aged

Volume 2

L–Z
Index

Editor-in-Chief
James E. Birren
Center on Aging
University of California, Los Angeles

ACADEMIC PRESS

San Diego   New York   Boston   London   Sydney   Tokyo   Toronto

Copyright © 1996 by ACADEMIC PRESS

Academic Press, Inc.
525 B Street, Suite 1900, San Diego, California 92101-4495, USA
http://www.apnet.com

Academic Press Limited
24-28 Oval Road, London NW1 7DX, UK
http://www.hbuk.co.uk/ap/

Library of Congress Cataloging-in-Publication Data

Encyclopedia of gerontology / edited by James E. Birren.
          p.   cm.
    Includes index.
    ISBN 0-12-226860-1 (set : alk. paper). -- ISBN 0-12-226861-X
(v. 1 : alk. paper). -- ISBN 0-12-226862-8 (v. 2 : alk. paper)
    1. Geriatrics--Encyclopedias.   2. Gerontology--Encyclopedias.
I. Birren, James E.
    [DNLM: 1. Geriatrics--encyclopedias.   WT 13 E563 1996]
RC952.5.E58 1996
612.6'7'03--dc20
DNLM/DLC
for Library of Congress   95-47195
                                                               CIP

PRINTED IN THE UNITED STATES OF AMERICA
96   97   98   99   00   01   EB   9   8   7   6   5   4   3   2   1

Contents

VOLUME I

About the Editors	xiii
Preface	xv
How to Use the Encyclopedia	xvii

A

Abuse and Neglect of Elders   I
Lynn McDonald

Accidents: Falls   II
Brian E. Maki and Geoff R. Fernie

Accidents: Traffic   19
Patricia F. Waller

Achievement   27
Dean Keith Simonton

Activities   37
John R. Kelly

Adaptation   51
Susan Krauss Whitbourne and
Erin L. Cassidy

Adult Education   61
Ronald J. Manheimer

Ageism and Discrimination   71
Thomas G. McGowan

Age Stratification   81
Matilda White Riley

Alcohol and Drugs   93
Edith S. Lisansky Gomberg

Allergic Reactivity in the Elderly   103
Truman O. Anderson

Arthritis   III
Elizabeth M. Badley and
Linda M. Rothman

Atherosclerosis   123
Michael T. Crow, Claudio Bilato, and
Edward G. Lakatta

Attention   131
David J. Madden and Philip A. Allen

Autonomic Nervous System   141
Stephen Borst

B

Balance, Posture, and Gait   149
Marjorie H. Woollacott

Behavioral Genetics   163
C. S. Bergeman and Robert Plomin

Bereavement and Loss   173
Dale A. Lund

Bioenergetics   185
Jon J. Ramsey and Joseph W. Kemnitz

Body: Composition, Weight, Height, and Build 193
Alice S. Ryan and Dariush Elahi

Bone and Osteoporosis   203
Dike N. Kalu and Richard L. Bauer

Brain and Central Nervous System   217
William Bondareff

C

Cancer and the Elderly   223
Michael L. Freedman

Cardiovascular System   245
Alvar Svanborg

Caregiving and Caring   253
Carol J. Whitlatch and Linda S. Noelker

Cell Death   269
Richard A. Lockshin and Zahra Zakeri

Cholesterol and Cell Plasma Membranes   279
Thomas N. Tulenko, David Lapotofsky,
Robert H. Cox, and R. Preston Mason

Cognitive–Behavioral Interventions   289
Helen M. DeVries

Cohort Studies   299
Peter Uhlenberg and Matilda White Riley

Comparative and Cross-Cultural Studies   311
Christine L. Fry

Conditioning   319
Diana S. Woodruff-Pak and
Richard L. Port

Consumer Behavior   329
Catherine A. Cole and
Nadine M. Castellano

Creativity   341
Dean Keith Simonton

Crime and Age   353
Edith Elisabeth Flynn

D

Death and Dying   361
Robert Kastenbaum

Decision Making and Everyday Problem Solving 373
Fredda Blanchard-Fields

Dementia   383
Ingmar Skoog, Kaj Blennow, and
Jan Marcusson

Demography   405
George C. Myers and Mitchell L. Eggers

Depression   415
   Harold G. Koenig and Dan G. Blazer, II

Diet and Nutrition   429
   Barbara J. Rolls and Adam Drewnowski

DNA and Gene Expression   441
   Jan Vijg

E

Economics: Individual   455
   Timothy M. Smeeding

Economics: Society   469
   Yung-Ping Chen

Endocrine Function and Dysfunction   477
   Felicia V. Nowak and
   Arshag D. Mooradian

Epidemiology   493
   Kenneth G. Manton

Ethics and Euthanasia   505
   Nancy S. Jecker

Evolution and Comparative Biology   509
   Michael R. Rose

Extracellular Matrix   519
   Karen M. Reiser

F

Folklore   531
   David P. Shuldiner

G

Gastrointestinal System: Function and Dysfunction   541
   David A. Greenwald and
   Lawrence J. Brandt

Gender Roles   555
   Sara Arber

Generational Differences   567
   K. Warner Schaie

Genetics   577
   Thomas E. Johnson, Gordon J. Lithgow,
   Shin Murakami, and David R. Shook

Geriatric Assessment: Physical   587
   Laurence Z. Rubenstein

Gerontechnology   593
   Max J. Vercruyssen,
   Jan A. M. Graafmans, James L. Fozard,
   Herman Bouma, and Jan Rietsema

Glycation   605
   Annette T. Lee and Anthony Cerami

Grandparenthood   611
   Helen Q. Kivnick and Heather M. Sinclair

Growth Factors and Cellular Senescence   625
   Vincent J. Cristofalo and Christian Sell

H

Health Care and Services   635
   Robert L. Kane and Bruce Friedman

Hearing   643
   Sandra Gordon-Salant

History of Gerontology   655
   James E. Birren

Home Care and Caregiving   667
Jennifer M. Kinney

Homeostasis   679
F. Eugene Yates

Hospice   687
Bert Hayslip, Jr.

Housing   703
Hal Kendig and Jon Pynoos

Human Factors and Ergonomics   715
Joseph H. Goldberg and R. Darin Ellis

Humor   727
Ronald J. Manheimer

I

Identity, Physical   733
Susan Krauss Whitbourne and
Lisa A. Primus

Images of Aging   743
Mike Featherstone and Mike Hepworth

Immune System   753
Sharon M. Papciak, Lijun Song,
James E. Nagel, and William H. Adler

Inhibition   761
Joan M. McDowd

VOLUME 2

About the Editors   xiii
How to Use the Encyclopedia   xv

L

**Language and Communication in Aging
and Dementia**   1
Loraine K. Obler and Martin L. Albert

Learning   7
Joel S. Freund

Leisure   19
John R. Kelly

Life Course   31
Tamara K. Hareven

Life Events   41
Jane D. McLeod

Life Review   53
Robert N. Butler

Life Satisfaction   59
Roger C. Mannell and Sherry L. Dupuis

Life Span Theory   65
William J. Hoyer and John M. Rybash

Literary Representations of Aging   73
Richard M. Eastman

Loneliness   79
Larry C. Mullins

Longevity and Long-Lived Populations   83
Kenneth G. Manton

M

Markers of Aging   97
Gerald E. McClearn

Memory   107
Anderson D. Smith

Memory Strategies 119
Judith A. Sugar

Mental Health 125
Bob Knight and Lauren S. Fox

Metabolism: Carbohydrate, Lipid, and Protein 135
Carolyn D. Berdanier

Migration 145
Charles F. Longino, Jr.

Models of Aging: Invertebrates, Filamentous Fungi,
and Yeasts 151
S. Michal Jazwinski

Models of Aging: Vertebrates 163
Edward J. Masoro

Modernization and Aging 171
Jacqueline Leavitt

Motor Control 177
Rachael Seidler and George Stelmach

Mythology 187
Judith de Luce

N

Network Analysis 197
Marjolein Broese van Groenou and
Theo van Tilburg

Neuromuscular System 211
S. D. R. Harridge and B. Saltin

Neurotransmitters and Neurotrophic Factors 221
Thomas H. McNeill, Timothy J. Collier,
and Franz Hefti

O

Organizations on Aging 229
Phoebe S. Liebig

Oxidative Damage 233
Arthur K. Balin and Michael M. Vilenchik

P

Pain and Presbyalgos 247
S. W. Harkins and Robert B. Scott

Pensions 261
Neal E. Cutler

Perception 271
Grover C. Gilmore

Personality 281
Jan-Erik Ruth

Pharmacology 295
William Edwin Fann

Philosophy 307
Gary M. Kenyon

Physiological Stress 317
Donald A. Jurivich and Joseph F. Welk

Political Attitudes and Behavior 325
Janie S. Steckenrider

Postponement of Aging 333
Alvar Svanborg

Premature Aging 341
Mitchell Turker

Prostate 355
William J. Aronson and Jean B. deKernion

Psychological Well-Being 365
Carol D. Ryff

R

Racial and Ethnic Diversity 371
Kyriakos S. Markides and Laura Rudkin

Reaction Time   377
Timothy A. Salthouse

Rehabilitation   381
Bryan Kemp

Religion and Spirituality   387
Susan McFadden

Reminiscence   399
Irene M. Burnside

Renal and Urinary Tract Function   407
Robert D. Lindeman

Research Design and Methods   419
Linda M. Collins

Respiratory System   431
N. S. Cherniack and M. D. Altose

Retirement   437
Robert C. Atchley

Rheumatic Diseases   451
Anders Bjelle

S

Self-Esteem   459
Roseann Giarrusso and Vern L. Bengtson

Self-Regulation, Health, and Behavior   467
Susan Brownlee, Elaine A. Leventhal, and
Howard Leventhal

Sexuality, Sensuality, and Intimacy   479
Ruth B. Weg

Skill Acquisition   489
David L. Strayer

Smell and Taste   497
Susan Schiffman

Social Networks, Support, and Integration   505
Toni C. Antonucci, Aurora Sherman, and
Hiroko Akiyama

Stroke   517
Philip B. Gorelick, Vijay Shanmugam, and
Aurora K. Pajeau

Suicide   529
Dan G. Blazer and Harold G. Koenig

T

Telomeres   539
Calvin B. Harley

Theories of Aging: Biological   545
F. Eugene Yates

Theories of Aging: Psychological   557
Johannes J. F. Schroots

Theories of Aging: Social   568
Victor W. Marshall

Thirst and Hydration   573
Margaret-Mary G. Wilson and
John E. Morley

Time: Concepts and Perceptions   583
Johannes J. F. Schroots

Touch and Proprioception   591
Janet M. Weisenberger

V

Vision   605
Charles T. Scialfa and Donald W. Kline

Volunteer Activity by Older Adults   613
Robert A. Harootyan

W

Widowhood and Widowerhood   621
Anne Martin-Matthews

Work and Employment   627
Jeanette N. Cleveland and
Lynn M. Shore

Contributors   641
Index   653

About the Editor-in-Chief

James E. Birren's many awards include the 1996 American Society on Aging President's Award, the Brookdale Foundation Award for Gerontological Research, the Sandoz prize for Gerontological Research, and the award for outstanding contribution to gerontology by the Canadian Association of Gerontology. Dr. Birren is currently Associate Director of the Center on Aging at the University of California, Los Angeles, and serves as an adjunct professor in medicine, psychiatry, and biobehavioral sciences. He is also Professor Emeritus of gerontology and psychology at the University of Southern California. Dr. Birren's previous positions include serving as Chief of the Section on Aging of the National Institute of Mental Health, founding Executive Director and Dean of the Ethel Percy Andrus Gerontology Center of USC, founding Director of the Anna and Harry Borun Center for Gerontological Research at UCLA, and President of the Gerontological Society of America, the Western Gerontological Society, and the Division on Adult Development and Aging of the American Psychological Association. Author of more than 250 scholarly publications, Dr. Birren's research interests include how speed of behavior changes with age, the causes and consequences of slowed information processing in the older nervous system, the effect of age on decision-making processes, and the role of expertise in skilled occupations. He has served as a delegate to several White House Conferences on Aging and continues to develop national priorities for research and education related to issues of aging.

About the Editorial Advisory Board

Victor W. Marshall is Professor of Behavioral Science at the University of Toronto and Director of its Centre for Studies of Aging. He served from 1990 to 1995 as Network Director of CARNET, the Canadian Aging Research Network, a Canadian federally funded, nationwide Network of Centres of Excellence. Professor Marshall is a fellow of the Gerontological Society of America and a founding member of the Canadian Association on Gerontology. He was Editor-in-Chief of *The Canadian Journal on Aging* for five years and is now on the editorial boards of the *Journal of Aging and Health* and *Ageing and Society*. More than 100 publications report his work from a broad social science perspective rooted in sociological training. Professor Marshall's work has covered such diverse aspects of aging as the family, long-term care, public policy, and death and dying, but it currently focuses on social theory of aging, independence and aging, and aging in relation to work and the life course. He directs a large multidisciplinary research program in the latter area funded by the Canadian government.

Thomas R. Cole's book *The Journal of Life: A Cultural History of Aging in America* (Cambridge, 1992) was nominated for a Pulitzer Prize. Another of his works, *The Oxford Book of Aging* (1994), for which he was Senior Editor, was noted as one of the most memorable books of 1995 by the *New Yorker*. Dr. Cole is Professor and Graduate Program Director at the Institute for Medical Humanities, University of Texas Medical Branch in Galveston, and a Fellow of the Gerontological Society. He has served as Chair of the Gerontological Society of America's Humanities and Arts Committee and on the editorial boards of *The Gerontologist, Generations,* and *Journal of Aging and Health.* Dr. Cole has published many articles and books on the history of aging and humanistic gerontology.

Alvar Svanborg was awarded the Thureus Prize for Research by the University of Uppsala, 1980; the Brookdale Foreign Award for distinguished contributions in gerontology, 1985; the Harold Hatch Award from Mount Sinai School of Medicine, New York, 1986; the Sandoz Prize for Gerontological Research, 1987; and the Third Age Award, XIV International Congress of Gerontology, Acapulco, Mexico, 1989. Dr. Svanborg is a Beth Fowler Vitoux and George E. Vitoux Distinguished Professor of Geriatric Medicine, Professor of Medicine, and Chief, Section of Geriatric Medicine, Clinical Director of Research in Gerontology, University of Illinois, Chicago. He has served as Scientific Advisor to the Swedish National Board of Health and Welfare, 1968–1988; Expert to the Supreme National Swedish Insurance Court, 1969–1988; and Swedish delegate at the United Nations World Assembly on Aging, 1982. Dr. Svanborg has been a consultant to the World Health Organization since 1970 and Special Advisor to the Director of the World Health Organization since 1984, in addition to serving as President of the Federation of Gerontology of the Nordic Countries from 1973–1988. Dr. Svanborg has been an advisor to the United States government, the Greek government, Hungarian authorities, the Israeli government, and the Polish government. He obtained his specialist license in internal medicine and cardiology in 1954 and in geriatric medicine in 1966. His research work has been focused in medical biochemistry, clinical physiology, internal medicine, medical gerontology, geriatrics, and long-term care medicine.

Edward J. Masoro was the recipient of the 1989 Allied-Signal Achievement Award in Aging Research. In 1990, he received the Geriatric Leadership Academic Award from the National Institute on Aging and the Robert W. Kleemeier Award from the Geron-

tological Society of America. In 1991, he received a medal of honor from the University of Pisa for Achievements in Gerontology, and in 1993, Dr. Masoro received the Distinguished Service Award from the Association of Chairmen of Departments of Physiology. In addition, he received the 1995 Irving Wright Award of Distinction of the American Federation for Aging Research and the 1995 Glenn Foundation Award. He served as President of the Gerontological Society of America from 1994–1995, as Chairman of the Aging Review Committee of the National Institute on Aging (NIA), and as Chairman of the Board of Scientific Counselors of the NIA. Dr. Masoro has held faculty positions at Queen's University (Canada), Tufts University School of Medicine, University of Washington, and Medical College of Pennsylvania. From 1973 through May of 1991, he served as Chairman of the Department of Physiology at the University of Texas Health Science Center at San Antonio. He currently continues his duties as Professor Emeritus in the Department of Physiology and is the Director of the newly created Aging Research and Education Center. Since 1975, Dr. Masoro's research has focused on the influence of food restriction on aging. He has served or is serving in an editorial role for 10 journals, and in January of 1992, he became the Editor of the *Journal of Gerontology: Biological Sciences.*

K. Warner Schaie has received the Kleemeier Award for Distinguished Research Contributions from the Gerontological Society of America and the Distinguished Scientific Contributions Award from the American Psychological Association. Dr. Schaie is the Evan Pugh Professor of Human Development and Psychology and Director of the Gerontology Center at the Pennsylvania State University. He also holds an appointment as Affiliate Professor of Psychiatry and Behavioral Science at the University of Washington. A fellow of the Gerontological Society and the American Psychological Association, Professor Schaie has served as president of the American Psychological Association Division of Adult Development and Aging and as Editor of the *Journal of Geronotology: Psychological Sciences.* Author of more than 250 scholarly publications of the psychology of aging, Dr. Schaie's interests include the life course of adult intelligence, its antecedents and modifiability, and methodological issues in the developmental sciences.

How to Use the Encyclopedia

The *Encyclopedia of Gerontology: Age, Aging, and the Aged* is intended for use by both students and research professionals. Articles have been chosen to reflect major disciplines in the study of gerontology and adult development and aging, common topics of research by professionals in this realm, and areas of public interest and concern. Coverage includes five major areas: the biology of aging, the psychology of aging, aging and the social sciences, health sciences, and the humanities and aging. Each article serves as a comprehensive overview of a given area, providing both breadth of coverage for students and depth of coverage for research professionals. We have designed the encyclopedia with the following features for maximum accessibility for all readers.

Articles in the encyclopedia are arranged alphabetically by subject. Complete tables of contents appear in both volumes. Here, one will find broad discipline-related titles such as "Demography" and "Pharmacology," research topics such as "Dementia" and "Creativity," and areas of public interest and concern such as "Abuse and Neglect of Elders" and "Ethics and Euthanasia."

The Index is located in Volume 2. Because the reader's topic of interest may be listed under a broader article title, we encourage use of the Index for access to a subject area, rather than use of the Table of Contents alone. For instance, Alzheimer's Disease is covered within the article "Dementia," and osteoporosis is covered in the article "Bone and Osteoporo-

sis." Because a topic of study in gerontology is often applicable to more than one article, the Index provides a complete listing of where a subject is covered and in what context.

Each article contains an outline, a glossary, cross references, and a bibliography. The outline allows a quick scan of the major areas discussed within each article. The glossary contains terms that may be unfamiliar to the reader, with each term defined *in the context of its use in that article*. Thus, a term may appear in the glossary for another article defined in a slightly different manner or with a subtle nuance specific to that article. For clarity, we have allowed these differences in definition to remain so that the terms are defined relative to the context of each article.

Each article has been cross referenced to other articles in the encyclopedia. Cross references are found at the first or predominant mention of a subject area covered elsewhere in the encyclopedia. We encourage readers to use the cross references to locate other encyclopedia articles that will provide more detailed information about a subject.

The bibliography lists recent secondary sources to aid the reader in locating more detailed or technical information. Review articles and research articles that are considered of primary importance to the understanding of a given subject area are also listed. Bibliographies are not intended to provide a full reference listing of all material covered in the context of a given article, but are provided as guides to further reading.

L

Language and Communication in Aging and Dementia

Loraine K. Obler

*CUNY Graduate School, and
Boston VA Medical Center*

Martin L. Albert

*Department of Veterans Affairs, and
Boston University School of Medicine*

I. Language and Communication in Normal Aging
II. Aphasia and Aging
III. Language in the Dementias
IV. Summary and Conclusions

Aphasia Loss of or impaired ability to speak, write, or to understand the meaning of words, due to brain damage.
Dementia Lasting deterioration of cognitive abilities resulting from any of a number of diseases affecting the brain.
Lexicon Words or the vocabulary of a language as distinguished from its grammar and construction.
Syntax The way in which linguistic elements (as words) are put together to form constituents (as phrases or clauses).

Age-related changes in **LANGUAGE AND COMMUNICATION** can be quite subtle, particularly when they are associated with healthy aging. Often they may be attributed to nonlinguistic factors both within the individual—such as memory or hearing changes—or external factors such as societal attitudes toward the elderly. In this article we treat the language and communication changes of normal aging first, to provide a baseline for the two brain-damaged older adult populations of interest: individuals with aphasia and those with dementia.

I. LANGUAGE AND COMMUNICATION IN NORMAL AGING

A. Definition

For our purposes *normal aging* means growing older into the sixties and beyond with no history of neurological or psychiatric incident, nor severe hearing or visual loss.

B. Language Production

The most studied aspects of normal language production in normal aging are lexical-semantic abilities, syntax, and discourse production. These three skills show some minimal to moderate decline with normal aging, as compared to other linguistic capabilities that remain intact: reading aloud, writing, phonology (production of appropriate sounds) and morphophonological production (appropriate use of suffixes), metalinguistic skills (the ability to manipulate language deliberately, as opposed to on-line processing), and pragmatics (the appropriate use of language in different situations).

1. Naming and Lexical Semantics
There is a clear age-related decline in the ability to recall names. Not only is it difficult for older people to remember the names of common nouns, but they also have increasing difficulties remembering the words for many verb labels (actions) and proper

nouns (names of people and places). The decline is subtle, but real, in the fifties to sixties, recent studies have demonstrated, and becomes more precipitous in the seventies. With cues, however, such as the first sound or syllable of a word, most older subjects can easily recall its name. This benefit from cuing strongly suggests that the age-related naming problem lies with locating or retrieving the word in storage (i.e., there is a lexical access or retrieval problem), but not with the actual storage of it. Further evidence that there are no age-related storage problems per se comes from the fact that a number of features that enter into lexical organization and storage remain equally effective with age. These include the ability to generate semantic associations, the ability to be primed when one sees a related word just before the target word, and the effects of frequency (whereby high-frequency words are easier to access for subjects of all ages than are low-frequency words) and concreteness (whereby concrete items are easier of access than abstract items).

A number of theories have been proposed to account for the lexical access difficulties of older adults. Some focus on the naming problem in the context of other memory decline. Some focus on naming tasks as controlled or conscious processes as compared to automatic ones. The Transmission Deficit Hypothesis of Burke and colleagues argues that word nodes are connected in the lexicon, and that these connections become weakened with age or infrequent use, particularly in the case of words with less rich semantic connections, such as proper nouns (e.g., people's names) and, perhaps, common nouns as compared to verbs. [See MEMORY.]

2. Syntax and Discourse

Discourse is extended speech or writing, consisting of more than one sentence unit. It can occur in a number of expressive modes, including conversation and narrative. With respect to the single sentence level, although syntax remains grossly spared in healthy aging, there are some indications that subtle changes may be taking place. In particular, although the full range of syntactic structures remains available to older adults, they are less likely to use highly complex syntactic structures in oral discourse.

At the paragraph level it is clear that task variables interact with the performance of older adults. Any task requiring substantial memory load is likely to provoke decline in older adults' communicative abilities; by contrast, conversational tasks with low memory load may show increased performance and, indeed, elaborateness of speech and even verbosity. The elaborateness may be reflected in additional details, in the form of, for example, prepositional phrases. Such elaborations tend to be "right-branching," that is, they elaborate on an item that has already been mentioned, rather than one that is about to be mentioned. The more complex embeddings tend to occur less with older adulthood. There remains debate as to whether discourse cohesion and coherence are spared with aging. A number of studies find no differences between older and younger adults, whereas others find subtle problems with use of such cohesive devices for cross-sentence linking as pronouns, or with coherence measures, such as keeping to the relevant theme or general topic.

Lexical production generally appears well spared in discourse (surprisingly, given its impairment on naming tasks), but subtle difficulties may be reflected in the increased speech errors associated with aging. Older adults are more likely to pause midphrase, or speak an unintended word, but they are as likely as young adults to correct such speech errors.

C. Language Comprehension

1. Syntax

Lexical comprehension is spared in healthy aging, assuming the subject has preserved hearing and vision. At the syntactic level, however, declines can be seen even as early as the sixties and into older aging. These problems arise with syntactically complex materials. More complex syntactic structures (e.g., double embeddings) cause progressively more problems with advancing age.

2. Discourse

When the task involves comprehending extended materials, whether through reading or listening, older adults have problems not at the sentence level but at the discourse level. In particular, when information is omitted in paragraph-length material and they are required to make inferences, older adults as a rule have more problems than younger adults. Moreover, memory for pertinent structurally crucial details is often retained, whereas that for peripheral details is more impaired in older adults than in younger adults.

D. Interacting Nonlanguage Abilities

Some, but not all, of the difficulty older adults have with language can be linked to nonlanguage cognitive deficits (problems with memory, both short-term and long-term, on paragraph recall tasks, for example), or cognitive slowing that renders comprehension or monitoring one's production difficult. Age-related hearing loss (presbycusis) affects performance on individual language tasks, and, not trivially, affects the amount of interaction that older adults may have and thus reduces opportunities for communication. Hearing loss occurs on at least two levels: not only at the pure tone level, reducing processing of higher pitched acoustic emissions (such as those used for fricatives: the sounds reflected by the letters *s, z, th, f, v*), but also at the auditory perceptual level that permits people to discriminate minimal pairs of words in language (e.g., *sip* vs. *sit*). [*See* HEARING.]

Age-related reductions in vision can mean less intake of information for use in the written mode. Problems with dentures can result in lower intelligibility in speech output.

E. Neurological Changes

Neurological changes associated with normal aging are well documented and include decreased brain weight, gyral atrophy, ventricular dilation, and changes in histological characteristics of fiber pathways. Neuronal cell loss affects those parts of the brain that are engaged in the functions of memory, speed of information processing, attention, and cortical arousal.

There should be no surprise, then, in the discovery of cognitive changes with normal aging dependent on the distribution of these anatomical changes. To the extent that these nonlinguistic cognitive changes influence language, the observed alterations of language in normal aging would be dependent on the above-described anatomical changes.

The question that remains, however, is the degree to which the neuroanatomical changes of normal aging have a direct influence on language. Insufficient research has been conducted to answer this question. The speculative hypothesis has been put forth that left temporal lobe atrophy may be linked to the naming difficulties of normal aging, but no firm data as yet support that hypothesis. Some early suspicions that

lateral organization for language may change in older adults have been quashed; there is no evidence of changes in left lateral dominance for aging, although increased automaticization within the left hemisphere language areas has not been ruled out.

F. Societal Factors

The decline of language and communication abilities in aging is linked to level of education. Scores on tests of naming, for example, correlate with education. Difficulties in equating the amounts and kind of education across different subject cohorts may contribute to different results from different studies, although longitudinal studies of language and aging often show a picture similar to that found in cross-sectional studies, and, obviously, years of education remain constant for the individual in a longitudinal study. It is unclear to what extent daily opportunities to communicate influence older adults. Some studies show that lessened "practice" with language results in decreased performance.

Little work has been done on cross-cultural aspects of language use in aging, although attitudes to the elderly vary across cultures, and communication opportunities may well differ in different communities. A discourse style called "elderspeak" has been identified in certain cultures. Younger adults tend to address elders in brief sentences with exaggerated intonation and simplified lexical choice, the assumption being that elders are not well able to understand normal adult discourse. Additionally, changes in acoustic aspects of speech enable listeners to identify older adults easily, and stereotypic responses to their voices have frequently been demonstrated (e.g., evaluating them as less positive and as less effective). In cultures with more respect for older individuals, elders may continue productive communicative lives for more extended periods.

II. APHASIA AND AGING

A. Definition

Aphasia is a language disturbance resulting from brain damage. In the Western world it currently occurs predominantly in older adults. The classic aphasias are the results of sudden injuries to the brain, such as those from war injuries or weapon injuries or stroke. Aphasias may be considered as being primarily "fluent" or primarily "nonfluent," depending on the language production of the aphasic individual, and the site of lesion. In particular, fluent aphasias have been associated with lesions in the more posterior regions of the cortical language area, whereas nonfluent aphasias have been associated with more anterior lesions in that area.

B. Age and Aphasia Type

Fluent aphasics tend to be older, by about a decade, than nonfluent aphasics, yet this finding is not entirely explained by differing lesion locations. It has been hypothesized that the increase in fluent aphasia types associated with age may be related to the increased verbosity and elaborateness reported in discourse in healthy aging, but no good explanation has been offered to date.

C. Age and Aphasia Recovery

There is controversy as to whether older adults recover as well as younger adults from aphasia. One set of studies finds no differences in recovery once lesion site and aphasia severity and possible dementia are controlled for. Another set of studies finds slight but consistent age-linked decline in ability to recover over the first half year and longer after the aphasia-producing incident. Potential reasons for decreased recovery associated with age, were it to be verified, could be the lesser education many older adults received, the memory declines associated with aging that would impinge on recovery of language and on any new learning strategies to circumvent aphasic problems, and the neurobiologic changes associated with normal aging.

D. Primary Progressive Aphasia

In the early 1980s Mesulam called attention to a clinical syndrome of progressive language deterioration that he called "slowly progressive aphasia without generalized dementia," subsequently labeled primary progressive aphasia. The syndrome may be defined operationally as a progressive disorder with prominent language deficits, preservation of other cognitive skills, and preservation of activities of daily living.

The pattern of language deficits exhibits considerable variability, although the more common patterns are nonfluent and resemble Broca's aphasia or transcortical motor aphasia. Of note is that this more common pattern is distinguished from the language disorder of Alzheimer's disease (AD), which is generally fluent. Nevertheless, cases of primary progressive aphasia have been reported with fluent aphasia. Variability in this syndrome is undoubtedly due to variability in etiology, which includes several different neurodegenerative disorders.

E. Societal Factors

In addition to the societal factors discussed in the section on normal aging, specific factors affect the individual with aphasia. These include cultural attitudes against the aphasic individual, which may affect whether this person takes advantage of rehabilitation services or not, and whether he or she is engaged in conversation by family members and friends. Socioeconomic factors associated with age as well as belonging to a particular subculture can also affect abilities and desire to make use of rehabilitation services. Poverty leads to such simple impediments as lack of transportation to rehabilitation, and marketing of these services may be more deliberately made to the majority population. Clinicians' assumptions about what is a desired rehabilitation outcome may also be limited by their own cultural experiences.

III. LANGUAGE IN THE DEMENTIAS

A. Alzheimer's Disease

AD is the most common dementing disease in the United States. At the beginning of the twentieth century, Alois Alzheimer reported the characteristic cellular changes associated with a peculiar language problem he called an *aphasia*.

In the early stages of AD, many individuals manifest an increase in problems with lexical access on naming tasks and in conversation (i.e., they cannot find the specific words they need). By the middle stages, discourse becomes empty, as meaningful words drop out of one's vocabulary, although as a rule the patient is voluble, even hard to interrupt. Comprehension is quite poor. In these mid and mid-to-late stages, the patient looks remarkably like a patient with Wernicke's aphasia, or, if repetition is relatively spared, like a patient with transcortical sensory aphasia. The ability to read aloud is preserved (except for low-frequency, irregularly spelled words). Syntax, however much produced, is spared, as in the fluent aphasias. Moreover phonology is well spared, and the patient remains intelligible at the level of the sound and word, even if the words and sentences produced make no sense in context. By mid-to-late stage, *neologisms* (i.e., newly created words that are structurally acceptable in the language but happen not to occur) can be found in speech output. Some aspects of pragmatics are remarkably spared at this time; for example, the patient will maintain eye contact and respond to questions and forceful interruptions appropriately. Overall in conversation, patients preserve the capacity for turn-taking until a relatively late stage, but they are less likely to initiate new topics or keep to their interlocutor's topics. However, more subtle aspects of pragmatics, such as appreciation of humor and inference, will be lost.

By the late stages of the disease, the patient is virtually no longer communicating at all. Each patient may have one or two spared pragmatic abilities (e.g., the ability to keep eye contact, or to speak formulaic phrases such as "I'm fine" when asked how he or she is). Neither reading nor writing are testable any longer.

Although this picture holds for the majority of patients with AD, it must be noted that there are other subpatterns that can be seen as well. In a sizable minority of patients, language problems are relatively mild, and concentrated mainly in naming, until quite late when communication is reduced. Originally, in earlier studies, it had appeared that individuals with later onset of AD demonstrated the milder pattern, but recently that opinion has been questioned.

Impairment on selected cognitive tasks such as memory for word lists has been noted as an early predictor of onset of AD. These cognitive tasks reflect the heavy contribution of nonlanguage abilities that decline with AD and influence language and communication performance. In particular, these are deficits in most types of memory, attention, and the ability to manipulate acquired knowledge.

There is substantial debate as to whether semantic memory storage *per se* becomes deficient in the course of AD, or whether the observed naming problems result from severe difficulty with lexical access. Some authors argue that subordinate categories may be spared while superordinate categories seem to lose their boundaries; others suggest that with alternate approaches, individual lexical items can be accessed in semantic memory in persons with AD. Experimental studies using priming tasks suggest that certain aspects of priming are spared relatively late in AD, although all possible relationships have been seen: increased priming, decreased priming, and no differences in priming as compared to normal age-matched controls. [*See* DEMENTIA.]

B. Pick's Disease

The location and precise cellular pathology differ in Pick's disease as compared with AD. Severe cell loss and atrophy affect primarily the frontal lobes and anterior and inferior parts of the temporal lobes. Depending on the precise starting point of the neuronal damage, and the rate of its progression and spread, language changes may vary. The few studies of language in Pick's disease have provided differing results.

A common finding in the language of Pick's disease is reduced output, increasing nonfluency, and finally mutism. Otherwise, reductions in syntactic structure and a pattern resembling transcortical sensory aphasia have been described. The degree to which semantic capacity may be preserved is an open question.

C. Multi-Infarct Dementia

Because the distribution of strokes in multi-infarct dementia (MID) (see article elsewhere in this volume) is variable across individuals, the language patterns are themselves quite different from individual to individual. Language problems typical of, although not invariably found, in MID, however, include the following: disorders of naming, fluency of output, preserved repetition, and impaired comprehension of complex or rapidly presented material.

IV. SUMMARY AND CONCLUSIONS

Declines in language performance with normal aging at the word and sentence level, especially for naming and word finding, have been demonstrated across many languages, both for production and, in the case of sentence and discourse levels, for comprehension. However, other language skills remain spared in healthy aging. Hemispheric lateralization for language does not change with age, although at the cellular level age-related changes may interact within the hemispheres producing the problems with lexicon that are seen. Other aspects of language change, such as impaired memory for paragraphs, are clearly language problems secondary to nonlanguage cognitive decline (such as failing memory) and cognitive slowing.

In AD problems with naming, and perhaps semantic storage, are manifested progressively with time, as are problems in comprehension, and pragmatics. Reading aloud is relatively spared but not reading for comprehension. Writing problems reflect those of oral language. In Pick's disease the principal language problems are associated with reduced output, whereas in MID they are quite variable.

Aphasia occurs primarily in older adults; its syndromes have been documented for over a century. Age interacts with type of aphasia (fluent aphasics being older on average than nonfluent aphasics) and with recovery from aphasia to a subtle degree.

Age-related changes in language and communication do not mean that age itself is the primary factor bringing about the changes. Rather, it is brain changes associated with aging that bring about these language changes. As automaticity increases with language usage and age, however, certain language abilities may become more tightly instantiated and resistant to change, particularly phonological shapes of words, the ability to read words aloud, and the ability to produce syntactically correct sentences. These language abilities then become resistant to disease, as well.

Societal attitudes toward aging and the diseases of aging contribute to communication difficulties, as elders may be treated like children despite the fact that the "regression hypothesis" has been demonstrably falsified for aphasia, as well as dementia, and certainly does not hold for the language changes of healthy aging.

BIBLIOGRAPHY

Bayles, K. (1995). Language in aging and dementia. In H. Kirshner (Eds.), *Handbook of neurological speech and language disorders* (pp. 351–372). New York: Marcel Dekker, Inc.

Kempler, D., & Zelinski, E. (1994). Language in dementia and normal aging. In F. A. Huppert, C. Brayne, & D. W. O'Connor, (Eds.), *Dementia and normal aging* (pp. 331–365). Cambridge: Cambridge University Press.

Light, L., & D. Burke (Eds.). (1988). *Language, memory and aging.* Cambridge: Cambridge University Press.

Lubinski, R. (Ed.). (1991). *Dementia and communication.* Philadelphia: B.C. Decker.

Obler, L. K., & Albert, M. L. (1984). Language in aging. In M. L. Albert (Ed.), *Clinical neurology of aging* (pp. 245–253). New York: Oxford University Press.

Ripich, D. (Ed.) (1991). *Handbook of geriatric communication disorders.* Austin, TX: Pro-Ed.

Learning

Joel S. Freund

University of Arkansas

I. Rationale and Theory
II. Nonverbal Tasks
III. Verbal Tasks
IV. Summary

Association An association between two events is inferred when a subject reliably produces one event when presented with the other.

Conditioned Response (CR) The learned response conditional upon presentation of the conditioned stimulus, and previous pairings of the conditioned and unconditioned stimulus.

Conditioned Stimulus (CS) Originally neutral stimulus that comes to elicit a response by being paired with the unconditioned stimulus.

Learning A relatively permanent change in behavior potential due to experience.

Paired-Associate Learning (PAL) A learning task involving pairs of stimuli. The subject is presented with the first item of each pair and is expected to produce the second.

Unconditioned Response (UCR) The response produced by the unconditioned stimulus.

Unconditioned Stimulus (UCS) A stimulus that has the ability to elicit a response without prior training.

LEARNING is often defined as a relatively permanent change in behavior potential as a function of successive experience with a task. Several of the terms in the definition need further explication. "Relatively permanent" is used to distinguish learning from other more transient changes due to habituation, motiva-tion, drugs, and so on. "Behavior potential" is used because nonlearning factors (e.g., motivation, opportunity to display the behavior) may not allow the changes to be expressed immediately. "Tasks" is an omnibus term encompassing a diverse set of activities that can and have been studied (for examples see Table I).

The area of learning must also be distinguished from its companion area, memory. It should be apparent that the difference between these two areas is often subtle, perhaps arbitrary, and certainly debatable. It is also true that they are inextricably linked: without learning there would be nothing to remember; without memory learning would be for naught. A working distinction, to be adopted here, is that one studies learning when the focus of the investigation is the acquisition process itself, whether the material or skill being acquired is novel or familiar. Operationally, the focus is learning when the time period between the study or practice phase and the test phase is equal to, or less than, the time taken for the study phase. An example might be useful.

In a typical learning experiment, a list of 35 common words is presented on a tape recorder at the rate of 1 word every 5 sec. After presentation, subjects are given 2 min to recall verbally as many of the words as possible. The list is then repeated, and again recall is attempted. This entire study–recall sequence is repeated five times. Although the list is composed of common words, that is, words already in memory, the focus of the study is the increase in recall (i.e., learning) across the five trials. Including a sixth recall trial 20 min after the fifth study–recall cycle would have added a memory component to the task.

I. RATIONALE AND THEORY

Psychologists are interested in the relationship between aging and learning for several reasons. On a practical level, the proportion of the population over 60 is growing, and psychologists need to determine in what ways the learning processes of older adults differ from those of younger adults. Knowledge of these differences will allow researchers to develop effective ways to teach older people new skills, for the workplace, for treatment of various physical or psychological problems, or simply to help people deal with, and get more enjoyment from, their retirement.

On a more basic research level, one way to understand a process is to compare the process under two conditions; when it is working efficiently, and when it is not. Careful comparison of those two situations may yield some insight into how the process works. Studying the effect of the aging process on learning may give us some insight into the learning process in general.

Finally, study of aging and learning allows psychologists to test theories of learning. Many theories of learning make predictions involving individual differences. For example, one theory might predict that physical activity is related to mental alertness. A preliminary test of the theory would be to determine if there was a correlation between some measure of physical activity and a measure of mental alertness. Although finding such a correlation would be only very modest support for the theory, not finding the correlation would likely doom the theory. Making different theoretical predictions for younger and older adults allows the testing of many different theories of learning.

Across the years many theories have been developed to explain the fact that elderly adults typically perform more poorly than younger adults on various tasks. Three different theoretical approaches to explain the typical age-related decrement in learning are actively being pursued. These three are briefly described here, and are mentioned where appropriate in the remaining sections. To anticipate somewhat, it should be clear that no one theory adequately explains all of the data concerning age changes in learning.

A. Response Slowing

As organisms age, various parts of the system slow down, including the speed at which nerve impulses are conducted, and motor movements are initiated and completed. Slower response mean many tasks take longer to complete or cannot be completed in the time available. Thus, on tasks that require speeded responses or faster pacing, elderly adults will be at a disadvantage relative to younger adults. The theory can also explain some Age × Complexity interactions. If a simple task requires only one component, then the age difference will be minimal, due to the age-related speed difference on that component. If a complex task requires three successive processes, and each is slowed by the same amount, the result will be a threefold age difference on the complex task, relative to the simple task; an Age × Task Complexity interaction.

B. Cognitive Capacity

Various theorists have argued that the capacity of working memory (i.e., the capacity to process information) is limited, and that humans allocate those limited resources to various tasks as required. Some tasks (for example, extracting frequency of occurrence information) require minimal capacity, whereas others (making visual images, learning a list of words) may require substantial cognitive resources. For whatever reasons, with age the capacity of working memory decreases. Thus, an effortful task that requires 80% of the processing resources of a young adult may require 95% of the resources of an older adult.

Although this approach has been useful in guiding research, different measures of working memory do not correlate with other measures of capacity, and do not consistently show age differences. In addition, other experimental results are not easily explained by this theory. [*See* MEMORY.]

C. Inhibitory Processes

A recent entry to the theoretical arena, this theory has as its basis the idea that the performance of many tasks may be complicated by the presence of extraneous or irrelevant stimuli, and to perform well on such tasks requires that responses to those stimuli must be eliminated or reduced. These irrelevant stimuli may be external, such as noises or voices, or internal, such as thoughts or feelings. Failure to inhibit attentional responses to these irrelevant stimuli leads to interference and subsequently to degradation in performance.

The theoretical assumption, based on research evidence, is that with increasing age comes a decreased effectiveness of these inhibitory processes. Thus, in situations where these irrelevant stimuli need to be inhibited to foster efficient learning, the elderly would be at a disadvantage. However, in situations where those previously irrelevant stimuli subsequently become relevant, the elderly might have an advantage. [*See* INHIBITION.]

II. NONVERBAL TASKS

The tasks in this section include classical or Pavlovian conditioning, operant, instrumental, and motor-skill learning. Because the contingencies to be learned in these tasks are easily acquired without instructions or the use of words, many of the studies in this category have used animals as their primary subjects.

A. Classical Conditioning

In classical or Pavlovian conditioning, the unconditioned response (UCR) is naturally elicited by the unconditioned stimulus (UCS). For example, an eyeblink is elicited by a puff of air to the eye; touching a hot object elicits a hand-withdrawal response. Conditioning occurs when control of the elicited response is transferred to a previously neutral stimulus, the conditioned stimulus (CS), so that presentation of the CS (e.g., a tone, sight of the stove) elicits the response (eyeblink, hand withdrawal). In a typical laboratory procedure the CS comes on about 500 ms before, and overlaps with, the UCS (puff of air). Both are terminated at the same time. After a number of CS–UCS pairings, the UCR, (blink) originally elicited by the UCS, would begin to occur at the onset of the CS, and prior to the UCS. (This statement is not meant to imply that the UCR and conditioned response [CR] are identical responses. There are many instances where the CR is very different, in fact the opposite of, the UCR. However, for the types of responses used in aging research, the CR and UCR are similar.)

Most of the research on aging and classical conditioning has been done with animals, and although generalizing from animals to humans is risky, the results in both areas lead to similar conclusions. Older adults acquire classical conditioning responses more slowly than younger adults. Although classical conditioning is sensitive to the effects of variables such as motivation and anxiety, which may be correlated with increasing age, it seems likely that differences in conditioning are not due to these factors.

Current theoretical accounts of classical conditioning revolve around the CS–UCS connection. Of particular import is the information value of the CS. When the CS is a reliable predictor of the UCS (i.e., the UCS always follows, but does not occur in the absence of the CS), conditioning is rapid. Reducing the strength of either of those correlations results in poorer conditioning. In fact, if conditions are arranged so that the CS is a reliable predictor of no UCS (i.e., the CS is never followed by the UCS), subjects can learn to withhold the CR when the tone sounds. Current theories stress the idea that subjects are abstracting the information value of the CS, or of the relative frequency of occurrence of stimulus events from their environment. Although the details of the theories are not relevant here, the implications for age differences are.

It is possible that elderly have decreased ability to learn the informational value of the CS or the nature of the CS–UCS contingency. According to one theory of classical conditioning, contextual stimuli become conditioned as part of the CS, thus reducing the strength of conditioning to the punctate CS, because the total associative strength is spread over all components of the CS. That is, the sights, sounds, and other external or internal stimuli in the situation may become conditioned as part of the CS. If the elderly are not as able to inhibit or suppress responses to these irrelevant stimuli, they will become conditioned as part of the CS, reducing its effectiveness as a predictor of the UCS, thus making learning more difficult. [*See* CONDITIONING.]

B. Operant Conditioning

Responses in operant conditioning, like those in classical conditioning, are of relatively short duration, and can be repeated many times without intervention by a researcher. Examples of these types of responses are presented in Table I. Unlike classical conditioning, these responses are emitted by subjects rather than elicited by stimuli, and are followed by the critical stimulus event. The goal of the stimulus event is to alter some attribute of the response, such as the rate

Table I Types of Learning and Examples of Research and Everyday Responses

| Type of learning | Research tasks and responses | | Everyday examples |
	Animal research	Human research	
Classical conditioning	Eyeblink Fear Taste aversion Salivation	Eyeblink Galvanic skin response	Desensitization therapy Phobias Prejudices Food aversions
Operant conditioning	Bar pressing (rats) Key pecking (pigeons)	Key pressing Digit-symbol substitution	Behavior therapies
Instrumental learning	Multiple-choice-point spatial maze	Multiple-choice-point paper maze	Navigate in a new environment
Motor-skill learning	None	Typing Pursuit rotor Mirror tracing	Typing Bike riding Playing golf Driving a car
Paired-associate learning	None	Learning a list of noun pairs or picture word pairs	Foreign language vocabulary Face-name learning

of emission, frequency, speed, or strength. Modification of the particular attribute may be accomplished by positively reinforcing (i.e., presenting a valued stimulus such as a candy bar, money, praise) when the desired attribute occurs, or negatively reinforcing (i.e., removing an aversive stimulus) when the response occurs. (Negative reinforcement might involve turning off an electric shock or noxious sound.) Another alternative might involve punishment of the response by taking away a desired stimulus (e.g., candy, privileges), or presenting an aversive stimulus (shock, insult, noise).

The paucity of studies with the elderly have involved enhancing the speed with which tasks like the digit-symbol substitution are performed, and indicates that both young and elderly benefit from reinforcement. There is some suggestion that the elderly may benefit more from the reinforcement than the young. To the extent that basic research on operant conditioning has indicated that the role of reinforcement is motivational or activational, reinforcement may result in age differences in performance rather than learning.

C. Instrumental Learning

Instrumental learning is similar to operant conditioning in that the behavior of interest is emitted and the desired responses are followed by reinforcement or punishment in order to produce modifications. It differs in that the responses may be more complex or of longer duration, and they typically involve discrete trials. That is, the responses in instrumental learning cannot easily be repeated without some external intervention. (In maze learning, the animal cannot repeat the maze until it is removed from the goal box and placed in the start box.)

Results of animal research indicate that on simple tasks, age differences are minimal, but on complex tasks, young subjects are more proficient (take fewer trials to learn, make fewer errors) than older subjects. These age differences may be reduced, but not eliminated, by factors such as guidance through the maze (not allowing incorrect choices) and individual-difference variables such as diet.

Partly because of its applied value, research employing more complex and real-world situations, such as learning to navigate in a new or strange environment, has been more frequent in recent years. Studies using simulated walks (via slides) in novel environments produced the familiar age-related decrement in learning, as well as revealing that the age difference was primarily due to a difference in learning route information. There was little age difference in extracting knowledge about landmarks on the trip. That is, elderly adults had more trouble than younger adults learning the turns in a route, but were about as good at recognizing landmarks.

D. Motor-Skill Learning

Motor-skill, or perceptual-motor learning requires coordinating fine motor skills with the perception of sequential stimuli. In many instances these skills are learned in youth and become very overlearned and automatic. A skill that has become automatic requires very little in the way of cognitive resources and thus can be maintained at reasonable levels even when cognitive resources have been greatly reduced, either by age or illness.

There is no doubt that increasing age brings with it a general slowing of responses. This slowing is evident in simple and choice reaction time tasks and other measures requiring speeded responding. Any theory of learning must be able to explain the generalized slowing with age, but also the fact that the slowing is even more pronounced for difficult or cognitively demanding tasks.

Research on motor-skill learning has used both real-world tasks (typing, computer skills, archery, etc.) and laboratory tasks. As in any area, use of real-world tasks allows for ready generalization of the findings to those tasks, but introduces a number of potential confounds that may be difficult to remove. Laboratory tasks, on the other hand, provide greater control over potential confounding variables, as well as permitting component analysis of the task. That is, with appropriate manipulations and theory, one can break a complex skill into its component processes. Examination of the separate processes allows for determination of those processes sensitive to aging, and those that might be less sensitive, or even age-insensitive.

Research using tasks that are sensitive to knowledge of results, and require discrete and precise movements, such as moving an object 80°, or moving one's hand a specified distance, show a main effect of age. Elderly start at a disadvantage relative to young subjects, but their rates of learning are comparable. As might be expected, when no knowledge of results is provided there are no age differences; there is little improvement in either age group.

Given the increasing importance of computers for everyday living, it is not surprising that there has been research in learning to use the computer. Basically, results indicate that the elderly can learn to use computers, but that the learning process takes longer and involves more errors in training than is true for younger subjects. Given the complexity of this task, it will take a substantial amount of research to isolate the important components.

Laboratory investigations have employed the pursuit rotor, mirror tracing, or problem-solving tasks involving motor skills. For example, in mirror tracing, the subject is to trace a figure (often a star) using only the information gained from the view of one's hand in a mirror. Tasks like mirror tracing produce larger age-related decrements than simpler tasks. It seems likely that the large age decrement may be due to the heavy cognitive component of the task. To trace an object using the mirror image requires that the subject mentally rotate the image and then translate that information into a hand movement. Thus the task is analogous to performing in a dual-task situation, where it has been consistently found that the age-related decrement on either task in a dual-task situation is greater than that for each task separately. These results are consistent with the idea that, relative to younger adults, elderly have reduced cognitive capacity to apply to various tasks.

Other research on the effects of expertise are also consistent with this theoretical explanation. A comprehensive study utilizing skilled typists ranging in age from 20 to 70 years found that when typing rate was measured by interkey interval, the regression line relating typing to age was essentially flat. There was no relationship between age and typing rate. For the same typists however, there was a strong positive relationship between age and choice reaction time. The typical age-related slowing was apparent in the choice reaction time task, but not on the typing task. Thus it appeared as if the subject's expertise led to an exception in the area of expertise. Because of the control afforded by the laboratory experiment, it was determined that the compensatory process responsible for this exceptional behavior was that older typists were more sensitive to characters farther in advance. Because the motor-skill portion of the task was automated, the older typists were able to commit some of their free cognitive resources to the task of translating letters into movements. Similar compensatory mechanisms may be seen in other areas where skills can become highly automated, such as reading, driving, or operating some machinery.

Because the typing tasks were performed under controlled laboratory conditions, there were few distractions. It is not clear how the results would have turned out had subjects also had to deal with distractions such as conversations or other noises. To the extent that subjects would have to use some of their cognitive resources to block out or otherwise deal with the extraneous stimuli, one might expect a decrement in typing speed, with a greater decrement for the elderly. By appropriate design of experimental conditions one could conceivably test different predictions generated by the cognitive resources and inhibition theories. [See MOTOR CONTROL; SKILL ACQUISITION.]

III. VERBAL TASKS

Because the use of words in spoken or written form is unique to human beings, all tasks reviewed in this section used human participants. The tasks used do differ on several dimensions, including the type of setting (laboratory, natural setting), and whether the focus of the research is more basic or applied. Tasks included here are paired-associate, serial, and free-recall learning.

A. Paired-Associate Learning

The classical associationist view that learning consists of the formation of individual stimulus–response (S-R) bonds or associations led to the use of paired-associate learning (PAL) as a standard task. In a typical associative-learning task, subjects are presented a list of pairs of events (often words), with one arbitrarily designated as the stimulus, and the second as the response. In the anticipation procedure, the stimulus is presented for some amount of time (e.g., 2 sec), during which the subject is to try to produce the response. At the end of this anticipation interval, the response (or the S-R pair) is presented for some amount of time (e.g., 2 sec) for study. One trial is completed when all pairs have been presented. After a brief interval a second trial begins, using the same procedure, but with the pairs, not the S-R units within the pair, in a different order. On the second and subsequent trials the subject must try to say the response aloud before it is shown. The entire process is repeated for either a fixed number of trials or until a preset performance criterion is reached. A concrete example might be useful.

A college student has created a deck of 3 × 5 cards with a Spanish word on one side of each card, and its German equivalent on the other side. The student goes through the deck of cards, looking at the Spanish word, trying to say the German word out loud. Whether or not she says the correct word she turns over the card and looks at it. After going through the list she shuffles the cards and repeats the procedure.

It is clear from a great deal of research with college students that PAL is composed of a number of different component processes, each of which may play a role in various situations. Because at least some of these processes may be age sensitive, a brief review of them is relevant.

Several processes deal with the stimulus terms. Stimulus differentiation is the process of discriminating among the various S elements in the list. When using meaningful and distinctive items such as words, this process is less important than when the items are meaningless and have overlapping physical features. A related process, stimulus selection, may be invoked when items have overlapping features, but one of which allows each stimulus to be uniquely identified. For example, if the stimuli in a list were JSF, SFJ, FJS, KLW, LWK, WKL, the subject could select the first letter of each trigram as the effective stimulus, and essentially ignore the remaining letters.

Similar processes are involved on the response side. Response learning refers to the acquisition of the responses (i.e., being able to report the responses irrespective of the S-R pairing). Acquiring the responses may involve response integration, or making the response a unit, especially when it consists of a series of unrelated letters.

The final set of components refers to the associations between stimuli and responses. The S-R, or forward association, is the ability to produce R when presented S. This association may be strengthened by rote rehearsal or mediation. The R-S, or backward association, is the ability to produce S when presented with R. The R-S associations develop incidentally, and often augment the S-R associations.

Results of cross-sectional and longitudinal studies indicate that increasing age is associated with less proficient PAL. Elderly subjects attain a lower level of learning after a fixed number of trials and take more trials to reach the same criterion. Although early studies suffered from serious methodological problems, more recent studies correcting these problems have produced similar results. Analysis of the learning curves (i.e., trial-by-trial performance data) of young and elderly indicates that both the intercept and the slope were affected by age. That is, not only do the elderly learn less on the first trial of PAL (which could be due to nonlearning factors), but their rate of learning (i.e., the number of additional items acquired on each trial), is lower than for younger subjects.

Although it is clear that there are substantial age effects in PAL, the more important question concerns the possible locus of those effects. As in motor-skill learning, where cognitive aspects of the task are more age sensitive than other aspects, it may be that some of the component processes are more age sensitive than others.

1. Response Slowing

There is ample evidence that at least part of the age-related decrement in PAL is due to the general slowing seen with age. Consistent with the idea that older adults are simply slower than younger adults is the finding that older adults make more omission than commission errors; they are more likely not to give a response than to give a wrong response, especially at faster presentation rates. Independent manipulation of the length of the study and anticipation intervals in PAL produces a significant Age × Anticipation Interval interaction, but a nonsignificant Age × Study Interval interaction. Short anticipation intervals are much more detrimental to elderly than to younger subjects, but there is a constant age difference in performance when the length of the study interval is varied. This pattern of results is consistent with the general slowing hypothesis. The process of producing a response is speed sensitive; therefore it should also be age sensitive. Processes involved in forming an association should be less dependent on timing, and thus should be less age sensitive. However, lack of an Age × Study Interval interaction does not imply that younger and older adults do not differ in the processes or methods used to form associations.

2. Response Learning

Research examining the role of response learning has compared conditions where response learning is required in PAL to conditions where it is not required. In one study, subjects learned the responses prior to PAL, whereas in another the responses were provided. Subjects simply matched the responses with the appropriate stimuli. Both manipulations greatly reduced

but did not eliminate the age decrement in PAL. Also, increasing the effect of the response learning phase by using nonsense syllable responses increases the age decrement. Thus, acquisition of the responses per se is important, but it is not the only important process.

3. Stimulus Learning

Stimulus learning is really a compilation of several subprocesses, including stimulus differentiation and stimulus selection. There has been no aging research addressing this aspect of associative learning, but several predictions are possible. Stimulus selection is one manifestation of a general mediational process, and to the extent that the elderly are less likely to spontaneously use mediational processes, they will be less likely to use this strategy. Finding age differences in stimulus selection would be interesting, but it would not be helpful in distinguishing between capacity and inhibition theories.

4. Backward Associations

One tests for the presence of the backward association by presenting the R terms and asking the subject to produce the S terms. In this situation, S-term recall is only a fraction of R-term recall, and the older subjects recall fewer S terms than younger subjects. This age difference may be explained as due to general slowing in the following manner. If R-S, or backward associations are strengthened as a result of incidental contiguity of the R and S terms during rehearsal of the pairs, then one would expect an asymmetry in recall of R and S terms. For example, rehearsing the pair (cot–gloomy) three times would result in a string of six words. In the string there would be three instances of S-R (cot–gloomy) contiguity, and only two instances of R-S (–gloomy cot–) contiguity. Because older adults rehearse more slowly than younger adults, in a given interval they would have fewer opportunities for the R-S association to occur, resulting in lower R-S recall.

5. Forward Associations

As in studying the role of response learning, one can look at the effect of age on association formation by comparing conditions requiring minimal associative learning with conditions requiring substantial associative learning. One way to make this comparison is to use pairs with preexisting associations, such as table–chair. Associatively related pairs should be much easier to learn (i.e., take less rehearsal) than unrelated pairs (slow–chair). If the elderly have difficulty forming associations, reducing the impact of that process should reduce or eliminate the age difference. Studies comparing learning of lists of associatively related pairs with unrelated pairs bear out this prediction. Acquisition of the S-R association is an age-sensitive process.

There are two methods of forming S-R associations; rote rehearsal and mediation. Although the associations can be learned by rote rehearsal, research comparing different types of rehearsal (elaborative, maintenance) indicates that it is a relatively ineffective method and a less preferred alternative, at least for college students. In one study, college students reported using mediators of various types on up to 75% of the pairs they studied. If younger and older adults rely differentially on rote rehearsal or mediational strategies, there will be age differences in PAL. Results of two early PAL studies indicated that older subjects were less likely to spontaneously use mediators of any sort, with 36% of the elderly and 68% of the younger subjects reporting mediator use. Also, young subjects reported using imaginal mediation (generating images or pictures) more frequently than verbal mediation (using sentences or connecting words), whereas elderly reported just the opposite. Basic research on mediation indicates that in general, imaginal mediation is more effective than verbal mediation. Thus, part of the age difference in learning S-R associations may be due to choice of mediational strategy.

Clearly mediational strategies produce faster learning, and younger subjects are more likely than older subjects to engage in mediation. However, the reason for the age difference in strategy has implications for possible remediation. If the age difference is the result of a "mediational deficit," that is, an inability to use mediators, then no amount of training or instructions in the use of mediators would reduce the age difference. However, if the age difference is the result of a "production deficiency," that is, simply not using mediators, then instructions and training should reduce or even eliminate the age difference.

In one study, subjects were given training both on the use and benefits of either imaginal or verbal mediators. Training in the use of imaginal mediators (relative to a no-training control) resulted in an 18% improvement for older and an 11% improvement for younger subjects. The older adults showed signifi-

cantly more benefit from training than younger subjects. However, training did not eliminate the age difference in PAL. In the no-training conditions, performance of the younger subjects (70% correct) was 35% better than performance of the elderly (35% correct). For those subjects receiving mediational training, the age difference was reduced to 28%. As might be expected from research on the generation effect, supplying mediators was less effective for both age groups than having subjects generate them. Results for conditions involving training in the use of verbal mediators were similar to those involving imaginal mediators. Training resulted in a 12% benefit for the older adults (35 vs. 47% correct) and a 1% benefit for the younger adults (70 vs. 71% correct). As before, training did not eliminate the age decrement in PAL, with age differences of 35 and 24% for the control and training conditions, respectively. It is possible that the elderly suffer from a production deficiency, but that the instructions and training were simply not sufficiently powerful to eliminate the deficit. However, it is also reasonable that other factors contribute to the deficit.

Use of mediational techniques, particularly the construction of images, is an effortful process, and part of the age differences in use of mediational strategies may be due to the effort needed to construct images. If the elderly are unwilling or unable to devote the necessary effort or capacity to this process, then they would be more likely to choose less capacity-demanding processes. At present, the data do not allow a choice among theories explaining aging effects. Statistical control of response time indicates that response slowing plays a role in the difficulty of constructing images, but there are no data relating to the other theories.

B. Transfer

Transfer effects are found when learning one task either facilitates (positive transfer) or interferes with, (negative transfer) learning the second task. Typically the first task is an explicit list learned in the lab, although sometimes the associations are assumed to have been learned as part of the participant's previous language experience. For example, learning the pair table–lamp in the lab might be made more difficult because of the strong association, table–chair that the subject had acquired outside the laboratory. Analysis of transfer in PAL has revealed two types of component processes, nonspecific and specific. Each will be discussed in turn.

1. Nonspecific Transfer Effects

Nonspecific transfer effects refer to improvements in performance on a second task that are independent of the specific content of the tasks. The only two types that have been identified, warm-up and learning-to-learn, both produce positive transfer. Warm-up is getting used to the particular pacing and timing procedures of the task, and is generally eliminated as a factor after a few trials. Although there is no research on this factor as related to aging, the response-slowing hypothesis would predict that it is most likely to become important as the rate of responding or the pacing of the task increases, with older adults requiring more warm-up time than younger adults.

The second factor, learning-to-learn (LTL) is defined as an improvement in performance on successive unrelated tasks. The amount of LTL can be substantial. One study with college students found a 2.75-fold increase in rate of learning as a function of extensive practice. These subjects learned 36 successive unrelated PAL lists (one list per day, every other day). Mean trials to criterion on the 10-item lists dropped from about 11 on the first list to 4 on the last list. No similar studies have been conducted with older adults, although some data do indicate that under self-pacing conditions the rate of improvement due to LTL is comparable for younger and older adults. However, results of other studies indicate that younger adults show a larger increase in LTL across lists than do older adults. Thus, no definitive conclusions are possible at this time.

2. Specific Transfer Effects

The study of specific transfer effects evolved from the component analysis of PAL, and research into the effects of various components. To examine these components requires two PAL lists with specific relations among the stimuli and responses. Some of the paradigms used in these investigations are summarized in Table II.

The paradigm used to control for the effects of warm-up and LTL is the A–B, C–D paradigm, where A refers to the stimuli and B to the responses in the first list. The stimuli and responses in the second list (C–D) are unrelated to the first list. Note that because

interest is in the learning of the second, or transfer list as a function of the *relationship* between the two lists, all paradigms have a common second list. Variations in the relationship between the two lists is accomplished by changing the stimuli or responses on the first list. Thus there are no possible confounds attributable to the different paradigms having different second lists; all groups learn the same second list.

3. Negative Transfer

Negative transfer results from several sources of incompatible or interfering forward associations, backward associations, or both acting together. Each of these sources can be examined by using the appropriate transfer paradigm. As seen in Table II, forward associations are the primary source of interference in the A–B, A–D paradigm. The associations formed during A–B learning are elicited during A–D learning and interfere with learning the second list. Results of various studies indicate that younger and older adults show about the same amount of negative transfer in the A–D paradigm, a finding somewhat at odds with what is expected if the elderly have more trouble inhibiting irrelevant responses (i.e., keeping them from intruding and interfering). Because this research was not designed to test the inhibition hypothesis, it may not have afforded an appropriate or sensitive test.

The role of the backward association in transfer is assessed through the A–B, C–B paradigm. To the extent that during C–B learning the B term elicits A, the first-list stimulus, it will interfere with the acquisition of the new backward association. As mentioned earlier, older adults have weaker backward associations (i.e., they evidence poorer R–S learning during acquisition of the A–B list). Thus, during C–B learning there should be less interference from the backward associations, and therefore less negative transfer for the older adults. However, methodological problems in those few studies using the C–B paradigm allow for no conclusions.

The A–Br paradigm involves interference from both forward and backward associations, and thus might be expected to produce large amounts of negative transfer. Studies using this paradigm have found that both younger and older adults show large amounts of negative transfer, and that older adults show substantially more negative transfer than younger adults. These results are consistent with both capacity and inhibition theories, but do not provide

Table II Transfer Paradigms in Paired-Associate Learning

Paradigm	First list (A–B) pairs Stimulus–response	Second list pairs Stimulus–response	Processes involved and transfer effects[a]
A–B, C–D (Control)	bug sleepy rug rural vat tranquil hat playful	cot gloomy kin insane gum dirty dam tearful	Warm-up + Learning to Learn +
A–B, A–D	cot sleepy kin rural gum tranquil dam playful	cot gloomy kin insane gum dirty dam tearful	Warm-up + Learning to Learn + S-R[b] association −
A–B, A–Br	cot insane kin tearful gum gloomy dam dirty	cot gloomy kin insane gum dirty dam tearful	Warm-up + Learning to Learn + S-R association − R-S association −
A–B, A–B′	cot dingy kin crazy gum sullied dam crying	cot gloomy kin insane gum dirty dam tearful	Warm-up + Learning to Learn + S-R association +/− (depends on mediation)
A–B, C–B	bug gloomy rug insane vat dirty hat tearful	cot gloomy kin insane gum dirty dam tearful	Warm-up + Learning to Learn + R-S association −

[a]Note: + indicates positive transfer; − indicates negative transfer
[b]S-R, stimulus–response; R-S, response–stimulus.

analytical comparisons to be able to distinguish between the two.

4. Positive Transfer

As can be seen in Table II, positive transfer over and above nonspecific transfer effects can be expected only in the A–B′ paradigm. In this paradigm the second-list responses are related (e.g., associatively, semantically, acoustically) to the first-list responses. To the extent that the subjects can use the first-list response as a mediator during second-list learning, transfer should be positive. Inability to recognize or use the B–B′ relationship would leave a nominal A–D, or negative transfer paradigm. Thus, one might expect less positive transfer for older than for younger adults. Limited data bear out this prediction, at least as far as initial performance on the second list.

IV. SUMMARY

Three general conclusions can be drawn from the research on the effects of normal aging on learning.

The most general conclusion might be "You *can* teach an old dog new tricks; it just might take a little longer." Normal aging produces decrements in almost all areas of learning, although the amount of the decrements will vary substantially across areas and individuals. Second, research psychologists have identified some of the age-sensitive component processes involved in various learning tasks, which should allow others to develop appropriate compensatory strategies. Finally, current theoretical accounts of age-related differences in learning offer additional insight into the aging process and to a better understanding of the learning process itself.

BIBLIOGRAPHY

Anderson, J. R. (1995). *Learning and memory: An integrated approach.* New York: Wiley.
Birren, J. E., & Schaie, K. W. (Eds.). (1985). *Handbook of the psychology of aging* (2nd ed.). New York: Van Nostrand Reinhold.
Birren, J. E., & Schaie, K. W. (Eds.). (1990). *Handbook of the*

psychology of aging (3rd ed.). San Diego: Academic Press.

Craik, F. I. M., & Trehub, S. (Eds.). (1982). *Advances in the study of communication and affect: Vol. 8. Aging and cognitive processes.* New York: Plenum Press.

Craik, F. I. M., & Salthouse, T. A. (Eds.). (1992). *The handbook of aging and cognition.* Hillsdale, NJ: Lawrence Erlbaum Associates.

Kausler, D. H. (1994). *Learning and memory in normal aging.* San Diego: Academic Press.

Kausler, D. H. (1991). *Experimental psychology, cognition, and human aging* (2nd ed.). New York: Springer-Verlag.

Lovelace, E. A. (1990). *Aging and cognition: Mental processes, self-awareness, and interventions.* Amsterdam: North Holland.

Poon, L. W., Rubin, D. C., & Wilson, B. A. (Eds.). (1989). *Everyday cognition in adulthood and late life.* Cambridge: Cambridge University Press.

Salthouse, T. A. (1991). *Theoretical perspectives on cognitive aging.* Hillsdale, NJ: Lawrence Erlbaum Associates.

Leisure

John R. Kelly
University of Illinois

I. Theory
II. Meanings of Leisure in Later Life
III. Leisure and the Later-Life Course
IV. Leisure and Community
V. Challenges to Functional Aging
VI. Programs, Resources, and Policy

Consumption   Use and possession of goods and services that in leisure produce experiences that are primarily dependent on the actions and products of others. Contrasts with existential or developmental leisure.

Development   The process of individual change in competence, identities, and selfhood. Development, involving a dilemma between security and challenge, is one dimension of leisure that has a life-course career.

Leisure   Usually defined as activity engaged in primarily for the experience itself. Leisure is defined inclusively as a multidimensional phenomenon with both personal and social meanings, more a dimension than a domain of life.

Roles   In the life course, roles are sequences of institutional positions or engagements—work, family, community, and leisure—that intersect in changing constellations of expectations, requirements, and opportunities.

Serious Leisure   High investment activity that is challenging and developmental, requires a consistent discipline of skills, and usually produces a social world of adherents.

LEISURE is activity focused on the experience rather than instrumental outcomes. It is not leftover time. For older adults, economic roles become less determinative of schedules, but leisure remains connected to the continuation of multiple family and community roles. Leisure involves dialectics between engagement and disengagement, existential action and social relationships. Older adults continue doing most of what they did before. Patterns of leisure incorporate considerable everyday activity that is informal and accessible. Leisure is multidimensional in its themes of personal expression and social interaction. Community and family roles are both the context and the content of much leisure. There are, however, dimensions of involvement, personal development, and social identity as leisure provides a context for maintaining a sense of ability, worth, and continuity of self. Limitations in resources and socialization are based in gender, social class, and other factors, including age itself. Older adults may also become more consumers of marketed leisure than actors engaged in continued active growth. Programs and policies should see older adults as being defined by abilities and resources rather than segregated by age in ways that limit their spheres of worthwhile action.

I. THEORY

When leisure is defined as a derivative of work, then it may seem irrelevant to a period of life in which work roles and commitments are largely left behind. If leisure is defined as the time remaining when all work obligations are completed and all maintenance functions satisfied, then retirement would seem to require a reorientation of the entire work–maintenance–leisure–rest scheme of the workday and its presumed 8–8–8 hourly division of time. A more realistic analysis of the web of life roles and requirements, however, suggests that such a simple design does not represent the variations and interpenetrations of obligation, expectation, and expression that ebb and flow through life with or without a central work role.

A. Approaches to Defining Leisure

Leisure has been defined in a number of ways that may be more complementary than conflicting. Even the classical approaches of Aristotle combine freedom from necessity and an application to activity that develops the self and enables the free citizen to exercise wisdom in social and political responsibility. Such freedom and development, of course, rested on the subjugation and service of slaves and women and the exclusion of the poor.

More recent approaches have each had a somewhat different focus. Leisure has frequently been defined as time, usually "discretionary time." The assumption has been that work obligates major and primary blocks of time and that other social roles also have time requirements. Leisure, then, is secondary and largely leftover. One problem with this approach is that research discovers relatively little such time because all obligations are seldom completed. Leisure as time is more often chosen as a temporal priority, even if only for rest and refreshment. When emphasis is placed on its discretionary nature, then leisure is part of the value system or temporal rhythm of life.

This approach raises the question of relevance for those who no longer have central work roles. Does leisure in retirement become central, replacing work, and primary rather than secondary? Can leisure replace work in the scheme of social time as well as of life meanings and satisfactions? Such a metaphor would call for a radical restructuring of life in its values as well as allocations. Most research on retirement, however, now suggests more continuity than change, more adaptation than disruption.

A second approach to defining leisure focuses more on the experience of the individual than time allocations. John Neulinger was a psychologist who emphasized the perceptions of freedom and noninstrumentality in activity undertaken primarily for its own sake. Mihaly Csikszentmihalyi refers to "flow" as the experience of immersion and involvement in action in which skill and challenge meet. A more common tactic is to define leisure as activity done primarily for the experience rather than extrinsic ends. Leisure, then, is activity defined by the primacy of the experience itself, of being done for its own sake. Such an approach is not in any way age-bound; nor does it require any special setting, time period, or form. It is not derived from any other role or meaning.

A third approach has a more existential theme. It focuses on the action of "doing something," even though the activity itself may be mental or imaginative as well as physical. It incorporates the form of the activity implying that the meanings of contemplation or daydreaming may differ from those of competitive sport or a wine-and-cheese party. Furthermore, this action metaphor has a longer time frame than a total concentration on the immediate experience. Leisure may be developmental in the sense of personal growth or social in relational bonding. Insofar as action creates meaning, such an approach incorporates what the actor becomes as well as experiences. Growth and development may be enhanced by an immersion in the experience and action. Leisure, then, is defined as action of any form engaged in primarily for the experience, autotelically rather than instrumentally.

The fundamental distinction may be whether leisure is seen as a domain of life or as a dimension. As a domain, it has parameters of time and space that are based in the social allocations of the society. Recognizing that people play in the workplace, build and express relationships on the playground, and learn and grow everywhere, the work–family–leisure boundaries may be fuzzy. Nevertheless, leisure and play are a domain of life that is central for the young, recedes to a secondary place when work and family roles are ascendent, and then gains in centrality in later life.

As a dimension of life, leisure is more of a theme that may be found in different forms anywhere and any time. There is off-task behavior at work, play in the kitchen, and expressive behavior anywhere. This approach may be especially responsive to the leisure of women that has tended to be less segregated in time and place from role-related activity. From this perspective, leisure is a theme that is part of the rhythm of life throughout the life span. In later years, life may be reallocated and restructured so that the expressive theme takes new and renewed forms. The playful dimension, however, of focus on the experience rather than products retains its meanings in later life. Leisure does not emerge simply as a replacement for lost roles.

B. Later-Life Changes

The stereotypes of later life may be negatively quite leisure related. Allegedly those who have dealt with the time pressures of multiple roles now are faced with a vast emptiness. Time scarcity is presumed to be replaced by time surplus. The first age of the life course is filled with learning and the second with productive activity, with work paid and unpaid. The third age is characterized by emptiness. Learning is for the young and valued production for midlife. The old are just filling in their remaining time. As a consequence, they have an abundance of time and a lack of meaningful engagement. The programmatic implication of this view is that they are sitting around waiting for someone to offer something that fills their emptiness. That something may be an age-segregated program of trivial and undemanding activity appropriate for their presumed incompetent state, or it may be the mass entertainment of home electronics with simplified and visible controls.

In the 1960s, the so-called disengagement theory was based on research findings that the geographical range, social circles, and activity repertoires of older persons tended to shrink. Age was associated with a disengagement—some forced as with age-based retirement, some based on age-graded expectations of withdrawal, some on diminished abilities or resources, and some on preferences. The theory proposed that such withdrawal was functional for the society and for the individual. Roles and their demands were often given up voluntarily. Disengagement might reflect priorities and preferences: a reassessment as well as lost opportunities and diminished resources.

Elaboration of disengagement soon pointed to its differential nature. Some roles are lessened or relinquished and others not. Family roles tend to remain central. Organizational ties vary stressing the community-producing dimension of membership. Although disengagement may be selective and reflect changing priorities as well as reduced resources, it is far from universal. From the perspective of leisure, it may be more one side of an engagement–disengagement dialectic than a process endemic to aging. The balance of leisure investment may shift in later life. There is no evidence, however, that developmental engagement is limited to the relatively young.

The analysis was based on evident role losses in the economy, the community, and even the family. Most older persons were assumed to no longer be primary caregivers for children. There was little recognition of the current reality that when they reach the age of 65 most adults still have a living parent, who often requires caregiving. Even leisure was assumed to be part of the overall decline in social involvement. The implication, however, was that in general this disengagement was appropriate and even satisfying for older persons. It was also implicitly a recognition of the social embeddedness of leisure. Negative social definitions of aging may discourage or even exclude older persons from engagement in an age-stratified society.

II. MEANINGS OF LEISURE IN LATER LIFE

It is hardly surprising that disengagement theory was soon countered by some sort of "engagement theory." To begin with, why should a diminution of one role alter a person's entire orientation to life? Most research has found that adults are more family-centered than work-centered. Family roles change, but for most continue in some form and context. Community roles, especially in organizations such as churches, are not cut off at an arbitrary age. Even work role changes may be anticipated and prepared for. Retirement may be a process over time rather than an abrupt trauma. Furthermore, leisure involvements may offer more continuity than change, even when there is some selective drawing back from particular settings and activities. One factor in such continuity is the multidimensional nature of leisure. As indicated above, leisure is not time left over from and residual to work as much as experience and action, a dimension more than a domain.

A. Dimensions of Leisure Meaning

It is the variety of leisure that is self-evident:

1. There are countless environments for leisure: natural and constructed, open and confining, quiet and clamorous, inviting and forbidding.

2. There are the social contexts of leisure: solitary and intensely interactive, silent and communicative, unstructured and rule-intensive, cooperative and competitive, exploratory and role-rigid, strange and familiar, comfortable and threatening, mass and intimate.

3. There are the mental states of leisure: relaxed and tense, detached and intensely involved, preoccupied and exhibitionist, free and conforming, excited and bored, seeking novelty and defensive, sensual and rational.

There is almost no activity that might not be undertaken primarily for the experience, and no experience that would be excluded, from high risk and challenge to withdrawal and self-protection. Many such meanings as they have been found in research on older persons have been categorized as experiential, developmental, and social meanings of leisure:

1. Experiential leisure: intrinsic satisfaction, solitude, diversion, relaxation

2. Developmental leisure: intellectual challenge, personal competence, health, expression and personal development, creativity

3. Social leisure: social interaction, social status, service

He further analyzes factors in the process of choice of leisure activity. Among them are temperament, environment, social learning, personality, and preference or taste. Over the life course, persons learn a repertoire of interests and skills. They make personal investments of time and energy, financial investments in equipment and resources, and social investments in associations and commitments. It is no wonder that such investments lead to considerable continuity in leisure that is not overturned by an event such as retirement. On the other hand, little is known about how those meanings of leisure may change as an individual moves into the later periods of the life span. The same kinds of activity may become more or less developmental or social. The multidimensional configurations of meaning may shift in subtle but significant ways. Even so, such investments are generally linked to consistencies of personality development and of self-definitions or identities. Such continuities are based on a history of satisfaction, especially when particular skills and associations are involved. Activities usually combine several meanings. For example,

persons engaged in amateur archeology have the experience of doing a dig in a natural environment, the intellectual challenge of recognition and classification, the development of learning with a consequent enhancement of selfhood, and the formation of associations with friends who share the experience. Such dimensions often persist through even radical life changes.

There are a number of models that focus on particular elements of leisure meaning. A line of research by the United States Forest Service has identified a set of "experience preference domains" based on recreation experiences in natural environments, including enjoying nature, physical fitness, reducing tension, escape, outdoor learning, sharing values, independence, family, introspection, achievement, stimulation, rest, leadership, risk, risk reduction, meeting new people, commodity use, and nostalgia. Note that some seem contradictory and suggest that combinations vary by locale, companions, and personal orientation. Furthermore, the same person may seek escape and solitude on one occasion and intense social interaction and communication on another. There is evidence that persons tend to seek a *balance* that may shift as role demands change.

Mihaly Csikszentmihalyi now has a cross-cultural research base for his concept of "flow." Flow is the experience of deep immersion in an activity in which skill and challenge are matched. When skill is too high for the challenge, boredom results. Too great a challenge produces anxiety. The key concept is challenge that requires an exercise of competence, usually developed over time through discipline and commitment. Throughout the life span, flow is accompanied by a sense of worth and ability as well as deep satisfaction in the experience itself. Recent research has demonstrated that the highest levels of satisfaction for older persons are correlated with high investment activity that produces the flow experience. Such experience is one side of a leisure dialectic that also includes disengagement and low intensity. Flow is a psychological component of leisure that is existential in the sense that it creates meaning. Existential approaches involve taking action that is significant to the self.

Other models of leisure emphasize social dimensions rather than individual. Television occupies the most time in what is usually low-intensity and low-communication consumption of entertainment. When questioned about the leisure that is most significant, however, two kinds of activity are commonly mentioned: the high investment activity requiring commitment and skill and activity done with other persons in a relationship of communication and sharing. Leisure is a context for the expression and development of relationships. Often the communication is more important than the activity context. Travel is not just getting away; it is usually getting away together.

There are, then, important dialectics of leisure. Leisure is both engagement and disengagement, existential and social, challenging and relaxing. One key to understanding the meanings of leisure in any life-course period is to ascertain the most satisfying balance of the dialectic. In no period, however, does one side disappear. As some of the role demands recede for older adults, then meanings of leisure that compensate for those losses may become crucial. Leisure may need to be more social as work associations diminish, more challenging and developmental as work tasks are left behind, and based on identities of worth and ability.

III. LEISURE AND THE LATER-LIFE COURSE

What do older people do as leisure? One answer, of course, is that they do pretty much what they have done before. There is no magic age at which they are transformed into quite different people with quite different interests and abilities. Especially the core of relatively low-cost and accessible activity continues much the same. Older people continue watching television, reading, interacting informally with family and friends, shopping, and just going on with home and community engagements.

A. Activity and Aging

There are, however, patterns of change. As indicated, core activities continue at least as long as older people live outside health-care institutions. In fact, the minority who move to recreation-based retirement communities may increase their levels of activity as they respond to the expectations and exploit the resources of the new environment. There is nothing inevitable about leisure in aging. Age itself is not a determinant of withdrawal.

On the other hand, aging is commonly accompanied by a pattern of activity constriction. Even the "active old" may experience decrements in energy and physical ability that may be associated with health conditions. Others lose some communication facility. Driving a car may become more limited in range and eventually given up entirely. Companions may drop out so that the social fabric of engagement is weakened or lost. Activities, locales, and associates may all become more constricted.

The stereotype of universal across-the-board dropping out, however, is not accurate. Studies in several communities do show an age-related overall decline in activity participation, especially in later years. For example, travel drops off significantly for those over 75, exercise and sport from age 45 on, and outdoor recreation, never at high levels, shows a linear decline in later years. On the other hand, community organization and church participation persists at levels close to 50%, social activities remain common, family leisure is reduced only for widows, cultural activity including reading continues, and other home-based activity is reduced only for those over 75. The pattern of constriction is selective, not universal. A life-course study in Houston found age-related reductions in dancing and drinking, movies, sports, outdoor activity, travel, and even reading, but no or small reductions in television viewing, talking with others, cultural consumption, entertaining, clubs, and home embellishment. Just as important, activities with developmental and creative components indicated little age-based declines. Solitary activity increased with age.

The point is that older adults continue activity that is appropriate, possible, and satisfying. There are changes, but not a total pattern of disengagement. Activity requiring high levels of physical exertion do decline as do those calling for costly or otherwise demanding travel. Both the social and developmental and existential components of leisure meaning remain important, however. Older persons demonstrate more continuity in leisure than once thought, in both activities and their meanings. [See Activities.]

B. Patterns of Constriction

What, then, are the elements of constriction in later-life leisure?

First, it is important to distinguish between the

active "young-old" and the frail. Age is only a rough indicator of activity and functioning. Frailty entails a loss of independence that is caused by a breakdown in one or more kinds of critical functioning. Most common for the "old-old"—usually those in their eighties or nineties—are mental and communicative losses. Others lose mobility. Significant for leisure is the ability to drive one's own car. Since 95% of those over 65 are not institutionalized and relatively few move to retirement communities, the stress here is on community-dwelling older persons with functional health and a viable income. Those lacking either or both of these prerequisites of viable aging are also limited in their leisure abilities and opportunities. All the "young-old" are not racing around in exciting leisure investment, but they are relatively able and active.

There are, however, a number of salient factors in activity constriction. Most often they combine to limit the range of activity. The first is economic. Income is quite limited for a high proportion of older persons. Many of the upscale offerings of travel packages, sun-belt second homes, and even special retirement housing developments are out of sight. A diachronic study of blue-collar retirees in the Midwest, however, found that on modest incomes they were able to continue most of the activity patterns developed in preretirement years. They were relatively satisfied with their opportunities and engagements as they aged in place until limited by health problems. Their pensions together with Social Security enabled them to support a modest leisure style that met their expectations. On the other hand, a high proportion of older persons, at or near poverty levels of income, find that they have little to spend on leisure, especially if they have demanding medical expenses.

A second set of constricting factors is based on health decrements. The ability to engage in rigorous physical activity may be diminished or lost due to chronic conditions that still permit relative independence in daily living. Strength, endurance, and agility may be lost. When such losses are accompanied by reductions in acuity of vision or hearing, the ability to engage in more demanding activity may be reduced or lost. Other leisure requires the ability to communicate, especially in a group setting, as well as mental quickness. Even if age is not a good predictor of functioning, later life sooner or later involves functional loss.

Third, there are also social factors in constriction. Significant companions may die, move away, or be unable to continue participation in joint leisure activity. The number of leisure companions who drive usually becomes gradually smaller. So much leisure involves sets of regular associates that such losses can have a major impact on participation.

C. Patterns of Continuity

Despite such constriction, there is also considerable continuity in leisure. As indicated above, informal social interaction and activity around the home do not have significant age-related reductions prior to frailty. The activities that fill the most time continue. At the same time, persons with major commitments to community organizations generally continue those affiliations, if on a modified schedule.

Less is known about continuity in the most demanding kinds of activity. When individuals have made a major commitment to skill-based leisure such as drawing, writing, musical performance, or even a physical proficiency, is there more likely to be continued engagement at some viable level than for activity that has been less central to one's life and identity? There is anecdotal evidence that central commitments in which older persons have a long-term investment are retained whenever possible. Such "serious leisure" involvements may even gain in salience when other roles are relinquished.

What are the leisure involvements that make the greatest difference in successful aging? Longitudinal studies find that activity outside the home, especially when it is physically active or socially involving distinguishes those with the highest later-life satisfaction. Other research has found that leisure with a continued commitment to activity that is challenging and deeply involving characterizes older adults with the highest levels of affect. The author has identified travel and cultural activity with the highest life satisfaction for those age 40–54 regardless of income, education, or other resources. Social leisure and exercise and sport also contribute moderately. For those aged 55–64, social, cultural, and travel activity contribute most with exercise and sport, outdoor recreation, and family interaction of moderate importance. For those aged 65–74, social leisure and travel are most salient along with cultural engagement. For those 75 and older, home-based and family activity contributed most to subjective well-being. Cultural leisure including reading and community organization participation (usually religious) also distinguish those who are most satisfied in those later years.

There seems to be a consensus that continuity is central. Furthermore, leisure is significant in later-life satisfaction even when income, health, and other resource factors are controlled. The kind of leisure, however, distinguishes those with the highest levels of subjective well-being as measured by several different scales. First, it is leisure that gets people out of the home and into interaction with other people. Also, the *quality* of the relationships is more important than their number. Second, leisure that provides some challenge and an opportunity to exercise continued competence contributes most. Such leisure is an opportunity to demonstrate to the self and others that one is still a person of worth and ability. Third, such leisure is usually built on a history of investment in skills, communities of common activity, significant relationships, and self-definitions. Leisure provides an opportunity for demonstrated continuity of self, what one researcher calls the "ageless self."

How does this emphasis on continuity square with findings of constriction and disengagement? Baltes and Baltes have proposed a pattern of "selective optimization with compensation." This approach has been analyzed in the context of leisure continuity. Selection is based on prior experience as environmental and personal resources are diminished. By focusing energy and resources on selected activities, even to the exclusion of others, the older adult can still achieve satisfying results. Compensation refers to adaptation to altered conditions and abilities to maintain as much continuity as possible. The focus is on the older person who remains an active agent in shaping and reshaping life. The older person is still the same person who has dealt with change in the past and takes existential action in later life.

D. Later-Life Issues

Of course, care must be taken to recognize that age-based cross-sectional research does not provide an adequate indication of how age cohorts may differ. Those who are in their forties and fifties now may be different in their seventies and eighties from those now in those age categories. They will have higher levels of education, demonstrated to be correlated

to a breadth of leisure interests and development of repertoires of skills. They may have somewhat greater financial resources, although the division between the comfortable and the deprived may be more pronounced. One basic question is whether they will be able to maintain a higher level of continuity with previous patterns of leisure, especially those requiring greater physical and mental ability.

A second set of issues revolves around economic change. One researcher has presented an argument that the requirements of a modern capitalist economy have created a time famine. Especially those with the dual roles of establishing economic careers and families are under considerable time pressure in what have traditionally been child-rearing years. This pressure is especially acute for single parents and women in dual-career marriages. Furthermore, those most central to productivity, such as research and development professionals, are called upon to put in extended work hours. At the same time, others are being declared marginal, either relegated to intermittent employment or involuntarily retired at a relatively early age. This means that some experience acute time shortages that impact leisure as well as family roles. Others have more time, especially in their fifties and sixties, but uncertain financial resources. For many, the time crunch is lessened in later years and leisure expected to take a more central place in time allocation. Just how this will affect traditional retirement is unclear.

For example, the stress on continuity may, for many, be rendered problematic by a life course with many changes and disruptions. Regular progressions of family roles are interrupted by divorce, work careers by shifts and periodic unemployment, and community roles by geographical mobility. Is leisure also disrupted by such changes, or does it provide possibilities of continuity in investment and identity amid change? One possibility is that activities may change more than their meanings. The persistent meanings of leisure—personal, developmental, and social—may endure when environments and forms change. If so, then "selective optimization with compensation" would characterize the most functional later-life leisure. Leisure may offer opportunity to adapt to change through the continuation of previous engagements that reinforce valued identities.

Third, are there developmental changes that influence the leisure of older adults? Such issues have been analyzed by distinguishing preretirement from the period from retirement to frailty. In preretirement the developmental themes of dignity versus control become more important than achievement and recognition. Leisure may bring acceptance and even affection from others, help to stave off despair, and restructure time. It is also a time in which generativity, supporting the development of others through mentoring, may become more salient. Mentoring, however, seems more a continuation than a new theme for women. In retirement the themes of autonomy and integration come to the fore. Meaningful integration refers to sharing and loving relationships, often expressed in leisure. With work roles largely past, leisure may also provide opportunity for effective decision and action. Valued identities may be maintained in leisure in a process of adaptation. This analysis supports the findings of the continued significance of social and family leisure as well as of activity that allows for personal development.

IV. LEISURE AND COMMUNITY

The "Kansas City" studies of adult life conducted in the post-World War II period gave special attention to leisure. Leisure in a community context was seen as interwoven with the roles of work, family, and community. The social stratification of the community was reflected in leisure associations and styles. Leisure was not a leftover, residual, or marginal aspect of life, but tied to and embedded in the total context of life.

Psychological approaches to leisure have tended to isolate the experience and separate it from the rest of life, even when it is located in the workplace and the home. Sociological approaches have tended to see leisure in community contexts and as having shifting meanings through the life course. For example, leisure is dramatically impacted by becoming parents, entering the paid workforce, and, consequently in later life by launching children and retirement. In the Kansas City study, middle-aged people were found to have high, medium, and low levels of leisure participation that were either balanced between home and community or primarily home-centered. All were tied to other gender-differentiated roles of work, parenting, spouse, homemaking, and citizen. The earlier community studies in "Middletown" demonstrated how the stratification system of the community was carried out in leisure styles. Such styles not only symbolized adults' place in the community, but also reflected economic conditions and resource limitations of the Depression.

In a more recent study of adults in Peoria, Illinois, the author found that almost half of the men and women balanced investments in work, family, and leisure in ways that were responsive to their sets of roles and related resources. About 20% were primarily family-focused with both work and leisure seen as largely instrumental. Almost none had either work or leisure alone dominant in their value orientations or resource allocations. Rather, the most common picture of leisure was of a significant domain of life that was consistently tied to other roles and that changed through the life course. Nevertheless, there were also leisure interests and commitments that retained salience through severe changes and disruptions.

The foremost of those ties to other roles is clearly with the family for most adults. The profoundly social nature of leisure makes primary relationships central to its meaning. Whatever the nature of the relationships, those in family or other committed relationships are the most common leisure companions. Furthermore, the meanings of the common activity usually involve the expression and/or development of that bonding. "Strengthening relationships" is one of the most common reasons given for valuing leisure choices. This close connection between primary relationships and leisure would seem to become even more important in later years. There are indications that men come to place greater value on friendships as they age. Women find their support systems in same-sex friendships when widowed. Those who are confidants also are usually leisure companions. Helena Zaniecka Lopata has described how social status and position are altered by becoming a widow, especially when a woman's social niche has been primarily defined by being a spouse. Leisure activities are one element in the process of adaptation, of recomposing a life, when women are drawn together. Even for those in the transition to frailty, caregivers and supporters are also primary leisure companions. Leisure is a context for the expressive and communicative aspects of significant relationships as well as for developing new connections after losses or environmental changes. [*See* SOCIAL NETWORKS, SUPPORT, AND INTEGRATION.]

There has been considerable attention given to the participation in voluntary community organizations by older adults. Several studies have found that only 15% of adults age 65 and above participate at some level in "senior" organizations. If older adults are in one organization, it is most likely to be the church. Those involved in community organizations, especially religious ones, are usually found to be healthier and happier. Such organizations provide a sense of continuity when other roles are lost. Those who are retired or relieved of familial caregiving can take positions of responsibility in churches in ways that provide a sense of continued worth. There is also a variety of avenues for volunteer service, although such engagement tends to drop off for those in their mid-seventies and older. It is clear that age-segregated organizations do not appeal to most older adults. Rather, community organizations that offer some continuity in relationships, responsibilities, and the exercise of abilities are most significant in later life. [*See* VOLUNTEER ACTIVITY BY OLDER ADULTS.]

Again, leisure is not a set-apart or leftover domain of life. Rather, it is linked with the entire complex of social roles. As those roles shift in later life, so leisure changes as well. It may become more salient to self-identification and provide continuities when other identities are altered. It may become more central to social bonds, to self-definitions of worth and ability, and to the ordinary round of life. Such increased salience, especially in retirement, does not imply that leisure is reserved for the last segment of the life course. Rather, satisfying engagement most often is based in previous experience. Some older persons may take up entirely new activities, perhaps something long desired and delayed. Most often, however, leisure remains woven into the ongoing fabric of life in ways that help maintain both selfhood and relatedness.

V. CHALLENGES TO FUNCTIONAL AGING

Does this mean that leisure is essentially a positive dimension of a seamless transition in later life, that its contributions to later life are incremental, at least until the decrements of frailty? Often that is the case as research correlating regular activity with life satisfaction and coping with changes indicates. There are, however, a number of challenges to this positive view

of leisure in later life. These challenges are based in both the nature of activity and in limits to access to resources.

Again, the challenges presuppose that leisure is not separate and easily manipulable. Rather, it is embedded in the full set of social roles and subject to threats related to those roles. For example, it is clear that a loss of employment in midlife impacts leisure in more ways than loss of income. The entire rhythm of life is upset so that leisure and family life both also have to be reconstituted. Later life commonly involves multiple significant changes, sometimes in sequence and "on time" and sometimes in traumatic and unanticipated clusters. Time and money allocations, the availability and expectations of companions, ability and mobility, community and natural resources, and even self-images are impacted by associated changes. The loss of a spouse may give a woman some freedom from expectations and responsibilities, but that freedom comes in company with losses that have profound social and psychological ramifications.

Also, it is important to remember that leisure is not just an undifferentiated set of things that some people do. Rather, different kinds of activity have different meanings and outcomes. Just doing something, filling time, does not yield the same outcomes of satisfaction as do regular engagements with other persons that offer an opportunity to demonstrate competence and worth. Just taking up some unchallenging entertainment does not provide the same sense of continuity and value as does an action seen as of value to and by others. "High investment" activity, "flow," and engagement connote possibilities that have been found to make a significant difference in any period of life, even the final one.

A. "Old Folks" Leisure

What are the stereotypes of "old folks'" leisure? Bingo, World War I singalongs, and lots of television may come to mind. The image is of low-demand, segregated, and low-quality activity. Older adults are viewed as being done for and even done to. They are not engaged, developmental, and active individuals who may be found almost anywhere doing almost anything.

Now the image is changing, partly due to education by social gerontologists and partly due to new marketing. Older adults, the active old, have been discovered as an important market for all kinds of goods and services. As aging is no longer associated with low incomes and younger cohorts become smaller, the purchasing power of the old is attracting more attention. But, for what?

Adults age 50 and above are the hot travel market with retirees especially targeted for off-season tourism. At one extreme is the rare "adventure," environmental, or educational tour that may challenge both the body and the mind. On that side of the spectrum there is also the remarkable Elderhostel worldwide program stressing education, the challenge of new environments on a budget, and social integration. At the other extreme is the common package tour in which everything is arranged so that older travelers can have a fleeting glimpse of a series of traditional attractions. Almost any trip, however, involves some stimulation, social interaction, and change.

Of more concern is the day-to-day fare of that most common entertainer, television. Older persons do watch more television than those engaged in multiple roles. Furthermore, they have the schedule flexibility to watch during the daytime hours dominated by a plethora of talk shows and soap operas. However formulated, such entertainment is low in demand, high in routinization, and filled with images of a consumptive lifestyle. There is little to challenge the mind and nothing to involve the viewers with real persons. It is, by design, just the opposite of the kinds of activity associated with higher levels of later life-satisfaction.

The problem is that little imagination has been put into anything other than drawing out the consumption propensities of older adults, even to the point of television "home shopping" networks on cable. The kinds of opportunities that are demanding of effort—physical, mental, or social—must generally be sought out or even developed by older persons who are too often seen as passive consumers of products, services, and programs. The kinds of opportunities provided by the market sector tend to be cost-intensive, requiring the expenditure of money more than focused effort. Functional aging calls for a variety of opportunities and engagements that are in an active rather than consumption mode, out of the home rather than situated in electronic ease.

B. Factors in Deprivation

Even though there is now no correlation between age and poverty, there remain many deprivations that are significant for later-life leisure. There remains a significant negative correlation between age and income, especially for single, widowed, or divorced women. For the most part, these are factors that have discriminatory impacts throughout the life course.

The first is gender. Women have come to later life with both a different set of socializing factors and deprivations. From childhood on, females are socialized more toward supporting and nurturing roles than males. Entering the later periods of life, such socialization combined with systematic work discrimination means that women alone generally have fewer financial resources in later life due to lower incomes and greater likelihood of erratic career trajectories. Those who enter later life in an intact marriage, on the other hand, are more likely to have social resources that fit their socialization. They often have placed greater emphasis on relationships as well as having developed skills in nurturing and supporting roles that remain available to older adults. There is only a start on research on the meanings of retirement for women, even now that most women are in the paid workforce. Furthermore, women are more likely than men to avoid going out, especially at night, due to fear of assault. Women in the cohorts now in their later years have had more limited opportunities than males, especially in regard to physical activity and sports. They are less likely to have a consistent history of physical activity that is built on school participation. On the other hand, they more often have developed skills and interests in the arts. Both cultural and physical activity are significant in higher satisfaction in later life. [See GENDER ROLES.]

The second factor is social class. The poor lack one of the prerequisites of successful aging, adequate income, and are more likely to lack the other, functional health. Activity combined with social integration characterize the most successful aging, but only when the economic and health base is present. Most of this analysis of later-life leisure presupposes income and health. Although 95% of older adults are community-dwelling and 80% are above the poverty line, access to opportunities in leisure often requires entry fees, reliable transportation, equipment, and other items of cost. Market provisions come at a higher cost, one reason why low-cost senior centers are disproportionately joined by those women with lower incomes. The increased reliance on the market sector in leisure will heighten the income factor in access to opportunity. [*See* ECONOMICS: INDIVIDUAL.]

The third factor is race and ethnicity. In a society that has persistently and arbitrarily discriminated against persons of color, an individual's entire history of leisure has been limited in both access and resources. Those now in their seventies and eighties were subjected to segregation in such facilities as swimming pools and theaters in their younger years and in access to lodging and food while traveling for much of their lives. The experiences taken for granted by middle-class Whites were not open, at first by law and later by custom, to African Americans and persons of identifiable ethnic origins. The development of a repertoire of skills and interests was limited. Now laws have changed, but more subtle negations of welcome and encouragement remain. [*See* RACIAL AND ETHNIC DIVERSITY.]

The overall point is that the opportunity structure of leisure is at least as discriminatory as is the economic opportunity structure, in parallel but distinct ways. As the constriction patterns of later-life leisure become manifest, current and past limitations become more acute. Both the prerequisites and the socialization histories for a full range of leisure engagements are lacking for a substantial proportion of the population. The challenge is to develop opportunities that are at least adequate for all and that are open, inviting, and stimulating for as many as possible.

VI. PROGRAMS, RESOURCES, AND POLICY

At the present time, there is no consensus in the United States that access to leisure resources and opportunity is fundamental to human welfare. Even the literature on aging is ambivalent. On the one hand, there are stories in *Modern Maturity* and other journals about the marvelous older persons who engage in exciting, demanding, and valuable activity. They are held up as examples to emulate. On the other hand, there is little support for research and programs with labels such as leisure, recreation, or even activity. The ideology of the culture seems to be that leisure is either peripheral to real life or is wholly the responsibility of the individual. It is a private rather than public matter, to be provided by the market sector and paid

for out of discretionary funds. As a consequence, the relatively few provisions targeted for older persons have tended to be at one end of the scale or the other. There are the high-end resort communities for those with quite high incomes and assets. Conversely, there are low-quality and low-cost programs, often in buildings abandoned by other users, for the poor elderly. Fortunately, there is every indication that the healthy and moderate-income middle class are able to fill their active later years with much the same activities they have engaged in most of their adult lives. Furthermore, resources that are not age-segregated such as libraries, parks, and churches offer possibilities of continuity.

A more detailed set of recommendations can be found in the article on "Activities" in this Encyclopedia. A summary follows:

1. Age designation should be avoided whenever possible. Older persons are not attracted by programs that require them to redefine themselves as "old." Retired persons can be targeted by scheduling and program descriptions without any need to limit ages or use labels such as "senior" or "golden."

2. Age segregation is equally unnecessary in most activities. Remember that the most "successful" community organization measured by the participation of older adults is the church, which includes a full range of ages. The experience and results of low-impact aerobics classes, for example, are not damaged by including both pregnant and retired women.

3. Place segregation is also unnecessary and unwelcome. Adult book clubs should be in the public library, not the senior center. Painting classes should be at the community college, sport and exercise at the recreation center, and volunteering at family services.

4. In general, older persons are attracted by quality. Programs should be offered in the locales and with the leaders that are associated with excellence.

5. Programs should have a social component as they are scheduled and organized.

6. There should be an adequate offering of opportunities that are developmental and challenging. Older persons need to learn and exercise skills as long as and as often as possible. There is so much evidence of the benefits of such activity that it is surprising that the old stereotypes still rule any plans.

7. Insofar as possible, capable older persons should be required to make their own priorities and organize their own programs.

As indicated in the overall analysis, there is now an adequate base of comprehensive research on which to base at least the principles of a public policy. In Europe there are terms such as "activation" that identify the basis for programs that support and enhance continued development and expression in later-life leisure.

BIBLIOGRAPHY

Kaplan, M. (1979). *Leisure: Lifestyle and lifespan.* Philadelphia: W.B. Saunders.

Kelly, J. R. (1995). *Leisure* (3rd ed.). Boston: Allyn and Bacon.

Kelly, J. R. (Ed.). (1993). *Activity and aging: Staying involved in later life.* Newbury Park, CA: Sage Publications.

Kleemeier, R. W. (Ed.). (1961). *Leisure and aging.* New York: Oxford University Press.

Osgood, N. (Ed.). (1982). *Life after work: Retirement, leisure, recreation, and the elderly.* New York: Praeger.

Life Course

Tamara K. Hareven

University of Delaware

I. The Life-Course Paradigm
II. Timing over the Life Course
III. Historical Changes in the Timing of
   Life Transitions
IV. The Cumulative Impact of Earlier Life Events on
   Subsequent Ones
V. The Subjective Life Course
VI. Conclusion

The **LIFE-COURSE PARADIGM** provides a way of examining the interrelationship between individual development and the family's development as a collective unit over lifetime and under changing historical and social contexts. The life-course approach emerged in the 1960s from the convergence of several strands of scholarship: research on social relationships, including family development and intergenerational relations, on age temporality and the aging and society paradigm, and on concepts of life-span development. Joining an earlier tradition of the study of lives in sociology and social psychology with new scholarship in the social history of the family, the life-course paradigm is developmental as well as historical. Unlike the individual "life cycle" and the "family cycle," the life-course paradigm is not concerned with a priori stages. Rather, it emphasizes the timing by which individuals and families make their transitions into and out of various roles and developmental tasks in relation to the social time clocks. The essence of the life-course paradigm is the synchronization of "individual time," "family time," and "historical time," and the cumulative impact of earlier life events as shaped by historical forces on subsequent life events.

I. THE LIFE-COURSE PARADIGM

Central to the life-course paradigm is the study of human lives situated in historical time and place, the timing of lives, the interdependence of lives, and human agency in its interaction with historical forces. The life-course paradigm encompasses individual development and collective development of the family, under varying social, cultural, and historical contexts. It focuses on individual life paths, as well as on the meshing of individuals' careers over their lifetimes with those of the family. It is especially concerned with the synchronization of several distinct roles in people's lives, such as work and family.

From a life-course perspective, the family is viewed as a constantly changing entity, rather than as a monolithic institution. The family serves as the arena in which various individual lives interact. Individual transitions into and out of different family roles, such as leaving home, getting married, setting up an independent household, becoming a parent, and in later life, entering widowhood are interrelated with the changes in the family as a collective unit. An understanding of these patterns also provides important insights into the process of decisionmaking within the family.

Underlying this concept of linked lives is the question of "Who travels with whom over life, and how do these configurations change?" The life-course approach has directed attention to the fluidity of life trajectories and to the interlocking and separation of career paths of couples, siblings, parents and children, other kin, and unrelated individuals. A life-course perspective thus adds an important dimension to the study of kinship by examining changing configurations of kin with whom individuals travel together over their lives. Such configurations are formed and reorganized over the life course. As people move through life, kinship networks change in their composition, as do family configurations and those of unrelated individuals. Whether networks of individuals who associate over certain periods of their lives consist of kin, surrogate kin, friends, or other kind of associates, a study of their changing configurations provides an understanding of how social supports are shared and exchanged and how networks formed earlier in life have an impact on the availability of supports in later life.

In its emphasis on interaction with historical time, the life-course approach provides an understanding of the location of cohorts in their respective historical contexts. The earlier life-course experiences of each cohort, as shaped by historical events, also affect the availability of resources for their members and their modes of assistance and coping abilities in later life. Specifically, the life course enables scholars and policy makers to understand the historical circumstances that have affected the lives of the members of different cohorts, and helps explain the differences in the historical experiences shaping their respective life histories. It thus provides an understanding of the ways in which earlier life experiences of older adults, as shaped by historical events and by their respective cultural heritage, have affected their values governing family relations, their expectations of kin supports, and the nature of their interaction with welfare agencies and institutions. Patterns of providing support and expectations for receiving support in old age are part of a continuing interaction among parents, children, other kin and institutions over their lives as people move through historical time. Relations of mutual support are formed over life and are reshaped by historical events, such as migration, wars, and the decline or collapse of local economies. [See SOCIAL NETWORKS, SUPPORT, AND INTEGRATION.]

Specifically, patterns of generational assistance are shaped by values and experiences that evolve or are modified over the entire life course and influenced by people's respective cultural milieus. For example, in the United States ethnic values that were carried over from premigration culture call for a more exclusive

dependence on filial and kin assistance than do more contemporary attitudes. The latter advocate a greater reliance on supports from government programs and community agencies. Such differences in values are expressed in the caregiving practices and attitudes of successive cohorts.

A life-course perspective thus provides a necessary dimension and an integrating framework for the study of generational relations because it is both developmental and historical. It enables one to understand how patterns of assistance and support networks were formed over life and were carried over into the later years, how they were shaped by historical circumstances and by people's cultural traditions, and what strategies individuals and families followed over their life course in order to secure future supports for their old age. Hence, generational relations and kin assistance in old age can be best understood in the context of the entire life course and of the historical changes affecting people at various points in their lives. They are molded by individual and familial experiences and by the specific historical events that have impinged on people's lives. Rather than viewing older people as a homogeneous group, a life-course perspective views them as cohorts moving through historical time, each cohort with its distinct life experiences shaped by the circumstances encountered earlier in life. [See CAREGIVING AND CARING.]

A cohort serves as a significant unit of analysis for understanding the context of social change that impinges on individual life histories. The life-course approach draws a distinction between *generation* and *cohort*, concepts which have been frequently confused in the gerontological literature, and provides insight into the interrelationship of these two concepts. Generation designates kin relationships (for example, parents and children or grandparents and grandchildren); it may encompass an age span, often as wide as thirty years. A *cohort* consists of a more specific age group that has shared a common historical experience. Most important, a cohort is defined by its interaction with the historical events that affect the subsequent life-course developments of that group. A generation may consist of several cohorts, each of whom has encountered different historical experiences that have affected its members' life course. Even though cohorts serve as excellent units for measuring social change, they should not be viewed as monoliths. Within cohorts, internal differences along gender, class, occupation, educational background, and ethnicity are important variables in explaining individual differences in adaptation among various cohorts. [*See* COHORT STUDIES; GENERATIONAL DIFFERENCES.]

II. TIMING OVER THE LIFE COURSE

The essence of the life-course paradigm is the interrelationship of several types of time: individual time, family time, and historical time. Underlying these concepts of timing are two major dimensions: (a) The timing of life transitions in the context of historical change; (b) the synchronization of individual life transitions with collective familial ones and their impact on generational relations.

The concept of timing over the life course involves the movement of individuals over their life trajectories from one state to the next, rather than the segmentation of the life course into fixed stages. Such movements have been defined in life-course research as transitions. "Timing" thus designates when a transition or an event occurs in an individual's life in relation to external events. It is a way of assessing whether a transition conforms to or diverges from societal norms of timeliness and how its timing relates to that of other people traveling with the individual through life. Thus the variables used in the examination of timing are relative rather than absolute chronological categories. They are perceptual as well as behavioral markers for the people undergoing them. In this respect, age, although an important determinant of the timing of life transitions, is not the only significant variable. Changes in family status, needs, and in accompanying roles are often as important as age, if not more significant. The life-course paradigm emphasizes social age, rather than calendar age.

Transitions are processes of individual change within socially constructed timetables, which members of different cohorts undergo. Many of the transitions that individuals experience over their work and family lives are normative; others are critical or, at times, even traumatic. Transitions are considered "normative" if a major portion of a population experiences them and if a society expects its members to undergo such transitions at certain points in their lives in conformity with established norms of timing. Under certain conditions even normative transitions might become critical ones and might be perceived as turning points.

A. The Timing of Individual Life Transitions

The timing of life transitions involves the balancing of individuals' entry into and exit from different work, family, and community roles over their life course, especially the sequencing of their work lives, and educational and family transitions in changing historical contexts. In all these areas, the pace and definition of "timing" hinge upon the social, economic, and cultural contexts in which transitions occurred, and the cultural construction of the life course in different time periods and in different societies.

Long-term historical change has a critical impact on timing over the life course in several areas. In demographic behavior the timing of marriage, fertility, and mortality patterns shape changing age configurations within the family. Similarly, external economic changes in the opportunity structure affect changes in the timing of entry into the labor force, and ultimately, retirement. Institutional and legislative changes, such as compulsory school attendance, child labor laws, and mandatory retirement, shape the work-life transitions of different age groups, and eventually influence their family life as well. Social and economic forces and cultural values that are prevalent in specific time periods converge and directly influence the timing of life transitions and the social construction of the life course. Cultural norms governing the timeliness of life transitions and familial obligations also shape individual and collective family timing. The meaning of timeliness depends, therefore, on different societies' cultural construction of the life course, especially around the question of whether a certain transition is perceived as being early, late, or on time. For example, by what age is a woman considered an "old maid" if she is not married?

Within the larger societal definitions of timeliness, individuals and families negotiate the timing of their life transitions in relation to their own needs and expectations and those of their family members, as well as in relation to institutional and legislative requirements. Economic and institutional factors also affected the timing of life transitions, especially transitions into the work life. The commencement of work for young people depends on the regulation of child labor and compulsory schooling; older people's exit from the labor force depends on the changing regulation of the work life; and the timing of leaving home, marrying, or setting up a separate household depends on the availability of work, on a young person's economic resources, and on the family of orientation's economic circumstances. For example, the concept of "disorderly cohorts" has been introduced as an explanation for the mismatch between the career plans of different cohorts entering adulthood in relation to changing opportunity structures.

The timing of life transitions is contingent on several factors: the place of such transitions in an individual's life in relation to other transitions; the relationship of an individual's transition to those experienced by other family members; and the historical conditions affecting such transitions. For this reason the differences among cohorts in experiencing and defining transitions is crucial for understanding the impact of social changes on the life course.

B. The Synchronization of Individual Life Transitions with Collective Family Transitions

A key concept of the life course is the interdependence of lives. Hence, the synchronization of individual timing with that of the family as a collective unit is a central aspect of life course analysis. Far from being an individualistic framework, the life course has captured the complexity of the synchronization of "individual time" and "family time" with the larger societal spheres. As one researcher put it: "Much like an interactionist, the life course analyst moves back and forth between the individual and group level. The resulting portrait depicts family in people and people in family."

The crucial question is how people time and organize their entry into various roles (education, family, work, and community) over their life course; for example, how they time their exit from school and entry to work, their leaving home, their marriage, their setting up of a separate household, and their transition to parenthood in relation to their family of orientation. The synchronization of individual life transitions with collective family timing involves the juggling of various family and work roles over the life course. Individuals engage in a multiplicity of familial configurations that change over their lives and that vary under different historical conditions. Accordingly, they time their transitions into and out of various roles differently. A question particularly related to women's lives is how they sequence and juggle their family and work transitions in the context of changing historical conditions, and under the impact of the cultural norms and social time clocks governing the timing of life transitions.

As people move over their life course, their individual roles and their functions vis-à-vis the family also vary significantly over their lives. Most individuals are involved simultaneously in several family configurations, fulfilling different roles in each. A married person is part of both his or her family of origin and family of procreation; in addition, such an individual also figures in his or her spouse's family of origin and in the spouse's kin network. In situations where remarriage follows a spouse's death or divorce, the new spouse's family enters the orbit of relationships, and the former spouse's family does not necessarily disappear. Thus, the multiplicity of familial relationships in which individuals are engaged changes over the life course, and along with them, individual members' transitions into various roles are also timed differently.

The synchronization of individual transitions with familial ones is a crucial aspect of the life course, especially where individual goals are in conflict with the demands of the family as a collective unit. Historically, because of the high integration of individual careers with the collective goals of the family, life transitions, such as leaving home, that were viewed as individual moves, were in reality closely connected to the family collectivity. Similarly, marriage, which today would be considered the joining of two individuals, impinges on at least three families: the husband's family of origin, the wife's family of origin, and the couple's newly founded family. In preindustrial society, when most educational, economic, and welfare functions were concentrated within the family, decisions on the timing of transitions were family-based and were regulated according to family needs. In the nineteenth and twentieth centuries, decisions on timing have been closely articulated to age norms, and to external economic and institutional factors.

The life course has thus provided an important way of linking human development to institutional change. Research on the timing of life transitions has identified the institutionalization of the life course that emerged as a historical process. As one researcher put it, "The emergence of a set of rules and preferences implicit in the organization of schools, labor markets, and retirement systems are viewed as creating a standardized life course, with which the subjective life course [of the individuals] resonates." At the same time, however, the ways in which people responded to institutional changes and to opportunities or constraints was also shaped by their cultural traditions. In earlier time periods, collective familial considerations took priority over individual preferences. The expectation that individuals subordinate their own choices to those of the family's collective needs, at times, caused tension and conflict in family relations. Because individual lives in the past were more integrated with familial goals, the timing of transitions that are today considered "individual," such as starting work, leaving home, and getting married, was governed by collective family strategies.

The synchronization of individual transitions with familial ones impinges directly on generational relations and on the status of older people, especially when individual goals are in conflict with the needs and dictates of the family as a collective unit. In the nineteenth century, the timing of young adults' life transitions often clashed with the demands and needs of aging parents. For example, it was customary among certain ethnic groups in the United States for parents to discourage the youngest daughter from leaving home and marrying so that she would continue to support them in their old age. Similarly, the timing of later-life transitions affected more than one generation. For example, as some researchers have found, in contemporary society the death of "old-old" parents enabled caregiving children, who were themselves old, to begin providing for their own old age, as well as helping their adult children or grandchildren.

III. HISTORICAL CHANGES IN THE TIMING OF LIFE TRANSITIONS

Over the past century, under the impact of demographic, economic, and cultural changes, the timing of the major transitions to adulthood in American society, particularly leaving home, entry into and exit from the labor force, marriage, setting up a separate household, and parenthood, has undergone significant changes. Underlying these changes has been an increase in age uniformity in the timing of life transitions. Over the twentieth century, the timing of these transitions has become more uniform, more orderly in sequence, and more rapid. Timing has become more regulated according to specific age norms, rather than in relation to the needs of the family. Individual life transitions have become less closely synchronized with collective familial ones, thus causing a further separation between the generations.

In the nineteenth century, these transitions to adulthood were more gradual and less rigidly timed. The time range necessary for a cohort to accomplish these transitions (leaving school, starting work, getting married, and establishing a separate household) was wider, and the sequence in which transitions followed one another was not rigidly established. As some researchers have found, the nineteenth-century pattern of transitions allowed for a wider age spread within the family and greater opportunity for interaction among parents and young adult children. Later age at marriage, higher fertility, and shorter life expectancy rendered family configurations different from those in contemporary society. The increasing rapidity in the timing of the transitions to adulthood, the separation of individuals' family of origin from their family of procreation, and the introduction of publicly regulated transitions such as mandatory retirement, have converged to isolate and segregate age groups and generations from each other in the larger society.

Since early and later-life transitions are interrelated, these changes in timing have affected the status of older people in the family and their sources of support, generating new stresses on familial needs and obligations. In the nineteenth century the timing of later-life transitions to the empty nest, to widowhood, and out of the headship of one's own household followed no orderly sequence and extended over a relatively longer time period. Older women did experience more marked transitions than men because of widowhood, although the continuing presence of at least one adult child in the household meant that widowhood did not necessarily represent a dramatic transition into the "empty nest." The residence of children in the parental household extended over a longer time period, sometimes over the parents' entire life. Most importantly, the nest was rarely empty, because usually one adult child was expected to remain at home while the parents were aging. Demographic factors account only in part for the phenomenon of the "empty nest" in the twentieth century. Even when sons and daughters were in their late teens and early twenties, at least one child remained at home to care for aging parents if no other assistance was available.

In a historical context, early-life transitions were bound up with later ones in a continuum of familial needs and obligations. Hence the life transitions of the younger generation were intertwined with those of the older generation. Specifically, the timing of children's leaving home, getting married, and setting up a separate household was contingent on the timing of parents' transitions into retirement, inheritance, or widowhood. This interdependence dictated the need for parental control over the timing of adult children's life transitions. The strategies that parents and children followed in determining exchanges and supports in relation to the timing of life-course transitions represent, therefore, important theoretical and empirical considerations that require further exploration.

The erratic timing of life transitions in the nineteenth century was governed by family needs and obligations, rather than by specific age norms. Familial obligations, dictated by economic insecurity and by cultural norms of kin assistance, took precedence over strict age norms. Over the twentieth century, on the other hand, age norms along with the legislative and institutional regulation of the life course have emerged as more important determinants of timing than familial obligations. As greater differentiation in stages of life began to develop in the twentieth century, and as social and economic functions became more closely related to age, a segregation emerged between age groups and with it an increasing separation among the generations. In American and European society, this separation occurred first in the middle class, and was only later extended to the working class. The pattern still varies considerably among ethnic groups and among black families in contemporary society.

Since the 1980s, more erratic and flexible patterns in the timing of life-course transitions have emerged

again. Young adult children in and out of the parental home has become more widespread. Young adults stay on, or return home after having previously left. This contemporary pattern, however, differs from that of the past in a fundamental way: In the late nineteenth century children continued to stay in the parental home, or moved back and forth in order to meet the needs of their family of orientation by taking care of aging parents or, in some cases, of younger siblings. In contemporary society, young adult children reside with their parents in order to meet their own needs, because of their inability to develop an independent work career or to find affordable housing. Another contemporary variant of the filling of the nest is the return of divorced or unmarried daughters with their own young children to the parental household. In this instance as well, even though the relationship may be reciprocal, the main purpose generally has not been for the daughter to assist her aging mother, but rather to receive help in housing and child care.

IV. THE CUMULATIVE IMPACT OF EARLIER LIFE EVENTS ON SUBSEQUENT ONES

Historical events experienced earlier in the life course can continue to influence an individual's or family's life path in different ways over their lives. Historical conditions not only have a direct impact on individuals' life course at the time they encounter them, but they continue to affect their work and family careers indirectly through life. Thus, the social experiences of each cohort are shaped both by the historical conditions its members encounter at a certain point in their lives, and by the historical processes that shaped their earlier life transitions. Early or late timing of life transitions affects the pace of subsequent ones. The life stage at which individuals encounter such events shapes their impact on subsequent life, as well. For example, researchers have found, respectively, that cohorts that entered the Great Depression at high school age had to drop out or forego high school education altogether, and experienced unemployment punctuated by occasional temporary, menial work. These cohorts suffered delays in starting work and in marriage and family formation. Some never achieved a regular work career and were unable to rise occupationally beyond the level of their parents.

The impact of historical events on the life course may continue over several generations. Each generation encounters a set of historical circumstances that shape its subsequent life history and transmits to the next generation the impact that historical events had on its life course. Thus one generation transmits to the next the ripple effects of the historical circumstances that affected its members' life history. For example, delays or irregularities in the parents' timing of their work and family transitions as a result of the Great Depression affected the subsequent timing of the children's life transitions. The children thus experienced the impact of historical events on two levels: directly, through their encounter with these events in early adulthood, and indirectly, in the transmission of these events across the generations.

Cohort experience should not be misconstrued, however, as cohort determinism. The impact of historical events on the life course is cumulative but not irreversible. This means that the negative impact of societal forces at one point in one's life could be modified or reversed later. The life-course approach has emphasized an interactive rather than a determinist process between individuals and historical events.

For example, researchers have examined the impact of World War II on the cohorts of young men in Berkeley, California and in Manchester, New Hampshire, in answer to the question, "Why did the Great Depression not produce a lost generation?" They found that military service during World War II had a major role in reversing or mitigating the negative impact of the Great Depression on the lives of these young men from disadvantaged backgrounds. There was, however, a significant difference between the Berkeley and Manchester cohorts. Most of the Berkeley men who started from a lower middle- and working-class base were able to advance far into the middle class. However, few members of the Manchester cohort managed to rise above their class origins. Rather than propelling them into the next level, military service prevented them from slipping below their parents' working class status. These differences in the life trajectories of the young men were closely linked to the differences in the occupational structures in the communities in which these men lived. They were thus the products of the interaction of *time and place*.

V. THE SUBJECTIVE LIFE COURSE

A life-course perspective illuminates the links between behavior and perception. Although the actual timing of life transitions can be reconstructed from demographic and behavioral data, the meaning of timing to the individual and family members undergoing these transitions hinges on the examination of qualitative, subjectively derived sources, such as interviews, memoirs, autobiographies, and other forms of personal testimony. In this respect it is an important goal of life-course analysis to relate formal, behavioral transitions to people's subjective perceptions of their lives.

A. Normative Transitions and Turning Points

A life transition is considered normative if it conforms to socially constructed timetables. Normative transitions are generally voluntary, except when people are coerced to follow prescribed patterns of timing such as starting work and retiring early, or marrying later than is their preference. Even when transitions are voluntary, their timing may be involuntary, if the age at which they are expected to occur is legally imposed. Not all transitions are normative, however. Transitions can be "off time" or out of sequence and can be in dissonance with established norms of timing. Certain people might perceive a transition as normative, whereas others might perceive the very same transition as a turning point. All transitions, normative or nonnormative, could potentially become turning points.

A *turning point* is a transition that individuals perceive and experience as a process, which continues to influence subsequent events over their life course. A turning point is perceived, therefore, as the alteration of a life path or as a "life-course correction," requiring certain strategies and choices. The duration or continuity of a turning point is dependent on various conditions such as individual personality, expectations, earlier life history, resources, cultural values, and the historical conditions affecting one's life. Not all turning points, however, are of long duration. Some are more limited in time and may cause no major alteration of life trajectories at the time of their occurrence. People might interpret them retrospectively, however, as turning points.

Turning points can be related to normative as well as nonnormative transitions. A normative transition can be transformed into a turning point under the impact of certain events or circumstances. It is important to distinguish empirically between those transitions that remain ordinary events and those that become turning points. Under what circumstances could a normative transition become a turning point? Individuals or families may experience turning points under the impact of internal family crises, such as the premature death of a close family member, illness or physical handicap, loss or damage of property, or loss of a job. Most crisis-related transitions are the result of internal family conflicts or personal breakdowns; others may be externally induced by historical circumstances or events. The Great Depression and World War II, for example, have caused critical turning points in the lives of the people experiencing them. Cohorts encountering certain historical events do not necessarily experience their impact uniformly. One would expect variations within a cohort in the experience of turning points, in relation to the social background, resources, and earlier life history of various members of the cohort.

Even without the influence of external events, a normative transition could become a turning point under the following conditions: (a) When it coincides with a crisis or is followed by an unexpected crisis. For example, the birth of a child could become a critical turning point when it coincides with the father's loss of a job or with the mother's death; (b) when a normative transition is accompanied by familial conflict, resulting from asynchrony between individual and collective transitions; for example, when a daughter's timing of marriage clashes with her parents' need for continued support in old age; (c) when a normative transition is "off time" for example, if one retires early or becomes a parent for the first time in one's forties; and in a more critical case, with the onset of early widowhood; (d) when a normative transition is followed by negative consequences, unforeseen at the time of the transition, as for example, when a marriage ends in divorce; and (e) when social adjustment is required in relation to an otherwise normative transition; for example, when leaving home involves migration from a rural to an urban area and therefore necessitates many consequent social adjustments.

An empirical examination of turning points raises several methodological problems, which are related to the subjective construction of the life course. Turning points are defined by the individuals undergoing them as they perceive these events. The retrospective construction of the life course involves a subjective life review process, during which people narrating their life history might report those transitions and turning points that they perceive as critical at the time of the interview, rather than in the way in which they perceived them at the time of their occurrence. A life review or life history interview often leads to a revision or reassessment of the significance of earlier life events as time goes on. Turning points that individuals perceive as critical at one point in their lives may not be viewed as such several decades later. Past critical events may fade in importance while earlier or later turning points may suddenly assume new importance.

The cultural definition of turning points also poses methodological problems. Individuals normally use the constructs of their own culture to interpret their life course. Yet life events that are considered normative in one society might be considered critical transitions in another. For example, divorce has become an almost normative life event for younger cohorts in American society, but it is still considered a critical turning point in other societies. One needs to understand, therefore, the cultural and historical context within which specific life transitions occur, in order to fully grasp individuals' interpretation of the transitions they undergo. For example, "midlife crisis" was a relatively recent invention by popular psychology in American society. It was applied to middle-class women in particular, to describe the problems connected to menopause and the "empty nest" in midadulthood. Its definition was actually subject to cultural stereotypes resulting from the social construction of age and gender. Similarly, "adolescence" was recognized as a distinct stage of life in a specific historic time period. This concept was developed to define the social and cultural characteristics accompanying stages of psychological development related to puberty in the late nineteenth century. But even though all teenagers undergo a psychobiological transition in puberty, the cultural and social phenomena associated with it were not uniformly experienced in all societies, nor did they receive the same recognition in the past prior to the "invention" and popularization of adolescence in the early twentieth century.

VI. CONCLUSION

Both the study of the behavioral and subjective aspects of the life-course paradigm has enabled sociologists, gerontologists, anthropologists, historians, and demographers to capture the complexity of interaction between individual transitions and collective family goals as both change over the individual's and the family's life. This interaction between individuals, the family and kin group over time and under changing historical conditions is the very essence of the life-course approach. The theoretical framework of the life course encompasses the temporal interdependence of the individual trajectory analyzed with other family members, both in the nuclear family and in the wider kin group; the interdependence of the individual life course with the collective one of the family; and finally the interdependence of all these with institutions and with the larger processes of social change.

The-life course approach has directed attention to the dynamic interaction of time and place in people's lives and in institutions. It's very metaphors such as "clocks," "trajectories," "transitions," and "convoys" emphasize movements and synchronization that reflect various aspects of appropriate timing or ill-timing. It has thus made an important contribution to the understanding of aging. Earlier life-course experiences affect changes in individual aging. As one researcher put it, cohorts age in different ways "because they follow different trajectories."

By focusing on the synchronization of various levels of timing, individual, familial, institutional and historical, the life-course approach has provided a way of examining the interaction of lives with the forces of social history and an understanding of how external historical events impinge on individuals and families. It has offered a way of capturing the complexity in the impact of social change on people, and conversely, the contribution of people to modifying social change.

BIBLIOGRAPHY

Bengtson, V. L., Cutler, N. E., Mengen, D. J., & Marshall, V. W. (1990). Families and aging: Diversity and heterogeneity. In R. B. Sloan, & J. E. Birren (Eds.), *Handbook of aging and the social sciences.* San Diego: Academic Press.

Chudacoff, H., & Hareven, T. K. (1978). Family transitions to old age. In T. K. Hareven (Ed.), *Transitions: The family and the life course in historical perspective.* San Diego: Academic Press.

Elder, G. H. (1974). *Children of the Great Depression.* Chicago: Chicago University Press.

Elder, G. H. (1995). The life course paradigm: Social change and individual development. In P. Moen, G. H. Elder, & K. Luscher (Eds.), *Examining lives in context: Perspectives on the ecology of human development.* Washington, DC: American Psychological Association.

Elder, G. H., & Hareven, T. K. (1992). Rising above life's disadvantages: From the great depression to global war. In J. Modell, G. H. Elder, Jr., & R. Parke (Eds.), *Children in time and place.* New York: Cambridge University Press.

Hareven, T. K. (1982). *Family time and industrial time.* Cambridge University Press: Cambridge, England. Reprinted 1994, University Press of America: Lanham, NY, London.

Hareven, T. K. (1991). Synchronizing individual time, family time, and historical time. In J. Bender, & D. E. Wellbery (Eds.), *Chronotypes: The construction of time.* Stanford, CA: Stanford University Press.

Hareven, T. K. (1994). Aging and generational relations: A historical and life course perspective. *Annual Review of Sociology, 20,* 437–461.

Hareven, T. K., & Adams, K. (1996). The generation in the middle: Cohort comparisons in assistance to aging parents in an American community. In T. K. Hareven (Ed.), *Aging and generational relations over the life course: A historical and cross-cultural perspective.* Berlin: Walter de Gruyter and Co.

Hareven, T. K., & Uhlenberg, P. (1995). Transition to widowhood and family support systems in the twentieth century, northeast U.S. In D. I. Kertzer, & P. Laslett, (Eds.), *Aging and the past: Society, demography and old age.* Los Angeles: University of California Press.

Hogan, D. P. (1989). Institutional perspectives on the life course: Challenges and strategies. In D. I. Kertzer, & K. W. Schaie, (Eds.), *Age structuring in comparative perspective.* Hillsdale, NJ: Lawrence Erlbaum Associates.

Hogan, D. P., Eggebeen, D. J., & Snaith, S. M. (1996). The well-being of aging Americans with very old parents. In T. K. Hareven (Ed.), *Aging, generational relations and the life course: A historical and cross-cultural perspective.* Berlin: Walter de-Gruyter.

Modell, J., Furstenberg, F., & Hershberg, T. (1976). Social change and transitions to adulthood in historical perspective. *Journal of Family History, 1(1),* 7–32.

Neugarten, B. & Datan, N. (1973). Sociological perspectives on the life cycle. In P. B. Baltes, & K. W. Schaie (Eds.), *Life span development psychology: Personality and socialization.* San Diego: Academic Press.

Riley, M. W., Waring, J., & Foner A. (1988). "The Sociology of Age," pp. 243–290. In *The Handbook of Sociology,* N. Smelser and R. Burt (Eds.), Newbury Park, CA: Sage.

Rossi, A. S., & Rossi, P. H. (1990). *Of human bonding: Parent-child relations across the life course.* New York: Aldine de Gruyter.

Uhlenberg, P. (1978). Changing configurations of the life course. In T. K. Hareven (Ed.), *Transitions: The family and the life course in historical perspective.* San Diego: Academic Press.

Life Events

Jane D. McLeod

University of Minnesota

I. Theoretical Background
II. The Methodology of Life Events Research
III. Research on the Consequences of Life Events
IV. Life Events, Age, and the Elderly
V. Challenges and Future Directions

Psychological Distress Feelings of dis-ease or discomfort that may be manifested in physiological changes, such as a rapid heart beat, or in mood changes, such as depression.

Stress Initially defined as the rate of wear and tear in the body, this term has come to represent the difference between the demands placed on an individual and his or her potential capacity to meet those demands.

Stressor An objective or subjective experience that has the potential to create physical or psychological distress.

Well-Being A state that encompasses any or all of positive mood, good physical health, and general life satisfaction.

LIFE EVENTS are objective life changes or transitions that prompt the need for adjustment. They disrupt or threaten to disrupt one's normal routines and activities and thereby threaten well-being. Life events are typically conceptualized as acute stressors, such as job loss or death of a spouse, in contrast to chronic stressors that are ongoing conditions that challenge adaptational capacities. However, life events and chronic stressors are related in two ways. Life events may create chronic stressors, as when job loss results in long-term financial problems. Life events and chronic stressors are also related because most presumably acute events happen over time. For example, retirement, which is often treated as a life event, may involve a series of decisions over time, with consequent entrances into and exits from the labor force. Life events have been linked to changes in physical health, mental health, and immune functioning. Much of the research on life events attempts to specify the conditions under which such changes will occur.

I. THEORETICAL BACKGROUND

A. Classic Works

Life events research is part of a broader program of research concerned with the causes and consequences of life stress. The work of three scientists was particularly influential in the early development of stress research. The first, W. B. Cannon, reviewed laboratory research on animals and case studies of medical patients to argue that emotionally provocative experiences, such as pain and fear, create physiological and bodily alterations that help animals cope with the experience. For example, heightened adrenal gland activity in the face of fear gives animals extra energy to fend off the potential threat. Cannon focused on the adaptive function of these physiological alterations, but he noted that, if they were not relieved in some way, they could prove pathogenic.

Adolf Meyer extended Cannon's argument in two ways. He suggested that normative changes, such as graduating from school or the birth of a child, require adjustment and thereby have pathogenic potential.

He also argued that the pathologies that result from life changes could be psychological as well as physical.

Finally, Hans Selye conducted extensive animal experiments that demonstrated that a variety of physical stressors (e.g., cold, pain) elicited the same syndrome of physiological reactions, which he called the General Adaptation Syndrome. This syndrome is characterized by stages of alarm, resistance, and exhaustion. Alarm is a stage of heightened physiological activity during which the animal responds to the potential threat. Resistance is a stage of adaptation during which the animal concentrates its energies on actively resisting the stressor. The final stage, exhaustion, does not follow inevitably, but occurs when the stressor overwhelms the animal's capacity to resist.

Within these works can be found the main tenets of stress research: that stress affects health by overwhelming adaptational capacities; that individuals vary in their capacities to adjust to stress; and that ordinary life changes can have pathogenic effects. Researchers applied these tenets to life events by arguing that life events have consequences for well-being to the extent that they disrupt the homeostasis of bodily and psychological systems. By extension, the more life change individuals experience, the more likely will their resistance be overcome and the more likely that disease will result. Because of its origins in research on physical and physiological responses, virtually all life events research focuses on pathological outcomes rather than on the potential of life events to contribute to positive outcomes like psychological growth and flexibility. Initial research in this area also paid little attention to the personal and social contexts in which life events occurred.

B. Subsequent Theoretical Developments

The theory linking life change to well-being has been elaborated over the years in an attempt to better specify the conditions under which life events have implications for well-being. Subsequent theoretical developments have maintained the fundamental belief that life events affect well-being by overwhelming adaptational capacities, but they differ from early theories in two ways: they argue that the subjective interpretation of an event is what determines responses rather than the amount of change the event creates; and they posit that the personal and social resources available to the individual influence the impact of events. [See PSYCHOLOGICAL WELL–BEING.]

The first theoretical elaboration involved the shift away from positing change per se as the relevant characteristic of life events towards the view that *undesirable* change has more potential to harm individuals than does desirable change. This perspective has been very influential in life events research. In fact, to the extent that desirable changes are even considered, they are usually seen as potentially ameliorative in the context of undesirable events, or as predictors of positive well-being. Because research on desirable changes is less well developed than research on undesirable changes, the relationship of desirable changes to well-being is poorly understood.

Social psychological theories of helplessness further specify the focus on undesirable change by arguing that undesirable events that are also uncontrollable have the most pronounced psychological effects. Individuals feel helpless in the face of such events, and helplessness generates psychological damage. Furthermore, uncontrollable events lead to greater impairments in immune functioning which, in turn, may lead to disease onset.

Following a similar logic, life span developmental researchers propose that the timing of events vis-à-vis life stage importantly influences their effects. According to this perspective, most major events occur according to a socially prescribed timetable. For example, employed persons can reasonably anticipate the age at which they will retire. Events that occur at unexpected, nonnormative times may provoke more psychological distress than expected, normative events because they afford less opportunity for anticipatory coping, and because social expectations for the appropriate timing of events may influence the responses of individuals, their friends, and their loved ones.

Other theorists, most notably Leonard Pearlin and George Brown, focus on the role context within which events occur as the determining factor in their effects. They argue that life events influence psychological distress only to the extent that the events create ongoing difficulties in enacting major social roles. For example, retirement would lead to increases in psychological distress only to the extent that it leads to enduring problems in one's role as a breadwinner. Role-based arguments have special relevance for the elderly inasmuch as many life events common to old age—retirement, death of a spouse, major illnesses—involve transitions into and out of valued social roles.

Related to role-based arguments are theories that propose that undesirable life events are emotionally distressing only when an individual's identity importantly derives from the domains of life in which those events occur (i.e., to the extent that the events are "identity-relevant"). The theory of identity relevance has been clearly articulated by Peggy Thoits. However, it has proven difficult to operationalize with standardized interviewing procedures in part because ratings of the salience of different life domains may change as a result of life events.

Identity-relevant events may have particularly potent effects on the elderly. Some theorists have proposed that, as people age, the challenge they face is learning to accept the person they have become over the years. Identity-relevant events have the potential to interfere with the process of integrating one's real self with one's ideal self by exposing discrepancies in those self-conceptions. Furthermore, changes in identity-relevant domains of life may erode feelings of mastery or control—feelings that are already challenged by the process of aging. [*See* IDENTITY, PHYSICAL.]

II. THE METHODOLOGY OF LIFE EVENTS RESEARCH

Research on life events has focused on the consequences of life events, although some studies of the origins of life events in social conditions have been conducted. Each area of inquiry can be subdivided in a number of ways, the most pertinent of which is the distinction between research on aggregate life events and research on specific life events. Most early studies of the consequences of life events considered the psychological effects of specific events, such as bereavement, or screened the histories of medical patients for evidence of stressful experiences. Beginning with the development of measures of aggregate life events exposure, research on the physical and psychological effects of multiple events became more common.

Research on aggregate life events has the advantage that it attempts to consider the full range of stressful experiences that individuals face as a predictor of well-being. It has the disadvantage that it offers little insight into the processes responsible for life event effects. In contrast, studies of specific life events provide rich detail about adaptation to those events, but they often offer little understanding of the broader context of stress in which those events occur, and of the general laws that govern their effects.

This article focuses on research involving measures of multiple events for three reasons: this type of research is more strongly identified with the life events rubric; methodological developments have been more extensive in this area; and other articles in this encyclopedia discuss the common life events of old age.

A. The Social Readjustment Rating Scale

The development of aggregate measures of life events parallels theoretical developments in the area of life stress. The first comprehensive measure of life events, the Social Readjustment Rating Scale (SRRS), was developed by Thomas Holmes, Richard Rahe, and their colleagues. They used U.S. Navy medical records to compile a list of 43 events commonly associated with the onset of disease or with injury. The list included experiences as disparate as "troubles with the boss," "death of a spouse," and "vacation." Events were then rated by a convenience sample of respondents for the amount of readjustment they implied, where readjustment was defined as "the amount and duration of change in one's accustomed pattern of life." Raters were asked to consider personal experiences as well as the experiences of others they knew to assign typical readjustment scores to each event. The scores ranged from 0 to infinity on a scale for which a standard readjustment rating of 500 was set for marriage.

The SRRS represents what is usually called a life events checklist or inventory. Respondents to whom it is administered check off or report the events they experienced during a given period of time. The readjustment ratings for those events are summed to create a measure of total life stress.

The SRRS has been criticized both for its content and for its use of uniform readjustment ratings. With respect to the former, the SRRS underrepresents events for women, the elderly, and children—a natural consequence of its origins in data from the U.S. Navy. Although researchers have attempted to create measures of life events that better represent the experiences of diverse groups of persons in subsequent studies, a central dilemma in these attempts is the difficulty of knowing when all relevant events have been identified.

In addition, the SRRS includes both desirable and undesirable changes, reflecting the assumption of its authors that change is the most relevant characteristic of life events for understanding their relationships with physical and mental health. As noted above, however, desirable changes may be less likely to have a damaging effect on health than undesirable changes. If that is true, measures that combine desirable and undesirable events would attenuate the relationship between life events and health.

The rating scheme of the SRRS implicitly assumes that events require the same amount of readjustment regardless of the circumstances under which they occur and the specific characteristics of the persons to whom they occur. Theorists who give a central role to the subjective interpretation of events in determining their effects find that assumption untenable. If these theorists are correct, by failing to take differences in interpretations of events into account, scales like the SRRS underestimate the relationship between life events and health.

In practice, the ratings that are assigned by the SRRS make little difference. Correlations of wellbeing with simple counts of life events are similar to the correlations using readjustment ratings. As a result, readjustment ratings are seldom used. Rather, attention has shifted to developing life events measures that distinguish between events that are thought to have stronger or weaker relationships with wellbeing. The dimensions that have been examined include desirability, controllability, expectedness, and severity.

B. Measuring Dimensions of Life Events

A key debate in the measurement of life events dimensions is the appropriateness of using self-reported ratings of these characteristics versus objective ratings determined by expert judges. Scholars who favor self-reports argue that stress is, by definition, a joint function of the objective stressor and the meaning that persons give that stressor. Thus, adequate measures of life stress must incorporate both components. Using this approach, for example, respondents are asked to report whether each event was desirable or undesirable, and separate counts of desirable and undesirable events are calculated. (In some cases, average desir-

ability ratings or other functions of self-reported ratings may be used.)

Opponents charge that using self-reports confounds measures of life events and well-being. (Confounding refers to a logical overlap in the meanings and measures of two concepts.) Specifically, psychological distress influences interpretations of life experiences. For example, depressed persons interpret their experiences more negatively than do nondepressed persons. Thus, any observed relationships between life events and depression based on self-reported characteristics of events could reflect bias in the ratings of events rather than the effects of events on depression.

Opponents of self-reported ratings propose, instead, that ratings of the characteristics of life events be made by expert judges based on a review of the circumstances surrounding those events. The most widely known example of this approach is the Life Events and Difficulties Schedule, developed by George Brown and his colleagues. In the context of a semistructured interview, respondents are asked whether or not they experienced any of 40 different events. Interviewers probe for the circumstances leading up to, surrounding, and following the events using unstructured questions. A group of researchers then reviews these descriptions and, in conjunction with information about the personal background and social characteristics of respondents, assigns ratings of the threat posed by the event (long-term versus short-term), the desirability of the event, and the extent to which the event is independent of the physical and mental state of the respondent. Through careful training and monitoring, Brown and his colleagues maintain high levels of consistency in ratings across raters.

Brown's approach has its limitations, however. It is an expensive procedure to use and extensive training is required. In addition, because the contextual ratings of events are made using information about the individual's life history and social characteristics, the ratings are not independent of those characteristics. Furthermore, although the ratings are intended to reflect only the objective circumstances surrounding the event, the respondent's account of the event may have already been colored by his or her response in ways that are difficult to identify and control.

Brown's work has made an important contribution, not only to the conceptualization and measurement of life events, but also by identifying an important concern in studies of life event effects: the possibility of reciprocal causation. That is, events may cause psychological distress, but psychological distress may also cause events. For example, a spouse's depression may be the result of marital conflict, but it may also be the source of that conflict. Failure to control for this possibility can lead to inflated estimates of the effects of life events on physical and mental health. There is widespread recognition of this problem among life events researchers. Brown's work represents the most systematic effort to address it.

Other researchers have attempted to capitalize on the strengths of Brown's approach to life events ratings while avoiding its limitations. Their scoring method, the Structured Events Probe and Narrative Rating Method, begins with a checklist of events, and uses detailed probes to elicit a narrative about the circumstances surrounding the event. Different probes are used for different events, and probes are applied systematically. Event descriptions are rated by two judges who evaluate the desirability and "fatefulness" of the event, where fatefulness is defined as the degree to which the event is outside of the control of the person (analogous to Brown's notion of independence). Events are also rated for the magnitude of change they imply, based on the standard of what a typical person would perceive. Personal characteristics are deleted from the narrative so as to minimize their influence on the ratings.

Rating procedures such as these have the potential to incorporate information about individual meanings of life events without risking the bias inherent in self-reports. They can meet that potential, however, only if they are sensitive to cultural differences in meanings and interpretations. Studies among the elderly raise questions about whether such sensitivity can be achieved in practice. For example, retirement is rated more positively by older persons themselves than it is by raters. Most raters tend to be young, and younger persons have difficulty inferring how a typical elder would respond to a given circumstance. Differences in ratings of events by the age of the rater have been observed in studies using Brown's rating scheme, suggesting that even sophisticated ratings by researchers may fail to incorporate sufficient cultural sensitivity. Similar problems may plausibly occur for other sociodemographic groups.

C. Reliability of Life Event Reports

Aggregate life events measures have low reliability. Test–retest correlations between life change scores are weak, and paired-respondent agreement (for example, between husbands and wives) on the occurrence of specific events is low. Reliability decreases with the length of the recall period and increases with the severity of the event. The low reliability seems to stem from respondents' forgetting to report events that occurred rather than from reporting fictitious events. Notably, reliability of life event reports does not seem to vary with age.

One response to this problem has been to use life event calendars to record the occurrence of major life events. These calendars record which events occurred on the vertical axis and the time of their occurrence on the horizontal axis. In addition, major annual events such as birthdays and holidays are included as reference points. The reliability of event reports seems to increase using these procedures, especially when they are used in conjunction with efforts to inquire about events in substantive sections of questionnaires that focus on the life domain in which they occurred (e.g., parenthood, marriage). Information about the timing of a broad range of events, and the contextual embeddedness of questions, improves respondents' abilities to remember events that occurred. This approach has not been used in samples of older adults but may represent a fruitful area for methodological development.

III. RESEARCH ON THE CONSEQUENCES OF LIFE EVENTS

A. Research Designs

Although questions about the causes of life events logically precede questions about their effects, the former have received much less research attention. Two research designs dominate research on the consequences of aggregate life events. In the first, random samples of persons are administered a measure of life events and a measure of well-being, and the relationship between the two is estimated statistically. The measures of life events ask respondents to report which of a list of events they experienced in the recent past (usually 6 months or 1 year prior to the interview); a summated score of the total number of events is calculated. Desirable events are usually excluded from the total, except when the effects of desirable events are a central concern of the research. Events are often disaggregated by the area of life in which they occur (e.g., financial, work) or by type (controllable vs. uncontrollable), although these disaggregations are less common in research on older adults.

Given the diverse approaches to life events measurement, it should come as no surprise that no single measure predominates. At least 15 life events scales for adults are well known; many others have been developed for individual research programs that draw on, but that are not identical to, the scales used by other researchers. Life events checklists developed specifically for the elderly include Kahana's Geriatric Life Events Schedule, Murrell's Louisville Older Person Event Scale, and Zautra's Research Inventory of Major and Small Events for Older Adults.

Measures of well-being include general scales of psychological distress, scales of specific symptoms (e.g., depression, anxiety), diagnostic measures of psychiatric disorders, scales of physical symptoms, and, for the elderly, mortality. Studies that focus on immune functioning use blood samples to measure the immune system's ability to respond to infectious agents.

The second approach to studying the consequences of life events compares samples of persons with a given disease (usually hospital patients) to matched samples of persons without the disease with respect to the number or type of recent life events they experienced. This approach has been used to study risk factors for stroke, hypertension, myocardial infarction, and other diseases among the elderly.

B. The Consequences of Life Events

Early studies of life change found significant, but weak, relationships with physical health, mental health, and immune functioning. Correlations were typically less than .30, indicating that life events explained only about 9% of the variation in well-being. Furthermore, the effects of life events diminished substantially with the passage of time.

The initial response to the low correlation between life events and well-being was to try to refine life events measures so that they might more accurately reflect the relevant variations in life stress as they pertain to health. Results from those studies suggest that *undesirable* events have stronger relationships with well-being than do life *changes*. Events occurring in salient social roles also have somewhat stronger effects on well-being than do other events. Results with respect to other dimensions of events have been less encouraging. Uncontrollable events predict depressive outcomes (depressive symptoms, clinical depression) more strongly than do controllable events, but the same does not hold true for other outcomes. Results with respect to the expectedness of events are inconclusive. Most importantly, regardless of which dimensions of events are considered, the correlations between life events and health outcomes show only modest improvement. Studies that consider critical combinations of types of events (e.g., fateful loss events) may hold some promise in improving predictions of well-being, but they also move further away from the realm of aggregate life events to more closely resemble studies of specific events, with all of the attendant strengths and limitations. [*See* DEPRESSION.]

One new line of work attempts to increase the correlation between life events and well-being by expanding the range of events included on life event checklists. Specifically, lifetime traumas are added to lists that typically include only recent events. The theory behind this addition is that current mental health is influenced not only by recent events but also by traumatic events that occurred in the past. Thus, measures of life events that purport to represent the full range of potentially stressful events should include major traumas regardless of the age at which they occurred. Empirical evidence bears this out. The prediction of psychological well-being improves considerably when lifetime traumas are included.

Some researchers contend that these and other innovations in the measurement of life events are doomed to failure because life events represent a limited range of the types of experiences that have distressing effects. These researchers argue that daily events and chronic stressors are stronger determinants of well-being than are major life changes. Daily events, sometimes called hassles, represent mundane experiences of daily life that nevertheless may provoke strong emotional responses. For example, depending on the context, an argument with a co-worker may trigger an episode of severe psychological distress. Chronic stressors are ongoing conditions that challenge adaptational capacities, such as financial problems. Chronic stressors and daily events serve as the context within which life events occur and represent potential sequelae of life events.

The relationships among these three sources of stress have been discussed theoretically but have not been satisfactorily examined empirically. One problem is that chronic stressors, daily events, and well-being are potentially confounded. Current levels of distress may influence reports of chronic stressors and of daily events. In addition, it is difficult to establish that chronic stress and daily events are causes of current and future distress rather than consequences of earlier distress (particularly when that distress takes the form of a diagnosable disorder). Even those researchers who advocate alternative conceptualizations of stress have not fully come to grips with the difficulties such a focus engenders. Nevertheless, given the low numbers of life events reported by the elderly (see below), studies which include more types of stress are warranted.

C. Modifiers of the Relationship between Life Events and Well-Being

Another approach to understanding the weak relationship between life events and well-being is to consider the social and personal resources that ameliorate or exacerbate the effects of those events. This research has its origins in the recognition that negative responses to life events will be strongest when individuals do not have sufficient resources to cope with the events; in other words, negative outcomes occur when there is a mismatch between the demands that stressors place on the individual and the resources that individuals have to address those demands.

Two main types of resources have been considered: social resources and personal resources. Social resources include socioeconomic resources, such as income, education, and occupational experiences, and social support. Personal resources include self-perceptions and coping behaviors.

I. Social Resources

Studies of socioeconomic variations in response to life events indicate that persons with low levels of income, education, and occupational prestige experience more distress in the face of life events than do persons with high levels of those resources. However, socioeconomic variations in response to life events differ across types of events (e.g., financial, love loss) and by the measure of socioeconomic status (SES) that is used. Thus, the relationship between socioeconomic resources and response to life events is not straightforward. Furthermore, none of this research has focused exclusively on samples of older adults. Although several scholars have identified low finances as an important aggravating condition for life events among the elderly, relevant empirical evidence is not available.

Studies of social support are similarly difficult to interpret. Social support refers broadly to the structure and content of social relations upon which individuals draw for help, advice, and understanding when faced with stress. Social support is relevant to the study of life events through its potential to "buffer" the effects of those events on physical and mental health. The buffering hypothesis proposes that, among those persons who experience undesirable life events, persons who also have access to supportive social relations will show fewer decrements in well-being than persons who do not have access to such relations.

Social support does appear to have a buffering effect in the general population and among the elderly. The buffering effect is stronger for emotional support (e.g., feeling that one is loved) than for practical support (e.g., help with concrete tasks, financial loans) and for measures of social integration (e.g., number of clubs, frequency of activities with friends). Among the elderly, in particular, supportive relationships appear to protect well-being, in part, by bolstering feelings of control and self-worth that are eroded by life events.

On the basis of these findings, many researchers have concluded that the availability of emotionally supportive relationships protects individuals from the potentially damaging effects of life events. Other researchers have challenged this interpretation, however. They note that the effects of social support are strongest when persons with no support are compared to persons with some support: Persons with no support react more negatively to life events than do persons with some support. Having no support can be conceptualized as a stressor itself, in which case, the buffering effect of social support may be better interpreted as evidence for the relevance of critical combinations of stressors when predicting well-being. The possibility that life events may cause changes in social support further complicates interpretations of the role of social support in responses to life events. Alternatively, lack of social support may signify the presence of a conflictual relationship. In that case, the buffering effect of social support could be interpreted as indicating that involvement in dysfunctional relationships impairs coping with stress. Neither alternative interpretation denies the critical role that social relationships hold in relation to well-being. What they challenge is the conclusion that help and support from loved ones can substantially reduce the stressful effects of life events. [See SOCIAL NETWORKS, SUPPORT, AND INTEGRATION.]

2. Personal Resources

Studies of personal resources focus on self-perceptions and on coping behaviors. With respect to the former, perceptions of mastery or control have received the most attention. Persons who perceive themselves as in control of their lives are less likely than persons who do not to experience psychological distress as a result of life events. The reasons for this are unclear. Sense of control may decrease subjective perceptions of stress or it may elicit more effective coping strategies. Older persons generally perceive themselves to have less control over their lives than do younger persons, suggesting a particular need for studies of stress and control among the elderly.

As is true for other modifiers of the effects of life events, relationships among life events, sense of control, and outcomes are complex. Perceptions of control may change as a result of life events, raising questions about whether the perception of control before or after the event most strongly determines the event's effects. (In fact, some researchers have argued that life events lead to negative outcomes because they lead to changes in perceptions of control.) In addition, perceptions of control are correlated with the stable dimensions of psychological distress (persons with high levels of distress report lower levels of control). It is therefore unclear whether the modifying effects of control actually reflect ameliorative effects of control or whether they reflect the exacerbating effects of prior distress.

Coping behaviors can be defined as specific actions or reactions that are intended to ameliorate a life stressor. To the extent that those actions are consistent across situations, one can speak of coping styles. Many different measures and categorizations of coping behaviors have been developed. One of the most influential is the Ways of Coping Checklist, which divides coping strategies into two broad categories: emotion-focused coping and problem-focused coping. Emotion-focused coping includes attempts to alter the meaning of the event (e.g., focusing on the positive implications of a generally negative experience) or to regulate one's emotional reaction. Problem-focused coping includes efforts to actively change the situation or to garner appropriate resources.

Coping strategies have been found to influence the effects of life events on physical and mental health. However, the effectiveness of different coping strategies varies by type of event. For example, active efforts to change the situation typically exacerbate the effects of uncontrollable events. Furthermore, most evidence for the ameliorative effects of specific coping strategies is amenable to an alternative interpretation: that distressed persons cope differently than nondistressed persons. Thus, although there is little doubt that the way in which individuals manage life events influences their responses, evidence about the specific processes through which that influence occurs is meager and not entirely persuasive.

One other personal resource that has received little research attention but that may be particularly important for the elderly is physical health. The elderly are thought to be vulnerable to stress because they do not have the physical stamina to withstand the physiological changes that result from life events. Although this hypothesis has been proposed, evidence to confirm or disconfirm it is lacking.

In summary, studies of the modifying effects of social and personal resources raise as many complexities as they resolve. Although these complexities stimulate theoretical and methodological advances, they have not as yet satisfactorily answered the question of why life events have only modest effects on well-being.

IV. LIFE EVENTS, AGE, AND THE ELDERLY

A. The Consequences of Life Events for the Elderly

I. Studies among the Elderly

Most studies of life events among the elderly have focused on specific events, such as widowhood and retirement, as they relate to physical or mental health. The few studies that have used aggregate measures of life events have yielded consistent conclusions. As was the case for general samples of adults, undesirable life events have small, but significant, negative effects on physical and mental health for older adults, whereas desirable events have smaller, but significant, positive effects. The effects of life events are generally transitory rather than persistent, although this conclusion may not hold for all types of events. Events that occur in salient areas of life have somewhat stronger effects on well-being than do events that occur in nonsalient areas of life. And, based on results from studies of specific events, events that are controllable seem to have fewer negative effects than do uncontrollable events.

As for modifiers of the relationship between life events and distress, buffering effects of social support are not consistently observed among the elderly. Some researchers have argued that social support is perceived in fundamentally different ways by older adults than it is by younger adults. Older adults have fewer resources to offer, so norms of reciprocity dictate that they use support less frequently and only when in severe need. In addition, older adults are less likely than younger adults to receive emotional support, and more likely to receive practical support, regardless of the demands of the situation. These age differences in the meaning and the receipt of social support may account for the inconsistent buffering effects in samples of elders.

As was the case generally, studies of life events and social support among the elderly have not adequately addressed the complexities of their interrelationship. Many of the events that are common to older adults, such as widowhood, imply changes in social networks. The confounding of these changes with life events, and the influence of these changes on responses to life events, have not yet received attention from researchers. [See WIDOWHOOD AND WIDOWERHOOD.]

2. Differences in the Effects of Life Events by Age

Although studies of life events among the elderly are of interest in and of themselves, elders' reactions to life events also serve as a useful baseline for understanding the role of life stage in shaping responses to stress. Two opposing theories have been proposed to understand elders' reactions to life events. The first theory proposes that life events would have stronger effects on older adults as compared to younger adults because older adults have cumulated stress over a longer period of time and because older adults have fewer personal and social resources to bring to bear on those events. In contrast, the second theory proposes that older adults would react less strongly to events because they are better able to face the challenges of those events. The current elderly represent a select, highly adaptive group of persons by virtue of the fact that they have survived to this point in time. Furthermore, older persons may be more mature and more resilient as a result of earlier efforts to cope with stress. These opposing theories reflect broader divisions among life events theorists as to whether events should be seen inevitably as harmful experiences, or whether the successful resolution of undesirable events has benefits.

Direct comparisons of the effects of life events and disaster experiences among persons of different ages suggest that life events cause less distress for older persons. This difference may result from any of the proposed processes: selection of nonadaptive elders out of the sample by death or severe morbidity, or age differences in maturity or resilience. It is also possible, however, that it reflects either of two additional alternatives: a lowering of aspirations with age, whereby older persons readjust their aspirations to reflect the likely state of their lives over their remaining years, or differences in the inherent stressfulness of the events experienced by older versus younger adults.

B. Differences in Numbers and Types of Events by Age

Older adults report fewer life events and rate life events as being less stressful than do younger adults. The age difference in number of life events may result, in part, from the content of life event checklists. Life event checklists tend to overrepresent events that are pertinent to younger persons (e.g., got married) and underrepresent events that are pertinent to older persons (e.g., became incontinent, lost driver's license).

Compared to younger adults, the undesirable events that are most commonly reported by older adults are death of a spouse, retirement, illness or hospitalization, and finances getting worse. Estimated 1-year prevalences for these events range from 1.5 to 3% for death of a spouse and for retirement, 30 to

55% for health-related events, and 10 to 15% for finances getting worse.

Relocation is another important event for the elderly. Relocation includes moves between home and an institution, between institutions, and between homes. Published studies report 1-year relocation rates of 3.5 to 7% in samples of elders. However, the samples for these studies did not include institutionalized elders and, therefore, would underestimate rates of relocation.

The life events that predominate in old age share three characteristics. They all result from role losses common to old age. They are usually not acute experiences (with the possible exception of death of a spouse) but rather they represent the beginning or ending points of sequences of experiences. And, they are all interrelated.

Widowhood often results in severe financial deprivation, particularly for older women. Researchers report an average decline in income of over 50% in the year after a husband's death. Retirement also results in a loss of income for most elders, although the loss is less severe than that associated with widowhood. Financial well-being influences physical health, and health-related events influence retirement decisions. The interrelationships among these events suggest that studies of their effects would benefit from an explicit consideration of the sequencing and timing of these events in relation to each other and in relation to well-being. The stress potential of events that overlap temporally may cumulate in nonlinear ways so that their overall effect is stronger than the sum of the effects of each. Limited evidence among adult samples supports this possibility, but comparable evidence for the elderly is not available.

Time clustering of events may also be relevant *within* categories of events. In particular, many elderly persons experience multiple losses of loved ones within a relatively short period of time. Whether repeated instances of an event help in coping with future events (sometimes called the "inoculation effect") or hinder such coping (due to the wearing down of resources) has not been evaluated.

C. Life Events as Explanatory Variables

Research on life events has the potential to illuminate sociodemographic patterns of health and illness through an examination of differences in exposure and vulnerability to life events. It has been argued that socioeconomic differences in psychological distress reflect both the higher levels of events experienced by persons in lower status positions and the greater responsivity of those persons to those events. Although this research relies on the possibly faulty assumption that life event checklists capture all relevant variation in life stress across sociodemographic groups, the notion of using stressors to illuminate sociodemographic variations in well-being has appeal.

Among the elderly, this approach has been applied to understanding socioeconomic variations in health. Older persons with high levels of SES recover more quickly from myocardial infarction than do older persons with low levels of SES. Some of this difference has been attributed to socioeconomic variations in exposure to life events and other stressors. In addition, the increasing socioeconomic disparity in health with age can be explained substantially by the greater exposure of persons from lower status groups to stressors, especially in middle age and early old age. Thus, life events may have important implications for understanding the health of elderly populations.

V. CHALLENGES AND FUTURE DIRECTIONS

Research on life events illuminates both the processes through which individuals cope with adversity and the ways in which societal positions influence the quantity and quality of adversity that individuals face. As such, it offers a unique opportunity to link the organization of societies to the well-being of their members. If that opportunity is to be realized, however, life events researchers must continue to tackle major conceptual and methodological challenges.

Life events, social support, coping, and well-being are confounded operationally and conceptually. This confounding is most obvious in the case of health-related events that are included in most life event checklists but which are also used as indicators of well-being. Other, less obvious examples of confounding are no less problematic. For example, deaths of loved ones are life events but they also represent changes in social support. Life events researchers have yet to resolve how to best conceptualize and disentangle the processes implied by these types of confounding.

Life events researchers also have not adequately addressed the problematic distinction between presumably acute life events and chronic stressors. Many experiences that are treated as life events unfold over long periods of time, and many experiences that are believed to be chronic embody a series of related acute events. Distinctions between potentially stressful experiences based on their presumed duration may have limited utility.

Concepts from life-course analysis offer one possible resolution to this problem. Life-course analysts conceive of life experiences as trajectories that include transitions into and out of roles and states of role occupancy. They analyze the relationships among the components of trajectories, and relationships across trajectories in different domains of life, to understand the way in which social structure and individual actions intersect to create individual life experiences. Applied to life stress, this conceptualization of life experience would move us away from an exclusive concern with the duration of stressors to consider other relevant aspects of temporality such as their rate and pace. This conceptualization could also incorporate concerns with the timing of stressors in relation to each other and in relation to well-being.

Applying this conceptualization to life events research would require methodological innovations in the measurement of stress. Given current measurement techniques, it is not clear that respondents can accurately report the relative timing of stressors, particularly in retrospect. Methodological studies of reports of health utilization and of criminal victimization may offer some guidance in modifying life events measures. However, the results of those studies suggest that procedures for improving recall do not always transfer from one type of event to another.

Life-course analysts offer another lesson to life events researchers in the central role they give to cohort and historical influences on individual development. Cohort and historical experiences importantly influence the meanings of events for the elderly. Since the early twentieth century, major policy changes in the United States have shaped the environment within which individuals cope with widowhood, retirement, ill health, and relocation. For example, the availability of Social Security has led to earlier ages at retirement and higher levels of voluntary retirement. Current elders rely on Social Security for approximately 40% of their aggregate income. In contrast, persons who will come of retirement age 20 years from now may face a very different economic and social environment, which will influence when they retire, the nature of their retirement, and the meanings that retirement has for them. Studies of the causes and consequences of life events cannot be complete without reference to the broader social context in which those events occur.

Finally, life events research among the elderly would also benefit from more analyses of the life experiences of racial and ethnic minorities, studied individually and in comparison to each other and to Whites. Studies of life event effects often include only white respondents, or small samples of racial or ethnic minorities. Whatever conclusions one can make about the effects of life events on older adults are confined to Whites for the most part. Studies suggest that social support, stress levels, and coping strategies vary by race and ethnicity as do interpretations of measures of well-being. Theories of life stress will become more robust as they acknowledge and include these variations.

BIBLIOGRAPHY

Coyne, J. C., & Downey, G. (1991). Social factors and psychopathology: Stress, social support, and coping processes. *Annual Review of Psychology, 42,* 401.

George, L. K. (1990). Social structure, social processes, and social-psychological states. In *Handbook of aging and the social sciences* (pp. 186–204). San Diego: Academic Press.

Murrell, S. A., & Meeks, S. (1991). Depressive symptoms in older adults: Predispositions, resources, and life experiences. *Annual Review of Gerontology and Geriatrics, 11,* 261.

Murrell, S. A., Norris, F. H., & Grote, C. (1988). Life events in older adults. In *Life events and psychological functioning* (pp. 96–122). Newbury Park, CA: Sage Publications.

Orrell, M. W. & Davies, A. D. M. (1994). Life events in the elderly. *International Review of Psychiatry, 6,* 59.

Zautra, A. J., Affleck, G., & Tennen, H. (1994). Assessing life events among older adults. *Annual Review of Gerontology and Geriatrics, 14,* 324.

Life Review

Robert N. Butler

The Mount Sinai Medical Center

I. Origin of the Theoretical Concept
II. The Nature of Memory
III. Life Review as Psychotherapy
IV. The Validity of the Life Review
V. The Value and Use of Oral History
and Autobiography
VI. Life Review and New Directions in Psychiatry
VII. Summary

Autobiographical Memory Refers to memories of specific events occurring in an individual's daily experience that are stored without the benefit of conscious memory goal activities on the part of the individual.
Guided Autobiography Topical approach to the collection of autobiographical data. Life review in a systematic manner.
Narrative (or Experiential) Gerontology The field of study by which the inner perspective of aging can be revealed.
Oral History Individual account that becomes a source of history.
Reminiscence The process of recollecting past experiences and events or the experiences or events recollected. One-on-one and group reminiscence can be therapeutic but not evaluative, thereby distinguishing reminiscence from life review.

The **LIFE REVIEW** is a normal developmental task of the later years characterized by the return of memories and past conflicts, which can result in resolution, reconciliation, atonement, integration, and serenity. It can occur spontaneously or can be structured. Structured evaluative life review is practiced for research and therapeutic purposes.

One key goal of early work on life review was to demonstrate that the process of life review in older people is not a pathological condition, rather a normal developmental task of the later years that may in certain cases contribute to psychological dysfunction and in other cases to psychological growth, including resolution of past conflicts, reconciliation with significant others, atonement for past wrongdoing, personality integration, and serentiy.

The concept of life review was used originally to refer to the older person's process of review and evaluation of their lives within the context of intensive psychotherapy and research interviews. The life review concept is distinguished from reminiscence. A related concept is guided autobiography.

I. ORIGIN OF THE THEORETICAL CONCEPT

In 1961, R. N. Butler postulated the universal occurrence in older persons of an inner experience or mental process he called the life review. He proposed that life review helps account for the increased reminiscence in the aged, contributes to the occurrence of certain late-life disorders, particularly depression, and participates in the evolution of such characteristics as candor, serenity, and wisdom among certain older persons.

Allusions to a life-reviewing process have been common in the literature of various historical periods, from Aristotle to Somerset Maugham. G. Stanley Hall adumbrated a somewhat similar idea in his 1922 work, *Senescence: The Last Half of Life*, and intima-tions of the life review can also be found in Gordon W. Allport's 1937 book, *Personality: A Psychological Interpretation*, in which he emphasizes the continuity of personal memories.

In contrast to the prevailing tendency, which at that time was to identify reminiscence in the aged with psychological dysfunction, and, thus, to regard it essentially as a symptom, Butler saw the life review as a naturally occurring, universal mental process characterized by the progressive return to consciousness of past experiences, particularly the resurgence of unresolved conflicts. Simultaneously and normally, these revived experiences and conflicts can be surveyed and reintegrated. Presumably this process is prompted by the realization of approaching dissolution and death and the inability to maintain one's sense of personal invulnerability. It is further shaped by contemporaneous psychosocial experiences, and its nature and outcome are affected by the lifelong unfolding of character.

The life review potentially proceeds toward personality reorganization. Generally, the more intense the unresolved life conflicts, the more work remains to be accomplished toward reintegration.

The life review is not synonymous with but includes reminiscence; it is one level or type of reminiscence. It can occur silently without obvious manifestations. In mild form, the life review is reflected in increased reminiscence, mild nostalgia, and mild regret. In severe form, it includes anxiety, guilt, despair, and depression. One case study presented by Butler describes a woman who in the course of reviewing her life became remarkably abusive, violent toward others, and physically damaging to herself. It became clear that past actions justified her sense of guilt. In such a case, a simple reassuring response is valueless. Discussing the events or situations that provoked the guilt reactions and confronting the feelings that are prompted by the life review are more productive responses. [*See* REMINISCENCE.]

In the extreme, life review may involve the excessive preoccupation of the older person with his or her past, and it may proceed to a state approximating terror and result in suicide. Thus, although the life review process may be universal and normative and contribute to a reconstruction of personality, its outcome can in extreme cases include psychopathology. The more severe affective and behavioral consequences tend to occur when the process occurs in

isolation in those who have been deeply affected by increasing contraction of life attachments and notable psychosocial discontinuities such as forced retirement and death of a spouse. The most tragic situation may be that of the person whose increasing but only partial insight into the past leads to a sense of total waste. Just as one is about to die, one may experience the horrifying feeling that one has never lived or see oneself realistically and in some sense inadequate.

Samuel Beckett's one-act play, *Krapp's Last Tape*, is a most compelling modern existential illustration of the life review. An old man listens uncomprehendingly to recordings he made as a young man in happier times. He is listening to a total stranger. The question is, can he be regarded as the same human being in youth and in old age? Novelists and poets have, of course, used reminiscence or life review in their works, such as the writings of Marcel Proust, James Joyce, Joyce Cary, and many others. Today, writers, poets, and teachers have deliberately used life review in their teaching, writing, and filmmaking. [*See* LITERARY REPRESENTATIONS OF AGING.]

People of all ages review their pasts at various times in life, especially when confronted with a crisis. Life review is common, for example, in middle age when one begins to see death at a closer distance. The philosopher Schopenhauer even remarked that middle age is that point in time when one begins to count backwards from death rather than forward from birth. However, one may ask, do all life reviews serve the same functions, regardless of when they happen? Or does life review in old age have particular characteristics, especially when it occurs in the face of death? As originally formulated, life review is defined as the latter.

II. THE NATURE OF MEMORY

Memory is a complex amalgam of the senses, perception, integration, and cognition. Memory, reminiscence, life review, autobiographical memory, life story, narrative, oral history, and related concepts may one day be understood from the neurophysiological and molecular–cellular perspectives. The neurotransmitter acetylcholine is especially crucial to memory, but memory, so important to adaptation, does not depend upon one neurotransmitter alone. Memory is apparently located in the hippocampus and the amygdala. The latter is associated with memories of fear. Gender may play a role in memory function, because estrogen and other hormones affect the brain. Corticosteroids have been associated with stress and "brain aging." In the 1940s, neurosurgeon William Penfield and others at McGill University in Canada demonstrated the human brain's information storage and retrieval capacity. With electrodes, they stimulated exposed temporal brain lobes of neurological patients under a local anesthetic. The process evoked vivid memories of isolated and even insignificant past events. [*See* BRAIN AND CENTRAL NERVOUS SYSTEM; ENDOCRINE FUNCTION AND DYSFUNCTION.]

Researchers still have much to learn about how the brain integrates and organizes information into categories. In *Remembering*, British psychologist, Sir Frederick C. Bartlett, argued that all new learning builds upon existing knowledge. A single stimulus can bring forth myriad memories, a fact novelist Marcel Proust poignantly illustrated in the "Combray" section of his book *Rememberance of Things Past*, when the protagonist experiences a flood of memories of his youth triggered by eating a cake he enjoyed as a child. However, there may not be a single bank or library of stored information that can be called up at any time. Special stimuli might be required to reveal what may be deeply repressed. On the other hand, some information might be easily recalled or retrieved when specific stimuli are provided. One researcher distinguished six types of reminiscence: integrative, instrumental, informative, narrative, escapist, and obsessive. By instrumental reminiscing, for example, he meant reviewing past experiences to solve present problems. Age and life stage may also be factors in memory (e.g., childhood amnesia). [*See* MEMORY.]

III. LIFE REVIEW AS PSYCHOTHERAPY

The life review and similar autobiographical concepts have been suggested as psychotherapeutic techniques. The Martin Method, in which the client is asked to relate his or her life history in detail; life review therapy; guided autobiography; and reminiscence and structured life review therapy are among the therapeutic techniques related to or using life review.

One can use family albums, scrapbooks, cherished possessions, and other visual images to evoke crucial memories. Genealogy, reunions, pilgrimages to one's ancestral home, and family archives have also been used therapeutically. Memories can involve all of the senses—taste, smell, vision, hearing, and touch—and each may be exploited to evoke memories of the past. One whiff of a paste would bring back the anguish of his early years to Charles Dickens. Music is a powerful stimulus for the flow of memories. The Hebrew Home for the Aged in New York City created in 1995 a lovely garden intended to trigger positive memories from the past. A porch swing evokes a bygone era, as does a water fountain made from a fire hydrant. The guided biography method proposed by Birren consists of creating a composition responding to topics such as "My Family of Origin."

Life review therapy or guided autobiography has been used with those who may not spontaneously report reminiscences. In structured life review, specific questions about one's life and conflicts are explored. Life review therapy may be conducted in group settings. For example, the family as a whole can participate in life review therapy. Such family life review has therapeutic advantages because it may lead to consensus and clarification of specific family issues.

Life review therapy has been used with institutionalized and demented older persons. Remote memory is not as affected in the early stages of dementia as much as recent memory is. Life review and reminiscence techniques are widely used by nurses in nursing homes and as part of hospice care. The life review has been used in caring for terminally ill young adults with AIDS as well as older people. The National Hospice Foundation has used the concept of the life review and created a comprehensive guide for persons of all ages. Such a review should be available for those dying patients who might wish to receive therapy that offers personal, existential, and spiritual help as well as palliative nursing and medicine. [*See* HOSPICE.]

Professionals in nursing, social work, occupational therapy, physical therapy, arts and music therapy, psychology, medicine, and psychiatry have advocated reminiscence and life review as ways to help patients achieve self-esteem. The life review may aid people to resolve conflicts in their lives. Part of the therapeutic value of life review therapy in older persons may be the simple fact that someone is listening to them and that approaching death, affording them little time, is a potent incentive for positive change, such as improvement in mood, increased self-esteem, and so on. [*See* SELF-ESTEEM.]

There is a moral dimension to the life review because one looks evaluatively at one's self, one's behavior, one's guilt. One stands in judgment of the life one has led. Atonement, expiation, redemption, reconciliation, and meaning in life are powerful potential positive outcomes of the life review. It is necessary to explore guilt, confess, and not deny it, as well as experience atonement and reconciliation especially at the end of life. With suffering may come resolution, new insight, and self-discovery.

Fears about time running out may be reduced and replaced with a sense of immediacy, or the here and now. The elemental things in life—children, friendship, nature, human touching (physical and emotional), colors, shapes—gain significance as people sort out the more important things in life from the less important.

IV. THE VALIDITY OF THE LIFE REVIEW

Although the concept of life review has become entrenched in both the literature and practice of gerontology, nursing, social work, and to some degree psychology and psychiatry, aspects of the life review have been called into question, and many questions remain unanswered. For example, how does one determine whether memories have a factual basis or are defensive distortions? How effective or even possible is external verification of memories? Studies show, for example, that even mothers' memories of the timing of the most simple events in their children's development, such as toilet training, are not always recalled with accuracy. What are the interconnections between emotions and memories? Personal myths emerge from childhood and may be held throughout life, affecting one's self-image and most certainly influencing reminiscences. How do self-representations change over time? What are the connections between memories and identity or self-definition? What is more important, that which is remembered or that which is forgotten, or both? How does one confirm some findings that people regret most the things that they failed to do rather than what they did do?

The life review helps both uncover and stabilize one's past selfhood. Tolstoy at age 81 said, "I remember very vividly that I am conscious of myself in exactly the same way now, at 81, as I was conscious of myself, my 'I' at five or six years of age." Consciousness is immovable. Due to this alone there is a movement which we call time. If time moves on, then there must be something that stands still, the consciousness of my "I" stands still. This is a common feeling, substantiated by extensive work at the National Institute on Aging's Baltimore Longitudinal Study of Aging.

There have been some careful studies that demonstrated the effect of life review on some dependent variables, such as depression and life satisfaction. It is true that much work still needs to be done to effectively operationalize outcome measures. But how does one "measure" meaning in life, guilt and expiation, redemption, and reconciliation?

It has been said that the life review may be specific to Western society because of its focus on individualism. However, there is an active program on reminiscence in Japan, for example, and meditation on death and the end of life is common in other Asian countries.

Is the life review a universal occurrence? Studies report that between 49 and 84.1% of older persons have reviewed their lives or are currently reviewing them. Of course, this does not preclude the possibility that all persons might eventually do so. One study showed that those closer to death showed significantly less reminiscence activity and significantly less introspection when compared with matched controls, but this could be consistent with the original theoretical formulation that suggested postreview serenity or ataraxia. Subjects in these studies were not always followed through to the time of death. Some individuals may only review their lives on their deathbed. A further complication is the difficulty of determining if the life review has already occurred because the process is not always a conscious one. The life review often occurs over a considerable period of time and only after a significant relationship has been established either with a mental health professional or a trained empathic listener.

One study reported asking questions such as, Some people review and evaluate their past in order to get an overall picture of their life. This is called the life review. Have you reviewed or are you currently reviewing your life? This question does not always give access to the life review, and it might not be immediately answerable by all individuals. Such a literal, objective, or conscious approach also contrasts with the context of intensive psychotherapy and intensive research interviews that led to the original formulation. This formulation assumed the existence of the unconscious, the division of the mind in psychoanalytic theory that contains memories or repressed desires, not subject to conscious perception or control but often affecting conscious thought and behavior.

V. THE VALUE AND USE OF ORAL HISTORY AND AUTOBIOGRAPHY

The need to engage in life review has prompted the writing of many major memoirs, autobiographies, and treatises summarizing the authors' life work, especially since the seventeenth century. People maintain diaries and write memoirs and autobiographies because they value their lives and feel that they have important ideas or information to convey to others or want to "set the record straight" or gain revenge against their enemies.

There are life review and family history training manuals and guides to help people collect on audio- or videotape their life stories to leave to their families and others. Several aging organizations have developed materials to help people create their autobiographies or life reviews. The American Association of Retired Persons, for example, conducts a reminiscence program and has created training materials. In Britain, Age Exchange, The Reminiscence Centre, has developed *A Practical Guide to Reminiscence*. Age Exchange focuses on "making memories matter." Its goal is to "improve the quality of life for older people by emphasizing the value of their reminiscences to old and young through pioneering artistic, educational, and welfare activities." Age Exchange has the only professional Reminiscence Theatre company in the United Kingdom, to which Londoners have given their memories of living through the blitz in World War II.

Autobiography is one literary genre that potentially gives everyone the opportunity to become "someone." This democratic process gives one the chance to speak about oneself which can, of course, lead to reinvention of the self, self-indulgence, shameless vanity and egotism, and defense and revenge, or offer a sensitive, valid portrait of oneself. In some measure whatever one writes, however biased or fabricated, provides, to a degree, information about the individual or his or her personality. External historical observations and the memories and commentaries of others may be available to evaluate the validity of the contents of autobiographies. Some public life reviews can be painful and controversial, such as Robert S. McNamara's *In Retrospect. The Tragedy and Lessons of Vietnam*, published in 1995.

Behaviorism brushed aside various subjective sources of information about personality. However, oral histories and autobiographies constitute a rich source for information in such fields as anthropology, history, and literature. For example, the popular *Foxfire* books of Eliot Wigginton, which recorded the lives of people living in Georgia, preserve cultural history as well as the lives and skills of everyday people. Another example is the 1993 oral history, *Having Our Say: The Delany Sisters' First 100 Years* by Sarah L. Delany and A. Elizabeth Delany with Amy Hill Hearth, was a best-seller and a Broadway play. It provides a firsthand account of what it has been like to live as an African American in the United States in this century.

VI. LIFE REVIEW AND NEW DIRECTIONS IN PSYCHIATRY

What will happen now that psychiatrists have moved further away from psychodynamics and the inner life to the use of psychoactive medications in their practices? Perhaps more people will feel good and healthier quicker. Painful feelings will be assuaged. But were medications utilized in the context of ongoing psychotherapy, self-understanding might also grow. There need not be a dichotomy here, for both psychoactive medications, such as antidepressants, and psychotherapy should be concurrent and reenforcing.

What about the fact that relatively few gerontologists and psychologists have spent significant amounts of time being with and listening to older people? They will lose opportunities to better understand the inner life if they depend upon drugs alone and if psychologists and gerontologists do not explore human personalities in depth. Researchers do not know how lasting either psychopharmacological or psychotherapeutic approaches are, but it is hard to believe a pill gets to the bottom of genuine guilt due to acts of commission or omission. Is there no place for some measure of human suffering? Is there not also a time for celebration when painful issues are successfully resolved?

The life review concept has contributed to a better understanding of late-life and end-of-life development as well as development across the life span. It has helped demonstrate the therapeutic value of reminiscence for older people and helped eliminate prejudice against those who reminisce. But people and their life stories are more complex than any presently available methods for their study allow. Therefore researchers must encourage further study of life span developmental psychology.

VII. SUMMARY

Memory is a great force for human adaptation in general and important to social evolution. The survival value of memory both to the individual and society cannot be denied. Life review is important in itself; in a sense, it is analogous to undifferentiated, basic research. It adds to self-knowledge per se, independent of consequences. And, by extension, one learns of the lives of others and how lives might be led. As virtue is its own reward, so, too, is the life review, for as Socrates said, "The life which is unexamined is not worth living." Put more positively, there are chances for pain, anger, guilt, and grief, but there are also opportunities for resolution and celebration, for affirmation and hope, for reconciliation and personal growth.

Although a majority of persons may undergo a life review, it may not be accessible and reportable in a significant minority. Memories may be deeply repressed. Moreover, life reviewers may be more introspective than those who do not appear to review. Studies of subgroups might help us to better understand such difference in personality.

It has been suggested that the life review might possibly not be universal or even exclusively precipi-tated by approaching death. Yet it is remarkably common among older people, and the prospect of death is one of its most common triggers. Only in old age with the proximity of death can one truly experience a personal sense of the entire life cycle. That makes old age a unique stage of life and makes the review of life at that time equally unique.

BIBLIOGRAPHY

Birren, J. E., & Deutchman, D. E. (1991). *Guiding autobiography groups for older adults: Exploring the fabric of life.* Baltimore, MD: Johns Hopkins University Press.

Birren, J. E., & Hedlund, B. (1987). Contributions of autobiography to developmental psychology. In N. Eisenberg (Ed.), *Contemporary topics in developmental psychology* (pp. 394–415).

Burnside, I. M. (1988). *Nursing and the aged* (3rd ed.). New York: McGraw-Hill.

Butler, R. N. (1963). The life review: An interpretation of reminiscence in the aged. *Psychiatry, 26,* 65–76.

Disch, R. (1988). Twenty-five years of the life review: Theoretical and practical considerations. *Journal of Gerontological Social Work, 12,* no. 3/4.

Haight, B. K., & Webster, J. D. (Eds.). (1995). *The art and science of reminiscing: Theory, research, methods, and applications.* Washington, DC: Taylor & Francis.

Lewis, M. I., & Butler, R. N. (1974). Life review therapy: Putting memories to work in individual and group psychotherapy. *Geriatrics, 29,* 165–69, 172–73.

Rubin, D. C., Wetzler, S. E., & Nebes, R. B. (1989). Autobiographical memory across the life span. In D. C. Rubin (Ed.), *Autobiographical memory.* Cambridge, UK: Cambridge University Press.

Ruth, J. E., & Birren, J. E. (1995). Personality and aging: Modes of coping and the meaning of stress. In A. Kruse, & R. Schmitz-Scherzer, (Eds.), *Psychologie des lebenslaufs Festschrift Hans Thomae,* Darmstadt: Steinkopf Verlag.

Staudinger, U. M. (1989). *The study of the life review: An approach to the investigation of intellectual development across the life span.* Berlin: Max Planck Institut fur Bildungsforschung, 1989.

Life Satisfaction

Roger C. Mannell

University of Waterloo

Sherry Dupuis

University of Guelph

I. Focus of Life Satisfaction Research
II. Constructs and Measures
III. Predictors and Correlates
IV. Promises and Prospects

Affect   A broad class of emotional processes, including feelings and moods.

Cognition   A general concept comprising all forms of knowing, including perceiving, imagining, reasoning, and judging.

Happiness   The extent to which positive feelings outweigh negative feelings. The relatively temporary affective feelings of the present moment. Often, the time period of the "past few weeks" is used to anchor the assessment.

Morale   A future-oriented optimism or pessimism regarding the problems and opportunities associated with living and aging. Morale refers to how well people feel they fit into their social and physical environments and their acceptance of those things they cannot change.

Satisfaction   Implies an act of judgment, a comparison of what people have to what they expect in terms of their whole life or some specific part of it. The more their achievements fall short of their aspirations, the greater the level of dissatisfaction. Satisfaction has a past orientation, an evaluation of how things have gone up to the present.

The quality of life for a society or group is often determined by using *objective* indicators such as gross national income, frequency of high-risk health behaviors, quality of the environment, and levels of crime, suicide, public violence, and family disintegration. An individual's quality of life can also be characterized on the basis of these types of objective factors. Alternatively, measures of subjective well-being were developed based on the belief that the psychological quality of a person's life cannot be understood simply from a knowledge of these objective circumstances. **LIFE SATISFACTION** is a popular *subjective well-being* measure of quality of life. People are typically asked to rate their satisfaction with life as a whole or some aspect of it.

I. FOCUS OF LIFE SATISFACTION RESEARCH

Life satisfaction is one of the oldest research issues in the social scientific study of aging. Initially, this research focused on pathology and coping, but later the issue became perceptions of the quality of life. Life satisfaction and other subjective well-being measures have been of increasing importance in gerontology. Researchers and policy makers are attempting to better understand the impact of disability on quality of life, changes in health status, bereavement, retirement, role loss, diminishing social networks, and modifications in activity involvement.

Two issues have dominated research on subjective well-being in the field of gerontology. The first concerns how best to conceptualize and measure subjective well-being. Life satisfaction is only one of several competing subjective well-being constructs, and researchers continue to work at developing appropriate measures. The second issue involves the identification of those factors in people's lives that influence subjective well-being. A substantial amount of research focusing on this issue and using the life satisfaction construct has been reported. The impact on life satisfaction of various interventions, programs, and policies directed at older adults has also been of interest. [*See* PSYCHOLOGICAL WELL-BEING.]

II. CONSTRUCTS AND MEASURES

In addition to life satisfaction, other popular constructs used to conceptualize subjective well-being in the study of older adults include happiness and morale. Paper-and-pencil scales have been developed to measure these constructs. Frequently used scales for measuring life satisfaction include Cantril's Self-Anchoring Scale, the Life Satisfaction Index, and modifications of it by Wood and colleagues, the Andrews and Withey Delighted–Terrible Faces Scale, and the Satisfaction with Life Scale. A number of single-item measures of life satisfaction have also been used in a variety of studies. The most frequently used happiness scale is the Bradburn Affect-Balance Scale, and morale is typically measured with The Philadelphia Geriatric Center Morale Scale.

A major problem with the subjective well-being research in gerontology has been the lack of consistency in defining, measuring, and using the terms *psychological well-being, happiness, life satisfaction,* and *morale.* In fact, these concepts and their measures have been used interchangeably. However, they appear to differ on a variety of dimensions. First, there is "time orientation." Satisfaction is seen to have a past, happiness a present, and morale a future orientation. Second, these constructs and measures vary in how enduring or temporary the state of subjective well-being is thought to be. Life satisfaction and morale scales measure more enduring and stable *cognitions,* whereas happiness scales measure more temporary and transient *affective* states. Third, the measures of these constructs differ to the extent that their items allow the assessment of both positive and negative life experiences as distinct aspects of subjective well-being. Some research evidence has been found to suggest that the positive and negative aspects of well-being are not opposite ends of a continuum but rather separate dimensions that reflect satisfaction with different components of life (e.g., external social conditions such as friends and activities versus inner psychological conditions such as self-esteem and health, respectively). Finally, the various measures used differ in terms of whether they assess global well-being or well-being in specific domains of life (e.g., work, family, leisure, and neighborhood). By examining satisfaction with each of these domains, some researchers believe that a more accurate picture of well-being can be obtained. Researchers examining different domains of life have primarily used satisfaction measures, and specialized areas of research have been developed on single domains, such as job and leisure satisfaction. [*See* LEISURE; WORK AND EMPLOYMENT.]

Substantial correlations have been found to exist between the satisfaction, morale, and happiness scales, suggesting that they measure the same underlying construct. These findings are not too surprising, given that the most popular measures share a number of scale items in common. However, these constructs and scales are not completely interchangeable; research has shown that they are related differently to the wide variety of predictors of subjective well-being studied.

Although researchers continue to examine empirically the internal structure of these measures, new approaches are being developed. For example, the Memorial University of Newfoundland Scale of Happiness and a shorter version, the Short Happiness and Affect Research Protocol, have been developed to measure both the enduring cognitive and the more immediate transitory affective dimensions of subjective well-being. As well, these scales systematically assess both the positive and negative content of people's life experience.

Another recent approach to conceptualizing and measuring subjective well-being takes a different tack. Several authors have proposed breaking with past work and reconceptualizing subjective well-being and successful aging by defining it as personal development and adjustment. They argue that measures of well-being based on the notions of satisfaction, happiness, and morale are too tied to concepts that were developed independently, and that attempts to integrate them into some superordinate subjective well-being construct fails to provide a strong theoretical basis for the development of better measures and future research. For example, researchers have developed a scale that reflects psychological health and well-being (e.g., self-acceptance, positive relations with others, autonomy, environmental mastery, purpose in life, and personal growth) based on major personality and life span theories such as those of Erikson, Rogers, and Maslow. Little research based on these constructs has been reported, and their success remains to be seen. [*See* LIFE SPAN THEORY.]

In spite of the difficulties of conceptualization and measurement, much research has investigated the factors that influence subjective well-being. Many researchers have conceptualized subjective well-being as life satisfaction.

III. PREDICTORS AND CORRELATES

A. Health Status and Functional Ability

Research has consistently demonstrated that individuals in poor health are less satisfied with their lives than those in good health. Subjective health perceptions are a better index of life satisfaction than number of actual health problems. Health has also been found to influence people's estimates of their future life satisfaction levels and changes in life satisfaction over time. However, health status may affect life satisfaction for some groups more than others. Perceived health is the best single predictor of life satisfaction for elderly Whites but may not be for elderly African Americans. Health problems also appear to be more important for females than for males, and for older than for younger adults.

Certain health problems are more strongly related to life satisfaction than others. Functional disorders that complicate daily living and interaction with others (e.g., control of bladder or bowel, seeing, and walking) have stronger negative correlations with life satisfaction than chronic disorders with established treatments. Long-standing illnesses or chronic health problems may have an indirect effect on life satisfaction by reducing activity levels. Declining health may lead not only to difficulties in performing everyday chores, but also to difficulties in maintaining social contacts and continuing valued leisure activities. It still remains unclear which aspects of health are more important and how other variables such as type of illness and time of onset influence life satisfaction.

Research is only beginning to identify those factors (e.g., coping strategies, support systems, treat-

ment programs, activities) that may play important roles in buffering the effects of decreased health status on life satisfaction. Positive cognitive coping (i.e., modifying the meaning of the problem) rather than direct action coping (i.e., behavioral approaches) has been shown to buffer the effects of health problems on life satisfaction. Formal support but not informal assistance has been found to reduce the deleterious effects of perceived health problems on life satisfaction. Involvement in adult day care programs has also led to significant improvements in life satisfaction for infirm older adults and their informal caregivers. [*See* SOCIAL NETWORKS, SUPPORT, AND INTEGRATION.]

B. Financial Satisfaction and Income

Overwhelming evidence from both cross-sectional and longitudinal studies suggests that adequacy of income, especially satisfaction with finances, plays an important role in the life satisfaction of older adults. Wealthier, older adults in a number of countries report higher levels of life satisfaction than poorer individuals. Financial problems appear to be a much more important factor in the well-being of older adults than younger adults, and of older men than women. Socioeconomic status (SES) in general appears to be a more important predictor of satisfaction for White than African Americans and for North Americans in comparison to other national groups. [*See* ECONOMICS: INDIVIDUAL.]

C. Education and Employment and Occupational Status

Evidence for the influence of education and employment status on life satisfaction is inconsistent, and relationships tend to be weak, often disappearing when other factors are controlled. Some researchers have found the relationship between education and life satisfaction differs for various age groups. Others have found that education may be more important to non-White population groups. Although some research suggests that education may play a more important role for women than for men, the opposite has also been found. Education likely has an indirect effect on life satisfaction through its influence on such things as retirement plans, current financial difficulties, satisfaction with finances, as well as perceived health.

Employment status appears to be more strongly related to life satisfaction than occupational status. For example, employment continuity has been found to be the most important factor after health in both assessments of present and future life satisfaction. Older workers, both male and female, have exhibited higher life satisfaction than homemakers or retirees. Being employed part-time is positively associated with life satisfaction among the urban elderly. Nonetheless, the relationship between employment status and life satisfaction tends to be weak and present among only specific groups of older people in the population. For instance, employment status has been found to be more important to life satisfaction for middle-aged women than for older women. However, it is unclear whether this difference holds for men. Past patterns of employment and homemaking do not appear to be related to current life satisfaction.

D. Age

Early studies found weak negative correlations between age and life satisfaction. However, once other variables associated with aging (e.g., declining health, decreasing financial resources, widowhood, loss of friends, and decreased activity) were introduced, the relationship between age and life satisfaction disappeared. Recent longitudinal studies tend to demonstrate the stability of life satisfaction over time. However, the pattern of life satisfaction over the life span is complex and may vary significantly as a function of gender. Furthermore, although different age groups may show similar life satisfaction scores, there may be important qualitative differences among them in the factors that affect life satisfaction. For example, the factors that contribute to the life satisfaction of older adult women have been found to be different from those that contribute to the life satisfaction of middle-aged women.

E. Gender

Few consistent patterns in life satisfaction can be attributed to gender alone. When direct relationships are found, they are generally weak and disappear when other variables are controlled. However, gender differences may interact with other factors such as race, SES, and age. Much work is still needed to determine how these variables interact and influence life satisfaction.

F. Marital Status

Marital status appears to be more strongly related to life satisfaction for older adults than younger adults. Married older adults typically have higher levels of life satisfaction than all nonmarried groups. For analysis, many studies, however, combine never-married, widowed, divorced, and separated older adults despite the fact that never-married older adult women have been found to report higher life satisfaction scores than widowed women. Never-married older women may have greater involvement in careers in comparison to widows, and this career involvement may account for some of the differences in life satisfaction attributed to marital status. The effects of being married on life satisfaction have been found to be more positive for African Americans than Whites. Marital and family satisfaction may be more important to life satisfaction than merely being married.

G. Race and Ethnicity

Race has been found to be more strongly related to life satisfaction for middle-aged compared to older adults. Some studies suggest that older African Americans have significantly higher levels of life satisfaction than older Whites. Others have found the opposite. It has been suggested that race differences in life satisfaction may be better explained by the influence of socioeconomic factors (i.e., educational attainment, economic retirement planning, present financial circumstances). Alternatively, black and white American life experiences may differ and, therefore, the predictors of life satisfaction may differ by race. Social support and integration appear to be important determinants of life satisfaction for Blacks. Religious participation and religiosity have also been found to be more important contributors to life satisfaction for Blacks than Whites. In addition, there may be cultural differences in the factors that influence life satisfaction when North Americans are compared to other cultures. For example, family and having love and affection appear to be more important contributors to life satisfaction next to health for West Germans compared to North Americans. [*See* RACIAL AND ETHNIC DIVERSITY.]

H. Activity and Social Interaction

Positive relationships between leisure activity patterns and the life satisfaction of older adults have frequently been found. In fact, some research suggests that activity levels may be better predictors of life satisfaction than health and income. Frequency of participation shows a stronger relationship with life satisfaction than amount of time spent participating, and leisure satisfaction is a better predictor of life satisfaction than rates of leisure participation. Activity levels, however, may be indirectly or directly influenced by such factors as income, health and functional ability, education level, perceived social competence, and opportunity.

Participation in some activities correlates more strongly with life satisfaction than participation in others. Social, outdoor, and sports activities have shown strong associations with life satisfaction. Formal activities such as voluntary association memberships also show a positive relationship to life satisfaction for older adults. Nonetheless, the types of activities that are significantly related to life satisfaction have been found to vary by age. Researchers have found that sports, travel, and outdoor activities were the most important predictors for those aged 55–64. Involvement in community organizations, culture and art activities, and travel were the most important activities for young older adults (65–74). Home-based activities and informal social activities were the most important contributors for those over 74. [*See* ACTIVITIES.]

Research on the importance of a person's social networks and support for life satisfaction is inconclusive. There is some evidence that social involvement may be more important to older adults than younger adults. For example, social involvement appears unrelated to life satisfaction among those aged 40–54, but is an important positive factor in the life satisfaction of older adults. The quality of social interactions is more important to life satisfaction than objective factors such as the frequency of contacts. Furthermore, spending time with family may be more related to global life satisfaction, whereas spending time with friends may have a strong influence on immediate happiness. Again, differences in these relationships have been found among various groups of older adults. For example, social support may be far more important to the life satisfaction of widowed older adults than the never-married.

I. Role Loss

Older adults who experience greater amounts of change and role loss in their lives have been found to have lower levels of life satisfaction, though this association may be stronger for men than women. Supporting the activity and continuity theories, much of this research suggests that role consistency, particularly a continued sense of usefulness in old age, is related to life satisfaction. Social integration also appears to be more important to African Americans than white Americans. [*See* GENDER ROLES.]

IV. PROMISES AND PROSPECTS

The research demonstrates that subjective rather than objective indicators are better predictors of life satisfaction. This finding may be in part due to *common method variance*, that is, similarities in the ways in which life satisfaction and the subjective indicators used to predict it are measured using paper-and-pencil self-report scales. Research is needed that examines the factors that mediate the relationship between the objective conditions of people's lives and their perceptions of the quality of those conditions. After all, interventions to improve the quality of life of older adults are typically aimed at changing objective living conditions. We should know how changes in these conditions translate into perceptions of satisfaction and quality. Although most of the research has been cross-sectional, longitudinal studies are being employed more frequently. This approach is an important step if the determinants of life satisfaction over the life span are to be successfully examined. Qualitative studies are all but nonexistent, and the detailed scrutiny that they could provide would also help improve understanding of those aspects of people's lives that are most meaningful for life satisfaction. Cross-cultural research and studies of people with lifelong disabilities are also needed.

Researchers recently have begun investigating the nature of the relationship between global life satisfaction and satisfaction with different domains of life using "bottom-up," "top-down," and "bidirectional" models. Evidence suggests that relationships between global and domain-specific satisfactions are bidirectional; however, they may vary across different types of life domains.

The relationship between life satisfaction and the various factors that researchers have examined is much more complex than simple correlations suggest. Research and statistical procedures that allow the reciprocal nature of these relationships to be examined are needed. Research is beginning to be reported that is based on more sophisticated multivariate analyses to determine the variables that are directly and indirectly related to life satisfaction and the direction of such relationships. However, as suggested earlier, these improvements and strategies will only lead to improved research when better conceptualizations of subjective well-being and their measures are developed. Happily, there is evidence that these types of developments are underway.

BIBLIOGRAPHY

Andrews, F. M., & Withey, S. B. (1976). *Social indicators of well-being.* New York: Holt, Rinehart & Winston.

Campbell, A., Converse, P. E., & Rodgers, W. L. (1976). *The quality of American life: Perceptions, evaluations, and satisfaction.* New York: Russell Sage Foundation.

Cantril, H. (1965). *The pattern of human concerns.* New Brunswick, NJ: Rutgers University Press.

Bradburn, N. M. (1969). *The structure of psychological well-being.* Chicago: Aldine Publ. Co.

Diener, E. (1984). Subjective well-being. *Psychological Bulletin, 95*(3), 542–575.

Diener, E., Emmons, R. A., Larson, R. J., & Griffin, S. (1985). The satisfaction with life scale. *Journal of Personality Assessment, 49,* 71–76.

Herzog, A. R., & Rodgers, W. L. (1986). Satisfaction among older adults. In F. M. Andrews (Ed.), *Research on the quality of life* (pp. 235–251). Ann Arbor, MI: University of Michigan.

Kozma, A., & Stones, M. J. (1980). The measurement of happiness: Development of the Memorial University of Newfoundland Scale of Happiness (MUNSH). *Journal of Gerontology, 35,* 906–912.

Lance, C. E., Lautenschlager, G. J., Sloan, C. E., & Varca, P. E. (1989). A comparison between bottom-up, top-down, and bidirectional models of relationships between global and life facet satisfaction. *Journal of Personality, 57*(3), 601–624.

Larson, R. (1978). Thirty years of research on the subjective well-being of older Americans. *Journal of Gerontology, 33*(1), 109–125.

Lawton, M. P. (1975). The Philadelphia Geriatric Center Moral Scale: A revision. *Journal of Gerontology, 30,* 85–89.

Mannell, R. C., & Dupuis, S. (1994). Leisure and productive activity. In M. P. Lawton, & J. Teresi (Eds.), *Annual review of gerontology and geriatrics* (vol. 14), (pp. 125–141). New York, NY: Springer Publishing Co.

Neugarten, B. L., Havighurst, R., & Tobin, S. (1961). The measurement of life satisfaction. *Journal of Gerontology, 16,* 134–143.

Ryff, C. (1989). Happiness is everything, or is it? Explorations on the meaning of psychological well-being. *Journal of Personality and Social Psychology, 57,* 1069–1081.

Stones, M. J., Kozma, A., Hirdes, J., Gold, D., Arbuckle, T., & Kolopack, P. (in press). Short happiness and affect research protocol (SHARP). *Social Indicators Research.*

Stull, D. E. (1987). Conceptualization and measurement of well-being: Implications for policy evaluation. In E. F. Borgatta, & R. J. V. Montgomery (Eds.), *Critical issues in aging policy* (pp. 55–90). Newbury Park, CA: Sage Publications.

Wood, V., Wyllie, M. L., & Sheafor, B. (1969). An analysis of a short self-report measure of life satisfaction. *Journal of Gerontology, 24,* 465–469.

Life Span Theory

William J. Hoyer

Syracuse University

John M. Rybash

Hamilton College

I. Emergence of Life Span Theory
II. What Is Aging?
III. Characteristics of the Life Span Approach
IV. Methods in the Study of Life Span Development
V. Implications for the Interdisciplinary Study of Aging
VI. Summary and Conclusions

Metatheory Refers to theorizing about theories. Life span theory is a metatheory in the sense that it refers to a variety of theories about development throughout the life span.

Ontogeny The study of the course of development of an individual organism. The term *ontogeny* emphasizes intraindividual change. From a life span perspective, ontogeny interacts with sociohistorical contexts in determining development.

Plasticity Refers to the extent to which change is possible within an individual. The term *plasticity* is frequently used to refer to the extent to which cognitive or physical performance can be improved by practice or intervention.

Primary Aging Refers to changes that occur with aging in the absence of disease. The effects of primary aging on physiological and behavioral functioning are relatively predictable for all members of a particular species. In contrast to many disease processes, primary aging occurs gradually and it eventually affects all systems.

Reserve Capacity Refers to the range of effective function that is available to the individual for responding to physical or psychological challenges. The amount of reserve capacity available for restoration of homeostasis when the individual is stressed is diminished with aging.

Secondary Aging Refers to the factors that influence the rate of senescence or primary aging. For example, factors such as stress, trauma, and disease serve to accelerate primary aging processes.

Senescence Refers to deterioration and declines in the structure and function of an organism that take place during the period of life when the mortality rate of a population is accelerated. Senescence is associated with a period in the life span when degenerative processes overtake regenerative processes.

LIFE SPAN THEORY is concerned with the description and explanation of how individuals change throughout the entire course of life. From a life span perspective, the study of any developmental period is best understood by considering that period within the context of the entire life of the individual. The study of aging from a life span perspective involves the study of age-related interindividual differences and age-related intraindividual change. Life span theory assumes that development occurs along multiple dimensions, and that there are both gains and losses in function along different dimensions throughout the life course. It is also assumed that aging depends on the interaction of a complex variety of biological, historical, and sociocultural influences, that the contributions of these influences vary for different dimensions of development and aging at different points in the life span, and that some combinations of influences are more synergistic or optimal with regard to effective functioning than others. It is also assumed that there are age-related interindividual differences and intraindividual differences in the plasticity of function throughout the life span, and in the extent to which the individual can actively determine the course of aging along some dimensions. Life span theorists generally take the view that the study of aging involves the integration of knowledge, methods, and perspectives across multiple disciplines and professions.

I. EMERGENCE OF LIFE SPAN THEORY

Life span theory represents a way of thinking about the development of individuals as they change throughout the entire life span. The view that development is a lifelong process is now widely accepted in the developmental sciences and gerontology. In the twentieth century, theorists and researchers have increasingly recognized that each period or phase of the life span is best understood by looking at it in the context of the entire life of the individual. Each developmental period may have its own distinctive characteristics and significance, but there are also similarities and continuity with earlier and later periods of the life span. In fact, one of the important questions in the study of life span development is the extent to which there are continuities and discontinuities across the life span. Life span theorists are interested in the nature of development itself, not just in cataloging or describing and explaining the changes associated with selected periods within the life span. For example, life span theorists are interested in *how* the processes and mechanisms of development in the early years of life are different from the later-life processes.

The life span perspective has stimulated new insights into the nature of human development. Many of the major empirical and theoretical advances in the developmental sciences in the past 25 years can be associated with the life span view. But specification of the limitations of the life span approach also benefits our understanding of human development and aging. Informal conceptions of the full course of the human life span reinforced the stereotype of development as gain during the early phases of life and that change is all for the worse in the later years. Innovative contributions by Charlotte Bühler, Erik Erikson, and others that took issue with the stereotypical view of the life course provided a basis for late twentieth-century writers, especially Paul Baltes, James Birren, Bernice Neugarten, Klaus Riegel, Matilda Riley, and K. Warner Schaie, to make major advances in the conceptualization and application of life span theory.

In recent years, life span theory has had a positive impact on the science and practice of gerontology by aiding the correction of negative stereotypes associated with particular age periods, such as overly pessimistic views of aging and the elderly. The life span approach will continue to evolve in light of new observations and theory-building efforts in the developmental sciences and gerontology.

II. WHAT IS AGING?

Many of the processes and mechanisms of aging are universal in that similar changes in human behavior can be observed at roughly the same age across persons. Many of these processes are controlled by "biological clocks." The term *primary aging* refers to changes that occur with aging in the absence of disease. The effects of primary aging on physiological and behavioral functioning are relatively predictable for all members of a particular species. In contrast to the consequences of many disease processes that are relatively abrupt and affect primarily one system or organ, the consequences of primary aging are more gradual, cumulative, and insidious. For example, there are gradual but reliable changes in all physiological systems and in physical appearance with aging. Furthermore, it is well established that the speed of information-processing abilities becomes gradually slower with advancing age.

Despite the ubiquity and universality of primary aging processes, one of the most remarkable characteristics of human aging is the wide range of heterogeneity in the expression of the consequences of aging. Secondary aging factors such as stress, trauma, exposure to toxins, and disease influence the rate of primary aging processes. In addition to heterogeneity in the expression of the consequences of aging, there are also individual differences in the interactive effects of aging and health on personality and ability functions. Furthermore, the circumstances and the sociocultural contexts associated with particular periods of historical time (e.g., World War II) are distinctly influential in producing interindividual differences within and across particular birth cohorts. [*See* COHORT STUDIES.]

In addition to large interindividual heterogeneity, there is also considerable age-related intraindividual variability across various dimensions of biological and behavioral function. Individuals become more unique as they grow older in part because of particular histories of life experience. During the life course, the repertoire of an individual is shaped by how that person invested time and energy in work and in human relationships. By deliberate selection and by circumstance, the developing individual is both a producer and a product of a myriad of developmental influences. Research and theory issues associated with the description and explanation of how individuals change as they grow older, and how different individuals show different patterns of change with aging are signature characteristics of a life span approach to the study of aging. [See LIFE COURSE.]

The study of aging has as its major goal the understanding of the orderly or regular time-related or age-related transformations that occur to representative organisms living under representative conditions. The main purpose of theory in the study of aging is to provide a context for describing and understanding such transformations. Theories serve the process of articulating meaningful patterns from observations that would otherwise be disconnected pieces of a puzzle and hence less meaningful. In the study of aging, theories are frameworks for connecting laboratory research findings as well as informal everyday observations with emerging themes in the field. [See THEORIES OF AGING: BIOLOGICAL; THEORIES OF AGING: PSYCHOLOGICAL; THEORIES OF AGING: SOCIAL.]

The study of aging can be approached in many different ways. In some areas of research inquiry, aging is equated with senescence. The term *senescence* refers to deterioration and declines in the structure and function of an organism that take place during the period of life when the mortality rate of a population is accelerated. Senescence is associated with late life when degenerative processes overtake regenerative processes.

In contrast, some researchers and theorists argue that aging begins at conception, and that the study of aging should not be limited to senescent processes. These writers see aging as a complex mix of interacting time-related biological processes and sociocultural influences. In gerontology, one of the aims of life span theory is to capture the full range of individual differences in age-related intraindividual change in functions that characterize the older population. Life span theory is usually considered to be a "metatheory" in that it is a set of themes for approaching the study of development and aging. Basically, life

Table I Summary of the Major Characteristics of a Life Span Approach to the Study of Aging

1. Aging is a lifelong process.
2. Aging is multidimensional and multidirectional in that there is variability in the rate and direction (gains and losses) of change for different characteristics within the individual and across individuals.
3. No age or period of life is any more important than any other age or period.
4. There is plasticity and resiliency in function throughout the life span.
5. There are age-related differences in the extent to which the individual is or can be active in determining the course of aging along some dimensions.
6. Aging is a product of the interactive effects of biogenetic processes and the historical and sociocultural contexts in which change takes place; the contributions of environmental and biological influences vary for different dimensions at different points in the life span. Some combinations of biogenetic and environmental influences may be uniquely synergistic.
7. The study of aging from a life span perspective involves the integration of knowledge, methods, and perspectives across multiple disciplines and professions (e.g., anthropology, biology, medicine and nursing, psychology, and sociology).

span theory offers a broadened approach to the study of aging. [See GROWTH FACTORS AND CELLULAR SENESCENCE.]

III. CHARACTERISTICS OF THE LIFE SPAN APPROACH

The characteristics of the life span approach are summarized in Table I. This list of characteristics is drawn from the work of Baltes and other leading theorists in life span developmental psychology, and the reader is referred to the citations listed in the bibliography for thorough discussions. The notion that aging is multidimensional and multidirectional is one of the basic tenets of a life span orientation to the study of aging. Consistent with evidence suggesting increased interindividual differences with aging in healthy adults, the experience of aging seems to produce cumulative differentiation within individuals along multiple dimensions. That gain or growth as well as loss or decline can be observed throughout the life course has provided a general framework for researchers to explore some of the positive attributes of aging. For example, the study of the characteristics of wisdom and of postformal styles of thinking, the maintenance or continue evolution of exercised cognitive skills and cognitive expertise in the later years, and the emergence of emotional maturity are areas receiving increased research attention. However, the research investigations aimed at describing the positive aspects and potentials of late-life functioning are far less frequent compared with the number of investigations in the literature aimed at description and explication of age-related deficit. Life span theorists seem to enjoy the challenge of chipping away at the prevailing views of aging in science and in society as monotonic deterioration, decrement, and loss. In their efforts to dispel overly negative views of aging, life span researchers tend to be critical of narrow or one-sided conceptions of aging. One line of evidence in support of a more balanced view is based on observations of ordinary lives in progress in real settings in contrast to age comparisons based on standardized tests and measures that are indigenous to youth and insensitive to the unique qualities of older adults. Another line of research evidence in support of a more balanced view is derived from studies that distinguish between the characteristics of normal aging, illness-free aging, and successful aging. Research on successful aging has as one of its aims to identify the personal attributes and contextual characteristics of individuals who minimize or escape the debilitating consequences of aging and disease. Considering the broad array of human capabilities; some show decline, some improve, and some remain the same across selected time periods. The advancement of a balanced view of the potentials and limits of aging is a main theme of life span theory.

The emphasis on age-related gains and losses along multiple dimensions implies that no age period is without advantages and disadvantages. No one age period should be glorified or valued as any "better" than any other age period. Throughout the life span, the individual is changing and at the same time adapting to change. As mentioned later in this article, such complex themes have resulted in the development of innovative methodological and statistical approaches for the analysis of multiple antecedents and multiple outcomes across age and time.

Referring to Table I, another main theme in life span theory is associated with the terms *plasticity, reserve capacity*, and *resiliency*. Plasticity refers to the potential for intraindividual change. Intraindividual plasticity is evident when there is variability in levels of performance across different kinds of tasks or when there is variability in carrying out the same task at different times or under different conditions. Life span researchers are interested in understanding developmental differences in the gap between observable behavior and underlying competence or potential. It is assumed that the potential for optimization is present throughout the life course. However, it is likely that the potential for intraindividual change becomes increasingly constrained as performance nears its upper limits at any point in the life span, especially near the end of the life span. Some researchers have suggested that there is diminished reserve capacity at the end of the life span, such that the individual is vulnerable to a variety of circumstances associated with mortality.

Individuals also exhibit varying capacities to protect themselves from impairment and insult associated with aging and disease, and to adapt effectively to the demands of stressful situations. The term *reserve capacity* refers to the individual's resources for responding effectively to challenging conditions. The term *resiliency* is similar in meaning and refers to a capacity for successful adaptation and recovery in response to stressful life events. Although the concept of resilience has been used mainly in reference to protective resources in children, recently some life span researchers have argued that resilience is useful concept for describing individual adaptation throughout the life span.

The concepts of plasticity and reserve hold promise for improving our understanding of the relationship between aging and behavior. Analogous to cardiovascular function, or muscular efficiency, healthy older adults usually function quite effectively in everyday nonstressful conditions, but their functioning is likely to be impaired under stressful conditions. That is, age-related deficits in behavioral efficiency are most prominent when systems that are critical to maintaining performance are challenged or stressed. The study of reserve capacity is useful for describing the effects of aging on a wide range of functions under stressed conditions. However, studies of reserve capacity and resiliency do not address how development can be enhanced in situations where there is optimal support.

Another main characteristic of a life span view is

the idea that development and aging is continuously and simultaneously influenced by a wide range of dynamic biological and social processes. Although it seems trivial to point out that aging has multiple causes, most theories of aging emphasize the ontogenetic and nonmalleable aspects of aging. The term *ontogeny* refers to the course of development of an individual organism. Ontogeny emphasizes intraindividual change. From a life span perspective, ontogeny interacts with sociohistorical context. As already mentioned, many of the antecedents and consequences of aging are universal and species-determined (e.g., graying hair, menopause), whereas other antecedents and consequences of aging are idiosyncratic or cohort-specific, culture-specific, or specific to a segment of historical time (e.g., happiness, wisdom). Furthermore, some of the biogenetic and sociocultural aspects of development and aging are gender-specific, and some of the biological and social aspects of development and aging are gender-invariant. Some of the environmental influences on aging are or seem entirely unique to individuals. The sources of variance that give rise to interindividual differences in the aging process probably involve different mechanisms than the sources of influence that give rise to species uniformity or universality in the aging process.

IV. METHODS IN THE STUDY OF LIFE SPAN DEVELOPMENT

Perhaps one of the most important methodological issues derivative of life span theory has been the distinction between age, cohort, and time of measurement as sources of influence in developmental research. In the study of aging, it is now well known that many observations of age differences in behavior are attributable to cohort factors (influences associated with time of birth) rather than to age factors per se. Work by K. Warner Schaie, for example, has demonstrated that cohort factors account for more of the variance than chronological age in some ability domains. The validity of inferences drawn from cross-sectional comparisons of different age groups is confounded by variability associated with chronological age differences and cohort differences. Furthermore, the validity of longitudinal comparisons across multiple times of measurement is confounded by variance associated with chronological

age change and the influences of changing sociohistorical circumstances. The significance of age, cohort, and sociohistorical factors as distinct sources of influence was not really acknowledged until development was conceptualized in a broad life span framework.

Another important methodological theme in life span theory has to do with the specification and meaning of the age variable. Although age-related change is usually described in terms of years since birth or calendar time, chronological age is a crude and unsatisfactory index of many aging phenomena. One theme of the life span approach is to replace chronological age with index measures that more accurately capture the sources of time-related or age-related change. For example, the effects of aging on behavior are sometimes irreversible, analogous to the irreversible consequences of chemical or nuclear reactions. The effects of aging on behavior can also be quantitative and continuous rather than qualitative, and reversible rather than irreversible. Furthermore, markers of elapsed time are insensitive to the meaning of time as a relative and subjective dimension. Indeed the experience of the passing of 365 days is likely not to be the same at different ages. There are also biological clocks based on biomarkers or measures of physiological time, and social clocks based on the socialization of age prescriptions.

Because age and time are not causes of change per se, an aim of aging research is to identify the mechanisms that are primarily responsible for age-related change. Successful explication of the mechanisms that produce aging would enable researchers to replace chronological age measures of time since birth with the real index variables and the real causal variables for which it is proxy. For example, there is some evidence to suggest that measures of brain reserve capacity can serve as more accurate measures of the effects of aging than chronological age.

It should also be mentioned that the multicausal and multidirectional themes in life span theory have driven the development of new methodologies and methods for the analysis of multiple antecedents and multiple outcomes across age and time. The life span approach has led to a number of significant advances in the way researchers think about the analysis of change. [See RESEARCH DESIGN AND METHODS.]

V. IMPLICATIONS FOR THE INTERDISCIPLINARY STUDY OF AGING

One consequence of acknowledging the multidimensionality and multicausality of aging is that life span researchers try to be both specialists and multidisciplinary generalists in their outlook. Although a high degree of disciplinary specialization is usually required in order to contribute meaningfully to the advancement of scientific knowledge about aging, life span researchers find it useful to also look for conceptual linkages across disciplinary barriers. Occasionally, such linkages lead to major changes in how we think about aging processes. For example, the idea that aging consists of multiple antecedent mechanisms and multiple outcomes and other main themes of life span theory discussed in this article are generally well accepted by researchers in the field. Furthermore, from the gains and losses perspective, to the extent that lifelong experience contributes to the construction of distinctive systems of knowledge for particular cohorts, the aging individual thinks and acts in ways that expand some opportunities and at the same time restrict other opportunities.

Significant advances in the study of aging and life span psychology often reflect multidisciplinary integrations of ideas. For example, recent work in the area of developmental behavioral genetics goes beyond the standard position on organism–environment interaction by calling attention to nonadditive synergistic effects. That is, there are unique combinations of nature and nurture that produce synergistic or optimal outcomes for development. As an example of a synergistic interaction between environmental conditions and heritability, it has been reported that there is a significant increase in the heights of second-generation Japanese persons raised in the United States compared with second-generation Japanese persons raised in Japan. Second-generation Japanese persons raised in the United States were over five inches taller than the American-reared sons of short Japanese fathers and the Japan-reared sons of tall Japanese fathers.

Finally, it should also be mentioned that a life span orientation complements the aims of research and practice in developmental and clinical intervention. How the aging individual compensates for age-related decrements is an important practical theme in life span theory. Some life span researchers maintain a focus on the optimization of aging in everyday situations. Several of the prevailing models of cognitive development in adulthood and aging emphasize such notions as knowledge encapsulation and selective optimization. Some life span researchers also emphasize the idea that individuals are active in constructing and modifying their own development throughout the life span.

VI. SUMMARY AND CONCLUSIONS

In conclusion, life span theory provides a basis for describing both gains and losses associated with aging. Life span theorists emphasize the potentials as well as limits of intraindividual change across the life span. Due to a combination of influences, many developmental outcomes are possible for each person, some outcomes are more likely than others, some outcomes can be made more likely, and some outcomes are not possible. The study of aging from a life span orientation emphasizes the idea that our understanding of human aging across domains (biological, biomedical, cognitive, and social) can be advanced by research that views aging as both a cause and a product of interactions among biological and sociocultural factors across time and age.

BIBLIOGRAPHY

Bäckman, L., & Dixon, R. (1992). Psychological compensation: A theoretical framework. *Psychological Bulletin, 112,* 259–283.

Baltes, P. B. (1983). Life-span developmental psychology: Observations on history and theory revisited. In R. M. Lerner (Ed.), *Developmental psychology: Historical and developmental perspectives* (pp. 79–111). Hillsdale, NJ: Erlbaum.

Baltes, P. B. (1987). Theoretical propositions of life-span developmental psychology: On the dynamics between growth and decline. *Developmental Psychology, 23,* 611–626.

Baltes, P. B., & Baltes, M. M. (1990). Psychological perspectives on successful aging: The model of selective optimization with compensation. In P. B. Baltes, & M. M. Baltes (Eds.), *Successful aging* (pp. 1–34). New York: Cambridge University Press.

Baltes, P. B., & Staudinger, U. M. (1993). The search for the psychology of wisdom. *Current directions in Psychological Science, 2,* 75–80.

Birren, J. E. (1959). Principles of research on aging. In J. E. Birren, (Ed.), *Handbook of aging and the individual* (pp. 3–42). Chicago: University of Chicago Press.

Birren, J. E. (1988). A contribution to the theory of the psychology of aging: As a counterpart of development. In J. E. Birren & V. L. Bengtson (Eds.), *Emergent theories of aging* (pp. 153–176). New York: Springer.

Birren, J. E., & Birren, B. A. (1990). The concepts, models, and history of the psychology of aging. In J. E. Birren & K. W. Schaie (Eds.), *Handbook of the psychology of aging* (3rd ed., pp. 3–20). San Diego: Academic Press.

Bronfenbrenner, U., & Ceci, S. J. (1994). Nature–nurture reconceptualized in developmental perspective: A bioecological model. *Psychological Review, 101,* 568–586.

Fries, J. F., & Crapo, L. M. (1981). *Vitality and aging.* San Francisco: Freeman.

Hoyer, W. J. (1985). Aging and the development of expert cognition. In T. M. Schlecter & M. P. Toglia (Eds.), *New directions in cognitive science* (pp. 69–87). Norwood, NJ: Ablex.

Hoyer, W. J., & Rybash, J. M. (1994). Characterizing adult cognitive development. *Journal of Adult Development, 1,* 7–12.

Lerner, R. M. (1991). Changing organism-context relations as the basic process of development: A developmental contextual perspective. *Developmental Psychology, 27,* 27–32.

Popper, K. (1959). *The logic of scientific discovery.* London: Cambridge University Press.

Riley, M. W. (1987). On the significance of age in sociology. *American Sociological Review, 52,* 1–14.

Rowe, J. W., & Kahn, R. L. (1987). Human aging: Usual and successful. *Science, 237,* 143–149.

Schaie, K. W. (1994). The course of adult intellectual development. *American Psychologist, 49,* 304–313.

Staudinger, U. M., Marsiske, M., & Baltes, P. B. (1993). Resilience and levels of reserve capacity in later adulthood: Perspectives from life-span theory. *Development and Psychopathology, 5,* 541–566.

Thompson, R. A. (1988). Early development in life-span perspective. In P. B. Baltes, D. L. Featherman, R. M. Lerner (Eds.), *Life-span development and behavior* (vol. 9, pp. 129–172). Hillsdale, NJ: Erlbaum.

Wohlwill, J. F. (1973). *The study of behavioral development.* New York: Academic Press.

Literary Representations of Aging

I. The New Importance of Literary Works That
   Depict Aging
II. The Arrival of a Literature of Aging
III. Sample Gerontological Concerns as Treated
   in Sample Literary Works
IV. A Cautionary Distinction: Literature as
   Gerontological Evidence versus Literature
   as Artwork
V. Practical Gerontological Applications of
   Literary Works
VI. Possible New Directions

Literature Works of fiction, poetry, drama, and biography (including autobiography) that represent the experience of fictional or actual characters. Literary essays are excluded as not meeting this definition.

The increasing aged population has led to an increased **LITERARY ATTENTION TO THE EXPERIENCES OF AGING.** Such attention is uniquely valuable because it helps readers to *feel* aging vicariously. It also helps to focus on behavior patterns that are often blurred in actual life. Thus it enriches the understanding of many gerontological topics. Both literary and gerontological scholars have worked and are working to make this asset more available through critical discussion, bibliography, academic courses, and wider availability of the relevant literary works.

I. THE NEW IMPORTANCE OF LITERARY WORKS THAT DEPICT AGING

A. The Increased Presence of Aging

Literature at the least reflects the dominant trends and values of a culture. Since the United States has increased its aged population twofold from 1900 to 1990, with another doubling expected by 2050 (with comparable global growth), aging will inevitably appear more and more in the characters and themes of novels, stories, plays, poems, and biographical writings. Aging also appears in the writers themselves, who will portray aging more and more from the inside. [*See* IMAGES OF AGING.]

B. The Prejudice against Age

From the nineteenth century the expanding presence of aging has provoked resistance through the prejudice now given the familiar name of "ageism"—the fear and dislike of aging and of older people, accentuated by what is often called the culture of youth. A growing number of elderly find the late years narrowed and saddened by the resulting ostracism. Sadly, they often absorb the prejudice themselves. They may dislike themselves; they may avoid the company of compeers; they may overlook the assets that a self-respecting old age can offer. [*See* AGEISM AND DISCRIMINATION.]

C. The Promise of Gerontology

As a rapidly growing cluster of disciplines, gerontology addresses such problems. Where gerontology struggled as a mere orphan of science in midcentury, scores of gerontology centers are now active. Courses and graduate degrees have opened up. Orientation in gerontology is often required of other professions: medicine, law, psychiatry, psychology, education. Some exposure to gerontology is now often expected of specialists in marketing and product development.

Encyclopedia of Gerontology
Volume 2

73

Copyright © 1996 by Academic Press, Inc.
All rights of reproduction in any form reserved.

D. What Literary Works Offer

All the more can gerontology benefit from the contributions of literature. Fiction, poetry, and drama do not aspire to scientific knowledge or discovery, but they can convey the *feel* of aging—the lived experiences of being old and relating to the old. They can also extract and select so that character patterns may emerge more clearly than are visible in the confusions of daily life. A masterwork of literature can do these things with greater concentration and intensity than is likely from case studies or patient surveys. What gerontologists can find in literature is compassion and insight for enriching their professional work. Literature has therefore begun to find a role in gerontological education. Courses on aging in literature are offered at many levels from undergraduate to doctoral. Within the humanities, scholars are examining these authors and works in order to define more clearly what they add to the total claims and concerns of literature itself.

II. THE ARRIVAL OF A LITERATURE OF AGING

A. Forerunners

Though traditional literature seldom concentrated on aging, sensitive treatments are to be found. Ancient Greece provided Sophocles' *Oedipus at Colonus*, showing the final journey and salvation of that tragic patricide. Shakespeare's *King Lear* centers on Lear's senile rage, downfall, madness, and ultimate rescue by his loving daughter. In the fantasy, *Gulliver's Travels* (1726), Jonathan Swift devoted one section to the wretchedness of extreme old age suffered by the immortal Struldbruggs. A century later, Alfred Tennyson voiced an old king's staunch adventurousness in the poem "Ulysses." Among other forerunners can be mentioned Cicero, Francis Bacon, Honoré de Balzac, Ivan Turgenev, Matthew Arnold, Robert Louis Stevenson, and Mary Wilkins Freeman.

B. Earlier Twentieth-Century Treatments

W. B. Yeats struck defiant and elegiac tones in such poems as "The Wild Old Wicked Man" and "Sailing to Byzantium." Arthur Miller still shocks theater au-diences with the wrenching crack-up of the troubled old Willy Loman in *Death of a Salesman*. In Ernest Hemingway's epic short novel, *The Old Man and the Sea*, Santiago's gallant but losing battle against the great marlin exemplifies a stoicism that has sometimes sustained the aging. Among other leading talents, Willa Cather, Edna Ferber, Katherine Anne Porter, and Victoria Sackville-West all provided fiction about the trials and triumphs of the aged.

C. The Abundance of Newer Writing

The poet-novelist May Sarton, herself old, has made the late years her special province. The novel *As We Are Now* exposes the horrors of elder abuse in a heartless nursing home. Such poems as "Gestalt at Sixty" and autobiographical works as "At Seventy" show a constant evaluation of what the years are bringing to her. The fiction of Richard Bausch explores aging in novel and story, with special vividness in the novella, *Rare and Endangered Species*, showing the radiating impact of a senior suicide. Gina Berriault's stories about age are well represented by "The Diary of K. W." on the last days of a starving but tender and poetic recluse. These names merely point up a much longer roster of authors: Maya Angelou, Louis Auchincloss, Charles Baxter, Michael Blumenthal, Susan Dodd, Elizabeth Jolley, Doris Lessing, Paule Marshall, Jack Matthews, Goffredo Parise, Linda Pastan, I. B. Singer, William Trevor, Mark Van Doren, Arturo Vivante, John Wheelock, to mention only a fraction.

III. SAMPLE GERONTOLOGICAL CONCERNS AS TREATED IN SAMPLE LITERARY WORKS[1]

A. Ageism

Edward Albee's one-act parable, "The Sandbox," shows Mommy and Daddy dumping Grandmother

---

[1]These illustrations should not be taken by any means as trying to show the whole range of a given gerontological concern. A full account of ageism, for instance, would need to show the various damages inflicted on the old and by the old upon themselves. It would also suggest the experiences and strategies by which ageism is countered. The illustrations are samples only.

into a sandbox (nursing home? hospice?) and with hypocritical regret leaving her to be claimed by the Angel of Death. The title of Lise Maclay's poem, "I Hate the Way I Look," speaks for itself as illustrating how ageism infects even the old.

B. Race

The strong female role in African-American family life is shown by the determined old black woman who trudges an enormous distance for her grandson's medicine in Eudora Welty's story, "A Worn Path." The poisonousness of racism appears in Alice Walker's story "The Welcome Table," where a feeble old black woman is turned away from a white church to die on the winter road following her vision of Jesus. [See RACIAL AND ETHNIC DIVERSITY.]

C. Gender

The male impulse to dominate does not easily succeed in old age, as shown in Shakespeare's King Lear, who thinks to retain all the honors of majesty after retirement. The female aspiration to establish an authentic, nonstereotyped identity is what projects Eva away from a long bad marriage and into a wholly different environment in Constance Beresford-Howe's novel *The Book of Eve*. [See GENDER ROLES.]

D. Family Conflicts

A conservative mother attacks the radicalism of her daughter in Phyllis Bentley's story "Mother and Daughter." Ironically, the daughter repeats the pattern a generation later, opposing her own rebellious daughter. Ben Brantley, the domineering father of Peter Taylor's story "Porte-Cochere," becomes enraged over a minor slight from his favorite son at the birthday party attended by his children. Just as Ben's own father had brutalized him in boyhood, old Ben ends the evening by whacking the empty chairs, calling them by his children's names.

E. Intergenerational (Nonfamily)

A retired accountant takes offense at a young blue-jeaned couple who enter a Bingo game and start cheating in Raymond Carver's story "After the Denim."

What will happen, he bitterly wonders, when these kids learn what life brings "after the denim"? A positive friendship between old and young is at the center of Lynn Schwartz's novel *Balancing Acts*, in which a feisty retired trapeze artist becomes mentor for an unruly teenaged girl.

F. Elder Abuse

Under the credential of welfare service, a Relief Inspector badgers an eccentric old slum woman in Sol Yurick's story "The Siege." He demands to check a certain room for concealed assets, not understanding that this room symbolizes her private memories. His forced entry becomes a kind of psychological rape. In Thyra Winslow's story "Grandma" a seventyish widow rotates through the homes of her three children, being in turn abused through being assigned to do drudgery, through being left to servants, and being found constantly at fault. [See ABUSE AND NEGLECT OF ELDERS.]

G. Dementia

A long personal memoir of her father-in-law's decline is furnished by Rosalie Honel in *Journey with Grandpa: Our Family's Struggle with Alzheimer's Disease*. For seven years the Honel family dealt with Grandpa's deepening disorientation. Although they suffered family strain and constant distraction from their own lives, they also found resources in themselves, in social agencies, and their church, which enriched them. Dementia as experienced from within is imagined in Marisa Labozzetta's story "Making the Wine" in which an Italian widow confusedly remembers her husband. [See DEMENTIA.]

H. Creativity

Storytelling, so often associated with older people, is an ingenious survival tactic for Nat, who develops various scenarios in coping with the violence around him in New York's Central Park, in Herb Gardner's play *I'm Not Rappaport*. A most productive period for the writer Elizabeth Gray Vining is related in her memoir *Being Seventy: The Measure of a Year*. A piano teacher refuses the security of a retirement home in order to continue giving music lessons to the children she loves, in the story "Ashur and Evir" by Annabel Thomas. [*See* CREATIVITY.]

IV. A CAUTIONARY DISTINCTION: LITERATURE AS GERONTOLOGICAL EVIDENCE VERSUS LITERATURE AS ARTWORK

The gerontologist may be tempted to wrench any possible illustration from a literary work regardless of how that detail fits the artistic whole of that work. Linda Loman, for instance, the protective wife of the ruined Willy in Miller's *Death of a Salesman*, could be lifted out as a gender study on the damage inflicted by a self-centered husband. But to do so without regard to the whole play would be to miss the larger relevance of Willy's own downfall as a tragedy of aging. The play is designed to focus on essential flaws in Willy's character—hypocritical congeniality, need to be petted, willingness to cheat—flaws that converge into an avalanche on Willy's plunge into forced retirement. Willy also has virtues—hard working, affection for wife and sons, longing for a simpler wholesome way of life. These draw the spectator's compassion. They accentuate the disasters of his downfall. The admitted pathos of his wife's helplessness should not be ignored. Willy's struggle offers the larger claim on the gerontologist's understanding.

If *Death of a Salesman* can be considered in this holistic way, one will see fruitful comparisons with other literary works that dramatize the pains and promises of retirement. There is Charley Newman, downgraded as "an old bird" on his part-time job so desperately needed in J. F. Powers' story "The Old Man: A Love Story." The horrors of functionless old age are magnified in Julio Ricci's fantasy story "The Concert," where an audience of oldsters is wretchedly paid to guffaw at the jokes of a stand-up comedian.

Positively, there is the former businessman Israel Danziger of I. B. Singer's story "The Hotel," who jumps out of a depressive idleness to join a new friend in a new commercial venture.

In these ways the gerontologist may find in literature a spectrum of illustrations to support the examination of any given topic.

V. PRACTICAL GERONTOLOGICAL APPLICATIONS OF LITERARY WORKS

A. Guidance from Literary Criticism

Humanistic scholarship has seized upon aging as it appears in literary works and as it affects the creativity of aging authors. Although some of this work speaks mainly to humanistic specialists, it has led to increased recognition both by gerontological professionals and by general readers. A major effort appears in the collection of critical essays, *Handbook of the Humanities and Aging*, edited by Thomas Cole, David Van Tassel, and Robert Kastenbaum. Other important writers include Andrew Achenbaum, Prisca Bagnell, Herbert Donow, Sally Gadow, Harry Moody, Donna Polisar, Patricia Soper, Kathleen Woodward, and Anne Wyatt-Brown.

B. Literature Anthologies for Use in Gerontological Study

An important collection whose editors combine literary and medical credentials has been *Literature and Aging* edited by Martin Kohn, Carol Donley, and Delese Wear. Altogether a dozen anthologies have appeared from 1980 onward, with some specialization in women's aging, African-American aging, aging through history, and aging worldwide. (See Bibliography for sample titles.)

C. Professional and Liberal Arts Courses in Literature

Close to forty academic courses can be listed at this writing, with many more probably not yet surveyed. Institutions offering them range from undergraduate to medical schools, to centers on aging, to theological seminaries. The sharing of curricular information is periodically provided by the Association for Gerontology in Higher Education, the American Society on Aging, the Gerontological Society of America, and by the newsletter *Aging and the Human Spirit*.

D. Courses in Creative Writing

Older persons often take readily to writing poetry and fiction which project their life review. An important project was reported by Kenneth Koch in *I Never Told Anybody: Teaching Poetry Writing in A Nursing Home.* Classes or study groups in autobiographical writing for seniors have sprung up in many campus and park district programs, on the generic topic, Writing Your Life Story.

VI. POSSIBLE NEW DIRECTIONS

Aging in literature can be increasingly taught in courses or course segments at all levels not excluding secondary education. As an element of liberal arts it can enlarge the student's enjoyment of literature as well as the student's appreciation of aging and readiness for it. Such study can continue into the private reading of adults of all ages. Here library guidance can play an important part. Bibliographical and critical surveys can be expanded and regularized to appear at set intervals in set form. Publishers, producers, and gerontology organizations can use contests and contracts to encourage new writing of fiction, drama, poetry, and biography.

BIBLIOGRAPHY

Bagnell, P. von D., & Roper, P. S. (1989). *Perceptions of aging in literature: A cross-cultural study.* Westport, CT: Greenwood Publishing Group.

Birren, J., & Deutchman, D. E. (1991). *Guiding autobiography groups for older adults.* Baltimore, MD: The Johns Hopkins University Press.

Cole, T., Van Tassel, D., & Kastenbaum, R. (Eds.). (1992). *Handbook of the humanities and aging.* New York: Springer Publishing Co.

Cole, T., & Winkler, M. G. (Eds.). (1994). *The Oxford book of aging.* New York: Oxford University Press.

Kohn, M., Donley, C., & Wear, D. (Eds.). (1992). *Literature and aging.* Kent, OH: Kent State University Press.

Rubin, R. J. (1990). *Of a certain age: A guide to contemporary fiction featuring older adults.* Santa Barbara, CA: ABC-CLIO.

Secundy, M. G., & Nixon, L. LaCivita (1991). *Trials, tribulations, and celebrations: African-American perspectives on health, illness, aging, and loss.* Yarmouth, ME: Intercultural Press.

Waxman, B. F. (1990). *From the hearth to the open road: A feminist study of aging in contemporary literature.* Westport, CT: Greenwood Publishing Group.

Yahnke, R., & Eastman, R. (1990). *Aging in literature: A reader's guide.* Chicago: American Library Association.

Yahnke, R., & Eastman, R. (1995). *Literature and gerontology: A guide to research.* Westport, CT: Greenwood Publishing Group.

Loneliness

Larry C. Mullins

Auburn University at Montgomery

I. Definitions and Theory
II. Loneliness Resulting from Social Isolation
III. Loneliness Resulting from Emotional Isolation
IV. Selected Findings from Recent Research

Emotional Isolation   The lack of person(s) to whom one feels attached (i.e., emotionally committed).
Loneliness   A psychosocial emotional condition that may stem from many factors, but is usually related to either social isolation or emotional isolation.
Social Isolation   The lack of, or a deficit in, the quantity of a social network.

LONELINESS is an affective emotional condition persons experience when they feel apart from others and apart from familiar social support networks. This sense of separation can lead to the realization that social contacts are either diminishing or lacking, or are not at a level, quantitatively or qualitatively, that is emotionally satisfying or supportive.

I. DEFINITIONS AND THEORY

Loneliness, an area of increasing concern to theoreticians and researchers in the study of older persons, is a complex psychosocial condition that is differentially experienced by persons in different cultures throughout the world. In the United States and Europe the percentage of community-dwelling older persons who experience loneliness appears to be 20% or less. Frequently, the terms *loneliness* and *alone* are used interchangeably, as if they refer to the same experience.

As numerous authors have noted, this is not the case; many isolated people are not lonely, and some integrated people are lonely.

There have been many conceptualizations of loneliness, which reflect numerous theoretical origins. The theoretical approaches can be broadly categorized as (a) the social needs approach, which has foundations in the neo-Freudian social developmental approaches and the social support perspectives; (b) the behavioral–personality approach; and (c) the cognitive processes approach. Common to these varied approaches are three essential points. First, loneliness is a subjective emotional experience that may be unrelated to actual social isolation. Second, loneliness is an aversive psychological condition. Third, the underlying root cause of loneliness is some form of social relationship deficit. Some authors take exception to this third point, contending that the internal state of the individual is a more important consideration than are interpersonal relationships.

II. LONELINESS RESULTING FROM SOCIAL ISOLATION

The idea of loneliness as social isolation has been related to a person's perceived isolation from those around him or her. Social isolation is the consequence of lacking a social network with peers. Subsequently, the emotional condition of loneliness has been examined as it is influenced by this deficit in the quantity of relationships, or by the lack of relatedness to the social environment. [*See* SOCIAL NETWORKS, SUPPORT, AND INTEGRATION.]

III. LONELINESS RESULTING FROM EMOTIONAL ISOLATION

Emotional isolation is related to the absence of an attachment figure, one with whom a person is emotionally committed. The resultant loneliness is a psychological state marked by feelings of loss, distress, separation, and isolation.

IV. SELECTED FINDINGS FROM RECENT RESEARCH

A. Spouse

Typically, results have indicated greater loneliness in the absence of a mate. Severe loneliness appears to be unusual among married men, somewhat more prevalent among married women, and quite prevalent among the unmarried of either sex. The marital relationship is viewed as a source of comfort and support as well as the focal point of everyday life.

B. Children

Empirical studies of the relationship between loneliness and contact with children have shown conflicting results. Most, but not all research, however, has found no association between frequency of contact with children and loneliness. The commitment in the relationship seems to be more important than the actual contact.

C. Friends

Research has shown that close friends exert a positive influence on the emotional well-being of older persons. Generally, older persons who have contact with their friends, and especially those who are satisfied with these relationships, are less lonely. Besides serving as confidants, friends provide numerous forms of social and emotional support that are valued, especially because the support is nonobligatory. [See PSY-CHOLOGICAL WELL–BEING.]

D. Health Conditions

Though most previous research has not looked at the distinction between objective and subjective physical health issues, the overall weight of the evidence points to a reasonably strong and consistent association between poorer health and greater loneliness. There is also concern with the relationship between the mental health and emotional condition of the older person and the loneliness they may experience. The evidence is not fully clear; nonetheless, loneliness should not be confused with depression, anxiety, or low self-esteem—these states and conditions are not correlative. [See MENTAL HEALTH.]

E. Age, Gender, Race and Ethnicity, Education, Urban or Rural

The conclusions from research that have examined background factors in their importance to loneliness are not in each instance definitive.

1. Age
There has been no clear pattern of relationship established between age and loneliness—results are mixed depending on whether the study was cross-sectional or longitudinal in design. Whether age is important seems to depend on the group being studied, and may vary due to cultural reasons, as well.

2. Gender
This is a more consistent predictor of loneliness than age. Generally, studies show that either gender has no effect on loneliness, or that women are more lonely than men.

3. Race and Ethnicity
This characteristic has not been systematically examined with regard to loneliness. Cross-racial, or cross-ethnic, comparisons of loneliness and its antecedents have not yet been conducted in a manner that lends any clarity to interpretation.

4. Education
Educational differences, also, have not been thoroughly examined. The little indirect evidence that does exist seems to be quite inconsistent. Some research shows some difference in the experience of loneliness by educational level, whereas other research does not show such results.

5. Urban or Rural Location
It is commonly held that urban elders are more lonely and socially isolated than their rural counterparts,

though research has not consistently confirmed this prevailing stereotype. The most recent examination of this found that rural and urban older persons shared relatively equally in social advantages and were about equally integrated into their respective communities.

BIBLIOGRAPHY

Andersson, L. (1986). A model of estrangement—including a theoretical understanding of loneliness. *Psychological Reports, 58,* 683.

Bowlby, J. (1969). *Attachment and loss: vol. 1. Attachment.* New York: Basic Books.

Hojat, M., & Crandall, R., (Ed.). (1989). *Loneliness—Theory, research, and applications.* Thousand Oaks, CA: Sage.

Johnson, D., & Mullins, L. (1987). Growing old and lonely in different societies: Toward a comparative perspective. *Journal of Cross-Cultural Gerontology, 1,* 257.

Jong-Gierveld, J. de, Kamphuis, F., & Dykstra, P. (1987). Old and lonely. *Comprehensive Gerontology, 1,* 13.

Marangoni, C., & Ickes, W. (1989). Loneliness: A theoretical review with implications for measurement. *Journal of Social Psychology, 116,* 269.

Mullins, L., & Mushel, M. (1992). The existence and emotional closeness of relationships with children, friends, and spouses. *Research on Aging, 14,* 448.

Peplau, L., & Perlman, D. (Ed.). (1982). *Loneliness: A sourcebook of current theory, research and therapy.* New York: Wiley.

Weiss, R. (1973). *Loneliness: The experience of emotional and social isolation.* Cambridge, MA: MIT Press.

Longevity and Long-Lived Populations

Kenneth G. Manton

Duke University

I. Definitions and Concepts
II. Models of Mortality
III. Evidence on Mortality Trajectories—A Need for a Paradigm Shift
IV. Future Changes in Life Expectancy and Longevity
V. Summary

Antioxidants Enzymes or micronutrients that counteract the effects of free radicals produced in metabolic processes.

Caenorhabditis elegans A nematode with a small number of cells (959 in the hermaphrodite) with well-characterized functions that have been used in genetic studies of life span and its modification.

Gompertz An English actuary who, in 1825, developed a model predicting adult human mortality increases as an exponential function of age.

Homeostasis The principal that biological organisms have a range of state variable values associated with high vitality and that there are mechanisms to return the organism to that range after environmental factors stress the organism.

Life Expectancy The average number of years members of a population are observed to live.

Life Span The potential number of years an organism might survive if exogenous conditions were ideal.

Longevity The biological potential for length of life.

Mortality Selection The loss of specific traits from a population due to those traits being associated with elevated mortality risks.

Risk Factors Measures of physiological factors associated with elevated morbidity or mortality risks.

Vitality The capacity of the organism to resist death in the face of environmental stresses.

LONGEVITY is the physiological capacity of an organism to live a specific amount of time. Longevity is a theoretical construct, and its measurable manifestation is the life expectancy, or the average number of years lived, in a population. Long-lived populations are groups that have genetic or behavioral traits that allow them to survive much longer, on average, than typical groups of members of the species. The study of long-lived populations is one way to determine what factors are associated with increased longevity.

I. DEFINITIONS AND CONCEPTS

There is confusion between longevity and several related concepts. Life expectancy, the average number of years a person can expect to live, is usually estimated from a cross-sectional (period) life table created from probabilities of deaths calculated from age-specific death and population counts for different populations (birth cohorts) assessed at a point in time. In populations where mortality is declining, cross-sectional age-specific life expectancy estimates are lower than estimates for the cohort defining a specific age group at a point in time. This is because the cohort from which an age-specific population is selected often has lower mortality rates at later times than the older cohorts from which mortality rates for later ages at the current time are generated. Period life tables and life expectancies are often calculated because they require only cross-sectional mortality and population data and because they reflect the current (though synthetic) status of mortality in a population. To calculate a complete cohort life table requires reliable data on age-specific mortality and population counts for a hundred or more years in the past. In a cohort followed from birth to the death of its last member, life expectancy is the mean age at death. Though cohorts reflect the age trajectory of mortality for a population of individuals, cohort analysis has the disadvantage that by the time a cohort's mortality is completed, its early experience is 100 years out of date. Confounding of cohort, age, and period mortality changes cannot be resolved solely from mortality data.

Life expectancy, the mean of the distribution of the ages of death, is used to compare mortality across populations. Life span is the number of years a person could potentially live. An empirical quantity, the "realized" life span, is the number of years an individual is observed to live. One can also discuss life span in terms of the potential number of years either an individual, or a population on average, could live. A species-specific *maximum* life span is a theoretical construct implying an age beyond which no member of a species survives—an intrinsic characteristic of the species' physiology. The theoretical "average" life span is the mean of life span potentials for a population. This suggests individuals have different biological potentials for the number of years they may live (i.e., there is a distribution of biologically determined individual life spans for which the species *characteristic* "life span" is the mean). Even if a mean life span exists for a species, there may be no fixed life span limit if the mean life span is the average length of life generated by stochastic processes determining the amount of time individuals live. In this case the highest age at death observed is determined probabilistically (i.e., achievement of a "higher" age is stochastically possible), though with a "vanishingly" small probability. In contrast, the "mean" characteristic life span for a species is more precisely determined as population size increases.

Longevity, the physiological potential for length of life, can be viewed as relating to realized life span as fertility (i.e., the realized number of births) relates to fecundity (i.e., the biological potential for reproduction). A difficulty in assessing longevity and life span, and their relation to life expectancy, is that data on processes governing the capacity to maintain physiological homeostasis at late ages have rapidly increased as (a) age-related diseases are distinguished from age-dependent physiological losses (e.g., the effects of Alzheimer's disease on cognitive function vs. general loss of neurological capacity due to "senescence"), and (b) as understanding of "aging" mechanisms improves at the molecular level, and for complex interactions of multiple organ, tissue, and hormonal systems. [*See* HOMEOSTASIS.]

An approach for assessing the effects of senescence on longevity was suggested by Simms. He studied how resistant rats of specific ages were to fixed physiological insults (e.g., the age-specific ability to survive the loss of a fixed amount of blood). In this and other studies, there is a tendency to assess longevity and the progression of senescence as the ability to resist death (i.e., to equate the rate of aging with the rate of dying). The ability to resist death is a proxy for the status of multiple physiological variables, with values that stochastically evolve with age and interact with the environment. A critical feature of this evolution is whether its deterministic components are linear or nonlinear. This arises in the theoretical justification of many models where mortality is assumed to increase exponentially while, at least in cross-sectional studies, many physiological functions, the integration of which determines an individual's vitality, decrease linearly. If linear, then many models imply a slowing in mortality at late ages—an empirical observation often made. However, even if physiological functions individually decline linearly, if they interact, they may imply nonlinear declines in "vitality," (i.e., the overall ability to resist death). To resolve these issues requires direct observation of both the time trajectory of state variables and age changes in mortality. Consequently, many studies attempt to identify measures of "functional" age and biomarkers of aging. These searches also result from a realization that physiological function has been partly disassociated from mortality, as the ability to artificially (i.e., exogenously) maintain homeostasis is advanced by biomedical innovations (e.g., renal dialysis; kidney transplants). Research should now focus on directly assessing physiological state changes, with less emphasis on associations with chronological age per se. [*See* GROWTH FACTORS AND CELLULAR SENESCENCE.]

Important for studying life span, and its relation to the physiological state of the organism, is the effect of mortality selection on populations—both experimental and human. Both measurement of the age-specific effects of risk-factor exposures and of the genetic predisposition to disease and mortality are affected by selection (i.e., the process by which organisms with poor survival traits are selected from a population by early death). Selection tends to reduce the effects of genetic factors on morbidity and mortality at late ages because persons with profound deficits in the genetic endowment for health, or longevity, die at early ages. This generates a population whose average survival traits are increasingly biased to more favorable values with advancing age. For example, longitudinal studies of coronary heart disease (CHD) mortality in monozygotic (MZ) and dyzygotic (DZ) twins show that the relative risk of either genetic or environmental factors are highest in middle age—and decline to parity about age 90—an age above which mortality in human populations has tended to a constant. The CHD mortality relative risk for MZ male twins in several studies was highest at ages 40 to 50 (e.g., as high as 15 to 1) and converged to 1.0 above age 85. Similarly, thyroid autoantibodies show increases from age 50 to 85. From age 85 to 100 their level decreases, with centenarians having the same levels as persons age 50. This was also found in a study of the prevalence of the apolipoprotein E4 allele in Finnish centenarians in 1991. The allele for Apo E4 decreased in prevalence from 22.7% at ages 20 to 55 to 8.4% in centenarians—apparently due to the elevation of circulatory and Alzheimer's disease risk in persons with the Apo E4 genotype. Persons with E2 and E3 genotypes were survival advantaged. Thus, a number of human studies empirically demonstrated the age effects of mortality selection on multiple health dimensions.

The effects of mortality selection for health and longevity in very elderly (e.g., above age 95) persons are now being identified in clinical studies as the number of very elderly survivors increases. It has been suggested that survivors to age 95 may be in better health on average than younger populations (e.g., in their eighties) because, to survive to 95, a person generally has to be in good health. Dynamically, a decreasing capacity to maintain homeostasis with age interacts with increasing chronic disease prevalence. Very elderly persons, after a serious disease onsets, have short remaining lifetimes (due to low homeostatic reserves), so the death rate of affected persons exceeds the age-specific disease incidence rate. Consequently, disease (or disability) prevalence may decline at late ages.

Numerous models have been proposed to explain species characteristic life spans. Most assume a specific physiological basis for senescence, and that when senescence reduces homeostatic capacity sufficiently, almost any environmental insult is sufficient to cause death. For example, a recent model focuses on the telomere that links chromosomes. It is suggested that when cells divide, a portion of the telomere is consumed to preserve the fidelity of the transmission of genetic traits. The rate of consumption of the telomere dictates, in probabilistic terms, the potential number of successful cell replications. This may explain the Hayflick limit (i.e., the maximum number of cell replications are biologically limited). However, though more specific physiologically, some of the same questions arise for the telomere model. In one study, the number of cell replications lost per year of life was 0.2 in humans from age 30 to 80. Thus, with 40–50 potential replications per cell, this would not limit currently observed life expectancies. Additionally, there are different cell division rates in different tissues—in complex organisms there are a wide variety of tissues. Furthermore, there is extensive biochemical communication and feedback between cells in different tissues. For example, there is a down regulation of skeletal muscle performance in persons with congestive heart failure (CHF) that is greater than the down regulation attributable to the lesser cardiac output available to sustain skeletal muscle activity. In addition, growth factors control cell growth and function both locally in specific tissues and globally in the organism. Examples of such factors are insulin like growth factor-1 (IGF-1), affecting smooth muscle growth in arterial walls, and angiotensin-converting enzymes, affecting peripheral vasodilation as well as intimal tissue growth. The telomere model, though useful at the cellular level leaves unanswered questions as to how complex, multiorgan biological systems with extensive biochemical feedback systems fail.

As the teleomere is exhausted as the cell replicates, not only is the risk of cell death increased, but so may be the probability of errors in genetic trait transmission. In some cells an enzyme (telomerase) is expressed that preserves the telomere, making the cell immortal. Thus, interest has emerged in telomerase, both as a promising area for new cancer therapies and possibly in altering longevity.

Another theory of senescence involves the role of free radicals in aging. Though oxidation (and the production of free radicals) is necessary to normal metabolism, and may be necessary for some immunological responses (macrophages may use free radicals to selectively kill cells), reactive oxygen subspecies can disrupt other cell functions. It has been suggested that the age-specific role of the production of antioxidant enzymes such as superoxide dimustase (SOD), and glutathione peroxidase has been studied as factors in physiological aging changes. In studies of *C. elegans,* it was found that a gene strongly affecting the nematode's life span may be involved in SOD production.

The telomere and free radical models are two examples of many biological theories of aging (e.g., macromolecular alterations [i.e., protein synthesis errors; cross linkage; altered protein turnover; DNA damage, repair, and somatic mutation]; free radicals; organ system theories; genetic programming of senescence).

II. MODELS OF MORTALITY

A major challenge is to translate the kinetics of physiological aging, as they are explicated by research at the cellular and molecular level, into models of the population dynamics of mortality. These are needed to describe changes in longevity and life span and to distinguish them from life expectancy changes. The need for such models is evidenced by population and experimental data that are inconsistent with classical models of human aging and mortality. For example, the most generally used model of adult mortality is the Gompertz function where mortality is an exponential function of age, for example,

$$\mu(t) = \alpha e^{\theta t}, \qquad (1)$$

where $\mu(t)$ is the age-specific mortality rate, θ is the percent increase in mortality per year of age (a parameter that can be viewed as the rate of aging), t is age, and α a scale factor representing the initial mortality level (i.e., when $t = 0$; $e^{\theta t} = e^0 = 1.0$). The Gompertz approximates (with different values of α and θ) the age dependence of human mortality between ages 30

and 90 in a number of populations. Finch found it described adult mortality in a number of animal species.

The Gompertz assumes that the rate of loss of "vitality" is proportional to the initial level of vitality over an age interval. The Gompertz has been rationalized in different ways. Strehler and Mildvan and Sacher and Trucco both developed models consistent with an exponential increase of mortality with age. These require stochastic endogenous or exogenous processes to generate random perturbations of the physiological state of individuals, which accumulate so that the individual's state moves closer with age to a region of state variable values associated with higher mortality. Sacher and Trucco's theory emphasized the random or stochastic component of the mortality process though individual differences, due to either past environmental responses or genetics, would have to be dealt with in a comprehensive model. Depending upon the distribution of random state fluctuations (Sacher and Trucco assumed a Gaussian distribution; Strehler and Mildvan a Maxwell-Boltzman distribution), and the form of the higher mortality region boundary, different relations of α and θ can be generated. Both models were evaluated by fitting a Gompertz function to mortality data and examining how α and θ changed over populations with different mortality levels. The development of both theories recognized that persistent (nonrandom) individual state differences could produce a slowing in the exponential age increase of mortality due to selection.

A second function used to describe the age dependence of mortality is the Weibull, where mortality increases as a power m of age and time,

$$\mu(t) = \alpha t^{m-1}, \qquad (2)$$

where m is the number of errors required to occur before the system fails and α is a scale factor derived from the product of the probability of those errors. Rosenberg and colleagues examined the relations of α and m in thermodynamic models of the survival potential of organisms, where denaturation of specific proteins at specific temperatures was the rate-limiting step in the death of an organism. In this model α was temperature dependent; m was not. α was viewed as a function of many variables, including genetic and environmental factors, in addition to temperature. This model allowed longevity (the entropy activation value) to be determined on a single dimension scaled as kcal/mole for multicellular organisms such as *Drosophila melanogaster*. It was speculated that the thermodynamics of death for poikilothermic multicellular organisms could be extrapolated to homeotherms.

Both the Weibull and Gompertz are applicable to (a) cohort mortality trajectories (unless there is no mortality improvement in a population, period, and cohort mortality trajectories are different) and (b) approximate homogeneous populations. Both functions generate what are referred to in the engineering reliability literature as "extreme value" distributions. Extreme value distributions have the property that there is a mathematical isomorphism of the times to failure of critical organ systems within organisms, and the distribution of times to death for individuals in a population. For example, when modeling carcinogenesis, the Weibull describes the shortest time it takes for m errors to accumulate in one of a population of cells in the target organ. The distribution of the times to this first occurrence (i.e., accumulation of m errors) in one cell in a population of N cells is consistent with the distribution of the times to disease onset under the Weibull model for a population of individuals.

Such isomorphism of individual component process outcomes, and the distribution of events in the population assumes a homogeneous population (i.e., every individual in the population has the same value for the Weibull or Gompertz parameters). This is inconsistent with evidence on mortality selection in very elderly populations. Thus, both the Weibull and Gompertz (and the Sacher and Trucco and Strehler and Mildvan theoretical rationales for a Gompertz-type function) have to be altered to reflect persistent individual differences in model parameters.

For example, the age-specific incidence of many cancers tend to slow at late ages. Usually it is assumed that m, the number of genetic errors incurred before a cell loses growth control, is a biological constant in a specific tissue (e.g., in the colon, $m = 5$ or 6). If exposures to carcinogens differ for persons, the probability of each of the m errors (whose product determines α) also differs. Consequently, the parameter actually estimated from age-specific population cancer risks is $\overline{\alpha}$—the mean of the distribution of the α_i. Because persons with high α_i values are more likely to die from the cancer, they are systematically re-

moved from the population. Because persons with high α_i values are lost, $\overline{\alpha}$ declines with age—slowing the rate of increase of tumor incidence at late ages. Heterogeneity would also cause a leveling off of mortality at extreme ages in the stochastic models of Sacher and Trucco and Strehler and Mildvan. Such a leveling off could also be due to the decline in vitality due to accumulation of damage from environmental exposure. When vitality reached the same level as the average environmental shock, the mortality rate would be constant.

One problem in developing models for heterogeneous populations is selecting the distribution of the α_is—which is generally unobserved and determined by multiple factors. This is important because the distribution assumed for α_i determines its coefficient of variation (i.e., the relation of the variance of α_i to its mean, $\overline{\alpha}$). The coefficient of variation of α_i will determine how rapidly $\overline{\alpha}$ declines as high-risk persons die. In heterogeneous population forms of the model, a Weibull, still describe age-related failure for individuals (i.e., for α_i fixed).

Similar adjustments can be made to the Gompertz (i.e., the scale factor α is assumed to be distributed). If the α_i are gamma distributed, the gamma mixed Gompertz approximates a logistic curve for the dependence of mortality on age, with mortality reaching a high, constant level at late ages. Actuaries found mortality at late ages often increased less rapidly than the Gompertz—in some human populations it reached a high constant value as in the logistic. Beard saw the logistic as resulting from a gamma-distributed mixture of Makeham mortality functions. The failure to identify when the Gompertz function is a biologically inappropriate model of mortality at extreme ages may be due to (a) sample sizes insufficient to statistically test alternative hazard functions with adequate power, (b) statistically inefficient procedures for parameter estimation, and (c) a failure to gather data on individuals who are truly of physiologically extreme ages for the species studied.

An assumption of heterogeneous population models is that the distribution of risks is fixed by the age at which one begins modeling the population. Such fixed frailty explains declines, or slower rates of age increase, in mortality at late ages, but it does not describe the effects of changes in individual risk differences. To do so, these models must be generalized to describe systematic age changes in individual characteristics by making α, in either the Weibull or Gompertz, a function of time-varying covariates, for example,

$$\mu(t, \underset{\sim}{x}_{it}, \theta) = \alpha_i(t)e^{\theta t} = (\underset{\sim}{x}_{it}^T B \underset{\sim}{x}_{it})e^{\theta t}, \qquad (3)$$

where mortality, μ, varies as a function of age (t), the physiological traits ($\underset{\sim}{x}_{it}$) of individuals (with a matrix of positive coefficients, B) and unobserved factors defining the age dependence of mortality ($e^{\theta t}$) conditional upon $\underset{\sim}{x}_{it}$. The Weibull is generalized,

$$\mu(t, \underset{\sim}{x}_{it}, m) = \alpha_i(t)t^{m-1} = (\underset{\sim}{x}_{it}^T B \underset{\sim}{x}_{it})t^{m-1}, \qquad (4)$$

where the quadratic term is again a function of time-varying covariates.

To estimate such models, data on time-varying covariates is needed (i.e., longitudinal data on multiple physiological variables). Thus, in equations for μ, α_i is a function of j state variables measured at time t for person i. To relate $\alpha_i(t)$ to covariates it is assumed to be a quadratic function of the time-specific trait profile $\underset{\sim}{x}_{it}$. By using a quadratic function one can use the property that the sum of quadratic forms produces a quadratic form to model cause-specific mortality by estimating a hazard for each of C causes.

Assessing the $\underset{\sim}{x}_{it}$ at each time of measurement in a longitudinal study does not describe how $\underset{\sim}{x}_{it}$ changes with age. Changes in $\underset{\sim}{x}_{it}$ can be described for survivors t to $t + 1$, as,

$$\underset{\sim}{x}_{it+1} = \underset{\sim}{u}_0(t) + A(t)\underset{\sim}{x}_{it} + B(t)\underset{\sim}{y}_{it} + C(t)(\underset{\sim}{x}_{it} \cdot \underset{\sim}{y}_{it}) + \underset{\sim}{e}_{it}. \qquad (5)$$

Values of $\underset{\sim}{x}_{it+1}$ are functions of individual trajectories $u_0(t)$, the prior state of the individual, $\underset{\sim}{x}_{it}$, with age-varying coefficients ($A(t)$) and exogenous factors, y_{it}, with time-varying coefficients $B(t)$. Interactions of exogenous ($\underset{\sim}{y}_{it}$) and endogenous ($\underset{\sim}{x}_{it}$) variables are modeled with time-varying coefficients, $C(t)$. These reflect interactions of the phenotypic expression of genetic traits on state parameters, with environmental factors. $\underset{\sim}{u}_0(t)$, represents the age track of a state variable caused by unobserved factors. Genetic traits expressed in $\underset{\sim}{u}_0(t)$ do not interact with exogenous factors but represent the genetic age dependence of each state variable. $\underset{\sim}{e}_{it}$ reflects uncertainty about the system's future (i.e., the covariance matrix of the $\underset{\sim}{e}_{it}$ represents diffusion in the J stochastic processes describing state changes). The function in (5) can be respecified in theoretically relevant ways. Higher order temporal lags could be included. One could also test whether

physiological functions are (a) linear or nonlinear functions of age, or (b) whether different variables interact in a compensating or reenforcing way to change vitality. Systematic state dynamics are not represented in Sacher and Trucco or Strehler and Mildvan's model because deviations of state variable values are exogenously randomly generated. The model represented by (3), (or (4) or (5)) describes both deterministic (drift) and random (diffusion) state changes interacting with a quadratic, multidimensional force of selection which is itself a function of state changes.

The mortality and dynamic equations are evaluated simultaneously (i.e., the values of $\underset{\sim}{x}_{it}$ in the quadratic function at t are generated from equation (5)). The mean and variance of the $\underset{\sim}{x}_{it}$ in (5) over time (for the population) will be regulated by the systematic mortality described by the age-dependent quadratic function in (3) (or (4)).

Such a two-component model has several advantages. First, the dynamic equations described age changes in the state of the physiological system. Second, the adequacy of the state descriptions can be assessed. In the mortality function, as information in $\underset{\sim}{x}_{it}$ increases, the effects of $e^{\theta t}$ (for the Gompertz form) declines. A decline of θ means that information in unobserved factors represented by θ are explicitly represented by the time trajectories of $\underset{\sim}{x}_{it}$. When $\theta = 0.0$, all information relevant to survival is represented by the trajectories of the $\underset{\sim}{x}_{it}$. In the dynamic equations, as $\underset{\sim}{x}_{it}$ and y_{it} become more informative, the dependence of $\underset{\sim}{u}_0$, A, $\underset{\sim}{B}$, and C on age–time per se declines— reflecting that the state variables are sufficient to describe the temporal evolution of the organism's state. Thus, one can test the adequacy of the state description of both aging and mortality processes— and their interactions. When the organism is well described one knows which state variables to change to increase life expectancy and how rate constants (dynamic coefficients) need to be changed to alter life span.

The state variables in the mortality and dynamic equations can be multivariate functions of other measures (e.g., $\underset{\sim}{x}_{it}$ could be descriptions of the functional status of persons. Functional status, assessed from the individual's capacity to perform a wide range of tasks, may better describe an organism's state than specific physiological parameters—an issue examined below.

III. EVIDENCE ON MORTALITY TRAJECTORIES—A NEED FOR A PARADIGM SHIFT

Experimental and human studies call into question classical models of the age dependence of mortality suggesting a need for new paradigms.

In a study of 1.1 million medflies (*ceratitis capitata*), mortality was found to be constant at "advanced ages" (after 90% of the population had died). Because the population was heterogeneous, this could be due to selection.

Mortality has also been found to be constant at late ages for genetically homogeneous fruitfly (*Drosophila melanogaster*) populations. However, because these populations were genetically homogeneous, selection is unlikely to explain the age pattern.

In a study of 180,000 isogenic *C. elegans* and 1,625 *C. elegans* of 79 genotypes heterogeneous for mean life span, the heterogeneous population mortality was constant from 17 to 60 days. In the isogenic population mortality continued to increase—though not exponentially.

Two genes (*daf*-2 and *daf*-16) have been found to be responsible for a doubling of the life span of *C. elegans*. Though life span doubled, the variability of ages at death did not decrease (i.e., heterogeneity in ages at death remained). The maintenance of variability in the age of death distribution for an experimentally controlled population suggests the length of life was increased not by eliminating exogenous forces of mortality but by manipulation of endogenous life span and longevity traits. As suggested above, the longevity gene in *C. elegans* may operate by controlling the production of an antioxidant enzyme (i.e., SOD).

Actuaries in the early twentieth century and most recent research has found that human mortality at late ages increases more slowly than predicted by a Gompertz. This is not represented in some Social Security Administration (SSA) life tables because mortality at late ages in those tables is fit to a Gompertz (i.e., mortality is assumed to increase at 5% per year past age 95 for males, and 6% per year for females) estimates from the charter cohort of Social Security beneficiaries (i.e., largely males age 65 in 1937–1939). It is unclear that cohort's experience, which terminated when the last member died at age 108 in about 1980,

describes mortality at late ages for males and females in 1995. Research suggests early nutritional status has effects on chronic disease risks. Civil War veterans passing age 65 in 1910 had more chronic morbidity than World War II veterans passing age 65 in 1985. Morbidity prevalence declined 6% per decade over the 75 years. Additionally, the education and economic status of new elderly cohorts has improved. This suggests continuing cohort mortality declines. There are four data sets where age is reported independent of census sources (which is subject to age-reporting errors) and mortality is followed to extreme ages, which can be used to examine recent mortality experience.

In a study that matched edited Social Security and Medicare records to death certificates for 1987, for Whites, age reporting on death certificates was consistent with that in the edited Social Security and Medicare records. It was also found that, consistent with several European countries, the U.S. centenarian population grew 7% per annum from 1980 to 1987. The peak period mortality rate estimate for 1987 was 52% at age 110.

In a French study, centenarians were examined who had preexisting relations with physicians. In this group, cross-sectional mortality rates from ages 100 to 109 averaged 44% per year.

The numbers of centenarians in these studies is limited and the data are cross-sectional. A data set where mortality at extreme ages can be examined in a large human population using ages recorded before death is a study of 50,000 persons passing age 75 between 1960 and 1987. These persons were the elderly portion of the American Cancer Society (ACS) Study of the health and health habits of one million U.S. residents. This population is, on average, better educated than the U.S. population and thus may have better than average mortality. Balancing their better education is the fact that the population's experience is drawn from a 27-year period during which there were significant mortality improvements at later ages.

In this population it was possible to estimate the percent change in mortality per year of age and mortality rates, above age 100. The average mortality probabilities per year of age from 95–109 were 34.3% for males and, for ages 100–109, 32.4% for females. This is lower than 1990 SSA period life-table estimates of average annual mortality probabilities of 39.7% for males, and 36.0% for females, aged 100–109. In the ACS study the per annum increase in mortality declined from 8.8% at ages 75–84 for males to 2.4% at ages 95–109. For females the decline was from 10.5% at age 75–84 to 3.4% at ages 100–109. Thus, there is a slower age increase in mortality for the ACS study than in SSA life tables where per annum increases of 5% (vs. 2.4%) for males and 6% (vs. 3.4%) for females were assumed above age 95.

Larger numbers of centenarians can be analyzed using U.S. mortality data to calculate extinct cohort life tables (i.e., life tables where the population at age x is the sum of all deaths observed after age x in a cohort). This has the advantage that (a) age reporting on death certificates is of as high quality as in edited SSA and Medicare records; (b) because numerators and denominators are consistent over age (the population is the sum of deaths past age x) age reporting errors balance out; and (c) mortality estimates are for cohorts.

Mortality (q_x) for U.S. and Japanese cohorts aged 70 in 1962 followed to 1990 are in Figure 1.

The q_xs in Figure 1 are smoothed using a 5-year moving average. Mortality is higher in Japan above age 70 with differences increasing to age 100. Past age 98 data from older cohorts were spliced in (e.g., from 99–108 the cohort aged 80 in 1962), so the convergence above 100 is due to smaller U.S. and Japanese differences in older cohorts.

Japan has the world's highest life expectancy at birth (i.e., in 1992, 83.0 years for females; 76.3 years for males). At age 65 Japanese life expectancy was 16.6 years for males and 21.1 years for females. Despite these values, health care, especially long-term care (LTC), for the elderly is poor in Japan. Because of a lack of LTC institutions, long hospital stays for elderly stroke patients are common. In 1987, 20% of 1.1 million hospital inpatients were 65+ with stays of 6+ months. Japanese LTC facilities also often lack physical and other rehabilitation therapies so 34% of residents are bedridden—compared to 6.5% in the United States and 4.2% in Sweden. Given poor quality of care for the elderly and oldest-old in Japan, it is not surprising that U.S. mortality at late ages is lower. Census Bureau 1993 period life expectancy estimates for U.S. Pacific Islanders and Asians are 86.2 years for females and 80.2 years for males—three years higher than Japan. Cohort life expectancy in populations with improving mortality is often 2 to 3 years higher than period estimates—potentially implying

cohort life expectancies of 89 years for females and 83 years for males in this U.S. subpopulation which should be crudely similar in racial admixture to the Japanese population.

Extinct cohort methods were applied to three U.S. cohorts aged 70, 80, and 90 in 1962. Mortality improved in the 20 years between cohorts. The mortality percent increases per year of age did not change over cohorts for males (i.e., for the two older cohorts it was about 2% per year above age 100). For females the mortality percent per year of age increases slowed from 3.2 to 2.6% for the two oldest cohorts. Both male and female estimates of age increases in mortality above 100 are lower than in SSA tables. Mortality estimates at age 100 for the cohort age 80 in 1962 (followed for 29 years to 1990) were roughly similar to those in the ACS study (followed for 27 years from 1960 to 1987) for ages 100–109 (i.e., 34.2% vs. 34.6% for males and 32.3% vs. 32.4% for females). Thus, extinct cohort and ACS analyses produce similar results and suggest U.S. cohort mortality estimates are lower than period estimates. The cohort q_xs are in Figure 2.

The q_xs at extreme ages (smoothed by a 5-year moving average) increase slowly—2 to 3% above age 100. This pattern may be characteristic of mortality dynamics for long-term survivors in any population (i.e., when the homeostatic potential of an individual reaches low levels almost any environmental insult can cause death). Thus at late ages, mortality risks and rates of aging reach an equilibrium. To examine late-age dynamics, different models and data (i.e., longitudinal studies with multiple assessments of physiological variables) are needed so that health and mortality dynamics can be modeled directly.

In modeling the trajectories of risk factors over 34 years in the Framingham Study the mean of many risk factors was predicted to plateau above age 95 as illustrated for vital capacity index (VCI) in Figure 3. This plateau effect is caused by the interaction of risk-factor dynamics and the age increasing (i.e., $\theta > 8\%$) quadratic mortality risk (i.e., persons with low VCI values die off more rapidly after age 95 than VCI function is lost through aging dynamics), producing an equilibrium in the population at (for VCI) age 100–105.

This model of risk factor trajectories and mortality can be used to estimate life expectancy using "ideal" risk-factor profiles in this model. With an ideal risk-

Males

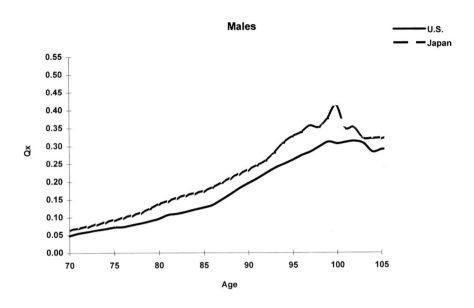

Females

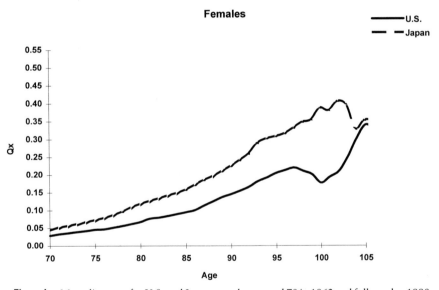

Figure I Mortality rates for U.S. and Japanese cohorts aged 70 in 1962 and followed to 1990.

factor profile, life expectancies of 100+ years were predicted. These are extreme in that they assume risk-factor profiles are maintained at optimal values. The model used to make estimates, however, did *not* assume (a) mortality changed below 30, (b) senescent-related increases in mortality are 0 (i.e., θ estimates were 8.05% for males and 8.12% for females conditional upon the risk factor trajectories), or (c) elimina-

tion of any cause of death. The results from the model can be compared to life expectancy estimates made from studies of select long-lived populations with good mortality characteristics and risk-factor profiles. In the select populations (Mormon High Priests; Mormon High Priests with healthy lifestyles; Almeada Study persons with healthy lifestyles; a Mormon-insured population; risk-factor-adjusted estimates for

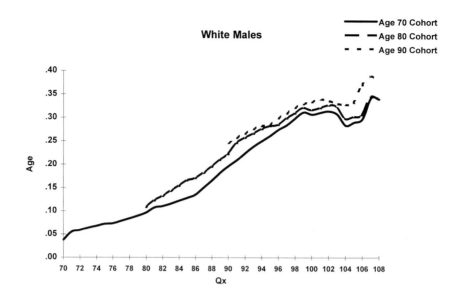

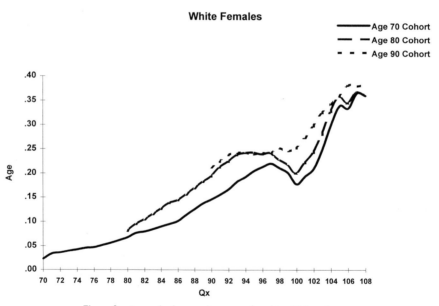

Figure 2 Smoothed mortality rates for three U.S. cohorts.

an active population; estimates from the 18-year follow-up of Almeada County study members; Longterm Seventh Day Adventists; Okinawans) life expectancy estimates (based on survivors to age 30) ranged from 79–98 years for males (averaging 88 years) and from 83.3 to 98.6 (averaging 89 years) for females.

Thus, the ideal risk-factor profile model produced a higher life expectancy (by 7+ years) than observed in long-lived U.S. populations. There may be further life expectancy to be gained in long-lived populations by manipulating known risk factors.

Recent evidence suggests risk factor effects on

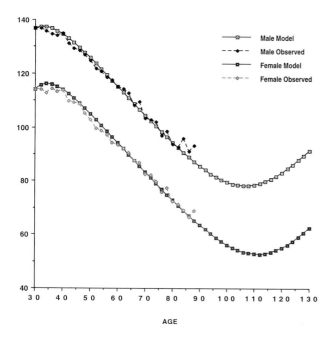

Figure 3 Vital Capacity Index risk factor means from the Framingham Study

health are underestimated when the attenuation of the relation of those factors to risk is not adjusted. For cholesterol the attenuation bias due to (a) regression (i.e., elevated risk-factor levels tend to regress to the mean), and (b) proxy effects (i.e., total cholesterol is modeled instead of low-density lipoproteins), could be as high as 60%. This would increase the estimated effect of cholesterol on survival in the risk-factor model calibrated to the ideal risk factor profile.

Mortality and disability age trajectories estimated from the 1982, 1984, and 1989 NLTCs are shown in Figure 4. The age decline in the average level of function (i.e., the "active") reverses about age 95, when the proportion of disabled starts to decline. This is due to mortality reaching high age-specific levels so that a relative risk above 1.0 for the disabled causes their higher mortality to dominate age increases in disability incidence. Overall mortality trajectories reach roughly the levels (30–40%) found in extinct cohort analyses, whereas risks for the disabled reach extremely high (80–90%) levels for both genders. Mortality for active females is much lower than overall mortality. Thus, late-age equilibriums of both physiological and functional dynamics with mortality can be illustrated in longitudinal data.

IV. FUTURE CHANGES IN LIFE EXPECTANCY AND LONGEVITY

A deficiency of past life expectancy forecasts is the failure to realize that, with respect to chronic disease, the U.S. is entering a historically unique period. U.S. research on chronic diseases started in earnest with the initiation of longitudinal studies of heart disease (e.g., the Framingham Heart Study in 1949–1950). Those studies began to identify CVD risk factors in the 1950s and early 1960s. National risk-factor prevention programs were begun in 1962–1963 (Surgeon General's report on health effects of smoking), 1972–1973 (National Hypertension Control Programs), and 1988 (the National Cholesterol Education Program).

Once chronic disease risk factors are identified, time is required to develop efficient interventions, and to disseminate them to the population. For example, the first antihypertensives were diuretics. A second class of agents were beta-blockers followed by calcium channel blockers and then angiotensin-converting enzyme II (ACE-II) inhibitors. Side effect profiles differed for each drug class as did cost–benefit ratios. ACE-II inhibitors not only control hypertension, but may control (and even possibly cause to regress) left ventricular hypertrophy (LVH), may be used to treat CHF, may slow atherogenesis (i.e., at levels lower than needed to control hypertension they block the growth-stimulating effects of angiotensin on smooth muscle cells) and the loss of renal function. The search for CVD risk factors is far from complete. Elevated homocysteine (due to folic acid deficiency) may be a risk factor as may be the effects of free radicals (and possibly body iron stores) on CVD. Postmenopausal gender differences in CVD may also be due to the interaction of atherogenesis and osteoporosis. Interventions include not only drugs, but also improved mechanical aids such as dual chamber, demand-controlled pacemakers.

Our knowledge of the effects of exercise and nutrition (and microsupplement use) on health at late ages is still in early stages. Physical activity can affect function and survival to very late ages (e.g., age 107). In very elderly (e.g., ages 86–96) frail populations, weight-bearing exercise and nutrition have been proven to increase function. Mortality forecasts do not yet adequately represent the effects of such factors. [See DIET AND NUTRITION.]

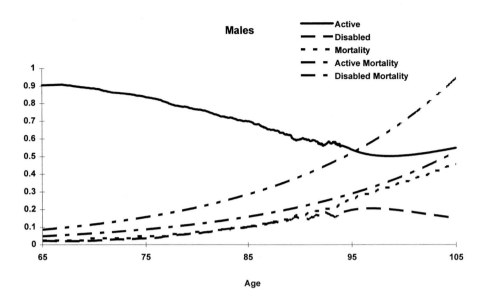

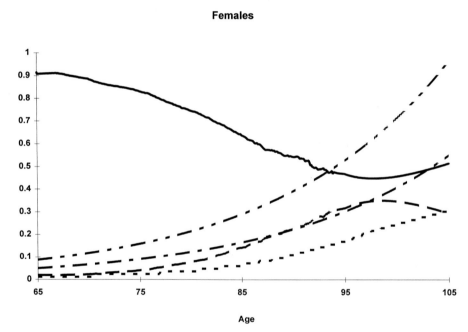

Figure 4 Mortality and disability age trajectories estimated from the 1982, 1984, and 1989 National Long Term Care Survey

Changes in longevity (and life span) require basic changes in human physiology. Here progress is just beginning. Tests of gene-altering interventions in genetically determined diseases (e.g., familial hypercholesteremia) have begun. Interventions affecting the subtle equilibrium of hormonal systems (e.g., ACE-II inhibitors in the renin, angiotensin, aldosterone system; human growth hormone and IGF-1) may extend life span. Increasing use of exogenous estrogens (from about 3 million women in 1985) raises the question whether such interventions, when affecting multiple risks (e.g., CVD, osteoporosis), possibly extend life span by influencing longevity. A synthetic "alteration" of the age at menopause to continue higher estrogen production might be viewed as a longevity change. The issue is whether that is different than ingestion of exogenous estrogens (possibly by delivery systems such as transdermal patches to closely mimic natural hormone bioavailability) to reduce fracture and CVD risks.

V. SUMMARY

The evidence suggests that there is great potential to increase life expectancy—the ability to increase longevity is just beginning as the understanding of the molecular and genetic basis of aging improves.

To better evaluate the potential to change life expectancy and to modify life span and longevity will require new data, concepts, and analytic models. For example, the U.S. centenarian population has increased over 7% per year from 1960 to at least 1987. Will this produce a less functional centenarian population because selection is decreasing? Or will health remain better at later ages because good general health is a prerequisite to survive to such late ages? To answer such questions mortality data and models of age at death distributions (in whatever form) are inadequate. Temporal changes in the physiological state and functional status of individuals have to be analyzed using models of state dynamics and mortality. Such data and models are necessary to resolve differences between population life expectancy and its limits, life span (and its limits), and to understand the longevity potential of human populations—and its relation to health changes at late ages. This resolution also requires that models fully exploit insights from biomedical research.

BIBLIOGRAPHY

Beard, R. E. (1963). A theory of mortality based on actuarial, biological and medical considerations. In *International Population Conference, New York, 1961, Proceedings* (vol. 1, p. 611). London: International Union for the Scientific Study of Population.

Brooks, A., Lithgow, G., & Johnson, T. (1994). Mortality rates in a genetically heterogeneous population of *Caenorhabditis elegans. Science, 263,* 668.

Carey, J. R., Liedo, P., Orozco, D. & Vaupel, J. W. (1992). Slowing of mortality rates at older ages in large medfly cohorts. *Science, 258,* 457.

Curtsinger, J. W., Fukui, H. H., Townsend, D. R., & Vaupel, J. W. (1992). Demography of genotypes: Failure of the limited-lifespan paradigm in *Drosophila melanogaster. Science, 258,* 461.

Cutler, R. (1991). Antioxidants and ageing. *American Journal of Clinical Nutrition, 53,* 373S.

Economos, A. C. (1982). Rate of aging, rate of dying, and the mechanisms of mortality. *Archives of Gerontological Geriatrics, 1,* 3.

Finch, C. E. (1990). *Longevity, senescence, and the genome.* Chicago: University of Chicago Press.

Fogel, R. W. (1994). Economic growth, population theory, and physiology: The bearing of long-term processes on the making of economic policy. *American Economic Review, 84,* 369.

IPSEN Fondation. (1991). Étude "A la récherche du secret des centenaires." *Sous l'égide de la fondation de France* (100 Tableaux pour 100 ans), (Document No. 1). Premiers résultats. Automne.

Johnson, T. E., & Lithgow, G. J. (1992). The search for the genetic basis of aging: The identification of gerontogenes in the nematode *Caenorhabditis elegans. Journal of the American Geriatrics Society, 40,* 936–945.

Kenyon, C., Cheng, T., Geusch, E., Rudner, A., & Tabtiang, R. (1993). A *C. elegans* mutant that lives twice as long as wild types. *Nature, 336,* 461.

Kestenbaum, B. (1992). A description of the extreme aged population based on improved Medicare enrollment data. *Demography, 29,* 565.

Lew, E. A., & Garfinkel, L. (1990). Mortality at ages 75 and older in the cancer prevention study (CPSI). *Cancer Journal for Clinicians, 40,* 210.

Lindsted, K. D., Tonstad, S., & Kuzma, J. W. (1991). Self-report of physical activity and patterns of mortality in Seventh-Day Adventist men. *Journal of Clinical Epidemiology, 44,* 355.

Manton, K. G., Stallard, E., & Tolley, H. D. (1991). Limits to human life expectancy: Evidence, prospects, and implications. *Population and Development Review, 17,* 603.

Manton, K. G., Stallard, E., Woodbury, M. A., & Dowd, J. E. (1994). Time varying covariates of human mortality and aging: Multidimensional generalization of the Gompertz. *Journal of Gerontology: Biological Sciences, 49,* B169.

Martin, G. M., Spaque, C. A., & Epstein, C. J. (1970). Replicative life-span of cultivated human cells: Effects of donor's age, tissue and genotype. *Laboratory Investigations, 23,* 86.

Perls, T. T. (1994). The oldest old. *Scientific American, 274,* 70.

Rosenberg, B., Kemeny, G., Smith, L. G., Skurnick, I. D., & Bandurski, M. J. (1973). The kinetics and thermodynamics of death in multicellular organisms. *Mechanisms of Ageing and Development, 2,* 275.

Sacher, G. A., & Trucco, E. (1962). The stochastic theory of mortality. *Annals of the New York Academy of Sciences, 96,* 985.

Simms, H. (1942). The use of measurable causes of death (hemorrhage) for the evaluation of aging. *Journal of General Physiology, 26,* 169.

Strehler, B. L., & Mildvan, A. S. (1960). General theory of mortality and aging. *Science, 132,* 14.

M

Markers of Aging

Gerald E. McClearn

The Pennsylvania State University

I. The Diversity of Biomarkers
II. Biometric Considerations
III. Biomarkers as Elements of Complex Systems
IV. Biomarkers in Changing Systems
V. Scale
VI. Summary

Biomarker A term for a descriptive or predictive variable intended to measure some aspect of some aging process.
Gerometric Biometric, psychometric, and sociometric applications to gerontology.
Reliability The proportion of variance in a measured variable that is attributable to variance in true scores as contrasted to error variance.
Validity The degree to which a measured variable represents the construct that it is intended to represent.

The term **BIOMARKER**, which is encountered with increasing frequency in the gerontological literature, is used with a variety of implicit or explicit definitions. In some contexts, a biomarker is expected to predict longevity; in other usages, it is expected to be correlated with physiological age; in still others, it is expected to be descriptive of a fundamental aspect of aging, and so on. This breadth of usage is so great that an argument can be made that the phrase, "biomarker of aging" is simply synonymous with "age-related variable."

When understood in this broad sense the only advantage of the label biomarker over the term "variable" might be the specific emphasis on biology

provided by *bio* and the reminder provided by *marker* that the variable in question is a proxy or surrogate variable. In the final analysis, whether it be labeled biomarker or age-related-variable, it is being used because one cannot measure biological age or aging directly.

In some contexts, the term biomarker is employed in a more restricted sense to refer specifically to variables being used in a multivariate attempt to define biological or functional age. In another, specialized usage, the biomarker label is reserved for outcome variables appropriate to assess the efficacy of an intervention designed to affect some aspect of aging processes. The desirability of a standard reference set of biomarkers in the latter sense has motivated a major program initiative of the National Institute on Aging.

In a recent evaluation of biomarkers, Arking has provided the following (paraphrased) list of desiderata, which may be regarded as a representative summary of current thinking in the field. Biomarkers should

1. change with time at a rate that reflects the rate of aging,
2. be monitoring some basic, important process,
3. be nonlethal, and preferably noninvasive and minimally traumatic,
4. be highly reproducible,
5. reflect physiological age,
6. display change over a relatively short period,
7. be crucial to the maintenance of health,
8. be measureable in a variety of species,
9. serve as predictor of life span, and/or
10. serve as a retrospective marker of aging.

As a further summary, it might be suggested that the desired attributes of biomarkers fall into three classes: pragmatic, ethical, and methodological. Pragmatically, biomarkers should be simple and inexpensive to measure. Ethically, they should be minimally intrusive, causing the least possible pain and stress. Methodologically, it is desirable that they be nondestructive (permitting longitudinal research); capable of demonstrating change over a relatively short portion of the life span; insensitive to effects of previous measurement; and robust over a large range of laboratory and experimental conditions. Of utmost importance is that they measure aging validly and reliably. The meaning of this last statement engages subtle issues, some of which will be elaborated later.

I. THE DIVERSITY OF BIOMARKERS

In the broadest usage described above, every attribute measured in a study of aging could reasonably be regarded as a biomarker. The range of applicability is nearly as great when more constrained definitions are used. In a conference reviewing the state of research at the onset of the biomarker initiative of the National Institute on Aging, genetic, molecular, cellular, tissue, and whole-organism variables were discussed. A few years later, the First International Congress on Biomarkers of Aging: Expression and Regulation was convened. Titles from the proceedings of that congress reveal a similarly wide array of measures. A sample of the domains within which putative biomarkers were investigated include neuroendocrine systems, degradation of altered protein molecules, lateral mobility of cell membrane proteins, DNA repair, molecular myocardial changes, membrane cholesterol, blood–brain barrier permeability, immune system alteration, heat shock proteins, activity levels, and cognitive functioning.

In a book on preventive intervention oriented toward the general reader, Evans and Rosenberg identified the following as pertinent biomarkers: muscle mass, strength, basal metabolic rate, body fat percentage, aerobic capacity, blood sugar tolerance, cholesterol or high-density lipoprotein (HDL) ratio, blood pressure, bone density, and ability to regulate internal temperature.

Obviously, neither a comprehensive review nor an evaluation of the degree to which each of these bio-

markers meets the specified criteria is within the scope of the present article. What follows is, therefore, a discussion of some principles that have general applicability.

II. BIOMETRIC CONSIDERATIONS

The definitions of biomarkers are quite varied, but all refer in one way or another to the measurement of age or aging. An appreciation of the purposes and requirements of biomarkers requires consideration of some basic issues of measurement in gerontology. Obviously, biomarkers must meet the same biometric, psychometric, and sociometric requirements as any other variable in biological, behavioral, or social sciences. In the dynamic context of change in aging there are some special, gerometric issues.

A. Limitations of Chronological Age as a Metric in Gerontological Research

At a cursory glance, gerontologists might be thought to possess a superb measurement instrument in the form of the calendar, for it is possible in principle to determine the chronological age of most human beings and animal subjects to a high degree of accuracy. For some purposes, this simple statement of chronological age—the number of days, months, or years that the individual organism has been alive—may suffice. For example, if the gerontological question concerns the relative longevity of different species, the relevant information may be provided by the average ages at death of people and mice, for example. Such facts of species differences in life span engage fundamental issues of evolution. For many purposes, however, calendar age is an unsatisfactory index, principally because, within species, individuals of the same chronological age may differ markedly in respect to a number of attributes that we associate with the aging process. Thus, there must be a process(es) at work that is somewhat, but not too closely, related to the passage of time, but that differs from individual to individual. To assign the same age value to a number of individuals, all of whom were born on a particular day in 1920, say, would omit information on the huge differences existing among them in functional competence, cognitive performance, memory capability, glucose tolerance, aerobic capacity, pulmonary functioning, cardiovascular health, body composition, and so on.

The facts of intraspecific variability in aging processes are of basic biological interest equal to those of interspecific differences. These individual differences are, of course, central to societal concern over the health and welfare of an aging population; it is expected that elucidation of the determinants of individuality in rate and pattern of aging will powerfully inform efforts to promote "successful aging" and extend the healthy life span.

If, as we have seen, individual differences reduce the descriptive and predictive value of chronological age, then measures must be employed that are capable of characterizing the individual differences of these features. The functional age of an organism may then be considered to be its relative rank among comparable individuals of the same chronological age with respect to these measures. Aging comes to be defined, then, as change with respect to these measures as a function of chronological time. The crux of the matter becomes the selection of measures, or, it may be said, of biomarkers of age and aging.

B. Validity: What Does a Biomarker Measure?

Perhaps the simplest definition of the concept of validity is that it is an index of the extent to which any empirical measure actually measures what it is alleged to measure. Under some circumstances, the entity or property under investigation could actually be measured directly, but the measure used is a substitute, (or proxy, or surrogate, or marker, or indicator) for it. In some cases, the marker is employed rather than the real thing because the marker is more convenient or less expensive. Though it might require considerable effort in practice, the determination of validity in these instances is conceptually straightforward. The *concurrent validity* of the marker can be evaluated by obtaining the correlation between it and the definitional "real thing" measured at the same time.

In other cases, the real thing will only exist in the future, and the objective is to predict it from the surrogate measurement. A familiar example of the latter situation is the attempt to predict success in college or in graduate school from standardized tests. Determining the correlation between the marker vari-

able and the outcome variable (when it later becomes available) is described as the predictive validity of the marker. Validity of this type is implied by the above-cited definitions of aging, which refer to the ability to predict longevity as a major criterion of biomarker status. Indeed, some investigators maintain that longevity is the ultimate validity criterion for a biomarker. A major difficulty in accepting age at death as the defining variable in gerontology is the loss of information concerning the highly variable differences in trajectory and pattern by which individuals arrive at the point of death. Thus, whereas longevity has high "face validity" (on the face of the matter, it seems that length of life must be related to aging), any claims that it enjoys superordinate status as the fundamental validity criterion for biomarkers of aging must be carefully and skeptically examined.

Circumstances abound in the life sciences where explanation invokes hypothetical constructs for which no single, unambiguous measure is consensually accepted by scientists as telling the truth, the whole truth, and nothing but the truth, about it. For constructs of this nature, of which age and aging are widely regarded as examples, there are several approaches to assessment of validity. Content validity, for example, refers to the extent to which a measure (or panel of measures, collectively) samples the domain under investigation. Obviously, to judge content validity, one requires an already highly developed understanding of the domain itself. Another approach is that of construct validity, which is the extent to which the biomarker behaves as predicted by formal theory or by expectation derived from a coherent body of empirical data. For example, although the limitations of chronological age have been discussed, it certainly appears that a valid biomarker of aging should have some relationship to it. Traditionally, this age relevance has been sought in the form of mean differences among groups of different chronological age, or of mean changes in longitudinal studies. The examination of mean values in this context is conceptually direct, but may overlook data of great value. For some purposes, systematic change in variances, covariances, kurtosis, and skewness should qualify a purported biomarker as age-relevant as definitively as would the conventional change in means.

From the perspective of construct validity, it might also be expected that a nominated biomarker of age should respond appropriately to an intervention, such as dietary restriction, which has been shown to increase life span. One problem in applying this criterion arises from the complexity of aging, discussed in more detail below. Different subprocesses of aging may proceed relatively independently and may be differentially susceptible to interventions. For example, research has shown that an antiaging treatment beneficial in one genotype may be harmful in another. Thus, legitimate measures of some aging processes in some animals might be rejected as biomarkers if tested with a different group of subjects. This observation epitomizes the general principle that the validity of a model system is a function not only of the biomarker employed, but also of the total context of its measurement, including the genotypes of the animal subjects.

C. Generalizability of Animal Model Results to Humankind

The types of validity discussed above concern the extent to which the measurement of some attribute of, for example, a mouse, is really assessing what it is intended to, *in the mouse*. In research that has the ultimate goal of illuminating aging processes in humankind, there is another level of concern about validity—the generalizability across the phyletic scale from animal model to human beings.

For some biomedical phenomena, the homology of human to animal condition may be apparent—blood pressure, glucose tolerance, renal function, muscle anatomy, body composition, immune system parameters, and so on. Even in these cases of high "face" validity of the animal model, however, there are often subtle differences that must be carefully evaluated.

In the realm of behavior the homology of animal to human phenotype is usually more difficult to demonstrate. The mouse equivalent of a test of fluid cognitive ability is not obvious, for example. However, this difficulty should not be regarded as totally prohibitive. Typically, the hope in utilizing the animal model is that there exists in the animal some system that has properties sufficiently similar to the human system that the former will be informative about *some* aspects of the latter. Of particular relevance to the topic of behavior are the parallels in the neurochemistry and neuroanatomy of humankind and research animals that have contributed immensely to the current understanding of the workings of the central nervous system (CNS). The existence of these parallels in CNS func-

tion justifies reasonable expectations that animal models can be valuable in the study of human behavioral aging. [*See* MODELS OF AGING: VERTEBRATES.]

D. Reliability of Measurement

A fundamental principle of measurement is that nothing can be measured with absolute accuracy. It is thus important to ponder the level of uncertainty associated with any biomarker measurement. The statistical model usually employed in such considerations posits the existence of a true value of the variate, with error-producing factors generating a normal distribution of measured values around the true value. That is to say, it is assumed that on any particular measurement occasion, for any given individual subject, there exists a real value of the attribute being measured. Inevitably, however, the measurement process will be affected by factors that cause the observed value to deviate from this true value. The model is particularly applicable when dealing with simple errors of observation—change in angle of view of a meniscus level, or parallax effects on a meter reading, or misscoring an item on a cognitive test, or misrecording of a value on a data sheet, or inaccuracy in mixing a solution. Within each discipline, standardized measurement protocols are intended to reduce such error. It is axiomatic that such error can only be reduced but cannot be eliminated.

Any particular single measurement must, therefore, be regarded as a single sample observation from a distribution of possible values. If the error distribution is narrow, then the number obtained on any one occasion of measurement will be close to the real, "true," value. If the error distribution is broad, the measure obtained for a single individual on one occasion might be quite far from the true value, and the particular value obtained will not be a very accurate representation of the "true" state of affairs. An obvious tactic in such a case is to take multiple measurements; the mean of such a series will be a more accurate estimator of the "true" value than will any single measurement. This direct course of action is not possible for many markers, however, which, by their nature, can only be measured once. The recourse usually sought is to shrug off the uncertainty about the precision of individual values and rely on reduction of the sampling error by employing larger numbers of subjects.

The general model of a true score with an error

distribution is also useful in circumstances involving factors that influence the measurement outcome but cannot be regarded as genuine error. Consider a biomarker employed to test the efficacy of some intervention in a rodent model. In addition to the effects of the intervention variable, the biomarker might be influenced by season of the year, time of day, temperature, time since last meal, constitution of the diet, techniques of the technician, previous measurements, time since importation into the laboratory, and so on. Each of these factors is, by definition, an independent variable that has influence upon the dependent variable whose value is being sought. In another context, each of these factors might be the object of investigation in its own right, but in the particular research context they are considered to generate unwanted variability. Thus, they are identified as contributing "error." The existence of such factors is well recognized within each discipline, of course, and procedures for minimizing their influence constitute the methodological lore of controlled variables within the disciplines. Naturally, these control procedures are effective only for "error" producers that are known.

There are logistical constraints on the amount of manipulated control that can be exercised in any experiment. Thus recourse to randomization is frequent. The effects of the randomized variables will add to the uncertainty generated by real error, increasing the aura of inconclusiveness to be associated with any empirically obtained measurement.

The concept of reliability addresses the issue of the proportions of variance in empirically obtained values that can be attributed to the variability of the true scores and to the magnitude of the error effects. If the locations of individuals in such an empirical distribution are mostly attributable to their true values, with little error (i.e., if the measurement is highly reliable), then a very similar distribution would be expected if all of them were measured again. The correlation of scores obtained on successive occasions is, in fact, one of the standard methods for estimating reliability.

III. BIOMARKERS AS ELEMENTS OF COMPLEX SYSTEMS

Appropriately for so dynamic a field of inquiry, many issues of gerontology are unsettled. There is good agreement, however, that aging is a complex process or set of processes. The consensus is well represented by Baker and Sprott (1988, p. 231): "It is also quite evident that there may be many processes of aging and that various systems (physiological, biochemical, and/or molecular-genetic) undergo alterations at differential rates."

It is apparent that a comprehensive view of aging will require representation of biological or functional age in terms of a complex nexus of interrelated variables constituting a system. Such a representation has important implications for what one can and cannot expect of biomarker variables.

Conceptual and analytical models for dealing with complex systems have long been the subject of intense intellectual effort. This effort has burgeoned in recent years, and considerations of complexity, dissipative structures, self-constructing systems, and so on, appear in an increasing range of both physical and life sciences. Yates and colleagues have urged and pioneered the application of systems principles to gerontological issues. It is probably accurate to observe, however, that gerontology has only begun to reap the benefits of systems perspectives.

A defining characteristic of a system is the interrelatedness of its elements. These interconnections can be hierarchical, with a one way flow of influence. On the other hand, there may be feedback. Indeed, some sort of feedback is implied in any system or subsystem that is subject to homeostatic or other types of regulation. The feedback loop blurs the meaning of cause and effect and severely limits interpretations based upon models of Newtonian, unidirectional causality.

A major consequence of network causality is that the influence of any element of the system is context-dependent. Whether or not some particular factor is influential, even the direction of its influence, is dependent upon other elements in the causal network. It may be somewhat discomfiting to conclude, therefore, that the significance of a biomarker may differ from one individual to another. The case cited earlier by Harrison and Archer will serve as a useful example here as well: the efficacy of dietary restriction is dependent upon genotype.

Another clear implication of great importance for the present topic is that no one marker can characterize a system; searching for a marker for all purposes is futile and misguided. The image of blind men describing an elephant is rather overworked, but is particularly apposite. A comprehensive representation emerges only when the diverse perceptions of tail, trunk, legs, ears, and so on are collated and interrelated. Inevitably, gerontology will require increasing sophistication with, and use of, multivariate (multibiomarker) methods as the limited information from each individual biomarker contributes to our understanding of age and aging.

It may be useful to reiterate by a Venn diagram as shown in Figure 1. Assume that the dashed circle represents all meaning of the concept of aging. No one has ever measured aging; they have simply been able to measure various manifestations of it. Assume a number of these operational measures of "aging": A, B, C, D, and E, shown in the figure as closed circles. It may be seen that all of these biomarkers tap some part of the "aging" system, and that none of them exhaustively assesses the total domain encompassed by the dashed circle. Furthermore, none of them measures only aspects of the domain; that is to say, some of the area of all of the closed circles lies outside the domain. (This means simply that there are things other than the aging processes that influence the biomarker.) Most measures are correlated (i.e., overlap) with others, but one (D) is completely independent. In one case (A and E), the correlation is only for elements outside the domain and is therefore meaningless with respect to aging. Relating this representation to the discussion of systems, it can be imagined that the degree of overlap of the Venn circles represents the extent to which the biomarkers share membership in "causal" routes within the "causal field." Inclusion of all of these empirical measures in an assessment of "aging" would tap much, but not all, of the total meaning of the concept. Some parts of the domain would be overmeasured, in that three of the measures overlap within the domain, but some would be left without representation.

Biological systems are usually composed of subsystems, often organized into hierarchies and subhierarchies. In a network or causal field of this sort, some elements will have more "connectedness" than others, in the sense that relatively more than average of the other elements of the system are related to them. The hoary notion of the "final common path" describes one type of such convergence of influences. Quite obviously, a biomarker that taps into such central "soft spots" can likely contribute more richly to description, understanding, or prediction than can a less well-connected element.

IV. BIOMARKERS IN CHANGING SYSTEMS

A system of the type discussed above cannot be maintained statically, but only dynamically. Thus, if some element in the system is perturbed, processes are set in motion to return the element to a set point or set range. This system responsiveness is familiar as homeostasis. Variants of the idea involve set points that are changing in developmental processes (homeorhesis or programmed rheostasis) or in response to environmental factors (reactive rheostasis). In a complex network, any such dynamic action can have widespread ripple effects, with elements of the same subsystem oscillating for some time before settling down. The interactions of a living organism with its environment (including others of its species) assure that at least some subsystems will be in an almost continuous process of displacement from set range and recovery toward it. In addition to the problem of error and uncontrolled variable sources discussed above in relation to reliability of measurement, there is this additional problem that an effort to characterize a biomarker is faced with a moving target. A biomarker of a labile system such as this might give different values on measurement occasions hours or even minutes apart. Somewhat paradoxically, if perfect or near-perfect reliability (in the sense of high test–retest correlation) is required of biomarkers, labile systems, which may be of high biological rele-

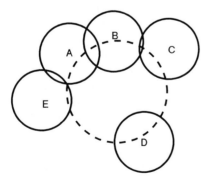

Figure 1 Partial representation of age or aging (dashed circle) by specific biomarker variables (solid circles labeled A–E).

vance, will be exempted from examination. [*See* Homeostasis.]

Intervals of sufficient duration to permit the occurrence of aging changes require a distinction between reliability and stability. If all individuals
change at the same rate in respect to some biomarker,
then, providing that the measurement is reasonably
reliable, their ordinal ranking on occasion *n + 1*
will be about the same as that on occasion *n*,
yielding a high correlation between occasions. If,
however, there are individual differences in rate of
change, the rank orders will differ on the two
occasions, and the correlation will be attenuated,
even though the biomarker is measured with high
reliability. A high correlation between occasions will
reflect both high reliability of measurement of the
biomarker and stability of the aging process of
which it is a marker. A low correlation between
occasions may not be a condemnation of the biomarker from a gerometric point of view, but simply
a reflection of individual differences in the pertinent
aging subprocess. Rejecting candidate biomarkers
because of low test–retest correlation across these
longer intervals might foreclose on the examination
of important processes.

In principle, it is remotely possible that all elements in a changing system would change in proportional ways in the same direction and at the same
rate. Given the evidence for differential changes in
age-related variables, this prospect is most unlikely
for gerontologically interesting systems. Thus one
may expect that aging of a system will be characterized by changes in the interrelationships among
elements in that system. Accepting that the meaning
of a variable can only be described by its relationships to other variables, the simple but profoundly
important implication is that the meaning of a
particular biomarker variable can change over the
life course. It might be describing central aspects
of some aging subprocess at one stage of the life
trajectory and be less related or even unrelated to
that same subprocess at another stage.

In multivariate research, through such issues as
degree of invariance in factor structure, the possibility
of change in the meaning of a biomarker is thrust
unmistakably to the fore. In univariate research, unfortunately, there is no obvious way to observe such
a change. Ignorance of changes in biomarker meaning
does not obviate their effects, however.

V. SCALE

A generally ignored matter, but one of substantial
methodological import, is the nature of the scale of
measurement of the biomarker. Four types of scale
are usually defined: nominal, ordinal, interval, and
ratio. The distinction among them is an important one
because the type of statistical analysis that is justified
depends upon the level of measurement that generated
the data. For the lowest level of measurement—
nominal—the data serve merely to identify individuals or to assign them to groups. Numbers on football
jerseys are often pointed to as exemplars of the former
application of a nominal scale. Assignment of individuals to the categories of male or female is an example
of the latter usage. Assignment of numbers on a nominal scale is an arbitrary matter, and, indeed any distinguishing symbols will work equally as well as numbers. About the only statistical procedures that can be
employed with nominal data are frequency analyses of
various sorts.

For a scale to be ordinal, there must be an implication of "greater than" or "less than" associated with
assigned numbers. For many, perhaps most, biomarkers in contemporary use, persuasive arguments can
be made that this requirement is met. Qualifying as
an ordinal scale permits the use of the median, percen-
tiles, order correlations, and similar nonparametric
statistical operations.

Unless a further criterion is met, however, one is
not entitled to the use of means, variances, product-
moment correlations, *t*-tests, analyses of variance,
and similar parametric statistics that constitute the
bulk of statistical treatment in gerontological science.
This additional requirement is that the numerical
difference between two values of the scale should
reflect the same magnitude of difference of the
attribute being measured at all positions on the
scale. A scale for which this attribute can be demonstrated is said to be an interval scale. Consider the
phenotypic domain of mouse activity, of which
numerous operational measures have been utilized
as biomarkers of aging. The interval-scalar criterion
requires that the difference in the underlying trait
being assessed (energy level, activity propensity, lack
of inhibition, degree of fear, or some combination
of these or other processes) between a score of 0
and one of 100 is the same as the difference in

underlying trait represented between a score of 5000 and one of 5100. In cases where the biomarker is one of convenience, substituting for a more expensive or difficult-to-obtain gold standard measure, appropriate comparisons between the two measures may demonstrate this equality of intervals. For those cases where no such gold standard exists (and such cases must be the rule rather than the exception in the gerontological literature), then demonstration of interval-scale status may be very difficult, if not impossible.

An even higher status of scalar adequacy is that of ratio scales in which there must be, in effect, a meaningful zero on the scale. Under such circumstances, it becomes possible to make comparisons such as twice as much as, one-third as much as, and so on. For ratio scales, one can legitimately utilize coefficients of variation and geometric means. Ratio scales are very rarely encountered anywhere in biological, behavioral, or social sciences.

Lack of interval-scale status may affect interpretation of life span differences or changes. Suppose that a change of x units in the lower ranges of a biomarker scale of "vitality" represents a greater change in the underlying attribute than does the same numerical change higher on the scale. If older people tend to have lower mean values than do younger people, it is impossible to determine if a change late in life is equivalent in magnitude to one earlier in life. Rarely is the function known by which the numerical scale maps onto the underlying variable. Usually, then, and strictly speaking, only ordinal inferences are warranted when relating biomarker status to chronological age. These same considerations suggest the logical difficulty of assessing whether different individuals are changing at the same rate if they differ in mean value of the biomarker.

Addressing issues of this sort requires systematic attention to scale properties, but scalar adequacy criteria are not universally recognized. Even when recognized, explicit demonstrations of scalar adequacy are seldom undertaken. The empirical robustness of parametric statistics in the face of failure to meet interval scale criteria is not very well known in respect to specific biomarkers of aging; much of what is regarded as reliable information about them should, therefore, be regarded with some reservation.

VI. SUMMARY

This review of biomarkers has recognized that there are multiple meanings of the term, but argues that all usages engage two central questions of measurement, which might be informally phrased as follows:

1. What is being measured?
2. How accurately is it being measured?

The theme has been one of caution. It has been asserted that there is no gold standard definition of age or aging, for the philosophically crucial reason that no one knows what aging is, only certain manifestations of it. Any single biomarker, it has been argued, can measure only some (probably very small) part of the total meaning of age and aging. Furthermore, the numerical value obtained for a biomarker must be considered as an approximation, no matter how exquisite the care with which the measurement is made. How crude the approximation will be depends not only upon error but also on the parameters of the regulatory system that responds to displacement of the biomarker from its set range. Even more important, the fundamental meaning of a biomarker will depend upon the values of other components of the subsystem of which it is an element, will almost certainly differ therefore from individual to individual, and may change from one part of the life trajectory to another. In short, at the present stage of gerontological science, it is

1. difficult to say definitively what a biomarker measures, or what it should be measuring, and
2. any particular measurement outcome is surrounded by an aura of indeterminancy, the magnitude of which is usually unknown.

But it must be made clear that the limitations and shortcomings dwelt upon here apply as well to the marker variables of any other biological, behavioral, or social science. Gerontology is not less well served by its variables than are other areas of investigation. Indeed, it must be concluded that they are quite robust to have supported the enormous strides that have occurred in the study of aging in the past few decades. Obviously no biomarker can be flawless in all respects. Equally obviously, consideration of the gerometric issues identified here might improve their incisiveness and utility.

BIBLIOGRAPHY

Arking, R. (1991). *Biology of aging: Observations and principles.* Englewood Cliffs, NJ: Prentice-Hall, Inc.

Baker, G. T. III, & Sprott, R. L. (1988). Biomarkers of aging. [Special Issue] *Experimental Gerontology, 23,* 223–239.

Evans, W., & Rosenberg, I. H. (Ed.). (1991). *Biomarkers: The 10 determinants of aging you can control.* New York: Simon and Schuster.

Harrison, D. E., & Archer, J. R. (1988). Biomarkers of aging: Tissue markers. Future research needs, strategies, directions and priorities. [Special Issue] *Experimental Gerontology, 23,* 309–321.

Johnson, T. E., Conley, W. L., & Keller, M. L. (1988). Long-lived lines of *Caenorhabditis elegans* can be used to establish predictive biomarkers of aging. [Special Issue] *Experimental Geronology, 23,* 281–295.

Licastro, F., & Caldarera, C. M. (Ed.). (1992). Biomarkers of aging: Expression and regulation. *Proceedings of the First International Congress on Biomarkers of Aging: Expression and Regulation.* Bologna, Italy: Editrice.

McClearn, G. E. (1989). Biomarker characteristics and research on the genetics aging. In D. E. Harrison (Ed.), *Genetic effects on aging II* (pp. 233–254). Caldwell, NJ: The Telford Press, Inc.

Reff, M. E., & Schneider, E. L. (Ed.). (1982). *Biological markers of aging.* (NIH Publication 82-2221). Washington, DC: USDHHS.

Sprott, R. L., & Baker, G. T. III (Ed.). (1988). Biomarkers of aging." [Special Issue] *Experimental Gerontology, 23.*

Wilson, D. L. (1988). Aging hypotheses, aging markers and the concept of biological age. [Special Issue] *Experimental Gerontology, 23,* 435–438.

Memory

Anderson D. Smith
Georgia Institute of Technology

I. Theoretical Perspectives to Aging and Memory
II. Moderating Effects of Other Variables
III. Interface of Cognitive Psychology of Aging with Other Areas
IV. Concusions

Episodic Memory   Storage and retrieval from long-term memory based on contextual information about original learning experience (internal diary).
Implicit Memory   Indirect effects of memory without conscious awareness.
Prospective Memory   Remembering to do something in the future.
Semantic Memory   Storage and retrieval from long-term memory based on the conceptual nature of to-be-remembered information (internal encyclopedia).
Short-Term Memory   Memory for recent events that have been maintained in conscious awareness prior to recall.
Working Memory   Type of short-term memory which involves maintenance of information at the same time one is engaged in an information-processing task.

It is clear that **MEMORY** changes with age. Serious memory decline is associated with many of the diseases of old age (e.g., Alzheimer's disease), but memory change is also characteristic of normal, healthy aging. [*See* DEMENTIA.] There are hundreds of research studies showing reliable age differences on a variety of different memory tasks. It is also true that not all memory changes with age in the same way. Whereas some memory tasks show large adult age differences (e.g., working memory or episodic memory), other tasks show little or no effects of age (e.g., semantic memory, implicit memory). The explanation for these differential effects of age on different memory performances depends on how one conceptualizes memory. Some theories suggest that age differences will be large if the task involves deliberate cognitive processing or cognitive resources. The more cognitive resources needed to adequately remember something, the larger the age differences. Other theories suggest that age effects are limited to specific memory processes or memory structures. It has also been suggested that memory differences between age groups are not memory effects at all, but rather reflect other confounding variables, such as motivational or differential experience effects.

I. THEORETICAL PERSPECTIVES TO AGING AND MEMORY

A. Memory Stage Theory

Memory stage theory separates memory into the sequential components of remembering. As shown in Figure 1A, information first has to be experienced at time-1 (i.e., encoding), then it has to be maintained over a retention interval from time-2 to time-*n* (i.e., storage), and finally it has to be reproduced at the time memory is tested at time-*n* (i.e., retrieval). Early researchers believed that adult age differences in memory were located primarily at retrieval, the final of the three stages of memory. For example, in the labo-

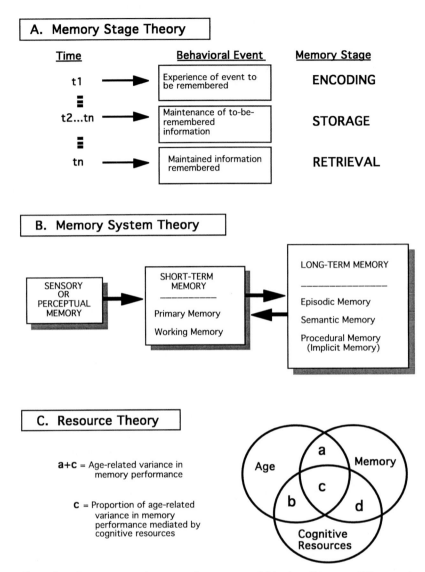

Figure 1   Three conceptualizations of memory useful in describing age differences in memory: (A) memory stage theory; (B) memory system theory; and (C) resource theory.

ratory it was demonstrated that age differences in free recall of a word list (with instructions such as, "Write down all the words you can remember having seen on the list earlier") were eliminated when recognition memory was used (with instructions such as, "Pick out the words from this list that you saw earlier"). Because the use of a recognition memory task is assumed to reduce the retrieval requirement of the memory task, it was then inferred that the locus of the age effect must be retrieval. When retrieval requirements are large such as in free recall, age differences are large; when retrieval requirements are minimal such as with recognition memory, age differences are small or even nonexistent. Such findings were prevalent in the 1960s and early 1970s. More recent research, however, has clearly demonstrated reliable age differences in recognition memory, and stage theory lost its appeal because of the methodological difficulties in isolating one memory stage from another in different age groups. In order to isolate retrieval, for example, everything must be held constant up until the time retrieval is tested. This is difficult to accomplish in aging research, however, because different aged adults may process information differently at one of the earlier stages, thus violating the requirement that all be held constant until retrieval.

One interesting phenomenon that is associated with the retrieval stage of memory is the "tip-of-the-tongue" state. There are many instances in everyday life when one cannot remember something even though one knows that he or she knows it. This tip-of-the-tongue state is simulated in the laboratory by having subjects read the definition of a word and then attempt to remember the word that goes with the definition. A tip-of-the tongue state occurs when retrieval is blocked and the subject cannot think of the word that goes with the definition, even though he or she is absolutely confident that the word is known. In fact, subjects can often remember specific information about the words (e.g., number of syllables, the beginning letter of the word) even though they cannot access the word itself. Research shows that older adults experience more tip-of-the-tongue states than younger adults. This difference, however, is probably not totally attributable to faulty retrieval processes because when given sufficient time to resolve the tip-of-the-tongue block, older adults eventually can come up with the words. They are simply slower at resolving the retrieval blocks. The same result occurs with name finding and picture naming tasks.

Memory research in the 1970s and early 1980s focused heavily on the encoding stage of memory. This focus on encoding was due to the development of a conceptual view of memory, the "levels-of-processing" framework, that proposed the ability to remember was determined by the extent of semantic processing engaged in during the encoding of the to-be-remembered information. For this reason most cognitive aging researchers during this period focused on encoding processes and aging. That emphasis may have been well placed for several reasons. First, the memory performance of older adults, relative to younger adults, is detrimentally affected by performing a divided attention task during the encoding stage of a memory task, but not if the divided attention task occurs at retrieval. Furthermore, recent data from neuroimaging studies with older adults suggest that age-related memory effects may be greater at encoding than at retrieval. By using positron emission tomogra-

phy (PET), researchers are able to determine which areas of the brain are active while subjects perform different cognitive tasks. A specific memory component (e.g., encoding or retrieval) is isolated by subtracting the brain activation seen in a control task from activation seen in a task containing the component of interest. In several laboratories, it is has been shown that more activation occurs in the left hemisphere during the encoding stage of a memory task and in the right hemisphere during the retrieval stage, a lateralization of encoding and retrieval in different regions of the brain. When PET studies are done with different aged subjects, the activation in the left prefrontal lobe seen in young adults during encoding is greatly attenuated in older adults. However, few age differences are detected in the level of activation in the right hemisphere when subjects are engaged in retrieving information from memory. This neurological evidence suggests that memory problems with aging may be more involved with encoding than with retrieval.

B. Memory System Theory

Another conceptualization of memory that has both behavioral and neurological support considers memory not as a unitary construct, but rather a collection of different component systems. As can be seen in Figure 1B, memory is typically broken down into sensory memory, short-term memory, and long-term memory. Short-term memory is further divided into primary memory and working memory, and long-term memory is divided into episodic, semantic, and procedural memory. These systems differ in the nature of memory representations and how these representations are maintained and retrieved. They also differ considerably in the effects of aging.

I. Sensory-Perceptual Memory

After experiencing an event, it is first represented briefly in the sensory-perceptual system. Here the information is represented as it is processed and analyzed by the perceptual systems. There has been very little work on this type of memory and aging, but some research does suggest that older adults are less efficient in this early type of processing, especially in the visual system. It should be pointed out, however, that differences in sensory-perceptual processing would be an unlikely candidate as an explanatory construct for memory differences found later in the system because later memory differences are not consistent but vary according to what system is examined. Adequate perceptual processing of the to-be-remembered stimulus would seem to be a requirement for all types of long-term memory, and the fact that some long-term memory systems are minimally affected by aging whereas others show large effects would not support an explanation that relied solely on faulty perceptual processing at the very early stage of processing the information.

2. Short-Term Memory

Short-term memory is conscious awareness. It consists of information that is currently in mind, a combination of incoming information being attended to from the sensory-perceptual system and information being retrieved from long-term memory to interpret and process the incoming information. For this reason, short-term memory is conceived as a complex information-processing system that involves a combination of storage (i.e., keeping things in mind) and processing.

The storage component, or how many things one can keep in mind at one time, is often called *primary* memory. The digit span test found on most intelligence tests is a measure of primary memory. Different strings of single digits are called out, and the subject has to repeat the digit strings. If the subject is correct, then an additional digit is added to the next string. Digit span is measured as the longest string of digits a person can repeat without making an error. When primary memory is tested by digit span tests with different aged subjects, no reliable age differences are found.

Age differences are found, however, on a measure of short-term memory that takes into account both processing and storage. *Working* memory, unlike primary memory, requires subjects to keep information in mind while engaging in another processing task at the same time. One commonly used working-memory task is called reading span. Subjects read a series of short sentences (e.g., "The boy ran with the dog.") and answer questions about the sentence (e.g., "Who ran?"). At the same time, subjects have to remember the last word in each of the sentences (e.g., "dog") and report the words when told to do so after all the sentences are presented. The number of sentences presented prior to recall of the words ranges from

two to seven and working-memory capacity is the longest list of sentences for which subjects can correctly report the words. Because working-memory tasks require simultaneous storage and processing, it is a better simulation of everyday information processing required to understand language, to solve problems, or to make decisions. Other working-memory tasks have been developed that involve different kinds of information processing such as arithmetical calculations (computational span), or spatial manipulations (spatial working memory). With all of these tasks, large reliable age differences are found. Therefore, although the more passive primary memory tasks, such as simple digit span, do not show age differences, differences are found with working-memory measures. As will be discussed later, working-memory capacity is considered by many researchers to be a fundamental mechanism for memory processing. Because of age differences in working memory, and because working memory is assumed to be a fundamental requirement of processing efficiently at encoding and retrieval, this measure has been considered an important factor in determining the complex age differences seen in long-term memory.

3. Long-Term Memory

Long-term memories are not kept in conscious awareness like short-term memories, but instead have to be retrieved when needed. Long-term memory is usually divided into episodic memory, semantic memory, and procedural memory.

a. Episodic Memory Episodic memories are those recollections that are actively retrieved from personal experiences. In other words, the contextual information about when and how an event was originally experienced is used to guide retrieval. "Where did I leave my keys?" "When did I last see Mary?" "What was I supposed to get at the grocery store?" Each of these questions involves remembering by reconstructing the context of the original experience.

Episodic memory has been studied extensively by cognitive aging researchers. Typically, a list of words, or some other to-be-remembered information is presented to subjects, and then later, after a retention interval, memory is tested. Because the words were already known to the subjects, the memory task is to remember the words in the particular context of the original list. Although the magnitude of age differences varies considerably among different memory tasks using different materials, older adults tend to have greater problems with episodic remembering than do younger adults. The variable that seems important in determining the magnitude of age differences is the degree to which the memory task involves deliberate processing by the subject. At both encoding and retrieval, the more intentional processing required to perform the task, the larger the age differences that will be found with that task.

For example, if the to-be-remembered materials are complex pictorial scenes such as those that might be found on picture postcards, older adults remember them as well on a later memory test as do younger adults. Because the pictorial images are rich in both semantic and visual context, little deliberate processing is necessary to encode the materials. This is called *environmental support*, because the task and materials themselves provide the cues necessary for optimal performance. When the pictures are depleted of their rich content at encoding, however, either by taking out perceptual details or by rearranging the components of the pictures to reduce meaningfulness, age differences emerge. Age differences can be increased by reducing environmental support and thereby increasing the requirement for deliberate processing on the part of the subject to adequately encode the information.

The same phenomenon is found for retrieval from episodic memory. The way in which the retrieval task is structured can influence the magnitude of age differences on the task. Earlier, it was mentioned that age differences in free recall are larger than age differences in recognition. In free recall, after seeing a list of common words, subjects are asked to recall as many of the words as possible. Other than the instruction to remember the words, no other cues are provided to the subjects, and age differences are typically very large on these free recall tasks. If recognition is used, however, age differences are considerably reduced. Instead of trying to remember the items though free recall, subjects in a recognition task only have to pick out the words they saw earlier on a longer list of words presented at test. Compared to free recall, a recognition task provides the very best retrieval cues, the words themselves, and little deliberate retrieval is required to perform the task. Thus, age differences are greatly reduced because of the environmental support provided at retrieval by the recognition procedure.

Because episodic memory is so dependent on contextual information, one of the reasons for older adults' poorer performance in these tasks is probably because of their inability to encode contextual information easily. Older adults, for example, do not do as well as younger adults in identifying the way in which information was presented to them. They do worse when asked to remember whether a word was presented in upper or lower case, presented auditorially or visually, spoken by a male or a female voice, in one color versus another, or in the upper part of a computer screen or the lower part. These tasks require subjects to remember contextual detail. Because older adults encode less contextual detail, they do not do as well on these tasks. In fact, because older adults encode less context, they are even less able to distinguish between events actually experienced from those just imagined, a process called "reality monitoring." In a typical reality-monitoring experiment, subjects either read words at encoding or generate words in response to some cue. Older subjects have greater problems in determining whether remembered events were the ones read or the ones imagined in response to the cue.

Because of the dependence of episodic remembering on context, an important principle in determining the level of performance is the *encoding specificity* principle. The encoding specificity principle states that the optimal condition for episodic remembering is when the contextual situation at retrieval matches the contextual situation that was experienced during the original encoding. Because older adults encode less contextual detail, they should be less influenced by the encoding specificity principle. Some studies, however, find that young and old subjects are affected in the same way by changing the contextual situation at retrieval, such as using different cues at retrieval from those used at encoding. Other studies offer conflicting findings that the older subjects are indeed less affected by contextual change from encoding to retrieval. The distinguishing feature of these studies seems to be the extent to which the context at encoding was integrated with the to-be-remembered information. Studies showing equal encoding specificity effects often involve cues and memory targets that are already integrated and do not require deliberate processing to relate them together. The studies showing less encoding specificity in older adults, on the other hand, involve situations when integration of the target with the context requires deliberate processing by the subjects. This supports the view stated earlier that episodic memory deficits in older adults are increased by increases in the processing requirements of the task.

One interesting type of episodic memory, *prospective memory*, involves remembering to do something in the future rather than remembering something from the past. "Don't forget to take your medicine at noon today." "When you see Bill, tell him I called." "Will you pick up the kids after work today?" All of these memory tasks require prospective memory or remembering to remember. Age differences are typically found with simulations of prospective memory tasks performed in the laboratory (e.g., press a key when the face has a beard, ask for a red pen when signing your name, or phone the laboratory at a certain date). With simple laboratory tasks, however, such as pressing a key when a certain word is presented, age differences in prospective memory are not found. Again, the determinant of whether age differences are found seems to be the degree of deliberate recollection required to perform the task.

In one study age differences were found when subjects were asked to press a computer key every 10 min while performing another computer cognitive task (time-based prospective memory), but not found when asked to press the key when a certain cue word appeared (event-based prospective memory). Because event-based prospective remembering involves less deliberate processing given the external cue, age differences were not found. When no external cue was provided to trigger remembering as in the time-based task, age differences emerged.

Older adults themselves commonly describe their episodic memory problems as limited to remembering recent events. "I can remember well what happened to me years ago, I just can't remember what I did yesterday." This anecdotal self-description of memory problems implies stability for remote memories coupled with loss of recent episodic memories. There are problems, however, in studying very long-term memories. Older adults remember events from their remote past, but it is difficult to judge the accuracy of these recollections. Furthermore, the recollections are typically of salient events from the past that would be remembered regardless of when they occurred. And finally, it is difficult to control for rehearsal (i.e., previous retrievals) during the long-term retention interval. When these variables have been controlled, research

has shown that remembering is directly related to retention interval. Unlike the conclusion reached in the self-description, memory performance gets worse as the time between the original experience and the subsequent retrieval increases. This has been shown by collecting memory data at high school reunions, examining memory for foreign language skills learned in school over the life span, testing memory for the names of grade school teachers, and by examining autobiographical facts from diaries over an 18-year period. In these cases, there is some control of salience, good criteria of accuracy, and better control of rehearsal over the retention interval. The conclusion is clear, the older the memory, the worse the performance. It should also be pointed out that although using retention intervals measured in years provides interesting data about remote memories, age is confounded with retention intervals in such studies. This constrains their interpretation in terms of understanding the effects of aging.

b. Semantic Memory   In order to remember something episodically, some aspect of the original encoding context has to be reinstated at retrieval. Often, however, one remembers information without reference to how or when it was originally learned. People have access to a great deal of world knowledge that has lost all connection to the context of its original learning. "Who was the first president of the United States?" "What fruit is yellow and good in cereal?" "What is your grandmother's maiden name?" Semantic memory is retrieved conceptually rather than contextually, and represents accumulated organized knowledge.

Measures of semantic memory are often considered "crystallized intelligence" on most intelligence tests. The general information test (answering questions such as "What was Mark Twain's real name?") and vocabulary test (providing definitions to words) on the Wechsler Adult Intelligence Scale, for example, measure access to conceptual knowledge. Few reliable age differences are seen on these tests assuming educational level between age groups and other demographic variables are held as constant as possible. In fact, older adults often do better than younger adults on vocabulary tests.

If young and old subjects were to differ in semantic memory, it most likely would reflect the way in which semantic memory was organized by the different age groups. There is little evidence, however, that the structure of organized knowledge differs between younger and older adults. One measure of semantic memory organization is the free-association test. For example, words are given one at a time, and subjects are asked to come up with the first other word that comes to mind. If the associative structure of semantic memory differed between age groups, then this would be indicated by differences in responses given on free-association tests. No age differences are found, however, in free associations to words, free associations to pictures, or in generation of category instances to a category name, such as *fruit*. As mentioned earlier, older adults do often take longer to retrieve semantic information, but the information in most cases can be ultimately retrieved.

c. Procedural Memory Often memory has its effect automatically without even conscious awareness. "Procedural memories" once acquired are automatic and do not require deliberate recollection at all. Once learned, people ride bicycles, type on computers, and understand language without devoting a great deal of attention to the task. Procedural memories involve motor and cognitive skills.

Ingenious laboratory procedures have been developed to examine *implicit* memory, tasks that show memory effects even when subjects are not aware that remembering is occurring. For example, subjects first examine a list of words while performing some cover task such as rating the words for pleasantness. They then perform a series of other tasks unrelated to the word list seen earlier. Finally, they are given a task to complete presented word stems with any words that come to mind (e.g., "por_____"). As compared to control subjects who did not read the words earlier, subjects who read the words earlier will produce a word seen on the initial list more often even though they are completely unaware that the word was presented earlier. If they are explicitly asked to use the word fragments to remember the words read earlier, large age differences are found. However, when asked instead to complete the fragments with any word that comes to mind and not implying a memory task, young and old show equal implicit memory. Age differences are typically not found on implicit memory tests, and when they are, they are very small as compared to explicit memory differences.

In summary, the memory systems approach has been very useful in describing when significant age differences in memory are found. It is also clear that even within one type of memory, age differences can vary considerably depending on the nature of the task and the nature of processing required to perform the task. For this reason, memory researchers have been searching for better explanatory power in accounting for age differences seen in memory.

C. Resource Theory

A third view of memory assumes that there is a limited amount of cognitive resources that can be devoted to any cognitive task. If aging is associated with a reduction in cognitive resources, then memory performance should be detrimentally affected. Investigators testing resource theory have adopted the correlational methods commonly used by individual-difference researchers. The typical approach of resource theory has been to identify resource mechanisms that can be independently measured, and then to determine their role in accounting for age-related variance in memory performance. The circles in Figure 1C represent the variance in measures of the three variables of interest: age, memory performance, and some measure of the cognitive resources. The overlap in the variance of age and memory performance is represented by the overlap in the two circles (i.e., $a + c$). The proportion of the age-related variance in memory accounted for by the cognitive-resource variable is represented by the letter c.

Several different theoretical cognitive resource constructs have been proposed. Several times the construct of deliberate processing has been discussed. Unfortunately, no independent measure of deliberate processing is available. Conceptually as a construct, it seems to be very useful in accounting for a multitude of age-related memory effects. To directly test deliberate processing as a cognitive resource, however, a reliable and valid measure of it would be required. Methodologically, in order to show that a cognitive resource mechanism can account for a significant proportion of age-related variance, the mechanism must be adequately measured at the same time memory is tested. Then statistical regression techniques can be used to relate the mechanism to age and memory performance as in the figure. To date there have been some beginning attempts to measure deliberate processing (e.g., the process dissociation approach), but more work is needed before it can be concluded that it can be measured reliably, and that it can account for age-related variance in a variety of different memory tasks.

A proposed cognitive resource mechanism that has been proven fruitful in accounting for age-related memory performance is the working-memory construct mentioned earlier. Assuming that working memory is a basic processing resource for engaging in remembering, then individual differences in working memory should account for individual differences in age-related memory performance. Regression analyses have shown that measures of working memory can account for over 50% of the age-related variance in a variety of different memory tasks (e.g., free recall, paired-associate learning, text memory).

An even more basic cognitive mechanism, perceptual speed, has proven to be even more effective in accounting for age-related variance in memory. Perceptual speed is the simple ability to perform simple perceptual-motor tasks such as deciding whether two digit or letter strings are the same or different, or placing digits next to the appropriate symbol on a sheet by using an answer key showing the correct pairings of digits and symbols. Many studies have shown that very little age-related variance in memory performance remains after controlling for perceptual speed. One typically used memory task is the paired-associate task in which a subject recalls a response word that goes with a particular stimulus word after seeing the stimulus–response pair earlier during encoding. In one study, only 1% of the age-related variance in paired-associate recall remained after controlling for perceptual speed. [*See* Perception.]

It should be noted that speed and working memory are not mutually exclusive, or even opponent mechanisms in the search for understanding age and memory. In fact, studies have shown that variance in working memory itself is largely accounted for by the speed construct. In one study, statistical techniques of structural equation modeling were used to test the relationship among perceptual speed, working memory, and episodic recall. Using this technique, the associative relationships among the variables and their directional strength can be determined. It was shown that age had no direct effect on episodic recall performance when speed and working memory were included in the model. Age influenced recall in two ways but only indirectly. Age first had an effect on perceptual speed,

which had a direct effect on recall. And second, age had an effect on speed that had a further indirect effect on recall through working memory. In other words, the best model in accounting for age-related differences in memory performance in this case included both the constructs of perceptual speed and working memory.

One final candidate for a contributing mechanism to age-related memory performance is *inhibition*, the ability to focus on target information by actively reducing attention to distracting, extraneous information. It has been suggested that as people grow older, they have increases in their failure to inhibit task-irrelevant information. The uninhibited information then reduces the available working-memory capacity available for processing of the memory task. Decreases in inhibition have been demonstrated in a variety of different tasks. For example, when asked to read a text passage that has irrelevant information in a different type font interweaved throughout the passage, older subjects have greater problems in reading and in processing the text. The "failure to inhibit" hypothesis is a promising one, but as with deliberate processing, reliable independent measures need to be developed that assess the construct. Attempts to do this so far have not produced adequate measures.

II. MODERATING EFFECTS OF OTHER VARIABLES

Even more active than the search for cognitive variables that can mediate the relationship between aging and memory performance has been the attempt to find variables that can serve as surrogates for the relationship. Because most cognitive aging studies are cross-sectional (comparison of different age groups at a point in time), variables confounded with different age groups are candidates for these surrogates. For example, because subjects in the different age groups were born at very different times and thus had very different life experiences, birth cohort is one such variable. To investigate this possibility, memory performance must be studied as change within the same subjects rather than differences across subjects. When cognitive abilities measured by psychometric intelligence tests are studied in this way, it is found that the cross-sectional age differences are typically overestimates of actual age change. Rarely, however, are cognitive age differences in cross-sectional studies completely eliminated when cohort designs are used. In fact, in the few studies that study age change in laboratory memory tasks using the same cohorts, identical findings to cross-sectional studies are found. [See COHORT STUDIES.]

More specific within-subject factors have also been examined as moderators of the age–memory relationship. Health, educational level, socioeconomic status, and occupation have all been measured in conjunction with age. To the extent to which these factors influence memory performance, they can influence the size of age differences on memory tasks. Controlling these factors, however, does not eliminate the age effects. Health status, for example, can influence how one performs on memory tasks. However, even though health can influence memory performance, studies have shown that age differences in memory are not reduced by controlling for self-reported health status. Even when more objective measures of health are used, such as the number of prescription medicines, only about 20% of the age-related variance in memory performance is reduced by controlling these factors. Controlling for health, therefore, can attenuate the relationship between age and memory, but not eliminate it.

One criticism of research on aging and memory has been its reliance on controlled laboratory tests of memory. It has been suggested that these tasks are contrived and do not overlap with everyday cognitive tasks performed by older adults. Laboratory tasks are not relevant to older adults and therefore do not adequately reflect their memory abilities. In other words, memory research has been accused of not being ecologically valid, because of the artificial, controlled nature of laboratory procedures. Laboratory memory tasks are seen as more like the formal remembering required in school settings and very unlike the everyday remembering engaged in by older adults. For this reason, younger adults may do better because of their familiarity with situations used in the laboratory to test memory rather than because of their age per se.

Because of this criticism, there have been a large number of ecologically valid, everyday memory tasks used with different aged subjects. Again, although using more familiar tasks can reduce age differences in memory performance, in most cases significant age differences are still found with everyday tasks. Such

memory tasks as remembering faces, remembering facts from written stories, remembering a route taken through a town, remembering performed activities, remembering and understanding prescription medication information, and remembering grocery items all show memory differences favoring younger adults.

Furthermore, other lines of research suggest that differential familiarity or differential experience is not the critical factor in determining age differences in memory. Even when student status is controlled by using older students and comparing them to younger students, age differences remain on a number of memory and cognitive tasks. There are also a number of memory studies using animals that show reliable age differences in memory performance, even though the different-aged animal subjects shared identical everyday experiences since birth.

The conclusion emerging from these studies is that successful aging is not the absence of change, but rather the adaptation to change across the life span. Memory change appears to be a normal consequence of the aging process, and although noncognitive factors such as motivation, health, or differential experiences can modify the magnitude of age differences in memory, rarely can these factors substitute for age itself in accounting for memory differences.

III. INTERFACE OF COGNITIVE PSYCHOLOGY OF AGING WITH OTHER AREAS

A. Individual Differences

As evidenced by the discussion of resource theory earlier, memory researchers are combining the methodologies of experimental cognitive psychology with the correlational techniques of individual-difference research. Correlational techniques of regression, path analysis, and causal modeling are being used to determine what mechanisms are responsible for age-related variance in memory performance. Because of the large number of subjects required to conduct such analyses, and the battery of different measures necessary to measure individual differences adequately, not many studies such as these have been conducted. The research so far, however, has been consistent in pointing out the importance of perceptual speed and working memory as important factors in producing differences in memory performance. Needed now are good measures of other theoretical constructs that can be used to understand the complex relationship between aging and memory.

These statistical techniques are not new and they have been used by individual-difference researchers for a long time. What is new, however, is the use of the techniques to test hypotheses that have been developed in the experimental cognitive psychology laboratory. This combination of research traditions brings new promise to the study of aging and memory.

B. Cognitive Neuroscience

The same conclusion can be reached about the new exciting field of cognitive neuroscience, the interaction between experimental cognitive psychology (laboratory studies of memory) and neuroscience (studies of brain structure and function). With the development of new neuroimaging techniques such as PET mentioned earlier and functional magnetic resonance imaging (fMRI), brain activation can be measured while subjects are actually performing memory tasks. For PET scans, radioisotopes with a short half-life (e.g., 2 min for oxygen-15) are injected into the subject. The radioisotope goes to the brain, and there the amount of blood flow reflects the level of activity in the brain. Different parts of the brain that differ in their level of activation could then be detected by PET. Because of the short half-life of the radioisotope, multiple scans can be made under different task conditions, and scans representing the different tasks can be compared. Typically, an experimental condition is compared to a control condition. The control condition matches the experimental condition in all aspects of task requirements except for the one task characteristic of interest. By subtracting control activation from experimental activation, the unique activation associated with the task characteristic of interest can then be estimated.

Because of the equipment and costs associated with these techniques, only a few studies now appear in the literature, especially studies that examine age differences in brain activation. Those that have, however, provide some validity for the behavioral data discussed so far.

For example, researchers have suggested that the prefrontal cortical areas of the brain are the locus for working memory. These parts of the cortex show unique activation when subjects are performing working-memory tasks. Furthermore, in one of the few studies comparing young and old subjects directly, older adults show differential patterns of activity in the prefrontal areas of the brain while performing a working-memory task.

Another area of the brain, the temporal cortical area (hippocampal area), is hypothesized to be responsible for deliberate processing in long-term episodic memory. This conclusion, however, comes primarily from the study of neurological studies of brain-damaged patients. These studies require autopsies before definitive evidence can be provided about the damaged brain areas that are responsible for the behavioral deficits. Lesion studies can also be misleading because of the possibility that disruptions in the circuits among different brain areas are produced by the lesion and these circuits are responsible for the behavior rather than the specific area lesioned. What is clearly needed are more neuroimaging studies, like the ones performed with working memory or in comparing encoding and retrieval discussed earlier, to test the hypothesis.

In summary, both individual-difference techniques and neuroscience techniques are expanding the methodological tools available for hypothesis testing by the research scientists studying aging and memory.

IV. CONCLUSIONS

In summary, memory changes as people grow older. The changes are selective, however, and primarily occur in working memory and in episodic memory. In general, the more self-initiated deliberate processing that is required to either encode or retrieve the information, the greater the age differences. Much of the age-related memory differences can be accounted for by simple cognitive mechanisms such as perceptual speed. Noncognitive variables, on the other hand, do not seem to account for age-related memory differences. To further understand the relationship between normal aging and memory, future research will use the statistical methods from individual-difference approaches and the brain imaging techniques of cognitive neuroscience to more completely identify the mechanisms responsible for memory changes with age.

BIBLIOGRAPHY

Craik, F. I. M., & Jennings, J. M. (1992). Human memory. In F. I. M. Craik & T. A. Salthouse (Eds.), *The handbook of aging and cognition* (pp. 51–110). Hillsdale, NJ: Lawrence Erlbaum Associates.

Kausler, D. H. (1994). *Learning and memory in normal aging.* San Diego: Academic Press.

Light, L. L. (1991). Memory and aging: Four hypotheses in search of data. *Annual Review of Psychology, 42,* 333–376.

Moscovitch, M., & Winocur, G. (1992). The neuropsychology of memory and aging. In (F. I. M. Craik & T. A. Salthouse (Eds.), *The handbook of aging and cognition* (pp. 315–372). Hillsdale, NJ: Lawrence Erlbaum Associates.

Salthouse, T. A. (1991). *Theoretical perspectives on cognitive aging.* Hillsdale, NJ: Lawrence Erlbaum Associates.

Smith, A. D. (1996). Memory. In J. E. Birren & K. W. Schaie (Eds.), *Handbook of the psychology of aging* (pp. 236–250). (4th ed). San Diego: Academic Press.

Smith, A. D., & Earles, J. L. K. (1996). Memory changes in normal aging. In T. Hess & F. Blanchard-Fields (Eds.), *Cognitive changes in adulthood and aging* (pp 192–220). New York: McGraw-Hill.

Memory Strategies

Judith A. Sugar

University of Nevada, Reno

I. Why Use Memory Strategies?
II. Types of Memory Strategies
III. Age Differences in Use of Memory Strategies
IV. Instruction in Memory Strategies

External Strategies Methods for remembering that make use of tangible, physical objects, places, or people, for example, writing out a list of items to buy at the grocery store.

Internal Strategies Methods for remembering that rely on internal mental processes, for example, creating mental images of items to buy at the grocery store.

Metamemory Perceptions, beliefs, and knowledge about memory functioning in general, and one's own memory in particular.

Method of Loci A formal memory technique (also called a mnemonic) in which a visual association is created between an item to be remembered and a location along a path through a familiar site (e.g., one's home).

Pegword System A formal memory technique (also called a mnemonic) in which a visual association is created between an item to be remembered and a keyword (*peg*) that has already been learned in a numbered sequence, one such sequence being "one is a bun, two is a shoe," and so on.

Prospective Memory Remembering to carry out intended actions.

Retrospective Memory Remembering events that occurred in the past.

Rote Rehearsal A method for remembering whereby items to be learned are repeated, silently or out loud, over and over again. Also called maintenance rehearsal.

MEMORY STRATEGIES are techniques or methods for increasing the probability of remembering events in the past (retrospective memory) as well as events that are to take place in the future (prospective memory). A critical issue for gerontology is the extent to which older adults can and do use effective strategies to remember. Knowing what strategies older adults *actually* use, and why they use them, can help one to understand potential effects of age, cohort, and historical events on human information processing, especially in late adulthood. What older adults *can do* is of interest from the point of view of the potential for improving older adults' quality of life, by decreasing perceived need for dependent living, increasing self-efficacy, and reducing health risks. Recent research has shown that even people with Alzheimer's disease can benefit from instruction to improve their memory. [*See* MEMORY.]

I. WHY USE MEMORY STRATEGIES?

A. Development of Memory Strategies

Human memory is fallible and people are generally bothered when they forget, especially as they age. Thus, memory strategies are important because, if effectively applied, they enable remembering things one wants to remember but might otherwise forget. When a person adopts strategies to remember an event, it indicates a high level of cognitive functioning. Proficient use of memory strategies is a sign of good cognitive management skills.

Throughout history, humans have devised innumerable methods for improving their memories. These methods generally depend on the kinds of materials that are available as well as prevailing conceptualizations and models of mental activity. Consequently, the variety and use of memory strategies have changed over time. For example, the method of loci, which dates back to at least the time of Cicero, is a formal memory technique (also called a mnemonic) in which a visual association is created between an item to be remembered and a location along a path through a familiar site (e.g., one's home). It is a strategy that was devised to aid memory long before materials such as paper and pencils were available for writing lists and notes.

Today, a burgeoning commercial enterprise is developing in the design, manufacture, and sale of technological devices to assist memory. Among these devices are reminder notebooks that include daily planners, calendars, expense records, and so on; electronic appointment books with programmable auditory and visual reminders, and pocket-sized electronic notebooks that can record spoken messages as well as respond to vocal requests to display stored information visually. And, some relatively new telecommunication devices are being used in novel ways to act as memory aids, for example, leaving messages for oneself on a telephone answering machine.

B. Relationship between Memory Strategy Usage and Memory Performance

Although details about the relationships between how good a person's memory is and the quantity and quality of strategies used have yet to be worked out, there is no dispute that effective strategies can significantly improve memory performance. This relationship has been demonstrated across a wide variety of memory strategies and materials to be remembered. Formal mnemonics, for example, have been shown to result in recall that is two to seven times better than rote rehearsal. Combinations of memory strategies can produce impressive feats of memory. For example, young and older adults have been shown to be capable of increasing their digit spans (the number of digits in a sequence that can be remembered) from a typical average between 7 and 11 digits to 72 or more by creating associations between their existing world knowledge and groups of digits; by chunking, or grouping, sets of digits; and by practicing these two

strategies together in multiple sessions over an extended period of time.

All theories of how memory works offer some explanations for the relationships between the use of memory strategies and memory performance, although they do so at a fairly global level. In one model of memory, for example, strategy use determines whether information will be passed from one stage of information processing to the next. Information not passed to the next stage of information processing is lost, or forgotten. Furthermore, better strategy use increases the likelihood of information being retrieved later. Thus, in the first stage of this "three-stage" model, paying attention to information leads to the information moving from the first stage to the second stage of processing. Rehearsal is necessary to maintain an item in the second stage and more elaborate processing strategies increase the chances that the item will be stored at the third stage for later retrieval.

According to another model, items that are processed at "deeper" levels (e.g., the semantic or meaning level) are much more likely to be retained than items processed at "shallower" levels (e.g., the phonemic level). This theoretical approach has helped to convince memory researchers that rhyming, which depends on surface characteristics of words, is not a terribly effective memory strategy.

II. TYPES OF MEMORY STRATEGIES

Strategies for remembering are typically employed when an event is deemed important enough to remember. Thus, more often than not, they are intentionally implemented, though with practice they may become quite automatic.

Memory strategies can be grouped in a number of different ways. Commonly used categories include formal mnemonics, image-based strategies, general internal strategies, and external strategies. Table I lists examples of each of these types of strategies.

A. Formal Mnemonics

Formal mnemonics are systems for remembering that must be learned through instruction, generally because they are complex systems built upon an acquired core of knowledge. Formal mnemonic systems are

Table I Types of Memory Strategies

Internal strategies	External strategies
Formal mnemonics	Lists
Method of loci	Reminder notes
Pegword method	Address book
Acronyms (e.g., HOMES for	Appointment book
Great Lakes)	Calendar
Linking items through a story	Diary
Imagery-based strategies	Timer
Bizarre images	Other people
Interacting images	Object placement
General internal strategies	Photographs
Alphabetical search	Tape recorder
Associations	Video recorder
Categorization	Bookmark
Elaboration	Recipe cards
Grouping	Medication organizer
Rehearsal	
Rhyming	

analogous to the scaffolding of a building on which the remainder of the house depends; they provide a framework on which to "hang," or incorporate, information to be remembered. Prototypical examples include the method of loci (previously described) and the pegword system. For the pegword system a visual association is created between an item to be remembered and a keyword (*peg*) that has already been learned in a numbered sequence, one such sequence being "one is a bun, two is a shoe," and so on.

Active memory researchers, who are presumably familiar enough with the theoretical and empirical underpinnings of memory research to be considered experts on memory, eschew formal mnemonics themselves and do not recommend them to others. Formal memory techniques require much effort to learn and constant practice to maintain. They are most readily applied to simple situations, such as learning a list of words, where, unfortunately, their use is often outmoded by present-day materials and technology. For example, using the pegword system to learn a list of items to buy at the grocery store is unduly cumbersome when a written list would serve the same purpose and be much more efficient. Thus, although formal memory strategies can significantly increase the amount of information a person can recall, they are impractical for meeting people's needs for remembering in real life.

B. Image-Based Memory Strategies

Image-based memory strategies are methods for remembering that rely on internal mental processes of visualization. Examples include the creation of bizarre images and visualizing interacting images.

Memory psychologists report that they seldom use image-based techniques for remembering and that these techniques are among the ones they are least likely to recommend to others. Image-based techniques are also not spontaneously used by older adults. In general, older adults do not like to use memory strategies that they perceive as silly, and many of them consider creating bizzare images of relationships between objects as silly.

C. General Internal Memory Strategies

General internal memory strategies are methods or techniques for remembering that depend solely on internal mental processes. Examples include making an association between something familiar and an item to be learned, and organizing items into categories of objects that are similar to one another.

Three general internal strategies—rehearsal, categorization, and elaboration—are among those most frequently used and recommended by memory researchers. For older adults, rote rehearsal is the only general internal memory strategy that they tend to use spontaneously and, in fact, it is their most preferred internal memory strategy.

D. External Memory Strategies

External memory strategies are methods or techniques for remembering that depend on tangible, physical objects, places, or people. Although external memory strategies are often called *aids* rather than strategies, both internal and external memory strategies rely on higher cognitive functions for effectively reducing instances of forgetting. Examples of external memory strategies that have wide applicability include lists, reminder notes, asking others for reminders, and object placement (placing objects where they will not be forgotten). Other external strategies are highly specific in their applications, for example, bookmarks, recipe cards, and organizers for sorting medications according to the days they need to be taken.

Memory researchers report extensive use of external memory strategies. In fact, their favorite memory technique is to write things down, which has been referred to as "the greatest memory strategy ever devised." Although older adults claim to use external strategies frequently, they tend to think of them as "crutches"; using techniques such as making a list is seen as "cheating."

III. AGE DIFFERENCES IN USE OF MEMORY STRATEGIES

A. Empirical Findings

Research comparing young and older adults' use of memory strategies demonstrates age-related differences in both the number and types of strategies people use. Compared to younger adults, older adults rely on a smaller repertoire of memory strategies. In addition to these quantitative differences, many studies report that the elderly tend to use fewer internal strategies and more external strategies than do younger adults. What is interesting about this latter age-related difference is that external strategies are especially helpful for prospective memory, that is, for remembering to do something in the future, and this is one area of memory where older adults seem to perform better than do younger adults.

Learning how to remember new information is *a* primary, if not *the* primary, foundation of schooling. Students learn memory strategies while they are in school, and being in school furnishes an ongoing opportunity to continue to learn and practice strategies for remembering. Not surprisingly, then, adults who are not in school rely on fewer, and less effective, memory strategies than those who are in school. Older adults who are not in school even reject as valuable those strategies, such as categorization and grouping, that are particularly effective for learning and remembering many kinds of information.

In the absence of being in school, other activities may provide an intellectually challenging environment that demands significant memory performance. Engaging in such activities, like the card game of bridge, may provide opportunities during later adulthood to continue to exercise the mental capacities required to learn and practice memory strategies. Also, research evidence suggests that older adults who

do engage in activities that have high memory demands perform better on memory tests than do older adults who do not participate in challenging activities. [*See* ACTIVITIES.]

B. Theoretical Considerations

When it comes to accounting for older adults' patterns of usage of memory strategies, theory is lacking. Studies have been primarily descriptive, reporting the results of surveys and questionnaires on older adults' ratings or rankings of lists of memory strategies in terms of how often they use them. While acknowledging that the elderly seldom spontaneously use some of the more effective strategies, such as categorization, researchers have turned their attention to determining possible benefits to older adults of instruction in how to use particular memory strategies. These studies demonstrate that elderly people can learn to use strategies that they do not typically bring to bear on a task, and that their memory performance can be significantly enhanced by applying such strategies. However, a remaining problem is that the effects in these studies are often transient.

One highly plausible reason for older adults' infrequent use of effective memory strategies that are very frequently used by today's young adults is that the older adults never learned them before memory researchers came along to teach them. Sophisticated information-processing strategies are generally learned through formal educational experiences. The primary technique today's older adults learned for remembering when they were children and young adults was rote rehearsal, and, as recent research shows, it is still their favored strategy for remembering.

For the first half of the twentieth century, memory research was dominated by a preoccupation with rote rehearsal and the serial learning of lists of verbal materials that were constructed to be as devoid as possible of meaning. Thus, it is not at all surprising that today's older adults, who were in school during the 1940s or earlier, learned that to memorize meant to practice rote rehearsal. In fact, it was in the 1950s that a significant body of experimental evidence began to accumulate confirming the positive effects of categorization and grouping strategies on recall of verbal materials. These important historical facts about the development of thinking and use of memory strategies must be recognized as critical factors in affecting the way today's older adults think about memory and the kinds of strategies they will tend to use when faced with a task requiring memory.

IV. INSTRUCTION IN MEMORY STRATEGIES

A. Features of Instructional Programs

Contemporary instructional programs for improving memory come in different forms. Self-help books and tapes are becoming more and more numerous, and they are very popular. It is important to note that these instructional materials are primarily directed, not at older adults, but at young and middle-aged people in the business world, suggesting that the perceived need to improve one's memory through better use of effective strategies is recognized well before late adulthood.

Typically these programs contain an overview of how memory works, followed by separate lessons on half a dozen or more memory strategies. Each lesson includes a thorough description of a specific strategy with examples, followed by an exercise or assignment for practicing the technique. The memory techniques that are taught are almost always internal techniques and seem to include at least one formal mnemonic system. Although many of the self-help products have been on the market for some time, they have yet to be subjected to careful scientific scrutiny to examine the extent to which they work, assuming their lessons are actually followed.

Scientific studies of instructional programs for memory improvement have generally focused on teaching a single memory strategy in small group sessions conducted in an atmosphere similar to a classroom over a period of no more than 4 or 5 weeks. These studies have demonstrated that older adults can learn new strategies and that their memory performance improves with the use of these strategies. On the other hand, the effects often seem to be relatively short-lived; older adults do not seem to continue to use these newly acquired strategies once outside the classroom.

Difficulties in demonstrating robust and lasting effectiveness of memory instruction may be primarily due to two factors: the types of strategies taught and the brevity of instruction relative to older adults' life-long beliefs and behavior pertaining to experiences of remembering and forgetting. Among the strategies most commonly taught to older adults is the method of loci, a formal mnemonic system. Despite its effectiveness with sufficient learning and practice, the method of loci, like other formal mnemonics, is not well suited to people's everyday needs for remembering because it requires much effort to learn and is not easily generalized to novel situations. Furthermore, the instructional period in scientific studies is usually brief relative to older adults' long history of relying only on a select few memory techniques. To develop proficiency with new strategies it is necessary to practice in sessions that are distributed over time, and to get extensive practice in generalizing the use of a specific strategy to situations other than the one(s) for which it was learned.

Rather than teaching one or two formal techniques and hoping they will be applied to many different situations, research on instructional programs suggests that it may be better to teach a large repertoire of strategies from which older adults can choose the ones that work best for them. Because many of the most effective strategies can be quite specific in their use (for example, medication organizers), teaching a large repertoire also enables older adults to have many different strategies to call upon in different situations. Refresher courses may also be valuable in helping older adults to modify techniques that are not working very well for them and in continuing to augment the repertoire of strategies. Computer-aided instruction may have a role in this regard, although the problem of accessibility will have to be resolved first.

Unfortunately, few instructional programs teach about the wide variety of highly effective external memory techniques available and how to use them. What little research has been done in this arena indicates that the value of these techniques in the daily lives of older adults can be demonstrated immediately. Instruction on external memory strategies would appear to be even more effective if introduced with a discussion to dispel older adults' notions that external strategies are inferior methods for improving memory.

Finally, a good repertoire of strategies may require not only learning new, effective strategies, but also getting rid of old, counterproductive strategies. One such strategy, frequently used by older adults, is the one of storing valuable or important objects in "special" places. This strategy results in significantly more forgetting that remembering. One reason is that the special place is specifically selected because it is a highly unlikely place for the object, which means that the person who put it there will, over time, be increasingly unlikely to think of looking for it in that location. Unfortunately, the fact that the special place is so unusual may also lead the person to be overly confident that they will certainly remember where they put the object. This overconfidence then leads to ignoring other memory strategies that could really aid memory.

B. Value of Instructional Programs

There are obvious advantages to older adults, as well as to society, of offering instruction in memory strategies. They are all related to improving the quality of life of older adults. Advantages include maintaining older adults' independent living; improving their self-efficacy; and reducing their health risks, for example, through increased medication compliance. Evidence just emerging in the research literature even suggests that instructing depressed and anxious people on how to improve their memory may help to alleviate their depression and anxiety. [See DEPRESSION.]

Too often, fears of family members and friends about an older loved one's perceived forgetfulness lead to premature, or unnecessary, institutionalization. Concerns about forgetting to turn off the stove, leaving the front door unlocked, or being stranded at night after headlights have drained the car battery, can worry older adults as well as their families and friends. Appropriate instruction in the use of memory strategies, and modern technology, however, can do much to alleviate these fears. Furthermore, instruction provides a more reasonable and economical alternative to institutionalization. For example, one can teach older adults how to use lists and reminder notes effectively to remember to carry out important actions in their everyday lives and to prevent memory failures that could jeopardize their safety. New products on the market furnish other means for reducing older adults' personal vulnerability: steam irons are now

available that shut themselves off after a short period of not being used, many car models come equipped with headlights that automatically shut off within a few minutes of the ignition key being removed, and medication organizers can make it much simpler to keep track of when to take medications.

Recent research has shown that even people with Alzheimer's disease can benefit from instruction to improve their memory. One research program is teaching Alzheimer's patients to remember the names of staff members in nursing homes by gradually lengthening the interval between learning and recall as the patient becomes successful at shorter durations. The application of these new techniques for helping Alzheimer's patients to improve their memories is all the more significant because progressive memory loss is such a devastating aspect of this disease. [See DEMENTIA.]

Such innovative and successful instructional programs are impressive and provide convincing evidence that research on the benefits of memory instruction for improving the quality of older adults' lives is just beginning.

BIBLIOGRAPHY

Camp, C. J., & McKitrick, L. A. (1991). Memory interventions in Alzheimer's-type dementia populations: Methodological and theoretical issues. *In* R. L. West & J. D. Sinnott (Eds.), *Everyday memory and aging: Current research and methodology* (pp. 155–172). New York: Springer-Verlag.

Herrmann, D. J., Weingartner, H., Searleman, A., & McEvoy, C. (Eds.). (1992). *Memory improvement. Implications for memory theory.* New York: Springer-Verlag.

Park, D. C., Smith, A. D., & Cavanaugh, J. C. (1990). Metamemories of memory researchers. *Memory & Cognition, 18,* 321–327.

Poon, L. W., Rubin, D. C., & Wilson, B. A. (Eds.). (1989). *Everday cognition in adulthood and late life.* New York: Cambridge University Press.

Scogin, F., & Prohaska, M. (1993). *Aiding older adults with memory complaints.* Sarasota, FL: Professional Resource Press.

Sugar, J. A., & McDowd, J. M. (1992). Memory, learning, and attention. *In* J. E. Birren, R. B. Sloane, & G. D. Cohen (Eds.), *Handbook of mental health and aging* (2nd ed., pp. 307–337). San Diego: Academic Press.

Mental Health

Bob Knight and Lauren S. Fox

University of Southern California

I. Populations of Elderly Needing Mental
   Health Services
II. Services Offered in the Mental Health System
III. Do Treatments Work?
IV. Models of Service Provision and Systems of Care
V. Payment Systems and Their Impact on
   Service Delivery
VI. Summary

Comorbid Disorders occurring together at the same time, such as a patient who is experiencing depression, hypertension, and heart disease.
Meta-Analysis A statistical method of summarizing primary studies in order to understand the average finding.
Psychotropic Acting on the brain's neurochemistry and meant to affect psychological or mental functioning; psychotropic medications are drugs given to alleviate psychological symptoms such as depression, anxiety, hallucinations, or delusions.

MENTAL HEALTH can be defined as freedom from mental illness. It can also be considered well-being or life satisfaction, which are covered in other articles in this encyclopedia. Our focus is on the system developed to provide services to alleviate psychological suffering in older adults. Mental health care of the older adult in its optimum form is interdisciplinary, involving psychology, social work, psychiatry, and other fields, intertwined in a mental health-care system that delivers a wide variety of services. To more fully describe the mental health system in the context of older adults, we will discuss the populations of

older clients in need of mental health services, what services are offered, the various systems set up to provide this care, and the financial incentives that shape mental health-care services for the elderly. [*See* LIFE SATISFACTION; PSYCHOLOGICAL WELL-BEING.]

I. POPULATIONS OF ELDERLY NEEDING MENTAL HEALTH SERVICES

There are various populations of older people who may need mental health services. Some client populations clearly have mental illnesses that would be diagnosable at a younger age, whereas others develop disorders in old age; some might not even be commonly labeled as "mentally ill" but can benefit from mental health care. The groups often need different types of services and settings for care.

A. The Severely Mentally Ill Elderly

The severely mentally ill elderly include older adults with schizophrenic and paranoid disorders as well as bipolar disorder and some severe or chronic cases of major depressive disorder. Diagnosis and severity does not necessarily predict the setting of care. Historically, older persons have tended to be overrepresented in inpatient psychiatric units and still account for about 16% of all psychiatric inpatients. The older patient has tended to remain on the inpatient unit longer as well, thus taking up an even more disproportionate amount of services. Stays average more than twice as long for geriatric inpatients in state and county psychiatric hospitals when compared to younger adult inpatients. This has typically been attributed to the rising prevalence of organic brain syndrome diagnoses in the later years of life; however depressive disorders make up a larger part of geropsychiatric admissions. Mentally ill elderly are also present in long-term care settings; about 30% of residents in nursing homes have a chronic mental disorder, excluding dementia.

B. The Acutely Distressed Older Adult

The psychological problems of this population are likely to include depression, anxiety disorders, phobias, adjustment disorders (a salient cause for the elderly being bereavement), and sleep disorders. These problems are also likely to co-occur with medical illness and may therefore complicate medical treatment and lead to unnecessary medical visits and costs. This population is generally assumed to be best served in outpatient mental health settings, although they most often present themselves to medical settings such as primary-care physicians. [See DEPRESSION.]

The elderly underutilize outpatient mental health services relative to their representation in the population. In 1983 the elderly comprised 11% of the population but only 6% of users of community mental health services and even lower percentages in other clinics and private practices. In recent years, more of the elderly have begun to use mental health services, possibly because more assertive outreach strategies are removing barriers between older adults and psychiatric or psychological treatment. On the other hand, older adult services are more likely to be dropped than added to community-based mental health programs.

C. The Dementing Elderly and Their Caregivers

The dementing elderly represent about 50% of nursing home residents and are present in large numbers in residential care facilities and in community-based long-term care for the elderly. Early-stage dementing older adults as well as caregivers of dementing elderly at all stages may benefit from outpatient services as well. Although the most widely recognized source of dementia is Alzheimer's disease (AD), it is important to note that dementia may be the result of many other conditions. Accurate neuropsychological assessment is crucial to differentiate among these disorders (and reversible sources of cognitive impairment such as delirium or severe depression). [See GERIATRIC ASSESSMENT.]

The increased number of cognitively impaired persons among older adults, many of whom suffer from irreversible brain impairment, poses the dilemma of whether they should be categorized as mental health or medical clients. This decision has varied state by state, as has the decision to separate the mental health service system from the systems for developmentally disabled and for substance abusers. The decision will have an impact in the type and scope of programming for the elderly. Given their different needs, older adults with dementing illnesses require distinct types of services from those with acute psychological disorders or psychoses. On the other hand, some dementing older adults develop behavioral problems in the middle stages of their decline for which the treatment consists of psychotropic medications and behavioral interventions. These treatments are typically provided in the mental health system to people whose brain impairment began earlier in life.

In addition, with the brain-impaired older person, as with others who are severely disabled, the caregiver may be in need of mental health services to be able to continue to care for the patient at home. One-third of caregivers are spouses, generally older adults themselves, who may experience a wide range of needs in response to the caregiving situation. Prevalence rates of depression, anxiety, and hostility are extremely high in this population; depression has been estimated to affect between 26 and 43% of caregivers. Helpful responses include respite care, behavioral management training (for the care of the demented elder), stress-reduction training, and therapy for depression. [See CAREGIVING AND CARING; DEMENTIA; HOME CARE AND CAREGIVING.]

D. Medically Ill Elderly

Certainly not all medically ill people require mental health care. The probability of physical disability and disease increases with age, creating patient populations with a high percentage of older adults, and many of these medical problems can cause psychological distress that is a legitimate focus of clinical attention. U.S. Senate figures from 1991 estimate that arthritis affects almost 50% of those over 65, hypertension about 38%, and hearing impairments and heart disease each about 28%. These figures are even higher for those above age 75. People over age 65 filled about 15 prescriptions per year in 1987 compared to 3.8 prescriptions for those under 65. In 1991, the 12% of Americans over 65 accounted for over one-third of total health-care expenditures in the United States. Depression is considerably more common among medical inpatients than in the population as a whole, affecting about one-fifth of patients. Illness is a good predictor of subsequent depression in community samples of older adults. [*See* ARTHRITIS; CARDIOVASCULAR SYSTEM; HEARING.]

The hospital is a setting for many geropsychologists involved in health psychology, who deal with issues such as pain management, behavior management in cardiac patients, the effect of depression and anxiety on medical symptomatology, as well as depression itself in medical settings, adjustment disorder, adapting to loss of physical or cognitive functioning (e.g., stroke patients), and sex therapy for patients whose sexual functioning is affected by surgery or illness. Coping with chronic conditions such as heart disease, cancer, and stroke, currently the three leading causes of death in individuals over 65, is a focus of therapy both inside and outside of the hospital setting. Mental health intervention in medical settings is of particular interest to cost-conscious medical care providers such as health-maintenance organizations (HMOs) because successful treatment of clients can reduce excessive and unnecessary medical visits. Attention to mental status also may affect recovery from medical ailment; for example, research has shown that patients with no depression recover from hip fractures much better than patients with depression, and cardiac patients without depression show better medication adherence than depressed patients. There is a complex interplay between psychological and medical origins of adjustment to and recovery from medical disorders.

E. Sexual Disorders

The sexual response changes with normal aging. Many older adults do not expect these normal developmental changes and misinterpret them, leading to a decrease in sexual activity and enjoyment. Psychoeducation can aid the older adult to understand and adapt to these normal age-related changes.

Many older adults also must cope with illness-related changes in sexual functioning. Prostate cancer, a disease that affects many older men, is often treated by prostatectomy, an operation that nearly always results in sexual functioning problems and often results in impotence. Medical and psychological factors interact in postoperative functioning; Corby and Solnick reported that counseling patients about what to expect postsurgery drastically reduced levels of impotence. However, some sexual dysfunction can only be treated medically, with medication or penile implants. Chronic disease-related pain (such as with diabetes or cancer) can also interfere with normal sexual functioning. Sex therapy can aid the older client to adapt to the losses in sexual functioning and maintain a satisfying sex life. A barrier to this is often the therapists' discomfort discussing sex with older clients or the misperception that the topic of sexuality is inappropriate with older adults. This is unfortunate because the majority of older adults welcome information and discussion and are not uncomfortable with the topic. Just as in younger adults, however, some older adults do exhibit sexual disorders of a deviant nature (exhibitionism, pedophilia, etc.), which are an appropriate target of intervention, either by the mental health-care system or the legal system. [*See* SEXUALITY, SENSUALITY, AND INTIMACY.]

F. Substance Abuse

Finally, substance abuse in later life can be considered an appropriate target for mental health system intervention. For example, alcohol abuse is a major problem among older men and is a legitimate mental health problem, as is the abuse of both illegal and prescription drugs. These problems are less prevalent in older adults than younger adults, possibly because substance abuse declines with maturation or because users die earlier than nonusers. Older adults commonly are on multiple prescription medications and experience side effects or drug interactions. Long-term use of alcohol may lead to behavior problems, exacerbation of previously existing personality disorder, or organic brain disorders, such as Korsakoff's syndrome, that can be distinguished from other dementing illnesses by comprehensive neuropsychological assessment. Misuse of over-the-counter (OTC) medications can cause problems in the elderly, who are more sensitive to medications anyway. The most common substance abuse disorder is tobacco dependence; it accounts for more medical disability and mortality in the elderly than all other substances combined. Polysubstance-use disorders may be a problem for many elderly who are using prescription medications, OTC medications, and/or alcohol. [See ALCOHOL AND DRUGS.]

II. SERVICES OFFERED IN THE MENTAL HEALTH SYSTEM

A. Psychological Testing

Assessments of cognitive functioning or personality are a specialty of clinical psychologists; those trained specifically to work with older adults are in a position to be able to accurately test and interpret results for this population with its higher frequency of sensory or other cognitive limitations and cohort differences. Assessments are done in response to a number of needs, such as diagnosis of any type of mental illness, differential diagnosis of depression or types of dementia, diagnosing functional abilities after stroke, or forensic work, such as establishing competence or incompetence for a court of law. Neuropsychological testing is often done with older adults; this type of assessment uses special tasks to try to determine functioning of cognitive abilities such as verbal and visual memory, speech, spatial ability, or reasoning. Different disorders or locations of brain injury show different patterns of deficit on the various tasks, which aid in diagnosis.

B. Psychotherapy

The most commonly recognized form of mental health-care services is probably the provision of individual psychotherapy in either the inpatient (hospital) or outpatient (clinic or private practice) setting, but there are many other forms of mental health care provided to the elderly. In the outpatient clinic or the inpatient psychiatric facility, individual therapy is only one of a number of therapy modalities such as group therapy, support groups, family therapy, and couples therapy. Some types of therapies that are not unique to but are more often used with older adults are life review and grief work. These services are provided by psychiatrists, psychologists, social workers, and counselors.

C. Medication

A large segment of mental health care is provided in the form of psychotropic medications, which are prescribed by psychiatrists or primary-care physicians. According to Lebowitz and Niederehe, most elderly present their symptoms to a primary-care physician; about 70% of physician visits by those 75 and older resulted in at least one prescription, and 44% received multiple medications. Ten percent of physician visits by those 65 and older resulted in a psychotropic drug prescription. Ninety-five percent of visits resulting in prescriptions for psychotropic medications were made to nonpsychiatrist physicians, mostly primary-care physicians. Additionally, over half of nursing home patients are prescribed psychotropic medications, 20% of these without recording of an appropriate diagnosis. Psychotropic medications are therefore not only prescribed by psychiatrists, but by nonspecialist physicians as well, highlighting the importance of effective coordination of care. Following a recent drive by some psychologists, specially trained psychologists may receive prescription privileges in the future, increasing the scope of the clinical psychologist's service delivery. Some interdisciplinary teams use clinical pharmacologists to advise proper medication usage due to their knowledge of medication action and interaction in the elderly. [See PHARMACOLOGY.]

D. Case Management

Case management is another form of mental health-care service to the elderly. This service helps the frail or cognitively impaired older adult with referrals to professionals in any field, coordination of service providers, household help, help with difficult decisions like legal or financial matters, and various other tasks. Case managers are often social workers, nurses, or gerontologists.

E. Social Services

Social activities and centers or services set up to provide seniors with social interaction are often organized and funded by aging-related agencies and sometimes staffed by mental health-care professionals or paraprofessionals. Examples of these are congregate meal sites, friendly visitor programs, and senior recreation centers.

F. Problem-Specific Services

Problem-specific services are also an important part of mental health-care delivery, especially to the elderly who most often experience specific challenges rather than general loss. Day care for dementia patients and respite programs for caregivers are two examples of programs tailored to the specific needs of older adults. Other types of specific services may concentrate on bereavement and widowhood counseling and support, or specific interventions designed to decrease geropsychiatric inpatient stays.

G. Health Psychology and Other Hospital-Based Services

Hospital-based mental health-care services cover a wide range of issues and modalities. To list just a few, hospitals and other medical settings often provide psychological and psychiatric services such as consultations, assessments (both neuropsychiatric and psychological), psychotropic medication, pain management, individual counseling on a wide range of medical or psychological issues, work on treatment adherence (most notably in cardiac patients), rehabilitation training, self-help groups or therapy groups for patients with specific disorders like breast cancer, social services, and discharge counseling.

III. DO TREATMENTS WORK?

Many of the services and treatments provided to older adults have been shown empirically to be effective. There is still a great need for studies validating treatments on special groups such as the elderly, but a number of meta-analyses (quantitative summaries of a number of studies on the same topic) have supported the use of psychological treatments such as cognitive-behavioral therapy, brief psychodynamic therapy, and pharmacotherapy for depression, as well as other interventions to aid caregivers of dementia patients. Nonquantitative literature reviews suggest that effective interventions exist for insomnia, the dementing elderly, and the severely mentally ill. The need for this type of outcome research will continue to grow as reimbursement agencies like insurance companies want support for the efficacy of services provided.

IV. MODELS OF SERVICE PROVISION AND SYSTEMS OF CARE

A. Long-Term Care for the Elderly

Appropriate placement of older adults, even when they have the same diagnoses as younger patients, introduces some complexities. In long-term care for the elderly, there are both the age-based system and the system for the mentally ill. Placement of the mentally ill elderly is a complex issue; are they best served in the mental health system or the aging care system? Older people often have complex chronic and acute medical needs. Nursing homes for older adults are equipped to handle chronic medical issues and some psychiatric issues, such as mild dementia, but are often not able to handle more severe behavioral problems, psychotic residents, or suicidal residents. Psychiatric facilities on the other hand are often not equipped to handle the complex medical needs of the older patient. The staff of psychiatric facilities often do not have the medical expertise to care for the elderly, and the staff of age-based long-term care facilities do not know about psychological or psychiatric issues; they do not effectively coordinate with each other either. This issue is also salient in assessing and interpreting assessments on older adults, who often perform differently on tests and require different norms than younger adults, especially when accounting for overlapping comorbid medical conditions or sensory limitations.

The notion of ranges of care within separate care systems can organize our thinking about the institutional environments for the elderly. It has been argued that two conceptually and legally separate systems of care for the elderly exist. The long-term care system for the elderly as defined by licensing regulations moves from independent living to residential care and locked residential care, intermediate care, skilled nursing care, and locked skilled nursing care. The psychiatric system could be viewed as including acute psychiatric hospitals, state hospitals, and locked skilled nursing facilities. Based on the preceding discussion of coexisting medical and mental health problems, the acute medical care system must also be considered as a third system of care through which older adults with psychological problems also move. The medical system provides an interesting example of care that is more integrated with the corresponding outpatient care and serves as a gateway to long-term care.

There are several problems in considering the range within any of these systems to be a progressive hierarchy. First, patients enter and leave the system and move from level to level in a wide variety of ways. The popularly accepted view may be that the elderly gradually deteriorate and progressively move up the scale, but reality fails to confirm this image. For example, dementia patients who also have behavior problems may move from independent living to high levels of locked care and then move to more "independent" levels of care as their physical condition deteriorates and they are no longer capable of causing trouble.

The rationale for movement within the three systems is also different. Movement within the aging long-term care system is based on physical frailty and functional ability in the activities of daily living (ADL) sense. Movement within the psychiatric system is based on the degree of acuity of the psychiatric disorder or the overtness of behavioral problems or both. Movement within the acute medical care system (and from acute to chronic or long-term care) is based on diagnosis, response to treatment, and intensity of need for nursing care. Thus three interlocking but conceptually distinct systems with built-in tensions exist and are bound together by serving some of the same patients and many similar patients. Mental health patients, former mental health patients, and the cognitively impaired inhabit all levels of care in all three systems. The ideal goal for the person who serves elderly clients is to seek the level and type of service required by the patient's condition and to avoid unnecessarily restrictive placement.

The concern with avoiding inappropriately restrictive and excessively costly treatment has led to a focus on community-based care. Although the distinction is more salient in some systems than others, for most services there is a dividing line between 24-hour care and community-based care systems.

B. Systems of Community-Based Care for the Elderly

During roughly the same time period as the development of community mental health services as an alternative to state hospital care for the mentally ill, a variety of community-based programs for older adults has developed that is funded by or at least encouraged by the Older Americans Act (OAA) and the set of planning and coordination agencies funded by that

act (the Administration on Aging, state Units on Aging, and Area Agencies on Aging). With a goal similar to that of the community mental health movement, this system and its funded services strive to keep older people independent and in the community. Senior recreation centers, multipurpose centers, congregate and home-delivered meals, social model day care for adults, legal aide, in-home supportive services, volunteer support, and the long-term care ombudsman programs are all part of this system. Although these programs are aging oriented, not mental health oriented, for the older adult these services can greatly improve the quality of life and therefore promote positive mental health.

The array of services is diverse and can be confusing to the outsider. There has been relatively little formal or informal cooperation between the aging services system and the community mental health system, although there are model programs that serve as exceptions to this general rule. In part, the problems are due to differences in definition of target populations in that mental health services are for people with diagnosable disorders, whereas aging services are based on age rather than need. The mental health professional working with older adults needs to be able to assess and refer intelligently.

Extending the argument of the previous section on institutional systems, a third community-based system of care for older adults is outpatient medical care, including physician's offices and outpatient clinics, outpatient surgery centers, and in-home health services. As is true within the institution-based systems, community-based medical care will depend on the patient's medical condition. Many older adults will be simultaneously moving through all of these systems of care.

Finally, recent years have seen the growth of yet another system of care: community-based dementia care. Although the need for segregated services for dementing elderly is far from clearly established, policy in many states and service systems in some states are moving toward a separate system of care for the dementing elderly. The extent to which dementia care will overlap with mental health care is not yet known but will depend in part on the policies and practices of the dementia care and mental health-care systems.

The issue of accessibility of services, long a cornerstone of the community mental health movement, is critical for a population with limited ability to get around. The aged need a facility close to public transportation, accessible to handicapped persons, and located in a safe neighborhood in which they feel at home. For those unable to come to the clinic, home visits are crucial. In many communities, the elderly may need an office in a location away from programs serving younger mentally ill or substance-abusing clients and away from the psychiatric hospital, quite often a key element in the fears of older people.

In summary, there are a number of potential subpopulations of older adults who need mental health services. These groups (and many other older adults who do not need mental health services) inhabit a complex service world that includes three systems of institution-based care and three or four systems of community-based care. The complexity is obvious and can be confusing even for professionals who work in the system. Clearly, the frail and confused older potential client cannot be expected to self-diagnose accurately and then enter the system through the right doorway. Hence, outreach with accurate assessment and valid referral is necessary.

C. Problems in Care Delivery That All Systems Must Address

What are some of the problems that prevent older adults from receiving care in the most appropriate location? Assessment of mental health problems in older adults is widely recognized to be complex due to the array of possible presenting problems and the high rates of comorbidity. Specialized training in assessment of older adults is desirable and can be obtained in graduate, postgraduate, or continuing education settings. Moreover, some elderly may simply not see their problems as psychological, or they may be unaware of the existence of outpatient therapy.

A second pervasive source of complexity is that older adults with mental health problems are embedded in a variety of distinct care systems at both institutional and community-based levels: medical care, long-term care for the elderly, mental health services, aging network services, and possibly dementia care services. Professionals need to be aware of other agencies' waiting lists and available services so that referred clients do not "fall through the cracks." Unfortunately, with limited resources and shrinking budgets, agencies are strict about who is eligible to receive services, and it may prove difficult to refer clients to services that can accept them, leaving gaps of need unfulfilled by any of the service providers. Difficulties in coordination of care may therefore be a function of economic pressures rather than planning failures. [*See* HEALTH CARE AND SERVICES.]

The complex needs of the older client will necessitate working with a range of professionals, such as aging network service providers, health-care providers, the legal system, and so on. This need for interdisciplinary and intersystem cooperation requires both conceptual understanding of how systems work together and practical training in manipulating complex systems for the good of the client. The interdisciplinary approach also requires a respect and understanding of other professionals in diverse fields. It should be common in the geriatric mental health team setting to find all members listening intently to valuable perspectives about clients offered by volunteers, nurses' aids, homemaker aides, and meal-site workers. In fact, the usual economies of health and social systems dictate that those with the least training and status will have the greatest actual exposure to the client and therefore the largest and best samples of behavioral observation (e.g., the client's physician sees him or her five to ten minutes a month, the home health nurse half an hour per week, the homemaker aide eight hours per week).

D. Program Principles in Mental Health and Aging

Fortunately there are guidelines available for providing more appropriate services to older adults. High-quality, community-based mental health services for the elderly share some common features:

1. All emphasize accurate diagnosis of older adults.
2. All are interdisciplinary and treatment focused.
3. All use active case-finding methods and community education approaches to bring clients in. They also collaborate actively with other agencies that serve older adults and in some cases with postal carriers, meter readers, and other "community gatekeepers."
4. All of them deliver mental health services to older adults at home.

These are key elements of successful community-based programs in mental health and aging.

The Veteran's Administration (VA) system provides a model for hospital-based care. Like the community-based programs, the VA emphasizes accurate assessment, active treatment, and interdisciplinary coordination of services. Many VA mental health services are provided in medical settings (acute wards, chronic care, nursing homes, etc.) as well as in distinct psychiatric units. Home-care services are also a part of the VA continuum of care. Furthermore, the VA has played a major role in developing training in geriatric mental health across the constituent disciplines.

Other model programs are those that focus on problem-specific outreach services for older adults. Specific problems are more salient than generic loss; programs that target specific needs and offer services to meet those needs are well utilized. At a program level, this schema for relating programs to needs and populations grows from the discovery that utilization of outpatient services in community mental health programs was uncorrelated with utilization of inpatient services by the elderly. Four programs that have been successful examples are senior outreach teams, family-based services for dementia care, intensive case management, and day treatment services for the older adult; these programs are tailored to the needs of the different subpopulations among the elderly who need mental health services. Throughout this range of programs, outreach principles of educating the clients, educating the providers, and improving the availability, accessibility, and affordability of services will help to assure that those in need understand and use effective mental health interventions.

The key issue in the continued development of services to older adults is their affordability. Until the last few years, most program development in mental health services for the elderly has taken place in contexts that do not rely entirely on fee for service or on Medicare funding. Other sources of funds have included state funding for mental health services, community mental health system funding, Veteran's Affairs funding, training grants, research grants, and various private, nonprofit agencies. These sources can be motivated by perceived client need, interest in creative program development, and training goals.

V. PAYMENT SYSTEMS AND THEIR IMPACT ON SERVICE DELIVERY

Since about 1980, there has been a privatization movement in mental health care characterized by an increasing reliance on private practice providers and organized for-profit systems that are driven by market forces such as demand for services and the need to make profit from service provision. Developments in health-care policy during this era have been described as leading to the development of a medical-industrial complex comparable to the military-industrial complex.

A. Fee for Service Medicare Reimbursement

The ultimate source of money for mental health services for the elderly is still government funding (75%, mainly Medicare and Medicaid). In 1988, $2.5 billion of total Medicare spending of $90.5 billion was spent on mental health care, $2.2 on Part A (inpatient services). This represents less than 3% of the Medicare budget as compared to 20–30% of private insurance spent on mental health. The National Institute on Mental Health (NIMH) estimated in 1984 that 51.2% of these services went to disabled adults under 65 years of age, so about 1.5% of Medicare funds paid for mental health services for the elderly.

The Omnibus Budget Reconciliation Acts (OBRA) of 1981, 1989, and 1990 have resulted in a lifting of the annual cap on reimbursement of outpatient mental health-care services and provided for direct payment of clinical psychologists and clinical social workers; however, certain services are still restricted. The 1989 OBRA changes have led to increases in Medicare spending in inpatient psychiatric care, including an expanding number of geropsychiatric inpatient units. Partial hospitalization services for older adults have exploded in recent years, increasing by 50% between 1986 and 1990. Outpatient mental health services have increased by 20% in the same 4-year period.

In terms of the principles of care outlined above, this program has the advantage of emphasizing assessment and of encouraging the development of services at several levels of care throughout the nation. The ability of fee-for-service Medicare to produce rapid changes in service delivery to older adults by a wide spectrum of service entities with minimal administrative overhead is its greatest strength.

On the negative side, Medicare regulations have tended to discourage home visits for mental health services, if not eliminate them altogether. Interdisciplinary cooperation is present to the extent that communication with the primary-care physician is encouraged, but this falls short of working in an interdisciplinary team setting. The emphasis on inpatient care would tend to exacerbate the existing imbalances of older adults in inpatient versus outpatient care, and is bad mental health policy in any case because outpatient care is generally more effective and less expensive.

The impact of Medicare through the fee-for-service reimbursement model seems to have been to expand mental health service delivery to older adults dramatically and to encourage the privatization of mental health care for older adults, with a built-in predilection so far for the encouragement of inpatient over outpatient options. This imbalance may have been corrected to an as yet unknown extent by the rapid growth of partial hospitalization programs and outpatient services since 1990, some of which serve older adults in nursing homes.

B. Managed Care Options

The rapid growth of fee for service medical care and the difficulties inherent in controlling quality and quantity of services reimbursed under this system have led to an increasing reliance on managed care models in general medical services and for medical services reimbursed under Medicare. These models are more recently beginning to affect mental health services for older adults.

Managed health options, especially health maintenance organizations (HMOs), have become a rapidly increasing part of the health-care coverage of older Americans since 1980. Approximately 10% of older Americans have opted to receive their Medicare-funded health care through HMOs. HMOs exist in order to provide overall health-care management for a defined population. Because the HMO is paid per capita rather than per visit, the HMO is motivated to achieve cost savings for the group of enrollees. These cost savings are based on several factors: (a) Because the care providers are not paid on a unit of service basis, there is no motivation to overprovide services; (b) there is a financial incentive to maintain the health of the population (i.e., to provide preventive services); and (c) less expensive services are substi-

tuted for more expensive ones (e.g., outpatient care for inpatient care, primary care for specialist care, nonphysician for physician, pharmacotherapy for psychotherapy).

A primary motivation for the inclusion of mental health services in HMOs from the provider's perspective is the potential for a cost-offset effect, the possibility that mental health services contribute to saving medical costs. This possibility is thought to be even greater in older populations due to pervasive comorbidity, prevention of institutionalization, and greater functional impact of mental health problems in the older population. Unfortunately, no evaluations of the effects of the managed-care system on services to older adults have yet been reported.

The potential strength of HMOs would be the high potential for interdisciplinary, coordinated care within a single managed health system. In principle, mental health and physical health care could be completely integrated, with shared recordkeeping, a single-source pharmacy for better medication coordination, and providers united by concern for the patient's long-term health. Another potential strength of the HMO model in application to older adults is their greater reliance on group and family therapy in the delivery of mental health services.

The weaker elements of HMOs in meeting the mental health needs of the elderly would come in specialized assessment of mental disorders in older patients, the need for outreach, the need for home visits, and the management of long-term severely mentally ill people. Although there is no systematically collected evidence on assessment of mental disorders in older patients in HMOs, the complexity of accurate assessment in older adults runs counter to the HMO's emphasis on use of nonspecialized service providers. HMOs are also not well suited organizationally for active outreach and case-finding approaches. When a guiding principle of an organization is cost containment, seeking out patients who are not actively seeking services is counterproductive.

VI. SUMMARY

The mental health system for older adults is new and still evolving. Although some differences in mental health care for older adults are due to specific problems (especially dementia), the largest differences lie in the mental health-care system itself: in specialty services provided to older adults, the dilemmas faced by elderly with comorbid conditions, and systems of payment for mental health services. The response to the needs of the elderly has included a number of specific services geared to this population and the extension of services developed with younger adults to the elderly via active outreach and case finding. The future of mental health services for older adults will be influenced by new knowledge and techniques from research and program development, the growing number of specialists in mental health and aging, and by the continuing evolution of mental health policy, especially changes in Medicare.

BIBLIOGRAPHY

Birren, J. E., & Schaie, K. W. (Eds.). (1990). *Handbook of the psychology of aging* (3rd ed.). San Diego: Academic Press.

Birren, J. E., Sloane, R. B., & Cohen, G. D. (Eds.). (1992). *Handbook of mental health and aging* (2nd ed.). San Diego: Academic Press.

Fogel, B. S., Furino, A., & Gottlieb, G. L. (1990). *Mental health policy for older Americans: Protecting minds at risk.* Washington, DC: American Psychiatric Press.

Gatz, M. (Ed.). (1995). *Emerging issues in mental health and aging.* Washington, DC: American Psychological Association.

Knight, B. (1996). *Psychotherapy with older adults* (2nd ed.). Newbury Park, CA: Sage.

LaRue, A. (1992). *Aging and neuropsychological assessment.* New York: Plenum Press.

Metabolism: Carbohydrate, Lipid, and Protein

Carolyn D. Berdanier

University of Georgia

I. Nuclear DNA
II. Mitochondrial DNA
III. Membranes
IV. Intracellular and Intercellular Communication
V. Fuel Fluxes

Adaptation Acquisition of a new steady state in response to environmental change.

Allosterism A regulatory mechanism that involves ligand binding. A cooperative interaction that occurs when a ligand binds at a site distal to the catalytic site and influences (inhibits or enhances) the activity of the catalytic or active site of an enzyme or receptor or transporter. In general, allosterism results from interactions among subunits of multiunit proteins, and these interactions determine the activity of the total protein.

Anabolism Reactions or reaction sequences that result in synthesis of macromolecules such as glycogen, proteins, triacylglycerols, and so on.

Apoptosis Programmed cell death.

ATP Adenosine triphosphate; a high-energy compound that functions in energy transfer within the cell.

Catabolism Reactions or reaction sequences that result in degradation of macromolecules to their smaller component molecules.

Citric Acid Cycle (Krebs Cycle) Cyclic series of reactions that enables cells to oxidize metabolites and that results in the production of reducing equivalents for use by the respiratory chain and citrate, which can be transported to the cytosol for hydrolysis to

oxalacetate and acetyl CoA. This cycle takes place in the mitochondria.

Gluconeogenesis Synthesis of glucose from two and three carbon metabolic intermediates. Gluconeogenesis is stimulated when the intake of glucose is deficient or when glucose is not being metabolized by cells. This occurs in the disease, *diabetes mellitus*. Gluconeogenesis takes place in the cytosol and shares many of its reactions with glycolysis.

Glycogenesis When more glucose is provided to the body than can be immediately used, some of this glucose is stored in the form of glycogen through a series of reactions beginning with glucose-6-phosphate and ending with a branched glucose polymer. Glucoses are joined by linkages between carbon 1 and carbons 4 or 6.

Glycogenolysis When the body is in need of glucose it raids its glycogen stores through glycogen hydrolysis.

Glycolysis The main pathway for the use of glucose by the cell. This use begins with the phosphorylation of glucose and, through a series of enzymatic steps in the cytosol, results in the production of the three-carbon molecule, pyruvate. If oxygen is in short supply, pyruvate is converted to lactate. If not converted to lactate, pyruvate enters the mitochondria for further use by the citric acid cycle.

Homeostasis A condition of constancy within the living animal characterized by the steady state maintenance of metabolism where anabolic and catabolic pathways counteract each other as appropriate for

Copyright © 1996 by Academic Press, Inc.
All rights of reproduction in any form reserved.

the nutritional, environmental, and hormonal condition of that animal.

Lipogenesis Synthesis of fatty acids from acetyl CoA and the esterification of these fatty acids to glycerol to make triglycerides. Lipogenesis occurs in the cytosol.

Lipolysis Cleavage of fatty acids from glycerol usually followed by the oxidation of these fatty acids and the reuse of glycerol. Lipolysis occurs in the cytosol, whereas fatty acid oxidation occurs in the mitochondria.

Membrane Lipid bilayer consisting of phospholipids and cholesterol. Proteins, which serve as receptors, carriers, or enzymes, are embedded in this bilayer, either wholly or partly.

Metabolic Control Regulation of metabolic processes with the result of optimal efficiency of energy and metabolite conservation.

Mitochondria Organelle responsible for energy transformation. The citric acid cycle, respiratory chain, oxidative phosphorylation, and fatty acid oxidation occur in this compartment.

Nucleus Organelle of the cell that contains the genetic material, DNA. Gene codes for almost all the proteins synthesized by the cell are in this cell component.

Pentose Phosphate Shunt When glucose is consumed in excess of need, some of the glucose is metabolized by way of this shunt. This series of reactions yields two reducing equivalents per molecule of glucose used. These reducing equivalents are used in the de novo synthesis of fatty acids. The shunt also produces ribose-5-phosphate, an important constituent of RNA, and three carbon intermediates, which can enter the glycolytic sequence. The shunt takes place in the cytosol.

Respiration and Oxidative Phosphorylation Series of reactions that results in the joining of oxygen to hydrogen to make water. Respiration produces energy, which is trapped (under closely regulated conditions) in the high energy bond of adenosine triphosphate (ATP); ATP, in turn, transfers this energy to the synthetic processes of the cell.

Steady State A characteristic of a living system in which all fluxes are maintained to optimize that system's survival. It is an open system that has maximum thermodynamic efficiency.

Ureogenesis Cyclic series of reactions for the synthesis of urea from ammonia.

Aging is a continuum of metabolic change from conception to death. As cells multiply and as differentiation occurs, the needs for specific nutrients (substrates) and fuels change. Hormones, genetics, and nutrients interact and affect the orchestration and regulation of this process called growth. Upon the attainment of full maturity, subtle changes in this regulation occur such that the system is maintained with little or no growth of new tissue. There are exceptions to this; adipose tissue fat stores can increase given an energy surplus and in the adult female, pregnancy and lactation are processes that inherently are characterized by the growth of new tissue. Of concern to this article is the regulation of metabolism in the postmaturation phase of life; that is, the postreproductive period of the female and the equivalent time period in the male.

The regulation of **CARBOHYDRATE, LIPID, AND PROTEIN METABOLISM** is an integrated process that occurs at many different levels in the body. Metabolic regulation is, in fact, the summation of all those processes and reactions that ensure a continuous supply of fuel and substrates necessary to sustain life. It includes both anabolic and catabolic processes that use or release energy and use or produce needed substrates or end products. Living organisms survive and thrive when all of these processes are interdigitated and synchronized. Characteristic of aging is a gradual, subtle, and not so subtle loss in this synchrony. How this loss occurs is the subject of much discussion. The pattern of loss is not the same in all individuals, although some similarities do exist. Genetic differences, gender differences, and species differences influence the gradual loss in metabolic control and the gradual loss in the homeostatic mechanisms that assure continuance of life.

I. NUCLEAR DNA

Although it is generally assumed that healthy life span is genetically dictated as well as modified by dietary conditions, no one gene or group of genes has been identified that is directly responsible for life span determination. Researchers interested in the aging phenomenon as well as those interested in the genetic aspects of age-related degenerative disease have found age-related changes in both nuclear and mitochondrial DNA. DNA, although a very large molecule, is also a labile one. When in solution, it decomposes at the labile N-glycosyl bond. In living systems this permits base substitutions and deletions (mutations) to occur, and if sufficient numbers of these occur, aberrant gene products will result that can explain in part, the age-related losses in particular cell functions. Nuclear DNA, although subject to hydrolysis, oxidation, and nonenzymatic methylation, can repair itself. Figure 1 illustrates where damage can occur. The base substitutions can be reversed by a series of reactions shown in Figure 2. In young animals this repair is quite efficient. However, one of the consequences of aging is a loss in DNA repair efficiency. It should be noted that these mutations are spontaneous and occur randomly. Not all cells or cell types are affected, nor does the process occur all at once. Losses in cell function occur cell by cell, and cell types differ in their vulnerability and in their repair capacity. Nonetheless, with age there are changes in DNA that result in functional losses. With this loss is a rise in the presence of methylated cytosines, base deletions, base substitutions, and strand breaks. All of these deviations from

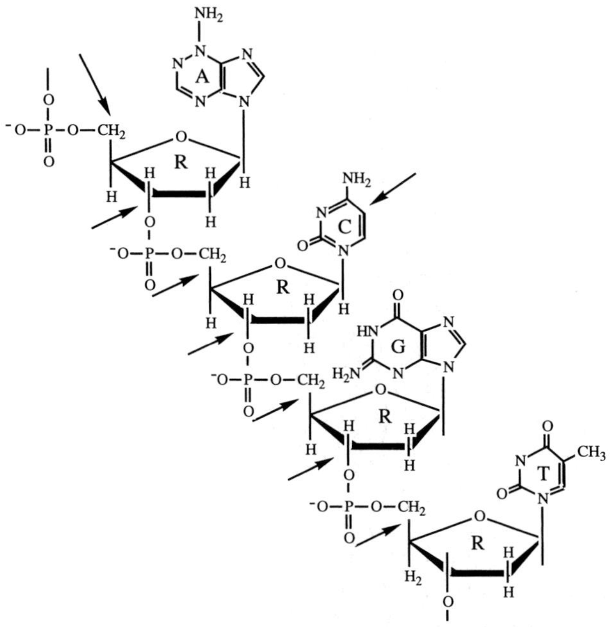

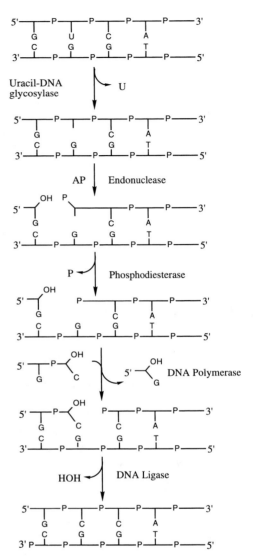

Figure 2 DNA repair. Shown here is the excision of uracil and the base-free deoxyribose phosphate, followed by replacement and correction of the missing residue by DNA repair synthesis. The glycosylases recognize the base substitution and remove it (Step 1). These enzymes also recognize bases that are methylated and oxidative damage. Cell viability is dependent on the presence of these glycosylases.

Figure 1 The bases that comprise the DNA polynucleotide chain are joined together by phosphodiester bonds using ribose as the common link between the bases. A, adenine; C, cytosine; G, guanine; T, thymine; R, ribose. Labile sites for DNA damage are indicated by arrows.

normal are biomarkers of aging. [*See* MARKERS OF AGING.] Of interest is the observation that food-restricted animals have fewer DNA aberrations than ad libitum fed animals of the same age. Food-restricted animals live longer than nonrestricted animals when both sets of animals are housed under the same conditions and are fed the same diet and are of the same genetic background. Should the genetic background differ, the difference in life span due to food restriction will also differ. In other words, although life span can be increased with food restriction, length of life will ultimately be controlled by the genetics of the consumer. Rats from short-lived strains will die sooner than rats of long-lived strains, and rats of both strains will live longer when food restricted. Those of the long-lived strain when food is restricted will live longer than those food-restricted rats of the short-lived strain. This probably also occurs in other species; however, there is the caveat of environmental control. Larger animals, and humans in particular, cannot be maintained in controlled environments where infections are minimized and climatic conditions are ideal. Furthermore, the complexity of human life with its social and economic demands does not lend itself to a stress-free environment.

II. MITOCHONDRIAL DNA

Nuclear DNA damage is forestalled in many instances by its protective histone coat. Mitochondrial DNA lacks this protection. Furthermore, mitochondrial DNA has limited repair capability. Mitochondrial DNA carries only a few messages when compared to nuclear DNA, yet should wholesale damage to this DNA occur, the results could be devastating. That damage occurs is without doubt, but seldom is the effect of this damage devastating. This is because each cell contains many mitochondria; the liver cell, for example, contains about 800. In addition, although cell turnover might be slow to nonexistent in some tissues, mitochondrial turnover is much more rapid. Thus, although mitochondrial DNA repair is limited, the large number per cell and turnover rate compensate for damage that might occur to a single mitochondrion or indeed to a group of mitochondria within a cell.

Normal aging is characterized by an accumulation of deletions in mitochondrial DNA. Different tissues accumulate these deletions at different rates. Deletions have been found in human skeletal muscle, liver, skin, neural tissue, and cardiac muscle. Skeletal muscle from humans shows a 10,000-fold increase in deletion over the course of a normal life span. In the rat, the increase in deletion is more rapid in hepatic and

cardiac muscle cells than in skeletal muscle cells. The deletion mutation in the mitochondrial genome has been attributed to free radical attack on the labile N-glycosyl bond. Free radicals can readily form in the mitochondrial because of its structure and function. The mitochondrion is comprised of two dual membranes that are rich in phospholipids, which contain a high percentage of fatty acids as polyunsaturated fatty acids. Because the mitochondria consume about 90% of all the oxygen consumed by the cell, and because this oxygen is usually in its ionic or charged state, there exists ample opportunity for free radical formation. With age, lipid peroxide levels rise in a variety of tissues from humans, mice, and rats. These very reactive substances attack the DNA, resulting in deletions. In turn, as the number of deletions accumulate, cell function and then organ or tissue function is compromised as the mitochondria lose their ability to respire and synthesize ATP. This sequence of events has been suggested as an explanation for heart disease, accelerated aging due to diabetes mellitus, renal disease, Parkinson's disease, and Alzheimer's disease.

III. MEMBRANES

The membranes serve as geographical boundaries of cells and cellular compartments. These structures are composed of phospholipids arranged in a dual layer with their hydrophilic aspects facing outward, and their hydrophobic aspects facing inward. Cholesterol is also part of the membrane and provides a measure of lipid structural stability. Four major phospholipids are found in these membranes: phosphatidyl choline, phosphatidyl serine, phosphatidyl ethanolamine and phosphatidyl inositol. Each of these phospholipids has fatty acids at carbons 1 and 2, and at carbon 3 of the glycerol backbone there is a phosphate group to which is attached either choline, ethanolamine, inositol, or serine. These structures comprise the charged portion or hydrophillic portion of the phospholipid. The fatty acids at carbons 1 and 2 comprise the hydrophobic portion of the molecules and provide the fluidity that is characteristic of a membrane. Fluidity is conferred by the ratio of saturated fatty acids to unsaturated fatty acids, and the ratio of these fatty acids to cholesterol. When the content of unsaturated fatty acids rises in a membrane, the membrane could become more fluid. This is compensated for by a rise in cholesterol. This compensation ensures a constancy in membrane fluidity. However, not all membranes are similarly regulated. The plasma membrane is carefully controlled in this way but the mitochondrial membrane is not. There is very little cholesterol in this membrane, thus this membrane can vary substantially. Diets rich in polyunsaturated fatty acids will affect the mitochondrial membrane to a greater extent than the plasma membrane. With age there is a gradual reduction in the fluidity of membranes as subtle shifts in the ratio of saturated fatty acids to unsaturated fatty acids occurs. This in turn affects those cell functions that are dependent on fluidity. [See CHOLESTEROL AND CELL PLASMA MEMBRANES.]

The membrane phospholipids create the environment for protein function. Just as these lipids are amphiphathic so too are the proteins. The proteins are distributed in a nonuniform fashion throughout the lipid bilayer. Some are anchored in the surface facing the plasma, others face the cytosol, and still others are inserted through the bilayer. Most of these peripheral and integral proteins do not interact directly with the phospholipids that surround them, yet these lipids can have effects on their function. In some instances these lipid effects are due to their fluidity. Proteins that function by changing shape would be less able to do so when surrounded by relatively rigid lipids. Changing membrane fluidity would thus result in changing the ease with which these proteins could change their conformation and hence activity. An example of this influence is the effect of plasma membrane fluidity on insulin receptor activity. Where the membrane is more fluid because of polyunsaturated fatty acids in the diet, the numbers of receptors available for binding and their binding affinity are increased. Another example relates to the mitochondrial membrane. In rats fed highly unsaturated (fish oil), moderately unsaturated (corn oil), moderately saturated (beef tallow), or very saturated (hydrogenated coconut oil) fat, mitochondrial respiration coupled to ATP synthesis is very efficient in the first group with gradual losses in efficiency observed in the subsequent groups. Both the enzymes of the respiratory chain and the many subunits of the ATP synthetase are embedded in the mitochondrial membranes and, in membranes that are very fluid, these proteins have optimal flexibility and function. Similarly, the transporters of the metabolites and adenine nucleotides that are required for optimized oxidative phosphorylation are likewise optimized in a more fluid environment.

Although the diet fat can have these influences, hormonal influences can be just as strong. Hypothyroidism is characterized by increased fatty acid saturation and decreased function of both plasma and mitochondrial membranes. Characteristic of hypothyroidism are derangements in carbohydrate use, notably a decrease in glucose oxidation, decreased protein synthesis, and accumulation of fat in the adipose tissue. Decreased thermogenic capacity characterized by an inability to maintain body temperature in a cold or chilly environment also characterizes hypothyroidism. Heat production results when ATP is synthesized. Thus, if ATP synthesis is reduced, so too is heat production. Providing a hormone replacement will reverse all these features. The membranes will become more fluid, and ATP synthesis will increase. Heat production will increase partly due to increased mitochondrial activity and partly due to an effect of ATP on protein synthesis that in turn has effects on skeletal muscle activity. Altogether, then, hormone replacement has a cascade of effects that appear related or integrated by the hormone's effect on membrane fluidity and function.

Other hormones likewise have effects on membrane phospholipid fatty acid saturation and fluidity. Growth hormone, the glucocorticoids, insulin, glucagon, the sex hormones, and some of the pituitary hormones (e.g., ACTH and thyroid-stimulating hormone have been found to influence membrane function through effects on membrane composition). In some instances, these effects are indirect. That is, the hormone in question stimulates the synthesis of fatty acids in the cytosol. Because these fatty acids rapidly exchange with those in the membrane phospholipids, there are effects on fluidity via this mechanism. Other hormones may stimulate the lipolysis. This results in a release of fatty acids from the stored triacylglycerides, which in turn can exchange with the phospholipid fatty acids in the membranes. Many of the catabolic hormones (i.e., glucagon, glucocorticoids, etc.) act in this way to influence membrane composition and function. [See ENDOCRINE FUNCTION AND DYSFUNCTION.]

Age has a profound effect on membrane lipid saturation and fluidity. As animals age the membrane fatty acids become more saturated, fluidity falls, and those enzymes, carriers, and signaling systems that depend on a fluid environment become less active. In addition to changes in fatty acid saturation, the cholesterol content rises, and this lends a further degree of rigidity to the system. Thus, age-related declines in membrane-associated reactions or pathways may be attributable in part to these age changes in composition without regard to diet or hormonal perturbations. The latter can modify the age changes either suppressing or magnifying them as described above.

In addition, there are age changes in free radical production and suppression. With age, there is a decline in oxidative phosphorylation efficiency. Mitochondrial respiratory activity declines with the result that there is greater opportunity for superoxides and fatty acid radicals to form. These very reactive substances can react with the mitochondrial DNA as well as with the various proteins in this organelle, causing damage and loss of function. Hepatic mitochondrial respiratory function has been shown to decline with age, as has the biosynthesis of mitochondrial inner membrane proteins. Mitochondrial DNA mutation has been shown to rise with age and increases in peroxidized lipids. These changes have cumulative effects on carbohydrate, lipid, and protein metabolism.

IV. INTRACELLULAR AND INTERCELLULAR COMMUNICATION

Hormones and their secondary messenger systems are the central integrators of the communications that exist between the brain and the rest of the body and between the different organs and tissues. With age there is a decline in the efficiency with which these communications are transmitted. This is due to a myriad of age-related structural and functional changes. Aging is associated with anatomical changes of the endocrine glands. Some glands, the ovary for instance, have a defined life span and the cells are programmed to cease functioning at midlife. Programmed cell death, apoptosis, is both genetically determined and nutritionally influenced. With age there is a general decline in gene expression (translation and transcription) with a related decline in the accuracy and efficiency of protein synthesis. In part this is due to the age-related accumulation in DNA mutations due to

free radical damage. Protein turnover also declines with increasing age, and this is manifested by an age-related increase in protein half-life. [See Cell Death.]

Many hormones are proteins, and as such one might expect that age will have effects on their synthesis, release, activity, and degradation. Best studied is the protein hormone, insulin. With age the pancreas becomes less responsive to signals for insulin release, and the target tissues become less responsive to its action. In part this may be due to age-related increased plasma membrane phospholipid saturation, but it is also due to age-related increases in fat cell size. As fat cells accumulate stored fat they become less sensitive to the action of insulin in promoting glucose uptake and use. Muscle cells likewise may have age-related changes in membrane fluidity that impair their response to insulin. As well, there is an age-related decrease in muscle use. Working muscles have little need for insulin bound to its receptor to facilitate glucose use. Altogether then, this decrease in muscle activity plus the increase in fat cell size has a negative effect on the insulin–glucose relationship. Glucose levels rise and the β cells of the pancreatic islets of Langerhans increase their output of insulin to meet the glucose challenge. However, this excess output does little good in reducing the blood glucose in the aging, overly fat, inactive individual, and it is not uncommon to have noninsulin dependent diabetes mellitus develop as a consequence. Age-related impaired glucose tolerance can be mitigated by food restriction and increased activity that reverses the above physiological state. Because insulin is one of the main regulators of intermediary metabolism and because its action is counterbalanced by the glucocorticoids, the catecholamines, the thyroid hormones, glucagon, and several other hormones, it should be no surprise that age changes in these hormones occur as well. Again, some of these changes can be attributed to age changes in membrane lipids, but some can be attributed to changes in hormone production and in the synthesis and activity of the receptors that mediate their action. Table I lists some hormones affected by age. The blood levels of most of these hormones decrease in the aging human and laboratory animal. A few pass through a phase where they are elevated above normal then fall below normal as aging continues. All of these hormones serve to regulate the metabolism of carbohydrate, lipid, and protein.

Table I Hormone Changes with Age

Hormone	Age effects
Serum thyroxine (T$_4$)	↓
Serum triiodothyronine (T$_3$)	↓
Thyroid-binding globulin	No change or ↑
Thyroid-stimulating hormone	↓
Insulin	↑ followed by ↓
ACTH	↓
Epinephrine	↓
Glucagon	↓
Growth hormone	↓
Estrogen	↓
Testosterone	↓
Cortisol (glucocorticoids)	↓
Pancreatic polypeptide	↑

↑, increase; ↓ decrease

V. FUEL FLUXES

Although all nucleated cells carry the same genetic messages for enzymes and cell constituents, many of these messages are not transcribed and translated. Thus, certain cells have special functions or processes that are their unique properties, whereas other cells appear to be more versatile. Adipose cells for example, synthesize and store triacylglycerols; kidney and liver cells synthesize glucose via gluconeogenesis; liver and muscle cells synthesize, store, and use glycogen as a fuel. Renal glomerular cells or tufts filter the blood, the central nervous system does none of the above and is unique as a central integrator of communication. Age has unique effects on each of these tissues and their respective metabolic processes. The pathways of intermediary metabolism are outlined in Table II. Each of these pathways has specific control points that in turn are affected by age. Although various studies have shown age-related declines in enzyme activities, it should be remembered that these are in vitro measurements in conditions where substrates and coenzymes are in optimal amounts to assure saturation. This rarely occurs in vivo. Hence, a decline in activity may not mean a decline in in vivo function. In a number of instances the age-related decline in activity of a pathway or reaction can be inhibited by chronic food restriction. This inhibition of aging effects on metabolism probably has to do with the decreased fat stores that are the result of food restriction. A decrease in fat store reduces the supply of fatty acid precursors to free radicals, and this may lead to a reduction in error rates in the genetic material as well as a reduction in protein damage with resultant loss of function. In addition, a reduced fat store has effects on peripheral cell responsivity to insulin vis á vis glucose use and of course, in the absence of hyperinsulinemia, there is a decreased release of the anti-insulin hormones. As described in section IV, age-related alterations in hormone balance do occur, and these alterations have an impact on carbohydrate oxidation, glycogen storage and mobilization, hexose monophosphate shunt, and gluconeogenesis.

As aging proceeds there is a rise in blood lipids coupled with a decrease in adipose tissue lipoprotein lipase. Adipocytes have a less competent lipid uptake system due to this decline in lipase activity. In normal aging animals the rates of cholesterol synthesis do not change; however, the uptake of this cholesterol as well as its oxidation and excretion declines. This has the result of an age-related increase in serum cholesterol levels. Genetics plays an important role in these age-related changes in serum lipids. Some genotypes are characterized by a sharper decline with age in lipid uptake processes than other genotypes. For example, those whose lipoprotein receptors are genetically aberrant will show a far earlier rise in srum lipids than those whose receptors are fully functional. Some may only have a decline in cholesterol uptake or triacylglyceride uptake, whereas others will have a decline in the uptake of both. Age-related declines in thyroid hormone production, thyroxine conversion to triiodothyronine, glucocorticoid release, and the insulin : glucagon ratio will have effects on fatty acid mobilization and oxidation. The results of this decline in hormone-stimulated lipolysis are observed as an age-related expansion of the fat stores. Although age has effects on fatty acid synthesis in rats and mice, these effects are minimal in humans consuming the typical Western diet. This is because this diet is relatively rich in fat, so the need for its synthesis is almost nonexistent. Humans tend to use the dietary carbohydrate as their primary fuel and the surplus dietary fat is transported to the adipose tissue for storage. Hence, de novo fatty acid synthesis is negligible. In rats and mice this is not the usual situation. The typical rodent diet is low in fat. Most of the energy comes from carbohydrate and deaminated amino acids (those in

Table II Effects of Age on Intermediary Metabolism and Its Control

Pathway	Control points	Effects of age[a]
Glycolysis	a. Transport of glucose into the cell (mobile glucose transporter)	↓
	b. Glucokinase	↓
	c. Phosphofructokinase	↓
	d. α-glycerophosphate shuttle	
	e. Redox state, phosphorylation state	
Pentose phosphate shunt	a. Glucose-6-phosphate dehydrogenase	↓
	b. 6-phosphogluconate dehydrogenase	↓
Glycogenesis	a. Stimulated by insulin and glucose	ND
	b. High-phosphorylation state (ratio of ATP to ADP)	ND
Glycogenolysis		ND
	a. Stimulated by catecholamines	ND
Lipogenesis	a. Stimulated by insulin	
	b. Acetyl-CoA carboxylase	
	c. High-phosphorylation state	
	d. Malate citrate shuttle	↓
Gluconeogenesis	a. Stimulated by epinephrine	
	b. Malate aspartate shuttle	↓
	c. Redox state	↑
	d. Phosphoenopyruvate carboxykinase	↓
	e. Pyruvate kinase	
Cholesterogenesis	a. HMG CoA reductase	
Ureogenesis	a. Carbamyl phosphate synthesis	↑, ↓
	b. ATP	ND
Citric acid cycle	a. All three shuttles	
	b. Phosphorylation state	↓
Lipolysis	a. Lipoprotein lipase	↓
Respiration	a. ADP influx into the mitochondria	↓
	b. Ca^{2+} flux	
	c. Shuttle activities	↓
	d. Substrate transporters	↓
Oxidative phosphorylation	a. ADP–ATP exchange	↓
	b. Ca^{2+} ion	
Protein synthesis	a. Accuracy of gene transcription	↓
	b. Availability of amino acids	↓
	c. ATP	↓

[a] ↑ —Increased as the animal ages; ↓ —decreased as the animal ages; ND, no data; NC, no change.

excess of need for protein synthesis). In the young animal there is considerable protein synthesis, and with age there is a decline in this synthetic activity. With an age-related decline in protein synthesis there is an increased need to rid the body of amino groups, as the surplus amino acids are deaminated for use in gluconeogenesis and lipogenesis. This means that if the protein intake is not reduced to accommodate the decreased need for protein, there will be an increase in the activity of the urea cycle. Studies in aging rats have shown that dietary intake excess of energy and protein are associated with an age-related increase in urinary protein and renal disease that is preceded by first an increase then a fall in ureogenesis. Food restriction or protein restriction ameliorates these age-related changes in renal function and urea synthesis.

All of these age-related changes in intermediary metabolism are linked together by age changes in mitochondrial oxidative phosphorylation. As discussed in sections II and IV, age carries with it a progressive change (increase) in mitochondrial membrane saturation, a progressive loss in ATP synthetic efficiency, and an increase in free radical damage to mitochondrial DNA and its translation products. These progressive changes mean a progressive loss in the tight control of intermediary metabolism exerted by the concentration and flux of the adenine nucleotides. In turn then, one might expect to find progressive changes as described above in carbohydrate, lipid, and protein metabolism in addition to and in response to the progressive changes with age in the endocrine system and the central nervous system.

BIBLIOGRAPHY

Bandy B., & Davison, A. J. (1990). Mitochondrial mutations may increase oxidative stress: Implications for carcinogenesis and aging? *Free Radical Biology & Medicine, 8*, 523–539.

Berdanier, C. D. (1988). Role of membrane lipids in metabolic regulation. *Nutritional Review 46*, 145–149.

Byrne, E., Trounce, I., & Dennett, X. (1991). Mitochondrial theory of senescence: Respiratory chain protein studies in human skeletal muscle. *Mechanisms of Aging & Development, 60*, 295–302.

Carlile, S., & Lacko, A. G. (1985). Age related changes in plasma lipid levels and tissue lipoprotein lipase activities of Fischer 344 rats. *Archives of Gerontology & Geriatrics, 4*, 133–140.

Coon, P. J., Rogus, E. M., Drinkwater, D., Muller, D. C., & Goldberg, A. P. (1992). Role of body fat distribution in the decline in insulin sensitivity and glucose tolerance with age. *Journal of Clinical Endocrinological Metabolism, 75*, 1125–1132.

Cohen, B. M., & Zubenko, G. S. (1985). Aging and the biophysical properties of cell membranes. *Life Sciences, 37*, 1403–1409.

Dempler, B., & Harrison, L. (1994). Repair of oxidative damage to DNA. *Annual Review of Biochemistry, 63*, 915–948.

Everitt, A. V., Porter, B. D., & Wyndham, J. R. (1982). Effects of caloric intake and dietary composition on the development of proteinuria, age-associated renal disease and longevity in the male rat. *Gerontology, 28*, 168–175.

Hass, B. S., Hart, R. W., Lu, L. H., & Lyn-Cook, B. D. (1993). Effects of caloric restriction in animals on cellular function, oncogene expression and DNA methylation in vitro. *Mutation Research, 295*, 281–289.

Mariotti, D., & Ruscitto, R. (1977). Age related changes of accuracy and efficiency of protein synthesis machinery in rat. *Biochem. Biophys. Acta, 475*, 96–102.

Marcus, D. L., Ibrahim, N. G., & Freedman, M. L. (1982). Age-related decline in the biosynthesis of mitochondrial inner membrane proteins. *Experimental Gerontology 17*, 333–341.

Meneilly, G. S., Minaker, K. L., Elahi, D., & Rowe, J. W. (1987). Insulin action in aging man: Evidence for tissue specific differences at low physiologic insulin levels. *Journal of Gerontology 42*, 196–201.

Moldave, K., Harris, J., Sabo, W., & Sadnik, I. (1979). Protein synthesis and aging studies with cell free mammalian systems. *Federation Proceedings, 38*, 1979–1983.

Mooradian, A. D. (1993). Mechanisms of age-related endocrine alterations. Parts I and II. *Drugs & Aging, 3*, 81–97, 131–146.

Nohl, H., & Kramer, R. (1980). Molecular basis of age-dependent changes in the activity of adenine nucleotide translocase. *Mechanisms of Aging & Development, 14*, 137–144.

Pardini, C., Mariani, L., Voliani, M., Rainaldi, G., & Citti, L. (1992). The ability of liver extracts from different aged rats to repair "mis instructive" and "non instructive" lesions of DNA. *Mutation Research, 275*, 1–6.

Randerath, K., Zhou, G-D., Hart, R. W., Turturro, A., & Randerath, E. (1993). Biomarkers of aging: Correlation of DNA 1-compound levels with median lifespan of calorically restricted and ad libitum fed rats and mice. *Mutation Research, 295*, 247–263.

Richardson, A., & Cheung, H. T. (1992). Relationship between age-related changes in gene expression, protein turnover and the responsiveness of an organism to stimuli. *Life Sciences, 31*, 605–613.

Shimokata, H., Muller, D. C., Fleg, J. L., Sorkin, J., Ziemba, A. W., & Andres, R. (1991). Age as independent determinant of glucose tolerance. *Diabetes, 40*, 44–51.

Simonetti, S., Chen, Z., DiMauro, S., & Schon, E. A. (1992). Accumulation of deletions in human mitochondrial DNA during normal aging: Analysis by quantitative PCR. *Biochemica Biophysica Acta 1180*, 113–122.

Venkatraman, J., & Fernandes, G. (1992). Modulation of age-related alterations in membrane composition and receptor associated immune functions by food restriction in Fischer 344 rats. *Mechanisms of Aging & Development, 63*, 27–44.

Wallace, D. C. (1992). Mitochondrial genetics: A paradigm for aging and degenerative diseases? *Science, 256*, 628–632.

Wei, Y-H. (1992). Mitochondrial DNA alterations as aging associated molecular events. *Mutation Research, 275*, 145–155.

Weirich-Schwaiger, H., Weirich, H. G., Gruber, B., Schweiger, M., & Hirsch-Kaufmann, M. (1994). Correlation between senescence and DNA repair in cells from young and old individuals and in premature aging syndromes. *Mutation Research, 316*, 37–48.

Yen, T.-C., Chen, Y.-S., King, K-L., Yeh, S.-H., & Wei, Y-H. (1989). Liver mitochondrial respiratory functions decline with age. *Biochemical Biophysics Research Communications, 165*, 994–1003.

Yen, T.-C., King, K-L., Lee, H-C., Yeh, S.-H., & Wei, Y-H. (1994). Age dependent increase of mitochondrial DNA deletions together with lipid peroxides and superoxide dismutase in human liver mitochondria. *Free Radical Biology & Medicines, 16*, 207–214.

Yu, B. P., Suescum, E. A., Yang, S. Y. (1992). Effect of age related lipid peroxidation on membrane fluidity and phospholipase A_2: Modulation by dietary restriction. *Mechanisms of Aging & Development, 65*, 17–33.

Migration

Charles F. Longino, Jr.

Wake Forest University

I. Introduction
II. Conceptual Issues
III. Migration

Interstate Migration The census definition is residence in another state five years before the census.
Retirement Migration Interstate migration of persons age 60 and over, some of whom may have become employed since moving.

Retirement **MIGRATION** is one aspect of a broader cultural happening that is very old. Winter palaces, the social season in the capital city, mineral springs, spas, and Italian villas for centuries have been part of the lifestyle of a European elite. Vacationing, seasonal migration, and retirement resettlement to a more healthful climate offering leisurely lifestyles is becoming a widespread phenomenon in America, but only after the development of a substantial middle class and transportation technology that made travel to distant places possible and affordable. Thus these activities have become common only in this century. Although the individual community histories of retirement settlement may extend back to the 1920s and 1930s in some places, retirement migration became more than a novelty only after World War II.

I. INTRODUCTION

In each decade between 1960 and 1990, both the number of Americans and the number of older Americans has increased, the latter increasing faster. Not surprisingly, the number of interstate migrants also grew in each decade. The proportion who moved in each 5-year period preceding the census, however, remained nearly constant, both for the population over age 5 (at about 9%) and the population over age 60 (at just under 5%). A trend that reaches back for four censuses is very stable.

Retirement migration is an alternative lifestyle. Most Americans over age 60 have not moved in any census-migration period. Roughly three-quarters are living at the same address as earlier; only one in ten has moved across county or state lines. Most tend to stay put when they retire. [*See* RETIREMENT.]

II. CONCEPTUAL ISSUES

A. Lifestyles and Place Ties

Asking why most people do not move is one way of getting at why some do move. People are tied to their environments by investments in their property, by the many community contexts in which they find meaning, by friends and family, by the experiences of the past, and by lifestyles that weave these strands together into patterns of satisfying activity. Any lifestyle requires a unique combination of environmental resources, and a retirement lifestyle is no exception to this rule. It is the combination of place ties, person ties, and resources that is the key to understanding what is behind a retirement move. The retirees who are most likely to relocate are those who have the fewest moorings; those whose desired retirement lifestyles are not compatible with their present community, neighborhood, and housing environments.

B. Person Ties

Lifestyle-motivated moves tend to be place-centered. When migration researchers focus on particular popular retirement destinations, they often see amenity-seeking migrants there. Person-centered motivations for moving are equally important. In a survey of residents of Sun City, Arizona, a decade ago, more than 40% of all households had at least one relative in the destination region.

C. Resources

If place and person ties often go undifferentiated when motives are assessed or inferred, it is equally true that place ties and resources are often confused. Retirees vary considerably in their possession of the resources needed to relocate—particularly their economic, health, and psychic resources. Psychic resources refer to the inner strength and freedom to take the risks involved in moving. Strong community moorings carry an emotional cost. They reduce the ability to mount the effort to move even if income and health resources are abundant.

D. Search Space

When a retired household is considering a move and begins looking for housing, geographers define the acceptable territory in which the couple will search for a new residence as *search space*. The search space of the couple is defined by their previously acquired knowledge. This knowledge, of course, is informed by earlier visits, discussions with migrants and travelers, and by reading. Rarely does one move to a place that was not previously unknown to the person making the move, unless the move was forced. The primary reason that people choose new locations where they have vacationed and visited is because they have gained the necessary knowledge base to make a choice.

Because the search space is conditioned by knowledge requirements and motivational factors, the size of the target area will vary from retiree to retiree. Migration flows, therefore, are not narrowly targeted because of varying amounts of search space.

E. Migration Motivation

Older migrants, like people in general, come in many types. The research literature tends to classify them into two major categories: dependency migrants and amenity migrants. Dependency migrants are typically forced to move due to deterioration of health or financial resources or the death of a spouse. Amenity migrants are looking for settings that will afford a new and better lifestyle. Communities located on or near lakes, beaches, and mountains, and those in temperate, tropical, or desert climates have an advantage in attracting this type of migrant, who tends to be recently retired, and therefore younger, usually married, and economically better off than many other retirees. Interstate migration streams to the Sunbelt are laden with amenity migrants.

F. Life-Course Models

One popular way of combining an analysis of place and person ties and resources is to examine the way that migration motivation tends to change during the retirement years. Litwak and Longino argued that long-distance movers during the retirement life course tend to fall into three categories. The first are recently retired amenity-seeking migrants. The pressure for the second type of move, however, occurs when people develop a disability that makes it difficult to carry out everyday household tasks, a situation often compounded by widowhood. Limited kin resources is the motive for the third basic type of move, from more or less exclusive care by kin to institutional care. Most movers that fit the third type are local, not long-distance movers. [See LIFE COURSE.]

III. MIGRATION

A. Patterns of Migration

1. Sunbelt

The earliest study of migration patterns of the elderly examined interregional moves between 1935 and 1940. In 1940, the Pacific Coast and South Atlantic regions were the most frequent destinations of older interregional migrants, and that migrants to the South Atlantic came mostly from east of the Mississippi. These findings have been remarkably stable over the intervening decades.

Biggar studied Sunbelt retirement migration during the 1965–1970 period, defining the region as the border states from Virginia southward to Florida and

Westward to California, adding two interior states, Arkansas and Missouri because they straddle in Ozarks area. She found that more than half (58%) of elderly interstate migrants moved to these 14 states. Furthermore, she found the 1970 pattern to have continued over the next decade; the same 14 states were capturing 59% of migrants age 60 and older in 1975–1980. The proportion was the same (59%) in the 1985–1990 period. The stability of Sunbelt retirement migration is quite remarkable.

2. State Flows and Streams

One of the defining characteristics of retirement migration is that migrants coming from all over the nation concentrate their destinations in a few states, forming highly channelized flows into these states. More than half arrive in just ten states; 60% in 1955–1960, 1965–1970, and 1975–1980, and 56% in 1985–1990. Although rankings shift slightly from decade to decade, Florida, California, Arizona, Texas, Pennsylvania, and New Jersey were among the top 10 in each census since 1960. Florida is in a class by itself as a destination state, receiving about one-quarter of all interstate migrants nationally in each of the past four censuses. Elderly migration is channelized both at destination and at origin. When the top 10 sending states are compiled, they collectively contribute 58–60% of all the migrants in 1965–1970, 1975–1980, and 1985–1990. There is also great stability among the top 10 sending states, with eight of the ten appearing in each of the past three censuses: New York, California, Florida, Illinois, New Jersey, Pennsylvania, Michigan, and Ohio. The two lists are not mutually exclusive. Three of the top four destination states, Florida, California and Texas, are also leading origins of migrants.

Migration streams have a specific origin and destination. Streams connect two places. When the large streams are examined, those that carry over 10,000 older migrants between two states, there are only five states receive three or more streams from noncontiguous states: Florida, California, Arizona, Texas, and North Carolina.

3. Counties of Origin

Out-migration, at least when it comes to large migration streams, is a metropolitan phenomenon with few exceptions. Two-thirds of the top 100 county-to-county streams across state lines originate in New York City, Chicago, and Los Angeles and their surrounding suburban counties. Each of the three cities provides a unique out-migration pattern. The New York City pattern is defined as having a favorite national destination and a favorite regional destination. All of the counties associated with the Greater New York City Metropolitan Area send streams to one, the other, or both of these destinations: Florida and New Jersey. Some other cities follow the New York pattern. Philadelphia, for example, divides its streams between the same two states, but favors New Jersey over Florida. Likewise, Massachusetts follows a modified New York pattern, substituting New Hampshire for New Jersey.

The Los Angeles pattern is very different from that of New York City. From 1985 to 1990, Los Angeles County sent nine large streams of retirees to its adjacent states: Arizona, Nevada, and Oregon. Adjacency, therefore, is the heart of the Los Angeles out-migration pattern. Some other cities follow the Los Angeles pattern. The large retirement migration streams from Washington, D.C., terminate in Maryland counties. In Kentucky and Tennessee, large streams go from Louisville and Memphis to counties immediately across the state line of the adjoining states.

From Chicago's vantage point, the popular sunbelt destination states all seem about the same distance away. New York loves Florida, but Chicago plays the field. Retired Cook County residents are nearly ubiquitous. They are as apt to show up in Southern California, Arizona, or Nevada as Florida. The only other city that follows Chicago's pattern is in Michigan. Metropolitan Detroit originates two streams, one to St. Petersburg, Florida, and the other to Phoenix, Arizona.

Why should it be surprising that most retirement out-migration to interstate destinations is from metropolitan counties? These are the places of economic opportunity. More city retirees can afford to move and more have been geographically mobile during their working years.

4. Receiving Counties

Nearly half of the top 100 county destinations for interstate migrants during the 1985–1990 migration period were in Florida. The single county that receives the largest number of such migrants, however, is Maricopa County, Arizona, the location of Phoenix and Sun City. When destination counties are ranked in their net migration, that is, in-migrants minus out-migrants, the regional migration destinations show up strongly. Some of these are coastal New Hampshire, Cape Cod, Massachusetts, counties in the Pennsylvania Poconos, and the West Virginia counties sandwiched between Maryland and Virginia. Further south, many of the mountainous and coastal counties of North Carolina, the coastal counties of South Carolina, and the mountainous north Georgia counties attract retirees from outside and within the region, as do the counties of the Ozarks region in Arkansas and Missouri. Counties on the Florida panhandle, on the eastern shore of Mobile Bay, and the Mississippi gulf coast and largely regional destinations. Counties in the Rio Grande Valley of Texas attract retirees from the Great Plains states. In other western states, Albuquerque, New Mexico, and the western slope counties of Colorado, have strong net-migration rankings. The counties containing Las Vegas and Reno, Nevada, the Pacific coast counties of Oregon, and the shoreline counties of Washington are attractive to retirees, particularly those from California. Florida counties, collectively, may receive the most interstate migrants from far away, but regional destinations are spread across the nation from New England to tropical Texas to Puget Sound.

B. Migration Selectivity

Biggar was the first to show that local movers over age 60 were generally not as economically and socially well off as nonmovers, and migrants were more so. Interstate migrants are the most positively selected. Later work extended her findings to decade comparisons, showing these differences to be relatively stable over time. Men and women are about equal in long-distance moves. Married couples predominate in this type of move, and the very old tend to move shorter distances. Migrants with the most education tend to move the farthest.

C. Seasonal Migration

The Census Bureau does not directly attempt to measure seasonal migration. There have been several surveys of seasonal migrants, however, that provide snapshots of older winter visitors at their destinations. The surveys have been conducted in Texas, Arizona, and Florida. They are accumulating and are beginning

to be compared, thereby providing a broader national picture. In this picture, the migrants are overwhelmingly white and retired. They are healthy, married couples in their mid- to late sixties with higher levels of income and education than the older population in general. One recent study compared samples of Canadians who wintered in Florida with U.S. citizens who winter in the Rio Grande Valley of Texas. The similarities between the two were impressive.

Climate is apparently a very strong factor in motivating seasonal migration. The propensity to seasonally migrate to Phoenix, Arizona, was highest in the northern plains and mountain states and bordering Canadian provinces. The trails that bring snowbirds south to Arizona or Florida are not strange or innovative. They follow the Sunbelt regional pattern. Perhaps the primary difference between seasonal and permanent migrants is that seasonal migrants sometimes travel farther, implying that the climatic change may be more important to them than to permanent migrants. The northward seasonal pattern from Florida and the desert states to cooler mountainous locations in North Carolina and New England in the east and to Colorado in the west have not yet been studied.

The dialogue among researchers concerning whether seasonal migration is part of a process leading to permanent migration has concluded that seasonal migration generates its own lifestyle and culture, different from that of permanent migrants, but equally valuable in its own right. Once having adopted the lifestyle, seasonal migration is likely to last for several years, finally interrupted and reluctantly terminated by a fluctuation or decrease in necessary resources. There are some who do settle down and stay, but those are often people who have strong person ties in and place ties to the host community. They have family members and others living permanently nearby who tend to anchor them.

D. Metropolitan and Nonmetropolitan Migration

One of the macrolevel processes that affects geographical mobility in our time is metropolitan deconcentration. The long-term trend of population movement to cities slowed and reversed in the 1970s. Older people were in the vanguard of migration to nonmetropolitan counties; the turnaround for them happened in the 1960s.

Most older migrants actually are moving from one metropolitan area to another, but they tend to step down to a smaller city, thereby increasing their quality of life by lowering the hassle factor. Although amenity migrants express a desire for a change of surroundings, they do not want to give up completely the comforts afforded by an urban lifestyle. Locations that are reasonably proximate to cities are especially attractive if the cultural and service amenities these migrants expect (e.g., museums, restaurants, theater, shopping, and an international airport) can be found in a city a couple of hours away. Sun City was built near Phoenix for a reason. And it is unthinkable that Cape Cod would have developed as it has without its proximity to Boston. One migrant described living on Cape Cod as "the best of both worlds," a place somewhere between the remoteness of rural living and the fast-paced life of the region's metropolitan centers.

E. Return Migration

It was once thought that retirees were likely to be returning to their home state. This popular myth was squashed by a paper in 1978 that shows the return migration rate of older migrants to be identical to that of all migrants, about 20%. More recent research shows return migration to be waning slowly among retirees. In 1990 the proportion declined to 17.5%.

All of the reports on older return migrants have found that some states and regions are more popular to return migrants than others. If one subtracts out all persons leaving their state of birth (because they cannot be return migrants), one-quarter of the nation's remaining migrating older population between 1985 and 1990 were returning to their home states. West Virginia and Iowa attract nearly two-thirds of their potential return migrants whereas Nevada, Arizona, Florida and Alaska attract less than 4%.

There is a popular ethnic explanation for return migration to the South and Southwest. It concerns the return migration of African Americans and Hispanics. Regional return migration involves a historical work cycle. Industrial states recruit workers from rural parts of the country. Streams of workers continue to tie these sending and receiving states together. However, over time, return migration streams develop that carry some of the retired workers back to their states of birth. These return streams build in a delayed but roughly proportional response to the earlier stream development for work. Although the principle applies to all, it is easier to discern when combined with ethnic identification.

F. Migration Impact

Retirement migration has been dubbed by some as the growth industry of the 1990s in small town America. Retirement migration to less urban areas is an economic boon because economic consumption increases, and the tax base is broadened. Economic conditions in nonmetropolitan counties tend to improve when they float on a cushion of Social Security, pensions, annuities, and asset income. The service sector is stimulated primarily.

The amount of income that is transferred between states through retirement migration is quite substantial. In 1990 there were 12 states that posted net gains of at least $100 million. Florida received a net gain of $6.5 billion in 1989 from retirees who had moved there since 1985, and New York experienced a net loss of $3.3 billion in 1989 from those who had left the state since 1985. Using the same measures, the actual income transfer in the one stream from New York to Florida was nearly $1.2 billion.

Not surprisingly, economic development agencies are mounting efforts to attract mature migrants. This is leading to sharpening competition among destinations for these migrants as new residents in the hope that advertizing by local communities about their amenities can influence future migration patterns and therefore the economic development of these retirement destinations. The impact of elderly migration as a social phenomenon has not yet generated enough research to provide definitive statements.

BIBLIOGRAPHY

Bennett, D. G. (1993). Retirement migration and economic development in high-amenity, nonmetropolitan areas. *Journal of Applied Gerontology, 12*(4), 466–481.

Biggar, J. C. (1980). Who moved among the elderly, 1965–1970: A comparison of types of older movers. *Research on Aging, 2*, 73–91.

Cuba, L. J. (1991). Models of migration decision making reexamined: The destination search of older migrants to Cape Cod. *The Gerontologist, 31*(2), 204–209.

Cuba, L. J., & Longino, C. F., Jr. (1991). Regional retirement migration: The case of Cape Cod. *Journal of Gerontology: Social Sciences, 46*, S33–S42.

Fagan, M., & Longino, C. F., Jr. (1993). Migrating retirees: A source of economic development. *Economic Development Quarterly, 7,* 98–106.

Haas, W. H. III, & Serow, W. J. (1993). Amenity retirement migration process: A model and preliminary evidence. *The Gerontologist, 33*(2), 212–220.

Litwak, E., & Longino, C. F., Jr. (1987). Migration patterns among the elderly: A development perspective. *The Gerontologist, 25*(3), 266–272.

Longino, C. F., Jr. (1995). *Retirement migration in America.* Houston, TX: Vacation Publications.

Longino, C. F., Jr., & Crown, W. H. (1990). Retirement migration and interstate income transfers. *The Gerontologist, 30,* 784–789.

McHugh, K. E., & Mings, R. C. (1991). On the road again: Seasonal migration to a sunbelt metropolis. *Urban Geography, 12,* 1–18.

Rogers, A. (1990). Return migration to region of birth among retirement-age persons in the United States. *Journal of Gerontology: Social Science, 45,* S128–S134.

Rowles, G. D. (1987). A place to call home. In L. L. Carstensen and B. A. Edelstein (Eds.), *Handbook of clinical gerontology* (pp. 335–353). Oxford, UK: Pergamon Press.

Models of Aging: Invertebrates, Filamentous Fungi, and Yeasts

S. Michal Jazwinski

Louisiana State University Medical Center and Center on Aging

I. Introduction: Why Study Aging in
   Lower Organisms?
II. Fungal Models
III. *Caenorhabditis elegans*
IV. *Drosophila*
V. Other Models
VI. Applications to Human Aging? Perspectives

Allele   An alternate form of a gene.
DNA   Deoxyribonucleic acid, the chemical from which genes are made.
Epistasis   An interaction between genes in which the action of one gene masks that of another.
Eukaryote   An organism whose cellular DNA is in a nucleus.
Gene   A unit of genetic information.
Genome   All of the genetic material of an organism.
Longevity-Assurance Gene   A gene that sets the limit (upper and/or lower) for longevity of an organism.
Mitochondrial DNA   The DNA constituting the genome of the ATP (adenosine 5′-triphosphate) generating organelle of the cell, the mitochondrion.
Mutant   A member of a species carrying an alteration (mutation) in one or more genes.
Phenotype   The entire set of physical characteristics of an organism.

This article reviews the major **MODELS FOR AGING** research among the lower eukaryotes. In these models a genetic approach is possible and has been applied with success. Special emphasis has been placed on common principles that have emerged: (a) the importance of developmental programs and environmental cues during development, (b) the significance of stress responses and associated signal-transduction pathways, and (c) the impact of metabolic capacity on the aging process. The idea that specific aspects of aging applicable to mammals, including humans, are revealed in studies with these lower eukaryotes is developed. In general, the terms *life span* and *longevity* refer to both mean and maximum life span unless indicated otherwise.

I. INTRODUCTION: WHY STUDY AGING IN LOWER ORGANISMS?

A. Simplicity

It would seem unnecessary to examine any biological process in an organism other than the human if one's focus was solely human health. However, one would find it very difficult and time-consuming in most cases. The experimental biologist attempts to simplify the analysis of biological phenomena by using experimental models. These models can constitute simpler organisms, which are called *lower organisms* if they are invertebrates. Parenthetically, they can be cells, extracts, or subcellular fractions from higher or lower organisms. The assumption inherent, but not necessarily substantiated at the outset of this model system approach, is that lower organisms are simpler. In one respect, they are usually simpler; namely, they are readily amenable to genetic analysis. This is the forte of these models, and thus the discussion here will be heavily slanted in this direction. Related to their utility in genetic analysis, lower organisms generally have considerably shorter life spans than higher organisms.

The decision to take the model system approach has certain consequences. One does not necessarily expect the information learned by their use to be totally and directly applicable to the human situation. On the other hand, researchers trust that the information obtained can be used to formulate specific and easily testable hypotheses in the human system. Furthermore, one expects to obtain the tools needed to identify the relevant components to humans, which will allow meaningful manipulation. Because researchers have already made a great leap in adopting a model system approach, it makes sense to choose a model that will be the most facile. Thus, there seems little reason to study chimpanzees, say, rather than humans, as a first choice of an experimental model.

Even a superficial analysis of the problem of aging suggests that the aging process will differ in its details between phylogenetic groups. An evolutionary analysis further bolsters this notion. Nevertheless, I venture there is much to learn from simple experimental models. Many organisms share certain aspects of aging; other aspects may be peculiar to closely related species. Thus, one might distinguish specific public and private aspects of aging. I would go further, however. The specific aspects of aging in any given species can be classified as major and minor. A major specific aspect should be more easily studied due to its significant impact on aging in that species. A major specific aspect in one species may be a minor one in another. Through a judicious choice of experimental models, one should be able to elaborate a variety of specific aspects of aging that are relevant for any species, including the human.

B. Genetics

The ability to carry out genetic analysis is a major strength of several lower organisms. The premier organisms from this perspective are the fruit fly *Drosophila*, the nematode or round worm *Caenorhabditis elegans*, the yeast *Saccharomyces cerevisiae*, and the filamentous fungi *Podospora anserina* and *Neurospora*. Three different genetic approaches can be used

in these organisms, although not all have been exploited to the same extent in each.

Quantitative genetic approaches have been used in both *Drosophila* and in *C. elegans*. The underlying assumption, which the quantitative approach indeed substantiates, is that many genes are involved in determining longevity. Some alleles of these genes are more conducive to a longer life than others, given the presence of certain alleles of yet other genes. The trick is to select from the different alleles of different genes extant in a population those that have a concerted effect on a phenotype of interest, in this case longevity. Given the fact that there are many ways in which it is possible to "muck up" the organism, the trend is to select for extended rather than attenuated life span. This can be done directly, or in a sense indirectly, by selecting for delayed reproduction.

By far, the best known and most typical method of genetic analysis is the isolation of mutants that display the phenotype of interest, which would be increased life span. This form of genetic analysis has been used successfully in both *C. elegans* and in *S. cerevisiae*. The power of this approach lies not only in the disregard of any assumptions as to specific processes involved in aging but also in the fact that the mutations "tag" the genes of interest, in stark contrast to the quantitative approach. The extent to which this tag is useful depends on the method used for mutagenesis. Transposon-tagged mutagenesis, for example, provides a physical tag that can be used directly to fish out the interesting gene. This feature, the tag, is what makes the mutational approach so powerful in comparison to the quantitative approach. Nevertheless, the mutational analysis may provide us with the tree and no forest. The quantitative approach in conjunction with the physiological analysis of resulting long-lived lines does the opposite, generating a picture defined by broad strokes with little hope for identification of individual genes. In practice, the mutational approach can be quite limited if the phenotype utilized for selection of mutants is not chosen very judiciously. This demon can rear its head if a phenotype secondary to or associated with the one of interest, longevity, is chosen for selection. In any case, verification of the results of selection is essential.

The third approach is the transgenic approach. It can also be called reverse genetics. Based on a set of criteria, a candidate for a gene affecting life span is identified. This candidate gene is tested by inserting it into the genome to effect expression or by mutating the gene in its chromosomal locus using knockout technologies. The important ingredient in this mode of genetic analysis is a stringent and imaginative set of criteria for the identification of candidate genes. The transgenic approach has been used with great success in *S. cerevisiae* and in *Drosophila*.

C. Physiology

It may seem surprising to list physiology as an important factor in the choice of lower organisms as experimental models of aging. After all, relatively little is known of the physiology of many of these organisms in comparison with mammals, especially humans. However, there are several selected areas in which physiological responses are well understood or at least relatively easily addressed in these models. The first is the area of developmental programs. Lower organisms possess the distinct capability of existing in several well-defined and easily recognizable developmental forms either transiently or more durably. The transitions between these forms, often called metamorphosis, frequently require certain environmental cues. In comparison with higher organisms, these developmental programs are highly orchestrated and quite exaggerated, making them easier to discern and to study. As will be seen later, these programs themselves or the conditions the organism encounters during development can have a profound impact on adult life span. This suggests that even in mammals the first environment the organism encounters, the uterus during gestation, will mold events that occur much later epigenetically with substantial influence on longevity.

This influence of development on longevity should not be viewed in the context of aging as an extension of a developmental program. I do not believe that aging, and death, are the result of a genetic program in the sense of a dependent sequence of genetically determined events leading from birth to death. Even phenomena such as programmed cell death may constitute a stereotypic biochemical response rather than a genetic pathway. This does not negate the role of genetically programmed events in the triggering of the response.

Two other facets of the physiology of lower organisms accentuate processes known throughout biology. These are responses to a variety of stresses and metabolic capacity. The response to stress encompasses biochemical events well known in higher organisms, but in the lower organisms these responses engage the entire organism even to the adoption of alternate developmental forms. Metabolic activity is often related to these responses. In any case, lower organisms seem to have the ability to alter their metabolic activity within rather broad limits. This feature is likely to have implications for the paradigm of caloric restriction that is known to strongly affect rodent life span.

II. FUNGAL MODELS

A. Filamentous Fungi

The filamentous fungi have been used as a model for aging for some 40 years. More is known about the etiology of senescence at the molecular level in these organisms than in any others. The major experimental models are *Podospora anserina* and *Neurospora crassa* and *Neurospora intermedia*. Senescence manifests itself as a progressive decline in the rate of growth of the fungal mycelium. The final length of the mycelium is one measure of life span. Chronological age at cessation of growth is another. Finally, the number of culture passages obtained by sequentially subcloning consecutive mycelial tips can also be the metric in some cases. The proximal cause of senescence is respiratory failure in these obligate aerobes.

The molecular events surrounding this respiratory failure involve the virtual disintegration of the mitochondrial genome. The mitochondrial DNA suffers extensive deletions and rearrangements. The initiating event in the generation of these aberrations varies depending upon the particular fungus. In *P. anserina*, excision of DNA sequences from various regions of the mitochondrial genome results in the appearance of circular DNA plasmids that undergo amplification. The precise manner in which the release of these plasmids from mitochondrial DNA occurs is not entirely clear. It has been hypothesized that this may involve an RNA intermediate. One of the plasmids that has been studied best does contain an open reading frame that encodes a protein homologous to reverse transcriptase. Recently, evidence has been presented in support of retrotransposition of the mitochondrial

DNA sequences that give rise to this plasmid. Subsequent events are more murky, but the mobility of the mitochondrial DNA sequences would result in an increase in recombinogenic activity, constituting the first step in the disintegration of this genome.

Certain strains of *N. crassa* (Mauriceville and Varkud) possess circular mitochondrial DNA plasmids. These plasmids can integrate into the mitochondrial genome. The plasmids encode a reverse transcriptase, and the integration appears to occur via an RNA intermediate in a retrotransposition process. The difference between these *N. crassa* strains and *P. anserina* is the fact that the plasmids in the former are not derived from the mitochondrial genome. *N. crassa* and *N. intermedia* strains can also possess linear mitochondrial DNA plasmids. These plasmids are called Maranhar and Kalilo, respectively. These linear plasmids possess many of the features of retrotransposons. In senescing strains, they integrate into the mitochondrial genome at various locations resulting in the instability of these sequences. The aberrant mitochondrial genomes come to predominate. Although the molecular mechanisms surrounding mitochondrial dysfunction in filamentous fungi are quite diverse, the physiological consequences are a predictable decline in respiratory capacity. Furthermore, it is possible that the dysfunctional mitochondria produce oxygen free radicals in increased quantities. This, in turn, could result in further cellular damage.

Both mitochondrial and nuclear mutants that show a postponed senescence have been isolated in *P. anserina*. Among the most interesting are the nuclear mutants *i*, *gr*, and *viv*. These mutants were originally isolated on the basis of morphological peculiarities. The double mutants *i gr* and *i viv* are immortal, revealing synergistic interactions between these genes. Recently, high-fidelity mutants in the EF-1α encoding gene have been identified that display an increased life span. In *N. crassa*, a nuclear mutant, *nd*, has been shown to display both a reduced life span and a decrease in mitochondrial DNA stability. Increased levels of recombination were found in the mitochondrial DNA of this mutant. The significance of all these nuclear mutations lies in the fact that they reveal the importance of the interaction between the nucleus and the mitochondrion in determining longevity. Although in detail they are distinct, the mitochondrial DNA abnormalities that lead to senescence in the filamentous fungi can be viewed as a paradigm for

the role of mitochondrial deletions in human disease and senescence.

B. Yeast

Individual cells of the yeast *S. cerevisiae* exhibit a finite replicative life span. They produce a limited number of progeny cells, swell, loose refractility, and die (lyse). The progeny start from scratch, having the capacity for a full life span. The yeast cell is the organism. As with any aging population of organisms, the individuals are mortal but the population is immortal. The fact that there is an aging process involved here is evidenced by the exponential increase in mortality rate with age and by the numerous morphological and physiological changes, some deleterious, that the yeast cell undergoes as it progresses through its life span. Normally, age is determined most accurately by the number of cell divisions the yeasts complete before they die. Indeed, yeasts can be stored for significant periods of time in a refrigerator, and they pick up where they left off, completing the same number of cell divisions.

Unlike the filamentous fungi, yeast aging does not appear to have a mitochondrial etiology. Isogenic yeast strains that differ by the presence or absence of a mitochondrial genome show identical life spans. Aging yeasts appear to accumulate a "senescence factor" that acts in a dominant fashion. In this way, yeasts resemble normal diploid fibroblasts in which the senescent phenotype is dominant. The nature of the senescence factor is not known at present, but it appears to accumulate until it overwhelms the yeast cell. The effects of the senescence factor extend to the progeny of old yeasts. However, these effects are transient in the progeny, unless they receive what appears to be an insurmountable "dose." These facts and others indicate that the senescent phenotype is not due to a permanent alteration in the yeast cell, such as a genetic mutation or a cell wall change. The essential questions in yeast aging are the nature of the senescence factor and the basis for the asymmetry between the yeast cell and its progeny. There is reason to suspect that the establishment and maintenance of cell polarity is important for yeast longevity.

More individual genes that are involved in longevity have been identified in yeast than in any other organism. Two approaches have been successful in identifying these genes. The first to yield results was the transgenic approach. Candidate genes were ferreted out by cloning genes differentially expressed during the yeast life span. These were then mutated or overexpressed to determine their role in longevity. This methodology has yielded eight genes. The prototypic yeast longevity-assurance gene, as the genes that play a role in setting the limits of longevity have been termed, is *LAG1*. *LAG1*, a novel gene, was the first gene cloned that determines longevity in any organism. When the gene is present and active it sets the limits for longevity. Its deletion from the genome increases the life span by fifty percent. The carboxy-terminal one-half of the Lag1 protein is responsible for extending life, while the amino-terminal domain moderates its effect. This constitutes a homeostatic device for yeast longevity. *LAG1* is preferentially expressed in young yeasts.

LAC1 is a recently identified homolog of *LAG1* on a different yeast chromosome. A null mutation in this gene has the same effect as the deletion of *LAG1*. The two genes have at least partially overlapping functions, because a double mutant is lethal. Another gene that affects yeast longevity is *PHB1*. This gene is a homolog of the mammalian prohibitin gene. The yeast gene is preferentially expressed in young yeasts. The biochemical function of prohibitin is not known. However, there are hints that it may be involved in signal transduction and in determining metabolic capacity. The Lag1 protein has several potential transmembrane domains, suggesting a location in the cell membrane. Thus, Lag1 could be at the beginning of a signal-transduction pathway.

RAS1 and *RAS2*, homologs of the mammalian signal transduction gene *c-ras*, are both preferentially expressed in young yeasts. They both determine yeast longevity, but they have opposite roles. *RAS1* limits life, whereas *RAS2* extends it. Thus, these genes constitute another homeostatic device in yeast longevity. The function of *RAS2* in yeast longevity may reveal a new signal transduction pathway for Ras2 protein in yeasts. Furthermore, *RAS2* points to the key role of stress responses in maintaining life. The Ras2 protein in yeast, like ras in mammalian cells, is essential for the response to ultraviolet (UV) radiation. This response does not involve DNA damage as a necessary component, and it is effected by posttranslational modification of the transcription factor Gcn4, a Jun homolog. We have determined that the resistance to

UV stress is biphasic as a function of yeast replicative age. It peaks at midlife and rapidly declines. The UV resistance profile coincides with the expression of *RAS2* during the yeast life span. This UV response is distinct from the response to DNA damage, which decreases monotonically as a function of age. These facts suggest that there is an advantage for the persistence of older yeasts in a population, because they can guarantee the survival of a clone under certain circumstances. Another thought that comes to mind from these data is that active life maintenance processes operate in yeast through midlife, after which the organism "coasts" on its life-maintenance reserves.

RAS is a central integrator of cell growth and cell division in yeasts (Fig. 1). It is also involved

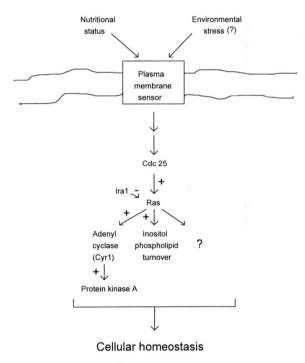

Figure 1   Role of *RAS* in yeast homeostasis. *RAS* is involved in sensing the nutritional status of the yeast cell. Its function is also essential for mounting a response to environmental stress. Cdc25 and Ira1 are positive and negative regulators of Ras, respectively. Ras functions along two known pathways: It stimulates adenyl cyclase (Cyr1) to synthesize cyclic AMP, an activator of protein kinase A, and it is also involved in stimulating inositol phospholipid turnover. Other pathways may be involved as well. Ras-mediated cellular homeostasis is achieved by integration of cell growth, cell division, and response to stress.

in cellular homeostasis by virtue of its role in the response to a variety of stresses, including UV, starvation, crowding, and heat shock, to name some. The gene plays an important role in carbon source utilization; yeasts prefer glucose. The activity of *RAS* plays an essential role in determining the metabolic capacity of yeasts. It is important to note that life extension by manipulation of *RAS2* or of *LAG1* is associated with the postponement of senescence and a marked increase in the metabolic capacity of the yeasts.

One way in which to view yeast aging is to postulate a stochastic trigger or threshold, set genetically, which represents the life-maintenance reserve. When this threshold is reached and surpassed a stereotypic response is evoked that is the proximal cause of senescence and death. This stereotypic response need not constitute a genetic program. The decreasing probability of a yeast cell continuing to the next cell division raises the possibility that there exists a "molecular memory" of previous cell divisions. I have proposed several mechanisms for such a molecular memory. One involves the inheritance of different regulatory states of chromatin. The silencing of gene expression at certain loci changes with a certain probability at every cell division. Yeast telomeres do not shorten with replicative age in the way they do in human diploid fibroblasts. (Yeast aging may thus provide a model for stem cell aging.) However, other components of the telomeric transcriptional silencing apparatus may be involved.

Recently, four additional genes have been implicated in yeast longevity using a mutational approach with selection on a secondary (surrogate) phenotype. One of these has been cloned and found to be identical to the yeast gene *SIR4*. This gene is part of a transcriptional silencing apparatus in yeasts. Mutations in *SIR4* have complex effects on yeast life span. However, these mutations invariably result in improved responses to a variety of stresses.

Yeasts can undertake several developmental programs. Signal-transduction pathways are involved in initiating these programs. Some involve alternative lifestyles, such as "foraging for nutrients" and "invasive" growth. These developmental programs are often initiated as a response to an environmental stress, such as starvation. It will be interesting to determine how much overlap exists between these programs and yeast life span determination. *RAS2*

already is known to be involved in both, implying that metabolic adjustments and resistance to stress operate.

III. *CAENORHABDITIS ELEGANS*

A. Quantitative Genetics

A limited amount of work has been carried out in *C. elegans* using the quantitative genetic approach. Two inbred laboratory strains of this nematode were bred to yield a collection of recombinant progeny that were then each easily inbred by virtue of the fact that this organism is a hermaphrodite. This generated recombinant inbred (RI) lines that displayed a wide array of characteristic life spans. A physiological analysis of the RI lines revealed that life span and other life history traits and physiological characteristics segregate independently. Only life expectancy and loss of general motor activity were correlated. Perhaps this should not be surprising, since general motor activity is used to determine death in this organism. Increased longevity resulted in postponed senescence in the RI lines. This is an important result, because extended life span need not be associated with postponed senescence. In other words, life extension may result in a longer period of senescence. This is a significant consideration, because the life extension obtained by mutation of *age-1* (see below) is not associated with a decreased rate of decline in general motor activity, implying no postponement of senescence.

A similar set of RI lines was generated with the goal of mapping major life span-determining loci in the nematode genome. Advantage was taken of the fact that the two parental strains differed dramatically in the content of transposon Tc1 in the genome. Longevity in the RI lines was correlated with certain Tc1 positional polymorphisms. These polymorphisms were detected using restriction fragment-length polymorphisms (RFLPs) and sequence-tagged sites derived from the Tc1 transposons. This approach has revealed at least five broad regions of the *C. elegans* genome that determine longevity. These regions await molecular dissection. Although most genetic contributions to *C. elegans* longevity appear to be additive, the quantitative approach stands a good chance to identify nonadditive effects as well.

B. Mutational Analysis

Mutational analysis has proven particularly fruitful in dissecting longevity in *C. elegans*. A bona fide screen for mutants exhibiting extended longevity has been attempted once and yielded the first mutant in a longevity gene. This gene is known as *age-1*. An apparent loss of function of *age-1* leads to extended life. The gene was initially thought to confer reduced fertility; however, the major fertility effect has been found to be associated with a closely linked gene. The *age-1* gene has been mapped genetically and physically to within about 100 kb of DNA on chromosome II. Cloning is in progress. It has been shown that *age-1* co-maps to a region on chromosome II that is involved in resistance to the free radical generator paraquat. This is not surprising, because it was shown that *age-1⁻* worms exhibit higher levels of Cu, Zn-superoxide dismutase, and catalase than wild type at all ages.

A most interesting finding has recently been made demonstrating that *age-1⁻* exhibits an increased intrinsic thermotolerance. This has several implications. Genes coding for oxidative defense enzymes and for heat shock proteins (hsp) frequently appear to be coordinately regulated. Deficits in the heat shock response as a function of age have been demonstrated in whole mammals as well as in isolated cells and in tissue culture. This deficit resides in the activity of the heat shock transcription factor (HSF) in old cells and organisms. The HSF is itself sensitive to oxidative stress. The heat shock response can be improved in aged animals that have been calorically restricted, the only treatment known to extend mammalian life span. The observations enumerated here clearly underline the significance of stress responses in organismal aging. They also raise the possibility that *age-1* is somehow involved in signal-transduction pathways that regulate stress responses.

Several additional genes involved in determining nematode life span have been identified by mutation recently. These accomplishments really represent the candidate gene approach more than the mutational approach inasmuch as the mutants had been known for quite some time previously in quite different functional contexts. The *spe-26* gene when mutated results in a 65% increase in longevity. This gene is involved in spermatogenesis. The initial conclusions from this study suggested quite surprisingly that spermatogenesis, as opposed to the more metabolically demanding oogenesis, might represent a life span trade-off for the nematode. It now appears that not all alleles of *spe-26* have the same effects on longevity, and it seems reasonable to suggest a separation between the effects of this gene on spermatogenesis and on longevity. It is not clear at present what the molecular mechanisms underlying the role of *spe-26* in *C. elegans* longevity are.

Recently, considerable excitement has been generated by the identification of an entire genetic pathway in *C. elegans* longevity. This pathway is complex with at least two branches. It is a developmental pathway that results in a detour of the L3 larva into a state of suspended animation of sorts, called the dauer larva. The triggers that result in dauer formation are environmental. They include starvation, heat, and crowding. The length of stay in the dauer state does not affect adult life span. The first gene in this pathway to be implicated in nematode life span was *daf-2*. A temperature-sensitive *daf-2* mutant enters the dauer larval state constitutively, even in the absence of the environmental cue. When *daf-2* mutants are shifted to nonpermissive temperature after passing the stage in development from which they can become dauers, they do not enter this stage but instead exhibit up to a doubling in adult life span. This effect on longevity occurs even when the gonads are ablated. Another mutant *daf-16*, defective in dauer formation, has no effect on life span. However, it prevents the *daf-2* effect on longevity; it is epistatic to *daf-2*. Thus, both dauer genes play a role in determining nematode life span, with *daf-16* acting downstream of *daf-2* in a genetic pathway.

It has now been shown that four other dauer genes, *daf-12*, *daf-18*, and *daf-23*, also play a role in *C. elegans* longevity. All these genes have been ordered provisionally in a pathway for nematode longevity (Fig. 2). There are several lessons to be learned from the elaboration of this pathway. Clearly, the dauer

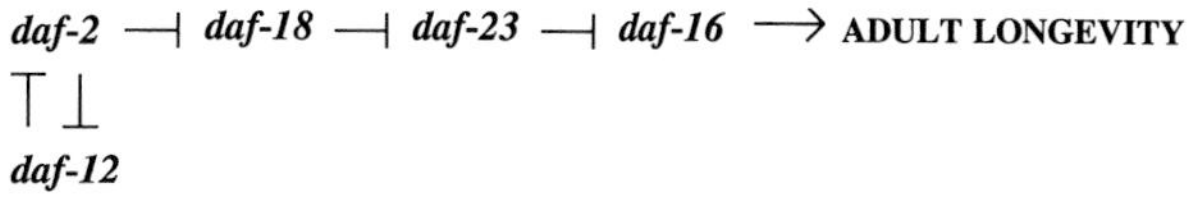

daf-2 —| *daf-18* —| *daf-23* —| *daf-16* —→ **ADULT LONGEVITY**

⊤ ⊥

daf-12

Figure 2 The *daf* genetic pathway in nematode longevity. *daf-16* is a positive effector of adult longevity in *C. elegans* (depicted by the arrow). The interactions of the wild-type gene products of the remaining *daf* genes are all inhibitory. The interaction between *daf-2* and *daf-12* is complex.

pathway represents a developmental program that responds to cues the developing nematode encounters. This might imply that environemntal factors during development may be crucial for longevity, and not only in nematodes. Although the molecular details of the dauer pathway are not yet fully known, some of the *daf* genes code for proteins involved in signal transduction. The environmental cues to which the dauer pathway responds are undoubtedly related to stress. It is also possible that the dauer response and the effect of this pathway on adult longevity are related to caloric restriction inasmuch as one of the signals for dauer formation is starvation. Indeed, caloric restriction is known to extend adult life span in *C. elegans* as it does in rodents. However, it should also be kept in mind that worms whose adult life is extended by the dauer response store food granules in their intestines. This food storage may be related to a general shift in metabolic activity and an adjustment in the metabolic capacity and efficiency of the animal. This does not differ that much from the effects in yeast of *RAS* on the life span and metabolism.

Unlike yeast, *C. elegans* is composed of postmitotic cells, if one disregards the gonads. In this way, this organism resembles postmitotic tissues, such as brain and heart, in the human. The accumulation of mitochondrial DNA deletions in these tissues has been noted earlier. Recently, it has been determined that *C. elegans* suffers such deletions as well.

At this point, it is worth underscoring the fact that in fungi and in nematodes large effects of single-gene alterations on longevity have been found. As we shall see, this is not the case in *Drosophila* and certainly not in higher organisms. Why is this the case? Several explanations might pertain. These two organisms are rather simple. Filamentous fungi exist as mycelia in which there is incomplete separation of the cytoplasm into individual cells. Yeasts, of course, are unicellular. *C. elegans* is composed of only 959 cells, all part of one large lineage. This simplicity may be the source for the enormity of single gene effects. Another possibility is the hermaphroditic nature of *C. elegans* and the largely clonal nature of fungi. This has led to an adaptation to an inbred state with attendant lack of accumulation of deleterious alleles. On this background, single gene changes may have a salutory effect on longevity without merely correcting recessive deficits.

IV. *DROSOPHILA*

A. Evolutionary Biology of Aging

The genetics of aging has taken a different turn in the fruit fly. The mutational approach has not proven very fruitful, likely due to the pronounced inbreeding depression encountered in *Drosophila*. Most of the work has been carried out using a selective breeding approach. Much of the impetus for this has been an attempt to test certain evolutionary theories of aging. Briefly, investigators have attempted to distinguish between the accumulation of deleterious mutations, due to lack of selection against such mutations in senescent organisms, and antagonistic pleiotropy. This latter mechanism denotes the selection for genes with positive selective advantages early in life and negative impact later in life. In both cases, the evolutionary theory holds that organisms have escaped the force of natural selection.

Selection for postponed senescence in *Drosophila* has been attempted a number of times. It has been successful when the flies are maintained at high larval density. This suggests that some level of environmental stress may be important. The success of the approach depends on using an outbred population of some size to start. With each step in the selection, eggs laid later and later during the life span are collected. Gradually, with each step, the longevity of the flies increases. A near doubling of life span has been obtained. The control flies are bred randomly. The long-lived lines obtained are stable, as long as this selection is maintained. However, the process is easily reversed. This approach works in *Drosophila*, because this organism breeds until late in life.

The extended longevity in the selected flies appears to be due to postponed senescence. A series of putative biomarkers for aging, events that characteristically occur or reach a certain level at certain points during the life span of the fly, has been identified. At least one of the lines displaying extended longevity shows the same characteristic sequence of appearance of these biomarkers; however, their appearance is delayed. Thus, the onset of aging is postponed, but aging takes the same course. The analysis of postponed senescence suggests a crucial period during the adult life span at about 5 days at which certain uncharacterized events occur that result in a delay in aging. Obviously, many alleles are selected from the diversity present in the starting population to generate extended longevity. These genetic factors are largely additive. Environmental factors also play a role in the extended longevity phenotype. High larval density during a narrow window of development spanning the late second and all of the third larval instar is required to elicit this phenotype in at least one line. As in *C. elegans*, it appears that developmental processes play an important role in setting the stage for longevity. Not all lines of *Drosophila* displaying extended longevity exhibit the same suite of associated phenotypic. changes. Thus, there are likely many routes to extended longevity.

The extended-longevity flies exhibit an enhanced response to a variety of stresses. Coselected responses include resistance to dessication, alcohol vapors, and starvation in one line. Significant further gains in longevity can be achieved when the long-lived flies are subsequently selected for resistance to starvation. These results suggest that postponed senescence is associated with the capacity to resist environmental stress. These flies store large amounts of fat in their abdomen, which might explain some of the aspects of their resistance to stress. This does not differ that much from the storage of food granules in the intestines of long-lived *daf-2* nematodes. It suggests an inherent change in metabolic capacity.

In another line of extended-longevity flies, an increase in paraquat resistance has been observed. This indicates an increase in resistance to oxygen free radical stress. The flies show increased levels of several antioxidant enzymes, including Cu, Zn-superoxide dismutase (SOD), catalase, glutathione-S-transferase, and xanthine oxidase. The mapping of the major longevity-determining loci in this line revealed a regulatory locus on chromosome III in the general vicinity of the SOD gene. However, the interval involved is very large, and there are loci on chromosomes I and II with modifying, nonadditive effects. The biochemistry of aging in *Drosophila* has amply demonstrated the association between metabolic capacity, oxidative damage, and aging in this organism.

B. Comparative Biology of Aging

The analysis of the existing lines of *Drosophila* that show an extended longevity phenotype clearly demonstrates that there is more than one specific aspect to aging in one organism. This is not surprising, espe-

cially in an outbred population. It is obvious that a comparison of aging in the two lines of flies can be quite informative with regard to the nature of the aging process. This conclusion can be enlarged to include the comparison of the aging processes in different species, even unrelated ones. Such comparisons can reveal both commonalities and differences. This provides the driving force for a comparative approach to aging.

C. Transgenic Approach

The free radical theory of aging has been argued, and correlative evidence has been shown in its favor. However, the first causal approach to this problem has been taken in *Drosophila* using a transgenic methodology. Transgenic flies carrying one or more copies of ectopic SOD genes have been created. A variety of levels of expression have been obtained dependent on both copy number and on chromosomal context. The DNA was introduced through P element (transposon)-mediated transformation. These genetic manipulations had very small, if any, effect on mean life span, and not on maximum life span. Similar lack of success was obtained by creating catalase transgenic flies. The trick turned out to be to obtain doubly transgenic flies with rather strictly balanced levels of both SOD and catalase overexpression. This strategy provided a 30% increase in longevity, suggesting that antioxidant defenses are limiting for longevity in the fruit fly. The increased longevity was associated with a longer mortality rate doubling time, lower level of protein oxidative damage, and delayed loss in physical performance. All of this despite the greater overall oxygen consumption during the life span of the transgenic animals.

The results with the transgenic flies seem to confirm the conclusions obtained with the flies selected for extended longevity in providing support for the role of antioxidant defenses, and thereby oxidative damage, in aging. There is one difficulty in this interpretation. The lack of catalase or the presence of only one copy of the SOD gene does not shorten life span in the fruit fly, indicating that these antioxidant enzymes are not limiting for longevity. This suggests that the extra SOD and catalase in the transgenic flies may be doing things in addition to protecting against oxidative damage. It is also possible that these flies have a new set point for longevity defined by the excess SOD and catalase. In any of these scenarios, one would have a distinct qualitative change rather than a quantitative one, something like a new species.

D. Enhancer Traps

In a genetic approach fundamentally similar to the one used in *S. cerevisiae*, a screen for genes that are differentially expressed during the *Drosophila* life span has been instituted. This has utilized enhancer traps. A reporter gene, encoding β-galactosidase, is randomly integrated at different sites in the fly genome with the aid of P element transformation. This gene has only basal promoter elements linked to it and depends for expression on integration in the close vicinity of an enhancer element. This results in a situation in which the reporter gene is expressed, and can be detected, only at times and places when the enhancer is active. Thus, the enhancer trap detects the expression of active genes, and the trick is to construct the experiment to identify genes expressed at various points during the life span of the fly. The expression of age-dependent genes can be detected quite easily in the whole animal.

Several genes that are differentially expressed during the life span of the fruit fly have been identified in this way, and they are in the process of being cloned. This approach identifies candidate genes that can then be assessed for their role as causal agents in determining longevity. During the course of studies utilizing the enhancer trap approach, it was found that some hsps are expressed in old flies, even without administration of heat shock.

The heat shock response occupies a particularly important position in the arsenal of protective devices available to the organism. It appears to play a role in protection of the organism from more than one stress. In addition to heat shock, it may be particularly important in protection from oxidative stress. Both heat shock response the response to UV are controlled by *ras* in both mammals and in yeast. As discussed earlier, a decline in the heat shock response with age is observed throughout phylogeny, and it is predicated upon changes at both the cellular and the organismal levels. These observations lend further support to the importance of stress responses in determining longevity. Furthermore, they indicate how comparative biology can decipher common mechanisms in aging.

E. Mitochondrial Biochemistry

Although *Drosophila* is composed almost entirely of postmitotic cells, a role for mitochondrial DNA deletions in aging has yet to be found. On the other hand, it has been shown recently that there is an age-dependent reduction in the expression of genes coding for mitochondrial proteins. This down regulation occurs in a coordinated fashion for genes encoded by both the nuclear and the mitochondrial genomes. The molecular basis for this phenomenon has not been identified. However, these results raise the fascinating possibility that the stochastic events of aging can result in a coordinated shutdown of an entire metabolic system. These results also bring to the fore the significance of metabolic capacity in the aging process.

V. OTHER MODELS

There are several other fungal and invertebrate models that have been exploited in aging research. Apart from the phylogenetic groupings already represented, such organisms as rotifers, protozoans, and ascidians have been utilized in aging research. Each presents unique opportunities to study certain specific aspects of aging. These organisms are not discussed here, however, because they have not attracted a substantial following. This is certainly due to the lack of robust genetics.

VI. APPLICATIONS TO HUMAN AGING? PERSPECTIVES

Studies with invertebrate and fungal models underscore the significance of stress responses in aging. Mammalian aging has been defined as a progressive decline in the ability to withstand stress, damage, and disease. Thus, it might not seem that the insight from these model systems is of great importance. Besides providing verification for these models, the identification of stress responses as components of the aging process in these model systems raises the perspective that the molecular mechanisms involved will be elaborated, and with this ameliorative measures will be defined. With this, an increase in healthy life span may readily be contemplated for our species.

Mammalian aging is also characterized by a decline in functional capacity. It is not always easy to define functional capacity at the physiological level in the model systems discussed here. However, one pattern that emerges is the increase in metabolic capacity associated with postponed senescence. This increase seems to be predicated on a more efficient utilization of caloric resources, and it may pull in tow a decreased generation of oxidative damage. In this regard, it is worth noting that in humans there is a decreased efficiency of clearance of glucose with age. This functional decline leaves in its wake the potential for tissue damage of various sorts. [See GROWTH FACTORS AND CELLULAR SENESCENCE.]

There is no one-to-one relationship between aging in any of these model systems and aging in humans. Nevertheless, each of these models highlights one or more specific aspects of aging that may apply to humans. Certain of these specific aspects repeat themselves over and over again in somewhat different guises. This reiteration is a persuasive argument for the potential universality of the specific aspect of aging under consideration. This conclusion in turn provides the impetus for the generation and testing of pointed hypotheses in the human system, with the ultimate goal of alleviation of some of the deficits of old age in our species.

ACKNOWLEDGMENTS

The research in the author's laboratory is supported by grants from the National Institute on Aging of the National Institutes of Health (U.S.P.H.S.) and from the Glenn Foundation for Medical Research.

BIBLIOGRAPHY

Arking, R., Dudas, S. P., & Baker, G. T. (1994). Genetic and environmental factors regulating the expression of an extended longevity phenotype in a long-lived strain of *Drosophila*. In M. R. Rose & C. E. Finch (Eds.), *Genetics and evolution of aging.* (pp. 145–160). Dordrecht, Netherlands. Kluwer Academic Publishers.

Calleja, M., Pena, P., Ugalde, C., Ferreiro, C., Marco, R., & Garesse, R. (1993). Mitochondrial DNA remains intact during *Drosophila* aging, but the levels of mitochondrial transcripts are significantly reduced. *Journal of Biological Chemistry, 268,* 18891–18897.

D'mello, N. P., Childress, A. M., Franklin, D. S., Kale, S. P., Pinswasdi, C., & Jazwinski, S. M. (1994). Cloning and characterization of *LAG1,* a longevity-assurance gene in yeast. *Journal of Biological Chemistry, 269,* 15451–15459.

Finch, C. E. (1990). *Longevity, senescence, and the genome.* Chicago, IL: University of Chicago Press.

Fleming, J. E., & Rose, M. R. (1996). Genetic analysis of aging. *Drosophila melanogaster.* In E. L. Schneider & J. W. Rowe (Eds.), *Handbook of the biology of aging* (4th ed.). (pp. 74–93). San Diego: Academic Press.

Griffiths, A. J. F. (1992). Fungal senescence. *Annual Review of Genetics, 26,* 351–357.

Jazwinski, S. M. (1993). The genetics of aging in the yeast *Saccharomyces cerevisiae. Genetica, 91,* 35–51.

Jazwinski, S. M. (1996). Longevity-assurance genes and mitochondrial DNA alterations: Yeast and filamentous fungi. In E. L. Schneider & J. W. Rowe (Eds.), *Handbook of the biology of aging* (4th ed.). (pp. 39–54). San Diego: Academic Press.

Kenyon, C., Chang, J., Gensch, E., Rudner, A., & Tabtlang, R. (1993). A *C. elegans* mutant that lives twice as long as wild type. *Nature, 366,* 461–464.

Larsen, P. L., Albert, P. S., & Riddle, D. L. (1995). Genes that regulate both development and longevity in *Caenorhabditis elegans. Genetics, 139,* 1567–1583.

Lithgow, G. J. (1996). The molecular genetics of *Caenorhabditis elegans.* In E. L. Schneider & J. W. Rowe (Eds.), *Handbook of the biology of aging* (4th ed.). (pp. 55–73). San Diego: Academic Press.

Orr, W. C., & Sohal, R. S. (1994). Extension of life span by overexpression of superoxide dismutase and catalase in *Drosophila melanogaster. Science, 263:* 1128–1130.

Osiewacz, H. D., & Hermanns, J. (1992). The role of mitochondrial DNA rearrangements in aging and human diseases. *Aging: Clinical and Experimental Research, 4,* 273–286.

Sun, J., Kale, S. P., Childress, A. M., Pinswasdi, C., & Jazwinski, S. M. (1994). Divergent roles of *RAS1* and *RAS2* in yeast longevity. *Journal of Biological Chemistry, 269,* 18638–18645.

Van Voorhies, W. A. (1992). Production of sperm reduces nematode life span. *Nature, 360,* 456–458.

Models of Aging: Vertebrates

Edward J. Masoro

University of Texas Health Science Center at San Antonio

I. Role of Animal Models in Aging Research
II. Criteria for Selection of Animal Models
III. Animal Husbandry Issues
IV. Vertebrate Species That Have Been Used
V. Current Issues and Status of Animal Model Use

Animal Models Animals used in experimental settings as surrogates for human subjects.
F₁ Hybrid Strain Progeny resulting from the mating of animals from two different inbred strains of the same species.
Genotype The genetic constitution of an individual.
Inbred Strain A population of individuals within a species with an identical or nearly identical genotype as the result of inbreeding.
Life Table A concise, standardized summary of population survival statistics in relation to age.
Mammals The class of vertebrate animals that are warm-blooded, possess hair, and suckle their young.
Species A taxonomic category of living organisms within which effective gene flow occurs or could occur.
Vertebrates A major subgroup of the phylum Chordata comprised of animals possessing an internal bony skeleton, particularly a backbone.

ANIMAL MODELS are used in aging research as a tool for the exploration of aging processes with the ultimate goal of uncovering the basic nature of human aging. In choosing a particular species or strain of a species as a model, certain criteria should be considered. The extent to which these criteria are met is an important factor in the success of a study using an animal model. In executing such studies, it is particularly important to pay careful attention to animal husbandry issues. Although many different vertebrate species have been employed as animal models for aging research, most studies have used mice and rats. There is great need for an increased diversity in species used as animal models for aging studies. Only through the use of diverse species can one acquire the knowledge needed to successfully meet the gerontologic challenge of the twenty-first century. Unfortunately, the growing public opposition to the use of animals in experimental biology poses a threat to the attainment of this knowledge.

I. ROLE OF ANIMAL MODELS IN AGING RESEARCH

Animal models are used in biomedical science as surrogates for humans. They enable studies that cannot be done in humans because of legal, ethical, economic, or technical considerations. The basic premise underlying their use is that what is learned will apply to the human condition. The validity of this premise for a particular model is often questioned, and new species are continuously being assessed in the quest for a model that closely mimics humans.

These issues also apply to the use of animal models for aging research, because human aging is the ultimate interest of most investigators. However, because of logistics peculiar to aging research, similarity to humans is often compromised when choosing a model for an aging study. For example, rodents, rather than nonhuman primates that are phylogenetically much closer to humans, are the mammalian models most often used in aging research because the cost of maintaining rodents and their relatively short lifespan make aging studies much easier to accomplish than with nonhuman primates. Scientific justification for making this choice is that basic aging processes are similar in all mammalian species, and there is some evidence to support this premise. However, recognition is growing of the great need to investigate the diversity of aging processes exhibited when a broad range of species is examined, including those far removed from humans. Indeed, studies with nematodes and fruit flies are yielding important new insights about the biology of aging. Of course, in part, this interest in diverse species relates to curiosity about the different mechanisms of aging that have evolved in living systems. However, in addition, mechanisms that are well developed and easily studied in a particular species may yield insights on aging processes in humans that may be expressed in a more subtle and less recognizable fashion. Therefore, although this chapter is focused on vertebrate, primarily mammalian, models, it should be noted that invertebrate species are also important to consider as models for aging research.

II. CRITERIA FOR SELECTION OF ANIMAL MODELS

In addition to relevance to the human condition, several criteria should always be considered when choosing a model because of their impact on the successful execution and interpretation of any aging study. Of course, no one model will be optimal in regard to all of these criteria; however, the extent to which a species or strain of species meets these criteria should be strongly considered, along with factors specifically relevant to the particular question being addressed by the study.

A. Availability of Life Table Data

Life tables contain information on the mortality characteristics of an animal population. From such tables, information on median length of life and age of tenth percentile survivors can be ascertained. Such informa-

tion is needed when designing an aging study, and without such data interpretation of the findings is not possible. For example, investigators using rats have often not been aware of the life table data for this species and have made gerontological interpretations based on studies with rats ranging in age from 1–6 months. Because the rat strains used had a median length of life of 24 months or so and age of tenth percentile survivors of 32 months or so, these gerontological interpretations are without merit. In these cases, life tables were available, and the ignorance of the investigators was the basic problem, which, of course, can be readily remedied by educating investigators. Unfortunately for many species, reliable life table data are not available; for example, such data are not available for rabbits, which is a particularly difficult problem because rabbits are a popular model for the study of atherosclerosis. The lack of reliable life table data precludes rabbit use to assess the relationship between aging processes and atherosclerosis. When an investigator has compelling reasons to use an animal model for gerontological research for which reliable life table data are lacking, gathering such data must be part of the research protocol.

B. Longevity Characteristics

The resources required to execute an aging study are to a great extent determined by the longevity characteristics of the animal model. Provided other factors are not compromised, the shorter the life span of the model the better because both the cost of animal maintenance and the time requirements of investigators are minimized. One reason that laboratory rodents are the most widely used model for aging research is their short life spans compared to most other mammalian species.

C. Availability of Data on Age-Associated Pathology

The prevalence of many diseases increases with advancing age, and much of this age-associated pathology is characteristic of a particular species or strain of the species. Whether this age-associated pathology is part of the aging process or a different entity is the subject of much debate. Irrespective of how this debate plays out, it is important for investigators to know the age-associated pathology of the model when designing a study using that model. Lack of such information impacts negatively on the experimental design process. It is also imperative that a pathological assessment be made on the animals used in a study whenever the design of the study makes this possible. In cross-sectional studies involving sacrifice of the animals, such analyses can almost always be done. In longitudinal studies, pathological analyses are possible only at the time of spontaneous death or at the end of the study when animals can be sacrificed.

D. Defined Genetic Characteristics

Ideally, the genetic characteristics of the animal model should be known and stable. The latter enables studies carried out at a later time or by another investigator to be executed with a model with unchanged genetic characteristics, thereby facilitating comparisons with earlier work. This criterion is readily met with rats and mice but is difficult, if not impossible, to realize with many other vertebrate species. Even with rats and mice, the investigator must take care to achieve this criterion. For example, outbred Sprague-Dawley strain rats are maintained by randomly mating members of the stock. However, the mating is often not sufficiently random and, as a result, Sprague-Dawley rats from different suppliers or from the same supplier at different times differ genetically. Investigators unaware of this problem when using rats of different ages from different suppliers or even from the same supplier may interpret differences between different age groups as being due to aging when in fact they are due to genetics.

Inbred strains of mice and rats have been used to assure uniformity and stability of genetic makeup. Presumably every animal in an inbred strain population has the same or nearly the same genotype as every other animal. Indeed, another reason for using inbred strains is the belief that inbreeding should maximize phenotypic uniformity within and between experiments. However, this putative advantage comes with a cost because of the phenomenon of inbreeding depression. F_1 hybrids, crosses between two inbred strains, circumvents the problem of inbreeding depression with animals that are as genetically defined as inbred strains. Moreover, for many phenotypic traits, F_1 hybrids have less variability among individuals than

do inbred strains. For these reasons, F_1 hybrids from a genetic perspective are the preferred model.

E. Availability and Cost of Animals

It is difficult to acquire animals of most species of a wide range of ages that have been carefully maintained, including a complete record of the husbandry. The alternative is for investigators to maintain the animals in their facility from birth until sacrifice or spontaneous death. Even for short-lived species, such maintenance is very expensive in monetary and space resources; and for long-lived species, for most investigators, it is prohibitively expensive. The National Institute on Aging has addressed this problem in the case of mice and rats by subsidizing the maintenance of eight mouse genotypes and four rat genotypes. On the downside, this subsidization has focused most research on aging on these species and strains and this lack of diversity of animal models is a serious problem that needs to be addressed. For species other than rats and mice, investigators have used a variety of approaches to obtain animals of a wide range of ages but in most cases have had to work with a less than well-characterized animal model.

III. ANIMAL HUSBANDRY ISSUES

The conditions under which animals are maintained markedly influence long-term studies, such as those carried out in aging research. A study with female C3H/HeJ mice that are prone to develop mammary tumors is a striking example. By 400 days of age, 65% of these mice maintained in a conventional holding facility developed these tumors compared to only 10% of the mice protected from the noise and odors of such a holding facility. Clearly, for most aging studies there is need to maintain the animals in a defined and optimal environment. With effort, this can be accomplished when the investigator maintains the animals in his or her own facility. However, it is difficult to address this issue with assurance when animals of various ages are obtained from a commercial supplier or other external source. The following factors are important for investigators to carefully address.

A. Housing

The size of the cage and the number of animals per cage have long been considered to be important considerations. Indeed, there are regulations about cage size relative to the size of the animals and the number per cage. Surprisingly, these regulations do not appear to be based on hard data. For instance, in the case of number of animals per cage, the published data have ranged from greatest longevity for singly housed rodents to just the opposite. Perhaps a high-density population entails stress as does isolation. Moreover, different species and different strains within species may vary in this regard. If so, and it seems likely to be so, optimal housing conditions will have to be known or determined for the particular model used. Moreover, the question being asked may determine the housing conditions. For example, if the study requires collecting data on the food intake of each animal, it is necessary to singly house the animals. Although there are still many questions concerning optimal cage size and/ or number of animals per cage, it is essential that investigators standardize this aspect of their study and clearly present this information when publishing the work. Failure to do so makes it impossible for others to repeat the study.

B. Microbiological Status

Infectious disease can distort an aging study. With mice and rats, this problem can be dealt with relatively easily by utilizing specific pathogen-free animals (i.e., free of murine pathogens) and by maintaining the animals in this state by housing them in a barrier facility. Barrier facilities vary in structure and complexity but all aim to exclude the entry of pathogenic organisms. Periodically, sentinel animals are removed from the facility to monitor for the presence of pathogens (i.e., to determine if the barrier has functioned effectively). Unfortunately, this problem is not easy to deal with when using most other mammalian species, which is a serious difficulty for investigators carrying out long-term aging studies with such species.

C. Diet

Studies with rodents have shown that diet can profoundly influence aging processes. Indeed, decreasing dietary energy intake by mice and rats markedly slows

the rate of aging in these species. Clearly, it is important to know and standardize both the composition of the diet and the amount eaten when rodents are the model used. It is not known whether diet has such profound influences on aging in other vertebrate species, but it seems likely that it does and until shown otherwise must be assumed to have such an action. Thus, diet is a factor that must be known and controlled in all aging studies using vertebrate species and reported in detail when publishing the research.

D. Exercise

The level of physical activity is another factor that is believed to influence aging. However, this factor is difficult to address in animal studies. The investigator can provide animals with the opportunity to exercise (e.g., provide rodents with running wheels) but the extent of physical activity is determined by the animal and not the investigator. Forcing animals to exercise is not an acceptable option because the procedure needed to do so stresses the animals. When publishing an aging study, all information on exercise (including the lack of exercise) should be reported.

E. Other Environmental Factors

Many other environmental factors have the potential to affect aging studies. Therefore, as far as possible the environment of the holding facility should be defined, controlled, and reported in publications of the research. The effects of noise and odors have already been mentioned. The intensity of light and the periodicity of the dark–light cycle need to be controlled. Ambient temperature is known to influence longevity and therefore should be maintained at an optimal level. Adventitious chemicals from bedding material or disinfectants or insecticides should be avoided because even low levels of these substances over a long period of time may markedly affect aging studies.

IV. VERTEBRATE SPECIES THAT HAVE BEEN USED

A. Fish

Although fish have been used as models in a few aging studies, remarkably little work has been done using these classes of vertebrates. This is unfortunate because the rate of aging varies greatly among fish species ranging from very rapid to imperceptible. Clearly, fish are a relatively untapped but potentially valuable source of animal models for aging research.

B. Birds

Another class of vertebrates that has been used to only a limited extent as models for aging research is birds. However, the fact that most bird species are dramatically longer lived than mammalian species of a similar size indicates that birds may be uniquely useful models. They may have specialized protective mechanisms against the damaging actions of aging processes. If so, studies with birds would offer insights for the development of medical interventions aimed at retarding aging in humans. Several commercially available bird species seem well suited to serve as models for aging research.

C. Mice

The mammalian species *Mus musculus* (the laboratory mouse) has been a widely used model for aging research. Indeed, it is the preferred mammalian model for the study of the genetics of aging because of the many genetically defined strains (more than 500 inbred plus many F_1 hybrids) and because of the richness of the genetic map available for the mouse. As stated earlier, eight mouse genotypes are available from a National Institute on Aging subsidized program. Also, the technology for the generation of transgenic mice is well developed. The longevity characteristics of many mouse strains are known and have been found to vary significantly among genotypes. The small size of the mouse impacts both positively and negatively on their use as an animal model for aging research. The space and other resources needed for their maintenance make mice relatively inexpensive for use in life span studies. However, the amount of biological material that can be obtained from a single mouse is small, and many physiological measurements are difficult to execute because of the small size of the animal. Husbandry is well worked out for mice, and for many strains there is much information on age-associated pathology.

D. Rats

This mammalian species is used more than any other species for aging research. As for mice, arrangements can be made with commercial vendors to supply laboratory rats of a wide range of ages. Also, as discussed earlier, the National Institute on Aging subsidizes the production of four rat genotypes; these animals are less expensive than those from unsubsidized commercial sources, and the investigator has assurance that the husbandry procedures are standardized and of high quality. Life table data are available for several rat strains and stocks, (e.g., the F344, BN, and WAG/Rij inbred strains and the Sprague-Dawley, Long-Evans, and Wistar stocks). The size of the rat enables physiological and pathophysiological measurements to be readily accomplished, and a single rat yields sufficient material for most biochemical and related analyses. Indeed, life span longitudinal studies involving periodic blood sampling or physiological measurements can be accomplished with rats without compromising longevity. The rat is less useful than the mouse for genetic studies because there is a lack of detailed genetic maps for rats; hopefully this deficit will soon be rectified. Husbandry procedures for rats are well developed, and much information is available on age-associated pathology of several rat strains and stocks.

E. Hamsters

Hamsters are mammals that have had significant use in aging research. The species used most is the Syrian hamster, *Mesocricetus auratus,* but the Chinese hamster, *Cricetulus griseus,* and the Turkish hamster, *Mesocricetus brandti,* have also been used. Syrian hamsters including several inbred strains are available from commercial sources. Although not studied as thoroughly as rats and mice, the husbandry information on hamsters is adequate for the execution of aging research. Life table data are available for Syrian hamsters, Turkish hamsters, and Chinese hamsters. The Chinese hamster is about the same size as the mouse and thus has the same size-related advantages and disadvantages. Syrian hamsters and Turkish hamsters are much larger than mice but are less than one-half the size of rats. Thus, these two species are more useful for physiological studies than mice. There is a sizable literature on the age-associated pathology of

Syrian hamsters and Chinese hamsters but not Turkish hamsters.

F. Cats

Cats are a mammalian species widely used for neuroscience research. Because nervous system dysfunction is a major problem encountered in human aging, cats are potentially very valuable as an animal model for aging research. However, very little use has been made of cats in aging research. A major reason for this is the lack of a readily available source of well-characterized cats of varying ages. Indeed, the only cat colony with the characteristics needed for the support of aging studies was one maintained by the British Medical Research Council at Mill Hill. However, that cat colony was not used for aging research. What little aging research that has been done utilizing cats was accomplished by investigators who pieced together a range of ages by obtaining cats from a variety of sources: university-maintained animals; commercial sources; pets made available by veterinarians with consent of the owners. Obtaining cats in this way clearly does not provide investigators with a reliable, well-standardized source of genetically defined animals. On the positive side, life tables and data on age-associated pathology collected on pets are available. Of course, cats are large and long-lived compared to rats and mice, which makes aging studies with cats expensive to execute.

G. Dogs

Dogs are widely used mammalian models for physiological studies but have not been a major animal model for gerontological studies for many reasons. A major reason is the fact that dogs of a range of ages are not commercially available. Indeed, much of the aging research on dogs has involved the dogs in the control groups of long-term radiation studies. Another issue is the fact that the genetics of the dogs that had been used in aging studies was not defined. However, a breeding program has been established for a beagle dog colony with a stable gene pool; clearly, such colonies are needed to supply dogs for aging research. On the positive side, life table data are available on beagle dogs maintained under laboratory conditions, and much is known about the husbandry and age-associated pathology of dogs. Dogs vary greatly in size depending on breed, but even small dogs are large compared to rodents, making them costly to maintain, particularly in regard to space requirements. For example, the beagle dog, which is the breed that has been most used for aging research, weighs about 10 kg (most rats weigh less than 1 kg and mice less than 0.1 kg.). Moreover, appropriate care of dogs requires attention be paid to their social environment, including an exercise program.

H. Nonhuman Primates

Because of the long life span of most primate species and the high cost of maintaining these mammals, it is difficult to execute aging research using nonhuman primate species. Nevertheless, there are at least two reasons why nonhuman primate models must be used for aging studies: (a) to make certain that gerontological findings observed in other vertebrates (primarily rats and mice) also occur in nonhuman primates (the assumption being that because of their phylogenetic closeness to humans, aging processes occurring in nonhuman primates also occur in humans); (b) to study age changes that occur only in humans and nonhuman primates. Government-sponsored primate laboratories tend to employ good husbandry and to maintain careful records on each animal. Commercial suppliers are also a source of these animals, but in many instances the quality of or information about the animals is less than might be desired. In the past, genetic characterization of the primate model has been nonexistent. However, breeding programs in government-supported primate centers and in other institutions with a mix of public and private funding are rectifying this problem. Also, advances in molecular biology are facilitating this characterization. For several nonhuman primate species, life table data are available. However, the quality of these data is often less than desirable, leading to the conclusion that the currently available information on longevity characteristics must be viewed as tentative. Nonhuman primate species vary greatly in size, with squirrel monkeys being in the size range of rats whereas other species exhibit a range of sizes similar to that seen with the various breeds of dogs. Husbandry for nonhuman primates is rather well developed, but there is still much to learn about the maintenance of old animals. Social environment is a major issue that must be addressed when using these species. A substantial literature is available on the age-associated pathology of several nonhuman primate species.

V. CURRENT ISSUES AND STATUS OF ANIMAL MODEL USE

During the past twenty-five years, there has been great progress in the development of rat and mouse models for aging research. Husbandry for these species is now such that the life span maintenance of these animals can be accomplished relatively easily.

The downside is that this progress in the use of rats and mice has resulted in these two species being the subjects of about 75% of all aging studies with the projection that their use, if anything, will increase in the future. This dominance by rats and mice is unfortunate, because diversity in the models used would almost certainly provide new, important insights on the biology of aging, including human aging.

Of course, it is important to make certain that when other animal models are used, the standards developed for rats and mice be adhered to. Unfortunately for most species, the information needed to meet these standards is not available, and in each case obtaining this information will be costly and time consuming. For example, obtaining reliable life table data for rabbits will require studies of a duration of many years. Similarly, determining the husbandry requirements for the maintenance of a previously uncharted species will require careful study of dietary needs, environmental temperature requirements, caging requirements, and many other factors. Also, information on the age-associated pathology must be developed for each species. The bottom line is that diversity in animal model use for aging studies is clearly needed but will require a substantial investment. To obtain the required fiscal support, the administrators of funding agencies and the members of scientific review panels must be made aware of the need. They must recognize that state-of-the-art molecular biology is of little value in the absence of appropriate animal models.

It is recognized that understanding the basic biological nature of aging will be necessary to successfully meet the gerontological challenges of the twenty-first century, and I hope this article has made evident the important role of diverse animal models in attaining this knowledge. However, it is regrettable that at this time many laypeople, including leaders in the arts and politics, condemn the use of animal models for biomedical research and moreover that these critics have had a significant negative impact on animal use.

Probably most of those opposed to the use of animal models are concerned about animal cruelty. Indeed, everyone should have this concern, especially those using animal models for aging research. Nothing is more damaging to the validity of an aging study than the maintenance of the animals in less than optimal environments. As is evident from this article, husbandry procedures must be employed that protect the animals from infection by pathogenic organisms, provide an optimal diet, and provide optimal environmental conditions. To do otherwise is counterproductive from an experimental standpoint, let alone humanitarian considerations. Of course, physiological measurements need to be made, and they may perturb the animal. However, the extent of this perturbation should be no greater than what humans experience when undergoing tests by physicians. To markedly perturb would be experimentally counterproductive. When sacrifice of the animal is required, it can and must be accomplished without pain.

Some critics feel that research using animal models is of no value. This is a surprising view because the history of biomedical research clearly shows the immense positive impact of the use of animal models. Examples are insulin, antibiotics, and vaccines, to name a few of those that required animal models for their development or ultimate medical use. Currently the most promising approaches to gaining an understanding of the basic biology of aging require animal models.

A small group of people object to the use of animal models because of the concept of animal rights. This concept is based on the premise that animals possess intrinsic value and are not to be used just for human purposes. Most people would agree that animals have intrinsic value but whether or not they should be used for human purposes has consequences that must be carefully considered. Because animals cannot provide informed consent, this concept rules out all use of animals for biomedical research. For the same reason, it precludes their use as a source of clothing, including the harvesting of wool, and of food, including milk, cheese, and eggs.

Many ask, Why use animal models for research when there are alternatives? One alternative is the use of cells in culture totally derived from consenting humans. However, the evidence that these cell culture systems are models of organismic aging is weak, and even those who champion their use feel that they are adjuncts to and not replacements of animal models. The other suggested alternative is the use of computer models. Given our current state of knowledge of the biology of aging, there is no way a computer model can replace animal models, although computer modeling is a powerful tool for optimizing the use of animal models.

BIBLIOGRAPHY

Finch, C. E. (1991). New models for new perspectives in the biology of senescence. *Neurobiology of Aging 12*, 625.

Holmes, D. J., & Austad, S. N. (1995). Birds as animal models for the comparative biology of aging: A prospectus. *Journal of Gerontology: Biological Sciences, 50A*, B59.

Masoro, E. J. (1990). Animal models for aging research. In E. L. Schneider & J. W. Rowe (Eds.), *Handbook of the biology of aging* (3rd ed.) San Diego: Academic Press.

Masoro, E. J. (1992). The role of animal models in meeting the gerontologic challenge of the 21st century. *The Gerontologist, 32*, 627.

Phelan, J. P., & Austad, S. N. (1994). Selecting animal models of human aging: Inbred strains often exhibit less biological uniformity than F_1 hybrids. *Journal of Gerontology: Biological Sciences, 49*, B1.

Weindruch, R. (1995). Animal models. In E. J. Masoro (Ed.), *Handbook of physiology, Section II: Aging* New York: Oxford University Press.

Modernization and Aging

Jacqueline Leavitt

University of California, Los Angeles

I. Modernization as Experienced by the Aging: Underlying Theory
II. Comparative Demographic Trends in Developed and Developing Countries
III. Other Trends Affecting the Future Quality of Life for the Aging
IV. Augmenting the Independent Household: The Neighborhood and Extended Family
V. Architectural and Planning Innovations
VI. Conclusions

Extended Households   Related or unrelated people sharing the same living quarters.
Independent Living   Nonfamily and family households who share living quarters in a unit that has a full bathroom and kitchen within the unit.
Neighborhood Families   Formal and informal support structures to households, with easy access to aging households, and replacing some functions that individual families provide.

MODERNIZATION is a process of social change, whereby developing nations seek to achieve and aspire to characteristics of developed nations (i.e., sustaining economic growth, including some level of public participation or democratic representation in political society; providing greater mobility for individuals; broader social service supports including social security, unemployment insurance, and health insurance; and increasing communication and adoption of societal norms). Changes include the transition from rural to urban settlements, increased introduction of technology into daily living (i.e., running hot and cold water, bathrooms within a unit, central heating); free universal education for men and women; the permanent entry of women, with and without children, into the labor force; declining fertility, increasing longevity, and smaller household sizes.

I. MODERNIZATION AS EXPERIENCED BY THE AGING: UNDERLYING THEORY

A. Background

Modernization is the process of social change whereby developing nations come closer to resembling developed nations in terms of reaching the level of economic growth, on a per capita basis; achieving some degree of public participation or democratic representation in politics; providing individuals with greater physical, social, and economic mobility; and using mass communication to influence society's adaptation of different norms. Government supports for social welfare may include social security, unemployment insurance, and health insurance. Women will be encouraged to pursue higher education, enter the wage labor force, and set up independent households; this will have repercussions on household size and values society holds about women's roles in that nation's structure. Industrialization and urbanization are indicators and reflectors of greater modernization, but primarily agrarian societies do not realize such aspirations by moving from traditional to transitional to modern at certain fixed intervals. Nor can one set of institutions, for example parliamentary republics or democratic republics, be transferred from one society to another without other institutions in place and a literate voting public. The nature and speed of modernization will be affected by prior patterns of settlement, such as colonialization; the existence of a strong military; the presence of a professional elite; the sophistication of the bureaucracy; the types of training and education available to the public; the existence of a middle class oriented to production, with the capacity to satisfy consumption, and the ability to respond to changes; relation to the timing of internal and external global events, including changes in immigration policies; and internal sustainability. Religious beliefs, attitudes to work, family, death, pleasure, and so on will influence whether change is resisted or accepted, and in what form.

Modernization has not equally benefited persons in developed or developing nations. The economist, Robert Heilbroner, has observed that in the post-World War II era, a widespread belief prevailed that sophisticated military technology would be converted for domestic purposes and improve everyone's lives. The optimism overshadowed the facts that uneven distribution of previous government benefits, through subsidized housing or civil service jobs, left out the poorest and persons of color. In the 1950s in the United States, the fruits of modernization for Whites were unattainable unless women in working class families, with and without young children, entered the labor force.

Women's entry into the labor force as well as greater access to higher education resulted in declining fertility rates overall along with decreasing average household size. Total fertility rates, or the level of reproduction that maintains population levels, for the 20 years between 1970 and 1990 closely resembled pre-World War II rates. In 1987, the total fertility rate moved upward as women began having more babies and women over 30 began having children. Such changes result in disruptions that are far more severe in countries where rising economic output is stifled; institutional change does not occur or is slow; and society reluctantly accepts a shift in values. Physical mobility of individuals may occur without social or economic mobility, as can be seen in squatter settlements and overcrowded urban areas of cities in developing nations around the world.

Modernization is characterized by individual households moving to urban areas, and more households gaining access to improvements in daily living, such as running hot and cold water, bathrooms within a unit, and central heating. For example, the extended household in colonial United States included family and nonrelatives, each of whom depended on the other members in order to survive. The person born around 1900 in the United States lived 49 years on average. Widespread electrification and indoor plumbing changed the quality of daily life. The individual no longer had to leave the house to gather firewood for heating and cooking purposes, make countless trips up and down tenement stairs for water supplies, or shop every day for groceries that would otherwise spoil without refrigeration. Social scientists noted that toward the end of life significant shifts in household arrangements had occurred. In modern society it had become obsolete for several generations to cohabit under the same roof. A notable exception in the 1960s was the popularity of intentional households composed of unrelated and related individuals who formed an economic unit informed by shared cultural and political values. In the 1970s, in areas where housing costs were high, the phenomenon was observed of grown children moving back to the parents' house.

II. COMPARATIVE DEMOGRAPHIC TRENDS IN DEVELOPED AND DEVELOPING COUNTRIES

The profile of aging in the United States informs the pattern associated with modernization. Household size decreases. In 1940, in the United States, the average number of persons per household for all ages was 3.67. After World War II, more young people, particularly women, entered the labor market, left their parents' home, and rented on their own or with roommates until forming families of their own. Parents maintained their households and continued to do so after spouses had died. By 1970 the average number of persons per household was 3.14, and steadily declined to 2.76 in 1980, reached 2.63 in 1990, and remained at 2.63 in 1993.

Life expectancy increases with modernization. In 1992, the average life expectancy in the United States was 75.7 years for all races; Whites with an average life expectancy of 76.5 years lived 6.7 years longer than AfricanAmericans although both populations experienced increases. Widows over the age of 65 outnumbered widowers. Over 65 years of age, between 1980 and 1994, increases were highest among those over 75 years, and especially in the 85 years and older category. Worldwide, Japan has been leading the developed world with a life expectancy of 79 years of age.

In contrast to the increasing older age profile in developed nations, youth dominate in developing nations where there is a greater birth rate and a lower life expectancy. Scientific breakthroughs, better nutrition, and improved health habits have helped to extend people's longevity in developed nations. Yet, in 1992, less than half the population of 20 countries, 17 of which are in Africa, had access to Western-style health care. In 1992, the shortest life expectancy was in Sierra Leone at 42 years of age. From one-third to the entire population lacked safe drinking water in countries of Africa as well as parts of Asia, South America, and Central America.

Declining fertility rates are another characteristic of modernization. Since the late 1960s, fertility rates have declined in developed countries such as Italy, which went from 2.5 to 1.5, and Spain, which dropped from 2.9 to 1.7. Developing nations have experienced a decline in fertility rates; on average, the range of births went from five to seven to three to six per woman. Yet, poor countries are expected to double their population in 30 years compared to the more than 162 years projected for developed countries. Between 1993 and 2025, 95% of the world's growth is projected to be in the developing world. The highest fertility rates remain in countries within Africa. By the year 2000, demographers expect that the largest urban areas will be in developing countries' already densely populated cities, such as Cairo, Lagos, Mexico City, Calcutta, and Shanghai. [See DEMOGRAPHY.]

Infant death rates decline with modernization. Developing nations have experienced declining infant mortality rates with greater access to immunization, antibiotics, and use of pesticides to reduce mosquito-borne malaria. Nonetheless, drought, civil strife, war, and the spread of AIDS have meant famines, murders, and more deaths, all of which tax the inadequate infrastructures of those nations. It is possible that if death rates increase, pressure to increase births will continue.

Fertility rates are found to decline when women's literacy rates increase. In turn, marriage and pregnancy are postponed and infant mortality rates are reduced. Countries in both the developed and developing world reveal exceptions. Mongolia has both high literacy among adult women and a high fertility rate. Sweden increased its fertility rate between 1983 and 1990, a result that is probably associated with social welfare provisions that included paid maternity and paternity leave and child care.

In developed countries with fewer social supports for old age, the elderly are more likely to be homeowners when compared to other age groups. Nonetheless, elderly homeowners in the United States are among the poorer groups of homeowners, and disparities exist between men and women. In 1992, of the 7.6 million single homeowners, age 65 and over, 79% were women. After age 65 women homeowners had a median income of $9,206 compared to $11,865 for men. In 1992, AfricanAmerican women homeowners age 55 to 64 were spending 27% of their income on housing compared to 17% for White women, and 12% for Hispanic women. AfricanAmerican male homeowners spent 12% and White men 8%. At 13%, only Hispanic male homeowners of the same age range were spending slightly more than women in the same group.

In developing nations, projections suggest a worldwide increase from 1990 to 2030 of low-income renters, from 1.780 million to 3.075 million, of whom more than one-half will be at least 80 years old. In both developed and developing countries, poverty will prevent home ownership. Increasing population and rising house prices will intensify in developing countries. This will lead to higher densities, including subdividing lots in squatter settlements, as well as using marginal land that may be vulnerable to flooding or landslides. In turn, this will impact on the supply of natural resources, and competitiveness for food, housing, and health care.

Homelessness became apparent in developed nations in the 1970s, giving rise to statements about third-world conditions in first-world cities. The risk of homelessness that the elderly face is possible because of their paying a high proportion of income to rent, failure to obtain health or nutrition subsidies, living in substandard conditions, and likelihood of evictions. Because the average age of death among the homeless in the United States is 52, the population over age 65 drops.

III. OTHER TRENDS AFFECTING THE FUTURE QUALITY OF LIFE FOR THE AGING

The elderly will continue to be polarized by income and place of birth within developed and in developing nations.

In developed nations this will become more visible as the numbers of people 65 and over are expected to increase in volume. Government policies have substantial potential to influence the quality of life for the poor. The Swedish government, as has the English, provided subsidies for retrofitting senior housing, adding elevators that made it easier for the old to leave their apartments and reduce isolation. The conservative political climate in the late twentieth century points to fewer programs as governments cut safety nets that include subsidized housing, utility and nutrition programs, and assistance in daily functions. In public and subsidized housing in the United States, in 1992, where tenants 65 and over had median incomes of $6,000 to $7,000, limited options will result in lower standards of living. Cutbacks in subsidies for supportive services in housing programs such as Section 202, where the average age was 74, may increase the likelihood for institutionalization. For those elderly with assets and resources, including equity in their houses, technology increases the possibilities for independent living. High-powered video magnifiers are one example; costing $3,000, they project onto television screens and compensate for poor eyesight. The "smart house," a fully integrated information and energy distribution system, uses electronic signals to manage all operations. In-home computer workstations, services such as the Internet, and integration of television with computers may be beneficial in reducing the amount of isolation the elderly face. [See GERONTECHNOLOGY.]

In developing countries, it is almost certain that technology in terms of consumer items will only be available to the relatively small number of elites who control the economy. A lag time exists in creating the infrastructure necessary for supplying running water and electricity to houses, as well as providing sewage disposal, all of which impact the health of the population and mortality rates. Governments that are economically able and politically committed to support more widespread technological development to sustain their younger populations will provide residual benefits for the already elderly. The next two sections focus on living arrangements for the aging in developed countries where modernization has occurred. These provide possible scenarios that may occur over time in developing countries.

IV. AUGMENTING THE INDEPENDENT HOUSEHOLD: THE NEIGHBORHOOD AND EXTENDED FAMILY

With modernization, and over time, many developing nations may come to resemble developed nations where the support network of the elderly among relatives has eroded. In the United States, the extended family is being replaced with what has been called substitute families—living arrangements that rely on nonfamily networks. Research among Chicana elderly who emigrated from Mexico to the United States as well as among Whites identified senior centers as examples of facilities that replaced family attachments with nonfamily relations. Other research highlights increased formal networks such as the official home help organizations in Sweden that provide aid in "cleaning, shopping and personal care ... meals on wheels, foot care, hair care, security, clearing away of snow, etc."—in effect, creating a "neighborhood family" system. [See SOCIAL NETWORKS, SUPPORT, AND INTEGRATION.]

Population growth in developed nations is expected to stem largely from immigration. Among some racial and ethnic groups, the extended family may survive, but the elderly grandparents may find circumstances have changed. Wives are in the paid labor force and do not stay at home, and the grandparents are babysitters for grandchildren who may distance themselves from the cultural values and norms of their heritage.

V. ARCHITECTURAL AND PLANNING INNOVATIONS

In developed nations, aging in place became a widely discussed topic in the 1970s as a means to address astronomically rising health costs and psychological factors brought about through displacement. Studies have varied as to the types of monetary savings actually realized but other benefits are less disputed. In-home care means not disrupting the accustomed routine of older people. Living arrangements that permit independence and the support of an extended family or nonfamily may be facilitated by various shared housing arrangements. Some programs match older people as roommates in existing units, or develop and operate congregate housing. Courtyard housing clusters individual units, anywhere from two to six, in order to provide easy access to companionship but also privacy. The Australian government purchases homes from the elderly, reconfigures lots, and mixes small and large houses with integrated age groups. This granny flat concept has been influential in the United States but within the private market. Additions and conversions to existing houses are typically regulated by municipal ordinances. Ordinances for accessory units specify who may reside in the primary residence, ages for those in the accessory unit, and or number of cars. These requirements reflect concerns that informal actions will alter the age profile, traffic, and density of residential neighborhoods that may cause de facto changes in zoning ordinances from singlefamily to multifamily residential.

Distinctions occur within developed countries as to the role government plays in assisted living, a hybrid concept that is halfway between congregate housing and skilled nursing. In European countries, as opposed to the United States, assisted living is more likely to be sponsored by public and nonprofit than by private sponsors. Personal care services are provided in a residential environment. Whereas the skilled nursing facility is modeled on the basis of hospital care, assisted living is tailored to the individual's needs and somewhat replicates the ways in which an extended family might manage aging relatives. [*See* HEALTH CARE AND SERVICES.]

For elderly homeowners in the United States who find it difficult to maintain their houses and who value their independence, new financing mechanisms have become available for home equity conversions. Instruments such as reverse annuity mortgages and split equity arrangements permit the house-rich but cash-poor the right to remain in their homes and neighborhoods, finance repairs, meet medical expenses, or make other consumption decisions. Older women homeowners, living alone, are found to be primary participants in these programs. In general, selecting

any financing mechanism is influenced by the values attached to homeownership weighed against the fear of losing one's home and independence. Regulatory protections have yet to become widespread to allay all these fears. [*See* ECONOMICS: INDIVIDUAL.]

VI. CONCLUSIONS

One researcher pointed out that the problems for an aging population do not differ greatly between developing and developed countries. Aging populations will experience modernization on the basis of individual and national poverty, and the timing and scale of modernization will create differential impacts. Changing demographics, competing political and economic strategies, and cultural values will continue to shape and define modernization.

BIBLIOGRAPHY

Facio, E. (1993). Gender and the life course: A case study of Chicano elderly. In A. De la Toree & B. M. Pesquera (Eds.), *Building with our hands: New directions in Chicana studies* (pp. 217–231). Berkeley: University of California Press.

Forsyth, A. (1992). *Changing places: Case studies of innovations in housing for older people.* Canberra, Australia: Department of Health, Housing and Community Services.

Kennedy, P. (1993). *Preparing for the Twenty-First Century.* New York: Vintage Books.

Pastalan, L. A. & Schwarz, B. (1993). The meaning of home and ecogenic housing: A new concept for elderly women. In H. Dandekar (Ed.), *Shelter, women and development: First and third world perspectives* (pp. 402–407). Ann Arbor, MI: George Wahr Publishing Co.

Sethi, R. (1993). Crossing Oceans: A Cross-Cultural Look at Elderly Immigrant Women in the United States and Elderly Women in India. In H. Dandekar (Ed.), *Shelter, women and development: First and third world perspectives* (pp. 408–413). Ann Arbor, MI: George Wahr Publishing Co.

Stucki, B. R. (1993). Housing and the creation of security in old age by rural women of Ghana: A development perspective. In H. Dandekar (Ed.), *Shelter, women and development: First and third world perspectives* (pp. 414–418). Ann Arbor, MI: George Wahr Publishing Co.

Tornstam, L. (1989). Formal and informal support for the elderly: An analysis of present patterns and future options in Sweden. *Impact of Science on Society, 153,* 57–63.

Zedlewski, S. R., Barnes, R. O., Burt, M. R., McBride, T. D., and Meyer, J. A. (1990). *The needs of the elderly in the 21st century* (Urban Institute Report 90-5). Washington, DC: Urban Institute Press.

Motor Control

Rachael Seidler and George Stelmach

Arizona State University

I. Introduction
II. Reaction Time
III. General Slowing of Movements with Age
IV. Determinants of Age Differences in Duration and Control of Movement
V. Reach-to-Grasp Movements
VI. Alterations in Handwriting Control
VII. Explanations of Declines in Motor Performance
VIII. Are the Observed Deficits Transistory in Nature?
IX. Conclusions

Motor Control   The integrative action of the nervous system in the control of posture and movement.

Motor Reaction Time   Time from the appearance of electromyographic activity until movement initiation.

Movement Preparation   Specification of certain movement parameters such as arm, direction, and extent of movement.

Neural Noise   Random neural background activity arising in the sense organs, neural pathways, and the brain.

Premotor Reaction Time   Time from onset of stimulus until appearance of electromyographic activity.

Reaction Time   The time from the onset of a stimulus until initiation of a volitional response.

Signal-to-Noise Ratio (SNR)   The ratio between the amount of modulation due to the invariant program component (signal) and the amount of unpredictable modulation (noise). A high SNR suggests a more reproducible movement.

Speed–Accuracy Trade-off   The well-known phenomenon that when a performer attempts to move more quickly, he or she becomes less accurate.

The elderly often exhibit impairments in **MOTOR PERFORMANCE** that can affect their everyday activities. Motor skills are influenced by deficits occurring before the movement, such as slowing in central processing speed, and by changes occurring during performance of the movement such as an inability to properly regulate force. Some of these declines can be partially mitigated with practice. However, speed, variability, and the kinematic profiles of motor responses usually do not reach levels seen in younger adults, suggesting that the declines may represent basic limitations in motor performance capacity for the elderly. The causes of these motor performance declines are not well understood. Regardless of the etiology of these declines, they can have a substantial effect on the independence of many elderly.

I. INTRODUCTION

Typically as individuals get older they experience substantial declines in sensorimotor processing. Motor performance often becomes slower and more variable. Research also has revealed that the elderly show (a) an increase in response initiation time; (b) an increase in movement duration; (c) a reduced capability for decelerating movements; and (d) an inability to calibrate appropriate force levels. Age-related changes in sensorimotor processing may lead to impairments in motor activities of daily living (ADLs); however, some deficits may be reduced with practice and/or familiar-

177

ization. The purpose of this article is to describe how aging alters the ability to initiate and regulate movement, and to document the manner in which such movements differ from those of younger subjects. As the topics are reviewed, we present several of the current theories of why such impairments occur.

II. REACTION TIME

Reaction time (RT), the time required to initiate a response following a stimulus, is a commonly used measure of performance. This measure is used to describe motor performance levels across age groups and to allow comparisons between healthy individuals and patients with various pathologies. Although RT is often used in aging research to decompose mental processes, response latency paradigms have also made important contributions in understanding why the elderly have delayed response latencies.

A. General Slowing

It is clear that the elderly are slower to initiate movements in response to stimuli. Their RTs are typically slowed by 15–30% in simple stimulus–response (S-R) paradigms. Several investigators have been successful in developing paradigms that have localized particular deficits in motor processes (see bibliography for examples).

B. Determinants of Age Differences in Response Initiation Times

There are several possible origins for the slowing of RT associated with aging within both the central and peripheral nervous systems. For example, decomposing RT into premotor and motor components provides information as to whether this slowing is central (an increase in premotor time) or peripheral (an increase in motor time) in origin. It has been shown that the elderly tend to exhibit greater increases in premotor rather than motor times. Because the premotor component consists of several central-processing operations such as stimulus identification and encoding, response selection, and response programming, these results only give a general impression of where some of the deficits may be localized. Thus

investigators have sought to explain some of the deficits seen in the elderly in more specific terms.

The ability to maintain preparation of an anticipated movement can be investigated by providing subjects with a movement-related precue stimulus, followed by a preparation maintenance interval of varying lengths prior to an imperative response stimulus. In such experiments, RT provides insight into how well the preparation is maintained. If a movement preparation is well maintained over the delay interval, RT should remain the same across delay intervals. For example, some research has shown that when the elderly are asked to maintain a movement preparation for a short amount of time, only minor differences are observed in comparison to young subjects. However, after a delay of 4 sec, the capability to maintain a movement preparation is reduced substantially for the elderly, as reflected in prolonged response latencies.

Another paradigm that has been used often to localize deficits in the elderly is an altered S-R mapping. When confronted with stimuli that do not contain a high degree of S-R compatibility, the elderly respond with prolonged RTs. In such experimental situations, the subjects must invoke a spatial motor translation in order to initiate the correct response. Thus S-R translations (i.e., initiating a response with the left hand when the visual stimulus was presented on the right visual field) are difficult for older adults. Experiments have shown that the elderly respond slower than the young at low and moderate levels of S-R incompatibility but are disproportionately slower at high levels of S-R incompatibility. These findings support the hypothesis that the elderly have difficulty making spatial-motor translations, with more substantial translations increasing the difficulty experienced.

The elderly have particular difficulty in initiating movements when the number of response choices increases. Increasing the potential number of response alternatives stresses the ability to make rapid response selections. RT performance follows a formulation as published by Hick: $RT = a + b \log N$, where N is the number of choices and a and b are constants. The effect of increasing the number of possible responses on RT is demonstrated in Figure 1. In choice RT tasks the elderly are 30–60% slower in response initiation than younger adults. Some investigations have observed the slope constant b to increase for the elderly compared to the young when the number of choices

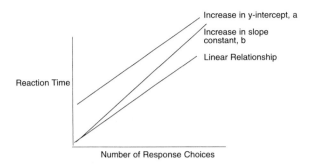

Figure 1 Choice reaction time (RT) and Hick's Law. The linear relationship shown reflects increases in RT with increasing number of response choices for the young. The other two lines represent slowing in response initiation for the elderly.

is increased. This means that stressing response-selection mechanisms affects the elderly disproportionately and implies a reduced information-processing capacity. Other investigators have found the y-intercept, *a*, to increase with increasing task complexity for the elderly. This suggests that the elderly use the same response-processing strategies as the young, but use them at a slower rate. Welford has suggested that the differing factor between the studies finding proportional increases and those finding disproportional increases appears to be related to the exposure time of the stimulus. Research protocols in which proportional increases were found provided a longer time for the subjects to make the appropriate selection. The implication of these results is that the elderly require more time to select the appropriate response. This is consistent with Welford's theory that neural noise increases with age (see section VII. Explanations). This increased neural activity is present throughout the central nervous system (CNS) and makes sensorimotor processing more difficult.

Experiments have been interested in whether the elderly can use precue information that informs them that they are more likely to make one type of a response compared to another. If the subjects use the information, they can preprogram a movement. Thus precues that are correct 75–85% of the time behave much like simple RTs where the probability of making a certain response is 100% (i.e., choice RTs get faster and become more like simple RTs—tasks with no choice component). Using such methods, both young and elderly subjects learn quickly to optimize on the validity of a precue. In other words, they quickly

learn to preprogram their movements based on the probability of the precue being correct. The major difference between age groups is that the elderly do not preprogram as effectively as young subjects. In other words, they do not take advantage of the precue to the same extent.

Response selection capabilities have also been studied in terms of documenting the time delays associated with specifying the dimensions of a movement. Movement specification capabilities can be investigated by providing subjects with either complete, partial, or no advanced information about an upcoming movement. This advanced information, in the form of a precue, allows the subject to preprogram certain aspects of a movement (arm, direction, extent, etc.) prior to the presentation of the stimulus. In complete information trials, the subjects do not have to specify any parameters at the time of the imperative "go" signal. However, in partial precue situations, the subjects must specify the unknown dimensions of the to-be-expected movement at the time of the imperative signal. It has been shown that the elderly are able to use the precue information, but, as displayed in Table I, they take longer than the younger subjects to specify such parameters as arm, direction, and extent of movement. These results suggest that the increases in RT seen in older adults may be partially due to an increased amount of time taken to specify certain movement parameters. Moreover, it has also been shown that the elderly specify the parameters of a movement in a serial (nonoverlapping) manner, whereas the younger subjects do this primarily in parallel.

If using valid precue information is a reflection of preprogramming capabilities, then responding to invalid precues is a reflection of reprogramming capa-

Table I Estimated Time Required to Specify Parameters of Movement for the Young and the Elderly[a]

Age group	Specification times (msec)			
	Extent	Direction	Arm	Mean
Young	18	34	23	25
Elderly	60	77	78	72

[a]Adapted from Stelmach et al. (1987). Movement specification time with age. *Experimental Aging Research, 13,* 39–46.

bility. Assuming that the subjects prepared a response to a high-probability precue, to respond to an invalid (low-probability) precue, they must discard their initial preparation and restructure their movement plan at the time of the imperative response signal. Studies have shown that not only do the elderly not prepare as well as the young, their efforts at restructuring a movement plan take considerably more time than for the young adults. Additional delays arise as more dimensions of a movement must be restructured. These types of paradigms have shown that the elderly are particularly disadvantaged by fully preparing for an anticipated movement as the time cost to modify it when necessary is substantial.

C. Summary

It is evident from the results reviewed in this section that the elderly are slower in response initiation. This slowing is central rather than peripheral in nature. The elderly are disproportionately slowed at high levels of S-R incompability and when confronted with an increasing number of response alternatives. In addition, they have difficulties in maintaining a response preparation and in changing a prepared response when necessary. [*See* REACTION TIME.]

III. GENERAL SLOWING OF MOVEMENTS WITH AGE

Time differences in RT alone do not capture all of the age-related declines in motor performance. Movement time, similar to the measure of RT, provides information regarding sensorimotor processing declines. In comparison to younger subjects, the elderly execute movements approximately 15–30% slower. In addition, they are disproportionately affected by increasing movement difficulty. An example of the effect of increasing difficulty is shown in Figure 2. In 1954, Fitts's law was formulated to establish the relationship between movement time and index of difficulty (ID) for aiming movements of varying amplitudes and target widths: $ID = -\log_2 2A/W$ bits/response, where W is target width and A is movement amplitude. Fitts demonstrated a linear relationship between the time taken to execute a movement and the logarithm of the required relative accuracy. Relative

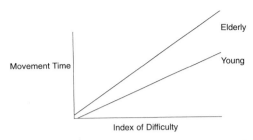

Figure 2 Fitts's Law: Movement duration increases as a function of the index of difficulty for the young and the elderly. The elderly show prolonged movement durations with increments in task difficulty.

accuracy was measured as twice the distance from the starting position to the target center, $2A$, divided by the target width, W. Movements of greater amplitudes to smaller targets take longer. More recently, performance speed for the young and elderly has been compared on tapping tasks requiring movements of three amplitudes and three target widths. The slope of the line relating movement time to index of difficulty increases with age, but not the y-intercept. As seen in Figure 2, the slowing is not in constant increments, but in increasing increments with age, implying that the elderly take considerably longer to execute movements that require greater precision. It is important to distinguish whether this effect represents a difference in movement strategies that might be eliminated by appropriate payoffs and/or training or whether the prolonged movement represents a fundamental limitation of the motor control system present in older adults. An increasingly popular approach to understanding such deficits in the elderly is to systematically examine the kinematics and kinetics that underlie a movement. These types of experiments are described in the next section.

IV. DETERMINANTS OF AGE DIFFERENCES IN DURATION AND CONTROL OF MOVEMENT

The speed–accuracy trade-off exhibited by the elderly and their inability to fully preprogram movements and maintain that preparation contribute to the observed slowing of limb movements. Kinematic analyses of movements further expose fundamental changes, not just slowing, in movement execution between the elderly and the young.

A. Kinematic Changes

As seen in Figure 3, the kinematics of aiming movements can be divided into two components: an acceleration phase, from movement initiation to peak velocity, and a deceleration phase, from peak velocity to the end of the movement. The deceleration phase is seen as a "homing in" on the target. Kinematic investigations have typically required subjects to perform aiming movements such as pointing at a target or using elbow flexion and extension movements to control a manipulandum that positions a cursor at different target locations. The most readily observable difference between the young and the elderly is seen in the velocity curve (Figure 3). Although the young subjects perform movements with symmetrical, bell-shaped profiles, the elderly spend a greater proportion of the movement in the deceleration phase. This effect is intensified as the accuracy requirements of a movement increase, consistent with a speed–accuracy trade-off strategy for the elderly. This lengthening of the deceleration time contributes to the increases in total movement duration. Although the acceleration phase of movements is assumed to be under open-loop control, with no need for feedback information, the deceleration phase is assumed to be under closed-loop control, where error detection and correction information from both motor and sensory systems are used. Because the deceleration phase of movement is lengthened with little changes appearing in the acceleration phase, this deficit may depend on the ability of the elderly to efficiently coordinate sensory and motor information.

In aiming tasks, young subjects typically perform the major portion of the movement as an initial, ballistic primary subcomponent and then employ a shorter, corrective secondary subcomponent to reach the target. Researchers have shown that elderly adults do not project the limb as far during the primary movement component and are therefore required to use a longer secondary subcomponent to reach the target accurately. It is not known why these components exhibit different time profiles for young and elderly subjects. This lengthening of the secondary component may reflect an inability to produce adequate force to rapidly move the limb during the primary component. It

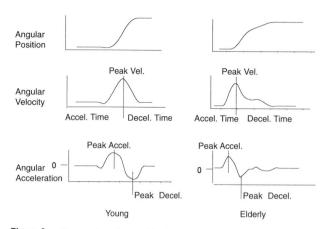

Figure 3 Kinematics of a rapid, aimed movement. Typical results for younger subjects are shown on the left while those for the elderly are on the right. It can be seen that the elderly exhibit a prolonged deceleration phase (time after peak velocity, middle trace) in comparison to the young.

also may be caused by a greater amount of time required to process sensory information regarding position of the arm with respect to the target.

B. Variability of Movements

Compared to younger subjects, the elderly have exhibited greater variability in their movements. Impulse variability theories maintain that discrete movement control consists of applying a sequence of force impulses to displace the limb to a target or object. Variability in the duration and amplitude of the force produces variability in the movement end point. If the initial force pulse does not take the limb to the target region, additional impulses must be applied until the target is reached. The successive episodes of acceleration and deceleration of the limb are referred to as submovements. For simple elbow movements, the elderly exhibit greater variability for short movement amplitudes where the deceleration phase of the movement contains several submovements. The occurrence of high variability in the deceleration phase suggests that the elderly need to make extensive modifications during this final movement.

Research has shown that removal of visual feedback during the movement reveals that the elderly have an increased dependency on visual information. When visual feedback is removed, the variability of the deceleration phase is increased for both young and elderly subjects; however, the effect is more substantial for the elderly. Such data support the notion that the elderly rely on feedback control during the deceleration phase of movements.

C. Scaling of Movements

When younger adults perform movements of differing amplitudes, the temporal features of the movement often remain invariant, thus the relative timing is preserved. It is normal for the motor system to increase acceleration for movements that have longer amplitudes. Thus, as movement duration increases, the ratio of peak velocity to mean velocity remains fairly constant. This suggests that the movement pattern remains invariant and is simply rescaled as the amplitude of movement changes. However, this does not appear to occur with the elderly. In a study requiring elderly subjects to perform elbow flexion and extension of varying amplitudes, the results showed that the elderly exhibited greater variation in the ratio of peak velocity to mean velocity, with the highest ratio values displayed for smaller amplitudes. This ratio is more variable for the elderly subjects, suggesting that the amplitude of their movements cannot be modified by a simple rescaling of the initial impulses.

V. REACH-TO-GRASP MOVEMENTS

In recent years, aging research has increasingly emphasized tasks involved in daily living. The appeal of these functional tasks, such as reaching to grasp an object, is that they stress goal-oriented behavior and are highly practiced. Thus, the data obtained provide a better approximation of how aging affects sensorimotor performance. Prehension research paradigms require subjects to reach and grasp objects using either a whole hand grip (thumb opposite all fingers) for large objects or a precision grip (thumb opposite the index finger) for smaller objects.

A. Inability to Calibrate Force Levels

To perform accurate movements, force production by the muscles must be coordinated with a proper onset timing and amplitude. For young subjects producing rapid aimed movements, the activation sequence used is an alternating cycle of agonist and antagonist mus-

cle activity. However, abnormal antagonist muscle activity has been observed in the elderly. It has been reported that antagonist activity is either not present or activated too early within the movement, leading to considerable cocontraction. In addition, it appears that the elderly use grip forces that are in excess of twice that of young subjects when lifting small objects. These high forces are well above the slip forces required for the objects (measured as the force at which the object begins to slip from grasp). The intertrial variability is higher for the elderly subjects, raising the possibility that intratrial variability of force control may play a role in the excessive grasp forces employed by elderly subjects. However, one researcher did not observe differences in intratrial variability of force between the elderly and the young subjects. The impairment observed appears to be an inability to calibrate afferent information such as tactile sensitivity. The overproduction of force observed undoubtedly impairs the elderly's ability to perform a variety of hand functions requiring dexterity and fine motor control.

B. Lengthening of the Deceleration Phase

Kinematics of both the transport action and the grip aperture of prehension can provide more information about the characteristics of the movement. It appears that, similar to the kinematics of arm aiming movements, the elderly spend a greater amount of time in the deceleration phase of reaching tasks, regardless of the type of grip employed.

C. Coordination of Transport and Manipulation

Coordination of transport and manipulation components in prehension tasks can be examined by correlation coefficients between the amplitude and temporal characteristics of wrist and grip. There is conflicting evidence regarding whether there is a breakdown of coordination in prehension in the elderly. One study has reported such correlations as higher for younger adults than for the elderly, suggesting that the coupling between the two components becomes less stable in older adults. However, another investigation has reported minor changes in coordination of the two components. Nevertheless, both studies showed that, when expressed as a percentage of movement duration, maximum grip aperture occurred earlier for the elderly. The slowing of movement and the longer deceleration times imply that the elderly may rely to a greater extent on on-line feedback, suggesting perhaps a greater emphasis on accuracy. This is further supported by the observation that some elderly subjects slightly close and then reopen the grip aperture during wrist transport. This suggests the elderly may place greater reliance on visual feedback during the reach, consistent with the finding that removal of visual feedback has more of a detrimental effect on the elderly than on the young.

VI. ALTERATIONS IN HANDWRITING CONTROL

The inability to properly modulate force production has also been observed in handwriting. Handwriting is a highly complex motor skill that requires coordination of the fingers, wrist, and arm in many combinations to create individual strokes. The small, rapid movements used are primarily controlled by ballistic muscle contractions and are not affected by inertial, frictional, or gravitational forces. These small amplitude movements do not require an excessive range of motion or high forces. Having subjects write on a digitizing pad allows the quantification of stroke characteristics such as size, duration, and acceleration.

As seen with a handwriting task in Figure 4, the elderly maintain accuracy of stroke size, but show reductions in peak accelerations and stroke durations. These declines suggest that the elderly are not able to produce necessary force levels. However, as the

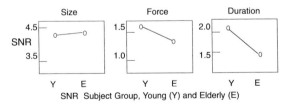

Figure 4 The accuracy (signal-to-noise ratio—SNR) of stroke sizes, peak accelerations (force), and stroke durations in young (Y) and elderly (E) handwriting ($N = 6$). (Adapted from Teulings & Stelmach, 1993). The elderly maintain stroke size (left panel) but show impaired force-generating capabilities (middle panel) resulting in lower stroke durations (right panel).

necessary force levels are quite small, it is not likely that the deficit lies in the inability to produce the appropriate force, but rather to correctly modulate the force production.

A. Summary

It can be seen from this review that, although elderly subjects do execute movements similarly to younger subjects, there are some fundamental differences. The elderly appear to rely more on feedback control, evidenced by longer deceleration phases and pronounced slowing when deprived of visual feedback. Reduced capabilities to produce adequate force levels are seen in handwriting and reaching tasks, although an overproduction of force occurs in precision grip tasks, presumably due to the reduced tactile input from the fingers. These data suggest that declines in motor performance for the elderly are due at least in part to a greater reliance on feedback monitoring, and/or a reduced capability to interpret required sensory information. They may also be further impaired by a decreased availability of sensory information.

VII. EXPLANATIONS OF DECLINES IN MOTOR PERFORMANCE

Explanations of slowing in older adults can be summarized into at least three main categories: (a) older adults produce slower movements in an attempt to minimize error; (b) with advancing age, there is an increase in perceptual noise in the system; (c) with advanced age there is an increase in motor noise in the system. These explanations are not mutually exclusive and probably overlap to some degree in explaining why the elderly make slower movements than younger subjects.

A. Minimizing Error

In all movement tasks, an individual must deal with the issue of speed versus accuracy. As the resulting speed of a movement increases so does the proability of making an error. Faster movements do not always end at intended target locations. For each task situation, a decision is made on how to optimize performance with respect to speed and accuracy. Speed–

accuracy relationships hold for all age groups but older adults choose higher accuracy levels for identical movement situations to minimize error.

B. Increased Perceptual Noise

Older adults are known to have relatively more noise in their visual processing system than younger adults. Such increases in noise are thought to inhibit visually guided feedback capabilities of movement-related information. In motor task situations where some visual guidance is expected, as in the deceleration (or homing in) phase of movement, there would be increased errors from imprecise monitoring and the ensuing corrective movements. This explanation postulates that older adults produce slow movements due to prolonged deceleration phases, a well-documented phenomena associated with movements in the elderly. [See VISION.]

C. Increased Motor Noise

Movement slowing has also been explained by decreases in signal-to-noise ratios (SNRs). This explanation of slowing is based on the assumption that motor noise increases with the amplitude of force generated. This hypothesis implies that when older adults produce a force of a certain level, the noise associated with it is greater than that observed in younger subjects. Thus this argument suggests that older adults produce slower movements than younger subjects because they must move more slowly to achieve the same level of accuracy.

The problem with these explanations is that they are not mutually exclusive. As is apparent, these hypotheses are interrelated and make very similar predictions about motor performance. This is perhaps why it has been so difficult to localize the exact cause of movement slowing in older adults.

VIII. ARE THE OBSERVED DEFICITS TRANSITORY IN NATURE?

Elderly subjects often perform worse on unfamiliar compared to familiar tasks. Such a finding raises the possibility that the observed age differences are not fundamental limitations of the motor system. These limitations should be thought of as transitory effects rather than primary deficits if practice can reduce or eliminate the observed age differences.

A. Reaction Time

RT has been shown to decrease for the elderly after practice; however, speed rarely approaches that of young subjects. Initially, latencies on a complex RT task are disproportionately slower as the task becomes more complex, but the elderly learn to respond faster when confronted with extended practice. After practice, their RT is typically slowed by constant increments as complexity of task increases rather than by increasing increments.

B. Variability of Movement

In some tasks, the elderly have been shown to reduce their variability of performance with practice. As an example, some research has shown that both elderly and young subjects became more accurate at a triangle tracing task that utilized opposition forces between the thumb and index finger over 3 days of practice. The elderly subjects did improve more than the young from day 1 to day 2, but then their performance stabilized by day 3. The young subjects, however, improved in a linear fashion across all three days. Moreover, the elderly have shown reduced movement to movement variability in an arm aiming task after practice. From these two examples it appears that the elderly can reduce the variability in their movements, but typically do not reduce it to the level exhibited by young subjects.

C. Movement Trajectories

There appear to be marginal effects of practice on many of the kinematic features of simple arm movements for the elderly. Young subjects exhibit a decline in the percentage of the movement spent in the deceleration phase and in the variability of arm position at the end of the acceleration phase with practice. The elderly, however, do not demonstrate changes in the acceleration to deceleration phase ratio, even after extended practice.

It appears that practice can be beneficial for improving the motor performance of elderly adults on some tasks. In some cases, the elderly improve at a faster rate than the young. However, performance levels often fail to reach those of younger adults, even after extended practice. This implies that the deficits observed in motor performance are a result of limitations in capacity of the aging motor system.

IX. CONCLUSIONS

It is evident that the elderly exhibit decreased motor performance abilities with advanced aging that may affect their capacity to perform everyday activities. The elderly have difficulties in selecting an appropriate response, specifying movement parameters, and restructuring motor plans when required, all of which contribute to the delays seen in RT. Age-related deficits also appear as a slowing of movement time and in alterations in control that suggest a greater reliance on feedback. An inability to precisely control and modulate force appears to be a limiting factor in a variety of activities such as discrete arm movements as well as complex tasks such as prehension and handwriting. Much of these data imply an increased reliance on feedback control by the elderly, and/or a decreased ability to interpret this feedback information. These reduced capabilities can be somewhat mitigated with practice, but in general performance levels seldom reach those of younger adults.

ACKNOWLEDGMENTS

The preparation of this paper was supported by grants from the Flinn Foundation and National Institutes of Neurological Disease and Strokes grants NS17421 and NS33173 awarded to George E. Stelmach. Dr. Stelmach is a professor of motor control in the Exercise Science Department at Arizona State University, and Rachael Seidler is a graduate student in the same program.

BIBLIOGRAPHY

Amrhein, P. C., Stelmach, G. E., & Goggin, N. L. (1991). Age differences in the maintenance and restructuring of movement preparation. *Psychology and Aging, 6,* 451–466.

Bennett, K. M. B., & Castiello, U. (1994). Reach to grasp: Changes with age. *Journal of Gerontology: Psychological Sciences, 49,* P1–P7.

Brogmus, G. E. (1991). Effects of age and sex on speed and accuracy of hand movements: And the refinements they suggest for Fitts' Law. *Proceedings of the Human Factors Society, 35,* 208–211.

Darling, W. G., Cooke, J. D., & Brown, S. J. (1989). Control of simple arm movements in elderly humans. *Neurobiology of Aging, 10,* 149–157.

Fitts, P. M. (1954). The information capacity of the human motor system in controlling the amplitude of movement. *Journal of Experimental Psychology, 47,* 381–391.

Haaland, K. Y., Harrington, D. L., & Grice, J. W. (1993). Effects of aging on planning and implementing arm movements. *Psychology & Aging, 8,* 617–632.

Hick, W. E. (1952). On the rate of gain of information. *Quarterly Journal of Experimental Psychology, 4,* 11–26.

Pratt, J., Chasteen, A. L., & Abrams, R. A. (1994). Rapid aimed limb movements: Age differences and practice effects in component submovements. *Psychology and Aging, 9,* 325.

Salthouse, T. A. (1985). *A theory of cognitive aging.* In G. E. Stelmach & P. A. Vroon (Eds.), Amsterdam: Elsevier Science Publishers.

Simon, J. R. (1967). Choice reaction time as a function of auditory S-R correspondence, age, and sex. *Ergonomics, 10,* 659–664.

Spirduso, W. W., & Choi, J. H. (1993). Age and practice effects on force control of the thumb and index fingers in precision pinching and bilateral coordination. In G. E. Stelmach & V. Homberg (Eds.), *Sensorimotor impairment in the elderly* (pp. 393–412). Dordrecht: Kluwer Academic Publishers.

Stelmach, G. E., Goggin, N. L., & Garcia-Colera, A. (1987). Movement specification time with age. *Experimental Aging Research, 13,* 39–46.

Teulings, H. L., & Stelmach, G. E. (1993). Signal-to-noise ratio of handwriting size, force, and time: Cues to early markers of Parkinson's disease? In G. E. Stelmach & V. Homberg (Eds.), *Sensorimotor impairment in the elderly* (pp. 311–328). Kluwer Academic Publishers.

Welford, A. T. (1984). Between bodily changes and performance: Some possible reasons for slowing with age. *Experimental Aging Research, 10,* 73–88.

Mythology

Judith de Luce

Miami University

I. Background to Mythology
II. Divine Old Age
III. Human Old Age

Apollodorus   The identity and dates for this Greek author are uncertain, but the *Library* of Apollodorus, which dates somewhere in the mid-first century CE, summarizes Greek mythology. (Ap.)

Apollonius of Rhodes   Third century BCE Greek author of the *Argonautica*, which tells the story of Jason and the Argonauts' search for the Golden Fleece. (Argon.)

Hesiod   (ca. 700 BCE) Greek author of the *Theogony*, a poem on the generations of the Greek gods, and of the *Works and Days*, a poem which includes the Five Ages and the story of Pandora. (Theog.; W and D)

Homer   (ca. 750 BCE) Greek author of the *Iliad*, which covers part of the last year of the Trojan War, beginning with the quarrel between Agamemnon and Achilles and ending with the death of Trojan Hector. (Il.) Homer's *Odyssey* follows Odysseus from Troy through ten years of wandering until he arrives home to find his house occupied by suitors after his wife Penelope's hand and his estate. (Od.)

Livy   (59 BCE–CE 17) Latin author of a history of Rome, the first five books of which cover Rome's earliest history from its founding to the Gauls' attack on Rome in 390 BCE. These books include some of the most important stories from Roman mythology and legend. (Livy)

Ovid   (43 BCE–CE 17) Latin poet whose *Metamorphoses* contains over 250 stories ostensibly focusing on transformation myths. The poem includes a significant proportion of Classical mythology. (Met.)

The *Fasti* is a calendar of Roman festivals and rituals. (Fasti)

Tragedy   Traditionally, Athenian tragedy was based on stories from mythology. The extant tragedies were composed by Aeschylus (524–456 BCE), Sophocles (496–406 BCE), and Euripides (485–406 BCE). (Aesch.; Soph.; Eur.)

Vergil   (70–19 BCE) Latin author of the *Aeneid*, which follows Aeneas from his escape from burning Troy to his landing in Italy where he is destined to establish the family which will found Rome. (Aen.)

Relatively few Greco-Roman **MYTHS** feature old characters of any significance or reveal anything about old age. That the gods are identified as ageless and deathless should suggest immediately how the Greeks and Romans regarded growing old. Substantially more old men appear in myth than old women, due in part to the preponderance of heroic sagas that feature male warriors. Four stories provide the most examples: the stories of Thebes, the Trojan War, the return of Odysseus, and Aeneas. On the basis of myths that either take aging as their theme or which present well-developed pictures of old persons, old age was primarily a time to be dreaded, a time marked by physical infirmity, loss, hardship, poverty, and grief. In some myths, it is not clear whether old age, gender, or class is the most salient factor in life; in some all three are intimately connected. Mythology provides examples of elders who are valued for their morality or their experience. Elders are often identified with prophecy, although it is not unusual to find their advice disregarded or belittled by their juniors, often to their peril. Myth also presents elders who call upon immense resources of strength and courage in crises, including old women capable of exacting extraordinary vengeance.

I. BACKGROUND TO MYTHOLOGY

A. Mythology, Legend, and Folktale

Mythology by its very nature provides a unique window onto a culture. Greek and Roman mythology not only reflects these two particular cultures, but many of the images of old age that occur in these myths have become part of Western tradition.

Originally, there was no sharp distinction between *mythos* (speech or narrative) and *logos* (argument or reason) but the dichotomy between the two developed between the eighth and fourth centuries BCE, helped in part by the change from oral to written literature. Within Western tradition, definitions of myth came to be stated in terms of what myth was not: myth was not true, myth was not logical. Yet myths are neither lies nor are they merely amusing stories of relatively little importance. On the contrary, myths often provide the truest and most serious accounts that a culture can give of itself. Moreover, myths reflect a culture's fears and expectations.

Although there is no absolute definition of myth to suit all occasions, a working definition is possible. A myth is a traditional story, a narrative set in the distant past that explains what cannot be explained any other way. It presents a model of the world and humankind's relation to it. The actors in a myth may be divine or superhuman. Like legends and folktales, myths tend to ignore the usual rules of time, space, and cause and effect. Because traditional stories are seldom the product of a single individual, one cannot identify an original author of a particular myth.

Legend and folktale are also traditional stories, but although they share some features with myth, they are also distinct from it. A legend is a narrative with a kernel of historical fact, although that kernel may be very small indeed. This kind of story focuses on human achievement and may be regarded by a people as part of their ancient history. A folktale is a story told in part to entertain. It often appeals to the underdog; the teller wants the listener to identify with the hero, who is often an ordinary person. Folktales often reflect social situations, although no one would claim

that the characters in folktale ever actually existed, unlike the characters in legend. Although all three kinds of traditional stories can be found separately, it is not uncommon for a single narrative to contain elements of all three.

B. Sources of Mythology

There are a variety of sources for Greek and Roman mythology. Archaeological remains and the visual arts provide some evidence for the popular traditions that gave rise to myths. Rituals may suggest the myths that provide the narrative for religious or secular observance. Ancient painting and sculpture frequently illustrate identifiable myths, although almost none of the myths depicted have anything to do with old age. In fact, with the exception of a few Greek vase paintings, some sculpture, and Roman portraits, representations of old age are almost entirely absent from extant Greek and Roman art. The most significant source by far is literary, from ancient mythology handbooks to every literary genre. [*See* IMAGES OF AGING.]

Many literary adaptations of mythology are so far removed from the original that the interpretation of the myths poses formidable challenges to the expert and general reader alike. One must distinguish between the actual myth and the literary expression of that myth. It is rarely the case in mythology that what you see is what you get, and even in antiquity a variety of interpretative models were developed. This article must rely almost exclusively on cataloging a variety of Greek and Latin literary adaptations of mythology with little regard for the differences in sources; the catalog must also be illustrative rather than exhaustive. This is not the place to attempt a full analysis of a literary work, to include multiple versions, or to attempt to distinguish the earliest version of a myth from its various incarnations. [*See* LITERARY REPRESENTATIONS OF AGING.]

C. Distinguishing Greek from Roman Myth

Finally, some distinctions must be made between Greek and Roman mythology. The greatest body of myth that matches the working definition belongs to the Greeks and was shared by the Romans. Greek mythology was itself influenced by stories from cultures that the Greeks encountered, including those in Africa and the Near and Middle East. The Greeks and the Romans were very different peoples with different languages and different cultures. Some scholars label Roman mythology "pseudo-mythology," in partial recognition of the striking differences between the stories that the Romans tell about themselves, and the Greek stories that they adopted. Roman mythology often does not involve stories about the gods or superhuman beings. Rather, it comes much closer to legend and folktale, often including a moral or a lesson on what it means to be a Roman. Roman myth is more self-conscious than Greek myth and often much younger; it is sometimes possible to identify when a Roman myth was actually started. Finally, Roman myth like Roman literature and much of Roman art tends to be intimately connected with Roman politics.

II. DIVINE OLD AGE

Although the gods are generally characterized as ageless and deathless, several gods are depicted as old, and some gods disguise themselves as old persons. The very few gods in the pantheon of either the Greeks or the Romans who are actually portrayed as old are almost exclusively male. Saturn, an ancient Roman god, is often equated with the Greek Cronus. In some accounts the Golden Age was also the Age of Saturn. Nereus and Proteus are each called the Old Man of the Sea. Nereus is regarded as kind and just; he is also prophetic and like other sea deities is able to change his appearance. Heracles seeks him out to find the way to the gardens of the Hesperides. Proteus, too, is famous for being able to change his shape at will; and like Nereus, he is prophetic. After the fall of Troy, Menelaus must wrestle with him in order to find out how to get home to Sparta. In Vergil's *Georgics 4*, 315–558 Aristaeus learns from him how to restore his swarm of bees.

Charon, the ferryman who takes the shades of the dead across the rivers in the Underworld is also an old god. When Vergil describes Charon as old in *Aeneid* 6.304 however, he says that the old age of a god is "green," that is, vigorous and vital. The comparison with the old age of a mortal is obvious if unremarked. Literary descriptions and visual representations of mortal old age tend to emphasize diminished strength, wasted muscles, unsteady gaits, wrinkles, gray hair, thin hair, diminished eyesight, and vulnerability.

Among the distinctly Roman gods, as opposed to the gods in the Roman pantheon who are derived in part from Greek models, Anna Perrenna personifies the yearly cycle. Depicted as an old woman, she was celebrated on the Ides of March with picnics, drinking, and girls singing ribald songs in her honor. According to one account, Anna was an old woman who baked and distributed bread to the starving people during the secession of the Plebs. In gratitude, they erected a statue to her. There is also a story that she tricked Mars, who was pressing her to persuade Minerva to marry him. As a mortal and in her worship as a god, Anna Perenna's vitality stands out (*Fasti* 3.523–542; 6.657–696).

The Erinyes or Furies are female avenging deities most closely associated with the protection of the family or clan and thus often closely associated with women. They are of a generation of gods older than the Olympians and may appear as old. Probably best known for their appearance in Aeschylus' *Eumenides*, they were feared for the horrible vengeance that they exact from those who violate the family.

The Graeae fit neither with the gods nor, really, with mortals. The two or three sisters are the daughters of Phorcys and related to such monsters as Echidna. Old from birth, they share one tooth and one eye. As with the old gods, the Graeae possess valuable information. The hero Perseus steals the eye and the tooth from them until they reveal to him the whereabouts of the nymphs who will provide him with the magic implements he needs to behead the Gorgon Medusa (Ap. 2.4.2).

Although not strictly gods, the Sileni are not strictly human either, because they are satyrs. One of them, Silenus, is the companion and in some versions the foster father of Dionysus. He is sometimes shown as a vigorous man in his prime, but more commonly he appears in art as a drunken old man, an opportunity for jokes, perhaps sleeping or falling off his donkey. Like Nereus and Proteus, he is also prophetic and is consulted by Midas (Ap. 7.5.4; Met. 11.89–101).

Throughout mythology the gods assume disguises. Athena dons the disguise of old age in the story of Arachne. When Arachne boasts that she is a better weaver than the goddess Athena, even refusing to acknowledge that she learned her skill from that deity, Athena disguises herself as an old woman and confronts the mortal. Presumably she is able to gain access to Arachne precisely because she is an old woman and therefore cannot be regarded as threatening, although there are enough vengeful old women in myth who might challenge this presumption. The gray-haired Athena warns Arachne that not everything associated with old age should be avoided. In fact, old age brings experience that the younger woman should pay attention to; she should not antagonize the god. But Arachne arrogantly dismisses the old woman, arguing that she has lived too long, that her mind has gone. She treats old age with disdain very much as the suitors in the *Odyssey* do. Rebuffed, the infuriated Athena reveals herself in her true form and the two enter into the weaving contest that will end in Arachne's transformation into a spider (Met. 6.1–145).

In a variation on the motif of the mortal woman raped by a god, Vertumnus, the Roman fertility god associated with the seasons, tries to win over Pomona, a deity of fruit trees, who has tried to remain a virgin and has resisted all proposals of marriage. He gains access to Pomona by disguising himself as a frail old woman, gray-haired, walking with the help of a stick. She advises Pomona to think carefully about her resistance to marriage and argues for Vertumnus's suitability as a spouse. Presumably Vertumnus adopted this disguise because an old woman would not be threatening to Pomona, and because she would not be surprised that an old woman would advise her about marriage. While Pomona does not attack or insult the old woman, as Arachne had done in a different situation, it is really the undisguised beauty of Vertumnus that wins her over in the end, not the old woman's advice (Met. 14.642–771).

In the *Homeric Hymn to Demeter*, the goddess, in deep mourning over the abduction of Persephone, disguises herself as an old woman and abandons the company of the gods. An old woman, Iambe or Baubo, tries to cheer up the grieving stranger by telling her ribald jokes and dancing obscene dances. In the few moments that Demeter laughs, the dormant earth begins to grow again until Demeter resumes her grief. At Eleusis, the daughters of the king take pity on the old woman and find her a job appropriate to her age and experience as nursemaid to their infant brother. Unlike Arachne, these young women respect the old woman's dignity and seek to relieve her suffering.

Hera disguises herself as an old woman to trick Semele, pregnant by the philandering Zeus, into demanding that he appear to her in his true form. When he complies, Semele is incinerated because he appears as a lightning bolt. As with other stories, the old woman clearly is a safe disguise because she is not regarded as a threat to anyone (Met. 3.261–286; Ap. 3.4.3).

III. HUMAN OLD AGE

A. The General View

In the *Works and Days* (109–201), Hesiod describes the history of humankind in terms of five ages or races. The Golden Age was the first and the best of the five. Humans lived comfortably. They did not have to labor for their livelihoods because the earth provided whatever they needed. "Wretched" old age did not exist. In fact, humans did not actually grow old and die. Rather, when it was time for them to die, they simply fell asleep. In the Silver Age, childhood lasted a century, and when humans had finally matured, they did not live very long. Hesiod says nothing about age in his description of the violent Bronze Age or the Age of Demigods, the time of the heroes who fought at Thebes and at Troy. Hesiod laments that he was born in the Iron Age, an age of violence and the destruction of traditional values. He predicts a final degeneration of humans to the point that children will be born already gray-haired. At the end of the Iron Age guests will not be safe from their hosts, and parents and children will conspire against one another. In fact, children will not honor their aged parents or repay them for the care they provided.

Ovid also describes the ages of humankind, reducing the total to four. His Golden Age is a time of eternal spring, and, following tradition, it is a time when humans do not have to practice agriculture, when there is no shipping or commerce. In his Iron Age, as in Hesiod's, things have deteriorated so much that greedy sons even plot the deaths of their fathers (Met. 1.89–150).

In the myth of Prometheus, Zeus created Pandora as a punishment for humans. Before Pandora, humans had been able to live off the earth's bounty without labor; they had been free of pain and sickness and old age. All that changed when the woman opened the jar given her by the gods, releasing all the ills of human experience including old age into the world (Theog. 510–610; W and D 47–105).

Vergil, too, counts old age among human cares

when he describes the vestibule in the Underworld, in the sixth book of the *Aeneid* (6.275). Vergil pictures "sad Age" along with grief, disease, dread, hunger, poverty, hardship, labor, and death.

The prevailing attitude toward old age underlies stories that view old age as punishment or which concern rejuvenation. For example, Zeus punishes Phineus with blindness and a long and painful old age. The Argonauts discover him starving to death because each time he tries to eat the food placed on his table, the Harpies foul the food so that it is inedible (Argon. 2.178–489).

Iolaus, the nephew of Heracles, was instrumental in his uncle's killing of the Lernaean Hydra (Ap. 2.5.2, 2.6.1; Met. 9.397; Eur., Heracleidae). After Heracles' death, the aged Iolaus tries to defend Heracles' children but must be rejuvenated or at least temporarily invigorated to enable him to do so. Medea avenges Jason's mistreatment at the hands of Pelias by persuading his daughters to kill Pelias and place their father's bloodless body in a cauldron of mage herbs (Ap. 1.9.26–27). Medea persuades the daughters with her claim that she can rejuvenate him. Clearly long life is not the problem, old age is.

Within the context of a tradition that regarded old age as hateful and that equated old age with death, Odysseus' rejection of Calypso's offer to make him immortal and ageless underscores his heroism. Given the choice of returning home to Ithaca at least, or remaining on Calypso's island forever, untroubled by toil or old age or death, Odysseus chooses to go home. In fact, Odysseus will enjoy a comfortable old age, as Teiresias predicts (Od. 5.136, 209–224; 11.119–137).

B. Physical Frailty

The motif of the grasshopper appears in several stories and suggests a metaphor for old age. Its sound, high-pitched and incessant, even annoying, emanates from a fragile insect; in some traditions the grasshopper was supposed to be especially short-lived. In the third book of the *Iliad*, Homer describes the old men of Troy, sitting along the city walls watching the battle. Homer says that the sound of their conversation was like the sound of grasshoppers; that is, they were not physically strong, perhaps, but their speech remained lively.

The image is closely tied to the story of the Trojan youth Tithonus who was loved by Eos, the amorous goddess of the Dawn. Eos asked Zeus that her mortal lover be made immortal but failed to request eternal youth for him as well. As he aged and grew increasingly feeble, the goddess lost interest in him and shut him away, although she continued to feed him ambrosia (Hom. Hymn to Aphrodite 5.218–238). Finally, all that remained of him emanating from the chamber was his voice. According to one tradition, he was finally transformed into a grasshopper (Scholiast to Il. 11.1).

Finally, in Petronius's *Satyricon*, Trimalchio recounts a youthful experience to his dinner guests. He claims to have seen the great Cumaean Sibyl, one of the most famous seers of Apollo. The Sibyl was supposed to have lived for one thousand years. Tradition says that Apollo sought her when she was a young woman and tried to bribe her by promising her a gift. She tricked Apollo by asking for as many years of life as grains in a handful of sand; however, she did not think to ask for lasting youth any more than Eos had. She was so old by the time Trimalchio saw her that she had shriveled up no bigger than a grasshopper and was hanging in a jar. When asked what she wanted, she said that she wanted to die (48.8).

C. Moral Strength

Mythology presents three noteworthy elderly couples: Baucis and Philemon, Cadmus and Harmony, and Priam and Hecuba. Of these, only Baucis and Philemon present a picture of an affectionate, lifelong relationship unmarred by tragedy. Jupiter and Mercury disguise themselves as humans and walk the earth to test humankind. In each house they are refused the hospitality that the rules of guest friendship require. Only Baucis and her husband Philemon welcome these strangers, unaware that they have received gods into their home. They are a poor couple, and frail, but entertain the gods from their meager supply of food. The gods drown the rest of the neighborhood but save these two and reward them by making them priests. They also grant the couple a wish. Because they have lived together for so long and because it would be too painful for one to survive the other, Baucis and Philemon request that they die at precisely the same moment. They not only die simultaneously, but they are transformed into an oak tree and a linden tree that continue to grow side by side (Met. 8.618–724).

D. Elders as Advisers

Elders are not the only ones to practice prophesy, but some old mortals are prophetic, as are some of the gods. For example, Pittheus, Theseus' grandfather and king of Troezen, was well known for his intelligence and his ability to interpret even the most ambiguous oracles.

The great Theban seer Teiresias usually appears as a blind old man, though his younger years spent as a woman are noteworthy. There is more than one version of the story explaining his blindness, his old age, and his prophetic power. Teiresias must deal with three arrogant, younger men who are kings of Thebes, who initially ignore his advice, and whose actions prove catastrophic: Oedipus probes into the death of Laius, the previous king of Thebes and Oedipus's actual father; Creon forbids the burial of Polynices and buries Antigone alive after Oedipus's death; and Pentheus forbids the worship of Dionysus in Thebes. Teirseias urges the young king to acknowledge the divinity of the Dionysus as Teiresias has, but Pentheus pays no more attention to Teiresias' warning than the others had (Soph., Oedipus Tyrannus, Antigone, Eur., Bacchae; Met. 3.513). Teiresias keeps his wits even in death in *Odyssey* Book 11; Circe instructs Odysseus to seek the shade of Teiresias for advice on how to get home to Ithaca. Although Teiresias never does give Odysseus all the specific information he seeks, the seer does tell him what his old age will be like.

Mythology often presents elders in the ambiguous position of enjoying respect for their experience and the traditions which they represent, but at the same time having their advice ignored or discounted. Peleus had entrusted the education of Achilles to the aged and childless Phoenix who accompanies Achilles to Troy. He is the third emissary sent to Achilles to try to persuade the young warrior to return to battle after he had withdrawn, insulted by Agamemnon. When Achilles refuses the embassy, Phoenix chooses to remain with him. That he was included in the embassy suggests the faith the Greeks had in the appeal he alone could make to Achilles even though the embassy failed (Il. 168–661; 17.553–566).

Nestor was supposed to have lived seven generations. In the *Iliad* he led Greek troops to Troy, where he not only compared that generation unfavorably with the earlier generations he had fought with, but where he acted as an adviser to the Greeks. Once back in Greece, he entertained Odysseus's son, advising Telemachus who has left Ithaca in search of news of his father (Od. 3). Although he clearly is not without honor and is respected for his accomplishments in the past, his long-winded advice is not always apt and there is no assumption with him or anyone else that elders are necessarily wise.

Aeneas's departure from burning Troy is especially famous as the intergenerational embodiment of the Roman virtue *pietas* (devotion to the state, the family, and the gods). The hero had left carrying his aged father on his shoulders and leading his young son by the hand. (Aen. 2.707–725) Anchises had carried statues of the household gods. Anchises died when they reached Sicily; Aeneas needs the guidance of his father even in death and in *Aeneid* 6 descends to the Underworld to see his shade. Anchises encourages his son, a reluctant hero at best, by showing him the future of Rome. Aeneas emerges from seeing his father arguably better equipped emotionally to fulfill his destiny.

E. Elders in Action

Although elders may not be as physically vigorous as they had once been, they may like Iolaus provide more than advice when action is required. In the latter half of the *Odyssey* the old goatherd Eumaeus, for example, plays a central figure in effecting Odysseus's vengeance on the suitors who are harassing his wife, have threatened the life of his son, and are eating up his wealth. Homer describes him in some detail, including the care he has taken to preserve and nurture the holdings of his master.

Eurycleia, Odysseus's old nursemaid, also aids him. She recognizes him in spite of his disguise as a beggar when she sees a telltale scar on his leg. Ferociously loyal to Odysseus, Eurycleia relishes the coming confrontation with the suitors, aids Odysseus in his plans, and informs on the maidservants who have betrayed their master's home (19.350–507).

Alcmena shares Eurycleia's enthusiasm for vengeance. After the death of Heracles, she joins Iolaus in his efforts to protect her grandchildren from Eurystheus, the king who had persecuted Heracles. In the accounts of Eurystheus's death, Alcmena's vengeance is brutal; she either gouges out his eyes after he was beheaded, or she demands his execution (Eur. Heracleidae).

Although the stories in the *Aeneid* rely on Vergil's manipulation of traditions from Greece as well as Rome, the Romans also tell stories that do not involve the gods and that serve as their ancient history. Most do not involve individuals who are old, but the story of Coriolanus includes an old woman acting in the interests of Rome. Her effectiveness may be due as much to her relation to a warrior as to her age. After the revolt of the people, which resulted in the secession of the Plebs, the arrogant Roman general Coriolanus had conspired with the Volscians against Rome. Coriolanus's wife and aged mother, accompanied by other women, sought to stop the ensuing war. Coriolanus's mother confronted her son, upbraiding him for his treachery against Rome. So chastened was he by his mother's courage and criticism, that he abandoned his attack on Rome and went into exile (Livy 2.33.5, 2.40.1–12). Coriolanus's mother acted very much within the tradition of Roman women, young and old, whose actions directly effect Roman politics.

F. Parents and Children

Regardless of whatever else they may be or do, elders often appear in their roles as parents; as parents, they appear most frequently mourning the deaths of their children. This motif underscores a number of things: the blighting of the promise of young people in the family; the horror of seeing one's own children die before oneself; the vulnerability of aging parents without children alive to provide them with care; in some cases the end of the family itself. The aged king of Athens, Aegeus, commits suicide when he thinks that his son Theseus has not survived the labyrinth and the Minotaur (Catullus 64).

Odysseus's parents suffer acutely from the war at Troy. When he goes to see the shade of Teiresias, Odysseus discovers the shade of his mother, Anticleia, who had been alive when he left Ithaca. She had died of grief while her son was at Troy (Od. 11). His father Laertes, unwell and grief-stricken at the death of his wife and at the failure of his son to return from Troy, had withdrawn to live in the country among his slaves. There he lived in squalor with a single slave to care for him. He had abandoned Odysseus's home, wife, and young son to the ravages of the suitors seeking

Penelope's hand in Odysseus's absence (Od. 11.195–196; 15.348–355; 16.142–145).

Scholars have often argued that the *Odyssey* is the epic of an old man, and that that may account for many of the differences between it and the *Iliad*. The frequency of aged persons in the epic may be related to the age of the author but also to the preponderance of folktale in the epic, because folktale tends to reflect social situations and involves the actions of ordinary people. The recurrence of old people and old age extends even to Odysseus's dog Argos. When Odysseus first arrives home, he does not go completely unrecognized. As Odysseus enters the courtyard of his house, he sees his old hunting dog lying on a dung heap, close to death. Argos, flea bitten and nearly blind, recognizes his master, lifts his head, and tries to wag his tail. Odysseus must pretend that he does not recognize the dog, because that would reveal his true identity, so he turns away just as the dog dies. The loyal dog had been grieving for his missing master just as Anticleia and Laertes had grieved for their missing son. The poignancy of Argos's death just as Odysseus returns reflects the sadness of old age, which appears throughout mythology (Od. 17.290–327).

In the course of Aeneas seeking allies in Italy, the Arcadian king Evander entrusts his young son Pallas to him so that the boy can learn to be a warrior, but Pallas is killed by Turnus (Aen. 8.454–607, 11.139–81). All of this may be an invention of Vergil's, but within the context of the second half of the *Aeneid*, it continues the motif of the enormous cost of founding Rome. The parents' presence and grief at the deaths of their children underscore the terrible loss as much as the vulnerability of aging parents without children to care for them.

The mourning parents in mythology tend to be fathers, but there are mourning mothers as well. Although the Trojans are fighting the Rutulians and their allies, proverbial friends Nisus and Euryalus set out on a dangerous night mission for Aeneas. No faint-hearted old woman, Euryalus's mother had dared to travel all the way from Troy to Italy with him. Before he leaves, Euryalus entrusts the care of his mother to Ascanius, Aeneas' son. Euryalus's death and the mother's grief reflects among other things the very real vulnerability of an aged mother alone in a strange land, without the support of a husband or a son (9.176–502).

Several of the myths have reflected what we know

from the laws of the Greeks and the Romans, that children, especially sons, were expected to provide care for their parents. The story of Alcestis provides a very different perspective on the relationship between parents and children and the obligations of each. The young king of Pherae, Admetus, was the eldest son of Pheres and famous for his piety. When Admetus fell seriously ill, Apollo promised him that he would not have to die if he could persuade someone to die for him. In Euripides' *Alcestis*, Admetus's father Pheres refuses to die for his son. Pheres argues that there is no law that says that a young man should die for his father, or a father for his son. Pheres rejects Admetus's argument that an old man who has already lived his life should give up what remains of that life in favor of a younger person. Admetus cannot persuade anyone to take his place; in the end his wife Alcestis determines to die for him in part to spare the old parents the loss of their son.

G. The Complex Picture of Old Age

Several of the myths that deal with old age provide portraits of some complexity. The aged Cadmus, founder of Cadmeia, later called Thebes, had made a name for himself well before he encountered Dionysus. All four daughters lived tragic lives, although his son fared well. His grandchildren were no happier than their mothers. Cadmus hands over the kingship of Thebes to his young grandson. Although he cannot persuade Pentheus to acknowledge the divinity of his cousin Dionysus, Cadmus himself joins Teiresias in worshipping the newly arrived god. Dionysus is not satisfied, however, and drives Cadmus into exile (Eur. Bacchae; Ap. 3.4.4). Cadmus and his wife Harmony abandon Thebes for Illyria, where they inspire the Encheleans in battle. At the end of their lives they become serpents.

In the *Aeneid*, Latinus, king of Laurentium, cannot receive Aeneas as son-in-law until the resolution of the war precipitated by his wife, who supports another man as husband for their daughter. The aged king cannot control the situation or do what he believes is right.

Priam and Hecuba display formidable courage as they face the fall of Troy. According to some accounts, Priam would have settled with the Greeks who came to retrieve Helen from Paris, but his sons were unwilling to make a deal.

In spite of their authority and status, Priam and Hecuba are as vulnerable as other aging parents. They witness the deaths of most of their children, including Hector who dies at the hands of Achilles. Tradition says that Priam finally went alone to the Greek camp to ransom the body of Hector from his killer (Il. 24). The grieving father appeals to Achilles' love for his own aged father, alive when he left Greece, and there are visual as well as literary representations of the old man kissing the hand of the man who had killed his son.

This scene mirrors the ransom scene that begins the *Iliad*, although this time the child to be ransomed is not dead. There, an elderly priest of Apollo, Chryses, unsuccessfully tries to negotiate with Agamemnon for the return of his daughter. Agamemnon's refusal to honor the old man's request leads to the quarrel with Achilles, which in turn sets in motion those events that will ultimately see Hector killed by Achilles and then, of course, Achilles' own death.

Priam's death is memorable as well, for it is the son of Achilles who kills Priam even as he clings to the altar of Zeus. Vergil's account of Priam's death is striking for the combination of the pathetic, Priam struggling into his armor as if a much younger man, and the courageous, as Priam upbraids Neoptolemus for his barbarism, so different from the integrity of Achilles himself (Aen. 2.506–558).

If Priam's ransoming the body of Hector captures much of the essence of his character and the precarious position in which he finds himself as an old man, Hecuba may be best characterized as mourning mother and fierce avenger (Met. 13.404, Eur. Trojan Women, Hecuba). She tries to dissuade Priam from approaching Achilles after Hector's death; indeed, in Homer she wishes she could tear Achilles' liver out with her teeth. She sees Priam murdered, her grandson thrown from the walls of Troy, her daughter Polyxena sacrificed on the tomb of Achilles, another daughter, the seer Cassandra, torn from the altar of Athena and taken as slave by the Greek leader Agamemnon. Her losses are not exclusively a product of her old age, although she has much to lose in part because she has lived long enough to acquire possessions and status. Not only has she lost her family, her city, her stature as queen, but she is given to Odysseus to be taken back to Ithaca as a slave. In Euripides, she provides comfort and leadership for the other Trojan women waiting to be taken as slaves to Greece. When Hecuba discovers the body of her remaining son Polydorus, who had been sent for safe keeping, along with considerable wealth, to a friend, her vengeance recalls that of Alcmena. Hecuba lures her "friend" Polymestor into her tent, where she blinds him and kills his infant sons. In the end, brutalized by the war and her losses, Hecuba turns into a howling dog. Hecuba represents the uncertainty of life as well as the Greek conviction that at the end of life terrible things can happen. She also represents the complexity of old age—its loss, vulnerability, danger, and hardship, but also its cunning, courage, and determination. Her transformation into a dog becomes a metaphor for the brutalization of war and for the grim realities of old age.

Oedipus may well be the best known old man from Greek and Roman mythology, in part because of the fame of Sophocles' plays about him, in part because his story is intimately connected to a riddle that has implications for a concept of the life span. According to tradition, the Sphinx sat outside of Thebes and asked passersby a riddle. If they could not answer the riddle, she killed and ate them. In its simplest form, the Sphinx asked: What has one voice and is four-footed, two-footed, and three-footed? What goes slowest when it has the most feet? Oedipus answered that the riddle fit human experience, because infancy goes on all fours, maturity on two feet, and old age with the help of a cane (the third "foot.") At hearing the correct answer, the Sphinx killed herself. The answer may imply that to some degree the human life span is circular; that is, it begins in dependency in childhood and returns to dependency in old age.

Oedipus himself does not match precisely the implications of the riddle. When the aged Oedipus finds his way to the Grove of the Eumenides at Colonus, outside of Athens, at the end of his life, he shows the strain of years of poverty in exile. He is feeble, sometimes querulous, utterly reliant on the aid of his daughter Antigone and the news and information provided by his second daughter, Ismene. Yet this Oedipus is still very much the man he was when he answered the riddle: he is smart, determined, staunchly protective of his daughters, and curses the sons who have done nothing to help him in his exile. The chorus in *Oedipus at Colonus* (1211–1248) reveals prevailing ancient attitudes that old age is above all a time of hardship, failing health, deprivation, and loss. Yet at the very end of his life, the lame, blind old man walks unaided to his death. Thus, the story of Oedipus embodies the complexity of the mythological representation of old age as a time of loss and vulnerability, but also a time of dignity and action.

BIBLIOGRAPHY

Falkner, T. (1995). *The poetics of old age in Greek epic, lyric, and tragedy.* Norman, OK: University of Oklahoma Press.

Falkner, T., & de Luce, J. (Ed.). (1989). *Old age in Greek and Latin literature.* Albany: State University of New York Press.

Falkner, T., & de Luce J. (1992). A view from antiquity: Greece, Rome, and Elders. In T. R. Cole, D. D. Van Tassel & R. Kastenbaum (Eds.), *Handbook of the humanities and aging.* New York: Springer Publishing Company.

Gardner, J. (1993). *Roman myths.* Austin, TX: University of Texas Press.

Powell, B. B. (1995). *Classical myth.* Englewood Cliffs, NJ: Prentice Hall.

Roscher, W. H. (1965). *Ausfuhrliches Lexikon der Griechischen und Romischen Mythologie.* G. Olms. Hidesheim (Rprt. 1884–1937. Teubner, B. G. ed. Leipzig.)

Rose, H. J. (1959). *A handbook of Greek mythology.* New York: E. P. Dutton & Co., Inc.

Tripp, E. (1970). *The Meridian handbook of classical mythology.* New York: Meridian.

Network Analysis

Marjolein Broese van Groenou and Theo van Tilburg

Vrije Universiteit, Amsterdam, The Netherlands

I. Aging and the Personal Network
II. Personal Network Delineation
III. Features of the Personal Network
IV. Full Networks
V. Methods of Network Analysis
VI. Summary and Conclusions

Anchor The central person within the network; the person providing information on who belongs to his or her network.

Full Personal Network Network in which information is available on all the network relationships; in most cases the information is collected from all the network members; also referred to as complete network.

Network Analysis Analytical methods used to compute measures of network structure and content.

Network Content The type of interaction that takes place within pairs of network members.

Network Delineation Procedure used to identify the personal network.

Network Structure Aspects of the total network derived from combining features of individual relationships and the linkages between these relationships.

Personal Network The group of persons (network members) with whom anchor has a direct relationship.

Star Personal Network Network in which information is available on relationships between network members and the focal individual; in most cases the information is collected from the focal individual; also referred to as egocentric network.

The personal networks of older people reflect their social opportunities and personal choices to maintain a specific set of relationships with relatives, neighbors, friends, acquaintances, and so on. **NETWORK ANALYSIS** is the method used to identify and examine the structural and functional features of the network of the older adult. The conceptualization and operationalization of the personal network depend on the subject of research. Five approaches to define personal network membership are presented and discussed. The five approaches differ regarding the part of the personal network that is mapped, and result in networks of different sizes and compositions. Regardless of the type of network delineation, a distinction can be drawn between the star network (data available on relationships with the focal person) and the full network (data available on all the network relationships). Features of the structure and content of both types of personal networks are presented. Finally, network analysis methods are presented and discussed, including ways to analyze hierarchical databases.

I. AGING AND THE PERSONAL NETWORK

A. The Personal Network of Older Adults: An Introduction

The personal network occupies an important place in the lives of individuals. The mere existence of a certain number of relationships has been shown to have beneficial effects; regular interaction with network members (children, relatives, neighbors, friends, and fellow members of organizations) enhances the feeling of being socially integrated and decreases feelings of loneliness. The positive effects of the network are also reflected in better health and a longer life. [*See* SOCIAL NETWORKS, SUPPORT, AND INTEGRATION.]

Old age has often been associated with loneliness and with social isolation. However, numerous studies have shown over the past decades that the large majority of older adults has at least a few relationships available. The networks of older people usually enclose both kin and nonkin with whom regular contact is maintained. In general, the core of the network consists of close kin (e.g., spouse and children, siblings, parents) and close friends. Depending on the identification method of the network, other network members as extended kin, neighbors, co-workers, acquaintances, members from organizations and so on, may also be identified. The younger old who are socially active in many parts of society and who experience few physical restrictions in general have large networks that are composed of a large number of nonkin. The oldest old, who often experienced life transitions as widowhood, retirement, and a decline in physical mobility, usually have smaller networks that enclose network members that are emotionally close (children, friends) or geographically close (neighbors). [*See* LONELINESS.]

In addition to the mere presence of relationships, interaction with others is important for daily functioning, coping with life events and maintaining well-being. Feelings, information, services, material goods, and so on can be exchanged between two individuals. These exchanges are often assumed to be supportive in nature. The support provided by network members helps protect individuals from experiencing negative outcomes, helps them in their efforts to improve their situation and helps them respond to adverse events. It has to be noted here that interactions with others may also be of a negative nature, existing, for example, of criticism and disapproval of one's behavior, or of episodes of conflict and quarreling. In particular these negative interactions are found to be related to loneliness and psychological distress. However, studies have revealed that these types of negative interactions occur relatively seldom within network relationships, and, when they do occur, it most often concerns strong and close relationships with the spouse or children.

Many studies on supportive relationships of older adults deal with the question, "Who provides what type of support to whom?" Within some studies this issue is closely related to the issue of caregiving and network relationships are categorized according to their capacity to provide either acute or daily long-term care to frail older adults. It has often been found that the spouse and the children (in particular the daughter) are the most important caregivers of frail older adults. When these types of relationships are not available, close kin (e.g., siblings), neighbors, and friends are the next preferred source of instrumental support. With respect to emotional support a same type of hierarchy in network relationships seems to exist, but relatively few studies have dealt with this type of support to older adults. Within support research gerontologists often perceived the older adult as a dependent person who needs to be taken care of. More recently, researchers take the perspective that older people are able to actively maintain their network relationships by negotiating balanced exchanges of support. The opportunities of older adults to remain active in providing support to others may be limited during the aging process, at least where the provision of instrumental support is concerned. The impact of aging on the structure and the supportive functions of the network are discussed more extensively further below (section I.C). [*See* CAREGIVING AND CARING; HOME CARE AND CAREGIVING.]

Social researchers have often studied the personal relationships of individuals without taking the linkages between various network members into account. However, network members do not function independently of each another. It is crucial to regard the interaction between the focal individual and one network member in relation to the interaction with other network members. For example, which of the adult children is to provide support for an elderly parent might be the outcome of a family meeting where it is decided to take turns in caregiving. The study of personal relationships evolves into the study of the personal *network* if relationships are viewed as part of a large network and if linkages between these relationships are also taken into account. By combining the features of individual relationships, one gains insight into the structural aspects of the network. Examples of structural aspects are size, composition (e.g., proportion of kin), and homogeneity (e.g., proportion of same-sex network members). Information regarding the content of the network can be obtained by aggregating the qualities of the individual relationships. Examples of network content are network interaction (e.g., number of network members contacted at least once a week) and support intensity (e.g., proportion of instrumentally supportive relationships). Features of the structure as well as the content of the network will be elaborated on in section III.

B. Determinants of Personal Networks

The development and maintenance of a personal network can be viewed as the outcome of social context combined with individual properties. The social context sets the opportunities to engage in social interaction and determines what sets of relationships are available to people. The conditions shaping the opportunities have been affected by the economic, demographic, and cultural changes of recent decades. For example, the rise in one-person households among the aged has forced a large number of elderly people to seek social contacts outside the home. Demographic developments have led to extensive changes in kin networks. Altered fertility and mortality patterns are leading to shifts in the number of intragenerational versus intergenerational ties, and in the balance of young and old in the family. Economic developments have led to changes in nonkin networks. The organization of the labor force requires greater geographic and job mobility. As a result, the fields from which relationships are recruited change, and there is a greater turnover in relationships during the life course. One implication of these developments is that greater efforts must be expended in initiating and maintaining nonkin relationships. [See DEMOGRAPHY; ECONOMICS: SOCIETY.]

Personal characteristics determine the sets of relationships that are developed within the opportunities set by society. Characteristics such as age, income, and health can restrict interaction with others as well as the provision of support to others. In addition, individual standards and decisions affect the choice of relationships. Individuals can take an active stand in determining which relationships they wish to develop and maintain and what quality standards these relationships have to meet with. Individual characteristics such as social skills, coping styles, and other personality traits are also relevant here.

C. The Impact of Aging on the Personal Network

The personal network is developed and shaped during the life course. From early childhood to old age, one is surrounded by a variety of persons with whom one develops relationships. During the life course some relationships end due to major transitions (divorce, death of the spouse) or minor transitions (moving, changing jobs, entering or leaving organizations), while others may last a lifetime. New members may enter the network as a result of marriage, a new job, becoming a parent, and so on. The importance of relationships also changes over time. For example, the function of parents differs at different stages of the life course. Likewise, the function of friends varies across the different social positions people occupy in the course of their lives. For elderly people, a personal network can be viewed as the result of earlier transitions affecting their opportunities and individual choices to maintain and develop relationships. [See LIFE COURSE.]

Aging is often associated with relationship losses. Usually persons from older generations (parents, uncles, etc.) are the first to be lost, followed by same-age associates (spouse, siblings, friends). Relationship losses have an immediate impact on kin and nonkin networks. [See BEREAVEMENT AND LOSS.]

The effects of other aging factors are more indirect. As people enter old age, they are generally in a position to exercise greater choices in their relationships. Unfettered by employment obligations and the responsibility for children at home, they generally have greater opportunities to organize and structure their social lives. Other changes that tend to come with age pertain to relational needs, for example due to increasing impairment. Older adults may become more dependent on others, lacking the ability to perform certain tasks themselves. The existing balance in their relationships may be disrupted, introducing strain and discomfort. Furthermore, a decline in health may impose restrictions upon older adults' capacities to engage in interaction with others. Hearing and memory problems can limit conversational exchanges. Reduced physical mobility can limit participation in shared activities. [See HEARING; MEMORY.]

It can be concluded that differences in the personal networks of older people are related to differences in situational and personal characteristics. A network is the result of macrosocial trends that create individual opportunities to maintain a personal network, but it also reflects individual transitions, relationship standards and personal characteristics. In studying the networks of elderly people, it is recommended to relate network features to situational as well as personal characteristics of the elderly.

II. PERSONAL NETWORK DELINEATION

A. Methods for Network Delineation

A personal network is defined in general as the group of persons (network members) with whom a focal individual (anchor) has a direct relationship. There are various methods to delineate the social network. Some methods are based on the content of the relationships, some on the affective value of the ties, and other methods use the formal role relationship as criterion for network membership. Research interests determine which method is used and which part of the larger social network will be identified.

With respect to the identification of networks of the aged, the following five major methods can be used: (1) the affective method, (2) the role relation method, (3) the exchange method, (4) the interactive method, and (5) the domain contact method. The 5 methods are conceptually unique and map different parts of the personal network. A general overview of these methods to delineate personal networks is provided below. Table I provides a summary of the main features of the 5 methods.

1. The Affective Method

a. **Conceptual Framework** The affective method identifies members who are of affective value to the focal individual, in other words, significant others or intimates. The underlying assumption is that these network members are potentially important sources of support for the focal individual. The method is commonly used by researchers who are interested in the "psychological network" defined by (among others) Milardo and Surra as "those persons to whom the focal person is committed emotionally and psychologically."

b. **Name Generator** Basically this type of network is identified by asking one question: "Who do you feel close to?" or "Who are the persons who are important to you?" Some researchers set limits to the number of names to be mentioned, others apply a time frame (e.g., within the past 6 months). Sometimes a distinction is drawn in the degree of importance or the level of closeness of the network members.

c. **Network Features** Typical of the affective network is a small size (about 5 to 9 members), a large proportion of (close) kin (about 50 to 80%), a large number of long-standing relationships, and many supportive exchanges within the ties. The stability of this type of network is high, mostly because relationships that are stable, as with close relatives and best friends, are cited.

d. **Evaluation** Crucial to this method is the subjective nature of the name generator. People are asked to evaluate relationships in terms of importance or closeness. This evaluation may be shaded by norms and obligations to mention relationships supposed to be important, for example with the spouse and children. One is less inclined to mention relationships that are potentially supportive but not very important to the individual, for example, with neighbors or colleagues. In addition, it need not be necessary to include persons with whom one interacts on a regular basis. As a result, this type of network cannot be used to indicate the degree of social participation or integration of the focal individual. This type of network is positively related to the degree of well-being and negatively to feelings of loneliness of the central person. The major advantage of this method is that it has proven to be a robust method by yielding similar types of networks in different samples.

2. The Role Relation Method

a. **Conceptual Framework** The role relation method defines network membership purely on the basis of the formal role relationship one maintains with the focal individual. Role relationships are derived from status variables such as marital status, employment status, type of living arrangements, friendship, and family status. The network accordingly includes the partner, children, co-workers, friends, and members of the household. The underlying assumption is that the formal role relationship reflects norms and obligations with respect to the con-

Table I Overview of Network Delineation Methods

	Affective[a]	Role relation[b]	Exchange[c]	Interactive	Domain contact[d]
Conceptual definition	Network of significant others (affect based)	Network of formal role relations (role based)	Network of relations in which significant interactions occur (content based)	Network of persons with whom social interaction exists (contact based)	Network of socially active and important relations (contact and affect based)
Name generator(s) (examples)	"Who do you feel close to?"	"Name your spouse, children, neighbors, colleagues, friends."	"Who do you discuss personal problems with?" and "Who helps you with daily chores?"	"Name the persons you have contacted today for at least 10 minutes."	For each role relation (e.g., children, neighbors): "Who do you have regular contact with and who is also important to you?"
Number of questions asked	1 or 2	Depending on the roles of interest: 5–7	3 to 20	1 (repeated every day for a certain period of time)	One for each role relation of interest (about 7)
Limits on period of time	No	No	Yes (past 6 months, past year)	Yes (2 weeks, one month etc)	No
Network size	Small (about 3–9)	Depends on the number of roles of interest	Large (10–22)	Large (16–26)	Medium (13–15)
Proportion of kin	Large (50–78%)	Depends on the roles of interest	Low (19–48%)	Low	Medium to large (66%)

[a]Kahn, R. L., & Antonucci, T. C. (1980). Convoys over the life course: Attachment, roles and social support. *In* P. B. Baltes & O. Brim (Eds.), *Life-span development and behavior* (pp. 253–286). New York: Academic Press.

Morgan, D. L., Schuster, T. L., & Butler, E. W. (1991). Role reversals in the exchange of social support. *Journal of Gerontology, 46,* 278.

Wellman, B., & Hall, A. (1986). Social networks and social support: Implications for later life. *In* V. W. Marshall (Ed.), *Later life: The psychology of aging* (pp. 191–232). London: Sage.

[b]Berkman, L. F., & Syme, S. L. (1979). Social networks, host resistance and mortality: A nine-year follow-up study of Alameda County residents. *American Journal of Epidemiology, 109,* 186.

Litwak, E., & Szelenyi, I. (1969). Primary groups structures and their functions: Kin, neighbours, and friends. *American Sociological Review, 34,* 465.

[c]Kendig, H. L. (1986). *Ageing and families: A social networks perspective.* Sydney: Allen and Unwin.

Tilburg, T. G. van. (1992). Support networks before and after retirement. *Journal of Social and Personal Relationships, 9,* 433.

Wenger, G. C. (1990). Change and adaptation in informal support networks of elderly people in Wales 1979–1987. *Journal of Aging Studies, 4,* 375.

[d]Tilburg, T. G. van. (1995). Delineation of the social network and differences in network size. *In* C. P. M. Knipscheer, J. de Jong Gierveld, T. G. van Tilburg & P. A. Dykstra (Eds.), *Living arrangements and social networks of older adults* (pp. 83–96). Amsterdam: VU University Press.

tent of the relationship. The mere existence of relationships is expected to protect one from social isolation, illness, and loneliness. There is very little focus on the content of the relationships.

b. Name Generator Researchers using this method do not always use a name generator. Inquiring after marital status, parental status, or job status will suffice if one is interested in the availability of a spouse,

children, or co-workers. Researchers interested in the additional features of the role relationships have to use name generators. Examples include "Who is your partner?" "Who is your best friend?" or "Could you name two of your neighbors/colleagues/fellow members of organizations etc?" The type of role relationship that is identified depends on the research objectives. Sometimes limits are set to the number of names to be mentioned.

c. Network Features The size as well as other features of the network are completely dependent on the name generators used. The stability of the role network is high, because formal role relationships are not likely to change over a short period of time.

d. Evaluation The advantages of this method are that it is very easy to administer and it uses an objective measure for the identification of network members. Researchers interested in the social integration of individuals will be able to use this method successfully. One disadvantage is that relationships that have no formal role but may nevertheless be important or supportive might be overlooked. Its use in studies on support networks may therefore be limited.

3. The Exchange Method

a. Conceptual Framework The exchange method assumes that the relationships in which significant interaction occurs with network members are among the most important ones. Within this significant interaction, a regular exchange of emotional support, instrumental assistance, and material goods takes place. This interaction is considered to be of a supportive nature. By asking about a large range of significant interactions, a broad and varied network is expected to be identified.

b. Name Generator The exchange method uses several questions (usually 6–10) to identify members with whom significant interaction occurs. Examples include "Who do you talk about personal problems with?" "Who do you discuss problems at work with?" "Who helps you with daily chores around the house?' "Who takes care of you if you are ill?" Often a limit is set to the number of names to be identified in response to each question. The number of questions asked is related to the number of persons to be identified, but there is a certain limit. It has been noted that asking 5 questions on different types of support (emotional and instrumental support and companionship) identified about 80–85% of the persons who are mapped with 10 questions. Some researchers distinguish between questions indicating the receipt of support ("Who helps you with daily chores?") and questions indicating the provision of support ("Who do you help with daily chores?"). This results in a larger number of identified persons compared to nondirective questioning about exchange relations.

c. Network Features The typical exchange network is rather large, varying from about 10 to 20 names. The proportion of kin within the network is rather low, varying from 35–50%. In general, the exchange network contains many relationships that are socially active at the time of measurement. A relatively large proportion of more superficial relationships are identified, based on a (temporary) sharing of the same workplace, organization membership, neighborhood, and so on. The stability of the exchange network is relatively low compared to the affective and role relation network, because many unstable nonkin relationships are identified.

d. Evaluation The exchange method is easy to administer and of a rather objective nature. The interactions are specific and not multi-interpretable. The exchange method can map different parts of the network. In contrary to the affective method, nonkin relationships are more likely to be identified. One disadvantage is that ties that are potentially supportive but not actually supportive at the moment are overlooked. In addition, persons one is socially involved with but with whom no significant interactions are exchanged (e.g., more distant relatives) are also excluded from this network. It is crucial to this method that it focuses on the content of a tie rather than the formal role relationship or the degree of contact frequency.

4. The Interaction Method

a. Conceptual Framework The interactive method identifies the persons one engages in social interaction within a given period of time (e.g., 2 weeks, 1 month). The assumption is that the interactive network indicates the degree of social participation. It is found to be unrelated to support or well-being.

b. Name Generator The interactive method requires a systematic recording of who one has contact with on a daily basis. Usually this is done by having respondents maintain a diary or by contacting them daily by telephone. Respondents have to indicate who they interacted with that day for at least 10 minutes.

c. Network Features The size of the interactive network depends on the period used for monitoring social interaction. The longer the period, the more different persons are identified. The interactive network may contain a large proportion of nonkin relationships, depending on the living situation of the respondent (married, employed, with children and so on). The interaction network is apt to be sensitive to changes in daily contacts. Many superficial contacts that are part of the interaction network in a given period may not be included in another period of time.

d. Evaluation The interactive network is a good indicator of the degree of social participation, because it records daily social interaction. Comparing this method to other methods reveals a very small overlap between the networks. The affective and exchange networks are far more psychological, and their members usually do not meet every day. However, enlarging the monitoring period of the interactive network will eventually decrease the differences with the exchange network. A major advantage of daily monitoring is that it provides a reliable picture of the social interaction of the respondents.

5. The Domain Contact Method

a. Conceptual Framework The domain contact method combines the different roles an individual performs with the frequency of contact and the importance of the relationships as criteria for the identification of network members. The main objective of this method is to identify the socially active relationships in the larger network. A central assumption is that this type of network constitutes the structural vehicle for the ties in which various types of support can be exchanged. In this line of reasoning, the potential or actual support exchanged is not a criteria for delineation, but an object of research on the delineation of the personal network.

b. Name Generator Network members are identified in various domains of the network, for example, household members (including the spouse), children and their partners, other relatives, neighbors, school or job acquaintances (including voluntary jobs), members of organizations (sport, church, political parties), and others (friends, acquaintances). All the household members are included in the network. As to the other domains, the respondents are asked: "Name the persons (e.g., in your neighborhood) you have frequent contact with and who are also important to you." No limits are set on the number of names to be mentioned.

c. Network Features The domain contact network is medium to large (an average of 13 members, ranging from 0–75), with about two-thirds of the relationships being with relatives. Because that contact frequency is used as a criterion for identification, the average contact frequency with these network members is relatively high, between about once every 2 weeks and weekly.

d. Evaluation Using several criteria for network membership leads to a medium-sized network (compared to the smaller affective network and the larger exchange network) that contains a large range of role relationships. The method combines objective (role relationship and contact frequency) and subjective criteria (importance) for the delineation of network relationships. As a result, the domain contact network indicates the actual degree of social participation as well as the availability of potentially supportive relationships.

B. Choices in Network Research

The examination of the personal networks of older adults requires several choices to be made by the researcher beforehand. The first choice concerns the type of method to be used for network delineation. This necessitates a clear description of the research objective. Usually two types of research objectives can be distinguished: (a) the network has to indicate the degree of social participation of older adults, and (b) the network has to reflect the actual support reservoir of older adults. The first type of objective requires the use of the role relation method, the interactive method or the domain contact method in the delineation of the network. The affective method and the exchange method are more appropriate if one has the second type of objective in mind.

The second choice within network research focuses on how many network members and relationships additional information will be collected on. In most network research (particularly large surveys), there is no time to collect information on *all* the network members who are identified. Some researchers have solved this time problem by setting limits to the number of names to be identified by the name generator. It is put forward here that limits of this kind distort the identification of the network because they leave uncertainty about the true size of the personal network. Because network size is crucial for the calculation of other structural and functional network features (e.g., proportion of kin), it is strongly recommended to set no limits on the number of persons to be identified. A better solution is to add an extra objective criterion such as contact frequency or traveling distance to the identification procedures. If interview time is of the essence, additional information can be asked about a selection of the network members. The selection criterion can either be objective (e.g., the 10 persons contacted most frequently) or subjective (e.g., the 6 persons who are the most important). The subjective option has the disadvantage that respondents have to choose between certain network members, which may be a difficult task.

The third choice in network research pertains to the type of information to be collected on some or all of the identified network members. Again this choice is guided by the research objectives. Yet, there seems to be a general consensus among network researchers that it is advisable to collect information on the type of relationship and sex of as many network members as possible. Researchers interested in the degree of social participation also inquire about the contact frequency with each network member, whereas support researchers are more interested in the support exchanged within the relationship.

A final choice the network researcher has to make involves who is to serve as a respondent in the study. Usually the information on network members and relationships is only obtained from the focal individual, the anchor of the network. The identified network is then called a star network, and information is only available on the ties between the anchor and his or her network members (Figure 1). Yet, it is also possible to

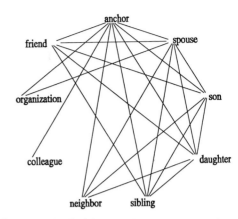

Figure 2 Example of a full network. Along with the focal individual, network members are included as respondents. Data become available on identified ties between all network members.

include network members as respondents and ask them about the tie characteristics with the anchor and with the other identified members of the network. If members of a personal network report about identified ties with other network members, data are available on a full network (Figure 2). The following two sections will elaborate on the characteristics of the star and the full network.

III. FEATURES OF THE PERSONAL NETWORK

In a star network, the older adult is the focal person, the anchor. All the features of the network and the relationships can be linked with his or her behavior and state of mind. An overview is provided below of features of the network structure and content that are associated with aging. As people age, these aspects of the network are subject to changes and are therefore relevant to the study of the networks of older adults. Tables II and III give examples of network structure and content based on information about relationship features.

A. Network Structure

The *size* of the network indicates how many relationships one is involved in, whether affect-based, role-based, or contact-based. Involvement in a larger network is associated with a larger degree of social participation and a greater exchange of support and

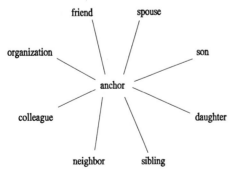

Figure 1 Example of a star network. Information is only available on the relationship between the focal individual (anchor) and other members of the network.

Table II Features of Network Structure

Network structure	Operationalization at the network level	Information on the dyad	Information on the network member
Size	Total number of identified network members	—	—
Composition	e.g., number of children, friends; proportion of kin	role or type of relationship	
Homogeneity	e.g., total number of females in the network; percentage of members within the same age category	Similarity between characteristics of anchor and nework member: e.g., same-sex or cross-sex	e.g., sex, age, race, partner status, employment status
Density	Total number of pairs who know each other of the total number of available pairs	—	How many of the other network members are known
Stability	Average years of network membership	Duration of the relationship	
Role complexity	Number of multiplex relationships	Number of different roles shared with the network member	
Geographical dispersion	e.g., number of persons living within 15 min; mean traveling time	Traveling time from anchor to network member	

well-being. A large network is considered a social resource. Older adults who want to reorganize their social life after retirement are better off with a large network, because it increases their chances of getting acquainted with new people. Network size varies widely among elderly people of different ages, types of living arrangements, and marital or parental status. Younger elderly people who live with a spouse and have children available usually have the largest networks, regardless of the delineation method used.

The network *composition* indicates the available proportions of kin and nonkin. The distinction between kin and nonkin is often too global, and it is wise

to differentiate between relationships with a spouse, children, other kin, neighbors, friends, and other nonkin. The impact of aging on the network composition is far larger in the other kin and other nonkin network sections, and smaller in the children, neighbors, and friends sections. Other kin are likely to be of the same generation (siblings, cousins) or of an older generation (parents, uncles, aunts) and become less available. Other nonkin are recruited from job sites, organizations, and so on, and participation in these social fields is greatly reduced in the oldest age groups. The composition of the network is strongly associated with marital and parental status. Elderly people who

Table III Features of the Network Content

Network content	Operationalization at the network level	Information on the dyad
Interaction	e.g., proportion of network members contacted at least weekly; mean frequency	Frequency of contact
Support intensity	e.g., total amount of emotional support received and given; proportion of ties with large social support intensity	Receiving and giving support (emotional, instrumental, social, material goods)
Support complexity	e.g., total number of multiplex relationships	Exchange of one versus more types of support
Reciprocity	e.g., average number of reciprocal relationships; proportion of unbalanced ties; ratio of given and received support	Balance between giving and receiving of support

have never been married or had children may have established bonds early in life with relatives (siblings or cousins) as well as neighbors and friends. These groups are used to recruit their contacts outside the home and benefit from these relationships until old age. Older women and men differ with respect to the composition of their network. Women are generally more involved with kin, neighbors, and friends, whereas men are more involved with other nonkin relationships.

If information on the personal characteristics of the network members is available, it is possible to compute the *homogeneity* of the network with respect to sex, age, parental status, and so forth. It has often been reported that individuals like to associate with people who have similar backgrounds and are assumed to have similar life experiences. In particular, nonkin network members are expected to exhibit marked similarities in sex, age, and level of education with the focal individual, resulting in a large homogeneous nonkin network. Relatives, however, are likely to be dissimilar with respect to sex, age, and parental status. Because of the increasing chance of the loss of a partner in old age and women living longer than men, the networks of the elderly will be relatively homogeneous with respect to sex and partner status, especially where intergenerational contacts are concerned.

The *density* of the network refers to the interconnectedness between network members. Large networks usually have a low overall density, meaning that fewer network members interact with each other without the anchor being present. Yet, large networks may also contain specific parts that are very high in density (neighbors or close relatives). Networks that are low in density are generally found with younger persons who are highly educated and participate in various social organizations, which are only loosely connected to each other, if at all. Small networks usually have a high density, and are generally more prevalent among elderly people with a relatively low level of education. Within dense networks, people often share the same norms and values. Being embedded in a dense network can be comforting for people who have recently lost a spouse. Yet, a dense network can also limit the widow or widower's capacity to rebuild and expand the network, which is a necessary step in adjusting to widowhood. Dense networks are generally composed of persons who have been inter-

acting for many years, indicating a high *stability* within the network. This stability may vary among different types of relationships. Relatives will have been around for a lifetime, while the widowed neighbor down the street may have entered the network only recently.

Network members may have more than one formal role relationship with the focal person. A neighbor may also be a friend, and a second-degree relative may also be a member of the same bridge club. At the network level, *role complexity* is indicated by the number of uniplex (one formal role) or multiplex relationships. Networks with a high role complexity are usually also small and densely knit.

The *geographical dispersion* within the network indicates the extent to which network members live in the same neighborhood or region by the proportion of network members who live less than half an hour's drive away. Networks of elderly people are generally largely locally based, although children and other relatives might live far away. How close network members live is of particular importance to elderly people who are in need of instrumental support. The geographical dispersion of the network may therefore be used to demonstrate the availability of potential supporters in the vicinity of the older adult.

B. Content of the Network

The overall *interaction* of the older adult with the network members is often used as a token of social participation. Network interaction may vary among different parts of the network. Interaction is higher with the spouse, children, and neighbors than it is with distant relatives and acquaintances. The more frequent one interacts with network members, the more likely the exchange of support.

The *support intensity* of the network refers to the exchange of support between all the network members and the focal person. Various types of support can be distinguished: emotional support, instrumental support, social support (companionship), material support, and so on. Furthermore, a distinction can be drawn between giving and receiving support. In general, elderly people are thought to be on the receiving end of support, in particular as they grow older, less mobile, or less healthy. Yet, they are also capable of giving support, specifically emotional support and financial support to their children. The types of support vary among the types of relationships, and among older men and women. Men are known to exchange instrumental support, whereas women are known to give and receive emotional support to an old age.

The exchange of two or more types of support within the network relationships indicates the *support complexity* of the network. Some network members provide emotional as well as instrumental support, whereas others only exchange material goods.

Lastly, the balance between the overall provision and receipt of support indicates the *support reciprocity* within the network. In general, elderly people receive more support than they provide. This is particularly the case after when they pass the age of 75 and there is a strong decline in their physical capacities. Giving and receiving support is usually more balanced for women than men. An unbalanced support network has a negative impact on the well-being of the elderly. The imbalance created by being in debt to many network members may lead to feelings of guilt, whereas providing support to many relatives and friends without receiving much in return can lead to feelings of being exploited.

IV. FULL NETWORKS

A. Advantages of Full Network above Star Network Data

In star networks, the elderly person occupies a central position as anchor of the network. This is why we focus completely on the world this one particular elderly person lives in, and explain, for example, his or her well-being on the basis of the features of the network as viewed by this elderly person. If one wants to gain insight into the structure and processes of the separate relationships and of the network as a whole, one can examine the relationships in which both of the persons within the relationship have been interviewed and collect data on both parties, and one can examine full networks, collecting data from all the network members on their relationships with each other.

In star networks, only the data of the elderly person are collected. Data on each relationship, such as the support exchanges within it, are then solely viewed from the perspective of the elderly person. Studies in which relationships are examined from both sides have shown that the perception of the network mem-

ber regarding the relationships frequently differs from the perception of the elderly person. This holds particularly true of more subjective information, for example, on giving and receiving emotional support. Differences in perception regarding the extent to which support is exchanged can be an important factor in the continuation of the support exchange.

If data are only collected from the elderly person, there is virtually no insight into the circumstances and attitudes of the network members. The support received by elderly people is not only influenced by the need and presumed need for support on the part of the elderly person, but also by how willing and able the network members are to give support. The poorer the health is of a network member, the less able he or she is to give instrumental support. It is possible to ask the elderly person to assess the health of the network members, though the validity of the data is questionable. The extent to which network members are willing to give support, particularly lengthy support, to an older person is not something the older person can easily be asked. Data on the circumstances and attitudes of network members should thus be gathered from the network members themselves.

In a full network, the relationships between the various network members are also addressed. The more support network members exchange with each other, the more likely they are to give support to an elderly person and the more organized it is apt to be. This is far less the case if the network members barely have any contact with each other. In the personal networks of older people, three of the structural aspects of the full network are important. *Support density* indicates the extent to which relationships are mutually supportive and serves as a supplement to the overall density. *Cliques* are indicative of the existence of subnetworks within which a great deal of contact and support is exchanged, and between which barely any contact or support at all is exchanged. *Network reciprocity* indicates the extent to which the total network is characterized by support reciprocity. In connection with this concept, patterns of exchange are distinguished within triads. The data from a star network might show that the anchor gives support to B, and C gives support to the anchor. The totality of the anchor's relationships are thus reciprocal even though the network need not be reciprocal. In the full network, the triad of the anchor, B, and C can be examined. Depending on whether B gives support to C, C giving support to the anchor can be viewed as the act that puts the equilibrium between giving and receiving support back into balance in the entire network. Network reciprocity touches upon the concept of generalized reciprocity, which indicates that the total balance within a network is more important than the balance within the relationships with one person, as they can be determined within the star network.

B. Data Collection on Full Networks

The data collection starts with the delineation of the network, as is explained in section II. The network members and their relationships with each other are the subject of the data collection. Because the number of network members and the number of relationships (maximum $N \times (N - 1)/2$) can be large, in many cases a selection will have to be made from the network members. The network members are then asked about their features (demographic data and data relevant to the specific study, such as attitudes) and about the features of their relationships with each other. Together with the data collected from the anchor, these data constitute the data set.

If a limited number of elderly people's networks are examined, the data can be collected in face-to-face interviews and dealt with in the usual case study manner. Studies of this kind have been conducted at various times. It has also proved possible to conduct large-scale studies on full networks. In a Dutch study, the networks of 500 elderly people were delineated in face-to-face interviews; the elderly people and 3,500 of their network members were then approached with mailed questionnaires. Because each network member was asked about his or her relationships with a unique set of other network members, the questionnaires were personalized; the study focused on a total of approximately 9000 relationships. As preparation for the production of the written questionnaires, in the face-to-face interviews with the elderly people with extent to which the network members had contact with each other was inventoried by way of a density matrix. This made it possible for the written questionnaires to only ask the network members questions about other network members whom they had contact with.

Collecting data on full networks requires a great deal of work. The advantage however is that the analysis can take place from three angles, the perspectives of the older person, the network member, and the structure of the network. Each of these angles is unique and supplements the other two.

V. METHODS OF NETWORK ANALYSIS

A. Data Storage

Network data is hierarchically constructed. There are two levels of star network data. The elderly person as the anchor of the network is the higher level with such characteristics as sex, age, network size, and well-being. Inside of it, characteristics of the network members, such as sex, and of their relationships with each other, such as traveling time and support received by the elderly person, are on the lower level. There are three levels of full network data: the network as a whole, for example its size, the characteristics of the network members including the elderly person, and the features of their relationships with each other. The data are stored in accordance with this hierarchic structure. They can either be stored in a hierarchic database or in different files for each level. If they are stored in different files, the levels can be linked to each other by giving each case in the files unique and shared identifiers. In the case of star networks, let us say the number 123 is attributed to the case of a certain elderly person and numbers 12301 to 12399 are attributed to this particular elderly person's 99 network members and his or her relationships with them. In the number 12301, the first three figures are the shared identifier and the last two figures are the unique identifier.

B. Analysis of Data of Star Networks

The data of star networks and the relationships within them can be analyzed on their own level. On the level of the elderly person, there is only one nonaggregated feature (i.e., the network size). The structural and functional features of the network referred to in section III are based upon the features of the separate relationships. The network size can serve as an explanatory variable for differences in the well-being of elderly people. In addition, the data can be analyzed on the level of the separate network members and the separate relationships with them. One can thus see whether there is any correlation between traveling time and the intensity of the support exchanges. One disadvantage of this analysis is that it violates an assumption of many analysis techniques, namely that the data of different cases are independent of each other, because the data on the relationships of an elderly person are all collected from and linked to the characteristics of one and the same elderly person. One way to study the correlation between traveling time and support without violating this assumption would be by randomly selecting one relationship of each elderly person. The procedure could be repeated for the remaining relationships.

One of the attractive things about being able to have network data at ones disposal is that data on different levels can be linked to each other. There are three methods for simultaneously analyzing the data on both levels: aggregation, disaggregation, and multilevel.

In aggregation, data from the lower level of the separate network members and/or relationships are transferred to the higher level of the elderly person. For each elderly person, one can take the mean of the contact frequency within his or her relationships and introduce the average contact frequency as variable in an analysis to explain the differences in the well-being of elderly people. In an aggregation of this kind, differences in the contact frequency between the network members of the elderly person are overlooked; if one wants to include them in the analysis, one can also calculate the variance in the contact frequency between the elderly person and his or her network members and include it in the analysis. A variant on the aggregation as the average frequency of contact across relationships would be to count the number of network members with whom there is contact at least once a week. Statistical software such as SPSS (Statistical Package for the Social Sciences) has capacities for aggregation of this kind. In aggregation, elderly people who have no network members are not given a score on the aggregated variable. One thus has to decide on substantive grounds whether these elderly people should be excluded from the analysis or what score should be attributed on the aggregated variable.

In disaggregation, data from the higher level of the elderly person are transferred to the lower level of the separate network members and/or relationships. To find out whether more support is exchanged in same-sex relationships than in cross-sex relationships, one adds a variable to the relationship data file that indicates for each relationship whether it is with an older man or woman. Using statistical software such as SPSS, this procedure is easy to implement. Then one can combine the sex of the elderly person and the network member in one variable and analyze whether the support differs for the values of this combined variable. In disaggregation it is also true that data from different cases are not independent of each other, so that one is violating an assumption of many analysis techniques.

An alternative for disaggregation is multilevel analysis. In this analysis technique, a linear regression equation is formulated for explaining variance in a variable on the lower level from the perspective of other variables on the lower level. The support received by an elderly person is then predicted on the basis of, for example, the age of the network member and the traveling time. A crucial aspect is that the magnitude of the effect of explanatory variables may differ between respondents. Therefore, the intercept as well as the slopes of the different independent variables in this equation are then explained with different regression equations from the perspective of independent variables on the higher level, such as the age and health of the elderly person. Multilevel analysis techniques are available as specific software (HLM, ML3, VARCL).

C. Analysis of Data of Full Networks

In star networks, it is possible to make data from different networks ready for analysis in one step. Techniques for the analysis of full networks analyze the data of one network at a time. To analyze the data of more than one network, the analysis has to be repeated. Then one collects the results of the analyses and includes them as network features in an analysis on the level of the elderly person. For a sample of elderly people, one can thus compare the network reciprocity of the full network with the anchor reciprocity as an aggregated feature of the star network. The UCINET program, which provides techniques for determining a wide range of network structural features, is available for analyzing full network data.

VI. SUMMARY AND CONCLUSIONS

This article provides an overview of network analysis with respect to elderly people. The article starts by describing the importance of the personal network for elderly people. The personal network is considered a social resource and is important for daily functioning, coping with life events, and maintaining well-being. The impact of aging on the personal network becomes evident in the changes within the structure as well as the content of the network. The personal network of the elderly can be studied from different perspectives. The focus can be on the content of the network (e.g., the relation between support and well-being), or on structural aspects of the network (e.g., the relation of marital status to its size, composition, and density). In every network study, several methodological choices are made beforehand: which network delineation method is to be used, whether additional information is to be collected on some or all of the identified network members, which information is to be collected, and who will provide this information (only the older adult or all the members of the network). With respect to the last choice, data will be available on either a star network or a full network. Five methods for personal network delineation are described, varying from affect-based, role-based, exchange-based, and interaction-based to domain contact-based. These methods are conceptually unique and map different parts of the personal network. Features of the network structure and content that are usually examined within star networks are described and related to features of the older population. Attention is devoted to the reasons for and methods of studying full networks. Finally, methods for storing and analyzing network data are described.

BIBLIOGRAPHY

Antonucci, T. C. (1990). Social supports and social relationships. In R. H. Binstock & L. K. George (Eds.), *Handbook of Aging and the Social Sciences* (pp. 205–226). San Diego: Academic Press.

Dykstra, P. A. (1990). *Next of (non)kin: The importance of primary relationships for older adults' well-being.* Lisse, The Netherlands: Swets and Zeitlinger.

Kendig, H. L. (1986). *Ageing and families: A social networks perspective.* Sydney: Allen and Unwin.

Knipscheer, C. P. M., & Antonucci, T. C. (Eds.). (1990). *Social network research: Substantive issues and methodological questions.* Lisse, The Netherlands: Swets and Zeitlinger.

Milardo, R. M., & Wellman, B. (Eds.). (1992). Social networks. *Journal of Social and Personal Relationships* (special issue), 9.

Sarason, I. G., Sarason, B. R., & Pierce, G. R. (1994). Social support: Global and relationship-based levels of analysis. *Journal of Social and Personal Relationships, 11,* 295.

Snijders, T. A. B., Spreen, M., & Zwaagstra, R. (1995). The use of multilevel modeling for analysing personal networks: Networks of cocaine users in an urban area. *Journal of Quantitative Anthropology, 5,* 85.

Starker, J. E., Morgan, D. L., & March, S. (1993). Analyzing change in networks of personal relationships. In D. Perlman & W. H. Jones, Eds., *Advances in personal relationships, vol. 4: A research annual* (pp. 229–260). London: Jessica Kingsley.

Wasserman, S., & Faust, K. (1994). *Social network analysis: Methods and applications.* New York: Cambridge University Press.

Wasserman, S., & Galaskiewicz, J. (Eds.). (1993). Advances in sociology from social network analysis. *Sociological Methods and Research* (special issue), 22.

Wenger, G. C., & St. Leger, F. (1992). Community structure and support network variations. *Ageing and Society, 12,* 213.

Neuromuscular System

S. D. R. Harridge and B. Saltin

Copenhagen Muscle Research Centre
Denmark

I. Properties of Skeletal Muscle
II. Properties of Aged Skeletal Muscle
III. Adaptability of Aged Muscle to Physical Activity

Contractile Proteins   Actin (thin filament) and myosin (thick filament) interact to form the sliding filament mechanism of muscle contraction. The myosin heavy chain isoforms are central in the regulation of muscle-shortening speed.
Contraction   Muscle can contract with (dynamic) or without (isometric) movement. During movement an active muscle can either shorten (concentric contraction) or lengthen (eccentric contraction).
Muscle Strength   The maximum force that can be produced by a muscle, which is specific to the type of contraction.
Plasticity   The ability of muscle to adapt to changes in usage. This can be at all levels, from changes in the expression of contractile proteins to its metabolism.
Power Output   The product of muscle force and speed of movement.
Sarcopenia   Age-related decline in muscle mass. The decline in muscle mass is most closely associated with the decline in muscle strength in old age.

Old age in both men and women is characterized by a reduction in muscle mass, which relates to both a reduction in the number and size of muscle fibers. This loss of contractile tissue is accompanied by a decline in muscle force production (strength) and power output. A loss of motor nerves in the spinal cord results in a reduction in the number of functioning motor units, and in those motor units remaining the number of muscle fibers is increased, as some of the fibers that have been lost become reinnervated. The proportion of fast myosin isoforms may be reduced in aged muscle resulting in a slowing in the speed of muscle movement, amplifying the decrease in power-producing capability. With only small changes in body mass, functional ability and mobility are reduced as the muscle power to body mass ratio decreases. Part of the age-related **NEUROMUSCU-LAR** phenomena relates to a decrease in the level of habitual physical activity, as muscle power and coordination can be reasonably maintained and improved, through strength training, even in the very old.

I. PROPERTIES OF SKELETAL MUSCLE

A. Types of Muscle Contraction

The three basic types of muscle contraction can be seen in Figure 1, which describes the force–velocity relationship of skeletal muscle. This relationship holds true for single muscle fibers, for whole muscles, as well for whole body movements generally. When a muscle is allowed to shorten or contract *concentrically*, mechanical work is performed, such as when a weight is lifted. The force–velocity relation dictates that if a contraction is performed at a high velocity then the force-generating capacity of the muscle is reduced, or alternatively, the heavier the weight the less quickly it can be lifted. The force-producing capacity of muscle thus reduces with increasing speed of contraction until a point is reached where no force

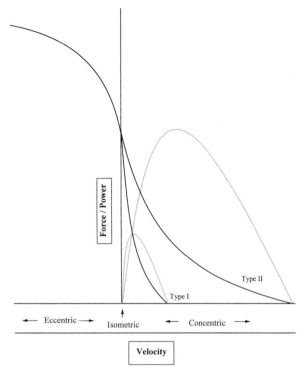

Figure I Schematic diagram showing the force (continuous line) and power (dotted line)–velocity relationship of skeletal muscle in slow (type I) and fast (type II fibers). For eccentric contractions only one fiber type is shown.

is generated and the velocity of shortening is at its maximum (V_{max}). If as opposed to shortening, a muscle is forcibly lengthened while it is active, the muscle will be stretched or contract *eccentrically*. An example of an eccentric contraction is the knee extensor muscles when walking downstairs. Under these conditions negative work is performed and it is possible to obtain greater force than during concentric contractions or during *isometric* contractions. Isometric contractions occur when the muscle is actively generating force, but does not lengthen or shorten. For example, to maintain posture the muscles of the lower leg are active and generating force, but not shortening or lengthening.

The product of force and velocity is *power*. As can be seen in Figure 1, power rises with increasing speed of movement until a velocity of shortening at approximately 30% of V_{max} is reached. Here peak power is obtained. Power then declines with further increases in the speed of movement. As all movements of the

body involve components of force generation and speed of movement, any changes in either of these variables will have an effect on the power that can be generated. Ultimately, it is the force and power-generating capacity of the muscle that will determine functional ability.

B. Structure and Diversity

Skeletal muscle is composed of elongated bands of single cells that can convert chemical energy (ATP) into force and movement. Muscle fibers do not work independently, but work simultaneously with other fibers innervated by the same motor nerve and are thus part of the same "motor unit." Muscle fibers are composed of bundles of myofibrils surrounded by a lace-like network of Ca^{2+}-storing sarcoplasmic reticulum (SR). Each myofibril is composed of a series of thick (myosin) and thin (actin) protein filaments aligned in parallel. Of particular importance in fiber diversity and the regulation of muscle contraction is the myosin filament. A myosin molecule consists of two identical heavy chains (molecular weight ~200 kD) components with a head region and a long tail region that intertwine to form an alpha helix. Attached to each heavy-chain component are two light-chain components (molecular weight ~50 kD each), one termed *regulatory* and the other *alkali*. It is this myosin complex that forms the cross-bridge mechanism responsible for force generation and which powers the sliding of the thin and thick filaments during muscle shortening.

With recent advances in immunohistochemical and electrophoretic techniques, a number of different myosin heavy chain (MHC) and myosin light chain (MLC) phenotypes, or isoforms, have been identified in mammalian skeletal muscle. Four isoforms of MHC have so far been identified in adult mammalian muscle, one slow MHC-I that corresponds to the beta slow isoform found in cardiac muscle and three fast isoforms MHC-IIA, MHC-IIB, and MHC-IIX (sometimes known as MHC-IID). In human skeletal muscle however, only two fast MHC isoforms have been identified, the MHC-IIA and what is commonly referred to as the MHC-IIB, although there is today strong evidence to suggest that MHC-IIB corresponds to the MHC-IIX in the rat and not MHC-IIB. However, for the purposes of this article the MHC-IIB nomenclature will be used. MLCs are also expressed as different fast and slow isoforms, which may modulate the contractile properties of the fiber.

C. Contractile Proteins and Function

The isometric force that can be generated during a contraction relates most closely to muscle or fiber size, specifically to its cross-sectional area. This in turn is a reflection of the number of myosin cross bridges that are working in parallel. However, there is evidence to suggest that type II fibers are capable of generating a higher force per unit area and thus have a higher specific tension. During movement the implications for fibers expressing different myosin isoforms are marked. Fibers that express MHC-I isoforms exhibit shortening speeds that are on average one-quarter to one-third slower than type II fibers (Fig. 1). In fast fibers a continuum of increasing V_{max} can be observed from MHC-IIA $\rightarrow$ MHC-IIX ($\rightarrow$MHC-IIB). Thus, type II fibers are capable of generating higher power outputs when compared to type I fibers. However, even within fibers that express the same MHC isoform there is considerable variability in V_{max}. In fast muscle fibers of the rat this has been attributed to differences in the expression of the alkali MLC isoforms. Individual muscle fibers may also possess more than one MHC isoform. Indeed the occurrence of fibers that express only MHC-IIB isoforms are relatively rare, with MHC-IIB isoforms usually coexisting with MHC-IIA isoforms. This coexpression has a marked influence on function, with MHC-IIA//IIB fibers having a higher V_{max} than pure MHC-IIA fibers.

D. Muscle Function in the Human Body

In intact muscle the force generated by a muscle is complicated by the interaction of the nervous and skeletal systems and by muscle architecture. For full force-generating capacity to be obtained all motor units must be recruited and activated at an optimal frequency. Muscle forces also act about the skeletal system, so the resultant external force applied is dependent on the mechanical advantage of the joint system about which the muscle is acting. In addition, muscles are rarely arranged in parallel, and the line of pull is rarely in a linear direction. Muscles can be arranged in a number of different ways (pennate and bipennate, etc.), a feature which, in many cases, allows a greater physiological cross-sectional area to be ob-

tained and thus greater force to be produced than if the muscle fibers are arranged in parallel.

Muscles are attached to the skeletal system via tendons and aponeuroses. These elements in series with the muscle fibers serve to dampen the response of the contracting muscle fibers while aiding in the speed and efficiency of movement by storing and releasing elastic energy.

In terms of power production (i.e., where muscle force is combined with movement) the composition of the muscle plays a key role. Human skeletal muscles are not homogeneous, but comprise a mixture of fast- and slow-contracting fibers depending on the isoforms that are expressed and thus show differences in their contractile characteristics. For activities that require the generation of large power outputs, a higher proportion of fast fibers would obviously be an advantage. Indeed, there are consistent observations that athletes who excel in power-based sports show a dominance of fast, type II fibers in the appropriate muscle (i.e., vastus lateralis muscle of the knee extensors and gastrocnemius of the plantar flexors), whereas those who excel in endurance events show a dominance of slow, type I fibers.

II. PROPERTIES OF AGED SKELETAL MUSCLE

A. Muscle Mass and Force Production

As the force generated by a skeletal muscle relates most closely to its size, a large decrease in whole muscle cross-sectional area will have a dramatic effect on muscle force production. Muscle cross-sectional area can be estimated using various techniques; ultrasonography, computed tomography scanning, magnetic resonance imaging, and whole body potassium and nitrogen content and the 24-hour excretion of creatanine have been used as markers of whole-body muscle mass. The numerous studies that have been performed in relation to increasing age clearly show that there is a marked decrease in muscle cross-sectional area and muscle mass (sarcopenia) of aged muscle (Fig. 2A). The similarity between the effects of disuse and those of aging on skeletal muscle has led to the suggestion that many age-related changes in muscle may relate to a disuse atrophy phenomenon. Indeed, the extent to which the decline in muscle mass

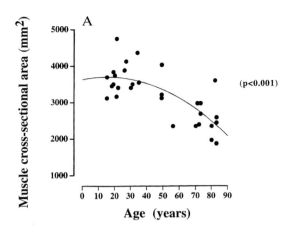

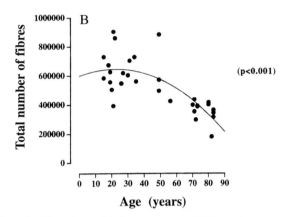

Figure 2 The relationship between age and (A) muscle cross-sectional area and (B) muscle fiber number. (Printed with permission from Lexell et al., 1988. *Journal of the Neurological Sciences, 84,* 275–294.)

results from a preprogrammed loss of contractile tissue, or a reduction in overall activity resulting in disuse atrophy, is one of the important questions still to be resolved in aged muscle. Recent studies that have analyzed whole sections of the vastus lateralis muscle indicate that the reduction in skeletal muscle size is due to both a loss of muscle fibers (Fig. 2B), and to a reduction in fiber size, particularly in the size of type II fibers. The latter factor however, plays a relatively minor role. Associated with this decline in muscle mass is a decline in muscle strength. Data in this regard have primarily come from cross-sectional studies where muscles from aged individuals have been compared with those of young and middle-aged adults. This method does have intrinsic limitations

given differences in nutritional status and health care between generations. However, the findings of numerous studies are reasonably consistent. These are that a decrease in strength can occur in muscles of the upper and lower limb, in both distal and proximal locations and that for both males and females the reduction in strength across the adult ranges trends towards being curvilinear with the onset of the seventh decade being a turning point for an accelerated decline. Between the ages of 30 and 80 years deficits in muscle strength have generally been found to be in the region of 30% for the arm muscles and 40% for the leg and back muscles (see Fig. 3).

It has been suggested that the decline in force production in elderly muscle may relate, in part, to the ability of elderly subjects to activate fully the total muscle mass during a maximum voluntary contraction. However, even when the muscle is activated by direct electrical stimulation, aged muscle has been shown to be markedly weaker than that of young muscle. Indeed, the decline in force production has been shown to be greater than the decrease in muscle

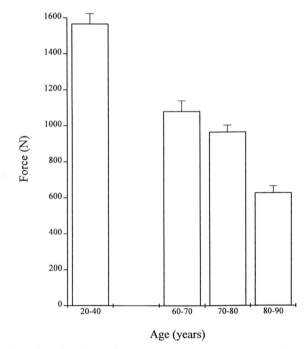

Figure 3 The effects of age on voluntary isometric plantar flexor strength (± S.E.) in males. (Data from Davies et al., 1986. *Acta Medica Scandinavica Suppl. 711,* 219–226, and unpublished observations).

mass. This decrease in specific tension has partly been attributed to the increased content of fat and connective tissue in elderly muscle resulting in overestimates of aged muscle cross-sectional area. In aged rodents there is evidence to suggest that the force loss is absent during stretching or eccentric contractions. There is also evidence that differences between elderly and young human muscle is least during this type of contraction, although the mechanisms underlying this phenomenon are as yet not clear.

B. Contractile Characteristics and Muscle Composition

The force–velocity properties of homogeneous muscles (comprising either virtually all type I or all type II fibers) of aged rodents have been reported to be essentially unchanged, but human muscles are far from homogeneous. Because the shortening properties of skeletal muscle are closely regulated by the MHC isoforms they express, a reduction in the relative proportion of the fast myosin isoforms will have a reducing effect on the velocity at which the muscle will contract. A reduction in the ability of the muscle to shorten quickly, coupled with a decline in muscle force production, will have a marked effect on the power-producing ability of the muscle. Muscle fibers are traditionally determined on the basis of their histochemical staining properties. The question as to whether there is a change in the distribution of histochemically determined fiber types with old age has been controversial. In recent studies where whole muscle cross-sections of the vastus lateralis have been examined, it is suggested that there is not a reduction in the proportion of slow, type I fibers, but a decrease in the area occupied by the fast, type II fibers. The histochemical technique, however, does not clearly show fibers that express more than one MHC isoform. Using single-fiber electrophoresis, elderly muscle has been shown to possess more of these "hybrid" fibers containing slow myosin, which together with the reduced fiber volume of type II fibers, means that the relative amount of slow myosin is elevated in the muscles of elderly people.

C. Implications for Changes in Contractile Function

A decrease in force production in old age coupled with a possible reduction in shortening characteristics

will have a dramatic effect on power production. This results in impaired functional ability reflected in increased difficulty in performing everyday tasks, such as rising from a chair or climbing stairs. As well as a decrease in power-generating capacity a slowing of contraction results in a reduced capacity for the rapid production of force in protective reflexes, thus amplifying the impact of muscle weakness on mobility and increasing the risk of falls. [See Accidents: Falls.]

As well as changes in the shortening properties of the muscle, a well-documented feature of the lower limb muscles is an increase in the isometric twitch-contraction time. The twitch (the mechanical response to a single electrical impulse) time course is an interaction of both the cross-bridge cycling and excitation-contraction coupling processes. With respect to the latter the Ca^{2+} release-repute kinetics are of critical importance. In this regard, studies have shown that there are alterations in the kinetics of Ca^{2+} release and reuptake by the SR in aged muscles of rodents. This slowing of muscle contraction may also contribute to the increased risk of injury with falls. One advantage of this phenomenon however, is the lower stimulation frequency required for a tetanic contraction to become fully fused, thereby making the muscle metabolically more efficient!

D. Changes in the Nervous System and Motor Unit Properties

A key question as regards aged muscle, is whether changes are of muscular or of neural origin. There is a reduction in the number of alpha motor neurones in the spinal cord, and nerve conduction velocity is known to decrease in the elderly, with the peripheral segment reflex loop being significantly delayed in aged individuals. Furthermore, impaired neuromuscular transmission and reduced muscle membrane excitability seem to be further consequences of old age. Electrophysiological evidence suggests that there is a loss of functioning motor units and an increase in the size of those motor units remaining (i.e., each remaining motor unit contains more muscle fibers that will affect coordination). This process contributes toward the changes that occur in proprioception with aging. [See Motor Control; Touch and Proprioception.]

The number of fibers that are reinnervated over a life span is very high. There is experimental evidence that in this reinnervation process there is preference for a specific fiber to be reinnervated by its own type of motor nerve. Type grouping is found in muscles of elderly humans (>~75 years), which is probably a sign of a less effective reinnervation procedure. Of note is the extent to which these neurological phenomenon vary between muscles, with the anatomically more distal regions seemingly most affected.

E. Skeletal Muscle Metabolism

Skeletal muscle endurance has not consistently been shown to be reduced in the elderly. Muscle fatigue is determined by a number of physiological and metabolic phenomena relating to the type and intensity of exercise. The activation of fatigued muscle, as indicated by neuromuscular transmission, does not seem to be a limiting factor in old age, although there is some evidence of a decrease in the amount of Na^+–K^+ pumps in elderly muscle, which might reduce the clearance of K^+ during exercise-induced hyperkalemia.

Oxygen availability to individual muscle fibers is determined in part by the degree of capillarization. Similar capillary densities are observed in elderly men and women as compared with young (Table I). During low-intensity exercise ATP production occurs from the aerobic metabolism of glycogen and fat. The enzymes responsible for the aerobic breakdown of glycogen in the Krebs cycle (citrate synthase, succinate dehydrogenase) and of fat through beta oxidation (3-hydrox Co-A dehydrogenase) have been shown to be unchanged, or in some instances only slightly reduced in old age (Table I). Enzymatic capacity is inextricably linked to activity pattern, making interpretation regarding the effects of aging per se difficult. In contrast to low-intensity exercise, the demand for ATP is greatly accelerated during high-intensity exercise,

such that its supply by aerobic metabolism cannot be maintained. During high-intensity exercise ATP is generated initially from the breakdown of phosphocreatine (PCr) and then by anaerobic glycolysis. The enzymes regulating PCr breakdown (creatine kinase) and glycolysis (phosphorylase, hexokinase, lactate dehydrogenase, phosphofructokinase) do not appear to be adversely affected by aging in sedentary humans. Moreover, the availability of the high-energy substrates (ATP, PCr) is similarly not affected. [See METABOLISM: CARBOHYDRATE, LIPID, AND PROTEIN.]

F. Mechanisms of Aging

The mechanisms underlying changes in skeletal muscle are unclear. Whether the aging process represents a cell- and organ-specific response to genetic preprogramming, or whether other factors relating to a decrease in usage, either coupled to a general reduction in physical activity per se, or to a reduction imposed by other factors not directly related to the neuromuscular system is not known. For example, changes in the amount or, sensitivity to different circulating hormones may be responsible for some of the alterations observed in aged muscle. It has been suggested that the decrease in muscle mass and thus force-generating capacity may be attributable to changes in the amount of anabolic hormones. Growth hormones (GH) are speculated to increase muscle growth and performance both directly and indirectly, by means of endocrine and paracrine insulinlike growth factor-I (IGF-1) production and possibly fuel utilization. A decrease in circulating GH is known to occur in aging. Furthermore, in women a significant decline in muscle force production has been shown to occur, which corresponds to the time of the menopause. This strength loss may possibly be offset by oestrogen replacement

Table I Capillary Density and Oxidative Enzyme Capacity in Muscle

| | Young | | | Elderly | | | |
| | | | | Sedentary | | Joggers (>60 yr) | Athletes (>70 yr) |
	Sedentary	Joggers	Athletes	(>60 yr)	(>80 yr)		
Capillaries (cap. fiber⁻¹)	1.2	1.6	2.7	1.4	1.5	1.7	2.5
Citrate synthase μmol g⁻¹min⁻¹	31	42	82	34	39	34	61
3-Hydroxyacl-CoA-dehydrogease (μmol g⁻¹min⁻¹)	27	36	76	29	32	32	58

therapy. The thyroid hormones may also be of importance, as in rats they have been shown to have a marked influence on the expression of myosin isoforms and on contractile characteristics. However, the extent to which the effects of aging per se and the effects of various experimental interventions reported in animals can be extrapolated to humans remains unclear. [*See* ENDOCRINE FUNCTION AND DYSFUNCTION.]

Aged skeletal muscle exhibits features of both neuropathy and myopathy with a predominance of neuropathic alterations. These neuropathic alterations include the presence of small angulated fibers and increased fiber-type grouping. Myopathiclike changes include dilation and proliferation of the SR-T system (sarcoplasmic reticulum and transverse tubuli systems), myofilament disorders, streaming of the Z band and rod formation, accumulation of lipofuscin and lipid droplets, infoldings of the sarcolema, aggregation of muscle nuclei, and alterations in the amount and structure of mitochondria.

Several hypotheses have been proposed for the deterioration of muscle and muscle function. These include the theory that as a result of random damage (wear and tear), errors occur in the duplication of DNA increase, so that when a significant number of errors accumulate, abnormal mRNA and protein molecules are formed that do not function normally. Another theory suggests that there is an inherent biological clock, just as some genes control embryonic development, so other genes program the aging processes. The changes associated with old age may thus result from the normal expression of a genetic program that begins at conception and ends in death. Given the large aerobic energy metabolism in working skeletal muscle, a further theory concerning that of oxygen free radicals may be of significance. Free radicals are produced from the oxidation of free fatty acids. These oxygen molecules that bear free electrons are highly reactive and can easily tie up and weaken proteins and cause damage to DNA.

III. ADAPTABILITY OF AGED MUSCLE TO PHYSICAL ACTIVITY

As mentioned above an unresolved question is whether the alterations observed in the muscles of elderly people are solely a function of age or whether usage of muscle when growing old also plays a role.

Human skeletal muscle is very plastic, and disuse and usage are critical determinants of both the size of a muscle fiber as well as its qualitative characteristics, such as the isoform pattern of contractile proteins, energy-related enzymes, and membrane-bound regulatory proteins. This plasticity appears to be present not only in muscles of the young, but also of the elderly.

A. Muscle Size and Strength

In 70-year-old men who have been physically active through strength (high resistance) training, muscle force is comparable to that of sedentary young adults. Muscle cross-sectional areas of both arms and legs can also be maintained in these elderly people. This is accomplished by a larger mean fiber size to compensate for a reduced number of muscle fibers. This effect of muscle usage on muscle fiber size is very specific. Endurance-based exercise such as walking, running, or swimming does not result in maintained muscle fiber size, and cross-sectional area and muscle strength is reduced in relation to the smaller muscle mass.

In recent years several well-controlled longitudinal studies have been performed to evaluate the effect of increased usage through strength training by elderly people. The general finding is that as with young adults, task-specific muscle function can be vastly improved in just a few months by regular training (Fig. 4). At the same time the changes in maximum isometric strength and muscle cross-sectional area as a result of training are not as impressive, suggesting that the elevation in, for example 1RM (one repetition maximum), is primarily a function of improved neural drive. These effects are similar in age groups from 70–90 years. A critical factor for obtaining these marked improvements is that the training is characterized by a regime of high resistance loading with few repetitions. Thus, the total time for training may amount to only 10 min per day. It appears favorable to use training loads exceeding 70% of 1RM. Such high muscle force developments can be sustained by elderly people. This has been shown repeatedly, not only in small studies with small numbers of selected elderly subjects, but also in population-based samples. In healthy elderly subjects nutritional supplementation does not add to the improvement in strength. Moreover, socialization and increased attention has also been shown not to cause elderly people to produce greater muscle forces.

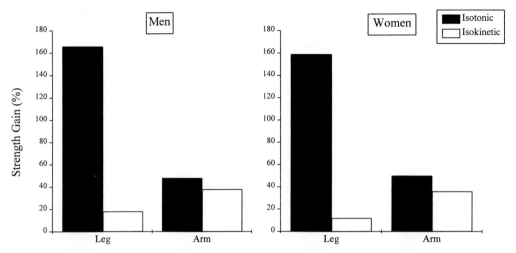

Figure 4 The effects of high-load isotonic (free weights) resistance training on the isotonic and isokinetic (constant speed at 30°s⁻¹) strength of the knee extensors and elbow flexors in elderly men and women aged 70–77 years. Note the similarity in responses between men and women, the greater improvement in isotonic, compared with isokinetic strength, and the greater improvement in the leg compared to the arm muscles, despite similar training loads (3 × 6 repetitions at 85% 1RM, 3 times per week for 11 weeks). (Data from Lexell et al., 1995.)

Muscle fiber size is enlarged when elderly people start to train, but the magnitude of change is small and usually in the order of 5–10%, an increase that in some studies does not reach statistical significance. Estimates of the increase in size of whole cross-sectional area of trained muscles are in the same range. A positive effect of combining strength training with GH supplementation has been noticed on muscle mass, but not on improved muscle strength.

B. Muscle Fiber Number

The role of physical activity for retarding the rate by which muscle fibers are lost with age is less clear. Indirect estimates based on measurements of cross-sectional area of the muscle and mean muscle fiber size suggest that active muscles of elderly people may contain more fibers (~15%). No thorough evaluation has been performed to estimate muscle fiber number with brief periods of training in elderly subjects. With small and similar changes observed in mean muscle fiber area, and whole muscle cross-sectional area, it is unlikely the training has an effect on the number of muscle fibers. It may, however, if the training period is extended. With daily strenuous muscle usage, muscle fiber number has been shown to be maintained at

a 30% higher level in active, as compared to inactive rats. Thus, slowing the rate by which muscle fibers are lost may be a significant factor in maintaining muscle mass in the elderly. It needs to be demonstrated whether the less marked loss of muscle fibers observed with muscle usage is due to the death of fewer spinal motor neurons, or to an increased reinnervation activity of the remaining functional peripheral motor nerves.

C. Muscle Fiber Types

Lifelong physical activity may affect muscle fiber type composition. Strength-trained elderly men have been shown to have the highest percentage of type II fibers, in both leg and arm muscles. In contrast, elderly joggers have the highest percentage of slow fibers in the leg muscles. Similar observations are available on elite master athletes who had been runners all their lives. Of note, however, is that muscles that have been dynamically active for a lifetime may have 20–30% more slow twitch fibers. More specific methods to characterize the isoform pattern of the contractile proteins, such as immunocytochemistry and single-fiber electrophoresis, give a similar pattern of change as the one described above.

Differences in muscle fiber composition comparing young and older sedentary people tends to be more marked in the leg compared to the arm muscles. Whether this is due to differences in muscle usage is not known. In a small number of very active elderly runners studied, the coexpression of MHC isoforms in the leg muscles was found to be similar to that found in young subjects. Whether an exercise stimuli aids in more proper regulation of gene transcription in the elderly is a possibility.

No change in muscle fiber types has been observed in longitudinal studies as a result of training, but that does not exclude the possibility that changes could occur, provided that the duration of the training is longer (many months) and more sensitive techniques other than traditional histochemistry are used to identify the MHC isoforms.

D. Capillaries and Mitochondrial Enzymes

Muscles of endurance-trained elderly men contain a very high number of capillaries, and their mitochondrial enzyme activity levels are high (Table I). Indeed, these men are at a similar level to young endurance-trained athletes. Less regular and strenuous endurance activities are also effective, although the absolute level of adaptation is smaller than in top-trained athletes, but nevertheless above that which is observed in young sedentary men.

Oxygen delivery to muscle during exercise is reduced in elderly subjects due to a drop in maximal heart rate and stroke volume. This also occurs even in very active elderly subjects, as the reduction in maximal heart rate is unaffected by the level of physical activity. With a maintained capacity of the muscle to receive a given blood flow and to utilize oxygen, there is a relative overcapacity for aerobic metabolism in the elderly muscle. The functional significance is a more favorable muscle metabolism during exercise, as indicated by a low blood lactate accumulation and a low respiratory exchange ratio (i.e., a large lipid oxidation), even at quite high exercise intensities.

Little is known about the effect of short-term training on aged muscles in humans as it has not been a focus of many studies. As the successful training programs to improve strength incorporate few repetitions and each session is of short duration, it is highly unlikely that muscle capillaries or mitochondrial enzymes would be enhanced. Rather, if there is fiber enlargement, a "dilution effect" may occur, with less capillaries and mitochondria present per unit area or volume.

In endurance-training studies on rodents, there is an increase in both the number of capillaries and mitochondrial capacity, clearly demonstrating that aged skeletal muscle maintains its capacity to adapt to demands in regard to aerobic metabolism.

E. Membrane-Bound Regulatory Proteins

Na^+–K^+ pumps and Ca^{2+} ATPase of the SR-system are affected by physical activity, and as for other muscle characteristics the effect is specific to the type of muscle usage. High-resistance activities during a lifetime maintain the Na^+–K^+ pump better than endurance activities, whereas the reverse is true for the Ca^{2+}–ATPase. These maintained capacities are likely to have a functional role by retarding the rate by which fatigue develops in high-intensity and endurance exercise.

Data from longitudinal training studies of humans are not available. In rodents a training-specific effect is observed for both Na^+–K^+ pumps and Ca^{2+} ATPase of the SR system, confirming the finding in cross-sectional studies. Resistance training is needed to affect the [^{3}H] ouabain-binding sites and repetitive monotonous activation affects the Ca^{2+} ATPase.

F. Conclusion

Skeletal muscle exhibits great plasticity and it is possible to maintain the capacity for adaptation in old age. The common alterations in aging skeletal muscle seem to be due largely to a lack of usage. This relates specifically to muscle fiber size, which can be maintained quite well in old age in people who undergo resistance training. The reduction in fiber number may, to a small extent, be retarded by usage. No major changes have been shown to occur in fiber-type composition either with age, or with training. A maintained muscle mass is reflected in maintained muscle strength and function, which translates into improvements in the performance of daily life activities.

Other qualities of skeletal muscle, such as capillaries, substrates, and energy-related enzymes in the elderly are kept at levels comparable to young adults, and the response to training is similar to that observed in young people. As with young people there is a very high degree of specificity in the response to training. High-load strength training affects mainly muscle fiber size and fiber number as well as ion pumps, whereas endurance training primarily affects capillary proliferation, mitochondria, oxidative enzyme activity, and the Ca^{2+} ATPase of the SR-system.

Finally, it is clear that several of the alterations that are observed in muscles of elderly healthy people relate to lack of muscle usage. However, there is a limit to how late in life skeletal muscle variables can be influenced by activity. This age limit definitely varies between individuals, but is probably not critical until an age above 75 years.

BIBLIOGRAPHY

Bassey, E. J., Fiatarone, M. A., O'Neill, E. F., Kelly, W. J., Evans, W. J., & Lipsitz, L. A. (1992). Leg extensor power and functional performance in very old men and women. *Clinical Science, 82,* 322–327.

Cartee, G. D. (1994). Aging skeletal muscle: response to exercise. In J. O. Holloszy (Ed.), *Exercise and sport science reviews,* American College of Sports Medicine series (vol. 22, pp. 91–120). Baltimore: Williams and Wilkins.

Fiatarone, M. A., O'Neill, E. F., & Ryan, N. D., Clements, E. R., Solares, K. M., and Evans, W. J. (1994). Exercise training and nutritional supplementation for physical frailty in very elderly people. *New England Journal of Medicine, 330,* 1769–1775.

Grabiner, M. D., & Enoka, R. M. (1995). Changes in movement capabilities with aging. In J. O. Holloszy (Ed.), *Exercise and sport science reviews,* American College of Sports Medicine series (vol. 23, pp. 65–104). Baltimore: Williams and Wilkins.

Grimby, G., Anianson, A., Hedberg, M., Henning, G-B., Grangard, U., & Kvist, H. (1992). Training can improve muscle strength and endurance in 78–84-year-old men. *Journal of Applied Physiology, 73,* 2517–2523.

Jones, D. A., & Round, J. M. (1990). *Skeletal muscle in health and disease. A textbook of muscle physiology.* Manchester, UK: Manchester University Press.

Klitgaard, H., Mantoni, M., Schiaffino, S., Ausoni, S., Gorza, L., Laurent-Winter, C., Schnohr, P., & Saltin, B. (1990). Function, morphology and protein expression of ageing skeletal muscle: a cross-sectional study of elderly men with different training backgrounds. *Acta Physiologica Scandinavica, 140,* 41–54.

Lexell, J., Downham, D. Y., Larsson, Y., Bruhn, E., & Morsing, B. (1995). Heavy resistance training in older Scandinavian men and women: short and long-term effects on arm and leg muscles. *Scandinavian Journal of Medicine and Science in Sports, 5,* 329–341.

Porter, M. M., Vandervoort, A. A., & Lexell, J. (1995). Ageing of human muscle: structure, function and adaptability. *Scandinavian Journal of Medicine and Science in Sports, 5,* 129–142.

Rogers, M. A., & Evans, W. J. (1993). Changes in skeletal muscle with aging: effects of exercise training. In J. O. Holloszy (Ed.), *Exercise and sport science reviews,* American College of Sports Medicine series (vol. 21, pp. 65–102). Baltimore: Williams and Wilkins.

Neurotransmitters and
Neurotrophic Factors

Thomas H. McNeill

University of Southern California

Timothy J. Collier

Rush-Presbyterian Medical Center

Franz Hefti

Merck Sharp and Dohme
Harlow, England

I. Introduction
II. Neurotransmitters and Neurotrophic Factors in
the Aged Brain
III. Neurotransmitters and Neurotrophic Factors in
Neurodegenerative Disease

Age-Related Neurodegenerative Diseases Diseases characterized by atrophy or death of nerve cells; examples are Alzheimer's disease and Parkinson's disease.

Neurotransmitters Chemicals mediating the contact between nerve cells at synaptic junctions.

Neurotrophic Factors Proteins regulating survival and morphological plasticity of nerve cells.

NEUROTRANSMITTER release and receptor mechanisms stimulated by them are key determinants of brain function. **NEUROTROPHIC FACTORS** are required for normal development and for maintenance of structural integrity of the nervous system. The function of neurotransmitters and neurotrophic factors changes during aging. However, such changes are selective and there is no evidence for a global decline. Neurotransmitters and neurotrophic factors are affected by neurodegenerative diseases and play a role in pathophysiology. Many current therapies and approaches to future therapy of such diseases are based on influencing neurotransmitter or neurotrophic factor mechanisms.

I. INTRODUCTION

A. Role of Neurotransmitters in Brain Function

The notion that the nerve cells function as independent units and must form physical contacts to facilitate intercellular communications was first proposed by neurohistologists at the turn of the century. This concept is termed the *neuron theory of brain function* and is based on the implicit assumption that nerve cells (neurons) do not form a contiguous labyrinth of intertwining processes but instead enter into close functional contacts to permit the transfer of information from one neuron to another. The site at which this transfer takes place is the synapse, and the chemical messenger that is used in the transfer of information is the neurotransmitter.

Synapses that use a chemical messenger to transfer information from one neuron to another are called chemical synapses. The distinctive feature of the chemical synapse is that information carried as an electrical impulse by an axon (presynaptic cell) is converted into a chemical signal at the axon terminal (Figure 1). The chemical signal (i.e. neurotransmitter) is released in small quanta from small membrane-bound vesicles (synaptic vesicles) at the axon terminal and crosses a physical space or gap (about 20 nm) between the two neurons, called the synaptic cleft. Upon arrival at the postsynaptic cell, the neurotransmitter combines with a protein embedded in the cell

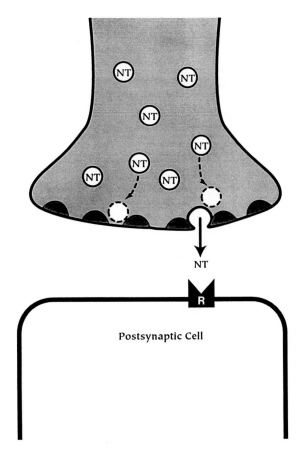

Postsynaptic Cell

Figure 1 Schematic drawing of a chemical synapse. Neurotransmitter (NT) is released in small quanta from synaptic vesicles at the presynaptic terminal. The neurotransmitter diffuses across the synaptic cleft and binds to the receptor (R) on the postsynaptic membrane.

membrane that is specifically designed to bind with that neurotransmitter. This protein, or receptor, induces an electrical signal in the target cell (postsynaptic potential) when the neurotransmitter binds to the receptor. Subsequently, the neurotransmitter is deactivated by a degrading enzyme or taken back up into the presynaptic nerve terminal. In this way the transfer of information between cells is carried out through unidirectional electrochemical transduction between the presynaptic and postsynaptic cell and does not involve the direct transfer of an electrical signal from one cell to another.

For both the central and peripheral nervous system there are a relatively small number of molecules that fulfill the criteria of a neurotransmitter. These include

the biogenic amines (dopamine [DA], norepinephrine [NE], epinephrine, serotonin, histamine), acetylcholine (ACh), gamma-amino butyric acid (GABA), glycine, and glutamate. In addition, over 100 small peptides that have been shown to be biologically active at the level of the synapse and to alter the electrophysiological state of the postsynaptic cell. Some of the peptides were demonstrated to act as neurotransmitters in a similar way as the small molecule transmitters.

Collections of neurons that contain a specific neurotransmitter can be clustered in specific nuclei (i.e., DA in the substantia nigra or ACh in the diagonal band of Broca) or can be distributed across many regions of the nervous system and serve as a common component of many neuroanatomical pathways (i.e., glutamate). In addition, based on previous clinical, neuropathological, and experimental research studies, it is clear that certain biological functions can be linked to neuroanatomical pathways that use a specific neurotransmitter to communicate information between neurons. Examples of this functional–biochemical correlation are found in the role of dopaminergic and GABAergic systems of the basal ganglia in the regulation of motor movement and cholinergic systems of the basal forebrain in learning and memory. The obvious corollary to this anatomical organization would be that damage to specific neuroanatomical pathways in the nervous system as part of aging or a neurological disease would lead to loss of selective neurotransmitter systems characteristic of the disease process. This is most readily seen in the loss of DA in Parkinson's disease and the loss of ACh in Alzheimer's disease (AD). However, it is clear that neurodegenerative diseases of the central nervous system (CNS) are not the result of the loss of a single neurotransmitter system but are a composite of multineurotransmitter deficits that result in the generation of specific sets of behavioral changes characteristic of a particular disease state. [*See* BRAIN AND CENTRAL NERVOUS SYSTEM.]

B. Role of Neurotrophic Factors in Nervous System Function

Neurotrophic factors are proteins that regulate developmental growth of nerve cells. Although the adult brain does not undergo significant morphological changes as a brain during development, most adult neurons retain the ability to change their morphology. This plasticity is regulated by neurotrophic factors similar to the regulation of developmental growth. Currently known neurotrophic factors include the neurotrophin family with nerve growth factor (NGF), brain-derived neurotrophic factor (BDNF), neurotrophin-3, and neurotrophin-4/5. Other factors are ciliary neurotrophic factor, midkine, heparin-binding neurotrophic factor, and glial cell-derived neurotrophic factor, which were purified based on their ability to promote the formation of axons and dendrites from embryonic neurons. Among previously known growth factors with neurotrophic actions are members of the fibroblast growth factor family, epidermal growth factor family, transforming growth factor (TGF)-β family, including glial cell-derived neurotrophic factor (GDNF), as well as insulin-like growth factors (IGFs). All these growth factors act by stimulating specific receptor molecules embedded in the cell membrane of responsive cells. A biological role is particularly well established for the neurotrophins in the development of the peripheral nervous system. This role has been most elegantly demonstrated by the creation of mutant mice in which genes coding for neurotrophic factors were deleted. Experimentally produced deletions of the genes coding for individual neurotrophins in mice produced animals that lacked specific subpopulations of neurons. In the brain, the cholinergic system of the basal forebrain, which undergoes degeneration in AD, failed to develop properly in animals lacking functional genes coding for NGF. The crucial role of neurotrophic factors in development and maintenance of function in the adult brain suggests that a gradual reduction in the efficiency of neurotrophic factor mechanism may be a responsible factor in the decline of neuronal function during aging.

II. NEUROTRANSMITTERS AND NEUROTROPHIC FACTORS IN THE AGED BRAIN

Two of the most prominent principles that underscore all gerontologic research are that (a) organisms age at different rates, as do different systems in their bodies; and (b) identifiable differences can be demonstrated between biological and chronological age among individuals of like age. This divergence between biological and chronological old age is most obvious in the human population but is not limited to the human experience. Functional variability with age is a consistent feature across species and is closely tied to the variability of biochemical changes found in different regions of the nervous system. In addition, research studies conducted over the past two decades have forced us to reevaluate the traditional view that age-related changes in the brain can be represented by simple cell loss that leads to functional decline. Rather it is now believed that the aging nervous system represents a composite of various adaptive responses that work together to preserve and repair neural networks against a background of ongoing cell death that is brain region, cell type, and species specific. A recent review of studies examining the neurobiology of aging rodents indicated that screening animals of life age for common behavioral characteristics, and correlating behavioral changes with the anatomical and biochemical changes found across the nervous system is an extremely useful approach for studying mechanisms of "usual aging," abnormal aging, and disease.

The degree to which age-related anatomical and biochemical changes occur in the neural circuitry of the nervous system is variable at best. Previous anatomical studies that have reported age-related morphological changes in neurotransmitter neurons of the nervous system of rodent brain have suggested that advancing age has a differential effect on cell loss and biochemical content of select populations of neurons in different regions of the brain. For example, in rodents, aging is associated with a decline in the number of nonDAergic neurons in the pars reticulate but not in dopaminergic neurons of the pars compacta of the substantia nigra. These data are consistent with previous biochemical studies that have reported small and inconsistent losses of DA and tyrosine hydroxylase activity in the nigrostriatal system of aged rodent brain. The decline in the DA content and tyrosine hydroxylase activity of the substantia nigra and striatum of aged rodents is not a consistent finding across rodent species and is generally smaller than that reported for postmortem human brain. In addition, although some studies have reported significant losses of DA content in the striatum of aged rodents, others have found only small changes that may or may not reach statistical significance. Although the reason for the variability in the loss of DA content of this brain region is unknown, it may be suggested that although DAergic neurons of the substantia nigra are not characterized by a generalized age-related cell loss or atrophy, some cells may show a decline in their ability to synthesize new protein, whereas others increase their rate of synthesis in order to compensate for the metabolic decline of neighboring DAergic neurons. This compensatory process, designed to maintain the DA content of the striatum within the normal range despite the metabolic decline in some cells, is similar to what has been reported following acute neurotoxic lesions of the substantia nigra using the selective neurotoxin 6-hydroxy-DA. These studies have reported that following an injection of this toxin some DAergic neurons show continual signs of neurotoxicity, atrophy, and cellular degeneration whereas others increase their rate of synthesis to offset the death of neighboring cells. It may be suggested that a similar compensatory phenomenon may occur in normal aging and that individual neurons within the substantia nigra may exhibit differential sensitivity to the effects of the aging process. In addition, based on these anatomical studies it may be suggested that age-related cell loss in the brain is both cell type and region specific, and that separate cell populations in contiguous regions of the same anatomical structure may be differentially sensitive to age-related declines in cell number.

Previous studies also suggest that neurons that contain the same neurotransmitter are differentially affected by age in different regions of the nervous system. For example, previous studies in the striatum have consistently reported a loss of cholinergic interneurons and activity of choline acetyltransferase, the rate-limiting enzyme for the synthesis of ACh, in aged mice, rats and humans; suggesting the cholinergic neurons may be particularly vulnerable to the aging process. However, age-related cholinergic cell loss is not a general characteristic for cholinergic neurons of the basal forebrain; a region of the brain particularly involved in learning and memory. Most revealing however, is the demonstration of the close association between functional and biochemical changes that occur in neurotransmitter neurons regardless of the age group examined. Previous studies have used a variety of behavioral tests to divide rats of like age into behaviorally impaired and unimpaired age groups and have correlated cell number and biochemical content for a number of neurotransmitter

systems with functional performance. Among the most robust relationships revealed by this approach has been the correlation between age-related changes in performance of spatial learning and memory tasks (e.g., Morris water maze, radial arm maze) and age-related changes in the hippocampus, in particular with age-related degenerative changes in basal forebrain cholinergic neurons. In addition, age-related impairments in learning and memory on inhibitory avoidance tasks have been correlated with the loss of NE from the locus coeruleus and deficits in motor performance, as assessed by performance on balance rod task have been linked with an age-related increase in the number of atrophic GABAergic neurons in the striatum. Consistent with this evidence is the premise that the variability in functional performance increases with age and that deficits in specific behavioral parameters may be correlated with alterations in selective neuroanatomical pathways in the brain. However, when data from neurogerontological studies are analyzed with age as the only independent variable, the ratio of functionally impaired versus unimpaired animals that constitute a specific sample population may directly confound the outcome of the experiment in regard to the relationship between performance and neurobiological substrates. Furthermore, neurobiological changes that do occur profoundly in some aged animals can be masked by the variability across old animals and can only be parceled out by relating neurobiological measures to behavioral performance.

Whether the patterns of cell loss within different neurotransmitter systems are similar between rodents, nonhuman primates, and humans remains an open question for most neurotransmitter pathways in both the central and peripheral nervous systems. For most regions of the brain, age-related cell loss is not a consistent feature across species, and interspecies comparisons are difficult because methodological procedures vary between studies. This seems particularly true for cell counts in the substantia nigra when comparisons are made between rodents and humans. For example, although it has been reported that normal aging is not associated with a significant decline in the total number of dopaminergic neurons of the substantia nigra in aged mice, controversy exists as to the degree of dopaminergic cell loss in the substantia nigra of humans. Although some studies have reported a decrease in the number of DAergic neurons with age, others have found no change in the number of DAergic neurons of postmortem human brain comparing data from young and old groups. In addition, recent studies in our laboratories using immunocytochemical staining to identify dopaminergic neurons in postmortem human tissue also support the later finding that aging is not characterized by a progressive loss of DAergic neurons of either nonhuman primates or humans. Discrepancies in age-related cell loss across species has also been reported for the locus coeruleus, a large NE-containing nucleus in the brain stem. Although previous studies have reported that cell loss in the locus coeruleus is a consistent feature of human aging the degree of noradrenergic cell loss varies between strains of aged mice and rats and is closely tied to functional performance but not necessarily chronological age.

The situation is further complicated by the existence of age-related changes at the level of neurotransmitter receptors. There is tentative evidence for changes in synthesis and function of specific receptors. For example, in the case of DAergic neurons, one of four known receptor molecules seems to be affected by aging. However, this field of investigation is still in its infancy, making it impossible to draw general conclusions.

Several findings suggest that mechanisms related to neurotrophic factors are involved in senescence. The decline in the proliferative capacity of certain cells in culture seems to be associated with alterations in their response to growth factors. For example, the expression and functional response of receptors mediating the biological actions of epidermal growth factor (EGF) declines during proliferative senescence of endothelial cells in culture. The investigation of neurotrophic factors during aging is still in its infancy and only initial findings are available. NGF synthesis remains constant or is only slightly reduced in the aged rat brain. Similar findings were obtained for BDNF and its receptor. However, several reports suggest a reduction in levels of a specific neurotrophin receptor, the low-affinity NGF receptor. Mice mutants in which its genes were disrupted show degenerative changes in the sensory nervous system during aging. There is indirect evidence that suggests that endogenous neurotrophins transduction mechanisms may be altered in the aged rat brain. Chronic NGF administration to aged animals stimulates the function of cholinergic neurons of the basal forebrain and improves performance in behavioral tasks, thus, counteracting age-related declines in cholinergic function. Taken together, these findings suggest the possibility that neu-

rotrophic factor-related mechanisms are altered during the aging process and that a reduced sensitivity to neurotrophic factors may be responsible for some of the age-related declines in neuronal and behavioral functions. [See MODELS OF AGING: VERTEBRATES.]

III. NEUROTRANSMITTERS AND NEUROTROPHIC FACTORS IN NEURODEGENERATIVE DISEASE

The question of how changes in the neurotransmitter systems that may be considered part of normal aging may contribute to the onset and progression of human neurodegenerative disease is the topic of much debate. Although it is well known that most neurodegenerative diseases of the brain have a characteristic age of onset, it is currently unclear what role natural age-related changes in the brain play in the onset of disease, or to what degree aging may effect different areas of the diseased brain. In addition, the question of how age-related changes in the morphological and biochemical properties of neurotransmitter neurons may contribute to the progression of human disease remains uncertain. What is clear, however, is the fact that neurodegenerative diseases of the brain are associated with a composite of multineurotransmitter deficits that are characteristic of a particular disease state and that classic neurodegenerative diseases of the brain, such as Parkinson's disease and AD, should not be considered the natural endpoints of normal aging but represent disease states separate from the normal aging process.

A second basic concept that is crucial for understanding the pathophysiology of neurotransmitter systems in human neurodegenerative disease is the notion that neurotransmitter neurons can compensate for disease-associated cell loss that can delay the onset of clinical systems for several decades after cell loss begins. The phenomenon of functional compensation was first observed in DAergic neurons of the nigrostriatal system in Parkinson's disease in the early 1970s when investigators reported that mild clinical symptoms were associated with a disproportionate large decrease (up to 80% loss) of striatal DA. Subsequent to this observation numerous investigators have developed various models and theories regarding the etiopathology of transmitter systems as a causal factor for the development of neurodegenerative diseases of the CNS. Common to all theories regarding the pathology of neurotransmitter systems and human disease are the hypotheses that (a) clinical symptoms become evident only when the neurotransmitter content of a critical brain region is substantially depleted (i.e., 80% in the case of Parkinson's disease); and (b) neurotransmitter cell loss, in the early stages of the disease, is offset by adaptive changes in both pre- and postsynaptic neurons that functionally compensates for the death of neighboring neurons. The notion that neurotransmitter neurons can functionally compensate for cell death has led to the suggestion that the onset and progression of human neurodegenerative disease can be characterized by two stages of the disease process. Stage 1 or presymptomatic disease spans the time from when disease-associated neurotransmitter cell loss begins (i.e., disease inception) to when cell loss and neurotransmitter depletion is sufficient to induce clinical symptoms (i.e., symptomatic threshold). As in the case of Parkinson's disease, presymptomatic disease can last as long as 20 to 40 years prior to when the disease becomes clinically manifest. By comparison, stage 2 or symptomatic disease is characterized by the progressive increase in the severity and complexity of clinical symptoms characteristic of the disease process and is positively correlated with the degree of neurotransmitter loss. Understanding the underlying mechanisms that relate to the loss of neurotransmitter neurons in human disease and how they relate to brain function is a prerequisite for developing new strategies to ameliorate age-related behavioral impairments and neurodegenerative diseases of the CNS.

Neurotrophic factors have been linked to neurodegeneration as it occurs in aged-related neurodegenerative diseases. Basic research indicating that these proteins regulate survival of neurons has created opportunities for using them therapeutically as neuroprotective agents. The field has reached the threshold of clinical application. There are ongoing clinical trials with neurotrophic factors in amyotrophic lateral sclerosis, peripheral sensory neuropathy, and AD. These and future trials are based on the anticipation that neurotropic factors will reverse atrophy of the nerve cell's synthetic machinery and atrophic synapses, stimulate the synthesis of proteins necessary for transmitter release and, perhaps, reestablish lost synaptic contacts (Figure 2).

The best known and most developed example of

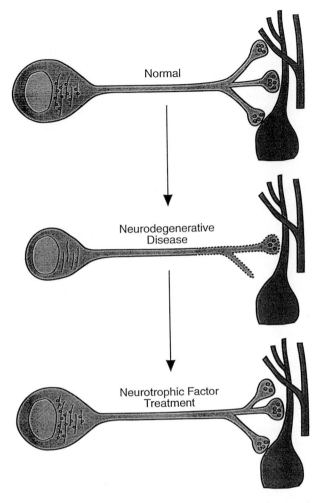

Figure 2 Schematic drawing depicting a nerve cell with synaptic contacts to target cells. In neurodegenerative diseases such as Alzheimer's and Parkinson's disease, there are atrophic changes in neuron, including shrinkage of the cell body and loss of synapses. Neurotrophic factor therapy is expected to reverse cell body and synaptic atrophy, to stimulate the synthesis of proteins necessary for transmitter release machinery, and, under special conditions, to reestablish lost synaptic contacts. (Reprinted with permission from Hefti, 1994.)

a therapeutic use of neurotrophic factors is that of NGF in AD. Intracerebroventricular administration of NGF to AD patients is based on the well-established trophic action of NGF on forebrain cholinergic neurons and the atrophy of these cells in AD. Although NGF presently is the most promising neurotrophic factor for the treatment of AD, its beneficial actions will be limited by their selective trophic effects on cholinergic neurons and the role of the cholinergic deficit in AD pathophysiology. Thus, current research focuses on identifying neurotrophic factors for non-cholinergic neurons affected in the disease. Besides potential side effects, a second major hurdle for the approach is the fact that neurotrophic factors do not cross the blood–brain barrier, making it necessary to administer directly to the brain. Strategies to overcome this significant limitation of neurotrophic factor therapy include intracerebral infusion devices, gene therapy, and the development of pharmacological agents that mimic the action on neurotrophic factors. [*See* PHARMACOLOGY.]

BIBLIOGRAPHY

Beck, K., & Hefti, F. (1993). Neurotrophic factor therapy of Alzheimer's disease. *Clinical Neuroscience, 1,* 219–224.

Collier, T. J., & Coleman, P. D. (1991). Divergence of biological and chronological aging: Evidence from rodent studies. *Neurobiology of Aging, 12,* 685–693.

Flood, D. G., & Coleman, P. D. (1988). Neuron numbers and sizes in aging brain: comparisons of human, monkey, and rodent data. *Neurobiology of Aging, 9,* 453–463.

Hefti, F. (1994). Neurotrophic factor therapy for nervous system degenerative diseases. *Journal of Neurobiology, 25,* 1418–1435.

Hefti, F., Hartikka, J., & Knusel, B. (1989). Function of neurotrophic factors in the adult and aging brain and their possible use in the treatment of neurodegenerative disease. *Neurobiology of Aging, 10,* 515–533.

Morgan, D. G., & Finch, C. E. (1988). Dopaminergic changes in basal ganglia: A generalized phenomenon of aging in mammals. *Annals of the New York Academy of Science, 515,* 145–160.

Snider, W. D. (1994). Functions of the neurotrophins during nervous system development: What the knockouts are teaching us. *Cell, 77,* 627–638.

Williams, L. R., Rylett, R. J., Ingram, D. K., Joseph, J. A., Moises, H. C., Tang, A. H., & Mervis, R. F. (1993). Nerve growth factor affects the cholinergic neurochemistry and behavior of aged rats. *Progress in Brain Research, 98,* 251–265.

Organizations on Aging

Phoebe S. Liebig

University of Southern California

I. Social Movement and Interest Group Theory
II. A Brief History of Organizations on Aging
III. Current Status and Characteristics
IV. The Future of Organizations on Aging

Advocacy Urging the larger society to attend to and act on the needs of elders. The aged can act as their own advocates, or others, such as service providers, can speak and act on their behalf.

Age Consciousness Identification of oneself with others by virtue of chronological age, as opposed to other kinds of group identification such as race, gender, religion.

Coalition An alliance, often temporary, of age-based groups with each other (the "aging coalition") or with nonage-based groups sharing similar concerns about a variety of issues, such as long-term care or transportation.

Interest Groups Organizations that seek collective benefits from policy makers through grass roots mobilization and lobbying. One part (or "player") of a complex political system, they are based on mass membership or private philanthropies or made up of professionals, business, or industry groupings. Also called special interest groups. The "gray lobby" denotes all age-based groups.

Politics of Aging Used to describe the process by which aging groups make demands on the policy-making system by bargaining, competing, or allying with other groups and sometimes threatening the re-election prospects of elected officials.

Public Policy for the Aged Policies that are enacted by governments to benefit elders. They include Social Security, Medicare, state tax preferences, and local zoning benefiting older persons.

Social Movements Mobilization of like-minded persons, often by a charismatic leader, to voice grievances. Often disorganized initially, they can evolve into interest groups. Examples include civil rights, women's, and seniors groups.

ORGANIZATIONS ON AGING are stable, non-profit collective entities that are distinguished by their emphasis on the betterment of older adults in society through research, education, and service. They are not necessarily identifiable by "aging" or "aged" in their names; the majority, however, do include those terms or related ones, such as *retired*, *older*, or *senior*. Several types exist. Mass membership groups composed of older persons are often driven by a sense of age consciousness. They and other age-based organizations composed of individuals and businesses providing services to the aged focus on ensuring that public policies benefit the elderly.

I. SOCIAL MOVEMENT AND INTEREST GROUP THEORY

Both social movement and interest group theory have been used to explain the rise and greater visibility of organizations on aging. Social movements involve collective actions to aggregate interests on a broad scale and are often characterized by two stages. The first, developmental stage consists of erratic expressions of grievances by individuals who feel left out or left behind by the larger society, in terms of economic or political

Copyright © 1996 by Academic Press, Inc.
All rights of reproduction in any form reserved.

benefits. These disgruntled feelings are often catalyzed by a populist leader into an ad hoc organization that focuses on political solutions to right perceived wrongs. The second or institutional phase consists of a large membership base and a stable organization with economic and political resources, division of labor and hierarchy, and connections with government officials. U.S. history is replete with such social movements from the midnineteenth century on, some of which have evolved into political parties or interest groups.

Interest group or pluralist theory posits that politics is characterized by dispersed power, competition and bargaining over specific goals by multiple groups or factions, and the responsiveness of decision makers to a wide range of societal interests and the voting public. Interest groups operate within a complex milieu of macroeconomic development, political parties, government officials, and policy professionals, as well as prevailing values and public opinion. [See POLITICAL ATTITUDES AND BEHAVIOR.]

II. A BRIEF HISTORY OF ORGANIZATIONS ON AGING

The history of organizations on aging can be divided into three periods: the 1920s–1950s, an incubation stage; the 1960s–1970s, a proliferation period; and the 1980s to the present, a consolidation era. The rise of these groups grew out of the state-level movement for old-age pensions, initially led by nonaging groups, such as the Fraternal Order of the Eagles. Between 1923 and 1933, 25 states enacted old-age assistance laws. The first age-based group was started in 1933 by Francis Townsend in California, a hotbed of old-age politics. He had a plan for a national pension of $200 per month to be paid to everyone age 60 and over, financed by a national sales tax. This plan led to a national movement, by early 1935, of more than 3000 clubs nationwide. After Social Security passed later that same year, the organization's membership and support declined because the law met some of the needs identified in Townsend's mass appeal. However, the Townsend movement went on to sponsor congressional candidates in 1938; 147 Townsend-endorsees were elected. After that peak, the movement subsided.

The passage of Social Security initiated a direct relationship between the federal government and the elderly, based on social insurance against the eco-

nomic risks of old age, as a matter of right. Despite this, the aged were still at a disadvantage. To raise the status of older people and provide benefits such as life insurance that were otherwise difficult to obtain, Ethel Percy Andrus established two age-based groups, the National Retired Teachers Association and the American Association of Retired Persons (AARP), during the late 1940s. She emphasized self-help and the contributions to be made by the aged to society, rather than influencing public policy to benefit elders. Until the 1960s the aging movement retained its popular, unstructured character.

The 1960s and 1970s ushered in a proliferation of interest groups in general and particularly age-based groups. It also gave rise to a "golden age" in the politics of aging. The Senior Citizens for Kennedy thrust age-related issues squarely into presidential politics. The 1961 and then the 1971 White House Conferences on Aging (WHCoA) provided a forum for discussing needs of the aged. New public policies benefiting the aged were enacted: Medicare, the Older Americans Act, Supplemental Security Income, and Medicaid. Although controversy exists over the extent to which age-based groups were primarily responsible for these entitlements, their ability to work in coalitions with other groups, especially labor unions, was an important factor. They also developed their own age-based coalitions to encompass the differing agenda of mass membership groups (e.g., AARP), professionals such as the National Council on the Aging and the Gerontological Society of America, and a wide array of groups such as the Older Women's League and the National Caucus and Center on Black Aged that were created to represent the interests of specific subgroups of the elderly, such as women and minorities. The growth in federal and state programs for elders also gave rise to trade associations and other organizations composed of industries, providers, and professionals serving the elderly, dubbed the "aging enterprise."

In the 1980s increases in the numbers of age-related groups slowed markedly, as did the earlier growth in programs for the aged. To ensure that the demands of age-based groups were more uniform, a coalition of those groups, the Leadership Council on Aging, was created. Despite this, the 1981 WHCoA lacked the impact of its predecessors, reflected in less funding for aging programs in housing and social services, taxation of Social Security income and changes in Medicare reimbursement that negatively affected elders. As the

1980s came to an end, a political backlash against elders surfaced and grew, signaling an end to the easy public policy gains of earlier decades and the need to consolidate those gains. In addition, the passage and subsequent repeal of the Medicare Catastrophic Care Act (MCCA) revealed the nonmonolithic advocacy stances of age-based groups. Nevertheless, national policy makers had come to view older people as a political force in their own right, beyond their high levels of participation in elections.

III. CURRENT STATUS AND CHARACTERISTICS

Today there are approximately 1000 age-based groups at the national, state, and local levels advocating for collective benefits for a highly diverse and growing old-age population. In Washington, many have achieved insider status, especially AARP, the Alzheimer's Association and Families/USA, which often join forces on issues such as long-term care. The "gray lobby" commands many resources necessary for access and influence: leadership stability, consistent sources of income, hierarchical structure, geographic dispersion, and skillful professional lobbyists and public relations capabilities. However, with few exceptions, age-based groups have not created political action committees (PACs) that increasingly affect electoral politics, and they have yet to develop the same kind of sophistication and influence at the state level as they have at the national level.

IV. THE FUTURE OF ORGANIZATIONS ON AGING

In the current policy climate of entitlement cutbacks and devolution to the states, organizations on aging will find it more difficult to promote major new programs, such as national insurance for long-term care. The resolutions emanating from the 1995 WHCoA, which were quite modest in comparison with the demands made in 1961, 1971, and 1981, reflected the realities of today's politics of aging. Even before the conference took place, age-based groups found it necessary to expend their energies on derailing proposals to merge nutrition programs for elders into a block grant for means-tested nutrition programs. Proposals to reduce funding and devolve more responsibility to the states in programs such as Medicaid, the major source of public funding for long-term care, also require blocking action by these groups, as do proposed cuts in Medicare. In addition, if more federal programs are funded through block grants to the states in such areas as housing, age-based groups will need to sharpen their organizing and lobbying skills at the state level. This kind of mobilization can be very expensive, especially for small organizations representing subgroups of the aged. Monitoring the implementation of block grants in 50 states will also require considerable effort. [*See* HEALTH CARE AND SERVICES.]

Organizations on aging, similar to other constituencies that have benefited from national programs, also will be challenged by the shift in party dominance in Congress and in many statehouses. The new Republican majority in Congress, with its emphasis on less government, may make it more difficult for the dominant age-based groups to expand collective benefits and to exercise the same kind of influence as they have in the past. Conservative organizations on aging that had little influence on the Democrats have found they have increased access in the policy process now that the Republicans are the majority party.

The strong showing of Republicans in state elections in 1992 and 1994 has resulted in party shifts that may lead to increased influence of traditional state interest groups such as business and industry, which are often at odds with the consumer focus of aging advocates. Term limits for state legislators may also result in age-based groups having less clout as legislators become less driven by the need to assuage older voters to get reelected. Term limits may also increase the influence of groups such as the insurance industry that, unlike the aging, contribute heavily to political campaigns.

Backlash against the aged at the national level has not subsided, with the likely result that age-based groups will increase their coalition-building activity with nonaging groups as they did in the late 1980s, when "greedy geezers" first became an issue. The ability of organizations on aging to forge strong links with other organizations may very well be the key to retaining current programs and to developing new programs at the federal and/or state level. Whatever the future holds for age-based organizations, programs that benefit only the aged are less likely to occur than in the past.

BIBLIOGRAPHY

Achenbaum, W. A. (1983). *Shades of gray.* Boston: Little, Brown.

Binstock, R. H. (1972, Autumn). Interest group liberalism and the politics of aging. *The Gerontologist, 12,* 265.

Day, C. L. (1990). *What older Americans think.* Princeton, NJ: Princeton University Press.

Liebig, P. S. (1992). Federalism and aging policy in the 1980s: Implications for changing interest group roles in the 1990s. *Journal of Aging & Social Policy, 4* (1/2), 17.

Pratt, H. J. (1976). *The gray lobby.* Chicago: University of Chicago Press.

Van Tassel, D. D., & Meyer, J. E. W. (Eds.). (1992). *U.S. aging policy interest groups.* New York: Greenwood Press.

Wallace, S. P., & Williamson, J. B. (1992). *The senior movement: References and resources.* New York: G. K. Hall.

Oxidative Damage

Arthur K. Balin

*Medical College of Pennsylvania
and Hahnemann University*

Michael M. Vilenchik

Longevity Achievement Foundation

I. Methodological Aspects
II. Chemical and Biochemical Aspects
III. Molecular-Physiological Aspects
IV. Pathophysiological and Gerontological Aspects
V. Summary and Conclusions

Enzymatic Antioxidant Defense System Enzymatic antioxidants (antioxidative enzymes) that provide protection against oxidative damage to biological molecules.

Free Radicals Any chemical species that contains one or more unpaired electrons in the outer atomic or molecular orbitals. Free radicals are normal metabolites and are usually very reactive. Biologically the most important are carbon-centered radicals, produced during lipid peroxidation; sulfur-centered, thiyl radicals; nitrogen-centered radicals; and, in particular, oxygen-centered radicals.

The Free Radical Theory of Aging Initially proposed by Denham Harman in 1954, this theory suggests that free radical-inducing and/or producing biochemical reactions can damage the tissue's major molecular components and that the damage is a cause of aging and is involved in the pathogenesis of some aging-related common chronic diseases. The terms *free radical, oxygen free radical,* and reactive oxygen species (ROS) are often employed in biological and medical publications as synonyms. Reactive oxygen species include the nonradical species H_2O_2 and singlet oxygen which can be produced through radical reactions and/or can produce free radicals, thereby contributing to oxidative stress.

Lipid Peroxidation A series of free radical reactions, which usually are initiated in membranes from the interaction of ROS with polyunsaturated fatty acids and that can result in a chain reaction producing aldehydes and hydroperoxides.

Nonenzymatic Antioxidants Hydrophilic or lipophilic molecules that when present at low concentrations (relative to the concentration of the important biomolecules targeted by ROS) significantly protect these targets against oxidation, usually through scavenging these ROS.

Oxidation and Reduction Oxidation is loss of an electron and reduction is gain of an electron by a molecule. Accordingly, oxidants and reductants are free radicals and nonradical species that abstract and gain electrons from biological molecules.

Oxidative Damage or Oxidative Injury Uncontrolled reactions of the ROS with the prime targets, bases in DNA, amino acids in proteins, unsaturated lipids in cell membranes. It is important to distinguish the oxidative *damage* randomly produced by certain ROS, from oxidative *modification* of certain enzyme, receptors, or transcription factors, which are used by mechanisms that control cell replication, differentiation, and the response to oxidative stress.

Oxidative Stress Usually dangerous disturbance of a dynamic oxidant–antioxidant equilibrium due to overwhelming the antioxidant defenses by excessive levels (load) of ROS in cells and tissues exposed to oxidants and/or due to an imbalance between the rates of ROS production and scavenging or dissipation of ROS. The state of such cells, including aged cells, can sometimes be referred to as a prooxidant state.

Encyclopedia of Gerontology
Volume 2

Oxygen-Centered Radicals or Oxygen Free Radicals   Superoxide Anion Radical, $\cdot O_2^-$; hydroxyl radical, $\cdot OH$; alkoxy radical, $RO\cdot$; alkylperoxy radical $ROO\cdot$; hydroperoxy radical, $HO_2\cdot$ are reduced forms of molecular oxygen that are produced during normal metabolism.

Reactive Oxygen Species (ROS) or Reactive Oxygen Intermediates   Include oxygen-centered radicals, singlet oxygen, and the H_2O_2 that is a nonradical product of incomplete reduction of molecular oxygen.

The Redox State of the Cell   The intracellular ratio of oxidizing to reducing equivalents.

A variety of reactive oxygen species (ROS) are produced during normal metabolism. They can react with proteins, DNA, and other biomacromolecules, either directly or through a chain of free radical reactions, which usually are initiated in the membranes by lipid peroxidation. **OXIDATIVE DAMAGE** to biomolecules are limited by antioxidant defenses. But the defenses are not 100% effective. Initial ROS such as superoxide radical and H_2O_2 have been found to escape from their deactivating enzymes. Additionally, certain levels of these reactive species are necessary for normal cellular function. Kinetically, ROS can escape from normal cellular metabolic pathways, particularly, if present in nonphysiological amounts. Thus ROS can induce various alterations, including difficult to repair damage to oxidizable biomolecules. These include key molecules, such as tumor-suppressor genes, mitochondrial DNA, transcription factors, and DNA repair enzymes, dysfunction of which may be involved in the pathogenesis of senescence and some of the common chronic diseases. At the moment, there is agreement among researchers in the fields of cancer and other chronic diseases connected with aging, that metabolic regulation of "free radical reactions" in the cell is an important cellular priority.

I. METHODOLOGICAL ASPECTS

A. History of the Concept and Underlying Theory

In 1944, the Russian nuclear physicist Evgenii Zavoisky measured, for the first time, a paramagnetic substance, using an electron spin resonance spectroscopy technique, in a nonbiological system. In 1954, a group of American scientists, led by biophysicist Commoner, made the first discovery in free radical biology by identifying the melanin radical in frog's eggs. At about the same time, Denham Harman developed the Free Radical Theory of Aging, which was presented in the fall of 1954. And also in 1954, Gerschman, Gilbert, Nye, Dwyer, and Fenn published the concept that oxygen radicals are major mediators of oxygen cytotoxicity, based on the similarity observed between oxygen poisoning and radiation toxicity. It is established now that high levels of oxygen tension generate an additional load of reactive oxygen species (ROS) that induce damage to cellular molecules, including DNA, and are similar to both aging-associated and radiation-induced lesions. Harman's free radical theory of aging has been seminal in laying the framework for the importance of free radical damage to living systems.

In 1986 Allen and Balin suggested that free radicals are involved in the mechanisms of differential gene expression and cell differentiation. As will be explained later, the cellular control mechanisms use some ROS for the regulation of expression of certain genes.

These concepts form a basis from which aging may be viewed as a multistep process of dysregulation of exogenous and endogenous oxidative stress-control mechanisms, thereby transforming useful ROS into detrimental ones. The problem is to avoid dysregulation in the use of ROS by cellular control mechanisms.

It has been established that the products of incomplete molecular oxygen reduction, including the most abundant of them, the superoxide radical, are more reactive than oxygen, because the reaction of oxygen with most biomolecules is kinetically forbidden. The enzyme superoxide dismutase destroys the initial reduction intermediate, superoxide radical. But dismutation of these radicals results in the formation of hydrogen peroxide, which can be the source of the hydroxyl radical. Hydroxyl radical can directly attack DNA and induce premutagenic DNA modification(s) and therefore is referred to as the ultimate ROS. Thus, there is a pathway of metabolism of ROS from the initial product of the incomplete reduction of oxygen to the ultimate endogenous mutagenic agent. This pathway may be looked upon as one of the atavistic, earliest, physicochemical endogenous mutagenic mechanisms that has been used as a mechanism of hereditary alterations catalyzing the process of evolution.

Oxidative damage to DNA is not only mutagenic, it is also carcinogenic if induced in such genes as proto-oncogenes and tumor-suppressor genes. During recent years, significant evidence has been obtained on both experimental and clinical levels that excessive production of free radicals and of nonradical reactive forms of oxygen is involved in the pathogenesis of some common chronic diseases connected with aging. The list of such diseases includes not only some cancers, but also degenerative diseases, including atherosclerosis, cataracts and macular degeneration, and some common neurodegenerative diseases.

Numerous radiobiological experiments and observational studies indicate that development of cancer and of some degenerative diseases, as well as of replicative cell aging in vitro and accumulation of DNA damage in vivo are accelerated in cells and tissues exposed to nonlethal low-level doses of ionizing radiation that can induce chronic oxidative stress. These observations suggest that the mechanisms that respond to oxidative stress are important in aging. On the other hand, Balin has shown that physiologic partial pressures of oxygen can modulate the growth and proliferative life span of human cells in culture. In recent years, mounting evidence indicates that ROS are involved in the mechanisms of cell replication, differentiation, and apoptotic cell death through selective processes that are activated in response to various stresses. Many cell strains and lines, as well as different tissues, respond to the stresses by activation of a group of transcription factors. These factors regulate transcription in animal and human cells by interaction with specific DNA sequences, the cis-regulatory elements. This interaction is changed in response to various ROS, as well as to ionizing radiation, UV light, tumor promoters, and some other factors, all of which are mediated by oxidative stress.

Different transcription factors, such as AP-1 (fosjun heterodimer), NFκB, and Sp1 bind their DNA cis-elements only if certain cysteine residues that are involved in these interactions are in the reduced state. Therefore, some oxidants, as well as antioxidants, regulate the transcription of specific genes, through modulation of binding of transcription factors with the DNA elements, because they can alter the cellular redox state. Genes that code for transcription factors and genes that are regulated by these factors are in-

volved in the control of the organism's capacity to adapt, which diminishes during aging.

In addition to oxidative damage, there are a number of other types of damage to cells and tissues that occur during aging. This damage includes depurination of DNA and glycation of proteins. Limited data suggest that, if each of these other types of damage is combined with oxidative damage, the combination can be difficult to repair and may accumulate in aged cells and tissues.

Thus it is appropriate to consider a new paradigm, which unifies elements of different concepts of stochastic and programmed theories of aging focusing on such specific interactions as (a) between ROS and certain macromolecules; (b) between different modifications produced in the same macromolecule; and (c) between different macromolecules that can respond to oxidative stress and/or to antioxidants interactively and/or in a certain sequence.

II. CHEMICAL AND BIOCHEMICAL ASPECTS

A. Important Sources and Mediators of Oxidative Damage

Established endogenous sources of superoxide anion radical and hydrogen peroxide include the mitochondrial electron transport chain, endoplasmic reticulum (microsomal electron transport chain), peroxisomes, nuclear and plasma membranes, and phagocytic cells. Cigarette smoke, sunlight, and some dietary factors such as certain metals and substances that oxidize glutathione are among the main exogenous sources of ROS production in the human body. The contribution of each of the ROS-producing cell compartments (cytosol, mitochondria, microsomes, and peroxisomes) into a total "ROS load," is dependent on the cell type. For example, the microsomal compartment is one of the main contributors in the rat liver.

Incomplete reduction products of oxygen are produced intracellularly during transport of electrons through the mitochondrial electron transport chain. ROS are additionally produced through other biochemical reactions, such as those catalyzed by cytochrome *P*450, or the peroxisomal enzyme xanthine oxidase, and the membrane-bound NADPH oxidases. ROS are also produced extracellularly. They are generated and used as microbicidal agents by polymorphonuclear cells where they are formed through the metabolic events that are related to an abrupt rise in the consumption of oxygen, called the respiratory burst, and production of $\cdot O_2^-$. It has been generally believed that only phagocytes can generate ROS through events catalyzed by a membrane-associated respiratory NADPH oxidase. But, NADPH oxidase-like enzymes, which can be activated by growth factors and which produce $\cdot O_2^-$, have been found in other cells, including human fibroblasts. Another important source of free radicals is the metabolism of L-arginine, which can result in the production of the free radical nitric oxide, $\cdot NO$.

There are three main types of radical reactions in vivo: (a) radical addition reactions, (b) electron transfer reactions, and (c) atom abstraction reactions. The chemical reactivity of the superoxide radical is relatively low in these reactions. The half-life of this radical varies from 0.4 μs up to 1 ms. For comparison, the half-life for hydroxyl radical is 0.3 ns.

Hydrogen peroxide is a weak oxidizing agent and is the most stable intermediate of the oxygen reduction products. However, H_2O_2 can oxidize sulfhydryl groups of enzymes and other proteins such as transcription factors. The effects of very low concentrations of H_2O_2 and $\cdot O_2^-$ are potentiated in the presence of transition metal ions, because extremely reactive hydroxyl radicals, $\cdot OH$ are generated from H_2O_2 by means of transition metal ion-catalyzed reactions called the Fe-catalyzed Haber-Weiss reaction or Fenton reaction.

$$Fe3(III) + \cdot O_2^- \rightarrow Fe(II) + O_2 \qquad (1)$$

$$Fe(II) + H_2O_2 \rightarrow \cdot OH + OH- + Fe(III) \qquad (2)(Fenton)$$

$$\cdot O_2^- + H_2O_2 \xrightarrow{Fe} \cdot OH + OH- + O_2 \qquad (3)(Haber\text{-}Weiss)$$

Additionally, $\cdot OH$ can be produced by the reaction of H_2O_2 with the complexes of Fe(II) or Cu(I) with DNA. This can result in DNA damaged by the hydroxyl radical at the sites of its formation:

$$DNA(Fe^{2+}) + H_2O_2 \rightarrow DNA(Fe^{3+})$$
$$+ \cdot OH + OH- \rightarrow DNA^*, \qquad (4)$$

where DNA* is DNA that contains oxidative damage,

such as 8-hydroxyguanine, and/or other chemical modification and/or single-strand breaks.

Catalysts of $\cdot OH$ radical production can be bound to proteins and membrane lipids and can initiate site-specific protein oxidation and lipid peroxidation, if H_2O_2 is formed and/or transported to these sites.

Methods of measurement of hydroxyl radical production in vivo remain under investigation. The difficulty in measuring free radicals is due to their extremely low levels and very short half-life. Therefore, although there is circumstantial evidence for the biological role of the $\cdot OH$ radical, quantitative evidence is lacking.

Singlet oxygen is an electronically excited form of oxygen and is a strongly electrophilic molecule produced in tissue as a result of dismutation of superoxide radical. In the skin, singlet oxygen is additionally produced as a result of various photochemical reactions. Until recently the importance of singlet oxygen was neglected. Only singlet oxygen, besides hydroxyl radical, can attack DNA directly. Also singlet oxygen can damage various enzymes through amino acid modification and may lead to oxidative damage in membranes and blood plasma, because it has high reactivity with double bonds in unsaturated fatty acids.

B. Primary Molecular Defense Mechanisms against Oxidative Damage

1. Enzymatic Antioxidants

Certain enzymes and many small water-soluble and lipid-soluble molecules can intercept and destroy free radicals and other ROS. Important components of cellular enzymatic protection include catalase, superoxide dismutase (Mn, Cu/Zn, extracellular), glutathione peroxidase, glutathione reductase, glutathione S-transferase, glucose-6-phosphate dehydrogenase, and thioredoxin reductase.

2. Nonenzymatic Antioxidant Proteins and Small Molecular Weight Antioxidants

There exist proteins that are not considered traditionally as antioxidants, but that have important antioxidant functions. Among them are metallothioneins, low-molecular weight sulfhydryl-rich Zn/Cd proteins, which are natural scavengers of superoxide and hydroxyl radicals. Important nonenzymatic macromolecular antioxidant defense mechanisms include metal-binding proteins that remove iron and copper ions because these ions can catalyze the production of ·OH and other ROS such as alkoxyradicals.

The antioxidant proteins are supplemented by a number of low-molecular weight molecules that protect against oxidative damage in tissue. These include (a) endogenous antioxidants, such as reduced glutathione, cysteine, and some other sulfhydryl-containing molecules; ubiquinol 10 in reduced state; bilirubin; uric acid and lipoic acid in reduced state; and (b) essential antioxidants, vitamin C (ascorbic acid), the principal and terminal scavenger of radicals in the aqueous phase; vitamin E (α-tocopherol), the principal chain-breaking antioxidant in membranes; vitamin A (retinol), a peroxy-radical and thyil-radical scavenger; beta-carotene, a precursor to vitamin A and a singlet oxygen quencher; and lycopene, the non-vitamin precursor carotenoid with extremely high singlet oxygen-quenching activity.

Among water-soluble scavengers, reduced glutathione (GSH) is one of the most abundant biological antioxidants that function to maintain redox homeostasis in vivo. Reduced GSH can scavenge various free radicals. Vitamin C also scavenges various oxy radicals, including thiyl radicals.

Thiyl radicals, RS·, are formed nonenzymatically by the reactions of thiol residues with superoxide anion radicals, transition metal ions, and allyl-type lipid radicals. Thiyl radicals can be produced through oxidation of GSH by peroxidases or by oxygen, catalyzed by iron and/or copper, or when GSH scavenges ·OH.

The function of the antioxidants is dependent not only on structures of ROS and the protected target, but also conditions of their interactions. For example, beta-carotene can protect membranes against oxidative damage, particularly at low oxygen tensions.

3. Repair of Oxidative Damage

These systems consist of several DNA repair pathways and a number of proteolytic enzymes and lipolytic enzymes. The most prevalent oxidative DNA damage is base damage, such as 8-hydroxyguanine, also referred to as 8-oxoguanine. Oxidatively damaged DNA is repaired through two pathways: base excision repair, referred to as "short patch repair", because it is connected with the resynthesis of only 1–3 nucleotides, and the nucleotide excision pathway, long patch

repair. Repair of oxidatively damaged DNA by base excision repair has been observed using 8-hydroxy-guanine-specific monoclonal antibodies and high performance liquid chromatography (HPLC)-electro-chemical detection. The repair is performed by (a) a glycosylase that recognizes and removes this damage, resulting in an abasic site; (b) an apurinic–apyrimidinic endonuclease that cleaves the phosphodiester backbone; and (c) DNA polymerase and (d) DNA ligase, which fills the nucleotide gap and seals it respectively.

In some cells, oxidized DNA base repair primarily occurs by this base excision repair pathway. This fact is important in order to properly interpret the results of measurements of 8-hydroxydeoxyguanosine in human and rodent urines. This nucleoside cannot be excised through the base excision repair pathway, because the glycosylase removes the base but not the nucleoside.

Proteases, such as a multicomponent protease, referred to as the proteasome complex, can degrade oxidatively damaged proteins, thereby removing oxidatively damaged proteins in mammalian cells. There are also mechanisms that can repair oxidatively damaged membrane lipids through selective cleaving of the peroxidized phospholipid and exchanging them for an undamaged one.

C. Methods of in Vivo Measurement of Free Radicals and Markers of Oxidative Stress

Stimulation of endogenous production of ROS, for example, in the liver by xenobiotics or in the skin by the sunlight; or decline of the antioxidant defenses (for example due to deficiencies of Vitamin C or alpha-tocopherol or GSH-inadequate dietary intakes), displace the intracellular oxidant–antioxidant equilibrium in favor of ROS. Transition metal ions can both initiate and mediate development of oxidative stress. Therefore, excess intake of these metals with foods can also result in oxidative stress.

In these situations, the oxidative stress results in a disturbance of the redox equilibrium, which must be restored through either a decrease in the production of ROS, and/or an increase in the antioxidant defense(s). These are controlled by a set of transcription factors and are reviewed in the next section.

An increase in the concentration of free radicals, measured using electron spin resonance (ESR) spectroscopy, can reflect the degree of oxidative stress. The ascorbyl free radical (AFR) arises when vitamin C scavenges a radical. AFR is relatively inert and therefore stable (resonance stabilized). Because AFR can be converted into vitamin C in vivo, its accumulation has been considered recently as a radical buffer or transient aqueous radical sink, or a Marker of Oxidative Stress. For example, free radical-mediated oxidative stress has been estimated in the skin in vivo by ESR measurements of ascorbyl free radical signal intensity. Recently, an in vivo ESR spectroscopy technique has been developed to measure free radical reactions in the whole animal noninvasively using nitroxide free radicals, which are sensitive to both redox state and ROS. Rates of penetration of nitroxide free radicals into the skin and their distribution in the skin have been measured by ESR technique. Thus, the generation and distribution of radicals, produced during normal metabolism, or induced after irradiation of the skin by sunlight can be measured, using nitroxide free radicals.

However, there are significant limitations to the use ESR to detect radical intermediates in association with oxidative damage in cells and tissues. Some radicals have very short lifetimes under normal conditions. These very reactive radical species will be less likely to accumulate, because the measured steady state concentrations of them are dependent on the rates with which these radicals react with surrounding molecules. Thus, more reactive radicals are less readily observed by standard ESR techniques. To measure concentrations of these radicals, spin-trapping agents such as alpha-phenyl-N-tert butylnitrone (PBN) or 5,5-dimethyl-1-pyrroline-N-oxide (DMPO) are used in vivo. But interpretation of the data concerning concentrations of the trapped radicals in vivo is complicated due to unknown mechanisms of metabolism of the spin traps and their respective radical adducts. The degradation of radical adducts of DMPO in cells can be very rapid.

There are specific markers of the attack of ·OH radical (DNA adducts, aromatic probes, amino acid hydroxylation, and salicylate hydroxylation products) that are used for measuring ·OH in vivo. Among these and other biomarkers that indicate target organ damage from hydroxyl radical and singlet oxygen, 8-hydroxyguanine (8-OHGua, 7,8-dihydro-8-oxoguanine), has become increasingly popular. The concentration of this stable and integral marker of oxidative

stress in cellular DNA, and in particular nucleoside 8-hydroxy-2′-deoxyguanosine (8-OHdG, 7,8-dihydro-8-oxo-2′-deoxyguanosine) can be analyzed in digests of DNA or other biological specimens, for the estimation of the level of the oxidative damage. Several laboratories have reported that 8-OHGua accumulates in the DNA of animal and human cells aged in vitro and in vivo.

Because 8-OHdG can be measured in the femtomole range in DNA digests containing nanomoles of intact deoxynucleotides, it is possible to estimate the level of this damage in a relatively small population of cells in the tissue. It has been established that carcinogens known to produce ROS induce a significant increase of 8-OHGua in the DNA isolated from the target organs of the exposed animals.

One of the most important pathways of oxidation of proteins by the ROS is conversion of side-chain amino groups to carbonyl derivatives, called protein carbonyls. The measurements of the levels of protein carbonyls in human body fluids have been used to estimate the levels of oxidative stress, in vivo.

Various tests have been developed to measure lipid peroxidation in human tissues and body fluids. Among them, the thiobarbituric acid (TBA) method is widely used, because it is an easy assay to perform. Recently an HPLC-based TBA assay has been used to avoid some of the artifacts of the standard TBA method.

Pentane is a product of lipid peroxidation in the human body. Because it is exhaled, pentane in the breath can be used as a measure of in vivo lipid peroxidation.

The capacity to accurately measure reactive oxygen species and oxidative damage and repair processes in vivo does not currently exist. Therefore many researchers in the fields of free radical biology and aging believe that accurate measures of oxidative stress in cells and tissues are important to develop.

Until recently, the effects of relatively high levels of exogenous ROS on cells have been studied in acute experiments, whereas aging and pathologies connected with aging are related to a low level of chronic oxidative stress. Many years ago it was established that chronic exposure of animals to ionizing radiation can accelerate the accumulation of some (but not all) age-dependent biophysical, biochemical, cellular, and tissue alterations, including DNA alterations. But one must be cautious in attempting simplified interpretations of results of not only the measurements of markers of oxidative stress but also its physiological consequences.

III. MOLECULAR-PHYSIOLOGICAL ASPECTS

A. Regulatory Role of Reactive Oxidants and Antioxidants

1. Response to Oxidative Stress and Sensitivity of Transcription Factors to ROS

Pretreatment of various cells, from bacteria to human lymphoid cells, with nondamaging concentrations of H_2O_2 protects these cells against different damaging effects, including oxidative DNA damage, induced by higher concentrations of H_2O_2. This effect, which is referred to as an adaptive response to oxidative stress, is similar to the adaptive response to low-level radiation, which has been documented to occur in various cells from bacteria to human cells.

About 45 years ago Barron suggested a redox mechanism of regulation in response to environmental stresses. Now there is significant evidence that modification of the redox state of certain transcription factors can contribute to or inhibit the formation of specific complexes between these factors and their cognate DNA elements in mammalian cells. This mechanism is similar to the mechanism of regulation of gene expression in response to oxidative stress in bacteria through a change in the DNA-binding specificity of the bacterial transcriptional regulatory protein, OxyR. This change is also dependent on the redox state. Thus, regulation by reduction-oxidation may be a general oxidative stress-control mechanism.

AP-1 is a DNA-binding protein and is composed of two transcription factors that are products of the proto-oncogenes *c-fos* and *c-jun*. In response to oxidative stress, such as H_2O_2 exposure, the *c-fos* and *c-jun* genes are activated. The concentration of *c-jun* mRNA decreases in mice during growth up to 12 months and then increases up to 24 months. This increase is a signature of oxidative stress to which *c-jun* can respond. Additionally, there are other pathways of response of transcription factors to the change of the cell's oxidative state, besides direct involvement of AP-1.

The transcription factor NFκB is a complex of two different proteins, p50 and p65. This complex is retained in the cytoplasm and kept in an inactive form by an inhibitory protein called IkB. Release of NFκB from IkB is induced in cells and tissues exposed to ROS and other agents, such as ionizing radiation, UV light, tumor necrosis factor, and phorbol esters, which all produce oxidative stress in the exposed cells and tissues. The release of NFκB results in its translocation into the nucleus and interaction with the cognate DNA cis-elements. Thus there are several pathways of regulation of transcription factors by ROS. ROS can activate NFκB by releasing it from its inhibitor. But ROS can also inhibit the function of NFκb by inhibiting its interaction with the cognate DNA cis-element by oxidation of the sulfhydryl residues of the protein involved in the interaction. Thus the control mechanisms for the response to oxidative stress are complex.

The human APE/Ref-1 protein has been known as a nuclear enzyme involved in the repair of apurinic and apyrimidinic sites in DNA. It has been discovered that it is also involved in the reactivation of the oxidized AP1 and has been given the name HAP1. This is one example demonstrating interdependences and/or coincidence of different functions: DNA repair and transcriptional activity; and DNA repair and antioxidant defense; transcriptional activity and antioxidant defense.

2. Intracellular Signal Transduction and Intercellular Signaling

There is evidence that formation of $\cdot O_2^-$ by reactions catalyzed by NADPH oxidase is used as an oxygen sensor by the receptors in the carotid sinus. A similar enzyme, which catalyzes conversion of molecular oxygen into superoxide radical, has also been found in the cytoplasmic membranes of fibroblasts. This process might be related to sensing and signaling in these cells and facilitates intercellular communication using the production of ROS. Another example is nitric oxide $\cdot NO$, which is used as a neurotransmitter for the regulation of vasomotor tone.

ROS and lipid peroxides are also utilized for the transfer of an intracellular message. Peroxidized fatty acids, released from membranes, can initiate the biosynthesis of eicosanoids, which are necessary for transduction of a signal that activates cell replication; for example, fibroblasts stimulated to proliferate by epidermal growth factor. Guanylate cyclase is activated following oxidation of its sulfhydryl groups by H_2O_2 and leads to the production of the second messenger, cyclic GMP for further signal transduction.

3. Cell Replication and Differentiation

Oxidants can regulate cell replication in a dose-dependent manner. Usually, low levels of exogenous oxidants stimulate cell replication, whereas high levels of oxidants inhibit it. Endogenously generated ROS, such as superoxide radical and hydrogen peroxide, can act in various cells as signals augmenting the proliferative response. Transcription factors and/or kinases involved in the growth signal transduction pathways can mediate these effects through regulation of the expression of genes and the activity of proteins that control the cell cycle.

Since Allen and Balin found that manganese superoxide dismutase (MnSOD) activity increased by as much as 46-fold during the differentiation of Physarum polycephalum, this enzyme has been found to increase as differentiation proceeds in various other biological systems. Moreover, transfection of rodent cells with MnSOD promotes their differentiation. Liposomes containing SOD can induce differentiation in some tumor cells, such as Friend erythroleukemia cells. Thus, factors controlling levels of the SOD, can be involved in the mechanisms of differentiation.

Paradoxically, not only the antioxidant enzymes, but the oxidant H_2O_2 can also induce cell differentiation in some systems. This paradox can be partially resolved if one remembers that SOD is involved in the mechanisms of production of intracellular H_2O_2. On the other hand, oxidative stress induced by H_2O_2 can result in an adaptive response connected with an increase activity of SOD.

IV. PATHOPHYSIOLOGICAL AND GERONTOLOGICAL ASPECTS

A. Primary Targets of Oxidative Injury, Physiological Aging, and Diseases Connected with Aging

1. Oxidative Damage to Nuclear DNA and Replicative Cell Aging and Initiation of Carcinogenesis

Even under normal conditions, the cell's DNA is bombarded by many ROS each minute. Most "spontane-

ous" oxidative DNA damage is removed by DNA repair systems. But, as shown in many radiobiological studies, these repair systems are not 100% effective. Thus oxidative damage to DNA, and in particular the difficult to repair complex DNA damage that can be produced by hydroxyl radicals, might accumulate during aging.

There is direct evidence that aging of some human and rodent cells and tissues is connected with an accumulation of various alterations in the human genome, including a major oxidative damage product, 8-OHGua.

Leonard Hayflick discovered that normal human fibroblasts in culture have a finite capacity to replicate. Cells are arrested at the G1/S boundary, when exposed to ionizing radiation and some other DNA-damaging agents. There is considerable, although not direct evidence that age-dependent accumulation of spontaneous (endogenous) DNA damage can activate mechanisms leading to the arrest of human cells aged in vitro. Levels of strand breaks and 8-OHGua are increased in nuclear DNA of human fibroblasts with their aging in vitro to levels that are higher than those that are induced by doses of ionizing radiation that inhibit cell replication. This indicates that the age-dependent accumulation of spontaneous (endogenous) DNA damage can result in the activation of mechanisms of the arrest of human cell growth at the G1/S boundary similar to the growth arrest induced by ionizing radiation.

8-OHGua has the ability to pair with A instead of C and this can result in G to T transversion. Such mutations have been found in some of the oncogenes and antioncogenes contained in the genome of human tumors at certain sites. There is a striking direct correlation between the presence of 8-OHGua in DNA and development of carcinogenesis. For example, treatments with certain carcinogens of rodent tissues induce high levels of 8-OHGua in the tissue that is transformed by this carcinogen. Thus, initiation of carcinogenesis can be associated with an accumulation of oxidative damage to DNA.

Correlations between the accumulation of 8-OHGua and the development of cancer have been observed in circumstances that are associated with oxidative stress. Therefore, these correlations can only be viewed reflecting one of many types of oxidatively induced damage to DNA as well as to proteins and lipids. Nevertheless, it is generally accepted by researchers in the fields of both spontaneous, chemical, ionizing radiation-, and UV light-induced carcinogenesis, that genetic alterations such as irreparable oxidative damage to the antioncogenes, is a critical event responsible for the initiation of carcinogenesis.

Some human cancer tissues show higher levels of oxidative damage to DNA, than nearby cancer-free surrounding tissue. For example, the number of molecules of 8-OHGua per 100 000 bases in cancer tissue versus its respective normal tissue are lung cancer 23, normal lung 7.3; stomach cancer 5.1, normal stomach 0.94; ovary cancer 9.2, normal ovary 3.1; colon cancer 4.4, normal colon 2.7; and human renal cell carcinoma 6.0, normal kidney 3.7. Thus, the average amount of 8-OHGua, measured in several laboratories, in cancer cells is at least 1.6 times higher than the average cancer-free respective tissue. This difference indicates increased oxidative damage to DNA of cancer cells, which can play a role at different phases of malignant evolution from initiation of carcinogenesis to tumor progression.

2. Oxidative Damage to Lipids, Proteins, and Lipoproteins and Promotion of Carcinogenesis and of Degenerative Diseases

The classical model of carcinogenesis has been operationally divided into initiation (mutation and formation of a transformed clone), promotion (expansion of clone) and progression (malignant evolution of tumor cells toward increased malignancy). It is established that H_2O_2 and some organic peroxides stimulate the promotion of skin cells to develop into papillomas. These oxidants can also stimulate progression of papillomas into carcinomas. Agents that generate ROS are also tumor promoters and/or can mimic the biochemical action of tumor promotors in a variety of other cells and tissues besides the skin. On the other hand, various antioxidants inhibit tumor promotion.

In addition, it is established that oxidative stress can modulate the expression of genes that are involved in the control of tumor promotion. At least some of these genes, such as the proto-oncogenes *c-fos* and *c-jun*, are related to cell growth and differentiation.

Lipid peroxides can function as a mitogenic intermediate in hormone receptor-mediated growth responses. The signal that triggers production of these intermediates can be bypassed by the generation of ROS induced by tumor promotors. This is one of the presumptive oxidative lipid-damage-mediated pathways of tumor promotion connected with oxidative stress.

Data obtained, using biophysical, biochemical, and histochemical methods, indicate that lipofuscin is a lipid-protein adduct complexed with metal ions, including copper and iron. These metals may be involved in the pathogenic mechanisms of age-dependent accumulation of lipofuscin by activation of lipid peroxidation. Direct or metal-catalyzed reactions of oxygen and unsaturated fatty acids also contribute to the age-related accumulation of lipofuscin. This accumulation may play a role in the functional decline of postmitotic cells.

One of the more serious end points of the activation of lipid peroxidation and the formation of oxidative damage to lipoproteins are the atherosclerotic lesions that develop in blood vessels. It is established that atherosclerosis can be accelerated in humans with elevated levels of low-density lipoprotein (LDL) and low levels of some antioxidants, especially vitamin E. A significant decrease in the activity of antioxidant enzymes, in particular superoxide dismutase and glutathione peroxidase has been found in atherosclerotic tissue.

ROS can induce oxidative damage to both the lipid and protein components of LDL and other lipoproteins. It is generally accepted by the researchers in the field of atherosclerosis that such modifications to lipids and proteins are involved and may be even obligatory in the pathogenesis of atherosclerosis in experimental animals and humans. Drugs, such as probucol, that are capable of inhibiting lipid peroxidation in LDL have turned out to be useful drugs for treating atherosclerosis.

The atherogenic potential of low-density lipoproteins is increased through the nonenzymic binding of glucose to the protein component; that is, by glycation of the protein. The combined effect of oxidation and glycation, which is exaggerated in diabetic individuals can foster the development of atherosclerosis.

Epidemiological observations, including research on vitamin E and other chain-breaking antioxidants such as probucol, confirmed a role of oxidative stress in the development of atherosclerosis in humans. Vitamin E treatment markedly reduces aortic atherosclerotic lesion development in the experimental model of atherosclerosis, Watanabe Heritable Hyperlipidemic Rabbits.

ROS can play a critical role in the pathogenesis of other cardiovascular diseases, such as ischemic injury associated with circulatory disturbance (section VIII). Endothelial cells can produce superoxide anion radical and oxidize lipoproteins extracellularly and may react with endothelium-derived relaxing factor, which modulates vascular resistance and thus the circulatory status of mammalian organism. During aging, a variety of proteins, not complexed with lipids, also undergo a nonenzymatic modification, including oxidation and glycation. The protein carbonyls content measured in numerous laboratories in several animal models and in human fibroblasts has been found to increase during aging by all groups (with the exception of one).

There is some evidence, obtained on preclinical models of Alzheimer's (AD), Parkinson's, and Huntington's disease, for the primary role of protein oxidation in the initial steps of these neurodegenerative diseases. Aging is a risk factor in the development of these diseases. Increase in oxidized proteins isolated from the brains of humans suffering from these diseases can reflect a mechanism of initiation of a cascade of biochemical events that results in the neurodegeneration. There is evidence that ROS formation results in oxidative damage to the central nervous system following stroke and neurotrauma. Lipid peroxidation or oxidative damage to proteins can be involved in the progression of the brain tissue injury, initiated by ischemic or traumatic damage, as well as in the pathogenesis of some aging-associated neurological deficits and neurodegenerative diseases. For example, symptoms, similar to those of amyotrophic lateral sclerosis, develop in mice that are transgenic to the mutant form of the familial amyotrophic lateral sclerosis gene that codes for copper and zinc SOD.

Brain regions that are the most sensitive to oxidative stress include the cortex, hippocampus, and striatum. These regions are the most vulnerable brain areas to age-related neurodegenerative diseases and ischemia-reperfusion insult.

There is biochemical and analytical epidemiological evidence that ROS formation is increased in the brains of patients with AD. Oxidative damage to proteins(s) can play a role in beta-amyloid accumulation, which is involved in the neurodegenerative cascades of AD. Iron is increased in the brain of patients with different neurodegenerative disorders, including the cortical regions in AD. The ROS, such as H_2O_2, pro-

duced through chemical oxidation of dopamine or accelerated metabolism by monoamine oxidase can be involved in the mechanism of death of cells in the substantia nigra. These cells are thought to die through apoptosis.

3. Oxidative Injury-Dependent Pathway of Programmed Cell Death

That the primary mechanism of programmed cell death (PCD) involves activation of a nuclease (called *suicide nuclease*) and DNA breakage during aging was initially proposed by the Russian researcher in the fields of free radical biophysics and aging, Vilenchik in 1970 (in Russian) and then in 1972 (in English). Since that time, different pathways of apoptosis, have been described. Many of the agents that activate PCD, such as ionizing radiation, high levels of H_2O_2, and factors that reduce GSH levels have in common the production of ROS or non-oxygen free radicals and the activation of DNA breakage mechanisms.

Some transcription factors are involved in the mechanisms of both apotosis and the response to oxidative stress. For example, oxidative stress can result in the dissociation of the NFκB–IkB complex thereby permitting translocation of the released transcription factor NFκB into the nucleus to bind to the cognate DNA cis-elements, some of which control other transcription factors. One of these is the tumor-suppressor p53 gene, whose protein is one of the regulators of PCD.

ROS-induced or ROS-mediated DNA damage can activate poly(ADP-ribosyl)polymerase (PARP), also referred to as ADP-ribosyltransferase, a nuclear enzyme which forms polyADP-ribose bound to proteins. If the levels of DNA damage are high, the enzyme consumes almost all of the intracellular NAD, because the ADP-ribose moiety of the NAD molecule is used for the production of poly-ADP-ribose. The depletion of cellular NAD and NADH pools leads to ATP depletion and cell death. Therefore, the apoptotic death of mammalian cells exposed to H_2O_2 can be prevented, if the drop in NAD levels is prevented by inhibiting the enzyme PARP with 3-aminobenzamide.

Another mechanism of PCD involves lipid peroxides that are formed in the cell's membranes, including mitochondrial membranes, and that lead to an alteration in cellular Ca^{2+} homeostasis. Thus, there are several pathways of PCD, in which ROS result in cell death.

In addition to the apoptotic form of cell death, a necrotic form of cell death exists. The degree of oxidative stress and certain concomitant factors can influence whether cell death occurs through apoptosis or necrosis. For example, moderate oxidative stresses, such as those associated with exposure of cells to relatively low levels of ionizing radiation, low concentrations of exogenous H_2O_2 or alloxan induce apoptotic cell death. But, cell death connected with severe oxidative stress induced by any of these agents can be of the necrotic type.

4. Oxidative Damage to the Intercellular Components of the Connective Tissue and Skin Aging

ROS, such as generated by activated macrophages or xanthine and xanthine oxidase, induce oxidative degradation of collagen in conjunction with proteases. ROS can target collagen molecules directly resulting in cross-linking. Collagen-associated fluorescence is increased with age in rat skin and tail tendon, indicating accumulation of oxidative damage to collagen molecules and of cross-links.

Oxidation of proteins, for example, glutamine synthetase, usually renders them highly susceptible to degradation by proteases, and some proteases have been found to exhibit selectivity for the oxidized form(s) of protein. Oxidative damage to skin elastin fibers can result in stimulation of proteolysis of the elastic fiber network that form a basis for skin elasticity. Thus oxidative damage to proteins may contribute to skin wrinkling.

5. Oxidative Damage to Mitochondrial DNA (mtDNA) and Limit of Life Span of Animals and Humans

Only the mtDNA is vulnerable to a direct attack of hydroxyl radical produced in the mitochondria, because hydroxyl radical has a very short half-life (0.3 ns) and can diffuse less than 10 molecular diameters before it reacts; therefore, this radical can induce DNA lesions only near its origin.

Superoxide radical or H_2O_2 can react with unsaturated lipids, which are enriched in the inner mitochondrial membranes. It is established that activation of lipid peroxidation in these membranes is connected with damage to mtDNA. Thus, mtDNA is placed in an inhospitable environment. The vulnerability of the

mtDNA to oxidative damage is amplified by a lack of histones, which can partially protect nuclear DNA in chromatin. The nucleotide excision DNA repair pathway, which could remove the oxidative damage, is absent in the mitochondria.

The content of 8-OHGua measured in mtDNA isolated from autopsied myocardium of Japanese patients increases exponentially with age and in parallel with the accumulation of mtDNA that contain a 7.4 kbp deletion. The age-dependent increase in both these mtDNA alterations are correlated with an age-dependent increase in the death rate in Japan.

An age-dependent increase in the proportion of mtDNA with a common 5-kb deletion compared to normal mtDNA has been found to occur in the skeletal muscles of American patients. This mDNA deletion increases exponentially and in parallel with the age-dependent increase in the human death rate in the United States. In all cases, the ratio of altered mtDNA to normal mtDNA and the death rate in both countries double each 7–8.8 years after age 30–40. Significant pathologic biochemical and molecular alterations, including higher levels of lipid peroxides, have been observed in the mitochondria isolated from the tissues of old animals. There is also a decline in the respiratory chain capacity of old cells, when measured at maximal stimulation of respiration.

Injection of mitochondria isolated from the liver of old rats into cultured normal human cells induces degeneration in the recipient cells after a few days. This does not occur when mitochondria are isolated from young rats and similarly injected. These observations suggest that there is an age-related increase in the mitochondrial production of ROS, which can induce toxic effects and that this increase could be responsible for the exponential age-dependent increase in the levels of mtDNA alterations.

On the other hand, it is established that mtDNA alterations are involved in the pathogenesis of several known mitochondrial diseases such as Kearns-Sayre syndrome and Chronic Progressive External Opthalmoplegia, which are connected with dysfunction of the muscle and/or nervous system.

The functions of the central nervous system and of skeletal and heart muscle are particularly dependent on oxygen consumption and on mitochondrial oxidative phosphorylation. Probably, therefore, mtDNA aging (mtDNAging) has been initially observed in these tissues, which are also particularly vulnerable to degenerative diseases connected with aging.

At the moment, it is generally believed that mechanisms limiting the proliferative life span of replicative cells involve telomere shortening. In this connection it is interesting that telomeric DNA (tDNA) is as mtDNA particularly vulnerable to various sources of spontaneous damage including free radical-induced damage. Moreover, there might be a deficiency in the repair of not only mtDNA, but also tDNA. The special features of instability and repair of these subsets of cellular DNA suggest the possibility that they may limit the life span of human postmitotic and replicative cells.

B. Oxidative Stress and Premature or Accelerated Aging

1. The Late Biological Effects of Ionizing Radiation

Exposure to ionizing radiation results in the increase of oxidative damage to DNA, protein, and lipids in a dose-dependent manner. This increase is mainly the result of the increased rate of production of ROS and their direct attack on other biomolecules.

Late biological effects of ionizing radiation include accelerated aging on different levels. For example, an increase in the rate of the age-dependent accumulation of DNA damage in brain cells and of cross-links in collagen molecules have been observed in rodent tissues many months after they were exposed to ionizing radiation. However, the role of oxidative damage in the radiation-induced aging of these molecules has not been studied.

2. Photoaging of the Skin and Accelerated Aging of Collagen Connected with Diabetes

The rate of aging of human skin is related to the combined effects of chronologic aging and actinic damage, referred to as photoaging. The destruction of several antioxidant enzymes, including SOD and catalase, occurs in UV irradiated keratinocytes in vitro and in the epidermis and dermis of skin exposed to UV light in vivo. Thus skin proteins are vulnerable to UV light, and this vulnerability is amplified by the decline in enzymatic antioxidant defenses.

Exposure of skin to UV light results in lipid peroxidation, connected with production of singlet oxygen.

In addition, UV-induced oxidative damage in human skin cells can be mediated by sensitized molecules including tryptophan, riboflavin, and pyridoxine. There is direct evidence, obtained by measurements of free radical signal intensity, using ESR technique, that UV radiation produces ROS and carbon-centered radicals in skin. Photochemically generated ROS induce various alterations, including cross-links in collagen that contribute to the molecular mechanisms of photoaging of mammalian skin.

The content of lipid peroxidation products is increased in the aged epidermis of animals and humans. In the senescence-accelerated mouse model an increase in the lipid peroxide levels in the skin precedes the accelerated senescent clinical signs of the mutant mouse skin. Tocopherol sorbate decreases the baseline radical formation in chronically UV-irradiated skin resulting in an antiwrinkling effect.

Skin senescense and aging-related skin diseases may be associated with a combination of oxidative modifications with the nonenzymatic glycation of skin proteins. Glycation of collagen is substantially elevated in diabetic patients as compared with age-matched controls. This phenomenon can be referred to as accelerated aging of collagen, because the collagen glycation increases almost linearly with normal aging also. The amount of the fluorescent imidazopyridinium compound pentosidine increased linearly with age in different tissues from diabetics faster than in normal tissues. Pentosidine is produced from ribose, lysine, and arginine. There is direct evidence for the role of oxygen, trace metals, and free radicals in the formation of the products of the oxidation of lysine residues. Collagen isolated from tissues of long-term diabetics is more stable compared with age-matched controls. Mechanisms of the stabilization of collagen molecules during normal and diabetes-accelerated aging include cross-linking of the molecules via glucose.

3. Hereditary Diseases Connected with Accelerated Aging

There are at least two hereditary progeroid syndromes, Werner's syndrome and Hutchinson-Gilford progeria. It has been reported that proteins isolated from cells derived from donors suffering from these syndromes contain more oxidative damage than normal cells derived from healthy donors of the same age. Some of the pathology associated with Down's syndrome, including symptoms of premature aging, can be connected with Cu-Zn-SOD overexpression in the response to oxidative stress.

There are a group of genetic diseases that can be linked with increased sensitivity of DNA to various agents. The general clinical abnormalities include increase of vulnerability to carcinogens and risk of spontaneous cancer; immunological dysfunctions; an usually high frequency of spontaneous chromosomal aberrations; skin photosensitivity; telangiectasia; and hyperpigmentation.

One such autosomal recessive disease is ataxia-telangiectasia (AT). Cells derived from patients with this disease are more sensitive than cells from normal donors to several agents that induce damage to DNA via ROS, as well as to ROS generated by neutrophils during inflammatory reactions. This is one of the pieces of evidence that the AT locus is one of the genes that control cellular response to oxidative stress.

Fanconi's anemia is another syndrome with instability of chromosomes. Cells derived from patients with this disease are highly susceptible to ROS. Such cells exhibit increased radiosensitivity and a several-fold higher sensitivity of their DNA to oxidative damage induced by H_2O_2.

Fibroblasts from patients with Bloom's syndrome constitute an example of a recessive disease with an increased frequency of chromosomal aberrations, including sister chromatid exchanges and increased radiosensitivity. A special feature of these cells is that they contain and secrete a clastogenic factor(s) that is strongly suppressed by superoxide dismutase. Thus the cells are not only deficient in the detoxification of ROS but also suffer from clastogenic activity, which is produced by reactions involving ROS.

Patients with AT, Fanconi's anemia, or Bloom's syndrome are at increased risk of cancer at certain sites. Skin cancer is dramatically increased in patients with Xeroderma pigmentosum, an autosomal recessive disease with a hereditary defect in DNA repair. Cultured fibroblasts derived from the skin of such patients have low catalase and SOD activity. Thus, there is an association of activities of two major molecular defense systems, DNA repair processes and those that are involved in the response to oxidative stress. Both defenses can be reduced in at least some patients suffering from different hereditary diseases. This association is similar to another association: the optimization of some of the DNA repair processes

during human evolution has been associated with an optimization of some of the antioxidant defenses. For example, repair of UV light-induced DNA damage is much more efficient in human skin cells as compared with rodent skin cells; and accumulation of beta-carotene in human plasma and skin is also many times more efficient than in short-living rodent plasma and skin.

C. Involvement of Oxidative Damage in the Pathogenesis of Ischemia and Reperfusion Injury

Ischemia and reperfusion injury is the damage to a tissue that occurs during the resumption of blood flow following a period of ischemia. This damage has been observed in many tissues, such as myocardium, lung, kidney, small intestine, and skin flaps. During ischemia there is a stepwise breakdown of adenosine 5'-triphosphate into xanthine, as the high-energy phospho diester bonds are used for energy. Upon reoxygenation (reperfusion), when the supply of oxygen to the ischemic tissue is restored, the enzyme xanthine dehydrogenase is converted to xanthine oxidase, which uses oxygen as its electron acceptor and has a high affinity for xanthine as substrate. This enzyme releases $\cdot O_2^-$ into the tissue.

The brains of older gerbils are more sensitive to ischemia and reperfusion injury when compared to younger gerbils. It is believed by many researchers in the fields of neurobiology of aging and neurodegenerative diseases that ischemia and reperfusion injury contributes to the mechanisms of development of brain disease initiated by ischemia, and of central nervous system disorders associated with aging. The activity of xanthine oxidase is significantly increased in patients with familial adenomatous polyposis, indicating the possibility that there is contribution of ischemia and reoxygenation to the mechanisms of carcinogenesis.

Thus ischemia and reperfusion injury can initiate molecular degenerative processes that could be related to both heart disease, neurodegenerative disease, and perhaps cancer, all connected with aging. Because certain brain regions, such as the hippocampus and the striatum, are very sensitive to both ischemia and reperfusion injury and age-related degenerative processes, ischemia and reperfusion might provide a good model for the screening of therapeutic agents that could protect against oxidative damage connected with brain aging.

V. SUMMARY AND CONCLUSIONS

Among the numerous modifications of various biomolecules induced by ROS, a few can be identified as oxidative damage associated with the process of aging. One of these oxidative damage products is 8-hydroxyguanine. Its steady accumulation with age in mitochondrial DNA of hearts and brains, and in nuclear DNA of replicative cells can be correlated with the age-dependent increase in the risk of chronic heart and brain disease and cancer, respectively. These observations lend credence to Harman's free radical theory of aging. But the picture that emerges is more complex than one simply due to damaged products.

First, different ROS can play a specific role in many processes from intracellular signal transduction to programmed cell death, which are necessary for both normal development and maintenance of adult health. Different ROS are endowed with different biophysical and biochemical characteristics, such as half-life, affinity to certain receptors, and chemical reactivity with certain groups in macromolecules including bases in DNA. These characteristics influence the physiological role of the different ROS.

Second, the physiological role of at least some of the ROS can be mediated by transcription factors, which are both sensors of the levels of ROS and/or of redox state and regulators of genes that determine cellular response to oxidative stress. These genes are among those that modulate cell replication and differentiation. This provides a mechanism where ROS are involved in both the mechanisms cell replication and differentiation and in pathogenesis of diseases connected with dysregulation of these processes.

Third, certain DNA repair enzymes are involved in the mechanisms of regulation of response to oxidative stress by transcription factors. Increased vulnerability to oxidative damage is associated with disturbance of DNA repair in cells of humans suffering from hereditary syndromes associated with accelerated aging and increased radiosensitivity. Other forms of accelerated aging, such as aging accelerated by low doses of ionizing radiation, also are connected with both oxidative stress and accumulation of DNA damage. Together these observations suggest an interplay between the decline of adaptability to oxidative stress and a decrease in DNA repair capacity in the cells of aged organisms. These observations suggest that a combination of agents, such as selected radioprotectors, which could decrease oxidative stress and increase DNA repair efficiency, might reduce the rate of aging and the risk of common chronic diseases synergistically.

BIBLIOGRAPHY

Ames, B. N., Shigenaga, M. K., & Hagen, T. M. (1993). Oxidants, antioxidants, and the degenerative diseases of aging. Proceedings of the National Academy of Science USA. 90, 7915–7922.

Asada, K., & Yoshikawa, T. (Eds.). (1994). Frontiers of reactive oxygen species in biology and medicine. Amsterdam: Excerpta Medica.

Halliwell, B., & Aruoma, O. I. (Eds.). (1993). DNA and free radicals. Chichester, OK: Ellis Horwood Limited.

Harman, D. (1994) Aging: Prospects for further increases in the functional life span. Age 17, 119–146.

Janssen, Y. M. W., Van Houten, B., Borm, P. J. A., & Mossman, B. T. (1993). Biology of disease: Cell and tissue responses to oxidative damage. Laboratory Investigation, 69, 3, 261.

Miyachi, Y. (1995). Photoaging from an oxidative standpoint. Journal of Dermatological Science 9, 79–86.

Packer, L. (Ed.). (1994). Oxygen radicals in biological systems. Part C and Part D, Methods in Enzymology (vols. 233 and 234). San Diego: Academic Press.

Sohal, R. S., & Dubey, A. (1994). Mitochondrial oxidative damage, hydrogen peroxide release, and aging. Free Radical Biology and Medicine 16, 621–626.

Stadtman, E. R. (1992). Protein oxidation and aging. Science, 257, 1220–1223.

Weindruch, R., Warner, H. R., & Starke-Reed, P. E. (1994). Future directions of free radical research in aging. In B. P. Yu. (Ed.), Free radicals in aging (pp. 269–295). Boca Raton, FL: CRC Press.

P

Pain and Presbyalgos

S. W. Harkins and Robert B. Scott

Virginia Commonwealth University

I. Introduction
II. Definition of Pain
III. Presbyalgos
IV. Types of Pain
V. Special Considerations in Assessment of
   Geriatric Pain
VI. Summary and Conclusion

Nociception Sensory properties of pain and pain perceptions. Determined, in part, by type, intensity, location, duration of the stimulus and resulting activity in nociceptive pathways in most cases. Central pain and other conditions involving referred pain, reflex sympathetic dystrophy, or causalgia are accepted as involving activity in nociceptive pathways. Sensory qualities of different nociceptive events may differ.

Nociceptor A receptor preferentially sensitive to a noxious stimulus or to a stimulus that would become noxious if prolonged or sufficiently intense.

Pain An unpleasant sensory and emotional experience associated with actual or potential tissue damage, or described in terms of such damage. Pain is always subjective. Activity induced in the nociceptor or nociceptive pathways by a noxious stimulus is not pain, which is always a psychological state.

Pain Affect Pain can elicit two distinct emotional components. One, the primary affective component, is associated with the immediate sensory/perceptual experience and is strongly related to cotemporal sensory pain experience (nociception). Another, the secondary affective component of pain, is determined more by past history of the painful experience, personality, cognitive appraisals,

and meaning of the pain to the individual. This dimension of pain can be equated with suffering. (see Table I).

Presbyalgos (*Presby*—old; *algos*—pain) A general term used to describe age changes in pain sensitivity, perception, affect, and behavior. It differs from the terms employed to describe age changes in vision (presbyopia: *opia*—vision) or audition (presbycusis—*cusis* or *acusis*—hearing), which are restricted to losses in sensory acuity. Presbyalgos includes sensory, cognitive, affective, and behavioral components and is not a generalized decrease in sensitivity to pain in old age, a phenomenon that likely does not exist. Social cohort influences on meaning of pain to the individual, individual differences in definition of pain and its properties, as well as individual differences in definition of acceptable pain behaviors must not be interpreted as age differences in nociception.

The topic of geriatric **PAIN** has not received attention in the field of gerontology until recently. This entry reviews what is currently known about pain in relation to age in the later years of life. Pain is defined and a preliminary definition of **PRESBYALGOS** is presented. The relations between old age and different types of the human experiences of pain are reviewed. These include: experimental pain, acute procedural and clinical pain, postsurgical pain, atypical pain, and chronic pain. Considerations for pain assessment in the geriatric population are discussed, and needs for future research to improve pain assessment in specific populations of elderly pain patients are suggested.

I. INTRODUCTION

There are at least four factors that might influence pain perception in the later years of life. These include loss of receptors for pain (nociceptors), changes in conduction properties of primary nociceptive (pain) afferents, changes in central mechanisms subserving the coding and sensation of pain, and psychosocial influences affecting the meaning of pain to the individual. The psychosocial influences that may differ between younger and older adults include those due to experiences with pain over the lifetime (developmental effects) and those due to social history or secular change (birth cohort effects). [See TOUCH AND PROPRIOCEPTION.]

Currently, it is unclear if pain perception is influenced by age in the later years of life. This is due in large part to confusions concerning not only the definition of what pain is, but also questions by some as to whether pain can be measured. As for pain, no discrete physiological markers exist for old age. Yet, this difficulty in definition and measurement of "age" has not deterred research related to the phenomena of biological, psychological, or sociological aging. Therefore, other reasons must account for the limited understanding of the effects of age on pain.

The field of pain research has expanded enormously in the past decade. This is in part due to (a) successful efforts to define the phenomenon of pain; (b) recognition that different types of pain exist (pain is not a unitary phenomenon); (c) a better understanding of some of the neural mechanisms of specific pain-related phenomenon; and (d) insights into both the impact of pain on the individual as well as the impact of individual differences (i.e., personality) on expression of pain symptoms and behaviors. Nevertheless, the psychophysical evaluation of the effect of age on pain has a history differing considerably from that of almost all other sensory modalities.

Although the physical, physiological, and psychological attributes of most sensory modalities have been carefully characterized, those defining pain are far less well documented. There are at least four reasons for the comparative lag in the understanding of the effects of old age on pain. The *first* reason relates to the precision to which stimuli that activate the various sensory modalities can be controlled and quantified. For example, in auditory or visual psychophysics, the ease of quantification and control of stimuli has facilitated precise definition of the effects of aging on hearing and vision. In contrast, quantification and control of stimuli that produce pain is far less precise. This is due, in large part, to the fact that these stimuli are potentially damaging, difficult to present repeatedly with the same effect, and many lack a natural physical counterpart (i.e., electrical shock).

The *second* reason relates to attitudes about pain. The human experience of pain has sensory-discriminative, motivational-emotional, and cognitive-evaluative dimensions. The operational definitions for measurement of these dimensions, however, remains a topic of considerable debate. Some, wrongly, even consider that pain is a private experience that is not measurable.

A *third* reason is the magnitude of the effort that has been directed toward the study of the other sensory modalities versus the study of pain in relation to age. The number of researchers exploring the effects of age on the psychophysics of other sensory modalities has been far greater than that devoted to the study of adult age differences in pain.

A *final* reason is that it is often simply assumed that age results in a loss of pain perception. In the clinical setting, particularly multidisciplinary pain clinics, it has also been assumed that the older adult with a chronic pain complaint is not a good candidate for treatment. Such ageist attitudes, combined with the view that pain is not measurable and the perceived difficulty in stimulus presentation and control, has limited advances in our understanding of adult developmental factors that may influence pain perception.

II. DEFINITION OF PAIN

Pain is defined according to Mersky and by the International Association for the Study of Pain as "an unpleasant sensory and emotional experience associated with actual or potential tissue damage, or described in terms of such damage" (Mersky, 1986, S217). It must be explicitly recognized that pain is an experience, not simply a response to a stimulus. Thus, "activity induced in the nociceptor and nociceptive pathways by a noxious stimulus is not pain, which is always a psychological state, even though we may well appreciate that pain most often has a proximate physical cause" (Mersky 1986. p S217). Two situations in which the proximate physical causes of pain are more clearly and quantifiably specified are in acute, procedural pain (e.g., injection, third molar extraction, etc.) and in experimental studies of pain in the laboratory. To our knowledge there are no systematic studies of age differences in procedural pain. A number of laboratory studies of the effects of age on pain sensation have been published, and these are reviewed below.

A. Dimensions of Pain

Human pain has been described as having sensory, emotional, and cognitive dimensions. The sensory components of pain are described in terms of location, temporal properties, quality, and quantity. Quantity in terms of pain intensity is the property most frequently studied, usually by verbal descriptor scales such as the widely used McGill Pain Questionnaire or by visual analog scales (VAS).

Effects of aging on the motivational-emotional dimension of pain has received less attention than the sensory-discriminative dimension. Recently it has been shown that two quite different emotional components of pain exist. One is associated with the immediate unpleasantness of pain. This emotional component (Stage 1 pain affect) usually does not exist in the absence of the sensory qualities of a painful event and is primarily, but not uniquely, determined by pain intensity. The second emotional component of pain (Stage 2 pain affect) is associated with broader feelings or moods that are in large part determined by interactions of the history of pain with cognitive-evaluative processes (meanings, expectancies, memories, social context, and pain-related limitations in activities of daily living [PRL-ADLs]). Stage 2 pain affect represents suffering that often occurs in the absence of the nociceptive event or that occurs for any threat to personal integrity. The effect of age on Stage 2 pain affect has not been systematically studied.

The cognitive-evaluative dimension of pain has received even less attention in relation to aging. The cognitive aspects of pain involve the meaning of the pain to the individual and expectancies concerning the pain, as well as the contexts in which it occurs, its impact on voluntary or obligatory ADLs (PRL-ADLs) and its effects on social, family, and occupational activities. The cognitive dimension of pain is now recognized to have a greater impact on the two emotional components than on the sensory dimension of pain, with a larger effect on Stage 2 than Stage 1 pain affect.

Figure 1 serves as a model to review the known effects of age on pain. The different dimensions of pain are illustrated in this figure. In this figure, a nociceptive event results in specific sensations that can be appreciated in terms of intensity, location, temporal quality, as well as other qualities. Cognitive appraisals, combined with the sensory quality of the nociceptive sensation(s) and autonomic arousal, condition the immediate unpleasantness of the painful event (Stage 1 affect). The second type of emotional response to pain, (Stage 2 affect in Figure 1), however, is mediated by more complex cognitive events that are influenced not only by the sensory quality and primary affective response but by the current context and past history with the same or similar pains.

III. PRESBYALGOS (*algos*—pain)

Table I summarizes possible age effects on the different dimensions of the human pain experience as shown in Figure 1. A common view is that the elderly have reduced sensitivity to pain that parallels the well-documented changes that occur in the major senses. Presbyopia (*opia*—vision) is the most common physiological marker for onset of old age for the eye. Presbyopia begins in the later fourth and early fifth decade of life and results in decreased ability to focus on near objects. It is due to loss of flexibility and accommodation ability of the lens. Presbycusis (*cusis*—hearing) is a decrease in hearing that is characterized psychophysically in terms of increased thresholds for pure tones. It is bilaterally symmetrical, progressive, irreversible, and affects higher before lower frequencies. Although presbycusis is, as presbyopia, almost universal, it affects men to a greater degree than women. Its onset, which is often a little later than that of presbyopia, indicates the beginnings of old age for

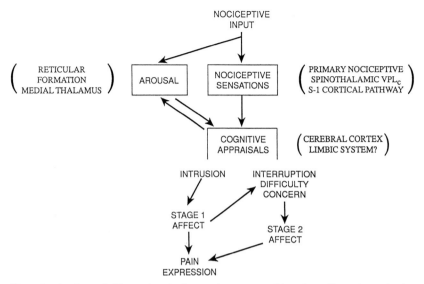

Figure I A schematic illustrating the interactions among the various dimensions of pain. Nociceptive input (a painful event) has specific sensory properties that are dependent on the type of pain. The perceived qualities of pain interact with cognitive evaluative processes influencing, to differing degrees Stage 1 (immediate unpleasantness of pain) and Stage 2 (pain-related suffering) pain affect. (From Price and Harkins, 1992a).

the ear. It is due to damage to the hair cells (cilia) of the cochlea and, likely secondarily, to loss of first-order neurons in the acoustic portion of the eighth cranial nerve (sensorineural hearing loss). [*See* HEARING; VISION.]

IV. TYPES OF PAIN

A phenomenon parallel to presbyopia and presbycusis that would adversely influence ability to perceived painful stimuli could be termed presbyalgos (*algos*—pain). However, a decrease in pain sensitivity with age and associated reduction in either nociceptors or in conduction properties of nociceptive afferents, has not been consistently demonstrated in experimental studies of pain.

A. Experimental Pain

The question, Does age influence the way in which pain is perceived? can be assessed in the laboratory. A number of studies have evaluated the effects of

aging on experimental pain, employing the psychophysical end points of threshold, reaction, tolerance, and discriminability. These studies are untidy. Some indicate that there is a loss of pain sensitivity with age, whereas others indicate that the elderly are more pain sensitive compared to younger adults. A third grouping of these studies indicate that age has no effect on pain sensitivity. These studies are summarized in Table II.

The various outcomes in experimental studies of pain (Table II) reflects a number of substantive differences between the studies. These studies vary in stimuli employed, psychophysical end point and method, the age and gender of subjects, as well as subject selection and screening criteria. The instructions and degree of practice on the psychophysical task also likely influence variability among these experimental studies.

It is likely that aging per se has minimal effect on sensitivity to superficial, acute pain. This conclusion is based largely upon recent studies employing contact thermal stimulation. This method of study of cutaneous pain in the laboratory has been demonstrated to be particularly powerful for assessing individual differences in acute pain sensitivity. Figure 2 presents

Table I Characteristics of Presbyalgos

I. Sensory Components: Nociception
   A. Characteristics:
      1. Determined by stimulus intensity, location, duration, type
      2. Sensory qualities differ for types of pain (e.g., superficial versus deep pain)
   B. Possible age effects:
      1. Increased pain thresholds (Not likely)
      2. Increased pain tolerance (Not likely)
      3. Reduced ability to discriminate between pain of various intensities (Not likely)
      4. Reduced ability to discriminate among different pains. (Difficult to assess)
      5. Increased frequency of atypical pain as a symptom of disease processes (Definitely)
      6. Increased frequency of chronic pain (Definitely)
II. Primary affective components: Stage 1 pain affect
   A. Characteristics:
      1. Strongly related to pain intensity and autonomic nervous system
      2. Related to appraisal of the present and short-term future
      3. Mediated by meaning and cognitive appraisal
   B. Possible age effects:
      1. Reduced unpleasantness of pain, due to reduced sensory intensity of pain in general (Not likely)
      2. Reduced unpleasantness of pain due to decreased arousal, exteroceptive (sight, sound), and interoceptive (startle, autonomic) responses resulting in reduced segmental responses to painful injury (No evidence exists for acute pain, may be true of chronic pain)
      3. Reduced general aversiveness of nociceptive stimuli (Unlikely)
      4. Decreased perception of threat, distress, annoyance associated with the intensity of the painful sensation and its accompanying arousal (Unlikely for acute pain)
      5. Differences or changes in cognitive appraisal (Likely)
III. Secondary affective components of pain: Stage 2 pain affect
   A. Characteristics:
      1. Related to past and long-term future
      2. Cognitive appraisal
      3. Related to or representative of suffering
      4. Not measurable in experimental studies of pain
      5. Stage 2 pain affect shares many properties of emotional suffering. Suffering is defined here "as the state of severe distress associated with events that threaten the intactness of the person." There is confusion between chronic pain and suffering because disease models dominate thinking concerning pain
      6. Unameliorated pain-related suffering (Stage 2 affect) requires different interventions than those traditionally used for control of the sensory intensity or the primary affective components of pain
   B. Possible age effects:
      1. No systematic studies exist concerning effects of age on the secondary affective component of human pain, but the results shown in Figure 5 suggest a reduction in Stage 2 Pain Affect with age

results from one of these studies. The results of this study indicated a significant, but trival, difference in pain ratings between younger, middle-aged, and older volunteer subjects.

Some earlier studies do indicate increased thresholds for radiant heat-induced thermal pain, whereas others indicated no effects of age (see Table II). We agree with those researchers who have found that pain intensity ratings are similar in older and younger adults if care is taken in subject selection, instructions, and practice. Instructions are critical. When they have

clearly indicated that responses are to be made to the pricking or first pain sensation in studies employing thermal stimuli no age effects have been found.

B. Acute Procedural Pain

As mentioned earlier there are, to our knowledge, no systematic studies of age differences in procedural pain in older adults. Procedural pain is defined here as pain resulting from a specific, limited, invasive procedure. Procedural pain has been systematically

Table II Laboratory Studies of the Effect of Age on Psychophysical Indices of Pain Sensitivity[a]

Stimulus	Source (Reference)	Psychophysical end points and findings
1. Thermal		
A. Radiant heat	Schumacher et al., 1940	Sensory thresholds No age effects
	Hardy et al., 1943	Sensory thresholds No age effects
	Chapman, 1944	Sensory thresholds Higher in elderly Reaction thresholds Higher in elderly
	Chapman and Jones, 1944	Sensory thresholds Higher in elderly Reaction thresholds Higher in elderly
	Birren et al., 1950	Pain sensory thresholds No age effects Pain reaction thresholds No age effects
	Sherman and Robillard, 1964a, 1964b	Sensory thresholds Higher in elderly Reaction thresholds Higher in elderly
	Procacci et al., 1970	Sensory thresholds Higher in elderly
	Clark and Mehl, 1971	Sensory thresholds Higher in 55-year-olds compared to younger adults
B. Contact Heat	Kenshalo, 1986	Sensory thresholds No age effects
	Harkins, Price, & Martelli, 1986	Magnitude matching Slight age effects (see text and Figure 2)
C. Cold Pressor	Walsh et al., 1989	Tolerance (time) Males: Lower with increasing age Females: Minimal increase with increasing age
2. Electrical shock		
A. Cutaneous	Collins and Stone, 1966	Sensory threshold Lower in elderly Tolerance Lower in elderly
	Tucker et al., 1989	Sensory threshold Higher in elderly
	Evans et al., 1992	Sensory thresholds No age effect in nondiabetics. Old diabetics higher thresholds than younger diabetics
B. Tooth	Mumford, 1965	Sensory threshold No age effects
	Mumford, 1968	Sensory threshold No age effects
	Harkins and Chapman, 1976	Sensory threshold No age effects

continues

Continued

Stimulus	Source (Reference)	Psychophysical end points and findings
	Harkins and Chapman, 1976	Discrimination accuracy Lower in elderly Response bias Age effects: variable Sensory threshold No age effects Discrimination accuracy Lower in elderly
3. Pressure A. Achilles tendon	Woodrow et al., 1972	Tolerance Lower in elderly
	Jensen et al., 1992	Muscle tenderness and pressure pain to age 65 Sensory thresholds Higher in older

[a]From Harkins et al., 1992, as modified from Harkins and Warner, 1980.

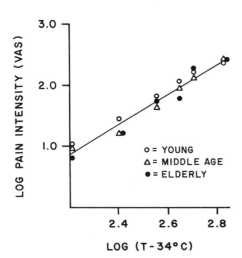

Figure 2 Psychophysical representation of reported pain intensity to brief heat pulses (43°C to 51°C; from an adapting temperature of 34°) in young (*M* = 25 years), middle age (*M* = 53 years), and older (*M* = 73 years) community-dwelling, healthy individuals. Stimuli were delivered to the inner surface of the forearm. Stimulus intensity in natural log units on the ordinate and pain intensity (by visual analog scales; VAS) on the abscissa. Statistical results indicated a significant groups effect with older individuals rating the intensity of the lower level stimuli as less intense compared to older subjects. At higher levels of stimulation age groups were not different in their pain ratings. The significant age effect at lower intensities accounted for less than 1% of the variance in VAS pain ratings. (Redrawn from Harkins et al., 1986.)

studied in evaluation of neonatal and pediatric pain (e.g., studies of reaction to heel prick in neonates or to allergy injections in young children). It is surprising that so little research has focused on this area in geriatric patients. There may well be significant hyperalgesia and allodynia in the frail elderly that would be demonstrable by carefully conceived and excuted studies of pain in the old-old and oldest-old.

C. Postsurgical Pain

Currently available information indicates that the intensity of postsurgical pain in different age groups is similar in quantity and quality. Some researchers, however, found that older adults received less analgesic than younger adults and that this may contribute to a longer hospital stay during postsurgery recovery in geriatric patients. Further research is sorely needed in this area and should focus on quality and quantity of procedural and postsurgical pain in relation to age in the later years of life. Long-term follow-up would indicate if the elderly are differentially at risk for postsurgical causalgia.

D. Cancer Pain

Cancer pain is a form of acute pain that is related to the type and status of the cancer. Pain in cancer patients occurs frequently. In the elderly cancer patient, any apparent decrease in sensitivity to pain is likely due to less effective report of pain than to actual losses of sensorineural processes subserving pain sensibilities. This impact of cultural inhibition on complaining of pain, and less effective reporting of pain in the old has not been systematically evaluated. Nevertheless, pain in the elderly is more likely to produce significant impairment of psychologic, social, and physical function than in younger individuals. [*See* CANCER AND THE ELDERLY.]

Management of cancer pain begins with efforts to control the underlying disease with standard modalities. An important principle of pharmacotherapy is to suppress the pain before it becomes severe, and to give continuous effective doses rather than to attempt to treat episodically. Elderly patients are more responsive to smaller doses than younger persons because of a somewhat diminished metabolism of the drugs (pharmacokinetic effects) and an enhanced effect at the cellular level in the central nervous system (pharmacodynamic effects). [*See* PHARMACOLOGY.]

In the elderly it is best to use drugs with a short half-life, prescribe one drug at a time, begin with low doses, and continue trial for an adequate period. In addition to the usual analgesics, other nonpharmacologic measures frequently used to aid pain control in younger cancer patients may be helpful. These include various forms of nerve stimulation, physical and occupational therapy, sectioning of nerves surgically, or psychotherapy.

E. Atypical Pain Presentation

Although the evidence is untidy concerning experimental pain sensitivity in old age, there is no question that important age differences exist with regard to acute pain as a symptom in the older patient. Silent or painless acute myocardial infarction (MI) occurs more frequently in the elderly (up to 30%) than in younger patients (23%). Pain consequent to MI develops when sufficient levels of afferent impulses are reached and when an appropriate activation of central ascending pathways has been established. In patients with a silent MI such levels are apparently not reached, perhaps because of insufficient stimulation of the myocardium, decreased capacity for cephalad transmission, or for other unknown pathophysiological reasons effecting peripheral transmission.

Such age differences in presentation of pain as a symptom have been cited as evidence for a general decline with aging in pain sensitivity. This is inappropriate. First, pain does occur with acute MI in the majority of older heart attack patients. Stress testing suggests that depression of the S-T segment, without pain, occurs relatively frequently in both young and elderly adults. Thus, silent MIs may well reflect individual differences or pathophysiological changes in processes subserving referred pain and not generalized age changes in mechanisms subserving pain. Pain from deep structures and superficial pain represent quite different phenomenon. Age differences in the one should not be generalized to the other without supporting empirical evidence.

Nonetheless, it is important clinically to recognize the increased prevalence of atypical presentation of pain as a symptom in the elderly. The direction of this is toward reduced not augmented pain. This reduction in incidence of acute pain, associated with certain conditions (e.g., myocardial ischemia) in the elderly does not appear to hold true for recurrent or chronic pain.

F. Recurrent and Chronic Pain

Chronic pain has been defined as a pain that has not responded to treatment and that, according to different authorities, has lasted at least 1, 3, or 6 months. Chronic pain can be defined as pain that outlasts the normal healing period following tissue damage by 1 month. A time of approximately 1 month is preferred because failure to intervene will, in some cases, result in irreversible changes, increasing the likelihood that the pain will not be successfully treated.

There are many conditions causing pain that are treatable only to a certain point. It has been suggested that any pain that recurs with some regularity (whether there is or is not evidence of associated pathophysiological process that may give rise to pain), that can be expected to recur, that responds only to a degree to currently available interventions, and that negatively impacts on the quality of life of the individual in pain should be considered chronic and appropriate for referral to a multidisciplinary chronic pain diagnostic and treatment center.

The pattern of painful conditions in relation to old age with population-based survey studies indicating that aging is associated with an increase in musculo-skeletal-related pains and a decrease in headaches and back pain typically seen in multidisciplinary pain clinical settings.

Figure 3 shows frequency of several chronic pains and Figure 4 the intensity of these pains in younger and older community-dwelling individuals. Although the elderly may underutilize the multidisciplinary pain clinic, the population-based findings, shown in Figures 3 and 4, indicate that older adults are at increased risk for chronic pain compared to younger individuals (Figure 3).

Herpes zoster and the associated risk for postherpetic neuralgia increase with age and represent a major source of suffering in the elderly. The pain associated with postherpetic neuralgia is thought to arise from peripheral neurons that were damaged during the herpes zoster eruption. Another source of pain of unknown etiology is associated with parkinsonism, a condition that increases with age in the later years of life. Approximately 50% of patients with parkinsonian's type movement disorders have significant pain, particularly in the lower limbs. Current thinking is that this pain is central in origin, but mechanisms and best modes of treatment are unclear.

There is no convincing evidence that pain systems are influenced by the major cause of dementia in later life, dementia of the Alzheimer's type (DAT). Given the widespread effects of this central degenerative disease and its impact on attention, memory, and semantic abilities it would not be surprising to find that perceptual aspects of pain were influenced by such disorders. More critical is the fact that ability to communicate is restricted in patients with DATs, and this will influence ability to communicate critical information concerning pain in these patients. [*See* DEMENTIA.]

The epidemiology of pain in patients with age-related neurological degenerative disorders or in older individuals in long-term care settings, particularly the frail elderly, have not been the subjects of focused

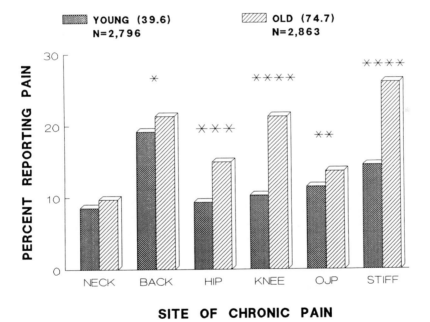

Figure 3 Chronic pain frequency in the general population in relation to age. Note that older individuals are at greater risk of pain from the back, hip, and knee compared to younger individuals. The older respondents also reported other joint pain (OJP) and stiff joints upon awakening compared to younger individuals. Chronic pain was defined here as a pain in the specified location lasting at least 1 month, which was present in the past week. (From Harkins et al., 1994.) (*$p < 0.05$; **$p < 0.01$; ***$p < 0.001$; ****$p < 0.0001$.)

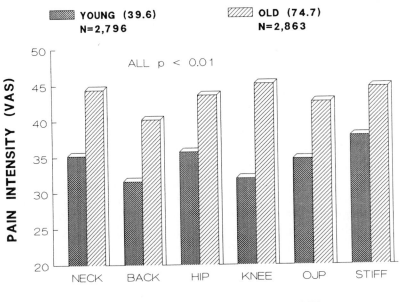

Figure 4 Chronic pain intensity in the general population in relation to age. Intensity ratings are for pains lasting at least 1 month that were present during the past week as in Figure 3. Pain intensity was greater in older compared to younger individuals (all *p* < 0.001). Pain intensity based on visual analog scale (VAS) labeled "No Pain" at one extreme and "Very Severe Pain" at the other extent. Pain severity ratings ranges from 0–60 and were recorded in this figure as percent (i.e., 0 to 100%) of the original scale. Individuals reporting 0 pain over the past week were eliminated from this analysis. OJP = other joint pain; Stiff = stiff or swollen painful joints. (Data from subjects as in Figure 3.)

study and merit attention. Considerable unnecessary suffering likely exists in these individuals.

The characteristics of presbyalgos (shown in Table I) can be summarized in terms of the sensory, affective, and cognitive dimensions of pain as follows:

1. *Sensory dimension of pain:* As indicated in Table II (see Figure 1), it is not likely that the elderly have increased thresholds, tolerance, and reactions, or decreased discriminability of pain intensity as determined in the laboratory. The elderly are at risk for atypical presentation of pain as a symptom and are more likely to suffer from chronic pain compared to younger individuals.

2. *Primary affective component of pain—Stage 1 pain affect:* Stage 1 pain affect in the model shown in Figure 1 and Table I is strongly influenced by the concurrent intensity of the noxious event, accompanying autonomic nervous system (ANS) activation (arousal), as well as a combination of situational and

predispositional factors. It is unlikely that the primary affective component of pain is reduced with normal aging. There have been no studies of age differences in ANS arousal to acute pain. Empirical demonstration of such age differences, however, would not be strong evidence for age differences in pain perception because both sympathetic and parasympathetic control of end organs differ with age. Demonstration of age differences in ANS response to nociceptive stressors and no such differences for nonpainful stressors, or vice versa, could lead to informative research in this regard.

Similarly, as indicated in Table II, it is unlikely the elderly have a generalized reduction in the immediate unpleasantness (Stage 1 pain affect) of a painful stimulus. That is, there is no substative evidence that the elderly can be characterized as "anhedonic" for pain.

It is more likely that there are age differences in perception of threat, resulting distress, and accompanying general arousal and anxiety for previously experienced pain that is mediated by age-related changes in cognitive appraisal. Such a change in the meaning of a pain, across a lifetime, likely accounts for the reduction in Stage 2 pain affect in elderly chronic pain patients discussed below (see Figure 5).

3. *Secondary affective component of pain—Stage 2 pain affect:* The characteristics and factors influencing Stage 2 pain affect (Figure 1) are summarized in Table II. As indicated, this secondary affective component of pain is a property of the suffering that accrues to a chronic pain. It is the distress associated with a threat to the intactness of the individual. This Stage 2 pain affect is not a component of experimental pain for obvious reasons. It must be, therefore, studied in the real world in relation to the stress and suffering associated with a pain problem.

There have been no systematic studies of this di-

mension of pain in the elderly. Preliminary evidence (Figure 5) indicates that the older chronic pain patients reports less Stage 2 pain affect compared to younger chronic pain patients. This occurs even when the intensity and Stage 1 pain affect are identical in younger and older chronic pain patients and suggests that there is a difference in meaning of the pain to younger compared to older chronic pain patients.

V. SPECIAL CONSIDERATIONS IN ASSESSMENT OF GERIATRIC PAIN

There are a number of issues that must be considered in geriatric pain assessment. Some of these are summarized in Table III. The major issues that merit attention are presence of comorbidities, mental status, depression, limitations in ADLs, medications, and the importance of family and other support systems. [*See* ACTIVITIES; DEPRESSION; SOCIAL NETWORKS, SUPPORT, AND INTEGRATION.]

Eighty percent of the elderly have at least one chronic, degenerative process. Many of these degenerative processes predispose one to chronic pain (i.e., osteoarthritis, osteoporosis, parkinsonism-type movement disorders, noninsulin-dependent diabetes mellitus). Additionally, these conditions exist in the presence of acute and other chronic morbidities that may interact with the pain-related degenerative disease.

An aspect often overlooked is the *functional* consequence of the pain in the older person. Older persons may have several limitations affecting their daily activities and the addition of pain may accentuate this. The elderly have less reserve capacity to adapt to functional stresses than do healthy young persons, and the consequence of pain on functional status may be very severe in an older person. The clinician must also be sensitive to the perceived needs of the individuals with differing wishes for the outcome of pain treatment. A patient at the end of life may wish only to die free of pain and even be heavily sedated by the medication, whereas another patient may prize the ability to effectively communicate with loved ones and want pain medications balanced so that sedation is minimized.

In dealing with the elderly patient, there is always the recognition that adverse effects of potent medi-

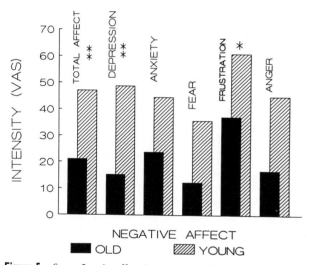

Figure 5 Stage 2 pain affect in younger and older chronic pain patients (see Figure 1 and Table I). Stage 2 pain affect defined here as depression, anxiety, fear, frustration, and anger specifically related to the chronic pain. Total affect is the sum of the individual domain-specific affect ratings. Ratings were made on 150-mm visual analog scales (VASs) for each emotion. VASs were labeled "No Depression" (or anxiety, etc.) on the left and "The most extreme depression imaginable" (or anxiety, etc.) on the right of the VAS. Care was taken to ensure patients were rating their mood or affect specifically related to their chronic pain. These results indicate that domain-specific affect related to chronic pain differs with chronological age in adults and is not due to age differences in pain intensity or immediate unpleasantness of pain (Stage 1 pain affect, in Figure 1 and Table I). Pain ratings made on the Virginia Commonwealth University Pain Inventory. (From Harkins et al., 1995.)

Table III Special Considerations in Geriatric Pain Assessment

1. General Considerations:
   a. Recognize that age itself does not reduce pain sensitivity.
   b. Recognize that there is no evidence that age, per se, influences qualitative properties of pain.
   c. Recognize the importance of encouraging patient to discuss the pain.
2. Comorbidity: Illness and symptom presentation in the elderly, particularly the frail and the old-old, is often characterized by multiplicity, duplicity, and chronicity.
3. Mental status: Assess for cognitive impairment: Dementia of the Alzheimer's type, pseudo-dementia secondary to depression, multi-infarct dementia. Refer if necessary.
4. Depression: Pain is likely a major source of depression in the elderly.
5. Activities of daily living (ADL): Differentiate between limitations caused by nonpain-related dysfunction and limitations in activities due to the fact that their performance is painful. Pain-related dysfunctions and limitation in ADLs is likely a significant source of depression in the old.
6. Medications: Assess all current and recent medications: (look in the "Brown Bag of Pills") Start low and go slow.
7. Family and social support systems: Maintain these systems in the physically or mentally impaired elderly.

cines are commonplace and the adage "Start low and go slow" must guide the treatment plan.

Although intensity and frequency of chronic pains, particularly those related to the musculoskeletal system, actually increase with age, presentation of pain in the very old is frequently characterized by multiplicity (multiple overlapping signs and findings), duplicity (unusual symptom presentation—particularly for acute pain of recent origin), and chronicity (new pains are especially suspicious in the elderly).

Mental status represents a challenging issue for pain assessment in the elderly. Between 50 and 60% of older individuals in long-term care setting have a dementing illness. It is also estimated that up to 40% of community-dwelling individuals 80 years of age and over score in the at risk for dementia range on mental status examinations. Social skills may be well maintained and the presence of a possible dementia only becoming suspected upon specific mental status evaluation. Screening instruments for evaluation of mental status exist, but because chronic pain reduces cognitive abilities, norms for such instruments are needed for older chronic pain patients.

Assessment of pain in patients with a clinical diagnosis of DAT represents a special challenge. No studies of the magnitude of this problem or the best methods for assessment of pain in dementia patients have been made. More is known about pain assessment and control in the very young than in the frail dependent or cognitively impaired elderly.

VI. SUMMARY AND CONCLUSION

Four factors were identified that may influence the perception of and reactions to pain across the life span. These included changes in receptors for pain, changes in primary nociceptive neurons, changes in central mechanisms subserving pain, and psychosocial influences. The information summarized indicates limited effect of age on perceived intensity of acute, superficial pain. This would suggest that changes, at least in cutaneous pain receptors, primary nociceptive afferents or central mechanisms subserving pain sensory processes, are not dramatically changed with age. The same cannot be said for deep or referred pains. As the mechanisms of pain from the viscera, joints, and muscle are better understood, control of pain associated with acute deep tissue injury and chronic degenerative processes in the elderly will improve.

The primary affective response (Stage 1 pain affect) to pain does not change with age. Stage 2 pain affect is less in older compared to younger chronic pain patients (Figures 1 and 5). This likely reflects experience of the patient with this or a similar pain as well as age–cohort effects.

The properties of *presbyalgos* are defined more by similarities between younger compared to elderly individuals (Table II). There is an increase in chronic pain in the old, and this is associated with greater pain intensity in the community-dwelling population, but not necessarily the pain clinic population, which is likely the result of self-selection and referral filters.

Considerable care must be exercised in evaluation and treatment of the older patient with significant comorbidity, particularly the metabolically compromised. Assessment of pain in the old-old and the frail individual is a particular challenge, which is made even more difficult if there is evidence of a dementing disorder. It is unfortunate that the very old, the frail elderly, the dementia patient, and the cognitively intact but physically challenged because of pain have not been systematically evaluated for pain and pain control. Considerable unnecessary discomfort, pain, and suffering currently exist in these subpopulations of geriatric patients.

BIBLIOGRAPHY

Birren, J. E., Shapiro, H. B., & Miller, J. H. (1950). The effect of salicylate upon pain sensitivity. *Journal of Pharmacology and Experimental Therapy, 100,* 67–71.

Bonica, J. J. (1990). *The management of pain,* (2nd ed.). Philadelphia: Lea & Febiger.

Bush, F. M., Harkins, S. W., Harrington, G., & Price, D. D. (1993). Analysis of gender effects on pain perception and symptom presentation in temporomandibular pain. *Pain, 53,* 73–80.

Bush, J., & Harkins, S. W. (1991). *Children in pain: Clinical and research issues from a developmental perspective.* New York: Springer-Verlag.

Chapman, W. P., & Jones, C. M. (1941). Variations in cutaneous and visceral pain sensitivity in normal subjects. *Journal of Clinical Investigation 23,* 81–91.

Clark, W. C., & Mehl, L. (1971). Thermal pain: A sensory decision theory analysis of the effect of age and sex on d', various response criteria, and 50 percent pain threshold. *Journal of Abnormal Psychology, 78,* 202–212.

Collins, G., & Stone, L. A. (1966). Pain sensitivity, age and activity level in chronic schizophrenics and in normals. *British Journal of Psychiatry, 112,* 33–35.

Crook, J., Rideout, E., & Browne, G. (1984). The prevalence of pain complaints in a general populations. *Pain, 18,* 299–314.

Evans, E. R., Rendall, M. S., Bartek, J. P., Bamisedum, O., Connor, S., & Glitter, M. (1992). Current perception threshold in ageing. *Age and Aging, 21,* 273–279.

Hardy, J. D., Wolff, H. G., & Goodell, H. (1943). The pain threshold in man. *American Journal of Psychiatry, 99,* 744–751.

Harkins, S. W. (1988). Pain in the elderly. In R. Dubner, F. G. Gebhart, M. R. Bond (Eds.), *Proceedings of the Vth World Congress on Pain* (pp. 355–357). Elsevier Science Publisher B.V. (Biomedical Dividison).

Harkins, S. W., & Chapman, C. R. (1976). Detection and decision factors in pain perception in young and elderly men. *Pain, 2,* 253–264.

Harkins, S. W., & Chapman, C. R. (1977a). The perception of induced dental pain in young and elderly women. *Journal of Gerontology, 32,* 428–435.

Harkins, S. W., & Chapman, C. R. (1977b). Age and sex differences in pain perception. In B. Anderson, B. Matthews (Eds.), *Pain in the trigeminal region* (pp. 435–441). Amsterdam: Elsevier/North Holland.

Harkins, S. W., Kwentus, J., & Price, D. D. (1990). Pain and suffering in the elderly. In J. J. Bonica (Ed.), *Management of pain* (2nd ed.) (pp. 552–559). Philadelphia: Lea and Febiger.

Harkins, S. W., & Price, D. D. (1992). Assessment of pain in the elderly. In D. Turk & T. Melzack (Eds.), *Handbook of pain measurement and assessment* (pp. 315–351). New York: Guilford Press.

Harkins, S. W., Price, D. D., & Braith, J. (1989). Effects of extraversion and neuroticism on experimental pain, clinical pain, and illness behavior. *Pain, 36,* 209–218.

Harkins, S. W., Price, D. D., Bush, F. M., & Small, R. (1994). Geriatric pain. In P. D. Wall & R. Melzack (Eds.), *Textbook of pain.* Edinburgh: Churchill Livingstone.

Harkins, S. W., Price, D. D., & Martelli, M. (1986). Effects of age on pain perception: Thermonociception. *Journal of Gerontology, 41,* 58–63.

Harkins, S. W., & Warner, M. H. (1980). Age and pain. In C. Eisdorfer (Ed.), *Annual review of gerontology and geriatrics,* (vol. 1, pp. 121–131). New York: Springer Publishing Company.

Harkins, S. W., Kwentus, J., and Price, D. D. (1984). Pain and the elderly. In C. Benedetti et al. (Eds.), *Advances in pain research and therapy* (vol. 7, pp. 103–212). New York: Raven Press.

Harkins, S. W., Price, D. D., Bush, F. M., & Small, R. (1995). Geriatric Pain. In R. Roy (Ed.), *Chronic pain in old age* (pp. 127–163). Toronto: University of Toronto Press.

Jensen, R., Rasmussen, B., Pedersen, B., Lous, I., & Olsen, J. (1992). Cephalic muscle tenderness and pressure pain threshold in a general population. *Pain, 48,* 197–203.

Kenshalo, D. R., Sr. (1986). Somesthetic sensitivity in young and elderly humans. *Journal of Gerontology, 41,* 732–742.

Knapp, D. A., & Koch, H. (1984). The management of new pain in office-based ambulatory care: National Ambulatory Medical Care Survey, 1980 and 1981. Advance data from Vital and Health Statistics, No. 97, DHHS Pub. No. (PHS) 84-1250. Public Health Service, Hyattsville, Maryland.

Marsland, D. W., Wood, M., & Mayo, F. (1976). Content of family practice: A statewide study in Virginia with its clinical educational, and research implications. New York: Appleton-Century-Crafts.

Melzack, R. (1973). *The puzzle of pain.* New York: Basic Books.

Melzack, R., Abbott, F. V., Zackon, W., Mulder, D. S., & Davis, M. W. L. (1987). Pain on a surgical ward: A survey of the duration or intensity of pain and the effectiveness of medication. *Pain, 29,* 67–72.

Merskey, H. (1986). Classification of chronic pain: Descriptions of chronic pain syndromes and definitions of pain terms. *Pain,* Suppl. 3.

Mumford, J. M. (1965). Pain perception threshold and adaptation of normal human teeth. *Arch Oral Biology, 10,* 957–968.

Mumford, J. M. (1968). Pain perception in man on electrically stimulating the teeth. In A. Soulairac, J. Cahn, J. Charpentier (Eds.), *Pain* (pp. 224–229). London: Academic Press.

Neri, M., & Agazzani, E. (1984). Aging and right-left asymmetry in experimental pain measurement. *Pain, 19,* 43–48.

Portenoy, R. K. (1992). Pain management in the older cancer patient. *Oncology, 6,* 86–98.

Price, D. D. (1988). *Psychological and neural mechanisms of pain.* New York: Raven Press.

Price, D. D., & Harkins, S. W. (1992a). The affective-motivational dimension of pain: A two-stage model. *American Pain Society Journal, 1,* 229–239.

Price, D. D., & Harkins, S. W. (1992b). A reply to the commentaries. *American Pain Society Journal, 1,* 256–258.

Procacci, P., Bozza, G., Buzzelli, G., & Della Corte, M. (1970). The cutaneous pricking pain threshold in old age. *Gerontologia Clinica, 12,* 213–218.

Procacci, P., Della Corte, M., Zoppi, M., Romano, S., Maresca, M. & Voegelin, M. (1974). Pain threshold measurement in man. In J. J. Bonica, P. Procacci, C. Pagoni (Eds.), *Recent advances on pain: Pathophysiology and clinical aspects* (pp. 105–147). Springfield, IL: Charles C. Thomas.

Schumacher, G. A., Goodell, H., Hardy, J. D., & Wolff, H. G. (1940). Uniformity of the pain threshold in man. *Science, 92,* 110–112.

Sherman, E. D., & Robillard, E. (1960). Sensitivity to pain in the aged. *Canadian Medical Association Journal, 83,* 944–947.

Sherman, E. D., & Robillard, E. (1964). Sensitivity to pain in relationship to age. *Journal of the American Geriatric Society, 12,* 1037–1044.

Sherman, E. D., & Robillard, E. (1964). Sensitivity to pain in relationship to age. In P. F. Hansen (Ed.), *Age with a future: Proceedings of the Sixth International Congress of Gerontology, Copenhagen, 1963* (pp. 325–333). Philadelphia: F. A. Davis.

Tucker, M. A., Andrew, M. F., Ogle, S. J., & Davison, J. G. (1989). Age associated change in pain threshold measured by transcutaneous neuronal electrical stimulation. *Age Aging, 18,* 241–246.

Walsh, N. E., Schoenfeld, L., Ramamurthy, S., & Hoffman, J. (1989). Normative model for cold pressor test. *American Journal of Physical Medicine and Rehabilitation 68,* 6–11.

Woodrow, K. M., Friedman, G. D., Siegelaub, A. B., Collen, M. F. (1972). Pain tolerance: Differences according to age, sex, and race. *Psychosomatic Medicine, 34,* 548–556.

Pensions

Neal E. Cutler

University of Pennsylvania

I. Introduction: Retirement Income and the Three-Legged Stool
II. From Employment to Pension Accumulation: Some Basic Concepts
III. From Pension to Retirement Dollars: Issues of Pension Plan Funding
IV. Defined Benefit versus Defined Contribution Pensions and the Need for More Personal Financial Literacy

Defined Benefit (DB) Pension The "traditional pension" in which the future retiree benefit defined in terms of dollars to be received, is defined or guaranteed in advance. The worker is told in advance what his pension will be at the time of retirement, based on salary level, age, number of years working, number of years covered, and similar factors. Because of this future "dollar output" obligation, the company has a current responsibility to plan for this future financial responsibility. As part of becoming and remaining eligible for ERISA's PBGC pension insurance the company must specify how the pension plan is organized and funded to guarantee these future benefits.

Defined Contribution (DC) Pension A pension plan in which the employer guarantees or defines only the "dollar input" into the employee's pension account, and not the future retiree-income dollar value of the pension. The DC pension creates a very different set of obligations on the part of the employer and the employee as compared to DB pensions. In the DB pension the employer guarantees what the employee will receive upon retirement, and so it becomes the employer's responsibility to make sure that the money is available to pay that guaranteed amount. In the

DC pension, by contrast, the employer guarantees only the monthly or annual "input" and it is the employee's responsibility to decide how the money is invested in order to grow into a future retirement income resource. Being vested in a DC pension means only legal ownership of the current funds in one's own account, not ownership of or rights to a guaranteed number of dollars. The future financial value of a DC pension is not insured by ERISA's PBGC insurance program.

The Employee Retirement Income Security Act of 1974. (ERISA) The primary federal program to protect private employer pensions. The central mechanism of this protection is a government-administered pension insurance program, the Pension Benefit Guaranty Corporation (PBGC), through which employers purchase insurance so that if the pension plan runs out of money the insurance makes the pension payments directly to the retiree. In order to become and to remain eligible to purchase this insurance the employer must meet a broad range of legal, administrative, and financial requirements. The ERISA regulations are not legally required of all employers or pension plans, but because the incentive to purchase this valuable PBGC financial protection is so substantial most large employers voluntarily join the program.

Pension Coverage Refers to employment in which the employer offers some form of pension plan. Coverage is only the first step in the path from employment to future pension income because, for example, not all employees who work in a covered job may be currently eligible to participate in the pension plan for reasons of age or job tenure. Or some covered employees may choose for financial or other personal reasons not to participate in their company's pension plan.

Vesting   Refers to the legal right of a pension plan participant to receive a specified amount of pension income, usually on the basis of a specific age, or age plus years on the job. Vesting is a worker's legal and economic protection that an earned pension will be paid, even if the worker leaves the job, whether voluntarily or involuntarily.

About two-thirds of middle-aged Americans are covered by some form of employer **PENSION**, and the percentage of total retirement income contributed by pensions is increasing. Alternatively stated, tomorrow's elderly are more likely to benefit from pension income in retirement than today's elderly. The path from employment to pension coverage to actual receipt of adequate pension income, however, is neither automatic nor inevitable, and is affected by a small number of key pension system concepts that are explored in this article, including: coverage, participation, and vesting; the basic pension plan alternatives of advance funding versus pay-as-you-go funding; the primary public policy pension protections found in the Employee Retirement Income Security Act (ERISA) and its Pension Benefit Guaranty Corporation. Finally, the article explores what may be the most important change in the American pension system, the historical shift from defined benefit pensions to defined contribution pensions. In turn this pension trend produces another fundamental change, the shift in the financial risk and responsibility for the future financial value of earned pension benefits from responsibility on the part of the employer or labor union to responsibility on the part of the individual employee. Overall, although the role of pensions as a component of retirement income among future cohorts of retirees may be increasing, so too is the need for more and earlier-acquired individual financial literacy on the part of today's preretirees.

I. INTRODUCTION: RETIREMENT INCOME AND THE THREE-LEGGED STOOL

Retirement income in the United States (and many economically-developed countries) is often described with the metaphor of a three-legged stool: Social Security, employer pensions, and personal savings. More recently a fourth source, or leg, has been added in many discussions, that of wages or earnings, as many retired persons work full- or part-time, either for the income, the psychological satisfaction, or both.

Although the retirement income component of Social Security (as distinct from the disability and Medicare and Medicaid health insurance benefits) is a form of pension, Social Security is such a pervasive aspect of the overall retirement income situation, both individual and public, that it is discussed in several other articles in this encyclopedia. This article focuses on the central concepts and basic descriptive data concerning employer pensions, and Social Security will be referred to only for purposes of comparison to pensions.

This overview begins with the basic question of the relative financial importance of pensions in the overall retirement income profile of older Americans. From this starting point some of the basic concepts necessary to understand the dynamics and controversies surrounding pensions as a component of retirement income are considered. For example, just because one works in a company that has a pension system does not mean that 20 or 30 years from now one will in fact receive a pension. This review of the basic concepts of coverage, participation, and vesting discusses the possible obstacles between current employment and future pension income. Finally, this article concludes with a brief introduction to a major shift in American pension policy, the shift from *defined benefit* (DB) to *defined contribution* (DC) pension plans, the related transfer of responsibility for the financial value of future pension income from employer to employee, and the new needs for individual financial literacy.

How important is the pension leg of the three-legged stool? Table I summarizes the income sources for older American households (age 65+), comparing 1976 with 1986, but the answer is not as clear as the data appear to suggest. Column 1 and Column 2 indicate that Social Security remains as the dominant source of retirement income, in that 90% of all older households receive Social Security income. Income from employer pensions (combining government civil service and military pensions with private pensions) has increased by over 10% in the 10-year period, but is still a notably less important source than is Social Security. [See RETIREMENT.]

Table I Profiles of Income Sources for Older Households[a]

| Income source | All households | | 1986 (older couples) | |
| | 1976 | 1986[b] | $5,000–$9,999 | $20,000 or more |
	(1)	(2)	(3)	(4)
Millions of households	17.3	21.6	1.17	4.04
Percentage with any retirement benefits	92%	94%	96%	94%
Social Security	89%	91%	95%	89%
Employer pensions (government or private)	31%	43%	15%	73%
Earnings	25%	20%	13%	49%
Income from assets	56%	67%	40%	93%

[a] Adapted from Employee Benefit Research Institute (1990), Table 3.23.
[b] The 1986 detail is for married couples with at least one person age 65+.

But the older population is not homogeneous, and the relative importance of various income sources is linked to the economic status of the older family. To illustrate this relationship, Table I compares less wealthy with more wealthy older couples in 1986. Social Security is important to both groups (95 vs. 89%) but is clearly the more dominant income source for the less wealthy couples. Income level does make a noticeable difference in the case of employer pensions, however; the wealthier the older household, the more important pensions are as a source of income (15 vs. 73%).

This might at first seem like a logical or even simply a definitional connection: If one has a pension in addition to Social Security, then of course one has more income! But the story is not quite that simple or direct. A more complete explanation of the connection between having a pension and being wealthier is that the kinds of employment that produce higher incomes are also the kinds of employment that are more likely to have pension plans associated with them. Thus, agricultural workers, laborers, service workers, many self-employed, and part-time workers are not only likely to earn lower wages, they are also less likely to work under conditions in which employer pensions are available.

Overall, among older couples (in 1986), only 43% of these retirees receive pension income. But the data on current retirees underestimate the future importance of pensions as a source of retirement income,

largely because employer pensions have become widespread only in the years after World War II, and key pension protections were not enacted until the mid-1970s (as discussed below). Consequently, more current, younger workers are earning future pensions, compared to current retirees whose work lives took place in an era when pensions were not as available as they are today. This is clearly suggested in the boxed age section at the top of Table II, which shows that although only 43.5% of persons age 65 and over are covered by a pension, 64% of people age 25–64 are covered. In other words, these younger "tomorrow's retirees" have higher levels of *pension coverage* than do current retirees.

II. FROM EMPLOYMENT TO PENSION ACCUMULATION: SOME BASIC CONCEPTS

The fact is, however, that not all the younger persons in Table II will get the pension income that they appear to be accumulating. The road from current employment to future pension income includes three fundamental steps, and the data in columns 2 and 3 of Table II describe only the first step. The three concepts, or steps, are *coverage*, *participation*, and *vesting*.

Table II Pension Coverage and Vesting, 1988[a]

	All workers	Covered		Vested	
	millions (1)	millions (2)	% (3)	millions (4)	% (5)
All workers	101.8	59.8	58.7%	30.0	50.2%
Age					
Under 25	18.3	6.9	37.7%	1.1	15.9%
25–44 years old	55.6	35.1	63.1%	16.9	48.1%
45–64 years old	25.6	16.8	65.6%	11.5	68.5%
65 years and older	2.3	1.0	43.5%	0.5	50.0%
Gender					
Women	47.0	26.6	56.6%	12.0	45.1%
Men	54.8	33.2	60.6%	18.0	54.2%
Employment sector					
Government	17.1	15.7	91.8%	9.3	59.2%
Private					
manufacturing	21.2	14.8	69.8%	8.0	54.1%
nonmanufacturing	63.5	29.3	46.1%	12.7	43.3%
Private Firms					
Less than 100 workers	34.1	9.1	26.7%	4.4	48.4%
100 or more workers	58.8	46.4	78.9%	24.0	51.7%
Union	19.3	17.3	89.6%	11.0	63.6%
Nonunion	82.5	42.5	51.5%	19.0	44.7%
Job tenure					
Less than 1 year	19.5	7.4	37.9%	0.7	9.5%
1–9 years	51.1	29.5	57.7%	11.5	39.0%
10 years or more	26.9	21.4	79.6%	17.5	81.8%

[a] Adapted from Employee Benefit Research Institute (1990) Table 3.1.

A. Coverage

In order to earn a future employer pension you have to work for an employer that offers a pension plan, and not all employers provide such coverage. As column 3 indicates, pension plan coverage is related to a number of employment circumstances. Governmental employers (federal, state, and local), for example, are much more likely to offer pensions than nongovernmental employers. Larger employers are more likely to offer pension plans than smaller, and unionized companies are more likely to offer pensions that nonunionized companies.

The point is that some employers offer pensions, and for whatever reasons or motivations, some do not. Thus, the first step in earning future pension income is to work for an employer that offers a pension plan. This situation is defined as *covered employment*, and simply means that there is a pension plan available in your work environment. Columns 2 and 3 of Table II are the data on coverage, (i.e., the number and percentage of workers whose employers or companies offer a pension plan).

B. Participation

But not all people who work in a covered job, (i.e., whose employers offer a pension plan) actually participate in that plan themselves. Why not? A company may only allow employees to participate after being on the job for a minimum of six months or a year; trainees and new employees, for example, may not be eligible to participate. Or, the legal and actuarial details of the pension plan may require a minimum age in order to participate. Or, only full-time employees may be eligible to participate. Thus, newer and younger employees, and employees with part-time or sporadic noncontinuous work may not be eligible to participate even though the company offers a pension plan. In many cases, nonparticipation may be only a temporary situation until the work history, tenure, or age requirements are met.

A second set of reasons for nonparticipation in pension-covered jobs is the worker's own choice. Some pension plans require the joint financial contributions of both employer and employee, and if the employee chooses not to contribute then the connection between coverage and participation is not established. Employees may choose other employment benefits, such as higher than minimum current health insurance or life insurance benefits, and forgo the future benefit of pension income. For whatever reasons, participation and coverage are not the same. In what are often called "cafeteria" employee benefit packages, the employee chooses from among a cafeteria selection of benefits, with pension benefits as only one of several options.

C. Vesting

The third step in the path from employment to actual receipt of pension income is vesting, which refers to the legal right of a pension plan participant to receive a specified amount of pension income, usually after a certain age, or age plus years on the job. Vesting is a worker's legal and economic protection that an earned pension benefit will be paid, even if the worker leaves the job, whether voluntarily or involuntarily. In previous years, without vesting rights, a worker could lose all pension benefits if he quit or was fired even on the eve of retirement after 20 or 30 years of participation in the pension plan. In the past two decades, however, legal protections and rules have been enacted that reduce the number of years that an employer can require as a precondition for vesting.

In the absence of a relatively brief vesting period, an employee could lose all the future pension benefits she has earned. For example, in the case of a 20-year vesting requirement, a worker who decides to change jobs after 17 years could lose all of her pension benefits. With vesting reduced to 5 years, she has much greater decision latitude about staying or changing jobs. Whether or not a worker should "hop" from job to job every 5 years is, of course, a separate question. Starting a new job, with pension benefits also starting over from "year one," may not be as financially wise as staying with one job and experiencing the growth

of pension benefits. Shorter vesting requirements, however, protect earned pension credits and give the employee more flexibility when deciding on whether to stay or change jobs.

Columns 4 and 5 in Table II show the number and percent of American workers who are likely to receive their pensions because they have met the vesting requirements of their employers and pension plans—in contrast to columns 2 and 3, which only show the number and percentage who work in *covered* jobs. As would be expected, older workers (e.g., those 45–64 vs. those 25 and younger) and those who have been on the job longer (10+ years vs. less than 1 year) are more likely to be vested. What this pattern optimistically suggests is that more workers will receive pension income in the future than current rates of retiree pensions suggest, simply due to the fact that more younger workers will be on the job long enough to meet the vesting requirements of their employers.

III. FROM PENSION TO RETIREMENT DOLLARS: ISSUES OF PENSION PLAN FUNDING

The mechanism by which the pension plan is *funded* identifies another set of issues that affects the financial safety and guarantee of a pension plan. In funding their pension plans, employers and their pension managers have two basic choices, known as *advance funding* and *pay-as-you-go funding*. Advance funding means that the pension plan managers deposit or invest enough money each year so that sufficient funds are available to pay all the pension costs of every employee who later retires. The key idea here is that the deposited funds plus the investment of those funds will produce sufficient money to continue to pay the pension costs for every retiree, for as many years as the retiree is alive (or even for the life of the retiree's survivors in some pension plans).

This goal constitutes a substantial financial challenge for several reasons. First, it requires calculations based on how much pension income each employee is scheduled to get upon his or her retirement. Second, it requires that the pension managers and their investment advisors choose investments that will be sure to produce enough future money to pay these calculated future obligations. Third, questions of how long the retiree is likely to live, and whether some form of future inflation protection will be added to the pension, also affect the amount of money needed for each future retiree. If investments do not produce as much funding as anticipated, or if pension obligations increase faster than predicted (e.g., if significantly more employees choose early retirement than anticipated), then the advance funding is not likely to be adequate, and additional sources of funds will have to be found.

At other extreme, the pay-as-you-go approach means that no money is put away for those future pension obligations. Rather, the company "simply" writes each month's pension checks to its current retirees out of its current operating budget. It should be kept in mind that in any given month (or year), a company has two sets of pension-funding obligations: obligations to workers already retired and receiving pensions, and accruing future obligations to current workers whose vested pensions will have to be paid in future years.

There is no problem with the pay-as-you-go approach as long as the company is financially healthy and has enough money to pay current salaries, current retirement obligations, current taxes, and other employee benefits, with enough additional money for business expansion, research, and dividends to stockholders. But what happens to the pay-as-you-go pension obligations when the company has major financial problems?

The most public pension default crisis came in the early 1960s when the Studebaker automobile company went bankrupt. Like most companies, the Studebaker pension plan used some advance funding along with substantial pay-as-you-go funding. As a result, workers and retirees alike lost virtually all their pension income. Those who were already retired each received a small amount, about $600 each, as their share of the small advance-funded portion of the pension plan. And those workers who were earning credits toward future retirement income, including those who were already vested and within just a few years of their retirement, got nothing.

The 1963 demise of the Studebaker Corporation and its pension plan was not the only instance of the absence of pension plan protection on a public policy level. The emerging, multiple problems produced several governmental investigations and, eventually, federal legislation. Although it took over a decade, the Employee Retirement Income Security Act (ERISA)

of 1974 was enacted. It has been called the single most complex piece of legislation ever enacted by the U.S. Congress. The complexity of its content and its politics reflect the fact that it is simultaneously a gerontology and retirement policy, and a set of intricate labor union and management issues, as well as a contract situation requiring substantial accountant and attorney involvements.

Among the key new protections that ERISA provided were administrative requirements concerning the advance funding of pension plans. Some pay-as-you-go funding is still allowable, but greater emphasis on advance funding is required along with more detailed analysis by companies and pension plans of such things as the age structure of the company's workforce—in order to more precisely estimate how much money will be needed to pay for all pension obligations during each future year. Armed with this kind of calculation plus estimates of the present and anticipated financial health of the company, a more rational assessment of how much pay-as-you-go funding can be tolerated is possible, with advance funding taking on a larger, more financially appropriate and protective role.

Although the Studebaker pension crisis reflected a corporate business failure, other pension plan failures were caused by the dishonesty and corruption of pension plan, labor union, and company officials. Consequently, a second set of ERISA protections focused on the legal and financial accountability of pension plan managers and their union and company colleagues.

The ERISA legislation uses a combination of legal requirements and financial "rewards" to encourage pension plan officials to conform to the new financial and legal administrative requirements. The primary financial inducement was the creation within ERISA of a federal agency to insure the financial viability of a company's pension obligations. The Pension Benefit Guaranty Corporation (PBGC) is a government agency that operates like a private insurance company. For each current pension plan participant (i.e., future retiree) the company purchases an insurance policy (or more accurately, a group policy covering all plan participants). Then, should the pension plan become unable to pay its obligations, the PBGC will pay the pension to the retiree.

The "catch" is that in order to qualify for this pension insurance the company and its pension plan has to be responsive to the various ERISA rules and requirements both in financial responsibility and legal-fiduciary rules. Thus, for example, the PBGC reviews and approves the pension plan's proposed mix of pay-as-you-go funding versus advance funding. If the PBGC estimates that the mix is too risky (i.e., that the company has not invested sufficient advance funding), then the PBGC can direct the pension plan to modify its financing if the company wants to continue to qualify for the pension insurance; the pension plan managers are likely to be responsive to the PBGC's directives.

Although it is a government agency, the PBGC operates to some extent like a private insurance company. Thus, just as drivers with bad accident records have to pay higher auto insurance premiums, the PBGC can raise the insurance premiums for companies and pension plans judged to be poor risks. Alternatively, it is in the pension plan's own best interests to conform to the various ERISA regulations, in order to lower its pension risk vulnerability, and therby keep its PBGC insurance.

ERISA and PBGC represent substantial protections for retirees and future retirees in the United States. Many of the changes in coverage, participation, and vesting rules of benefit to workers have come from ERISA. Employers are willing to implement these regulations in order to acquire and maintain their PBGC pension insurance. ERISA and PBGC are a mixed blessing however. Two sets of problems should be mentioned, although detailed discussion of them is beyond the scope of this article. First, the financial obligations on the shoulders of the PBGC has grown substantially. Like other insurance companies, if a significant number of policyholders get into trouble in a short period of time, the assets of the insurance agency may not cover its liabilities. Because the PBGC is a government program rather than a private insurance company, however, if it does get into financial difficulty because of pension plan defaults, it is the American taxpayer who will be called upon to pay the bills.

Second, the rules and regulations imposed by ERISA and PBGC are complex, just as the financial accounting and arithmetic required to estimate current and future pension obligations are complex. As a result, it has been argued that companies are less willing to establish new pension plans precisely because the administrative procedures have become so costly, especially for smaller and midsize companies. One argument, therefore, is that although ERISA was enacted to protect the retirement income of American workers, if new pension plans are not being established or if companies are simply not extending pensions to new employees, then the cause of the American worker's retirement income may not be well served after all.

IV. DEFINED BENEFIT VERSUS DEFINED CONTRIBUTION PENSIONS AND THE NEED FOR MORE PERSONAL FINANCIAL LITERACY

These issues—the public liability of the PBGC and the possible "reverse" impact of ERISA administrative requirements—are the occasion of complex and large-scale public policy debates, each with both technical and ideological aspects. Nonetheless, there is one substantial change in the American pension system that to some degree can be seen as a response to the increased cost and complexity of traditional pensions (whether those costs and complexities are the consequence of ERISA or other forces remains an open question).

Our discussion to this point has focused on traditional pensions, which are usually referred to as *defined benefit* (DB) pension plans. In this kind of pension, it is the *dollar benefit* to be received by the retiree that is defined, or guaranteed, in advance. The worker is told, in advance, what his pension will be at the time of retirement, given his salary, age, number of years working, number of years covered, and similar factors. It is because these dollar benefits are defined (i.e., obligated) in advance that the company or pension plan has a responsibility to allocate current dollars for this future obligation, or invest current dollars so that the return on investment will cover (fully or partially) the future pension costs, or have enough money in the company's current treasury now and in the foreseeable future to fund the pension obligations on a pay-as-you-go basis.

The alternative to the DB pension is the *defined contribution* (DC) pension. In this alternative the employer still provides pension resources to the employee, but it is only the current contribution into the employee's pension account that is guaranteed *and not the future, retirement-years' value of that pension.* The two kinds of pension imply very different obligations on the part of the employer and the employee. In the DB plan the employer guarantees to the employee what he or she will receive upon retirement. *It is then the employer's responsibility to make sure that the money is available to pay that guaranteed amount.*

In the DC plan, by contrast, the employer guarantees only the "input," the amount contributed into the retirement account each month or year. In many cases the contribution into the retirement account is made by both the employer and the employee. However, *it is then the employee's responsibility rather than the employer's responsibility to make the key decisions about how the money is invested, how it will grow into a future retirement income resource.* That is, the output is not the employer's responsibility.

In most cases the employer is still an active participant in the administration of the pension plan. For example, the employer typically arranges for several kinds of investment options, from relatively low-risk but low-return savings-account types of investments, to higher risk but potentially higher return stock market funds. Although the employer provides opportunities, information, and even financial counseling, the DC plan has the following characteristics: (a) it is the employee rather than the employer who makes the guiding investment decisions; (b) it is the employee rather than the employer who assumes the risk for the future value of the pension, and (c) no one guarantees the success of the pension's investments. If the employee makes poor financial choices, or just has bad luck, then 20 years later all the DC could have low or no value.

DC pension plans have a number of features that are attractive to the employer. In financial terms, once a contribution is made into the employee's account the financial responsibility is completed. There may administrative obligations as well as fiduciary protections involved, but the employer does not have to guarantee a future dollar output amount. Administratively the DC pension plan is also easier. The company does not have to keep track of all its former employees over a long period of years for purposes of mailing out pension checks to retirees. The pension investment

Defined Contribution vs. Defined Benefit Pensions Plans

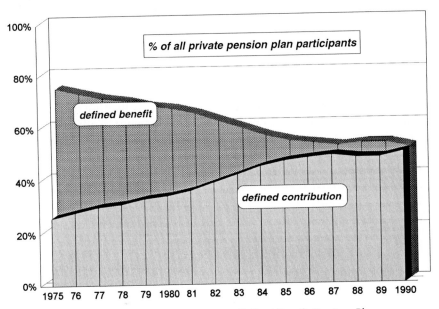

Figure 1   Defined contribution versus Defined Benefit Pensions Plans.

accounts belong to the employee, and in most cases can be moved when the employee moves. Overall, the administrative machinery as well as the financial investments required are less burdensome than in the case of the more traditional DB pension.

Figure 1 shows the 15-year trend, 1975 to 1990, in the two types of pension plans. The decline in number of participants in traditional DB pensions is mirrored by the growing popularity of DC plans. The largest share of new plans, in other words, are the easier to administer and financially less burdensome (to the employers) DC plans. The connection between this trend and financial literacy is clear. In DC plans the first-order responsibility for the investment of retirement funds belongs to the individual employee. Even though the employer offers a choice of professionally managed investment options with alternative profiles of risk and return, the choice from among these options is made by the employee.

From the employee's perspective, DC pensions have both advantages and disadvantages. One advantage is immediate vesting, in that the contributions into the retirement account belong to the employee immediately. For parallel reasons, because the money typically belongs to the employee, the pension-loss risks associated with the business failure of the employer are minimized. If each Studebaker employee and retiree had been given his or her own savings account, then the company's failure would have caused future payments to cease, but the earned pension benefits would have already been placed into those accounts.

But there are disadvantages as well. Where the PBGC can insure a DB pension, no one guarantees the future value of a DC investment account. In the traditional pension someone else both makes the investment decisions and guarantees that, one way or another, the defined pension benefit will be there (although it was the abuses and failures of that system that produced ERISA and the PBGC).

The burdens of making investment decisions for DC pensions rest with the individual employee. The need, therefore, is for increased financial literacy. This does not mean that people should make these retirement investment decisions on their own. As investment options and alternatives expand, seminars, books, magazines, software, and professional advisors are all part of an increasingly complex environment. And financial literacy is the necessary gateway to that environment.

In sum, although the precise combination of the causes of the changes in the American pension system—gerontology, demography, economics, bureaucracy—is not clear, the consequences of these changes are fairly clear. More and more people are more and more responsible for their own pension income investment decisions. Furthermore, these decisions will increasingly be made in the early years of a person's wealth span, and will have direct and significant impact on the size of retirement income many years later. The key to success and survival, consequently, is financial literacy—to be acquired at earlier ages than was necessary in previous historical periods.

BIBLIOGRAPHY

Cutler, N. E. (1994). Who's responsible for my pension now? The need for more financial literacy at younger ages. *Journal of the American Society of CLU & ChFC, 48* (January), 31–36.

Cutler, N. E., Gregg, D. W., & Lawton, M. P. (Eds.). (1992). *Aging, money, and life satisfaction: Aspects of financial gerontology.* New York: Springer Publishing.

Doyle, R. J., Tacchino, K. B., Kurlowicz, T., Schnepper, J., & Cutler, N. E. (1992). *Can you afford to retire?* Chicago: Probus Publishing.

Employee Benefit Research Institute [EBRI]. (1990). *EBRI databook on employee benefits.* Washington, DC: Employee Benefit Research Institute.

Gregg, D. W. (1992). *The human wealth span: A life-span view of financial well-being* [the 1992 Boettner Lecture]. Philadelphia, PA: Boettner Institute of Financial Gerontology, University of Pennsylvania.

Salisbury, D. L., & Jones, N. S. (Eds.) (1994). *Pension funding & taxation: Implications for tomorrow.* Washington, DC: Employee Benefit Research Institute.

Schultz, J. H. (1995). *The economics of aging,* (6th ed.) Westport, CT: Auburn House.

Perception

Grover C. Gilmore

Case Western Reserve University

I. Data Limitations
II. Impact of Perceptual Deficits on Higher
   Order Processing
III. Conclusion

Contrast   The difference in intensity between an object and its immediate surroundings.

Global Precedence   The tendency for observers to detect and identify a whole object before its component parts.

Masking   The obscuring of a target stimulus by stimuli that precede or follow it.

Perceptual Span   The amount of information that an observer can apprehend in a single glance.

Sensitivity   The capability of the biological system to respond to stimulation; the inverse of threshold.

Stimulus Persistence   The phenomenon that after stimulus offset there is continued activity in the sensory system causing the stimulus to be perceived as having a longer duration.

Threshold   The minimum amount of stimulation needed to detect a stimulus or to discriminate among stimuli.

Useful Field of View   The spatial extent of a visual display within which highly accurate stimulus detection and identification can be performed.

The study of **PERCEPTION** has a broad base, from the examination of sensory systems to the analysis of higher-order processes of attention. This article will focus on how adults use the information acquired by their senses to gain an initial understanding of their immediate world.

I. DATA LIMITATIONS

The amount of information that the adult perceiver has available is limited first by the sensory systems. As reviewed in the chapters on the sensory systems, there are marked changes with aging in the ability of the senses to respond to physical stimulation. Several examples from the vision literature will illustrate this point. [*See* VISION.]

A. Light Sensitivity

At some time in our younger years most people have had an adult, perhaps a grandparent, encourage them to turn on more lights. "How can you see in that light?" the grandparent may have exclaimed. The dutiful response was to turn on the lamp but many wondered why the grandparent thought the room to be dimly illuminated. The simple reason is that light sensitivity decreases with age in adulthood. The most commonly used method to determine light sensitivity requires a person to sit in the dark for varying periods of time. As the period of time in the dark lengthens, the observer grows more light sensitive. After about 45 min in the dark, a person has reached their maximum level of light sensitivity. After the third decade of life there is a remarkable reduction in maximum light sensitivity, which is highly correlated with age ($r = .895$). Indeed, starting with age 20 years the intensity of illumination must be doubled for every increase of 13 years for a light to be just seen by the fully dark-adapted eye.

This reduction in the response to light is also seen in a physiological response of the visual system. When

Encyclopedia of Gerontology
Volume 2

an observer views a reversing checkerboard pattern each reversal elicits an electrocortical potential. By attaching electrodes at appropriate positions on the scalps of observers the electrical activity of the cortex can be recorded in an electroencephalogram (EEG). By averaging the data associated with the presentation of the visual event, evoked potentials (EP) with characteristic latencies and amplitudes can be extracted. The latency of these visually EPs (VEPs) have been shown to be related to the age of the observers, with older adults showing longer VEPs. That is, the time for cortical registration of a visual event is notably longer in older adults. Interestingly, the age-related delay in responding to visual stimuli is linked to the luminance of the display with little age-dependent delays in the VEP at high levels of luminance. The latter finding suggests that although older adults are less sensitive to light, their cortical response may approach that of younger adults when the stimuli are at a high intensity. The latter is an important observation, for it suggests a means by which one source of elementary age differences may be compensated.

B. Acuity

From common experience one is aware that the use of optical corrections is widespread among adults. These lenses permit a person to resolve detail. However, there is an apparent limit associated with age to the acuity that a person may achieve. Visual acuity, defined as a measure of the smallest spatial detail that a person can resolve, has been shown to decline throughout adulthood in individuals with normal, healthy eyes. Researchers have reported that acuity was best for a sample of adults in their late twenties and then gradually became worse with increasing age. It is noteworthy that the latter study was careful to test persons while they wore their optimal refractive correction. Thus, older adults even with corrective lenses can be expected to perform more poorly on tasks that require the resolution of spatial detail.

C. Spatial Contrast Sensitivity

The measurement of acuity assesses the ability to resolve small details at a high level of contrast. In the assessment of spatial contrast sensitivity the minimum contrast required to resolve stimuli of different sizes is determined. Typically, the stimulus is a grating in which the contrast is sinusoidally modulated. At high-contrast levels, the grating appears to be composed of fuzzy stripes alternating from dark to light across the display panel. The width of the stripes is also varied to permit the determination of contrast thresholds for different-sized stimuli. The variation of stimulus size is described in terms of spatial frequency, where the number of light bars per unit area on the retina is a measure of the spatial frequency of the stimulus.

The measurement of spatial contrast sensitivity has emerged as an important tool in understanding visual processing. It has been demonstrated that there are multiple neural channels in the visual system that respond to different bands of spatial frequencies. The pattern of response characteristics of the channels, including the lag and duration of the response, dictate the initial development and formation of visual representations. Although it had been common to consider the initial stage of visual information processing to be a passive, static recording of visual stimulation, it has now become reasonable to consider that the flow of visual information that arises in the nervous system is continuous from the onset of the stimulus. The information needed to detect or identify various aspects of a stimulus develops at different rates following stimulus onset as the neural channels respond successively to spatial frequency characteristics. The multichannel model of visual processing holds much promise of offering a new view of the early stages of perception; it permits new questions to be raised regarding the availability of information to the perceiver.

The dominant measure of the status of the multiple neural channels has been the measurement of spatial contrast sensitivity. As would be expected from the acuity literature, elderly adults do have reduced contrast sensitivity to high spatial frequencies (thin stripes). In addition, older adults require higher contrasts than do young adults to detect lower spatial frequencies (bigger stripes). Furthermore, as the luminance of the display is reduced, the contrast required by the elderly adults to detect the stimuli increases at a greater rate than it does for younger subjects.

It also has been demonstrated that the spatial contrast sensitivity of persons diagnosed with Alzheimer's disease (AD) is significantly poorer than healthy elderly adults. Contrast sensitivity can decline quite rapidly. A longitudinal study showed that the sensitivity of AD patients declines in as little as 6 months, particularly for low spatial frequencies. Thus, elderly adults have been shown to have a weak response to a broad range of spatial frequencies, particularly under low levels of stimulus luminance. The implication of these findings is that the information carried by the spatial frequencies will be more weakly represented in the perceptual constructions of elderly adults and particularly persons with AD. [See DEMENTIA.]

D. Stimulus Persistence

Following a stimulus event there is a phenomenal continuation of the stimulus for a brief period of time. For instance, if the reader closes his eyes, he will find that the image of the page persists briefly. The phenomenon of stimulus persistence has been studied in a variety of paradigms. Relevant to our discussion it has been found that there is an inverse relationship between the duration of the persistence and the luminance, contrast, and duration of the stimulus. That is, brighter, longer visual events lead to shorter periods of visible persistence. Short persistence is advantageous in visual information processing for it permits the system to be cleared before the presentation of successive events.

Elderly adults have been shown to experience longer visible persistence than young adults. It has been argued that this prolonged neural stimulation may be at the root of a number of perceptual deficits reported for elderly observers. For example, if a series of light pulses are presented with varying dark periods between the pulses, subjects will report seeing a flickering light at low rates of pulsing. However, when the pulse rate is increased, the subject will report that the series of lights have fused into a steady light. The pulse rate at which this fusion occurs is referred to as the critical flicker fusion (CFF) threshold. Elderly adults have lower thresholds than do young adults. This finding suggests that the temporal integrity of the stimulus event has been diminished in the older observers. That is, the neural stimulation continues for a prolonged period of time causing the elderly subjects to perceive the dark interval as being filled with light.

The existence of this phenomenon was cleverly demonstrated using a form integration task. The task of the subject was to read a word presented for a brief period of time. The unique aspect of the stimulus presentation was that the stimuli were fragmented and split over two displays. The separate displays appeared to be simply a jumble of lines. However, if the displays were overlapped, then the complete word could be read. The displays were presented successively to the subjects and were separated by a brief time interval. Success at reading the word indicated that the subjects were able to integrate the separate stimulus events. Interestingly, the elderly adults were superior to the young subjects at reading the words. Furthermore, there was an inverse relationship between stimulus duration and accuracy with both groups of subjects doing better in the 20-msec than in the 40-msec condition. The short duration stimuli led to longer persistence and better form integration. The implication is that the elderly subjects experienced even longer visible persistence than did the young subjects.

In 1985, researchers used a type of form integration task in which the observer was required to detect the appearance or disappearance of a small light in the midst of a larger array. It was argued that the persistence effect was related at least in part to the antagonistic interactions of the ON- and OFF-center relay cells of the lateral geniculate nucleus (LGN). The ON cells respond to the onset of visual stimulation. Because of antagonistic inhibition, the OFF cells become hyperpolarized at light onset. The resultant inhibition gradually decays, and after the offset of the stimulus the OFF cells burst into activity. The time period between the firing of the ON and OFF cells dictates the duration of visible persistence. However, the latency of the OFF cells to respond to the offset of stimulation is inversely related to the duration of the stimulus. That is, both the neurophysiological event of the firing of the OFF cells and the perceptual phenomenon of visible persistence are inversely related to the duration of the stimulus. Researchers demonstrated that the age-related performance differences in the integration task could be accounted for by positing that the elderly adults had OFF cells that took longer to respond to the offset of a stimulus event. Furthermore, they empirically demonstrated that the differences between the age groups could be eliminated by presenting the stimulus to the elderly adults for a slightly longer period of time. The longer duration stimulus presumably led to both a reduction in the latency of the OFF cells and of the persistence of the stimulus in the elderly observers. Thus, the study demonstrated that the persistence phenomenon could be linked to a specific neural event, and furthermore that a simple intervention, the increase in the duration of the stimulus, could eliminate the age-related effect.

There are few situations outside of the laboratory in which the integration of forms over a long period of time would be advantageous. More often the perceiver deals with a series of images, each of which carries unique and perhaps critical information. So, it is relevant to ascertain the ability of an individual to obtain information from a single event embedded in a series of stimulus events. This question is addressed by masking studies. In the typical visual masking study a stimulus, such as a letter, is presented for a brief period of time followed by a blank interval of variable length and finally by another stimulus that may be a plain lighted field or a patterned stimulus. In general, masking studies have shown that elderly adults are less accurate than young adults in recognizing the first stimulus in the series. Recently, however, it has been demonstrated that the age-related deficit in the masking studies can be eliminated by an adjustment in the luminance of the target stimulus display. Thus, by applying the principle that stimulus persistence is inversely related to stimulus luminance, researchers were able to shorten the persistence of the elderly observers and improve their performance to the level of the young subjects.

The examination of effects related to stimulus persistence has demonstrated two important findings. The first is that the age-related performance decrements associated with the persistence phenomenon may be linked to specific delays in the latency of firing of the OFF-center cells. Second, and perhaps more importantly, the relatively poor performance of the elderly observers may be improved significantly by using slightly brighter or longer duration stimuli.

E. Motion Discrimination

The detection and discrimination of motion is an elementary ability that is critical for daily tasks, such as driving. Yet, there has been little study of the motion-discrimination capabilities of older adults. The studies that have been conducted have demonstrated in general that elderly adults experience more difficulty in detecting and discriminating simple motion. Researchers have reported that there is a steady decline in motion sensitivity across the age range. It has been

argued that this deterioration of visual function suggests age-related neurodegeneration in the visual pathways. Other researchers have found that only elderly women showed a reduction in motion sensitivity. The source of such an age-by-gender effect has not been suggested in the literature. Further work is needed to determine the basis of this intriguing effect.

Another study of motion perception in adults is noteworthy for its finding that the performance of elderly adults can be improved. It has been found that although elderly adults consistently perform more poorly than young adults their performance can be improved through training. Indeed, after a short period of experience with the motion-discrimination task the level of performance of the elderly adults reached the initial level of the young adults in the pretraining condition. This finding underlines two important factors. First, experience in making perceptual judgments may play an important role in age-related performance differences. If the older participants have had less experience or are less familiar with the testing environment, then they may perform more poorly than the younger subjects. Secondly, training in perceptual judgments may be used to remediate age-related visual losses in visual guidance of locomotion and mobility. Thus, further study in this area is warranted to determine the extent to which such remediation can be effective in improving the performance and quality of life of elderly adults.

F. Perceptual Span

It is clear from the above review that there are limitations in the sensory systems that affect the responsiveness of elderly adults to environmental stimulation. A direct measure of the impact of these limits on the construction of a percept can be made through the measurement of the amount of information that a person acquires in a brief glance at a stimulus. This brief visual storage buffer has been labeled iconic memory. It is apparent that the visual system of young adults is able to hold a large amount of the information presented to it for a very brief period of time. For example, it has been demonstrated that young adults presented with an array of 12 letters can capture the name and location of at least 9 of the letters in their sensory store. The capacity of this sensory store is affected by the light-adapted state of the eye and the strength of the stimulus. Furthermore, the information held in the store is volatile and is not available for further processing after about one-quarter of a second. Thus, the observer must transfer the information to more permanent stores during this short period of time.

Given the sensory limitations of elderly adults one might expect that their iconic memory would be smaller than that of young adults. The initial investigations into this quesiton were met with the frustrating finding that elderly adults could not be tested with the partial-report method, which was the classic method for assessing the capacity of iconic memory. The failure of the elderly adults was taken as a measure of both their severely inadequate iconic memory and their poor attention abilities.

Iconic memory capacity has been successfully measured by modifying the stimulus paradigm from that used by other aging investigators. Auditory cuing has been used to avoid age-related visual masking effects associated with the use of visual cues. Other researchers have presented stimuli at longer durations for the elderly adults to compensate for the ocular factors that reduce the stimulus energy for elderly adults. The result was that not only could all of the elderly adults perform the partial-report task but also there were no significant differences in the capacity of iconic memory for the two age groups. When a portion of the stimulus is projected outside the foveal region, elderly subjects perform more poorly than their young counterparts. This finding illustrates several points. First, the success of the elderly subjects demonstrates that there is not an attentional limitation in this age group for performing the demanding partial report task. Second, the iconic memory capacity of the elderly, like the young, is linked to the sensitivity of their visual system. Finally, adequate compensation for the reduced sensitivity of the older adults can lead to the achievement of "young" performance levels.

In the absence of stimulus compensations, it is apparent that elderly adults capture less information in a brief glance than do young adults. That is, given an array of letters or a complex scene the older observers will not perceive as many elements accurately. This limit on the perceptual span may be linked to what has been identified as the useful field of view (UFOV). Operationally, the UFOV has been defined as the spatial extent within which highly accurate stimulus detection and identification can be performed. It is ap-

parent that elderly adults have a UFOV that is up to three times more restricted than young adults. That is, older observers can sample only small chunks of visual information, whereas younger persons can accommodate larger areas of data.

The limit on the size of the perceptual sample was evident in the study of global precedence and aging. When arrays of letters are arranged so that they form a single large letter (for example, multiple instances of the letter *F* would be presented on a stimulus card to form a shape identifiable as the letter *G*), the task for the subject is to either identify the large or the small form, depending on the instructions. The typical finding of young adults was that subjects were faster at identifying the larger form than the smaller component letters. Such a finding suggests a precedence for the processing of the larger or global form. The elderly subjects however, showed the opposite pattern. The elderly adults were faster in identifying the small component letters, suggesting a local precedence effect. It appears that when observers are presented with a large, complex array of visual information, young subjects are capable of capturing large chunks of information. Older observers must sample small chunks of data and construct the whole pattern from these parts. Thus, a consequence of the limited perceptual span may be that older observers are required to engage in the spatial integration of the small chunks of visual information to a greater extent than are younger perceivers. Such a requirement will further slow the visual processing of the older adult.

The limit on the perceptual span may also lead to different perceptual constructions by young and old adults. An ambiguous figure is one that may be interpreted to have more than one form depending on the stimulus features that are salient to the observer. Elderly adults tend to perceive the form that is comprised of fewer features and requires less spatial integration. Thus, the sampling of a small number of features in a limited area causes the elderly observers to construct a percept that is different from that reported by younger subjects who sample and integrate a broader area of the visual stimulus.

A test used in the assessment of perceptual style, the Embedded Figures Test may also be affected by the perceptual span of the participant. The test was designed in part to assess how easily an individual could disembed a simple figure from a complex background. A subject is shown a simple figure and is then required to find it in the midst of a complex array. Strong age-related changes on the test have been reported with older subjects being less able to find the simple figures and requiring a longer period of time to complete the test. Given that the perceptual span has been linked to the strength of the visual stimulus, it would be expected that a manipulation of signal strength would affect performance on the Embedded Figures Test. The performance of young adults is affected negatively by viewing stimuli through filters that simulate some of the ocular deficits of the elderly, such as yellowing of the lens and reduced retinal illumination. This finding provides an important link in the argument that it is the limited perceptual span of elderly adults, with the concomitant sampling of small chunks of visual information, which is at the heart of the elderly adults' difficulties in dealing with embedded figures.

G. Perceptual Noise

The above presentation has emphasized the reduction in the strength of the signal in the processing system of elderly adults. It is logical to infer from both psychophysical and neurophysiological measurements that demonstrate age-related changes in thresholds and neural latencies that there are reductions in the strength of the neural signals available in the processing system. It also must be considered that these signals occur in the midst of random neural activity or neural noise. That is, the signal must be evaluated against the background noise of the system.

The direct measurement of noise in perceptual studies has proven elusive. However, it has been argued that the poor performance of elderly subjects in perceptual tasks may be attributed not only to weak signal strength but also to an increase in internal noise. The arguments posed by investigators in this area are compelling in part because they offer a fuller picture of performance that is governed by both signal and noise strength. However, a difficulty with the noise measurement is that it is indirect. Noise levels must be inferred from the variability of the subject's performance, and the pattern of results among test conditions. Until an accepted empirical method for varying internal noise has been developed, the conclusions derived from noise studies will not carry the impact that they may deserve.

II. IMPACT OF PERCEPTUAL DEFICITS ON HIGHER ORDER PROCESSING

The quality of the percept that is constructed by the perceiver is related to the quantity and quality of the sensory information that has been captured. Several examples have been given above to illustrate how the manipulation of signal strength has been shown to affect the detection of stimuli as well as perceptual judgments. In this section, we will consider the effect of low-level sensory problems on a variety of higher order tasks, including object recognition, reading, and intelligence test tasks.

A. Effect of Acuity Deficits

The most striking and perhaps far-reaching research is on the impact of sensory deficits on intelligence test performance. Intelligence tests involve a broad range of tasks that tap a variety of information-processing skills and capacities. There is little evidence that the performance of young and middle-aged adults on intelligence tests is related to simple sensory deficits. However, evidence has been accumulating that the poor performance of elderly adults is related in part to their poor sensory acuity. A recent study indicates that the visual and auditory acuities of the elderly accounted for 49% of the variance in intelligence and 93% of the age-related variance. These striking findings strongly suggest that sensory capabilities are important mediators of intellectual performance in older adults.

There are several interpretations of the link between acuity and intelligence test performance. First, the subjects with poorer acuities may not adequately see or hear the material that is part of the tests and consequently cannot fully appreciate and respond to the test items. In this way, the poor acuities are mediating factors that affect the validity of the test instruments. The intelligence tests in this view would not be accurate measures of the intellectual competence of the subjects. The second point of view is that the acuity deficits are a reflection of the physiological and neurological changes occurring throughout the nervous system. That is, it is assumed that there is a common biological cause for deterioration in all aspects of the nervous system, which is reflected in general poor performance. The third account is the only one that attributes the poor intellectual performance at least indirectly to the acuity loss. It has been argued that the reduced sensory capabilities associated with advancing age cause a long-term reduction in the stimulating interactions that a person has in his or her environment. For example, if it becomes a little harder to read then one might read less and not be afforded the intellectual stimulation. Thus, the mild, long-term sensory deprivation of limited sensory acuity may lead to a dulling of intellectual functions. The studies to date cannot resolve whether one of these accounts or others are correct. However, the research does illustrate the importance of intact sensory abilities for capturing information necessary for efficient higher order processing.

B. Effect of Spatial Contrast-Sensitivity Deficits

As noted earlier, there is an age-related loss of spatial contrast sensitivity. It may be argued that poor spatial contrast sensitivity creates weak visual signals that are ineffectively processed by the higher order visual areas. Indeed, it has been argued that a contrast-sensing deficit could masquerade as a higher order disability, such as object recognition. Research has demonstrated that a portion of the problem that elderly adults have with face perception can be linked to their low contrast sensitivity. Furthermore, the detection and identification of signs and other objects is related directly to the contrast sensitivity of adults. Recently, the limitations experienced by elderly adults in reading small or large text has been linked to their relatively minor contrast-sensitivity deficits. Thus, with age the ability to see faces, road signs, text, and other common objects is diminished.

Work with younger adults who have spatial contrast-sensitivity deficits is instructive for demonstrating that a manipulation of contrast can lead to improved performance. For example, low vision patients, who typically suffer from a loss of moderate-to high-spatial frequency contrast sensitivity, significantly improve their reading speed and face recognition performance when they view material in which the contrast has been enhanced. Reading disabled children, who suffer a reduction in sensitivity to low spatial frequencies, also benefit from a modification of contrast. Thus, by increasing the contrast of a display not only will the detectability of the elements be increased but also the use of these elements in higher

order processes, such as reading and object recognition, will be improved.

The relatively greater loss of spatial contrast sensitivity by AD patients suggests that they may have problems with reading and recognition tasks independent of their memory-related deficits. Indeed, difficulty with reading and the recognition of objects is a common complaint of persons who have been diagnosed with AD. Although AD patients are able to read aloud accurately, their reading speed and comprehension are poor. Also, AD patients perform quite poorly when asked to identify drawings of common objects. Because of the AD patients' good acuity, it has been assumed that their poor performance is due to a linguistic and/or memory deficit rather than a visual perception problem. This position has been challenged by researchers who argue that the very poor spatial contrast sensitivity of the AD patients can be expected by itself to lead to poor performance on any task or endeavor involving the perception of visual stimuli. This position has been supported by two recent studies. In the first it was shown that both healthy young and elderly adults will do poorly on an object naming task when they are presented with stimuli that have been degraded to simulate the visual experience of AD patients. That is, the simple contrast degradation of the stimuli led the healthy adults to exhibit Alzheimer-like test behavior. In the second study, AD patients read briefly presented letters as quickly as healthy elderly adults, when the stimuli had a sufficiently high contrast. Compensating for the weak contrast sensitivity of the AD patients by presenting very strong stimuli eliminated their letter-reading speed deficit. Thus, the studies with AD patients clearly illustrate the powerful impact of a contrast-sensitivity deficit on higher order tasks and demonstrate that a manipulation of contrast can be used to improve performance.

To argue that the visual deficits of both healthy elderly adults and AD patients may influence their higher order information processing is consistent with recent theories of information processing. It is clear that manipulations of physical characteristics of the stimulus, such as its size or spatial frequency content or its duration, can have direct impacts on the processing speed and accuracy of young subjects whose visual systems are intact. The degradation of a stimulus may have both a main effect on performance by slowing sensory acquisition and encoding processes and also an interactive effect with higher order decision and processing stages. It is suggested here that if manipulations of the distal stimuli can influence information processing, then alterations of the proximal stimulus by a deficient visual system can create similar processing burdens.

C. Effect of Motion Perception Deficits

It is clear that the ability to move efficiently through the environment and to respond appropriately to moving objects depends on the ability to detect and discriminate motion. As noted above, motion perception like the other sensory-perceptual abilities changes with age. The importance of these changes for the performance of higher order tasks is illustrated by recent studies of vehicle motion. In a study that had young and old observers judge the speed of cars that sped past the stationary observers, older observers were less sensitive to differences in velocity and relative to the young subjects tended to overestimate the velocity of slow-moving vehicles. This finding would suggest that older subjects may judge that vehicles moving towards them, as at an intersection, will arrive rather quickly. In fact, elderly men are as accurate in their judgment of the time of vehicle arrival as young adults, but elderly women yielded significantly less accurate judgments. It has been suggested that the marked overestimation of speed by elderly women may account for the observations that older women drivers tend to wait before turning into traffic even when they have ample time to do so. These studies demonstrate that the perception of motion is a critical age-related skill in describing the driving performance of adults.

III. CONCLUSION

The chapter has reviewed evidence of the sensory-perceptual changes that are associated with aging. It has been further shown that these low-level effects are associated with the performance of older adults in higher order tasks, such as object and face recognition, reading, and intelligence test tasks. The point is made that the perceptual world that is constructed by elderly adults may be quite different from that of young adults.

Acknowledgment of a relationship between ele-mentary processing and perceptual-cognitive judgments is critical for two reasons. First, recognition of the impact of sensory-perceptual factors on general performance may bring about a different outlook on the slow performance of elderly adults. To argue that a person is slow or error prone because of limited light sensitivity has a different impact from saying that the performance is due to a centrally mediated slowing in the nervous system. The latter view suggests a deterioration of the nervous system that may not be reversed through behavioral interventions. The sensory-perceptual locus of behavioral slowing offers the hope that environmental interventions may be helpful for improving the daily lives of elderly adults. Second, and perhaps most important, the recognition of the role of sensory factors suggest specific methods of intervention that may be used to improve the performance of elderly adults. As has been noted above, simple increases in the luminance and contrast of visual stimuli can reduce or eliminate age-related task differences. Further work is needed to determine if such interventions may be effective in improving the effective performance of elderly adults on a broader range of higher order tasks.

ACKNOWLEDGMENTS

I thank Cindy Lustig for her assistance in library research.

The author was supported in part by National Institute on Aging (NIA) Grant AG11549 during the preparation of the article.

BIBLIOGRAPHY

Botwinick, J. (1978). *Aging and behavior: A comprehensive integration of research findings (2nd Ed.)*. New York: Springer Publishing Co.

Cristarella, M. C. (1977). Visual functions of the elderly. *The American Journal of Occupational Therapy, 31*, 432–440.

Gilmore, G. C., Wenk, H., Naylor, L., & Stuve, T. (1992). Motion perception and aging. *Psychology and Aging, 7*, 654–660.

Lee, A. J., & Pollack, R. H. (1978). The effects of age on perceptual problem-solving strategies. *Experimental Aging Research, 4*, 37–54.

Lindenberger, U., & Baltes, P. B. (1994). Sensory functioning and intelligence in old age: A strong connection. *Psychology and Aging, 9*, 339–355.

Sands, L. P., & Meredith, W. (1989). Effects of sensory and motor functioning on adult intellectual performance. *Journal of Gerontology: Psychological Sciences, 2,* P56–P58.

Schiff, W., Oldak, R., & Shah, V. (1992). Aging persons' estimates of vehicular motion. *Psychology and Aging, 7,* 518–525.

Walsh, D. A. (1975). Age differences in aging learning and memory. In D. S. Woodruff & J. E. Birren (Eds.), *Aging: Scientific perspectives and social issues.* New York: Van Nostrand.

Walsh, D. A., & Prasse, M. J. (1980). Iconic memory and attentional processes in the aged. In L. W. Poon, J. L. Fozard, L. S. Cermak, D. Arenberg, & L. W. Thompson (Eds.), *New directions in memory and aging.* Hillsdale, NJ.: Lawrence Erlbaum.

Walsh, D. A., Till, R. E., & Williams, M. V. (1978). Age differences in peripheral perceptual processing: Monoptic backward masking investigation. *Journal of Experimental Psychology: Human Perception and Performance, 4,* 232–243.

Welford, A. T. (1981). Signal, noise, performance, and age. *Human Factors, 23,* 97–109.

Personality

Jan-Erik Ruth

Kuntokallio, Center for Gerontological Training and Research, Finland

I. Introduction
II. Theoretical and Research Approaches to Personality
III. Findings from Research on Personality and Aging
IV. Conclusions

Neuroticism　The (basic) tendency to react with anxiety, hostility, or obsessive-compulsive behavior in interpersonal relationships or faced with demanding situations in life.

Psychogerontology　A scientific field of inquiry focused on psychological development and aging. Psychogerontology addresses questions of cognitive aging (intelligence, learning, memory) as well as questions of personality development and mental health.

Phenomenology　A method for describing the individual's primary experiences of events. Phenomenology often refers to the perceptual, evaluative, and meaning-giving processes within the individual.

Projective Test　A standardized psychological measurement whereby personality attributes are measured indirectly. Projective tests consist of ambiguous stimuli (persons and situations) onto which the individual projects internal motivations and dispositions.

Self-Concept　Self-awareness, or the way the individual views him- or herself (in relation to others). The self-concept consists of the motivations, attitudes, and behaviors that are relevant to self-definition.

Transactional Processes　Interactive processes between the individual and his or her environment, in which human consciousness (personality) is seen as an ongoing stream and the adapting acts of the individual are in focus.

PERSONALITY can be defined as the individual characteristics of a person in the way he or she reacts to events. The construct of personality pertains to the internal character as well as the external behavior that differentiates one person from another. Personality psychologists differ remarkably in which aspect of personality they stress. There are those who point to the inner awareness or reflectivity of an individual, called the *self*, as the core of personality. Others stress outer factors such as learned expectations or the repertoire of learned behaviors. And there are those who are interested in the structure of mind and the profile of personality traits, as well as those who advocate that personality can be observed only from the individual's life as a whole.

I. INTRODUCTION

Three interrelated themes characterize the field of personality and aging. One theme is the various theoretical and research approaches to the concept of personality. Second is the analysis of whether personality changes over the years, and if so, which aspects show stability and which aspects change. A third theme is the question of how aging individuals can cope with the daily hassles and the major life events that old age brings about. These themes are reflected throughout the sections that follow.

II. THEORETICAL AND RESEARCH APPROACHES TO PERSONALITY

The metaphor *personality* that psychologists have created is a nebulous construct encompassing a multitude of theoretical concepts, research issues, and methods. The three major traditions in personality research—the trait model, the developmental model, and the experiential-contextual model—were created long ago but are all still alive and well. These three models differ widely in their definitions of the concept of personality as well as in their ways of measuring it.

The three traditions also differ in the balance between theory and empiricism. The developmental tradition is characterized by more theorizing, whereas the trait tradition is more empirically oriented. In the experiential-contextual tradition some models of person–situation interaction have been formulated, and research data in support of these models are gradually emerging.

A. The Trait Model

The trait model has, for some time now, been one of the dominant personality research traditions. This model aims at uncovering the basic dimensions of descriptive adjectives of personality found in natural language. There is both a lexical and a questionnaire approach to traits, however. Personality traits are measured by tests and self-report instruments, with the dimensionality of the measures validated by factor analysis.

Personality is inferred in the trait model from the metrical representations of self-reports. It can be argued that the behavior of variables in the metric space is studied in this research tradition, rather than the behavior of persons in real life. The critics of this vigorous research tradition point to its mechanical and abstract way of measuring personality and they question the validity of the sampling of personality constructs used in the instruments. A central question here is how well the tests cover the behavior of the individual in everyday situations. The main issue, thus, is the ecological validity of the tests. Multitrait multimethod (MTMM) analyses linking together self-report measures, peer ratings, and behavioral measures have produced a rather delineated picture of the main personality constructs of the trait tradition and their validity, however.

B. The Developmental Model

According to the second dominant research tradition, the developmental model, there are either qualitative shifts, such as stages or phases found in the development of personality, or there is a more continuous development around certain themes throughout life. The development model, along with the trait model discussed above, has generated the majority of empirical research findings within the field of personality.

In the developmental model, the level of development is mapped by measuring instruments (some of which are trait-oriented) or by observation of behavior in social roles or around developmental tasks. In some developmental theories, stages or periods of life are postulated representing qualitative shifts in behavior (such as the development of generativity in middle age and integrity in old age, as in Erik Erikson's theory). In these models the stages follow each other in fixed succession, advancing from more immature to more mature levels. In other developmental theories, timetables are postulated that are closely linked to chronological age (such as the succession of stable phases and transitions in the life structures, as in Daniel Levinson's model). These theories are mostly based on Freudian reasoning, focusing on the development of the ego and the defense mechanisms the ego uses to protect itself from feelings of distress through life.

In the theories that pertain to a more continuous development, certain developmental themes considered typical for a life period (such as middle age) are investigated. Carl Jung, for instance, focuses on the midlife transition, where the balance of extraversion versus introversion shifts and where an individuation process leads to increased maturity in old age. For the general developmental model the interesting question is how changes vary in an orderly way, regardless of the direction of change. The general developmental model can depict decline, and decrement with compensation, as well as growth in personality-linked issues.

The *stage* theories, such as Erikson's, are criticized because they do not seriously take situational and cultural factors into consideration but rather presuppose universal developmental stages for a human being, seemingly irrespective of context. Although the *stage* and *phase* theories were conceived long ago they have not initiated much empirical research that would test their credibility. Daniel Levinson's model can be criticized for making general statements about development for the two genders, although his original research sample consisted only of men, and for a rigid chronological time structure that does not take into account sociohistorical change.

C. The Experiential-Contextual Model

Lately, the experiential-contextual model, which was initiated in the 1960s and constitutes the third tradition in personality research, has grown strong again. In this model the evolving lives of persons and the meaning people ascribe to life events are in focus. The trajectory of personality change is mapped over extended time intervals, and social and historical factors are considered as important as individual ones.

Within the existential-contextual model, the *constructionist* approach emphasizes the situations and contexts in which persons create their own selves and those of others. If stability or change are found in personality across the years, this research tradition looks for explanations in the sociocultural and historical context. Accordingly, another characteristic of this approach is to see old age as basically produced and shaped by social factors; there is thus a research interest in uncovering "the social construction of aging," for example in Glen Elder's studies on developmental conditions during the Great Depression.

In the *life story* approach, another direction within this model that is also based on a life span perspective, personal accounts are studied in order to get a picture of development and aging "from within" through the stories the self narrates at different points in time. In the life story approach, the phenomenology of the narrator is in focus, and the sociohistorical factors are seen through the interpretations of those factors given by the narrating person. The accounts of lives are collected and analyzed concerning life events, developmental tasks, life projects, turning points, life demands, traumata, life stress, and daily hassles (e.g., the studies by Susan Whitbourne on identity formation, and by Dan McAdams on the making of the self, both of which were based on life stories).

Retrospective and prospective data as well as accounts of the present situation are considered useful in this research tradition. The level of analysis can vary from the study of single cases to the study of groups, and from cohorts to subcultures and cultures of aging individuals.

The experiential-contextual model seems promising in its ability to combine individual and sociohistorical (internal and external) factors and to study their interrelations in time. In this tradition the management of the self in demanding life situations can be studied, as well as the possibilities of the self proactively creating and changing life circumstances. This method has not yet, however, produced enough data to allow evaluation of its scientific significance within the field of personality.

III. FINDINGS FROM RESEARCH ON PERSONALITY AND AGING

A. Results from Research in the Trait Tradition

I. Traits

Costa and McCrae have in several rather extensive studies addressed the question of whether personality "sets like plaster" at some point during the life span and then remains unchanged, or if change can be found with time. Their studies have been based on a five-factor model of *personality traits:* Neuroticism (N), Extraversion (E), Openness (O), Agreeableness (A), and Conscientiousness (C). In some of the studies, a revised, N, E, O Personality Inventory (NEO-PI-R, with full-length measures of the five factors) has been used. The five constructs in a rather systematic way organize hundreds of personality traits proposed by theorists using adjectives that emanate from natural language to describe personality features.

The N scale measures anxiety, hostility, depression, and other variables that refer to maladjustment and psychopathology. N is an important concept because it has been shown that neurotic elderly individuals do not cope as effectively with stressors like severe losses in old age, and that a close relationship exists between low scores for N and subjective well-being. E pertains to external activity, positive emotionality, gregariousness, and assertiveness. O includes intellectual curiosity, active fantasy, and differentiated feelings. A consists of tender-mindedness and compliance. C consists of orderliness, self-discipline, and need for achievement.

Both cross-sectional and longitudinal methods have been employed in the N, E, O, A, and C trait studies. The cross-sectional studies tend to show small declines in N, E, and O and small increases in A and C in older age groups. One of the studies was based on a substantial sample of 10,000 men and women aged 35–84. Similar results have been obtained with smaller samples in other studies. The problematic nature of cross-sectional designs makes the interpretation of these results difficult, however. It can be questioned whether we are seeing in these results the personality features of the different generations under comparison, or if we are really seeing systematic changes in personality with advancing age.

The longitudinal and cohort-sequential studies based on mean levels show another picture: no change or very modest change in personality traits across the years. A 6-year longitudinal study by Costa and McCrae did not show systematic changes in N, E, and O. In overviews of the research on general anxiety, a stability has been reported, but this pertains only to trait anxiety. For more contextual anxieties and fears it is clear that the aged show higher levels of fear, for example, fear of becoming a victim of crime or elder abuse. [See ABUSE AND NEGLECT OF ELDERS.]

The picture of no, or little, change in personality traits by age is further strengthened by stability estimates (retest correlations) of individual differences. The Costa and McCrae research group, as well as other research groups, have in several studies showed considerable stability effects in comparing the rank order of individuals in their personality traits over time. When the studied correlation coefficients are corrected for estimated error of measurement they reach as high as .90, which indicate substantial stability. In a study using the Social Introversion Scale of the Minnesota Multiphasic Personality Inventory (MMPI), a stability coefficient of .74 has been reported for a follow-up from middle adulthood (30 years) into late middle age.

Correlations across personality components have shown the greatest instability during the formative years, especially in late adolescence to early adulthood. Around age 30, personality presumably takes its final, fully developed form, staying roughly the same over the life span. Stability in personality traits is typical of older adult ages, according to many studies. If correlations among personality components are extended over very long time periods, (i.e., over 50 years), a decline in consistency is evident, however, indicating the possibility of some change. But the decline, when it occurs, is generally modest.

In longitudinal studies of persons aged 21–84, based on Cattell's Sixteen Personality Factor Questionnaire (16 PF), Warner Schaie has shown that excit-

ability of emotions is the only trait that increases over the years. Some of the traits in the 16 PF did show age differences in cross-sectional analyses, indicating that they were actually cohort effects.

According to Freudian reasoning, old age should be accompanied by increased rigidity of the ego. In some longitudinal studies by Schaie and his associates this assumption was not confirmed, however. Their studies showed stability both in behavioral and in attitudinal flexibility over the years.

The measuring instruments of personality concepts in the main longitudinal studies within the United States vary widely. This hampers the comparison between projects considerably. On the other hand, generalizability is much enhanced when a robustness in results and resemblances among factors measured in different studies can be found. When the constructs used in the studies are factor analyzed, they do produce factors with reasonable resemblance to Costa and McCrae's N, E, O, A, C model. These results give additional support to the principle of structural invariance in personality over the adult life span.

2. Motives

Other theorists within the differential psychological research approach have postulated conceptions other than trait as the fundamental unit of personality. According to the Murray tradition, *motive* is such an unit. Three basic motives—achievement, affiliation, and power—have been studied in depth, within a life span perspective. Projective tests (such as the Thematic Apperception Test—TAT) have been used for indirectly assessing motives (defined as dispositions to find a class of incentives attractive). Studies linking the N, E, O, A, and C traits of Costa and McCrae with motivational factors from other types of research have appeared, suggesting that the Murray motives can possibly be conceptualized as motivational traits.

Researchers with a motive approach have challenged the stability claim that has arisen from the N, E, O, A, C studies. Longitudinal studies using the Edwards Personality Preference Schedule (EPPS) have found increases in the achievement and dominance motives and decreases in the abasement and affiliation motives by age, possibly indicating maturational changes in adulthood. Another study has indicated that the need for achievement decreased for employed women who did not get promotion in midlife, and that the power motive was highest for men in midlife.

There are also other longitudinal data implying some personality change from adulthood to middle age. The indication is, therefore, that there are personality constructs that do show changes over time in adult life. It is a challenge to further research to identify these more change-prone aspects of personality.

3. Control Beliefs

Julian Rotter's *locus of control* idea has initiated some studies that map stability and change in control beliefs over the life span. This research tradition goes back to learning theories that postulate the existence of generalized expectancies concerning behavior possibilities, based on reinforcement. Thus the individual's feelings of outer control from the caregiving parents would be typical of the childhood years, whereas feelings of increasing inner control in young adulthood will grow out of newly gained independence. Decreased internality of control beliefs is postulated again in old age, when advancing frailty might lead to an increased need for assistance and care.

The research group led by Margy Gatz has generated most of the longitudinal data concerning this issue. In a cross-sequential study with a follow-up of 20 years there seems to be strong evidence for continuity of internality over the adult years. The mean levels of personal control actually became more internal in all the young, middle-aged, and old-age groups followed in this study, a finding that probably reflects changing contextual factors in the culture. At the same time the oldest women showed more outer control, most probably a cohort effect. In addition to the gender difference, the researchers point out the great individual differences found concerning this attribute.

According to some researchers, the inconsistency in some other longitudinal research projects on this issue can be explained by the unidimensional way of defining *control* (as inner or outer control). Multidimensional approaches might thus be needed. The European researcher Jochen Brandstädter has shown in a cross-sequential study of developmental goals that self-perceptions of autonomous control became more pronounced in middle and late adulthood. This control concerned the domains of health and physical well-being, assertiveness, self-assurance, intellectual efficacy, self-development, mature understanding, and wisdom. Recently researchers have started to stress the need for studying personality-linked concepts such as control, self-efficacy, or autonomy as transactional processes rather than as personality traits. Where these concepts are studied as processes, the relation between the aging individual and his or her environment will be the focus of the research.

4. Beliefs Concerning the Future

A positive future outlook on life has favorable influences on health-related factors, and the existence of hope has favorable effects on psychological well-being. *Future time perspective* has been defined as the outcome of cognitive and emotional interactions in the aging person. The European gerontologist Hans Thomae has shown that the existence of a positive future time perspective is related to lifestyle, open-mindedness, emotional responsiveness, active coping, and good adjustment. Those aging individuals who did not attain an inner locus of control, as well as those whose control was lost late in life because of severe illness, exhibit more negative outlooks for the future.

These trends have been confirmed in studies of elderly married women. Women who showed a negative attitude toward the future were socially isolated and devalued by their husband and children, and this detracted not only from their feeling of being needed, but from their satisfaction with life in general.

A pattern of beliefs in the possibility of changing one's life has also been investigated. The beliefs pertain to the possibility of improving conditions in old age. It has been shown that those with higher income, better subjective health status, and stronger feelings of being needed by others more often show these kind of beliefs. The stronger the self-perceptions of autonomous control over individual developmental goals are, the more optimistic is the individual's outlook on aging. With a decreasing sense of personal control of life circumstances in old age, symptoms of resignation and depression may emerge. [*See* DEPRESSION.]

B. Results from Research in the Developmental Research Tradition

1. General Developmental Conceptualizations

Research on the themes of middle age has produced optimistic as well as pessimistic descriptions. Middle age has been depicted both as a period of increasing maturity and individuation and as a crisis-prone period of life characterized by turbulence and transitions.

According to Jung, a young person will be more extraverted than an old person. After middle age there is a shift in the introversion–extraversion balance. An old person will show increased introversion, and his or her reflectivity on the life he or she has lived will help the individual to develop wisdom. Jung stressed also the process of individuation in midlife, in which the individual becomes increasingly aware of the masculine and feminine features that both men and women show in their personalities. Another aspect of the individuation process is the recognition of both good (moral) and bad (immoral) features of one's personality.

Bernice Neugarten stresses the increased capability of steering one's own life and mastering one's social environment instead of just adapting to it, as in earlier periods of life. The middle-aged cohort has been described as at the top of its capacities and powers. It has also been described as dominating other age cohorts. Studies show that middle-aged men, compared to younger and older men, have the most positive self-concept. Men seem to value career roles highly in this period. At the same time they evaluate their marriages as more satisfying than women do. Women in middle age have been described as possessing a larger and more flexible role repertoire than men. A defense mechanism of rejecting feelings of possible problems and misery seems to add to the feelings of life satisfaction among middle-aged men. The early middle-age period in particular has been seen as a period of active mastery of life themes.

According to Roger Gold, middle age is also a period of reevaluation of earlier assumptions and expectations concerning self and significant others. There are pushes for a reevaluation linked to an arrested career development, the empty-nest issue, and changes in roles. Also, insight on a limited time for life planning as well as insight on the restriction of one's own capacities push for change. Only through a series of transformations will growth toward an increased inner directedness be possible.

Middle age is also a period characterized by an increase in divorce rates, health problems, and psychiatric disorders. Another sign of being middle-aged is that friends and colleagues fall ill and die, perhaps activating thoughts of one's own mortality. The efforts to master these major life events often take the form of personal crises. According to studies, the feelings of loss, reevaluation, and depression are widespread at the peak of a crisis. But when the peak is over, these feelings are gradually replaced by feelings of accepting the realities of life and feelings of the necessity of reorientation.

Large individual differences exist concerning the smoothness versus abruptness of development in middle age. The middle-age transition may pass almost unnoticed by some, whereas individuals who resist change or cannot accept losses or occasional failures seem to be the most crisis prone, according to Levinson.

Earlier it was believed that old age was characterized by increased rigidity and dogmatism. Longitudinal studies show that this usually is not the case. An increased cautiousness (i.e., a lesser willingness to take risks) is still presumed for the aged, however. Studies have suggested that older individuals comply more to social norms and are less aggressive than younger age groups. Neugarten labels the change from active to passive mastery that is typical for the oldest of the old as *interiority*.

Increased interiority (or even magical mastery) is a male-specific aging phenomenon, however, as David Gutmann found in his comparative anthropological studies. For women, the developmental trend would be the opposite, from passive mastery to an even aggressive mastery. This developmental shift has been seen as a liberation from sex role stereotypes in late old age. [See GENDER ROLES.]

2. Levinson's Model of Developmental Periods

Levinson's model describes the developmental periods of early adulthood to late adulthood (the ages 17–65). The central concept in this model is *life structure*. The life structure consists of three levels: the sociocultural level (social contexts of class, ethnicity, religion, and political system); the personal level (the self and realization or inhibition of self themes); and the behavioral level (individuals' participation in the world, in significant roles—occupational, familial, and societal). Levinson's own study of 40 men as well as a few other studies seem to affirm his theoretical formulations.

The life structure, according to Levinson, evolves through a relative orderly sequence during the adult years and this sequence is bound to chronological age (this assumption has been much debated). The developmental task of a life period is crucial for the evolution of the period. (In what follows only the midlife transition will be presented. The other period with significance for aging is the late adult transition, but this period has not been described in detail in Levinson's presentations.)

The developmental tasks of the midlife transition (ages 40–45) are connected with a review and termination of early adulthood, with the initiation of middle adulthood, and with dealing with four polarities in life (mentioned below). There is a need for reevaluation of the relation to the spouse, to the job and one's superiors, to one's mentor, and to one's own values and strivings. Levinson reports that 80% of the men in his study experienced a repeated questioning of and a struggle with these life themes. The need for change will be felt in some areas, and experimentation with new solutions and modification of the life structure will thus start.

The four polarities whose resolution are considered the principal tasks of midlife individuation are young–old, destruction–creation, masculine–feminine, and attachment–separateness. The most important one is the young–old polarity, which is repeatedly raised throughout life. The middle-aged period of life is experienced as "in-between," and the developmental task is to restructure the polarities. *Old* represents maturity, good judgement, self-knowledge, and getting a perspective on life; *young* is a symbol for play, initiation, openness, energy, and potential.

In Levinson's theory of developmental periods the concept of life structure is centered on the boundary between self and world. The theory gives equal weight to the self and the world as aspects of life lived. Erikson's theory, which is presented below, is likewise concerned with how the self is engaged with the world, but the focus in this theory is on developmental change within the person.

3. Erikson's Epigenetic Stage Theory

The *stage theory* of Erikson is the only developmental theory that covers the complete life cycle, but only the last two stages (out of a total of eight) will be considered here. The first versions of the theory were created as early as 1950 but it has later been elaborated on many times. The most recent presentation is from 1986 and specifically concerns old age.

Three organizational principles constitute the basis for development and change: the biological, psychological, and sociocultural processes. The concept of *epigenesis* is used for linking the somatic development to the psychological (psychosexual) and social. The concept of *ritualization* signifies predicted repetitious behavior typical of a certain stage of life. The development of new life stages arises out of the demands of the biological, psychological, and social areas during critical time periods in life.

The critical time periods in life that induce development of a person's identity are conceived as crises in Erikson's theory. The crises can be solved by finding a balance between two opposite developmental trends. A sign of a successful completion of a developmental crisis is the occurrence of new, age-typical rationalizations.

In middle age the crises are focused on the polarity of generativity versus self-absorption, and the adaptive strength that can grow out of this crisis is care. Generativity presupposes reproduction, production, and creativity. An adult person cares for children, work-related products, and ideas. By this behavior the adult takes responsibility for the major concerns in his or her life at that time; that is, the adult takes responsibility for self and for younger generations. The age-typical patterns of behavior, the rationalizations, include the parental and the educational roles, as well as productive and nurturant behavior. [See CREATIVITY.]

In old age the dominant crisis evolves around the opposites *integrity versus despair*, and the final identity strength that may develop is called wisdom. The last crises of the life cycle accompany the visceral and muscular decrement in the somatic area, the diffusion of the border between past and present and other memory changes in the psychological area, and lost responsibilities in the social area. The major ritualization that grows out of a positive solution of the crisis is a philosophical stance toward one's own life, toward humankind, and toward death.

Wisdom is seen in the development of closeness to persons of earlier times and other cultures, representing other ways of life. But the feeling of integrity is also tied to one's own self with its positive and negative features, and to the life lived with its bright and dark periods. When an acceptance of the self and the life lived is possible, the individual is also ready, without fear, to accept death as the final event of life. The negative developmental path of this stage leads into despair. In this case the aging individual is unable to accept and finalize his or her life, but rather feels disgust and repulsion toward other human beings, toward life, toward aging, and toward his or her own self.

The generativity typical of the preceding stage may take on an enlarged function in old age and may develop into engagement, if the solution of the crisis is positive. The increasing life expectancy of modern times presupposes new rationalizations based on vital involvement in old age, something not seen before.

Empirical studies of those parts of the theory pertaining to middle age and old age are rather scarce. A test (Erikson Psychosocial Inventory Scale—EPSI) has been developed, however, to measure resilience to the life crises depicted in the theory. Research based on this test shows that those who have succeeded in solving earlier crises also tend to solve later crises in a positive way. Qualitative studies, by McAdams and others, give delineated accounts of some of the generativity and integrity themes told by the middle-aged and aging self.

Erikson's theory shows rather visible normative underpinnings, based as it is on American norms of development from the period of the 1950s through the 1980s. Thus it remains to be seen how well the stages cover the development of both men and women today as well as persons from different cultures.

4. Synthesized Developmental Models

Recently two humanistic, existential models of positive psychological functioning in old age have been proposed: Carol Ryff's successful aging and well-being model and Lars Tornstam's model on gero-transcendence. Both models draw heavily on earlier theorizing in the field (by Gordon Allport, Charlotte Buhler, Carl Jung, Erik Erikson, Bernice Neugarten, Carl Rogers, Abraham Maslow, and many more). The models are creative reconstructions, but seem promising in their own right.

a. Successful Aging and Well-Being Ryff has criticized research on successful aging for only collecting research data without drawing up models or theories for explaining them. Many researchers routinely use ready-made instruments in research without questioning how well they cover the central constructs in well-being. Some of these measuring instruments are biased against finding evidence of change by including only basic tendencies of personality and by discarding

from the scales items sensitive to change. The earlier research on well-being is said to be too focused on illness rather than "wellness" in old age, and on finding problems rather than resources.

In an effort to integrate mental health, clinical, and life span developmental theories, Ryff has proposed a model for multiple positive psychological functioning based on the following dimensions:

- Self-Acceptance. A high scoring individual on self-acceptance shows a positive attitude toward the self, acknowledges and accepts multiple aspects of self (including both good and bad aspects), and evaluates his or her past life positively.
- Positive Relations with Others. The person has trusting, satisfying, and warm relations with others and cares for them; shows feelings of empathy, affection, and intimacy; and gives and takes in human relationships.
- Autonomy. The person shows self-determination and independence and is capable of resisting social pressure in ways of thinking and acting. The person regulates behavior from within and evaluates self by personal standards.
- Environmental Mastery. The person is competent in managing the environment and has an inner sense of mastery. The person can control a complex array of external activities, makes use of surrounding opportunities, and can choose or create contexts corresponding to personal needs and values.
- Purpose in Life. The person has goals in life and a sense of directedness; experiences meaning in past and present life; holds beliefs that give purpose; and has aims and objectives for living.
- Personal Growth. The person has a sense of continuous development with a growing and expanding self and increased self-knowledge over time; is open to new experiences; and has a feeling of realizing his or her own potential.

In the presentation above only the positive criteria for well-being were presented. In the self-report scale that Ryff has constructed, characteristics of low scorers on these dimensions can also be found. The model does give a positive outlook on aging, but seems to describe late middle age or early old age better than late old age.

b. Gero-Transcendence A new theory suitable for describing the last part of the life span is Tornstam's theory of gero-transcendence. The theory is a reformulation of the disengagement idea, advocating the quest for reaching a metaperspective on life for the oldest of the old. The theory is still tentative, and research to confirm the claims made by the theory has only recently started.

The shift in metaperspective toward gero-transcendence includes the following:

- An increasing feeling of cosmic union with the spirit of the universe.
- A redefinition of the perception of time, space, and objects.
- A redefinition of the perception of life and death and a decrease in the fear of death.
- An increased feeling of affinity with past and coming generations.
- A decrease in interest in superfluous social interaction
- A decrease in interest in material things.
- A decrease in self-centeredness.
- An increase in the time spent in meditation.

Some evidence for these ideas can be found in the work of Robert Peck who studied the crises faced by aging businessmen. The crises were centered around ego differentiation versus job preoccupation, body transcendence versus body preoccupation, and ego transcendence versus ego preoccupation. In an initial study Tornstam found some evidence for the differentiation between gero-transcendence and depression and the differentiation between gero-transcendence and unsuccessful coping. The question of whether gero-transcendence presupposes a religious revival is left unanswered, however, and the theory can be criticized for its metaphysical conceptualizations.

C. Results from Research in the Experiential-Contextual Tradition

I. Personality Types, Developmental Trajectories, and Ways of Life

In a classic study of adjustment of elderly men to retirement, conducted in the early 1960s by Susanne Reichard, Florine Livson, and Paul Petersen, extensive measurements and self-reports were used in obtaining the data. The researchers found five different personality types that differed in their adjustment. The *mature* men accepted their own selves and had positive attitudes toward aging. The *rocking chair* type quietly adapted to aging, enjoying their new freedom from responsibilities. The *armored* men, however, were not ready for retirement yet; they used overactivity as a defense. The *angry* men were clearly not well adjusted to retirement; they showed bitterness and blamed others for their predicament. The *self-haters* turned their aggressiveness inward, and were disappointed and depressed.

In another by now classic study Neugarten and her collaborators, using a multidimensional approach that included an index of life satisfaction, found four types. The *integrated* and the *armored* showed high life satisfaction, the *unintegrated* showed low life satisfaction, and part of the *passive-dependent* were satisfied and part dissatisfied with their life in old age.

The two studies described above use many of the traditional personality tests of the trait tradition, but also use some more open measures, such as interviews that are typical of the experiential-contextual tradition. The researchers' efforts to describe personality as a strategy of adaptation or an integrated whole (or type) are features of the experiential-contextual tradition.

In present-day research it has been suggested that a way of measuring core identity changes would be to focus on the ideas and perceptions the individual has about his or her life span development. According to Whitbourne, it is fruitful to focus on two components, the scenario and the life story. The scenario consists of a person's expectations on how his or her life will unfold. The life story will reveal the course of identity formation, and individual values and motives, as well as normative developmental expectations in society for the cohort to which an individual belongs.

Elder has shown that only by describing developmental paths is it possible to reach an ecologically relevant perspective on individual development. The paths, or trajectories, should be examined in the context of time, locality, and social group. Elder, who studied developmental trajectories that took place during the Great Depression, points out that many of the central choices in life, such as career, can be understood only when analyzed along with the individual's personality and social background and the time during which the choices were made.

Ravenna Helson studied lives through time by focusing on normative change (change related to personality patterns and to role sequences). Helson studied a cohort of women attending college in the late 1950s. She found that "the feminine social clock" (the developmental schedule for this cohort of women) produced self-controlled, tolerant, and responsible women, most of whom were mothers as young adults. But approaching middle age, when those women who followed the "masculine occupational clock" has gained in independence and dominance, those who followed the feminine social clock had become increasingly overcontrolled. Thus the effect of the homemaker role was to make these women subordinate their own needs to the needs of other. These data give a more delineated pattern of when and why change occurs and the form it takes in different periods of the life span.

In a recent Finnish study Jan-Erik Ruth and Peter Öberg studied individuals' ways of life and adaptation to old age by using life stories and thematic interviews. Six ways of life were found: *the bitter life, life as a trapping pit, life as a hurdle race, the devoted, silenced life, life as a job career,* and *the sweet life.* In these ways of life, earlier life events such as sociohistorical background, marriage, and other human relationships were handled in quite different ways. The sense of locus of control as well as the self-image varied in all of the ways of life. The life lived, clearly, had a substantial impact on the emotional tone of old age.

In the two most negative ways of life, the bitter life and life as a trapping pit, severe losses (such as health problems) and problems in human relationships and career had a negative impact on the respondents' lives and resulted in a dysfunctional old age. There were two gender-specific ways of life: the devoted, silenced life that consisted of caretaking and adherence to the needs or others (typical of daughters at home), and life as a job career where the life story was like a curriculum vitae, with little room for family values (typical of well-educated men). These two ways of life had led up to a satisfactory life or a good life in old age. In the sweet life resources like intimate relations with parents, spouse, and children as well as a good education and economy contributed to a healthy lifestyle that resulted in a happy old age.

2. Coping

The coping studies can be classified according to different conceptual frameworks. In some studies personality measures from the trait tradition are used and in some a developmental vantage point is taken. Most coping studies, however, belong clearly in a phenomenological framework, where the perception of stress and the experience of mastering a stressful situation are central. Thus, the results are considered as emanating from an experiential-contextual tradition.

In the work by Lazarus, one of the founders of research on coping, coping consists of the constantly changing cognitive and behavioral efforts to manage specific external or internal demands that the person appraises as taxing or that exceed the resources of the person. The cognitive processes in coping pertain to primary and secondary appraisal. *Primary appraisal* is the person's assessment of a life situation as stressful or benign and *secondary appraisal* is the person's perceived ways of mastering the situation.

The ways of coping have been divided into problem-focused or emotion-focused (palliative); active-passive coping; and approach-avoidance coping. Research data show that the more active coping strategies lead to a successful mastering of the threat in most situations, resulting in increased life satisfaction. The more passive coping strategies such as minimization of the threat, resignation, or avoidance are considered less successful.

In earlier gerontological studies, old age was depicted as rather stressful, and as a period of multiple losses. The loss of roles, income, health, and even friends and spouse were said to lead to increased distress and to a state of learned helplessness because of an increased inability to master these cumulative losses.

The results from several recent longitudinal studies of the effect of major life events in old age has altered this picture, however. In an American follow-up study of persons aged 40–70, the effects of the empty nest, retirement, retirement of the spouse, medical problems, and widowhood were examined. None of these transition events from middle age to old age was experienced as overriding the individual's capacity to cope. According to recent data, old age is generally not an unhappy period of life, or a period of low morale. [See RETIREMENT; WIDOWHOOD AND WIDOWERHOOD.]

Persons aged 60–70 were followed over a 10-year period in the Bonn Longitudinal Study. It was found that the ways of adaptation differed for persons and situations, but a pattern of constancy, rather than decrement, nevertheless constituted the major finding of the study. In a study in Jerusalem, which spanned about 20 years, this trend was confirmed. No changes in coping patterns (from active to passive) were found across the years. According to this study, coping styles were related to personality dispositions, and a variety of styles were found, from active integrative coping and failing overcoping to dependent passive coping and self-negated undercoping.

The most taxing life events in old ages are, according to research findings the death of a close person, one's own illness, the illness of a close person, and giving up activities because of medical problems. But research data also show that only about half of these events occur for the first time in old age. Medical problems, for instance, usually arise in middle age. Small problems and daily hassles may constitute another source of distress in old age, however. Research shows that the coping mechanisms used by the aged are more event specific and more differentiated than was assumed earlier. Seeking social support is, for example, often used in coping with death of a close person, but seldom in coping with involuntary relocation and giving up activities.

All adults, however, including the aged, have many resources, external and internal, to draw upon in distressing situations. *External resources* such as high education and high socioeconomic status usually result in coping based on logical choice and flexibility rather than on irrational and rigid solutions. Older individuals with support from the social network, such as family support, are also less likely to use the avoidance coping that is associated with lower levels of well-being. [*See* SOCIAL NETWORKS, SUPPORT, AND INTEGRATION.]

Some studies have suggested that accepting the situation as such, seeking emotional support based on intimacy and friendship ties, and seeking help from religion are used more by women than by men. Men use more information seeking and rely more on instrumental support and camaraderie. These differences between the genders may be cohort specific, and dependent on time-bound and culturally determined behavior expectations.

Internal resources useful in coping are tied to experience or maturation, personality dispositions, and motivation. It has been shown that younger copers rely on denial and projection as a defense mechanism in taxing situations, whereas older copers are more

likely to use sublimation, suppression, and humor. An easy-going disposition and optimism are favorable personality dispositions in coping, whereas neuroticism negatively affects perceptions of stress and coping possibilities. Self-efficacious individuals and those with a disposition of commitment, control, and challenge (called *hardiness*) are more active and successful copers.

The above-mentioned active, and even competitive, ways of coping may be best suited for middle-aged persons and the newly retired, however. Old persons may be better served by accommodating to negative life events, like severe illness, and reassessing the events in a more positive way, or by lowering their own aspiration level. For the frail elderly, the behaviorally oriented coping mechanism may be replaced by more psychological ones, such as relying more on acceptance coping in situations in which they genuinely have little control.

3. Management of the Self

Lately a change can been seen in gerontological research in approaches toward the construct of the *self*. A more active, creative, and competent self emanates from recent findings. In studies of coping, presented above, there is an increased consideration of resources available for the aging individual. The self is thus no longer seen only as a passive, reactive agent battling life stress induced from outside. In the process-oriented, narrative research tradition there is a possibility of change, in reconsideration and revision of previous history and future plans.

The self-concept is made up of the attitudes, goals, and behavior relevant to self-definition and the meaning of life. This is an enlargement of the former perspective of studying only the actual self, ideal self, and self-esteem, as proposed by Rogers. Now a variety of actual and possible future selves are the focus of research: the good, the bad, the hoped for, the not-me, the ought-to selves. [*See* IDENTITY, PHYSICAL; SELF-ESTEEM.]

Persons of all ages have a tendency to perceive themselves as loving, competent, and good. If they cannot perform a role well, they have a tendency to devalue its importance and put emphasis on other roles that add to their feelings of competency and self-esteem. Another principle of self-concept management is downward social comparison (i.e., a comparison of the self with those even worse off).

Other possibilities are attributing failures to external, unyielding causes, and deemphasizing the importance of unattainable goals and emphasizing more attainable ones. Research data show that in old age the discrepancy between the actual self and the ideal self decreases. Old individuals also stress the need to accept change and lower their expectations in life in order to achieve continued well-being.

Earlier studies show that elderly women report more health problems and report feeling more lonely than men. Many old men are still living in intact marriages, but even those men who live alone do not report feeling as lonely. Recent data indicate, on the other hand, that a sense of aloneness resulting from multiple bereavements might be compensated for by a feeling of special status as long-term survivors, for both women and men. Data including many age groups also show that deep feelings of loneliness may occur in many phases of the life span (such as in the teens), rather than only in old age.

The resilience of the self in old age is based on interpretive processes such as reappraisals and social comparisons, but when the self encounters challenges of frailty, a difficulty in identifying possible future selves may occur. It is also more difficult to use selective interaction and feedback from others to formulate new selves. The social interaction is then used for reconfirming the old self and for maintaining hope. Institutionalized elderly often strive to keep their life story intact, and defend against including problems connected to institutionalization in it.

4. Thomae's Cognitive Theory of Adjustment to Aging

Gerontology is data rich but theory poor, according to James Birren. In recognition of that criticism this review ends with some recent theoretical formulations, the first of which is created by Thomae.

Thomae's *cognitive theory* of aging, which was formulated in 1970, falls under the experiential-contextual framework. In the Bonn Longitudinal Study of Aging (BOLSA) many aspects of the theory have been empirically verified over the years.

In this theory, fixed personality traits are of no interest, but personality is viewed as a process, with the cognitive representations of life situations in focus. According to Thomae both cognitive maintenance and cognitive restructuring are possible in the individual's adjustment to different situations in life.

Central concepts in this theory are the perceived situation as well as the perceived self. The perception of a life situation, rather than its objective characteristics, is related to behavioral change. The situation, the resources of the individual, and the possibilities for change are perceived according to the needs of the individual at the moment.

Three postulates are basic to this theory:

- Perception of change rather than objective change is related to behavioral change. This also concerns perception of present, past, and future life and its impact on behavior.
- Changes and situations are perceived and stored in the memory based on the dominant concerns of the individual. This acknowledges both emotional and motivational factors in the cognitive representations.
- Adjustment is dependent on achieving a balance between the cognitive and motivational structures or systems of the individual. This postulate focuses on the cognition–motivation interaction in adjustment to problems in old age.

The interrelation between the aging person and his or her environment has been stressed in the research based on this theory. Complex competence models including both situation-specific and person-specific areas of social competence have been advanced. In a concept such as social competence both the individual's capacity to meet social (and biological) demands and society's capacity to meet an aging individual's needs have to be considered concomitantly.

Situation–individual interaction patterns have been found in studies on stress and coping in old age, where the specific demands of the situation are met with a specific way of adaptation. The distressing situation can be dealt with cognitively, for example, by accepting what has happened, attaining a distance, or focusing on the bright side of the situation. But adaptation to the situation can also be behavioral, such as adapting to the needs of others or actively establishing new social contact that can provide help. In Thomae's BOLSA studies, the individual has been depicted as an active decision maker, not as just passively adjusting to life stress.

5. Selectivity Theories

Three models based on the *selectivity principle* have recently been created within psychogerontology:

Laura Carstensen's socioemotional selectivity theory, the selective optimization with compensation model of Paul and Margret Baltes, and Powell Lawton's press-competence model. The conceptualizations differ considerably in their scope, however, and are presented below by moving from the most limited to the most general case.

a. Socioemotional Selectivity Theory In Carstensen's socioemotional selectivity theory the decline with age in initiating new social contacts is explained. It is argued that less social interaction in old age is deliberately chosen by the individual and is not a sign of social disengagement. According to this theory, social interaction has three basic features: information acquisition; development and the maintenance of identity; and regulation of emotion.

It is argued that in the earlier phases of life increasing social contacts will give access to needed information about life and provide a multitude of developmental models and opportunities. As people age, the need for different kinds of information is reduced and becomes increasingly specialized. Other sources than social contacts (e.g., books and data files) can provide information.

During the life course individuals use a considerable time negotiating their identities with significant others. When the self-conceptions are getting more fixed later in life, only close social partners of long duration can have this self-confirmatory function. Many social partners will not share enough history to verify identity. Close family members and long-time friends, however, provide this function. Thus these social contacts are selectively chosen and preferred over the overcrowding of social partners in milieus like retirement homes.

The cultivation of a social environment to maximize potential for the experience of positive emotions and minimize negative ones is a deliberate way of regulating affect. In old age, contrary to earlier expectations, no emotional flattening occurs. According to recent research findings old age seems to bring an improved understanding of emotional contexts and meanings.

b. The Selective Optimization with Compensation Model Paul and Margaret Baltes's principles for selective optimization with compensation constitutes a general model for successful aging. The model has

grown out of the ideas of plasticity and self-resiliency and out of recognition of increasing heterogeneity among individuals in old age.

Persons may be engaged in a process of selective optimization with compensation throughout life, but this process takes on a specific significance in old age, because of lessened biological, mental, and social reserves. By selectively specializing in those areas the individual values highly, the limitations brought on by age can be overcome. This theory resembles Carstensen's socioemotional selection theory, but depicts the psychological adaptation process in aging more generally.

The model is based on three principles:

- The selection principle is seen in a restriction of the individual's world to fewer domains of high priority. The selection process presupposes an adjustment of an aging individual's expectation of satisfaction and control.
- The optimization principle makes it possible for aging individuals to enrich and augment their general reserves and maximize their effectiveness within their chosen life course.
- The compensation principle becomes operative when specific behavioral capacities are reduced or lost and the individual is using a great deal of time or effort to maintain a high level of performance.

A good example of these three principles is provided by Baltes and Baltes who describe how the aging pianist Artur Rubinstein conquered the weakness in his piano playing in the following way: First, he reduced his repertoire by selective choice of those piano pieces he knew best. Second, he optimized his performance by practicing these pieces more often than when he was younger. Third, he compensated for his increasing slowness by retarding his playing prior to fast passages, which gave an impression of movement in the appropriate passages.

c. The Press-Competence Model The two previous models based on the principle of selection resemble a third, even more general model: the press-competence model created by Lawton. This model depicts the interaction of persons and environments in producing adaptive or maladaptive aging. The older person is said to construct appropriate environments by selection. An extraverted individual functions best in a stimulus-rich and even stressful environment, whereas in introverted individual functions best in a stimulus-poor and less stressful environment.

Motivation differs by temperament, and neural activation may push an individual toward the external environment (extraversion) or toward internal processes (introversion). In the ideal case, environments match individual competencies. Through the choice or construction of a more suitable environment, the restrictions of old age can, at least partly, be overcome and an optimal fit between person and environment can be achieved.

IV. CONCLUSIONS

This review points to the importance of how personality constructs are conceived and measured in psychogerontology. If personality is defined as basic tendencies or traits, as in the N, E, O, C, A five-factor model of personality, the results in longitudinal studies will show stability or only minor change over the years. In the trait tradition, the self is not considered as an active and purposeful agent in a person's life but as an epiphenomenon that passively mirrors the basic tendencies (traits) and the dynamic processes between them and adaptation to life situations.

According to the developmental tradition, personality is defined as motives, commitments, and roles, which represent more transient units than traits; hence, there is possibility for change across the years. In the developmental tradition the research focus is on the development of the self and its defense mechanisms. The developmental stages or periods depicted in some developmental theories presuppose change in a regular or time-bound order for a positive solution of developmental crises met by the individual throughout life.

In the experiential-contextual tradition adapting is conceived as subjective biography, or as mastering based on perception, evaluation, and meaning-giving in the situations encountered by the proactive self; change in personality will not only be possible, but probable throughout the life span. The models and theories within this tradition conceive personality as transactional processes characterized by continuous calibrations in the person–situation interaction.

BIBLIOGRAPHY

Atchley, R. C. (1991). The influence of aging or frailty on perceptions and expressions of the self: Theoretical and methodological issues. In J. E. Birren and I. Lubben (Eds.), *The concept and measurement of quality of life in the frail elderly* (pp. 207–225). San Diego: Academic Press.

Baltes, P. B., & Baltes, M. M. (Eds.). (1990). *Successful aging: Perspectives from the behavioral sciences.* New York: Cambridge University Press.

Birren, J. E., Kenyon, G., Ruth, J.-E., Schroots, J. J. F., & Svensson, T. (Eds.). (1996). *Biography and aging: Explorations in adult development.* New York: Springer.

Costa, P. T., & McCrae, R. R. (1994). Set like plaster? Evidence for the stability of adult personality. In T. Heatherton and J. Weinberger. (Eds.), *Can personality change?* Washington, DC: American Psychological Association.

Funder, D. C., & Parke, R. D., Tomlinson-Keasey, C., & Widaman, K. (1993). Studying lives through time. Washington, DC: American Psychological Association.

Kogan, N. (1990). Personality and aging. In J. E. Birren and K. W. Schaie (Eds.), *Handbook of the psychology of aging* (3rd ed., pp. 300–346.) New York: Van Nostrand Reinhold Co.

Ruth, J.-E., & Coleman, P. (1996). Personality and aging: Coping and the management of the self in later life. In J. E. Birren & K. W. Schaie (Eds.), *Handbook of the psychology of aging* (4th ed., ch. 17.) San Diego: Academic Press.

Ruth, J.-E., & Coleman, P. (in press). *Personality and aging.* Blackwell Publishers. Oxford, England.

Schaie, K. W., & Willis, S. (1995). Personality development: Continuity and change. In K. W. Schaie & S. Willis (Eds.), *Adult Development and Aging,* (4th ed.) New York: Harper Collins.

Thomae, H. (1992). Emotion and personality. In J. E. Birren, B. Sloane, & G. Cohen (Eds.), *Handbook of mental health and aging* (2nd ed., pp. 355–375) San Diego: Academic Press.

Pharmacology

William Edwin Fann

Baylor College of Medicine

I. Introduction
II. Pharmacokinetics
III. Pharmacodynamics
IV. Drug Interactions and Side Effects

Enzyme A biochemical which catalyzes reactions between other biochemicals without itself being consumed.

Ester Linkage The chemical bond formed in the reaction between organic bases and acids uniting them into organic salts called esters.

Glucuronic Acid A naturally occurring organic acid used in bodily processes to denature drugs and render them excretable through the kidneys.

Hydrolysis An enzymatic inactivation of an esteric drug. Hydrolysis breaks the ester linkage and returns the compound to its acidic and basic constituents.

PHARMACOLOGY is a discipline concerned with the study of therapeutic medications, their effects on the body and, conversely, the effects of the body on the medication itself. As a science, it provides the theoretical substrate for the rational prescription of therapeutic agents and is an important element of the physician's training and knowledge base. A cognate discipline, toxicology, the study of the toxic effects of a multiplicity of chemicals, including therapeutic compounds, is sometimes included in Pharmacology.

I. INTRODUCTION

Pharmacology's goals are to pursue an understanding of the mechanisms by which drugs exert their therapeutic effects and adverse consequences, and to provide theories for development of safer and more effective agents. The pioneer medicinal chemist, Dr. Paul Ehrlich, called the ideal drug "the silver bullet": it would act rapidly, act only on the targeted disease, organ, or system for which it is administered, and be completely curative. Dr. Ehrlich's aphorism remains the unwritten standard for pharmacologists who work today as his successors. Sadly, despite many astounding advances in the discovery and development of therapeutic chemicals, there is no medicinal agent that approaches this ideal. Medications are usually given to achieve one effect on a target disease, but all cause additional effects beyond the one for which they are prescribed. These effects are unwanted, sometimes unanticipated, and can be disabling and even fatal. Despite a host of undesirable nontherapeutic effects, for the majority of patients to whom they are prescribed, drugs continue to help, and even cure. But they remain problematic for many, especially elderly patients, and the physicians who prescribe for them.

For a drug to be effective, it must appear at its intended site of action in adequate amounts. The degree and rapidity with which the body is able to absorb, transport, metabolize, and excrete an administered medication may determine that medication's efficacy, therapeutic effects, unwanted side effects, and ultimately the success or failure of the treatment. The ability of the body to perform these functions is, of course, determined by the functional state of the organ systems subserving them, organ systems which may be altered by age and/or disease. The body's ability to handle a drug may be adversely affected by both age and illness, but the relative strength of these two variables is difficult to specify. To help overcome this quandary, an expanding number of studies conducted in groups of healthy older volunteers are contributing important data by which to formulate a general pharmacology of the older patient. Moreover, premarketing evaluation of therapeutic compounds, traditionally carried out in relatively small populations of selected younger adults, increasingly includes studies performed on geriatric populations. While the elderly are by no means a homogeneous group, such studies provide the manufacturer, regulatory agencies, and ultimately the practitioner with data reflecting the distinctive requirements of the older patient. With data from tests of such parameters as effective dose, absorption, metabolism, distribution, excretion, onset of action, and side effect profile, predictions can be made of the drug's actions as affected by the altered physiology and special circumstances found in many elderly patients. Health-care professionals have long known, through observation and anecdote, that because of age-related changes in organ physiology and multiple-system decompensation, the elderly are likely to show increased sensitivity to medications, and are at risk for adverse reactions. The growing body of theoretical and experimental pharmacology from this special population largely substantiates these empirical notions and provides a database to better inform and guide the health-care professionals who care for the elderly patient.

The increasing size and special pharmacological requirements of the geriatric subpopulation energizes the thrust for developing a pharmacology for this special group. Not only is the group increasing in absolute size but the elderly also characteristically visit physicians, are admitted to hospitals, and are prescribed medications at a rate greater than other subpopulation groups. They are more likely to be administered several medications at once (polypharmacy) and for longer periods of time. All of these factors collectively contribute to one of the more vexing pharmacological problems in the elderly, that of noncompliance. Upwards of one half of elderly outpatients reportedly do not take their medications as prescribed, with underutilization being the predominant deviation. Causes for noncompliance include forgetfulness, misunderstanding of verbal directions, inability to purchase the medication, trouble with side effects, difficulty in swallowing larger capsules and tablets, and for the frail and arthritic, inability to open some medication containers. For many elderly patients, the sheer numbers of concommitant prescription medications is the problem; it is not unusual to observe an elderly patient arriving at an appointment carrying his or her medications in paper bags. Many elderly are under the concommitant care of more than one physician and purchase medications from more than one pharmacy; they often accumulate as many as 10–15 simultaneous medicaments for themselves. The majority of drugs for elderly outpatients are to be taken orally and each on a two to four times per day schedule. Such numbers make the patient (or caregiver) responsible for administration of twenty to thirty, or more, dosages each day. Under these circumstances, perfect compliance cannot reasonably be expected. Of course, not every alteration in regimens of medication self-administration are necessarily detrimental or contraindicated: in some instances changes are made because of side effects and toxicity, wherein lowering the dose is the sensible course to follow. Conversely, the dose of a medication may be increased above the prescribed level when the patient correctly perceives an absent or reduced therapeusis. The patient's adherence to a medication regimen is crucial to the prescribing physician's ability to correctly assess the effect of the medication; any alteration in the regimen should be reported by the patient or caregiver. Such cooperation may be vital to a successful treatment outcome. Unfortunately, the actual effect of incomplete compliance and the magnitude of any deleteriousness to the health of the elderly have not received the research attention they obviously deserve.

This article is intended to outline some basic principles of the discipline of Pharmacology and to comment on how these principles apply in the special circumstances of the elderly patient. Emphasis will be given to the important determinants of Drug Absorption, Distribution, Metabolism, and Excretion. Particular attention will be given to Pharmacokinetics, the correlation between a drug's effect and its level in the blood, and to Pharmacodynamics, the study of a drug's effects and the bodily mechanisms through which it exerts the effects.

II. PHARMACOKINETICS

Pharmacokinetics is concerned with the association between the pharmacological effects of a drug and its concentration in the blood. By studying the drug's blood level, a more accurate estimation can be made of the amount of the drug actually in the body than can be obtained from measuring the oral dose, even if given on a dose-per-body-weight basis. The drug circulating in the blood is one step closer to the target, and its concentration more closely correlates with concentration at the target tissue. The drug's half-life also allows predictions about time required after multiple doses to reach a steady state level. Where considered necessary, information for hepatic and renal clearance, and volume of distribution for a drug can be obtained by specialized pharmacological procedures and tests, and may be of utility in severely compromised patients undergoing intensive and prolonged therapy.

A. Drug Absorption

The most common route for medication administration for all patients is by mouth, with subsequent absorption from the gastrointestinal (GI) tract, through the wall of the stomach and/or intestine. In special situations drugs may also be administered by intramuscular or subcutaneous injection or intravenous infusion; or intrathecally, intraperitoneally, sublingually, rectal suppository, transdermally, inhalation (gases and aerosols through pulmonary membranes), or instillation of the eye; or topically on mucous membranes and the skin. This discussion will concentrate on the fate and actions of drugs entering the body through the GI tract, with exceptions noted. Absorption from the GI tract is mainly by passive diffusion, but certain drugs may be actively transported by cells in the lining of the tract that ordinarily absorb molecules from digested food. [See GASTROINTESTINAL SYSTEM: FUNCTION AND DYSFUNCTION.]

Almost all medications are either weak acids or bases, which may exist in solution in both ionized and un-ionized forms. They can be further divided into two categories on the basis of their solubility. The lipid soluble (also called nonpolar or lipophilic) drugs are not soluble in water, and thus, unless specially prepared, cannot be given via routes (e.g., intravenous), which may require an aqueous transport medium for administration. They pass easily through most biological membranes, however, and are thus readily absorbed through the GI tract. The more un-ionized the drug, the more lipid soluble (nonpolar) it will be. The water-soluble drugs (also called polar or

hydrophilic) when dissolved in water, tend to dissociate into negatively and positively charged ions. These characteristics may influence how well a drug is absorbed and distributed in the body and, ultimately, how much reaches the target site.

The acid (low pH) environment of the stomach may affect absorption of drugs in several ways. Weak acids will reman mostly in an un-ionized (more lipid soluble) form and be more readily absorbed through the stomach wall membrane. A weak base, on the other hand, often becomes more highly dissociated into its ionized (more polar and less lipid soluble) form and hence not easily absorbed through the gastric wall. Once the drug reaches the basic (higher pH) environment of the small intestine, converse conditions may prevail: weakly acidic drugs often show an increased ionization and become less absorbable, while the weakly basic drugs are frequently less ionized and more absorbable.

While some drug absorption takes place in the stomach, the thickness of its wall, its mucosal lining, small surface area, and strong electrophysiological resistance render it a less than optimal organ for absorption of most drugs. It is important, therefore, that the drug pass quickly from the stomach into the small intestine: the more rapid the stomach emptying time, the more rapid the absorption of the drug. The inner surface area of the intestine is much greater, its wall thinner, with a lining that promotes passive absorption. The epithelium that lines the intestinal wall also contains cells with mechanisms which actively transport certain drugs out of the intestinal lumen. In any case, the rate of absorption from the intestine is much more rapid than from the stomach, even for a drug remaining largely un-ionized in the stomach. Some drugs may be inactivated or destroyed by the stomach's highly acidic juices, so that the manufacturer may give a particularly susceptible drug a coat which resists decomposition in the stomach, allowing it to pass undissolved until it reaches the intestinal tract. There are also slow-release forms which may be prescribed to prolong the effect of a particular drug, or allow it to be given on a once or twice daily regimen.

With age, the pH of gastric juice increases (becomes less acidic), the stomach's emptying time is longer, the GI wall becomes thinner, and there is some loss of the absorptive and transporting epithelium. All of these conditions may exert an effect on a drug's chemical dissociation phenomena and alter the rate of its absorption. While these age-related changes are of theoretical interest, there is no compelling evidence that they exert a meaningful effect on drug absorption from the GI tract or have clinical significance for the elderly patient.

B. Drug Distribution

Drugs enter the circulating blood by injection, or after absorption from the GI tract and begin a process of distribution into the fluids within and between cells of body tissue, two of several so-called compartments of the body. The distributed drug goes first to various bodily organs in proportional amounts: the amount of drug an organ receives is determined primarily by the amount of blood it receives. The brain, kidney, liver, heart, and other well-supplied major organs receive most of the first few minutes' dispersion, but within the following minutes to hours, the viscera, muscle, fat, and skin are infused to the same general level. This early phase of drug distribution is a function of cardiac output and blood flow and may be diminished or prolonged by the reduced output of a diseased or aging heart. Another important factor is the drug's solubility. Lipid-soluble drugs which cross biological membranes easily will be more widely distributed than nonlipid soluble ionized ones. Except for small elemental ions, such as lithium, most biological membranes are impervious to ionized drugs.

During the time they are within the vascular system, many drugs are bound to circulating blood proteins, leaving only the unbound portion of the drug free to diffuse into tissues, other compartments, and ultimately to the target site of its action, the drug's receptor. The binding of drugs to these proteins imposes a limit on the circulating drug's availability for further distribution and the speed with which it reaches its intended site of action. The bound drug is in a dynamic equilibrium with the unbound drug population, and is released from binding as the unbound portion is diminished as a result of its leaving the circulation to be further distributed, metabolized, and excreted. The more strongly bound the drug, the less accessible it is for distribution to cells and other body compartments outside the vascular system. In such a case the drug's pharmacological action may be restricted and its metabolism and excretion slowed. There may be an age-related decrease of the blood

proteins which bind the drugs, resulting in a smaller bound portion of the circulating drug and a larger portion of it in the unbound state. Figure 1 demonstrates this phenomenon comparing the bound and free ratios for a hypothetical drug in a young adult to that in an older patient. Since the unbound portion is that part of the dose which carries out its effects, a small alteration in the amount of unbound drug may cause a large percentage change in the functional dose of the drug, and is one mechanism postulated to underlie an increase in drug sensitivity and adverse effects in the elderly.

Drug distribution is further influenced by the small differences in pH between fluids inside and outside the cells. A drug rendered more lipid soluble by the slightly higher pH of the extracellular fluid might easily traverse the cell membrane but become less lipid soluble in the lower pH of the intracellular fluid, and could not then easily diffuse out of the cell. In this manner, the drug could accumulate in a tissue: More would be entering than leaving its cells. Highly lipid-soluble drugs accumulate in fat tissues. Diffusion into tissues where the drug has no pharmacological activity is one of the body's drug-inactivation processes, but may also affect drug action in other ways. An accumulation of a drug in a tissue or compartment may be-

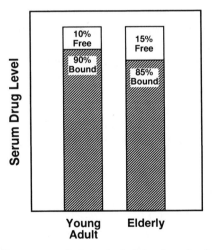

Figure 1 Percentages of a hypothetical drug's molecules circulating free and bound to plasma proteins, comparing a young adult and an elderly patient. In comparison to the young adult, the elderly patient has a lower concentration of blood proteins to bind the drug, leaving a greater percentage of the circulating drug unbound. Note that a 5% increase in the unbound portion represents a 50% increase in this, the functional portion of the circulating drug.

come a repository from which the drug, after its administration has been stopped, diffuses back into the general circulation and, in some cases, continues to act pharmacologically. Some examples of the manner in which these principles are manifest in clinical practice would include the following instances: Many highly lipid-soluble agents, such as phenothiazines, are stored in fatty tissues, and after chronic dosing can be detected in the patient's serum 6 months after the last dose. One of the highly lipophilic barbiturates given for anesthesia rapidly disperses from serum into the brain, where it acts quickly but transiently if given for only a brief period but becomes longer acting after repeated or prolonged infusion causes saturation of fatty tissue storage sites. With the storage sites filled, this rapid diffusion–storage mode no longer predominates, and the slower processes of metabolism and excretion become the major mechanisms terminating pharmacological activity. The slower elimination results in continued circulating therapeutic levels and longer pharmacological activity for the barbituate. This latter instance also illustrates how various pharmacological mechanisms, all of which must be taken into account and understood in the prescription of a medication, contribute to that medication's actions, side effects, and idiosyncrasies.

Only lipophilic drugs are able to diffuse from the blood into the central nervous system (CNS). Ionized compounds, on the other hand, are unable to breach the blood–brain-barrier, a factor which must be considered in choosing an agent in particular clinical situations. Many drugs, sold over-the-counter (OTC) or prescribed to the elderly, possess the ability to block the effects of the neurotransmitter acetylcholine (ACh) in the CNS and the peripheral nervous system (PNS). Such drugs (commonly called anticholinergics) may in high doses cause delirium, agitation, and hallucinations (CNS symptoms); other effects may include tachycardia, constipation, and urinary retention (PNS symptoms). The elderly, who are particularly sensitive to these effects, may become poisoned by accidently overdosing on such a drug or drugs and require emergency treatment. The antidote, physostigmine, which easily traverses the blood–brain barrier, will reverse all of the anticholinergic effects. Neostigmine, a strongly ionized congener of physostigmine, which does not enter the CNS, is sometimes mistakenly selected in such cases by the treating physician. In this situation only the PNS symptoms are reversed. The patient would therefore continue to be delirious, hallucinated, and agitated until the mistake were discovered and physostigmine administered. [See BRAIN AND CENTRAL NERVOUS SYSTEM.]

Drugs may accumulate in other cells, tissues, and fluids in sufficiently high concentrations to promote a reservoir effect as the plasma level of the drug decreases. For instance, some of the drugs bound to blood proteins may act as a reservoir when displaced from their binding sites by other drugs.

C. Drug Metabolism

Once a drug has been absorbed and distributed, the body begins processes to inactivate and eliminate it. How thoroughly and rapidly the body eliminates a drug is a strong determinant of that drug's duration of action, its efficacy, and toxicity. In any given patient population, there are very large interindividual variations in the rate of these processes. These differences are frequently genetically based and constitute the subject of a subdiscipline called pharmacogenetics. A patient who metabolizes a drug rapidly would maintain a low circulating blood drug level and may require larger than usual doses for therapeutic effect. Another, who metabolizes slowly, causing a higher than expected blood drug level, may become toxic on an average dose of the drug. These elimination processes begin immediately, and variations in their rate must be considered by the prescribing professional when formulating a therapeutic regimen for the individual patient. In most elderly patients these processes are slowed, and unless this fact is recognized, and the usual daily adult dose modified to meet the special requirements of the elderly, the blood drug level may reach toxic amounts. For this reason, in order to reduce the incidence of adverse reactions, the homely dictum "Start low and go slow" is applicable when prescribing for the older patient. The physician must also monitor the patient carefully, however, to ascertain that a therapeutic effect is obtained. After "starting low," care must taken to raise the dose sufficiently; unless therapeutic amounts are given, the drug may not reach adequate blood levels, exposing the patient to risk of adverse effects without providing therapeutic benefit. [See METABOLISM: CARBOHYDRATE, LIPID, AND PROTEIN.]

Once in circulation the drug is subjected to the degradative actions of a variety of bodily enzymes.

Most of the enzymes which metabolize drugs are found in the liver, but several types are found in kidney, lung, and GI tract as well. Because most of the absorbed drugs are lipid-soluble, they must first be converted to water-soluble forms in order to be excreted by the kidneys. Lipophilic drugs, which diffuse easily out of the kidney and back into circulation, are conjugated with polar molecules provided by the host to make water-soluble products, which are then excreted in the urine. Other types of enzymatic actions result in altered forms, called metabolites, of the drug. These forms may be rendered pharmacologically inactive, but some have as much (occasionally even more) potency than the parent molecule. If the metabolite has pharmacological activity, it will be transformed further to an inactive form, conjugated, and excreted.

After absorption from the GI tract, a drug enters the veins of the hepatic portal system and is transported to the liver, through which it must pass before entering the general circulation. Certain drugs are subjected to the combined effects of enzymes in the GI wall and the liver, which may prevent a clinically significant amount of the drug from gaining entry to the general circulation. This is called the *first pass effect*. While the water-soluble drugs are not well extracted by the liver, highly lipophilic drugs are avidly taken up and transformed. This first pass process may be so efficient that only 5–10% of the drug dose will pass through into the systemic circulation. The term *bioavailable* describes that portion of the drug reaching systemic circulation, which then transports it to the site of action. The bioavailability of a drug that is highly extracted by the liver may be markedly increased by a modest reduction in the efficiency of this first pass effect. Thus, if a drug ordinarily is 95% removed in this process, only 5% of the dose will become bioavailable. If the extraction value were to be reduced to 92%, bioavailability will increase by more than 50%. This would generally have the effect of administering a 50% larger dose of the medication to the patient. If not accounted for, this increase may result in serious side effects normally associated with drugs administered at much higher dosages. Physiological changes, which cause a reduction in this important hepatic function, are reported to occur in otherwise healthy people, but are more prevalent, and to a greater degree, in those elderly who are frail and with organs decompensated by disease. Many drugs,

particularly cardiovascular agents, prescribed for the older patient are affected by these changes. Propranolol is a beta-adrenergic blocking agent given for the treatment of cardiac arrhythmias and hypertension. The first oral dose of propanolol is almost completely removed by the extraction activity during its first pass through the liver. It is not until subsequent doses partially or completely saturate the degradative enzymes that sufficient unchanged drug passes through to the general circulation, and raises propranolol to clinically effective blood levels. Even so, for propranolol, the average bioavailable amount is only 25% of the administered dose.

Upon extraction from the blood, the drug enters the hepatic cells. The liver enzymes (and other bodily enzymes as well), many of which are in the microsomal organelles within the hepatic cells, begin transformation of the drug by a variety of enzymatically catalyzed reactions which will determine its fate. One such reaction is conjugation, combining the drug molecule or its metabolite with another compound, usually a substance found naturally in the body, such as a carbohydrate, amino acid, sulfate, or acetic acid. These conjugations, also called synthetic reactions, commonly utilize the carbohydrate glucuronic acid, but other substances such as the acetyl and methyl molecules, glycine, and sulfate are extensively used. After conjugation, the lipid-soluble drug becomes water-soluble and may now be excreted by the kidneys. Part of the dose is converted by a variety of other biochemical actions to inactive (or pharmacologically active) metabolites. Whether active or inactive, those metabolites that remain lipid-soluble will be subsequently conjugated and excreted.

In addition to conjugative metabolism, liver enzymes subject drugs to multifarious other reactions. Oxidative metabolism, an important method for inactivating drugs, is performed by multiple enzyme systems, including heme peroxidases, amine oxidases, alcohol dehydrogenase, and xanthine oxidase. The largest group of oxidases, which are responsible for the breakdown of a multiplicity of drugs, is a family of related forms (isoforms) called cytochrome P_{450}, found in organelles within the cell. Many therapeutic agents induce or inhibit these enzymes, and a growing body of literature is elucidating important drug–drug interactions at this vector. Table I lists several types of drugs metabolized by just three isoforms of the P_{450} enzyme. The frequency with which these drugs are

Table I Drugs Metabolized by Cytochrome P$_{450}$[a]

Antiarrhythmics	Immunosuppressant
Lidocaine	Cyclosporine
Metoprolol	Antihypertensives
Propafenone	Diltiazem
Propranolol	Nifedipine
Quinidine	
Timolol	Antianxiety and Sedatives
	Alprazolam
Antidepressants	Midazolam
Desipramine	Triazolam
Nortriptyline	
	Antihistaminic
Analgesics	Terfenadine
Codeine	

[a] A partial list of drugs metabolized by three isoforms of the cytochrome P$_{450}$ enzymes. A drug which inhibits these enzymes would raise the blood level of the affected drugs and increase their pharmacological effects. An agent which induced these enzymes would, conversely, lower the blood levels of these drugs and reduce their pharmacological activity.

prescribed to the older patient dictates that drug–drug interactions will inevitably occur.

Imipramine, a tricyclic antidepressant used to treat depression and anxiety states, is initially metabolized by oxidative removal of one of the two methyl groups from its side-chain nitrogen, forming the pharmacologically active metabolite, desmethylimipramine. This molecule is, in turn, further oxidized to its inactive 2-hydroxy metabolite, glucuronidated, and excreted. Other tricyclics undergo similar side-chain demethylations, but with varying sites of oxidation of the ring structure before conjugation. Chlorpromazine, an antipsychotic given in the treatment of such conditions as schizophrenia and manic-depressive disorders, is transformed into as many as 26 different metabolites. Some of these may be more toxic than the parent drug. It is possible that a patient whose enzymes idiosyncratically form more of the toxic metabolite would experience more toxic adverse effects than someone whose enzymatic systems transformed chlorpromazine mainly to other less toxic forms. Such variation in underlying enzymatic mechanisms might explain the wide differences in side-effect profiles seen in patients treated with chlorpromazine.

Enzymatic chemical reduction of nitrogen atoms within the molecular complex of a drug, through addition of hydrogen to their azo and nitro forms, is an-other inactivation pathway. Other metabolic enzymes destroy certain drugs by the process of hydrolysis. Physostigmine, which enhances central and peripheral cholinergic action by preventing the breakdown of the neurotransmitter ACh, is itself hydrolyzed at its ester linkage by cholinesterase enzymes. Breaking the ester linkage splits the physostigmine molecule, ending its pharmacological action. This process is rapid: most of an administered dose of physostigmine is inactivated in 2 hours.

Although activity of drug-metabolizing enzymes is a consistent determinant of drug action, there are a variety of chemicals that enhance or retard their ability to act on particular drugs. Enhancing an enzyme's effect is commonly called induction. Increasing activity of a drug-metabolizing enzyme increases its actions, and reduces the amount of the circulating drug. Inhibition of an enzyme reduces its degradative activity, resulting in higher blood levels of the drug. Chemicals that inhibit or induce the biochemical activity of the enzymes include other medications, toxins, and ethyl alcohol. Such agents given before or during a drug's administration might cause an acceleration or diminution of that drug's metabolic breakdown, thus raising or lowering the anticipated blood level. Since the broad range of enzyme-inducing and -inhibiting agents include many commonly prescribed medications, the responsible physician must give cognizance to these interactions when recommending more than one drug at a time for any patient, but especially the more vulnerable older patient. Physiological changes, such as age-related shrinkage of liver mass and reduction in hepatic blood flow, also affect drug metabolism. Reducing hepatic blood flow reduces the amount of circulating drug presented for uptake into the liver cells, whereas loss of liver mass would reduce the amount of that organ's enzymes available for action.

D. Drug Excretion

The end point of the foregoing operations is the elimination of the administered drug from the body. The final pathway for elimination is the process of excretion, which is conducted mainly by the kidneys with several other organs and routes playing less significant roles. Orally administered drugs which have not been absorbed, or which have been excreted into the intestine in bile, are passed out with the feces. Drug metabolites formed in the liver may be excreted into the intestine through the biliary tract, and are reabsorbed to be excreted by the kidneys or pass with the feces. Excretion by the lungs is limited almost exclusively to gases and volatile agents. Excretion through tears, sweat, and saliva is relatively insignificant. Salivary drug levels may correlate well with plasma levels (and are sometimes used to measure a drug's concentration when other body fluids are not available): they are generally swallowed and reabsorbed, and only a miniscule amount excreted.

The excretory function of the kidney involves three intrinsic processes of its nephron: filtration of drugs through the glomeruli, secretion through the tubules, and passive reabsorption into the tubular cells. In the service of maintaining the narrow limits of the body's internal milieu, the kidney is very active in the excretion and reabsorption of a variety of molecular materials, including water and electrolytes, body wastes, and foreign compounds such as drugs and poisons. Once filtered, the fluid containing the drug and/or its metabolites enters the renal tubules where the metabolites may be reabsorbed or pass into the urine. For a drug to be readily excreted by the kidneys it must be water soluble. This most important variable determines that lipid-soluble drugs must be rendered polar (water soluble) before they will be excreted into the urine. A nonpolar (lipid-soluble) drug, particularly a weak acid or a weak base, in the glomerular filtrate will be almost completely passively reabsorbed through the cells of the proximal and distal tubules of the nephron. The sum total of filtration, reabsorption, and excretion determines the renal clearance of a drug. How tightly bound the drug is to blood proteins also affects its renal excretion, because the bound portion is not readily available for glomerular filtration, and lowers its renal clearance rate. Because tubular cells are not as permeable to ionized drugs as to the un-ionized ones, passive reabsorption of water-soluble drugs becomes dependent in part on the pH of the tubular fluid. In the presence of a more alkaline tubular fluid (higher pH), weakly acidic drugs are more ionized and more rapidly excreted. The opposite occurs when the tubular urine is more acidic (lower pH): a weak acid would remain un-ionized and more readily reabsorbed. For weakly basic drugs the converse of these conditions would hold true: their excretion would be enhanced in the more acidic tubular fluid but inhibited in the presence of a more alkaline fluid. [See RENAL AND URINARY TRACT FUNCTION.]

Clinicians sometimes take advantage of this renal physiology by manipulating urine pH to accelerate the excretion of a drug that may be present in moderate overdose or causing unwanted effects. Drugs such as ammonium chloride render the urine more basic; ascorbic acid causes a more acidic urine. This principle would be salutary in the management of toxic levels of such drugs as a salicylate (i.e., aspirin). Raising urinary pH (rendering it more alkaline) will accelerate elimination of the salicylate in the older patient without having to resort to invasive measures, such as renal dialysis. In order for this treatment to be effective, however, the change in pH must be made to persist until the drug blood level is reduced. An overdose that is very large or is life-threatening would, of course, be treated by more heroic measures, such as renal dialysis, and other appropriate supportive therapy.

An important measurement of a drug's kinetics is its serum half-life (also called half-life and elimination half-life), determined by serial measurements of the drug's blood level after a single dose, and often indicated by the symbol T½. As illustrated for a hypothetical agent in Figure 2, a drug's half-life is defined as the time required to reduce its blood level to one-half of its single-dose peak blood level. The data obtained from the time required for the rise and fall of a drug's

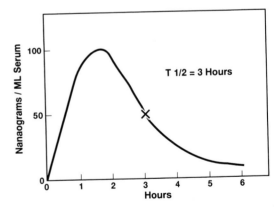

Figure 2 Illustration of the derivation of a drug's serum half-life. In this depiction an oral dose of a hypothetical drug was given at time "0." The drug's blood level rises to a peak of 100 nanograms per ml of serum. As it is distributed, metabolized, and excreted, its blood level falls. The drug's half-life (T½) is considered to be the time required for its serum level to reach one-half its peak value. Here, one-half of the peak value (denoted by the X in downslope) is reached in 3 hours.

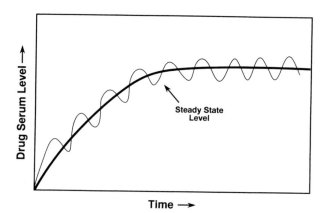

Figure 3 In this illustration repeated oral doses of a hypothetical drug are given beginning at time "0." Subsequent doses are given at approximately the drug's elimination half-life, resulting in a rising drug blood level. In between each oral dose the drug's blood level rises and falls. At a time between four and five of the drug's half-life, its serum level reaches a steady state. The unwavering line represents the rise of the drug's serum level to steady state during intravenous administration.

blood concentration also reflect rates of its distribution, bioavailability, and clearance. From these data the pharmacologist can infer how long the drug remains in blood after an acute dose, how much time is required to reach a steady state level, and how long the drug will remain in the blood after the last dose. The length of time the drug stays in the blood is a function of its clearance, which is a corollary of all the mechanisms previously discussed. Because it is multifactorally determined, the drug's half-life cannot be used alone as the only measure of its disposition, or to specify an alteration in any one of the bodily functions that subserve it.

When a drug's dose is repeated and each subsequent dose is given at an interval approximating its elimination half-life, the drug will accumulate, its blood level will rise, and a steady state blood level will build. In between each dose the drug's blood concentration rises and falls, with the steady state level usually being calculated at a midpoint between the upper and lower blood level values from the individual doses. At the point where the amount of drug entering into the blood equals the amount being eliminated, a steady state level is attained. Note that Figure 3 demonstrates that the time required to reach a steady state level is approximately four of the drug's elimination half-lives. When drug blood levels are reported for the usual clinical practice situation, it is

the steady state value that is used. Many drugs have a "therapeutic window," by which is meant that there is a steady state blood level below which it will not be effective, and a level above which it is toxic, with a midrange wherein it will exert its therapeutic effect with minimal or no toxicity. Figure 4 shows the therapeutic window for a hypothetical drug as the cross-hatched area. Where a therapeutic window has been established for a particular drug, the physician is able to utilize this information and determine from one drug blood level value, whether or not the patient's blood level is too high or too low before ordering adjustments in the dose. For many drugs laboratories have established ranges of drug blood level values to assist the physician in adjusting adequacy of the therapy. In elderly patients, many of whom have reduced tolerance to adverse drug effects, it may be difficult to differentiate whether worsening symptoms are due to the primary disease or adverse drug effects. In such cases, drug blood levels may be discriminatory and of definitive clinical value. These same kinetics apply to drugs given intravenously: the blood drug level will rise and reach a steady state at approximately four of its elimination half-times, though the accumulation will be smoother and not show the fluctuations characteristically seen with orally administered doses.

Blood level data and knowledge of a drug's pharmacokinetics may be especially valuable where its therapeutic effects are difficult to judge from observa-

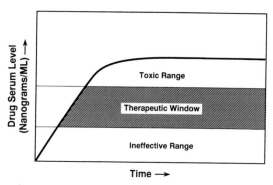

Figure 4 Illustration of a drug's therapeutic window. As a drug's serum level rises it reaches a value at which it becomes therapeutically effective. As the level continues to rise it remains effective until it reaches a value above which it begins to exert more toxic than therapeutic effects. The range of the drug's serum level values between the ineffective and the toxic is called the drug's therapeutic window.

tion, its dose must be raised quickly as treatment necessity, or it has a very narrow dose range (i.e., where there is a small range of values between its therapeutic and toxic levels). Though not foolproof (the patient can go off the medication and restart it shortly before the blood sample is drawn), blood levels offer one of the most reliable methods for ascertaining the patient's compliance with the prescribed medication. Lithium, an important agent in treatment of affective disorders, has a narrow therapeutic range. In treating a patient with a manic–depressive disorder which has persisted into old age, the physician may order repeated serum lithium levels early in the therapy to establish the oral lithium dose required to maintain the blood level between 0.5–1.4 milliequivalents per liter of serum. Such monitoring is necessary in all patients, but is especially important in the older patient, who may have a reduced renal clearance for lithium. Even if given a lower than usual starting dose, an elderly person can quickly accumulate toxic levels of this ion, making regular blood level determinations mandatory.

III. PHARMACODYNAMICS

Pharmacodynamics is concerned with drug effects and the body's physiological and biochemical mechanisms through which the drugs exert these effects. Pharmacodynamic data are derived from studies of drug receptor sites, cellular activity, intracellular mechanisms, and structure–activity relationships of the drug itself. Though cellular, molecular, and clinical pharmacology are contributing to a growing body of research in pharmacodynamics, there remains a paucity of data specific for the elderly subpopulation in this area.

Drugs typically begin their pharmacological activity by interacting with a cell as specialized proteins called receptor sites, in its plasma (outer cell wall) membrane, or on channels in the membrane through which ions pass in and out of the cell. They may also act on receptors within the cell or on other proteins or chemical moieties which comprise intracellular mechanisms. The cell wall receptors are typically agonized or antagonized by a variety of endogenous substances (called agonists and antagonists), which transform the receptors, sending a signal into the cell, and stimulation or inhibition of the cell's activity. Drugs

are designed to mimic, exaggerate, or interfere in some way with the body's own physiologically active substances (ions, transmitter substances, enzymes, hormones). Stimulation of a cell's receptor site typically causes a cascade of intracellular events which embrace a multiplicity of mechanisms and lead ultimately to cellular activity (e.g., signaling another cell, contraction, secretion of a substance, or genetic activity).

There is an age-related decrease in some types of receptor sites and a decrease in physiologic cellular and organ activity. These changes may lead to an altered sensitivity to medication effects. While there is evidence of an age-related decrease in sensitivity to many medications, others, such as the anticoagulant warfarin, may show an increased effect in the older patient. In general, the elderly are more susceptible than younger patients to the adverse events attendant on drug therapy. Because there is no "silver bullet," drugs all act at multiple sites and cause multiple and often unwanted effects, in addition to their action at the target site. Thus, an antidepressant given to treat depression in an elderly patient would cause the down regulation of the beta-adrenergic receptor as part of its antidepressant effect. At the same time it antagonizes the muscarinic cholinergic receptors, producing urinary retention, constipation, dry mouth, blurred vision, and such a degree of discomfort to the patient as to merit stopping the drug, despite its salutary action in lifting the patient's depression.

IV. DRUG INTERACTIONS AND SIDE EFFECTS

The physician must individualize the elderly patient's therapeutic regimen. Appropriate therapy for the elderly includes careful consideration not only of Pharmacokinetics but also Pharmacodynamics. Because the elderly patient is often administered multiple drugs, the physician must note that significant interactions can and will occur. The elderly are particularly sensitive to the effects of blocking the body's ubiquitous muscarinic cholinergic receptors. Antimuscarinic actions are therapeutically useful in instances such as relaxing spasmodic smooth muscle (i.e., intestine, urinary bladder) or for parkinsonism, but they are more commonly encountered as unwanted side effects. The United States Pharmacopeial Drug Information (USP DI) Review includes a selected list of more

Table II Antimuscarinic Effects[a]

Blurred (near) vision
Urinary retention
Constipation
Dry mouth
Thirst
↓ Sweating
Tachycardia
Palpitation
Restlessness
Delirium
Hallucinations

[a] A partial list of effects caused by blocking the muscarinic receptors of the various body organ systems. These are also referred to as anticholinergic or atropinic effects. Some of these effects, especially the bottom three, may be misdiagnosed as a psychiatric illness.

than fifty drugs which possess antimuscarinic activity in addition to their primary therapeutic actions. In a regimen of polypharmacy, the side-effects of several drugs may be interactive and additive, further slowing an age-related GI tract hypomotility, causing severe constipation. Drug-induced urinary retention, even where mild, is problematic for all older patients, but can become emergent in the elderly male, who may require prompt catheterization due to a prolonged inability to void. Table II lists several of the more prominent signs and symptoms associated with antimuscarinic effects (often synonymously called atropinic or anticholinergic effects). In addition, the restlessness, delirium, and hallucinations may be misdiagnosed as a psychiatric illness. Prescription of a psychiatric drug, nearly all of which possess inherent antimuscarinic properties, may be contraindicated in such an instance because they may additively aggravate this critical drug-induced situation.

Though many drug–drug interactions have been identified by experiential observation and careful clinical pharmacological research, there is a potential for many others between the hundreds of prescription agents and OTC remedies available to the elderly. A complete cataloging of known interactions is not possible here, but some representative examples might include the following:

1. The antibiotic neomycin can abolish intestinal bacteria which are responsible for the metabolic transformation of certain drugs. Without these bacteria the ingested drug in question would not be metabolized at its usual rate and its pharmacological actions may be reduced, or greater than expected. Drugs such as L-Dopa, salicylazosulfapyridine, and digoxin would be examples of agents affected in this manner.

2. Ion exchange resins (administered to reduce blood cholesterol levels) and gel antacids physically adsorb many concomitantly administered drugs, and may thereby reduce or delay their absorption.

3. Guanethidine, an antihypertensive, must be taken up by the adrenergic neuron's norepinephrine reuptake pump in order to reach its site of action. Drugs which block this pump, such as tricyclic antidepressants and phenothiazines, prevent the uptake of guanethedine and antagonize its antihypertensive actions.

4. Ethyl alcohol is involved in multiple interactions and may variously affect the pharmacology of other drugs through such actions as delaying gastric emptying time, changing gastric pH, delaying drug absorption, or denaturing the drug itself.

5. Probenecid inhibits the renal tubular secretion of penicillin and is often used in a therapeutic interaction to raise the blood level of this antibiotic.

6. Metabolic breakdown of the oral hypoglycemic tolbutamide is inhibited by sulphaphenazole. This interaction raises the blood level of tobutamide causing hypoglycemic attacks in patients whose diabetes had been well controlled before the second drug was given.

7. Dicoumarol, an oral anticoagulant requiring careful attention to proper dosing and frequently prescribed to elderly patients, is subject to interactions by a variety of other drugs. Drugs which accelerate its metabolism would lower dicoumarol's blood level and reduce its therapeutic action. A drug which inhibits dicoumarol's metabolism would raise its blood level and increase its therapeutic effects.

The extent of potential problems caused by unwanted effects of prescription drugs may be inferred by reference to the USP DI Review which lists, in addition to anticholinergically active drugs, an extensive (but not inclusive) compilation of medications which may cause other problems as well. These adverse reactions include such categories as blood dyscrasia, blocking thyroid function, depressing the bone marrow, depressing the CNS, stimulating the CNS, inducing hepatic P_{450} enzymes, inhibiting various hepatic enzymes, extrapyramidal reactions, antagonizing folic acid, hemolysis, hepatotoxicity, hyperkalemia, hypokalemia, hypotension, hypothermia, methemoglobinemia, nephrotoxicity, neurotoxicity, ototoxicity, and blood platelet aggregation. Each of these categories contain from approximately twenty to more than fifty prescription drugs, making is probable that the elderly patient will have some exposure to the potential hazards. Information such as this on prescription medications is regularly disseminated in the USP publications, as well as in continuing medical education forums sponsored by various medical institutions, and is available to professionals and others who care for the elderly.

ACKNOWLEDGMENTS

The author thanks Patricia F. Bouteneff and Lynn C. Yeoman for their critical reading of the manuscript and helpful suggestions.

BIBLIOGRAPHY

Benet, L. Z., Mitchell, J. R., & Sheiner, L. B. (1990). Pharmacokinetics: The dynamics of drug absorption, distribution, and elimination. In A. G. Gilman, T. W. Rall, A. S. Nies, & P. Taylor (Eds.), *The pharmacological basis of therapeutics* (pp. 3–32). New York: Pergamon Press.

Ross, E .M. (1990). Pharmacodynamics: Mechanisms of drug action and the relationship between drug concentration and effect. In A. G. Gilman, T. W. Rall, A. S. Nies, & P. Taylor (Eds.), *The pharmacological basis of therapeutics* (pp. 33–48). New York: Pergamon Press.

Salzman, C., Satlin, A., & Burrows, A. B. (1995). Geriatric psychopharmacology. In A. F. Schatzberg & C. B. Nemeroff (Eds.), *Textbook of psychopharmacology* (pp. 803–822). Washington, DC: American Psychiatric Press.

United States Pharmacopeial Convention, Inc., 15th ed. (1995). *Drug information for the health care professional* (vol. I). Taunton, MA: Rand McNally.

United States Pharmacopeial Convention, Inc., 15th ed. (1995). *Advice for the patient: Drug information in lay language* (vol. II). Taunton, MA: Rand McNally.

Vestal, R. E., Montamat, S. C., & Nielson, C. P. (1992). Drugs in special patient groups: The elderly. In K. L. Melmon, H. F. Morrelli, B. B. Hoffman, & D. W. Nierenberg (Eds.), *Clinical pharmacology* (pp. 851–874). New York: McGraw-Hill, Inc.

Philosophy

Gary M. Kenyon

St. Thomas University
Canada

I. Introduction
II. Ontology
III. Epistemology
IV. Ethics

Biography   The life story of a person as written or told by another person. The term also refers to various types of biographical materials used in gerontology.
Epistemology   The study of the origins, process, and limits of human knowledge.
Ethics   The study of human values, moral concepts, and systems of morality.
Existentialism   A philosophical perspective that emphasizes the role of the human person in creating and discovering meaning in life and in the face of finitude.
Ontology   The study of basic assumptions and images of human nature and/or the cosmos.

The contribution of **PHILOSOPHY** to gerontology is evident in three of the main subject areas of philosophy, namely, ontology, epistemology, and ethics. Under ontology, the discussion centers on the various interpretations or meanings of aging and human nature that are contained in historical and contemporary perspectives, including scientific theories of aging. Ontological inquiry is also concerned with proposing new metaphors or interpretations. The central topics under epistemology are methodological issues including importantly the experimental–interpretive, or quantitative–qualitative debate, the analysis of theories from an analytical and logical perspective, and the analysis of the process of knowledge acquisition in gerontology. Finally, ethical discourse in gerontology focuses on values and the process of decision making in various areas of research and intervention, including mandatory retirement, long-term care, and advance directives. These issues and others are addressed at both the level of personal ethics and social ethics.

I. INTRODUCTION

The contribution of philosophy to gerontology is multifaceted. A useful way to describe this contribution is to outline the main branches of philosophy as they apply to the study of aging. Three of the four main branches of philosophy are relevant to the present discussion; namely, metaphysics or *ontology*, *epistemology*, and *ethics*. The fourth branch, logic, will not be considered, except as it is implied in methodological issues in the section on epistemology. It is interesting to note at the outset that philosophical contributions to gerontology originate in many disciplines, which reflect the thoroughgoing interdisciplinary character of the field of aging, and therefore are not exclusively the focus of professional philosophers.

In moving to the first major theme, ontology, the discussion centers on the different images, interpretations, and meanings of aging and human nature that are contained in selected philosophical positions, both historical and contemporary. Reference is made to such views as those of ancient Greece and Rome in the Western tradition and to Buddhism and Confucianism in the East. In addition to this, an outline of current philosophical thinking about aging is undertaken.

Second, with respect to epistemology, the central issues fall under the general themes of philosophy of science and methodology. There are three significant topics in this area. The first consists of an inquiry into the components of gerontological knowledge. The second concerns philosophical analysis of theory in gerontology. Examples in this area include the current discussion of the notion of a critical gerontology, and the commentary on the possibility of a grand theory of aging, one that would reach across disciplines. The second significant epistemological topic is that of the philosophical contribution to the so-called quantitative–qualitative debate. A useful focus for this discussion is the intense interest in the area of aging and *biography*. In fact, a focus on biography is relevant to all three main areas of concern in philosophy and gerontology.

Third, the area of ethics and aging has grown very rapidly recently. Important topics in this context include biomedical issues concerning research and practice with older persons, and social issues such as ageism, mandatory retirement, and institutionalization. Another very important issue here concerns end-of-life decisions, including the debate about living wills and advance directives. These ethical issues in gerontology are addressed both at the micro- and macrolevel, that is, at the level of both personal and social ethics. [*See* AGEISM AND DISCRIMINATION; ETHICS AND EUTHANASIA; RETIREMENT.]

II. ONTOLOGY

The contribution of philosophy to gerontology from an ontological perspective is best explicated through a focus on *meaning*. The meaning of life and death, the meaning of aging and being older, and the implications that these meanings have for human beings in terms of how to live an authentic or good life, are questions that have been addressed by philosophers throughout history, that is, across time, cultures, and persons. This rich source of knowledge and experience is being integrated by contemporary researchers and applied to present and future aging people and issues.

A. Philosophy and Aging: Selected Traditional Perspectives

Although gerontology is a new field, philosophers and others have reflected on the meaning of life and aging

throughout history and across cultures. To begin with Western culture, the ancient Greeks, represented by Socrates, held that "the unexamined life is not worth living." It is interesting to note that this might constitute a motto for the contemporary interest in biography, to be discussed later. In general, the ancient Greeks' ontology of aging can be characterized by ambivalence. On the one hand, physical aging was often demeaned and not valued. On the other hand, if someone did manage to live longer, then the appropriate task and potential ability connected with being older was to contemplate such things as the divine cosmos and to seek wisdom. For example, it was the view of Plato that one should study philosophy, the vehicle to overcome the illusions of life, only after the age of fifty. This view about the second half of life has a modern counterpart in the work of Carl Jung.

Aristotle's philosophy also contained a view of a good life in old age; namely, a kind of integration of self over time that was based on an expression of distinctly human qualities. For Aristotle, the expression of these qualities presupposed such external elements as good character, friends, and economic security.

In the Roman world, the Stoic philosophers, such as Cicero, argued that a long life should be characterized by self-discipline and self-possession. This view would be in contrast to that of Aristotle, for example, as the Stoic emphasis was on internal sources of integrity and meaning in the face of life's vicissitudes and the losses associated with aging. These sentiments are echoed today in the work of Erik Erikson, as well as existentialist philosophers, including Jean-Paul Sartre, Maurice Merleau-Ponty, and Gabriel Marcel. Incidentally, philosophers of aging in the ancient world discussed aging from a subjective as well as objective perspective in the sense that they were a long-lived group.

A final philosophy of aging that deserves attention is that represented by the Native North American tradition. This tradition emphasizes reverence for the earth as a sacred and therefore deeply meaningful reality to be cared for and nourished. It has been argued that older persons in this tradition had and have a vital role to play as carriers of a preindustrial, tribal ethos, which provides important sources of meaning throughout the life span in modern and postmodern society.

In addition to Western traditional approaches to philosophy and aging, there are two Eastern perspectives that are increasingly of interest in contemporary gerontology. Among the important views are those of Confucianism and Buddhism. The ontological image that is dominant in the Confucian philosophy of aging is that of the family, as manifested in the concept of *filial piety*. Filial piety or duty to the family is said to be the main guiding moral principle and one that defines the very meaning of being in the world. With respect to aging, it is a duty of children to respect and honor parents and other elders in a family. In this Chinese and Korean tradition, death is not held to be a source of sadness for older people. Meaningfulness in life is measured by the amount of good an older person does for family and society, and from serving as a good example for the younger generation.

Although Buddhism may be treated as a religion, it is commonly practiced as a way of life or a spiritual path apart from its religious affiliation. The Buddhist philosophy of aging is based on the idea that it is possible to discover meaning in suffering and loss and to develop a healthy detachment to possessions, whether they be physical, mental, or emotional. Contrary to many interpretations of this philosophy, Buddhism does not advocate the denial of everyday life or an escape from it. Rather, it emphasizes acceptance of the basic conditions of human life in its transitoriness, an acceptance that is said to bring a form of freedom from anxiety and confusion. A cornerstone of this view is the practice of meditation.

Aging itself has profound value for the Buddhist. It represents the bodily record of the passage of time and a life of experiences. Aging reflects a movement toward more and not less life. Such an outcome is not automatic, as it requires that a person be willing to look at that life in meditation and thereby make friends with all that one is within. In this way, the Buddhist tradition offers the older person a way to see the future and to realize meaning in a long life. [*See* HISTORY OF GERONTOLOGY.]

B. Philosophy and Aging: Selected Contemporary Views

As the foregoing discussion indicates, some of the questions regarding aging and meaning are timeless; however, others are contemporary. For example, as the expectation of physical life extends further and

further, a new question concerns the purpose of that longer life. Other questions involve identifying the elements of a meaningful or worthwhile life, such as health, meaning itself, work, and companionship.

The question of meaning can be addressed from various points of view, or at different levels of discourse. Underlying these different perspectives is the insight that aging or growing older is, on the one hand, a "process," based on the fact that human beings are embodied and are therefore subject to biological conditions. However, aging is also an "experience," a personal set of events lived out in a particular social, cultural, and historical context.

An ontological metaphor that is employed in discussing the notion of aging and meaning is that of the *journey*. This metaphor has a long history and has received significant attention by gerontologists. One reason for this that has been suggested is that viewing a life as a journey facilitates a consideration of human aging simultaneously from individual, social, and cosmic perspectives. Philosophical analysis of the journey metaphor takes at least three forms. First, one can explicate the dimensions or aspects of the notion of a journey itself, that is, in its effectiveness as a metaphor for human life. Second, one can focus on the various ways in which the journey of life has been and is characterized in various traditions. Third, in addition to understanding these different descriptions of the meaning of life and aging as contained in the journey metaphor, philosophers are also interested in reflecting on the ideal or most appropriate rendering of that journey given the human condition. At this point there is an overlap between ontology and ethics or human values.

In this regard, a major philosophical issue in contemporary gerontology centers on the discussion of meaning and the purpose of aging, at both the individual and cultural levels of discourse; in other words, the elements of the journey in the modern and postmodern world. The basic concern here is that currently this is a world that looks to science for answers to most of its problems, rather than to religion or philosophy. The emergence of a problem initiates a search for a technique or technological solution.

On the basis of this dominant cultural image or metaphor, one attempts also to seek an answer or solution to the "problem" of aging, the meaning of life, and death. The urgent philosophical question is whether science is at all capable or even possesses the language to deal with the fundamental existential and moral issues surrounding the meaning of human aging and the purpose of life beyond biological reproduction and economic productivity, as the former is defined in contemporary society.

Science is an important component of an ontology of aging in today's world. The question is whether science and professional techniques can constitute a reliable guide on the human journey, which can be characterized by the existentialist dictum as the search for love and meaning in the face of death. The implicit or explicit ontological image by which most people live is characterized by a lack of relatedness, or conversely, separatedness, a condition that, for some philosophers of aging, contributes to the widespread spiritual malaise and meaninglessness that is evident in contemporary Western society.

This condition is said to manifest itself in several ways. First, there is a separation from transcendental sources of meaning. The contemplative aspects of life contained in traditional philosophical and religious systems have been replaced by an exclusive emphasis on the *via activa*. Along with this occurrence, the human life span has been divided up into pieces or boxes and is managed from a policy point of view: the boxes of education, work, and retirement. Furthermore, the contemporary or postmodern society is said to emphasize privatism or individualism. This means that people understand themselves as separate, both from other persons and from any collective sense of the meaning of aging and life. The meaning of life is equivalent to the meaning of *my* life as a unique individual.

As indicated earlier, philosophers of aging are concerned with describing historical and prevailing ontological images and metaphors, such as the one just outlined. However, they are also interested in reflecting on the ways in which individual and cultural meanings of life and aging are or are not effective in permitting human beings to express an "abundance of life." In this respect, the scenario just described is claimed to produce only negative outcomes and meaninglessness, as manifested in what has been called the culture of narcissism and, one could add, the culture of ageism. A future task for philosophy in gerontology, one that has just begun, will be to create and discover new viable ontological metaphors that can restore meaning to the wholeness of life, and to the later stages of human ontogeny.

C. Life Story as Ontology

A contemporary example of the search for new meanings of aging is the focus on life as story. Interest in this approach involves researchers in several disciplines within the field of aging including, philosophy, psychology, sociology, literature, and anthropology. The basic assumption of this approach is that human beings not only have a life story, but *are* stories or narratives. That is, people understand and perceive themselves and their world on the basis of storytelling. Furthermore, stories are also the basis for action. Gerontologists who are interested in the narrative approach, an approach that has a distinctly philosophical ethos, claim that it allows one to gain insight into the meaning of aging from the inside. This is important for several reasons. First, an emphasis on narratives puts the pieces of the older person back together and facilitates an understanding of aging at different levels in the same person; physical, social, psychological, and spiritual.

In this way, the narrative approach attempts to restore relatedness in our vision of human nature and aging. For example, a life story is theorized to contain social and cultural elements, as well as the creative and unique personal dimension. In other words, the story of my life is only partly my own. It is constructed and expressed in a particular context and reflects the ontological view that human beings are interpersonal entities and not isolated individuals. The life story metaphor is also sensitive to the existential or meaning-giving dimension of human nature, per se. Finally, the volitional aspect of life stories makes it an effective approach on the basis of which one can search for and facilitate optimistic, creative, and positive meanings of aging.

Statements such as the foregoing underlie the ontological view that human beings are not in control of everything and that an explication of the meaning of aging must take this into account. From this point of view, the meaning of aging is both created and discovered. It is created in part through scientific activity; however, it is also both created and discovered by aging persons as they reflect on their journey or the story that they are. It is the openness to and reflection on what amount to the mysteries of human existence, mysteries that have to do with cosmic issues, everyday relationships, and one's inner life, that allow people to accept aspects of life and aging that are opaque, that is, not transparent and self-evident.

An important outcome of the ontology just outlined is that the philosophical investigation of the meaning of growing older has crucial implications for science itself, for medicine, education, public policy, and even for discussions of religion and spirituality. This is the case in so far as it is deemed necessary to develop cultural and personal meanings of aging that reflect appropriate ontological images, with the goal of creating a society that values human beings as persons throughout the life span.

III. EPISTEMOLOGY

The second major area of interest in the consideration of philosophy in gerontology consists of the epistemological issues. Epistemology is characterized by a concern with the ways in which knowledge of aging is acquired or constructed by researchers, interveners, and older persons in general. In this regard, three topics are particularly significant: namely, the components of gerontological knowledge, theories of aging, and methodology in the field of aging.

A. Knowledge of Aging: Components

With respect to the first topic, researchers increasingly argue that knowledge of aging as it is formulated in science and practice is significantly influenced by the ontological images just discussed. This means that all theories and formal intervention strategies concerned with aging and older persons reflect specific meanings of human nature and aging. These meanings or images can be explicit or implicit; however, it is claimed that they are always operative. There is an interesting role for philosophers to play in facilitating a dialogue with physical, social, and behavioral gerontologists, as well as interveners, towards the explication and interpretation of these ontological assumptions.

The view that gerontological science and practice contain ontological images is based on the idea that all knowledge is made up of more than facts that can be automatically established so long as one follows the scientific method. From the postmodern perspective, there is an hermeneutic, interpretive, or biographical dimension to all knowledge. This means that researchers and interveners bring their own meanings to their professional situation, and those meanings and values are important components of what comes to count as knowledge of aging. Whereas from the modern or logical positivist perspective knowledge is based solely on objective facts, the postmodern view is that knowledge contains both subjective and objective dimensions, as it is constructed in an interpersonal context.

One of the interesting issues of concern both to philosophers of science and to sociologists of knowledge in the field of aging is the determination of the relativity of scientific knowledge. That is, the concern here is to inquire as to whether truth is whatever a group claims it to be, or whether truth is contextual and established on the basis of a dialogue and therefore not totally socially constructed. The work of the philosopher Hans Gadamer has given impetus to this type of inquiry in gerontology.

Another example of research concerning the components of knowledge of aging, which is inspired by the work of Jurgen Habermas, is the perspective of critical gerontology. This view calls upon the humanities to offer alternative assumptions regarding theories of aging. These alternative images would question the instrumentalist values that dominate current theory, practice, and method in gerontology and which are said to consequently rigidify human nature. It is interesting to note that this view goes beyond the position of multidisciplinary coexistence in gerontology and argues that philosophy and the other humanities have a distinct role to play in gerontology. This role includes forging new relationships between academics and practitioners, with the ultimate objective of liberation from the meaning and or meaninglessness of old age that informs modern culture.

B. Knowledge of Aging: Theory

In addition to the foregoing, philosophers contribute to theory in gerontology by explicating the meaning of many technical concepts employed in the field. These concepts include life satisfaction, disengagement, leisure, cognitive growth and decline, along with intelligence and wisdom, and meaning and spirituality. There is an important collaborative activity in this context as scientists and practitioners go about the business of operationalizing their variables.

For example, a particular scientific instrument may inadvertently restrict the meaning of a phenomenon in its attempt to exhibit consistency with its chosen theory. Philosophical reflection can contribute to pointing out the strengths and weaknesses of implicit or explicit assumptions that are contained both in the theory and its operationalization. This occurs by reference to historical perspectives and also by way of providing a hermeneutic dimension to contemporary analysis. Finally, this hermeneutic activity can also contribute new metaphors for future theorizing. It is important to indicate that an authentic philosophy of aging is also informed by science and practice in that hermeneutic circle.

The role of philosophy in this context can be highlighted by reference to the current increase of interest in the phenomenon of *wisdom*, on the part of both humanists and social scientists. Philosophical inquiry contributes to the understanding of wisdom and aging through an explication of historical definitions of wisdom that derive from many traditions, both Eastern and Western. These interpretations of wisdom can be compared with current attempts to define and operationalize wisdom, and to measure it.

For example, important distinctions need to be made between wisdom and other phenomena, such as cleverness and specialized forms of intellectual competence, which are accessible through standard scientific methods. In many traditions, wisdom is reserved for those who may or may not be cognitively gifted, but in any case are capable in thought and action of knowing and doing the good. It follows that an understanding of wisdom may require a thorough evaluation of the meanings that different people place on situations and a subtle assessment of interpersonal encounters, including the intentions that different people bring to these encounters.

Although the study of wisdom as a potentially positive outcome of aging should be encouraged, it is important to question the possibility to define and observe instances of wisdom, and to ask whether it is one phenomenon or many. Wisdom is a concept with a rich history, and one that may represent a significant challenge to gerontologists, in its analysis and perhaps in the possible facilitation of its expression in an aging population.

Beyond the discourse concerning concepts and methods in general, philosophy has a role to play with respect to two further questions. The first centers on the scientific adequacy of theories of aging, and the second deals with the plausibility of a grand *theory* of aging. With respect to scientific adequacy, researchers have pointed out that, for example, disengagement theory would be given high marks on logical adequacy, that is, by virtue of its explicit statements concerning constructs and linkages. However, the theory is significantly weaker in view of its unfalsifiability and lack of empirical support. This type of analysis of a theory is both a scientific and philosophical enterprise, and extends to a reflection on the meaning of disengagement as contained in the theory and then compared to other possible meanings of that phenomenon.

Finally, philosophers contribute to the debate concerning the possibility of a theory of aging that would cross levels of discourse, disciplines, and dimensions of the aging person. Such "grand theories" exist in the biology of aging, and there is no reason to rule them out in the broader context. In fact, perhaps increased theorizing at aggregate levels should be encouraged in the new field of gerontology as a way to facilitate the context of discovery.

C. Knowledge of Aging: Methodology

With regard to the third theme, a contemporary methodological issue in gerontology centers on the quantitative–qualitative debate. Increasingly, the positivist or logical empiricist perspective, which is based on the scientific method in the natural sciences, is being perceived as insufficient or incomplete in providing adequate descriptions and explanations of various aging phenomena. In many contexts, ranging from health issues to intellectual and memory functioning, to social behavior to spirituality, the search for valid knowledge of aging is being seen to involve something more than standard modern scientific instruments and assessment tools. It is this movement towards new methods to which philosophy has a contribution to make. This contribution can be clarified, for example, by focusing on the increasing use of biographical materials in gerontology.

As indicated in the section on ontology, the philosophical basis for aging and biography is the central importance of lived experience or the life world of a person. This life world is both the source and object of human science research. Researchers working in this area argue that the preferred methods for such an agenda are descriptions of experience, such as are found in life stories, interpretations, self-reflections, and critical analyses. It is further argued that the outcome of this approach is a more complete understanding of human aging, because biographical approaches are effective in capturing subjective or inner aspects of aging, at the level of the individual older person. However, these approaches are also effective in reflecting the social and cultural contexts of meaning in which personal storytelling is embedded.

From a methodological point of view, such questions as sample size and the accuracy and truthfulness of the data are a function of the purpose of the study. In one context, one might be interested in a detailed rendering of the meanings of one life as it is expressed in a life story. In another context, the purpose might be to understand how a group of older persons experiences widowhood or family life. There is a philosophical dimension to this approach to the science of aging that is operative at the level of ontology, epistemology, and methodology. That is, reflection, interpretation, and even intuition are elements of the design, implementation, and outcome of a study of this kind, to a much greater degree than is evident in studies that depend only on standard instruments and assessment strategies, such as statistics and survey questionnaires.

As a final remark, some researchers argue that multiple approaches are often most appropriate for the investigation of aging phenomena, and it is precisely the problem or phenomenon that should guide the choice of method. However, it remains a contemporary philosophy of science issue that gerontologists are primarily trained in only one paradigm, and that paradigm reflects the values of logical empiricism and traditional quantitative methods.

IV. ETHICS

The third major area of interest in the discussion of philosophy and gerontology is that of ethics. An aging population gives rise to many important moral issues; some of which are more specific to older persons, such as mandatory retirement and rights to intimacy in an institution, and some that are relevant in a life span perspective as, for example, euthanasia and advance directives. Thus, ethical discourse in the field of aging usually has implications for both present and future older persons.

In essence, ethics is a form of reasoning. It is a reflective process that attempts to answer the basic question: What should I do in *this* situation, all things considered? It is important to emphasize that ethics involves reasoning not just for its own sake, as one

might theorize, say, about the origin of the universe. The domain of ethics is the domain of action; moreover, action that is concerned directly with our own life or other people's lives. Thus the phrase, What should I *do*. Ethics usually involves a concern for feelings and also often involves the will: ethical decisions, once thought out, often presuppose courageous behavior in order to carry out what one knows is the right course of action.

There are two interrelated branches of ethical discourse: theoretical or normative ethics and practical or applied ethics. Theoretical ethics emphasizes such things as the investigation of concepts and the analysis of principles that guide decision making in various areas such as scientific research, international business, and medicine. Practical ethics focuses on the resolution of specific ethical dilemmas, that is, what is the best course of action here and now, in this situation. Applied ethical decision making can be very complex and requires careful attention to specific idiosyncracies and subtleties, particularly in cases such as euthanasia, which deals literally with life and death.

One example of the the relationship between theoretical and practical ethics would be the following. One might want to know more about the differences between the principles of individualism and collectivism in deciding on health-care policies for an aging population. In this exercise of theoretical ethics, one might analyze the history and definition of the principles to discover how they guide action and decision making in a particular society; that is, one wants to show how policy in a particular society proceeds or should proceed to balance, on the one hand, individual freedom or *autonomy* (that is, choice and self-determination) and, on the other hand, *beneficence* or providing collectively for the needs of vulnerable people, such as the frail elderly. Research on the allocation of health care resources is an example of how theoretical ethical thinking is applied to the issues raised by an aging society.

Similarly, as one attempts to resolve specific ethical issues with respect to, say, a 75-year-old woman who has an urgent need for kidney dialysis, one draws on practical ethics. The immediate question may be whether it is the woman's responsibility as an individual to pay for dialysis or whether there is a collective right to such treatment, regardless of age. Through this practical ethical problem one may gain a more refined insight into the theoretical meaning of the principles of autonomy and beneficence.

The distinguishing feature of ethics is that it is a very broad form of reasoning, and one that is intended to include and be complementary to political, economic, and other forms of reasoning. It takes into consideration the interests of all persons directly or indirectly involved in a situation or affected by a course of action and ponders the possible outcomes of actions, again for all those involved, including society as a whole. This is what is meant by the phrase, "All things considered."

The aging of the world is creating fundamental changes at the level of the individual, the family, and society. Ethical reasoning is necessary to deal humanely with the challenges posed by this unprecedented demographic change. Questions about the rights of older persons to various kinds of social services, about the allocation of health-care resources, the forms of professional service society is obligated to provide, and about the responsibilities older persons are expected to assume are all primarily moral issues.

Furthermore, as the discussion of contemporary ontological images pointed out, Western society remains, in many important ways, an ageist society. For example, the Supreme Court of Canada upholds a policy of mandatory retirement that discriminates against workers on the basis of age. Furthermore, to the extent that eligibility for health care is discussed in relation to age, there is a danger of age discrimination. These examples, along with many others, point to an urgent need for people to be better informed about both ethics and the process of human aging. A more accurate understanding of what it means to be older is needed to make decisions for an aging society.

Often decisions are made that reflect "old" ontological assumptions or metaphors concerning what it is to be an older person. These decisions and policies are not informed by the "all things considered" aspect of moral reasoning bcause they are based on incomplete or false information. The common metaphor of aging as decline, degeneration, and incompetence, albeit a stereotype, leads to mandatory retirement policies in the workplace. There is an important role for philosophical reflection, in addition to scientific activity in this context, a reflection that involves the relationship between "is" and "ought." That is, a consideration of what constitutes a person ontologically can contribute to ethical discourse regarding the

desires to be fulfilled and the goods that society ought to provide in an aging society.

This is a significant issue because intervention decisions, whether at the level of social policy, institutions, or in a family setting, are made on the basis of the perspective held by the decision makers, either knowingly or unwittingly. From an ethical standpoint, as well as the earlier discussed epistemological perspective, it is important to acknowledge that one is always working explicitly and implicitly from a particular perspective, with a particular set of assumptions or metaphors. The ethical territory is characterized, on the one hand, by the fact that choosing one perspective on aging or another is inevitable, and, on the other hand, by the presence of multiple and often competing interpretations of aging, human nature, and human development. Thus, it becomes a problem for decision makers and service providers to decide which alternative is most accurate, correct, or true about older people. Interveners often find themselves in an ambiguous situation: pragmatically, decisions and hard choices must be made concerning older persons at the individual and the social levels, but there are no clear and adequate criteria upon which to base decisions.

The first step in resolving this problem is to bring it into the domain of moral reasoning by recognizing that it exists, regardless of how confusing the situation may appear. The crucial point here is that choices and decisions have implications whether or not one chooses to acknowledge their existence. Ethically, to do nothing is still to do something. Furthermore, there are three guidelines for working with this ambiguous situation, each of which presuppose a partnership among philosophy, the science of aging, and interveners.

First, current gerontological knowledge should make one cautious regarding general statements of later-life function, such as "all older people decline" or, conversely, "all older people continue to grow." The main problem with subscribing to such blanket statements is their exclusivity. As they age, people do decline, grow, and often do both at the same time. When exclusive claims are taken to be universal, they often lead to well-intentioned but misguided attempts to ensure that everyone conforms to a particular model or set of characteristics, for example, the "what do you expect at your age" syndrome. What is required is a critical evaluation of the knowledge base employed in guiding decisions, an evaluation that extends to training in gerontology as a necessary condition for morally informed action.

Second, in addition to developing a critical attitude toward the evolving body of gerontological knowledge, decision makers and service providers need to be sensitive to their own assumptions, images, and beliefs about aging and older persons. As discussed earlier, these images or stories form part of how people perceive each other, whether they know it or not. Problems arise when these images are adopted unthinkingly as a basis for action. Developing sensitivity to personal meanings of aging is crucial although difficult to implement, in the sense that emotional resistance and ambivalent feelings are encountered when one tackles images and projections of aging and death. This is the case in so far as the predominant ontological assumptions about aging in North American culture are negative, and positive images such as wisdom, meaningfulness, and spiritual growth are considered much less likely outcomes.

The third suggestion is that intervention be guided by a view of the elderly as older persons. The term *person* is significant here because it has a particular philosophical connotation. To see aging individuals as persons means that one should explicitly acknowledge all aspects of human functioning, including *inner aging*. Inner aging refers to the idea that human beings are engaged in an activity of choosing, valuing, and placing meaning on their situations at the same time as they are influenced by environmental constraints and social or cultural pressures. Therefore, how one understands one's own aging from the inside—the inside story—can be very different from the outside story—the images of one's aging received from the outside—images that include the way one is treated by others.

For example, some researchers note that from the point of view of aging and biography, discussed earlier, a focus on subjective meaning or personal stories facilitates an environment whereby the larger social and intersubjective story that is co-authored in a research or intervention situation will include all relevant components, that is, all things considered, minimize isolation and separation, and enhance communion and community. The discipline of philosophy is particularly suited to the implementation of such an agenda in contributing to the clarification of various contexts. This activity takes place by way of humanities research in aging, reflective forms of practice, and by way of ethics committees.

A. Selected Issues in Ethics and Aging

There are two ethical issues in gerontology that deserve further attention as they are of significant and increasing interest to researchers and practitioners. These issues are *informed consent* and *competency*.

A basic ethical requirement of any research or intervention in the field of aging is said to be the establishment of informed consent. In many contexts, professional codes of practice are not likely to provide sufficient guidelines to achieve this end. For example, in situations where qualitative approaches are being employed, informed consent, according to some researchers, amounts to a prolonged negotiation based on mutual trust. This notion goes far beyond the securing of a signature on a consent document. Informed consent also involves an ongoing awareness on the part of the intervener or researcher to ensure privacy and confidentiality, and to ensure that no harm comes to an informant as a result of the activity.

Another aspect of informed consent is that it be given voluntarily or freely. Recent research suggests that there is a significant interpretive or hermeneutic activity connected with this ethical requirement. For example, it has been noted that residents of nursing homes and other institutions are increasingly being offered opportunities to complete living wills and advance directives. Although there is agreement that these documents are intended to ensure autonomy and dignity, there is a danger that they can be implemented inappropriately. In other words, older persons are vulnerable to inadvertent coercion in these situations, through such things as fear of reprisal by their caregivers. It has been suggested that there is an ethical imperative to educate older persons regarding the implications of their decisions and to allow authentic choices to arise through reflection.

An interesting example of research in this area is the argument that in many situations, informed consent is more properly termed *negotiated* consent. This view suggests that although autonomy is a basic right of a human being, this does not mean that a person can always satisfy their individual desires in an intervention situation, such as a nursing home or a family context. The idea here is that human beings are not isolated individuals; rather, ontologically, they live out their stories with other people and in physical environments. Therefore, when one says that one is respecting autonomy, one is respecting the primacy of a personal story and personal decisions; however, decisions are based on an evaluation of the entire situation and include all those who have vested interests in that situation. Nevertheless, it is important to note that in some situations, a person does have a right to make their own decisions, such as in cases of refusing medical treatment, even to the point of putting themselves at risk.

With respect to the notion of competency or decisional capacity, a contemporary research issue centers on the problem of avoiding two extremes. For example, it is unethical to rule out as research subjects, a priori, older persons with diminished capacity through such conditions as dementia. On the other hand, a person's capacity to make informed decisions needs to be assessed, and that assessment needs to be based on more than standard instruments, because those instruments themselves may be morally questionable in terms of their impact on a person. That is, the assessment of competency itself may cause a person anxiety and loss of dignity. The suggestion is that this delicate issue requires sensitivity to and interpretation of particular situations.

A final issue concerning competence concerns the contemporary shift away from all-or-nothing definitions of this concept. In the past, older persons have been considered either competent or incompetent, and to either retain or relinquish their autonomy as a result of decisions made about them in this area. This exclusive disjunction is increasingly being understood to constitute an unethical situation, due to the fact that research is indicating that competence is a contextual and even personal phenomenon. Moreover, even frail persons may demonstrate forms of competence in nonverbal ways, or even through a significant other. For example, studies based on existentialist assumptions that highlight the primacy of meaning have indicated the complexity of the notion of competence and the fact that it seems that all human beings, including severely dementing persons, have a story to tell as long as they are alive.

As a concluding remark, philosophical contributions to gerontology help to explicate the richness and complexity of a field that involves many disciplines in both the natural and human sciences. These contributions invite a dialogue concerning the basic assumptions of extant perspectives on aging, whether they originate in science, society, or in individual stories. Philosophical reflection also introduces new possibilities into our understanding of aging and later life. Finally, philosophy contributes to the intense, complex, and urgent agenda concerning cultural values and ethically responsive decision making in an aging world.

BIBLIOGRAPHY

Achenbaum, A., & Bengtson, V. (1994). Re-engaging the disengagement theory of aging: On the history and assessment of theory development in gerontology. *Gerontologist, 34, 6,* 756–763.

Birren, J. E., & Bengtson, V. (Eds.). (1988). *Emergent theories of aging.* New York: Springer Publishing.

Birren, J. E., Kenyon, G., Ruth, J. E., Schroots, J. J. F. & Svensson, T. (Eds.) (1996). *Aging and biography: Explorations in adult development.* New York: Springer Publishing.

Cole, T. R. (1992). *The journey of life.* New York: Cambridge University Press.

Cole, T. R., & Gadow, S. (Eds.). (1986). *What does it mean to grow old? Reflections from the humanities.* Durham: Duke University Press.

Cole, T. R., Van Tassel, D. & Kastenbaum, R. (Eds.). (1992). *Handbook of the humanities and aging.* New York: Springer Publishing.

Gubrium, J. F., & Sankar, A. (Eds.). (1994). *Qualitative methods in aging research.* Thousand Oaks, CA: Sage Publications.

Jecker, N. (Ed.). (1991). *Aging and ethics.* Clifton, NJ: The Humana Press.

Kenyon, G. (Ed.). (1993). Special issue: The humanities in gerontology. *Canadian Journal on Aging, 12, 4.*

Kenyon, G., Birren, J. E., & Schroots, J. J. F. (Eds.). (1991). *Metaphors of aging in science and the humanities.* New York: Springer Publishing.

McKee, P. (Ed.). (1982). *Philosophical foundations of gerontology.* New York: Human Sciences Press.

Minois, G. (1987). *History of old age.* Chicago: University of Chicago Press.

Thornton, J., & Winkler, E. (Eds.). (1988). *Ethics and aging.* Vancouver, BC: University of British Columbia Press.

Tiso, F. (Ed.). (1982). *Aging: Spiritual perspectives.* Lake Worth, FL: Sunday Publications.

Physiological Stress

Donald A. Jurivich and Joseph F. Welk

Northwestern University Medical School

I. Molecular Responses to Stress
II. Age-Dependent Changes in the Stress Response
III. Conclusions

Heat Shock   Exposure of cells or organisms to elevated temperatures, usually 4–5°C above basal or core temperatures.
Heat Shock Genes   A class of genes preferentially expressed during cellular stress. Classes of heat shock genes are designated by the size (molecular weight) of the proteins that they encode.
Heat Shock Proteins   A collection of proteins also known as molecular chaperones that have multiple and vital functions. These include shuttling proteins from within and without the cell, disaggregating damaged proteins, tagging proteins for degradation, protecting newly synthesized polypeptides, folding new and old proteins, enhancing enzymatic activity during stress, and acting as molecular brakes for transcription (e.g., glucocorticoid receptor).
Physiological Stress   Any condition, including perturbations in heat, that creates an unfavorable environment for survival of cells, organs, or organisms.

A fundamental question in gerontology is how age might affect responses to **PHYSIOLOGICAL STRESS.** A broad spectrum of unfavorable conditions can affect cells, tissue, or whole body, and survival is often determined not only by the severity of stress but also by the response of living organisms to stressful stimuli. Physiological stress can occur with perturbations in the ambient environment such as temperature fluxes or oxygen deprivation. Alterations in the macroenvi-

ronment can also occur with accumulation of noxious gases or toxic agents. Physiological stress can also occur when cells or organs experience local perturbations in homeostasis. Examples of microenvironmental problems include nutrient deprivation, osmotic shock, radiant energy, infection, and inflammation. Obviously there are limits to survival when environmental conditions are extreme, but fortunately there are numerous adaptive responses to physiological stress that increase the chance of weathering aberrant conditions until they subside. Furthermore, chronic physiological stress may evoke a long-term adaptive process called tolerance. Thus, acute and chronic responses to physiological stress can potentially be altered by the aging process. With increased knowledge about basic responses to physiological stress, it has become increasingly apparent that age-dependent changes can alter this fundamental response at the cellular and molecular level. With this in mind, an overview of what is known about the cellular stress response is a prerequisite to understanding the mechanism of age-dependent changes in adaptive processes.

I. MOLECULAR RESPONSES TO STRESS

The cellular stress response was first dubbed the *heat shock response.* At least three decades ago, an Italian scientist working with fruit flies discovered that heat elicited a unique pattern of chromosomal puffing. Later, these changes in chromosomal structure were found to be associated with increased expression of a class of genes called the heat shock genes. These genes were dispersed amongst several chromosomes and exhibited multiple family members. Attempts to knock out or delete these genes were unsuccessful because cells apparently depended upon them under normal conditions as well as during stress. Even though the initial observations were made in fruit flies, it has been found that heat shock genes are conserved in all living organisms. Given the importance of these genes, investigators have inquired about the function of proteins encoded by messenger RNA (mRNA), which in turn is produced from heat shock gene expression, and they have worked towards an understanding of how these genes are regulated. As will be seen later, age alters regulation of heat shock gene expression, thus suggesting that senescence is most apparent during inducible rather than constitutive molecular responses.

The reason that the so-called heat shock response has given way to a more comprehensive term, the cellular stress response, is because numerous inducers of heat shock and other stress-related genes have been discovered. Specific responses have been found for ultraviolet light exposure, oxidant injury, DNA damage, and glucose deprivation. Some overlap with the heat shock response, and others appear unique. Table I lists by category many known inducers of the cellular stress response. An intriguing aspect of this list is how so many divergent factors trigger a common cellular response. The net result is enhanced cellular protection from otherwise lethal conditions. Curiously, one stressor can lead to cellular protection from other stressors. For example, heavy metal exposure will result in a response that will confer protection from heat. Both of these stressors are thought to induce protein damage, which somehow acts as a signal for a cell to shut down usual transcriptional and translational activities and to switch toward expression of heat shock and other stress proteins.

Triggering the cellular stress response requires activation of an intracellular protein called the heat shock factor (HSF) that has the capacity to bind to DNA, which in turn increases RNA polymerase activity associated with the cellular stress genes. The heightened RNA polymerase activity results in higher levels of mRNA encoded by the stress genes, and ribosomes preferentially translate these stress mRNAs into stress proteins. Stress proteins serve multiple functions and historically have been referred to as heat shock proteins (hsp). These proteins are classified according to their size or molecular weight. Broadly, hsp are

Table I Categories of Environmental Problems and Examples of Inducers of the Heat Shock Response or Its Equivalent

Ambient energy
  Heat
  Ultraviolet light
Toxins and metal accumulation

Heavy metals	Herbamycin A
Ethanol	Sodium azide
Hemin (iron)	Dinitrophenol
Nicotine	

Lipid perturbations
  Arachidonate
  Synthetic prostaglandins
  Sphingosine
Protein damage
Nutrient deprivation
  Hypoglycemia
  Hypocalcemia
  Amino acid analogs
Pharmacological agents
  Sodium salicylate
  Indomethacin
  Alkylating agents
Pathogens
  Viruses: adenovirus, herpes, influenza
  Bacteria: actinobacillus

comprised of high-, middle-, and low-molecular weight species, the most common of which is the heat shock protein 70 (hsp70) (molecular weight = 70 kD). Most hsp exist under normal conditions and their levels increase during stress.

Hsp have multiple functions during normal conditions that assume greater importance during stress. One of the functions of cellular stress or hsp includes a chaperoning function whereby other proteins are shuttled from one cellular compartment to another. Stress proteins earmark damaged proteins for degradation. They help disaggregate and possibly even refold damaged proteins. Stress proteins protect newly synthesized proteins and help them fold into a functional form. Certain enzymatic activities may be protected or enhanced by stress proteins during aberrant conditions, and in some instances the stress proteins will function as molecular brakes for gene expression. Although ongoing studies may reveal additional functions of cellular stress proteins, there is no information available whether age alters the function of these proteins either under normal or stressful conditions. Lack of information does not presuppose a qualitative dysfunction of cellular stress proteins with age, but primary interest in gerontology has been in the quantitative expression of these proteins.

One of the key features of the cellular stress response is that it is a paradigm of inducible gene expression, thus offering a fairly well-understood system to examine the question whether age affects transcriptional controls. Pivotal to induction of the cellular stress response is the heat shock transcription factor. Several HSFs have been isolated in various species, but HSF1 appears to be the primary mediator of heat shock gene expression. Figure 1 depicts a model of how HSF1 functions in human and many eukaryotic cells. Basically, HSF1 exists in the cytoplasm and nucleus of cells as a horse shoe-shaped molecule folded upon itself. Through some signal induced by stress, the cytoplasmic HSF1 trans-

locates to the nucleus, possibly facilitated by hsp. HSF1 unfolds and associates with other molecules of HSF1, forming a trimeric structure capable of binding DNA. The activated HSF1 trimer binds to heat shock elements located in the promoter region of heat shock and other genes. The heat shock elements are composed of repetitive nucleotide sequences guanine, adenosine, and adenosine (GAA). Interactions between HSF1 and the GAA sequences in the promoter region of the heat shock genes appear to be insufficient to fully increase heat shock gene expression. The exact modification of HSF1 that enhances heat shock gene expression is not known, although HSF1 phosphorylation and perhaps HSF1–protein–DNA complexes are thought to affect RNA polymerase processivity and the rate of mRNA production. [*See* DNA AND GENE EXPRESSION.]

A curious aspect about HSF1 binding to the pro-

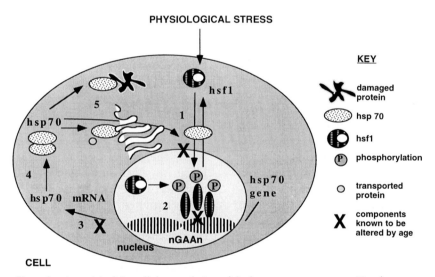

Figure I A model of the cellular regulation of the human stress response. Numbers correspond to the various transcriptional and translational steps necessary for induction of the stress response. (1) HSF1 under homeostatic conditions is folded upon itself in the cytoplasm and nucleus. Environmental stress triggers its unfolding and HSF1 accumulates in the nucleus as a homo-trimeric complex that binds to cis-acting elements in the promoter region of heat shock and other "stress genes." (2) During the course of acquiring DNA binding potential, hsf1 becomes increasingly phosphorylated and drives RNA polymerase II activity to a higher level. (3) Single exon mRNA for heat shock genes such as the hsp70 gene accumulate and are preferentially expressed by the translational apparatus. (4) Heat shock protein levels increase, and the dimeric form of hsp70 dissociates and forms complexes with other proteins. (5) Hsp70 and other molecular chaperones serve multiple functions, including protection of newly synthesized proteins, disaggregation of damaged proteins, protection of essential enzymes, and regulation of specific transcription factors.

moter region of heat shock genes is that despite continuous stress, HSF1–DNA binding is attenuated. How HSF1 falls off the promoter and resumes its inactive form as a monomeric molecule is not clear. In yeast a single phosphorylated residue on HSF has been implicated in down regulation, and there may be some function of hsp70 in disassembling multimers of HSF1. There is no transcription of the HSF1 gene itself during stress, so this relatively long-lived transcription factor appears to be regulated by posttranslational controls. After recovery from an initial stress, HSF1 may be less sensitive to reactivation by further stress unless it is more vigorous than the first. This change in HSF1 sensitivity to stressful stimuli may have importance to the aging process. For instance, prolonged exposure to stress such as might occur when neuronal cells are chronically exposed to neurotoxic amyloid could very well change the set point of the cellular stress response.

II. AGE-DEPENDENT CHANGES IN THE STRESS RESPONSE

Several models of senescence have demonstrated that heat shock gene expression is altered with time (see Table II). One of the original observations concerning the cellular stress response was by A. Y.-C. Liu who found that late-passage, fetal lung-derived fibroblasts (IMR-90) did not express hsp in response to a 42°C heat shock, whereas early-passage cells did. Both the early- and late-passage cells expressed the same class of hsp after heat shock, but cells of population doubling level (PDL) 51 produced significantly less hsp than PDL 18 cells when incorporation of ^{35}S-methionine into newly synthesized proteins was analyzed by autoradiography of proteins separated by SDS-polyacrylamide gel electrophoresis. Both the initial rate of synthesis and the absolute amounts of many hsp were reduced in the late-passage cells when compared to the early-passage cells during heat shock. The basal levels of hsp at 37°C did not appear to be altered with serial passage of the IMR-90 cells, thus emphasizing the loss of inducible gene expression as cells become senescent. The basal expression of hsp did not change with serial passage of other human diploid cell lines such as TIG-1.

Both Northern blot and nuclear runoff analysis confirmed that the *decreased* induction of hsp in late-

passage cells was due to a transcriptional problem. Maintenance of constitutive gene expression such as the β-actin gene within late-passage cells indicated that there is not a general perturbation in the RNA polymerase activity over time. Rather, signaling of heat shock gene expression is somehow disrupted.

Thus far, attenuated heat shock gene expression in senescent fibroblasts appears to be due to decreased levels of HSF–DNA binding activity. This loss of inducible HSF–DNA binding activity has been attributed to either a negative regulator of HSF or posttranslational modifications that prevent DNA binding. "Mixing" experiments whereby extracts from late-passage cells are added to extracts from early-passage cells seem to reduce the HSF–DNA binding activity in early-passage cells, thus suggesting a dominant negative inhibitor of DNA binding produced in senescent cells. These experiments are not a robust means to confirm a senescent-dependent inhibitor of HSF–DNA binding activity, and alternative results have been obtained in rat hepatocytes. Because there are several HSFs, it is possible that senescence leads to production of a modified HSF that exhibits reduced DNA binding after stress. This could occur through alternative splicing or proteolysis of pre-existing HSF.

The relationship of the cell cycle to induction of HSF may have some relevance to aging. Serum-starved or quiescent cells also seem to lack HSF–DNA binding activity after being stressed by factors other than heat. Thus, the mechanism by which late-passage fibroblasts lose heat-inducible HSF–DNA binding activity is subject to continued investigation.

Even though an altered heat shock response has been identified in senescent fibroblasts, a primary concern is whether other models of aging exhibit a similar perturbation. The issue here is whether universal, age-dependent changes exist in gene expression. N. Holbrook and A. Richardson each have contributed extensively towards our understanding of how the cellular stress response is potentially altered by age in rodents. Growing fibroblasts isolated from young and aged donor rats were found to have comparable levels of heat-inducible heat shock gene expression; however, when cells became confluent, little to no hsp70 gene expression occurred in old donor fibroblasts. After examining over 20 individual animal cultures, it was concluded that age led to approximately a 50% decline in hsp70 mRNA levels after heat shock. This

Table II Representative Studies That Examined Age-Dependent Changes in Heat Shock
Gene Expression

Model of senescence	Type of stress	Old versus young response
Human peripheral blood mononuclear cells (Kishimoto)	42°C heat shock	~30% reduction of maximal hsp70 transcription rate relative to young donor cells.
Human diploid fibroblasts IMR-90 (Liu)	42°C heat shock	~30% reduction in levels of hsp70 mRNA in late passage cells.
Aged rats (Holbrook)	Whole animal exposure to 40°C	Core body temperature of aged animals is lower than young animals. 60–75% reduction in hsp70 mRNA levels in old rat brain, lung, and skin. No changes noted in whole liver.
Rat hepatocytes (Richardson)	42.5°C heat shock	40% reduction in hsp70 mRNA levels in old donor hepatocyes.

decline in hsp70 mRNA levels appeared to occur in both skin and lung fibroblasts, with the largest age-dependent difference in hsp70–mRNA levels manifested in skin fibroblasts. Whole tissue analysis of inducible hsp70 mRNA levels showed results similar to cultured cells. Importantly, there was no age-dependent decline in β-actin mRNA, thus confirming that quantitative decreases in hsp70 mRNA after stress are specific and not general, age-related problems with RNA polymerase activity per se.

In contrast to the human senescent fibroblast model, cultured fibroblasts from aged rats apparently demonstrated a selective defect in hsp70 gene expression. mRNA for the high- and low-molecular weight hsp did not show an age-dependent decrease in their expression after heat shock. The reason for this discrepancy is not clear. Differences in culture conditions and the fact that the aged-donor rodent fibroblasts retain their proliferative potential, whereas the late-passage human fibroblasts do not, suggest that the growth state of cells somehow intersects with the aging process. The fact that the vast majority of tissue exists in a postmitotic state also suggests that age-dependent changes in gene expression during stress are likely to be most apparent in nonregenerative organs.

Investigations on the stress response in the human and animal populations have been substantially more difficult than tissue culture studies. An interesting result of whole animal studies and physiological stress is that physical restraint of male Wistar rats induces

a neurohormonal stress response resulting in elevated heat shock gene expression. Although there may be strain-specific variations in this response, age causes nearly a 75% reduction of inducible mRNA levels in adrenal tissue of restrained rats. The induction of hsp70 mRNA seems to be linked to ACTH because hypophysectomized animals did not exhibit increased hsp70 mRNA levels after restraint. Paradoxically, cultured adrenal cells do not exhibit a stress response when exposed to various concentrations of ACTH; thus other circulating factors may be involved or neurohormonal stress may sensitize the adrenal glands to hypoxic damage, which in turn activates the stress response. This paradox represents one of the difficulties in correlating *in vivo* findings with observations from tissue culture experiments. Nevertheless, induction of the heat shock response in restrained Wistar rats is an encouraging observation regarding the biological relevance of heat shock gene expression, especially because many tissue culture studies employ heat shock temperatures that generally are not encountered *in vivo*.

In addressing the issue of whether HSF1–DNA binding can be triggered by physiologically relevant elevations in temperature (39–40°C), D. Jurivich found that exposure of cells to inflammatory modulators such as arachidonate can activate HSF1–DNA binding at temperatures that normally do not do so. Recently, this investigator found that HSF1–DNA binding could be detected in the peripheral blood mononuclear cells from a febrile human donor (unpublished data). Activation of HSF1 by 42°C in cultured cells appears to be recapitulated by febrile temperatues *in vivo* and thus reinforces the link between *in vitro* research models and actual human responses to heat.

Mechanistically, several possibilities exist that may account for altered heat shock gene expression during senescence. Because the expression of many other genes such as β-actin does not appear to be affected by senescence, altered heat shock gene expression is likely to result from age-dependent changes in the signaling of the stress response. A putative candidate in the signaling cascade is HSF itself. Most studies to date indicate that aging is accompanied by a diminution in HSF–DNA binding activity. The lower levels of HSF–DNA binding activity have been documented in a gel shift assay that utilizes a short, synthetic piece of DNA, so it is not entirely certain whether decreased levels of HSF–DNA binding activity are actually reflected *in vivo*. That is, does loss of HSF–DNA binding activity as seen in a gel shift assay mean that protein–DNA binding activity is altered in the nucleus of intact cells? Thus far, no one has clarified how HSF–DNA binding levels dictate the rate of heat shock gene expression. Furthermore, D. Jurivich has found that HSF–DNA binding alone is insufficient for maximal heat shock gene expression. Thus, in addition to altered levels of HSF–DNA binding, senescence may be associated with a partially activated transcription factor.

The diminished HSF–DNA binding with age may be due to an inhibitor. This inhibitor has been proposed by some investigators who find extracts from old donor or senescent cells partially block HSF–DNA binding in extracts from young donor cells. Others have not found an inhibitor in these mixing experiments, but this is not surprising since known inhibitors of other transcription factors are not revealed by this method. No one has purified a senescent inhibitor of HSF–DNA binding activity, and with the exception of hsp70–HSF1 interactions, there is no evidence of specific protein–HSF1 interactions that might interfere with the ability of HSF to interact with DNA. Posttranslational modifications of HSF1 during senescence may render it less capable of binding to DNA. In yeast, phosphorylation of a specific amino acid residue will attenuate HSF–DNA binding; thus the possibility exists that age-dependent modifications of HSF1 alter its capac-

ity to bind to the promoter region of the heat shock genes. Initial studies suggest that some aged human donor lymphocytes contain a factor that prevents maximal induction of HSF1 multimerization. Thus a new line of investigation posits an inhibitor of HSF multimerization rather than DNA binding.

Stress-induced transient modification of HSF1 by one or more protein kinases has been observed in cultured cells. The purpose of HSF1 phosphorylation is not entirely clear, although in yeast it is thought to contribute to enhanced expression of the heat shock genes. Currently, there is little information on whether age is associated with altered HSF1 phosphorylation. A handful of stress-inducible kinases have been identified, and the author has found at least one of these to have a lower activity in aged donor cells during heat shock.

Although age-dependent perturbations in the regulation of HSF1 are likely to account for changes in heat shock gene expression, there are other possibilities that may disrupt inducible gene expression. Protein–protein interactions in the promoter region of the heat shock genes may be altered during senescence, and proteins constitutively bound to the heat shock promoter may be modified in a fashion that does not fully support transactivation of the genes. Consistent with these possibilities, mitogen activation of heat shock gene expression was found to be reduced in elderly donor peripheral blood lymphocytes. This observation might infer that control of the proximal heat shock promoter is affected by age. Whether age-dependent changes in the DNA binding proteins in the proximal promoter of the heat shock genes have any role in the diminished production of hsp mRNA during stress is not known.

As investigators seek the mechanism for altered heat shock gene expression, it is important to ask whether there is a functional consequence of age-dependent changes in this response. One question is whether altered gene expression leads to changes in the basal or inducible levels of one or more hsp. Thus far, both the human senescent fibroblast model and rodent models of aging reveal that hsp levels are not affected by age in the nonstressed state. Experiments consistently show inducible hsp70 levels are diminished with age. The affect on other hsp is less clear-cut, and in one instance there appeared to be an increase in the number of hsp in old fruit flies. Whether this observation was due to increased expression of new hsp or degradation of preexisting ones is not known. Nevertheless, changes in hsp70 levels or other hsp could alter the sensitivity of aged-donor cells to injury and death. Research has found that growing primary fibroblasts and lymphocytes from aged donors exhibit a slightly higher sensitivity to heat-induced cellular death when compared to cells from young donors, but there is very little information at large about the functional consequence of an attenuated heat shock response during aging. The growth state of the cell clearly has an impact on its sensitivity to stress, and growing cells, especially those in the mitotic or DNA synthesis phase of the cell cycle, are the most sensitive to stress-induced injury and death. Quiescent cells show a resistance to stress-induced cellular death, and factors other than hsp may mediate this cytoprotection. Some investigators cite hsp phosphorylation as a means to confer cytoprotection rather than the accumulation of hsp. The idea that increased levels of hsp contribute to cytoprotection comes from experiments where hsp are overexpressed in a cell line after transfection with a plasmid. The cell line then becomes resistant to cell death induced by extreme heat or by cytokines, such as tumor necrosis factor. Based upon these studies, a potential goal in clinical gerontology would be to enhance the human heat shock response during aging by elevating hsp levels.

Efforts to manipulate the heat shock response during senescence could take several routes. The author has found that nonsteroidal anti-inflammatory drugs (NSAIDs) have the capacity to affect HSF1 and to alter the set point for induction of this transcription factor by heat. Based upon current information, salicylate could act as a protein-binding moiety that potentially disrupts a putative inhibitor of HSF1–DNA binding or somehow alters its conformation. Regardless of how salicylate and other NSAIDs affect the transcriptional regulation of the heat shock response, the author has found that pretreatment of cultured epithelial cell lines will enhance their resistance to thermal stress. This effect needs to be examined in clinical studies, but the data do encourage pharmacological approaches towards reconstituting the cellular stress response in the elderly. In addition to pharmacological approaches, there may be gene or hsp infusion therapy that may enhance the heat shock response in certain clinical settings, such as ischemic heart or central nervous system disease.

III. CONCLUSIONS

In summary, the molecular response to physiological stress appears to be altered by the aging process in several models of aging examined thus far. The diminished induction of hsp70 gene expression during senescence is likely due to perturbations in triggering the transcription factor responsible for the increased expression of heat shock genes. Other undetermined factors also may contribute to a less efficient production of hsp mRNA. The functional consequence of altered heat shock gene expression during aging is still to be investigated. The levels of hsp are tightly regulated in cells, and during periods of stress a suboptimal response in senescent cells could result in higher accumulations of damaged protein than in young cells. Usually cellular functions such as growth are temporarily arrested by stress. This suspended state may be prolonged in senescent cells after stress or they may never recuperate. The prolonged accumulation of damaged proteins may also act as an endogenous toxin, such as has been suggested in the accumulation of amyloid. A maladaptive stress response would further decrease the chances of cellular survival in aged-donor organs.

From an evolutionary point of view, perturbations in the cellular stress response with aging may be a genetic means to heighten cellular or whole organism death due to environmental stress, thus assuring a continuous turnover of a population. It is curious that long-lived strains of nematodes and yeast appear to have higher levels of hsp than the wild-type strains, thus suggesting a critical link between longevity and stress proteins.

Finally, a recent observation that hsp reverse prion protein malformations in yeast suggests that clinical strategies to up-regulate hsp in the human population could be a valuable adjunct to neurodegeneration disorders associated with age. Additional knowledge of basic molecular responses to physiological stress potentially can lead to new clinic interventions that help reverse age-dependent decrements in cytoprotection. [See Cell Death; Growth Factors and Cellular Senescence.]

BIBLIOGRAPHY

Blake, M. J., Gershon, D., Fargnoli, J., & Holbrook, N. J. (1990). Discordant expression of heat shock protein mRNAs in tissues of heat stressed rats. *Journal of Biological Chemistry, 265*(25), 15275.

Deguchi, Y., Negoro, S., & Kishimoto, S. (1988). Age-related changes of heat shock protein gene transcription in human peripheral blood mononuclear cells. *Biochemical and Biophysical Research Communications, 157*(2), 580.

Fawcett, T. W., Sylvester, S. L., Sarge, K. D., Morimoto, R. I., & Holbrook, N. J. (1994). Effects of neurohormonal stress and aging on the activation of mammalian heat shock factor 1. *Journal of Biological Chemistry, 269*(51), 32272.

Fleming, J. E., Walton, J. K., Dubitsky, R., & Bensch, K. G. (1988). Aging results in an unusual expression of Drosophila heat shock proteins. *Procedures of the National Academy of Science USA 85,* 4099.

Heydari, A. R., WU, B., Takahashi, R., Strong, R., & Richardson, A. (1993). Expression of heat shock protein 70 is altered by age and diet at the level of transcription. *Molecular & Cellular Biology, 13*(5), 2909.

Jurivich, D. A., Sistonen, L., Kroes, R. A., & Morimoto, R. I. (1992). Effect of sodium salicylate on the human heat shock response. *Science, 255,* 1243.

Liu, A.-Y., Lin, Z., Choi, H. S., Sorhage, F. & Li, B. (1989). Attenuated induction of heat shock gene expression in aging diploid fibroblasts. *Journal of Biological Chemistry, 264*(20), 12037.

Political Attitudes and Behavior

Janie S. Steckenrider

Loyola Marymount University

I. General Trends and Misconceptions
II. Political Attitudes of Seniors
III. Seniors as Voters
IV. Seniors as Political Partisans

Cohort or Generational Effect Age differences reflecting the historical experiences and socialization events occurring for each generation. A cohort experiences a different slice of history that provides a similarity of outlook or behavior for its members but one that may be different from other age groups.

Group Benefits Perspective The orientation toward a political issue or public policy based on the individual's personal stake or gain as a member of a particular group. For example, farmers tend to support agricultural subsidies.

Intensity of Partisanship The strength of a person's loyalty to a particular political party. It can be either strong or weak.

Life Cycle or Maturational Effect Changes that occur as an individual gets older due to the aging process or movement through the life cycle.

Low-Stimulus Elections Nonpresidential-type elections. These elections include the off-year congressional elections, state elections, and local elections, such as city council, school board, and water district. Media coverage is minimal and local issues dominate. Voter turnout in these elections is considerably lower than in presidential elections.

Party Identification An individual's self-proclaimed preference for a particular political party.

Voter Turnout The percentage of the eligible vo-

ting population that participates (votes) in a particular election.

The **POLITICAL ATTITUDES AND BEHAVIOR** of older persons confirm that they are actively engaged and influential participants in politics. Linked by common political concerns and the collective benefits of government age-related programs, the elderly have similar political attitudes on some issues. Most issues, however, are not distinguished by age, with older persons pitted against younger persons; instead senior citizens fall into all attitudinal categories of the political spectrum. The elderly are a heterogeneous group, and their diverse political attitudes reflect their varied group identifications based on income, education, party identification, gender, occupation, ethnicity, religion, or political ideology. Any of these characteristics may be more politically important than age. Even on age-related political issues, these group identities can be more salient as the elderly are often less supportive of increasing old-age benefits than other age groups. The political behavior of seniors reveals the highest voter registration of any age group and the highest voter turnout, especially in low-stimulus elections. This increased political participation with age is a maturational effect. The elderly are also more likely to identify with a political party and have stronger partisan loyalties than younger persons. The current elderly population identifies more with the Democratic Party, although elderly cohorts of previous decades had stronger ties with the Republican Party. These contrasting patterns of the elderly's identification with a particular political party reflect generational or cohort effects.

I. GENERAL TRENDS AND MISCONCEPTIONS

A. General Trends

The political influence of the elderly is a given in our political system. The elderly are beneficiaries of two of the largest governmental programs, Social Security and Medicare. By their political participation and activism, both through old-age political organizations and at the grassroots level, seniors have mobilized to defend old-age programs from the sizable reductions besieging other governmental programs over the last decade. The repeal of the Medicare Catastrophic Coverage Act in 1989 after intense political lobbying and protests of senior citizens indicates their influence. [See HEALTH CARE AND SERVICES.]

Political candidates and officeholders act on the belief of the elderly's potential power and are reluctant, if not unwilling, to take political stands that seniors might oppose. Politicians fear seniors will mobilize as a bloc to punish them at the polls. Older persons do turn out to vote at substantially higher rates than other age groups, but seniors rarely vote as a monolithic block or differ markedly in their vote choice from other ages. However, seniors are politically well organized and are represented by numerous advocacy groups who make their positions known to politicians. Yet some of the elderly's political power is aptly described as "an electoral bluff," where the organizations have convinced elected officials of the elderly's potential for collective action.

B. Misconceptions about the Elderly's Political Attitudes and Behavior

There are four basic misconceptions about the political attitudes and behavior of the elderly that research has dispelled. First is the myth that the elderly are a monolithic bloc and speak politically with one voice. Although the elderly do share common concerns due to age, the reality is the older population is a heterogeneous group with diversity in wealth, education, political ideology, religion, and health status. Thus, how seniors think and act politically reflect these differ-

ences. The second inaccurate assumption about older persons is that they are inherently more conservative than younger people. It is true that on some political issues, seniors hold more conservative views than younger adults, but this is not because older persons become more conservative as they age. Early research did support this notion of a conservative change with age, but current research recognizes these age differences are the result of the historical socialization patterns of different generations.

The third myth is older persons tend to withdraw or disengage from politics. Again, current research rejects earlier theories and finds older persons *remain* involved and interested in political activities well into their later years. In fact, with the increased leisure time in retirement, the involvement with senior citizen advocacy organizations, and the stake in preserving government benefits, old age is often a time of increased political activity and interest. [See LEISURE; RETIREMENT.]

Fourth, a currently popular assumption is that older persons are entirely self-interested and opposed to public policies benefiting other generations. This notion of generational conflict has labeled the elderly as the Greedy Geezers. Although older persons are concerned about their government benefits and have flexed their political muscles to protect their programs, studies find seniors are supportive of programs for families and children. Surveys on support for old-age programs often find that younger people are more supportive than the elderly who would receive the benefits. The diverse group identifications of the elderly extend to generational issues, and it is a rare issue distinguished by the elderly versus younger persons.

II. POLITICAL ATTITUDES OF SENIORS

A. Political Ideology and Issue Positions

A key question in examining political attitudes of seniors is, Do older persons hold different positions on political issues than other age groups? The answer is sometimes, and the existence and extent of such age differences depend on the issue. However, on most issues the elderly, like the young and middle aged, are distributed across the political spectrum from liberal to conservative. Their issue positions reflect their social, economic, and political diversity.

When age differences in political attitudes do occur, there are two possible explanations. One explanation is that people change their attitudes as they get older. This is a maturational or aging effect emphasizing the inherent change as an individual moves through the life cycle. The second explanation is that age differences in attitudes are a reflection of the historical experiences and socialization events occurring for each generation. A cohort experiences a different "slice" of history, which provides a similarity of outlook for its members but one that may be different from other age groups. These age differences, which are not age changes, reflect generational or cohort effects. Both approaches must be considered when explaining age differences in political attitudes.

The stereotype of political attitudes of seniors takes a maturational approach and assumes that people become more conservative with age. This myth is not supported by the elderly's self-described political ideology. When asked in a 1992 survey to identify themselves as liberal, moderate, or conservative, older persons did not describe themselves as significantly more conservative than other age groups. Table I shows that persons ages 65–74 and aged 75 and over are the least liberal, but the middle aged (36–49 and 50–64 age groups) are the most conservative on this measure. Instead of conservatism, these data highlight the trend toward political moderation in old age. This measure supports no clear-cut pattern of age differences and indicates the age groups are divided across the ideological spectrum.

Another way to examine political attitudes is to explore the positions of seniors on various issues. The evidence is older persons are more conservative on some issues but have the same concerns and beliefs as other age groups on many issues. Survey data indicate older persons tend to be more conservative than younger adults on many social issues including women's rights, abortion, drug legalization, pollution, civil rights, and law and order. Table II displays survey results of attitudes toward social issues and shows a tendency for more conservative views among the older adults. People over 50 are more likely to favor restrictions on abortion, to oppose government protection from job discrimination for gays, to oppose allowing homosexuals to serve in the military, and to favor allowing school prayer. But the differences between the age groups are often slight, and no clear pattern of a steady increased conservatism with age appears on any issue.

This slight conservatism on social issues is likely due to generational or cohort effects not maturational effects. Older persons do not necessarily become more intolerant or rigid with age, the age differences may reflect the younger generations' socialization experiences during the current environment of varied lifestyles. Many of these issues, such as women's rights or gays in the military, were not even on the political agenda when the older cohorts were socialized as young adults, and they are not as comfortable with the recent social changes.

B. Group Benefit Trends

Much of the inquiry since the mid-1970s into political attitudes of the elderly has centered on the extent of their support of aging policies or whether they take a self-interested perspective to politics. The group benefits approach based on the self-interest principle assumes people choose those issue positions that benefit them personally. For example, taxpayers generally prefer proposals for lower taxes, farmers favor congressional candidates who endorse agricultural subsidies, and teachers tend to support gubernatorial candidates who emphasize funding for education. In turn, older persons would be expected to adopt political attitudes on aging issues and policies that further their own interests, such as increased government spending for old age programs like Social Security and Medicare.

The popular assumption of a strong group benefits perspective among the elderly has prompted current

Table I Self-Described Ideology by Age[a]

Ideology	Age				
	17–35	36–49	50–64	65–74	75+
Liberal (%)	31	33	21	19	21
Moderate (%)	32	25	33	40	40
Conservative (%)	37	43	46	42	40
Total[b]	100	101	100	101	101

[a]Source: American National Election Study, 1992. Data provided by the Inter-university Consortium for Political and Social Research.

[b]Totals may not add up to 100% due to rounding.

Table II Attitudes toward Social Issues: Percentage in Each Group Who Agree[a]

	Age				
	17–35	36–49	50–64	65–74	75+
Abortion should not be restricted.	49	52	39	42	38
Gays should be protected from job discrimination.	61	63	58	59	57
Homosexuals should be allowed to serve in the military.	61	64	51	53	51
Death penalty should be used for murder convictions.	79	78	82	81	79
School prayer should be allowed.	32	35	37	36	50

[a]Source: American National Election Study, 1992. Data provided by the Inter-university Consortium for Political and Social Research.

attention among journalists, politicians, and researchers to the notion of generational conflict. Claims that the elderly are receiving more than their fair share of government benefits is increasingly coming from various quarters and have even sparked organized groups such as AGE (Americans for Generational Equity). Popular assumptions aside, generational conflict does not appear in attitudes toward old-age programs, as support is strong among all age groups. Recent surveys find little evidence of widespread generational conflict where older persons are pitted against younger generations in a battle over government benefits. In fact, it is often older persons who are less supportive of increased benefits in old-age programs than younger people. [See GENERATIONAL DIFFERENCES.]

Instead of indicating generational conflict, attitudes toward old-age government benefits demonstrate widespread popular support among all age groups, as seen in Table III. There are few age differences in opposition to taxing Social Security benefits and in support of expanding Medicare to cover nursing home care. Between 80 and 90% of all age groups share a common attitude on these issues. Interestingly, views toward the level of Social Security benefits actually show the opposite of generational conflict, as over 60% of the younger age groups (ages 17–35 and ages 36–49) feel the current level is too low whereas only 51% of those aged 65–74 and 41% of those over age 75 feel it is too low. Most of those over age 65—those who are receiving Social Security benefits—are satis-

fied with the current level. Almost no one of any age feels the benefit level is too high. These patterns show anything but generational conflict in attitudes toward age-related programs.

The lack of age differences in attitudes toward aging policies can be explained by three intervening factors that mitigate the group benefits principle. First, it is in the self-interest of younger persons to expand old-age government programs if it means

Table III Attitudes toward Government Benefits for Older Persons by Age[a]

	Age				
	17–35	36–49	50–64	65–74	75+
Level of Social Security benefits (%)					
Too low	66	63	57	51	41
About right	30	34	41	48	57
Too high	4	3	2	1	2
Total	100	100	100	100	100
Favor taxes on Social Security benefits (%)					
Favor	13	13	12	15	10
Oppose	87	87	88	85	90
Total	100	100	100	100	100
Expand Medicare to cover nursing home care (%)					
Favor	88	85	84	88	87
Oppose	12	15	16	12	13
Total	100	100	100	100	100

[a]Source: American National Election Study, 1992. Data provided by the Inter-university Consortium for Political and Social Research.

less responsibility in their care of an aging relative. Old-age benefits are in the self-interest of all generations, not just older persons, leading to little variation in attitudes, as all age groups favor these programs. Second, the entire self-interest model may be flawed and should be used with caution because it assumes age is more important to the senior than any other characteristic. The elderly person is a composite of other identifications including gender, economics, partisanship, ethnicity, family status, health, religion, and education. These other characteristics are generally long-enduring, strong, and as salient in the political attitudes of the elderly as for younger persons. Lastly, self-interest might not create considerable age differences toward aging policies because the elderly population itself is quite heterogeneous. Given seniors' diversity, it may be impossible even to speak of the elderly's self-interest or of a single group benefits perspective.

III. SENIORS AS VOTERS

A. Voter Registration

The first hurdle in the voting process in the United States is registering to vote. Older persons have the highest level of voter registration, as shown in Table IV which traces voter registration from 1966 to 1992. Over three-quarters of persons over age 65 are registered to vote compared to just half of the 18–24 age group. Looking at voter registration over the past decades, much of the historical trend is an increase

with age and a slight drop-off in registration among the elderly. Since 1988, however, older persons have the highest level of registration of any age group, and the drop-off in old age has disappeared. Another trend in voter registration shown in Table IV is the relatively stable level of voter registration among those over age 65, whereas it has decreased among other age groups since the late 1960s.

B. Voter Turnout in Presidential Elections

Political participation encompasses a broad range of activities including precinct work, monetary contributions, working for a candidate, contacting elected officials, and serving on community boards, but a basic form of political participation is going to the polls and voting in an election. Older persons are active political participants and have the highest turnout in both presidential and congressional elections (see Table V). Like voter registration, age differences in turnout appear as the younger age groups have a much lower propensity.

Voter turnout in presidential elections is higher overall than off-year congressional elections, because more voters are mobilized by the importance of the office and the extensive media attention. The elderly have consistently exercised their right to vote in large numbers, and voter turnout increases steadily with age. In the 1992 presidential election, 70% of those over age 65 voted compared to only 43% of the 18–24 age group. Like voter registration, the pattern over the past few decades is increasing voter

Table IV Percentage of Registered Voters by Age—1966–1992[a,b]

	Presidential elections							Congressional elections						
	1992	1988	1984	1980	1976	1972	1968	1990	1986	1982	1978	1974	1970	1966
18–24	53	48	51	49	51	59	56	40	42	42	41	41	41	44
25–44	65	63	67	66	66	71	72	58	61	62	60	60	65	68
45–64	75	76	77	76	76	80	81	71	75	76	74	74	78	79
65+	78	78	77	75	71	76	76	77	77	75	73	70	74	74
Overall	68	67	68	67	67	72	74	62	64	64	63	62	68	70

[a]In the years prior to 1972, the 18–24 age group includes persons 18–20 years old in Georgia and Kentucky, 19 and 20 in Alaska, and 20-year-olds in Hawaii.

[b]Source: U.S. Bureau of the Census, 1993. Current Population Reports, Series P-20, Nos. 192, 253, 293, 322, 344, 370, 383, 405, 414, 440.

Table V   Percentage of Voter Turnout by Age—1964–1992[a,b]

	Presidential elections								Congressional elections						
	1992	1988	1984	1980	1976	1972	1968	1964	1990	1986	1982	1978	1974	1970	1966
18–24	43	36	41	40	42	50	50	51	20	22	25	24	24	30	31
25–44	58	54	58	59	59	63	67	69	41	41	45	43	42	52	53
45–64	70	68	70	69	69	71	75	76	56	59	62	59	57	64	65
65+	70	69	68	65	62	64	66	66	60	61	60	56	51	57	56
Overall	61	57	60	59	59	63	68	69	45	46	49	46	45	55	55

[a]In the years prior to 1972, the 18–24 age group includes persons 18–20 in Georgia and Kentucky, 19 and 20 in Alaska, and 20-year-olds in Hawaii.

[b]Source: U.S. Bureau of the Census. Current Population Reports, Series P-20, Nos. 174, 228, 293, 344, 383, 393, 414, 440.

turnout among older persons, while turnout has declined among all other age groups (see Table V). Since 1964, seniors have consistently outpaced overall voter turnout.

The age differences of increased voter turnout seen in Table V are recognized as maturational or aging effects. The low turnout of the 18–24 age group is attributed to their overriding concerns with the nonpolitical aspects of their lives, such as school, job, career, marriage, and family which distract them from political participation. As individuals move through the life cycle, they become more integrated into the community and more concerned with electoral decisions. With age and the additional roles the individual assumes, such as homeowner, parent, and taxpayer, comes a heightened concern about public policies. Other factors leading to the age differences in voter turnout are the increased leisure time older persons have to devote to politics and the elderly's desire to protect their expanded stake in governmental programs. The continuation of governmental benefits and services provided to the elderly is an important impetus to voice their electoral choices.

C. Low-Stimulus Elections

Another key age difference in voter participation is found in low-stimulus elections. These are nonpresidential-type elections when state and/or local issues and candidates are determined, media coverage is minimal, partisan labels are often nonexistent, and the overall psychological identification with voting as a civic duty is less intense. It is not a surprise that the turnout rate for all age groups exhibits considerable drop-off from the presidential election, as only the more interested, more partisan, and more involved participate. Table V compares the turnout in presidential elections with congressional elections, one form of low stimulus elections. Older people, however, have far less drop-off in congressional elections than other age groups and consistently outpace younger voters. Voter turnout by the elderly in the 1990 congressional election was 60%, which was three times the 20% turnout of the 18–24-year-olds.

The participation of older persons in low-stimulus elections increases their political clout because they consistently vote regardless of the type of election. Using a ratio of those who voted in 1992 to those also voting in 1990, there is a consistent pattern of

Table VI   Turnout Drop-Off in Low-Stimulus Elections by Age[a]

	Turnout ratio, 1990 to 1992
18–24	.47
25–44	.71
45–64	.80
65+	.86
Overall	.74

[a]Source: U.S. Bureau of the Census, 1993. Current Population Reports, Series P-20, Nos. 174, 192, 228, 253, 293, 322, 344, 370, 383, 393, 405, 414, 440.

Table VII Percentage of 1992 Presidential Vote by Age[a]

| | Age | | | | |
	18–35	36–49	50–64	65–74	75+
Bush	34	32	37	32	40
Clinton	43	49	48	54	52
Perot	23	19	16	14	8
Total[b]	100	100	101	100	100

[a]Source: American National Election Study, 1992. Data provided by the Inter-university Consortium for Political and Social Research.

[b]Note: Totals may not add up to 100% due to rounding.

an increased ratio of turnout with age, as displayed in Table VI. The 1990–1992 ratio is .86 for the elderly and only .47 for the 18–24 age group. This pattern is instructive because it demonstrates the voting influence of older persons may be even greater in off-year elections when overall voting interest is low and seniors make up a higher proportional share of voters. Seniors' consistent turnout in low-stimulus elections suggests their potential political strength goes beyond their higher voter registration and higher turnout.

D. Elderly Vote in the 1992 Presidential Election

Voting behavior of the elderly in national elections differs little from other age groups, and their electoral choices in the 1992 presidential election is indicative of this (see Table VII). Older persons, like all other age groups, cast most of their votes for Clinton, which is not a surprise given the Democratic leanings of the older population and the fact that Clinton received the most votes overall. Although the historical tendency is generational similarity in vote choice with only a few percentage point differences between the age groups, the 1992 election with the candidacy of Ross Perot produced interesting age patterns. People over 65 cast the majority of their votes for Clinton compared to only 43% of the 18–35 age group, and those over age 75 were also the most supportive of Bush. The most obvious difference in vote choice, however, is the age pattern of the Perot vote. Only 8% of those age 75 and older rejected the two major party candidates to vote for Perot compared to 23% of the 18–24

years olds. This age pattern toward the third-party candidate parallels the weaker partisan ties among younger voters.

IV. SENIORS AS POLITICAL PARTISANS

A. Political Party Identification

Political party identification is an individual's psychological attachment to a political party and is measured on the dimensions of partisanship versus party independence, the specific party affiliation, and the intensity of party loyalty. Older persons are more likely to identify with a political party, whereas younger persons are inclined to claim partisan independence, as shown in Table VIII. Three of four persons over age 75 claim a party identification compared to just over half of those persons aged 17–35. The movement with age from political independence to partisanship is attributed to life cycle or maturational effects. As individuals age, their political ideas come into clearer focus and their partisan activities increase.

Generational effects, however, explain the age differences in the pattern of identification with a particular political party. The current elderly generation identifies more with the Democratic Party and less with the Republican Party than younger persons (see Table IX). The Democratic leanings of older persons trace back to their early adult years of socialization during the political climate of the De-

Table VIII Percentage of Partisan Loyalty by Age[a]

| | Age | | | | |
	17–35	36–49	50–64	65–74	75+
Partisanship					
Identify with party	55	61	65	67	75
Independent	45	39	35	33	25
Total	100	100	100	100	100
Strength of partisanship (party identifiers only)					
Strong partisans	37	46	54	61	61
Weak partisans	63	54	46	39	39
Total	100	100	100	100	100

[a]Source: American National Election Study, 1992. Data provided by the Inter-university Consortium for Political and Social Research.

Table IX Percentage of Party Identification by Age[a]

			Age		
	17–35	36–49	50–64	65–74	75+
Democrat	29	37	39	44	44
Independent	45	39	35	33	25
Republican	26	24	26	23	31
Total	100	100	100	100	100

[a]Source: American National Election Study, 1992. Data provided by the Inter-university Consortium for Political and Social Research.

pression and Franklin Roosevelt's leadership with New Deal programs. As young persons coming of age during this political era, they developed a loyalty to the Democratic Party and have retained these partisan ties into their old age.

Further support of the generational effects involved in political party identification comes from earlier decades when older persons had strong ties to the Republican Party. Initially, researchers believed that the consistent age differences were maturational effects and concluded people not only naturally became more Republican as they got older but also more conservative as well. Later research utilizing cohort analysis to follow cohorts across time found no evidence of change toward Republican Party identification with age and recognized the generational effects. Contrasting the current Democratic ties of today's elderly with the Republican loyalties of earlier generations of older persons illustrates that partisan ties reflect a generation's early political socialization experiences. The research on political party identification points out that age differences do not always mean age changes. [See Cohort Studies.]

B. Political Party Intensity

Political party identification is also examined in terms of strength of partisanship or how intensely the individual describes his attachment to a specific political party, as strong or weak. Older persons have strong attachments to their political party, and most describe themselves as strong partisans, as shown in Table VIII. Younger persons claiming a political party identification, on the other hand, are far more likely to describe their party loyalty as weak. This increasing partisan strength with age is attributed to maturational effects that individuals become stronger partisans as they get older.

BIBLIOGRAPHY

Binstock, R. H. (1992). Older voters and the 1992 presidential election. *The Gerontologist, 32*, 601–606.

Button, J., & Rosenbaum, W. (1990). Gray power, gray peril, or gray myth? The political impact of the aging in local sunbelt policies. *Social Science Quarterly, 71*, 25–38.

Day, C. L. (1990). *What older Americans think: Interest groups and aging policy*. Princeton, NJ: Princeton University Press.

Day, C. L. (1993). Older Americans' attitudes toward the Medicare Catastrophic Coverage Act of 1988. *Journal of Politics, 55*, 167–177.

Day, C. L. (1993). Public opinion toward costs and benefits of Social Security and Medicare. *Research on Aging, 15*, 279–298.

Rhodebeck, L. A. (1993). The politics of greed? Political preferences among the elderly. *The Journal of Politics, 55*, 342–364.

Rosenbaum, W. A., & Button, J. W. (1993). The unquiet future of intergenerational politics. *The Gerontologist, 33*, 481–490.

Postponement of Aging

Alvar Svanborg

University of Illinois at Chicago

I. Introduction
II. Exogenous Factors Influencing Aging
III. Conclusion

Cohort A group of individuals sharing a statistical characteristic, (e.g., date of birth) who are used in epidemiologic or other statistical studies of disease.

Estrogens A generic term for estrus-producing steroid compounds; the female sex hormones. In humans, estrogen is formed in the ovary, the adrenal cortex, the testis, and the fetoplacental unit, and it has various functions in both sexes.

Exogenous Growing by additions to the outside; developed or originating outside the organism.

Idiopathy A morbid state of spontaneous origin; one neither sympathetic nor traumatic.

Morbidity The condition of being diseased or morbid.

Osteoarthritis (OA) Noninflammatory degenerative joint disease occurring chiefly in older persons characterized by degeneration of the articular cartilage, hypertrophy of bone at the margins, and changes in the synovial membrane.

Osteoporosis Abnormal rarefaction of bone, seen most commonly in the elderly; may be idiopathic or secondary to other diseases such as thyrotoxicosis.

Overdiagnosis When manifestations of aging have been understood as symptoms of disease.

Progestin Name originally given to the crude hormone of the corpora lutea. It has since been isolated in pure form and is now known as progesterone. The name progestin is used for certain synthetic or natural progestational agents.

Proteoglycans Any group of glycoproteins present in connective tissue and formed of subunits of disaccharides linked together and joined to a protein core; the proteoglycans that include the mucopolysaccharides with their protein moiety, serve as a binding or cementing material.

Reactivation Here used to identify rehabilitation of frail older persons whose condition requests special knowledge in geriatric medicine and treatment through geriatric team efforts.

Underdiagnosis When symptoms of disease have been understood as manifestations of aging.

Indirect evidence has accumulated indicating or showing that **POSTPONEMENT** of some important manifestations of aging-related functional decline is possible. There are, however, not yet available systematic perspective lifelong intervention programs providing scientific evidences for how and to what extent preventive interventions might be successful. Knowledge is accumulating indicating that preventive or postponing measures would be meaningful also when starting at ages when aging-related morphological and functional decline has become obvious, and that intervention efforts should in the future become a part of good public health practice. This article gives examples on possible intervention measures.

I. INTRODUCTION

When Cicero in 54 B.C. wrote his song of praise to old age, "De Senectute," he was 63-years-old—a very high age at that time. Since then the average longevity has increased from around 20 to 75 years in similar

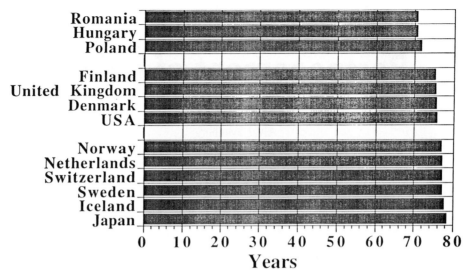

Figure I   Life expectancy at birth in 1990.

populations. During recent decades marked change in longevity has been observed also in a shorter perspective (i.e., between age cohorts born with only a few years interval). Some parts of the more than threefold increase in longevity since Cicero's days, and the ongoing faster accelerating changes in longevity during the twentieth century, are obviously related to a growing understanding of the nature and importance of hygiene, nutrition, biomedical advancements, as well as lowering risks for disease or introducing treatments, and on socioeconomic developments.

There are, however, reasons for questioning to what extent these remarkable improvements in vitality and health also mirror a *postponement* of aging itself.

Variations in longevity exist between countries with similar socioeconomic structure, occurrence of disease during the life span, and availability of medical care. This is the case, for example, in the Nordic countries of Denmark, Finland, Iceland, and Sweden (Fig. 1). Such variations also trigger questions about the extent to which differences in aging itself might contribute to differences in longevity.

Detailed longitudinal population studies of aging and health have provided information indicating that a considerable proportion of older persons (at least up to 75–80 years of age) are without symptoms that can be referred to as known diseases. These findings have allowed a sharpening of diagnostic criteria and

separate studies of manifestations of aging also at ages when morbidity becomes common. Results of such studies indicate that exogenous factors summarized in terms as lifestyle, environment, and availability of medical care are influencing not only medical health, but also morphological and functional manifestations of aging.

The aim of this article is to summarize certain observations demonstrating or strongly indicating that, besides genetic factors, personal lifestyle, living circumstances, and availability of adequate medical care are, in fact, influencing aging *per se*. As a consequence, the possibilities for efforts to postpone negative consequences of aging-related morphological and functional decline and to prolong creativity and independence has to be brought to the forefront for realistic and relevant considerations.

II. EXOGENOUS FACTORS INFLUENCING AGING

A. Health

The Framingham studies, the Alameda County studies, the Baltimore Longitudinal Studies in the United States, and the longitudinal study of 70-year-olds in Gothenburg, Sweden, as well as the functional assessments of men in Jyväskylä, Finland, are examples of population studies that have illustrated age-related change in manifestations of aging *per se* as well as possible influences on aging of exogenous factors. Attempts to identify aging itself from morbidity imply detailed medical examination and, especially in older population samples, longitudinal follow-ups to reveal initially subclinical morbidity or overdiagnosis. The evaluation of exogenous influences on aging requires not only detailed longitudinal information in the fields of biology and health, but also about social and psychological well-being.

Aging-related functional decline reflects itself both as lowered resistance to disease and lowered ability to mobilize reserves when needed. Diseases often have also an indirect negative effect on performance through decline in appetite, inadequate intake of fluid and food, lowered muscle strength and balance, and so on. Early and correct diagnosis and treatment has, therefore, been found to be even more important for old frail people than in younger individuals in order to prevent unnecessary functional decline. Intervention studies have demonstrated that older person's main fears concern their health, and that careful and detailed health surveys are highly appreciated. There are many reasons to believe that adequate health care should be one factor postponing not only decline in health, but also age-related dysfunction.

B. Cognition and Sensory Deprivation

Several studies indicate that when abnormal conditions are carefully identified older healthy persons show mainly a decline in psychomotor speed, which also is the main reason for change in cognition in general. As far as personality traits are concerned the previous traditional view that the old persons's mind should become more rigid has apparently not been verified as a cause of aging in itself. From the perspective of possible interventions to postpone aging, the main considerations thus include awareness of change in speed and adapting the methodology to suit the slower old person. Studies have indicated that psychomotor speed often can be "trained" or accelerated by systematic activation in people above age 75–80. In general, however, usage can obviously only postpone a functional decline in psychomotor speed. Practical experiences also indicate that the possible personality change caused

by aging *per se* is not a significant hindrance for intervention directed to already old persons. This is exemplified by the high participation rate in a broad medical–social intervention study added to the longitudinal study of 70-year-olds in Gothenburg, Sweden. The general clinical experience is, on the contrary, that when older people begin to feel functional decline, they usually become an interested audience for health promotion and disease prevention. The problem is more to change their often too negative attitudes toward the existence of possibilities for a postponement of manifestations of aging. They also fear that participation in activities that tax them physically, intellectually, or emotionally might constitute dangerous stressful events. Realistic information that is effectively mediated and illustrated about possible gains and risks are essential components of intervention measures.

Changes in vision and hearing are common. Modern illumination techniques allowing more light without causing light reflexes and glaring can in most older persons compensate for vision problems caused by aging *per se*. Another practically important aging-related visual change concerns the lengthening of the time it takes to adapt from light to darkness. Coming out in a dark street or driving into a dark tunnel might mean much longer time of adaptation than at a younger age. There are no reports indicating that aging-related visual decline can be preserved through interventions directed towards the individual. Postponing measures have to focus on compensation through technical aids and be directed toward prevention of negative events caused by aging-related dysfunction.

Aging-related hearing changes are common, causing not only communication problems, but also increased risk for social isolation, inactivity, and accidents. The ability to localize sounds (e.g., those coming from behind) is very efficient indeed when we are young. The ability of the two ears to register the short difference in time sounds reaching them become less efficient with presbycusis (i.e., aging-related decline in hearing). A considerable proportion of hearing defects at old age are due also to other factors than aging itself (e.g., by increasing age, longer exposure to noise, and nerve-damaging effects of drugs and other compounds). There is no clear evidence that hearing deficits caused by aging itself can be actively counteracted.

C. Striated Muscles and Joints

As described elsewhere, the number of muscle fibers and their functional efficiency decline during aging, and especially after around age 60. There is a greater reduction of fibers with the ability to twitch fast, implying a reduction of the speed of contraction. Several studies have shown that systematic strength training can improve muscle strength and also speed of contraction. A comparison of the effects of extremity muscle training in physically inactive young and old individuals indicated that the improvement is proportionally the same, although older persons start lower and can never reach the same performance level as the young ones. This ability both to regain a better muscle function and postpone decline seems to prevail still at ages above 80 (Fig. 2). The importance of a good muscular performance for quality of many components of life is obvious. A common disastrous event is falling and fractures. Strength and speed of muscle contraction is crucial for prevention of falls.

The range of motion of extremity joints has been shown to be in general well preserved in older people without joint abnormalities, although increased stiffness in joing capsules and ligaments is common. In general, aging-related changes in joint motion do not cause limitations for the use of arms and legs. Back problems have been reported by one-third of 70-year-olds, and constant back pains by approximately 10%. In the vast majority such pains or other problems were due to, for example, osteoarthrosis or sequelae of traumatic injuries. In the back, and especially in the cervical area, the range of motion is, however, somewhat restricted in older people, and stiffness often causes functional limitations. Many older persons have, for example, difficulty turning the head sufficiently when attempting to put a car in reverse. To what extent back stiffness might be reversible or preventable, and how, needs to be studied systematically.

D. Osteoarthritis

Osteoarthritis (OA) is common in older persons. It is, however, not clear to what extent, if any, OA is a consequence of aging itself. Such degenerative disorders have been considered to a great extent to be due to aging. Biochemically, aging-related changes in, for example, water content and alterations in proteoglycans in cartilage have been shown to be different that changes in OA. OA is presumably the result of many different factors that still have to be fully characterized. The pathways leading to OA and the risk factors

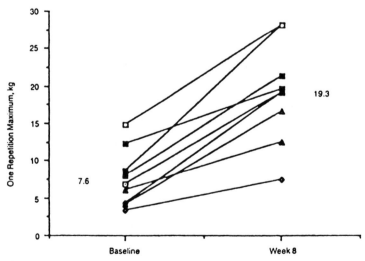

Figure 2 Effects of weight training on knee extensor strength. Maximum left knee extensor strength before and after 8 weeks of high-intensity progressive-resistance training in nine subjects aged 87–96 years ($p < .0001$ compared with baseline). Similar strength gains were seen in the right leg. Symbols represent individual subjects. (From Fiatrone, M. A., Manks, E. C., Ryan, N. D., 1990. High intensity strength training in nonagenarians. *JAMA, 263,* No. 22, 3029.)

involved are also different for different joints and have yet to be fully characterized. To what extent aging of cartilage is at all even a contributing factor for OA is thus not clear. This is the case also for a possible influence of the ordinary wear-and-tear of joints over the life span. Repetitive traumatic injuries (e.g., in sports) has been linked to permanent cartilage damage and other joint injuries causing joint instability and symptoms similar to "idiopathic" forms of OA. On the other hand, there is evidence that a certain degree of loading of joint cartilage is necessary to maintain healthy cartilage. Practical experience also indicates that well-trained muscles are crucial to the maintenance of joint stability. Even if cartilage in the old joint will be shown to be less resistant to loading, there is no proven evidence that a reasonable loading of joints should increase the risk for OA. Marked obesity, especially obesity that influences the mechanics of the knee joints, however, should be a principal target for prevention. It is known that obesity is accompanied also by increased prevalence of OA in the finger joints, which is one observation indicating that obesity involves metabolic changes with causal relationships to OA. Avoidance of certain extremes such as obesity and traumatic injuries can thus be expected to postpone joint changes leading to this type of joint problem in old age. In general, however, proven knowledge about measures to prevent or postpone the most common forms of OA is not yet available.

E. Skeleton

Osteoporosis (low bone mass) is one of the important negative consequences of aging, causing compression fractures of spine and fractures due to traumatic injuries. Several epidemiological studies have demonstrated a nonage-related progressive increase in the hip fracture incidence in northern Europe (Fig. 3). In Gothenburg, Sweden, where the frequency of hip fractures more than doubled between 1965 and 1983, only 20% of the cases could be explained on the basis of age factors. Age-standardized incidence of hip fracture in rural areas was found to be significantly lower than in big cities. The conclusion is that a difference in bone quality is caused by lifestyle factors, and possibly dfferences in the social structure. There is, thus, no evidence that such regional differences are due to any disease, but to differences in the rate of development of osteopenia. Osteopenia and osteopo-

rosis are related in most cases to aging and not to disease. Osteoporosis and concomitant increase in risk of bone deformation and fractures is thus influenced both by aging and exogenous factors (e.g., by lifestyle). Aims to postpone osteopenia should consider, for example, that reasonable physical loading has been demonstrated to slow down the loss of bone mass also at ages above 70–80 not only by increasing the nutritional intake of energy and nutrients such as calcium, vitamin D, and proteins involved in the metabolism of the matrix of the skeleton, but also through other mechanisms working on the skeleton. "Skeletal" training through physical activation does not imply a recommendation to suddenly start heavy lifting and other heavy loading body-building activities. Available information indicates that less heavy activation (e.g., systematic loading in the form of daily walking) would give skeletal stimulation without obvious risk for skeletal injuries. As previously mentioned, tobacco smoking (Fig. 4) and alcohol abuse have been shown to negatively influence density of the skeleton. Smoking females also get their menopause 1.5–2 years earlier than nonsmokers. Several studies indicate that substitution therapy with estrogens, or estrogens in combination with progestins, has a significant positive influence upon the development of osteoporosis and slows its rate of development. To what extent the side effects of such a treatment in older females outweigh the positive effects and therefore would hinder a more general recommendation, or restrict the recommendation to certain individuals, remains unclear.

F. Urinary Incontinence

Urinary incontinence is common in older people and can be a manifestation of aging itself. This is especially the case in females; advanced incontinence problems appear to exist in about 10%, and lower degree of leakage, which creates social life problems, occurs in another 30% of the population at age 70 and above. "Hidden" forms of urinary incontinence can often become worsened by the prescription of drugs that directly influence bladder and urethral function. Immobility is also commonly associated with incontinence. The use of estrogens has been shown to have beneficial effects in many women and can markedly postpone incontinence when it is dependent on aging-related atrophy of surface membranes in the urethra.

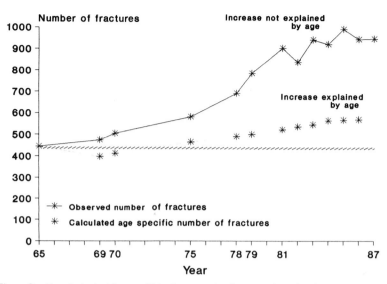

Figure 3 Trends in incidence of hip fractures in the city of Gothenburg in Sweden. (Zetterberg et al., personal communication.)

Intervention efforts to prevent or postpone aging-related urinary incontinence should thus primarily be directed toward stimulation of general physical fitness, and hormone therapy directed toward a postponement of surface membrane atrophy in the pelvic area.

G. Social Contacts

Absence of social interactions, contacts, and relationships has been shown to negatively influence vitality, the old individual's self-evaluation of health, and consequently the request for medical service. The risk for older persons of losing their spouse is also well documented, causing a sudden increase in mortality and morbidity compared to those of the same age still living with their spouse. Attempts to actively support newly bereaved older persons have been made, although studies proven to show to what extent external support really can postpone decline and dysfunction and prolong life is not yet available.

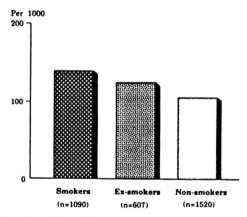

Figure 4 Estimated number of fractures per 1000 women among smokers, ex-smokers, and nonsmokers in the 1930 and 1940 birth cohorts. The fracture risk was greater among smokers than nonsmokers ($p < 0.01$, Pitman's permutation test). (From Johansson et al., 1991; *Maturitas* 14:65–74).

H. Clinical Medicine

In clinical medicine, pediatrics has for decades been actively involved in understanding not only children's disease, but also growth and maturation and how to support successful growth. Adult medicine, on the other hand, has only recently through the introduction of geriatric medicine started to understand aging as a phenomenon distinguished from morbidity and how to contribute to postponement of negative manifestations of aging. The importance of an improvement in diagnostic criteria and a better understanding of how to differentiate manifestations of aging from symptoms of definable disease has become evident especially through longitudinal population studies. The aging-related lowering of organ and organ system reserves underscores the importance of more early diagnosis, correct diagnosis, and earliest possible treatment intervention. Furthermore, many studies have demonstrated that too many older persons after episodes of disease and also after curable disease, lose so much of their functional ability that they cannot regain their previous level by themselves. They might have recovered to a healthy state but without having regained the level of activity they had before acquiring the disease. Such a stepwise decline in function is not uncommon, especially in the latter part of life. Careful but systematic and relatively longer-lasting help to regain functional performance (i.e., reactivation) than currently available in the majority of hospitals is needed to postpone unnecessary decline in functional performance during aging. Unfortunately, the shortening of stays in hospitals and earlier discharge too often implies a discharge of patients "quicker and sicker," as emphasized in the 1990 *White Paper on Elderly Health* by the American Medical Association. This might imply a negative trend for coming generations of older people. Interventions to counteract such stepwise decline are available and must be established in our health-care system.

III. CONCLUSION

This article does not cover all aspects of how the rate of aging might be postponed and has not dealt with more basic concepts of possibilities to intervene at the level of genetic mechanisms or into other basic cellular processes influencing aging. Such perspectives are directly or indirectly illustrated in other chapters of this encyclopedia.

Adequate physical activity, intellectual performance, emotional engagement, and social integration are examples of factors that can preserve vitality. Personal lifestyle has significant influence on aging-related changes in vitality and health. There is evidence that this influence becomes even more pertinent at ages when the reserve capacity has declined.

Early detection of diseases and introduction of treatment is often crucial for a preservation of performance in older persons.

Interventions to postpone aging-related decline should identify not only medical risk factors but also risk situations more common in the elderly, such as social isolation and bereavement, which both have proven negative effects on vitality and health.

Many frail older persons are left without adequate help to regain functional performance after medical events, resulting in stepwise functional decline after episodes of curable diseases. To understand aging would mean also to be aware of the ability to regain functional performance after events threatening vitality (such as disease, loss of spouse, etc.).

Finally, it should be emphasized that this article has not dealt with manifestations of aging that, according to present knowledge, have not been proven to be influenced by exogenous factors! Examples are such important tissue structure changes as the connective tissue becoming stiffer during aging, and the neuroconductive system of the heart crucial for the regulation and coordination of the sucking and pumping heart.

BIBLIOGRAPHY

American Medical Association White Paper on Elderly Health (1990). Report of the Council on Scientific Affairs. *Archives of Internal Medicine, 150,* December, 2459–2472.

Aniansson, A., & Gustafsson, E. (1981). Physical training in elderly men with special reference to quadriceps muscle strength and morphology. *Clinical Psychology, 1,* 87.

Berg, S., Mellström, D., Persson, G., & Svanborg, A. (1981). Loneliness in the Swedish aged. *Journal of Gerontology, 36,* 342.

Eriksson, B. G., Mellström, D., & Svanborg, A. (1987). Medical-social intervention in a 70-year-old Swedish population. A general presentation of methodological experience. *Comprehensive Gerontology, 1,* 49.

Fiatarone, M., Marks, E. C., Meridith, C. N., & Lipsitz, L. A.

(1989). High intensity strength training in nonagenarians: Effects of skeletal muscle. *Clinical Research, 37,* 330A.

Grimby, G., & Saltin, B. (1983). Mini-review: The aging muscle. *Clinical Physiology, 3,* 209.

Heikkinen, E., Arajarvi, R-L., Era, P., Jyha, M., Kinnunen, V., Leskinen, A. L., Masseli, E., Pohjolainen, P., & Rahkila, P. (1984). Functional capacity of men born in 1906–10, 1926–30, and 1946–50. A basic report. *Scandinavian Journal of Social Medicine, 33,* 1.

Institute of Medicine, National Academy of Sciences, Division of Health Promotion and Disease Prevention, *The Second Fifty Years,* Washington, D.C. (1990). National Academy Press. [Provides background and insights into 13 health priority areas for older people and makes recommendations for improvements in policy and practice relevant to each priority area.]

Kannel, W. B., & Gordon, T. (1980). Cardiovascular risk factors in the aged: The Framingham Study. In S. G. Haynes & M. Feinlieb (Eds.), *Second Conference in the Epidemiology of Aging* (No. 80-969). Bethesda, MD: National Institutes of Health. [Provides an overview of the on-going Framingham study of the significant risk factors for the development of CVD and their additive or multiplicative effects.]

Longeran, E. T. (Ed.). (1991). *Extending life, enhancing life. A national research agenda on aging.* Washington, DC: National Academy Press.

Maddox, G. L. (1972). Interventions and outcomes: Notes on designing and implementing an experiment in health care. *International Journal of Epidemiology, 23,* 339.

Mannius, S., Mellström, D., Oden, A., Rundgren, Å., & Zetterberg, C. (1987). Incidence of hip fracture in Western Sweden 1974–1985. *Acta Orthopaedic Scandinavian, 58,* 765.

Mellström, D., Rundgren, A., Jagenburg, R., Steen, B., & Svanborg, A. (1982). Tobacco smoking, ageing and health among the elderly. A longitudinal population study of 70-year-old men and an age cohort comparison. *Age and Aging, 11,* 45.

Rundgren, A., Aniansson, A., Ljungberg, P., & Wetterqvist, H. (1984). Effect of a training programme for elderly people on mineral content of the heel bone. *Archives of Gerontology and Geriatrics, 3,* 243.

Schaie, K. W., & Parham, I. A. (1977). Cohort-sequential analyses of adult intellectual development. *Developmental Psychology, 13,* 649.

Shock, N. W., Greulich, R. C., Andres, R., David Arenberg, Paul T. Costa, Jr., Edward G. Lakatta, Jordan D. Tobin. (1984). *Normal human aging: The Baltimore Longitudinal Study of Aging.* (NIA, NIH, PHS, USDHHS. NIH Publication No. 84-2450). Washington, DC [Provides a detailed description of the major components of the Baltimore Longitudinal Study of Aging including design and operation, tests administered, and cross-sectional and longitudinal analysis.]

Suominen, H., Heikkinen, E., Liesen, H., Michel, D. J., & Hollman, W. (1977). Effects of 8 weeks endurance training on skeletal muscle metabolism in 56 70-year-old sedentary men. *European Journal of Applied Physiology, 37,* 173.

Suominen, H., Heikkinen, E., Vainio, P., & Lahtinen, T. (1984). Mineral density of calcaneus in men at different ages: A population study with special reference to life-style factors. *Age and Aging, 13,* 273.

Svanborg, A. (1988). The health of the elderly population: Results from longitudinal studies with age-cohort comparisons. In D. Evered and J. Whelan. (Eds.), *Research and the aging population. Ciba Foundation Symposium* (pp. 3–16). New York: Wiley & Sons.

Svanborg, A. (1993). A medical-social intervention in a 70-year-old Swedish population: Is it possible to postpone functional decline in aging? *Journal of Gerontology, 48,* 84.

Premature Aging

Mitchell Turker

University of Kentucky

I. Overview
II. Model Systems
III. Premature Aging in Humans
IV. Conclusion

Allele   One of a group of genes that occurs alternatively at a given locus.

Autosomal Dominant   An inheritance pattern in which a single mutant allele produces a phenotype.

Autosomal Recessive   An inheritance pattern in which two mutant alleles are required for a phenotype to be observed.

Genomic Instability   A situation in which mutations accumulate at a high rate within a cell.

Helicase   An enzyme that separates the strands of duplex DNA.

Homozygosity   When both alleles of a given locus are identical.

Locus   The position in the chromosome of a particular gene or allele.

Mutant   An individual bearing a mutation.

Mutation   An alteration in the primary structure of DNA.

Mutator Phenotype   A cell type that exhibits an elevated rate of mutations.

Nucleotide Excision Repair (NER)   The excision of a short stretch of damaged DNA and its replacement with undamaged DNA by polymerization.

Oxidative Damage   Macromolecular damage caused by highly reactive oxidants.

Senescence   The process of becoming old.

Aging represents a gradual decline in most functions during the postdevelopmental life of an organism. The rate of aging varies markedly among species and to a lesser extent among individuals within a given species. The term **PREMATURE AGING** is commonly used to define a situation in which one or more of the aging processes occurs at a rate that is increased significantly over that which is considered to be the norm for the species. Premature aging of an individual can result from genetic or environmental effects, or a combination of both. The study of premature aging, although interesting in its own right, provides an important opportunity for gerontologists to dissect out processes that play causal roles in aging and to determine the underlying mechanisms.

I. OVERVIEW

A. Background

1. What Is Premature Aging?

Premature aging represents an acceleration in the rate of aging for one or more target systems within an individual. Although premature aging will frequently lead to premature death, these terms are not always interchangeable. An important criterion for premature aging is that it must mimic at least one aspect of aging that is normal for the species. Death, therefore, would result from the accelerated decline that occurs and not simply a single lethal event. This chapter will cite a number of putative examples of premature aging in humans and in model systems and use them to dissect out some of the processes that, in total, comprise the complex phenotype of aging.

2. What Is Aging?

A discussion of premature aging is not possible without a firm understanding of the biology of aging. Although many aspects of the biology of aging will be covered in detail in other chapters, those aspects that are pertinent to this chapter will be considered briefly in this section and in several ensuing sections. Aging represents a progressive decline in organismal viability that occurs as a function of time and ultimately results in death. This decline results from both degenerative and proliferative alterations. Examples of the latter class of alterations include cancer and atherosclerosis. For a given individual, the decline in viability is the sum total of a large number of events that are collectively expressed as the aging phenotype. The number of genes that underlie the aging process in humans is not known. Estimates have ranged from as low as seven to as many as several hundred. Moreover, it is quite possible that for a single locus polymorphic alleles exist that have slightly different effects on aging. Regardless of the true number of loci that affect aging, it is likely that the tremendous variation in age-related changes occurring in humans is the result of a complex mix of genotypes and environmental factors. Even identical twins do not age in an identical fashion. [See BEHAVIORAL GENETICS.]

3. What Causes Aging?

A vast literature is available that describes the molecular, biochemical, cellular, and organismal changes that accompany biological aging. Unfortunately, we are still left to ponder the causes of aging. For the purpose of this chapter, it will be assumed that the underlying cause of aging is alterations in the structure and functions of the macromolecules that comprise each individual. This is not meant to be a definitive statement, but instead will serve as a context for discussing premature aging based on the available data. Therefore, a bias in this chapter will be given to theories of aging that consider damage to macromolecules to be causal to aging. Damaging agents include free radicals generated from oxygen (Figure 1) or ionizing radiation, ultraviolet (UV) radiation from the sun, and natural-occurring chemical mutagens, such as phenolic compounds in edible plants. Affected molecules include lipids, proteins, and DNA. Of these, many authors assume that progressive DNA damage is most deleterious. The evolution of systems that detoxify damaging agents (see Figure 2 for enzymes

$$O_2 + e^- \longrightarrow O_2^-$$
$$O_2 + e^- + 2H^+ \longrightarrow H_2O_2$$
$$H_2O_2 + e^- + H^+ \longrightarrow H_2O + \cdot OH$$
$$\cdot OH + e^- + H^+ \longrightarrow H_2O$$

Figure 1 Pathway of production of high-energy oxygen (O_2) species. Reduction of O_2 occurs in four steps. e^-, electron; H^+, proton; H_2O, water; H_2O_2, hydrogen peroxide; O_2^-, superoxide radical; $\cdot O_2$; hydroxyl radical. (Figure reprinted with permission from Bernstein & Bernstein, 1991.)

that scavenge free radicals) or repair the damage that they cause provides evidence for the harm these agents can inflict on an unprotected individual. Additional evidence can be obtained from the reports of individuals with genetic deficiencies in one or more of these protective systems. [See DNA AND GENE EXPRESSION.]

4. Why Do We Age?

This question is better left to evolutionary biologists for a complete consideration, or perhaps to those who wish to explore the interface between religion and science. However, a brief consideration of this issue is necessary for an analysis of premature aging. A consensus among evolutionary biologists is that aging has not been specifically selected for, with a few exceptions such as semelparous species (which will be discussed later). Instead, the forces of natural selection may be reduced at later ages, particularly after the reproductive life of the individual has ceased. A reasonable explanation is that it is not necessary or cost effective to evolve systems that will protect an individual indefinitely. Therefore, systems that have evolved to protect an individual, or more specifically its somatic cells, from the effects of intrinsic cellular processes and from our environment will have inherent limitations. The result will be damage accumulation over the lifetime of the individual. Moreover, species that reproduce at earlier ages should have evolved less-efficient protective systems and therefore accumulate damage at higher rates than long-lived species. Both concepts have been verified experimentally. Although it is not appropriate to state that a mouse ages prematurely as opposed to a human, it is fair to say that the evolutionary path each species has taken provides a genetic basis for the rate at which it ages.

$$2O_2^- + 2H^+ \xrightarrow{\text{superoxide dismutase}} H_2O_2 + O_2$$

$$2H_2O_2 \xrightarrow{\text{catalase}} 2H_2O + O_2$$

$$H_2O_2 + 2GSH \xrightarrow{\text{glutathione peroxidase}} 2H_2O + GSSG$$

$$GSSG + NADPH + H^+ \xrightarrow{\text{glutathione reductase}} NADP^+ + 2GSH$$

Figure 2 Enzymatic defenses against active oxygen (O_2) species. Reactive species are metabolized by several enzymes, including those shown here. O_2^-, superoxide radical; H^+, proton, GSH, reduced glutathione; H_2O_2, hydrogen peroxide; GSSG, oxidized glutathione; NADPH, nicotinamide adenine dinucleotide phosphate; NADP, reduced form of NADP. (Figure reprinted with permission from Bernstein & Bernstein, 1991.)

II. MODEL SYSTEMS

The study of aging in humans has two inherent limitations: an inability to do controlled experiments and the long life span of our species. Therefore, experimental gerontologists often turn to model systems to unravel basic mechanisms of aging. As long as one accepts that there are certain universal principles to the aging process, the use of model systems is valid. Model systems that have relevance to our discussion of premature aging will be considered in this section. License will be taken to include systems in which accelerated aging is normal within the species, but still can be considered premature by demonstrating that such aging is not mandatory within the species or by comparison with closely related species. [See MODELS OF AGING: INVERTEBRATES, FILAMENTOUS FUNGI, AND YEASTS; MODELS OF AGING: VERTEBRATES.]

A. Semelparous Species

Semelparous species are those that reproduce only once and then undergo very rapid aging and death. Death can occur shortly after breeding or after the young have been successfully raised. Although rare in mammals, most of which are iteroparous (i.e., reproduce more than once per an individual's lifetime), semelparity is common among bacteria, invertebrates, and plants. It is also found in approximately 1% of fish species. At least for multicellular organisms, the existence of semelparity is considered evidence of nat-

ural selection for programmed aging. An interesting aspect of semelparity is that programmed aging can be blocked by experimental manipulation. For example, the rapid death of Pacific salmon that follows spawning can be prevented by castration. The result is an approximate doubling of the life span. Landlocked salmon are also known to breed successfully for several years. It is important to note that pathological lesions that occur at first spawning in migratory salmon, such as arteriosclerosis of coronary arteries, become progressive in older fish that reproduce in subsequent years. Such lesions, however, are not causal to death, which instead is mediated hormonally. Therefore, the Pacific salmon can undergo a "normal" aging process or an induced process that results in rapid death after spawning. Rapid senescence of the female *Octopus cyanea*, which results in death several days after the brood is hatched and approximately 1 month after mating, can be blocked by removing the optic glands. These glands stimulate gonadal development in *Octopus*.

The segmented worm *Nereis diversicolor* is an interesting model system for the study of hormonal effects in the life cycle of a semelparous species. *N. diversicolor* is found in intertidal mud regions where it matures slowly over a 2-year period. Upon maturation, the individual ceases feeding, spawns, and then dies. Mature individuals also lose the ability to regenerate ablated segments. It is known that segment regeneration and gametogenesis are dependent upon a hormone produced by the cerebral neuroendocrine system. This hormone is also required to inhibit maturation. Normally, as the organism grows the hormone level drops, resulting in maturation, cessation of feeding, spawning, and death. A restoration of hormone levels and a resultant inhibition of programmed death can be achieved by implanting cerebral ganglia from 1-year-old (immature) animals into 2-year-old animals. This reversal of the "aging" process can still occur after the animals have ceased to feed (and results in a resumption of feeding), but not after spawning has commenced. Interestingly, the implanted animals will go on to mature, spawn, and die in the subsequent year (year 3), unless implanted again. In this case, a fourth year can be added onto their life. Experiments have not been conducted to determine how many times the process of rejuvenation can occur, allowing a determination of the timing and causes of noninduced aging in N. diversicolor.

A final example of semelparity that will be considered are marsupial mice (genus Antechinus). Males of this species disperse from the maternal nest in May (the fall season in Australia), establish their territories, and become sexually mature. In August, the females come into estrus and a hectic period of mating occurs. Within 2 weeks of mating (at 11 months of age), all the males are dead following a period of rapid weight loss and illness. Most females die after raising their first litter, although a few will live to breed for a second season. The causes of rapid senescence in the male are complex, but partly understood. The sexual organs rapidly regress with the testes being replaced by connective tissue. Other pathological changes that have been noted include hypertrophy of the adrenals, hepatic necrosis, infection, stomach and intestinal hemorrhage, anemia, and infection. The infections that occur may result from low levels of circulating immunoglobulins, which in turn may result from increased levels of corticosteroids in the plasma. As with the other species mentioned above, rapid senescence in the marsupial mice species is not an obligatory event and can be prevented in several ways. One is to simply capture male mice during the breeding season, which results in a life span extension up to 2 years. The degree of life span extension is dependent upon the condition of the animal at the time it was captured, suggesting that the physical toll exacted on the animal during the breeding season also contributes to its death. It is also interesting to note that the captive males exhibit an annual cycle of weight loss and re-

gression of the sexual organs that occurs in the wild. Sexual function is not regained, and the animals remain sterile for the remainder of their life span, as opposed to N. diversicolor (discussed previously), which can go on to spawn in subsequent years. The annual cycle of weight loss can be blocked by castrating the males, implying a hormonal effect mediated by the sex organs similar to that shown for salmon.

In total, the semelparous species teach us that, where advantageous to the species, rapid aging can be mediated hormonally. Although rapid senescence is a normal part of the life cycle of these organisms, it is not obligatory. By the definition given at the start of this article, therefore, rapid aging in these species is not strictly premature aging because it is the norm. Nevertheless, semelparous species appear to have evolved from iteroparous ancestors and demonstrate premature aging when compared to a prototype ancestor. Further studies are required to determine more fully the aging phenotype of semelparous individuals in which accelerated senescence associated with reproduction has been eliminated and to compare these results with aging studies from closely related iteroparous species.

B. Senescence in Fungi

Ascomycete fungi, most notably *Podospora anserina* and several Neurospora species, have proven to be excellent models for premature aging caused by mitochondrial dysfunction. For Podospora, cultures maintained in growth tubes exhibit a finite life span characterized by a juvenile phase of steady growth and a senescent phase of slow growth and eventual death (as defined by an inability to grow further). Although senescence of Podospora is common in culture conditions, this event does not occur in the wild, most likely due to mating-related rejuvenation. In the late 1970s and early 1980s, senescence in Podospora was correlated with disintegration of the wild-type mitochondrial genome, which is approximately 100 kb (kilobases) in size, and the emergence of one or more types of mitochondrial plasmids. Each plasmid, commonly called a senDNA, is derived from the wild-type mitochondrial genome and consists of a series of covalently closed head-to-tail multimers of the excised monomeric unit. The most common plasmid is α-senDNA, which is a 2.5-kb sequence that represents the first intron of the gene for subunit 1 of cytochrome oxidase (CO1). It is a group II intron that may code for a reverse transcriptase molecule. An increase in the level of reverse transcriptase-like activity has been noted in senescent cultures of Podospora. Therefore, it has been proposed that the α-senDNA is formed by reverse transcription of its sequence followed by autonomous replication. A second class of senDNAs have also been noted in Podospora, but these appear to have a different origin than α-senDNA. These senDNAs, which can arise from a variety of genomic locations, have in common a directly repeated sequence at the apparent excretion sites. Interestingly, many of the excision sites have an 11 base pair consensus sequence, suggesting that the mitochondrial excision events are "programmed" in the genome, with major variables being the consensus sites used and the timing of the excision events.

Senescence in natural populations of Neurospora also involves the mitochondrial genome, although via a mechanism that is opposite to that observed in Podospora. During Neurospora senescence, linear mitochondrial plasmids, which usually replicate autonomously, integrate into various locations of the mitochondrial genome. There is no homology between the free form of the plasmid DNA and the wild-type mitochondrial genome.

It is clear for both Podospora and Neurospora, that disruptions of the wild-type mitochondrial genomes occur during senescence, and it can be assumed that these disruptions play a causal role. Although in both cases aging appears to be programmed, plasmid integration in Neurospora clearly hastens this process because laboratory strains that lack these plasmids are immortal. A number of immortal laboratory strains of Podospora have also been reported, with many of them exhibiting a deletion of the intron that gives rise to α-senDNA. Therefore, although noting that disruption of mitochondrial function can contribute to premature aging in fungi, we should further note that the underlying mechanism is loss of integrity of the mitochondrial genome.

C. Senescence in *Drosophila melanogaster*

The fruit fly *Drosophila melanogaster* has also yielded insight into the process of premature aging. This species offers the advantage of a relatively short average life span (30–60 days) and the ability to breed and score a large number of progeny. Drosophila has the added advantage of a vast supporting literature and the availability of a large number of mutant strains. A caveat with Drosophila, however, that will also complicate discussion of premature aging in humans is a difficulty in separating those mutations that simply increase mortality (i.e., short-lived mutants) from those that truly hasten senescence. Environmental factors have also been shown to hasten senescence in Drosophila. For example, an inverse relationship between adult life span and ambient temperature has been observed. Although the exact cause of this relationship is still not known (except that it does not appear to be a simple function of metabolic rate), the use of different temperatures has led to the identification of temperature-sensitive mutants that die rapidly at elevated temperatures. One of these mutants, 1(1)adl-16ts, appears to have a hastened senescence at 27°C that is due to physiological dysfunction in the central nervous system, including the brain and central ganglia.

Motor defects and decreased life span, in addition to UV sensitivity, have also been observed for viable flies with mutations at the *haywire* locus. This locus encodes a protein that exhibits significant homology to the human ERCC3 protein, which has been implicated in nucleotide-excision repair. The functions of the haywire and ERCC3 proteins are not known, but the amino acid sequences suggest a helicase function. It has been suggested that Drosophila *haywire* mutants provide a useful model for two human genetic diseases, Xeroderma pigmentosum and Cockayne's syndrome. (Both diseases will be discussed in Section III.C).

Other studies with Drosophila have implicated enzymes that protect against oxidative damage as playing important roles in determining life span. One of the better characterized systems is catalase deficiency. Mutants homozygous for null alleles have markedly reduced average life spans (<10 days) as compared with controls (approx. 45 days). A normal life span can be restored by introducing one or more copies of the catalase gene, but an additive effect for transgene copy number that increases life span was not noted. It is important to note that mutants with small amounts of catalase activity (3–8%) do not exhibit reduced life spans under normal laboratory conditions. However, if these mutants are stressed by the addition of hydrogen peroxide (H_2O_2) to the culture medium, mortality is enhanced significantly. This result indicates that only a small amount of catalase is sufficient under ideal conditions, but that it is insufficient during conditions of stress. Null mutants for superoxide dismutase have also been reported, but they live less than a day before dying and therefore cannot be considered to have aged prematurely. Finally, it has been shown recently that senescence of female Drosophila is hastened by a product of the male accessory gland. Once this factor is isolated, it will be interesting to determine how it functions and to compare it with hormones isolated from the semelparous species.

D. *Mus musculus*

The common laboratory mouse, *Mus musculus domesticus,* has proven to be one of the most useful animal models for experimental gerontologists interested in human aging. *M. domesticus* has a relatively short life span of 3–4 years and, like humans, is a mammalian species. Like Drosophila, a vast literature exists for *M. domesticus* and a large number of mutant strains are available. Moreover, using transgenic technology it is possible to produce strains that express or lack expression of genes that are believed important in controlling life span. In this section, only naturally occurring mutations and agents will be considered. Where appropriate, transgenic mouse models of premature aging will be considered with their human counterparts.

The most extensively studied mouse models for premature aging are the SAM (senescence-accelerated mouse) strains developed by researchers at Kyoto University in Japan. Work with SAM mice began with the observation that certain litters of AKR/J mice exhibited a shortened life span that was accompanied by a number of hallmarks of aging. Breeding experiments showed that premature aging in these mice was heritable, and a number of substrains were derived. Aspects of premature aging that have been observed in SAM mice include senile amyloidosis, cataracts, senile osteoporosis, short-term memory loss, and a decline in immune function. Cultured fibroblasts from SAM mice have also been observed to age prematurely, as defined by the number of population doublings prior to culture crisis and transformation. Unfortunately with a single exception, it has not been possible to link a specific genetic alteration with the SAM phenotype of accelerated aging. This has severely limited the utility of the SAM mouse as a model to understand the underlying molecular genetic causes of premature aging. The one exception is the finding that premature senile amyloidosis is linked to an amino acid substitution in the structure of the apolipoprotein (apo) AII. This substitution is genetically encoded, but it appears to be a naturally occurring variation in several mouse strains instead of a *de novo* mutation in the SAM mice. Thus, there still may be one or more underlying genetic defects in the SAM mice that promote deposition of the apoII protein in the SAM mice in addition to the other aspects of premature aging in these mice.

Wild populations of *M. domesticus* have also proven useful in understanding the causes of premature aging. One example will be given in which the triggering agent was ultimately linked to a retrovirus. In a large study using over 10,000 animals, representing 15 different populations in Southern California, individual mice were allowed to age to obtain life tables for each population. In most populations, only a few tumors occurred late in life. The majority of tumors were lymphomas that arose after the animals were 2 years of age. Antigens to murine leukemia virus (MuLV) were present in these tumors, indicating that virus-induced tumors could occur during aging in wild mice. Detectable levels of virus were not found in other tumors or in the circulatory system, indicating that the mice did not have a systemic lifelong infection. The virus was apparently transmitted vertically as a milk-borne infection. In 3 of the 15 populations, an earlier incidence of lymphoma (one year of age) and/or paralysis of the hind limbs was observed. Other tumors were also observed. These characteristics were ultimately traced to a second milk-borne MuLV that was restricted to the three populations and that led to a lifelong systemic infection. Interestingly, about 15% of the infected populations were virus free due to inheritance of a provirus allele that, although not producing infectious virus, did produce a protein that competed with the infectious virus for its cell surface receptor. This large study with wild mice teaches us two important lessons about aging. First, infectious agents can induce one or more of the hallmarks of aging. Second, virulent forms of these infectious agents can hasten the process.

III. PREMATURE AGING IN HUMANS

The previous section on model systems began with a brief consideration of the limitations of using our species as a model system to study aging. This does not mean, however, that a great deal of insight cannot be gained by studying premature aging in humans. In fact, there are some major advantages that such studies possess, including descriptions in the literature of virtually every genetic disease known to afflict humans and the ongoing work to clone most of the genes responsible. Moreover, the long life span of humans allows an accurate characterization of disease and aging progression within a single individual over a relatively long period of time. Finally, the ability to make mouse models for most significant human genetic diseases offers the opportunity to ask questions about these diseases in experimental systems.

This section will be devoted to describing interesting and relevant mutations in humans that accelerate one or more aspects of the aging phenotype, particularly those for which the underlying genetic and/or biochemical defect has been elucidated. As above, the purpose will be to use these examples to learn something about normal aging: its causes and the mechanisms that are used to retard its progression. (The term *normal aging* is a bit of a misnomer because everyone ages differently and what is considered to be normal in one population may not be considered normal in another. Nonetheless, this term will be used here to highlight the accelerated events of premature aging.) Wherever possible, the focus for each disease will be on the underlying molecular defect. One classic example of premature aging will also be given, although the responsible genetic defect is still unknown. Relevant characteristics of the human diseases discussed are summarized in Table I. The examples given in this section are meant to be representative rather than all inclusive. Environmental agents that hasten aging such as tobacco, alcohol, and human made mutagens will also be omitted from discussion.

A. Hutchinson-Gilford Syndrome

Hutchinson-Gilford (HG) syndrome (Figure 3) represents one of the rarest and more remarkable genetic syndromes in humans. It is the one genetic disease that is commonly called *progeria*. As of 1990, only 17 cases of this disease were known throughout the world. At birth HG patients appear normal, but by about 1 year of age severe growth retardation is seen. There is a rapid loss of subcutaneous fat and hair, resulting in a prominent display of the scalp veins. Other distinctive characteristics include a high-pitched voice, bone resorption, an elevated basic metabolic rate, and a shuffling gait. Most HG patients have normal to above normal intelligence. The median age of death is 12 years, with most deaths resulting from heart attacks or congestive heart failure. Wide-spread atherosclerosis, which is histologically indistinguishable from that observed during normal aging, is found in all patients at autopsy. Other cardiovascular (CV) degenerative changes include calcification of the heart rings, cardiomyopathy, arteriosclerosis, and arterial aneurysms. Therefore, HG is an excellent model for CV disease, which accounts for over 70% of all deaths for persons aged 90–94 (i.e., very old populations). A prominent biochemical abnormality that is found in HG patients is a 7–14-fold increase in the excretion of hyaluronic acid, which could account for altered angiogenesis. Increased excretion of hyaluronic acid is also observed in normal aging. Unfortunately, the molecular genetic defect responsible for HG is unknown. Attempts to locate an HG gene are complicated by the rarity of this disease, which only occurs as the result of a *de novo* mutation that is expressed in a dominant manner. Therefore, HG remains an interesting example of accelerated aging in humans, but it has not been useful in understanding fundamental mechanisms that are important in the aging process.

B. Werner Syndrome

Werner syndrome (Figure 4) is an autosomal recessive disease that is sometimes referred to as "progeria of the adult." It is first manifested as a failure to undergo the usual adolescent growth spurt, although it is rarely identified at that time. By the early twenties other changes are noted, such as hair loss, graying of the hair, atrophy of the skin, and cataracts. The skin changes often lead to large ulcers later in life. Diabetes and osteoporosis are additional changes that occur during the life span of many Werner syndrome pa-

Table I Relevant Characteristics of Premature Aging Syndromes[a]

Syndrome[b]	Inheritance[c]	Chromosome	Gene[d]	Defect	Instability[e]
Aging	complex	many	many	??	Yes
HG	AD	??	??	??	No
WS	AR	8	WRN	Helicase	Yes
BS	AR	15	BLM	Helicase	Yes
FA	AR(4)	??	??	DNA repair	Yes
CS	AR(2)	10	ERCC6(B)	Strand specific NER (helicase?)	No
XP	AR(7)	19	ERCC2(D)	NER	Yes
		2	ERCC3(B)	Helicase?	
		16	ERCC4(F)		
		13	ERCC5(G)		
DS	AD	21	??	??	Yes
ALS	AD	21	SOD	Gain of function	No
FAD	AD	21	APP	Amyloid deposition	No
	AD	14	PS-1	??	
	AD	1	PS-2	??	
	AR(?)	19	APOE4(?)	Amyloid deposition(?)	
MD	Maternal	Mitochondria	Many	Reduction in OXPHOS	No
Diabetes	Complex	Several	Several	Hyperglycemia	No

[a] See text for more details.

[b] HG, Hutchinson-Gilford (progeria); WS, Werner's syndrome; BS, Bloom syndrome; FA, Fanconi anemia; CS, Cockayne syndrome; XP, Xeroderma pigmentosum; DS, Down's syndrome; ALS, atrophic lateral sclerosis; FAD, familial Alzheimer's disease; MD, mitochondrial disease.

[c] AD, autosomal dominant; AR, autosomal recessive; number in parentheses indicates number of complementation groups.

[d] ERCC, excision repair cross complementing; letter in parentheses indicates specific complementation group; SOD, superoxide dismutase; APP, amyloid precursor protein; APOE4, apolipoprotein E.

[e] Instability defined by an increased propensity for cancer.

tients. Like HG, Werner syndrome is characterized by an elevated level of hyaluronic acid excretion. Death usually occurs in the late forties from CV complications or from neoplasia. Approximately 10% of Werner syndrome patients acquire cancers, with a disproportionate number of them being sarcomas or meningiomas. Fibroblast cells from Werner syndrome patients have a strikingly short life span in cultures. Whereas normal human diploid fibroblasts will divide approximately 50 times in culture prior to senescing (as defined by the loss of proliferative potential), those from Werner individuals will only survive for approximately 10–15 doublings.

Cytogenetic and molecular genetic studies have suggested that Werner syndrome is due to a loss in the maintenance of genomic stability. These studies have shown an unusually high frequency of reciprocal chromosome translocation and of single-gene mutations in cells derived from patients. The latter phenomenon is frequently referred to as a *mutator phenotype,* and in the case of Werner syndrome, the resultant mutations are frequently due to relatively large, submicroscopic deletion events. A similar observation of a mutator phenotype due to deletion events has been noted in cells isolated from patients with Fanconi anemia. This autosomal recessive disease, which is characterized by progressive bone marrow failure, developmental abnormalities, a predisposition to leukemia, and high levels of chromosome breakage, is due to a defect in DNA repair that is manifested as hypersensitivity to cross-linking agents. It is also interesting to note similarities between Werner syn-

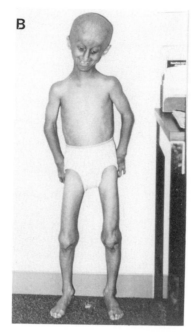

Figure 3 Example of patients with Hutchinson-Gilford syndrome. (A) Ten-year-old female. (B) Thirteen-year-old male. (Photos kindly provided by Dr. Ted Brown.)

drome and another autosomal recessive disease, Bloom syndrome, which is characterized by a high frequency of cancers and short stature in affected individuals. Cells from Bloom syndrome patients also display a high rate of chromosomal abnormalities, a mutator phenotype, and a shortened in vitro life span. Interestingly, the genes for both Werner syndrome and Bloom syndrome have been cloned recently and both syndromes appear due to defects in helicase proteins. In total, examples like Werner syndrome, Fanconi anemia, and Bloom syndrome indicate the critical requirement for genomic stability in somatic cells for maintaining a normal life span.

C. Xeroderma Pigmentosum and Cockayne's Syndrome

These are rare autosomal inherited diseases that are linked by common phenotypes in some individuals. Of the two, Cockayne's syndrome (CS) has significantly more progeroid features. Relevant aspects of the phenotype, for which there are two complementa-

tion groups (CS-A and -B), include growth retardation that occurs after several months to several years of life, photosensitivity, optic atrophy, deafness, intracranial calcification, progressive ataxia, mental retardation, and demyelination-associated neurodegeneration, which ultimately leads to death of patients in the second or third decade of life. CS patients do not appear to be at an increased risk of cancer despite the observation that their cells are moderately sensitive to UV radiation due to a defect in preferential repair of the transcribed strand of active genes. Such repair, which is induced by UV and other genotoxic agents, is a conserved function that utilizes the nucleotide excision repair (NER) pathway. Despite their inability to perform strand-specific repair, CS cells are not deficient in NER.

Xeroderma pigmentosum (XP) is characterized by extreme sensitivity to UV radiation, which is most dramatically exhibited as a several thousandfold increase in the risk of skin cancer presumably due to sun exposure. XP patients are also at approximately a 10-fold increased risk for cancers that do not appear to be induced by UV radiation. There are at least seven complementation groups for XP (XP-A-G), all leading to NER deficiency. It is interesting to note that XP patients whose defects map to several of the complementation groups (XP-B, -D, and -G) will sometimes exhibit clinical features of CS.

Molecular cloning and identification of the biochemical lesions for some of the XP and one of the CS complementation groups has shed light on the apparent linkage of these two genetic deficiencies and an unexpected biochemical linkage between DNA repair and transcription. The XP-B protein, which represents the *ERCC3* locus (the *haywire* locus in Drosophila), was found by independent investigators to be required for both NER and transcription. Similar to Werner syndrome and Bloom syndrome, the ERCC3 protein may be a helicase that, in this case, could promote transcription and nucleotide excision by virtue of its DNA-unwinding activity. Helicase function has also been proposed for the CS-B protein, which is encoded by the *ERCC6* locus. These observations have led to the intriguing hypothesis that the clinical phenotype of CS may be due to defects in transcription rather than strand-specific NER. This hypothesis would also explain the presence of individuals with a mixed XP/CS phenotype. If true, a defect in transcription may be a previously unrecognized

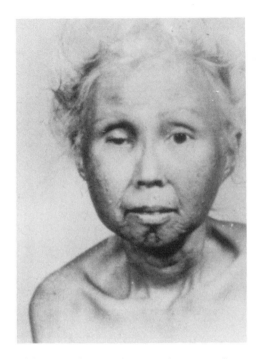

Figure 4　Example of patient with Werner syndrome. Photo at left taken when patient was in her teens. Photo at right was taken when patient was 48. (Figure reprinted with permission from Epstein et al., Werner's Syndrome: A review of its symptomatology, natural history, pathological features, genetics and relationship to the natural aging process. 1966, *Medicine, 45,* 177–221.)

mechanism that can predispose an individual to premature aging.

D. Down's Syndrome

Down's syndrome (DS) is a well-recognized disorder that is most commonly associated with trisomy for chromosome 21. In a classic study published in 1978, Dr. George M. Martin compared 162 human genetic disorders with features of premature aging and came to the somewhat surprising conclusion that DS exhibited the greatest number of characteristics associated with aging in normal populations. These characteristics, which implicated chromosome 21 in the aging process, included a decline in the immune function, an increased frequency of neoplasms, amyloid deposition, cataracts, degenerative vascular diseases, and nonconstitutional chromosomal aberrations. Of particular note is the observation that virtually 100% of DS patients will obtain the pathological hallmarks of Alzheimer's disease (AD) if they live past the age of

40. The critical region for the DS phenotype, but not necessarily premature aging, has been mapped to 21q22.1-3. Nearby, at 21q21.2 are two loci that have been implicated in premature aging syndromes (see below), amyloid precursor protein (APP) and Cu,Zn superoxide dismutase (SOD). As seen in Figure 2, H_2O_2 is a product of SOD enzymatic action. Although both catalase and glutathione reductase can act on H_2O_2, it can also react with transition metals to form hydroxyl radicals. Thus, increased levels of SOD protein could conceivably lead to increased rather than decreased levels of highly reactive oxidized molecules and therefore oxidative damage. Overexpression of *SOD* in transgenic mice has tended to support the notion that increased levels of protein could lead to significant pathology. However, overexpression of this gene alone clearly did not bring forth the complex phenotype of DS in the mouse. Other work with mice trisomic for chromosome 16 (the mouse equivalent of human chromosome 21) suggests that gene dysregulation plays an important role in establishing the DS

phenotype. Clearly, more work will be necessary to identify the absolute minimal region required for DS as well as to identify syntenic genes that contribute to the severity and complexity of this genetic disease.

E. Amyotrophic Lateral Sclerosis

Amyotrophic lateral sclerosis (ALS) (also known as Lou Gehrig's disease) is a progressive paralytic disorder that strikes middle-aged adults and is usually fatal within 5 years of diagnosis. Approximately 10% of ALS cases are inherited as an autosomal dominant disorder; the remainder are sporadic. Paralysis is due to degeneration of the large motor neurons of the brain and spinal cord. The molecular defect in many of the familial cases has been shown to be base pair substitutions in the chromosome 21-encoded *SOD* gene discussed previously. These mutations do not result in amino acid substitutions in the catalytic domain of the protein, but instead are located in regions that are important for maintaining the three-dimensional structure. Regardless, the mutations result in decreased enzymatic activity, which led to speculation that decreased levels of SOD protein could lead to ALS. Surprisingly, work with transgenic mice has suggested that it is a change of function in the altered SOD protein, rather than decreased function, that is important for the ALS phenotype. This conclusion is based on the observation that transgenic mice made with mutant human or mouse *SOD* genes develop weakness and neuronal degeneration similar to that observed in ALS patients. Because the two endogenous (and wild-type) mouse *SOD* alleles are unaffected in the transgenic lines, it would not appear that a reduction in SOD levels is causal for ALS. Instead, a dominant gain of function seems to be the culprit. The exact mechanism involved remains to be elucidated. It also remains to be determined why a specific neuronal cell type is the main target for a mutant gene that is ubiquitously expressed.

F. Alzheimer's Disease

AD is the most common form of senile dementia and the fourth leading cause of death in developed portions of the world. It is characterized by neuritic plaques, which contain a central region of β-amyloid (βA) deposition and neurofibrillary tangles. Although most cases of AD appear to be sporadic, over 200 families have been identified in which AD is inherited with an autosomal dominant mode of transmission. These cases will be referred to as familial AD (FAD). At least three lines of evidence have implicated chromosome 21 in some cases of FAD. First, as discussed previously, patients with DS invariably suffer from the pathological hallmarks of AD, if they live long enough. Secondly, the APP gene that gives rise to the βA found in the neuritic plaques is located on chromosome 21. It should be noted that βA deposition occurs in many mammalian species, including humans, as a function of normal aging. It is believed that abnormal processing of APP leads to amyloid formation and that this process is hastened in AD. Finally, base pair substitutions within APP predispose affected individuals to early-onset FAD (defined by mean age of onset before the age of 60), presumably by favoring the abnormal processing reaction. Recent studies with transgenic mice have demonstrated that strains overexpressing the mutant form of the APP gene will develop the characteristic plaques.

Despite the clear association of chromosome 21 and some FAD, it is not the only chromosome implicated in this disease. The vast majority of early-onset familial cases have been mapped to a recently cloned gene of chromosome 14. Moreover, a group of pedigrees from the Volga region of Russia (Volga Germans) has been identified that exhibits early onset due to mutations in a recently cloned gene located on chromosome 1. Interestingly, the chromosome 14 and 1 FAD genes are highly homologous, although their functions are not known. Families that exhibit late-onset FAD have been linked to a locus on chromosome 19. It is possible that this locus is apolipoprotein E (APOE) because a strong association has been made with homozygosity for *APOE4* allele, but not with the more common *APOE3* allele. It should be noted, however, that the *APOE4* allele is neither sufficient or necessary for AD, but instead may be an age-of-onset modifying allele. Recent data have shown that the APOE gene product is an inhibitor of βA formation and that the E3 protein is a more efficient inhibitor than the E4 protein. This result suggests a possible molecular mechanism for the association noted for the APOE4 allele, but clearly more work is necessary to prove or refute this notion. Similarly, it will be important to determine if the chromosome 14 gene product also contributes to βA formation, which will help establish that this deposited protein is the true cause of AD. [*See* DEMENTIA.]

G. Mitochondrial Diseases

Mitochondrial diseases are maternally inherited, with affected individuals having a mixture of mutant and wild-type mitochondrial genomes. Most inherited forms of mitochondrial diseases have age-related onsets of expression, representing premature aging of the affected targets. The exact organ systems affected is dependent upon the underlying mutation. For example, Leber's hereditary optic neuropathy (LHON), which is due to point mutations in mitochondrial genes necessary for oxidative phosphorylation (OXPHOS), frequently results in blindness, whereas mutations that affect mitochondrial protein synthesis will often affect muscle tissue, including cardiac muscle. Deletions of portions of the mitochondrial genome are associated with adult-onset diabetes and deafness.

An important issue that the study of inherited mitochondrial diseases allows us to address is the mechanisms underlying age-related onset of phenotypic expression. Simply put, why is phenotypic expression of a mutation delayed until adult life? There are several factors that may contribute to the age-related onset of expression of inherited mitochondrial diseases. The first is an age-related decline in OXPHOS that occurs normally. It is believed that this decline is due to the accumulation of oxidative damage in the mitochondrial genome that occurs over the life span. The high rate of accumulation of 8-oxo-2'-deoxyguanosine (oxo^{8}dG) residues results in approximately 0.5–1% of all guanine residues being modified in sensitive organs, such as muscle and brain, in elderly individuals. Coupled with high levels of mitochondrial DNA damage is a second contributing factor, inefficient repair of mitochondrial DNA damage. This, in turn, leads to a third factor, an age-related increase in mutations. In particular, mitochondrial DNA genomes containing deletions will accumulate as a function of age, perhaps because such genomes replicate faster than the wild-type genome. Similar to the fungal systems discussed earlier, mitochondrial deletions in humans often occur at directly repeated sequences that are dispersed throughout the genome. Figure 5 demonstrates a hypothetical model for the age-related onset of optic atrophy in patients with different point

mutations resulting in LHON. As seen in this model, the age-related decrease in OXPHOS will result in the energy production for affected individuals going below a threshold that is necessary to sustain the optic nerve. The age at which an individual will experience blindness is influenced by the severity of the initial mutation, the rate at which OXPHOS capacity falls, and in certain cases, environmental exacerbation. Therefore, even if the proportion of mutant mitochondrial genomes does not change as a function of age, the individual will still be at an increasing risk for blindness as he or she ages.

H. Diabetes

Diabetes is a widespread condition that results in increased levels of circulating glucose (hyperglycemia). It exists in two forms. Type 1 (juvenile-onset and insulin-dependent) due to autoimmune destruction of the insulin-producing pancreatic β cells and Type 2 (adult-onset and insulin-resistant). Although insulin therapy for diabetic children has proven to be an effective therapy, many lifelong complications that resemble premature aging occur as the affected individuals grow older. These complications, which also affect Type 2 diabetics, include retinopathy, nephropathy, neuropathy, and vascular disease. The genetics of diabetes is complicated. Mutations in specific genes such as glucokinase and the glucagon receptor have shown to contribute to some cases of adult-onset diabetes, as do mitochondrial mutations. Juvenile-onset diabetes has been linked to the human leukocyte antigen (HLA) region on chromosome 6 and to a polymorphic region near the insulin gene on chromosome 11. This region may regulate the level of insulin transcription.

Despite control with insulin therapy, juvenile-onset diabetic individuals suffer from a hyperglycemic condition that many investigators believe is responsible for the long-term complications of this disease. Glucose can form glycosylation products with proteins (Schiff bases) in a chemically reversible reaction that is proportional to its concentration. The Schiff bases can then go on to form more stable compounds termed *Amadori products*. Like Schiff bases, the Amadori products are chemically reversible and are considered to be early glycosylation products that will dissociate when hyperglycemic conditions are reversed. However, some of the early glycosylation products will un-

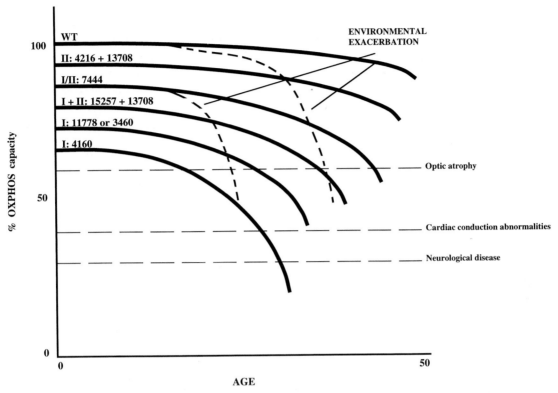

Figure 5 A model for explaining the variable expression and late onset of Leber's hereditary optic neuropathy (LHON) mutations. Patients with in-born oxidative phosphorylation (OXPHOS) defects due to mitochondrial DNA mutations have lowered OXPHOS capacities relative to normal (WT) individuals. Because OXPHOS capacity declines with age, patients cross a disease threshold earlier than normal individuals, resulting in tissue dysfunction. Nongenetic factors such as the environment can further influence LHON expression. I and II indicate class I and class II mutations, respectively. Numbers indicate relative position of mutation on mitochondrial genome. See reference for more details. (Reprinted with permission from Brown et al., 1992. Leber's hereditary optic neuropathy: A model for mitochondrial neurodegenerative diseases. *FASEB Journal, 6,* 2791–2799.)

dergo a slow series of reactions that will result in irreversible advance glycosylation end products (AGE) that can accumulate over the lifetime. Some targets of AGE are collagen, myelin proteins, and long-lived proteins of the vessel wall. This can explain some of the pathology of diabetes. Although AGE proteins will accumulate more rapidly in diabetic individuals, they are also found in normal individuals and are specifically recognized by a receptor on monocyte-derived macrophages. The macrophages remove the AGE proteins and then signal other cells to perform tissue remodeling. Some investigators believe that the increased levels of AGE proteins found in diabetics and in aged individuals upset the normal balance of tissue removal and remodeling, leading to further complications. AGE receptors may also be present on other cell types such as

T lymphocytes, endothelial cells, and fibroblasts, suggesting additional pathways for pathological lesions induced by these abnormal proteins. Although more research is required to elucidate the mechanisms by which AGE proteins cause diabetic complications, the lesson to researchers is that glucose-mediated damage may play a significant role during aging in nondiabetic individuals, and that it hastens this process in diabetic individuals.

IV. CONCLUSION

After undergoing a remarkable set of developmental changes that result in the mature individual, each human wages a solitary battle to maintain the integrity of his or her soma. This battle is influenced by genes, environment, and to a certain extent, by luck. Although the timing will vary for each person, the end result will invariably be the same; a slow progressive decline resulting in death (if one is fortunate enough to have survived long enough to age). This decline may be ultimately due to a lack of selection by evolution for the postreproductive individual, which may seem unfair until one considers those examples in which nature has targeted the postreproductive individuals of semelparous species. The major lesson learned from a review of the premature aging syndromes in humans and the other model systems that were presented is that a large number of protective systems are required to allow one to age slowly, if not always gracefully, and that removal of even a single component of one system may hasten this process.

BIBLIOGRAPHY

Arking, R., & Dudas, S. P. (1989). Review of genetic investigations into the aging processes of Drosophila. *Journal of the American Geriatrics Society, 37,* 757–773.

Bernstein, C., & Bernstein, H. (1991). *Aging, sex, and DNA repair.* San Diego, CA: Academic Press.

Finch, C. E. (1994). Latent capacities for gametogenic cycling in the semelparous invertebrate *Nereis. Proceedings of the National Academy of Sciences (USA), 91,* 11769–11770.

Gardner, M. B. (1993). Genetic control of retroviral disease in aging wild mice. *Genetica, 91,* 199–209.

Griffiths, A. J. F. (1992). Fungal senescence. *Annual Review of Genetics, 26,* 351–372.

Hanawalt, P. C. (1994). Transcription-coupled repair and human disease. *Science, 266,* 1957–1958.

Martin, G. M. (1978). Genetic syndromes in man with potential relevance to the pathobiology of aging. In D. Bergsma & D. E. Harrison, (Eds.), *Genetic effects of aging. Birth defects, original articles series* (pp. 5–39). New York: The National Foundation March of Dimes.

Martin, G. M., & Turker, M. S. (1994). Genetics of human disease, longevity, and aging. In W. R. Hazzard, E. L. Bierman, J. P. Blass, W. H. Ettinger, Jr., & J. B. Halter, (Eds.), *Principles of geriatric medicine and gerontology* (pp. 19–36). New York: McGraw-Hill, Inc.

Rose, M. R. (1991). *Evolutionary biology of aging.* New York: Oxford University Press.

Shigenaga, M. K., Hagen, T. M., & Ames, B. N. (1994). Oxidative damage and mitochondrial decay in aging. *Proceedings of the National Academy of Sciences (USA), 91,* 10771–10778.

Takeda, T. (1994). *The SAM model of senescence.* Amsterdam, The Netherlands: Elsevier Sciences B.V.

Vlassara, H., Bucala, R., & Striker, L. (1994). Pathological effects of advanced glycosylation: Biochemical, biologic, and clinical implications for diabetes and aging. *Laboratory Investigation, 70,* 138–151.

Wallace, D. C. (1992). Mitochondrial genetics: A paradigm for aging and degenerative diseases. *Science, 256,* 628–632.

Prostate

William J. Aronson and Jean B. deKernion

University of California, Los Angeles, School of Medicine

I. Anatomy
II. Physiology
III. Prostatitis
IV. Benign Prostatic Hyperplasia
V. Prostate Cancer
VI. Conclusion

Autocrine Pathway in which a cell responds to the same peptide growth factor that it simultaneously produced.

Exocrine Gland A gland that releases a secretion external to the surface of an organ by means of a canal or duct.

Paracrine Pathway in which a peptide growth factor is elaborated by one cell type but affects a different neighboring cell type.

The **PROSTATE** functions as a reproductive exocrine organ and functions to prevent urinary tract infections. However, the prostate is most noted for the frequency with which it is the origin of benign and malignant neoplasms and infectious diseases in aging men. The most important of these diseases are prostatitis, benign prostatic hyperplasia, and prostate cancer. This article will review the prostate in health and disease with an emphasis, where possible, on the gerontological aspects of prostate disease. [*See* RENAL AND URINARY TRACT FUNCTION.]

I. ANATOMY

The adult prostate gland weighs an average of 20 g, is approximately the size of a walnut, and surrounds the urethra just below the bladder neck as shown in Figure 1. The posterior surface of the prostate can be palpated by a digital rectal exam. The prostate is composed of tubuloalveolar glands and stroma. The fluid produced by the prostate glands drains into 20 to 30 ducts that enter the urethra at or distal to a bulge in the distal prostatic urethra called the verumontanum. On each side of the verumontanum are the ejaculatory ducts, which are the conduits for sperm from the testicles and seminal fluid from the seminal vesicles. The prostate stroma surrounds the prostate glands and is made up of smooth muscle and fibroblasts.

II. PHYSIOLOGY

A. Reproduction

The prostate is an exocrine gland (excretes fluid) and has no known endocrine (hormonal) function. The exocrine secretions make up 15% of the ejaculate volume, but this fluid in itself is not necessary for fertility. The prostate along with the bladder neck and prostatic urethra play a critical role in coordinated antegrade sperm delivery during ejaculation. At the time of ejaculation, sympathetic nerve fibers innervating the $\alpha1$ receptors in the smooth muscle in the prostate, bladder neck, and vas deferens cause emission of seminal fluid and sperm into the prostatic urethra, and closure of the bladder neck and prostatic urethra. This closure prevents the sperm and seminal fluid from going into the bladder during ejaculation and is necessary for normal ejaculation.

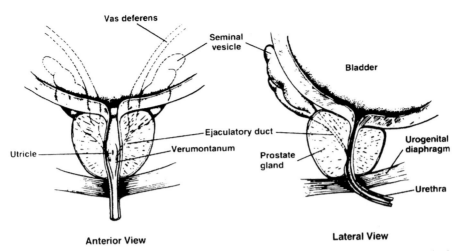

Figure I The prostate surrounds the urethra just below the level of the bladder neck. Fluid from the vas deferens and seminal vesicles drains into the ejaculatory ducts that enter the prostatic urethra just lateral to the verumontanum. The verumontanum is a midline bulge at the distal prostatic urethra. (From Goluboff, E. T., Stifelman, M. D., & Fisch, H., 1995. Ejaculatory duct obstruction in the infertile male. *Urology, 45(6)*, 925. Used by permission.)

B. Infection—Host Resistance

The prostate glands produce numerous substances that are continuously released into the urethra. These include zinc, citric acid, calcium, phosphoryl choline, prostatic acid phosphatase, and prostate-specific antigen (PSA). The prostatic fluid has the highest concentration of zinc in the body, and zinc is known to be an antibacterial factor. Ongoing release of zinc by the prostate may play a role in preventing urinary tract infections. There is a great deal of popular literature purporting that intake of zinc is beneficial in preventing urinary infections and prostate disease, but this is unsubstantiated.

III. PROSTATITIS

Prostatitis, or inflammation of the prostate, is a term used to describe infectious and noninfectious inflammatory conditions of the prostate. Prostatitis may occur in men from puberty through adulthood. Patients may present with a variety of symptoms, including pain in the perineum, low back, and suprapubic area, painful ejaculation and urination, and a decrease in the force of the urinary stream. There are four different types of prostatitis that are described herein.

A. Etiology

A variety of theories have been proposed to explain the cause of prostatitis. These include urinary reflux into prostatic ducts, alterations in the secretory products of the prostate, and the presence of infected prostatic calculi. Unfortunately, we do not understand why men develop prostatitis, and as a result, physicians are frequently unsuccessful and frustrated in their attempts to treat patients. Not surprisingly, patients also have a poor understanding of their disease and are frequently unhappy with treatment results.

B. Bacterial Prostatitis

The most common organism causing bacterial prostatitis is *Escherichia coli*, which is also the most common pathogen causing urinary tract infections. Indeed, bacterial prostatitis is the most common cause of urinary tract infections in older men. Other organisms causing bacterial prostatitis include Proteus, Klebsiella, Enterobacter, Pseudomonas, Serratia, and less frequently, Enterococcus.

C. Acute Bacterial Prostatitis

Acute prostatitis is an acute febrile illness associated with constitutional symptoms as well as the prostatitis symptoms previously described. On examination patients are acutely ill and the prostate is exquisitely tender and should not be palpated with any force. Pathologically the prostate is infiltrated with neutrophils. These patients require admission to the hospital and intravenous antibiotics. If patients have urinary retention or severe obstructive voiding symptoms, a suprapubic tube is placed into the bladder to drain the urine to avoid traumatizing the prostate with a urethral catheter. If the infection fails to resolve then studies are performed to rule out a prostatic abscess, which may require drainage. Treatment for acute prostatitis is quite successful, and subsequent urologic studies are directed towards identifying a source for the infection.

D. Chronic Bacterial Prostatitis

A diagnosis of chronic bacterial prostatitis is based on positive cultures of prostatic fluid obtained by digitally massaging the prostate and culturing the expressed fluid that exits the meatus. Microscopy on this fluid shows >10–20 white blood cells per high power field. A small volume of urine is voided after the prostate massage, and the bacterial count of this culture exceeds that of the urine voided prior to the prostate massage. Treatment consists of 1 month of oral antibiotics based on bacterial sensitivity testing. The ideal antibiotic must have good coverage of gram-negative bacteria and must be lipid soluble to penetrate the prostate tissue. The quinolone antibiotics have these characteristics and are effective in the majority of cases of bacterial prostatitis. For reasons that are unknown, some infections persist and do not respond to treatment.

E. Chronic Nonbacterial Prostatitis

The diagnosis of chronic nonbacterial prostatitis is based on the expressed prostate fluid showing >10–20 white blood cells per high power field but no documentation of any bacterial infection. These patients present with symptoms of prostatitis, but the etiology of the inflammation is unknown. Physicians explain to these patients that there is inflammation of the prostate the causes of which are not understood. In general, physicians will try a course of empiric oral antibiotics, usually the quinolones, for 1 month. If symptoms do not resolve then treatment becomes dif-

ficult because the etiology of the disease is not understood. Treatment options include frequent hot sitz baths, anti-inflammatory agents, and in some patients, diet alteration may be helpful if they find that their symptoms are exacerbated by spicy foods, caffeine, or alcohol.

F. Prostatodynia

Prostatodynia, literally prostate pain, is a diagnosis given to patients with prostatitis symptoms but no evidence of infection or inflammation in the prostate fluid. Typically these patients are young to middle aged and suffer a great deal from their symptoms. Empiric antibiotics and supportive treatment as described in the chronic nonbacterial prostatitis section are prescribed with varying results. In some of these patients, nonrelaxation of the pelvic floor muscles and hyperplasia of the bladder neck has been documented. Urodynamic studies to measure the pressure generated in the bladder during voiding may be indicated in patients with prostatodynia, and if bladder outlet obstruction from bladder neck hyperplasia is documented, these patients may benefit from incision of the bladder neck. Thermotherapy of the prostate is also being studied for patients with nonbacterial prostatitis and prostatodynia, and uncontrolled trials have shown some success with this treatment. Unfortunately, the etiology of prostatodynia remains quite speculative.

IV. BENIGN PROSTATIC HYPERPLASIA

Benign prostatic hyperplasia (BPH) is the most common benign tumor of adult men and is a major factor affecting the health of older men. BPH is a pathologic term referring to growth of the glandular and stromal elements in the prostate. With this growth of the prostate, men can develop bothersome urinary symptoms and complications resulting from bladder outlet obstruction. This section will review the etiology, physiology, and clinical aspects of BPH.

A. Incidence

Men begin to develop BPH in their thirties, and the incidence increases with age as shown in Figure 2. Over 50% of men older than age 50 have BPH, and

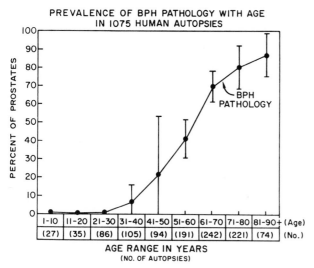

PREVALENCE OF BPH PATHOLOGY WITH AGE
IN 1075 HUMAN AUTOPSIES

Figure 2 The prevalence of benign prostatic hyperplasia (BPH) as assessed in autopsy specimens. As men get older the prevalence of BPH increases. (From Berry, S. J., Coffee, D. S., Walsh, P. C., et al., 1984. The development of human benign prostatic hyperplasia with age, *Journal of Urology, 132*, 474. Used by permission.)

75% of men in their eighth decade have BPH. The urinary symptoms caused by bladder outlet obstruction, termed prostatism, occur in 25% of men 55 years of age and occur in 55% of men aged 75.

B. Etiology

The two conditions necessary for BPH to develop are the aging process and testosterone production from the testicles. Men who receive an orchiectomy before puberty do not develop BPH. Testosterone produced by the testicles is converted to dihydrotestosterone in the cytoplasm of the prostate stromal and epithelial cells. Dihydrotestosterone then binds to an androgen receptor, and this complex binds to specific DNA sites in the nucleus and causes protein synthesis and cell growth. As further evidence of the role of testosterone in the development of BPH, 5-α reductase inhibitors, androgen receptor blockers, and orchiectomy all cause a decrease in prostate size.

As men age, their testosterone levels decrease. The ongoing growth of the prostate can be explained in part by an increase in number of androgen receptors in the prostate with age. More recent experiments support the role of stromal and glandular interactions

via growth factors in causing BPH. Basic fibroblast growth factor (FGF) and transforming growth factor (TGF) beta have been shown in tissue culture to act as autocrine and paracrine factors leading to BPH. Researchers are just beginning to understand the causes of BPH in aging men.

C. Physiology

Benign prostatic hyperplasia occurs in both the glandular and stromal elements of the prostate. The enlarging prostate can cause bladder outlet obstruction by physically blocking the prostatic urethra, termed *static obstruction*. In addition, contraction of the smooth muscle in the prostate stroma and capsule causes dynamic bladder outlet obstruction. This contraction is under the influence of sympathetic nerve fibers innervating the α1 receptors in the smooth muscle. Pharmacologic therapy that blocks the α1 receptors is extremely effective in alleviating symptoms of BPH and will be discussed later.

With bladder outlet obstruction from BPH, men may develop obstructive voiding symptoms including a decreased force of their urinary stream and difficulty emptying their bladder. In response to the bladder outlet obstruction, the smooth muscle in the bladder wall hypertrophies and the bladder wall thickens. This causes a decreased functional capacity of the bladder, and men develop the so-called irritative voiding symptoms that include urinary frequency, urgency, and nocturia. These irritative symptoms are usually more bothersome to patients than their obstructive symptoms, and can interfere with their daily activities and their sleeping.

A small percentage of patients will develop complications from their BPH including recurrent urinary tract infections, gross hematuria, urinary retention, and obstructive uropathy. These patients usually require surgical rather than medical management of their BPH.

D. Diagnosis

The diagnosis of benign prostatic hyperplasia is based on clinical assessment and does not require a biopsy of the prostate tissue. The history begins with assessment of the presence and severity of the obstructive

Table I Prostatism Symptoms

Obstructive	Irritative
Difficulty initiating stream	Frequency
Slow force of stream	Urgency
Hesitancy (stream starts and stops)	Urgency incontinence
Straining to urinate	Dysuria
Feeling of incomplete bladder emptying	Nocturia

and irritative voiding symptoms shown in Table I. To this end, the American Urologic Association (AUA) developed the AUA Symptom Score shown in Figure 3, a scientifically valid and reproducible questionnaire to assess the severity of prostatism symptoms and to assess the efficacy of treatment. The AUA symptom score can be quite helpful in managing patients with BPH. The symptom score also has limitations in that it does not diagnose prostatism, and any number of causes of voiding dysfunction can cause an elevated AUA symptom score. In addition, the AUA symptom score does not assess the degree of bother that patients have as a result of their symptoms, and some patients have a high AUA score but are not troubled by their symptoms and do not want any type of treatment.

The history of patients with suspected BPH is also directed at elucidating any other etiologies for the patient's voiding dysfunction. The differential diagnosis for voiding dysfunction is extensive and includes malignancy, infection, neurologic diseases, other causes of bladder outlet obstruction, such as urethral stricture disease, and side effects of various medications on the bladder and bladder outlet.

Physical examination includes a careful digital rectal exam of the prostate to assess for any nodules suggestive of malignancy and to rule out prostatitis. A common misconception is that the size of the prostate correlates with urinary symptoms or with the need for some type of intervention. In fact, the size of the prostate does not correlate with the incidence or severity of prostatism symptoms and in no way correlates with the risk of malignancy. The physical exam also includes palpation for a distended bladder, examination of the meatus to rule out meatal stenosis as a cause of bladder outlet obstruction, and a thorough neurologic exam.

All patients with prostatism symptoms should have a urinalysis to rule out infection and microscopic he-

The AUA symptom index

Question	Not at All	Less Than 1 Time in 5	Less Than Half the Time	About Half the Time	More Than Half the Time	Almost Always
1. During the last month or so, how often have you had a sensation of not emptying your bladder completely after you finished urinating?	0	1	2	3	4	5
2. During the last month or so, how often have you had to urinate again less than 2 hours after you finished urinating?	0	1	2	3	4	5
3. During the last month or so, how often have you found you stopped and started again several times when you urinated?	0	1	2	3	4	5
4. During the last month or so, how often have you found it difficult to postpone urination?	0	1	2	3	4	5
5. During the last month or so, how often have you had a weak urinary stream?	0	1	2	3	4	5
6. During the last month or so, how often have you had to push or strain to begin urination?	0	1	2	3	4	5
	None	1 Time	2 Times	3 Times	4 Times	5 or More times
7. During the last month, how many times did you most typically get up to urinate from the time you went to bed at night until the time you got up in the morning?	0	1	2	3	4	5

AUA symptom score = sum of questions 1 to 7.

Figure 3 The American Urological Association Symptom Score is a standardized questionnaire that gives a numeric value to the severity of voiding symptoms. Voiding symptoms are considered mild if the score is 0–7, moderate if the score is 8–19, and severe if the score is 20–35. (From Barry, M. J., Fowler, Jr., F. J., O'Leary, M. P., et al., 1992. The American Urological Association symptom index for benign prostatic hyperplasia. *Journal of Urology, 148*(5), 1549. Used by permission.)

maturia, and a serum creatinine to rule out renal failure. There is ongoing debate concerning whether a PSA is necessary in all patients with suspected BPH. In general, we obtain a PSA in all of our patients with prostatism symptoms because the PSA appears to be more sensitive than the digital prostate exam in detecting prostate cancer. Moreover, if prostate cancer is present it would greatly change our management.

E. Medical Treatment

Once we establish the diagnosis of BPH, we explain to our patients about their condition and reassure them that there is no evidence of malignancy. We also explain that, unfortunately, symptomatic BPH appears to be a normal part of aging. Usually, patients are reassured to hear that there is no evidence of prostate cancer, and if their voiding symptoms are not bothersome, they will frequently elect watchful waiting and periodic checkups. If the prostatism symptoms are bothersome to the patient, we usually first offer pharmacologic treatment consisting of either α1 blocking agents or 5-α reductase inhibitors.

The selective α1 blocking agents (doxazosin, terazosin) exert their effects by relaxing the smooth muscle in the prostate stroma, capsule, and bladder neck, and thus decrease the dynamic component of the bladder outlet obstruction. In prospective randomized double-blind trials, these agents have been shown to give patients symptomatic improvement and to increase the urinary flow rate. Whereas placebo is effective at improving symptoms in about 40% of patients with BPH, α1 blockers are effective in about 75% of patients. Patients can notice improvement within several weeks of beginning therapy, and they must continue to take these drugs on a daily basis or else their symptoms will recur. Because α1 blocking agents are also effective for treating hypertension, in some patients this one medication can treat two problems at once. These agents are tolerated well by normotensive as well as hypertensive patients, and side effects include dizziness, fatigue, and hypotension.

The other medical therapy available to treat prostatism is finasteride, a 5-α reductase inhibitor that blocks the conversion of testosterone to dihydrotestosterone. This drug causes the prostate to decrease in volume by 25% and causes a 50% reduction in the PSA at 6 months. Prospective randomized blinded trials have demonstrated that finasteride gives symptomatic improvement and causes a modest increase in urinary flow rate after at least 6 months of treatment. Side effects include impotence, decreased libido, and decreased ejaculatory volume in less than 5% of patients. Prospective, randomized studies comparing the efficacy of α1 blockers, finasteride, and the combination of these two drugs are in progress.

F. Surgical Treatment

Surgery is indicated for BPH when there is documented obstructive uropathy (kidney failure), urinary retention, recurrent urinary tract infections secondary to high postvoid residuals, or gross hematuria secondary to BPH. Surgery is also indicated for symptomatic improvement especially if pharmacologic treatment is insufficient. The gold standard technique that gives the best improvement in urinary flow rate and the best symptomatic improvement is the transurethral resection of the prostate (TURP). In this procedure the obstructing prostate tissue is resected using a cautery-wire loop through a cystoscope in the urethra. This procedure requires an anesthetic and several days of hospitalization after the procedure with an indwelling foley catheter in the bladder. The catheter is removed prior to discharge from the hospital. Several weeks of convalescence are required to allow the surgical site to heal. Most patients have retrograde ejaculation following a TURP in which the ejaculate goes into the bladder instead of out the penis during the sexual act. Other side effects are rare and include incontinence, impotence, stricture, and bleeding requiring a blood transfusion. In patients who require surgery and have extremely large prostates in excess of 100 g, an open prostatectomy is performed. In this procedure the benign obstructing prostate tissue is removed through a lower abdominal incision, while the peripheral prostate tissue and capsule are left behind.

There is a great deal of ongoing research investigating other surgical procedures to remove obstructing prostate tissue. The most promising of these techniques involves use of laser energy to either coagulate or vaporize the obstructive tissue. Laser surgery offers advantages over TURP, including less hospitalization time and less bleeding complications as well as a decreased incidence of retrograde ejaculation. TURP, on the other hand, continues to give better improvement in the urinary flow rate compared to the laser. Until more data are available concerning the type of laser energy used, the power level, and the duration of laser exposure, we continue to use the TURP for patients requiring surgical treatment of BPH.

Another technique that is actively being investigated is transurethral vaporization of the prostate, which uses a steel rollerball device to transmit high-power electrical cutting current to the prostate. This technique is purported to require less hospitalization, cause less bleeding, and be technically easier than a TURP, but controlled studies are not yet available.

V. PROSTATE CANCER

A. Incidence

Adenocarcinoma of the prostate is the most common internal cancer of males in the United States and is the second most common cause of cancer deaths, second only to lung cancer. The incidence of prostate cancer continues to rise each decade. In 1995 it is estimated that there will be 244,000 new cases of prostate cancer and 40,000 deaths from prostate cancer in the United States. Overall, men in the United States have a 9.5% lifetime risk of developing prostate cancer and a 2.8% lifetime risk of dying of prostate cancer. Clearly, prostate cancer is a major health problem in aging males. [See CANCER AND THE ELDERLY.]

B. Etiology

As men age, the incidence of prostate cancer increases. There is a great disparity between the incidence of clinical carcinoma of the prostate (CAP) and the incidence of prostate cancer found at autopsy (occult cancer) in men who die of other causes. Autopsy studies reveal that 30% of men in their seventh decade, 40% of men in their eighth decade, and 50% of men in their ninth decade have subclinical prostate cancer. Of great interest is that only a small percentage of these men go on to develop clinical prostate cancer. The factors that cause subclinical prostate cancer to progress to clinical prostate cancer are presently under intense investigation.

Although the autopsy incidence of prostate cancer is equal in Japanese and American men, clinical prostate cancer is uncommon in Japanese men. However, when Japanese men move to the United States, the incidence of clinical CAP approaches that of whites in one to two generations. The reason for this is not known, but research is focusing on the difference in dietary habits of Japanese and Americans. In Japan, unlike America, the usual diet is low in fat and high in soybean. Studies in tissue culture and in mice have shown that low fat and high soybean confers protection from growth of established prostate cancer. Other environmental factors may also play a role in converting latent prostate cancer to clinical prostate cancer. [See DIET AND NUTRITION.]

Race also plays a significant role in the development of clinical CAP. Whereas the autopsy incidence of CAP in Blacks equals that of Whites in the United States, black men have a higher incidence of clinical prostate cancer than Whites, and these cancers present at more advanced stages and have a higher mortality in Blacks. These statistics hold even when controlling for age, socioeconomic status, and the geographic area. Access to medical care, diet, and genetic factors may all play a role, and research in this area is ongoing. [See RACIAL AND ETHNIC DIVERSITY.]

In a subset of men, genetics also plays an important role in the development of prostate cancer. Men with first-degree relatives with prostate cancer have a 2- to 3-fold increased incidence of developing prostate cancer, and this risk increases with the number of family members affected. Therefore, inquiry into a family history of prostate cancer should be made in every man undergoing a routine history and physical examination, and patients with a positive family history need more careful follow-up.

C. Prostate-Specific Antigen

PSA is presently the most unique marker in cancer biology, and its discovery has revolutionized the detection, diagnosis, and treatment of prostate cancer. PSA is a glycoprotein normally produced by prostate epithelial cells and it functions to hydrolyze the coagulum of the ejaculate. Prostate cancer as well as inflammation, BPH, and prostate trauma can cause increased amounts of PSA to be released into the bloodstream. An abnormally elevated serum PSA has been shown to be more sensitive than the digital prostate exam in detecting prostate cancer. With the discovery of PSA, physicians are now detecting many more prostate cancers, and there is now a sensitive marker to measure the effectiveness of treatments.

However, up to 20% of men with clinical prostate cancer have a normal PSA level, thus emphasizing the importance of the digital prostate exam.

D. Screening

With the discovery of PSA, numerous screening programs have been set up with the hope of detecting prostate cancer earlier. Although physicians are now detecting more early and advanced stage prostate cancers, to date there is still no evidence that prostate cancer screening has decreased the mortality from prostate cancer. This may be partly because many prostate cancers appear to be slow growing, and patients often die of other causes than their prostate cancer. Conclusions on the effectiveness of screening for CAP are forthcoming, but at this time the American Cancer Society and the AUA are recommending yearly PSA measurements and prostate exams in men beginning at age 50, and beginning at age 40 in patients with risk factors for prostate cancer.

E. Diagnosis and Staging

Patients suspected of having prostate cancer from an abnormal digital prostate exam or an elevated serum PSA undergo biopsy of the prostate. This is accomplished by advancing a biopsy needle transrectally into the prostate with either ultrasound or finger guidance and obtaining cores of tissue from the prostate. Transrectal ultrasound allows accurate sizing of the prostate and helps in directing the biopsy needle to specific areas in the prostate. Volumetric measurement of the prostate with ultrasound is especially important because a large volume of BPH can sometimes explain an increase in the PSA.

Once the diagnosis of CAP is made, the tissue is graded pathologically by the Geason scale, with grade 5 being the most poorly differentiated and grade 1 being well differentiated. Staging is based on the size and extent of the palpable cancer and on the metastatic workup, which includes a chest X ray, bone scan, blood count, and liver function tests. The prostatic acid phosphatase blood test is also frequently used; elevation of the enzymatic acid phosphatase usually means the prostate cancer is advanced and cannot be cured by surgery or radiation therapy.

F. Treatment

The appropriate treatment depends on a broad range of factors including tumor grade and stage, the patient's 10- to 15-year life expectancy and general health, and most importantly, the patient's preference. A great deal of controversy exists regarding the best treatment for prostate cancer, and numerous ongoing studies are attempting to address this issue.

G. Expectant Management

Expectant management for prostate cancer consists of regular clinic visits, monitoring for the complications of prostate cancer, and treating patients for symptoms if they arise. This is the primary management used for prostate cancer in some parts of Europe and Scandanavia. Several prospective studies show that the majority of patients treated by expectant management die of causes other than their prostate cancer, and the cancer does not impact on their life expectancy. This is because many prostate cancers grow slowly and may take decades to spread or cause symptoms. Expectant management has come under harsh criticism because a significant percentage of patients in expectant management studies go on to develop locally advanced or metastatic disease. Also, many of the patients in these studies have lower grade, less aggressive tumors to begin with. At present, we are participating in a prospective randomized trial comparing expectant management to radical prostatectomy for localized prostate cancer, and hopefully some important questions will be answered by this study.

H. Radical Prostatectomy

Radical prostatectomy consists of removing the entire prostate and seminal vesicles. After the prostate is removed, the bladder neck is sutured to the urethra over a urethral catheter. Patients are hospitalized for about 3–4 days and are required to wear the urethral catheter for 2 weeks at home. Radical prostatectomy cures 60–80% of patients and is a good option in patients with a 10- to 15-year life expectancy. The cure rate of radical prostatectomy approaches 90% if the cancer is confined to the prostate gland on pathological examination. Potency can be preserved in a select group of younger patients with small tumors by sparing the nerves that run along each side the prostate. A significant number of patients suffer from impotence and periodic urinary incontinence after the surgery, and this can impact negatively on their quality of life. On the other hand, radical prostatectomy offers the possibility of a cure of a potentially deadly cancer. If impotence and incontinence develop, various treatments are available that deal successfully with these complications.

I. Radiation Therapy

Radiation therapy either by external beam or by interstitial seed implantation also offers the chance for cure in patients with localized prostate cancer. Although retrospective studies suggest that surgery may offer a better chance for cure than radiation therapy, there still has not been a good prospective randomized study comparing these two treatments. It may be that many patients receiving radiation therapy in these studies are poor surgical risk patients and have more advanced disease than the patients in the retrospective surgery series, thus making these studies invalid for comparison. Although patients who receive radiation therapy suffer less impotence and urinary incontinence than patients who receive surgery, these as well as other side effects, including bowel and bladder irritation, can occur from radiation treatment.

J. Hormonal Therapy

The growth of prostate cancer is partly dependent on androgens produced by the testicles and adrenal glands. By either removing the testicles (orchiectomy), or giving drugs that inhibit the production of or action of androgens, prostate cancer can be put into a remission for up to several years. Unfortunately, this effect is only temporary and eventually the prostate cancer becomes independent of androgens and continues to grow.

Patients with advanced prostate cancer usually receive some form of hormonal treatment. This consists of either bilateral orchiectomy or medical therapy. The leutinizing hormone (LH)-releasing agonists leuprolide and goserelin act by preventing the release of LH from the anterior pituitary. These medications ultimately stop the production of testosterone by the testicles and are as effective as orchiectomy. Another agent, flutamide, blocks androgen receptors and pre-

vents the binding of androgens produced by the adrenal glands and the testicles. These hormonal treatments are extremely effective in putting advanced prostate cancer into a remission for a variable period of time. Side effects of these agents include hot flushes and, most notably, impotence.

K. Cryotherapy

More recently, numerous medical centers are attempting to cure clinically localized prostate cancer by freezing the prostate via special probes placed in the perineum under ultrasound guidance. Patients go home the same or next day. Although many patients develop an undetectable PSA after cryotherapy, the side effects can be significant. Long-term results of cryotherapy are needed before we can recommend this treatment.

L. Recent Advances in Prostate Cancer

A number of recent discoveries concerning PSA deserve mentioning here. Age-specific reference ranges are now being established for PSA. As men age, the upper limit of normal for PSA increases. Whereas a PSA of 4 ng/ml was previously the upper limit of normal for the Hybritech PSA test, now for men in their seventies, a PSA of 5 or 6 ng/ml is probably within normal limits. Hopefully, this will help relieve the great anxiety these older men experience when they are told that their PSA is elevated and will prevent some unnecessary prostate biopsies from being performed.

Further technology in PSA measurement may help us better predict which patients with an elevated PSA require a prostate needle biopsy. Many men with a PSA between 4 and 10 ng/ml (normal Hybritech range 0–4 ng/ml) have a PSA elevation secondary to their BPH and undergo needless prostate biopsies. PSA can now be measured in both a free and bound form, and it appears that the fraction of the bound PSA to the total PSA may help distinguish which of these men may have a higher likelihood of having prostate cancer and require a biopsy.

Another recent advance is in the area of molecular staging of prostate cancer. With gene amplification techniques, physicians can now detect a single PSA-producing prostate cancer cell in the bloodstream. This technology may help physicians to better detect or stage prostate cancer, and may help them evaluate better the effectiveness of various treatments of prostate cancer.

VI. CONCLUSION

A number of prostate diseases including prostatitis, BPH, and prostate cancer are having a major impact on the health of aging men. For reasons that are not understood, these diseases develop as men get older. In fact, BPH and prostate cancer seem to be a normal part of aging, and many men live with mild symptoms or occult cancer and die before these diseases have a significant impact on their quality of life. Part of the art of medicine is determining when to treat patients and subject them to the side effects of medications and surgeries, and when to observe patients without any active interventions.

BIBLIOGRAPHY

Barry, M. J., Fowler, Jr., F. J., O'Leary, M. P., Bruskewitz, R. C., Holtgrewe, H. L., Mebust, W. K., & Cockett, A. T. (1992). The American Urological Association symptom index for benign prostatic hyperplasia. The Measurement Committee of the American Urological Association, *Journal of Urology, 148*(5), 1549.

Gillenwater, J. Y., Conn, R. L., Chrysant, S. G., Roy, J., Gaffney, M., Ice, K., & Dias, N., for the Multicenter Study Group (1995). Doxazosin for the treatment of benign prostatic hyperplasia in patients with mild to moderate essential hypertension: A double-blind, placebo-controlled, dose-response multicenter study. *Journal of Urology, 154*, 110.

Gillenwater, J. Y., Grayhack, J. T., Howards, S. S., & Duckett, J. W., (Eds.) (1991). *Adult and pediatric urology* (2nd ed.). St. Louis: Mosby-Year Book, Inc.

Gormley, G. J., Stoner, E., & Bruskewitz, R. C. (1992). The effect of finasteride in men with benign prostatic hyperplasia. The Finasteride Study Group. *New England Journal of Medicine, 327*, 1185.

Johansson, J., Adami, H., Andersson, S., Bergstrom, R., Holmberg, L., & Krusemo, U. B. (1992). High 10-year survival rate in patients with early, untreated prostatic cancer. *Journal of the American Medical Association, 267*(16), 2191.

Lepor, H., Auerbach, S., Puras-Baez, A., Narayan, P., Soloway, M., Lowe, F., Moon, T., Leifer, G., & Madsen, P. (1992). A randomized, placebo-controlled multicenter study of the efficacy and safety of terazosin in the treatment of benign prostatic hyperplasia. *Journal of Urology, 148*(5), 1467.

McConnell, J. D., Barry, M. J., Bruskewitz, R. C., et al. (1994). Benign prostatic hyperplasia: Diagnosis and treatment. Clinical Practice Guideline, Number 8. (AHCPR Publication No. 94-0582). Rockville, MD: Agency for Health Care Policy and Research, Public Health Service, U.S. Department of Health and Human Services.

Steiner, M. S. (1995). Review of peptide growth factors in benign prostatic hyperplasia and urological malignancy. *Journal of Urology, 153*, 1085.

Trapasso, J. G., deKernion, J. B., Smith, R. B., & Dorey, F. (1994). The incidence and significance of detectable levels of serum prostate specific antigen after radical prostatectomy. *Journal of Urology, 152*, 1821.

Walsh, P. C., & Donker, P. J. (1982). Impotence following radical prostatectomy: Insight into etiology and prevention. *Journal of Urology, 128*, 492.

Walsh, P. C., Retik, A. B., Stamey, T. A., & Vaughan, Jr., E. D. (Eds.). (1992). *Campbell's urology* (6th ed.). Philadelphia: W. B. Saunders Co.

Psychological Well-Being

Carol D. Ryff

University of Wisconsin—Madison

I. Historical Perspectives on Well-Being in Later Life
II. A Multidimensional Model of Psychological Well-Being
III. Understanding Variations in Well-Being
IV. Future Directions in Research on Psychological Well-Being

Autonomy A component of psychological well-being in which one is self-determining and independent, able to resist social pressures to think and act in certain ways, regulates behavior from within, and evaluates self by personal standards.

Environmental Mastery A component of psychological well-being in which one has a sense of mastery and competence in managing the environment, controls a complex array of external activities, makes effective use of surrounding opportunities, and is able to choose or create contexts suitable to personal needs and values.

Happiness A frequently investigated dimension of subjective well-being, typically operationalized as the balance between positive and negative affect, or as the response to single-item questions about frequency or intensity of happiness.

Life Satisfaction The most frequently investigated dimension of well-being in later life. Components from original construct include zest versus apathy, resolution and fortitude, relationships between desired goals and achieved goals, self-concept, and mood tone.

Personal Growth A component of psychological well-being involving feelings of continued development, seeing one's self as growing and expanding, being open to new experiences, having the sense that

one's potential is being realized, seeing improvement in self and behavior over time, and being able to change in ways that reflect more self-knowledge and effectiveness.

Positive Relations with Others A component of psychological well-being in which one has warm, satisfying, trusting relationships with others; shows concern for the welfare of others; is capable of strong empathy, affection, and intimacy, and understands the give and take of human relationships.

Purpose in Life A component of psychological well-being that includes having goals in life and a sense of directedness, feeling there is meaning in one's present and past life, holding beliefs that give life purpose; and having aims and objectives for living.

Self-Acceptance A component of psychological well-being that includes having a positive attitude toward one's self, acknowledging and accepting one's good and bad qualities, and feeling positive about one's past life.

POSITIVE PSYCHOLOGICAL FUNCTIONING in later life has been of interest to social gerontologists for nearly half a century, although philosophers have written about the positive and negative aspects of old age since classical antiquity. Scientific studies of successful aging are traceable to scholars at the University of Chicago who orchestrated the Kansas City Studies of Adult Life. The strengths and limits of these early efforts are summarized and juxtaposed with a recent formulation of well-being based on the integration of multiple theoretical domains. Six key dimensions of positive functioning emerge from the synthesis, and an empirical model of them is described.

Encyclopedia of Gerontology
Volume 2

365

Variations in well-being linked with sociodemographic factors (age, sex, class, culture) and with particular life experiences are summarized. Future inquiries are needed to address life history profiles of well-being as well as the connections between mental and physical health.

I. HISTORICAL PERSPECTIVES ON WELL-BEING IN LATER LIFE

What it means to be well in later life has engaged thinkers across the ages. Nearly 2000 years ago, Cicero wrote about the force of character and judgment that comes with age, and importantly, of the need to adopt a regimen of health to guard against the infirmities of age. This, he stressed, was not simply a matter of attending to the body (eating moderately, getting exercise), but also of caring for the mind and soul for "they, too, like lamps, grow dim with time, unless we keep them supplied with oil" (see Chandler, 1948). When questioned about the burdens of old age, Cicero replied "to those who have not the means within themselves of a virtuous and happy life, every age is burdensome." His portrayal provided stark contrast to Aristotle's detailed elaboration of the defects of old men.

Scientific investigation of positive aging began at the University of Chicago in the 1940s with a group of scholars interested in exploring the meaning of personal and social adjustment in old age. The Kansas City Studies of Adult Life carried the Chicago tradition forward and articulated the original conception of successful aging, which included the amount of activity in which the individual engaged, the ability to disengage, satisfaction with life, and maturity or integration of the personality. Of these, life satisfaction became the most frequently investigated dimension of successful aging. This construct included component of zest versus apathy, resolution and fortitude, relationship between desired goals and achieved goals, self-concept, and mood tone. Over the next 30 years, enormous empirical research was generated on age profiles of life satisfaction. [See LIFE SATISFACTION.]

Along the way, researchers elaborated the meaning of successful aging to include other dimensions such as happiness or affect balance, morale, subjective well-being, and optimal interplay between individual and environment. Some of these grew out of a specific focus on old age, whereas others were imported from separate empirical domains and applied to the later years. The broad array of indicators expanded knowledge of the many ways to operationalize well-being and dispelled entrenched myths, such as the view that old age is a time of unhappiness and low morale. Attempts to explain why some people were happy, satisfied, and adjusted in old age, whereas others were not, met with limited success—factors such as health, marital status, socioeconomic status, and social activity accounted for generally less than 10% of the variation in well-being.

Overall, an absence of theory surrounded many of these initial studies of successful aging. The omission was due in part to the historical emphasis on applied research in social gerontology and accompanying concerns for problem solving and program development. Neglect of theory, however, led to elusive conceptual definitions, which hindered efforts to translate the guiding constructs to valid and reliable empirical measures. There was an implicit negativism as well, consistent with the general scientific tendency to focus on illness rather than wellness, which led to studies of anxiety, depression, worry, anomie, loneliness, and somatic symptoms. Such "mental health" research reflected an impoverished conception of well-being that ignored individuals' potential for achieving high levels of functioning and paid little attention to unique resources and possibilities for continued development in later years. [See DEPRESSION; MENTAL HEALTH.]

II. A MULTIDIMENSIONAL MODEL OF PSYCHOLOGICAL WELL-BEING

Three literatures offer theoretical guidance for articulating the meaning of psychological well-being. Developmental psychology, particularly life span developmental psychology, conceives of wellness as progressions of continued growth across the life course. Included are Erikson's model of the stages of psychosocial development, Buhler's formulation of basic life tendencies that work toward the fulfillment of life, and Neugarten's descriptions of personality change in adulthood and old age. Clinical psychology also offers multiple formulations of well-being, such as Maslow's conception of self-actualization, Roger's view of the fully functioning person, Jung's formulation of individuation, and Allport's conception of maturity. Finally, the literature on mental health, although guided largely by absence of illness definitions of well-being, includes significant exceptions, such as Jahoda's formulation of positive criteria of mental health, and Birren and Renner's conception of positive functioning in later life.

Points of convergence in the above theories comprise the key components of a multidimensional model of well-being. The six dimensions include self-acceptance, positive relations with others, autonomy, environmental mastery, purpose in life, and personal growth. Definitions of those who possess these qualities are provided in the glossary (original publications also describe those who lack such features). Taken together, these dimensions encompass a breadth of wellness that includes positive evaluations of one's self and one's life, a sense of continued growth and development as a person, the belief that life is purposeful and meaningful, the possession of quality relations with others, the capacity to manage effectively one's life and surrounding world, and a sense of self-determination. Little gerontological knowledge had been amassed on these theory-based components of well-being, particularly older persons' reported levels of purpose in life or personal growth.

Structured self-report scales were written to operationalize these six dimensions. The validity and reliability of the measures has been documented with extensive psychometric data across multiple studies. Recently, the proposed six-factor structure of the well-being model was empirically supported with a national probability sample. The sociodemographic correlates of the various aspects of positive functioning are addressed next.

III. UNDERSTANDING VARIATIONS IN WELL-BEING

Do profiles of psychological well-being vary across the life course? Are men and women different in their avowed well-being? Does socioeconomic status or cultural background influence positive functioning? In addition to these questions, researchers have also probed the role of adults' actual life experiences and their interpretations of them as factors that affect their well-being profiles.

A. Age Patterns

Cross-sectional studies show incremental patterns with age for certain aspects of well-being, such as environmental mastery and autonomy (particularly from young adulthood to midlife). Other dimensions, such as personal growth and purpose in life, show decremental patterns, especially from midlife to old age. Still other aspects, notably self-acceptance, shows no significant age differences across the three age periods. Positive relations with others varies between showing age increments and no age differences. These overall patterns recur with replicative consistency in select community samples as well as nationally representative samples. Taken together, the findings point to a differentiated life-course story in which some aspects of well-being appear to improve with time, some seem to decline, and some appear stable. [See LIFE COURSE.]

Longitudinal studies are necessary to clarify whether these patterns reflect developmental changes or cohort differences. Whatever the explanation, the recurring reports of lower ratings of purpose in life and personal growth among the aged warrants attention. Such patterns point to possibly important challenges of later life, and related arguments that contemporary social structures lag behind the added years of life many people now enjoy. That is, opportunities for continued growth and development and for meaningful existence be limited for present cohorts of older persons. It might also be that older persons place less value on personal growth and purpose in life than younger age groups, but research on the ideals of midlife and older adults refutes the notion that the aged place little value on continued self-development or purposeful living.

B. Gender Differences

With regard to gender, multiple data sets have shown that women of all ages consistently rate themselves higher on positive relations with others than do men, and in several studies, women tend to score higher than men on personal growth. The remaining four aspects of psychological well-being consistently show no significant differences between men and women. These findings offer new evidence to mental health research, which repeatedly documents a higher incidence of certain psychological problems, such as depression, among women. When the positive end of the mental health spectrum is considered, however, women are shown to have greater psychological strengths compared to men in certain aspects of well-being, and comparable profiles with regard to other dimensions. To miss such findings is to tell an incomplete story about the psychological functioning of women.

C. Class Differences

Whether socioeconomic status, typically defined in terms of education, income, and occupational standing, is linked with profiles of psychological well-being has been recently examined in the Wisconsin Longitudinal Study of educational and occupational aspirations and achievements. Based on a sample of midlife adults who have been studied since their senior year in high school, the research shows higher profiles of well-being for those with higher occupational standing. Higher well-being is also evident among those with greater educational attainment, with such differences most evident in reported levels of purpose in life and personal growth (for men and women). Viewed in the context of the growing scientific literature that links social class standing to health, these findings suggest that low social status not only increases the likelihood of negative outcomes, but also decreases likelihood of positive well-being, which may provide important protective factors in the face of life stresses.

D. Cultural Variation

How culture bears on fundamental conceptions of self and self in relation to others is an increasingly prevalent theme in social scientific inquiry. Much current discussion involves contrasts between individualistic and independent cultures with those that are more collectivistic and interdependent. Following this distinction, self-oriented aspects of well-being, such as self-acceptance or autonomy, might be expected to have salience in the Western cultural context, whereas other-oriented dimensions of well-being, such as positive relations with others, might have greater significance in Eastern, interdependent cultures. Midlife adults from the United States and South Korea showed higher profiles of well-being in the United States, a finding consistent with formulations of underlying cultural differences in self-presentation (Westerners

are more likely to attribute positive qualities to themselves). Despite these main effects, analyses within cultures revealed that Koreans showed highest self-ratings on the measure of positive relations with others, and lowest ratings for self-acceptance and personal growth. Among U.S. respondents, personal growth was rated highest, especially for women, whereas autonomy, contrary to the purported emphasis on self-determination in our own culture, was rated lowest. Sex differences were the same in both cultures—women rated themselves significantly higher than men on positive relations with others and personal growth. Qualitative data showed that Koreans placed greater emphasis on the well-being of others (e.g., children) in defining their own well-being than did Americans.

E. Life Experience and Interpretive Mechanisms

Understanding who does and does not possess high profiles of well-being can also be examined via proximal investigation of the actual substance of people's lives, that is, their life experiences and the meaning they give to them. We have studied a series of life experiences, ranging from the having and raising of children, to growing up with an alcoholic parent, to educational and occupational achievements in midlife, to health problems and relocation experiences in later life. The experiences thus vary by their location in the life course, by the nature of the challenge or task posed, and by their typicality (whether the experience is shared by many or few, whether it is expected or unexpected). Our formulation of how experiences are interpreted draws extensively on social psychological theory, such as how people make sense of their life experiences by comparing themselves with others (social comparison processes), by evaluating the feedback they perceive from significant others (reflected appraisals), by their understanding of the causes of their experiences (attributional processes), and by the importance they attach to such experiences (psychological centrality).

Collectively, the studies demonstrate that life experiences and how they are interpreted provide useful avenues for understanding human variation in well-being. The research on midlife parenting shows, for example, that considerable variability in adults' reported levels of environmental mastery, purpose in life, self-acceptance, and depression is accounted for by perceptions of how their grown children have "turned out" and how these children compare with themselves. In later life, we find that the physical health problems of aging women, combined with their assessments of how they compare with other older women, explain substantial variation in reports of personal growth, positive relations with others, autonomy, depression, and anxiety. Importantly, this work shows that older women in poor physical health who engage in positive social comparison processes have comparable psychological well-being to that of women in good physical health. Research on relocation among aging women shows how changes in self-concept can enhance well-being during a life transition. Thus, multiple experiences and diverse avenues for interpreting them point to gains or losses in psychological well-being through time.

IV. FUTURE DIRECTIONS IN RESEARCH ON PSYCHOLOGICAL WELL-BEING

To understand psychological wellness in old age will become ever more important with the population shift toward greater numbers of long-lived persons. Prior studies have delineated diverse components of positive psychological functioning, and future inquiries must address how individuals achieve and maintain such desired ends. Cicero's wise admonition that a positive old age has its foundation well established in youth points to the need for more longitudinal research that tracks long-term life histories and how they culminate in psychological fulfillment versus despair. Cicero warned that an intemperate and indulgent youth delivers to old age a body that is all worn out, but at the same time, he elevated the practice of virtue, which when cultivated in all periods of life, brings forth "wonderful fruits at the close of a long and busy career." Social scientific investigations need to explicate the array of prior factors (individual, social structural, experiential) that contribute to psychological well-being in the last decades of life. Studies that simultaneously monitor sociodemographic factors and their role in facilitating or hindering rich life experiences, along with individuals' framing of what has transpired, will be richly poised to explain who, in the final acts, remains purposeful, deeply connected

to others, open to continued insight from life, and contented with self. A further critical agenda will address the influence of these positive states of mind on the aging body. Connections between wellness of mind and vitality of body constitute a most provocative challenge, philosophically and scientifically, for those who would unravel the mysteries of well-being in later life.

BIBLIOGRAPHY

Chandler, A. R. (1948). Cicero's ideal old man. *Journal of Gerontology, 3,* 285–289.

Cutler, N. E. (1979). Age variations in the dimensionality of life satisfaction. *Journal of Gerontology, 34,* 573–578.

George, L. K. (1979). The happiness syndrome: Methodological and substantive issues in the study of social-psychological well-being in adulthood. *Gerontologist, 19,* 210–216.

Herzog, A. R., Rodgers, W., & Woodworth, J. (1982). *Subjective well-being among different age groups.* Ann Arbor: University of Michigan, Institute for Social Research.

Larson, R. (1978). Thirty years of research on the subjective well-being of older Americans. *Journal of Gerontology, 33,* 109–125.

Lawton, M. P. (1984). The varieties of well-being. In C. Z. Malatesta & C. E. Izard (Eds.), *Emotion in adult development* (pp. 67–84). Beverly Hills, CA: Sage.

Neugarten, B. L., Havighurst, R., & Tobin, S. (1961). The measurement of life satisfaction. *Journal of Gerontology, 16,* 134–143.

Ryff, C. D. (1995). Psychological well-being in adult life. *Current Directions in Psychological Science, 4,* 99–104.

Ryff, C. D. (1989a). Beyond Ponce de Leon and life satisfaction: New directions in quest of successful aging. *International Journal of Behavioral Development, 12,* 35–55.

Ryff, C. D. (1989b). Happiness is everything, or is it? Explorations on the meaning of psychological well-being. *Journal of Personality and Social Psychology, 57,* 1069–1081.

Ryff, C. D., & Essex, M. J. (1992). Psychological well-being in adulthood and old age: Descriptive markers and explanatory processes. In K. W. Schaie & M. P. Lawton (Eds.), *Annual review of gerontology and geriatrics,* (vol. 11, pp. 144–171). New York: Springer.

Ryff, C. D., & Keyes, C. L. M. (1995). The structure of psychological well-being revisited. *Journal of Personality and Social Psychology, 69,* 719–727.

Sauer, W. J., & Warland, R. (1982). Morale and life satisfaction. In D. A. Mangen & W. A. Peterson (Eds.), *Research instruments in social gerontology: Vol. 1, Clinical and social psychology* (pp. 195–240). Minneapolis: University of Minnesota Press.

Stock, W. A., Okun, M. A., & Benin, M. (1986). Structure of subjective well-being among the elderly. *Psychology and Aging, 1,* 91–102.

Williams, R. H., & Wirths, C. G. (1965). *Lives through the years: Styles of life and successful aging.* New York: Atherton Press.

Racial and Ethnic Diversity

Kyriakos S. Markides and Laura Rudkin

University of Texas Medical Branch

I. Studying Racial and Ethnic Diversity
II. Physical Health
III. Mental Health and Psychological Well-Being
IV. Social Relationships
V. Economic Status
VI. Conclusion

Ethnic Groups Social groups that are distinguished on the basis of national origin, race, or religion.
Ethnic Minority Groups Groups that suffer discrimination and subordination within society on the basis of their racial or ethnic background.
Racial Groups Social groups that are distinguished on the basis of biological factors such as facial features and skin color that are thought to derive from a common heredity.

Gerontologists have recently given increasing attention to the heterogeneity of the aged population, especially with respect to **RACE, ETHNICITY, AND MINORITY STATUS.** This interest is based to a large extent on the tremendous growth in the numbers and proportions of people of color and diverse ethnic origins in the United States, Canada, Australia, the United Kingdom, as well as in other Western societies. In the United States, non-Hispanic Whites accounted for 80% of the 65 and older population in 1980. This figure dropped to 74% in 1995, and is projected to be only around 67% by the year 2050.

Although African American elderly are the largest component of minority elderly population, they are projected to show only modest increases in their numbers in the foreseeable future. On the other hand,

Hispanic elderly should outnumber African American elderly by the year 2020 and one in six elderly Americans are expected to be of Hispanic origin by the year 2050. The fastest growing segment of the elderly population are Asian and Pacific Islanders who are expected to grow from 2% of the older population in 1995 to 7% by 2050.

What is often neglected both by researchers and policy makers is the great diversity within the above ethnic categories, especially among Hispanics and Asian Pacific Islanders. In 1990, for example, 49% of Hispanic elderly were of Mexican origin, 15% of Cuban origin, 12% of Puerto Rican origin, and 25% of Central American and other Hispanic origin. Among Asian Pacific Islanders, 30% were of Chinese origin, 24% Japanese, 24% Filipino, 8% Korean, 5% Asian Indian, and 5% of other Asian and Pacific Islander origin. Although Hispanics share a common linguistic background and the overwhelming majority are Roman Catholics, they nevertheless vary widely by such characteristics as educational levels, poverty status, geographic concentration, and immigrant status. Asian and Pacific Islanders are from a variety of linguistic, religious, and cultural backgrounds. Finally, Native Americans originated from roughly 500 tribes differing in cultural, social, and economic characteristics. This great diversity makes generalizations to the status and well-being of Hispanic, Asian Pacific Islander, and Native American elderly often inappropriate. In addition there is substantial ethnic diversity in the non-Hispanic white elderly population that remains understudied and unappreciated.

As we look toward the twenty-first century, the growing ethnic diversity of the United States elderly population poses challenges to both gerontologists and policy makers. In this article we attempt to provide a brief overview of what is known about the status and well-being of America's ethnic elderly, focusing on such important areas as health, mental health, social relationships, and economic status. We begin by outlining a historical overview of the field of ethnic and minority aging and conceptual approaches to studying ethnic diversity.

I. STUDYING RACIAL AND ETHNIC DIVERSITY

Much of the field of gerontology has grown without adequate attention to the population's racial and ethnic diversity. Serious attention was first given to aging among African Americans in the 1960s when certain advocacy groups highlighted the disadvantages of older African Americans in health, income, life satisfaction, and housing. Attention to Hispanics, mostly Mexican Americans, began in the 1970s and it was not until the 1980s when Asian and Pacific Islanders, Native Americans, and European-origin ethnic groups received substantial attention. The last three broad categories continue to be understudied. As mentioned earlier, great within-group diversity makes studying these groups more difficult. Small numbers have added to these difficulties.

Examination of the historical development of the field of ethnic minority aging will reveal the centrality of the concept of inequality in its conceptual development in the form of the double jeopardy hypothesis and the larger multiple hierarchy stratification system. Although the focus on the growing disadvantages of ethnic minority groups with aging has guided the field for over two decades, widening ethnic and racial differences with age in health, income, and psychological well-being have not typically been found in the literature. Although differences between minority groups and the majority are clearly evident, such differences appear to be even greater in middle age. These findings give greater support to the "aging as leveler hypothesis," which argues that aging subjects people to various influences that cut across ethnic and racial lines. It has also been suggested that declining differentials in old age result from higher early mortality in disadvantaged populations, which lead to greater selective survival into old age.

Researchers have suggested that the double jeopardy hypothesis and the emphasis on inequality reflect ways of thinking dominant in the 1970s. They argue that this emphasis did little to advance the field because it gave disproportionate attention to between-group differences at the expense of within-group cultural variation.

Within-group cultural variation has received limited attention from perspectives following the modernization and acculturation theories of aging. Modernization theory emphasized the declining status of the aged in ethnic groups of immigrant origin who find themselves transplanted in a complex, modern society. Acculturation theory has argued that the acculturation of younger generations into the larger society has created frictions between the generations that have negatively affected the well-being of the elderly. Unique cultural characteristics of ethnic groups and how they influence the aging process remain understudied. One of the great challenges of the field is the better specification of the influence of such characteristics and of the immigrant experience on the health and social relationships of the elderly of diverse ethnic origin. [See MODERNIZATION AND AGING.]

II. PHYSICAL HEALTH

A. Mortality and Life Expectancy

The most common indicators of health differences employed in the literature have been mortality rates and life-expectancy figures. Estimates for 1993 indicate a continuing disadvantage of African Americans who had a life expectancy at birth of 70.4 years compared with 76.6 years for Whites. Figures for Hispanics, Native Americans, and Asian Americans no longer support a disadvantage of these groups, especially people of Asian origin who were estimated to have a life expectancy at birth of 82.9 years. However, the quality of mortality estimates for these groups is more questionable than those of African Americans and non-Hispanic Whites.

Although African Americans have traditionally had higher mortality rates than Whites, these differences have been observed to decline with age, to the point of a reversal at very advanced ages. Although lower mortality rates of African Americans at advanced ages have been challenged on methodological grounds, there is agreement that the African American disadvantage at a minimum declines in old age, probably because of greater selective survival among African Americans.

Although estimates of the life expectancy of the Hispanic populations have been questioned, accumulating evidence since around 1980 suggests a life expectancy at birth at least equal to that for non-Hispanic Whites. This has been observed for all three major Hispanic populations: Mexican Americans, Cuban Americans, and Puerto Ricans. This paradoxical phenomenon, at least with respect to the socioeconomically disadvantaged Mexican Americans and Puerto Ricans appears to result from low death rates from diseases of the heart and cancer, especially among men.

The apparent favorable mortality profile of Hispanics has been attributed to certain protective cultural factors and selective immigration. Recent data have suggested that immigrants at any age are healthier than nonimmigrants.

Selective immigration may very well be the prime reason behind the favorable mortality situation of most Asian origin populations. Another factor is the relatively favorable economic situation of most Asian origin groups.

The life expectancy of the Native American population has also increased to the level of the general population, although again these estimates are of questionable quality. At a minimum, Native Americans have exhibited remarkable progress in recent decades owing a great deal to the success of the Indian Health Service in controlling infectious diseases and providing acute care.

B. Morbidity and Functional Health

Mortality statistics tell only part of the story. Also important are data on prevalence of chronic conditions and disabilities and other morbidity indicators. Among the main ethnic minority populations, only data for African Americans have been available in a systematic way, especially at the older ages. These data have shown for some time that with respect to highly prevalent conditions such as hypertension, diseases of the circulatory system, and diabetes, African Americans aged 45 and over have excess prevalence relative to Whites, but this excess declines steadily

with age. Nevertheless, elderly African Americans are disadvantaged relative to elderly Whites on most chronic disease indicators as well as several disability indicators and self-ratings of health. [See EPIDEMIOLOGY.]

Does the favorable mortality situation of Hispanics translate into a favorable morbidity situation in old age? The picture here is not very clear, principally because of the absence of adequate data. Most evidence suggests that Hispanic men have lower prevalence of heart disease and major cancers, but it is not clear why. With the exception of Cuban Americans, Hispanics are clearly disadvantaged socioeconomically, have very high rates of diabetes and obesity, and engage less in exercise. In addition, recent data from a large study of Mexican American elderly show that hypertension is at least as prevalent among them as it is among the general elderly population. Smoking and alcohol consumption rates among Hispanic males are also high. Any advantages in diseases of the heart and cancer among Hispanic males cannot be explained by known risk factors and may very well be related to selective immigration. [See ALCOHOL AND DRUGS; CARDIOVASCULAR SYSTEM; CANCER AND THE ELDERLY.]

The picture is quite clear with respect to diabetes, which is considerably more prevalent in Mexican American men and women than in non-Hispanic men and women at any age. Recent data on Mexican American elderly mentioned earlier show that both male and female diabetes rates decline significantly from ages 65 to 74 to ages 75 and over, a situation that is not present among non-Hispanic Whites. This underscores the great negative consequences of diabetes in early old age among Mexican Americans and the high rates of mortality it is associated with.

In addition to mortality and disease prevalence, indicators of functional health are also especially important among the elderly. Recent data suggest that the functional health of Mexican American elderly in terms of needing assistance with activities of daily living (ADLs) appears to be better than the functional health of African American elderly but slightly worse than non-Hispanic white elderly. With respect to four instrumental ADLs (IADLs) (meal preparation, shopping, using the telephone, and performing light housework) elderly Mexican Americans appear to be more impaired than either non-Hispanic Whites and African Americans. [See ACTIVITIES.]

Diversity in functional status has been observed across elderly Hispanic subgroups. In one study, older Cuban Americans were found to have the lowest rates of limitations in ADLs and IADLs, while Puerto Ricans reported the highest rates. Older Mexican Americans had rates of limitation similar to Cuban-origin elders for ADLs but similar to Puerto Ricans for IADLs. The prevalence of functional limitations among these groups confirmed that their functional health tends to be worse than that of the general population of elderly persons.

The poorer functional health of African American, Mexican American, and Puerto Rican elderly is consistent with data on self-assessed health, which show poorer self-assessments than non-Hispanic white elderly. In light of the socioeconomic, health, and access to care disadvantages of minority elderly, the poorer self-assessments appear to be realistic and not pessimistic because of certain cultural factors that predispose them to report poorer health.

With respect to Asian and Pacific Islander elderly, it could be expected that they should have favorable morbidity and functional health profiles given their apparent favorable mortality profiles as well as their relatively favorable socioeconomic profiles. However, there are not as yet systematic data on these populations' health, especially functional health and disability. If the evidence supporting better health among immigrants at any age is correct, it could be expected that the health of most Asian-origin populations in old age would be favorable given the high rates of immigrants among them. On the other hand, immigrant status has been associated with poorer access to health care because of lower Medicare coverage as well as linguistic and cultural barriers. Clearly more systematic data are necessary before researchers can gain a clear understanding of the health situation of the elderly in the various Asian and Pacific Islander populations.

We know even less about the health of Native American elderly, although there is some suggestion that those alive today are survivors of higher mortality at earlier years and are relatively healthy. Yet, as the population's mortality rates at younger ages have fallen in recent years, it could be predicted that a greater concentration of health problems at older ages can be expected in the years ahead. In addition, despite progress in access to health care, many Native American elderly remain socioeconomically disadvantaged and isolated from health and social services. Again, much remains to be learned about the health situation of the elderly from various Native American tribes.

III. MENTAL HEALTH AND PSYCHOLOGICAL WELL-BEING

Although the area of mental health and psychological well-being broadly defined has been central to the development of gerontology, our understanding of how ethnic and minority elderly fare in this area remains limited because of the absence of systematic data. The literature has predicted disadvantages among ethnic and minority elderly because of greater difficulties adjusting during old age given their disadvantaged situation in the larger society. Yet the evidence does not consistently support this prediction. Because most research is based on subjective evaluations of psychological well-being that are made with important reference groups in mind, inequalities in objective conditions do not always translate into inequalities in subjective assessments. [See MENTAL HEALTH; PSYCHOLOGICAL WELL-BEING.]

Even when research has focused on relatively more objective measures of psychological well-being, such as measures of depressive symptomatology, no clearcut differences have been observed between African Americans and Whites at any age. The same is the case with respect to Mexican Americans, except that older Mexican American women appear to have relatively high rates of depressive symptomatology. In addition, there is some evidence of lower depressive symptomatology among the foreign-born, which supports the "healthy migrant" effect also observed with regard to physical health. [See DEPRESSION.]

There is also inconclusive evidence with regard to the mental health and well-being of the elderly from the various Asian Pacific Islander groups. Although some evidence suggests greater problems among recent immigrants, other evidence suggests that older immigrants experience more problems with the passage of time because of increasing isolation from the larger society as well as the increasing acculturation of the children. The latter appear to fare better with the passage of time as they become assimilated and acculturated into the host society.

Systematic assessments of the mental health of Native American elderly are also lacking, although there is indication of high rates of depression among older women that are related to personal losses, social isolation, and acculturative stress. Kunitz and Levy found no differences in the prevalence of depression between elderly Navajo and the general population. They did find, however, that persistent depression was more prevalent among Navajo elderly women, although they acknowledged difficulties in assessing depression among men because it may be obscured by alcohol use, an observation also relevant with respect to the general population.

IV. SOCIAL RELATIONSHIPS

Conventional wisdom suggests that elderly in ethnic minority populations are advantaged in their social relationships, particularly family and intergenerational relationships. African American, Hispanic, Asian American, and Native American elderly all have been found to benefit from higher rates of coresidence with adult children and from social support from their extended families. Yet coresidence is often a matter of survival among these groups rather than simply a cultural preference. At the same time, lower coresidence among non-Hispanic Whites is evidence of their greater socioeconomic independence from their children. Research has shown over the years that although elderly in ethnic and minority populations have closer relationships with their children, they nevertheless report higher rates of unfulfilled expectations of filial responsibility than is the case among non-Hispanic white elderly, who appear more satisfied with what their children do for them. Clearly, availability of family members in the household or in close proximity is a great support to ethnic and minority elderly who have few other resources, but it is not always a sign of an advantage in intergenerational relationships. [See SOCIAL NETWORKS, SUPPORT, AND INTEGRATION.]

V. ECONOMIC STATUS

Underlying much of the variation among the elderly from various ethnic origins is their great diversity in economic status. Clearly, relative to non-Hispanic white elderly, significantly higher proportions of Afri-

can American elderly, most Hispanic elderly, and Native American elderly live in poverty and have lower incomes. These differences reflect differences in educational background, occupational status, and past discrimination. Economic status differences are even greater with respect to wealth measured by net worth.

On the other hand, most Asian Pacific Islanders are more secure economically, although family incomes in these groups are spread over a larger number of family members than is the case among non-Hispanic Whites. At the same time, given their greater proportion of foreign-born people, the economic status of Asian Pacific Islander elderly is negatively influenced by lower Medicare coverage. Finally, much economic variation exists among the various Asian Pacific Islander groups that is little understood. [See ECONOMICS: INDIVIDUAL.]

VI. CONCLUSION

The elderly population of the United States and other Western societies is becoming increasingly diverse ethnically primarily because of high rates of immigration from a variety of national origins. This trend in the United States is particularly evident among Hispanics and Asian Pacific Islanders. This diversity has not been adequately studied or understood, although research in this area of gerontology has increased markedly in recent years.

Although the field of ethnic and minority aging is growing it has not shown adequate conceptual development, which has focused more on inequalities between groups than within-group ethnic and cultural diversity.

Examination of ethnic differences in health suggests wide, continuing disadvantages of African American elderly but not among Hispanic elderly, at least with respect to mortality. Native Americans have also narrowed the mortality gap, but little is known about their morbidity and functional health status. The mortality situation of most Asian Pacific Islander elderly appears to be favorable and may very well reflect a "healthy immigrant" effect also thought to operate among Hispanics.

Much less is known about mental health and psychological differences between groups because of a scarcity of data, especially on more objective indicators. With respect to social relationships, ethnic and minority elderly appear to be advantaged because of higher coresidence rates and greater contact with adult children; this coresidence and contact often signify a lack of options relative to non-Hispanic white elderly.

There is no question regarding the lower economic status of African American, most Hispanic, and Native American elderly. Low incomes are compounded by even lower levels of net worth, which can be so important to the economic security of the elderly.

Although we have emphasized the importance of understanding within-group diversity, much of our discussion has focused on between-group differences in health, mental health, social relationships, and economic status. Clearly adequate data are not available to understand within-group diversity, especially among Asian Pacific Islanders and Native Americans. National surveys that include adequate numbers representing the various subpopulations are impractical because of cost considerations. Although large studies of the elderly in the largest of these groups are possible and needed, smaller and more intensive ethnographic studies of the smaller groups will go a long way to give an understanding of the characteristics and needs of the elderly.

Finally, research on ethnic and minority elderly needs to give greater attention to the immigrant experience and how it influences the elderly, both positively and negatively. Elderly immigrants from a variety of ethnic and cultural backgrounds face a number of similar experiences that have not been adequately understood or incorporated into our conceptual frameworks.

BIBLIOGRAPHY

Burton, L. M., Dilworth-Anderson, P., & Bengston, V. L. (1992). Creating culturally relevant ways of thinking about diversity and aging: Theoretical challenges for the twenty-first century. In E. P. Stanford & F. M. Torres-Gil (Eds.), *Diversity: New approaches to ethnic minority aging*. Amityville, NY: Baywood Publishing Company.

Chen, Y. (1992). Improving the economic security of minority persons as they enter old age. In *Minority elders: Longevity, economics, and health*. Washington, D.C.: The Gerontological Society of America.

John, R. (1991). The state of research on American Indian elders' health, income security, and social support networks. In *Minority elders: Longevity, economics, and health*. Washington, D.C.: The Gerontological Society of America.

Kunitz, S. J., & Levy, J. E. (1991). *Navajo aging*. Tucson: The University of Arizona Press.

Markides, K. S. (1994). Gender and ethnic diversity in aging. In R. J. Mannheimer (Ed.), *Older Americans' almanac*. Detroit: Gale Research Inc.

Markides, K. S., & Black, S. A. (1996). Race, ethnicity, and aging: The impact of inequality. In R. H. Binstock & L. K. George (Eds.), *The Handbook of Aging and the Social Sciences* (4th ed.) San Diego: Academic Press.

Markides, K. S., Rudkin, L., Angel, R. J., & Espino, D. V. (in press). Health status of Hispanic elderly in the United States. In Racial and Ethnic Differences in Health in Later Life B. Soldo (Ed.). Washington, DC: National Academy of Sciences.

Ramirez de Arellano, A. B. (1994). The elderly. In C. W. Molina & M. Aguirre-Molina (Eds.), (pp. 189–208). *Latino health in the U.S.: A growing challenge*. Washington, D.C.: American Public Health Association.

Treas, J. (1995). *Older Americans in the 1990s and beyond*. Population Bulletin, Vol. 50, no. 2. Washington, D.C.: Population Reference Bureau, Inc.

United States Bureau of the Census. 1993. *Racial and ethnic diversity of America's elderly population. Profiles of America's Elderly*; (no. 3). Washington, D.C.: U.S. Bureau of the Census.

Reaction Time

Timothy A. Salthouse

Georgia Institute of Technology

I. Historical Background
II. Importance

Choice Reaction Time   The time between the presentation of one of several stimuli and the occurrence of one of several responses. It is termed choice reaction time because a discrimination has to be made between two or more stimuli and a different response made depending on which stimulus was presented.
Cognition   Mental or intellectual abilities, typically assessed with special psychometric or experimental tests.
Neurological Status   The level of one's health with respect to the central nervous system.
Perceptual Speed   A cognitive ability usually assessed with simple paper-and-pencil tasks requiring search or discrimination tasks.
Slowing   The decrease in speed in many RT and perceptual speed tasks associated with increased age.
Speed   The rate at which an individual can carry out many processes. Typically assessed with choice reaction time and perceptual speed tasks.

REACTION TIME is typically measured in terms of the time elapsing between the presentation of a stimulus, which is often a brief visual or auditory signal, and a discrete response such as the press or release of a response key, the initiation of a movement, or the emission of a vocal response.

I. HISTORICAL BACKGROUND

The first systematic assessment of the relations between adult age and reaction time (RT) was by Galton in the late 1800s, although analyses of his data were not published until much later. There were sporadic investigations of the relations between age and RT until about 1950, when interest in this topic increased because of an assumption that an individual's RT might be informative about the status of his or her neurological system. A number of studies then appeared in which RT per se was the focus of the research.

Beginning in the 1960s, there was an increase in the use of RT as a primary dependent variable because it was assumed to reflect the duration of interesting mental processes. RT measurement in the context of mental chronometry has been a valuable tool in the information-processing perspective on cognition, and a very large number of studies have been reported within this tradition. In recent years a major issue in RT research has been the extent to which RT measures reflect general or specific age-related influences.

II. IMPORTANCE

There are three major reasons why RT is an important topic in gerontology. First, the speed with which a simple response can be produced is a very elementary behavioral measure, and therefore may function as a relatively direct indicator of an individual's neurological status. Second, studies of RT have revealed moderately large age relations, and these relations are among the most consistent and robust in all of the behavioral sciences. And third, RT measures have been found to be related to measures of higher cognitive functioning. In fact, measures of speed are actually included in

Copyright © 1996 by Academic Press, Inc.
All rights of reproduction in any form reserved.

several intelligence test batteries. These three points are elaborated in the following paragraphs.

A. Indicator of Neurological Status

RT has been considered a reflection of neurological status because a rapid response to an external stimulus not only requires intact sensory and motor processes, but also an efficient system of communication between input and output processes. There are clearly many neurological conditions that could exist with little effect on RT, but at least at a very gross level, it seems reasonable to assume that factors related to intactness of neural connections contribute to the efficiency of responding to environmental stimuli.

Unfortunately, although RT has been assumed to have sensitivity to certain neurological conditions, its specificity is unknown. That is, because all the factors responsible for slowed RT have not yet been identified, slow RT is not necessarily informative about the specific types of neurological impairment that might exist. Among the neurophysiology factors that have been mentioned as possible contributors to age-related slowing are loss of neurons due to vascular complications, reductions in degree of myelination, extent of dendritic branching, or in the quantity of certain

neurotransmitters. Until these alternatives can be discriminated, RT may have limited value as an indicator of particular types of neurological impairment.

There is some evidence that age-related slowing is not simply mediated by poorer health because slower RTs with increased age are still evident in samples of adults who report themselves to be in good to excellent health. However, it has recently been reported that the age-related slowing was greater for individuals reporting incidents of head trauma or general anesthesia, and thus this conclusion should probably be considered tentative until more data are available.

B. Robustness of Age Relations

In an earlier review of adult age differences in speeded performance, it was found that the median of over 50 correlations between age and a variety of speed measures was .45. The magnitude of the relations between age and measures of RT can also be illustrated with results of several recent studies. For example, in a study similar to that of Galton RTs were obtained from visitors to a public exhibition. In a sample of 2190 adults age 20 and older, simple RT to a single stimulus increased approximately 0.7 ms per year.

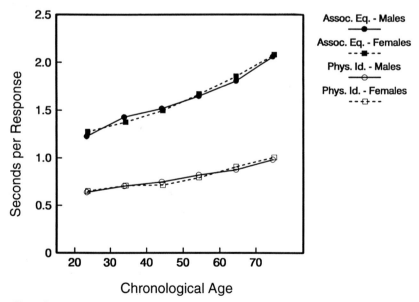

Figure I   Mean reaction time for physical identity and associational equivalence decisions as a function of age.

Comparisons of simple RT and choice RT are also interesting because the difference between the two times can be interpreted as the time to discriminate between stimuli. That is, choice RT involves a different response for each stimulus, and simple RT consists of the same response to all stimuli, and thus the additional time needed for the choice RT response can be assumed to reflect the duration of the added process. In another study, both simple and choice RT tasks were administered to 1265 adults (833 males, 432 females) between 20 and 90 years of age. The regression equations in this sample indicated an increase of about .5 ms per year for simple RT, and an increase of about 1.7 ms per year for choice RT. Because the age trends are greater in the measure requiring stimulus discrimination, results such as these suggest that age-related effects on RT are not simply attributable to slower sensorimotor processes.

Age relations have also been investigated in more complex RT tasks. For example, a wide range of tasks can be created in which one response (depression of one key) is made when two stimuli are the same in some dimension, and another response (depression of a different key) is made when the two stimuli are different. To illustrate, in one version of the task the stimuli can be pairs of digits, with the decision based on physical identity, and in another version of the task the stimuli can be pairs of digits and symbols, with the decision based on whether the digit-symbol pair was equivalent according to a code table displayed simultaneously with the stimuli.

Figure 1 illustrates means by decade for these two measures in a sample of 583 males and 776 females, with between 70 and 152 individuals in each decade. Notice that the age trends are monotonic and nearly continuous, and that the patterns are nearly identical for males and females. However, the average RTs are greater, and the age-related effects are larger for decisions based on associational equivalence (i.e., digit-symbol) compared to those based on physical identity (i.e., digit-digit). Regression analyses for the physical identity RT measure revealed an increase of approximately 6.4 ms per year, whereas those for the association RT measure had an increase of about 15 ms per year.

The pattern of larger age-related effects on measures in which greater amounts of cognitive processing seem to be required is consistent with a large amount of data in the gerontological literature. That is, when the task is merely to make a predetermined response to a single stimulus the age effects are rather slight (e.g., less than 1 ms per year); when the task requires a choice between different stimuli with a different response to each stimulus, the age effects are somewhat larger (e.g., about 1.5 to 2 ms per year); when the task requires two stimuli to be compared the age effects are larger (e.g., about 6 ms per year); and when stimuli are to be compared on the basis of an association then the age effects are even larger (e.g., about 15 ms per year).

Because similar patterns of age relations have been found with other speed measures, such as paper-and-pencil tests merely requiring simple motoric responses (e.g., connecting lines, copying digits) or also requiring cognitive operations (e.g., comparison or substitution), RT measures have been interpreted as reflections or indicators of a more general processing speed construct. Age relations on four paper-and-pencil tests hypothesized to reflect sensorimotor speed (i.e., connecting lines—Boxes, or copying digits—Digit Copying), and perceptual comparison speed (i.e., comparing letters—Letter Comparison, or comparing patterns—Pattern Comparison) are illustrated in Figure 2. Notice that the age trends are relatively slight (i.e., about 5 ms per year) for the two sensorimotor tasks, but larger (i.e., approximately 20 and 56 ms per year) for the two perceptual comparison tasks.

In addition to similar patterns of age relations, speed measures from paper-and-pencil tasks have also been found to have moderate correlations with RT measures. For example, in two recent samples of 372 adults, the correlations between the paper-and-pencil Pattern Comparison measure and the digit symbol RT measure were .60 and .61.

C. Relation to Cognition

As noted earlier, speed measures have been incorporated into several widely used cognitive test batteries. The fact that paper-and-pencil speed measures have been found to be moderately correlated with more traditional measures of cognitive functioning indicates that some relation exists between speed and cognition. Moderate relations between RT and paper-and-pencil speed measures and a variety of cognitive measures have also been found in several experimental

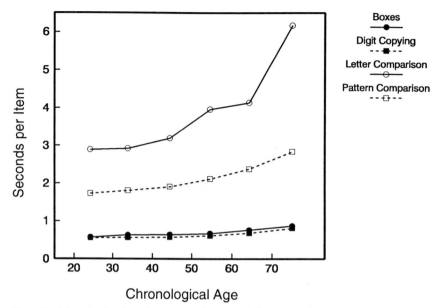

Figure 2   Mean levels of performance in four speeded paper-and-pencil tasks as a function of age.

studies, including some in which the cognitive tests were administered under self-paced conditions with no external time limits.

In several of these studies statistical control analyses have been conducted in which statistical procedures were used to equate people of different ages on an index of speed before examining the relation between age and measures of cognitive functioning. The typical outcome from these analyses has been that the age relations on cognitive functioning are greatly reduced after statistical control of speed. Moreover, with certain combinations of speed and cognitive measures the statistical control procedure has resulted in the complete elimination of the age-related variance in the measure.

Results such as these imply that RT and other speed measures reflect something that is important for the age differences in cognitive functioning. What is not yet obvious is the exact nature of the processes or factors assessed by speed measures that contribute to the age-related variations in cognitive functioning.

BIBLIOGRAPHY

Earles, J. L., & Salthouse, T. A. (1995). Interrelations of age, health, and speed. *Journal of Gerontology: Psychological Sciences, 50B,* P33–P41.

Fozard, J. L., Vercruyssen, M., Reynolds, S. L., Hancock, P. A., & Quilter, R. E. (1994). Age differences and changes in reaction time: The Baltimore Longitudinal Study. *Journal of Gerontology: Psychological Sciences, 49,* P179–P189.

Houx, P. J., & Jolles, J. (1993). Age-related decline of psychomotor speed: Effects of age, brain health, sex, and education. *Perceptual and Motor Skills, 76,* 195–211.

Koga, Y., & Morant, G. M. (1923). On the degree of association between reaction times in the case of different senses. *Biometrika, 15,* 346–372.

Salthouse, T. A. (1985). Speed of behavior and its implications for cognition. In J. E. Birren & K. W. Schaie (Eds.), *Handbook of the psychology of aging* (2nd Ed.; pp. 400–426), New York: Van Nostrand Reinhold.

Salthouse, T. A., Kausler, D. H., & Saults, J. S. (1990). Age, self-assessed health status, and cognition. *Journal of Gerontology, 45,* 156–160.

Wilkinson, R. T., & Allison, S. (1989). Age and simple reaction time: Decade differences for 5,235 subjects. *Journal of Gerontology: Psychological Sciences, 44,* P29–P35.

Rehabilitation

Bryan Kemp

Rancho Los Amigos Medical Center
University of Southern California

I. The Relevance of Rehabilitation to Aging
II. Unique Aspects of Geriatric Rehabilitation
III. The Practice of Rehabilitation
IV. Outcomes of Rehabilitation
V. Emerging Issues
VI. Summary

Activity of Daily Living (ADL)   The basic skills required to live at home independently: toileting, dressing, bathing, eating, transferring, mobility.

Deconditioning   Loss of strength, endurance, flexibility, fitness, and coordination due to lack of sufficient activity.

Disability   Dysfunction at the task level due to a temporary or chronic impairment and the difficulties of the task.

Handicap   Dysfunction at the social level of participation for people having a chronic disabling impairment; caused chiefly by societal barriers.

Impairment   Dysfunction at the organ level that decreases functioning of the organ. May be temporary or permanent.

Instrumental Activities of Daily Living (IADL)   Skills needed to live independently in the community: transportation, money management, taking medicines, shopping, household chores, safety.

Pathology   Dysfunction at the cellular level that kills, damages, or disrupts cellular function of an organ.

Rehabilitation   The process of restoring or improving function to people with a disabling illness or injury.

REHABILITATION is the process of improving or restoring functional ability to individuals who have sustained a disabling illness or injury. It rests on the belief that maximization of functional capacity is more important than cure, particularly for permanently disabled individuals. Geriatric rehabilitation takes into account the principles of rehabilitation, ranging from medical stabilization to societal integration, and incorporates the unique aspects of geriatrics. Rehabilitation for older individuals is successful when properly carried out. These services are available in a variety of locations including rehabilitation hospitals, community hospitals, nursing homes, adult day health-care centers, and home.

I. THE RELEVANCE OF REHABILITATION TO AGING

As people age, the prevalence of chronic disabling illnesses increases dramatically. Such conditions place older individuals at great risk for loss of independence, disengagement from society, and lifelong dependency. Up to the age of 18, the prevalence of such disabling conditions is about 10%; in adulthood, it is about 20%; in the 65–75 age group it is about 40%; and in the 75+ age group it is about 60%. By contrast, the prevalence of acute recoverable illnesses (such as infections) is actually not too different across the life span, although older individuals tend to have more serious episodes and more complications from them. A common accompaniment to aging is *chronic* illness, and many chronic illnesses cause permanent disability. Rehabilitation is the process of maximizing abilities after a disabling event. Geriatric rehabilitation is the application of rehabilitation practices to older individuals, taking into account their unique age-related differences. The majority of rehabilitation approaches are concerned with permanent disabling conditions, although rehabilitation procedures are also used when someone sustains a serious but reversible injury or illness. There is also a large and growing number of people who acquired disabilities in early or midlife and who are surviving into old age. Today, millions of people with mental retardation, spinal cord injury, polio, cerebral palsy, schizophrenia, arthritis, and other conditions are living to late life. As they age, many develop new medical, functional, and social problems requiring further assistance. They, together with aged people who acquire a disabling condition in late life, amount to between 15 and 18 million people in need of rehabilitation assistance.

In order to better understand rehabilitation, it is helpful to understand four commonly used terms: *pathology, impairment, disability,* and *handicap. Pathology* refers to cell dysfunction or cell death within an organ or organ system. Pathological changes are caused by genetic disease, illness, or injury. Death of cells in the retina of the eye, for example, can be caused by macular degeneration, diabetes, or glaucoma. Polio virus kills cells in the efferent neurons of the spinal column. Osteoporosis is the pathological loss of bone density. When an organ or organ system sustains enough pathological change, it will result in an *impairment,* which is a loss in function of the organ system. Not all pathology causes impairment. A person can lose millions of brain cells without impairing the functioning of the brain and can lose density in the bones without causing significant changes in the skeleton's ability to support a person's weight. This is because most systems have *excess capacity,* that is, a surplus of cells and/or the capacity to replace damaged or dead cells (the main exception is the nervous system). Impairment is measured by the organ's ability to carry out its functions. Thus kidney impairment is measured by the ability to filter impurities from the blood; muscle impairment is measured by strength; cardiac impairment is measured by the ability of the heart to pump blood. Impairment can be temporary or permanent (e.g., a broken leg vs. blindness) and can cause disability or not (e.g., hyperten-

sion vs. amputation). [*See* BONE AND OSTEOPOROSIS; CELL DEATH.]

Disability refers to dysfunction at the level of being able to carry out a task. Tasks are made up of a series of interrelated, sequenced skills. Walking, shopping, driving, and working are examples of these complex activities. In rehabilitation, the most important tasks are grouped into two kinds: Activities of daily living (ADLs) are those required to care for oneself at home (mobility, transfers, dressing, toileting, bathing and eating), and Instrumental ADLs (IADLs) are those required to live in the community (shopping, transportation, home chores, money management, making appointments, taking medicines, and handling emergencies). The level of disability can be measured by how many tasks a person can do and with what degree of independence. Usually, each task is measured on a simple scale: the person can do it (a) independently, (b) with supervision, (c) with minimal assistance from others or equipment, (d) with moderate, or (e) maximum assistance, and (f) unable. Numerous scales exist to assess disability from these vantage points, including the Functional Independence Measure, the Barthel Index, and the Katz Index. Disability is not an *absolute* measure of the person's abilities. Rather, it is a *relative* measure of the person's abilities compared to the demands of the task. Viewed this way, it is possible to reduce a disability by either increasing the person's ability or by decreasing the task demands (often through simplification or redesign). Both approaches are used in rehabilitation. Another important aspect of the term disability is that it is not determined solely by physical characteristics of the person. Task performance is also highly influenced by the person's psychological status and social situation. Thus, a person with a stroke who is depressed will be less functional than if he or she is not depressed; a person who lives on the second floor of an apartment house with no elevator will be less mobile than someone who lives on the ground floor. This *biopsychosocial* view of disability is one of the most critical concepts in rehabilitation. Giving emphasis to what a person can and cannot do and determining the biological, psychological, and social causes of it is sometimes referred to as the *functional approach.* This approach places greater emphasis on performance than on diagnosis and on care than on cure for determining everyday living capabilities. The importance of a functional approach can be seen by the fact that functional ability, but not diagnosis, predicts nursing home placement, life satisfaction, and quality of life in geriatric patients. Common late-life disabling impairments include stroke, hip fracture, chronic obstructive pulmonary disease, heart failure, Alzheimer's disease (AD), Parkinson's disease, rheumatoid arthritis, blindness, severe osteoporosis, and most cancers. [*See* ACTIVITIES.]

A *handicap* is defined as dysfunction at the social role level of performance. These roles may include worker, spouse, community participant, parent, and volunteer. The generally accepted position in American rehabilitation is to view handicap as a function of the environment rather than as a function of the person. For example, a person with a disability will be less "work-handicapped" if an employer has positive attitudes toward people with disabilities or if greater accommodations are made at work. Older people with disabilities would not be so socially handicapped if communities had fewer architectural barriers.

II. UNIQUE ASPECTS OF GERIATRIC REHABILITATION

Older individuals face many unique problems that can complicate rehabilitation and lead to treatment failure if not properly understood. Perhaps most importantly, many professionals and many older persons themselves do not believe it is possible to improve functioning after a disabling condition. Rehabilitation is not free of ageist attitudes. Because older people are not expected to improve, they often are not given an equal opportunity to engage in rehabilitation. Yet, there is no empirical evidence to indicate that older people do worse than younger persons in rehabilitation. Despite this, investigators have found large age differences in expectations and treatment. Older individuals also typically suffer from several interrelated chronic and acute illnesses. By contrast, the younger person usually has one or two illnesses. The net result of this difference is that older people can take longer to achieve their maximum benefits in rehabilitation. For example, an older person may have a stroke, some arthritis, and diabetes. He or she may also have a urinary tract infection and uncontrolled hypertension. Medical management of these conditions takes time and may slow participation and improvement in rehabilitation programs. A related difference is the fact that older individuals, due to normal age changes, have lost functioning in critical organ systems. The cardiovascular (CV) system, renal system, and musculoskeletal system may be functioning at only 40% of their capacity compared to when the person was younger. CV changes make an important difference in terms of how fast a person can progress in treatment because it is not safe to exceed cardiopulmonary capacity and that, in turn, limits musculoskeletal progress. [*See* CARDIOVASCULAR SYSTEM.]

The older person is at risk of becoming severely deconditioned as a result of the above changes. In addition to functional consequences, deconditioning also produces CV changes and demineralization of bone. Deconditioning occurs very rapidly in older persons. They may lose up to 2–3% of musculoskeletal and CV function per day when subjected to bedrest. Thus an older person in bed for 2 weeks may lose 25–40% of functional capacity. If the older person was already at only 60% of "maximum" conditioned state due to a sedentary lifestyle, then a 40% additional loss would place that person at such a low level that even basic mobility would be impaired. Unfortunately, this is exactly what is observed in many older persons. Moreover, the older person takes a very long time to reachieve his or her prior state of conditioning. For every day of bedrest, it may take 2–3 days of active treatment to reverse the process. In addition, the discouragement associated with rapid loss of function and slow recovery can affect rehabilitation motivation. Fortunately, specific rehabilitation intervention can reverse these changes, even in octogenarians. Older people themselves are often surprised at what can be accomplished through rehabilitation intervention!

III. THE PRACTICE OF ACUTE REHABILITATION

The goals of rehabilitation for older persons are to improve the level of functioning in ADLs, IADLs, and specific functions (such as speech), promote continued social integration, and to maintain living in the most independent circumstances possible. Even an increase in function from a "maximum assist" prerehabilitation level to a "partial assist" level after rehabilitation can make the difference between staying at home, with family help or paid assistance, and living in a residential care facility or a nursing home. Usually, in order to achieve improvement in ADLs, it is necessary to address even more basic abilities, including strength, endurance, range of motion, and coordination. In addition, many patients need treatment for communication and swallowing difficulties, particularly after a stroke. Many individuals also require assistance with pain management, perceptual difficulties, motivation, depression, and family problems in order to be able to attain ADL and IADL improvements. On average, a patient is involved in 3–4 hours of therapy daily in an acute rehabilitation program.

In order to achieve these goals, a multidisciplinary team is usually required, because no one professional can provide all the necessary kinds of care. A team typically consists of a physician, nurse, physical therapist (PT), occupational therapist (OT), speech therapist, social worker, and psychologist. Ideally, these people have advanced training in geriatrics within their specialty. In addition, the team may be complemented with a neurologist, psychiatrist, orthotist, prosthetist, recreation therapist, dentist, audiologist, pharmacist, podiatrist, and dietitian because older people often have problems requiring these other disciplines.

The physician is usually a specialist in physiatry (physical medicine and rehabilitation), internal medicine, or family medicine. The physician's orientation toward functional outcomes, the team approach, and a biopsychosocial perspective are more important than his or her specific training. The physician usually directs the patient's care and guides team care. Nursing addresses the patient's basic needs in the hospital, administers medicines, and educates the patient about self-care (e.g., skin care, urination, etc.). The PT addresses strengthening of major muscles, endurance, coordination, mobility, ambulation, transfers, wheel chair use, and the need for orthoses (braces) and prostheses (artificial limbs). The OT usually addresses basic ADL and IADL functioning directly, through training in dressing, eating, bathing, grooming, cooking, shopping, driving, and home chores. Both PT and OT make home evaluations and may extend their therapies to the home environment to promote follow through and determine specific problems at home. Speech therapists or communication therapists help patients with expressive or receptive language (the cognitive part of communication) or speech (the motor production of language). Language problems arise because of injury or disease in the primary or secondary language cortices of the brain. Speech problems can occur with or without language problems if parts of the speech motor system are impaired. Therapists may retrain speech or language ability and devise alternative communication methods such as through electronic or mechanical means. [*See* LANGUAGE AND COMMUNICATION IN AGING AND DEMENTIA.]

The social worker addresses problems related to the patient's finances, family and support issues, adjustment to illness, and discharge circumstances. Determining the patient's insurance coverage and basic economic situations are critical to care in the hospital and to determining availability and types of assistance after the hospital. Family issues, including their need to be involved in the rehabilitation process, and education for future care is vital to success. Without support of the family, the older person does not fare as well after discharge. Helping families to solve their own problems related to the older person's disability is therefore very important, and the majority of families will have a problem significant enough to affect the patient's care or outcome. The psychologist has the main responsibility for assessing and treating mental health problems in the rehabilitation context and for assisting the patient with issues such as discouragement, coping with the changes brought about by the disability, exploring new roles, and helping to solve motivational problems in rehabilitation. The most common mental health problem is depression. Usually this is treated by medication prescribed in consultation with the physician, through psychotherapy, and through the process of rehabilitation itself.

A. Rehabilitation in Other Settings

Rehabilitation can and does occur in many different settings. Typical settings include an acute rehabilitation hospital as described above, the rehabilitation section of a general or community hospital, in a long-term care facility such as a nursing home, in an outpatient setting, or home. It is most important that the setting match the person's needs. Intensive rehabilitation (3, 4, or 5 hours a day) is needed when a person's functional needs are great in terms of very limited ADL and IADL ability in several areas, and the expectation for improvement is at least fair. An outpatient setting may suffice for a person who has one or two ADL deficiencies. A skilled nursing facility can provide rehabilitation services to long-term residents to help maintain their function. Today, because of growing emphasis on diagnostic-related groups (DRGs) for reimbursement of acute hospitalization, many patients are transferred to skilled nursing facilities for rehabilitation.

Rehabilitation extends far beyond the doors of the rehabilitation setting. In order to be fully successful, it must include the home and community environments as well. An older person could be very successful in the inpatient setting and be very unsuccessful after discharge. Ensuring adequate help and environmental modifications at home is therefore also important.

IV. OUTCOMES OF REHABILITATION

Rehabilitation is designed to improve ADL and IADL performance primarily. At the same time, medical, psychological, and social problems may be, and may *have* to be, addressed to make rehabilitation successful (e.g., managing congestive heart failure, depression, or lack of housing), but the intended outcome is still functional performance. Hopefully, this functional gain results in improved living on a larger scale, such as greater community independence, a higher quality of life, or a return to social roles. How well does rehabilitation accomplish these goals for older persons? Overall, improvement occurs for about two-thirds to three-quarters of participants. The more specific the outcome (e.g., strength) or the more restricted the kind of primary impairment (e.g., stroke), the better the overall success rate. Results from controlled randomized trials indicate that older people who receive rehabilitation care from a geriatric specialist do better than with care received from a nongeriatric specialist. Many studies illustrate the benefits of rehabilitation treatment on specific abilities of older people even into their nineties. It is generally accepted that age itself is not a predictive factor of rehabilitative success.

V. EMERGING ISSUES

As more people age and a higher percentage of people live into their seventies, eighties, and nineties, more people are going to need rehabilitation services. A higher percentage of the national health-care dollars will need to be spent on rehabilitative care. This means that the percent available for acute care, particularly the part spent on expensive life-sustaining care in the last years of life (a high-expenditure item), may need to be reexamined in terms of quality of life benefits.

Another issue is the high percentage of older people enrolling in health maintenance organizations (HMOs) for their care. HMOs provide health care to older people and do so at a reasonable cost in an efficient manner. As the person's health problems grow more complex, however, HMOs may not provide costly but necessary care as readily. For example, researchers have found that 33% of people enrolled in an HMO had less physical therapy and lower ambulation abilities and were more likely to be discharged to a nursing home after hospitalization for a hip fracture than were non-HMO patients.

VI. SUMMARY

Rehabilitation for older persons attempts to improve abilities needed for daily living. Such care is often complicated owing to medical, psychological, social, and functional problems affecting the older person. Multidisciplinary care is therefore usually required. Despite having complex problems, older people fare very well in rehabilitation, and it is a health-care service that should be made easily available.

BIBLIOGRAPHY

Brody, S., & Ruff, G. (Eds.). (1986). *Aging and rehabilitation: Advances in the state of the art.* New York: Springer.

Brummel-Smith, K. (Ed.). (1993). *Clinics in Geriatric Medicine, 9,* Philadelphia: W. B. Saunders.

Fitzgerald, J. F., Moore, P. S., & Dittus, R. S. (1988). The care of elderly patients with hip fracture: Changes since implementation of the prospective payment system. *New England Journal of Medicine, 319,* 1392–1397.

Kauffman, T. L., Albright, L., & Wagner, C. (1987). Rehabilitative advances after hip fracture in persons 90 years old and older. *Archives Physical Medicine and Rehabilitation, 68,* 369–371.

Kemp, B. J., Brummel-Smith, K., & Ransdell, J. (Eds.) (1990). *Geriatric rehabilitation.* San Diego, CA: Pro-ed Publishing.

Kennie, D. C., Reid, J., Richardson, I. R., Kiaman, A. A., & Kelt, C. (1988). Effectiveness of geriatric rehabilitative care after fracture of the proximal femur in elderly women: A randomized clinical trial. *British Medical Journal, 297,* 1083–1085.

Kvitek, S. D. B., et al. (1986). Age bias: Physical therapists and older patients. *Journal of Gerontology, 41,*702–706.

Manton, K. G. (1989). Epidemiological, demographic, and social correlation of disability among the elderly. *Milbank Memorial Fund Q67,* (Suppl. 2, part 1), 13–58.

Pope, A., Mand Tarlov, A. R. (Eds.). (1991). Disability in America: Toward a national agenda for prevention. Institute of Medicine, Washington, DC: National Academy Press.

Religion and Spirituality

Susan H. McFadden

University of Wisconsin—Oshkosh

I. Early Studies of Religion and Aging
II. Religious Gerontology
III. Studying Religion and Spirituality
IV. Religious Participation of Older People
V. Religion and Well-Being
VI. Religious and Spiritual Development
VII. Summary and Conclusion

Extrinsic Religiosity An instrumental, utilitarian orientation toward religion adopted to provide personal and social well-being; religion used as a means to an end.

Intrinsic Religiosity An internalized religious orientation in which faith is integrated into beliefs, behaviors, and feelings; religion lived as an end in itself.

Spirituality A motivational-emotional phenomenon associated with a sense of meaningful integration within the self, with other persons and the world, and with the divine.

For many older persons today, religious involvement is an important component of their overall adaptation to the experiences of aging. Although the **RELIGIOUS AND SPIRITUAL CONCERNS** of older persons have been studied since midcentury, only recently has this topic attracted attention from persons working in disciplines ranging from theological and religious studies to medicine and the behavioral and social sciences. Some gerontologists who study well-being in later life and the developmental processes that continue through old age include measures of religiosity in their research. In addition, questions about the meaning of a long life are prompting inquiry into the spiritual component of late-life experience.

I. EARLY STUDIES OF RELIGION AND AGING

In the late 1940s, the Federal Council of Churches in America commissioned Paul Maves to conduct a study of ministries to older persons sponsored by religious organizations. The three books that resulted from this work encouraged clergy and national judicatory bodies to develop congregational programs as well as alliances between religious bodies and social agencies in order to deliver services to older persons. These books raised issues about aging that had previously gone unaddressed both by older people and religious leaders. Maves's work represented the first organized attempt to raise questions about religion and aging for a national audience.

Maves continued to lead the effort to increase awareness about religion and aging among religious groups and gerontological researchers. His article, "Aging, Religion, and the Church," published in the 1960 edition of the *Handbook of Social Gerontology*, presented a comprehensive view of the significance of religion for an aging population both in terms of personal piety and the kinds of services offered by religious organizations. In this article, he noted the challenges of studying religion and aging due to the range and variety of religious groups, the differences among local religious organizations, the diverse sociocultural backgrounds of American religions, and the variety of religious experiences and types of affiliation found among older persons. In other words, Maves articulated the need for recognition of heterogeneity among older persons and their ways of being religious. Moreover, his review of the research of the time on religion and aging contradicted popular notions that people become more religious with age. His observations about the need for multidimensional measures of religiosity as well as longitudinal studies of aging persons remain key concerns of contemporary researchers.

A perennial question for behavioral and social scientists concerns the effects of religiosity upon the adjustment of older persons to the exigencies of aging. The pioneering research on this issue was conducted by sociologist David Moberg, whose 1951 doctoral dissertation was titled "Religion and Personal Adjustment in Old Age." Throughout his career, Moberg and his colleagues conducted studies to determine if older persons with active religious lives showed greater adjustment than persons who had little or no religious involvement. Moberg found that church membership alone had no effect upon adjustment; rather, the types of religious activities and beliefs were related to adjustment. Moberg cautioned that his correlational data did not show that religiosity caused good adjustment or, conversely, that good adjustment led to greater religious involvement. Nevertheless, his work strongly suggested that involvement in religious activities can buffer much of the stress of older persons and that aspects of religiosity are associated with positive adaptations to the challenges of later life.

In many ways, these early studies of religion and aging existed on the margins of both gerontology and American religious life. From the 1950s on, research on aging grew exponentially, but little attention was paid to religion as the medical, psychological, and social dimensions of the aging process received increasing scientific scrutiny. Despite the fact that gerontological research was accumulating at a rapid rate between 1950 and 1980, American religious bodies continued to focus most of their attention on younger persons in their program development and training of clergy.

Although scientific gerontology largely ignored religion, a few concerned researchers and religious professionals continued to urge that interest be paid to the religious dimensions of aging. Led by Moberg, these individuals drafted a statement on "spiritual well-being" for the 1971 White House Conference on Aging. They later defined spiritual well-being as "the affirmation of life in a relationship with God, self, community and environment that nurtures and celebrates wholeness" and argued that America's policy makers needed to design programs and assign resources for the purpose of preserving the dignity and integrity of older people. The National Interfaith Coalition on Aging (NICA)—now a part of the National Council on Aging—was born out of these efforts to introduce religious and spiritual issues into the national debate on how best to address the concerns of an aging population.

II. RELIGIOUS GERONTOLOGY

Gerontology has always been strongly interdisciplinary both in research and in practice. As religious and spiritual issues have emerged as a component of gerontology, persons from many diverse disciplines are contributing to their study. Theologians reflect upon how aging brings the paradoxes and polarities of life into focus. They examine how various religious traditions understand the meaning and purpose of a long life and the opportunities presented for religious and spiritual growth in old age. Jewish, Christian, Islamic, Hindu, and Buddhist conceptions of aging have all been studied for the insights they offer about elderhood.

Religious professionals such as clergy, pastoral counselors, chaplains, and religious educators seek additional education about the biological, psychological, and social aspects of aging in order to design programs for an older population. These training programs are offered through professional societies as well as by seminaries. For example, Luther Seminary in St. Paul, Minnesota, has recently established the Center on Aging, Religion, and Spirituality with a grant from the Retirement Research Foundation. In addition, the Robert Wood Johnson Foundation has supported the development of interfaith approaches to caregiving by laypeople and religious professionals.

In health-related fields, doctors, nurses, epidemiologists, medical ethicists, and others examine the ways religious and spiritual concerns affect well-being and decisions about care. Research about morbidity and mortality among religious and nonreligious older persons is supporting efforts to develop whole-person approaches to medical treatment. Religious perspectives on the meaning of suffering are being studied as issues like physician-assisted suicide receive increasing attention from the public. [See ETHICS AND EUTHANASIA; PSYCHOLOGICAL WELL-BEING.]

Public policy planners working in a time of reduced governmental support for aging programs are seeking creative alliances with religious institutions. Congregational networks already in place and highly trusted by many older individuals can be active players in the design and delivery of programs for housing, meal-delivery, transportation, home maintenance, health care, and counseling and psychotherapy. Partnerships are forming between religious professionals, social workers, and others involved with the comprehensive care of older adults with a variety of needs. These include elders living independently in the community as well as residents of long-term-care facilities.

Academics who study aging, including those in the humanities and the behavioral and social sciences, have also contributed to the development of religious gerontology. They debate the meanings of religion and spirituality and how these phenomena can best be studied in an older population. Researchers investigate forms of religious involvement in late life as well as predictors and outcomes of that involvement. They study religion's contribution to quality of life and its role in older adults' coping processes. They seek insight into the continuities and discontinuities in religiosity and spiritual experience through adulthood. The remaining sections of this article examine these concerns in detail.

III. STUDYING RELIGION AND SPIRITUALITY

A. Religion

Is belief in a deity the essential component of religion? What is spirituality and how does it relate to religiosity? Can a person be spiritual and not religious or vice versa? Given the multidimensional nature of religion, how can it be studied? Is spirituality a concept closed to scientific scrutiny? These questions—whether implicitly or explicitly acknowledged—represent a backdrop for the emerging study of religion, spirituality, and aging.

The scientific study of religion has tended to employ two different approaches to definition. The *functional* approach defines religion in terms of its role in providing a comprehensive and meaningful worldview, patterning individual behaviors, and co-

ordinating and stabilizing social groups. For some scholars, this means that the Rotary Club or the Democratic Party could function as religions in people's lives. In gerontology, functional approaches to religion guide studies of its effects upon physical and mental health in older persons. A *substantive* approach to defining religion emphasizes belief in a sacred realm of a god or gods known to humans through experiences of transcendence. This approach is evident in gerontological research that examines older adults' cognitive, emotional, and behavioral responses to the numinous dimension of experience. How religion is conceptualized can influence the ways researchers frame questions, design studies, and interpret data.

Instead of debating which approach to definition is more appropriate, some scholars assert that both are necessary to provide a complete understanding of religion as a complex human phenomenon. For example, one psychologist has noted that religion is best conceptualized in terms of its function and its substance. Religion's narratives, symbols, rituals, and belief structures function as guides for humans seeking meaning, personal significance, and social organization. Religion also defines what has been called "destinations of significance"—the sacred realm that encompasses the substance of religion. Clearly, the complexities of religion offer many challenges to researchers whose work involves measures of individual religiosity.

The earliest measures of religiosity date to the early 1900s. By the 1970s, over 70 different scales had been devised and studied by sociologists and psychologists of religion. Many of these tapped the five dimensions of religion defined by sociologist Charles Glock: ideological (belief), ritualistic (practice), intellectual (knowledge), experiential (feeling), and consequential (effects). Although factor analytic studies of scales measuring these dimensions differ in their conclusions about their interrelations, behavioral and social scientists continue to support the notion that religion is multidimensional. On the other hand, some scholars also argue that there may also be a single factor uniting these dimensions, reflecting a common core of religiousness that for some individuals permeates all the dimensions. In other words, religion may be both multidimensional and unidimensional, a paradox that creates considerable challenge for scientists attempting to measure it. A question that requires further research attention is whether the dimensionality of religion changes with age.

For psychologists, one of the most fruitful approaches to understanding religiosity originated with Gordon Allport, who argued that people vary in their ways of being religious and that the same types of religious behaviors can be motivated by very different underlying needs. Some individuals articulate an extrinsic form of piety in which religion is employed as a means to an end. A typical example of this is the apparently devout individual who participates in organized religious activities as a way of seeking social status or business contacts. The intrinsic orientation, on the other hand, is found in individuals for whom religion functions as the master motive in life; religion for these persons is, as Allport stated, lived and not used.

Several measures of extrinsic and intrinsic religiosity have been developed and widely studied, although considerable disagreement exists among researchers regarding the scales, the intrinsic–extrinsic dimension itself, and the usefulness of this approach in predicting social attitudes and behaviors. In general, researchers have found that persons scoring high on intrinsic religiosity experience greater well-being as indexed by various measures of physical and mental health.

Undoubtedly, psychologists and sociologists interested in religion in later life will continue to employ psychometric approaches in studies of religion as a predictor of various behaviors and as an outcome of different attitudes and personality structures. Nevertheless, psychometric research is limited to the extent that it cannot completely depict the heterogeneity of the older population and the variability in older people's attitudes and experiences of religion. Recently, phenomenological and hermeneutical studies of aging have presented alternative approaches that reveal the spiritual dimensions of the aging process. These studies show that for some older persons, spirituality is intimately connected with religious beliefs and behaviors, whereas for others, spirituality is experienced apart from religiosity.

B. Spirituality

Both popular and scholarly works on spirituality have proliferated in recent years, and some of the impetus for an emerging interest in spirituality lies in the age shift occurring in American society. Many older per-

sons wonder about the meaning of their own long lives; they question how their self-understanding as well as their relations with others and the world around them can continue to be meaningful given the many losses and difficulties encountered in late life. Religious persons ask whether the faith embraced in youth is sufficient for meeting the challenges of old age. In response to these questions, some practitioners and researchers in gerontology are seeking to understand the spiritual dimension of late life, the kinds of spiritual crises peculiar to old age, and the ways these crises can be addressed in a pluralistic society where most aging services are organized by secular agencies.

One way of understanding spirituality is to view it as a motivational-emotional phenomenon. Victor Frankl implied this when he spoke of spirituality as the human drive for meaning and purpose in life. The motivation to seek this sense of meaning and purpose can be associated with a variety of experiences, all of which are signaled by emotions subjectively experienced as supporting a sense of connectedness or integration. Spiritual experiences of God, the world, other persons, and even of the self are usually described as involving feelings of unity and transcendence of the ordinary subject–object distinction. Sometimes these experiences take on mystical or other worldly qualities; at other times, they are woven into common, everyday activities that are grasped as providing a sense of meaning and fulfillment.

Like religion, spirituality is complex and multifaceted. Scholars have argued that attempts to capture it with psychometric instruments fail to appreciate both its diversity and its ineffable character, although some gerontologists have found measures like the Spiritual Well-Being Scale—a widely used instrument developed by Paloutzian and Ellison—to be useful. Others, however, seek an understanding of spirituality in the stories that older people tell about themselves and their life experiences. They assert that a nursing home resident describing her caring, empathic concern for others is revealing an aspect of her spirituality. Similarly, an older man who finds meaning in his ongoing relationship with the natural world demonstrates a form of spirituality. One researcher's studies of creative elders have shown how they often express the inward turn of spirituality in depicting their journeys of aging. Thus spirituality can be expressed in many different ways, some of which have little relation to the organized beliefs and behaviors of religion.

On the other hand, some religious older people experience their organized and nonorganized activities as suffused with spirituality. It is possible, however, that a deepened sense of spirituality can direct elders away from earlier religious commitments. The religious formalism of youth may fade or be actively rejected even as the motivational and emotional processes of spirituality are increasingly integrated into efforts to adapt to the processes of aging. People take different spiritual pathways through later life, an observation that is only now beginning to be systematically examined by gerontologists. Unfortunately, insights into the dimensions of spirituality and the experienced relation to religious traditions may not be revealed in research that asks a series of structured questions with limited possible responses.

Narrative analysis and other phenomenological approaches aimed at grasping the essence of spiritual motivation and emotion represent a different way of knowing. With increasing involvement in gerontological study by scholars from various disciplines in the humanities, interest in qualitative approaches to gerontology is growing.

Another way of addressing spirituality in later life examines the spiritual needs of older persons, particularly those who experience physical illnesses of various kinds. One psychiatrist has outlined fourteen spiritual needs of physically ill elders. These needs include some sense of meaning and hope in the face of suffering, the transcendence of the circumstances of multiple chronic difficulties, the feeling of continuity within the self despite life-altering changes such as the loss of sensory capacities and mobility, the affirmation of personal dignity by others, the opportunity to forgive others and be forgiven of past wrongs, and preparation for dying and death. In addition to these intrapersonal, interpersonal, and transcendent aspects of spirituality, older persons need to maintain their meaningful attachments to the world even as they prepare for death. This spiritual need is expressed in their desires to remain in their homes or, if forced to reside in long-term care, to retain certain precious possessions and interests such as music or access to the natural world.

Some clergy, social workers, nurses, and others working with older persons have begun to assess individual spiritual needs and to determine whether they are being met. Structured interviews conducted with elders and their families can reveal these needs. Care plans can then be designed to insure that older persons retain a sense of wholeness and dignity no matter what their particular physical or mental circumstances might be.

IV. RELIGIOUS PARTICIPATION OF OLDER PEOPLE

Many early studies of religion and aging measured religiosity by asking older persons how often they attended religious services. Reports from cross-sectional research indicated a drop in religiosity with age when religiosity was measured with the single variable of religious attendance. However, the functional status of elderly persons was probably affecting their ability to engage in public, organizational religious activities. Gerontologists realized that they needed to employ multidimensional measures of religion in order to more accurately represent older adults' religious participation.

Studies published in the 1970s and 1980s utilizing cross-sectional as well as longitudinal designs indicated that for some individuals, nonorganizational behaviors rise in later life, as if in compensation for decreased public religious activity. Such private, nonorganizational behaviors include prayer, reading the Bible and other religious literature, watching religious television programming or listening to religious radio programs.

Studies that measure organizational and nonorganizational religious participation as well as subjective religiosity report high levels of religious involvement among older persons. For example, recent surveys indicate that that over three-quarters of persons aged 65 and older say that religion is very important in their lives. About 50% attend religious services at least once a week; nearly a quarter of the older population prays three times a day and about the same percentage reads the bible on a daily basis. More than half of all older persons watch religious television programs at least occasionally. These data about religious involvement among older persons are derived from national studies conducted by organizations such as the National Opinion Research Center and the Princeton Religion Research Center.

These levels of religious activity are corroborated in numerous smaller, more localized studies, such as one in which older persons attending a geriatric outpatient clinic were surveyed. Over 80% of those surveyed considered their religious faith to be the most important influence in their lives. Other studies have indicated that older people most often spontaneously name religion as their primary way of coping with difficult life events.

One limitation of research using samples of convenience limited to a particular region of the country or to one or two religious denominations is the lack of generalizability to the whole population of older persons. It is well known that people living in various geographical regions show different levels of religious involvement. For example, one study noted that less than half of persons 85 and older living in San Francisco agreed that religion was important in their lives. Differences between urban, suburban, and rural environments also need to be noted. Changing populations in urban regions have forced the closing of some churches and synagogues, leaving older persons without access to their religious communities. Additionally, reductions in the numbers of Catholic priests have caused the consolidation of parishes in rural areas, a situation that creates difficulties for older persons without access to transportation.

In studying religion and aging, researchers need to be aware of local issues that influence religious participation, and they also need to continue to utilize data from large, national probability surveys in order to obtain accurate information about the older population as a whole. It is equally important that researchers not treat all persons over 65 as a homogeneous group. In addition to age, functional status, and geographic location, other important influences on religious participation include gender, race and ethnicity, and the content of religious belief systems.

A. Gender

A consistent finding in research on religion and aging has been that older women show significantly higher levels of religious behaviors and subjective religiosity than men. Women rate their own religious activities of all types as more meaningful to them, and they also are more likely to turn to religion as a way of coping with life's difficulties.

Several ways of explaining this gender difference have been advanced by psychologists and sociologists.

For example, some have suggested that because women are socialized to respond to the emotional nuances of life, they are more comfortable with religious feelings aroused both in public ritual observances and in private meditation. Others point to women's traditional roles as nurturers within families and their acceptance of responsibility for socializing children in matters of values and personal faith. Also, because older women adopt caregiving roles more often than older men, many rely upon religion for social support and as a way of moderating the stress associated with caregiving.

Some researchers argue that men's identification with their work prevents their involvement in religious activities or at least diminishes the centrality of religion in their lives. There is some evidence that religious organizations reduce men's participation by designing their educational and social missions based on the availability of women who are not working outside the home. It is ironic that some religious communities fail to minister to the religious and spiritual needs of men despite the predominance of patriarchal images and leadership structures. Given the repeated observation that religiosity remains fairly stable across the adult life span, it is likely that lower participation by men in later life is an outgrowth of patterns established in young and middle adulthood. [See GENDER ROLES.]

B. Race and Ethnicity

In 1994, an important study in the *Journal of Gerontology: Social Sciences* reported on four large-scale, national probability surveys of older men and women, Blacks, and Whites. Consistent with previous research, the study found significantly higher levels of religiosity among women. A significantly higher level of religious involvement among older Blacks than among older Whites was also reported.

These data support the findings of other studies that have indicated the importance of religion to the present cohort of older African Americans and their high degree of involvement in both organizational and nonorganizational religious activities. They turn to the church in times of life stress, finding within that institution a wide variety of personal and social supports. The integration of the church into many arenas of life in the Black community has enabled it to offer both formal and informal responses to the life conditions faced by older persons.

Researchers have also noted high levels of religious involvement among other ethnic and minority elders, particularly Hispanics. These individuals, whose early years were shaped by poverty and discrimination, often found within religious organizations the psychological and social support needed to survive in a society that systematically excluded them from most routes to opportunity. Their ties to their faith communities have remained strong in old age.

Those who study Native American elders have noted the diversity of their religious traditions. Some older persons remain wholly committed to the Christianity adopted in youth; others merge Christian and native religious beliefs and practices; still others have embraced native practices as a way of restoring a sense of cultural identity, with Christianity rejected as a religion forced upon them by the dominant white culture.

In general, African Americans affiliate with Protestant denominations and independent Protestant churches; Hispanics most often embrace Catholicism; some Native Americans who are Christian identify themselves as Protestant while others are Catholic. Although they share some core beliefs, traditions, sacraments, and Scriptures, Christian denominations differ widely in historical origin, polity, doctrine, norms of participation, and behavioral expectations. Therefore, it is unwise to treat religion as generic when considering its role in the lives of racial and ethnic minority elders. Further systematic research is needed to determine the impact of religious affiliation on older persons' well-being and psychospiritual development. [See RACIAL AND ETHNIC DIVERSITY.]

C. Religious Pluralism

Religion is a multidimensional phenomenon incorporating beliefs, behaviors, and feelings. Religious traditions vary in their emphasis upon these and these differences have important consequences in shaping the role of religion in the lives of older persons. For example, a frail elderly Catholic woman who has become increasingly homebound may experience a

greater disruption to her religious life than a similarly incapacitated Presbyterian who can turn to nonorganizational religious activities to compensate for the inability to attend religious services. The Catholic woman, on the other hand, embraces a religious faith centered in sacrament and ritual and thus her inability to participate may produce a more profound sense of loss. Similarly, a Jewish elder living in a long-term-care facility that fails to recognize the significance of Sabbath observances may experience a religious dislocation not felt by a person who has never ordered time through religious behaviors. That individual may be quite satisfied to attend occasional chapel services on weekday afternoons.

Religious traditions that emphasize personal piety expressed in prayer shape the ways older persons cope with life stressors. Research has shown that elderly Baptists are significantly more likely to employ prayer in coping with physical illness than non-Baptists. Moreover, they are also more likely to believe that illness can represent a test of faith and possibly even a punishment for sin. The ways that individuals conceptualize illness affect their use of the health-care system and thus their own physical well-being. Also, religious traditions differ in their prescriptions and proscriptions regarding health-related behaviors such as the consumption of alcohol, diet, and the use of alternative healing practices. These influence not only how older persons respond to physical difficulties in later life but also the types of problems they experience.

In addition to structured beliefs articulated in various religious traditions, the ways people personally and privately relate to whatever they call divine affects their adjustment to life circumstances. Some people understand and experience a God who is wrathful and judges human failing harshly. An older person in a caregiving situation who holds this belief might be inclined to feel guilty and ashamed for not living up to what she believes about religious expectations of selfless giving. Others embrace a God image that assures them of divine love and caring intercession into the lives of human beings. A caregiver with this attitude might find himself sustained by acts of prayer and his belief in divine responses to prayer. Still other persons envision a God that is essentially detached from human affairs. These individuals would probably tend not to utilize religious responses in coping with adversity. Finally, some older people do not believe in a god at all, and others are essentially apathetic or indifferent about the issue. The relation between the God image and responses to life circumstances in old age requires further systematic study. [See CARE-GIVING AND CARING.]

Behavioral and social scientists have only recently begun to examine the effects of varying beliefs on coping behaviors and overall adaptation in later life. Studies of the differential outcomes of specific religious beliefs, behaviors, and feelings promise to reveal important insights into the role of religion in the lives of aging persons.

V. RELIGION AND WELL-BEING

Gerontologists have studied many objective indicators of well-being in later life. The most commonly cited are good health, social support, and financial security. However, gerontologists have noted the problems with relying upon objective indicators alone because older persons actively interpret each by comparing present life circumstances to the personal past and to the situations of others. Thus the individual judged as being in poor health according to an index of health problems might recognize health problems while at the same time maintain an overall sense that life remains meaningful and good. Often, religious beliefs and behaviors support this subjective sense of well-being regardless of the objective indicators. Increasingly, researchers are attending to the relation of religion to well-being and the ability to cope with stress.

One researcher has determined that there are statistically significant relations between religion and health variables such as cardiovascular disease, hypertension and stroke, cancer, general health status, numerous specific illnesses, and self-rated health. Although it is noted that correlational data do not indicate causation, a number of hypotheses regarding these salutary religious effects are suggested. These include the health-promoting behaviors encouraged by certain religious traditions, the psychosocial effects of social support, and the psychodynamics of religious belief systems, rituals, and faith. A multifactorial explanation employing some or all of these is probably the best approach to understanding the relation of health status and religiosity.

Research on older adults' mental health has shown that religious beliefs, attitudes, and ways of coping contribute to significantly higher levels of adjustment as indexed by depression, suicide rates, anxiety, and alcohol abuse. A longitudinal study of male patients associated with the Durham VA Mental Health Survey has shown an inverse relationship between turning to religion and depressive symptoms and major depressive disorder. Other studies have shown a moderately strong relationship between measures of religiosity and morale. Furthermore, older adults with high levels of religious commitment feel significantly more satisfied with their lives than persons who experience little or no sense of religious belonging or religious meaning. Even controlling for age, education, race, marital status, and perceived health does not change the positive effect of religious salience on an overall sense of life meaning and purpose. [See MENTAL HEALTH.]

Anecdotal evidence from nursing home chaplains and social workers indicates that religious rituals developed for leaving one's private residence and entering a long-term-care facility may generate more positive feelings about relocation. Other kinds of life transitions experienced by older persons—notably the deaths of loved ones—are often accompanied by religious observances that convey meanings that moderate the effects of loss. One study of rural elders found that although their scores on a standard measure of well-being were depressed by recognition of the difficulties wrought by late-life losses, nevertheless the individuals who appealed to a "transcendent standard" were more likely to affirm that their lives had meaning.

Some longitudinal research demonstrates significant positive correlations between religious measures and happiness, feelings of usefulness, and personal adjustment, thereby leading to the conclusion that religion increases in its importance for personal adjustment as people age. However, this finding is challenged by data from another longitudinal study that showed little relation between religious attendance and life satisfaction when dropouts were analyzed.

One area of research related to the well-being of elders that has attracted considerable attention recently concerns the variety of coping responses to stressful life conditions. One researcher who has published widely on the ways religious adults of all ages employ their religious beliefs and behaviors in the service of coping notes that increasing age may be associated with a change in religious coping styles. Although younger adults may adopt an active, self-directing coping style that assumes their God grants them agency in dealing with life's difficulties, older persons may substitute a more deferring style in which they wait upon God's grace. Recognition of the ways that religious coping can be deleterious is urged, particularly when it promotes beliefs and behaviors that restrict people in creatively responding to stressors.

Recent research has suggested that the salutary effects of religion can be explained largely as the result of religious behaviors and beliefs acting as buffers against late-life stress. One study showed that religious people may be less susceptible to the damaging effects of stress upon feelings of self-worth and mastery. Another found that although there is no direct effect of religious attendance on mental health, attendance nevertheless reduces the adverse effects of psychological distress on well-being.

Clearly, the multidimensional nature of religion makes comparison of these studies difficult because they tend to use different definitions and measures of religiosity. Nevertheless, as others have noted, there does seem to be a salutary effect of religion in later life. Caution is needed however in interpreting these data because some of the relationships are small though significant and may not account for enough variance in measures of well-being to be meaningful. Explanatory mechanisms are doubtless complex and overlapping. In addition, it is important that behavioral and social scientists who study religion in late life investigate the negative effects religion can have upon well-being. Religion can evoke maladaptive coping behaviors such as inappropriate levels of financial commitment in return for promises of well-being.

VI. RELIGIOUS AND SPIRITUAL DEVELOPMENT

With the exception of some longitudinal studies with waves of data collected throughout adulthood, research on religion and well-being seldom examines developmental issues. Therefore, many important questions remain to be answered. For example, have the individuals for whom religion functions protectively against life stressors always experienced such

an effect? Or, given the fact that aging often depletes personal and social resources, do people employ religious coping more later in life than they did at younger ages? These questions point to what one psychologist has called the central problem for gerontology: to determine how behavior becomes organized and changes over time.

Unfortunately, much of the research on religion, spirituality, and aging has employed cross-sectional designs that confound age and cohort. The present cohort of older persons were socialized into religious life during a time of high rates of active participation in religious institutions. Therefore, their evaluation of the importance of religion and their high levels of religious activity may be a function of their membership in a cohort that came of age when religious institutions and their leaders were highly regarded, a time of wide acceptance of religion in public and private life.

Social scientific research has produced mixed results in attempting to answer the question of whether today's elders have experienced an increase of religiosity with age. Longitudinal data from a number of studies indicate considerable stability of religiosity, with religious beliefs and attitudes showing little change over adulthood. Functional health, however, affects some older persons' religious behaviors by leading to a reduction in organizational activities that is often offset by an increase in nonorganizational activities.

One reason why a clear portrait of religious development has failed to emerge may be due to the kinds of questions asked of many research participants. If only religious behaviors and specific beliefs are indexed, then important information about changes in people's modes of knowing may be lost. Some research has demonstrated that many aging persons undergo a developmental shift that results in a greater ability to integrate thinking and feeling. In other words, the fundamental way in which they know themselves and the world changes to produce a more reflective, emotionally shaped response to the self and others. The wisdom of older persons reflects this integration of cognitive, affective, and intuitive qualities. Wisdom does not necessarily produce answers to life's vexing problems; rather it can promote a different way of interpreting their significance along with a greater appreciation for and acceptance of mystery.

The potential for the emergence of wisdom in later life has important implications for the consideration of religious development. Some aging persons may discover that formerly held religious beliefs need to change and perhaps even be rejected in light of this new way of knowing. Rigid, logical-analytical conceptions of religion may yield to a more integrated, holistic response that for some might even be called mystical. Although older adults who have experienced this kind of personal transformation may continue to engage in the same forms of religious behaviors of earlier years—attending religious services, praying, reading Scriptures and the like—nevertheless their subjective experience of these activities may change. Thus, in considering religious development, it is important to acknowledge both continuity and discontinuity and the possibility that both can be experienced at the same time. Aging produces paradoxical juxtapositions of change and stability, engagement and disengagement, attachment and detachment, clearer insight and greater appreciation of mystery. It is reasonable to expect that religious development would reflect this.

Religious development might be very subtle for some persons (although one should not discount the possibility of late-life conversion experiences). The objective, quantified measures typically used by behavioral and social scientists may not be adequate to assess important subjective shifts. Increasingly, gerontologists are turning to the interpretation of narrative to gain insight into developmental processes in later life.

Sources such as autobiographies, journals, oral histories, and folklore can reveal themes of religious and spiritual development. For example, it has been shown how stories told in many cultures portray the spiritual journeys of aging. These elder tales reveal universal themes of personal transformation. They convey the challenges older persons experience as they move toward the ultimate encounter with mystery. The confrontation with decline and loss prepares older persons to evaluate their own dark side. Out of this experience comes wisdom and "emancipated innocence," a liberation from social customs and ways of thinking that lock so many adults into rigid patterns of belief, behavior, and feeling. One philosopher referred to this as a "second naïveté," an outlook on the world that can support both religious and spiritual development in later life. Through this process, elders are able to reclaim a sense of wonder about their lives

and their worlds. The final step in spiritual development that may be discerned from elder tales requires that older people reveal to youth some of the insights they have grasped in their journeys of aging. This generativity, once affirmed and supported by many cultural institutions, is essential for the growth and development of young people.

Phenomenological and hermeneutical approaches promise to reveal much about how older people develop religiously and spiritually. For some elders, religious and spiritual development is synonymous; others experience a deepening spiritual life with little or no connection with religious beliefs, symbols, rituals, narratives, or institutions. Certain older persons are indifferent about religion and the existential questions raised by attention to spirituality. Others display hostility toward religion and religious institutions. This heterogeneity means that researchers must continue to study the normative trends that seem to indicate stability in religiosity and spiritual experience; they also need to employ qualitative approaches in discerning the themes revealed in the individual pathways taken by aging persons.

VII. SUMMARY AND CONCLUSION

In general, older persons today demonstrate high levels of public and private religiosity. This broad statement must be tempered, however, with recognition of the many forms of religious belief, behavior, and feeling and their differential effects upon adaptation to the contingencies of later life. For many older persons, religion functions positively in the service of greater well-being and a sense of meaning and purpose in life. Religious and spiritual resources support their adaptation to changed environments and physical conditions. Additionally, the cognitive and affective changes that accompany the aging process present possibilities for spiritual development that for some persons is associated with shifts in religiosity.

Increasingly, gerontologists are finding that acknowledgment of late-life religion and spirituality has important implications both for practice and research. Many studies have shown that after the family, older persons turn to their churches and synagogues for support and assistance in times of change and loss. Therefore, opportunities exist for creative alliances between religious institutions and public and private agencies serving older persons. Applied research on the outcomes of programs that meet the religious and spiritual needs of both independent and dependent elders can support these kinds of initiatives. More basic research on the ways religiosity and a spiritual sense affect self-regulation of biological, psychological, and social processes can also contribute to improved services for older adults. Finally, careful study of the religion and spirituality of elders can support the creation of metaphors of wholeness, integration, and the value of a long life. These new ways of organizing significant ideas and feelings about aging may help to restore personal and social meanings to old age by countering biomedical images of decline.

BIBLIOGRAPHY

Bianchi, E. (1994). *Elder wisdom: Crafting your own elderhood.* New York: Crossroad.

Cole, T. R., Van Tassel, D. D., & Kastenbaum, R. (Eds.). (1992). *Handbook of the humanities and aging.* New York: Springer Publishing Co.

Kimble, M. A., McFadden, S. H., Ellor, J. W,. & Seeber, J. J. (Eds.). (1995). *Aging, spirituality, and religion: A handbook.* Minneapolis: Fortress Press.

Koenig, H. G. (1994). *Aging and God: Spiritual pathways to mental health in midlife and later years.* New York: Haworth Press.

Levin, J. S. (Ed.). (1994). *Religion in aging and health.* Thousand Oaks, CA: Sage Publications.

Thomas, L. E., & Eisenhandler, S. A. (Eds.). (1994). *Aging and the religious dimension.* Westport, CT: Auburn House.

Wulff, D. M. (1991). *Psychology of religion.* New York: John Wiley & Sons.

The contours of our memories are much like the
features of a distant landscape: we cannot be sure if what
we think we see is what is really there.
—Jon Hendricks

Reminiscence

Irene M. Burnside

San Diego State University

I. Introduction
II. Historical View
III. Typologies
IV. As a Treatment Modality
V. Techniques
VI. Benefits of Reminiscence Group Themes
VII. Protocols
VIII. Importance of Past Experiences
IX. Summary

"Flashbulb" Memories Memories that cause instant recall during reminiscence for persons living at that time, for example, for the assassination of President Kennedy.

Genograms Diagrammed sets of boxes much like a family tree, with data about the client's ancestors, usually including date of birth and death and what caused the relative's death.

Long-Term Memory Recall or recollection of persons or events occurring in the earlier life of the person. This is the focus for reminiscence therapy.

Props Objects brought to the group by the leader or members with the intent of eliciting memories.

Short-Term Memory Recall or recollection of persons or events occurring within a recent time frame.

Themes and Topics Subjects for discussion selected by the leader or members for a reminiscence therapy group.

Time Lines Personal or historical chronological listings of events important in the older person's life or during a specific time frame for a specific country.

Triggers Words or phrases or expressed thoughts that help other members recall similar memories, or memories in some way related; for example, the reminiscer will often begin, "That reminds me of ..."

It is difficult to find a universally accepted definition of **REMINISCENCE** in spite of the fact that the concept has been studied consistently for the past 30 years. A general definition of reminiscence is the process of recalling past events or experience; the process can be silent or oral. When reminiscence is verbal, it may be achieved through one-to-one interaction or in a group.

I. INTRODUCTION

Over the past three decades, reminiscence has become a popular concept for aging research, as well as a treatment modality for older adults. The roots of reminiscence lie in a seminal article about life review written by Butler in 1963.

Memories are also used to elicit an autobiography or oral history. Guided autobiography groups were pioneered by James Birren in the 1970s.

This article is about reminiscence as a therapeutic modality. However, the bibliography provides a listing of recent books that discuss all aspects of reminiscence theory, practice, and application. The bibliography includes books from the United Kingdom to provide a broad perspective.

Memories are both sad and happy and sometimes bittersweet. Studying the literature leaves one with the impression that only happy memories are elicited. However, many leaders say that it is almost impossible to have only pleasant memories for an entire session, whether in the one-to-one situation or group. The caregiver eliciting the reminiscence must, therefore, be prepared to listen to the sad, the tragic, and even painful memories of exploitation. The Holocaust is a prime example.

Reminiscence as a modality is differentiated from life review by the intent and the criteria for the process. Some practitioners feel that to truly conduct a life review, the person eliciting the review needs to help the older person synthesize the life experiences and evaluate his or her life. Other writers use the term *life review,* when in fact autobiography, oral history, or simple reminiscence might better describe the process. Life review is increasingly viewed as a major psychosocial task for older adults. [*See* LIFE REVIEW.]

Although it is true that some reminiscers may on their own synthesize and evaluate the meaning of their life, simple reminiscence does not include those criteria. It is generally agreed that life review also requires special skill on the part of the practitioner eliciting the review, whereas laypeople have been taught to successfully conduct reminiscence. However, there is not agreement in this regard either, because some writers have described teaching life review techniques to nurse's aides. Volunteers have been taught to use reminiscence, both in the nursing home and the community.

The American Association of Retired Persons (AARP) offers a reminiscence program begun in 1983. There is also a Reminiscence Training Kit available for volunteers through interlibrary loan. With the current shortage of personnel in long-term care settings, volunteers may increasingly provide this psychosocial intervention.

A reminiscence group may also be quite different from guided autobiography groups, which have a different format and different goals. The themes, for example, may be quite different for the two groups. Leaders need to have the goals clearly in mind before they begin a group.

II. HISTORICAL VIEW

The importance of memories dates back as far as Aristotle's pessimistic commentary in his "Treatise on Rhetoric." Early anecdotal and later research reports indicate that reminiscence is to be enjoyed by most people; however, measurable benefits have not been consistently demonstrated. This inability to document benefits may be due in part to the methodological limitations of some studies; for example, many studies have relied on small convenience samples. Likewise, many of the studies lack control groups. Most studies did not describe type of reminiscences. The functions of the life review, oral history, autobiography, or a simple reminiscence session were not described.

Until recently there has been little information about older individuals' different needs for reminiscence. Perhaps individuals need to focus on positive and happy memories, especially if the older persons have lived through trauma. Residents in drab, boring environments may escape into the past to cope with their present life, and find reassurance and peace of mind with happy memories.

Writers in the 1970s noted that negative views about reminiscence prevailed. Some gerontologists viewed reminiscence as pathological and felt it was used to avoid the present, or worse, that it indicated a loss of recent memory. Others (including health professionals) felt it to be absolutely boring, particularly if the older person told the same story repeatedly, and wrote off older reminiscers as garrulous.

It has long been thought that reminiscence was specific only to older persons. However, there is now a body of evidence that challenges this assumption. Few of the early published studies included adults of all ages. The literature offers little about the role of gender in reminiscence, though there is some evidence that women generally reminisce more frequently than men.

The earliest article by Butler discussed reminiscence as used in the life review process. It was originally described from the perspective of individual therapy; only later did Butler and Lewis write about group life review therapy. Butler recently wrote in a foreword that at the time his seminal article was published it never occurred to him that it would have such a great impact on the various disciplines. He now fears that interventions such as those described in this chapter may lose ground under pressure to contain health-care costs. The trend may be shifting towards using more medication instead of psychosocial interventions. Omnibus Budget Reconciliation Act (OBRA '87) regulations do demand that psychosocial interventions be considered. Still, health professionals will have to be on guard to prevent substituting medications as quick fixes that may have drastic side effects. Fortunately, no equivalent deleterious side effects have been reported with the use of reminiscence as an intervention.

One of the earliest studies of reminiscence found that older veterans who thought about the past were less likely to be depressed. That article laid the foundation for many subsequent articles promoting reminiscence techniques as an intervention for depression. Nurses, social workers, and psychologists in particular have included reminiscence as a therapeutic intervention in depression, and numerous studies have been published, but results are inconclusive. [*See* DEPRESSION.]

III. TYPOLOGIES

Through the years researchers have identified many types of reminiscence. Some categories clearly overlap, although they have different names. See Table I for a list of types of reminiscence.

Only recently have detailed typologies of reminiscence that include implications for practice been available. The benefits of reminiscence depend not on reminiscence itself, but rather on the type of reminiscence occurring in the process. Reminiscence can be viewed as a valuable resource and each type can be used to enhance the well-being of older people, in either an individual interaction or in group.

Haight and Webster have designed "a taxonomy of recall" and their list includes (a) identity, (b) problem solving, (c) teach/inform, (d) conversation, (e) boredom reduction, (f) bitterness revival, (g) death preparation, and (h) intimacy maintenance. Included in their table are functions of each one on the list. They suggest that these more recent classification systems differ from earlier approaches because they are more comprehensive, and both encompass and add to the early types listed in Table I. The typologies explain the variance in the reminiscence process and should be of help to neophyte practitioners as they incorporate reminiscence into their practice.

The literature indicates that reminiscence groups are implemented for a variety of reasons. One very early therapeutic group was formed by a nurse to reduce apathy and confusion in long-term care resi-

Table I Typologies of Reminiscence: 1964–1991[a]

1964	Storytelling Material for life review Defensive reminiscence[b]
1974	Simple reminiscence Life review Informative reminiscence[c]
1976	Affirming style Negating style Despairing style[d]
1980–1981	Informative reminiscence Evaluative reminiscence Obsessive reminiscence[e]
1982	Flight from past reminiscence Informative reminiscence Ruminative reminiscence Idealized reminiscence Integrative reminiscence[f]
1984	Simple reminiscence Informative reminiscence Life review Grief work[g]
1991	Integrative reminiscence Instrumental reminiscence Transmissive reminiscence Escapist reminiscence Obsessive reminiscence Narrative reminiscence[h]

[a]Source: Burnside and Schmidt, *Working with older adults: Group process and techniques,* (3d ed.). © 1994 Boston: Jones and Bartlett Publishers. Reprinted with permission.

[b]McMahon, A. D. V., & Rhudick, P. J. (1964). Reminiscing: Adaptational significance in the aged. *Archives of General Psychiatry, 10,* 292–298.

[c]Coleman, P. (1974). Measuring reminiscence characteristics as from conversation as adaptive features of old age. *International Journal of Aging and Human Development, 5*(2), 281–295.

[d]Fallot, R. D. (1976). The life story through reminiscence in later years. Unpublished doctoral dissertation, Yale University, New Haven, CT.

[e]Lo Gerfo, M. (1980–1981). Three ways of reminiscence in theory and practice. *International Journal of Aging and Human Development, 12,* 39–48.

[f]Bliwise, N. G. (1982). Reminiscence: Presentations of the personal past in middle and late life. Unpublished doctoral dissertation, The University of Chicago, Chicago, IL.

[g]Walker, L. S. (1984). The relationship between reminiscing, health state, physical functioning, and depression in older adults. Unpublished doctoral dissertation, The Catholic University of America, Washington, DC.

[h]Watt, L. M., & Wong, P. T. P. (1991). A taxonomy of reminiscence and therapeutic implications. *Journal Gerontological Social Work, 16*(1/2), 35–57.

dents. As stated, some studies indicate that therapeutic reminiscence groups reduce depression.

Two types of reminiscences seem to hold promise for an effective therapeutic approach with depressed older persons. The integrative approach focuses on a constructive reappraisal of the older person's past, and the instrumental approach is centered on the past problem-solving abilities and the coping activities. Other goals of reminiscence include (a) increasing life satisfaction, (b) improving morale, (c) increasing self-esteem, (d) tapping into creativity, (e) increasing feelings of control over the environment, (f) measuring ego integrity, (g) facilitating social interaction, and (h) offering mutual social support. Reminiscence is currently viewed as a viable treatment modality.

IV. AS A TREATMENT MODALITY

As stated earlier, reminiscence is used both in one-to-one interaction and as a group modality. Reminiscence groups are viewed as one facet of overall program therapy in nursing homes, retirement homes, adult senior centers, and adult day care centers. Also as stated earlier, educators also introduce reminiscence as a teaching strategy by having students conduct reminiscence as part of a practicum experience. There is evidence that both students and older persons benefit from such experiences.

Reminiscence has been implemented by members of a variety of disciplines: clergy, nurses, occupational therapists, physical therapists, physicians (including psychiatrists), social workers, and psychologists. Each discipline may have a different approach because of background and training. Because so many disciplines implement reminiscence, the literature offers an interesting variety of approaches.

Current literature lacks guidelines to help the practitioner decide when to implement reminiscence, life review, or autobiography. The goals for the client or the group must be carefully considered. But other factors must also be taken into account. The following list of questions may be helpful.

1. What is the time frame?
2. Who will be selected (particularly if it is a group)?
3. Is there memory loss? If so, how will that affect the reminiscence? What strategies will help the practitioner focus on long-term memory?

4. What is the cost of conducting one-to-one intervention versus group? (Cost includes materials, personnel, transportation, supervision, etc.)
5. Is there support from agency and personnel?
6. Is transportation for older persons a problem? (Transportation both within the institution or from the community.)
7. If the person is dying, and life review is judged to be the appropriate intervention, is there available energy and how much pain is present?

The latter is added because the literature does indicate that life review is frequently the modality of choice for dying persons, and nurses particularly are ones who listen and elicit life reviews during the later stage of a patient's life. Such life reviews are usually done in the one-to-one interaction.

A. One-to-One-Interaction

Although one-to-one reminiscence may be introduced for many reasons, two common ones are (a) to obtain information for a history and (b) therapy for an older person who cannot tolerate a group experience; for example, loners and those too weak or debilitated to attend group meetings.

In the face of so many losses, stress reductions may be a goal. Hendricks states that both reminiscence and life review will "undoubtedly be used by mental health professionals as they attempt to help their elderly patients deal with their sources of stress" (p. 4).

The vast amount of information elicited during reminiscence can be an advantage (and sometimes a disadvantage) for the health-care worker eliciting reminiscence. If the professional is seeking information only about health-related events, it may be quite difficult to keep such a focus. This is particularly true in a person who rambles, or one how has lived 80, 90, or 100 years and has lots to tell. Guiding the very old person in reminiscence provides a real challenge to the health-care worker, or even the researcher.

Finding an appropriate technique for the interview may be problematic. Adams in Bornat's book, described such a difficulty. He described his interviews with older persons in a hospital ward in London. At the time he believed "reminiscence was a straightforward activity that involved asking a series of questions" (p. 86). That technique seemed to fail, and he felt he had lost control of the interview. He returned to the question format later and he credits Watt and Wong for helping him incorporate knowledge of the taxonomy into his practice. A knowledge of the taxonomy is also helpful for the leaders of group reminiscence.

B. Group Reminiscence

A recent overview of reminiscence literature indicates group reminiscence is more often described in articles than dyad reminiscence. As stated earlier, the goal will determine the selection of members for the group as well as the techniques to be chosen. The one-to-one reminiscence interaction may be easier for the new practitioner than group leadership. The group modality has many variables for the leader to juggle. This is particularly true if the group is large and there is only one leader. From experience, I have found six to eight to be the ideal number in a group. But if one is working with individuals with memory loss, a group of four to six is best. If there are more than six the leader may have problems attending to all the needs of the group. Less than four or five puts the spotlight on a few members and may be stressful for them and they will drop out. The leader must carefully screen members. Some of the criteria for screening a member for the group might include the following:

- The personality of the potential member
- Assessing physical improvements, especially hearing and vision loss as well as mobility
- Assessing the cognitive ability of each person

However, there are some individuals who could make the group endeavor difficult for a leader (especially a neophyte leader):

- Disturbed, hyperactive, and wandering persons
- Incontinent persons
- Persons with a psychotic depression
- Persons with a bipolar disorder
- Hypochondriacal persons

Failure to do so can put the leader in the position of dealing with difficult group members.

Coleadership is a luxury that rarely can be afforded in most facilities, but two leaders can manage a much larger group, and the leaders can learn from one another. Two leaders also help to cover the group from week to week in the event one leader is absent.

The wide array of settings for reminiscence has been previously noted. The setting itself will influence the type of members available. For example, the leader should anticipate frailty among groups of nursing home residents. Severe sensory deficits and memory loss provide a challenge for the leader. So does lack of mobility.

Finding a room for reminiscing that ensures privacy should be of paramount concern to the group leader. Lack of space is a pervasive problem in both community places and in institutions. A sense of privacy is important in both one-to-one and group interactions.

Confidentiality is another concern of many group members. The leader may have to emphasize the importance of confidentiality. Group members will drop out if they feel they cannot trust the group or the leader. Confidentiality, of course, is one of the requirements of any research being conducted. The leader must practice confidentiality as well. In rare cases, the leader may need to suggest a referral, or share information with the attending physician. An example might be a person who is mentioning suicide, even in veiled terms. [See SUICIDE.]

The practitioner may hit snags in the selection of members. It is not always easy to get the desired number of members. Refusals to join a group should be studied carefully, and refusers should be given a second chance. To my knowledge, there are no studies that focus on those persons who have refused to reminisce. Persons with a very low self-esteem often refuse to join a group. Loners, the paranoid, severely depressed, and Holocaust survivors also may refuse. Affluent older adults may not wish to reminisce because they hold such a pejorative attitude about reminiscence. They often have such busy schedules traveling, golfing, playing tennis, or playing bridge that they will not devote the time to attend such a group. If it is a reminiscence study, the word *research* may also scare off potential subjects. Persons with dementia may refuse because they do not quite understand what is being asked of them. [See SELF-ESTEEM.]

C. Reminiscence with Persons with Dementia

Reminiscence has been the basis for a therapeutic modality for both alert and confused older persons in the hospital and the community. Practitioners from several disciplines have taken general aspects of reminiscence and applied it to their care of people with dementia. Reminiscence has been recommended for persons in the early stages of dementia because they may become anxious and depressed as they become more aware of their memory loss and the problems associated with it. [See DEMENTIA.]

When using reminiscence with persons with dementia, who are usually very sensitive about their memory loss, the practitioner must focus on long-term memories. These persons have failed many mental status questions and are often asked about recent memory, so they may decline participation. It is helpful to obtain the background of the older person if he or she cannot present it fluently. The high level of anxiety is also a factor to consider with these persons, especially those with Alzheimer's disease (AD).

AD is the most well-known form of dementia, and currently there are special units for persons for AD. Because it is a progressively deteriorating disease, any intervention is welcomed that will halt some of the deterioration or improve the quality of life. Reminiscence may be viewed as therapy or simply stimulation for the group. Boredom is generally viewed as one of the problems for residents on special care units. Approximately one third of long-term residents receive benefit and/or satisfaction from reminiscence groups.

Groups can provide a support and camaraderie that more often appears to be in nonverbal behaviors than verbal. For example, watching a couple walk to a group meeting hand-in-hand without conversation.

The implementation of reminiscence for the person with dementia requires that the caregiver know something about the person to facilitate the memory sharing. It is necessary to pace the sessions to the energy and willingness of the older person. For example, in one adult day care center, the after-lunch reminiscence group was not successful because the members usually fell asleep. The time was changed to morning hours and that improved the situation.

Artifacts or props that can be touched, smelled, and/or tasted are particularly effective with individuals with dementia. Music can also stir memories and be a source of pleasure. A strictly verbal approach with these persons is very difficult, and insight is an impossible goal.

Regarding reminiscence research, it should be noted that "pure" reminiscence is usually not done in groups. There are a variety of activities combined with the reminiscence. The literature indicates that props (food-tasting being a popular one), touching, poetry, music, films, and pets can all be incorporated in a group to elicit reminiscence. Then the question is, What provided the therapeutic gain? Was it the reminiscence, the additive, or the combination?

Reminiscence with persons with dementia requires patience, skill, and time. They cannot be hurried, as rushing only makes them flustered or agitated. They need a stable environment—quiet and very supportive. Touch can often be used as an adjunct to reminiscing with them; holding a hand often helps them continue a memory by reducing anxiety or agitation.

It is nearly impossible to reminisce with persons in advanced states of dementia. For example, wanderers will not sit still long enough to listen or share. Persons with aphasia may be self-conscious because they cannot share. And others may be just too frightened of a stranger or a new activity introduced into their regular routine.

One has to remember that most persons with dementia had an interesting life, even though they cannot convey it. The quality of their life may be vastly improved by the endeavors of one person to reminisce with them and be with them. The presence of a caring person is powerful. This is beautifully portrayed in the children's book, *Wilfred Gordon McDonald Partridge* by Mem Fox, which is an excellent teaching tool. Woods and McKiernan in Haight and Webster provide a detailed list of practical considerations to take into account for leading reminiscence groups with persons with dementia; there are specific group reminiscence techniques described in the literature.

V. TECHNIQUES

The literature reveals that several strategies are used in current practices to elicit reminiscence in older persons. All of these techniques, except triggers, may be used in either the one-to-one or the group modalities. Triggers are common in the group setting:

1. *Flashbulb memories:* An event or person that instantly elicits memories. In one group of six older

women who lived in a retirement home, three of the group had been to a parade honoring Charles Lindbergh when he returned from his historic flight to Paris. A more recent flashbulb memory is the assassination of John F. Kennedy. Most older persons remember exactly what they were doing at the moment that tragedy occurred; they can vividly describe where they were, and how they reacted.

2. *Genograms:* A diagram of family members, much like a family tree, which was originally used by health professionals to discern medical problems and/or cause of death of relatives. Social workers and nurses have been the professionals to implement this technique.

3. *Props:* Objects brought either by the older person or the helping professional that will help evoke memories or events from an earlier time. The items may be antiques, old newspapers, pictures, music, and so on. Generally, props are chosen by the person eliciting reminiscence; however, the literature notes that a few leaders encouraged group members to bring items to stimulate memories.

4. *Themes:* A leader-chosen or a member-chosen subject of discourse and discussion, which is a unifying dominant idea for a reminiscence group. Rationale for the choice of themes in groups is not discussed in the literature.

5. *Time line:* A personal time line could also be designed by the older person for important events in his or her life. It could be marked by decades: 1910–1920, 1920–1930, 1930–1940, and so on, and significant events recorded for each time line.

6. *Triggers:* Triggers are words or phrases expressed by one member that calls to mind a memory of another member. Triggers are most helpful to a leader in a reminiscence group because they increase the group process and interest. One person will say, "Oh that reminds me of . . .". The leader can capitalize on triggers and sit back and encourage the words or ideas presented to help group members recall events. Triggers really do make the group leadership much easier, and leaders need to be sensitive when they occur.

Although the above techniques are mentioned in the literature, there is rarely detailed information on how to implement them and, more importantly, how successful they are when used as adjuncts to the reminiscence process.

VI. BENEFITS OF REMINISCENCE GROUP THEMES

Weiss described the benefits of using group themes with older adults. Even though the leader introduces a theme, the members are still in control of the discussion. They also have a choice regarding which direction their sharing will go. There is a commitment to the older person because the preselected themes are intended to focus on them. Furthermore, the themes may provide continuity because members can pursue this theme later on their own. If only one or two themes are introduced, it provides for an in-depth, detailed discussion by the group. The themes help increase the confidence of the members because they are likely to select themes with which they are most comfortable sharing. Themes provide structures for meetings and could reduce anxiety because the members would be more clear about the content and purpose of the meetings. Finally, themes could help to reduce the ambiguity because they are not expected to discuss their entire lives. The latter is in direct contrast to a life review session. Preselected themes help reduce the anxiety of a new leader. Sometimes such themes may be found in a protocol.

A protocol is a plan of an experiment or treatment. A protocol helps guide the reader. For example, a list of the themes for a group, or questions for a one-to-one interaction would be helpful.

VII. PROTOCOLS

Protocols are occasionally found in research reports; however, they are still lacking in practice. There is just now beginning to be an effort to describe reminiscence techniques in the way that Birren has for guided autobiography groups. For neophytes, the use of protocols could help them organize and streamline the intervention, although one should never lose sight of the importance of spontaneity in the reminiscence process. Spontaneity is such an important component of reminiscence groups.

VIII. IMPORTANCE OF PAST EXPERIENCES

Older people use past experiences to help them cope with the present. The problem-solving skills learned during the Depression years, for example, may surface as they struggle with present problems. They will say, for instance, "Well I survived that, and I'll make it through this, too." This would be an example of instrumental reminiscence.

As they describe their life it helps them to understand both their past and the present. When they receive feedback from other group members, they often realize how strong they have been and how well they coped with a traumatic life. Sometimes when they compare their life to others in the group, they feel they have been fortunate to have had such a good life. The act of comparing their life to others often seems to have a positive effect. This is an example of integrative, or positively reappraising their past life.

In ways not always understood, the group may also help the members think about and/or prepare for their future. A frail 85-year-old woman, who daily visited her 105-year-old mother in a nursing home, wrote after eight reminiscence group sessions, "I am more positive about my future." The weaknesses of her changing body had not kept her from being active in the reminiscence group, and her mind certainly was active through it all.

Reminiscence helps provide continuity as they move through the time phases, but leaders who are bent on keeping them continually focused on the past may struggle and feel frustrated.

Reminiscence is an experience that gives meaning, lets the participant select the memories, as well as the time they occurred and to organize and express those memories to help give meaning to their lives. The benefits of reminiscence intervention may vary according to the setting in which it occurs. For example, the boring, monotonous routine of institutional life may make reminiscence an intensely enjoyable experience, but it may be less so for active community-based older persons.

IX. SUMMARY

The literature reveals that many disciplines implement reminiscence. Continual refinement of research has occurred; however, the results of reminiscence as a therapeutic modality have produced inconclusive results according to several reviewers. And although reminiscence is a widely used modality, researchers still lack precise definitions and protocols or guidelines. Some researchers clearly feel that reminiscence is adaptive in later life. There is a wide range of methodologies of research and variables. At the present time, there is little qualitative research to further the understanding of this fascinating concept, but that appears to be on the increase. The positive aspects of reminiscence for older persons makes it a viable therapeutic endeavor for volunteers, students, and health professionals.

BIBLIOGRAPHY

Birren, J. E., & Deutchman, D. E. (1994). *Guiding autobiography groups for older adults: Exploring the fabric of life.* Baltimore: John Hopkins Press.

Bornat, J. (Ed.). (1994). *Reminiscence reviewed: Evaluations, achievements, perspectives.* Philadelphia: Open University Press.

Burnside, I. (1993). Themes in reminiscence groups with older women. *International Journal of Aging & Human Development, 37*(3), 177–189.

Burnside, I., & Haight, B. K. (1994). Reminiscence and life review: Therapeutic interventions for older people. *Nurse Practitioner, 19*(4), 55–61. (Article contains protocols).

Butler, R. N. (1963). The life review: An interpretation of reminiscence in the aged. *Psychiatry, 26,* 65–76.

Haight, B. K., & Webster, J. D. (1995). *The art and science of reminiscing: Theory, research, methods, and applications.* Washington, DC: Taylor & Francis.

Hendricks, J. (1995). (Ed.). *The meaning of reminiscence and life review.* Amityville, NY: Baywood Publishing.

James, A., & Gilkes, C. (1994). *Reminiscence work with old people.* Oxford, UK: Chapman & Hall.

Sherman, E. (1991). *Reminiscence and the self in old age.* New York: Springer.

Thorsheim, H., & Roberts, R. (1990). *Reminiscing together.* Minneapolis: Comp Care Publishers.

Weiss, C. R. (1993). Capture the moments: Preserving the memories of older adults. *JoPERD, 64* (April), 41–44.

Weiss, C. R. (1989). Therapeutic recreation and reminiscing: The pursuit of elusive memory and the art of remembering. *Journal of Therapeutic Recreation, 23*(3), 7–8.

Renal and Urinary Tract Function

Robert D. Lindeman

University of New Mexico School of Medicine

I. Introduction
II. Age-Related Changes in Kidney Structure and Function
III. Age-Related Changes in Renal Control of Fluid and Electrolyte Homeostasis
IV. Aging and Kidney–Urinary Tract Disease
V. Lower Urinary Tract Dysfunction with Aging

Effective Renal Plasma Flow (ERPF) (Para-Aminohippuric Acid [PAH] Clearance) A measure (in ml or cc per minute) of the volume of plasma flowing through the kidney. This can be measured by the para-aminohippuric acid (PAH) or diodrast clearance as low concentrations of these substances are cleared completely by tubular secretion each pass through the kidney. Approximately 92% of plasma perfusing the kidney secretes its PAH into the tubular system so it can be excreted. Renal blood flow (RBF) can be calculated as,

$$RBF = \frac{ERPF \times \frac{100}{92}}{1 - \frac{hematocrit}{100}}$$

The PAH clearance is normally four to five times the glomerular filtration rate.

Glomerular Filtration Rate (GFR) (Inulin or Creatinine Clearance) A measure (in ml or cc per minute) often corrected to body surface area (meters^2), of the volume of filtrate formed by the kidney glomeruli. The most accurate measure is the inulin clearance, but this requires a constant infusion. Endogenous creatinine clearance provides a much simpler, clinical measure that approximates inulin clearance. The normal valve is 100–120 ml per minute; blood urea nitrogen and serum creatinine concentrations begin to increase above normal when this clearance falls below 30 ml per minute.

Urine Osmolality (mOsm/L) (Concentrating and Diluting Ability) The serum and urine osmolality per kilogram of water or liter is a measure of all solute particles per unit of volume and can be used to measure ability to concentrate urine when water is restricted and to dilute urine when water loaded.

Cross-sectional studies of healthy populations show a decrease in **KIDNEY FUNCTION** that approximates 1% per year after the age of 40 years, as measured by glomerular filtration rates (inulin or creatinine clearances) and other measures of kidney function that parallel this measure. However, longitudinal studies show there are some elderly individuals who, when followed for periods of up to 20 years, show no decrease. This suggests that loss of renal function is not an inevitable involutional process, but may be the result of pathologic processes in selected individuals. Studies of structural changes with age, on the other hand, demonstrate an increasing prevalence of ischemic obsolescence of glomeruli and glomerulosclerosis with age. The ability of the kidney to conserve sodium (salt) and water and an impaired thirst mechanism increases the susceptibility of older individuals to dehydration (hypernatremia). An increased sensitivity to osmotic stimuli with release of antidiuretic hormone increases the susceptibility to hyponatremia. Kidney and urinary tract diseases are not different in the elderly compared to the young, but frequency and prognosis are altered. Finally, urinary tract dysfunction with age is generally not life-threatening, but does affect quality of life.

I. INTRODUCTION

Studies in rats have shown the development of proteinuria and impaired renal function during the course of aging associated with significant structural changes in the kidney. The most striking anatomic features are focal and segmental glomerulosclerosis, increases in mesangial matrix, and glomerular and tubular basement membrane thickening. Whether the proteinuria is the cause or an effect of those structural lesions remains unclear; immunological and/or environmental factors may play a prominent role.

In otherwise healthy individuals, the aging kidney also is associated with structural and functional changes. In both cross-sectional and longitudinal studies, mean values of kidney function decrease with age. Results from the Baltimore Longitudinal Study on Aging, however, suggest that the loss of renal function with age is not inevitable and that decreases in mean values may be primarily the result of superimposed pathology (e.g., undetected glomerulonephritis or interstitial nephritis secondary to infections, immunologic insults, drugs, or other toxic exposures; atherosclerotic vascular occlusions with resultant ischemic injury; and urinary tract infections or obstruction). The terms *successful* and *usual* aging have been used to distinguish between individuals who age without loss of organ function and the usual cross-section of any aging population where mean values are tabulated. The latter must include individuals with asymptomatic, or at least undocumented, pathology.

A variety of lesions can be observed by the pathologist in patients with impaired renal function. These can be divided into glomerular, tubulointerstitial, and vascular pathologies. For clinical purposes, in this article we have divided the renal disorders into acute renal failure (ARF), nephrotic syndrome, chronic renal failure, and urinary tract infections (UTIs).

Lower urinary tract dysfunction in the elderly, although responsible for a number of medical concerns, is rarely life-threatening with the exception of malignant disease and unrelieved obstruction. These dysfunctions affect quality of life and many require medical management. Urinary incontinence, for example,

is one of the most frequent reasons elderly persons are placed in nursing homes. It occurs in more than 50% of nursing home residents. The involuntary loss of urine severe enough to cause social and hygienic problems is seen in 15–30% of community-living elders, especially women. Benign prostatic hypertrophy is another example of a medical concern that develops in virtually all men if they live long enough.

II. AGE-RELATED CHANGES IN KIDNEY STRUCTURE AND FUNCTION

A. Changes in Renal Morphology with Age

Both kidney mass and function decrease after the third or fourth decade of life at the rate of approximately 1% per year so that there is a reduction in renal mass up to 30% by the eighth decade. There is a 30–50% reduction in the number of glomeruli, with a substantial number of the rest developing focal glomerulosclerosis. The number of mesangial cells increases, thereby decreasing the filtering surface while the percentage of epithelial cells decreases, and the mesangium increases from 8 to 12% of the total glomerular volume. Although the number of glomerular tufts per unit area decreases, as does the number of glomerular and tubular cells, the size of surviving cells increases with age. There also is a significant increase in connective tissue in the medulla. Thickening of the glomerular and tubular basement membranes becomes apparent. Finally, diverticula of the distal nephron begin to appear and may be the cause of the cysts frequently seen in the elderly, but not in the young.

The loss of renal mass is principally from the cortex and is primarily vascular in origin, with the most significant changes occurring at the capillary level. Normal aging is associated with sclerotic changes in the walls of the larger renal arteries, but these lesions generally do not encroach on the lumen sufficiently to produce functional changes. Smaller vessels are relatively spared in nonhypertensive elderly subjects with only a small percentage of senescent kidneys showing arteriolar changes. The incidence of sclerotic glomeruli increases with advancing age, from less than 5% of the total glomeruli at 40 years to 10–30% of the total by the eighth decade. One study reported a strong direct correlation between the number of sclerotic glomeruli and the severity of atherosclerotic disease. Furthermore, when the percentage of sclerosed glomeruli was less than 5%, the distribution between cortex and medulla was relatively uniform, but as the percentage increased, the distribution became predominantly cortical.

Several investigators have compared ischemic obsolescence in cortical and juxtamedullary glomeruli. Initially, in both, there is a progressive collapse of the glomerular tuft with wrinkling of the basement membranes, followed by simplification and reduction in the vascular channels. Hyaline is deposited within both the residual glomerular tuft and the space of Bowman's capsule. Identifiable structures rapidly disappear so that the obsolete glomerulus may be reabsorbed and disappear completely. Reabsorption is suggested by the scantiness of the cellular response and the residual scar. In the cortical glomeruli, there is obliteration of the afferent arterioles with complete atrophy of the glomerular tuft; in the juxtamedullary glomeruli, there is spiraling of the arterioles with subsequent shunting of blood from the afferent to the efferent arterioles. This produces a redistribution of blood flow from the cortical to the juxtamedullary portions of the kidney with age.

B. Changes in Renal Function with Age

Most data on changes in renal function with age come from cross-sectional studies, because they are easier to perform and can be accomplished over relatively short periods of time. Potential misinterpretations can be introduced by cohort differences and selective mortality, problems that can be avoided only by much more costly, time-consuming, longitudinal studies.

1. Glomerular Filtration Rate

Cross-sectional studies have shown an age-related decrease in renal function after age 30–40 years. Four decades ago, researchers observed a 50% reduction in inulin clearances between 30 and 90 years of age. Data was subsequently collected from 38 studies where individual inulin clearances and ages were recorded and found an accelerating decrease in glomerular filtration rate (GFR) with increasing age in both men (Figure 1) and women. The rate of decline was more rapid in men. Rowe and co-investigators, reporting on results from the Baltimore Longitudinal Study on Aging, showed a similar rate of decline in mean creatinine clearances in normal male subjects

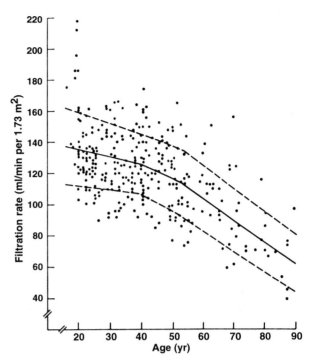

Figure 1 Glomerular filtration rate (inulin clearances) per 1.73 m² in normal male volunteers plotted against age from 38 studies. Solid and broken lines represent mean ± one standard deviation. (Reprinted by permission of Wesson, L. G., Jr. (Ed.), Renal hemodynamics in physiologic states. In Wesson, L. G., Jr., Ed. Physiology of the Human Kidney, 1969, Grune and Stratton, New York, pp. 98–100.)

followed over a 10-year period with clearances obtained every 12 to 18 months.

Although mean true creatinine clearances fell from 140 ml/min/1.73m² between 25 and 34 years of age to 97 ml/min/1.73m² between 75 and 84 years of age, mean serum creatinine concentrations rose insignificantly from 0.81 to 0.84 mg/ml. This shows that mean creatinine production falls at essentially the same rate as mean creatinine clearance, paralleling the decrease in body muscle mass with age. Serum creatinine concentrations in older individuals must be interpreted with this observation in mind when used to determine or modify dosages of drugs cleared totally (e.g., aminoglycoside antibiotics) or partially (e.g., digoxin) by the kidney.

A subsequent report from this study showed that the mean decrease in this volunteer cohort followed over a 23-year period was 0.87 ml/min/year in all subjects and 0.75 ml/min/year in the individuals free of renal and urinary tract disease and not under treatment for hypertension. This is very close to that observed in the above-mentioned cross-sectional analyses. One-third of these subjects, however, had no decline in creatinine clearance, as illustrated by six subjects followed for 15–21 years (Figure 2). These observations suggest that the decline in renal function seen with age in cross-sectional analyses is not the result of a universal chronic involutional change, but more likely is a result of intervening pathology in a portion of each population: for examples, (a) undetected glomerulonephritis or interstitial nephritis secondary to immunological insults, infections, drugs, and other toxic exposures; (b) vascular occlusions with resultant ischemic injury; and (c) UTIs or obstruction. One of the variables that affects the rate of decline in renal function is blood pressure, as hypertensive individuals exhibit a more rapid decline in renal function when compared to normotensive subjects.

2. Renal Blood and Plasma Flow

The effective renal plasma flow (ERPF), as measured by quantifying para-aminohippuric acid (PAH) clearance, decreases from a mean of 649 ml per min during the fourth decade to a mean of 289 ml per min during the ninth decade. Since the extraction ratio (ERPF/

RPF) at low arterial PAH concentrations is not affected by age (92% in young and old subjects), PAH clearance can be used to reflect changes in renal blood flow with age. The ERPF decreases more rapidly than the GFR, resulting in an increase in the filtration fraction.

The decrease in renal blood flow with age without a parallel decrease in blood pressure could be explained by either the presence of intraluminal vascular pathology (e.g., atheromata or sclerosis) or by increased renal vascular resistance caused by arteriolar vasoconstriction. Two studies have examined this issue, one suggesting that there is a greater resting vasoconstriction in older subjects, and the other suggesting there is a greater resting vasodilation in older subjects. The latter study, using xenon washout techniques, also reported that perfusion of the outer cortical nephrons fell more with age than perfusion of corticomedullary nephrons.

3. Maximum Tubular Transport Capacity

The tubular maximum for PAH secretory transport decreases with age at a rate paralleling the decrease in inulin clearance. The tubular maximum for glucose reabsorption decreases similarly with age. Although reductions in the secretory and reabsorptive tubular maxima with age could be explained by a progressive

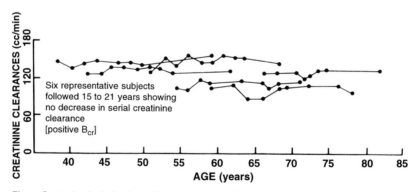

Figure 2 Individual displays of serial creatinine clearances plotted against age in years for six representative subjects from the Baltimore Longitudinal Study of Aging. These six subjects were followed from 15–21 years and showed no decrease in creatinine clearances over this period of time (positive slope of creatinine clearance plotted against time in years). This was representative of the one-third of the 254 normal subjects followed who showed no decline in renal function over the 23 years the study was being conducted. (Reprinted by permission of Lindeman, R. D., Tobin, J., Shock, N. W., 1985. Longitudinal studies on the rate of decline in renal function with age. *Journal of the American Geriatric Society, 23,* 278–285.)

loss of functioning nephrons, animal studies suggest that tubular cells in old compared to young kidneys have fewer energy-producing mitochondria, lower enzyme concentrations, lower concentrations of total or sodium-potassium-activated adenosine triphosphatase (ATPase), decreased sodium extrusion and oxygen consumption, and decreased tubular transport capacity. Because these studies were performed on tissue slices, it is difficult to be sure that these decreases are not attributable to a higher proportion of nontubular mass in old compared to young kidneys.

4. Concentrating and Diluting Abilities

A decrease in urine concentrating ability with age is well documented. In the Baltimore Longitudinal Study on Aging, 12 hours of water deprivation increased mean urine osmolality to 1109 mOsm/l in young subjects (mean age 33 years), 1051 mOsm/l in middle-aged subjects (mean age 49 years), and 882 mOsm/l in older subjects (mean age 68 years). The decrease in concentrating ability could not be related to an increase in solute load in surviving functioning nephrons, but most likely appears explainable by an increase in medullary blood flow that reduces medullary tonicity due to washout of solute that occurs with age.

Maximum urine osmolality following infusions of large doses of pitressin is decreased in older subjects first undergoing a water diuresis. Elderly subjects, however, respond normally to infusions of pitressin insufficient to maximally concentrate the urine, further supporting the hypothesis that the decrease in concentrating ability observed in older individuals is the result of a decrease in medullary tonicity rather than any defect in the ability of the tubule to respond to antidiuretic hormone.

Maximum diluting ability, as measured by minimum urine osmolality achieved with water loading, also decreases with age. When one compares maximum free water clearance per unit of nephron mass (GFR), there is little difference between young and old individuals, suggesting no basic defect exists in the ability to produce a diluted urine.

5. Excretion of Acid

To maintain systemic acid–base balance, the kidney must excrete a quantity of hydrogen ion equal to that generated by metabolism. Under basal conditions, the blood pH, pCO_2, and bicarbonate of older persons without significant renal disease do not differ from the values observed in young subjects. However, the decreases in blood pH and bicarbonate concentrations following ingestion of an acid load (e.g., 8 g of ammonium chloride) persist longer in elderly persons. The minimum urine pH achieved after an acid load is comparable in young and old individuals. A much larger percentage of the ingested acid load, as measured by total acid excretion (ammonium plus titratable acid minus bicarbonate) is excreted over an 8-hour period by the young subjects; however, if total acid excretion is factored by GFR, similar rates of excretion are observed. Young subjects excrete a higher percentage of total acid as ammonium, whereas older subjects have a higher percentage as titratable acid, presumably because they have an increase in urinary buffers per unit of GFR. This limitation in the kidney's ability to excrete acid in older individuals may predispose them to the development of metabolic acidosis and delay their recovery from it.

6. Glomerular Permeability

Functional studies of glomerular permeability show no change with age. Although the incidence of clinical proteinuria increases with age, glomerular permeability to free hemoglobin and a spectrum of different molecular weight dextrans does not differ between young and old subjects. Glomerular basement membrane does thicken with age.

C. Pathophysiology of the Decrease in Renal Function with Age

Whether the decrease in renal function with age is the result of a progressive involutional process with loss of nephron units and a loss of cellular function similar to the glomerulosclerosis observed in rodents, or is the result of a variety of pathological processes, often undetected, producing acute or chronic damage, or both, remains unresolved. Although results from the Baltimore Longitudinal Study on Aging showed that one-third of the male volunteers (some followed for over 20 years) failed to show any decrease in renal function over the period studied, anatomic studies show a progressive increase in the number of sclerotic glomeruli with advancing age. The former data suggest that there is no inevitable progressive involutional change with age, at least not in all individuals, and support the concept that the decrease in renal function with age observed in cross-sectional studies is the result of superimposed pathology in a portion of the population under study. Anatomic studies, however, suggest there is a sequence of events that results in sclerosis and loss of function in glomeruli that parallels the severity of atherosclerosis elsewhere in the body. An alternative possibility is that as glomeruli become sclerotic, there is a hyperplasia and hypertrophy of cells in remaining glomeruli, perhaps stimulated by circulating growth factors, that compensates and maintains renal function much as observed after unilateral nephrectomy and in diabetes mellitus and hypertension.

A number of examples of undetected pathology causing reduced renal function in the elderly can be cited. For example, one study utilizing scanning techniques to localize defects in kidney function in elderly patients (mean age 75 years) without a history of renal disease found abnormal scans in 25 of 35 (71%) subjects with a mean creatinine clearance of 53 ml/min. Sixteen (46%) showed focal areas of diminished uptake, which were felt to represent ischemic or infarcted areas. Significant pyuria was present in 37% of the patients, and intravenous pyelograms were interpreted as normal in all cases. These findings suggest that vascular occlusions, interstitial infection (pyelonephritis), or both contribute to the decrease in renal function observed in any aging population.

Once a critical level of renal functional deterioration is reached in individuals with kidney injury from any cause, progression of the damage occurs, even if the initiating event or condition is resolved. This is due to a progressive glomerulosclerosis. A vast literature has been generated on the role of hyperperfusion and hyperfiltration in the progression of declining renal function as it has been observed in rodents. It has been hypothesized that high glomerular pressures and plasma flow rates created by high protein intakes contribute to the development of glomerulosclerosis, resulting in a progressive decline in renal function with age alone, as with primary renal disease, renal ablation, diabetes mellitus, and hypertension.

III. AGE-RELATED CHANGES IN RENAL CONTROL OF FLUID AND ELECTROLYTE HOMEOSTASIS

Under normal circumstances, age has little or no effect on serum sodium and potassium concentrations or the ability to maintain normal extracellular fluid volumes. The extrarenal mechanisms responsible for maintaining volume and composition of the extracellular fluids, however, often become impaired in the elderly, especially when stressed by acute and/or chronic illness.

A. Control of Sodium Balance

Older subjects fail to conserve sodium as efficiently as young subjects when subjected to rigid salt restriction. They have consistently lower plasma renin concentrations and urinary aldosterone excretions on both restricted and unrestricted salt diets and in both supine and upright positions. These decreased plasma renin concentrations and urinary aldosterone excretions in the elderly may be related to the impaired responsiveness to β-adrenergic stimulation observed in the elderly because one of the effects of β-adrenergic stimulation is to increase levels of circulating renin and aldosterone. The decrease in aldosterone at least partially explains the decreased ability of the elderly to conserve sodium when challenged with a low-salt diet.

Two other factors may affect the ability of the elderly to conserve sodium. Circulating atrial natriuretic factor (ANF) levels, although very variable, are increased in the elderly, increasing the salt-losing tendency of the kidney, both directly by its natriuretic effect and indirectly by suppressing renin and aldosterone synthesis and release. Also, as renal function decreases with age, assuming food and salt intake are maintained, the solute load in each residual functional nephron increases, thereby producing a relative osmotic diuresis and a decreased ability to conserve sodium and water.

B. Control of Potassium Balance

The low renin and aldosterone levels described earlier also could account for the greater tendency of older individuals to develop hyperkalemia when challenged with an increased exogenous (potassium supplements, potassium-containing medications) or endogenous (tissue catabolism, blood in the intestine) load of potassium. Because the distal nephron has such a large capacity for secreting potassium, even in patients with markedly reduced renal function, hyperkalemia generally develops only with one or more additional factors (e.g., excess endogenous or exogenous potassium) or introduction of a drug or disease that affects distal tubular secretion of potassium. Drugs that interfere with this aldosterone-dependent tubular secretion of potassium include the potassium-sparing diuretics (spironolactone, triamterene, amiloride), the β-adrenergic blockers, the angiotensin-converting enzyme (ACE) inhibitors, and the nonsteroidal anti-inflammatory drugs (NSAIDs). Elderly persons with a chronic interstitial nephritis, especially diabetics, develop a more pronounced hyporeninemic hypoaldosteronism (type IV renal tubular acidosis) with hyperkalemia.

C. Susceptibility of Older Individuals to Dehydration (Hypernatremia)

The increased tendency of the older individual to lose both sodium (salt) and water (concentrating defect) contribute to the more rapid development of dehydration and hypernatremia. Another factor that might accelerate the development of dehydration is an impaired secretion of antidiuretic hormone (arginine vasopressin, AVP) associated with the hypoangiotensinemia (decreased renin-angiotensin-aldosterone) commonly seen in the elderly. This would result in an inability to concentrate the urine and thereby conserve water.

More important, however, is the impairment in the thirst mechanism that develops with age. In one study reported, older subjects following 24 hours of water deprivation had increased serum osmolalities and plasma AVP levels and decreased urine osmolalities (concentrations) compared to younger subjects. The younger subjects, however, reported much more thirst, and at the end of the study rapidly drank water to restore plasma osmolality to normal. The older individuals, in contrast, drank little water and still had not corrected the hyperosmolality after 2 hours. If older persons had a normal thirst response to water deprivation, the inability to conserve salt and water would be compensated for by an increased fluid intake.

D. Susceptibility of Older Individuals to the Development of Hyponatremia

Surveys of older individuals in both acute and chronic care facilities show a high incidence of hyponatremia. Chronically hyponatremic individuals show an impaired ability to increase urine volume and decrease urine osmolality when challenged with a water load. The most frequent etiology is a normovolemic hyponatremia consistent with the syndrome of inappropriate antidiuretic hormone (SIADH) release. Other etiologies included primary salt depletion (hypovolemia), dilutional hyponatremia (hypervolemia, as seen in congestive heart failure (CHF), cirrhosis, nephrotic syndrome) hyperglycemia, and renal failure. In one study of elderly, hospital-acquired hyponatremics, nonosmotic (baroreceptor) stimulation of vasopressin release was a major factor in the development of this electrolyte disorder, regardless of cause. Elderly patients, under a variety of stressors, are much more likely to develop hyponatremia than younger subjects (e.g., postoperatively and following diuretic and sulfonylurea [chlorpropamide] therapy).

Antidiuretic hormone activity in the serum or plasma tends to be higher in older persons when compared to younger persons under comparable conditions. Following infusions of a standardized hypertonic saline infusion designed to raise serum osmolality to 306 mOsm/l, older subjects had more than a twofold greater rise in serum AVP concentrations. In contrast, ethanol infusions, known to inhibit AVP secretion, produces a more prolonged decrease in serum AVP concentrations in young than in old subjects. These two observations suggest an increasing osmoreceptor sensitivity with age with a greater release of AVP and thus more water retention in response to any given osmotic stimulus. Subsequent studies designed to determine if this was a consistent, age-related increase in vasopressin responsiveness or was specific only for osmotic stimuli showed that older subjects, following periods of quiet standing, failed to increase serum AVP concentrations as much or as consistently as younger subjects. Because these subjects had an intact norepinephrine response to orthostasis, the age-related defect was felt to be distal to the vasomotor center in the afferent limb of the baroreceptor reflex arc. Furthermore, it was suggested that the contrasting influence of age on the vasopressin response to osmolar and volume-pressure stimuli, in at least some elderly, might be related to impaired baroreceptor input to the supraoptic nucleus, which in turn might remove constraints on the response to osmotic stimuli.

IV. AGING AND KIDNEY–URINARY TRACT DISEASE

The inability of the kidney to excrete, through the process of formation of a glomerular filtrate and selective reabsorption and secretion in the tubular system, the normal load of metabolites produced by the body can be separated into ARF or chronic renal failure. When one discusses ARF, and, to a lesser extent chronic renal failure, a further distinction needs to be made between prerenal, renal, and postrenal azotemia. Useful in categorizing these broad groups is calculation of the blood urea nitrogen (BUN)/serum creatinine ratio. With prerenal azotemia, there is either a decrease in renal perfusion (dehydration, hypotension, CHF) or an increase in nitrogen production (bleeding into the gastrointestinal tract) so that the BUN/serum creatinine ratio increases to over 20 to 1. The decreased perfusion associated with prerenal azotemia enhances tubular urea reabsorption disproportionately, raising BUN to serum creatinine concentrations. In one study of ARF in the elderly (>70 years of age), nearly one-half was prerenal in origin (over half of these due to dehydration). The increased hydrostatic pressure transmitted to the tubular fluid in postrenal (obstructive) azotemia also creates a disproportionate reabsorption of urea compared to creatinine increasing the BUN/serum creatinine ratio. These changes are in contrast to azotemia resulting from intrinsic renal disease, where the BUN/serum creatinine ratio ranges between 10 and 14 to 1.

A. Acute Renal Failure

Of the renal causes of ARF in the elderly, glomerular, tubulointerstitial, or vascular pathology may be causative. The tubulointerstitial nephropathies [acute tubular necrosis (ATN), acute interstitial nephritis (AIN)] are the most common etiologies; the ATN can either be ischemic or nephrotoxic in origin. Most of the acute tubular necrosis of ischemic origin in the elderly is associated with surgical procedures and problems, including pre- and postoperative sepsis. Medical illness such as pneumonia, sepsis, and ischemic heart disease, especially those that produce hypotension, can cause ischemic ATN. Causes of nephrotoxic ATN include the aminoglycoside antibiotics (gentamicin) and intravenous contrast agents used in pyelography, angiography, and computerized tomog-

raphy (CT). Beside age, factors that increase risk of ATN include diabetes mellitus, preexisting renal insufficiency, multiple myeloma, renal hypoperfusion (dehydration), hypertension, and hepatic disease. A review of prognosis in older patients with this type of ARF suggests age does not appreciably affect survival rates, but older patients need more time to recover renal function and recovered less fully.

Drug-induced AIN has become an increasingly common cause of ARF in the elderly; AIN can also be seen as a complication of infections or systemic disease. Over 40 drugs have been implicated as potential etiologic agents with the penicillins, most commonly methicillin, and NSAIDs being the most frequently incriminated. Patients commonly develop fever, rash, and eosinophilia–eosinophiluria along with nonoliguric, progressive azotemia. [See PHARMACOLOGY.]

Acute glomerulonephritis, generally regarded as a cause of ARF in children and young adults, also is more common in the elderly than generally believed. The essential clinical features of hematuria, proteinuria, sodium and fluid retention, decreased renal function, and hypertension are not different in the elderly but are obscured by the presence of preexisting cardiovascular disease and a low index of suspicion. It may be difficult clinically to distinguish patients with poststreptococcal or postinfectious glomerulonephritis from patients with rapidly progressive (crescentic) glomerulonephritis or glomerulonephritis related to systemic disease (lupus erythematosus, vasculitis, subacute bacterial endocarditis, etc.)

B. Glomerular Disease (Nephrotic Syndrome)

The nephrotic syndrome is defined by the urinary excretion of protein in excess of 3 g per day and other features that are the consequence of this protein loss (e.g., hypoalbuminemia, hyperlipidemia, edema, and a hypercoagulable state). Hypertension and renal insufficiency may or may not be present. The nephrotic syndrome can result from primary glomerular disease, neoplastic disease, or multisystem disease. Studies of nephrotic syndrome in the elderly suggest it is at least as common as it is in younger persons. Several reviews of histologic diagnoses indicate that over one-third of the biopsied patients have a membranous nephropathy with the next most common diagnoses being minimal change disease, primary amyloidosis, mesangial proliferative glomeulonephritis, and focal/segmental glomerulosclerosis. The incidence of membranous nephropathy and amyloidosis was higher than in younger adults, proliferative glomerulonephritis was much lower, whereas minimal change disease was comparable but lower than in children. The incidence of IgA nephropathy and rapidly progressive (crescentic) glomerulonephritis appears to be low in the elderly. Several authors have reported on the increased incidence of underlying malignancies (5–10%) in patients found to have membranous glomerulopathies on biopsy.

Glomerulopathies resulting from systemic disease are more common in the elderly because of the increased incidence of such underlying diseases as diabetes mellitus, amyloidosis (dysproteinemias), vasculitis, and scleroderma. In one review, a secondary cause was found in one-third of the cases. Diabetic nephropathy is the most frequent cause of glomerular disease associated with systemic illness in the elderly (diabetic glomerulosclerosis); however, because many of these patients have an obvious etiology for their nephrotic syndrome, documentation in biopsy series tends to be low and to underestimate the prevalence of this lesion, especially in the elderly. All elderly nephrotics should have urine and serum electrophoreses performed as amyloidosis is the most frequent cause of nephrotic syndrome secondary to systemic disease in biopsied patients.

C. Chronic Renal Failure

Chronic renal failure results from irreversible damage to both kidneys from a wide variety of glomerular, tubulointerstitial, and vascular causes. Up to 90% of kidney function may be lost without significant morbidity. Progression of the renal lesions can be delayed by managing hypertension, infection, obstructive uropathy, heart failure, and dehydration.

Occlusive arterial disease can cause either acute or chronic renal failure. Bilateral renal artery stenosis due to atherosclerosis may cause, in addition, accelerated hypertension. Renal cholesterol embolization is a geriatric disorder that may occur spontaneously or in association with aortic surgery or angiography in patients with diffuse atherosclerosis. Hypertensives may develop benign or malignant nephrosclerosis. Systemic vasculitis, polycystic renal disease, and

scleroderma are other diseases that can cause chronic renal failure without sufficient glomerular disease to cause nephrotic syndrome. [*See* ATHEROSCLEROSIS.]

The high frequency of arthritis and arthralgia in the elderly increases the risk of long-term use and abuse of NSAIDs and analgesics. The NSAIDs, because they inhibit vasodilatory prostaglandins, reduce medullary blood flow and inhibit the hexose monophosphate shunt that leads to oxidative injury of medullary cells and frequently cause chronic interstitial nephritis and ultimately papillary necrosis. Phenacetin is the most frequently incriminated analgesic, but salicylates and acetaminophen also may be implicated.

D. Urinary Tract Infections

Pyelonephritis is a serious infection, being the most common cause of gram-negative bacteremia in elderly hospitalized patients. *Escherichia coli* causes approximately two-thirds of the episodes of infection, with Klebsiella, Enterobacter, Citrobacter, Enterococcus, Proteus, and Pseudomonas accounting for most of the rest.

Acute symptomatic pyelonephritis often offers a greater diagnostic challenge in elderly than in younger patients, where the classic irritative voiding symptoms make diagnosis readily apparent. Patients with neurological disease (dementia, cerebral vascular disease, parkinsonism) especially have an increased incidence of infection and often present only with altered mental status (somnolence, confusion), tachypnea, loss of appetite, and vague abdominal pains that may suggest pneumonia, diverticulitis, or intestinal obstruction as alternative diagnoses. Fever and leukocytosis may be absent. Pyuria and bacteriuria are seen with both pyelonephritis or infections limited to the lower urinary tract (cystitis) which are common in the elderly, especially women. It is often difficult to determine whether or not infections are limited to the bladder and urethra alone or extend up to involve the kidney. High fever and back (costovertebral angle) pain and tenderness suggest the latter.

Asymptomatic bacteriuria (pyuria and bacteria in the urine greater than 10^5 organisms per ml on clean voided examination) is increasingly prevalent with advancing age, being present in one-third of patients in long-term care facilities. Although these patients with asymptomatic bacteriuria, have an increased mortality rate, it remains unclear whether this is an independent risk factor for shortened survival or merely a marker for severe underlying disease. It does not appear that antibiotic therapy has been useful in prolonging survival or preventing recurrent bacteriuria or symptomatic infection, so the prevailing philosophy seems to be to leave asymptomatic bacteriuria untreated until it becomes symptomatic. This also may prevent emergence of resistant organisms.

V. LOWER URINARY TRACT DYSFUNCTION WITH AGING

A. Effect of Age on the Lower Urinary Tract

Aging affects the lower urinary tract in a number of ways, but incontinence is not a normal consequence. Bladder capacity, the ability to postpone voiding, bladder compliance, and urinary flow rate appear to decline in both sexes, and maximum urethral closure pressure and urethral length appear to decline in women. The number of uninhibited contractions of the detrusor (bladder) probably increases with age, and postvoiding residual volume may increase but probably to no more than 25–50 ml. Although none of these age-related changes causes incontinence, each can predispose one to incontinence, especially because older persons are prone to additional problems that increase the likelihood of this dysfunction.

B. Transient Incontinence

A number of medical, functional, and cognitive problems superimposed on an elderly person can lead to the development of incontinence. Resnick has used the mnemonic DIAPPERS (with a double P) (Table I) to describe these problems.

Delirium is an acute confusional state, often precipitated by an acute medical problem such as pneumonia or heart failure, that affects one's ability to react appropriately when the bladder becomes distended. UTIs promote a sense of urgency that precipitates voiding. Atrophic vaginitis (urethritis) in elderly women, due to estrogen deficiency, presents with dysuria, dyspareunia, urgency, and incontinence. A number of medications are capable of causing incontinence, most notably those with anticholinergic properties that can impair emptying, especially in those individuals with partial obstruction (e.g., men

Table I Common Cause of Transient Incontinence

Mnemonic designation	Cause
D	Delirium or confusional state
I	Infection, urinary tract
A	Atrophic urethritis or vaginitis
P	Pharmaceuticals (sedative hypnotics, loop diuretics, anticholinergics [antipsychotics, antiarrythmics, antiparkinsonism medications], α-adrenergic agonists and antagonists, calcium channel blockers)
P	Psychological disorders (depression)
E	Endocrine disorders (hypercalcemia, hypokalemia, hyperglycemia)
R	Restricted mobility
S	Stool impaction

with benign prostatic hypertrophy). Psychological disturbances, most notably depression, can lead to incontinence. The endocrine causes listed all can cause polyuria, and reduced mobility and stool impaction also can contribute to the development of incontinence. Many times in the elderly, the cause of incontinence is multifactorial, with confusion, medications, and mobility all playing roles. [See ENDOCRINE FUNCTION AND DYSFUNCTION.]

C. Established Incontinence

There are essentially four ways that the lower urinary tract can malfunction to produce incontinence. The detrusor (bladder) muscle either contracts when it should not (detrusor overactivity), leading to urge incontinence, or fails to contract as well as it should (detrusor underactivity), leading to overflow incontinence. Also, outlet resistance can be either persistently high, as seen with obstructive lesions such as prostatism, leading to overflow incontinence, or persistently low, as in the outlet incompetence seen with stress incontinence, usually in women with a history of multiple or difficult deliveries, or men following transurethral resection of the prostate (TURP).

Detrusor overactivity is a condition in which the bladder contracts precipitously with little warning and often empties itself completely. This can occur with normal or impaired contractile function and can result from damage to the central nervous system inhibitory centers (e.g., cerebrovascular accident, Parkinsonism, or Alzheimer's dementia), or it can result from local irritative pathology (e.g., cystitis, bladder carcinoma, or bladder stone) which impairs the ability of the normal brain to inhibit bladder contraction. Both outlet obstruction and outlet incompetence can predispose to detrusor hyperactivity.

Detrusor underactivity can result from damage to the nerves supplying the bladder (disk compression, tumors) or from an autonomic neuropathy (diabetes, alcoholism, pernicious anemia, tabes dorsalis). It can also result from replacement of bladder muscle by fibrosis and connective tissue, as seen with chronic obstruction (prostatism), whereby the bladder is no longer able to empty normally.

BIBLIOGRAPHY

Beck, L. H. (1994). Aging changes in renal function. In W. R. Hazzard, E. L. Bierman, J. P. Blass, W. H. Ettinger, Jr., & J. B. Halter (Eds.), *Principles of geriatric medicine and gerontology* (3rd ed.) (p. 615–624). New York: McGraw Hill.

Levi, M., & Rowe, J. W. (1992). Renal function and dysfunction in aging. In D. W. Seldin, & G. Giebisch (Eds.), *The kidney: Physiology and pathophysiology* (2nd ed.) (pp. 3433–3456). New York: Raven Press.

Lindeman, R. D. (1990). Overview: Renal physiology and pathophysiology of aging. *American Journal of Kidney Disease, 16,* 275–282.

Lindeman, R. D. (1992). Renal and electrolyte abnormalities. In: E. Calkins, A. B. Ford, & P. R. Katz (Eds.), *Practice of geriatrics* (2nd ed.) (pp. 436–453). Philadelphia: W.B. Saunders Co.

Lindeman, R. D., Tobin, J., & Shock, N. W. (1985). Longitudinal studies on the rate of decline in renal function with age. *Journal of the American Geriatric Society, 23,* 278–285.

Lindeman, R. D., & Goldman, R. (1986). Anatomic and physiologic age changes in the kidney. *Experimental Gerontology, 21,* 379–406.

Resnick, N. M. (1988). Urinary incontinence—A treatable disorder. In J. W. Rowe, & R. W. Besdine (Eds.), *Geriatric medicine* (2nd ed.) (pp. 246–265). Boston: Little, Brown.

Rowe, J. W. (1992). Nephrology and the genitourinary system. In J. G. Evans, & T. F. Williams (Eds.), *Oxford textbook of geriatric medicine.* (p. 423–431). Oxford: University Press.

Research Design and Methods

Linda M. Collins

The Pennsylvania State University

I. Fundamentals of Design for Research on Aging
II. A Brief Introduction to Statistics
III. A Brief Introduction to Measurement

Design The plan for carrying out a research study. This plan specifies every detail of the study including (but not limited to) what are the variables to be studied and how they are defined and measured; who are the individuals who will be participating in the study; what treatment will be administered to which participants, and how it will be decided which participants receive which treatment; and what statistical analyses are to be used.

Measurement The procedure by which variables in a study are quantified so that they will be amenable to statistical analysis and in order to form a basis for comparison of results across scientific studies.

Statistical Analysis A set of procedures by which a researcher uses information gathered from a sample in order to draw more general conclusions applicable to a larger group or population.

Science is about studying causes and effects through **RESEARCH DESIGN and METHODS** in order to draw conclusions and thereby provide knowledge about the world. When researchers carry out gerontological research, they are trying to establish the causes of certain phenomena that have been observed to be associated with aging. Much of the time it is difficult to determine the independent causes of these phenomena. Possible causal factors such as biological changes, preprogrammed genetic influences, environmental insults including drug and alcohol abuse and workplace exposure, education, and cultural and historical influences not only coexist, but influence each other as well as the aging process.

Disentangling which factors cause the phenomena observed and which merely accompany aging is a difficult task. Sometimes, the factors cannot be disentangled completely. But if the issues surrounding causation are carefully thought out, a researcher can usually carry out a study so as to narrow the list of alternative possible causes dramatically. This is done by paying careful attention to the design of the study, statistical analysis, and measurement.

I. FUNDAMENTALS OF DESIGN FOR RESEARCH ON AGING

A. The Role of Theory

Every scientific study starts with a hypothesis, which is a specific statement about what the scientist expects to find out by conducting the study. In the social sciences in general and in aging research in particular, it is very important that the hypotheses stem directly from a clearly and thoroughly specified theory. The theory must incorporate prior research relevant to the topic of interest, and must make predictions that can be tested in an empirical study.

B. The Concept of Causation

A great deal has been written about the meaning of causation, what constitutes evidence of causation, and how to infer causation in social science research.

Covering this literature thoroughly is well outside the scope of this contribution. Here we will simply mention several aspects of causation that are important to keep in mind, without claiming to have done justice to this important topic. First, a cause always precedes an effect, even if only instantaneously. An effect never precedes a cause. Second, an effect may have several causes. These causes may each be sufficient but not necessary, as when any one of several causes operating alone can trigger an effect; or they may each be necessary, but each alone is not sufficient, as when several causes occurring together are needed to trigger an effect. Third, manipulation of a cause results in manipulation of the effect. This property of causation is the basis of scientific experimentation.

C. Subject Sampling

A population is the entire universe of individuals to which a research question or finding pertains. The theory upon which a study's hypotheses are based specifies the population. The population may be the entire human race, or all individuals over the age of 50, or all individuals over the age of 50 with at least a high school education, or any group of people of interest to the researchers. Except for the rare instances where resources and subject availability permit collection of data on the entire population, it is necessary to select a manageably sized subset of individuals from the population who will participate in a study. Sampling is the method by which these individuals are selected.

Once the population has been identified, the next step is to identify a sampling frame. The sampling frame specifies the exact pool from which a study's sample is to be drawn. Although in an ideal study the sampling frame would be identical to the population, in practice this is rare. For example, a sampling frame may be confined to a particular geographic area, or to those who have telephones, or to those who will not be moving during the time period the study is to be conducted. It is important to make every effort to identify a sampling frame that is as close as possible to the population of interest, and to be specific about the differences between the sampling frame and the population so that the implications of these differences for the study's results can be carefully considered. The third step in sampling is to draw a random sample of study participants from the individuals in the sampling frame.

In much research in the social sciences "convenience" sampling is used. In other words, rather than starting with a defined population, identifying a sampling frame, and then drawing a random sample, researchers use samples of individuals who are available for study participation but are not drawn from a population defined a priori. There are many reasons why circumstances force researchers into this less than optimal way of collecting data. In general, although drawing a random sample is unarguably the most scientifically sound approach, it is difficult and expensive, particularly if the study involves much more participation than answering a few questions over the telephone. For these reasons and others researchers are much more apt to draw a sample from a group made up of individuals who are likely to agree to participate (alumni of the university sponsoring the study, for example) even if the group is not completely representative of the population of interest. This nonrandom sampling procedure has important implications for the external validity of research, which is discussed below.

D. Variables

As the name implies, variables are quantities that can vary across the individuals in a study. For example, one variable that appears frequently in aging research is age itself, when the individuals taking part in the study are of different ages. Often the variables in a study can be categorized as independent and dependent variables. In traditional laboratory experimentation, the independent variable is the putatively causal variable manipulated by the experimenter, and it has an effect on the dependent variable. With the advent of field experimentation and quasi- and nonexperimental designs (see below), variables are often referred to as independent even if their relationship with the dependent variable is only predictive rather than causal per se. Sometimes the terms *exogenous* and *endogenous* are used in place of independent and dependent, respectively. These are relative terms; a variable may be independent in one context and dependent in another.

E. Operational Definitions

An operational definition is an exact description of how a variable is to be defined and measured for the purposes of a study. For example, if a study is to compare middle-aged and older adults, it is necessary to have an operational definition of what range of ages constitutes "middle age" and what range of ages constitutes "older." Whenever a standardized instrument, such as an IQ test, is used the test score serves as an operational definition of the variable of interest. In the case of IQ tests, the test score is an operational definition of intelligence.

F. Laboratory Experiments and Control

Causal factors can be isolated most convincingly by means of an experiment. An experiment is distinguished from other types of scientific studies by the use of random assignment to treatment. The logic behind an experiment is to establish groups that on average are identical, and then to expose one or more of the groups to a treatment. Usually one of the groups is left untreated so that it can serve as a baseline or *control* group. If *the groups start out identical* and then a treatment is administered *under carefully controlled conditions*, any differences between the groups that are observed can be attributed to the treatment.

There are two parts of the previous sentence that should be elaborated on. First, how does the researcher ensure that the groups start out identical? This is where random assignment, the distinguishing feature of an experiment, comes in. If a scientist decides randomly which group a participant will be in, then on the average (across many studies) the groups will be comparable. Random assignment can be carried out by tossing a fair coin, rolling a fair die, or using a computer program to generate random numbers for use in assignment. It should be noted that the use of random assignment does not guarantee that comparability has been achieved in any particular study. If it is known that balance on certain subject characteristics is desirable, it is wise to stratify the random assignment accordingly. For example, if gender balance across groups is necessary, the experimenter can conduct random assignment separately for males and females.

Second, what is meant by "carefully controlled conditions?" This means that when the independent variable is manipulated, *only* the independent variable accounts for differences across groups, rather than any other aspect of the study. For example, suppose a scientist wishes to conduct an experiment to study the effects of a particular drug on cognitive performance in the elderly. In this case the independent variable is drug dosage. Participants are randomly assigned either to a group receiving the drug or to a control group receiving a placebo (inert substance). Thus the independent variable can take on two values, either some prespecified dosage of a drug or no exposure to the drug. The dependent variable is cognitive performance. It is operationally defined as performance on a set of several cognitive tasks.

After the drug dose is administered, the participants are given the cognitive tasks to perform. Now suppose all those who receive the drug are tested in the morning hours and all those who receive the placebo are tested in the late afternoon. Thus the time of day that testing takes place differs substantially between the group receiving the drug and the group receiving the placebo. If the group that receives the drug performs better on the cognitive task, it may be because these subjects were fresher and more energetic than the placebo group rather than because of the effects of the drug. A better approach would be to bring all of the subjects into the laboratory at the same time of day, or to make sure that drug and placebo condition subjects are equally likely to participate in a morning or afternoon session.

G. Field Research and Quasi-Experiments

Although excellent control can be achieved in the laboratory, it is not a very realistic setting. Sometimes the behavior people exhibit in the laboratory does not generalize very well to the world outside the laboratory. In addition, there are many interesting and important questions that cannot be investigated by means of a laboratory study. Questions about such topics as workplace performance and ability to carry out activities of daily living, as well as many others, can often be addressed most directly by venturing outside the laboratory and observing behavior in its natural setting.

Ideally, field research is experimental, that is, it uses random assignment. These are the conditions under which the strongest conclusions can be drawn from a field study. However, in practice random assignment often cannot be used in field settings. More often questions must be addressed by means of a quasi-experiment. The term *quasi-experiment* refers to a study where there are treatment and control groups, but random assignment is not used. There are many problems associated with drawing causal inferences from quasi-experimental studies, all of which stem from the initial nonequivalence of groups. If random assignment is not used, the groups are usually not comparable at the outset. Often the existing differences between the groups provide alternative explanations for any results that are observed. For example, suppose a researcher desires to examine the effects of retirement on health. The independent variable is thus retirement, and it can take on two values: retired or still in the workforce. The dependent variable is health, in this case operationally defined as score on a self-report health questionnaire. The researcher takes a sample of people of retirement age, records who is retired and who is not, and has them complete the self-report questionnaire. Suppose it is found that the retired respondents report, on average, poorer health than the respondents who are still in the workforce. Can it be concluded that retirement causes poorer health? No, there is an important alternative explanation. There may be a tendency for the individuals who are in poorer health to choose to retire, while the healthier individuals stay on the job longer. In other words, retirement does not cause poor health; instead, poor health causes retirement. A more definitive study could be done if individuals would agree to be randomly assigned to retire or to stay in the workforce. This is impractical for obvious reasons. Another, more practical approach would be to start with a group of older adults who are still in the workforce but nearing standard retirement age, and observe them over a period of several years. In this way an important question can be addressed: Is declining health followed by retirement, or is retirement followed by declining health? The answer to this question is necessary but not sufficient to allow an inference about which variable, if either, is causal.

The term *nonexperiment* refers to a study where there are not treatment and control groups per se; instead, the relations among two or, usually, more variables are passively observed with no direct manipulation of an independent variable. The difference between a quasi-experiment and a nonexperiment is a matter of degree rather than kind. The main difference

between the two approaches is that a quasi-experiment involves a comparison between clearly defined groups. But in neither case does the experimenter use random assignment, so neither design provides inherently stronger causal inference than the other.

H. Age, Cohort, and Time

Most behavioral research investigates interindividual differences, or differences between people. In research on aging, as well as in all developmental research, researchers are also interested in investigating intraindividual differences, or change within an individual across time; and interindividual differences in intraindividual differences, or differences between people in the nature and amount of individual change over time. There are three broad classes of predictors of intraindividual change over time: age, cohort, and time. Age refers to each individual's chronological age at each observation; cohort refers to the birth cohort or generation, in a sociological sense, to which an individual belongs; and time refers to the time that an observation is made on an individual. These are not independent, because any two of them determine the third. For example, if the time of measurement and an individual's age are known, that individual's cohort can be determined. [*See* Cohort Studies; Generational Differences.]

For many years there were two primary approaches to studying aging: the cross-sectional design and the longitudinal design. In a cross-sectional design, data are collected on individuals of different ages at a single time. Comparisons are then made across ages. The cross-sectional approach has the advantage of being relatively inexpensive and fast. However, the conclusions about aging that can be drawn from a cross-sectional study are limited. First, the existence of differences across groups defined by age does not necessarily imply that individuals undergo corresponding change as they age. Second, the cross-sectional approach confounds age and cohort. In a cross-sectional study, all of the individuals who are a particular age belong to a particular cohort. It can be argued that any observed age differences are in reality due to cohort membership, and that if individuals from different cohorts were involved the results would be different.

In the longitudinal approach, data are collected on individuals repeatedly across time. Longitudinal studies are more expensive and time-consuming, but this design offers the ability to observe intraindividual growth over time. However, with traditional longitudinal designs only a single cohort is studied. Thus it is impossible to determine whether the results will hold for another cohort.

Somewhat more elaborate versions of these designs have been devised in order to address these concerns. In the cross-sequential design, cross-sectional data are collected in two different years. The first year is a traditional cross-sectional study, where people of several different ages are included in the sample. In a second year, data are collected on independent samples from the same cohorts (who are now older) and on individuals who are the same age as the participants were in the first year, but are members of different cohorts. This permits the comparison of age differences with several different pairs of cohorts involved. In the cohort-sequential design, a longitudinal study involves several cohorts simultaneously. The data collection is arranged so that data are collected on the same ages in each cohort. This allows the comparison of results across cohorts.

I. Internal Validity

The internal validity of a study is the confidence with which causation can be attributed to the independent variable and not to some other uncontrolled aspect of the study. A few of the possible threats to the internal validity of aging studies are listed below. This is by no means an exhaustive list.

1. Testing

This can be a problem in longitudinal research if participants are given the same tests or asked to complete the same questionnaires frequently. Scores on tests can go up because of increased familiarity with the test rather than because of any real growth in skill or ability, or participants may become bored or irritated and stop paying attention, leading to a decline in test scores.

2. Instrumentation

If a test or questionnaire has different meanings at different points in time in a longitudinal study, this can pose a threat to internal validity. A frequently occurring example of this is floor and ceiling effects. A floor effect is when a test is not sensitive at the low end of the range, usually because it is too difficult and many individuals in a sample score zero on it. Correspondingly, a ceiling effect is when a test is not sensitive at the high end of the range because it is too easy. In aging studies where decline over time may be of interest, floor effects can create a problem.

3. Differential Subject Attrition

It is almost inevitable in longitudinal studies for some participant dropout to occur. Of course, the investigators should do everything possible to keep this to a minimum. Subject attrition becomes a threat to the internal validity of a study when treatment-group dropouts are a different kind of person than control-group dropouts. For example, suppose a study has taken a random sample of older individuals for a study on the effects of cognitive exercises on memory. Participants are randomly assigned to a treatment group that is taught the exercises or a control group that is not taught any exercises. Suppose the individuals most in need of the memory exercises drop out of the control group, because they know they need help and decide to seek it elsewhere. This would leave only the least impaired individuals in the control group. This pattern of subject dropout can make a treatment look less effective than it really is or even ineffective. Other patterns of subject dropout can make a treatment look more effective than it is in reality.

J. External Validity

External validity is the extent to which the results of a study can be generalized to a clearly defined and theoretically interesting population. Internal validity is a logical prerequisite for external validity, because if a study has poor internal validity it makes little difference whether or not it is generalizable.

The results obtained from a sample can be generalized to a population with a high degree of confidence when the sample was drawn randomly from the population. Thus studies that use careful subject sampling procedures and enjoy good participant retention have the best external validity. However, many studies in the social sciences use convenience sampling, as described above. When a convenience sample is used, the investigator is in a considerably weaker position with respect to generalizability, because the convenience sample is not a random sample. Nonrandom subject attrition also has a deleterious effect on external validity, even in the rare cases where it does not affect internal validity. Those who choose to drop out of a study are nearly always different from those who choose to continue. They may be involved in more competing activities, less patient, more transient, lower or higher in socioeconomic status, or different in a wide variety of other ways. When the individuals who drop out of a study are different from those who remain, the remaining sample is no longer a random sample, and the results of the study may not be generalizable to the population from which the researchers originally sampled. Severe nonrandom subject attrition can even transform a random sample into essentially a convenience sample, with a corresponding reduction in external validity.

III. A BRIEF INTRODUCTION TO STATISTICS

A. Descriptive Statistics

Descriptive statistics are numbers used to describe a sample or population. Usually descriptive statistics computed on samples are intended as estimates of the corresponding population quantities, called parameters. One type of descriptive statistic is the measure of central tendency. There are three measures of central tendency in widespread use: the mean, median, and mode. The mean is what is commonly called the average, computed by summing up all the values of a variable and dividing by the number of individuals. The median is the 50th percentile of the distribution, in other words, the point at which half the distribution is above and half is below. The mode is the most frequently occurring score. Although all three measures of central tendency are used to describe distributions, statistical inference (see below) makes much more extensive use of the mean than either the median or the mode.

Another type of descriptive statistic is the measure of dispersion, which conveys a sense of how much variability there is in a sample or population. The simplest and most intuitively obvious measure of dispersion is the range, commonly computed by subtracting the smallest value occurring in a sample or population from the largest. However, the largest and smallest values in a sample tend to be among the least stable, so the range is itself an unstable measure of

dispersion. Statisticians prefer the variance, which for populations is defined as the average squared deviation about the mean. The sample-based estimate of variance is computed slightly differently.

B. Statistical Inference

Research is conducted on samples so that conclusions can be drawn about populations. In fact, researchers are interested in a sample only as a means to an end. The end is drawing conclusions about the population, which contains all the individuals that are ultimately of interest. If it were possible, researchers would study the entire population. However, constraints imposed by time, money, and subject availability preclude this in most cases, except where resources are extensive or the population is small. The purpose of statistical inference is to provide guidelines to the researcher for drawing inferences about a population based on information gathered from a sample.

For purposes of illustration, suppose researchers are interested in whether 40-year-olds differ from 60-year-olds in performance on a cognitive task. In classical statistical inference, one begins with a null hypothesis and an alternative hypothesis. These hypotheses refer to the population, not to any particular sample. The null hypothesis is a statistical straw man, stating that the mean performance on the cognitive tasks is the same in the two populations. The alternative hypothesis is simply that the null hypothesis is not true, in other words, the two populations have different mean performance on the cognitive task. (When the direction of the difference between groups is not specified, as in this example, the hypothesis is *two-tailed*. When the direction of the difference is specified, the hypothesis is *one-tailed*.)

Suppose data on performance on the cognitive task have been collected on a suitable sample of 40-year-olds and a suitable sample of 60-year-olds. Sample means and the difference between the sample means have been computed. Because sample means are usually not exactly equal to population means, even in a case where the population means are identical, there usually will be a difference between the 40-year-old sample mean and the 60-year-old sample mean, due to chance. Over repeated sampling, relatively small differences will occur frequently, whereas larger differences occur less frequently. The logic of hypothesis testing is as follows:

Assume for the moment that the null hypothesis is true, that is, the means are identical in the 40-year-old and 60-year-old populations. Then ask the question: If the null hypothesis is true, what is the probability of observing a difference between sample means of a magnitude at least as extreme as the one obtained in this study? If a difference between sample means at least as large in absolute magnitude as the one observed in this study occurs very commonly when the null hypothesis is true, then the researcher concludes that there is no basis for rejecting the null hypothesis. However, if results at least as extreme as these are very rare when the null hypothesis is true, then the researcher concludes that the null hypothesis is probably incorrect in this case.

The decision about whether or not to reject the null hypothesis hinges on the answer to the question about the probability of obtaining results at least as extreme as those observed, conditional on the null hypothesis being true. The answer is found by referring to one of the many tabled distributions found in statistics books. Depending on the statistical analysis done, the researcher refers to a *t*, *F*, chi-square, or some other distribution. If the statistical analysis is done by computer, the researcher instead refers to the computed probability conveniently appearing on the output.

It is important to understand that statistical hypothesis testing is a decision accompanied by the risk of making an incorrect decision. When the null hypothesis is in reality true, in a certain proportion of cases extreme results will occur by chance, and the researcher will mistakenly conclude that the null hypothesis is false. Concluding that the null hypothesis is false when it is in fact true is known as a Type I error. On the other hand, when the null hypothesis is in reality false, in a certain proportion of cases results will occur by chance that will lead to the conclusion that the null hypothesis should not be rejected. Concluding that the null hypothesis is true when it is in fact false is known as a Type II error.

The Type I error rate, designated by the Greek letter α, can be controlled very easily simply by defining what is meant by "extreme" results. For example, if it is decided ahead of time that the null hypothesis will be rejected only if the probability of results as least as extreme as those obtained is .01 or less, then the Type I error rate is .01. However, all else being equal, any measures taken to reduce the Type I error rate will increase the Type II error rate, sometimes to unacceptable levels.

Statistical power is an important aspect of research that is often not given sufficient consideration. Statistical power refers to the probability of rejecting the null hypothesis given that it is in fact false. It is 1 minus the Type II error rate. Statistical power is a function of three aspects of a study: The Type I error rate chosen, the true effect size, and the sample size. All else being equal, larger values of any of these quantities results in an increase in statistical power. In practice, a Type I error rate of no larger than .05 is considered acceptable in scientific research, and in many cases (although by no means all) the effect size cannot be influenced by the researcher. Thus, in most situations the researcher tries to obtain the largest sample size possible in order to maximize statistical power. Whenever a study concludes that the null hypothesis cannot be rejected, a careful look should be taken at the study's statistical power. If the statistical power is low (i.e., the Type II error rate is high), this means that the study was not an adequate test of the hypothesis.

C. Statistical Procedures

There are many statistical procedures that are used extensively in research on aging, including the following:

1. Independent groups *t*-test: compares means from two independent samples to infer whether the corresponding population means are different.

2. Related groups *t*-test: examines the difference between means from two related samples to infer whether in the population this difference is zero.

3. Analysis of variance (ANOVA): compares means from two or more independent samples to infer whether at least one of the corresponding population means is different from the others. Usually accompanied by further examination of differences between means, by means of either a priori or post hoc procedures. A factorial ANOVA may involve more than one independent variable, which allows the examination of interactions. An interaction occurs when the effect of one independent variable depends on the level of the other.

4. Analysis of covariance (ANCOVA): an extension of ANOVA that allows a statistical elimination or "partialling out" of the effects of a variable under certain circumstances.

5. Correlation: estimates the extent of linear relation between two variables.

6. Regression: closely related to correlation. Uses one or more independent or predictor variables to build a linear prediction model for a dependent variable.

7. Contingency table analysis: a broad class of procedures involving categorical variables. These procedures are roughly analogous to *t*-tests, correlation, regression, and ANOVA, but they involve all categorical variables. In this category are procedures such as the chi-square test for independence and log-linear models.

8. Multivariate analysis of variance (MANOVA): An extension of ANOVA for situations where there are many related dependent variables. The procedure finds one or more linear combinations of dependent variables that provide maximum differentiation among groups, subject to the provision that the linear combinations are uncorrelated.

9. Discriminant analysis: Exactly the same as MANOVA, but often treated as if it is different. In discriminant analysis the emphasis is placed on using the dependent variables to predict the category of the independent variable.

10. Canonical correlation: the most general multivariate procedure. Canonical correlation starts with two batteries of variables, and then finds the linear combinations of the variables that produce the largest correlation, subject to the provision that the linear combinations are uncorrelated.

11. Growth curve modeling: A relatively new approach that is likely to become widely used in aging research. In growth curve modeling an individual growth trajectory is fit for each participant in a longitudinal study, allowing examination of individual and group differences in growth.

12. Factor analysis: A general set of procedures for empirically determining whether a large set of manifest variables can be represented by a smaller number of latent variables.

13. Covariance Structure Modeling: A procedure by which models involving latent variables, including regressions between latent variables, can be estimated and tested.

III. A BRIEF INTRODUCTION TO MEASUREMENT

Measurement is a set of rules by which numbers are assigned to objects. In research, the "objects" are usually research participants, often called subjects. Measurement is something commonly done in everyday life. When one measures his or her height with a yardstick, the yardstick is the set of rules by which a number is assigned to height. In much the same way, an IQ test provides a set of rules for assigning a number to an individual's intelligence, a grade point average provides a set of rules for assigning a number to a person's scholastic achievement, and a questionnaire provides a set of rules for assigning a number to an individual's attitude.

Measurement is one of the most significant challenges facing social science researchers. Unlike research in the natural sciences, where quantities can usually be measured directly with a caliper, scale, and so on, research in the behavioral sciences is faced with measurement of quantities that cannot be seen directly. These quantities are called *constructs*. Constructs such as intelligence, temperament, opinions, cooperativeness, and ability to perform a task must be measured by means of subject self-report, subject test performance, or observations by others. Because of this, extensive work on measurement theory has been done in the behavioral sciences. Measurement theory provides guidelines for evaluating the quality of an approach to measurement, and for how to develop a high-quality measurement instrument.

A. Measurement Validity

Validity is the most important goal in measurement. It is the extent to which an instrument measures the construct it is intended to measure. This is a broad concept, and there is not one single widely accepted method for determining measurement validity. Instead, there are several aspects of validity that should be addressed. In any particular situation, some aspects of validity will be more relevant than others.

I. Criterion Validity

This is the extent to which an instrument can be demonstrated to be related to a variable that serves as a criterion. There are two types of criterion validity, concurrent and predictive. Concurrent validity is established by demonstrating a relationship with a variable measured at about the same time as the measurement instrument being evaluated. For example, a researcher may wish to establish the validity of a shorter self-administered measure intended to replace a lengthy interview. Concurrent validity can be established by collecting data using the self-administered measure along with the interview data, and then computing the correlation between the two measures. A large correlation is evidence for concurrent validity. Predictive validity is established by demonstrating that the instrument in question is a useful prospective predictor in a longitudinal design.

2. Content Validity

Content validity is the extent to which the items or questions making up a measurement instrument are representative of the construct being measured. Good content validity does not require that the items exhaust every aspect of the construct, but it does require that no important aspect is left out.

3. Construct Validity

This has to do with the extent to which the measure is theoretically meaningful. There are many ways to demonstrate this, with the most appropriate way depending on the research questions of interest. One widely used way of demonstrating construct validity is by means of the multitrait multimethod (MTMM) matrix. This framework involves multiple constructs, or traits, all of which are amenable to measurement by a set of several different methods. For example, sociability, extroversion, and altruism might all be measured by means of a self-report questionnaire, reports of friends, and behavioral observation. Data are collected measuring each of the traits by means of each of the methods, and all possible correlations are computed. If there is good construct validity, it is expected that the correlations between different methods measuring the same trait will be large (this is referred to as *convergent validity*) and that correlations between the same method measuring different traits will be low (this is referred to as *discriminant validity*). Today the MTMM matrix is often analyzed by means of covariance structure modeling.

B. Measurement Precision

Another very important aspect of measurement is its precision. The various measurement theories in the behavioral sciences offer somewhat different definitions of measurement precision. One of the most widely used measurement theories is classical test theory. It offers a definition of measurement precision known as reliability. A new approach to assessing measurement precision, known as generalizability theory, is beginning to be widely used.

1. Classical Test Theory and Reliability

According to classical test theory, every observed score on a test or measure, denoted X, can be divided up into two components: a true score, T, and an error component, E.

$$X = T + E \qquad (1)$$

There are several important assumptions made. First, this relationship is additive, in other words, X is the sum of $T + E$, it is never the product. Second, T and E are independent of each other. Third, the error component, E, is random, so it is independent of any other measure, any other true score, or any other error component. Fourth, if an individual is measured repeatedly the true score T is unchanging, but the error component E may change. It follows from these assumptions that the variance of X can be divided into two components: the variance of the true score and the error variance.

$$\sigma_X^2 = \sigma_T^2 + \sigma_E^2 \qquad (2)$$

It is important to note that the true score variance can be further divided into valid and invalid variance. Valid variance is variance due to the underlying trait the instrument is intended to measure. Invalid variance is true score variance that is not due to the underlying trait the instrument is intended to measure. Instead, it is due to some other trait or quantity. Thus it is a type of error variance, but it is systematic rather than random error. In some ways the term *true score* is a misnomer, because true scores are not necessarily a "true" reflection of the construct being measured.

Measurement reliability is defined as the proportion of observed score variance that is made up of true score variance:

$$\frac{\sigma_T^2}{\sigma_X^2} \qquad (3)$$

All else being equal, a large reliability is desirable in a measurement instrument. When reliability is large, it means that a relatively small proportion of the observed score variance in an instrument is made up of random error. However, a large reliability does not imply that the instrument is valid. In fact, it is possible for an instrument to have a large, even perfect reliability but zero validity, if the true score variance is made up exclusively of invalid variance. Validity, the proportion of observed score variance made up of *valid* true score variance, cannot exceed reliability.

2. Methods for Assessing Reliability

In most measurement situations only the observed score is known. The true score and the error score are unknown. Thus one cannot directly determine reliability. However, there are several methods for approximating reliability.

a. Test–Retest Reliability   Test–retest reliability of an instrument is computed by measuring subjects at two distinct occasions on the instrument and then computing the correlation. If the correlation is large, this is considered evidence for good test–retest reliability. However, the test–retest procedure makes the assumption that the construct being measured does not change over time. In life span developmental research, this assumption is usually unwarranted. If the subjects in a study undergo change on the construct at different rates between the first and second occasions, the correlation between the two occasions can be low even if the measurement instrument is highly precise.

b. Split-Half Reliability   Split-half reliability is computed by administering an instrument at a single occasion, randomly dividing the items into two subsets, and correlating the two subtests. The idea is that if the instrument is highly precise, any two halves should be highly correlated. A problem with the split-half approach is that the assessment of reliability can differ considerably depending on which of the many possible divisions of the items is used.

c. Cronbach's Alpha   Cronbach's alpha is a way of assessing reliability by comparing the amount of shared variance, or covariance, among the items making up an instrument to the amount of overall vari-

ance. The idea is that if the instrument is reliable, there should be a great deal of covariance among the items relative to the variance. Cronbach's alpha is equivalent to taking the average of all possible split-half reliabilities. Most computer packages for statistics in wide use today can compute Cronbach's alpha. Often it is helpful to examine what the Cronbach's alpha becomes after a particular item is deleted. If Cronbach's alpha goes up considerably upon deletion of an item, the item may not belong in the measure.

3. Generalizability Theory

Generalizability theory focuses on identifying and assessing the effects of various possible sources of error in measurement. According to this approach, each measurement situation involves one or more facets. One facet is usually test or questionnaire items. Other facets may be raters, times, or any of a number of possible aspects of a measurement design. (Although times may be a facet, it is important to note that generalizability theory assumes that the quantity being measured is unchanging.) Usually the items, raters, or times are sampled from the larger population. For example, a test contains a sample of items, not an exhaustive list of all possible items. Generalizability theory poses the question, How generalizable is the score on the instrument to other samples of items, raters, times, and so on? In order to perform a generalizability study, it is necessary to collect data on the instrument in question. Then ANOVA is used to partition the variance in the instrument into components. Some of the variance is attributable to individual differences among the subjects, whereas other variance is attributable to differences within a facet, such as differences between raters. All else being equal, good generalizability is reflected in a larger proportion of variance due to individual differences between subjects and a smaller proportion due to a facet.

A generalizability analysis can provide a great deal of useful information. Because it partitions error variance, it allows the researcher to study the sources of error in a study. The results of a generalizability study give the researcher the information necessary to decide what to do to reduce error. Often increasing the number of elements of a facet, such as increasing the number of raters or the number of items, can reduce the amount of error. Furthermore, the analysis can help the researcher to assess the costs of reducing the length of an instrument or using fewer raters.

C. Behavioral Observation

Sometimes asking individuals to report on their own behavior is not desirable or even feasible. For example, very young children are not capable of completing self-report questionnaires or responding to in-depth interview questions. Or, it may be desired to measure certain aspects of interpersonal interactions, such as grandparent–parent discussions about child rearing, as they are taking place so that a sequence of conversational statements and responses can be determined. In these situations and many others data are collected by behavioral observation. Trained observers watch behavior, either as it occurs or recorded on videotape, make judgments about what is going on, and record the instances of whatever behavior is of interest. There are several important procedures to follow when collecting behavioral observations. First, a detailed and explicit system for coding the observed behaviors must be developed and pilot tested before data collection begins. Second, the observers should be thoroughly trained in the behavioral rating system. Third, it is critical to have more than one observer rating behaviors simultaneously. Fourth, where possible the observers should be kept uninformed about the study hypotheses or any expectations the experimenter has about the outcome, so that this information will not bias their interpretation of what they see. (They can be briefed about the study after data collection has been concluded.)

There are several methods used to establish measurement precision of behavioral observation. Often the correlation between raters is called interrater reliability. Technically this quantity is not a reliability, although it may be useful information. When the rating involves choosing among qualitatively different categories, Cohen's kappa is an informative measure of interrater agreement and is recommended over the more commonly used percent agreement. For most research the method of choice for assessing measurement precision of behavioral observations is generalizability theory, because it allows the investigator to distinguish among, and ultimately act upon, different sources of measurement error.

BIBLIOGRAPHY

Baltes, P. B., Reese, H. W., & Nesselroade, J. R. (1988). *Life-span developmental psychology: Introduction to research methods*. Hillsdale, NJ: Lawrence Erlbaum Associates.

Collins, L. M., & Horn, J. L. (1991). *Best methods for the analysis of change: Recent advances, unanswered questions, future directions*. Washington, DC: American Psychological Association.

Cook, T. D., & Campbell, D. T. (1979). *Quasi-experimentation: Design and analysis for field settings*. Boston: Houghton Mifflin.

Pedhazur, E. J., & Schmelkin, L. P. (1991). *Measurement, design, and analysis: An integrated approach*. Hillsdale, NJ: Lawrence Erlbaum Associates.

Shavelson, R. J. (1988). *Statistical reasoning for the behavioral sciences* (2nd ed.). Boston: Allyn and Bacon, Inc.

Shavelson, R. J., & Webb, N. M. (1991). *Generalizability theory: A primer*. Newbury Park, CA: Sage Publications.

Vogt, P. W. (1993). *Dictionary of statistics and methodology: A nontechnical guide for the social sciences*. Newbury Park, CA: Sage Publications.

Respiratory System

N. S. Cherniack and M. D. Altose

Case Western Reserve University

I. Normal Operation of the Respiratory System
II. Effects of Aging on Lung Function
III. Effects of Aging on Respiratory Muscle Function
IV. Effects of Aging on the Regulation of Respiration
V. Breathing during Sleep in the Elderly
VI. The Effects of Aging on Respiratory System Defenses

Alveolar Capillary Membrane The alveolar epithelium, interstitial tissue, and capillary endothelium separating gas in the alveoli from the blood in lung capillaries.

Carbon Dioxide Response Slope The change in ventilation per minute produced by a change in arterial partial pressure of CO_2.

Elastic Recoil of Lung or Thoracic Cage The elastic force that returns the lung or thoracic cage to its resting condition.

Functional Residual Capacity (FRC) The volume of air in the lungs at the end of a normal expiration with the respiratory muscles at rest.

Mucociliary Blanket Hairy cells with covering mucus that lines the airways of the lungs.

Oxygen Response Slope The change in ventilation per minute produced by a change in arterial partial pressure of O_2.

Oxygen Saturation The amount of oxygen combined with hemoglobin as a percent of the maximal amount that can be so combined.

Partial pressure The escaping tendencies of dissolved gas in the blood (e.g., PO_2, partial pressure of O_2, PCO_2, partial pressure of CO_2).

Residual Volume (RV) The volume of air remaining in the lung after a maximal expiration.

Vital Capacity (VC) The maximal volume of air that can be expired after a maximal inspiration.

The metabolic processes of the body require O_2 and produce CO_2. The **RESPIRATORY SYSTEM** operates so that sufficient amounts of O_2 are brought into the body and CO_2 removed to allow the partial pressure of O_2 and CO_2 (PO_2, PCO_2) in the arterial blood to remain within fairly narrow limits.

I. NORMAL OPERATION OF THE RESPIRATORY SYSTEM

Breathing is an involuntary rhythmic act controlled by respiratory neurons in the brain primarily in the medulla and pons. These neurons direct the muscles of the thorax and abdomen to contract and relax, altering the pressure around the lung so that air enters the air passages during inspiration and is expelled during expiration. The incoming air is brought to body temperature humidified, and particulate matters (>5 u) removed with passage through the nasal and oral cavities and the larynx, (the upper airways) and then down through the trachea, bronchi, and bronchioles (the lower airways). The lower airways are lined by a mucous layer and cilia (mucociliary blanket), which help to remove particulate matter.

Air makes contact with the blood in microscopic air sacs of the lung called alveoli. Here O_2 enters and CO_2 leaves the blood by diffusion. The pumping action of the right ventricle propels blood returning from body organs and tissues through the pulmonary artery and its branches to the capillary bed. The pulmonary veins bring blood enriched in O_2 and with lower levels of CO_2 back to the left side of the heart where the left ventricle pumps the now arterialized blood to the tissues. Oxygen is carried in the blood mainly in combination with hemoglobin but also as dissolved O_2. Carbon dioxide is carried in the blood mainly in the form of bicarbonate but also as CO_2 in solution.

Sensors in the arterial blood (peripheral chemoreceptors) and in the brain (central chemoreceptors) monitor CO_2 and O_2 levels and send signals to the respiratory neurons in the brain, which activate the respiratory muscles. A decrease in PO_2 or a rise in PCO_2 excites these sensors and in turn increases the activity of brain stem respiratory neurons. Contraction of the respiratory muscles becomes more vigorous and ventilation (the volume of air entering and leaving the lung) increases. Neurons in the brain stem, primarily in the medulla and pons, also coordinate the operation of the respiratory and cardiovascular systems so that tissue metabolic requirements are met. Increased metabolism, for example, results in increased ventilation and increased blood flow to the tissues where the rise in metabolism is occurring. When the respiratory system is functioning normally, the O_2 supplied at the gas–blood interface in the lung (the alveolar–capillary membrane) and the CO_2 removed is sufficient to maintain oxygen tension (PO_2) in the arterial blood at sufficiently high levels (>90 mmHg) so that the hemoglobin is nearly saturated with O_2. The partial pressure of CO_2 (PCO_2) kept near 40 mmHg is usually adequate to maintain acid-base balance near normal (as measured by arterial pH about 7.40.)

Even though rhythmic breathing occurs virtually continuously and over a lifetime the alveolar gas-exchanging surface is brought into contact with more than 60 million gallons of air, which may contain harmful particulate matter and noxious gaseous elements; the deterioration of respiratory function with aging itself, although measurable, is relatively small. Although impairment of respiratory system function can be a major problem in the elderly, this mainly results from smoking, atmospheric pollution, and disease rather than from the wear and tear associated with the aging process itself.

In large part, respiratory function is preserved by an intricate protective system that includes the laryngeal and pharyngeal muscles, which prevent aspiration of foreign material into the lungs, the mucocilary blanket of the airways, which clear particulate matter from the tracheobronchial tree, and immune cells in the blood and lymphatic systems of the lung, which remove microbes and other harmful microscopic inhaled matter and help neutralize toxic chemicals released in the lung by infectious material and air pollutants.

II. EFFECTS OF AGING ON LUNG FUNCTION

With aging, there is a significant decrease in the elasticity of the lung. Alveolar diameters widen and the alveolar surface area per unit of lung volume decreases. These structural changes are a consequence of biochemical alterations in the elastic fiber network of alveolar walls.

Changes in lung elasticity with age affect lung volumes. With the respiratory muscles (both those that cause inspiration and those that produce expiration) at rest and not actively contracting, lung volume is determined by the balance between the elastic recoil tendency of the lung to collapse and the opposing elastic recoil tendency of the thoracic cage to expand. This resting lung volume, the volume at the end of a normal quiet exhalation, is termed the *functional residual capacity* (FRC). Because the elasticity of the lung decreases with age, FRC is larger in the elderly than in the young. This increase in volume would be even greater were it not for the decrease in thoracic wall elasticity that also occurs with aging.

Peripheral airways are essentially tethered to the parenchymal lung tissue. Lung tissue pulls outward on the airway walls, and the airways are kept open by the elastic recoil of the attached alveolar walls. The loss of lung elastic recoil with age decreases this tethering effect, resulting in a narrowing of peripheral airways. With narrowing, airway resistance increases. The resistive properties of the airways are commonly assessed from measurements of airflow rates out of the lungs during rapid, forceful expiratory maneuvers. Following a maximum inspiration, the volume exhaled during the first second of a subsequent forced expiratory maneuver is termed the FEV_1 (forced expiratory volume in 1 sec). The reduction in airway caliber that accompanies the loss of lung elastic recoil with advancing age results in a decline in FEV_1 that averages about 30 ml/year from age 25 to 65 years. FEV_1

continues to fall after age 65 years but at a somewhat reduced rate of 20 ml/year. The annual rate of decline in FEV_1 is considerably accelerated in cigarette smokers.

As lung volume decreases from total lung capacity (TLC) (i.e., the volume of air contained in the lungs at the end of a maximum inspiration) to residual volume (RV) (i.e., the volume of air remaining in the lungs after a maximum expiratory effort), the airways normally shorten and narrow. Near RV, some airways particularly at the lung bases actually close. With reductions in elastic recoil of the lung with advancing age, airways tend to close at higher and higher lung volumes, trapping alveolar gas behind them and raising residual volume. Also, the vital capacity (VC), the difference between TLC and RV, decreases with age.

Changes in lung elastic recoil properties with advancing age are not uniform in alveoli throughout the lung. This nonuniformity of pulmonary mechanical properties results in unevenness in the distribution of ventilation usually without adequate compensatory readjustments in the distribution of pulmonary blood flow. As a result there is a mismatch in the ratio of ventilation to perfusion in some gas-exchanging areas of the lung, and blood leaving those alveoli may not be fully oxygenated. Some, but not all, investigations suggest impaired diffusion of gas across the alveolar-capillary membrane with aging, but abnormalities in diffusion probably do not contribute significantly to changes in oxygenation with age. Overall, arterial O_2 saturation falls only slightly with age, and there are no significant changes in arterial PCO_2 that can be ascribed to aging alone.

Exercise capacity as measured by maximal O_2 uptake decreases progressively with age in adults. In the elderly there is greater stress on the respiratory system to accommodate the increase in metabolic rate during exercise. There is a greater increase in ventilation for a given increase in exercise workload in the elderly as compared to young adults. This likely is the result of compensation for age-related increases in physiological dead space. Additionally, the force-generating capacity of the respiratory muscles is reduced in the elderly due to a loss of muscle strength. Increased FRC in the elderly, particularly at high levels of ventilation required during severe exercise, may place the respiratory muscles at a mechanical disadvantage such that a greater level of central respiratory motor output is required to achieve a given muscle force. On the other hand, the increase in FRC stretches the expiratory muscles and allows them to expire air with greater force.

However, the decrease in the ability of the elderly to achieve as high levels of exercise as younger people is largely due to changes in the cardiovascular system and in the fiber composition of the skeletal muscles rather than to changes in the elasticity of the respiratory system. Both the maximal heart rate and maximal cardiac output that can be achieved during exercise fall with advancing age. The kinetics of changes in cardiovascular variables and O_2 consumption as well as maximal ventilation decline with age. However, the elderly may be able to perform for long periods of time at a higher percent of maximum O_2 consumption than the young. [See CARDIOVASCULAR SYSTEM.]

III. EFFECTS OF AGING ON RESPIRATORY MUSCLE FUNCTION

Changes with age in the respiratory muscles contribute to decrements in respiratory function. Respiratory muscle strength is less in the elderly reducing the maximal pressures that can be exerted during inspiration and expiration. Maximal inspiratory pressure decreases progressively after age 20 years, whereas the loss in maximal expiratory pressure accelerates past age 50 years. These reductions in maximal respiratory pressures correlate with age-related reductions in the strength of other muscles, such as, the trunk flexor and the hand grip muscles. Moreover, there is suggestive evidence that the respiratory muscles may be more fatigueable in the elderly than in the young.

The diaphragm in mammals is the main inspiratory muscle. Studies in hamsters show that there are decreases in both the rate of contraction and relaxation of the diaphragm with age. Tensions per cross-sectional area of the diaphragm is reduced and the velocity of its shortening is slowed. These functional changes may reflect less activated actinomycin cross-links in older animals, decreases in rates of cross-bridge cycling, and reduced actinomycin ATPase activity.

IV. EFFECTS OF AGING ON THE REGULATION OF RESPIRATION

Arterial chemoreceptors in the carotid and aortic bodies are responsible for the changes in ventilation that accompany alterations in blood O_2 content. Central chemoreceptors located in the medulla primarily mediate the ventilatory responses that occur with changes in PCO_2. These chemoreceptors are critical for homeostasis and for the maintenance of normal body oxygenation and acid-base balance. The sensitivity of the chemoreceptors is assessed from measurements of the ratio of changes in ventilation to changes in blood gas composition.

The effects of age on respiratory chemoresponses remain uncertain. Several published reports describe age-related decreases in the respiratory responses to chemical stimuli. Other studies, however, have failed to note any significant differences in the responses of young and elderly people. On the average, the ventilatory responses to hypercapnia are usually lower in older as compared to young subjects. However, the interindividual variability in responses are so great that group differences are usually not statistically significant.

Similarly, the results of studies of the effects of aging on hypoxic ventilatory responses vary. Some studies have reported attenuated ventilatory responses to hypoxia in elderly adults. A decrease in Type I cells, the O_2-sensitive cells in the carotid body, has been reported in the elderly. In contrast, other investigations indicate that hypoxic ventilatory responses, particularly when measured at normal resting PCO_2 levels, are actually higher in the elderly as compared to young people.

There is an important synergistic interaction between the responses to hypercapnia and hypoxia and the strength of the interaction may vary with age. Whereas in the young there is a multiplicative interaction between hypoxia and hypercapnia (i.e., hypercapnic ventilatory response slopes are higher during hypoxia compared to hyperoxia), in the elderly hypoxia has only an additive effect on hypercapnic responses with no change in CO_2 response slopes.

This alteration in respiratory regulation in the elderly is probably due to age-related changes in central respiratory neuronal activity. Changes in ventilatory system mechanical properties and respiratory muscle strength found in the elderly are not sufficiently severe to account for changes in ventilatory chemoresponses.

In addition to chemoreceptors, there are other systems that provide information to the central respiratory controller about the state of the lungs and the respiratory muscles. Vagal receptors, including stretch receptors, irritant receptors, and J-receptors, report volume, flow, and pressures within and around the airways and lungs. Respiratory muscle receptors including muscle spindles, and tendon organs monitor muscle length and tension. Nonchemical reflexes involving these mechanoreceptor inputs control the pattern of breathing and mediate adjustments in breathing when the mechanical properties of the lung are rendered abnormal by disease. For example, some diseases may increase the fibrous tissue in the lung (many occupational lung diseases) making the lungs stiffer. Other diseases (asthma) narrow the airways and increase the resistance to airflow. In both instances, greater muscular force is required for ventilation, and the activity of respiratory muscle receptors may be altered.

Respiratory mechanoreceptor afferents transmitted to higher brain centers may also subserve some of the sensations associated with the act of breathing. Changes in the elastic and resistive properties of the lung can be simulated with externally applied devices that can be perceived consciously. Psychophysical studies of respiratory sensations have shown that the perceived magnitude of externally applied elastic and resistive ventilatory loads is reduced in the elderly. This impairment of ventilatory load sensation is consistent with other age-related changes in perceptual sensitivity. Advancing age is associated with a reduced ability to detect changes in joint motion, vibration, and heaviness of lifted weights. This suggest that blunted respiratory sensation in the elderly is due to a generalized loss of kinesthetic sensibility.

V. BREATHING DURING SLEEP IN THE ELDERLY

Breathing during sleep becomes more variable with aging. Sometimes breathing during sleep ceases momentarily but repeatedly during the night. These episodes of sleep apnea occur more frequently in older than in younger individuals. Apneas are of two types; central, where respiratory effort seem to stop, and obstructive, where respiratory efforts continue but no air enters the lungs because of blockage in the upper airway. Both types of apnea occur more often in the elderly. Periodic breathing, a waxing and waning of respiration during sleep, is also more common in the elderly and contributes to the occurrence of apneas.

The explanation for the frequency of occurrence of sleep apneas in the elderly is still uncertain. A number of different mechanisms may be involved.

Sleep consists of two distinct stages; rapid eye movement (REM) sleep, which is generally associated with dreaming and REMs, and non-REM sleep (NREM). Responses to hypoxia and hypercapnia diminish during NREM sleep and even more during REM sleep. A study in dogs demonstrated no changes in the ventilation response to CO_2 during sleep with age, but the response to hypoxia was not studied. Responses to mechanical stimulation of the upper airways are generally diminished during sleep, but the effect of aging on these responses is not known.

The patency of the upper airway during sleep depends on the activity of the upper-airway muscles. Many of the laryngeal and pharyngeal muscles in addition to their protective function display a respiratory rhythm that during inspiration serves to stiffen and dilate the airways. With inspiration the pressure in the airways become subatmospheric. Animal studies demonstrate that the upper airways tend to collapse with the negative pressure produced in the pharynx and larynx during inspiration if these muscles are not appropriately activated. Like the diaphragm and the intercostal muscles that move the ribs, the activity of the upper-airway muscles increase with hypoxia and hypercapnia. The tongue muscles, which widen the pharynx, and the laryngeal abductor muscles, which widen the laryngeal aperture, contract more forcefully when CO_2 is raised or O_2 levels are decreased. Sleep has a much greater depressant effect on the activity of these upper-airway muscles than on the thoracic muscles. Thus, airway obstruction is more likely to occur during sleep than it is during wakefulness. Snoring is a result of partial obstruction of the upper airways.

Cyclic changes in the activity of upper-airway muscles and the diaphragm have been observed during periodic breathing. Discoordinated activity of the upper-airway muscles and the inspiratory muscles like the diaphragm, particularly during periodic breathing, may be an important cause of both central and obstructive apneas in the elderly.

Although there have been very few studies of the upper airways in the elderly, differences from younger individuals in the ability of the upper-airway muscles to respond to chemical or reflex stimulation have not yet been found. No anatomical differences in upper airway diameters between young and old were found in one study in humans that used computerized axial tomography (CAT) scanning to assess upper-airway cross-section.

VI. THE EFFECT OF AGING ON RESPIRATORY SYSTEM DEFENSES

The elderly are at increased risk for viral and bacterial pneumonia and lung cancer, conditions that suggest possible deficiencies in lung defense mechanisms and immune function.

The clearance of particles in the airways of the lung occurs by movement of cilia in the airway that are embedded in a lining layer of mucus. Mucociliary clearance is diminished with aging. Ultrastructural changes have been observed in the tracheal glands, and the composition of the mucous blanket is changed so its viscosity is increased with age. The lower airways contain receptors that allow them to constrict or dilate when stimulated via the autonomic nervous system. Generally, the responsivity to such stimulation is less in the elderly. Responses to skin antigen are decreased in the elderly but not reactivity to antigens in the inspired air.

Recent studies have also found important changes in the function of immune cells that occur with the aging process. Polymorphonuclear leukocyte function seems to be well maintained in the elderly except for some decrease in chemotactic ability in those over 80. Alveolar macrophage immune capacity is also not changed appreciably with age. However, there are substantial deficiencies in the activity of T and B lymphocytes. B lymphocytes are able to produce less immunoglobulin, but the ability to produce autoantibodies has been reported to be greater. This may lead to poorer immune regulation by suppression in the elderly. T cells show less proliferative response to antigens or to mitogens like plant lectins. The production of cytokines (chemicals important in the immune response) by T lymphocytes is also reduced with decreases in both interleukin 1 and 2 formation. Tumor cell lysis is less, as is natural killer cell activity. There is an age-related expansion of undifferentiated lymphocytes. These T cell changes appear to be related to reduced secretions of thymic hormones. [*See* Immune System.]

In summary, the lungs are constantly exposed to

injurious material in the inspired air, and the respiratory system must be able to compensate for the acute change in respiratory function with age. The effects of aging itself on the respiratory system are small and often require tests of maximal performance to be detected.

BIBLIOGRAPHY

Akiyama, Y., Nishimora, M., Koboyashi, S., Yamamoto, M., Miyamoto, K., & Kawakami, Y. (1991). Effect of aging on respiratory load compensation and dyspnea sensation. *American Review of Respiratory Disease, 148,* 1586–1591.

Bruschi, C., Cerveri, I., Zola, M. C., Fanfolla, F., Florentini, M., Casali, L., Grassi, M., & Grassi, A. (1992). Reference values of maximal respiratory mouth pressures: A population-based study. American Review of Respiratory Disease, 146, 790–793.

Burr, M. L., Phillips, K. M., & Hurst, D. N. (1985). Lung function in the elderly. *Thorax, 40,* 54–59.

Carskado, M. A., & Dement, V. C. (1981). Respiration during sleep in the aged human. *Journal of Gerontology, 36,* 420–423.

Chanag, S-C., Chang, H-F., Liu, S-Y., Shiao, G-M, & Peray, R-P. (1992). The effects of body position and age on membrane diffusing capacity and pulmonary capillary blood volume. *Chest, 102,* 139–142.

Chapman, K. R., & Cherniack, N. S. (1987). Aging effects on the interaction of hypercapnia and hypoxia as ventilatory stimuli. *Journal of Gerontology, 92,* 202–209.

Frank, W. R., Mead, J., Ferris, B. G., Jr. (1957). The mechanical behavior of the lung in healthy elderly persons. *Journal of Clinical Investment, 36,* 1680–1687.

Gillooly, M., & Lamb, D. (1993). Air space size in lungs of lifelong non-smokers: Effect of age and sex. *Thorax, 48,* 39–43.

Gyetko, M. C., & Toews, G. B. (1993). Immunology of the aging lung. *Clinics in Chest Medicine, 19,* 379–391.

Mahler, D., Cunningham, L., & Curtman, G. (1986). Aging and exercise performance. *Clinical Geriatric Medicine, 2,* 433–452.

McElvaney, G., Blackie, S., Morrison, M. J. (1989). Maximal static respiratory pressures in normal elderly. *American Review of Respiratory Disease, 139,* 696–702.

Pfitzenmeyer, P., Brondel, L., D'Arthis, Lacrox, S., Didier, J., & Gaudet, M. (1993). Lung function in advanced age: Study of ambulatory subjects aged over 75 years. *Gerontology, 39,* 267–275.

Rizzato, G., & Marrazzini, L. (1970). Thoracoabdominal mechanics in elderly men. *Journal of Applied Physiology, 28,* 457–460.

Rubin, S., Tack, M., & Cherniack, N. S. (1982). Effect of aging on respiratory responses to CO_2 and inspiratory resistive loads. *Journal of Gerontology, 37,* 306–312.

Tack, M., Altose, M. D., & Cherniack, N. S. Effect of aging on the perception of resistive ventilatory loads. *American Review of Respiratory Disease, 126,* 463–467.

Zhang, Y., & Kelsen, S. G. (1990). Effects of aging on diaphragm contractile function in golden hamsters. *American Review of Respiratory Disease 146,* 2396–1401.

Retirement

Robert C. Atchley

Miami University

I. The Importance of Retirement to Society
II. Concepts
III. History of Retirement
IV. Current Retirement Trends
V. Effects of Retirement on Individuals and Households
VI. Explanations of Retirement
VII. The Future of Retirement

Retired Person   Someone with a lengthy work history who has experienced a substantial reduction in employment, accompanied by retirement pension income.

Retirement   (a) The institutional arrangements that provide retirement pensions and rules of eligibility for retirement. (b) The transition between a position of employment and the position of retired person. (c) The life stage following retirement from the labor force.

Retirement Pension   A periodic payment, usually linked to past earnings and years of service and provided to those who meet retirement eligibility rules, usually age and/or years of service.

For society, **RETIREMENT** is a social institution consisting of rules of permissible and required exit from the labor force based on age or length of service and the financial arrangements for creating and delivering retirement pensions. For individual workers, retirement is the transition to a life stage that does not require employment. As an individual attribute, retirement is characterized by withdrawal from the labor force and support from one or more retirement pensions.

I. THE IMPORTANCE OF RETIREMENT TO SOCIETY

Industrial societies today have well-developed financial and social arrangements for the orderly withdrawal of aging and older people from the labor force. Although the specifics of retirement policies and financing differ considerably across countries, more than 90% of the population age 65 and older is retired in a large majority of industrial nations. In addition, nonindustrial nations have adopted features of the retirement institution in selected areas of their economics, especially in civil service and in the military.

Although retirement is quite similar from one industrial society to another in terms of the proportion of elders who are retired, eligibility rules and financing mechanisms vary considerably, and forces influencing retirement policies are often culture-specific. Exploring international variations in retirement is beyond the scope of this discussion. Instead, the development of retirement in the United States is used as a case study to illustrate various concepts and theories concerning retirement's origins, functions, and development.

As a social institution, retirement revolves around two important sets of social policies: (a) rules establishing eligibility for retirement pensions, and (b) policies that gather the financial resources to pay retirement pensions. As a result of the development of retirement, industrial societies allocate about 10% of gross domestic product to public social-security-type retirement pensions alone. In addition, 20–30% of all stocks, bonds, and government securities in the

United States are held by employer pension programs. [*See* PENSIONS.]

Individuals usually see retirement as an emancipatory life stage, one in which the individual is free to decide for him- or herself what goals to pursue. At retirement, individuals see themselves as shifting from working for someone else to working for themselves. Employers see retirement as an effective labor management device that allows them to reduce their labor force or replace less desirable (older) workers with more desirable (younger) workers. Legislators and administration policy makers, however, tend to be ambivalent about retirement. On the one hand, they see it as an appropriate individual reward for lengthy employment service and as a significant social achievement. On the other hand, they view retirement as a social problem that "wastes" potentially productive human resources and places an economic "burden" on society.

Few in this cast of characters understands the basic underlying function of retirement: controlling unemployment in high-energy industrial societies. In industrial societies, most physical work is done by machines, which continue to displace people in the economy at a breathtaking pace. For example, in the United States in 1930, electric power delivered to commerce and industry provided energy equivalent to the work of 365 million people. By 1980, the use of electric power by industry was equivalent to the energy that could be provided by 6.9 *billion* human beings. Today computerized "expert systems" displace professional and technical employees as well as clerical workers and industrial wage laborers.

High unemployment has always been a major source of political instability in industrial societies, and various social policies evolved that on the surface addressed the public welfare but also had the important function of reducing the size of the labor pool competing for available jobs. Child labor and compulsory education laws removed young people from labor competition, and retirement removed older people. Enormous public expenditures go to provide the educational institutions that keep young people well occupied. Likewise, public revenues are usually a major source of retirement income in all industrial democracies. Industrial societies need well-educated workers, and elders certainly benefit from having a period of retirement following a lengthy working life, but the important relation between re-

tirement and the need to control unemployment is the mostly invisible engine that drives the need for retirement. Accordingly, retirement policies become more liberal in times of high unemployment and more stringent in times of labor shortages. For example, Social Security retirement eligibility age was dropped from 65 to 62 in direct response to high unemployment. Conversely, retirement incentive plans disappear when there are labor shortages. The benefits of industrial production are many, but there are costs, and retirement is an important and necessary cost of living in industrial societies. [*See* WORK AND EMPLOYMENT.]

II. CONCEPTS

Retirement pensions provide the means for carrying out retirement. Pensions come in many varieties: public social insurance retirement pensions such as Social Security; employer pensions that provide a defined benefit (DB) amount per month, usually tied to years of service and earnings; employer pensions based on defined contributions (DC) by the employer, the employee, or both, which can often be taken as a lump sum or as a monthly annuity; and self-initiated retirement annuities, many of which are encouraged by tax shelters.

In essence, *retired person* is an individual status earned by years of service in the workforce. It is morally approved and economically supported as a legitimate earned right. At the same time, the status of retired person is presumed to be voluntary. Operationally, a retired person can be defined as someone with a lengthy work history who has experienced at least partial withdrawal from the labor force, accompanied by retirement pension income earned through prior employment. Retired Person can also be a subjectively assigned personal attribute and in addition is sometimes used as a euphemism for an older person. However, as a legitimate status attribute, retired person is an achieved status, not an ascribed status based solely on age.

Determining retirement status is relatively easy for people who work continuously for 40 years or more and then retire completely, but other categories are more ambiguous. For example, people who "retire" from one job only to take up another job full-time may consider themselves retired and may receive a

pension, but are they "really" retired? What about people who only worked sporadically and do not qualify for a retirement pension but who see their Supplemental Security Income check (a means-tested public welfare benefit) as a retirement pension and label themselves as retired? As the idealized pattern of long work career followed by abrupt and complete retirement becomes less and less common, defining who is retired becomes more complex and more difficult.

Retirement is also a life transition during which a person moves from full-time employment to no employment. Retirement pensions usually begin when employment is substantially reduced. For some, this transition is abrupt, but an increasing number of people experience "bridge employment" at fewer hours or weeks of employment, often at lower pay and occupational status, for some period of time before they withdraw completely from the labor force. A broader definition of the retirement transition includes a period of preparation for retirement and a period of adjusting to retirement. By either definition, retirement transitions vary greatly in length and may span a considerable period of time. However, by age 75 all but a very small proportion of adults have retired completely from the labor force.

Retirement is also a life stage that follows a lengthy period of reasonably continuous employment during adulthood. Here the emphasis is on a lifestyle that includes an array of social roles appropriate to a person who is no longer required to be part of the labor force. Retirement is literally a "do-it-yourself" life stage in that the only cultural expectation of retired people is that they avoid competing for full-time jobs, and even this norm is only half-heartedly applied. Retirement lifestyles can be built around a wide variety of activities such as sports, travel, community service, church activities, maintaining a home, landscape or vegetable gardening, spiritual contemplation, or taking care of grandchildren. However, the "busy ethic" requires that retired people remain productively engaged in some way. [See ACTIVITIES; LEISURE.]

Retirement is also a social institution made up of a cultural rationale for retirement and a complex array of social policies that establish the rules under which people are allowed or encouraged to retire and that provide mechanisms for financing retirement. *Ageism*—prejudice against aging or older people—is at the heart of the cultural rationale for retirement as a social institution. All industrial societies espouse a widespread cultural belief that by late middle age, aging has profound cognitive and physical effects that interfere with an aging person's capability to engage in productive employment. This often erroneous belief legitimates employment policies that discriminate against middle-aged and older people seeking jobs and that encourage retirement long before the onset of old age, if old age is defined symptomatically in terms of significant physical or mental incapacity. [See AGEISM AND DISCRIMINATION.]

However, industrial cultures also contain a long-standing norm of caring for elders, which means that simply discharging middle-aged and older workers is not a morally acceptable option. In order to discriminate against older workers and at the same time preserve the illusion that no harm comes to them from this practice, retirement pensions were developed to prevent elders displaced from employment from becoming destitute. The extent to which pension systems are designed to provide pensions that will support preretirement lifestyles depends in large measure on the robustness of the economy, the proportion of elders in the population, the availability of employer pensions, and organized political advocacy on behalf of retirement pensions.

The underlying rationale for retirement may be cultural, but specific retirement policies are managerial and political. In most cases, employer retirement policies are designed to move workers into retirement at the earliest age possible given the level of funding of the employer pension program. By not allowing pensions to increase with service beyond the minimum retirement age or service requirements, employer pensions often contain very strong economic incentives to retire. Employers use pensions as bargaining tools in negotiations with employees, even in the absence of unions, particularly as a way of deferring wages into the future. Unions favor retirement and bargain for pensions as a means of making way for younger, presumably more action-oriented members to replace older workers, who are seen as a more conservative element.

Public retirement programs are governed by policies developed through a political process. Elements of public retirement policies include the proportion of the population covered, funding mechanisms, minimum retirement age, length of service requirements, relation of eligibility and/or benefits amounts to age, retirement tests, links between benefit amounts and career earnings, special provisions for unhealthy occupations, pension supplements for dependents of retirees, indexing of benefits to offset inflation, and the extent to which benefits are expected to replace preretirement earnings from employment. This large complex of interrelated policies is manipulated legislatively to maintain the functioning of the retirement institution within an area bounded by unemployment rates, levels of poverty in old age, adequate pension replacement rates, and public willingness to finance retirement. [*See* ECONOMICS: SOCIETY.]

Each of these elements is in turn influenced by a wide array of factors, chiefly the robustness of the economy, the proportion of elders in the population, and the extent to which the political process is open to influence by class and interest group organizations. The goals of public retirement policies are (a) to keep unemployment down by manipulating retirement levels; (b) to minimize the proportion of older people in poverty; (c) to provide at least 60% replacement of preretirement earnings, particularly for low-income workers, in order to minimize the individual financial hardship connected with retirement, and (d) not to exceed the public's willingness to pay. To balance these constantly changing factors, most retirement systems are continually under adjustment in response to feedback, especially from business cycles. When the complex of factors that influence employer and self-initiated retirement income programs are included alongside issues shaping social-security-type public retirement systems, retirement can be a very complex social institution indeed.

III. HISTORY OF RETIREMENT

Retirement is a creature of modernization, the sociocultural shift that began in the late 1700s and brought new ways of thinking about how to pursue material progress, particularly in the form of more and better goods and a higher general level of living. Key aspects of modernization included the rise of science as a way of knowing, technology as a means of production, hierarchical bureaucracy as a form of organization, universalistic law as a means of social control, individualism as a moral philosophy, communication as a means of generating agreement, and geographic and social mobility as means of matching people with jobs

in an increasingly complex division of labor. As an *ideal*, a modern society is dominated by techno-scientific rationality, universal education, mass organizations and communications, cosmopolitan urban populations, and political democracy.

But what was it about modernization that caused older people to be singled out for exclusion from the labor force through the development of retirement? The rise of science as a way of knowing, technology as a way of production, and impersonal bureaucratic rules as a way of deciding are all aspects of modernization that played a key role in excluding elders from the pool of workers defined as desirable and in the development of retirement as a method of insuring society against widespread personal hardship and political instability that could be expected to accompany the wholesale exclusion of elders from the workforce in the absence of retirement pensions. [*See* MODERNIZATION AND AGING.]

Early science was crude in both measurement and research design. The first studies of physical and mental aging focused on mean age differences and paid almost no attention to dispersion around the mean. Thus, early medical texts stressed the sharp declines observed in mean level of functioning for various bodily systems and organs. Early psychology texts stressed mean age differences in cognitive functioning. Little or no attention was paid to the enormous variation in functional capability *within* age groups, and no studies were based on longitudinal research designs that looked at actual age changes over time. In addition, differences in functioning were only compared across age categories, not against a benchmark level of functioning necessary to sustain a normal level of adult activity. As a result, outrageous generalizations were made and believed about the scientific "evidence" concerning the negative effects of aging. For example, William Osler, physician-in-chief of Johns Hopkins University Hospital, gave a widely reported address in 1905 in which he contended that aging had such profound effects on human creativity and productivity that men above 40 could be considered benign but relatively useless workers, and men above 60 were so useless that they represented a drain on an organization and absolutely had to be retired. Although Osler's view was extreme, it was endorsed in milder forms by the scientific community, and it was adopted by influential industrial leaders. This belief in the relative worthlessness of older people as workers

remains strong today, and it forms an important part of the belief system that sustains retirement.

Technology increased productivity enormously, but at a tremendous cost in terms of a net loss of jobs. For example, mechanization of agriculture began to displace farmers and farm workers from the land in large numbers after the American Civil War. Rapid cycles of technological change led to wide short-term fluctuations in urban industrial employment. Unrest and mob violence associated with cycles of very high unemployment led employers, labor leaders, and politicians alike to search for ways to moderate the unemployment effects of business cycles.

Retirement was a potential solution to the problem of excess workers, but so long as work organizations were small and proprietary and the relatively few older workers who had to be assigned to lighter work could be paid lower wages, personal relationships insulated older workers from ageism to a great extent. Older workers tended to be dealt with as individuals rather than as members of an age category. However, with the growth of corporate management forms and impersonal, bureaucratic organizational policies, it became possible to justify and implement universalistic policies based on assumed characteristics of age categories. Individual characteristics no longer mattered, nor did variation within age categories.

But so long as retirement was not accompanied by pensions, employers were reluctant to simply throw out older workers. The spread of employer pensions in the 1920s and the passage of Social Security legislation in 1935 provided a basic model for retirement financing. In the 1950s, changes in labor and tax laws allowed collective bargaining to rapidly expand employer pension coverage. These changes combined to provide a financial foundation for the adoption of retirement as a universal social expectation.

In summary, scientific ageism, displacement of workers by technology, and bureaucratic impersonality all combined to devalue older workers and to justify their exclusion from the labor force. The development of Social Security and employer pensions provided the stimulus that attracted older workers to retirement.

IV. CURRENT RETIREMENT TRENDS

In the United States, the average age of first retirement began to decline in the late 1950s, the decline accel-erated in the 1970s, and then leveled off in the late 1980s. Most of these changes are a product of two forces: increased desire for retirement on the part of workers and liberalized pension eligibility rules. In 1950, for example, most men in the United States felt that retirement was morally justified only if the individual was physically unable to continue working, but by 1960 most men said that retirement was legitimate if the individual wanted to retire and had a pension to support it. By 1975, a large majority of American workers had very positive attitudes toward their own retirement.

Meanwhile, pension programs were maturing, pension amounts were becoming more generous, and eligibility rules were liberalized. For example, in real dollars, the average monthly Social Security benefit increased from $90 in 1965 to $233 in 1975. The minimum retirement age under Social Security was dropped from 65 to 62 for women in 1959 and for men in 1962. These "early" benefits were actuarially reduced, but as Social Security benefits became more adequate in the 1970s, more and more workers opted for early retirement. There has also been a general reduction in age of eligibility for employer pension benefits, and private pension programs have increasingly used early retirement incentive programs to deal with massive reductions in the commercial and industrial workforce since 1980.

However, early first retirements are not necessarily complete retirements. In the 1980s, labor force data began to reveal a pattern of "bridge employment," a period of continued employment, often full-time, that bridged the point at which the individual began to draw a private pension benefit and the point at which the individual could receive Social Security benefits. By 1980, more than half of men who retired completely were retiring from bridge jobs.

Retirement is becoming an increasingly diverse set of patterns: (a) continuations into retirement of occupational inequalities in income and health-care insurance, (b) different age patterns of retirement, and (c) divergent meanings of retirement. Although Social Security provides nearly universal access to retirement pensions to residents who work at least 10 years, the pension formulas used to compute benefits dramatically favor those who have worked at least 35 years and disadvantage those who have spent significant portions of adulthood out of the labor force. Sporadic work histories are most common among women, particularly those who drop out of the labor force for child rearing or other caregiving, and among minorities and those with less education.

Gender, social class, and minority group differences in access to adequate public retirement pensions are compounded by the fact that women, less well-educated men, and minorities also tend to be concentrated in employment sectors where employer pensions and continuation of health benefits into retirement are seldom provided. As a result, for most working-class people, Social Security is their sole source of retirement income and Medicare their only source of health-care coverage. The average retirement benefit for these workers was less than $650 per month in 1993. Middle-class workers are much more likely to have worked for large employers or for government, where employer pensions are both more common and more generous. Upper middle-class workers (e.g., professionals, upper-level managers, senior government officials, scientists, and engineers) tend to be the most advantaged in that they are much more likely to have multiple retirement income sources: Social Security retirement pensions, generous employer pensions, and self-initiated retirement income.

Thus, today's mature retirement income systems are designed to produce income inequalities in retirement that closely match the very broad range of income inequalities that exist during the employment years. This is quite a contrast to the situation in the 1960s, when immature retirement income systems resulted in more income compression, a lower range of inequality in retirement income, and a much higher proportion of retirees living in poverty.

Age patterns of complete withdrawal from the labor force have also become increasingly diverse. Whereas 65 was by far the dominant retirement age in the 1970s, by the 1990s there was much less noticeable heaping of retirement around age 65, even though 65 remained the minimum age for full retirement benefits under Social Security. The most advantaged segments of the labor force were those most likely to retire abruptly and completely in their fifties; the most disadvantaged were most likely to remain in the labor force past age 70. Women were especially likely to remain employed into their seventies out of economic necessity. However, most people still retired in their early to mid-sixties.

Retirement lifestyles have also become increasingly diverse. For some retirement means a life of leisure, which can take an enormous variety of forms. For others, retirement represents a new beginning; the opportunity to become self-employed. Others retire into community service. An increasing number retire into the family by taking on responsibilities for care of their grandchildren as more middle-class mothers stay in the workforce. Still others retire to care for older members of the family. Many retire into a life of couplehood. As people live out retirement as a life stage, they may experience several of these different lifestyles. Increasingly, retirement is coming to be seen as an active life stage that occurs between the cessation of employment and the onset of the frailties associated with old age. When frailty becomes a dominant influence on lifestyles, the concept of a retirement lifestyle becomes less salient, even though the person is still retired and getting income entirely from retirement income sources.

V. EFFECTS OF RETIREMENT ON INDIVIDUALS AND HOUSEHOLDS

Early gerontologists thought retirement had a great number of negative effects. In addition to financial difficulties, retirement was said to cause demoralization and a loss of self-esteem, reduced activity levels, increased isolation and loneliness, increased feelings of uselessness, and declining physical and mental health. Most gerontologists thought that the root of these negative outcomes was psychic damage caused by the loss of an occupational identity. It is true that demoralization, low activity levels, and so on could be found among retired people, but most of these unfortunate outcomes observed in the 1950s were apparently caused by low retirement incomes rather than loss of occupational roles.

By the 1970s, retirement incomes had become much more adequate, and retirement research was following people through the retirement transition rather than looking at age differences and attributing all of the negative characteristics of later life to retirement. Study after study showed that retirement had little or no effect on physical or mental health, overall activity levels, social participation, or life satisfaction. It became increasingly clear that depression attributable to retirement was a rare outcome. In short, retirement research since the 1970s has shown clearly that

most adults adjust very well to the life changes associated with retirement.

Likewise, early literature on retirement assumed that retirement represented a major upheaval for most married-couple households, particularly the invasion of a traditional "wife's domain" by newly retired husbands. Again, research showed a different picture. Although there are certainly adjustments that must be made when a working household becomes a retired household, most of these adjustments are seen as relatively minor by retired couples themselves. Those couples who have troublesome relationships in retirement tend to be those that had troublesome relationships in earlier life stages as well.

Why is retirement such an easy adjustment for most people? First, given adequate retirement income, people can relax about the adjustment process because they do not have to worry about securing their next month's income. Second, most people anticipate retirement and have watched others retire before them. As a result, they do not feel that they are stepping off into unmapped territory. There are many clearly marked paths and effective role models. Third, retirement is a morally sanctioned life change. The cultural life course concept in industrial societies defines retirement as an earned reward financed from the productivity of an economic system that individual workers helped create through their lengthy employment, a reward that individuals ought to feel good about accepting. Fourth, as a cultural life stage, retirement still requires individuals to have goals and to engage in productive work even though it may not be for pay. This expectation of continued productive activity maintains the sense of self as competent and worthy.

Although a large majority of people who willingly retire accomplish the transition with minimal stress and find a satisfying retirement lifestyle within a relatively short time, the small proportion who are coerced into retirement are more likely to experience difficulty. For example, though the practice is illegal, some workers are given two unattractive choices: retire before they are ready or see their jobs be terminated. Most choose retirement over unemployment, but some cannot be happy about the circumstances under which they retired. They may still have unfinished occupational goals, retirement earlier than expected may result in lower retirement income than they see as adequate, and they may not be ready to relinquish an occupational identity. Nevertheless,

within a year or two, most reluctant retirees have either found another full-time job or have adjusted well to life in retirement.

Another category of unhappy retirees consists of those who retired for health reasons. If health deteriorates to the point of being so disabling that it forces an individual to retire, no one should be surprised that disability and the constraints on activity that come with it continue into retirement. In these cases, disability, not retirement, is the cause of constricted life space and any attendant psychological distress. Fortunately, the proportion of people retiring for health reasons has dropped dramatically since the 1960s.

VI. EXPLANATIONS OF RETIREMENT

Why does retirement exist? What factors have been responsible for the rapid evolution of retirement and the directions this evolution has taken? What accounts for the rapid public acceptance of retirement, especially in work-oriented societies? Why has retirement been called into question by the very economic and government interests that gave rise to it in the first place? These central questions have stimulated social gerontologists to develop a number of explanations.

Why does retirement exist? The idea of retirement from the pressures of economic and social life in one's sixties to lead a life of contemplation and spiritual growth can be traced back over 4,000 years to the Hindu Vedas. A few medieval farmers deeded their land to their sons or to the church in exchange for food and shelter in retirement. Wealthy merchants could retire and live on the proceeds of their wealth. But retirement has been an economic possibility for most workers only since the advent of modern industrial societies. Why did we create such ambitious and effective systems of financing to provide retirement for the masses?

Explanations center around functionalist and exchange theories. *Functional theory* presumes that retirement is caused by functional needs, specifically the need to control unemployment. As mentioned, industrial societies have historically had difficulty providing full employment, and retirement serves an important unemployment control function by systematically removing a sizable segment of the adult population from labor market competition. However, in democratic societies, retirement must primarily be done by persuasion and incentive rather than by coercion. Thus, retirement pension systems must provide pensions generous enough to attract large numbers of older workers out of the labor market and therefore alleviate unemployment.

Exchange theory argues that retirement is a result of *age discrimination*. According to this theory, employers want to hire workers who will give the greatest value in exchange for wages. People in the labor market are not viewed as individuals with unique talents and skills; instead, employers sort potential employees into categories and arrange these categories into a hierarchy of relative desirability in terms of the resources they are assumed to bring to the exchange. In this context, "older" begins at about age 50. Older workers are widely believed to bring fewer resources to the employment transaction in comparison with other categories of adults. Older workers are assumed to have less energy and stamina, less up-to-date education, less ambition, and less creativity. They are assumed to cost more, bring a lower return on training investment, derive less benefit from training, and resist new technologies. Research evidence indicates that many of these beliefs are inaccurate, but what matters is that managers and policy makers act on these beliefs as if they were true and do not want or need proof in order to act.

Thus, organizations are motivated to create ways of keeping to a minimum the number of employees in the older worker category. They do not hire older workers if they have other alternatives and they seek ways of moving workers out of the organization as soon as possible once they enter the older category. To many managers, the only good older worker is a retired older worker. Retirement was developed to provide a means of humanely disposing of workers presumed to be less effective. Again, in free societies, incentives are preferred over coercive policies. This preference for subtle rather than heavy-handed age discrimination is revealed by the fact that in 1978, when mandatory retirement rules were declared illegal for most jobs in the United States, pension incentives for retirement were being used to the greatest extent in history, and retirement ages were still dropping.

Functional and exchange theories of retirement complement one another. Both accept the notion that older workers are seen as a category that can legitimately be excluded from the labor force. Functional theory focuses on effects of this exclusion on unemployment in the economy as a whole, whereas exchange theory focuses on the presumed benefits of this exclusion for employer organizations. The widespread acceptance of cultural myths about the negative effects of aging on employability are foundational assumptions for both theories. These theories also help to explain why retirement is encouraged long before the frailties of old age become prevalent in a population cohort.

Some functionalists argue that retirement serves the function of humanely removing people disabled by aging from the labor force. But as a social institution, retirement is not primarily concerned with disabled elders. Retirement is designed to encourage older workers, who are assumed to be less effective but who are usually not disabled, to withdraw from employment. Elders who are physically or mentally unable to work can be dealt with through disability pensions, so retirement pensions are not needed for this function.

Other functionalists argue that retirement arose to meet workers' desires for leisure. But here there is a substantial causal order problem, because retirement pension systems were developed long before a majority of industrial workers began to see retirement as a legitimate individual goal.

But if retirement's major function is to simply remove workers from the labor force, how does one explain the fact that the retirement institution in most societies delivers pensions more generous than would be needed simply to allow people to survive outside the labor force? For example, evidence indicates that a large number of workers can be attracted from the labor force with pensions amounting to only 40% of preretirement earnings, but many public retirement systems in the industrial world provide 60% or more earnings replacement. The theoretical answers to this question come from political economy theory, moral economy theory, and social justice theory.

The *political economy theory* of the dynamics of retirement as an institution starts from several basic assumptions: most industrial societies are capitalist, capitalist economies exploit workers unless confronted by organized opposition from labor, most industrial societies are democracies, and democratic politics provides a vehicle through which labor, organized or not, can achieve just treatment in the form of adequate retirement benefits. In this frame of reference, the adequacy of retirement benefits is a function of the political power of wage and salary workers. This power can be exercised in one of two ways: through direct negotiations between organized labor and management and/or through the capacity of advocates for the interests of labor to influence the legislative process through which public pension formulas are set and rules governing employer pensions are made.

Moral economy theory assumes that raw economic power or political power are not enough to explain the generosity of retirement pensions. Moral economy theory holds that the economy is not just a matter of financial obligations and that for a highly interdependent industrial economy to function, there must also be moral commitments that go beyond simple payment of wages. These extended commitments provide the sense of security needed for industrial workers to concentrate on doing their jobs productively. Thus, moral economy theory assumes that current wages and other benefits do not fully compensate workers for their labor, and that a part of their just compensation consists of moral commitments by the society to provide both security against unemployment and income in retirement. It is on the basis of this accumulated moral capital that retiree claims for adequate retirement benefits can be most effectively made.

Social justice theory is based on the concept of civil rights. It assumes that eligibility for socially adequate retirement benefits is a right earned by all residents who participate in the workforce throughout a major portion of their adult lives. The rationale here is that in affluent industrial societies, there is no justification for retirees to be disadvantaged by being forced to survive on less than adequate retirement pensions. This perspective helped fuel the movement for better Social Security pensions and protection of benefits against inflation in the late 1960s, when a large proportion of Social Security pensioners were living below the poverty level.

Note that the issue is not whether retirement should exist. That tends to be taken as a given by political economy theory, moral economy theory, and social justice theory. The issue is the adequacy and fairness of the compensation retirees should receive in return for leaving the workforce. Evidence indicates that each of these perspectives has merit when applied to specific eras in the development of retirement.

The nature of industrial capitalist economies and of democratic politics may explain why retirement is needed by society and how retirement benefits come

to be at least adequate if not generous. But why does such a large majority of individuals go willingly into retirement, especially if retirement is not mandatory? This question is addressed by theories of individualism and human development.

Individualism as a personal philosophy is at the heart of industrial societies. Young people are socialized to pursue their own individual talents and ambitions and aggressively seek opportunities in the complex postindustrial division of labor. Individual freedom and self-determination are held up as the highest rewards possible. Retirement may have been created as a way to institutionalize age discrimination in employment, but so long as the payoff is adequate, many employees are quite willing to take even a sizable pay cut in exchange for the level of freedom and self-determination that retirement represents.

Adult development theory also offers explanations for why individuals might be attracted to retirement. Career ladders do not extend infinitely. In fact, the concept of career probably poorly describes the succession of jobs most people occupy. For those stuck in career or job plateaus, switching job fields is constrained by age discrimination in employment. And even if new jobs are available, the person is still at the mercy of another boss. Retirement is a growth option because it offers a secure income and a chance to become one's own boss.

Movement away from a focus on material acquisition and social position represents another developmental support for individual acceptance of retirement. Many adults find that the preoccupation with material acquisition and social position that characterized young and middle adulthood becomes less satisfying over time. They see more meaning in the quality of everyday life, and retirement gives them more control over that quality than they can achieve if they are still integrated into employer organizations, particularly in a time of growing employer pressures for increased individual productivity. For example, as leisure time contracts in the face of job demands, many adults experience a degradation in their quality of life, and they see retirement as an attractive way to restore a better balance of both control and life quality. They also have experienced material acquisition and achievement of social position and find them overrated as sources of ongoing life satisfaction. They increasingly find themselves drawn to what they see as a more relaxed and humane pace of life, more control over their personal life goals, and more time for personal relationships and satisfying activities. The informal friendship networks of retired people often resemble a congenial extended family, and the lifestyles of most retired people revolve around meaningful and satisfying activities.

The advantages of retirement have become institutionalized through the packaging, marketing, and advertising of retirement as prepaid leisure. Industries that have formed around individual retirement needs include retirement planning, retirement personal finance, and retirement housing.

Thus, adults go willingly into retirement even though it represents a decline in social status and nothing less than institutionalized age discrimination because for them the benefits, in the form of freedom and enhanced quality of life at the personal level, far outweigh the costs in terms of abstract social status.

Why has retirement been called into question by business and government? Since 1976, the institution of retirement has been under a sustained political and managerial attack in the United States. Part of this assault is based on philosophical opposition to government operations in areas where private enterprise sees potential business opportunities. Thus, Social Security is criticized on the grounds that private retirement programs could bring workers a better "return on investment." That Social Security is social insurance and not intended to be an investment is ignored. These critics also usually ignore survivor, disability, and health benefits that are part of Social Security and imply that retirement benefits are the only return workers get for their Social Security taxes. These arguments are put forward by a financial services industry made up of insurance companies, banks, and securities firms who want to "privatize" all or part of Social Security in order to increase their own business opportunities.

Employers also want to reduce their Social Security tax liabilities. Corporate income taxes have fallen much faster than individual income taxes since 1970, whereas the employer's 50% share of Social Security payroll taxes increased from 3% of earnings up to $4,200 per year in 1960 to 7.65% of earnings up to $60,600 in 1994. Reducing the Social Security tax is a major policy objective of the business community. Employers want Social Security to continue to draw older workers out of the labor force, but employers do not want to pay their share of the cost of this benefit.

The financial services industry and business advocates joined forces to mount a well-organized campaign to convince the public that Social Security could not be sustained. According to their argument, the rapid increase in the older population that will come with the entry of the baby boom population into retirement is bound to bankrupt the system; therefore, people who are currently paying Social Security taxes are unlikely to get a Social Security pension. This argument flies in the face of dozens of studies showing that under current benefit formulas, providing Social Security pensions for the baby boomers will require only very modest changes to the system under any likely economic scenario. Nevertheless, the propaganda campaign has been very successful in that a large proportion of younger workers thinks that Social Security will not be there when they reach retirement age, even though a very large majority of workers wants the program to remain and expresses willingness to pay higher taxes to maintain it. But as more and more younger workers come to believe that the collapse of Social Security is inevitable, resentment of those who currently enjoy Social Security benefits rises and willingness to pay Social Security taxes falls.

Understanding the multidimensional assault on Social Security retirement demands a *conflict theory* perspective. The history of the United States is a history of conflict between opposing philosophies of government. At one extreme are those who feel that the best government is the least government. A procedural state that allows for peaceful resolution of disputes and a common monetary system are about all that is necessary in this view. A less extreme but still conservative position would add armed forces, police and fire protection, and perhaps education to the list of public institutions. At the other pole are those who wish a strong national government to protect the public interest in a number of areas including pensions, health care, housing, education, science, commerce, banking, environmental protections, public welfare, and transportation. The assault on Social Security should be seen in the context of a general social movement to scale back the resources going into national government. This movement is being vigorously opposed by those who believe that there are certain functions such as national retirement pension systems that only government can perform adequately.

The power of membership organizations made up mainly of retired people to assert a voice in favor of

Social Security is unclear. On the one hand, the media frequently refer to the American Association of Retired Persons (AARP) as "the most powerful lobby in Washington." But AARP is a large and diverse organization made up of over 30 million members with all sorts of political orientations. Most members did not join AARP to become part of a social movement; they joined to take advantage of AARP's insurance, financial, travel, and pharmacy services. To protect its nonprofit status, AARP cannot give financial support to political candidates or Political Action Committees. AARP does not participate in setting political agendas, but instead reacts to political initiatives. In the 1970s, AARP and other membership organizations were effective in shaping the agendas of a sympathetic congress and administration. But the climate of the 1990s is no longer sympathetic to issues such as Social Security. Two decades of propaganda charging Social Security with "generational inequity" and ignoring the intergenerational benefits of Social Security have increased anxieties about Social Security. As yet, there is no sign that AARP or any other membership organization of elders will mount an active grass-roots movement to set the record straight and to advocate for preserving the Social Security retirement program in its current form. [*See* POLITICAL ATTITUDES AND BEHAVIOR.]

The weight of the evidence suggests that regardless of political or economic philosophy, industrial nations generate policies that move a very large proportion of their older populations into retirement. Therefore, political conflict tends to be about the relative generosity of national pensions, not whether or not to have them. The intergenerational social contract whereby public retirement systems institutionalized economic support of elders by the younger generations is being called into question. There is no reason to expect that the long-standing conflict between strong-government and weak-government advocates will abate, and as this ongoing conflict focuses on public pension generosity, social security-type retirement systems will change.

VII. THE FUTURE OF RETIREMENT

The future of retirement is uncertain. It will emerge from the interaction of a number of opposing economic, political, demographic, and social policy concerns. The key question is whether retirement is or even should be sustainable.

At the turn of the twenty-first century, industrial economies are not the robust forces that they were in 1960. Worldwide decentralization of industrial production has destabilized wages and benefits for large segments of the labor forces in industrial nations. Demassification processes have drastically reduced the scale of many types of economic activity, particularly in the types of professional, managerial, and technical jobs that formerly carried access to adequate retirement benefits. Retirement institutions are no longer shaped by negotiations among representatives of monolithic labor unions, corporations, and national governments. In the United States, as a result of declines in organized labor, reductions in availability of pension coverage, shifting of pension plans from defined benefit to defined contribution plans, shifting of pension plan contributions from being an employer responsibility to being an employee responsibility, and rules that allow employees to withdraw their funds from pension programs when they change employers, access to adequate employer pensions among young adult workers is becoming increasingly problematic. Because of this fragmentation of retirement policy, young workers have little confidence in retirement as a social institution.

The longevity revolution is rapidly increasing the proportion of the population surviving beyond age 85. The retired population begins chronologically as early as age 45, but most people retire in their sixties. This means that retirement income programs must be designed to deliver secure retirement income for up to 25 years on average and for up to 50 years in many cases. Policy makers have generally advanced two scenarios for responding to the impending masses of retirees: keep aging people in the workforce longer and plan to reduce benefits.

There is no sign that age discrimination in employment will be reversed or that elders will be welcomed to remain employed. The increase in the number of complaints under the Age Discrimination in Employment Act from 8,000 in 1988 to over 15,000 in 1993 point in the opposite direction. Labor shortages resulting from continued low birth rates among the middle and upper classes are more likely to be offset by increased immigration or by increased use of technology than by creating more job opportunities for older workers. However, if benefits are reduced, many older people, especially those under age 75, may be forced by economic circumstances to stay in the labor force, where for the most part they will compete with the nation's youth for minimum-wage jobs in fast-food restaurants and retailing. In any case, keeping more elders in the labor force is not likely to be a satisfactory solution should the increased size of the older population outstrip the nation's capacity to provide retirement income.

The other possibility is to reduce benefits. Currently those elders whose retirement incomes are mainly from Social Security live just over the poverty level. Benefit cuts would push this population into eligibility for public assistance, which would simply shift the liability for their income from one government program to another. Sharp reduction of Social Security retirement benefits for middle- and upper-income retirees would reduce the revenues needed to sustain Social Security retirement, but middle- and upper-income retirees feel that they earned their pensions and they expect to receive them. They also have the economic resources and educational background to mount effective political action.

The sheer number of future elders in the baby boom generation scares policy makers, who picture a huge phalanx of older baby boomers taking to the streets to demand adequate retirement benefits. To head off this possibility, two major actions were taken in 1983: the age for full Social Security retirement benefits was scheduled to increase gradually from 65 to 67 and the scheduled increases in Social Security taxes were advanced in order to build up a sizable surplus in the retirement trust fund that could be used in conjunction with taxes to pay pensions for the baby boomers. But because projections of survival rates among the old have consistently underestimated the number of future elders, the Social Security system has consistently experienced shortfalls in projected income to benefits ratios that have required periodic increases to tax rates and/or benefit reductions.

Each year, the Social Security Trustees are required by law to review the short- and long-range economic and demographic assumptions and actuarial projections for each trust fund. Thus, the system's capacity to look ahead and make needed adjustments well in advance of financial difficulty is a strength, but this process of continual adjustment also gives opponents of Social Security an opportunity to claim that the system is "flawed" and "will be bankrupt," which

further reinforces the widespread image among the young that Social Security is not so secure.

The long-term financial viability of public social-security-type retirement programs depends on the continued voting support of national legislators. For many decades legislative support for Social Security programs has been unwavering, but in recent years economic pressures have caused legislatures to back away from many programs that have traditionally received strong support. The lack of a clear-cut set of legislative priorities makes the long-term viability of Social Security retirement seem less predictable and therefore less secure. This insecurity is heightened by political rhetoric inaccurately portraying reductions in Social Security as inevitable.

At the same time, public demand for retirement has shown no signs of diminishing. The concept of retirement as an earned right and prepaid leisure is widespread. People continue to desire the freedom and autonomy of retirement and to feel that they have earned the opportunity.

Public and employer pension policies are on opposite courses. The political rhetoric advocating changes in Social Security emphasizes keeping people in the labor force longer and reducing retirement benefits. But employer pensions, nearly all of which are subsidized by tax shelters, are geared toward encouraging older workers to exit the labor force at the earliest age possible. These conflicting philosophies reflect a national ambivalence about retirement. On the one hand, most people who retire could continue to work. On the other hand, there is not likely to be enough work to go around. The question is whether the political process will adequately compensate elders for leaving the workforce, force them into a lower-income retirement, or require them to stay in the labor force and risk an open struggle between the young and the old for jobs on the margins of the economy.

What is the alternative to retirement? Legislators and administration policy makers cannot expect the voting public to sit quietly by and watch barely adequate retirement benefits be replaced by predatory employment or poverty. As retirement becomes more problematic, political conflict over retirement will intensify. Nevertheless, if only because of its unemployment control function, retirement will remain an important social institution in postindustrial or high tech societies.

BIBLIOGRAPHY

Atchley, R. C. (1982). Retirement as a social institution. *Annual Review of Sociology*, 8, 263–287.

Ekerdt, D. J. (1986). The busy ethic. *The Gerontologist*, 26, 239–244.

Graebner, W. (1980). *A history of retirement: The meaning and function of an American institution.* New Haven, CT: Yale University Press.

Kohli, M. (1987). Retirement and the moral economy: An historical interpretation of the German case. *Journal of Aging Studies* 1, 125–144.

Marmor, T. R., Mashaw, J. L., & Harvey, P. L. (1990). *America's misunderstood welfare state.* New York: Basic Books.

Myles, J., & Quadagno, J. (Eds.). (1991). *States, labor markets, and the future of old-age security.* Philadelphia: Temple University Press.

Quadagno, J. (1988). *The transformation of old age security.* Chicago: University of Chicago Press.

Ruhm, C. J. (1990). Career jobs, bridge employment, and retirement. In P. B. Doeringer (Ed.), *Bridges to Retirement* (pp. 92–110). Ithaca, NY: ILR Press.

Schulz, J. H. (1995). *The economics of aging* (6th ed.). New York: Auburn House.

Social Security Administration. (1994). *Annual statistical supplement to the Social Security Bulletin, 1994.* Washington, DC: U.S. Government Printing Office.

Williamson, J. B., & Pampel, F. C. (1993). *Old-age security in comparative perspective.* New York: Oxford University Press.

Rheumatic Diseases

Anders Bjelle

Gothenburg University

I. Musculoskeletal Tissues
II. Immune System
III. Locomotor Function
IV. Pain
V. Epidemiology
VI. Health Care
VII. Therapy
VIII. Diseases

Rheumatic Diseases   Diseases of the musculoskeletal system and the connective tissues.
Arthritis   Inflammatory condition of joint structures.
Crystal Arthritis   Joint inflammation caused by microcrystals.
Osteoarthritis   Degenerative diseases of articular cartilage.
Vasculitis   Inflammatory condition of the blood vessels.

RHEUMATIC DISORDERS affect individuals of all ages, although both the incidence and prevalence vary between age groups. Furthermore, the diagnosis and management of the same rheumatic disease may be very different at different ages. Because of the high prevalence and the specific diagnostic and therapeutic problems of rheumatic disorders in the elderly, it is important that both specialists and general practitioners recognize this problem.

I. MUSCULOSKELETAL TISSUES

A special feature of many musculoskeletal tissues is their dependence on physical forces and their remark-

able ability to change in response to altered functional demands. Thus, changes with aging in the elderly are often a result of a complex interaction between decline of function and decreased physical demands. Normality values relating to age groups for physical and organ function are helpful, but an increased individual variation with aging due to different rate of functional decline of cells, tissues, and organs creates diagnostic difficulties. There will be a risk of underdiagnosis because symptoms or signs are misinterpreted as reduced function due to age, and of overdiagnosis because symptoms or signs are taken for disease instead of a result of the aging process (Table I).

A number of age-related changes occur in the musculoskeletal system and in other tissues of importance to the rheumatic disorders.

A. Muscle

Skeletal muscle is not a homogeneous tissue, and its function is dependent on trophic influences from, for instance, the nervous, vascular, and endocrine systems, which in turn are influenced by the aging processes. A number of changes occur in the skeletal muscle with aging (Table II).

The fiber composition in adults does not change until late in life, but the variation among individuals increases with age. An important fact is that muscle function remains trainable even into advanced age. Thus, the potential to retain and regain muscle function warrants a more active approach to the treatment of disability from musculoskeletal disorders in the elderly.

Some muscle diseases have an association with high

Table I Diagnostic Errors in the Elderly

Overdiagnosis
  When comparing the elderly with young individuals
Underdiagnosis
  When dysfunction is misinterpreted as aging

---

age (e.g., polymyositis associated with malignancy). Inflammatory rheumatic diseases involve muscle tissue to a varying extent. Inflammatory changes, myositis, are less common than noninflammatory, nonspecific myopathy. This condition is frequently overlooked by the clinician in rheumatoid arthritis or ankylosing spondylitis despite the obvious muscle wasting and weakness caused by these diseases. [*See* NEUROMUSCULAR SYSTEM.]

B. Bone

Changes in the geometry of long bones reflect the body's ability to adapt in the most biomechanically useful way. Continuous remodeling of bone takes place throughout life. The importance for degenerative joint diseases in late life is apparent for malalignments, but more has to be learned about the interaction between bone formation and cartilage.

The peak bone mass occurs around 30–40 years of age and somewhat earlier in trabecular than in cortical bone. The individual variation in bone mass is considerable and dependent on a number of factors: genetic, nutritional, hormonal, and social. After the age of 40 the mineral content of the skeleton decreases by about 0.5% per year for men and 1% for women. This is also reflected in the incidence of fractures, which is higher in women, and fractures are a major cause of disability in the elderly. [*See* BONE AND OSTEOPOROSIS.]

Table II Muscle in the Elderly

Reduced
  strength
  endurance
  coordination
  muscle mass
  aerobic capacity
  fast/slow (type II/type I) fibers

Table III Articular Cartilage in the Aged and in Osteoarthritis

	Aging	Osteoarthritis
Water	decreased	increased
Chondroitin sulfate	normal	decreased
Chondroitin sulfate 4/6	decreased	increased
Keratan sulfate	increased	decreased
Proteoglycans		
Extractability	decreased	increased
Aggregation	normal	diminished
Monomer size	decreased	increased
Enzyme activity	normal	increased

Interestingly, smoking and stomach ulcer surgery have more influence than aging on the mineral content of the skeleton. The negative influence of exogenic factors like smoking and the positive influence of physical activity indicate that preventive measures against the development of osteoporosis are possible.

C. Cartilage

Changes characteristic of aging as opposed to osteoarthritis (OA) are now being described at the molecular level of proteoglycans (Table III). Because the nutrition of articular cartilage from the bone is closed at adolescence, its capacity for repair in later life has been denied. However, advancing knowledge on cartilage metabolism gives hope that a regenerative capacity of cartilage tissue in the adult can be stimulated.

D. Ligament and Fascia

The tendon consists of bundles of fine filaments with sparse cells within a sheath of connective tissue. It is bound to the bone by transition zones of unmineralized and mineralized fibrocartilage. This is the weakest point, which usually breaks in trauma. It is also a site of inflammatory reactions in ankylosing spondylitis and in reactive arthritides following infections, although these diseases are rare in the elderly.

Degenerative changes with age due to altered nutrition are most apparent in the rotator cuff tendon of the shoulder joint. This tendon is highly susceptible to tears after middle age, when the local blood supply is reduced. This also results in degenerative changes with calicifications causing inflammatory reactions.

Undiagnosed and untreated shoulder complaints of clinical significance are common in the elderly population. Although the cellular components in adults are few, the fascia has a reactive capacity illustrated by the occurrence of inflammatory conditions, fasciitis.

II. IMMUNE SYSTEM

It has been discussed whether *immunosenescence* is a general failure of cell function in the elderly or is secondary to other factors, like nutritional factors with zinc or glutathion deficiencies, other illnesses, or even iatrogenic causes. A number of changes in the immunological responses have been described in the elderly (Table IV). The thymic function decreases from the age of 40, but an impaired delayed hypersensitivity reaction is not observed until several decades later. There is some evidence of a decreased balance between T-cell helpers and suppressors and a decrease of Interleukin 2 (IL-2) receptors and of IL-3 production with aging. Resistance to infection is also dependent on other components of the defense system (e.g., reduced integrity of the skin and mucous membranes and reduced function in the respiratory and urinary tracts in the elderly). This may explain why the total defense against infections does not decline until high age despite the gradual decline in adult life of immunocompetent lymphocytes and a reduced ability to react to newly presented antigens.

Parallel to the reduced capacity to react to new antigens, the amount of autoantibodies increases with aging. The increased number of individuals with "false positive rheumatoid factors" in the elderly can produce some diagnostic confusion in those who think the rheumatoid factor test is a disease-specific test. [*See* IMMUNE SYSTEM.]

Table IV Immune System in the Elderly

Reduced cell-mediated response
Reduced antibody immune response
Increased incidence of plasma cell dyscrasias
Increased IgA and IgG levels
Increased antibodies

III. LOCOMOTOR FUNCTION

Joints can be regarded as an organ system, both in the study of joint biology and in the assessment of functional status. Components like range of motion, muscle strength, or dexterity give insufficient information on how a limb functions for the individual. Even a standardized assessment of activities of daily living may not reflect the demands of the individual.

Range of motion decreases with age. This fact is important to consider in the clinical situation when one is trying to retain normal function in the joint afflicted by a rheumatic condition. The individual variation is considerable, however. Thus, in the assessment of normal functions in the individual patient, it is more important to compare with the contralateral side than with normality values.

Locomotor function is closely linked to concepts of global health and quality of life. It has a wide range depending on the demands, which can only be set by the individual. It is apparent that these demands will vary greatly with age and the individual's social situation. With the growing number of elderly people, it is becoming increasingly important not only to treat but also to prevent locomotor dysfunction to maintain quality of life of the individual. Another important objective is to save money for society by keeping the elderly person mobile and self-supported. [*See* MOTOR CONTROL.]

IV. PAIN

Pain is the most common symptom bringing patients with diseases of the locomotor system to seek medical advice. The clinician uses patients' pain as important guidance for therapeutic interventions. In old people, however, pain may be misinterpreted because of concomitant depression.

Cutaneous pain thresholds in healthy volunteers gradually increase up to 25 years of age, followed by a plateau up to 75. After 75, the threshold increases, with a widening range of threshold values observed at ages over 80. Increased pain threshold values have been observed in patients with arthritis. Sedatives, hypnotics, and antihistamines, but not analgesics produce an elevation in threshold values. [*See* PAIN AND PRESBYALGOS.]

V. EPIDEMIOLOGY

The prevalence of chronic disorders will increase with age unless they are associated with an increased mortality, like rheumatoid arthritis (RA) and the systemic rheumatic disorders. The incidence of some musculoskeletal disorders increases with age and is even typical of the higher age groups (eg., OA, the crystal arthropathies, polymyalgia arteritica, and osteoporosis).

In one study of 70–79-year-olds, around half of the women and 30% of the men reported current joint and/or back complaints. Musculoskeletal complaints tended to decrease with age in women and were more constant with age after 70 in men. The majority of current complaints in 79-year-olds were localized to the knee joints (17%), followed by the shoulder (16%) and hip (12%) joints. Few reported complaints of finger joints. No complaints were reported by over half of the persons with restricted range of motion, and restricted range of motion was only associated with functional disability in hip and knee joints. One-third used walking aids, one-third needed handicap transport, and one-third needed assistance with housekeeping. [See EPIDEMIOLOGY.]

VI. HEALTH CARE

Both geriatric and rheumatological care vary among and within countries, due not only to different traditions, but also to different density of geriatricians and rheumatologists. Geriatric care is sometimes coordinated with primary care, and rheumatology can establish collaboration on a regular consultant basis with the aim of preventing the development of unnecessary disabilities due to musculoskeletal disorders in the elderly. In this way, geriatric rheumatology can emerge for the elderly just as pediatric rheumatology has already evolved in close collaboration with pediatric care.

The spectrum of rheumatic disorders in the elderly is different at different levels of health care. A study of regional health care in Sweden showed that the number of patients over 65 years of age per age-specific group was lower than in younger age groups among both out- and inpatients in the rheumatology departments. In the departments of internal medicine at the local hospital level, patients over 65 were more

frequent than patients below that age. Men were seen less after retirement age in primary care for rheumatic disorders, mainly due to fewer consultations for back disorders. Women had an increased number of consultations in primary care after 65 years of age, mainly due to OA and soft tissue rheumatism.

In a nursing home, the prevalence of joint problems was 78%, and around 50% of the patients reported symptomatic joint complaints affecting mobility (Table V). However, joint diseases were only recorded as the main diagnosis in 6% and as contributing to hospitalization in 26% of the patients. It is interesting to note that joint diseases caused dysfunction that was unrecognized by the staff in 19% of the patients.

This set of data reflects the low priority of rheumatic disorders in the care of the elderly. It also indicates that discussions on priority in the care of the elderly will be difficult in the coming years. Unless rheumatology can make an impact by showing a positive outcome with improved management of rheumatic disorders in the elderly, these aspects of health will continue to be neglected.

VII. THERAPY

By and large the same drugs are used for the rheumatic diseases at all ages. Drug treatment in the elderly entails some particular problems. One is that polypharmacy is common and interaction between drugs is thus an important issue. The slower metabolism of drugs may require lower dosages in the elderly. This is particularly important since the risk of side ef-

Table V Musculoskeletal Disorders in Nursing Home Patients

Feature	%
Joint disease	78
affecting mobility	52
symptomatic	52
Hip fractures	15
Hip replacement for osteoarthritis	5
Joint disease as the main diagnosis	6
contributing to hospitalization	26
affecting function	48
unrecognized dysfunction	19

fects increases (e.g., the risk of gastrointestinal side effects from nonsteroidal anti-inflammatory drugs [NSAIDs]). Over one-third of Swedish women over 85 were prescribed an NSAID during a 1-year period, mainly due to OA. Information to prescribers about such misuse of drugs in the elderly is thus important.

Two other kinds of drugs are of special interest in the elderly. One is glucocorticoids, particularly in the treatment of giant cell arteritis. It has recently been shown that low-dose prednisolone (<7.5 mg/day) in long-term use does not affect the bone mass in women with this disease, in contrast to what has been feared. The other important drug problem is the overuse of allopurinol in elderly persons with moderate hyperuricemia, particularly in patients on thiazide diuretics. They very rarely develop gout or any other symptom from their uric acid level. They are often poorly informed about the reason why they are supposed to take this drug and thus take it irregularly and sometimes as a painkiller. [*See* PHARMACOLOGY.]

VIII. DISEASES

Late manifestations of diseases like complications of some chronic inflammatory disorders are more frequent in the elderly (e.g., amyloidosis, vasculitis, and Sjögren's syndrome). The onset of inflammatory rheumatic diseases may differ in the elderly (e.g., in RA and systemic lupus erythematosus [SLE]), but this has so far attracted little attention in clinical practice. Furthermore, concomitant disorders are prevalent in the elderly and may render both the diagnosis and the therapy more complicated than in younger patients.

A. Rheumatoid Arthritis

RA in the adult has a peak onset between 35 and 55 years of age but there are now reports that the peak age has increased, which may imply a change in the expression of this disease. There are also indications of a different sex ratio between the young and the elderly. Before 60 years of age there is a great female dominance, but over 60 the ratio is reduced to about 2 : 1 (females : males).

The course of late-onset RA may be extremely severe, with rapidly deteriorating cartilage as well as many other characteristics of a general disease. However, in larger patient series subsets with a better prog-

nosis than in earlier onset have been identified, the majority of whom go into remission. A more acute onset in the elderly than in the younger age group has also been reported. A "polymyalgia-like" onset of RA in the elderly has been debated and may be due to frequent symptoms of myopathy. A special differential diagnosis, besides polymyalgia, in the elderly is arthritides secondary to malignancy. [*See* ARTHRITIS.]

B. Systemic Lupus Erythematosus

The peak onset of SLE is 15–25 years (e.g., earlier than for RA), and the mean age of diagnosis is around 30 years. The vast majority of patients are women, although the sex ratio is more equal in patients with onset of SLE at postmenopausal age.

The disease manifestations are as varied in the elderly as in younger adults, and the onset may even be more easily mistaken for other diseases in the elderly than in the young. In a series of 361 SLE patients, lymphopenia was found more frequently with increasing age, whereas rash, proteinuria, and hypocomplementemia were found less frequently. Age associations were found for the prevalence of 16 of 24 clinical features, including arthritis, serositis, psychosis, nephrotic proteinuria, renal failure, hemolytic anemia, and leukopenia. The overall prognosis did not seem to change with age of onset.

Because of the dominance of early-onset SLE, this disease tends to be forgotten in the elderly. A report from England of 19 patients with onset over the age of 60 showed a frequent insidious onset with different patterns of organ involvement compared to younger age groups. Pulmonary disease was more prominent, and the patients had an increased incidence of Sjögren's syndrome compared with early-onset patients. Symptoms of myositis may in this age group be mistaken for polymyalgia.

C. Ankylosing Spondylitis

In the elderly the disease is rarely active. Late complications of aortitis, amyloidosis, and osteoporosis are not frequent.

D. Crystal Arthropathies

The occurrence of primary gout closely follows the levels of serum uric acid in the population, which are

Table VI Causes of Hyperuricemia

	Increased synthesis	Reduced excretion
Primary	Idiopathic Enzymatic defects	Idiopathic Tubular defects
Secondary	Myelo- and lymphoproliferative Disseminated carcinoma Chronic hemolytic anemia Damages of renal tubules Psoriasis Drug induced (e.g., cytostatics, diuretics)	Renal insufficiency Lead poisoning

Table VII Treatment of Gout[a]

Inflammation and pain
  NSAIDs in high dosage
Prevention of attacks
  NSAIDs in low dose following an attack
  Allopurinol or uricosuric drugs to reduce the concentration of
    uric acid in the chronic case
  Allopurinol prior to high-dose cytostatic regimens
  Treatment of secondary causes of hyperuricemia

[a]NSAIDs, nonsteroidal anti-inflammatory drugs.

highly age dependent. A gouty attack in an adolescent male or a premenopausal female would thus probaby be either an enzymatic defect or secondary to a severe condition. The introduction of allopurinol has radically changed the therapy and prognosis for patients with gout. Regardless of the cause (Table VI), allopurinal is the drug of choice. However, a problem is the rather too frequent prescription of this drug (Table VII).

Pyrophosphate arthropathy is rare before the age of 60 but is the most frequent cause of acute arthritis in the elderly. It is clearly associated with aging of the articular cartilage, although so far the nature of this association has not been clarified. It is important to recognize the more chronic and sometimes polyarticular forms, which may be misinterpreted as RA or OA. In some elderly patients it may be part of hyperparathyroidism, and it seems to be more fre-

quent in elderly persons bedridden by some acute illness. After an operation, mild fever, pain, and swelling of the knee and leg may easily be misinterpreted as thrombosis.

Pyrophosphate arthropathy occurs in different forms (Table VIII) (e.g., in the rare instances of familial pyrophosphate arthropathy). Another rather rare cause of "pseudogout" is hemochromatosis. However, the majority of individuals with pyrophosphate calcifications in articular cartilage or menisci will never experience any symptoms of arthritis. Other calcium phosphate crystal deposits in cartilage (e.g., apatite) are also associated with aging and with the degenerative joint diseases.

E. Vasculitis

Many forms of vasculitis are age-related (Table IX). The most common is giant cell arteritis or polymyalgia

Table VIII Characteristics of Pyrophosphate Arthropathy

Type	Age at Onset	Sex	Occurrence	Joints No.	Joints Site	Prognosis	Differential diagnosis
Acute	>65	o ≥ °	Common	One	Large	Good	Gout, sepsis thrombosis
Chronic	≥65	o ≤ °	Common	One or few	Large	Good	Osteoarthritis, rheumatoid arthritis
Familial	20–40	o − °	Rare	Few to many	Large & small, spine	Poor	Rheumatoid arthritis, osteoarthritis, ankylosing spondylitis, reactive arthritis
Destructive	≥65	o < °	Rare	One	Large	Poor	Osteoarthritis, neuropathic arthropathy, avascular necrosis
Asymptomatic calcifications	≥65	o = °	Common	One or few	Knee menisci & cartilage	Good	Apatite arthropathy

Table IX Classification of Osteoarthritis

Primary
  A. Localized
  B. Generalized
Secondary
  A. Trauma
  B. Congenital diseases (e.g., hip dysplasia)
  C. Other joint diseases (e.g., rheumatoid arthritis, septic arthritis)
  D. Endocrine (e.g., acromegaly)
  E. Neuropathic (e.g., Charcot joints)
  F. Environmental (e.g., Kashin-Becky disease, caisson disease)

Table X Age at Onset in Systemic Vasculitis

Age at onset	Vasculitis	Male/Female
20–40	Takayashu's syndrome	1/9
50–60	Wegener's granulomatosis	3/1
	Periarteritis nodosa	2.5/1
	Lymphomatoid granulomatosis	
	Churg-Strauss' angiitis	1.3/1
60–70	Cryoglobulinemia	1/2
>70	Giant cell arteritis	1/2
All age groups	Hypersensitivity angiitis	
	Serum sickness	
	Vasculitis associated with infection, tumor, or rheumatic diseases	

rheumatica or arteritica, all dependent on the most common symptoms. It is now believed that people with symptoms of polymyalgia also have giant cell arteritis, and a few of them certainly develop blindness.

Polymyalgia symptoms often develop rather acutely and are localized to proximal large muscles. Morning stiffness is typical. In contrast to patients with fibromyalgia, polymyalgia patients have no typical pain on palpation of trigger points but a general soreness. The erythrocyte sedimentation rate and the levels of acute phase reactants (e.g., C-reactive protein), are usually high but both may be normal. Temporal artery biopsy may also fail, particularly due to the segmental distribution of changes. Plasma viscosity may prove to be a test of choice to follow patients, but so far there is no diagnostic laboratory test. A rapid and rather dramatic response to 10–15-mg prednisolone is strongly suggestive of polymyalgia and is sometimes used to confirm the diagnosis. In patients with clinical signs and symptoms of temporal arteritis, indications for higher doses of prednisolone are evident, but different schedules are applied for those with polymyalgia only. It is not unusual to start these patients also on rather high doses, 30–40 mg/day, and reduce the dose during 2 weeks to 5–7.5 mg/day and maintain this dose for many months.

F. Osteoarthritis

Degenerative changes of articular cartilage are already found from the second decade and by the age of 40, 90% of all persons have such changes in their weight-bearing joints. Radiographic OA increases rapidly from the age of 50 until 70–75 years of age but seems to be rather constant thereafter. These findings are contradictory to the steep increase of OA at ages below 70 reported earlier. No increased mortality from OA was found to explain this finding, and cohort differences were not observed.

The association between symptoms and radiographic or macroscopic signs of OA is weaker than expected. This is particularly the case with Heberden's nodes, where few patients of high age have complaints despite the very high prevalence of radiographic changes in the population. In the oldest groups the prevalence of joint complaints seems to decrease, which may have many other explanations than a decreased prevalence of the joint diseases.

The cause is unknown (primary) in the majority of patients with OA (Table X). A few families are now known with inborn errors of cartilage matrix metabolism, and an understanding of differences between aging and OA processes is emerging (Table XI).

Table XI Prevention of Osteoporosis

Adequate calcium intake
Outdoors in daylight × 2–3/week
Regular physical activity
Stop smoking
Avoid large alcohol intake

G. Osteoporosis

There seems to be an inverse correlation between OA and osteoporosis (i.e., those with low bone density do not suffer from OA). The reason for this is unknown but the lively, thin elderly woman bent by her vertebral fractures and maybe with a walking stick after her hip fracture but with no other joint complaints is almost an archetype. Fractures due to osteoporosis are a common threat to the ability of elderly women to live a normal life and are costly to society. It is apparent that hormonal factors are very important, and adequate estrogen intervention has even been suggested for postmenopausal women concerned about osteoporosis. A number of other risk factors than hormonal have been identified and should be avoided (Table XI). With modern techniques for bone density measurements, it has been shown that regular exercise in the elderly can improve the bone density.

BIBLIOGRAPHY

Brooks, P. M. (Ed.). (1992). *Slow-acting antirheumatic drugs and immunosuppressives. Balliere's Clinical Rheumatology. Vol 4 (No 3)*. Philadelphia. Balliere Tindall.

Gardner, D. L. (1992). *Pathological basis of the connective tissue disorders*. London: Edward Arnold.

Lane, N. E. (Ed.). (1994). *Osteoporosis. Rheumatic diseases of North America* (Vol 20, No 3). Philadelphia: W.B. Saunders Co.

McCarty, D., Jr. (Ed.). (1993). *Arthritis and allied conditions*. Philadelphia: Lea & Febiger.

Svanborg, A. (1988). Practical and functional consequences of aging. *Gerontology, 34* (suppl. 1), 11–15.

S

Self-Esteem

Roseann Giarrusso and Vern L. Bengtson

University of Southern California

I. Does Self-Esteem Change across the Life Course?
II. Theoretical Approaches to Self-Esteem and Aging
III. Methodological Issues in Studying Self-Esteem and Aging
IV. Empirical Studies of Self-Esteem and Aging
V. Future Directions

Cohort   Individuals born in the same time period: either the same year or the same decade.

Cohort-Sequential   A design in which individuals from more than one birth cohort are studied at more than one time point. This design allows for a separation of the effects of aging, cohort membership, and social and cultural events.

Cross-Sectional   A design in which a group of individuals is studied at only one time point. Age effects are assumed when age differences are found between individuals in the group. However, age and cohort effects are confounded in this study design.

Longitudinal   A design in which a group of individuals is studied at more than one time point. Age effects are assumed when the same individuals demonstrate change from one time of measurement to another. However, if this study design is used with a single cohort then age is confounded with time of measurement.

Repeated Cross-Sectional   A design in which different groups of individuals from the same birth cohort are studied at different times. Aging effects are assumed if differences are found between groups at different time points.

Role   Expectations regarding the rights and duties of an individual holding a certain status position in society.

SELF-ESTEEM is the positive or negative evaluation an individual makes regarding the "self" as an object. William James counterposed the terms the *I* and the *me* to describe the ability of the self to act simultaneously as both subject and object. The phenomenological self, I, is capable of thinking about the object self, me. High self-esteem results when the evaluation is positive; low self-esteem when the evaluation is negative.

To place self-esteem in a broader context—it is the evaluative component of the self-concept. The self-concept refers to the *totality* of one's attitudes toward the self as an object. Like other attitudes, the self-concept is made up of three parts. In addition to the evaluative component, it also contains cognitive and conative components.

The cognitive component of the self-concept refers to the way individuals identify themselves in terms of the roles they play or the characteristics that describe them. The evaluative component of the self-concept reflects the extent to which individuals like or dislike this self-defined identity. The conative component refers to individuals' motivations to maintain or change themselves as a result of discrepancies between their real selves and their ideal selves.

The majority of the empirical work on the self-concept is on self-esteem. The least researched aspect of the self-concept is the conative component.

I. DOES SELF-ESTEEM CHANGE ACROSS THE LIFE COURSE?

Of concern to gerontologists is the extent to which self-esteem remains stable across the life course. That is, does self-esteem change with aging? Or is it determined by the time an individual reaches adulthood? Does the aging process have a negative impact on self-esteem? If self-esteem does change over the life course, is the pattern linear or curvilinear?

The question of whether self-esteem changes over the life course should be considered within the larger ongoing debate in gerontology as to whether personality changes with aging. The extent to which personality changes or remains stable is a long-standing question in the social psychology of aging. It is instructive to consider self-esteem and aging within this context because many of the methodological and theoretical issues with regard to stability are the same.

Until the 1970s, most social scientists believed that by the age of 30 personality was set and did not change. Traditional personality trait theory was widely accepted. However, in the 1970s the life span developmental approach challenged this notion by showing that there were age differences in personality across stages of adulthood. At the same time, leading personality theorists such as Walter Mischel began to criticize the notion of traits, pointing out the importance of the situation in predicting behavior. The movement away from personality traits was also furthered by the growing popularity of B. F. Skinner's theory of behaviorism and its emphasis on the environment.

The stability versus change debate grew even more heated in the 1980s when ardent supporters of a contemporary version of personality trait theory waged a backlash movement. Previous versions of this theory had been set back by methodological and conceptual problems that made it difficult to draw firm conclusions. However, armed with data from longitudinal studies and a redefinition of traits, this new contingent was able to demonstrate stability on a number of dimensions of personality across a substantial part of the life course.

Four different longitudinal studies using different methods found little evidence of age-related changes in personality during the adult years. The pattern of continuity discovered suggested a five-factor (NEO-AC) model of personality known as the "Big Five" which includes: neuroticism, extraversion, openness to experience, agreeableness, and conscientiousness. Although these studies used pencil-and-paper measures of personality, suggesting that their findings might simply reflect the stability of individuals' per-

ceptions of their personality, other research using ratings by multiple observers over time also found consistency in five traits similar to the Big Five. [*See* PERSONALITY.]

Like the debate regarding personality and aging, resolving the question of self-esteem and aging may also have to wait for longitudinal studies. Although longitudinal studies did not end the controversy regarding the stability of personality across the life course, these studies did serve to narrow and focus the debate.

The purpose of this article is to outline questions relevant to examining stability and change in self-esteem across the life course. First, what theories are helpful in guiding research on self-esteem across the life course? Second, what are the methodological challenges in examining self-esteem across time? Third, what empirical evidence exists? Does it answer questions regarding stability or change in self-esteem? Fourth, what directions should future research take?

II. THEORETICAL APPROACHES TO SELF-ESTEEM AND AGING

The question of whether self-esteem changes with aging can be approached from a variety of theoretical perspectives. These perspectives do not provide a clear set of propositions to be tested; rather, they suggest whether and when self-esteem would be expected to change, and if so, the direction of that change over the life course. The theoretical approaches include (a) personality trait psychology, (b) life span developmental psychology, (c) role theory, and (d) contextual models.

A. Personality Trait Theories

Personality traits were traditionally defined as the tendency of individuals to behave consistently across situations. Traits could only be measured with projective tests or observations of *behavior* by trained observers. However, contemporary definitions of personality traits were broadened to include cross-situational consistencies in individuals' *thoughts and feelings* as well. Consequently, researchers were able to obtain reliable measures of traits with surveys and questionnaires in studies with large samples and longitudinal designs.

Thus, contemporary personality theorists most commonly measure traits by making inferences from respondent's self-reports on a number of scaled survey items. Consequently, the methods used to measure personality became the same as those used to measure self-concept. This enabled the research on personality to be integrated with the research on the self-concept.

Although self-esteem refers to the affective or evaluative component of the self-concept, personality represents the cognitive component. Despite this important distinction, many researchers view self-esteem as a personality trait. Because personality traits are assumed to be stable, at least once the individual reaches adulthood, trait theorists would predict that self-esteem would remain stable across the life course.

B. Life Span Developmental Theories

Developmental life span psychology grew out of the work of Freud, Erikson, and Piaget. These theories share the notion that development, due to its biological basis, is universal and occurs in a sequence of stages generally corresponding to age.

Erikson's eight-stage theory was the first to include adult stages of development. During the sixth stage, "intimacy versus isolation," individuals are involved in mate selection, family formation, and career development. Once resolved, individuals move on to the seventh stage, "generativity versus stagnation," a time when individuals are concerned with productivity, creativity, and guiding the younger generation. During the last stage, "ego integrity versus despair," individuals become less concerned with achievement and more accepting of their life as meaningful.

More recent life span developmental theorists suggest a similar sequence of development. Early and middle adulthood are dominated by a concern with the self, power, accomplishments, and control. Conversely, late adulthood is characterized by a reduction in ego concerns and an increase in self-acceptance. Theories of the stages of adult development suggest that aging is associated with a growing acceptance of self and others.

The life span developmental perspective implies that aging, rather than being merely problematic, is also a positive process. Individuals potentially progress from high levels of ego involvement and self-serving activities in early and middle stages of life to high levels of altruism and interiority in late life. These types of developmental changes lead to a less critical evaluation of self. Thus, based on this perspective, one would predict that self-esteem would progressively increase over the life course. [See LIFE SPAN THEORY; THEORIES OF AGING: PSYCHOLOGICAL.]

C. Role Theories

Sociologists are critical of theories of life span development for ignoring the contribution of social structure to stability and change across the life course. From a sociological perspective, age-related roles are more important than chronological age for a variety of behaviors and attitudes, including self-esteem.

Roles serve as the link between the individual and society. According to role theory, individuals develop a sense of who they are through interaction with others in the variety of roles they play. Because role relationships are relatively enduring and organized, roles can be a source of stability in self-identity. And because roles are closely connected to the norms and values of society, having roles not only integrates the individual with society, it makes life meaningful.

Throughout the different stages of life, individuals are engaged in the process of role acquisition, role transition, and role loss. Age can influence, if not determine, role access and egress. During early and middle adulthood, individuals acquire and transition into many new roles, such as occupational, marital, and parental roles. Involvement in multiple roles provides the individual with many opportunities for social rewards and feelings of competence and achievement. Involvement in social roles results in high levels of self-esteem during these stages in the life cycle. However, during late adulthood individuals experience role loss, such as retirement, widowhood, empty nest, and declining health. Consequently, individuals are less integrated with society and have fewer opportunities for social rewards and feelings of competence and achievement. Lack of involvement in social roles would be predicted to lead to low self-esteem toward the end of the life cycle.

This is the same prediction that would be made by activity theory. Activity theory is one application of role theory to the elderly. According to activity theory, social interaction is important for the maintenance of self-esteem. Because the elderly lack formal roles and statuses within the main institutions of society, it makes it difficult for them to maintain a positive self-evaluation. Continuity theory, another offshoot of role theory used in gerontology, makes a slightly different prediction. It suggests that a reduction in role activity does not lead to a decrease in self-esteem as long as the individual maintains some continuity between past roles and current interests and behaviors.

From the role perspective, there are two additional reasons why self-esteem would be expected to decline with increasing age. First, the youth-oriented culture in which people live has promoted the development of negative stereotypes of the old. To the extent to which older adults believe and accept these negative expectations, they are cast in unattractive roles. This in turn leads to lower self-esteem. Second, rapid technological advances and social change sometimes make it difficult for older adults to keep pace with society. [See THEORIES OF AGING: SOCIAL.]

D. Life-Course and Other Contextual Perspectives

Proponents of contextual models argue that any analysis of individuals must take into account the sociocultural and historical context in which the individuals live. Macroevents, such as the Great Depression, major wars, and various social and political movements, interact with the micro age-graded role transitions of individuals from different birth cohorts. Different birth cohorts presented with the same events may experience those events in different ways. For example, individuals of draft age during the Vietnam War may have experienced the role transitions of graduation, occupational attainment, marriage, and parenthood differently than individuals who were a decade younger. Both birth cohorts lived during the same historical period yet the effect of the historical period on the major role transitions of members of each cohort was very different.

This interaction between person and situation can have long-lasting effects and can result in different life-course trajectories. This would require studies that compare different birth cohorts across long periods of time in order to separate the age, period, and cohort effects.

The importance of this perspective for the study of self-esteem is that it suggests that the level of self-esteem for individuals from a particular birth cohort may, due to sociocultural or historical events, start out lower or higher than other birth cohorts. These events may maintain their influence on the level of self-esteem across the life course and act as a source of stability in self-esteem. For example, individuals born during the Great Depression may have lower self-esteem than individuals who were born after, and this suppression effect on self-esteem may evidence itself across the life course of this cohort. On the other hand, depending on the stage of life during which the macroevent occurs, and whether additional events occur at later stages of life, the events could be a major source of change in self-esteem. The direction of the change on self-esteem, either positive or negative, would depend on the event and how it interacted with the age-graded role transitions that were experienced. [See COHORT STUDIES.]

III. METHODOLOGICAL ISSUES IN STUDYING SELF-ESTEEM AND AGING

Four methodological issues present challenges to those wishing to study stability and change in self-esteem across the life course. These issues are the same as those confronted by researchers interested in life span personality. They include problems of (a) definition and measurement, (b) research design, (c) statistical analysis and data interpretation, and (d) population sampling.

A. Definition and Measurement of Self-Esteem

Because the majority of the literature on self-concept deals with self-esteem, the terms are often (incorrectly) used interchangeably, leading to a lack of conceptual precision. Similarly, researchers also refer to self-esteem by a variety of other terms such as self-regard, self-respect, and self-confidence. Without clear definitions, measures cannot adequately represent the constructs under study.

Many studies develop their own unique measure of self-esteem rather than use standard scales. Not only do researchers fail to use the same instruments, they rarely examine the validity or reliability of these one-shot measures. The practice of using different measures generally produces different information about stability and change in self-esteem across the life course, making it difficult to draw conclusions.

Several standard scales are available to measure self-esteem, the most popular among them being the Total Positive Scale from the Tennessee Self Concept Scale, the Rosenberg Self-Esteem Scale, and the Monge Semantic Differential Scale. The problem with these scales for age-based analyses is that their validity and reliability, although established on young age groups, has rarely been calculated for older age groups. Without these statistics and evidence of factorial invariance across age groups, intercorrelations between self-esteem and age are difficult to interpret. Low intercorrelations may mean there is no relationship between age and self-esteem, or alternatively, that the scales are inappropriate for use with older age groups.

B. Issues of Research Design

The fundamental problem with cross-sectional studies of self-esteem is that maturation and birth cohort effects are confounded. Thus, it is impossible to determine if age differences in self-esteem actually represent changes in self-esteem over time or whether they represent cohort differences. In longitudinal designs the same individuals are studied over a period of time, thereby controlling for intercohort differences.

Although longitudinal studies of self-esteem would be a substantial improvement over cross-sectional studies, several issues still need to be considered. The few existing longitudinal studies of self-esteem have focused on younger age groups to the exclusion of older age groups. Furthermore, these longitudinal studies followed their respondents for relatively short periods of time. To adequately study the effects of aging on self-esteem, mature adults should be included for study, and individuals should ideally be followed across several stages of the life course.

However, even longitudinal designs that span several life stages cannot rule out all alternative explanations. In longitudinal studies of single cohorts, age changes would be confounded with the effects of time of measurement. Furthermore, the unique historical experience of the birth cohort under study (described more fully above in the section on contextual analysis) and the possibility of selective attrition could also make the interpretation of aging effects in self-esteem ambiguous.

No design can provide completely unambiguous results regarding the stability of self-esteem across the life course because aging, time of measurement, and birth cohort will always be confounded in any design that is used. However, the optimal method for studying self-esteem and aging would be to use a cohort-sequential design. In a cohort-sequential design, more than one birth cohort would be followed over the same developmental time span but different historical time spans, in order to separate out the effects of aging, cohort membership, and social and cultural events on self-esteem. Currently, there are no published cohort-sequential studies of self-esteem.

C. Issues in Statistical Analysis

There are four ways to assess stability or change in self-esteem: (a) structural invariance, (b) correlational stability, (c) mean level stability, and (d) ipsative stability.

Before other types of stability in self-esteem are assessed, it is necessary to establish that there is structural invariance. Structural invariance refers to the stability in the structure, organization, or dimensionality of self-esteem, typically assessed through factor analysis or cluster analysis. Structural invariance is established when the measure of self-esteem displays the same dimensions and relationships among component elements over time and/or across birth cohorts.

Correlation, the most frequently used method for calculating stability, is a measure of constancy or change in an individual's rank order position on self-esteem over time. Pearsonian, Spearman, or Kendall correlation coefficients are computed between measures of self-esteem at different time points for the same group of individuals. These statistics indicate the extent to which individuals retain their position on self-esteem relative to others from one time of measurement to another.

However, there is no set standard for evaluating whether the level of the coefficients obtained actually represents stability. Consequently, a correlation coefficient of .50 may be interpreted by some as an indication of substantial stability in self-esteem, whereas others may interpret it as an indication of substantial change.

Mean level stability is the constancy or change in the group level of self-esteem over time. In longitudinal designs, mean scores on self-esteem are compared for the same group of individuals between different time points. Attention is paid to increases or decreases over time in both group mean scores and group variances. No change on group mean scores would indicate stability only if there was also no change in group variances. If there were no change in group mean scores but the variance increased, this would indicate increased individual differences in self-esteem. Change in mean level stability can also be assessed using a repeated cross-sectional design. Aging effects for self-esteem are examined by comparing group means on self-esteem for the same cohorts at different times.

As with correlational stability, there is no agreed upon standard for deciding whether a statistically significant change in mean level scores is actually substantively significant. That is why a measure of effect size that is independent of sample size should also accompany analyses of mean level or normative stability.

Ipsative stability, a measure of intraindividual continuity in self-esteem, is the least frequently investigated. Based on profile analysis, it provides information as to whether an individual's attributes change their relative position over time.

Depending on the method used to assess stability, the results are likely to be different. Stability using one method does not imply stability using another method. Each method provides different information and likely leads to different conclusions regarding stability or change in self-esteem across the life course. Ideally, studies should report results using all the methods and try to explain any inconsistencies that are found.

D. Issues of Population Sampling

Substantial heterogeneity exists within the populations sampled for studies of self-esteem. Although respondents vary in sociodemographic characteristics, health, and birth-cohort membership, and so on, the extent to which these factors contribute to stability or change in self-esteem over the life course is rarely considered. Furthermore, cross-sectional studies that examine age differences in self-esteem do not represent the full spectrum of adulthood among their respondents. For example, some studies compare young adulthood to middle adulthood, whereas others compare the old to the oldest old. Longitudinal studies have not followed individuals for long periods of time. Without the inclusion of respondents from all age groups or the examination of the same individuals across a large number of life stages, studies can lead to incomplete findings regarding the pattern of stability and change in self-esteem across the life course.

IV. EMPIRICAL STUDIES OF SELF-ESTEEM AND AGING

Over the last 40 years there have been literally thousands of studies published on self-esteem. Given the preponderance of research on this concept, it is surprising how few studies have examined the relationship between self-esteem and aging. There are only 33 studies that have investigated the effect of age on self-esteem. The majority of these studies used a cross-sectional design to look at age differences.

There are no longitudinal studies of stability or change in self-esteem across the life course. The few existing longitudinal studies of self-esteem have focused on younger age groups to the exclusion of older age groups, and have followed their respondents for relatively short periods of time. To date there is only one longitudinal study of mature adults that includes information on self-esteem across a 10-year period.

Of the 33 studies, 22 showed a positive relationship between age and self-esteem, 9 showed no age differences, 1 showed a negative relationship between age and self-esteem, and 1 showed a curvilinear relationship. In total, these studies suggest that self-esteem increases from early adolescence through the remainder of the life course. However, because the majority of the studies used a cross-sectional design in which age and cohort effects are confounded, no definitive conclusions can be drawn.

V. FUTURE DIRECTIONS

In the beginning of this chapter, it was suggested that it would be instructive to consider the question of stability and change in self-esteem within the debate on personality and aging. Several longitudinal studies of personality found continuity on five traits across the life course. However, other longitudinal studies have found evidence of change in other aspects of personality over the life course.

Researchers using longitudinal studies are coming

to accept that there are several possible sources of stability and change in personality. Those aspects of personality that are most likely to be stable are those that are genetically based. However, some social structural factors are so influential that they also can lead to stability in personality. Furthermore, role changes or life events such as divorce or death of a family member may lead to change that is long-lasting and hence promote stability. Finally, there may be some aspects of personality that are developmental and not the result of social structure or life events. An example of this is recent findings of increased interiority toward the end of life.

Thus, there is a growing trend among those interested in personality and aging to rely on what they term an *interactionist perspective*—a perspective that can accommodate both the person and the situation. Researchers are concluding that continuity and change can coexist. Some traits are stable and others respond to changing situations and roles.

Although the vast majority of the studies of self-esteem focus on global self-esteem, researchers have recently begun to recognize that self-esteem is multidimensional. The dimensions of self-esteem are hierarchically ranked based on their importance to the individual. Because self-esteem is multidimensional and hierarchically ranked, specific components of self-esteem may change over time in response to situational or role changes, whereas other components may remain stable.

The extent to which changes in any of these specific components affects global self-esteem is not known. Components that are central may affect global self-esteem, whereas changes in other less central components of self-esteem may have little impact on global self-esteem. Thus, like personality, self-esteem may incorporate both stability and change.

The main focus of this article has been on stability in levels of self-esteem across long periods of time. The objective was to find out whether aging influences the long-term stability of self-esteem. However, it may be equally important to know if aging influences the short-term stability of self-esteem. Recently, researchers have begun to examine individual differences in short-term stability in self-esteem as a dimension in its own right.

To measure instability, an innovative study had respondents wear a pager for days at a time in naturalistic settings. Whenever respondents were paged, they filled out a measure of self-esteem. It was found that the self-esteem of some individuals was stable while others was quite unstable. Short-term stability in self-esteem was found to be independent of the respondents' level of self-esteem. Furthermore, short-term stability was a better predictor of certain types of behaviors than was the respondent's level of self-esteem. Instability was related to anger and aggression, especially among high self-esteem individuals.

These types of studies provide important information about substantive and methodological directions for future research. First, future research should examine whether the aging process results in decreased day-to-day instability in self-esteem and how this relates to long-term stability or instability. Second, future research might be able to use the technique of having respondents fill out a measure of self-esteem upon being paged to better understand the situational and social conditions that influence both specific and global self-esteem across the life course. The paging technique could be used periodically with respondents in a longitudinal design that spanned long rather than short periods of time.

Self-esteem may fluctuate day to day or from situation to situation but still retain a stable core. The question for future research should not only be whether self-esteem is stable across the life course but also under what conditions it is stable and under what conditions does it change?

Little is known about the developmental, social structural, and contextual processes that influence stability and change in self-esteem across the life course. Future research should be directed at studying how the timing and sequencing of developmental maturation, role change, and life events influences self-esteem over time. In addition, research should be conducted on how the sociocultural and historical context affects the self-esteem of different birth cohorts.

As with the research on personality and aging, those interested in self-esteem and aging must await longitudinal studies. Ideally, the longitudinal studies will have a cohort-sequential design. An integrated approach combining aspects of all theoretical perspectives would allow for the most fully developed examination of self-esteem and aging.

It should be noted that due to space limitations a second issue of interest to gerontologists related to self-esteem and aging was not covered in this chapter: the extent to which successful aging is mediated through self-esteem. Researchers are beginning to find that self-esteem may be an important factor in such things as health behaviors, coping, and well-being.

BIBLIOGRAPHY

Bengtson, V. L., Reedy, M. N., & Gordon, C. (1985). Aging and self-conceptions: personality processes and social contexts. In J. E. Birren & K. W. Schaie (Eds.), *Handbook of the psychology of aging* (2nd ed.). New York: Van Nostrand Reinhold Co.

Demo, D. D. (1992). The self-concept over time: Research issues and directions. *Annual Review of Sociology, 18*, 303–326.

Gove, W. R., Ortega, S. T., & Style, C. B. (1989). The maturational and role perspectives on aging and self through the adult years: An empirical evaluation. *American Journal of Sociology, 94*, 1117–1145.

Field, D. (1991). Continuity and change in personality in old age—Evidence from five longitudinal studies: Introduction to a special issue. *Journal of Gerontology, 46*, P271–274.

Helson, R., & Wink, P. (1992). Personality change in women from the early 40s to the early 50s. *Psychology and Aging, 7*, 46–55.

Kernis, M. H. Grannemann, B. D., & Barclay, L. C. (1992). Stability of self-esteem: Assessment, correlates, and excuse making. *Journal of Personality, 60*, 621–644.

Kogan, N. (1990). Personality and Aging. In J. E. Birren & K. W. Schaie (Eds.), *Handbook of the psychology of aging* (2nd ed.) New York: Academic Press.

Markus, H. R., & Herzog, R. A. (1991). The role of the self-concept in aging. In K. W. Schaie & M. P. Lawton (Eds.), *Annual review of gerontology and geriatrics* (Vol. 11, pp. 110–143). New York: Springer.

Rosenberg, M., Schooler, C., Schoenbach, C., & Rosenberg, F. (1995). Global self-esteem and specific self-esteem: Different concepts, different outcomes. *American Sociological Review, 60*, 141–156.

Self-Regulation, Health, and Behavior

Susan Brownlee

Rutgers University

Elaine A. Leventhal

Robert Wood Johnson School of Medicine

Howard Leventhal

Rutgers University

I. Introduction
II. Questions from a Life Span View
III. Models for Intervention
IV. Conclusion

The belief that **BEHAVIOR** affects **HEALTH** provides a comforting sense of control over life and death. Evidence is minimal that the adoption of health-promotive and risk-avoiding behaviors will achieve such desired ends. Each behavior must be considered in terms of its impact on the biology of an array of diseases with vastly different developmental histories, in addition to its possible effects on the nondisease aging process. In addition, motivation to adopt new and eliminate ongoing behaviors will differ as a function of the perceived relationship of the behavior to the presumed health threat and the motivational structure of the individual at a specific point in the life span. These relationships are best understood within a **SELF-REGULATION** framework that makes room for age-related changes in motivation for health behavior over the life span. This approach makes clear that age is not a psychological variable and life span changes can best be understood by treating age as a moderator of the self-regulation process. [*See* LIFE SPAN THEORY.]

I. INTRODUCTION

Most, if not all, people believe that behavior has a major impact upon health. Adequate rest, a diet rich in fruits and vegetables, and exercise are seen to protect against disease and enhance health, whereas cigarette smoking, a high-fat diet, excessive alcohol consumption, and a stress-filled existence are perceived to cause illness. Although epidemiological data are supportive of some of these perceptions, most of the evidence is from studies that compared individuals engaging in a particular behavior with those not doing so. The data, therefore, are correlational and it is not known whether *interventions to change and enhance* health-promoting behaviors or to *change and reduce* risk-inducing behaviors will improve health. Were we to proceed by summarizing the literature for each of the health and risk behaviors mentioned, our article would be replete with details and endless qualifications. Even for quitting cigarette smoking and engaging in exercise, two behaviors where experimental and quasi-experimental data show positive health effects, one may need to qualify the benefits as a function of the time of life at which the behavioral changes take place and the specific benefit that can be expected. In addition, such a summary would not address a major concern of the gerontologist, which is to identify the special issues that emerge when examining the effects of behavior on health from a life span perspective. As we believe this concern is critical for understanding when and how behavioral factors might affect health, the remainder of the article will elaborate upon a number of themes that emerge when one looks at the relationship of health to behavior from a self-regulation model framed within a life span perspective.

II. QUESTIONS FROM A LIFE SPAN VIEW

Although the issues are vast and underinvestigated, the following questions will help to clarify them. The biological issues are as follows:

1. Will behavioral change affect the disease process?
2. For each of the many possible behaviors that may be identified as health-promoting and/or disease-generating, what specific diseases do they affect?
3. At what point in the developmental history of the individual and the disease are these effects most visible?
4. Does the behavior affect susceptibility to disease (senility) or does it affect the basic, aging process (senescence)?
5. Can one identify the individual-difference factors that moderate these processes (e.g., gender, genetic susceptibilities?).

The social psychological issues are as follows:

1. How is the behavior represented? Is it perceived to be a cause of disease or a way of avoiding disease? For what disease(s) are these threats and/or benefits perceived?
2. What are the perceived costs and barriers to performing the behavior, and is it seen as within the competence and/or resources of the individual and his or her support network?
3. Are there life span changes in the perceived effectiveness of the behavior or the perceived barriers to its adoption? Are these changes specific to the behavior or part of more general views of aging, health, and the availability of resources (personal and social) for the prevention and treatment of disease and the enhancement of quality of life?

Although we touch on items 2 and 3 of the biological set, this article will focus primarily on the social psychological issues.

A. Selecting an Appropriate Outcome

Both social and biological changes associated with the life course produce an increasingly differentiated elderly population. Although it is not always possible to distinguish between aging-related changes due to senility (the impact of physical and mental disease) from those caused by senescence (the normal process of aging), the distinction does direct attention to the wide range of criteria that may be considered as outcomes of health and risk behaviors. For example, smoking and excessive alcohol use can lead to diseases such as lung cancer and cirrhosis of the liver, and they also appear to speed the aging of musculoskeletal and pulmonary tissue. The evaluation of health benefits from changes in these and other such behaviors may require, therefore, multiple and partially overlapping criteria. For example, is it reasonable to expect aerobic exercise programs to increase longevity and to reduce coronary disease, or only the latter? And are exercise programs useless if they increase feelings of vigor and involvement in social and other everyday activities, but fail to affect "hard end points" such as longevity and coronary disease?

In short, researchers must assess a broad range of physical, psychological, and social criteria to determine the effects of each of many behavioral factors. But the selection of measures should be rational and theory-driven (i.e., there should be plausible biological and psychological arguments underlying each choice). One may need different criteria to assess the effects of the very same intervention (e.g., exercise, low-fat diets, smoking cessation) for participants of different ages. For 20-year-olds, these may be lipid values and body mass indices; mortality would be added for those over 65. Assessment should not proceed in a shotgun manner. In an ideal world, multiple interventions would be available to enhance a broad range of health behaviors and eliminate risky ones, resulting in a modest increase in longevity associated with a greatly reduced period of senility prior to death, a further "squaring of the curve."

B. Selecting a Time and an Approach for Intervention

Biological and social psychological factors set the optimal window for behavioral interventions, and that which is optimal will vary with the behavior and the physiological system targeted for change. For example, atherosclerotic changes likely begin during adolescence and possibly earlier. Thus, dietary interventions for reduction of risk to this biological system may be best achieved by the careful shaping of tastes and eating habits early in life. Life-protecting interventions by means of cholesterol-reducing drugs, on the other hand, are recommended for young adults suffering from familial hypercholesteremia and middle-aged adults with elevated lipids. Cholesterol reduction is far less likely to be life-protective in men and women 80 years and older who show few signs of cardiovascular disease. By contrast, smoking cessation makes good sense at most anytime in life. Although cessation may prove less effective at restoring pulmonary function and reducing risk of lung disease and cancer for over 65-year-olds who have a 30–50-year history of heavy cigarette consumption, cessation will reduce the risk of coronary episodes. Thus, each biological system and each of the many diseases of that system have a developmental history that determines the optimal behavior and time for interventions to reduce health risks for specifiable outcome criteria. [*See* CARDIOVASCULAR SYSTEM; DIET AND NUTRITION.]

Social psychological factors also play a major role in the adoption of healthy behaviors and the elimination of risky ones. First, social psychological factors can act as facilitators or barriers to change. For example, although vigorous walking may be heart healthy, it may be difficult and even dangerous for an older person if s/he is crippled with arthritis or lives in a neighborhood that is no longer safe. Substantial differences may obtain among older persons with regard to the financial and social resources needed to make critical changes in health-related behaviors. Second, stereotypic views of aging can be barriers to change. Perceiving problems as intrinsic to age and unalterable can lead older persons to accept rather than combat disabilities that are potentially correctable. For example, although weight-bearing exercise has been shown to increase muscle mass and functional ability, it is likely that it will be rejected by many elderly persons because it is seen as age inappropriate. It may prove difficult to convince the older person that these stereotypic beliefs are false if these views of aging are held and expressed by family, friends and medical providers.

The older person's psychological state represents a third set of factors important for successful intervention. Depressed mood due to the accumulation of physical illnesses and the loss of important others can result in a sense of helplessness and loss of purpose that lead to decreased participation in daily activities, poor sleep, inadequate diet, and excessive drinking.

Elderly persons who are well integrated in family and community networks will likely be buffered from the adverse effects of accumulated losses, whereas those who are isolated will suffer the risk of behaviorally related health changes driven by declines in vigor and the replacement of positive with depressed emotion and mood. Although many specific factors affecting health and risk behaviors can be placed in one or another of our three categories (environmental resources; age stereotypes; emotional and motivational), others have multiple effects and are less easily classified. For example, factors such as retirement, death of a spouse, and cognitive decline affect resources and emotional and motivational states and generate stereotypes, all of which will affect the motivation and skills needed to discard old behaviors and acquire new ones. Given the complex impact of biological and social psychological factors on health-promoting and risk-inducing behaviors, a comprehensive theoretical framework is essential for guiding inquiries in this area. [*See* DEPRESSION; RETIREMENT; SOCIAL NETWORKS, SUPPORT, AND INTEGRATION.]

III. MODELS FOR INTERVENTION

Medical epidemiology and behavioral psychology have offered a number of models for approaching the conceptualization and linking of health-promoting and risk-inducing behaviors to health outcomes. We will first describe the medical definition and orientation toward three types of prevention. After that we will focus upon a self-regulation framework that can encompass the medical view and, in addition, be integrated with a life span perspective for guiding research and practice in the modification of health-relevant behaviors. [*See* EPIDEMIOLOGY.]

A. Primary, Secondary, and Tertiary Prevention: A Medical View

Preventive medicine distinguishes three types of intervention: primary prevention, which includes behavioral practices designed to block the occurrence of disease; secondary prevention, which centers upon behavioral practices for early detection and interventions to treat and hopefully cure or impede progression to a full-blown disease state; and tertiary prevention, which focuses on the treatment and control of disease to maximize the duration and quality of life. It is probably fair to say that for the past half century, medical practice has been focused upon tertiary prevention (i.e., the development of new technologies for disease treatment). Although this orientation has generated and will continue to generate the many miracles of modern medicine (e.g., heart transplants to gene therapies), it has also been the major force behind the rapid increase in health-care costs. Although it has been suggested that primary prevention may be a way to reverse this trend, it is clear that the possibility of altering behavior to prevent disease is viewed with great skepticism by medical practitioners.

For many chronic diseases, the above three categories of preventive activity are not discrete. For example, cardiovascular disease may begin with atherosclerotic changes that are eventually detected clinically by tonic elevations of blood pressure, eventuating over time in life-threatening strokes and coronary thromboses. These are different manifestations of an underlying, systemwide pathology, though it is likely that only a few laypersons are aware of the connections among these separately named conditions. Because these "diseases" are manifestations of a common underlying pathology, seemingly different health-promoting and risk-creating behaviors can be foci for intervention at multiple points in the developmental history of this systemic disorder. Failure to fully appreciate such basic, biological facts may be a deterrent to involvement in the adoption and performance of healthful action over the life span. The self-regulation model here proposed provides a life span orientation that may be helpful toward understanding these issues and generating useful interventions.

B. A Self-Regulation Model for the Management of Health Threats

1. Self-Regulation and the Representation of Disease Threats

Over the past 25 years we have been developing a self-regulation model for health-promoting and risk-inducing behaviors that can be used to generate research questions and procedures for interventions designed for cohorts at different periods of the life span. A central assumption of the model is that the adoption and maintenance of a health-promoting or a risk-inducing behavior is a function of the individual's *representation* of the threats and gains associated with the behavior (i.e., the representation establishes the goals or targets that motivate and direct action) (Figure 1). For example, there is absolutely no reason to expect adolescents or young adults to engage in health-promoting behavior to prevent the onset of hypertension or lung cancer if these diseases are perceived to have the following values on each of the five attributes of illness representations: (a) genetically caused (causal attribute); (b) develops over a short period of time in old age, a perceived time line that is similar to that for infectious diseases that are caused by pathogens and are sudden in onset; (c) illness identifiable by presence of physical symptoms (symptom identity), suggesting that action can be delayed until the appearance of somatic signs; (d) treatable by modern technology (controllable), plus someone else will manage it; and (e) not serious or life-threatening (consequences). The "commonsense" implication of these suggestions is that preventive action can wait until one is old enough to attend to and detect the factors causing the disease or any somatic signs of their presence, at which point a preventive or curative action is available.

There is a simple and important feature of illness representations that is insufficiently appreciated by investigators and practitioners: virtually every attribute of an illness representation contains both abstract and concrete components. The identity of a disease consists of its label and its symptoms (e.g., *high blood pressure* is both hypertension and headaches and a flushed face; *cancer* is a disease name and a palpable tumor; and the label *flu* is accompanied by symptoms such as headache, running nose, and fatigue). The abstract feature of the time line is the knowledge of the time for each aspect of a disease (i.e., known time for onset, progression, and recovery), whereas the concrete, "experiential" aspect of time is expressed in terms such as "It took so long for the medicine to work," "It took so long to get back on my feet," and so on. What is striking about the bilevel nature of representations is the extraordinary power of the concrete, symptomatic identity of a disease, its felt time, perceived consequences, and so forth, in driving procedures for coping and emotional reactions. During illness, the abstract takes a backseat to the concrete.

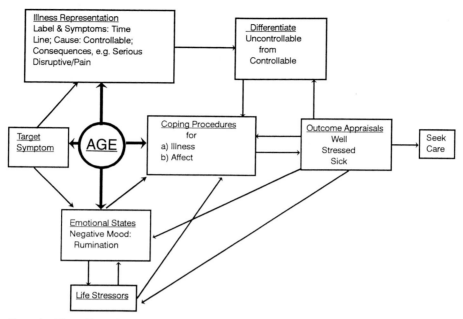

Figure 1   The self-regulation model illustrates the translation of a target symptom (or sensation) into a multiattribute, bilevel representation (the perceptual-concrete and abstract features of each attribute are not depicted) of a disease threat. The representation generates and shapes the selection and performance of procedures in efforts to identify and regulate the controllable features of the disease. The process is iterative: outcomees can lead to care seeking, to emotional upset, and become a major source of life stress. Chronological age acts as a moderator of the process, affecting target symptoms, the way symptoms are interpreted and represented, coping procedures, and emotional reactions. The figure does not show all possible interactions.

2. Self-Regulation and Action Plans

Second, we propose that representations will lead to action, such as the adoption of a health-promoting behavior or the discard of a risk-inducing one, only when the representation is linked to an action plan, that is, to a specific set of action alternatives each of which is perceived as more or less effective in preventing the disease threat (response efficacy) and is within the capabilities of the actor (self-efficacy) and his or her support system (lay and professional efficacy). The third assumption is that the individual appraises the effects of his or her actions and assesses whether they move toward a desired target or criterion (e.g., symptom removal, improved function, etc).

Although concepts of self-efficacy and self-responsibility date back to Hippocratic medicine of the pre-Christian era, the concepts take on richer meaning within the self-regulation context. One key facet is the proposition that behavioral output (i.e., action)

depends upon the combined activity of both the representation and the action plan; neither alone is sufficient for action. A second is that the representation and action plan form an integrated whole (i.e., the perceptions of response efficacy and self and professional efficacy are shaped and/or defined by the representation). The anthropological literature is filled with such examples. For instance, the commonsense procedures for treating life-threatening dehydration in infants suffering from diarrhea are pressure to the soft palate, inverting and shaking the infant, and so on. These procedures make sense with respect to a key symptom of advanced dehydration (i.e., the depression of the soft spot or fontanelle). The passion of elderly persons for cholesterol-reduction and low-fat diets to protect against hypertension and stroke is likely reinforced by the ease with which older persons can imagine the accumulation of fat in arteries, given their lengthy history of seeing fats in meat. Both examples reflect the gestalt-like relationship of the representation to procedures for threat management: it just sounds and looks right to eat less fat to avoid atherosclerosis.

The fourth assumption is that emotional reactions such as fear, anger, and depression are elicited by the representation of the threat and the status of the action plan. For example, if a disease is seen to be life-threatening and painful, if the time line for these consequences is drawn out rather than brief, if the disease is seen as uncontrollable, and if the criterion for perceiving movement toward risk reduction is ambiguous, the representation will evoke strong, negative affect, and very likely depression when the assessment of self-efficacy and response-efficacy are negative. The pattern of these cognitive, representational, and efficacy variables elicits different emotional responses. And once emotional reactions are brought into play, they will feed back to and alter the individual's cognitions. The bidirectionality of the affect–cognition relationship can have critical effects upon the performance of preventive actions. The sense of loss and hopelessness comprising the cognitive component of depression militates against future goal setting: Why set goals when all is lost and hope is absent? The difficulty of acting is inhibited further by the sense of anergy and fatigue that comprise the somatic substrate of depressed mood. The cognitive and somatic features of depression are so inhibiting of action that the depressed individual is not even likely to generate the random responses that might, by accident, suggest that all is not lost and change is possible. Similarly, although the threat of a serious disease such as lung cancer will generate fear and motivate preventive action in individuals with a strong sense of self-efficacy, the same level of fear can undermine the sense of self-competence and inhibit performance in less self-confident persons. Fear of cancer may produce these contrasting effects as follows: fear may increase the perceived magnitude and proximity (time line) of the threat, which will increase the perceived need for risk-controlling action; or, it may stimulate feelings of hopelessness in the path of an onrushing and overwhelming threat if it focuses attention on the consequences of disease, of cancer as a deadly, uncontrollable disease associated with endlessly painful treatments, rather than focusing attention on procedures for avoiding threat. [See CANCER AND THE ELDERLY.]

3. The Life Span as a Context for Self-Regulation

The way in which contextual factors, in particular, changing views of the self over the life span, moderate self-regulation for health promotion and risk reduction is a critical area for further theoretical development. As people view sickness as an outcome of a struggle between environmental pathogens and their physical resources, concepts and measures need to be developed to take into account the various ways in which representations of the self moderate the self-regulation system. For example, people vary in the degree to which they view their bodies as able to resist disease and able to tolerate medication. An optimistic outlook on life affects how one recuperates following myocardial infarction, and optimism affects people's judgments of their health status and moderates how accurately they predict their mortality. It is useful to speculate for a moment on how the elaboration of contextual factors, such as perceptions of self, will further differentiate this model from other frameworks for the analysis of health-promoting behavior.

The theory of planned behavior is regularly used for the analysis of health actions ranging from contraceptive use to tooth brushing. It proposes that performing a health action involves the formulation of an intention to act and the perceived ability to perform the desired action (self-efficacy). Intentions, in turn, are a product of two sets of factors: (a) attitudes toward the action, which are a product of the perceived likelihood of the action satisfying the individual's values; and (b) perceived norms, (i.e., the perceived value placed on the action by others and the importance the individual places on holding opinions that others value). Thus, normative cognitions, which are a contextual factor, have a direct effect on intentions, though normative factors could also operate indirectly via their effects upon attitudes and values.

Both the theory of planned behavior and the self-regulation model view health behavior as a product of multiple variables acting through direct and indirect (i.e., mediated) pathways. They differ, however, in the following important ways. First, the self-regulation model identifies specific attributes of illness threats that shape coping behaviors. Examples include labels as identifying health threats, symptoms as guides to action, time lines as setting a framework for action and evaluating outcomes, controllability as a property of the threat, causes as perceived targets for action, and consequences as intensifiers of the motivation for action. Such attributes are ignored in the theory of planned behavior. Second, the self-regulation framework postulates that emotional reactions are generated by a parallel set of processes and that these reactions have multiple functions within the self-regulation system. One of the most important of these functions is that emotions form a separate set of goals for action (e.g., fear can create a need for fear control, undermine self-efficacy, and alter perceived time frames and consequences, etc.). Emotional reactions are given little weight in the theory of planned behavior.

Finally, the self-regulation model treats contextual factors such as the physical experience of the disease and the perception of personal resources as having direct effects on the representation of disease and action plans for disease management. Thus, although contextual factors can have direct effects on health actions, many of their more interesting and important effects will occur via their effects on the disease representation and procedures for disease management. Contextual factors are expected to serve as important moderators of the processes involved in the adoption and maintenance of a health-promoting or risk-inducing behavior, though the representation of the threat and its associated procedures for threat management are the primary factors in control of action. For example, is cancer treatable if detected early? Is the treatment more frightening than the disease? Are the detection procedures effective and are they manageable? The self-regulation model treats chronological age in the same way (i.e., as a contextual or moderating variable that can alter the representational, procedural, and appraisal processes of the self-regulatory system) (see Figure 1). For example, chronological age leads to changes in the biological system that moderate the sensory properties of disease symptoms. It introduces knowledge elements that affect the interpretation of symptoms (e.g., whether they are represented as indicators of illness or signs of normal aging). And chronological age may also affect the strategies that people use in selecting specific procedures for threat management. Thus, it is the *representation* of the self and the disease threat and the *procedures for the management* of the self and the disease threat that mediate the effects of chronological age on health-promoting and risk-inducing actions.

4. A Chronological Approach

Though we have argued that chronological age should be treated as a contextual or moderator variable, the literature is replete with findings comparing age cohorts on rates of performance of a number of health-related behaviors: we call this the "chronological approach." The question is whether data of this type will lead to generalizations that deepen our understanding of the way in which age affects health behavior and, at a practical level, whether this data will identify biological targets and social psychological procedures for health improvement? A brief survey of the empirical literature should help us to address this question.

Survey data show that older cohorts (over 65 years of age) are more likely to report engaging in preventive behaviors (e.g., eat a balanced diet, avoid salty foods, get medical check-ups, avoid contaminated water and air, and avoid emotional stress and negative affects—anger, depression, etc.). People over 65 years of age are less likely to fail to take their medication or quit hypertension treatment, are less distressed during chemotherapy treatments for cancer, and less likely to think about dropping out of treatment. Myers and colleagues found the elderly were more responsive to cancer screening: they completed fecal occult blood tests at a higher rate than did younger cohorts, did not need follow-up contacts to complete the tests, and were more likely to continue testing in the following year than the younger members of a large health maintenance organization. One is tempted to conclude, therefore, that the elderly are motivated to engage in primary (prevention), secondary, and tertiary (treatment adherence) prevention.

Not every comparison, however, is so favorable to older cohorts. For example, although increased rates of exercise have been reported from pre- to postretirement (respondents 60–66 years of age), the more general finding is for decreases in vigorous physical activity with increasing age, and women over 65 years of age are more likely to be physically inactive than women 18–34 years of age (42.1 vs. 25.6%), though self-reports that one is more active than one's peers are more likely among older than younger persons. Even though it is not yet certain that the beneficial effects of vigorous exercise training will persist, the decline in participation in exercise with advancing age and the data showing that vigorous exercise and resistance training leads to gains in physical strength, improved muscle mass, and increased participation in daily activities strongly suggest that it would be desirable to encourage older persons to participate in such programs. We could, therefore, qualify our earlier empirical generalization to state that, with the exception of vigorous exercise, the members of older cohorts are more likely to engage in health-promoting behaviors than the members of younger cohorts. The question is whether this reformulated, empirical generalization has deepened our understanding sufficiently to serve as a guide for larger scale trials of exercise and other health-promotive behaviors using more diverse samples of elderly participants.

A careful reading of the methods section of the exercise studies reveals one area in which this reformulated rule is insufficient: it provides little or no help with recruitment. Fully 21% of the presumably healthy and highly motivated elderly dropped out of the experimental exercise condition in one study, and further inadequacies of this rule emerge when we compare different age groups on their rates of engaging in behavior for detecting cancer risk. Older women were more likely to have had a mammogram and a clinical breast examination in the prior 2 years in comparison to younger women. But this age-related increase held only until 80 years of age: the frequency of both mammography and breast self-examination declined sharply for women over 80. Although this effect may reflect implicit rules guiding medical practice as well as the reluctance of the old-old to engage in risk detection, it is clearly a further limit on the validity of our generalization that with the exception of vigorous exercise, the elderly engage in more health-promoting actions. As we examine data for different health and risk behaviors for different age groups, the empirical picture will become more complex and still more difficult to summarize with a simple, recallable generalization. As another example, the proportion of smokers is lower among older than younger women, a welcome finding as smoking has an especially adverse effect upon lower body vasculature, which in turn impacts mobility. But older women who were smokers were found to be less accepting of the idea that smoking is harmful to health. These older smokers may, of course, represent a survivor subgroup that is particularly resistant to change.

That that complexity would be the norm was clear from the early studies which found only correlations of 20% or less from health-promotive behaviors such as the use of blood pressure screening and seat belts to tooth brushing. It is clear, therefore, that one can expect yet more complexity when examining other risk behaviors and can anticipate that it will be impossible to summarize the results in terms of a simple, age-related generalization. The conclusion we draw from this is that chronological age should not be treated as a psychological variable! Age is a contextual variable associated with a diverse set of factors that affect the risk of illness, the perceptions of the risks and benefits associated with specific health-promoting and risk-inducing actions, and the possibility of generating motivation to adopt the former and eliminate the latter. We believe it will be possible to address these important, motivational issues by placing age in a self-regulation framework.

5. A Self-Regulation Approach to Life Span Change

Placing age in the self-regulation model alters our view of both the biological and psychological problems associated with behaviorally generated improvements in health (see Figure 1). Age impacts every component of the self-regulation system. Indeed, age affects the very base of the representational process as it alters the somatic sensations associated with disease processes: the very same diseases present differently in the sensorium of the older person. Comorbidities add complexity at the somatosensory level: the symptoms and threat to life of a disease that can be managed by a younger, less sick body may be life-threatening to the elderly. Interpreting or assigning meaning to symptoms is complicated by these somatosensory changes, and is made yet more complex by the interaction of age with the presence of comorbidities (i.e., should a slowly developing symptom be regarded as benign and non-life-threatening or as potentially malignant?). The possibility and the risk of error is greater in the older, compromised system. As the perception of control wanes with the increase in the number of persistent, chronic conditions and the level of threat increases, the perception of death may loom behind each somatic twitch. What procedures for threat management are reasonable for these later years?

Biological and social psychological changes over the life span clearly influence the self-regulation process. For example, the economic and social changes that occur with the transition from the state of freewheeling young adult to the young, married adult with children, and the further transitions to middle or older age and the roles of grandparent, reshape the individual's views of the self and the role of health and health-related behaviors for the self and its social relationships. The vigorous adolescent is little motivated for health promotion as he believes he can eat junk food that would damage a middle-aged adult, and the middle-aged adult may share the belief. The transition to parenthood introduces concerns with the health, diet, and physical activities of the child, and the self as the parent must be both a good example and a healthy wage earner to fulfill his responsibilities to the child: the risk-taking orientation of single life is inappropriate for a parent. And as retirement approaches and one moves from the fifties and sixties to the seventies and eighties, increasingly large numbers of friends and family bear the marks of chronic illness and an increasing number exit from the stage of life. These visible, external changes in combination with the visible and felt changes of aging (i.e., the increase in girth, deconditioning due to an increasingly sedentary life, reduction in energy and endurance, loss of muscle mass and physical strength) heighten the individual's awareness of his or her potential frailty and the need to act to retain physical and mental vigor. It is no surprise, therefore, that the 65 and older cohorts have been characterized as risk averse (i.e., quick to avoid threats to their physical well-being), and conserving (i.e., eager to restore and strengthen their personal physical and mental resources). This orientation, however, is visible to different degrees in different elderly cohorts, and its impact will differ depending upon the particular disease threat and health action.

One area in which the adoption of an overall strategy of risk-averse and self-conserving procedures has been studied is the time frame used by older adults for evaluating symptoms. For example, a comparison of delay in seeking medical care for symptoms self-rated as mild, possibly serious, or definitely serious showed that the time from symptom onset to seeking expert medical advice was shorter for the over-65-year-old cohort than for the cohort 45–55 years of age. To obtain a more detailed look at this age difference, the delay period was divided into two component parts: *appraisal delay*, the time from first noticing a symptom to deciding one was ill, and *illness delay*, the time from deciding one was ill till calling for care.

The pattern that evolved showed that the older cohorts were quicker to appraise their symptoms as signs of illness at all levels of perceived seriousness, but the difference between the age groups was smallest for symptoms regarded as definitely serious. Illness delay, the time from deciding one was ill to calling for care, introduced the threat of a potentially serious diagnosis that led to a more complex pattern. Differences in illness delay were negligible for mild and definitely serious symptoms. But for symptoms judged as possibly serious, the middle-aged cohort waited over a week before calling, whereas the elderly barely waited a day. This difference in illness delay, plus the absence of differences in reported barriers to care seeking and the admissions of avoidant and denial-like thinking on the part of the middle-aged cohort support the hypothesis that older persons are unwilling to bear the threat and stress of an unknown risk: they are risk-averse and energy-conserving.

The strategy of conserving self in a risk-filled world provides a somewhat different way of viewing the elderly's willingness to adopt specific health actions. If one views health-promoting actions such as exercise, low-fat or high-fiber diets, and so on, through the lens of this adaptive strategy, one can see why there may be reluctance to adopt vigorous exercise whereas dietary changes are willingly accepted. Exercise is enervating: it feels as though it depletes rather than increases the body's energy store, and the self-regulative system is extremely sensitive to concrete, perceptual feedback. Indeed, if aging produces a decline in abstract cognitive capacity, one can anticipate that the feel of an activity, its immediate sensory properties, will be increasingly potent relative to abstractly defined, more long-term outcomes. By contrast, although low-fat and high-fiber diets may have little or no benefit with regard to extending the life span, they are typically easy to do and they provide immediate sensory feedback; low fat, especially if it involves reducing dairy products, can minimize gaseous bloating, and high fiber can be helpful with bowel function: immediate perceptual experiences that paint these practices as effective health promoters.

This risk averse view of self-in-world is not, however, held by all older persons, nor is it likely to increase in frequency or remain stable as people move from their sixties and seventies into their eighties and nineties. As chronic illnesses impact the perception that one's health is poor or fair, as memory loss and failing physical vigor become more pronounced, and as these events convince one that he or she is indeed old, the emphasis is on passive preservation rather than active avoidance. And there will come a time when reversing disease threats is felt to be impossible or fruitless when the concrete perceptions of costs involved outweigh the expected benefits for the older, compromised body (i.e., the effort for action exceeds perceived resources, and the time line for the experience of benefits extends only for weeks or months). These changing views will affect whether illness is accepted as an integral part of aging, something to be endured rather than an imposition to be combatted, thereby deferring efforts to adopt new, health-promoting actions.

IV. CONCLUSION

The domain of health promotive and risk-creating behaviors ranges across virtually every area of human activity. An individual's health is affected by behaviors involved in every basic human function from procreation, through eating, to recreation, whether or not the culture and the individual are aware of the linkage. This complexity, along with genetic variability, leads to an increasing diversity in the elderly population making it impossible to formulate one or two simple, empirical generalizations either to understand or guide health-promotion programs to improve the health of older persons. Both the biological effects of an intervention and the ability to attract and sustain active involvement will vary across behaviors and persons. Complexities of this sort can lead to despairing confusion (i.e., the world or prevention is like a pretzel and a rather weirdly shaped one at that), or to the adoption of a process model that is both sufficiently comprehensive and simple to allow researchers to analyze the possible ways that age-related changes in the self and social environment will affect health-promotive action and health outcomes. Our objective here has been to illustrate the viability of such an approach. Although it is always reasonable to assert that the adequacy of one's vision will be tested by future theoretical and empirical development, the tension between the theoretically motivated investigator and the public health person susceptible to political pressure for results "now" and at a low price may prevent substantial advances in understanding health behav-

ior and improving practice. There is little evidence that the human species is averse to random behavior or willing to examine history with a dispassionate eye in order to avoid the errors of prior generations.

ACKNOWLEDGMENTS

Preparation of this chapter was abetted by support by Grant AG03501 from the National Institute on Aging.

BIBLIOGRAPHY

Backett, K. C., & Davison, C. (1995). Lifecourse and lifestyle: The social and cultural location of health behaviours. *Society, Science, and Medicine, 40,* 629–638.

Blair, S. N., Kohl, H. W., Gordon, N. F., & Paffenbarger, R. S., Jr. (1992). How much physical activity is good for health? *Annual Review of Public Health, 13,* 99–126.

Fiatarone, M. A., O'Neill, E. F., Ryan, N. D., Clements, K., Solares, G. R., Nelson, M. E., Roberts, S. B., Kehayias, J., Kipsitz, L. A., & Evans, W. J. (1994). Exercise training and nutritional supplementation for physical frailty in very elderly people. *New England Journal of Medicine, 330,* 1769–1775.

Kottke, T. E., Trap, M. A., Fores, M. M., Kelly, A. W., Jung, S., Novotny, P., & Panser, L. A. (1995). Cancer screening behaviors and attitudes of women in Southeastern Minnesota. *Journal of the American Medical Association, 273,* 1099–1105.

LaCroix, A., Lang, J., Scherr, P., Wallace, R., Cornoni-Huntley, J., Berkman, L., Curb, D., Evans, D., & Hennekens, C. (1991). Smoking and mortality among men and women in three communities. *New England Journal of Medicine, 324,* 1619–1625.

Leventhal, H. (1970). Findings and theory in the study of fear communications. *Advances in Experimental Social Psychology, 5,* 119–186.

Leventhal, H., Leventhal, E. A., & Schaefer, P. (1991). Vigilant coping and health behavior: A life span problem. In M. Ory & R. Abeles (Eds.), *Aging, health, and behavior* (pp. 109–140). Baltimore: Johns Hopkins.

Leventhal, E. A., Leventhal, H., Schaefer, P., & Easterling, D. (1993). Conservation of energy, uncertainty reduction and swift utilization of medical care among the elderly. *Journal of Gerontology: Psychological Sciences, 48,* P78–P86.

Leventhal, H., Prohaska, T. R., & Hirschman, R. S. (1985). Preventive health behavior across the life span. In J. C. Rosen & L. J. Solomon (Eds.), *Prevention in health psychology* (Vol. 8, pp. 191–235). Hanover, NH: University Press of New England.

McCartney, N., Hicks, A. L., Martin, J., & Webber, C. E. (1995). Long term resistance training in the elderly: Effects on dynamic strength, exercise capacity, muscle and bone. *Journal of Gerontology, 50A,* B97–B104.

Midanik, L. T., Soghikian, K., Ransom, L. J., & Tekawa, I. S. (1995). The effect of retirement on mental health and health behaviors: The Kaiser permanente retirement study. *Journal of Gerontology, 50B,* S59–S61.

Myers, R. E., Balshen, A. M., Wolf, T. A., Ross, E. A., & Miller, L. (1993). Adherence to continuous screening for colorectal neoplasia. *Medical Care, 3,* 508–519.

Orleans, T. C., Jepson, C., Resch, N., & Rimer, B. (1994). Quitting motives and barriers among older smokers. *Cancer, 74,* 2055–2061.

Park, D. C., Morrell, R. W., Frieske, D., & Kincaid, D. (1992). Medication adherence behaviors in older adults: effects of external cognitive supports. *Psychology and Aging, 7,* 252–256.

Prohaska, T. R., Keller, M. L., Leventhal, E. A., & Leventhal, H. (1987). Impact of symptoms and aging attribution on emotions and coping. *Health Psychology, 6,* 495–514.

Prohaska, T. R., Leventhal, E. A., & Leventhal, H., & Keller, M. L. (1985). Health practices and illness cognition in young, middle-aged, and elderly adults. *Journal of Gerontology, 40,* 569–578.

Striegel-Moore, R., & Rodin, J. (1985). Prevention of obesity. In J. Rosen, & L. Solomon (Eds.), *Prevention in health psychology* (pp. 72–110). Hanover & London: University Press of England.

Sutton, S. (1989). Smoking attitudes and behavior: Applications of Fishbein and Ajzen's theory of reasoned action to predicting and understanding smoking decisions. In T. Ney, & A. Gale (Eds.), *Smoking and human behavior* (pp. 289–312). London: John Wiley & Sons.

Wallston, K. A., Wallston, B. S., Smith, S., & Dobbins, C. J. (1987). Perceived control and health. *Current Psychological Research and Reviews, 6*(1), 5–25.

Wolinsky, F. D., Stump, T. E., & Clark, C. O. (1995). Antecedents and consequences of physical activity and exercise among older adults. *The Gerontologist, 35,* 451–462.

Sexuality, Sensuality, and Intimacy

Ruth B. Weg

University of Southern California

I. Myths and Stereotypes of Sexless Old
II. Exploding the Myths and Stereotypes: Science and Research
III. Intimacy: The Core of Loving Human Relationships
IV. Growing Older Sexually
V. Sexual Dysfunctions and Therapies
VI. Summary

Climacteric That period of multidimensional change for both men and women occurring between 40–50 years, duration of 5–10 years; the range of changes include circulatory, emotional, neuronal, and psychosocial.

Homosexuality A sexual orientation directed toward individuals of the same sex; the orientation is more than an erotic focus and involves lifestyle, love, commitment, companionship, and trust.

Intimacy Involves an affectionate bond composed of mutual caring, responsibility, trust, and open communication.

Libido Sexual desire under the biological control of the male sex hormone, testosterone, for both men and women.

Menopause A particular multidimensional stage in the female climacteric characterized by a cessation of menses and therefore usually cessation of release of eggs, marked by a continuing diminution in estrogen and progesterone, which have effects on both genital and nonsexual tissues and functions.

Orgasm A climax of excitement in the sexual response cycle characterized by whole-body heightened sensation; the sensate focus is generally genital, but can be initiated in other areas with radiating waves of contractions to other organs of the body.

Refractory Period A time after resolution of orgasm during which another erection and orgasm are difficult to experience, ranges from 1–2 minutes in the young male and from 2–24 hours in the older male.

Sex Hormones Steroids, estrogen and progesterone, female sex hormones synthesized and released from the ovary; testosterone, male sex hormone synthesized and released from the testes. The adrenal gland synthesizes and releases androgens in both female and male.

There is finally a growing acceptance among health professionals, educators, and older persons themselves that sexual interest, capacities, pleasures, and libido remain throughout the life span into the ninth and perhaps tenth decades. The loveless, sexless label for older persons has been widespread in the society at large during most of this century.

This stereotype is a penalty for the old, the young, and the middle aged. It is no surprise that age has become the enemy to be ignored, feared, and rejected. Contrary to any myths and stereotypes still extant among ageists and those in society who cling to ignorance, older persons are sexual human beings, with persistent sexual desires, fantasies, and sexual expression to meet their needs. The multidimensional nature of SEXUALITY, SENSUALITY, AND INTIMACY beyond the genital has been acknowledged more recently, with attention to intimacy, trust, touch, love, friendship, play, and caring as significant aspects of the life span, personal choice, and whole personhood. Because sensual and sexual behavior is largely learned, it is recognized that education and other therapeutic interventions are increasingly available for unlearning stereotypic behavior and learning anew more appropriate behavior.

Health professionals, to whom elders turn for help with sexual feelings, frustrations, and questions, have often been among the worst offenders. Its apparent that even in society today, some physicians suggest to older patients remarks such as, "You don't need to bother about such things at your age." Such mistaken, misleading advice may be correlated with physicians' discomfort with their own sexuality. Medical schools have only recently introduced courses appropriate to the changing realities of older persons, including sexuality.

It is an unfortunate commentary that this society, enlightened in a number of ares, cannot completely shed the fears of aging and ageist socialization, which are translated into deliberate and/or unconscious barriers to healthy, normative sexual expression among older adults.

I. MYTHS AND STEREOTYPES OF SEXLESS OLD

The asexual image of aging and the old has ancient origins reinforced by culture, ignorance, religion, states, families, and peers through the centuries. With the maturation of the human family beyond the most primitive, there developed the acceptance of marital, procreative sexuality to the exclusion of all other sexual activities. This led to regarding the later, barren years as asexual, especially for women.

Religious influences varied: Judaism found that "sex" was more than the duty of procreation, that pleasure through sexual expression should be enjoyed by both man and woman in the sanctity of marriage. The early Greeks, pleasure-oriented and identified with sex-positive attitudes, still perceived women primarily as "gyne" or childbearers. As Christianity developed, the idealization of celibacy and perception of "sex" as evil predominated. Concurrent and contrasting Islamic, Hindu, and Oriental sexual philosophies and practices were more approving and relatively free of taboos. Finding "sex" not sinful and little virtue in celibacy and chastity awaited the Renaissance and Protestant Reformation. Nevertheless, women were still childbearers and sources of satisfaction for men's sexual desires.

In the 1840s Victorianism began a long period of contradictions, modesty, prudery, and reserve (particularly among women), degrees of which persist into the twentieth century. Prostitution was legal, but the first antipornography law was passed. Masturbation was considered the cause for a range of physical illness and insanity. Evaluation of women remained one of disadvantage: "less" than men cognitively, physically, minimally libidinous, with little capacity for sexual response. Virginity was expected of women (virgin prostitutes were special), and sexual athletics was expected from the men. During these eras, sexuality was identified as pleasurable or procreative, natural or evil, health promoting or debilitating. Generally, sexual expression was discussed in genital terms—intercourse, orgasm, and conception, devoid of whole-person connotations.

II. EXPLODING THE MYTHS AND STEREOTYPES: SCIENCE AND RESEARCH

A. Early Search for Facts

Two pioneers in the scientific exploration of human sexuality were Sigmund Freud and Havelock Ellis, both of the late nineteenth and twentieth centuries. Freud's conclusions were drawn from his psychiatric patients. He designated sexuality and sexual expression as the driving force of all human behavior and major basis for neuroses. Havelock Ellis came to his conclusions related to average persons, and conceived of sexuality as a natural drive. He rejected the illness and insanity mode that masturbation had earned, and the declaration of professionals that homosexuality was degenerate. Despite the views of the majority of his colleagues, Ellis stated that women also had sexual desires and pleasures, and that many sexual dysfunctions were psychogenic in origin.

Kinsey and his team documented a massive survey of sexual behavior of about 11,000 American men and women in 1948 and 1953. To ensure scientific acceptance of inquiries into sexuality, the focus was on "objective" measurement of genital sexuality. Their report recorded the number of encounters and orgasms resulting from self-stimulation, heterosexual, homosexual, bisexual, fellatio, cunnilingus, or fantasy. Although the methodology and nonrandom population deserved criticism, Kinsey's study did elucidate the variation and range of human sexual-genital behavior. However, a negative aspect of the Kinsey Report was the omission of the quality and meaning of human relationships and sexual expression—the desires, feelings, needs. A quantitative emphasis continues to create a narrow, genital perception of sexual expression, especially troublesome for older persons.

B. Contemporary and Recent Inquiries

The work of Masters and Johnson initiated in the 1960s and into the 1970s launched a more open and direct series of investigations about the nature of sexuality. Forthcoming information in an heretofore untouched area on the physiology of sexual arousal and response during different stimuli was a removal of mystery and taboo. Their major study provided unequivocal support for the same physiological nature of clitoral and vaginal orgasm. Millions of women who had been condemned by Freud as inadequate and immature for not always choosing vaginal orgasm during intercourse were freed of that burden. Just as Kinsey's survey gave primacy to the genital dimensions of sexuality as the only important reportable data, Masters and Johnson studies also emphasized the genital response but with new, useful information. In addition, their work supported the earlier Kinsey findings for persons over 65. "There is no time limit drawn by the advancing years of female sexuality," and the male maintains "a capacity for sexual performance that frequently may extend to and beyond the 80-year-old age level."

American longitudinal studies of aging are among the most dependable sources of reliable information. In the assessment of all physical, mental, and emotional changes with time, sexual behavior was also explored. The Duke Center for the Study of Aging and Human Development began one such study in 1954. Data confirmed the continuation of social and sexual interests and capacities into the ninth decade for those older persons in moderately good physical and psychological health. Questions attended not only to the genital quantitative data, but also to the issues of current and past interest and pleasure in sexual expression in the later years. Significant information of older men and women included. Earlier interest, frequency, and enjoyment were reliable predictors of active sexuality in the later years. Furthermore, any decline with age appeared related to death or illness of partner. The Baltimore Longitudinal Study has added

data regarding its study population of urban white, married, well-educated men aged 25–85. Like the Duke study, findings indicated a decrease in frequency of sexual expression—62% of men in their seventies reported coital activity dropping to 23% masturbatory behavior between 70 and 79 years.

C. Nonlongitudinal Varied Studies

In addition to longitudinal data using survey techniques, there have been fruitful inquiries into sexual capacities and behaviors of older persons. One American survey of 800 adults between 60 and 91 from all regions of the country produced findings similar to those already noted. Interest in sexual activity continued; beliefs in the benefits of sexual activity to mental and physical health prevailed. There was no embarrassment, reluctance, or anxiety in discussing sexuality. Moreover sex was perceived as better in the later years. Researchers also found the respondents unexpectedly comfortable with oral sex as well as extramarital sexual encounters.

Another survey using a self-administered anonymous questionnaire of 202 men and women, 80–102 years old living in a retirement community in Northern California, found ongoing sexual activity. Even in this community with potentially excessive constraints it was found that sexuality remained significant in their lives.

Late-life sexuality was again confirmed in a nonrandom survey of 4246 adults from 50 to 93 years under the guidance of Brecher and the editors of *Consumer Reports*. *Consumer Reports* published a questionnaire concerning sexuality. The response of the readership was confirming of interest, frequency, and desire. This inquiry was unique because it departed from the quantitative data so far accumulated. There were open-ended questions, which explored feelings, beliefs, desires, and needs. For the first time, there was documentation beyond genital behavior, as the older readers reflected on the importance of relationships, sexual and sensual activities, enjoyment, quality, and meaning. It is clear that growing older does not inevitably lead to the removal of sexual interest, libido, and pleasure.

In face-to-face interviews with singles over 65, sexually active older adults (average age for men, 67; for women, 65 years), noted passion and romance are important in their lives. Dating was a viable alternative to marriage, a welcome protection against fear and loneliness as well as an emotional and sexual outlet.

The role and interaction of exercise and its psychological benefits for sexual interest and activity was presented at a 1987 meeting of Sexuality Information and Education Council of the United States (SIECUS). In an investigation of 160 competitive swimmers, aged 40–80 years, it was found that older swimmers were as sexually active as persons 20–40 years younger. Eighty-eight percent of the 60+ men reported high levels of enjoyment and satisfaction.

What about institutionalization, too frequently the last resort for older persons? What impact does it have on their sexual natures? Because public lounges or corridors are the usual potential for human contact, any sexual behavior is monitored and restrained. Married couples are frequently separated. A survey of 42 skilled nursing homes found that staff had admitted difficulty in getting beyond the taboos regarding sexuality and older persons, thereby adding to further dehumanization. However, some nursing homes have established privacy rooms or other means for men and women to be together. Individual personal sexual desires and needs do not evaporate upon institutionalization. Education for families, staff, and older persons is remiss if reality of late-life sexuality is omitted from essential, basic information.

D. Similar Findings in Other Countries and Cultures

Other countries in which inquiries have been undertaken report familiar findings with small differences, probably a function of the particular culture. Eighty-five percent of Italian men between 62 and 81 years were coitally active, with frequency decrease but sexual satisfaction after 60 years the same as or greater than that experienced in earlier years. Active women reported little difference in frequency from sexually active men; fewer women (53%) were coitally active.

As part of an older population health study (166 men and 266 women), Sweden's analysis of sexual activities of 70-year-old men and women found that 46% of men and 16% of women were still enjoying sexual intercourse. Marriage was one of the factors that exerted a positive influence on frequency. Men characterized with good mental health had a more positive attitude toward sexual activity among older people. Women who remained sexually active had younger husbands, low levels of anxiety, and better mental and physical health than those who were not active, and they evaluated their marriage as happy. They had positive attitudes towards sexual expression among older persons and evaluated their past and present sexual intercourse as enjoyable.

In Denmark there were similar data, a decrease in coital activity among older men from their sixties beyond 80 years old. Masturbatory activity also declined but more gradually. There were fewer studies that included women, but in general, the findings report a decline in frequency of coitus and orgasmic response.

A more recent study than those already noted reported on the sexual activity of aging men and women in Israel. These findings also echo aforementioned inquiry results. This investigation examined the impact of psychosocial factors on sexuality. Again, marriage resulted in more activity among men and women. The sexual activity of aging women was largely dependent on three factors: marital status, perceived health, and desire. For men, the importance order was different: sexual desire, marital status, and health. Earlier sexual expression appeared to exert greater effect on men's rather than women's sexual behavior. The fact that findings in this recent (1990s) study are comparable to earlier inquiries (1960s, 1970s) in the United States suggests that factors predicting sexual activity in the later years are cross-culturally valid and comparable over time as well. Because the first factor for older women was marital status and sexual desire among older men, an investigation into the impact of sex role socialization would provide insight into the possible basis for the difference.

III. INTIMACY: THE CORE OF LOVING HUMAN RELATIONSHIPS

Perhaps one of the most basic human needs is for affection, caring from and about another person. Whether young or old, well or ill, the human being who denies or is denied the touch, affection, and trusting human connection slowly deteriorates and dies emotionally and/or physically. Intimacy, the quality that enables each person to be open, trusting, accepting, and caring also enables self-revelation and loving. The significance of intimate relationships for each older person is the enhancement of self-esteem, a reason for being, and the assurance that someone will be there for them as they are needed to be there for someone else.

There is some confusion about the meaning or achievement of intimacy. Men still appear to have greater difficulty with openness, self-revelation, and reaching out—all part of establishing intimacy. Women on the other hand have been practicing this behavior most of their lives. Differential socialization encouraging bravado and loner behavior in boys and truth telling, friendliness, and group behavior among girls has contributed to the adult differences that are found. Intimacy is not always within reach in relationships that are characterized by more than average sexual activity.

Intimate relationships within and outside of marriage are protection and support against the feelings of loneliness and diminishing demonstration of affection that may accompany many years of being together. Increasingly, older persons make efforts to establish ties with friends and confidants, intimate connections that can become emotionally, intellectually, spiritually, and potentially sexually (physically) satisfying and energizing. Some elders may be more vulnerable than others to a lack of intimacy because activities of other parts of their lives have diminished. Resultant increasing isolation puts self-love and self-image at risk.

IV. GROWING OLDER SEXUALLY

A. The Climacteric and Beyond

Among many professionals the climacteric had long been associated with menopause, and therefore a so-called feminine experience. However, with continued research, the climacteric is identified as a period of change for both men and women occurring between 40 and 50 years, with a duration of 5–10 years. Individuals experience a range of changes: circulatory, emotional, hormonal, neuronal, and psychosocial. These tend to be symptomatic in men about 8–10 years later than in women. Men and women do experience this period differently. Not all men report the aforementioned changes, and among those who do, they indicate variable levels of diminished libido,

weakness, fatiguability, increased irritability, intermittent loss of potency, listlessness, poor appetite, weight loss, and problems with concentration. A determination of subnormal plasma testosterone is a clinical suggestion that the climacteric is the causative factor. The use of successful hormone replacement therapy effectively eliminates other contributing factors such as anemia, depression, and malignancy. The hot flush, generally associated with menopausal women, may be missing or less frequent in men, probably related to the constancy of estrogen concentration and resulting vasomotor stability.

In women, there is a group of changes that indicate the climacteric is underway and within a few years menopause will be a fact of life. Fertility decreases, menses become irregular, for some the hot flush does occur, a mark of vasomotor instability. Hormonal changes contribute to urogenital atrophy, altered body contours, diminished muscle tone, and skin elasticity.

There are subjective and objective symptoms that are said to be typical of climacteric women. However, recent inquiries report that, in fact, perimenopausal and postmenopausal women live through a highly individual experience. There is no "menopausal syndrome" inevitably characterized by all the symptoms attributed to menopause. Some women report a few or more varied complaints: anxiety, loss of appetite, depression, dizziness, headache, palpitations, high blood pressure, and insomnia. Some women report no negative symptoms. It is important to note that many of the symptoms listed can also have other etiologies not derivative of menopause. There is little consensus among researchers and clinics regarding the psychogenic and biological contribution for depression, anxiety, and headaches.

This author searched the literature on menopausal median age from classical through modern eras, in different countries and cultures, and 50–51 years remains the most noted. Also noteworthy are the sources of the data, American and European industrialized countries, Caucasian women. Non-European women have a lower median age, among whom poor nutrition may be a critical factor. The non-Western cultures have a positive view of menopausal women in terms of roles, privileges, and improved status. Unfortunately, there are fewer inquiries into pre- and postmenopausal women of color.

Menopause, the cessation of menses and loss of

fertility, is one phase of the female climacteric. Like the climacteric, it is multidimensional so that biomedical and psychosocial factors all impact on the nature of the individual menopause. The Women's Health Initiative, a National Institutes of Health's longitudinal study, will be producing overall health data of late-life women, investigating controlled lifestyle factors. This study will be pursuing a number of variables and therapies, consequences of natural and surgical menopause (often unnecessary), which will put real and assumed complaints into appropriate perspective. One particular inquiry involves the effects of hormonal replacement therapy, still a matter for controversy. In the past, the hot flush was considered a necessary accompaniment of every woman's menopause. Current facts contradict this feared vasomotor instability easily minimized by estrogen replacement.

B. Older Persons as Sexual Partners: Physical Changes

In no other body system is sexism more apparent than within perceptions of the sexual system. Men, middle aged and older, may be grey, paunchy, and out of shape, yet they are considered vital, attractive into their seventies and beyond. However, panic may set in when and if they experience a few episodes of impotence and/or ejaculatory retardation. Response to these occasional threats to sexual vigor may include a withdrawal from sexual activity or a choice of young partners for reinvigoration, female or male, depending on sexual preference. Impotence or other sexual dysfunction with age are not inevitable. Dysfunctions may be a consequence of other major systemic disorders, long-time interruption of activity, alcoholism, workaholism, excessive eating, and difficulties feeling desire for a long-time partner.

Women in their climacteric years have been perceived as less attractive, and in their later years, they become wrinkled, with grey hair, an angular shape, thus neutered. Recently, increasing numbers of women in their sixties and seventies are relatively healthy, vigorous, working, and remaining more attractive to themselves and others, thus more active sexually.

One researcher compared female and male sexual responsiveness in the 1970s and found they were out of phase. For the female, socialization has resulted in minimal sexual responsiveness in her teens, peaks in her thirties and forties, and remaining at this level into her later years. Only opportunity and societal support may be lacking. Menopausal and postmenopausal women have been stereotypically labeled as sexless. In such an environment, some older women with fragile egos find themselves unlovable. Yet, many of late middle-aged and older women report enhanced libido and activity, possibly a result of the diminished estrogen and unopposed testosterone, the libido hormone in both women and men. Changes in patterns of sexual activity among elders become noticeable in the middle years—sexuality like all of life is part of a continuum. The nature of desire also changes. It may be necessary to optimize the circumstance and romance in lovemaking to stir desire appropriately.

I. The Older Woman, Lovable and Loving

Small changes in genital and other body anatomy and physiology do occur. Associated with sex hormone decrease, neuronal responsiveness and circulatory efficiency diminish. Breasts eventually become less full and firm. Lower tissue elasticity, muscle tone, and diminution in fat and glandular tissue all contribute to breast appearance. None of these relate directly to sexual capacity. No changes occur suddenly, and estrogen and progesterone decreases are gradual—perhaps involving 6–10 years postmenopause before any significant, measurable difference. A surgical menopause and the complete hysterectomy would, of course, result in more abrupt changes unless estrogen or hormonal (estrogen and progesterone) replacement therapy is begun. Some women are upset by appearance alterations putting self-image at risk. As a matter of fact, there are decreases in vulval tissue, uterus, and ovaries, but a neglible change in the clitoris and its responsiveness so important in stimulation to excitement, lubrication, and orgasm. The changes in the vagina represent the most significant for the physical and emotional consequences the woman may experience. Vaginal circumference and length diminish, mucosa thins, and rugal pattern of younger years gradually flattens. Estrogen deficiency may lead to vaginitis, slower and less lubrication, thinning, dry vaginal walls, mild bleeding, and some problems with penile intromission. With the years, both bladder and urethra also reduce in size, which may complicate genital tissue symptoms. Frequency of urination and burning may occur with and after intercourse. Coitus may not be as comfortable or inviting as in the past. Pleasurable uterine contractions become less so, spasmodic, and possibly painful.

What real changes exist in the phases of genital responsivity? The clitoris remains as the sensate focus, lubrication usually takes longer, depending on the kind and period of stimulation, elevating and flattening of the anterior border of symphysis. All these stages of response enhance the ease of intercourse and potential orgasm. Orgasm is noticeably shorter between the fifth and seventh decade. Resolution, the final recognizable stage, is more rapid and may also be a function of diminished sex steroids. Most importantly, there is no loss of women's earlier multiorgasmic capacity. Furthermore, as mentioned earlier and contrary to the mythology of menopausal consequences, there is no loss of interest and capacity as a loving sexual partner after a hysterectomy. There have been many who report enhanced arousability, desire, interest, and a relatively intact sexual system responsivity.

Yet, too many older women find it difficult to keep sexually active. It is now known that women in their sixties and seventies have vital sexual feelings but few means for expression. Witness the skewed demography. In 1993, there were ratios of 147 females to 100 males aged 65 and older, and 256 women to 1 man for those over 85. This gender differential is based on a number of factors: older widowers marry quickly to younger women; single older men frequently choose younger women as partners, yet most older women outlive men by about $7\frac{1}{2}$ years. According to 1993 data, 77% of older men compared to 42% of older women are married. References exist documenting the feelings of frustration, guilt, and even shame among some women. Vague illness and nonsexual symptoms are presented to health professionals. They include insomnia, anxiety, depression, phobias, as well as physical symptoms such as back pain and bowel and vaginal discomforts. It is fair to say that there are older women who, if still married or single, welcome a retreat from the expression of genital sexuality, an experience that does not conjure up loving exchanges. For those older women who are still with an ill, withdrawn mate, they could be in emotional and physical need for loving. Although masturbation may represent a physical release, it is acknowledged that many older women in their seventh, eighth, and ninth decades were socialized to view masturbation as a "no-no." Moreover, this release is no substitute for an affectionate exchange between loving partners.

2. The Older Man, Loving, Lovable

Unlike the eventual loss of female fertility 2 or more years postmenopause, men can maintain fertility and spermatogenesis into the ninth decade. Nevertheless, hormonal and tissue changes do occur. Early in the 1970s there were studies that reported a gradual decrease in testosterone, and other inquiries claimed no decrease or a possible increase. The range of tissue and organ changes is comparable to that of older women. Muscle tone, strength, and stamina diminish, especially with the lack of exercise. Genital changes are gradual and include smaller testes and increased penile flaccidity; the prostate gland enlarges, hardens, and evidences weaker contractions. The force of ejaculation is diminished, the volume of the ejaculate is less, as is the viscosity of the seminal fluid.

The nature of intercourse changes gradually. It may be less frequent, decreased in intensity, requiring longer time to reach an erection. With heterosexual older couples this may even be an advantage, since the reduction in ejaculatory demand fits with the older woman's need for more time to reach the excitement phase. There is more time for arousal for both. Most older men are helped to reach engorgement and erection with more caressing and direct stimulation of the penis. In many older men, erections can be maintained longer, but in some orgasm is shorter and return of the penis to a flaccid state is reduced to seconds compared to minutes or the hour of a younger male. Perhaps even more disturbing is the lengthening of the refractory phase, extended from 2 min to 12–24 hours. There is no comparable refractory period in the older female who is advantaged. She maintains whatever capacity and pattern of orgasmic response that was typical of younger years.

In summary, the gradual, small changes in physiology and/or anatomy of the sexual system in older persons leaves little doubt of remaining capacities for responsivity and pleasurable behavior as sexual partners. Increasing current documentation for heightened vitality among older persons in their seventh, eighth, and ninth decades is accompanied by stated sexual interest, desires, needs, and expression. Perhaps it is more important to note that loving, genital, sensual, and intimate exchanges are not only possible but enjoyable even with weaker ejaculations and less erect penis among older men in their later decades. Loving, sexual genital interactions, sensual pleasure, and intimate sharing are part of the late years in support of the excitement of being alive.

3. The Older Homosexual, Gay and Lesbian

Few studies focus particularly on sexuality and age, and even fewer on gay and lesbian sexuality. As a matter of fact, older lesbian sexuality is given the least attention and may be a function of discrimination against age, gender, and sexual orientation. Despite the increase in studies of sexuality in older men and women, homosexuals (10% of each group) have been essentially ignored. Whatever studies of older homosexuals do exist report high levels of life satisfaction and acceptance of growing older. This is so despite predictable difficulties that are part of this sexual orientation and aging. It has been further noted that being involved in the gay community is a definitive plus in acceptance of one's own aging. Some researchers suggest there is greater flexibility with gender roles among gays and lesbians, which could contribute to aging changes.

Most studies appear to involve active gays for whom sexual orientation constitutes a lifestyle, and the subjects chosen through community networks of older gay and lesbian adults. An urban bias exists relative to the sites from which subjects were selected—locations in New York, San Francisco, or Los Angeles. It has also been pointed out that older persons with working-class backgrounds and ethnic and racial diversity were underrepresented. There is research underway to include African American aging gay males and to study gay and lesbian adults in rural areas. Another identified methodological difficulty stems from early studies in which gay men and lesbians were grouped as one study cohort. The assumption that homosexuality resulted in more similarity between these men and women than gender made them unique was probably incorrect. However, in a very recent study, significant gender differences were found in community participation, living situation, housing, friendship, and in gay and lesbian organizations. It is clear that gender differences would remain unknown unless specifically designed for in the research paradigm.

Much has been written recently in the scientific and popular literature about the genetic basis for homosexuality in some individuals, so that psychosexual therapy with reversal purpose would have minimal success. Controversy does continue on the validity of the biological or psychogenic basis. The common definitions of homosexuality usually emphasize the erotic attraction to persons of same sex. It is significant that both female and male homosexuals maintain that this definition omits very important aspects, such as love, commitment, companionship, trust, and lifestyle. The fear that has been voiced by heterosexuals that children who live in households of gays and lesbians will invariably grow up gay or lesbian has little basis in fact. Most of today's older gay and lesbian adults had early socialization in heterosexual families, brought up in traditional feminine and masculine roles. Most desire steady love relationships, not choosing casual liaisons. Compared to younger gay males, older gay partners have fewer sexual partners, lower frequency of genital activity, less cruising, and maintain longer relationships. Poor quality of kinship support for the homosexual lifestyle stimulates strong friendship ties, gay males with other gay males, lesbians with other lesbians. It is noteworthy that most sexuality and age literature, with all of its shortcomings, acknowledges the range of sexual behavior among older adults, which includes hetero-, homo-, and bisexuality.

V. SEXUAL DYSFUNCTIONS AND THERAPIES

Successful aging, which grows more widespread every day will delay or eliminate some of the disorders often consequent to uninformed lifestyles: nutrition, exercise, stress management, and control of life's decisions.

A. Chronic Diseases

There has been ample evidence that these disorders interfere with desire and phases of genital activity. They include coronary heart disease, cerebrovascular accidents, diabetes, pelvic disorders, and arthritis. Long-time diabetes will finally lead to male impotence (rarely true for female diabetic) and minimize female lubrication. Coronary disease and atherosclerosis do affect circulation and reduce penile engorgement and erection. Both older men and women with cardiac difficulties may withdraw from sexual activity for fear of heightening death risk.

B. Drugs

Prescribed and over-the-counter drugs used in treatment of these systemic diseases are identified as the culprits in diminishing libido, capacity for erection, lubrication, and orgasm. Other drug abuse—alcohol, marijuana, and tranquilizers—makes erection more difficult and can delay ejaculation. Antihypertensive medication not only results in the foregoing of sex but diminishes libido as well as conscious withdrawal from sexual activity for fear of intensifying the illness. Drug researchers and clinicians must find substitute drugs, when needed, with less serious side effects that drain desire, pleasure, and connection with loving mates.

C. Pelvic Surgeries

Many older men and women have ended their sexual activity after pelvic and breast surgeries—hysterectomies, prostatectomies, colostomies, ileostomies, and mastectomies. These surgeries affect libido and all phases of intercourse, and prostate enlargement, fairly common in older men, is often benign but can be cancerous. Chemotherapy and radiation have made significant headway providing choice and thus avoiding the necessity for surgery. Though technically improved over the last 20 years, prostatecomy still leaves a significant number of patients incontinent and impotent. Hysterectomies have been the most frequent, unnecessary surgery among middle-aged and older women. Women now ask more questions and vigorously seek to exert control over this decision; the numbers are therefore decreasing. Despite some reports of depression of desire and orgasmic capacity after pelvic surgery in men and women, these results are not inevitable.

D. Human Immunodeficiency Virus and Acquired Immune Deficiency Syndrome

The epidemic began in earnest in the United States by 1982. Most people were surprised, but from the beginning, about 10% of adult infections were found in persons 50 years or more, 25% were over 60, and 4% were over 70. Data from Europe do differ in specifics, not in trend: 11% of acquired immunodeficiency virus (AIDS) among older adults over 50; 42% 60+. These facts reinforce the urgency of lifelong sex education including the emphasis on the value of safe sex and the use of condoms in the later years.

AIDS is now considered a chronic disease and requires, as do other chronic disorders, early diagnosis, ongoing care and treatment, and modification as the nature of the infection changes (e.g., opportunistic infections). New medications are being developed and tested but generally with younger patients. The older American population is now described as remaining relatively well and vigorous into eighth and ninth decades, most of the chronic disorders are increasingly delayed. The kind of long-term care of the old-old is a topic for discussion and deliberation. For those who become infected at younger ages—long-term care becomes a necessity. For the aging and those elders with AIDS, the ethical and psychological factors are compounded. There is little that has been pursued concerning the effect of this infection on the sexual behavior of older adults.

E. Disabilities and the Physically Challenged

Among those elders with significant physical disabilities or challenges (e.g., paraplegia, stroke and paralysis), there are possibilities and potential for fulfilling sexual desires and needs. As with the majority of contemporary psychosexual therapies, partners working together achieve the best, most satisfying results.

F. Therapies

Generally, sexual dysfunctions are thought to be either biologic, psychogenic, or both in origin. For most of the dysfunctions noted, even if biologic in origin (circulatory, drug, or other systemic disease) a psychological overlay is almost always present. Therapy, therefore, includes medication, surgery, radiation and diet where necessary and psychotherapy as support for attitude and behavior changes.

Penile prostheses via surgery have been in use for at least two decades. A cooperative and supportive partner is central to its successful use. The last few years have provided a number of injectable drugs for males who are incapable of erection for a variety of reasons. There appears to be reasonable success, in the use of papaverine and the most recent caverject both injected directly into the penis, intracavernosa. The procedure may be instructed by a physician but is then taken over by the patient. Time to reach and maintain the erection are variable and no side effects have been reported.

In the last 15–20 years sexual therapists in conjunction with primary-care health professionals have been available to work through whatever sexual problems older persons present. Results depend not only on the capable therapist but on the motivation and basic mutual affection the couple may still enjoy.

Systemic disease almost always affects sexual, sensual, and intimate behavior. If the effects are not a direct result of the disease itself, the therapy, whether drugs, surgery, or radiation, frequently have negative results for the sexual system: libido, phases of sexual responsiveness, confidence, self-image, and positive attitudes.

VI. SUMMARY

Age can be considered irrelevant as a major barrier in the expression of sexuality, sensuality, and intimacy in the later years. The greatest barrier to successful loving relationships among the aging are the attitudes and practices of health professionals and society-at-large. Older adults today are increasingly vigorous and relatively well, and need opportunity and societal emotional support to remain active, sexual beings. For many older persons the genital aspect remains important, but for all older adults there is more to a loving relationship than genitalia—intimacy, sensuality, companionship, and friendship. Sexual behavior confirms each individual's personhood and nurtures the love of life till the end.

BIBLIOGRAPHY

Buss, D. M. (1994). *The evolution of desire: Strategies of human mating.* New York: Basic Books.

Butler, R. N., & Lewis, M. I. (1993). *Love and sex after 60* (rev). New York: Ballantine Books.

Guam, J. K., & Whitford, G. S. (1992). Adaptation and age-related expectations of older gay and lesbian adults. *The Gerontologist, 32*(3), 367–374.

Hodson, D. S., & Skeen, P. (1994). Sexuality and aging: The Hammerlock of myths. *Journal of Applied Gerontology, 13*(3), 219–235.

Hunter, M. S. (1990). Emotional well-being, sexual behavior, and hormone replacement therapy. *Maturitas, 12*(3), 299–314.

Kaplan, H. S. (1990). Sex, intimacy, and the aging process. *Journal of the American Academy of Psychoanalysis, 18*(2), 185–205.

Kimmel, D. C. (1992). The families of older gay men and lesbians. *Generations, 16*(3), 17(3), 37–38.

Kronenberg, F. (1994). Hot flashes. In R. Loblo (Ed.), *Treatment of the postmenopausal woman: Basic and clinical aspects* (pp. 99–117). New York: Raven Press, Ltd.

Rose, M. K., & Soares, H. H. (1993). Sexual adaptations of the frail elderly: A realistic approach. *Journal of Gerontological Social Work, 19*(3/4), 167–178.

Sandowski, C. (1993). Responding to the sexual concerns of persons with disabilities. *Journal of Social Work and Sexuality, 8*(2), 29–43.

Weg, R. B. (1996). Biomedical aspects of menopause. In G. L. Maddox, (Ed.), *The encyclopedia of aging* (2nd ed.). New York: Springer Publishing Company.

Skill Acquisition

David L. Strayer

University of Utah

I. Definition of Skill
II. Strategic Components of Skill
III. Automatic Components of Skill
IV. Strategies for Reducing Age-Related Differences in Skill Acquisition
V. Conclusions

Associative Learning The process of strengthening the associative link between a stimulus and a response that underlies automatic processing.

Consistent Practice A type of practice in which the stimulus–response associations are consistently maintained throughout training.

Part-Task Training A training procedure whereby the consistent components of a task are practiced separately from the whole task.

Priority Learning The process of modifying the attention-capturing properties of a stimulus leading to the automatic capture of attention.

Proactive Interference A situation in which prior learning interferes with learning new material.

Variable Priority Training A training procedure whereby subjects are trained to flexibly share attention between two tasks performed concurrently.

One of the most important components of human behavior is the **ABILITY TO ACQUIRE SKILLS** that allow us to perform very complex tasks quickly and accurately with little thought or effort. Given the centrality of this ability, a critical question concerns how normal aging affects the acquisition of new skills. A related issue concerns cognitive strategies that may facilitate skill acquisition and thereby minimize any age-related differences. These issues are becoming increasingly important in everyday life as technology is changing at an ever increasing pace. For example, the introduction of the personal computer into the workplace has necessitated the acquisition of a new class of complex skills for a large segment of the population. The purpose of this article is to examine the effects of normal aging on skill acquisition and to suggest training strategies that may reduce age-related differences in the acquisition of skill.

I. DEFINITION OF SKILL

Skill is thought to involve the coordination and integration of a number of component automatic processes with strategic knowledge about when and how to use these automatic procedures. It is well documented that *consistent practice* is necessary for the development of the automatic processes underlying skill. Moreover, there appear to be important contextual influences that affect the acquisition and deployment of the strategic components of skilled performance. The level of skill achieved in any task is the result of a synergistic interaction between these strategic and automatic components of skill. Therefore, understanding age-related differences in skill acquisition necessitates identifying which, if any, of these components differ as a function of age.

A. Possible Age–Skill Relationships

It is commonly believed that the acquisition of skill follows a power function, such that the improvements in performance are greater early in training than later in training. The generalized power function is

$$T = a + b(x)^{-c}. \quad (1)$$

In equation 1, response speed, T, is a monotonically decreasing function of the number of trials of practice, x, raised to the power $-c$, times the total amount of improvement, b, plus a constant reflecting the asymptotic lower bound of T, a. Using equation 1, it is possible to generate a set of theoretical relationships between the acquisition of skill in younger and older adults. Figure 1 illustrates several of these theoretical relationships. The functions are plotted on log-log coordinates, transforming the negatively accelerated learning functions into linear functions. Curve A represents the theoretical performance of younger adults. The remaining curves represent the theoretical performance of older adults. Notice that in each of the cases, older adults are initially slower than younger adults, consistent with the ubiquitous age-related slowing of behavior with senescence. Curve B represents a situation in which older adults learn the same amount and learn at the same rate as younger adults (i.e., parameters b and c of equation 1 are not age-sensitive). Curve C represents a situation in which older adults learn the same amount as younger adults, but older adults learn at a slower rate (i.e., parameter b is not age-sensitive, whereas the absolute value of the

parameter c is smaller for older adults than for younger adults). Curve D represents a situation in which older adults learn less than younger adults, but older adults improve at the same (relative) rate as younger adults (i.e., parameter b is smaller for older adults than for younger adults, whereas parameter c is not age-sensitive). Finally, curve E represents a situation in which older adults learn less and improve at a slower rate than younger adults (i.e., the absolute value of parameters b and c are both smaller for older adults than for younger adults).

The possibilities illustrated in Figure 1 represent a small, but theoretically important subset of the possible effects of aging on skill acquisition. The pattern of data illustrated in curve B would suggest that there are no age-related differences in skill acquisition and that any initial performance differences are preserved throughout training. The pattern of data illustrated in curve C would suggest that providing extra practice for older adults would eliminate any age-related differences in skill acquisition. Curve D would suggest that there is some limit on the amount of learning for older adults, but that both younger and older adults improve at the same (relative) rate. Finally, the pattern of data illustrated in curve E would suggest that there is a limit on the amount of learning for older adults, and that older adults take longer to learn this information. These curves were derived from the equation that describes skill acquisition over extended practice. To better understand the process of skill acquisition we need to be aware of two components of skill: the strategic component and the automatic component. These two components will be discussed in turn.

II. STRATEGIC COMPONENTS OF SKILL

Across a variety of perceptual, cognitive, and motor tasks, there is a systematic slowing of behavior with senescence. This can be readily observed by examining speed–accuracy trade-off functions, which are generated by cross-plotting reaction time (RT) with response accuracy at a number of levels of speed–accuracy instruction. Figure 2 presents idealized speed–accuracy trade-off functions for younger and older adults. The solid line represents the hypothetical speed–accuracy trade-off function for the younger adults, and the dashed line represents the hypothetical speed–accuracy trade-off function for the older

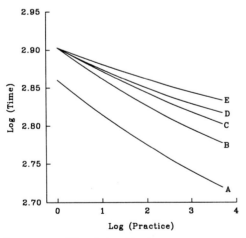

Figure I Four possible relationships between younger and older adults in skill acquisition. Curve A represents the performance of younger adults. Curves B–E represent the theoretical performance of older adults (see text for additional details). The data are plotted in log-log coordinates.

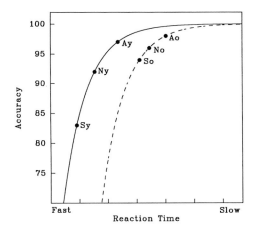

Figure 2 Theoretical speed–accuracy trade-off functions for younger subjects (solid line) and older subjects (dashed line). The points labeled S, N, and A refer to speed, neutral, and accuracy stress, respectively. The Y and O subscripts refer to younger and older subjects, respectively.

adults. Inspection of the figure reveals a monotonic increase in RT as accuracy increases. Thus, performance becomes slower as accuracy increases. The curves are negatively accelerated, indicating that a change in accuracy will produce a greater change in RT when subjects are operating at high levels of accuracy (e.g., 95%) than when they are operating at intermediate levels of accuracy (e.g., 75%). [*See* REACTION TIME.]

There are several important things to note in Figure 2. First, the curves are identical with the exception that the curve for older adults is shifted to the right of the curve for the younger adults. This suggests that if younger and older adults operate at similar points on their respective speed–accuracy trade-off functions that older adults will be systematically slower than younger adults. Another important point illustrated in Figure 2 is that younger and older adults typically do not operate at the same point on their respective speed–accuracy trade-off functions. The performance of older adults tends to fall in the upper righthand portion of the curve where small changes in accuracy lead to large changes in RT. For example, points N_y and N_o represent a "neutral" situation in which accuracy and speed are equally stressed for younger and older subjects, respectively. Note that N_o is closer to the asymptote of the older subjects curve than N_y is to the asymptote of the younger subjects curve. This

is indicative of a *conservative bias* to emphasize response accuracy over response speed in older adults. Finally, when given equivalent speed–accuracy instructions, older adults tend to operate over a more restricted range of their speed–accuracy trade-off function than do younger adults. For example, points A_y and A_o represent performance of younger and older subjects when they are given instructions emphasizing accuracy. Similarly, S_y and S_o represent performance of younger and older subjects when they are given instructions emphasizing response speed. Note that the spread between points A_y and S_y in younger adults is greater than the spread between points A_o and S_o in older adults. This is indicative of a less flexible information-processing style in older adults.

The pattern of data represented in Figure 2 is consistent with the hypothesis that older adults have adopted a more conservative response bias than younger adults. One interpretation of this is that older adults tend to evaluate more (or different) information before making a response than do younger adults. There are several possible reasons for this conservative response bias. First, the conservative bias may be the result of deliberate caution, which may carry over to other tasks. In many real-world tasks, the rewards for responding rapidly are often outweighed by the costs of making errors. Second, older adults may find it more difficult to dynamically modify their response criteria, which could result in older adults operating over a restricted range of their speed–accuracy trade-off function. Finally, older adults may engage in excessive monitoring of their performance, which would tend to make their performance very accurate at the expense of response speed.

When considering the effect of the conservative response bias of older adults on the acquisition of skill, it is important to make a distinction between learning and performance. It is possible that the conservative response bias of older adults may interfere with learning of the strategies necessary to facilitate skilled performance. Support for this interpretation has been obtained with younger adults who adopted response biases similar to those of older adults. These younger adults exhibited sustained deficits in the level of skill that they achieved, despite the opportunity to adopt and deploy more efficient response strategies. It is also possible that the conservative response bias of older adults affects performance, but does not directly affect learning. There is recent evidence suggesting that age-related differences can be reduced by requiring younger and older adults to operate at similar points along their respective speed–accuracy trade-off functions. Thus, it appears that the cautiousness of older adults may have at least two consequences. First, it may interfere with learning strategic knowledge that is necessary for skilled performance. Second, it may exacerbate any existing age-related differences in skill acquisition.

As illustrated in Figure 2, older adults do not trade speed for accuracy to the same extent as younger adults. This finding is consistent with a general trend for a loss of flexibility in older adults. Older subjects have also shown deficits in flexibly switching attention between auditory and visual modalities and in a number of dual-task paradigms in which they were required to flexibly share attention between two tasks. This reduction in flexibility in older adults may also serve to limit the information-processing strategies that are explored during the acquisition of skill. If the strategic parameter space that older adults explore is reduced relative to younger adults, then this would also contribute to age-related differences in skill acquisition. This possibility is supported by recent evidence that encouraging older adults to adopt a more flexible information-processing style facilitates skill acquisition. [See ATTENTION.]

In summary, older adults do not adopt and deploy the same cognitive strategies as younger adults; older adults tend to be more cautious and less flexible than younger adults. While the cause of these differences deserves further investigation, it is clear that these strategic differences contribute to the age-related differences in skill acquisition.

III. AUTOMATIC COMPONENTS OF SKILL

A cornerstone of skill is the automatic components of performance that underlie the task. Consistent practice is essential for automatization of the component processes within a task. A critical question is whether there are age-related differences in the development of automatic processing that would place limits on skill acquisition. As described above, the answer is complicated somewhat by the fact that older and younger adults typically do not operate at the same point on their respective speed–accuracy trade-off functions. However, through a combination of in-

structions, feedback, and payoffs, it is possible to reduce or eliminate age-related differences in strategic bias. In the remainder of this section, only studies that have controlled for the age-related conservative response bias will be considered.

Researchers have used a variety of laboratory and real-world tasks to examine age-related differences in automatization. One laboratory paradigm, commonly referred to as *visual search*, involves having subjects search visual displays for target stimuli. With younger subjects, consistent practice searching for one or more targets leads to an improvement in target detection, such that performance becomes insensitive to the size of the target set or the number of distractor stimuli on the display. Older subjects also show an improvement with consistent practice; however, the performance of older adults remains sensitive to both the size of the target set and the number of distractor stimuli on the display. These age-related deficits in visual search have been interpreted as reflecting a deficit in *priority learning*. Priority learning refers to a modification of the attention-capturing properties of a stimulus. Consistently attending to a stimulus leads to an increase in the attention-capturing properties of that stimulus, whereas consistently ignoring a distractor stimulus leads to a decrease in the attention-capturing properties of that stimulus. This modulation of the attention-capturing properties of the stimulus permits a rapid segmentation of the world on the basis of the salience of the stimuli. With advanced levels of practice, younger subjects often report that consistently attended targets appear to "pop-out" from the field of distractors, yielding highly efficient visual search performance. The age-related deficits in priority learning suggest that the mechanisms underlying the automatic capture of attention are deficient in older adults.

Another laboratory paradigm, commonly referred to as *memory search*, used to study age-related differences in automatization involves presenting one or more items in a set to be memorized. A series of probe stimuli are then presented and the subjects must decide whether the probe stimulus was one of the items in the memorized set. Younger subjects improve with consistent practice such that performance becomes insensitive to the number of items in the memorized set. Older subjects also improve with consistent practice, but older subjects do not improve as much as younger subjects, and older subjects improve at a slower rate than younger subjects. These age-related deficits in memory search have been interpreted as reflecting a deficit in *associative learning*. [*See* LEARNING; MEMORY.*]

Associative learning refers to the learning of associative relations between a stimulus and response. According to the modal view, when there is a consistent relationship between a stimulus and a response, the associative link between a stimulus and a response is strengthened. With high levels of practice, the stimulus–response (S-R) association will become so strong that little or no effort (i.e., attention) is required to perform the task. Under these high levels of practice, younger subjects often report that the response comes to mind automatically, without having to think of the solution. In fact, the dual-task literature suggests that the automatic components of a task can be performed even when subjects are actively attending to another task. The age-related differences in associative learning suggest that the mechanisms underlying the process of strengthening the S-R associations is deficient in older adults.

Several researchers have examined skill acquisition in more real-world situations. Although it is more difficult to control for the strategic and automatic components of skill, these studies generally arrive at the same conclusion as laboratory investigations. Interestingly, it appears that skills that were acquired as a young adult are maintained in older adults as long as these skills continue to receive practice. For example, there appears to be age-related sparing in real-world tasks such as chess, cigar rolling, pillar drilling, handwriting, mathematics, typing, and telegraphy if these skills were acquired early in life and were practiced throughout the life span. These findings may indicate that highly practiced skills may override age-related deficits in performance. Unfortunately, there is a natural confounding of the amount of practice on a skill and the age of the individual. This confounding makes it difficult to determine if the "sparing" is due to the retention of previously acquired skills or to the additional practice that older adults have received in the task.

In summary, the evidence points to at least two sources of age-related deficits in the automatization of the component processes underlying skill acquisition: priority learning and associative learning. Older adults do improve with consistent practice; however, age-related differences persist after training. In fact,

under some circumstances, the age-related differences may actually be greater after training than before training.

A. Possible Mechanisms for Age-Related Differences in Automatization

There have been few attempts to explain the mechanisms underlying these age-related learning differences. However, there are several potential reasons for these deficits. One possibility is that the age-related differences in learning may be related to neuronal cell loss. With senescence, there is a decrease in brain volume of about 2% per decade beginning at the age of 50. Older adults tend to exhibit atrophies of frontal and temporal cortices and also show a decrease in metabolic function in the frontal lobes. In neural-network computer simulations, it has been shown that the amount of material that an associative network can learn decreases, and the amount of practice necessary to learn the associative relations increases as the number and/or connectivity of neural-like units in the network decreases. Thus, the neuronal cell loss account would predict that the rate and amount of associative learning should decrease as a function of age. [*See* CELL DEATH.]

A second possibility for the age-related differences in learning is that there is a reduction in the neuronal plasticity of the system with increasing age. If associative and priority learning are mediated by neural substrates with reduced plasticity, this is likely to account for some portion of the automatization deficit. Note that the plasticity account differs from the neuronal cell loss account in that the former assumes that the processing units are modified less easily with training, whereas the latter assumes that there is a loss of processing units in the network. It is likely that both accounts contribute to the age-related differences in automatization.

Another account of the age-related differences in learning ascribes these differences to *proactive interference*. In this context, proactive interference refers to a situation in which material learned earlier in life interferes with the learning of new associative relations. Older adults have learned more material in their life than younger adults; therefore older adults are more likely to suffer from proactive interference than their younger counterparts. Unfortunately, because the amount of material learned through life naturally covaries with age, any simple method of equating younger and older adults is precluded. Consequently, the proactive interference interpretation may prove difficult to falsify.

IV. STRATEGIES FOR REDUCING AGE-RELATED DIFFERENCES IN SKILL ACQUISITION

The pattern that has emerged in this article is that older adults do not adopt the same strategies as younger adults and that there are age-related differences in priority and associative learning that interfere with skill acquisition. Overall, this pattern is most consistent with curve E presented in Figure 1: Older adults learn less and improve at a slower rate than younger adults.

There are several approaches that can be used to minimize the age-related differences in skill acquisition. First, encourage older adults to adopt strategies similar to those of younger adults. For example, it is possible to reduce the excessive cautiousness observed in the elderly through instructions, feedback, and payoffs. When these techniques are employed, age-related differences in skilled performance are diminished. There are likely to be other strategic differences between older and younger adults that interfere with skill acquisition, and many of these strategic differences will be task dependent. The framework developed in this article suggests that a fruitful approach will be to identify the strategies that younger adults adopt and encourage older adults to also use these strategies.

A second approach to minimize age-related differences is to provide practice on the consistent components of the task. Although there are age-related differences in priority and associative learning, older adults do improve with practice. One efficient means to facilitate the automatization of components processes is to use *part-task training*. Part-task training is a procedure in which the consistent components of a task are practiced separately, providing more practice on the individual components of a task than would be achieved by practicing the task in entirety. As long as the strategies in the part and whole task are similar, part-task training can be effective in reducing age-related differences in skill acquisition. In particu-

lar, part-task training can be used to provide additional consistent practice for older adults so as to compensate for differences in the rate of learning new skills.

A third approach that has proven to augment the acquisition of skill in older adults is *variable-priority training*. The variable-priority training procedure is derived from the dual-task attention literature in which subjects are required to perform two tasks concurrently. For example, given two tasks, A and B, subjects would be instructed to allocate a $p\%$ of their attention to task A and $q\%$ to task B, where $p + q = 100\%$. Variable-priority training involves requiring subjects to flexibly share their attention between the two tasks, such that p and q vary across blocks of trials. In contrast, a control group of subjects is instructed to maintain p and q at 50% for the duration of the training period. There are a number of transfer tasks that can be used to assess the effectiveness of variable-priority training. First, both groups can be given allocation instructions at transfer that hold p and q at 50%. In these situations, the performance of the variable-priority training group often exceeds that of the fixed-priority training group, despite that fact that the fixed-priority training group received more training at the 50/50 prioritization level than the variable-priority training group. Second, both groups can be transferred to novel tasks to determine if the attentional strategies transfer beyond the specific task combinations used during training. In novel transfer tasks, the variable-priority training group typically outperforms the fixed-priority training group, suggesting that subjects learned a task-coordination strategy that transfers to novel task combinations. Finally, both training groups can be evaluated in the context of real-world skill acquisition. It has been shown that subjects who receive variable-priority training on a video game have had lower dropout rates from flight school than subjects who receive fixed-priority training. Similar studies have shown decreased traffic accidents for subjects who have received variable-priority training. In short, variable-priority training appears to facilitate resource management strategies that transfer beyond the training session.

One recent study contrasted variable-priority training with fixed-priority training in both younger and older adults. Subjects were initially trained on a visual monitoring and alphabet arithmetic task and then transferred to two novel tasks: A scheduling task and a running memory task. Consistent with the earlier work, there was an advantage for the variable-priority training group. Moreover, older subjects who received variable-priority training actually *outperformed* younger subjects who received fixed-priority training. In addition, both younger and older adults showed similar transfer to the novel stimuli. This latter finding is encouraging because it suggests that the strategies used to coordinate the dual tasks were similar for both age groups. Thus, the variable-priority training procedure shows promise as a training strategy for minimizing age-related differences in skill acquisition.

V. CONCLUSIONS

Older adults do not acquire new skills as readily as younger adults, although older adults do exhibit significant improvement with consistent practice. The age-related deficits appear to be due to a combination of differences in strategic processing and to differences in associative and priority learning. A number of approaches were discussed to minimize the age-related differences in skill acquisition, including (a) encouraging older adults to adopt the same strategies as younger adults, (b) providing additional practice for older adults in the form of part-task training, and (c) using a variable-priority training procedure to facilitate the coordination and integration of component automatic processes underlying skill.

BIBLIOGRAPHY

Charness, N., & Bosman, E. A. (1990). Expertise and aging: Life in the lab. In T. M. Hess (Ed.), *Aging and cognition: Knowledge organization and utilization* (pp. 343–385). New York: Elsevier.

Charness, N., & Cambell, J. I. D. (1988). Acquiring skill at mental calculation in adulthood: A task decomposition. *Journal of Experimental Psychology: General, 117,* 115–129.

Fisk, A. D., & Rogers, W. A. (1991). Towards an understanding of age-related memory and visual search effects. *Journal of Experimental Psychology: General, 120,* 131–149.

Kramer, A. F., Larish, J. F., & Strayer, D. L. (1995). Training for attentional control in dual-task settings: A comparison of young and old adults. *Journal of Experimental Psychology: Applied, 1,* 50–76.

Strayer, D. L., & Kramer, A. F. (1994). Aging and skill acquisition: Learning-performance distinctions. *Psychology and Aging, 9,* 589–605.

Smell and Taste

Susan Schiffman

Duke University Medical Center

I. Introduction
II. Anatomy and Physiology of Smell and Taste:
   Change with Age
III. Perception of Smell and Taste: Losses with Age
IV. Compensation for Chemosensory Losses
   in the Elderly
V. Conclusion

Chemical Senses Smell and taste are chemical senses.
Olfaction Sense of smell.
Transduction Mechanism The biochemical process by which stimuli (in this case, chemicals) stimulate the receptors to induce a signal.

SMELL AND TASTE are chemical senses that are important in food selection, nutrition, and protection from toxins. Smell and taste sensitivity decreases with advancing age, and these losses result from normal aging, diseases, medications, and environmental pollution. For smell, the losses are due mainly to anatomical and physiological changes associated with normal aging; for taste, medications and medical conditions play a far larger role in sensory decrements than age-related anatomical losses. Alterations in the anatomy and physiology of the olfactory system are especially severe in Alzheimer's disease (AD). The majority of elderly persons has losses in the chemical senses of smell or taste or both. These chemosensory decrements can reduce the enjoyment of food and the quality of life. Recent studies indicate amplification of food with volatile compounds that stimulate the olfactory nerve can increase the intensity of the odor of food, improve intake, and amplify the immune system.

I. INTRODUCTION

The majority of elderly persons have losses in the chemical senses of smell, taste, or both. These chemosensory decrements can reduce the enjoyment of food and the quality of life. They may also cause health problems resulting in nutritional deficiencies, exacerbation of disease states, and impaired immunity. Disorders of smell and taste that occur with advancing age include anosmia (absence of smell), hyposmia (diminished sensitivity of smell), dysosmia (distortion of normal smell), ageusia (absence of taste), hypogeusia (diminished sensitivity of taste), and dysgeusia (distortion of normal taste). Smell and taste losses tend to begin around 60 years of age with a progressive decline with increasing age. Olfactory losses are due to anatomical and physiological changes in the olfactory system associated with normal aging as well as disease states and use of medications. For taste, medications and medical conditions play a far larger role in sensory decrements than anatomical or biological losses that result from normal aging. The drugs and medical conditions that alter smell and taste perception are given in Tables I and II. Over 250 drugs can alter the chemical senses, which indicates the enormity of the problem. The sites of action for most pharmaceutical compounds that induce smell and taste losses are not known, but medications can act at several levels including peripheral receptors, chemosensory neural pathways, and/or the brain. Drugs are secreted into the saliva, and salivary concentrations of many drugs are high enough to exert adverse effects on taste sensations, either by modifying taste transduction mechanisms or by producing a taste of their own. Little is

Table I Drugs That Interfere with the Smell and Taste Systems

AIDS- and HIV drugs
Didanosine
Zalcitabine
Zidovudine

Amebicides & anthelmintics
Metronidazole
Niclosamide
Niridazole

Anesthetics
Benzocaine
Cocaine and tetracaine hydrochloride
Dibucaine hydrochloride
Euprocin
Lidocaine
Procaine hydrochloride
Propofol
Tropacocaine

Anticholesteremics and antilipidemics
Cholestyramine
Clofibrate
Fluvastatin sodium
Gemfibrozil
Lovastatin
Pravastatin sodium
Probucol
Simvastatin

Anticoagulants
Phenindione

Antihistamines
Chlorpheniramine maleate
Loratadine
Terfenadine and pseudoephedrine

Antimicrobial agents
Allicin
Amphotericin B
Ampicillin
Atovaquone
Aztreonam
Bleomycin
Carbenicillin indanyl sodium
Cefamandole
Cefpodoxime proxetil
Ceftriaxone sodium
Cefuroxime axetil
Cinoxacin
Ciprofloxacin
Clarithromycin
Clindamycin phosphate
Clofazimine
Enoxacin
Ethambutol hydrochloride
Griseofulvin
Imipenem-cilastatin sodium
Lincomycin

Antimicrobial agents (*continued*)
Lomefloxacin HCl
Mezlocillin sodium
Norfloxacin
Ofloxacin
Pentamidine isethionate
Piperacillin and tazobactam sodium
Rifabutin
Streptomycin
Tetracyclines
Ticarcillin disodium and clavulanate potassium
Tyrothricin

Antiproliferative, including immunosuppressive agents
Aldesleukin
Azathioprine
Carmustine
Cisplatin
Carboplatin
Doxorubicin and methotrexate
Fluorouracil
Interferon alfa-2a
Interferon alfa-2b
Vincristine sulfate

Antirheumatic, antiarthritic, analgesic-antipyretic and anti-inflammatory
Auranofin
Aurothioglucose
Benoxaprofen
Butorphanol tartrate
Choline magnesium trisalicylate
Colchicine
Dexamethasone
Diclofenac potassium/diclofenac sodium
Dimethyl sulfoxide
Etodolac
Fenoprofen calcium
Flurbiprofen
Gold
Hydrocortisone
Hydromorphone HCl
Ketoprofen
Ketorolac tromethamine
Levamisole
Morphine sulfate
Nabumetone
Nalbuphine HCl
Oxaprozin
D-penicillamine and penicillamine
Pentazocine lactate
Phenylbutazone
Piroxicam
Salicylates
Sulindac

Antirheumatic, antiarthritic, analgesic-antipyretic and anti-inflammatory (*continued*)
Sumatriptan succinate
5-thiopyridoxine

Antiseptics
Hexetidine

Antispasmodics, irritable bowel syndrome
Dicylomine HCl
Oxybutynin
Phenobarbital + hyoscyamine
SO_4 + atropine SO_4 + scopolamine hydrobromide

Antithyroid agents
Carbimazole
Methimazole
Methylthiouracil
Propylthiouracil
Thiouracil

Antiulcerative
Clidinium bromide
Famotidine
Glycopyrrolate
Hyoscyamine sulfate
Mesalamine
Misoprostol
Omeprazole
Propantheline bromide
Sulfasalazine

Antiviral
Acyclovir
Foscarnet sodium
Idoxuridine
Interferon alfa-n3
Interferon beta-1b
Rimantadine HCl

Agents for dental hygiene
Sodium fluoride
Sodium lauryl sulfate
Chlorhexidine digluconate mouthrinses

Bronchodilators and antiasthmatic drugs
Albuterol sulfate
Beclomethasone dipropionate
Bitolterol mesylate
Cromolyn sodium
Ephedrine HCl + phenobarbitol + potassium iodide + theophylline calcium salicylate
Flunisolide
Metaproterenol sulfate
Nedocromil
Pirbuterol acetate inhalation aerosol
Terbutaline sulfate

continues

Continued

Diuretics, antiarrhythmic, antihypertensive, & antifibrillatory agents
Acetazolamide
Adenosine
Amiodarone HCl
Amiloride and its analogs
Amlodipine besylate
Benazepril HCl and hydrochlorothiazide
Betaxolol HCl
Bisoprolol fumarate and bisoprolol fumarate with hydrochlorothiazide
Captopril and Captopril/hydrochlorothiazide
Clonidine
Diazoxide
Diltiazem
Doxazosin mesylate
Enalapril
Esmolol
Ethacrynic acid
Flecainide acetate
Fosinopril sodium
Guanfacine HCl
Hydrochlorothiazide
Labetalol HCl
Metolazone
Mexiletine HCl
Moricizine HCl
Nifedipine
Procainamide HCl
Propafenone HCl
Propranolol
Ramipril
Spironolactone
Tocainide HCl
Triamterene/hydrochlorothiazide

Hyper and hypoglycemic drugs
Diazoxide
Glipizide
Phenformin and derivatives

Hypnotics and sedatives
Estazolam
Flurazepam HCl
Midazolam HCl
Quazepam
Triazolam
Zolpidem tartrate

Hypnotics and sedatives (*continued*)
Zoplicone

Muscle relaxants and drugs for treatment of Parkinson's disease
Baclofen
Chlormezanone
Cyclobenzaprine HCl
Dantrolene sodium
Levodopa
Methocarbamol
Pergolide mesylate
Selegiline HCl

Opiates
Codeine
Hydromorphone hydrochloride
Morphine

Psychopharmacologic including antiepileptics
Alprazolam
Amitriptyline HCl
Amoxapine
Buspirone HCl
Carbamazepine
Chlordiazepoxide + Amitriptyline HCl
Clomipramine HCl
Clozapine
Desipramine HCl
Doxepin HCl
Felbamate
Fluoxetine HCl
Imipramine HCl and Imipramine pamoate
Lithium carbonate
Maprotiline HCl
Nortriptyline HCl
Paroxetine HCl
Perphenazine-amitriptyline HCl
Phenytoin
Pimozide
Protriptyline HCl
Psilocybin
Risperidone
Sertraline HCl
Trazodone HCl
Trifluoperazine
Trimipramine maleate
Venlafaxine HCl

Radiation therapy
Radiation to head

Sympathomimetic drugs
Amphetamines
Benzphetamine HCl
Dextroamphetamine sulfate
Fenfluramine HCl
Mazindol
Methamphetamine HCl
Phenmetrazine theoclate with fenbutrazate hydrochloride
Phendimetrazine tartrate
Phentermine

Vasodilators
Bamifylline hydrochloride
Dipyridamole
Isosorbide mononitrate
Nitroglycerin patch
Oxyfedrine

Others (indication)
Acetylcholine-like substances
Allopurinol
Antihemophilic factor
Antithrombin III
Bepridil HCl
Calcitonin
Etidronate
Etretinate
Gadodiamide
Germine monoacetate
Granisetron HCl
Histamine phosphate
Iohexol
Iron sorbitex
Leuprolide acetate
Levamisole HCl
Mesna
Methazolamide
Methylergonovine maleate
Nicotine
Nicotine polacrilex
Pentoxifylline
Potassium iodide
Sermorelin acetate
Strychnine
Succimer
Terbinafine
Ursodiol
Vitamin D/Calcitriol
Vitamin K_1/Phytonadione

known about the concentrations of drugs in olfactory mucous secretions.

Smell and taste can play a role in the control of food intake and metabolic processes in the elderly. First, the chemical senses serve as monitors of a food's caloric and nutritional value. Thus, when chemosensory systems are compromised, smell and taste signals may not be adequate cues for caloric and nutritional value of food, and inadequate intake of essential macro- and micronutrients may result. Second, smell

Table II Medical Conditions That Affect Smell or Taste

Classification/Condition	Smell	Taste
Nervous		
Alzheimer's disease	X	X
Bell's palsy		X
Damage to chorda tympani		X
Down's syndrome	X	
Epilepsy	X	
Familial dysautonomia		X
Guillain-Barre syndrome		X
Head trauma	X	X
Korsakoff's syndrome	X	
Migraine	X	
Multiple sclerosis	X	X
Parkinson's disease	X	
Raeder's paratrigeminal syndrome		X
Tumors and lesions	X	X
Nutritional		
Cancer		X
Chronic renal failure	X	X
Liver disease including cirrhosis	X	X
Niacin (vitamin B_3) deficiency		X
Thermal burn		X
Trimethylaminuria	X	
Vitamin B_{12} deficiency	X	
Zinc deficiency		X
Endocrine		
Adrenal cortical insufficiency	X	X
Congenital adrenal hyperplasia		X
Cretinism		X
Cushing's syndrome	X	X
Diabetes mellitus	X	X
Gonadal dysgenesis (Turner's syndrome)	X	X
Hypogonadotropic hypogonadism (Kallman's syndrome)	X	
Hypothyroidism	X	X
Panhypopituitarism		X
Primary amenorrhea	X	
Pseudohypoparathyroidism	X	X
X-linked ichthyosis due to steroid sulfatase deficiency	X	
Local		
Adenoid hypertrophy	X	
Allergic rhinitis, atopy, and bronchial asthma	X	
Crouzon's syndrome	X	
Facial hypoplasia	X	X
Glossitis and other oral disorders		X
Leprosy	X	X
Oral Crohn's disease		X
Ozena	X	
Paranasal sinus exenteration	X	
Sinusitis and polyposis	X	

continues

Continued

Classification/Condition	Smell	Taste
Local (*continued*)		
Sjögren's syndrome	**X**	**X**
Viral and Infectious		
Acute viral hepatitis	X	
HIV infection	X	
Influenza-like infections	X	X
Other		
Amyloidosis and sarcoidosis	X	X
Cystic fibrosis	X	X
Familial (genetic)	X	
High altitude		X
Hypertension		X
Laryngectomy	X	X
Major depressive disorder		X

and taste sensations can induce gastric and pancreatic secretions as well as preabsorptive insulin release. Thus, chemosensory losses may compromise the body's preparation for influx of nutrients. Third, the irreversible declines in smell and taste acuity that occur with age may contribute to impaired immunity among the elderly. Recent data suggest that flavor enhancement of food for the eldely can improve immune status. [*See* IMMUNE SYSTEM.]

Demographic studies suggest that the number of persons with chemosensory losses is increasing worldwide. International population studies have reported that a dramatic increase in both the proportion and absolute numbers of elderly persons is occurring in all countries. In 1980 the number of persons worldwide aged 60 years or more was 36 million. By the year 2025 this number is expected to reach 1.21 billion. This increase presents a global health challenge given the number of persons who will suffer from chemosensory losses that contribute to nutritional deficiences and impaired immunity.

II. ANATOMY AND PHYSIOLOGY OF SMELL AND TASTE: CHANGE WITH AGE

In order to understand the alterations in smell and taste functioning that occur with age, it is helpful to be familiar with the anatomy and physiology of these systems. The receptors for olfaction are located in the pigmented upper part of the superior turbinate, the adjoining nasal septum, and the intervening roof between them. Olfactory receptors are specialized bipolar neurons with cilia that protrude into the mucus covering the epithelium. The specialized receptor portion of the bipolar neuron undergoes continuous renewal with an average turnover time of 30 days. This process of renewal can be affected by nutritional and hormonal states, therapeutic radiation, and pharmaceutical agents. The axons of bipolar neurons are very thin and travel in bundles to the olfactory bulb coursing through small holes in the cribriform plate of the ethmoid bone. In the olfactory bulb, they synapse in bushy masses called glomeruli. With age, glomeruli degenerate and the olfactory bulb takes on a moth-eaten appearance as fibers disappear.

There are major connections between the olfactory bulb and parts of the brain termed the "limbic system" which not only processes olfactory information but mediates emotions in humans as well. This portion of the brain frequently degenerates earlier than other structures, and it is here that age-related neurofibrillary tangles and senile plaques are first seen. The brain structures that are involved in efferent connections from the olfactory bulb to the brain as well as centrifugal inputs from the brain to the olfactory bulb include the anterior olfactory nucleus, piriform cortex, hippocampus, olfactory tubercle, lateral entorhinal cortex, amygdala, and hypothalamus. With age there are anatomic and physiological losses in most of these structures associated with the olfactory system. [See BRAIN AND CENTRAL NERVOUS SYSTEM.]

Alterations in the anatomy and physiology of the olfactory system are especially severe in Alzheimer's disease (AD) with morphological and neurochemical changes that are prominent in the olfactory epithelium, olfactory bulbs, anterior olfactory nucleus, olfactory tubercle, amygdala, prepiriform cortex, hippocampus, entorhinal cortex, uncus, and subiculum. Most of the histopathological changes seen in olfactory pathways (except the olfactory epithelium) are neuritic plaques, neurofibrillary tangles, and granulovacuolar degeneration. In olfactory epithelium, abnormal masses of neurites (axonal and dendritic processes of neurons) and compositional changes in subunits of neurofilament proteins are found. Reduced choline acetyltransferase (CAT) levels have been reported in olfactory tubercle.

The impairment of olfactory and limbic structures

of the temporal lobe in AD produces decrements in the ability to identify, recognize, and remember odorants. Impairment closer to the periphery produces losses in the ability to detect the presence of odorants. One theory of AD is that the olfactory system is the site of initial pathology with the causative agent acting through a nasal route. There is evidence for transneural transport in the olfactory system for such diverse materials as viruses, dyes, gold, aluminosilicates, and wheat-germ agglutinin-horseradish peroxidase conjugate. These compounds may be transported from the external environment via olfactory receptor neurons to the olfactory bulb and beyond, disrupting the functioning of neurons known to be associated with AD and produce long-term changes or degeneration in these regions. [See DEMENTIA.]

A. Taste

Taste sensations are mediated by taste buds that are comprised of approximately 50 cells arranged to form a pear-shaped organ. Taste cells are derived from dividing epithelium that surrounds the bud. Taste cells, like olfactory receptors, are in a constant state of continuous renewal but with a turnover time that averages $10-10\frac{1}{2}$ days. Like smell receptors, this process of renewal can be affected by nutritional and hormonal states, therapeutic radiation, and pharmaceutical agents.

Taste buds are located on the tongue, soft palate, pharynx, larynx, epiglottis, uvula, and upper third of the esophagus. Lingual taste buds are situated on small structures called papillae, which are classified into three types: fungiform (found on anterior $\frac{2}{3}$ of the tongue), circumvallate (arranged in the shape of a V on the posterior tongue), and foliate (folds on the lateral border of the tongue). The fungiform papillae are innervated by a branch of the seventh cranial nerve called the chorda tympani. The circumvallate papillae are innervated by the ninth cranial nerve called the glossopharyngeal. The foliate papillae are innervated by both the chorda tympani and the glossopharyngeal nerves. Taste buds on the epiglottis and the larynx are innervated by the tenth cranial nerve called the vagus nerve. The glossopharyngeal and vagus nerves also appear to innervate taste buds on the pharynx.

Gustatory information from all three nerves is transmitted to the nucleus of the solitarius in the medulla and ultimately to the thalamus and cortical taste area as well as the lateral hypothalamus, which is the feeding center in the brain. Free nerve endings of the fifth cranial nerve called the trigeminal nerve are found on the anterior tongue and the oral cavity. Lesions along any of these pathways can alter the perception of taste. Disorders that reduce the input from taste buds can amplify the awareness of the trigeminal components of spicy foods and carbonated beverages, which can be irritating and even painful.

There is scientific disagreement about the biological mechanisms responsible for age-related taste losses. Medications, medical conditions, and possibly environmental pollutants may play a far larger role in taste decrements than anatomical or physiological losses resulting from normal aging. Although some studies have found reductions in the number of papillae and/or taste buds with age in humans and animals, other studies have not confirmed these losses. Some investigations suggest that taste losses are due to changes in taste cell membranes. Another possible cause of taste (as well as smell) loss is age-related deficits in neurotransmitters, including glutamic acid, acetylcholine, serotonin, somatostatin, noradrenaline, and dopamine. The loss in neurotransmitters may be especially important in the gustatory losses found in AD.

III. PERCEPTION OF SMELL AND TASTE: LOSSES WITH AGE

A. Olfactory Thresholds

Psychophysical studies of smell consistently find significant olfactory losses at threshold concentrations in elderly subjects. Elevated threshold levels (detection and/or recognition thresholds) have been reported for a broad range of compounds including *n*-butanol, coal gas, coffee, citral, menthol, pyridine, thiophene, citralva, food odors, and many other purified odorants.

B. Suprathreshold Odor Perception

Magnitude estimation experiments in which numbers are assigned to smells in proportion to their perceived intensities reveal losses for a broad range of pleasant, foul, and neutral odorants. The elderly also have reduced ability to identify odors. Multidimensional scaling experiments in which odors are arranged in a spatial map based on their perceived similarities indicate that the elderly have reduced capacity to discriminate the degree of difference between odors of different qualities. The elderly are also more prone than young adults to olfactory adaptation.

C. Taste Thresholds

Most psychophysical studies have found increases in both the detection and recognition thresholds (decreased sensitivity) in the elderly. Elevated thresholds have been reported for salty, sweet, sour, and bitter tastes as well as for tastes of amino acids and weak galvanic current. Recent studies suggest that medications and medical disorders contribute substantially to these losses. For simple (primary) tastes, such as sodium chloride (salty), sucrose (sweet), citric acid (sour), and quinine hydrochloride (bitter), taste decrements due strictly to normal aging alone in the absence of disease and medications are small. This conclusion comes from psychophysical tests of 140 very healthy individuals (20 subjects per decade) who had no present or previous illnesses and were taking no over-the-counter or prescription drugs. However, far greater losses in threshold taste sensitivity occurred for elderly taking medications. The average detection thresholds for relatively active but medicated elderly persons were 11.6 times higher for sodium salts; 4.3 times higher for acids; 7.0 times higher for bitter compounds; 2.5 times higher for amino acids; 5.0 times higher for glutamate salts; and 2.7 times higher for sweeteners compared with young subjects. Retrospective analysis of medication use in these subjects revealed that the average subject was taking 3.4 medications. Thus medications (and medical conditions) clearly account for a significant proportion of losses at threshold level, especially for primary tastes. Medications may also play a role in the nonuniform losses with age that occur within a chemical group; for example, far greater losses with age are found for sodium succinate, sodium tartrate, sodium citrate, and sodium sulfate than for sodium chloride. [*See* PHARMACOLOGY.]

D. Suprathreshold Taste Perception

Most suprathreshold experiments, like threshold experiments, have found taste losses in the elderly. Magnitude estimation techniques suggest that the elderly perceive a broad range of tastes including sweeteners, glutamate salts, and bitter compounds as less intense than the young. The mean ratio of the slope of the concentration–response function for young compared to the elderly is approximately 2–2.5. The elderly have less ability to discriminate among different intensities of the same tastant. Suprathreshold taste losses can be especially troublesome for certain subsets of the elderly population such as those with diabetes and those with hypertension. Impaired sweet taste perception can make elderly subjects with diabetes vulnerable to the adverse effects from excess consumption of sugar. Impaired salt taste perception can make it difficult for hypertensive patients to comply with a low-sodium diet.

IV. COMPENSATION FOR CHEMOSENSORY LOSSES IN THE ELDERLY

Compounds that stimulate the olfactory nerve have been added to food for the elderly to amplify the intensity and improve intake. In one study, flavors such as simulated bacon and beef flavors were added to some but not all foods at meals in a retirement home. For 3 weeks elderly subjects ate an institutional diet (Unenhanced). During another 3-week period, the same subjects ate identical foods to which intense flavors were added (Enhanced). The subjects were tested in two groups. For Group 1 the Unenhanced food period preceded the Enhanced food period. For Group 2 the order was reversed. The amount of each food was measured every weekday throughout the study, and the nutritional composition of the diet was analyzed. Biochemical measures of health status were obtained at the beginning of the study (Baseline) and following both the Unenhanced and Enhanced periods. These measures included somatomedin-C/insulinlike growth factor I, transferrin, total T and B lymphocytes, and routine blood chemistries. Weight, height, midarm circumference, and triceps skinfold thickness were also measured. Handgrip strength and pinch strength were measured in Group 1. The results of the study showed the elderly ate more of flavor-enhanced foods and less of unenhanced foods resulting in consumption of the same number of calories

and nutrients on the Enhanced and Unenhanced arms of the study. However, intake of flavor-amplified foods produced an increase in T-cell and B-cell counts, in spite of the fact that it did not alter total dietary intake and other biochemical measures. Thus, three major conclusions emerged from this study: (a) elderly persons will eat more food when it is flavor-enhanced; (b) consumption of flavor-enhanced food appears to improve immune function, which is not attributable to altered nutrient intake or biochemical status; and (c) improved grip strength in both hands was evident after 3 weeks' consumption of flavor-enhanced foods.

Four potential factors may account for the improved immune status produced by flavor enhancement. First, there are direct neural-immune connections between the limbic system in the brain, which subserves olfaction, and the immune system. Thus olfactory stimulation may directly boost immune function. Second, the increased flavor levels may produce greater release of digestive enzymes, which leads to better absorption of nutrients. Third, there may be compounds in the flavors that directly improve immunocompetence due to their biochemical actions. Many phytochemicals, such as allium compounds, are known to have immunological actions. Fourth, the improved immunity from flavors may be a psychoimmune response because flavor enhancement improves the palatability of the food. Improved palatability and enjoyment of food could improve mood leading to reduced circulating cortisol. Cortisol is known to suppress the immune status.

Compounds that stimulate the taste nerves, such as monosodium glutamate (MSG), have also been found to improve both preference and intake, although direct measures of nutritional and immune status have not been reported. Addition of MSG to familiar foods in a group of institutionalized elderly persons was found to facilitate long-term intake in elderly persons. The selection of MSG-flavored diets can be explained by sensory means with no appreciable effects on preference by postingestive consequences.

V. CONCLUSION

Losses in smell and taste occur with age, and these losses may contribute to nutritional and immune deficiencies found in the elderly. Recent studies have shown that flavor amplification of diets for the elderly can improve intake and increase the number of T and B lymphocytes.

BIBLIOGRAPHY

Mattes, R. D., & Cowart, B. J. (1994). Dietary assessment of patients with chemosensory disorders. *Journal of the American Diet Association, 94,* 50–56.

Physicians' Desk Reference (49th ed.). DesMoines: Medical Economics; 1995.

Schiffman, S. S. (1983). Taste and smell in disease. *New England Journal of Medicine, 308,* 1275–1279, 1337–1343.

Schiffman, S. S. (1991). Drugs influencing taste and smell perception. In T. V. Getchell, R. L. Doty, L. M. Bartoshuk, J. B. Snow (Eds.), *Smell and taste in health and disease* (pp. 845–850). New York: Raven Press.

Schiffman, S. S. (1992). Food acceptability and nutritional status: Considerations for the aging population in the 21st century. In P. Leathwood, M. Horisberger, & W. P. T. James (Eds.), *For a better nutrition in the 21st century* (pp. 149–162). New York: Raven Press.

Schiffman, S. S. (1993). Perception of taste and smell in elderly persons. *Critical Review of Food Science and Nutrition, 33,* 17–26.

Schiffman, S. S., Crumbliss, A. L., Warwick, Z. S. & Graham, B. G. (1990). Thresholds for sodium salts in young and elderly subjects: correlation with molar conductivity of anion. *Chemical Senses, 15,* 671–678.

Schiffman, S. S., & Warwick, Z. S. (1993). Effect of flavor enhancement of foods for the elderly on nutritional status: food intake, biochemical indices and anthropometric measures. *Physiology and Behavior, 53,* 395–402.

Schiffman, S. S., & Warwick, Z. S. (1992). The biology of taste and food intake. In G. A. Bray & D. H. Ryan (Eds.), *The science of food regulation: Food intake, taste, nutrient partitioning, and energy expenditure.* Pennington Center Nutrition Series. (vol. 2) (pp. 293–312). Baton Rouge: Louisiana State University Press.

Social Networks, Support, and Integration

Toni C. Antonucci, Aurora M. Sherman, and Hiroko Akiyama

The University of Michigan

I. Theoretical Issues
II. Measurement Issues
III. Data Sources
IV. Social Support and the Health Continuum
V. Family and Friendship Relationships
VI. Social Exchange and Reciprocity
VII. Gender Differences
VIII. Cultural Differences
IX. Social Relations and Well-Being
X. Summary and Conclusion

Buffering Effects Describes the hypothesized indirect effect of social support on well-being (i.e., the degree to which receiving social support helps the individual cope with stress, life events, or crises, and thus has a positive effect on that individual's quality of life, well-being, or health).

Convoy Model of Social Relations Argues that individuals move through time, age, and history, effecting and being effected by others who have fundamental influences on the individual's development and well-being.

Equity Theory Builds on the basic notion of the norm of reciprocity, the societal norm that assumes that there should be an overall equal amount of support provided as received. In addition to reciprocity, one can also overbenefit (i.e., receive more support than one provides) or underbenefit (i.e., provide more support than one receives).

Exchange Rule Refers to the societal or culturally assumed norm of exchanges among different people, groups of people, or generations. Thus, in some cultures the exchange rule is that younger people should always provide older people with support, whereas in other groups or cultures the reverse might be assumed.

Continuum A specific way to conceptualize health along a continuum that includes the premorbid, predisease state, through a crisis or disease event, followed by a recovery, rehabilitative, or adaptation stage.

Life Span Developmental Theory Describes a theoretical perspective that argues that it is critical to understand the effect of inter- and intraindividual development over time in order to truly understand the individual at any one point in time.

Main Effects of Social Support Describes the hypothesized direct effect of social support on well-being (i.e., the degree to which receiving social support improves an individual's quality of life, well-being, or health).

Reciprocity In the social support literature used to refer to reciprocal exchanges, that is, exchanges that are seen as equal with the same amount of support provided and received by each participant. Of course, exchanges can also be nonreciprocal.

Social Integration Describes the degree to which an individual is blended into the group, organization, or community. This term can be thought of as one that considers the centrality versus marginality of the individual to the comparison group.

Social Networks The term used to describe the structural characteristics of an individual's social relations. Social networks include the objective aspects

Copyright © 1996 by Academic Press, Inc.
All rights of reproduction in any form reserved.

of these relationships such as their number, age, sex, relationship, and frequency of contact.

Social Relations An umbrella term used to encompass the large number of concepts and measures involving interpersonal interactions and transactions.

Social Support This term describes the exchange of resources, goods, or services between or among social network members and has been used to describe both the provision and receipt of these exchanges.

Social Support Exchanges Emphasizes that the interpersonal interactions known as social support involve both the provision and receipt of support by different people.

Socioemotional Selectivity Theory Takes a life span perspective of social relations and argues that as people age they become increasingly select about the number of and specific persons with whom they would like to maintain a close, interpersonal relationship.

Support Bank In keeping with the general norm of reciprocity, it is proposed that people build up nonequitable relationships by providing more support than they receive (i.e., making support deposits into the support bank) so that support will be available to them at some time in the future when and if they are in need.

The importance of social relations has been increasingly recognized as a critical element in the adaptation, adjustment, and well-being of older people. In the past 20 years the theoretical basis for the study of **SOCIAL NETWORKS, SUPPORT, AND INTEGRATION** has expanded considerably, significantly advantaged by an accumulation of empirical evidence. In this article we provide an overview of the theoretical and conceptual issues that have guided the research, a consideration of methodological limitations and advancements, and illustrative examples of the empirical research now available in the field.

I. THEORETICAL ISSUES

Although a great deal of empirical research examining social networks, support, and integration was essentially conducted without any theoretical basis, several conceptual and definitional issues have received a great deal of attention. The terms themselves must be specified. Early research frequently blurred the distinctions between these concepts thus limiting the theoretical advances that could be made. The term *social network* refers to the structural or objective makeup of the social relationships maintained by the individual. Examples of social network concepts include the number of people in the network, their relationship to the older person, their age, frequency of contact or interaction, and the degree to which members of the social network know each other, as well as the older person. Networks can be dense, as is the case when the social network consists mostly of relatives who all know each other. A network might not be very dense at all, as is the case with a network consisting mostly of friends who know the older person but not each other. Another concept relevant to social networks is multiplexity. Individuals within a social network can serve multiple roles for the older person, as is often the case with relatives, or single roles, as might be the case with a bridge partner or church member. Social support, on the other hand, refers to the actual exchange of something within the relationship and is also called functional support. It might be tangible or intangible. One often thinks of giving or receiving emotional support or instrumental aid from people with whom one feels close. This is what is commonly meant by the term *social support*. And finally, *social integration* refers to the degree to which the individual, by virtue of social relations with others, feels integrated into the community and society more generally. Social integration is the exemplification of adaptation, adjustment, and general well-being and might be considered an outcome of optimally existing social networks and social support.

The term *social relations* is sometimes used as an umbrella term for the three previously outlined concepts. An important issue when considering the role of social relations in the lives of the elderly is the processes through which social relations might operate. Two major approaches have been outlined and labeled the main effects and the buffering effects positions. Both approaches have implications for maximizing the benefits of social relations in the lives of older people. The concepts are relatively simple. In the main effect explanation, the presence of close and important others, and their constant positive interactions or provision of support, provides the individual with a sense of self-worth and positive well-being. Having friends and family who think highly of one, makes one feel good about oneself and thereby contributes in fundamental ways to adjustment, adaptation, well-being, and mental health. A second, slightly more complicated explanation of how social relations might operate suggests that friends and family help the individual, either through direct tangible, instrumental support or specific emotional support, cope with problems or crises they might encounter. Thus, support from others buffers the impact of negative events, crises, or stresses in the individual's life, thereby also improving their adjustment, adaptation, well-being, and mental health. Empirical evidence has supported both explanations.

An integrative theoretical explanation has been proposed that argues that the most comprehensive explanation of the role of social relations is one that incorporates a life span perspective. Over time individuals accumulate relationships as well as specific support exchange histories, both of which influence their perspective on current relationships. Recent research on attachment as a life span concept and the convoy model of social relationships takes this perspective. Although it is not likely that early relationships predetermine later relationships unmodifiably, it does seem to be the case that people develop styles of relationships and expectations about them. There appears to be a cumulative element to important, close, enduring relationships that permits the development of expectations concerning long-term reciprocity of exchanges. Similarly, although there is a tendency to assume that social relations have both long- and short-term positive effects, it is important to recognize that these relationships, and expectations about them, might also be negative. Thus, an older person who becomes ill might expect help and support from a spouse or daughter, or, based on previous experience, the older person might consider their relative an unreliable source of support, especially in times of crisis.

There is now some developing consensus that a long-term or life span view of social relations provides a promising theoretical perspective from which to understand social relations. A life span perspective also allows the integration of both main and buffering effects of support. As individuals mature, their ongoing social relations have (optimally) positive effects on general well-being and life satisfaction, but when specific crises emerge, social relations can buffer their impact on specific outcome events.

II. MEASUREMENT ISSUES

There are several measurement issues that have been inadequately considered in the empirical study of social relations. Because they fundamentally effect the quality of the data and the understanding of how to interpret those data, they merit at least a brief consideration. In the same way that researchers have been inconsistent and nonspecific in their definition of social relations terms, they have been nonspecific in measurement. Network measures have been considered support measures, and questions that ambivalently assess support concepts have been interpreted definitively. Thus, for example, a network question that establishes marital status is interpreted as evidence of social support (i.e., the receipt of emotional support from a spouse). However, having a spouse does not guarantee that the spouse provides support. An older person might have a spouse, but that spouse might be too sick to provide any type of support. Measures might be role driven or affect driven, and the reliability of these measures can be quite different. Research has shown that role-based measures of social relations are the most reliable. Obviously, if a person is asked whether they have children, the answer is not likely to change substantially over time. However, affectively based measures can be less stable. Asking how close one feels to one's adult child, for example, may change over time. The child might move out of state, the two might have an argument, or the child might disagree about a specific health-care or lifestyle choice being made by the elder. Under these conditions, how close the older person feels to his or her child could change radically and thus give the appearance of unreliability.

Even though the difference in results between network and support measures might be considerable, it should not be assumed that this problem has a simple solution or that an optimal or absolutely correct measure of these concepts exists. In fact, the most correct or appropriate measure is best chosen not based on any absolute criteria but rather on a consideration of the overall purpose of the empirical investigation or intervention. Thus, if the purpose is to assess the relative number of social contacts or network linkages the elderly have, for example, to assess the potential for social interaction, simple network assessments are most appropriate. However, if the purpose is to propose an intervention strategy or assess the supportive potential of specific relationships, it would be critical to assess both the affective as well as instrumental aspects of the relationship. An elderly poststroke individual needing an intense rehabilitation program and temporary but significant assistance with daily living needs not only the existence of children but children with whom they have a positive affective relationship and who can provide transportation to the outpatient rehabilitation center. Knowing that the older person has ten adult children does not necessarily answer the question of their availability, either emotionally or instrumentally, to provide support. For the most part, researchers now understand that there are different types of measures of social relations and that they should not be globally aggregated into a single construct. It is also important to recognize that the optimal measure to be used depends heavily on the research questions being asked.

III. DATA SOURCES

Social relations interest scientists from a wide variety of disciplines, each of which use diverse approaches to study design and sample development. Anthropologists, sociologists, psychologists, epidemiologists, psychiatrists, and gerontologists have all studied social relations across the life span and among older people specifically. Thus, major studies in the field incorporate very different types of samples, a fact that is fundamentally important when assessing both the quantity and quality of what is known about social relations. Anthropologists have used ethnographic techniques to study social relations among select groups of people, whereas epidemiologists have studied thousands of people who are randomly selected to represent designated portions of the population. Clinically based samples might study people being treated for a specific disease or inpatients with a specific psychiatric diagnosis. Some samples are very small but are studied intensely, others are exceedingly large with only a few questions addressing the topic of support relations. Similarly, a body of empirical evidence is now accumulating concerning mothers and infants, school-age children, and young and middle-aged adults, as well as older people. It is not established and certainly should not be assumed that evidence based on small nonrepresentative samples of

certain subpopulations should be applied to specific issues of concern among the elderly. Although there may be some lifetime continuity in relationships, knowing that a school-age child is most advantaged by instrumental support from parents may provide general information about the importance of family, but cannot be assumed to be generalizable to the elderly or to a specific older person. Whereas the young might feel very comfortable receiving, for example, financial support from their parents, the elderly might not feel comfortable receiving money from their children. It might be considered a signal of failure to need to take money from one's children rather than being able to provide it. Similarly, knowing that the social relations of those suffering from schizophrenia are characterized by certain patterns of social relations may or may not provide information that is useful in understanding the social relations of older nonschizophrenic people.

In sum, application and relevance of previous research to the elderly should be assessed with an awareness of both sample quality and population characteristics of the previous research. These issues effect the degree to which research findings are applicable to the elderly or any specific population of interest.

IV. SOCIAL SUPPORT AND THE HEALTH CONTINUUM

A final conceptual issue is important to consider before reviewing current empirical evidence. Although specific concerns regarding definition and methodology have been raised and highlight the potentially critical flaws in empirical research currently available, it is also the case that interest in specific aspects of health or different points on the health continuum can fundamentally influence the characteristics of optimal support relations or the types of support that would be of greatest interest.

Consider health among the elderly as the focal outcome. Although health is a major concern among the elderly, the elderly range from very healthy with few or no health problems to terminally ill with significant comorbidity. This enormous diversity of health status has been labeled the health continuum. There is a great deal of research that argues that social support influences health and well-being. However, it is not appropriate to assume that the same type of social support will meet the needs of the elderly at all points on the continuum. The healthy elder might need a companion to share an exercise regimen, whereas the terminally ill might need someone to provide emotional support and help with the final disposition of their affairs. Elders in an acute health crisis might need someone to recognize the crisis (e.g., a heart attack as opposed to indigestion) and provide the instrumental support of a ride to the hospital. Similarly, postmyocardial infarction patients might best be supported by individuals who tell them they are tough and able enough to complete the rehabilitation program as well as able to successfully adopt the lifestyle changes required. These examples emphasize the importance of social support as a main versus buffering effect. Although general positive feelings from close and important others are likely to promote overall well-being, in the face of a specific crisis or event, specific types of support, no doubt from specific others, are likely to be the most effective resources. This point is made to emphasize once again that the most appropriate methodology for any study must be specific to the goals and needs of that study. There can never be one specific measure that can assess the social relations, network, support, or integration under all circumstances for all elders.

The next section considers the empirical evidence currently available concerning social relations among the elderly. Five bodies of empirical evidence are considered: Family and friendship relationships; social exchange and reciprocity; gender differences; cultural differences; social relations and well-being.

V. FAMILY AND FRIENDSHIP RELATIONSHIPS

The study of social relations in adulthood and old age has frequently been divided into family relations versus friend relations. Although early work often described the broad inclusive categories of "family, friends, and neighbors," most current work pays more careful attention to the specific relationship, whether family or friend. In such work, the function of a person in a support network is often shown particularly to impact the well-being of the older adult. For example, it has been found that having a spouse meant that formal supports (such as home nurse care or

Meals on Wheels) are needed less often. Although it is clear that the families of older adults play important roles in the lives of elderly people, providing sometimes extraordinary caregiving efforts and instrumental help, friends are also invaluable resources. Indeed, research initially designed to examine the impact of family members alone often finds that the friendship networks of their study participants are frequently mentioned as significant supports.

Initial studies documented the structural characteristics of social networks. It is known from early cross-sectional studies, for example, that younger respondents have more frequent contact with network members than older respondents, whereas older respondents have known members of their networks longer. Most networks of older people consist of family members, primarily spouses, children, and siblings. Friends, however, make up a significant portion of their networks.

Generational differences in women's network structure and support patterns have also been examined. Older respondents include more family members in their networks, whereas younger adults include more friends. Close family members are named as closest network members, with friends and more distant relatives named as somewhat less close. Significantly more support from friends is often reported by younger than middle-aged respondents, who in turn report more support from family. However, research has shown that when nuclear family members are not present in the social networks of older adults, other close relationships seem to be substituted. This especially appears to be the case for instrumental support.

Reviews of the general definitions of friends and the level of friendship maintenance in adults over 60 provides some interesting insights concerning the social relations of the elderly. Sixty-eight percent of one sample reported long-term friendship ties throughout their lives, although the levels of continuity differed slightly by gender. More than half the women who reported having a close friend in childhood or adolescence indicated they were still friends, whereas men showed high levels of continuity with close friendships developed at midlife.

There seem to be constraints on and changing definitions of friendships among the "oldest-old." In one sample of people over 85 years old, it was found that over half still had at least one close friend, and three-fourths were in weekly contact with people considered to be their friends. Furthermore, almost half reported that they had made new friends after age 85, though the criteria for those friends differed from the establishment of relationships earlier in their lives. The respondents had given up some expectations for intimacy and shared history in order to count people as friends.

Studies of support from kin and friends have highlighted the importance of assessing various relationships. Although research focused on the exchange or receipt of social support is more limited, differing degrees of support appear to be provided depending upon the closeness of the relationship. Partners are usually rated as most supportive, but best friends and children are rated a very close second, and above all other categories. Compensation for the loss of major support persons has also been investigated. It has been found that children, friends, and acquaintances compensated for the loss of a spouse with increased emotional support to the widow. Some protection from loneliness is provided by children and friends, at least for respondents without partners.

Although spouses provide the most support overall, and adult children often give instrumental support, siblings may have a distinct place in the lives of older adults by bridging aspects of both family and friend relations. Continued sibling contact provides opportunities for life span socialization. An interesting race difference is evident among white and African American sibling pairs. White sibling relationships appear to range from very positive, intimate, and congenial to quite negative and hostile. African American sibling pairs, however, exhibit primarily positive interaction patterns. Other studies of siblings indicate that a large number of older people consider their sibling a very close friend. Sibling ties are the most egalitarian and most friendlike of all family relations, though there are important differences between siblings and friends.

Although specific studies are available indicating that most elderly receive sustantial support from others, there is some indication of a pattern suggesting that more support is received from fewer people as the individual gets older. This has often been interpreted as resulting from increased physical or functional limitations. Recent theoretical perspectives, however, have offered additional explanations.

Several studies have indicated that there are age differences in how family and friends are valued, with older respondents indicating that friendships increase in importance as compared to younger respondents. Adequate longitudinal data are not yet available to address the question of the changing value of relationships over time, though there are at least two theoretical positions that are suggestive. Socioemotional selectivity theory and the convoy model both predict that close and important friends and family relationships will remain so into old age, whereas more superficial relationships are likely to dissipate. Alternatively, because life transitions often provide different opportunities and circumstances for relations, some ties, especially those with friends and siblings, may take on renewed importance as individuals emerge from earlier obligations.

One consistent, almost universal, finding should be mentioned with regard to the reported quality of social relations among family and friends. Older people are much more satisfied with the support they receive and with their their support network more generally than are younger people. One possible explanation is that as people get older they are more likely to evaluate various aspects of their environment positively. Indeed, survey researchers have noted that older people show consistent increases in life satisfaction with age but a leveling off or plateauing of affective responses such as happiness. The socioemotional selectivity theory would suggest that as people get older, they only maintain relationships with people they want to and with whom they feel they have a good relationship. Clearly, both family and friends fall into this category, but with age their numbers are increasingly select.

VI. SOCIAL EXCHANGE AND RECIPROCITY

A significant portion of the social support literature is concerned with the examination of social exchanges and reciprocity. Equity theory has provided a theoretical basis for much of this research. This theoretical perspective proposes that reciprocity is the most equitable status of exchange. It is argued that overbenefitting (i.e., receiving more than providing) and underbenefitting (providing more than receiving) are both less than optimal, often resulting in guilt or resentment. A life span perspective adds the possibility of assessing reciprocity either in explicitly contemporary terms or in longitudinal terms. There is evidence in support of both types of assessment. Reciprocity within superficial or recent relationships is more likely to be short-term and immediate. On the other hand, among relationships that have endured over many years, older persons are more likely to use a long-term accounting system. In the former case, one might return a cup of sugar after the next trip to the grocery. In the latter case, however, one might provide intense sick care for a spouse and expect no immediate return but feel assured that if a similar need arose in the distant future that spouse would provide the same care when needed. It has been suggested that people maintain an unconscious Support Bank, much like a savings account, where they keep track of who owes them and to whom they owe various types of support. Interestingly enough, in this culture most people, even old people, report that they give more than they receive. It appears that the preferred state is what exchange theorists would term the underbenefitted state, but the Support Bank perspective would consider significant savings or deposits.

Dramatic increases in life expectancy during the past decades have resulted in a rapid growth of the oldest-old (aged 80+) population. This segment of the population continues to grow. From an exchange theory perspective, the problems of the oldest-old are essentially problems of scarcity in exchange commodities. The oldest-old, as a statistical aggregate, suffer from lower income and poorer health than younger people. Consequently, they are physically and financially limited in entering into exchange situations. They may no longer be able to afford to exchange holiday gifts with children and grandchildren in the way they used to do or to babysit grandchildren in return for the help that they receive from their daughters or daughters-in-law. Many have very little of any instrumental value to exchange.

How do such limitations affect their social relations? Currently, there appear to be no commonly accepted rules for support exchanges involving the oldest-old. Some older people withdraw from exchange situations altogether. This is clearly a coping strategy used by some older persons to maintain reciprocity. They simply choose not to enter exchange situations, thus preventing the nonreciprocal relationships that would result because they do not have the resources to reciprocate. Other older people apply the long-term reciprocity notion of a Social Support Bank, in the face of diminishing commodities. Thus, they can receive a great deal of support from close and important others, potentially for an extended period of time, and yet feel relatively unindebted. In this case older people can assume that they are simply receiving support due from people to whom they have provided support in the past. Some exchange theorists argue that even in this contract-oriented society, noncontractual relationships are not completely absent. No longer bound by the norm of reciprocity, older people sometimes benefit from the norm of beneficence (i.e., the provision of support from people with more resources to those with less resources). A continuous growth of the oldest-old population urges modifications of the conventional support exchange rules and the emergence of new rules that are more suitable to the aging society.

VII. GENDER DIFFERENCES

Empirical evidence has been accumulating over the years concerning gender differences in social relations. Originally, these gender differences were assumed to favor women. However, additional research has suggested that the question might be considerably more complicated. There tend to be relatively few gender differences in the support networks of men and women. Greater similarity is likely to be obtained if the assessment method focuses on close and supportive others. This is the case because most people list family members (i.e., parents, spouse, and children) as their close and supportive others. However, even these structural characteristics tend to become slightly female-biased as one focuses on the elderly because of the significantly greater life span of women.

Greater controversy, or at least complexity, arises with the provision and receipt of social support. When considering specifically who provides what, to whom and how much of it, greater gender differences are likely to arise. The findings can be summarized as follows. Men tend to report receiving from and providing support primarily to their wives. Women, in addition to support exchanged with spouse, also tend to provide and receive support from a much larger array of people including children, other relatives, and friends.

A similarly interesting gender difference exists in terms of the interpretation or perception of support interactions. Women appear to feel greater involvement with most of the people in their networks and to feel a greater sense of responsibility concerning the resolution of needs or conflicts among their support-network members. Thus, although there is a tendency towards same-sex friendships, both men and women are more likely to mention women as confidants. Such gender differences in the nature of relationships, which are observed across the life course, are directly linked to sex roles in this society and indicate a lifelong impact of socialization on the social relations of men and women. Other research has shown that even when data are from both members of the same older couple, reporting on the provision and receipt of support between them, it is clear that there are significant differences in what these men and women experience as support exchanged with their spouse.

These support differences and the discrepancy in the life expectancy of men and women portend important differences in the social relations of older men and women. On the one hand, men are much more likely to be married when they get older. If married, their social relationships are likely to remain relatively stable and intact. On the other hand, if an older man becomes widowed or has never married, he may find himself in a particularly precarious position with regard to social relations. Single men are much more likely to be social isolates than single women, and are much less likely to replace or be able to sustain the relationships previously maintained by their spouse. The single exception to this, of course, is if the widowed man remarries. Demographics suggest that older women are quite likely to be widowed but will have the skills to continue to maintain relationships as they had previously. They may turn to other family members and friends to assist with difficulties that emerge, such as the physical limitations and illnesses that sometimes accompany old age. Nevertheless, older women of today have lived a relatively traditional lifestyle, which might mean that in old age they find themselves with less money and less access to powerful others or community status than they did as the respected wives of men well established in their community. One can assume that this will change as women begin to enter old age with a lifetime of experience as members of the labor force with greater independence in their general lifestyle.

VIII. CULTURAL DIFFERENCES

The literature has documented some variation in social network and social support across different societies. Different social structures across societies result in variations in the support networks of older persons. Most notably, different family structures directly affect the social networks of older persons. For example, in societies where large extended families live together, an entire support network often consists of family members who provide all the support an older person needs. In societies such as the United States, where a larger proportion of the elderly live with their spouse or alone, friends and neighbors also comprise a vital part of the support network. In most societies, women of younger generations provide support to the elders, but the focal support person may vary by society. Thus, in the United States this person is usually a daughter, whereas in Japan, due to the structure of their family and living arrangements as well as tradition, this person is likely to be the daughter-in-law.

Different societal norms influence support exchanges. Reciprocity is the basic rule of support exchanges in most societies. However, specific applications of the norm of reciprocity vary among societies. For example, the primary exchange rule of middle-class Americans prescribes exchange of support in kind and of equivalent value in a relatively short period of time. This rule suppresses one-way transactions of support and thereby reduces the development of dependence, which often leads to the disturbance of stable relationships in the United States.

By contrast, the exchange rule in close relationships in Japan inhibits complete repayment in support exchanges, therefore maintaining indebtedness and dependence. It consequently serves to sustain the relationships based on dependence. This illustrates how the general norm of reciprocity regulates support exchanges in the two societies in quite different ways, yet serving the same goal of maintaining the solidarity of support networks. Data are also available concerning reciprocity among the French elderly. They, too, maintain a norm of reciprocity. In fact, a slightly higher percentage of French elderly report reciprocal relationships than American elderly. However, if a relationship is reported to be nonreciprocal, the French elderly are more likely to say they receive more support than they provide, whereas American elderly tend to report they provide more support than they receive. These findings suggest that there are cultural differences in the optimal level of balance between provision and receipt of support even among Western societies. American elderly appear to consider it most desirable to maintain slightly overproviding relationships both because "being a giving person" is valued and reinforced in American society and because it ensures having someone available to provide support in case of need in the future, "a deposit in the Support Bank." Under the French norm, however, it appears to be more acceptable to overbenefit (i.e., to receive more than you provide) in old age.

Data examining subgroups within the United States indicate that many more African American than white elderly report reciprocal relationships. Among nonreciprocal relationships, the majority of African Americans report that they receive less support than they provide. Although subgroup differences in perceptions of reciprocity within the United States might have seemed large when only American data are considered, when considered within the context of Japanese and French data, the degree to which culture influences reciprocity and dependency norms is noteworthy.

IX. SOCIAL RELATIONS AND WELL-BEING

Among the most important and impressive research in this area is that documenting an association between health or well-being and social relations. Substantial evidence has accumulated over the years indicating that people who have larger social networks, more social supports, and are better integrated into the social fiber of their community are less likely to die. Similarly impressive research has documented the association between social relations and various forms of morbidity including cardiovascular diseases, depression, symptom severity, hospital and emergency room utilization, preventive health behaviors, and successful rehabilitation. Controversy exists concerning the exact nature or characteristics of social relations that are important. As noted earlier, many studies have simply documented the existence of social ties (i.e., the social network characteristics) and demonstrated a statistical association of these measures

with health and well-being. However, some researchers argue that the measure of the existence of these ties simply offers a proxy measure of support exchanges and, by implication, support satisfaction. Thus, being married often suggests that a significant other exists with whom the older person has a close, supportive and qualitatively superior relationship. Nevertheless, it is important to recognize that this is not always the case; not all spouses offer that kind of support. Researchers have now begun to consider what specific characteristics of support relationships are most important. It is reasonable to assume that each characteristic of a support relationship offers some insight into the nature and functioning of that relationship. Knowing that an individual is married is helpful. Also helpful is knowing whether the partners exchange support (i.e., give and receive different types of support such as emotional and instrumental support from each other). But perhaps the most important measure we have of the effect of social relations on well-being is the individual's evaluation, perception of, or satisfaction with, that relationship. Although some reviews indicate that size of network is the best predictor of well-being, other research evidence suggests that although objective measures such as social network characteristics are useful, the most predictive measures are those that assess the individual's subjective evaluation of the relationship. Research exists on both American and French elderly representative populations indicating that although both objective and subjective measures of support are significantly related to depressive symptomatology, subjective measures, such as satisfaction with the quality of the relationship, have a greater inhibiting effect on depression than more objective measures, such as number of social ties.

Additional evidence suggests that family and friends may function quite differently, although both play important roles in the well-being of the elderly. Family relationships, under normal circumstances, make an important contribution to well-being when conflict is minimal and normal positive relationships are maintained. Under these conditions, older people report relatively stable levels of well-being. When such relationships either do not exist or are conflictual, a negative impact on well-being is usually evident. Another long-standing finding in the literature is that friend, but not family, relations have significant positive effects on the mental health of the elderly. A number of investigations concluded that family relations, although critical, are assumed, that is, their presence and the support therein provided are normatively expected. When present, no extraordinary positive effect is apparent. However, when absent or conflictual, their negative impact is substantial. The opposite appears to be the case for friendship relations. When not present, few significant negative effects are evident, but the presence of close supportive friendship relations has a significant, positive effect on well-being.

Some have discussed the findings on family versus friend support in terms of the volitional versus obligatory nature of the two types of relationships. Although family ties are often proscribed by roles and expectations, friends are free to enter into a relationship, as well as leave it, at any time. Family members are expected to provide support, therefore when they fail to do so or are unavailable, there is a significant negative impact. Friends, however, are not necessarily required by the relationship to be available for support, thus support from friends is perceived more positively. Also, in contrast to family relationships, friends are chosen rather than ascribed, and most often chosen on the basis of similarity of interest, experience, or personality. The act of choosing one another also brings with it feelings of being admired and liked over others, which also enhances emotional well-being.

Gender differences in the role of social relations and their effect on well-being should also be noted. The well-being of men is much more positively effected by marriage than is the case for women. Men seem to garner significant benefits from the marital relationship, but women do not. In fact, women, much more than men, appear to be at risk for the negative impact of this relationship, should the marital relationship be of poor quality. Furthermore, it is clear that there is a significant gender difference in the role of social relations that transcends the marital relationship. Women's generally high sensitivity to the effect of poor quality of social relations effects their mental and physical well-being. At the same time, an intriguing finding suggests that although women report many more sources of support in their network than most men, the effect of larger numbers of close relationships is negative in that these women report being less happy. It appears that although women have many more intimate relationships from which they receive support, they also are more emotionally involved with and feel a need to provide more support to each of their relationships.

As this latter point suggests, it is important to note that there may be negative, as well as positive, consequences of social interaction. Negative social relations are evident in relationships that are tarnished by conflict or negative affect; or in exchanges where positive support is provided to a degree that it is overwhelming and smothering. Similarly, social relations can be assumed to be negative or to have a negative effect on well-being when support is provided for maladaptive behaviors, such as smoking, drinking, avoiding health care, or not taking medications. Thus, the study of social relations must take into account that convoys of close friends and family members may be both pleasant and unpleasant, both supportive and unsupportive. These differences, of course, result in fundamental differences in patterns of outcomes.

X. SUMMARY AND CONCLUSION

In conclusion, it should be recognized that social networks, social support, and social integration can play a significant role in the maintenance of the health and well-being of an elderly individual. At the same time, social relations represent only one of many important factors contributing to the well-being of the elderly. Biological and physical factors also play an important role. However, neither exist in isolation and bidirectionality of influence appears to exist. While a great deal of research in recent years has improved our knowledge of both the conceptual and methodological characteristics of social relations, it must be recognized that because of the idiosyncratic nature of social relations, there are no absolutely correct singular conceptualizations or measures. Research thus far suggests that social relations can improve the overall quality of life of healthy elder persons and can serve to improve the experience of the elderly as they face the physical and psychological challenges of aging.

BIBLIOGRAPHY

Adams, R. G., & Blieszner, R. (Eds.). (1989). *Older adult friendship: Structure and process.* Newbury Park, CA: Sage Publications.

Akiyama, H., Antonucci, T. C., & Campbell, R. (1990). Exchange and reciprocity among two generations of Japanese and American women, In J. Sokolovski (Ed.), *Cultural context of aging: Worldwide perspectives* (pp. 127–138). Westport, CT: Greenwood Press.

Antonucci, T. C. (1994). A life-span view of women's social relations. In B. F. Turner & L. E. Troll (Eds.), *Women growing older* (pp. 239–269). Thousand Oaks, CA: Sage Publications.

Antonucci, T. C., & Akiyama, H. (1987). An examination of sex differences in social support among older men and women. *Sex Roles, 17* (11/12), 737–749.

Antonucci, T. C., & Akiyama, H. (1995). Convoys of social relations: Family and friendships within a life span context. In R. Blieszner & V. Bedford (Eds.), *Handbook of aging and the family* (pp. 355–371). Westport, CT: Greenwood Press.

Antonucci, T. C., Fuhrer, R., & Jackson, J. S. (1990). Social support and reciprocity: A cross-ethnic and cross-national perspective. *Journal of Social and Personal Relationships, 7*(4), 519–530.

Antonucci, T. C., & Jackson, J. S. (1987). Social support, interpersonal efficacy, and health: A life course perspective. In L. L. Carstensen & B. A. Edelstein (Eds.), *Handbook of Clinical Gerontology*. New York: Pergamon Press.

Antonucci, T. C., Kahn, R. L., & Akiyama, H. (1989). Psychological factors and the response to cancer symptoms. In R. Yancik & J. W. Yates (Eds.), *Cancer in the elderly: Approaches to early detection and treatment* (pp. 40–52). New York: Springer Publishing Co.

Berkman, L. F., & Syme, S. L. (1979). Social networks, host resistance, and mortality: a nine-year follow-up study of Alameda County residents. *American Journal of Epidemiology, 109,* 186–204.

Carstensen, L. L. (1992). Social and emotional patterns in adulthood: Support for socioemotional selectivity theory. *Psychology and Aging, 7*(3), 331–338.

Gold, D. (1990). Late-life sibling relationships: Does race affect typological distribution? *The Gerontologist, 30*(6), 741–748.

Johnson, C. L., & Troll, L. E. (1994). Constraints and facilitators to friendships in late late life. *The Gerontologist, 34*(1), 79–87.

Lee, G. R., & Shehan, C. L. (1989). Social relations and the self-esteem of older persons. *Research on Aging, 11,* 427–442.

Silverstein, M., & Waite, L. J. (1993). Are blacks more likely than whites to receive and provide social support in middle and old age? Yes, no, and maybe so. *Journal of Gerontology: Social Sciences, 48*(4), S212–S222.

Umberson, D. (1992). Gender, marital status and the social control of health behavior. *Social Science Medicine, 34*(8), 907–917.

Stroke

Philip B. Gorelick, Vijay Shanmugam, and Aurora K. Pajeau

Rush Medical College

I. Introduction
II. Stroke Epidemiology
III. Stroke Classification and Pathophysiology
IV. Diagnostic Studies
V. Treatment and Prevention
VI. Consequences of Stroke

Antiplatelet Agents Medications such as aspirin and ticlopidine that reduce stroke risk by preventing platelets from clumping or aggregating.
Carotid Endarterectomy A surgical procedure to reduce stroke risk by removal of atherosclerotic blockage in the carotid artery.
Risk Factors Antecedent physiologic (genetic), lifestyle, or dietary factors that increase the likelihood of developing a disease.
Stroke The sudden or subacute onset of neurologic deficit caused by occlusion or rupture of a cerebral artery.
Stroke Subtypes Specific pathophysiologic mechanisms that underlie cerebral ischemia or hemorrhage.
Vascular Dementia Dementia caused by strokes.

STROKE is the sudden onset of neurologic deficit caused by occlusion or spontaneous rupture of a cerebral artery. Stroke is the third leading cause of death in the United States and ranks as the most common disabling and lethal neurologic disease of adult life. It is estimated that there are 400,000–500,000 new strokes, 3 million stroke survivors, and 150,000 deaths attributable to stroke annually in the United States. Furthermore, the direct and indirect health-care costs are estimated to total $30 billion yearly.

I. INTRODUCTION

Stroke is unique among neurologic diseases as it has a high prevalence and burden of illness, high economic cost, and safe and effective prevention measures. Although stroke may occur at any age, it is most common among the elderly. There is an exponential rise of stroke with age that leads to an approximate doubling of stroke frequency in each successive decade from middle age onward. Thus, the elderly, the most rapidly expanding segment of our society, are most likely to be afflicted by stroke and its disabling complications.

This chapter will review stroke epidemiology, classification and pathophysiology, treatment and prevention, and consequences. Topical discussions will emphasize how stroke affects the elderly.

II. STROKE EPIDEMIOLOGY

Epidemiology is the study of the distribution and determinants (causes) of disease in our population. Epidemiologic study helps answer scientific questions relating to who is most likely to be afflicted by a disease, why the disease has occurred, and if there will be an epidemic of the disease. The distribution of disease refers to its prevalence and incidence. Prevalence is the number of persons with the disease in a defined population at a given point in time. Incidence is the number of new cases of disease that develops in a defined population during a specified period of time. Prevalence alerts us about the magnitude of a disease in our society and aids public health planners in making decisions about allocation of health-care resources for the disease. Incidence is an indicator of risk or who is most likely to develop the disease. Finally, disease determinants or risk factors are antecedent physiological, dietary, or lifestyle habits that increase the likelihood of developing a disease. The presence of a risk factor increases the probability of disease. However, not every person with the risk factor will develop the disease, nor will the absence of the risk factor ensure absence of the disease. As a group, the elderly are unique as they often have multiple stroke risk factors. [See EPIDEMIOLOGY.]

A. Mortality

Stroke death rates have shown a steady decline in the United States since the early 1900s with about a 1% per year decline. In the late 1960s and early 1970s death rates from stroke began to fall by 5–7% per year, and the greatest decline has been in the older age groups. However, since 1979 the annual rate of decline of stroke mortality began to slow considerably. Overall, stroke death in the United States increases with age, is higher among men than women except in the oldest age group, and is highest among African Americans.

The reason for the accelerated stroke mortality decline in the United States in the early 1970s has been debated. Possible explanations include improved antihypertensive therapy, declining stroke incidence, improved stroke survival, reduction in the severity of stroke, or some other factor. The precise explanation for the deceleration in stroke mortality trends since 1979 remains uncertain, but it parallels decreasing social and economic conditions for many and a leveling off of a national trend for continued improvement in blood pressure control.

B. Prevalence

In general, stroke prevalence increases exponentially with advancing age. Stroke prevalence is estimated to range between 500–600 per 100,000 in the West but is generally higher in the East.

C. Incidence

Stroke incidence increases with age and approximately doubles in each successive decade. In general, the incidence of stroke is higher in men than women

Table I Average Annual Stroke Incidence per 1000 Persons by Age (Framingham Study 36-Year Follow-up)[a]

Age[b]	Atherothrombotic brain infarction		Stroke—all types	
	Men	Women	Men	Women
45–54	0.8	0.7	2.2	1.2
55–64	2.1	1.2	4.5	2.8
65–74	4.3	3.7	9.3	8.0
75–84	8.5	6.8	19.2	15.0

[a]With permission W.B. Saunders Company, *Neurologic Clinics 1992*; 10(1), 179.
[b]Age in years at Biennial Exam.

and is substantially higher in U.S. Blacks as compared to Whites. The relative risk of brain infarction is higher among African American women when compared to white women, and African Americans have a higher incidence of brain hemorrhage. Table I demonstrates the exponential rise in annual stroke incidence with age according to the Framingham Study.

Over time (1950–1979) stroke incidence has declined substantially. However, more recently (1979–1984) it has been noted that stroke incidence may be increasing. Among persons with ischemic heart disease, this may be due to increased survival. Further information is needed about the effect of increased detection of stroke by up-to-date neuroimaging techniques, levels of blood pressure of treated and non-treated persons, and treatment of other cardiovascular disease risk factors.

D. Risk Factors

There is a substantial body of epidemiologic knowledge about stroke risk factors. Such factors may be classified as modifiable and nonmodifiable and well-documented and less well-documented. The following discussion will emphasize major host risk factors that are well established and potentially modifiable. These factors are listed in Table II. Previously mentioned nonmodifiable risk factors such as race, sex, and age will not be reviewed.

I. Hypertension

Hypertension is considered to be the most important treatable risk factor for stroke. The risk of stroke rises

Table II Stroke Risk Factors That May Be Modified

1. Hypertension
2. Heart disease
   a. Coronary heart disease[a]
   b. Congestive heart failure[a]
   c. Left ventricular hypertrophy[a]
   d. Atrial fibrillation
3. Diabetes mellitus[a]
4. Cigarette smoking
5. Alcohol consumption[b]
6. Hyperlipidemia[a,b]
7. Asymptomatic carotid stenosis
8. Transient ischemic attack

[a]Treatment feasible but benefit for stroke prevention as yet established.

[b]Classified as less well-documented risk factor for stroke.

with increasing blood pressure, and the relative risk of stroke among hypertensives is about 3–4 times greater than nonhypertensives. Systolic, diastolic, or combined systolic and diastolic hypertension confer substantial stroke risk.

The prevalence of hypertension increases with age. In the Framingham Study, 38.2% of those 50–59 years had hypertension, whereas 71.6% of those 80–89 years were hypertensive. Although hypertension remained an important risk factor for stroke, there was a decline in its estimated relative risk and the number of strokes attributable to it with advancing age. Isolated systolic hypertension is highly prevalent with advancing age, and there is at least a twofold increased risk of brain infarction among those 65–84 years with systolic pressures greater than 160 mmHg and diastolic pressures consistently below 95 mmHg.

2. Heart Disease

Coronary heart disease, left ventricular hypertrophy, congestive heart failure (CHF), and atrial fibrillation are all independent risk factors for brain infarction. The prevalence of these factors also generally increases with advancing age but does not attain the magnitude of prevalence in the elderly as does hypertension. However, the estimated relative risk and number of strokes attributable to atrial fibrillation substantially increases with age such that by age 80–89 years atrial fibrillation may increase stroke risk

by 4.5 times and account for almost 24% of strokes. [See Cardiovascular System.]

3. Diabetes Mellitus

Diabetes mellitus is an independent risk factor for brain infarction. According to the Framingham Study the relative impact of diabetes may be greater in women than in men, and its impact on the risk of brain infarction does not diminish with advancing age. Rigorous treatment of diabetes retards some vascular complications but has not been proved conclusively to prevent stroke.

4. Cigarette Smoking

Stroke risk increases in a stepwise manner with the number of cigarettes smoked. With cessation of cigarette smoking, stroke risk may reverse after 2–5 years. Cigarette smoking is less prevalent in the elderly, and its impact as a risk factor in the aged may be less obvious. This was the case for men in the Framingham Study. However, women aged 65–94 years continued to have a substantial effect from cigarette smoking relative to those 35–64 years.

5. Alcohol Consumption

Epidemiologic study suggests that moderate alcohol consumption reduces the risk of brain infarction. Whereas abstention or infrequent alcohol use may increase risk slightly, heavy consumption may increase risk substantially. For brain hemorrhage it seems that the risk of stroke increases directly with the number of daily drinks. The risk of brain hemorrhage may reverse with reduction in heavy alcohol consumption.

There is a paucity of information about the role of alcohol consumption as a risk factor for stroke in the elderly. It is likely that this factor makes a much smaller relative and absolute contribution toward stroke occurrence in the elderly compared to, for example, hypertension and atrial fibrillation. [See Alcohol and Drugs.]

6. Hyperlipidemia

There is mounting evidence to link blood lipids to risk for brain infarction. Further study will be required to clarify this relationship. Hypercholesterolemia is an important modifiable risk factor for coronary heart disease. However, lower levels of serum cholesterol are associated with an increased risk of brain hemorrhage. The effect of blood lipids on stroke risk may be less substantial in the very old.

7. Asymptomatic Carotid Atherosclerosis

With advancing age there are degenerative cerebral vessel wall changes termed *atherosclerosis*. These atherosclerotic deposits or plaques cause the larger cerebral arteries to narrow and may compromise blood flow to the brain. With increasing severity of atherosclerosis in the carotid artery, there is an associated increased risk for stroke and heart attack, and death due to stroke, heart disease, or other vascular cause. Recently, it has been shown that removal of high-grade carotid atherosclerotic plaque by a surgical procedure called carotid endarterectomy may reduce the risk of stroke and death in patients who have had no prior stroke symptoms. [*See* ATHEROSCLEROSIS.]

8. Transient Ischemic Attact

Transient ischemic attack (TIA) is a transient focal neurologic deficit lasting less than 24 hours that is referable to diminished perfusion to a focal area of the brain. It is estimated that the 5-year risk of stroke following TIA is about 33%. Most strokes occur within the first year of TIA with up to 21% in the first month, one-half within 3 months, and two-thirds within 6 months. The occurrence of TIA increases with advancing age.

III. STROKE CLASSIFICATION AND PATHOPHYSIOLOGY

Stroke is not a homogeneous disorder. Rather, it is a group of syndromes with definable subtypes and distinct pathophysiology. The discovery and recognition of stroke subtypes have been one of the leading advances in stroke research. The classification scheme for major stroke subtypes is listed in Table III. The following discussion will review the pathophysiology of individual stroke subtypes. One must keep in mind that stroke-related terms such as TIA, reversible ischemic neurologic deficit (RIND) (partial neurologic deficit that lasts more than 24 hours but resolves completely or almost completely within several days), and completed stroke (focal stroke deficit that comes on abruptly, stabilizes, and does not progress) provide information about the time course of stroke and the

Table III Classification of Stroke by Pathophysiologic Mechanism

Ischemia
  Atherothrombotic brain infarction
    (cerebral thrombosis)
  Lacunar brain infarction
  Cerebral embolic brain infarction
    Cardiogenic
    Artery-to-artery
  Infarct of undetermined cause
  Nonatherosclerotic brain infarction
Hemorrhage
  Subarachnoid hemorrhage
  Intraparenchymal hemorrhage
  Nonatherosclerotic brain hemorrhage

extent of the neurologic deficit, but little information about the way in which cerebral blood vessels have become affected. More specific terms that indicate the pathophysiologic mechanism are preferred (see Table III).

Stroke may be broadly divided into ischemic and hemorrhagic pathophysiologic subtypes. Ischemic stroke occurs when there is blockage of a cerebral artery by in situ clot (thrombus) or embolism (clot from an artery or the heart, or fragments of the atherosclerotic vessel wall that travel distally to occlude the artery). Brain hemorrhage occurs when a major cerebral vessel ruptures and blood leaks into the brain tissue or surrounding areas. With both ischemic and hemorrhagic stroke, the brain is deprived of blood that carries needed nutrients such as glucose and oxygen. Neurologic deficits such as weakness (hemiparesis), sensory signs and symptoms, visual loss, speech impairment, and language dysfunction (aphasia) may occur. Of the two major stroke subtypes, ischemic stroke constitutes about 85% of cases and hemorrhagic stroke about 15%.

A. Atherothrombotic Brain Infarction

Atherosclerosis is a degenerative vessel wall disease that results in narrowing of major cranial and systemic arteries. The primary pathology is the atherosclerotic plaque. The plaque contains fat deposits, smooth muscle hyperplasia, and other elements that lead to occlusion of the vessel lumen. As cerebral atherosclerosis progresses, signs of cerebral ischemia (i.e., lack of blood flow) may develop as the narrowed artery thromboses or as embolic debris dislodges and travels downstream. Atherosclerotic plaques have a predilection for major arterial bifurcations and branch points such as the internal carotid artery origin, junction of the vertebral and basilar arteries, and initial segments of the middle and posterior cerebral arteries.

A leading theory proposes that atherosclerosis occurs in the setting of elevated blood cholesterol and hypertension. The blood vessel wall is damaged by hypertension, and this leads to deposition of fat components from the bloodstream and other atherosclerotic changes. Atherosclerotic plaques are common in the elderly and increase with age.

B. Lacunar Brain Infarction

In contradistinction to atherothrombotic brain infarction, in which large cerebral artery pathology underlies the stroke, lacunes result from occlusion of deep penetrating branches of the larger cerebral arteries. The infarct (small "lake") may measure only several cubic millimeters. The vascular pathology underlying this syndrome, lipohyalinosis, differs from atherosclerosis. Lipohyalinosis is a degenerative disease in which lipids and hyaline form in the vessel wall to block blood flow. Lacunar infarction may also be caused by microatheroma that obstructs the orifice of a small penetrating artery at its origin from the large parent artery. In addition, lacunes may be caused by microembolism or other arteriopathies.

Lacunar infarction is often encountered in the clinical setting of sustained hypertension. Multiple lacunar infarction may be an important cause of stroke (vascular) dementia in the elderly.

C. Cerebral Embolism

Cerebral embolism may arise from two major sources: The heart and the arterial blood vessel wall. Certain cardiac conditions such as atrial fibrillation, myocardial infarct, and cardiomyopathy lead to stasis of blood and clot formation in the major heart chambers. A portion of the clot may dislodge and travel into the cerebral or systemic circulation to cause ischemia. Cardiac valve disease (e.g., rheumatic heart disease) can also serve as a source for cardiac embolism. Finally, atherosclerotic debris (fragments of cholesterol, thrombus, and fibrin-platelet material) from the aorta

or carotid artery may embolize to cause cerebral ischemia.

Cardiac source embolism is now considered a major cause of cerebral ischemia (causing up to 30% of cases) and has reached this status with modern advances in cardiac diagnostic technology. Nonvalvular atrial fibrillation (i.e., atrial fibrillation not related to valvular heart disease) is the most important source of cardiac embolism to the brain and is an important risk factor for stroke in the elderly.

D. Infarct of Undetermined Cause

Despite advances in stroke diagnostic technology, a disproportionately high percentage of cases cannot be classified as one of the traditional stroke subtypes. Infarct of undetermined cause (IUC) includes both those cases of undetermined cause with extensive stroke diagnostic workup and those with less extensive work-up. This category of stroke may include up to 40% of cases. Some are thought to be caused by a nonatherosclerotic stroke mechanism, and many are probably a form of occult cerebral embolism.

E. Nonatherosclerotic Brain Infarction

This type of stroke usually occurs when there are underlying systemic disorders that cause stroke by secondary mechanisms. The secondary mechanism may be a systemic illness with associated cerebral arteriopathy, vasculitis, cardiac involvement, or hypercoagulable state. Brain infarction associated with street-drug abuse and consequent cerebral arteriopathy is such an example. Infarction or hemorrhage may occur. These disorders are generally more prevalent in young adults and have less importance in the elderly.

F. Subarachnoid Hemorrhage

The most common cause of primary subarachnoid hemorrhage (SAH) is ruptured intracranial aneurysm. The usual type of aneurysm is saccular in form and projects as a tiny outpouching or blister-like structure from the cerebral artery. Most saccular aneurysms arise from the carotid artery at the level of the posterior communicating artery, the anterior communicating artery region, or the middle cerebral artery bifurcation. The cerebral territory bound by these blood vessels and some from the vertebrobasilar circulation has been collectively called the circle of Willis.

Clinically, the onset of SAH is abrupt and associated invariably with headache. Blood under arterial pressure ruptures into the subarachnoid space (the protective cerebrospinal fluid-filled space bound by a thin membrane) or adjacent brain tissue and causes neurologic damage. The major cerebral arteries that course through the blood-laden subarachnoid space may develop "vasospasm" that leads to cerebral infarction.

The incidence of aneurysmal SAH rises with age. However, when compared with ischemic stroke subtypes, there is a disproportionate number of aneurysmal SAH among women and the young.

G. Intraparenchymal Hemorrhage

Intraparenchymal hemorrhage (IH) arises commonly from deep penetrating cerebral arteries affected by lipohyalinosis, microaneurysm formation, and arteriosclerosis with severe degeneration of medial smooth muscle cells. As blood extravasates from the ruptured artery, neurologic deficit arises as adjacent brain tissue is disrupted, displaced, and compressed. The sites of predilection for IH are similar to those of lacunar infarction as in both cases the deep penetrating arteries are involved. These sites include commonly the putamen, thalamus, pons, and cerebellum.

IH usually occurs in the setting of chronic hypertension. In the elderly it may also occur in association with cerebral amyloid angiopathy (CAA). CAA is characterized by deposits of amyloid in the media and adventia of small and medium-sized cerebral arteries usually located in the superficial layers of the cerebral cortex and leptomeninges. The resultant cerebral hemorrhage is usually located superficially in one of the major brain lobes (so-called lobar hemorrhage). Lobar hemorrhage may also occur with other conditions including hypertension, bleeding disorders, and arteriovenous malformation. CAA increases with advancing age and is associated with histopathologic and clinical features of Alzheimer's disease.

IV. DIAGNOSTIC STUDIES

An elderly patient who has had a brain infarct, TIA, RIND, or brain hemorrhage will undergo a stroke diagnostic workup to define the underlying stroke mechanism. Once the underlying cause of stroke is determined, stroke treatment can be tailored appropriately. There are different levels of diagnostic stroke workup based on the risk associated with the procedure. One usually proceeds in a stepwise manner ordering noninvasive tests before invasive ones. The goal is to avoid higher risk invasive procedures if possible. Before obtaining stroke diagnostic studies in the elderly, one must weigh the following questions: (a) Is the patient's stroke condition so severe that an extensive battery of stroke-diagnostic studies would be contraindicated or would not alter one's treatment plan? (b) Are there comorbid conditions that would contraindicate stroke diagnostic or therapeutic modalities? (c) Are the patient and caregiver aware of and in agreement with the proposed diagnostic and treatment options given the inherent risks and benefits?

The vigorous or well-selected geriatric patients are good candidates for stroke diagnostic procedures and treatments. However, discretion must be exercised by the clinician before embarking on an aggressive and extensive stroke diagnostic workup in these patients.

Table IV lists stroke diagnostic studies by ischemic and hemorrhagic stroke subtype and level of invasiveness. Cranial computed tomography (CT) is usually performed on an emergent basis as it is an excellent tool for distinguishing infarct from hemorrhage. Once this distinction is made, the workup may proceed according to the algorithm in Figure 1. Magnetic resonance imaging (MRI) of the brain is generally more sensitive than CT in stroke diagnosis but may not diagnose hemorrhagic stroke until well after its onset.

V. TREATMENT AND PREVENTION

Treatment of stroke may be divided into three stages: (a) the hyperacute period; (b) the secondary prevention period; and (c) the primary prevention stage. The hyperacute period encompasses the earliest stage and generally includes the time from onset of cerebral ischemia or hemorrhage through the first 7 days. During this stage the brain is vulnerable to cerebral ischemia. A window of opportunity exists to rescue marginally functioning brain cells in the "ischemic penumbra" (i.e., the brain tissue at risk in the shadow zone of the compromised cerebral blood flow). The exact therapeutic window of opportunity for hyper-

Table IV Stroke Diagnostic Studies

	Invasive?
Brain infarction	
Neuroimaging	
Cranial computed tomography (CT)	No
Magnetic resonance imaging (MRI)	No
Magnetic resonance angiography (MRA)	No
Single photon emission computed tomography (SPECT)	No
Conventional cerebral angiography	Yes
Carotid duplex ultrasound	No
Transcranial doppler (TCD)	No
Cardiac studies	
Ambulatory electrocardiogram (EKG)	No
Echocardiography	
Conventional (transthoracic)	No
Transesophageal (TEE)	Yes
Procoagulant blood studies and other studies	
Lupus anticoagulant, anticardiolipin antibodies, proteins S and C, antithrombin III, homocysteine	No
Lumbar puncture	Yes
Brain Hemorrhage	
Neuroimaging	
CT	No
MRI	No
MRA	No
Conventional Cerebral Angiography	Yes
Other Studies	
Lumbar puncture	Yes

acute cerebral treatment is debated, but may be less than 12–24 hours. After the hyperacute period efforts are aimed at preventing recurrent stroke (secondary prevention) and at rehabilitation. During the hyperacute and early secondary stroke prevention phases, high-quality medical, nursing, and rehabilitative management is critical to prevent aspiration pneumonia, deep venous thrombosis and pulmonary embolism, urinary tract infection, cardiac complications, and other medical consequences of acute stroke. These are listed in Table V. The primary prevention stage aims to prevent a *first* stroke by dietary, lifestyle, and medical strategies designed to alter the community's and individual risk of stroke.

The following discussion will focus on acute treatment and prevention of ischemic stroke. The reader is referred to several excellent references for a review of treatment and prevention of brain hemorrhage. (See Mayberg et al., 1994, Broderick, 1994, and Longstreth, 1994).

A. Hyperacute Treatment

Acute loss of blood flow to the brain results in synaptic transmission failure when blood flow drops to about 18 ml/100 g/min and membrane pump failure and cell death at about 8 ml/100 g/min. The mainstay of hyperacute management is administration of medication to protect the neuron against cell death or improve brain blood flow and delivery of oxygen, glucose, and other nutrients. Most hyperacute agents are classified as pharmacologic or cell protectants, antithrombotics, thrombolytics, or hemorheologic treatments based on their mechanism of action. Many are still undergoing clinical trial testing. As of yet there is only one hyperacute stroke treatment, tPA when given within 180 min of ischemic stroke onset, that has been proved conclusively to reduce stroke morbidity or death. Most experts believe that hyperacute stroke treatment should be administered as soon as possible ("Time is brain") and no later than 6–8 hours after stroke onset.

Table VI summarizes key hyperacute stroke treatments and their status with regard to clinical testing. Should these agents prove to be effective, the future of hyperacute treatment may include combination therapy.

B. Secondary Prevention

There is substantial clinical trial literature on antiplatelet agents and recurrent stroke prevention. It is widely held that the risk of recurrent stroke or death is reduced significantly in TIA or mild stroke patients who take the antiplatelet agents aspirin or ticlopidine. In the first 2 years of treatment, ticlopidine may be more effective than aspirin in secondary stroke prevention; however, its adverse event profile may be less favorable. The latter factor plus cost and monitoring considerations have engendered controversy about the indications for ticlopidine based on risk–benefit analysis. There is also controversy about the proper dose of aspirin for secondary stroke prevention. Some experts argue for lower doses (e.g., 75–325 mg), whereas others adhere to higher dose regimens (500 mg or 975–1300 mg).

The anticoagulant warfarin is beneficial for the prevention of stroke in patients with nonvalvular atrial fibrillation. Carotid endarterectomy, a surgical procedure to remove atherosclerotic plaque from the carotid artery, is the treatment of choice when there is

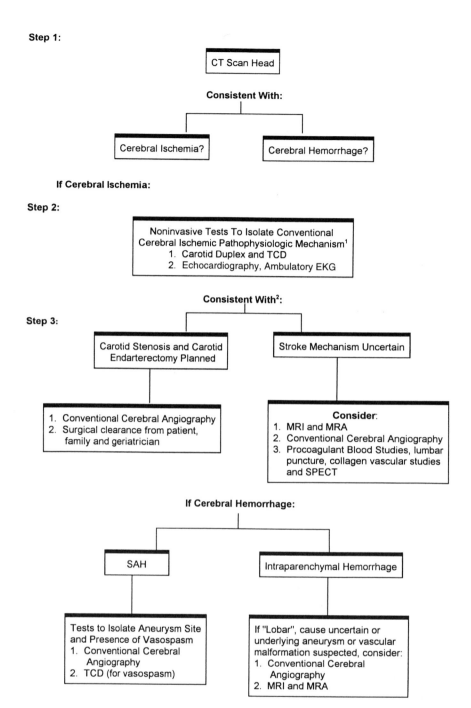

Step 1:

CT Scan Head

Consistent With:

Cerebral Ischemia?   Cerebral Hemorrhage?

If Cerebral Ischemia:

Step 2:

Noninvasive Tests To Isolate Conventional
Cerebral Ischemic Pathophysiologic Mechanism[1]
1. Carotid Duplex and TCD
2. Echocardiography, Ambulatory EKG

Consistent With[2]:

Step 3:

Carotid Stenosis and Carotid
Endarterectomy Planned

Stroke Mechanism Uncertain

1. Conventional Cerebral Angiography
2. Surgical clearance from patient,
   family and geriatrician

Consider:
1. MRI and MRA
2. Conventional Cerebral Angiography
3. Procoagulant Blood Studies, lumbar
   puncture, collagen vascular studies
   and SPECT

If Cerebral Hemorrhage:

SAH

Intraparenchymal Hemorrhage

Tests to Isolate Aneurysm Site
and Presence of Vasospasm
1. Conventional Cerebral
   Angiography
2. TCD (for vasospasm)

If "Lobar", cause uncertain or
underlying aneurysm or vascular
malformation suspected, consider:
1. Conventional Cerebral
   Angiography
2. MRI and MRA

Figure I   Stroke diagnostic algorithm. If CT is negative for SAH, perform lumbar puncture to isolate blood in cerebrospinal fluid if clinical presentation is consistent with SAH; MRI and MRA may be performed but are not the most sensitive procedures to isolate aneurysm site. Routine blood studies should include a screen for bleeding diathesis; MRI is useful as a follow-up study to rule-out underlying lesions such as neoplasm and to chart the course of hemorrhage resolution. [1]To be performed in conjunction with routine blood studies, electrocardiogram and chest X-ray. Some experts would consider MRI and MRA as Step 2 tests. [2]Carotid duplex and TCD are used to define high-grade extracranial and intracranial large artery atherosclerotic occlusive disease. Echocardiography and ambulatory EKG define cardiac source embolism. Lacunar infarction is generally diagnosed in the absence of atherosclerotic mechanism or cardiac source embolism and in the presence of a typical lacunar syndrome (e.g., pure motor hemiparesis, pure sensory stroke, clumsy-hand dysarthria, ataxic hemiparesis).

Table V Medical Complications of Acute Stroke and Their Prevention

Complication	Prevention measure
Aspiration pneumonia	1. Frequent oral-pharyngeal suctioning if indicated 2. Swallow evaluation and appropriate diet 3. Frequent turning and positioning 4. Protect airway and intubate if indicated.
Loss of cerebral autoregulation	1. Maintain mild to moderate arterial hypertension. 2. Avoid rapid lowering of blood pressure unless a vital organ is compromised.
Dehydration	1. Maintain hydration status with 0.45 or 0.9 normal saline. 2. Avoid hypotonic fluids or those containing glucose.
Skin breakdown/decubitus ulcer formation	1. Regular examination of skin, especially dependent portions, for evidence of breakdown 2. Special pressure mattress and frequent turning of patient
Urinary tract infection	1. Avoid indwelling urinary catheters
Venous thromboembolism	1. Pressure-gradient stockings or pneumatic-compression stockings 2. Anticoagulant if not contraindicated
Seizure	1. Observe for occurrence of seizure. 2. Anticonvulsant administration if seizure occurs
Cardiac arrhythmia	1. Ambulatory electrocardiogram

high-grade (70–99%) ipsilateral symptomatic carotid stenosis in patients with TIA or minor stroke. For low-grade carotid stenosis (0–29%), the surgical risks outweigh the benefits, and antiplatelet therapy is recommended. For medium-grade carotid stenosis (30–69%), the answer is as yet uncertain but is the focus of ongoing study.

Secondary stroke preventatives have been studied most extensively in those in the 60–65-year age range. Clinical trial experience in the very elderly is limited. It has been shown that aspirin may not be an effective stroke preventative in patients over 75 years of age with atrial fibrillation, yet warfarin may be dangerous in this group. Carotid endarterectomy may be safely performed in well-selected older patients.

C. Primary Prevention

Generally, stroke, a chronic disease, has a long latent period, and primary prevention is possible. Public health strategies to prevent stroke by modification of risk factors amenable to medication, diet, or other interventions include the mass and high-risk approaches. The mass approach emphasizes lifestyle modification to achieve modest reductions in the level of the risk factor in all individuals in the population. The high-risk approach identifies individuals with high levels of a risk factor or multiple risk factors, and

medication is usually prescribed to achieve substantial reductions in the risk factor(s).

There is substantial primary prevention data to show a major benefit for treatment of hypertension and use of warfarin in atrial fibrillation. More recently it has been shown that carotid endarterectomy is safe and effective in patients with high-grade (50 or 60–99%) asymptomatic carotid stenosis. Observational epidemiologic studies support the contention that cessation of smoking and heavy alcohol consumption is beneficial in reducing stroke risk. Debate exists about the efficacy of treatment of hypercholesterolemia and other blood lipid abnormalities.

There is clear evidence for substantial stroke risk reduction by treating isolated systolic hypertension in the elderly. However, in the very old the window of opportunity for primary prevention may have lapsed in regard to treatment of some modifiable risk factors. Cerebrovascular disease may be too far advanced, treatments are not safe or effective, or the absolute benefit for risk factor modification is small, as the risk factor has low prevalence and relative risk in the very old.

VI. CONSEQUENCES OF STROKE

It is estimated that more than half of stroke survivors have significant residual physical disability and func-

Table VI Major Hyperacute Stroke Therapies

Type	Results of clinical trial testing
Cytoprotectants	
Calcium channel blockers	No major benefit
Opiate receptor antagonists	No major clinical trial underway
Barbiturates	No established benefit
N-methyl-D-aspartate antagonists	Clinical trial testing underway
Antithrombotics	
Heparin	No established benefit
Heparinoids	Clinical trial testing underway
Prostacyclin	No major benefit
Thrombolytics	
Streptokinase	No established benefit
Tissue-type plasminogen activator (t-PA)	Established benefit with administration within 3 hr
Urokinase	Clinical trial testing underway
Hemorheologic Treatment	
Hemodilution	No major benefit
Ancrod	Clinical trial testing underway
Pentoxifylline	No major benefit
Other	
Ganglioside (GM_1)	No major benefit

tional impairment. Among long-term survivors in the Framingham Study the following deficits were observed: decreased vocation function (63%), decreased socialization outside the home (59%), limitations in household tasks (56%), decrease in interests and hobbies (47%), decreased ability to use outside transportation (44%), decreased socialization at home (43%), dependence in activities of daily living (32%), dependence in mobility (22%), and relocation to a nursing home or other institutional setting (15%).

Age is an important predictor of functional prognosis in stroke. Although age does not preclude good functional outcome, it is associated with shorter survival, more comorbidity, and adverse psychosocial conditions. The most powerful determinant of functional outcome in stroke seems to be specific neurologic deficit. Severity of stroke deficit and comorbidity (medical and psychosocial) are crucial to functional outcome. Other factors that may play a role include sex, race, marital status, etiology of stroke, educational level, vocation status, financial status, and other "intrinsic" factors such as family support and available community services.

Dementia is an important consequence of stroke. It is estimated that vascular dementia is the second leading cause of progressive and irreversible dementia, accounting for approximately 10–20% of cases. The frequency of vascular dementia rises exponentially with age. It is generally held to be more common among men than women and may be more prevalent than Alzheimer's disease in Asia and among the very old in some countries (e.g., Sweden). In addition to age and possibly education, risk factors for vascular dementia seem to be those cardiovascular determinants that underlie stroke.

At present, vascular dementia is the only preventable form of dementia of late life. As stroke leads to vascular dementia, the prevention of stroke by modification of treatable risk factors is anticipated to result in a significant reduction in vascular dementia. However, once vascular dementia is diagnosed, there is no proven secondary preventative to reduce its debilitating cognitive effects. [*See* DEMENTIA.]

BIBLIOGRAPHY

Epidemiology

Gorelick, P. B. (1994). Stroke prevention: An opportunity for efficient utilization of health care resources during the coming decade. *Stroke, 25,* 220–224.

Sacco, R. L. (1994). Ischemic stroke. In P. B. Gorelick, & M. Alter (Eds.), *Handbook of neuroepidemiology* (pp. 77–119). New York: Marcell Dekker, Inc.

Wolf, P. A., Abbott, R. D., & Kannel, W. B. (1991). Atrial fibrillation as an indepenent risk factor for stroke: The Framingham Study. *Stroke, 22,* 983–988.

Wolf, P. A., Belanger, A. J., D'Agostino, R. B. (1992). Management of risk factors. *Neurologic Clinics, 10,* 177–191.

Stroke Classification and Pathophysiology

Mohr, J. P. (1994). Classification of stroke: Experience from stroke data banks. In W. Dorndorf & P. Marx (Eds.), *Stroke prevention* (pp. 1–13). Basel: Karger.

(1987). Stroke and Other Brain Disorders: In D. B. Hier, P. B. Gorelick, & A. G. Shindler (Eds.), *Topics in behavioral neurology and neuropsychology. With Key References* (pp. 205–223). Boston: Butterworths.

Diagnosis

Adams, H. P., Jr, Brott, T. G., Crowell, R. M., Furlan, A. J., Gomez, C. R., Grotta, J., et al. (1994). Guidelines for the management of patients with ischemic stroke. A statement for health care professionals from a special writing group of the Stroke Council, American Heart Association. *Stroke 25,* 1901–1914.

Brown, R. D., Evans, B. A., Wiebers, D. O., Petty, G. W., Meissner, I., Dale, A. J. D., for the Mayo Clinic Division of Cerebrovascular Disease. (1994). Transient ischemic attack and minor ischemic stroke: An algorithm for evaluation and treatment. *Mayo Clinical Proceedings, 69,* 1027–1039.

Mayberg, M. R., Batjer, H. H., Dacey, R., Diringer, M., Haley, E. C., Heros, R. C., et al. (1994). Guidelines for the management of aneurysmal subarachnoid hemorrhage. A statement for health care professionals from a special writing group of the Stroke Council, American Heart Association. *Stroke, 25,* 2315–2328.

Mohr, J. P. (1992). Overview of laboratory studies in stroke. In H. J. M. Barnett, J. P. Mohr, R. M. Stein, F. M. Yatsu. *Stroke: Pathophysiology, diagnosis and management* (pp. 149–154). New York: Churchill Livingstone.

Treatment and Prevention

Antiplatelet Trialists' Collaboration. (1994). Collaborative overview of randomized trials of antiplatelet therapy—I: Prevention of death, myocardial infarction, and stroke by prolonged antiplatelet therapy in various categories of patients. *British Medical Journal, 308,* 81–106.

Biller, J. (1992). Medical management of acute cerebral ischemia. *Neurologic Clinics, 10*(1), 63–85.

Broderick, J. P. (1994). Intracerebral hemorrhage. In P. B. Gorelick & M. A. Alter (Eds.), *Handbook of neuroepidemiology* (pp. 141–167). New York: Marcell Dekker.

Brott, T. (1992). Thrombolytic therapy. *Neurologic Clinics, 10*(1), 219–232.

van Gijn, J. (1992). Aspirin: Dose and indications in modern medicine. *Neurologic Clinics, 10*(1), 193–207.

Gorelick, P. B. (1995). Stroke prevention. *Archives of Neurology, 52,* 347–355.

Hobson, R. W. II, Weiss, D. G., Fields, W. S., Goldstone, J., Moore, W. S., Towne, J. B., Wright, C. B., & the Veterans Affairs Cooperative Study Group. (1993). Efficacy of carotid endarterectomy for asymptomatic carotid stenosis. *New England Journal of Medicine, 328,* 221–227.

Longstreth, W. T. (1994). Nontraumatic subarachnoid hemorrhage. In P. B. Gorelick & M. A. Alter (Eds.), *Handbook of neuroepidemiology* (pp. 123–140). New York: Marcell Dekker, Inc.

Stroke Prevention in Atrial Fibrillation Investigators. (1994). Warfarin versus aspirin for prevention of thromboembolism in atrial fibrillation: Stroke Prevention in Atrial Fibrillation II Study. *Lancet, 343,* 687–691.

Consequences

Alexander, M. P. (1994). Stroke rehabilitation outcome. A potential use of predictive variables to establish levels of care. *Stroke, 25,* 128–134.

Gorelick, P. B., Roman, G., & Mangone, C. A. (1994). Vascular dementia. In P. B. Gorelick & M. A. Alter (Eds.), *Handbook of neuroepidemiology* (pp. 197–213). New York: Marcell Dekker, Inc.

Gresham, G. E. (1992). Rehabilitation of the stroke survivor. In H. J. M. Barnett, B. M. Stein, J. P. Mohr, & F. M. Yatsu (Eds.), *Stroke: Pathophysiology, diagnosis and management* (2nd ed.) (pp. 1189–1201). New York: Churchill Livingstone.

Ottenbacher, K. J., & Jannell, S. (1993). The results of clinical trials in stroke rehabilitation research. *Archives of Neurology, 50,* 37–44.

Skoog, I., Nilsson, L., Palmertz, B., Andreasson, L- A, & Svanborg, A. (1993). A population-based study of dementia in 85 year olds. *New England Journal of Medicine, 328,* 153–158.

Suicide

Dan G. Blazer and Harold G. Koenig

Duke University Medical Center

I. Introduction
II. Epidemiology of Suicide in Late Life
III. Risk Factors for Suicide in Late Life
IV. Evaluating the Potentially Suicidal Older Adult
V. The Clinical Management of the Suicidal Older
   Adult—Intervention as Prevention
VI. Ethical and Legal Issues

Chronic Suicide The hastening of death by willful actions over extended periods of time, such as failure to eat, sustained drug and alcohol abuse fully knowing the risks for death, and refusal to use life-sustaining medications.

Euthanasia Literally, an easy or painless death. Now used to describe the putting to death of a person suffering from an incurable illness with the full compliance of the person put to death.

Hemlock Society A group of individuals who actively support euthanasia.

Physician-Assisted Suicide A form of euthanasia in which a physician actively assists an individual in killing herself or himself, usually with the preparation of a lethal drug that can be self-administered by the person seeking suicide.

Suicide The voluntary termination of one's life. Suicide is not a mental illness but rather a behavior.

SUICIDE, by definition, is the voluntary termination of one's life. Suicide, therefore, is not a mental illness but rather a behavior. That behavior is frequently (but not exclusively) associated with psychiatric disorders. Even so, suicide is best understood as a transient psychological state leading to a constriction of affect and intellect. Constriction of thinking leads the individual to a dilemma. Either there is a solution to life or life should be brought to an end. Intolerable psychological pain and frustrated psychological needs lead to a feeling of hopelessness and helplessness in which the purpose of suicide is to resolve the dilemma and that resolution is a cessation of consciousness in order to avoid pain.

I. INTRODUCTION

A. The Association of Suicide with Late Life

Suicide has been associated with late life since antiquity, Seneca, the personal teacher of the Emperor Nero, said:

> For this reason, but for this alone, life is not an evil—that no one is obliged to live. If life pleases you, live. If not, you have a right to return whence you came. I will not relinquish old age if it leaves my better part intact. But if it begins to shake my mind, if it destroys its facilities one by one, if it leaves me not life but breath, I will depart from the putrid or tottering edifice. I will not escape by death from disease so long as it may be healed, and leaves my mind unimpaired. I will not raise my hand against myself on account of pain, for so to die is to be conquered. But if I know that I must suffer without hope of relief, I will depart, not through fear of the pain itself, but because it prevents all for which I would live. (Lecky, 1869, pps. 219–220)

Seneca's response to suicide, however, was anything but a rational decision. Having fallen out of favor with Nero, Seneca was given a choice later in his life to take his own life or to have it taken by someone else. He chose the former and therein lies the dilemma facing clinicians and, indeed, society, when it confronts the specter of suicide in late life. Is suicide among the elderly rational, a disorder, or a response to a disorder? In this entry, we argue that suicide is, in most cases, an irrational response to severe psychological pain that results from diagnosable psychiatric disorders. Even so, however, there are other factors that associate suicide with late life and, perhaps, lower the threshold for committing suicide in late life. Albert Camus believed whether one should commit suicide to be the only serious philosophical problem. He struggled with thoughts of suicide through much of his life, and though he did not actively commit suicide, many believed the automobile accident that led to his death was, in fact, an indirect suicide. He described his struggle with the problem of suicide in the *Myth of Sisiphysus*. The philosophical question raised by Camus is no more acute than it is among older persons. For example, older persons are more likely to experience severe physical illnesses which inevitably lead to death. Therefore the issue of physician-assisted suicide has involved older persons more than others. In addition, many older persons fear becoming burdens to themselves, friends, and society. The spectre of chronic, debilitating illnesses, such as Alzheimer's disease (AD), with the concomitant impact upon families leads some elders to justify suicide. Finally, older persons recognize that they have lived the vast majority of their lives, accomplished most of what they wished to accomplish, and therefore see little future compared with past memories, whether those memories be pleasant or unpleasant. Seneca's reflections upon suicide in late life, therefore, are as applicable in the latter twentieth century as they were 2000 years ago.

B. The Scope of Suicide

I. Acute versus Chronic Suicide

When one considers the concept of suicide, one usually reflects upon the acute, decisive actions that lead to death. These include shooting one's self, hanging one's self, overdosing on medications, crashing one's automobile in a single-car accident, or asphyxiation with carbon monoxide or some form of toxic gas. These methods of suicide are usually easily identifiable and are the causes of death that are generally used to compile statistics regarding suicide in late life. Our ability to predict a suicide, even acute suicide, is not

easy, however. For example, the older person involved in a single-car accident, such as crashing into a tree, would rarely be assumed to have committed suicide, though the likelihood that this accident was in fact a suicide may be quite high. Older persons found dead in their homes may not be subjected to a thorough medical examination to rule out all possible self-inflicted causes of death, in part because older persons are "expected" to die from conditions such as cardiac disease. Medical examiners are reticent to embarrass the older person and the family if no evidence of participation by another person in the death can be found.

Far more difficult for the clinician working with older adults is chronic suicide. By far the most common form of chronic suicide is failure to eat, therefore leading to slow but definite starvation. Other forms of chronic suicide include sustained drug and alcohol abuse, refusal to use life-sustaining medications (such as insulin), and self-neglect. Carl Menninger, in *Man Against Himself*, explored in detail the potential for chronic suicide in society, and this is perhaps more applicable to older persons than persons of other ages.

2. Direct versus Indirect Suicide

Indirect suicide is closely associated with chronic suicide but some differences do emerge. Direct actions to take one's life, such as self-inflicted gunshot wounds and overdoses of medication, are the most noticeable attempts of suicide. Nevertheless, a number of indirect approaches to suicide are prevalent in our society. Some older persons submit themselves to dangerous, even reckless situations. For example, an older person may attempt a wilderness hike with inadequate preparation, submitting their safety to the elements. Others refuse adequate medical care for a potentially fatal condition that could be prevented. For example, an older adult may suffer from a significant and severe cardiac arrhythmia that can be controlled by medications, yet refuse to take the medications, therefore increasing the likelihood that she or he will die from the arrhythmia.

3. Euthanasia and Physician-Assisted Suicide

Voluntary suicide, often with the assistance of someone else, has taken place since antiquity. These voluntary approaches of taking one's life, are counter to a culture that views suicide as a "mental illness" and have received considerable attention in the press in recent years. Euthanasia has been a topic of many conversations recently stimulated in large part by the foundation of the Hemlock Society and is closely connected with physician-assisted suicide. Physician assisted-suicide has made headline news during the 1990s since Dr. Jack Kevorkian assisted Mrs. Janet Adkins to end her life while parked in a van later found in a Michigan suburb. She was hooked to a so-called suicide machine provided by Dr. Kevorkian. Mrs. Adkins had been diagnosed as suffering from probable AD (in its early stages) and made the decision to end her life rather than undergo the slow decline in her cognitive abilities. (The ethics of physician-assisted suicide will be discussed at the end of this article.)

4. Suicidal Ideation, Attempts, and Completed Suicides

Suicidal ideation is relatively common throughout the life cycle. In a large survey of older adults in the community, 6.1% expressed thoughts about death within 2 weeks before the time of the interview, and 4.4% at some point in their life expressed a desire to die, with 1.2% expressing this desire within the 2 weeks before the interview. Three and one-half percent reported that *they* had contemplated suicide at some point in their lives. In the entire sample (persons 18 and above), 7.5% reported having thoughts of suicide sometime during their life. [*See* DEATH AND DYING.]

Suicide attempts range widely, and some individuals have categorized these attempts. From a clinical perspective, these categorizations are of little value, for categorization is generally based on the concept that some "attempts" are more serious that others. In reality, all suicide attempts are serious, even if the intent of the gesture is not to die but perhaps to call for help. Suicide attempts range from taking a few pills that are highly unlikely to lead to death to a self-inflicted gunshot wound from which a person miraculously survives. Reports of attempted suicide are less frequent in late life (less than 1% report an attempt at some time in their lives) compared to younger persons where the lifetime frequency of attempted suicide is between 1 and 2%.

As noted above, completed suicides are not always easy to identify. Even so, there is little doubt that completed suicides are more frequent in late life than at other stages of the life cycle, but this is almost entirely due to an increased frequency of suicide deaths among older white males.

II. EPIDEMIOLOGY OF SUICIDE IN LATE LIFE

A. Suicide Rates in the United States by Demographic Characteristics

Suicide rates in the United States have averaged 12.5 per 100,000 persons per year during this century. From a high of 17.4 observed during the economic depression in 1932, suicide rates dropped to a low of 9.8 in 1957 and have climbed steadily to a rate of 12.3 in 1990. Suicide rates are highest among older persons, being 21.5 in 1986. The trend overall in age affects on suicide nevertheless is changing. Suicide rates for elderly persons decreased from 1950 to 1980 but exhibited a 25% increase from 1980 to 1986. The overall increased rates of suicide since the 1950s have been associated with a decline in the medium age of suicide victims from 47.2 years of age in 1970 to 39.9 years in 1980, however.

Suicide rates vary significantly by gender, race, and ethnicity among older adults. Rates for white males in 1986 were 45.6 per 100,000 persons, 16.2 for black males, 7.5 for white females, and 2.4 for black females. Even so, the rates for black males are increasing at a much faster pace than for white males.

The methods used for committing suicide also vary by age and gender. Two-thirds of suicides among the elderly are committed by use of firearms (compared to 57% among persons under the age of 65). In 1986, 75% of male victims over the age of 65 died of gunshot wounds compared to 61% of male victims under the age of 65. During the same year, only 31% of female suicides over 65 died of gunshot wounds compared to 41% under the age of 65. The use of drugs and poisons are more common methods of committing suicide among older women.

Though suicide rates have increased among older persons in the United States, rates are not as high as among other industrialized societies. For example, the suicide rate among persons 75 plus in Austria between 1974 and 1988 averaged 87.3 compared to 43.8 for persons in the United States. Sweden, West Germany, France, Denmark, Switzerland, Portugal, Belgium and Japan all had higher rates among elders than found in the United States. Even so, between 1974 and 1987 there were increases in male suicide rates in the United States at a faster pace than for the remainder of the industrialized world.

B. Cohort Analyses

Birth cohort appears to be a strong predictor of suicide rates. Persons born between 1900 and 1920 have experienced lower suicide rates at every age than persons born prior to 1900 and persons born after 1920. This in part explains the decline in suicide rates among older persons from 1950 to 1980 and the subsequent upswing in rates since 1980. Why do some birth cohorts suffer from higher rates of suicide than others? Suicide rates may be related to the relative size of birth cohorts compared with other cohorts within the population. For example, successively younger birth cohorts are facing a more competitive job market, increased social stress, delayed marriage (and therefore delayed establishment of close relationships), fewer children, and smaller social networks. More frequent divorce rates, secularization, and perhaps a subsequent feeling of alienation may also explain the increased suicide rates in younger birth cohorts. These are theories only and can scarcely be tested using national suicide data. Even so, tracing suicide rates by age through the twentieth century is most useful to understand the relative well-being of older persons compared to the remainder of society through time. [See COHORT STUDIES.]

C. Gender Difference in Suicide

Gender is one of the most important predictors of suicide in older persons, for older women do not experience an increase in rates with age as do older white men. One possibility for explaining these gender differences in suicide mortality is that women exhibit differences in coping that protect them from suicide compared to men. In contrast to men (at least through most of the twentieth century), women tend to experience several role shifts during adulthood. In addition to a period of mothering, women have traditionally moved in and out of the workforce depending upon their age. Men, in contrast, have tended to follow a relatively stable course. The change from work to retirement for men, therefore, may be more difficult, and men may not have developed the coping skills

necessary for such changes, which in turn increases their likelihood of suicide. Women are also more likely to maintain close relationships outside the marriage relationship than are men, and this may explain part of the difference. Finally, men are more likely to use violent means of suicide, such as gunshot wounds, which tend to be more fatal than taking pills. [See RETIREMENT; SOCIAL NETWORKS, SUPPORT, AND INTEGRATION; STRESS.]

III. RISK FACTORS FOR SUICIDE IN LATE LIFE

A. Demographic Factors

As described above, increased age is a risk for suicide throughout life, irrespective of birth cohort effects. This increased risk does not plateau at age of 65, but rather persons, 85 years of age have the highest rates of suicide in our society. The association of age and suicide is explained exclusively by the association of age and suicide among males in the United States, in that rates of suicide among females (both White and non-White) change relatively little across mid- and late life. Males are much more likely to commit suicide than females, and Whites have higher suicide rates than non-Whites, though among older persons, rates for black males are increasing at a faster pace than for white males. Suicide rates are also higher among persons single, separated, divorced, or widowed compared to persons who are married at all ages. This is especially true for males. Suicide rates usually increase during troublesome economic times and decrease during times of prosperity. Suicide rates also exhibit age-specific temporal cycles. For example, day-of-the-week effects are found almost exclusively in middle-aged suicide. On the other hand, older persons are more likely to commit suicide during the summer months, whereas teenagers are more likely to commit suicide during the winter months. [See DEMOGRAPHY.]

B. Psychiatric Disorders

Psychiatric disorders are the most important risk factors for suicide, especially depression and alcohol abuse and dependence. In one study, 80% of persons who had attempted suicide and were later admitted to an adult psychiatric inpatient unit had experienced a major depression of late onset, especially a psychotic depression. In another study, suicide attempts were made by 8.7% of older depressed persons after hospital admission. Alcohol abuse is a known risk factor of suicide, though the impact of alcohol abuse on suicide rates in older persons is debated. [*See* ALCOHOL AND DRUGS; DEPRESSION.]

C. Physical Illness and Functional Disability

Chronic physical illness as a risk factor for suicide has received significant attention in the press during recent years. The prospect of living many years with chronic pain or disability and subsequently becoming dependent upon the health-care system and/or family members is especially difficult for older persons who have traditionally accepted an independent lifestyle and cling to our society's valuation of self-sufficiency. Some have suggested that physical illness may contribute to suicide in over one-third of older persons. The illnesses most frequently cited are diseases of the central nervous systems (especially AD), malignancies, cardiopulmonary conditions, and urogenital diseases in men. [*See* BRAIN AND CENTRAL NERVOUS SYSTEM.]

D. Previous Suicide Attempts

A previous history of a suicide attempt is well known to contribute to the risk for future suicide attempts. Each attempt increases the risk of a successful suicide in the future. In some ways, having made a suicide attempt breaks through a psychological barrier to suicide and therefore decreases the threshold for future suicide attempts. Clinicians must be especially vigilant in working with older persons who have made suicide attempts, given that, in general, older persons do not attempt suicide as frequently as younger persons, even though their rates are higher for completed suicides.

E. Psychological Factors

The association of hopelessness with suicide is intuitive, and in recent years, the relationship between hopelessness and suicide attempts in older persons has been demonstrated. Persons experiencing recurrent major depression and treated with standard psychotherapy and pharmacotherapy are of a higher risk for a suicide attempt if they exhibit a higher degree of hopelessness. In addition, loss of pleasure or interest,

significant cycling of mood, which can lead to severe experiences of depression following periods of well-being, can also contribute to an increased risk for suicide. As noted above, coping styles also may increase the risk for suicide. For example, older persons who tend to act out their conflicts and psychological pain, as opposed to expressing them to confidant, are at greater risk for suicide.

F. Biological Susceptibility

In recent years, two areas of psychobiological research have been related to suicide: the hypothalamic-pituitary-adrenal (HPA) axis and the serotonin system. For example, HPA dysfunction has been associated with significant changes in cognitive function, such as confusion, which may contribute to the propensity to suicide. Decreased levels of 5-HIAA (a metabolite of serotonin) have been found in a number of studies of persons who have either died of violent suicide or showed an increased propensity to attempt suicide. Decreased levels of serotonin have been associated with increased aggressiveness, which in turn may lead to an increased risk of suicide. These findings may be especially relevant to the elderly (though studies that clearly associate these findings with older persons have not been completed), for older persons do show some propensity toward dysregulation of the HPA axis. There is no evidence that in normal aging, the serotonin system is changed.

IV. EVALUATING THE POTENTIALLY SUICIDAL OLDER ADULT

The evaluation of the potentially suicidal older adult can be divided into the evaluation of the direct and indirect risk of suicide. Neither of these approaches to an evaluation is highly predictive of suicide, primarily because suicide is such a rare evident. Therefore suicidal risk is, by its very nature, subject to overestimation. Even so, given the tragedy of suicide, this overestimation may be helpful. Early intervention to prevent suicide based on the assessment of the potential for suicide could save the lives of many older persons. Unfortunately, the degree to which these efforts are successful will never be known, primarily because of the rarity of the event. In other words, one would have great difficulty in performing a "controlled study" of interventive prevention in a high-risk group of suicidal patients compared to a controlled group in order to determine the effectiveness of that intervention.

A. Direct Assessment

The direct assessment of suicide occurs in the interview with the potentially suicidal older adult. Many clinicians feel uncomfortable asking older adults directly about their intentions to harm themselves. A fourfold, layered approach to assessment is useful in obtaining the necessary data without disrupting the therapeutic relationship with the potentially suicidal elder. The first inquiry should be, "Have you ever felt life is not worth living?" As noted above, this question is answered affirmatively in a significant minority of older persons. Among depressed older persons the frequency of a positive response is much greater. Yet many older persons who wish they were dead would never act upon that wish. The reasons vary from moral and/or religious prohibitions to fears of the pain of killing oneself.

The second inquiry, if the first is positive, is, "Have you ever thought of hurting or harming yourself?" Though this question does not specifically inquire about suicide, the elder will almost always interpret the question accurately and will usually provide an honest response in return. If the elder states that he or she has not considered inflicing personal harm, then the inquiry can cease and the older person may be considered, at least from the perspective of direct assessment, at low risk for suicide.

If the answer to the second question is positive, however, the clinician should inquire, "Have you considered specific methods for harming yourself?" Many elders who have thought of harming themselves have only thought so in general terms. Others, however, have considered specific means by which they might harm themselves, such as shooting themselves, taking medications, or refusing necessary medical therapies. If an individual has considered a specific method for inflicting personal harm and that method is readily available to the elder, for example, an older person states that he will shoot himself and possess a gun, then a critical threshold has been crossed and a risk of suicide is much higher.

Finally, the clinician should inquire, "Have you ever made a suicide attempt?" The importance of suicide attempts as part of the overall risk-factor profile of the potentially suicidal older adult has been emphasized. Yet "attempts" vary in severity. Some persons will simply walk to the medicine cabinet to determine if they have sufficient medicines for an attempt. Others, however, have actually taken guns from their bureaus within the bedroom, loaded their guns and placed the gun to their heads, only to decide, at the last moment, not to pull the trigger. Still others have actually made attempts, either taking medications or wounding themselves in an attempt at suicide.

In summary, the direct assessment of the potential for suicide ranges from suicidal ideation in broadest terms to serious attempts to end one's life. The more severe the attempt, or the more specific the ideation, the greater the risk for suicide.

B. Indirect Assessment and Risk Factors

Given the rarity of completed suicides and the difficulty of establishing a clear relationship between direct assessment of suicidal risk and suicide over short periods of time (for example, a few days), clinicians treating persons at risk for suicide would do well to emulate physicians in their approach to reducing the risk for myocardial infarction. Direct assessment of risk should be coupled with known indirect risk factors, as described above: older age; male gender; white race/ethnicity; physical illness; psychological factors such as hopelessness; previous suicide attempts and psychiatric disorders such as depression and alcohol abuse. Clinicians can then develop a risk-factor profile. This profile is analogous to that for cardiovascular disease, which includes obesity, hypertension, cholesterol and lipid levels, lack of exercise, as well as demographics such as age, gender, race or ethnicity, and lifestyle.

Even though suicide and myocardial infraction at first glance exhibit little in common there are similarities in the approach to preventing these two tragic events. First, both are isolated and severe events that decrease life expectancy among persons at greater risk. Studies abound that demonstrate that, among the depressed, life expectancy is decreased in large part by suicide just as studies abound demonstrating that persons with a high risk for myocardial infarction have a shortened life expectancy. A second similarity is that death is usually not the outcome of the event. Most persons experiencing a myocardial infarction do not die, as is the case with most persons who make a suicide attempt. Those persons, however, are known to be at especially high risk for future fatal events regardless of the presence or absence of other risk factors. Therefore preventive efforts are especially directed toward persons who have experienced a nonfatal event. Third, risk for both suicide and myocardial infarction derive from a combination of risk factors rather than any single factor. Therefore, an aggressive, generic approach to prevention is more appropriate than an isolated specific approach. The clinician must call on all of her or his resources in order to decrease the risk of suicide as much as possible.

V. THE CLINICAL MANAGEMENT OF THE SUICIDAL OLDER ADULT—INTERVENTION AS PREVENTION

The management of the older person at risk for suicide consists of intervention strategies directed at preventing future suicide attempts. In other words, intervention is preventive. The intervention can be conveniently divided into two phases, crisis intervention and treatment of underlying problems. These strategies are not always successful, however, and clinicians must also be prepared to assist family and health-care workers when an older adult commits suicide.

A. Crisis Intervention

Crisis intervention consists of three phases. First, and perhaps foremost, is protection of the person at significant suicidal risk. These persons come to the attention of the clinician, perhaps because of a suicide attempt that was unsuccessful but also through an expressed desire to end their lives conveyed to, perhaps, a family member or the clinician herself or himself. When a clinician deems the risk for suicide at crisis level, then extraordinary measures are indicated. These measures include involuntary hospitalization. If the older person refuses voluntary hospitalization, around-the-clock vigils by family members and 24-hour-a-day availability by the clinician may substitute for involuntary hospital-

ization. The crisis of suicide generally is short lived, for suicide by its very nature tends to be an impulsive act. Therefore protecting the older adult through the period of crisis is paramount.

A second phase in crisis intervention is the suicide contract. If an older adult expresses the intent to commit suicide, the clinician often can obtain a promise from the older person that he or she will not make a suicide attempt without contacting the clinician and speaking to the clinician about her or his specific intent. For a suicide contract to be effective, the potentially suicidal elder must be cognitively intact, and the clinician must be available either by telephone or by immediate visit to a clinic facility. Older persons in the latter twentieth century in the United States are generally faithful to their word and therefore the suicide contract, if it can be negotiated, is an effective means for deterring suicide through the period of crisis. Why would an older person intent upon harming himself submit to a contract with the clinician? The intent to kill one's self is, by its very nature, ambivalent, for the desire to live is clearly present if the elder is still alive. The clinician therefore takes advantage of this ambivalence through the crisis period.

In the midst of the crisis of suicide, the clinician must involve the family. First, if the older person is not hospitalized, the responsibility is placed upon the family for vigilance during the period of increased risk for suicide, then the family must be instructed as to what they should do to assist in preventing a suicide. For example, family members must be told to remove any potentially harmful instruments from availability to the older person, such as guns and knives, and also should be instructed to take responsibility for medications. Frequent checks by the clinician with the elder during the period of crisis as well as family members or friends who stay with the elder should be a part of the family support as well.

The use of families in preventing suicides during the crisis period will probably become of more importance in the future, given the decreased resources for hospitalizing older persons. Families must be cautioned, however, that even their best efforts may prove ineffective, and this is no different than what could be expected in a hospital setting. Older persons, even in the best of medical facilities, have managed to successfully commit suicide. In other words, families must not be given the "responsibility" (or it should not even be suggested that families can take the responsibility) to prevent an older person from harming herself or himself. If families cannot manage to garner the necessary support or show significant ambivalence regarding the management of an older adult during a suicidal crises, then that older person must be hospitalized.

B. Treating the Underlying Problem

The crisis of suicide is short-term. In contrast, the problems leading to the crisis generally build up over a considerable period, are complex, and multifactorial. Once the crisis has abated, the clinician should aggressively address the problems that may have contributed to the crisis, whether those problems be the treatment of a major depressive disorder, treatment of alcohol abuse and dependence, or assisting the older person to adjust to a recent loss. Some problems can be addressed more easily than others, for a chronic and progressive illness such as cancer or AD cannot be reversed. In these situations, the clinician can only work with the older person to help the elder adjust to the problem presented. Though in some cases, even the clinician may deem a suicide as "rational" given the alternatives available to the elder, the clinician has a responsibility from the outset to assume that suicidal thoughts and behavior are abnormal and therefore deserve the best medical and psychiatric intervention available.

C. If a Suicide Occurs

Arnold Toynbe, in his book *Man's Concern with Death* said "There are always two parties to a death; the person who dies and the survivors who are bereaved ... and in the proportionment of suffering, the survivor takes the brunt." If an older person commits suicide, then clinicians who treated that elder should assist the family. Families often feel guilty and tend to project that guilt onto the health-care profession, despite the best efforts of the profession to instruct the family of its limitations. Lawyers often suggest that, if a suicide occurs, clinicians have little if any contact with family. However, it is the responsibility of the clinician to provide family members with an opportunity to vent their anger and frustration. The clinician may also vent her or his frustration (without suggesting that he or she made a mistake) in preventing a suicide. [*See* Bereavement and Loss.]

Both families and physicians must recognize that suicide, in the last analysis, cannot always be prevented. Even the best efforts of clinicians and family members, even the most compulsive procedures directed toward preventing suicide cannot be assumed to always be effective. Families express many concerns, not the least of which is embarrassment, over the fact that a valued family member has committed, according to some, an unpardonable sin. Family members feel guilt that they did not provide an environment that could rescue the elder from a sense of profound hopelessness and helplessness. Family members need to talk, and that talk must cover a spectrum of suicide, from the specific details of the actual event to the ethical and religious issues surrounding suicide. Each of these needs felt by family members are also felt by clinicians who have worked closely with older persons who commit suicide.

Both those professionals who have worked with the elder and family members must work through their grief. Initially, they may share this work but ultimately, the grief work must be individual. Any clinician who has treated an older person who has committed suicide cannot easily dismiss the outcome of that treatment. Clinicians should never become comfortable with an unnatural death and this is especially true when that death is voluntary. Suicide therefore challenges the existential core of those persons left behind.

VI. ETHICAL AND LEGAL ISSUES

The phenomena of suicide spans many fields of inquiry, not just the psychiatric or the medical. As noted above, many physicians and other health-care professionals, clergy, and scholars support the free choice of an older person to "death with dignity." In Greek society, both the Stoics and Epicureans viewed suicide as not only acceptable but especially relevant for escaping the problem of pain and old age. In recent years, the Hemlock Society, which accepts suicide as an acceptable solution to certain human conditions such as painful illness, has grown in membership dramatically. Even so, the recognition that suicide, more often than not, is usually an irrational act and the strong beliefs by others that suicide is unacceptable under any circumstances render societal discussions of elderly suicides especially relevant. Three issues related to the ethical and legal parameters of suicide are discussed below. [*See* ETHICS AND EUTHANASIA.]

A. Societal Intervention

As noted above, firearms are a favored means of committing suicide by many older adults, especially males. Given that suicide is often irrational and impulsive, the lack of the instruments to commit suicide is one means for its prevention. Just as arguments have been made that violent crimes can be decreased by gun control, equally cogent arguments have been made that suicide can be limited by gun controls as well. A parallel example suggesting that suicide rates can be lowered, at least for a time, by removing an instrument of suicide has been demonstrated in England. During the early 1960s, a toxic form of cooking gas was replaced by a nontoxic form. A favorite means of suicide in England at that time was placing one's head in an oven and turning on the gas. At approximately the time nontoxic cooking gas replaced toxic gas, suicide rates dropped dramatically, especially among elderly white males.

B. Rational Suicide on the Grounds of Old Age

Despite the optimistic approach to aging among many gerontologists, the concept of an old age relatively free of illness for the vast majority of elders is not a reality and not expected to be a reality in the future. Though persons are living longer and have achieved greater economic security during this century, more elders who are subsequently relegated to a discouraging dependence, frequently during years lived in a nursing home. This fact has led many to suggest that suicide is a rational alternative to frailty in late life. These advocates of rational suicide are not simply advocating the voluntary withdrawal of life supports when a medical condition is hopeless and/or cognitive functioning is severely impaired. They have revived an interest in legally facilitating older persons to make a choice regarding life supports under certain circumstances

in the future, as evidenced by a new law that requires hospitals to present older persons admitted an opportunity to provide "advance directives" regarding life supports in the future.

The debate regarding rational suicide transcends the science of gerontology, much less the practice of the mental health professionals. If the issue were to remain as, simply, an ethical debate in society, then the subject could be relegated to the ethicists and the theologians. With a rise of physician-assisted suicide, which has an impact upon the laws of our society and the practice of medicine, "rational suicide" becomes an issue of central importance to all who work with older adults.

C. Physician-Assisted Suicide

Physician-assisted suicide has received much attention throughout the lay press in recent years, predominantly through the activities of the Michigan physician Jack Kevorkian. As noted above, Kevorkian constructed a device for intravenously administering a lethal chemical that permits an apparent painless death at the choice of an individual who seeks the assistance of the physician. At times, Dr. Kevorkian has been present when the lethal chemical was administered, and at times he has been absent. He has been arrested on more than one occasion but has not been incarcerated for an extended period.

Kevorkian has confronted society with the necessity of making legal decisions regarding physician-assisted suicide. Society, in turn, has exemplified its ambivalence toward physician-assisted suicide through its circuitous legal approaches. Recently, the state of Oregon established a law permitting physician-assisted suicide, the first such law in this country. That law has been challenged in court, however. Surveys of persons in our society, both physicians and nonphysicians, reveal a relative acceptance of physician-assisted suicide, more than half of persons surveyed in most cases. When physicians are specifically asked about their willingness to assist a person in committing suicide, however, the likelihood of a positive response drops significantly. It is not known at this point whether physicians hesitate on the basis that physician-assisted suicide in most states is illegal or "questionably illegal" or whether the hesitation relates to the physicians' own ethical and moral values. Regardless, society has been forced to confront physician-assisted suicide as a phenomena and make decisions accordingly.

BIBLIOGRAPHY

Alexander, V. (1991). Grief after suicide: Giving voice to the lost. *Journal of Geriatric Psychiatry, 24,* 277.

Blazer, D. (1991). Suicide risk factors in the elderly: An epidemiological study. *Journal of Geriatric Psychiatry, 24,* 175.

Blazer, D. G., Bachar, J. R., & Manton, J. G. (1986). Suicide in late life: Reviewing commentary. *Journal of American Geriatric Society, 34,* 519.

Camus, A. (1955). *The myth of Sisiphysus.* London: Penguin.

Canetto, S. S. (1992). Gender and suicide in the elderly. *Suicide and Life Threatening Behavior, 22,* 80.

Conwell, Y. (1994). Suicide in elderly patients. In L. S. Schneider, C. F. Reynolds, B. D. Lebowitz, A. J. Friedhoff (Eds.), *Diagnosis and treatment of depression in late life* (pps. 397–418). Washington, DC: American Psychiatric Press.

Durkheim, E. (1951). *Suicide.* New York: Free Press.

Fawcett, J., & Busch, K. A. (1993). The psychobiology of suicide. *Clinical Neuroscience, 1,* 101.

Hendrin, H. (1982). *Suicide in America.* New York: W. W. Norton Company.

Lecky, W. E. H. (1869). *History of European morals from Augustus to Charlemagne* (2 vols). New York: Appleton & Co.

Lyness, J. M., Conwell, Y., & Nelson, J. C. (1992). Suicide attempts in elderly psychiatric inpatients. *Journal of American Geriatric Society, 40,* 320.

McCleary, R., Chew, K. S. Y., Hellscen, J. J., & Flynn-Bransford, M. (1991). Age-sex-specific cycles in the United States suicides, 1973–1985. *American Journal of Public Health, 14,* 94.

Meechan, P. J., Saltzman, L. E., & Sattin, R. W. (1991). Suicides among older United States residents: Epidemiologic characteristics in trends. *American Journal of Public Health, 81,* 1198.

Menninger, K. (1938). *Man against himself.* New York: Harcourt.

Moody, H. R. (1991). "Rational suicide" on grounds of old age? *Journal of Geriatric Society, 24,* 261.

Osgood, N. J. (1991). Prevention of suicide in the elderly. *Journal of Geriatric Psychiatry, 24,* 293.

Pritchard, C. (1992). Changes in elderly suicides in the U.S.A. and the developed world 1974–1987: Comparison with current homicides. *International Journal of Geriatric Psychiatry, 7,* 125.

Rifai, A. H., George, C. J., Seack, J. A., Mann, J. J., & Reynolds, C. F. (1994). Hopelessness in suicide attemptors after acute treatment of major depression in late life. *American Journal of Psychiatry, 151,* 1687.

Schneider, L. S., Reynolds, C. F., Lebowitz, B. D., & Friedhoff, A. J. (Eds.) (1993). *Diagnosis and treatment of depression in late life: Results of the NIH Consensus Development Conference* (p. 397). Washington, DC: American Psychiatric Press.

Schneidman, E. S. (1991). Key psychological factors in understanding and managing suicidal risk. *Journal of Geriatric Psychiatry, 24,* 153.

Seneca [as quoted in Lecky, W. E. H. (1869). *History of European morals from Augustus to Charlemagne (2 vols).* New York: Appleton & Company. (pps. 219–220).]

Tsuang, M. T., Simpson, J. C., & Fleming, J. A. (1992). Epidemiology of suicide. *International Review of Psychiatry, 4,* 117.

Zweig, R. A., & Hinrichsen, G. A. (1993). Factors associated with suicide attempts by depressed older adults: A perspective study. *American Journal of Psychiatry, 150,* 1687.

Telomeres

Calvin B. Harley

Geron Corporation

I. Replicative Senescence in Human Somatic Cells
II. Telomeres, the End-Replication Problem, and Telomerase
III. Telomere Loss in Aging and Telomerase Reactivation in Cancer
IV. Implications
V. Summary

Cell Senescence The deleterious aspects of a cell's phenotype at or approaching the end of its replicative capacity.

Hayflick Limit A somatic cell's replicative capacity: the maximum number of divisions it can undergo prior to permanent arrest.

Telomerase The RNA–protein (ribonucleoprotein) enzyme complex that has a DNA polymerase activity capable of extending telomeres with the specific telomere repeat sequence characteristic of the species.

Telomere The genetic element at the two ends of each linear chromosome in a eukaryotic nucleus. The telomere is composed of a specific DNA sequence and associated proteins.

Terminal Restriction Fragment (TRF) The last fragment of DNA at each end of a chromosome generated by cleaving genomic DNA with restriction endonucleases.

TELOMERES are essential genetic elements capping the ends of chromosomes. In most immortal eukaryotic cells, replication of telomeres cannot be completed without telomerase, a novel DNA polymerase that synthesizes the characteristic telomere DNA repeat (TTAGGG, in humans). In the majority of normal somatic cells and tissues, the enzyme telomerase is absent, and telomeres gradually shorten with age due to incomplete replication. In contrast, telomerase is present, and telomeres are stably maintained in reproductive tissues and most tumor cell lines and cancers. Thus, telomeres are critically involved in cell mortality and immortality, and hence in aging and age-related diseases, including cancer. In essence, telomeres provide a mitotic clock for somatic cells that undergo replicative aging, whereas aberrant reactivation of germline telomerase accounts in part for the immortal characteristic of cancer cells. Measurement or manipulation of telomeres and telomerase has important applications in research and medicine.

I. REPLICATIVE SENESCENCE IN HUMAN SOMATIC CELLS

Hayflick first described the limited replicative capacity of normal human fibroblasts in culture as a manifestation of cellular senescence in the early 1960s. As cells become senescent, they fail to divide in response to a variety of normal growth stimuli after a characteristic number of divisions, but they do not die. Instead, they remain metabolically active, but with an aberrant and generally deleterious pattern of gene expression. In the past 30 years, numerous other somatic cell types, including epithelial cells, endothelial cells, myoblasts, astrocytes, and lymphocytes, have also shown evidence of a clock that limits their division capacity. This clock relies upon cell divisions as the unit of time rather than chronological or metabolic age, and hence has been called a "mitotic clock." The maximum division capacity ex vivo of human somatic cell populations from a young, normal individual varies significantly from donor to donor, site of biopsy, and cell type to cell type. However, it typically falls in the range 50–100. This limit generally decreases as a function of donor age, presumably reflecting the replicative history of the cells in vivo. Somatic cells from other vertebrate species also have a limited proliferative capacity, and a positive correlation can be drawn between species longevity and cell life span. Within humans, a substantial amount of data now indicates that telomeric DNA at the ends of chromosomes is the "mitotic clock" of aging in somatic cells. [*See* CELL DEATH.]

II. TELOMERES, THE END-REPLICATION PROBLEM, AND TELOMERASE

Telomeres are essential genetic elements stabilizing the ends of linear eukaryotic chromosomes and protecting them from degradation and abnormal recombination. They are comprised of telomeric DNA and associated proteins. In all vertebrates studied to date, the telomere sequence is composed of hundreds or perhaps thousands of repeats of the hexamer duplex (TTAGGG:CCCTAA) arranged such that the G-rich strand runs 5′–3′ towards the end of the chromosome and sometimes extends beyond the 5′ end to generate a single-stranded (TTAGGG)$_n$ overhang. However, the linear DNA ends cannot be fully replicated by the conventional DNA polymerase complex, which requires a labile RNA primer to initiate DNA synthesis (Figure 1). Without a mechanism to overcome the "end-replication problem," organisms would fail to pass their complete genetic complement from generation to generation. In fact, without a special system for telomere maintenance, eukaryotic cells that would otherwise be immortal go through a number of doublings while their telomeres gradually shorten prior to cell-cycle arrest and/or death. Hence, all species must possess at least a germline mechanism to circumvent incomplete replication of their genome. Telomeres are typically analyzed by digestion of genomic DNA with restriction enzymes and analysis of the size distribution of the terminal restriction fragments (TRF) in gels following hybridization to a radioactive

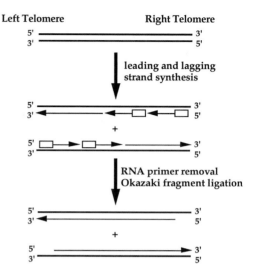

Figure I   The end-replication problem. A schematic of a simple linear parent duplex (heavy lines, top diagram) is shown. The middle diagram shows the expected intermediates of replication (thin lines) and the polarity of synthesis (arrows) arising from a single origin of replication near the middle of the parent molecule. Lagging strand synthesis is discontinuous, consisting of Okazaki fragments that initiate with a labile RNA primer (box). Leading strand synthesis is continuous, proceeding in the 5′–3′ direction to the very 5′ end of the template strand. After RNA primer removal and Okazaki fragment extension and ligation, the most 5′ Okazaki fragment will remain incomplete because the RNA primer cannot be replaced (bottom diagram). If the 5′ terminal Okazaki fragment does not initiate directly opposite the 3′ end of the template DNA, there will be additional bases incompletely replicated. The net effect is the loss of a small amount of DNA at the 5′ end of the newly synthesized DNA. (Adapted from Harley, 1991.)

telomeric oligonucleotide. [*See* DNA AND GENE EXPRESSION.]

Most eukaryotic species utilize a novel enzyme, telomerase, to generate telomeric DNA de novo, thus compensating for, rather than avoiding, terminal deletions. Telomerase is a complex of protein components and an integral RNA component. The RNA component of the human enzyme has been cloned and found to contain a short region complementary to ≈1.5 repeats of the human telomere sequence. This "template region" interacts in the catalytic region of the enzyme to direct the synthesis of the telomeric sequence. The mechanism of telomerase action involves the positioning of the G-rich, 3′ end of the chromosome near the active site of the enzyme, base paired to an alignment domain of the template region (Figure 2). Then, the RNA-dependent DNA polymerase activ-

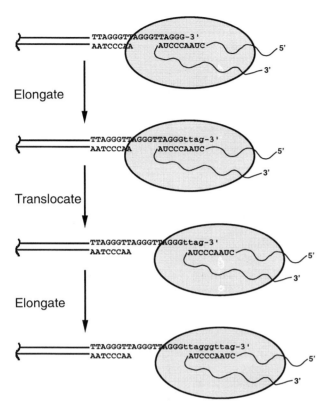

Figure 2 Model of processive telomerase action in immortal human cells. The template region of the RNA component of human telomerase (5'-CUAACCCUA-3') is shown schematically within the protein component(s) of the ribonucleoprotein complex (shaded oval). A chromosome end with a 3' overhang is shown aligned against the template region in the top figure. This primer-template configuration allows extension of the telomere (lower-case letters) in the first round of elongation until the extended product reaches the 5' end of the template domain. Translocation then moves the extended DNA back one repeat relative to the template region, positioning it for another round of elongation in which a full repeat (ggttag) is added to the 3' end of the chromosome. (Adapted from Greider & Blackburn, 1989.)

ity of the telomerase protein component(s) catalyzes the extension of the DNA 3' end. Cycles of elongation and translocation of the DNA back to the alignment region allow telomerase to processively extend the 3' end of chromosomes with GGTTAG repeats. As of this writing, the cloning of the protein components of the human enzyme or antibodies to human telomerase had not been reported in the scientific literature: all measurements of telomerase have been based on activity measurements, or, more recently, the presence of the RNA component. Because the RNA component

of telomerase does not correlate perfectly with telomerase activity, the best determination of whether a cell population or tissue contains active telomerase is by analyzing extracts for the extension of telomere-like oligonucleotides with GGTTAG repeats.

III. TELOMERE LOSS IN AGING AND TELOMERASE REACTIVATION IN CANCER

The telomere hypothesis of cell aging and immortalization in human cells and tissues (Figure 3) is built upon three basic observations. First, telomerase activity is easily detected in both male and female reproductive tissues, and long telomeres are stably main-

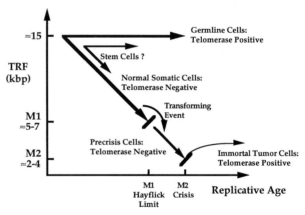

Figure 3 The telomere hypothesis of cell aging and immortalization. Telomerase is active in germline cells, maintaining long stable telomeres (terminal restriction fragment [TRF] ≈ 15 kbp), but is repressed in most normal somatic cells, resulting in telomere loss in dividing cells (≈50–200 bp/cell doubling), until mortality phase 1 (M1, or the Hayflick limit) (TRF ≈ 5–7 kbp). At M1, critical telomere loss on one or perhaps a few chromosomes possibly signals irreversible cell cycle arrest. The mechanism that signals this arrest is not known, but could involve a damaged DNA response or an alteration in gene expression near telomeres. Telomerase activity and telomere length have not been well characterized during embryonic and fetal development, or for true somatic stem cells, hence this part of the schematic is marked with a "?". Transformation events such as oncogene expression or tumor suppressor gene inactivation allow somatic cells to bypass M1 without activating telomerase. When telomeres become critically short on a large number of chromosomes, cells enter crisis (M2) at a time when a large increase in genetic instability is observed. Rare clones that activate telomerase escape M2, stabilize chromosomes, and acquire an indefinite growth capacity. (Adapted from Harley, 1991.)

Table I Telomeres and Telomerase in Human Cells and Tissues[a]

Source	Phenotype	Cell type or tissue source	Telomere dynamics	Telomerase activity
Cultured cells	Mortal dividing	Fibroblasts	Shorten	Negative
		Epithelium	Shorten	Negative
		Endothelium	Shorten	Negative
		Lymphocytes	Shorten	Weakly positive
	Mortal nondividing	Fibroblasts	Stable	Negative
Normal tissues	Immortal	Testes	Stable	Positive
		Ovaries	Not done	Positive
	Mortal dividing	Dermis	Shorten	Negative
		Epidermis	Shorten	Negative
		Vascular intima	Shorten	Negative
		Gut mucosa	Shorten	Negative
		Peripheral blood	Shorten	Weakly positive
		Bone marrow	Shorten	Weakly positive
	Mortal nondividing	Brain	Stable	Negative
Tumor tissues	Assumed immortal	Lung, breast, prostate, colorectal, brain, ovary, liver, kidney, blood, others	Generally short, but variable; most are stable	≈85% of ≈1000 biopsies tested positive
Stem cells	?	Hematopoietic	Long, but slowly shorten	Weakly positive, transient

[a]These data apply to postnatal and adult tissue. Telomere dynamics and telomerase expression during embryogenesis and fetal development is not well established for specific cell types and tissues, although telomerase generally can be detected in various fetal tissues.

tained in germline cells. Second, telomerase activity is absent and telomeres gradually shorten with age ex vivo and in vivo in essentially all postnatal somatic tissues and cells examined. And third, telomerase is again easily detected in almost all tumor biopsies and tumor cell lines examined. These observations have been supported in a variety of studies of cultured cells and normal and tumor tissues in vivo (Table I).

Thus, telomerase is developmentally repressed early in life, perhaps to confer a finite life span to somatic cells as a protective mechanism against the runaway expansion of transformed and growth-deregulated cells. One consequence of this is that some normal somatic cells that divide throughout life may acquire critically shortened telomeres and hence reach the end of their replicative capacity. Such cells would contribute to age-related pathology in tissues through their inability to respond to growth signals and their altered pattern of gene expression. Telomerase repression thus has beneficial early effects as an anticancer mechanism but has detrimental late effects due to the mortality of normal somatic cells. Moreover, telo-

merase repression is not perfect, because this enzyme becomes aberrantly reactivated in nearly all biopsies from all cancers studied. The opposing forces of selection that control the balance between longevity and cancer are reflected in a comparison of telomerase regulation in mice and humans: mice have a much higher frequency of cancer on a per cell, per year basis, and have a dramatically weakened stringency of telomerase repression in their normal somatic cells and tissues.

A further refinement to the telomere hypothesis of cell aging and immortalization is revealed by considering the effects of cell transformation on telomere dynamics (Figure 3). In somatic cells transformed by viruses or viral oncogenes (for example SV40 T antigen, HPV E6/E7, or EBV), telomerase is absent, and telomeres continue to shorten in the "extended life span" between the normal Hayflick limit (M1, or senescence) and a second mortality point (M2, or crisis). No combination of oncogene activation or tumor-suppressor gene inactivation tested to date has been demonstrated to directly activate telomerase.

When the transformed cell population reaches crisis with critically shortened telomeres on perhaps all chromosomes, there is strong selection for cells that escape lethal genomic instability through the activation of telomerase. Thus, telomerase is detected and telomeres are stably maintained (at usually a short length) in most postcrisis (immortal) transformed and tumor cell lines.

A direct demonstration that telomerase activity and maintenance of telomeres are essential for continued proliferation of cancer cells was demonstrated through expressing antisense copies of the telomerase RNA in human tumor cells in culture. Cell populations in which telomerase was inhibited by the antisense RNA had a reduced telomere length after a period of cell doublings and a "crisis" phenotype: the vast majority of cells in the population died. Similar evidence pointing to the essential nature of telomerase expression for most immortal cells was also obtained through manipulation of telomerase or telomere dynamics in simple eukaryotes such as protozoa and yeast. However, these organisms indicate that alternative, less efficient mechanisms for telomere maintenance can also exist.

IV. IMPLICATIONS

Telomere loss is clearly linked to replicative senescence of somatic cells on the one hand, whereas telomerase reactivation is linked to cell immortalization and cancer on the other. Thus, an exciting aspect of telomere research in cell mortality and immortality is the potential application of this knowledge to novel methods for diagnosis and treatment of diseases of aging, including cancer. Replicative senescence, reflected not only in the loss of division capacity, but also in deleterious patterns of gene expression, is believed to occur with age in a variety of tissues, contributing to, for example, reduced wound healing in skin (dermal fibroblast aging), immune dysfunction (T-cell aging), and cardiovascular diseases (endothelial cell aging). It also seems clear that escape from replicative senescence permits many tumors to progress to a malignant or metastatic state. Thus, measurements of telomere length and telomerase activity should be clinically useful diagnostic markers of normal aging and cancer, respectively. More importantly, delaying criti-

cal telomere loss through transient reactivation of telomerase or slowing the rate of telomere loss should extend cell life span and delay the onset of replicative senescence, whereas inhibition of telomerase should provide a safe and effective therapy for many, if not all, cancers. [See CANCER AND THE ELDERLY.]

V. SUMMARY

In summary, telomeric DNA is gradually lost with replicative aging of human somatic cells both in culture and as a function of donor age in vivo. The cause of this loss appears to be the incomplete replication of the 3′ ends of linear chromosomes in the absence of telomerase. Critical telomere loss on one or more chromosomes likely triggers a signal for cell cycle arrest at senescence, although other mechanisms could be involved. Analysis of cell transformation in culture, and tumor cells and tissues in vivo, indicates that the ultimate immortalization of cells is tightly linked to aberrant reactivation of telomerase. These observations provide the framework for the discovery and development of novel therapeutic agents to treat age-related diseases, including cancer.

BIBLIOGRAPHY

Feng, J., Funk, W. D., Wang, S.-S., Weinrich, S. L., Avilion, A. A., Chiu, C.-P., Adams, R. R., Chang, E., Allsopp, R. C., Yu, J., Le, S., West, M. D., Harley, C. B., Andrews, W. H., Greider, C. W., & Villeponteau, B. (1995). The RNA component of human telomerase. *Science, 269,* 1236–1241.

Greider, C. W., & Blackburn, E. H. (1989). A telomeric sequence in the RNA of *Tetrahymena* telomerase required for telomere repeat synthesis. *Nature, 337,* 331–337.

Harley, C. B. (1991). Telomere loss: mitotic clock or genetic time bomb? *Mutation Research, 256,* 271–282.

Harley, C. B., Kim, N. W., Prowse, K. R., Weinrich, S. L., Hirsch, K. S., West, M. D., Bacchetti, S., Hirte, H. W., Counter, C. M., Greider, C. W., Wright, W. E., & Shay, J. W. (1994). Telomerase, cell immortality, and cancer. *Cold Spring Harbor Symposium on Quantitative Biology, 59,* 307–315.

Kim, N. W., Piatyszek, M. A., Prowse, K. R., Harley, C. B., West, M. D., Ho, P. L. C., Coviello, G. M., Wright, W. E., Weinrich, S. L., & Shay, J. W. (1994). Specific association of human telomerase activity with immortal cells and cancer. *Science, 266,* 2011–2014.

Kipling, D. (1995). *The Telomere.* Oxford: Oxford University Press.

Rhyu, M. S. (1995). Telomeres, telomerase, and immortality. *Journal of the National Cancer Institute, 87,* 884–894.

Theories of Aging: Biological

F. Eugene Yates

University of California, Los Angeles

I. Time, Aging, and Senescence

II. The Paradox

III. Three Views of Senescence

IV. Life Trajectory of Individual Organism

V. "Aspect Theories" of Senescence

VI. New, General Theory for Senescence

VII. Determinants of Senescence Rates (**r**)

VIII. Evolutionary Biology of Aging

IX. Summary

Aging Any time-dependent change in an object or system. The change may be good, bad, or indifferent as judged by an observer.

Biomarkers (of Aging) Hoped for but so far fictitious age-related changes that predict remaining life span. No age-related changes are predictors of life span in humans. Even in colonies of inbred animals under laboratory conditions efforts using physical, chemical, or biological measures have so far failed to predict individual life spans in any species.

Component Failure Death Failure of a complex system of many nodes and connections and levels when some local or particular part or region ceases to have the dynamic range required for its contribution to the stability of the whole system. In medical and pathological terms one says, for example, that the patient died of renal failure.

Degrees of Freedom (Dynamical) The statistical meaning of this term is not relevant here. A system has one degree of freedom for every variable whose value must be specified to define the state of the system. It is the number of independent variables in a system. A simple physical example is the gas

law $PV = nRT$. R and n are parameters (constant in any particular instance); P, V, and T are variables. Degrees of freedom equal the number of variables (here three) minus the number of laws or rules that bind the variables (here one)—thus two. When any pair of P, V, and T is specified the remaining variable is no longer free, but determined by the rule. In a complex system, when structures are added they act like rule constraints and reduce degrees of freedom. Paradoxically, the behavior of the system may be enriched. A gasoline spill burning in air has many degrees of freedom, but little behavior. When that burning is confined by the geometrical constraints of engine blocks and valves, torque can be applied to roadways through wheels and the possibilities enlarge. When structural genetic constraints bear on carbon chemistry degrees of freedom are drastically reduced, but system behavior enlarges.

Maximum Life Span Potential A statistical extreme value for a population of members of the same species and birth cohort, under similar circumstances, that estimates the duration of life of the last to die. It is a random variable, not precisely determined by genotype or phenotype. (Caution: the statistics of extreme values is underdeveloped.)

Mortality Rate, m(t) As a function of age, $m(t)dt$ is the fraction of the surviving population that dies between t and $t + dt$.

Mortality Rate Doubling Time In preference to the constant hazard term in the exponent of the Gompertz equation, which varies inversely with life span potential, the doubling time is a more natural unit for mortality rate acceleration because it is in the same direction as the life span and is measured in the same units of time. It is given by $ln2/C$, where C is the Gompertz exponent constant. (See Eq. 3.)

Negentropic (Process) Any process occurring in a system not at equilibrium, which leads to a local increase in order (decrease in entropy), usually manifested as the appearance of a new structure. (The risk of confounding entropy and information is great, and invited by the similarity between the Shannon formulation for selective information and Boltzmann's statistical entropy. That confusion will not be dealt with here!)

Process Any time-dependent series of changes. The current condition may or may not depend on past conditions, depending on the type of process.

Senescence Progressive loss of stability arising from the cummulative effects of byproducts of otherwise normal, salubrious processes that increase the probability of system failure. It may be accelerated by interaction with or addition of other processes that are deleterious (e.g., smoking.)

Specific Metabolism Total energy conversion rate (a unit of power) per unit of mass of the active tissues and organs. In the case of mammals, for example, connective tissue, bone, and fat are often excluded, and the residue, a virtual lean body mass is used as reference total mass.

System Death Failure of a complex system when all its parts, though compromised, are individually still within viable limits or specifications. A loss of connectivity is often involved.

SENESCENCE is distinguished from aging and is viewed from three perspectives: (a) evolutionary biology, (b) population mortality kinetics, and (c) life trajectory of an individual organism. Twenty-three "aspect theories" of senescence are introduced. A more general theory, that senescence results from a changing balance between competitive anabolic (negentropic) and catabolic (entropic) processes is illustrated. The senescence rate for an individual healthy human being is estimated to be an average loss of 0.5% per year of capacity at age 30, until age 80, after which the senescence rate accelerates to 1% per year, leading to a catastrophic failure when only 30% of initial (age 30) capacity is left.

I. TIME, AGING, AND SENESCENCE

A. Time Effects: Aging

The passage of time may or may not be causal with respect to change. If lightning strikes a golfer on the green across the way, it is treated as an isolated event having nothing to do with time itself. In contrast, people monitor carefully the ripening of the bananas bought when green, lest the aging changes wrought by time go past the desired endpoint before one can eat them. *Aging* is a term that can be applied to *any* changes dependent upon the passage of time, whether those changes are judged to be good, bad, or indifferent at any moment. Time-dependent changes are processes, and in general they may be slowed or stopped by freezing, which in effect stops their flow of time. (In many but not all cases they can resume on rethermalization.)

B. Time Effects: Senescence

Although *senescence* in familiar usage refers merely to growing old, it is helpful to give it a more technical denotation specifically reserved to those time-dependent changes in living systems that have cumulative, deleterious effects ultimately and inevitably leading to death—if accident, diseases, or predation do not kill the organism first. There is a further restriction: senescence in the above sense has meaning only for organisms or cell lines in which throughout their life spans there is a substantial investment of metabolism in repair and maintenance. Thus, the death of cells by apoptosis during morphogenesis or after certain challenges, the seasonal dropping of leaves from deciduous trees in the fall, the death of those insects that do not eat in their brief adult stage (and may even lack mouth parts or gastrointestinal tracts), the sudden death of semelparous reproducers, or the elimination of nonnucleated human erythrocytes after several months are processes that here do *not* qualify as senescence. This article addresses biological theories of senescence as it is defined above and coins *senesce* as an intransitive verb. Because senescence is time-dependent, the chronological age of an organism will always be one very relevant estimate of the progress of its deterioration, although the rates of senescence vary among individuals and species, as will be discussed.

II. THE PARADOX

In an appropriate environment, individual living systems are self-organizing, and either continuously throughout their life spans or in some stage of it they invest heavily in maintenance and repair of form and function, as well as in growth, development, differentiation, and reproduction. There is no obvious reason that with this repertoire of anabolic, negentropic processes they should grow old, become frail, senesce, lose their resilience, and die. The challenge for a theory of senescence is to account for mortality in organisms that earlier in their lives were increasing in robustness.

III. THREE VIEWS OF SENESCENCE

Data holding clues to the nature of senescence come from three major sources: (a) evolutionary biology, (b) demographics of populations of a given species, and (c) life trajectories of individual organisms, including experimental manipulations that increase longevity. These varied sources do not necessarily encourage the same styles of theorizing. Because demographics is the statistical science of the number, distribution, and life spans of populations of individuals, a single theory might be able to account for the kinetics of mortality in both populations and individuals, just as microscopic statistical mechanics can account for macroscopic, classical field thermodynamics. It is less clear that evolutionary biology can provide specific insights into (for example) the mortality of human beings, though it is reasonable to suppose that it might. Its contributions to understanding senescence will be discussed at the end of this article.

IV. LIFE TRAJECTORY OF INDIVIDUAL ORGANISM

A. Three Stages

In organisms that senesce (described in section VIII) there are three broad stages of life trajectory: (a) start-up (growth and development), (b) nearly steady-state maturity, and (c) accelerated, terminal decline to frailty, dependency (in the case of human beings), and death. Of course the trajectory can be aborted by inborn errors of metabolism or other genetic defects incompatible with reaching full maturity, or by diseases, predation, or accidents.

B. Sustaining Processes

During all three stages some set of the following (not necessarily independent) processes support the continuing existence of the organism: (a) healing, (b) protecting DNA or RNA, (c) guaranteeing fidelity of replication of DNA, (d) degrading aberrant protein molecules, (e) eliminating free radicals generated by respiration or other cellular processes, (f) detoxifying, (g) immunologically defending against threats, (h) inducing protective mechanisms against environmental shock, such as the heat shock response, (i) maintaining activity of specialized genes in differentiated cells and repressing activity of other genes to be expressed only at other stages or in other cell types, (j) assuring chromosomal integrity, and (k) defending the *milieu interieur*.

V. "ASPECT THEORIES" OF SENESCENCE

We do not expect that any single, overarching, predictive theory of senescence will ever be found for humans, because aging human beings undergo changes in all domains of their lives: genetic, biochemical, metabolic, physiological, psychological, social, and, for some, even spiritual. Although age-related decrements in function have been described in nearly every system examined, there is no common program of functional decline with age in the absence of recognizable disease. In view of individual variability, these decrements cannot be considered as biomarkers of either aging or mortality if such markers require that aging and mortality have exactly the same specific bases in all subjects. Almost all bodily functions in every person are found to decline with increasing chronological age even in the absence of clinical diseases, but the rate of decline, which partly determines life span potential, differs even between closely related species, individuals, or processes. It has been suggested that persons who are unusually long-lived and live past 100 years do so not because they age more slowly, but because they age more uniformly, as will be assumed in the model presented below, by lumping all senescence processes into one rate term, r, with a value of -0.005 (to be explained). [See MARKERS OF AGING.]

A. Partial Listing

A narrow theory of senescence can be based on the assumed failure of any one of the repair and maintenance processes listed above, if an organism normally exhibits the process. These are the "aspect theories" of senescence and they are numerous. Unfortunately, pluralism in theory building in gerontology has distracted from the development of a comprehensive, theoretical structure. Aspect theories arise because specialized investigators with different disciplinary backgrounds perceive many diverse growing points for the development of theories about senescence. Unfortunately, there is a tendency for each aspect theory to become transformed from a theory *about* an aspect of aging into a general, all-comprehending theory *of* senescence. Table I presents a partial list of aspect theories of senescence.

B. Shortcomings

Each of the aspect theories shown has advocates, critics, and data for and against it. Each is interesting in its own right, but at present it is clear that none provides a universal or general theory of senescence, and some have been withdrawn by their authors (e.g., Orgel's error catastrophe theory). Even so, the rich marketplace of aspect theories has led to certain modest generalizations about senescence and what phenomena must be explained by a theory. Sacher and Duffy, looking for longevity-related processes, found that four factors could account for 80% of variation in species life span: brain weight, body weight, specific metabolism, and body temperature. DNA repair capacity and activity of superoxide dismutase enzyme constellations have also been shown to be correlated with species life span. None of these has yet proven to be absolutely fundamental to senescence. The diversity of aspect theories does not express incompatibility so much as the fact that senescence is a multifaceted problem. It occurs concurrently at different levels of organization from molecules to societies, a fact accounted for more plausibly by stochastic and dynamic processes than by genetic mechanisms. Regardless of the degree of genetic homogeneity of a population, individuals die across an enormous range of ages.

These facts imply that although stochastic processes have effects that depend within limits on the genotype, the course of stochastic damage is so sensitive to small perturbations that the genotype of an individual within a species is not a very useful indicator of his or her life span potential. The predominant causes of death or age-correlated impairments of function can be species-specific. In human beings the most dangerous age-correlated impairments are atherosclerosis, cancer, diabetic complications, and neurologic diseases. The immune system certainly does senesce, and that senescence can contribute to the increasing morbidity from cancer, but it is not obvious how it would lead to atherosclerosis, Type II diabetes, or neurological diseases. (Even in cancer, an altered expression of oncogenes over time might be a better explanation.)

It is universally agreed that senescence leads to a reduced ability of older individuals to respond adaptively to environmental changes. There is a slowing down of many processes, even before there is detectable degradation of the mean operating point.

Caloric restriction, within limits, can extend life span of some species. Masoro and Yu have shown that specific metabolic rate (oxygen utilization per unit of lean body mass) in members of a particular species may not be the measure or determinant of senescence rate, contrary to some expectations. If correct, this is an important fact that any rate-of-living theory of aging must digest. Austad and Fischer examined the rate-of-living theory across species using a database consisting of body mass and maximum recorded longevity for 580 mammalian species gleaned from standard sources. They pointed out that the gold standard against which life spans of particular mammalian groups are usually measured—the linear logarithmic relationship between body mass and maximum longevity—does not fit bats or marsupials. Bats have maximum life spans at least three times those of nonflying eutherians—a trend resulting from neither low basal metabolic rate, the ability to enter torpor, nor large relative brain size. On the other hand, marsupials live only about 80% as long as nonflying eutherians despite an average lower basal metabolic rate. These data show no effect of heterothermy or relative brain size on longevity and directly conflict with predictions of both rate-of-living and brain-size-mediated theories of aging. They are, however, consistent with an evolutionary theory that posits exceptionally long

Table I Kernels of Some "Aspect" Theories of Senescence[a]

1. Hysteretic Disinhibition
Neuroendocrine negative feeback systems have their feedback detectors ultimately destroyed by the very hormonal agents they are detecting and regulating. ("Use it and lose it.")

2. Wear and Tear
Activities of being, such as growth, development, reproduction, feeding, fighting, moving, and maintaining, all tax a living system and ultimately bring it down by unspecified means. ("Use and lose it.")

3. Biological Life Events
There are cumulative life events, such as the number of times one has undergone general anesthesia or been injured, that leave trace effects that accumulate and lead to increasing fragility.

4. "Throw Away" Soma: Antagonistic Pleiotropy
These perspectives imagine that biological systems are designed to invest their resources more in reproduction than in maintenance so that repair falls behind the requirement of ongoing operations. Some traits presumably have been selected over evolutionary time to increase fitness by increasing reproductive potential at the expense of postreproductive survival.

5. Error Castastrophe
One version is a stochastic theory supposing that although error-containing molecules do not ordinarily accumulate, nevertheless, if an erroneously synthesized protein happens to be involved in the synthesis of the genetic apparatus, then there will be amplification of the error until an error catastrophe causes death of the individual. (This idea has been withdrawn by its originator.)

6. Defective Proteins—Glycation, Racemization, Deamidation. . . .
Genetic errors are one source of defective proteins, but blood sugar, oxidizing free radicals, and other reactions acting over a lifetime can lead to alterations of proteins that favor irreversible cross-linking and other interferences with structure and functions.

7. Decreased or Aberrant Immune Function
This viewpoint is an example of a somatic mutation theory. It supposes that intrinsic mutagenesis leads to forbidden clones in the immune system and that these in turn invite autoimmune disasters.

8. Clonal Senescence—Telomeric Shortening
Normal mitotic cells under optimal culture conditions do not divide forever. One limitation may be that the telomeres of their chromosomes lose a repetitive fragment, TTAGGG in humans, at each cell cycle. This repeated sequence normally has a stabilizing effect on chromosome structure, and in many human mitotic cells telomeres shorten in length by deleting repetitions of this fragment with each division of the cell. Chromosomes thereby supposedly become unstable or inoperative. The data correlate with observed senescence, but do not yet prove causation.

9. Somatic Mutations
This theory belongs to the class of stochastic theories of aging that assumes that an accumulation of environmental insults eventually reaches a level incompatible with life, primarily because of genetic damage.

10. Free Radicals
Oxidative metabolism and some syntheses (e.g., of dopamine in the brain) necessarily produce free radicals. These evanescent, but highly reactive chemical species damage DNA or proteins and degrade system structure and function.

11. Failure of DNA Repair
DNA repair capacity decreases with time in many systems studied, presumably leaving an animal more vulnerable to certain cancers and formation of abnormal proteins. However, there are many contrary data.

12. Rate of Aging
Among the hominid ancestral descendent sequence leading to Homo sapiens, life span appears to have increased at a maximum rate of about 14 years per 100,000 years. These data have been interpreted as indicating that a gene regulatory process governs aging rate and that this rate has decreased. The chimpanzee supposedly ages at twice the rate that humans do, living only 50 years instead of 100.

13. Rate of Living
This old idea supposes crudely that there is a certain number of calories or heart beats allotted to an individual and the faster these are used the shorter the life.

14. Dysdifferentiation
Over time the ability of specialized cells to suppress genetic information irrelevant to their specialization may become weakened, and therefore they lose their differentiation. There is not yet much evidence for this effect.

15. Membrane Stiffening
This hypothesis supposes that membrane fluidity decreases with age, and that this physical change affects the disposition and action of membrane receptors. Phospholipases may be key factors in the changes, along with lipid peroxidation.

16. Gerontogenes
This view imagines that there are programmed "death gene" instructions determining how long an individual shall live. (Note, however, that apoptosis is not senescence.)

17. Diffusion Limitation
Changes in basement membranes or extracellular matrices increase diffusion resistance for metabolites in the pathways between blood and parenchyma so that metabolizing cells become slowly strangled.

18. Desynchronosis
With senescence come alterations among various circadian and other rhythms. There are phase changes, losses of amplitude, and a loosening of coupling among internal clocks.

19. Storage Disease
Senescent cells accumulate or are surrounded by various forms of "garbage," including intracellular lipofuscin and extracellular amyloid. Glycation of proteins and DNA adducts participate.

20. Programmed Aging
This deterministic view supposes that the central nervous system (or the genome) has a pacemaker for senescence.

continues

Continued

21. Fluctuation Theory

As time passes, because of various internal changes a living system becomes more vulnerable to large, random fluctuations in the internal or external environments.

22. Counterpart Theory

These ideas belong to the class of theories that supposes that senescence is a continuation of a trajectory of growth, development, and maturation.

23. Hormonal Deficiency

In human beings (as example) aging is associated with declines in plasma levels of dehydroepiandrosterone (DHEA) and its sulfates, primary sex hormones (estradiol in women, testosterone in men), melatonin, growth hormone, and so on. In the elderly a deficiency disease requiring hormonal replacement arises.

*[a]*This list of our paraphrases is neither detailed nor complete. For that reason we do not give sources. Furthermore, every idea or claim listed has been severely criticized by competent scholars. We offer the list only to highlight the great variety of partially formed ideas addressing senescence. The various theories addressed are not all independent.

life spans among mammals with reduced environmental vulnerability.

VI. NEW, GENERAL THEORY FOR SENESCENCE

A. Competition between Anabolic (Negentropic) and Catabolic (Entropic) Processes

Figure 1 illustrates an hypothesis that supposes that there is a lifelong competition between constructive metabolic processes (growth, development, repair, maintenance) and destructive metabolic processes. Both are operating throughout life, but in the start-up stage the genetic initial conditions and the immediate environmental potentials support anabolism over catabolism. As new structures arise by differentiation, energy throughput meets new constraints consequent to the "freezing out" of dynamic degrees of freedom by the formation of these structures. Paradoxically, the process repertoire then increases, but at the cost of domination of anabolism by catabolism. From that point of crossing over and beyond, senescence begins to manifest itself. By about age 30 in human beings, after the crossing over at about puberty, the gap between destructive and constructive metabolic effects becomes roughly constant. So does the *rate* of senescence, which is thereafter uniform until approximately 80 years, after which it accelerates (see next section).

B. Rates of Senescence

From studies on changes in DNA repair in skin not exposed to sunlight, from records of athletic perfor-

mance of trained participants, and from detailed physiological studies of particular functions, such as maximum heart rate, it is found that there is an approximately linear decline in healthy subjects according to the model in equation 1a.

$$y_x = -\mathbf{r}(x - x_0) + 1 \quad (30 \leq x \leq 80) \quad (1a)$$

In this model:

$x_0 = 30$ years

x = chronological age rounded to nearest year ($30 \leq x \leq 80$)

y_x is fraction of capacity at age 30 that is left at age x

Capacity at age 30 is 1.0

$\mathbf{r}$ = fractional loss per year

W. Bortz has collected data from numerous sources indicating that an average value for the rate of senescence $\mathbf{r}$ is a loss of 0.5% of capacity at age 30, per year, until age 80. That means that at age 80 75% of the initial capacity (age 30) will be left and 25% lost, as calculated from equation 1b:

$$y_x = -0.005(x - 30) + 1 \quad (1b)$$

Of course, depending on a person's genetic initial condition and his or her life experiences, the value of $\mathbf{r}$ may not be identical for all internal biochemical and physiological processes. Here I merely postulate a fundamental, global average with a small dispersion, to simplify the model. If $\mathbf{r}$ is much larger for one process or subset of processes than for others, the individual will die a "component failure death," such as atherosclerotic stroke. If the values of $\mathbf{r}$ have small dispersion across all processes, then the individual will die a "system death," and the medical opinion is likely to be that the "cause" was "old age" (not a

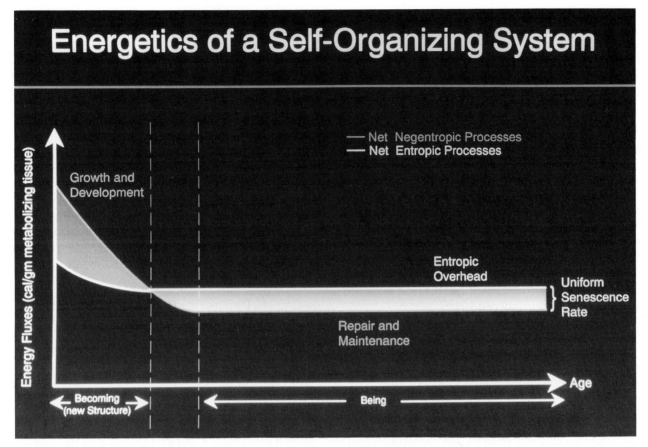

Figure I Idealization of the competition between constructive (growth, development, repair, maintenance) processes (thin line) and dissipative consequences of metabolism (thicker line). The vertical dashed lines indicate a transition zone (in humans, ages 15–30 years) from anabolic dominance (negentropic) to catabolic dominance (entropic). The postulated uniform senescence rate operates from ages 30–80 years in humans.

formal diagnostic category, which are typically organ or disease oriented.)

The fundamental, underlying, rather uniform rate of senescence in healthy individuals may be modified by diet, drugs, and exercise, but it does not accelerate with the passage of time until the later years are reached. Caloric restriction has been shown to reduce the value of **r** in some insects, spiders, *C. elegans*, and some laboratory mammals. In human beings alcohol or other drug abuse, smoking, dietary extremes (either direction), or a sedentary disposition can increase the value of **r** to perhaps 2% per year, starting in midlife or even earlier. For those individuals the senescence model is as shown in equation 2:

$$y_x = -0.02(x - 30) + 1 \quad (x \geq 30) \qquad (2)$$

Because biological systems are full of control operations, it is to be expected that the consequences of ongoing senescence will in many instances be subtle or even undetectable over long stretches of time because of masking by compensatory actions. But the compensatory processes themselves must inevitably succumb to the metabolic dissipations and pay the degradative consequences.

C. Piecewise Linear Model

Empirical, deterministic models fitting population mortality data for most species so far studied use a single, monotonic, exponential function to fit the midrange data, but the fit may fail at the extremes (start-up and terminal decline epochs). In the case of human populations the Makeham-Gompertz model for mortality fits data well for the 50-year period from ages 30–80 years. That famous model is repeated below.

$$m(t) = A + B \exp C(x - 30) \quad (30 \leq x \leq 80), \quad (3)$$

where $m(t)$ is mortality rate, A is an age-independent, but environment-dependent mortality rate, B is an age-independent initial or intrinsic mortality parameter to some extent environmentally dependent, C is the Gompertz hazard parameter, which is age-independent over the range of applicability of the model (in human beings from age 30–80) and is almost environmentally independent (but caloric restriction under special circumstances can diminish it).

For some species there is evidence that B and C are at least weakly correlated, whereas the standard model assumes their independence.

D. Acceleration Threshold

I propose that the model of equation 1 for an individual fits the range of years (approximately 30–80) in which the Gompertzian hazard for the population is constant, and mortality increases monotonically. For the epoch beyond age 80–85 years, when the Gompertz model no longer fits human population data well, I suggest that the model of equation 4 applies. The structure of the model is the same, but the senescence rate parameter has increased from 0.005 to 0.010. Thus, to cover the trajectory for the full range of adult life, I use a piecewise linear approach. Of course I expect that the increase in senescence rate from 0.005 to 0.010 may occur gradually, but the function is not known, so the piecewise linear approach suffices as an approximation of an unknown function.

After 25% of initial capacity at age 30 is lost, an individual becomes less resilient and less able to correct or adapt to further assaults from a fluctuational environment, including its social aspects. The losses include connections or communication pathways among interacting elements and processes, and the resulting increased isolation of subsystems accentuates their vulnerability (mutual support and compensation is lost), and on that basis the senescence loss rate increases to 1% per year. The model becomes as

shown in equation 4. At age 125 years only 30% of initial capacity (age 30) will be left.

$$y_x = -0.01(x - 80) + 0.75 \quad (x \geq 80) \quad (4)$$

E. Death Threshold

In this piecewise linear model (equations 1a,b and 4), when two-thirds or more of initial capacity has been lost, vulnerability has become so severe that almost any fluctuation can cause death. The apparent maximum life span potential for human species (which is not a fixed genetically determined parameter) will thus be a narrow statistical dispersion of ages around 120–130 years. At present the longest lived individual with documented birth record is a 120-year-old woman in 1995. Genes plus environment set the threshold.

F. Diminishing Gompertzian Hazard Function: Heterogeneity Effects

In the model shown in equation 3, the value of the exponential parameter C for the population decreases after age 80. It is necessary to reconcile that slowing down of population mortality increase with the postulated acceleration of the rate of individual senescence at that same age indicated by the piecewise linear model (equations 1 and 4). I believe that the explanation lies in the heterogeneity of senescence rates in populations. The piecewise linear model assumes senescence rates between −0.5% and −1.0% per year for the *healthiest* members of the population. Therefore these are minimal rates for the species as a whole. For many in a population, because of suboptimal diets, drug use, smoking, plagues, and/or physical inactivity, the loss rate will be nearer to −2% per year. In their case diseases, trauma, inadequate diets, smoking, and so on, may be thought of in two different ways. Either they *add* a new loss term to the basic senescence **r**, or they *modulate* the same basic **r** and accelerate it. At present it is not clear which "mechanism" (if either) is correct. They are not mutually exclusive. The life span potential for those persons with r = −0.02 per year will be only about 65 years on average if the factors increasing their rate from the healthy baseline of −0.005 per year operate continuously from age 30 on. The early elimination of this fast-enfeebling group from the population will result in an apparent slowing of mortality rate for the population of survivors, even though individually their senescence rates are increasing after age 80 with respect to their own earlier rates.

VII. DETERMINANTS OF SENESCENCE RATES (r)

A. Evaluating the Rates

W. Bortz has assembled data from many sources justifying the choice of $r = -0.005$ per year as the fundamental, average senescence rate for the healthiest human beings. Because median life expectancies are less for men than for women in the populations of developed countries, it may be that the value is not the same for both sexes. This remains to be determined. Bortz examined data from the Masters' Track and Field Organization in the 100-yard dash and the marathon, as well as swimming data for the 1500-m event from the U.S. Masters' Swimming Congress. He also examined data on declines in maximum oxygen consumption over time. In fit individuals the rate of loss of VO₂ max is 0.5% per year. That loss rate applies also to division of human skin fibroblasts, the length of their telomeres, cerebral metabolism, maximum pulse rate, the rate of nail growth, numbers of muscle cells in the thigh, and appendicular bone calcium. The 0.5% per year loss rate closely approximates declines in cognitive competence by certain measures reported by Schaie. Although there is no reason to believe that a senescence rate of -0.5% per year is universal for all processes and functions in a healthy person, it appears to represent some kind of central tendency.

B. Possible Underlying Mechanisms Determining r

The modeling discussed above has used the life trajectory of individual human beings as exemplar, but with different chronological time scaling the model could be general. Different species will of course have different values of **r** if the time base of years is used for all. The wide range of **r** values that result can be narrowed by using a normalized time base as percent of maximum life span potential for the species, if known, but that presents the difficulty that the maximum life span potential is itself a stochastic variable, not a parameter.

For a particular species (s) consisting of individuals (i) a uniform theory of senescence rate would be a theory of r_{si}. Species may senesce at different rates and on different bases. If geophysical time is used as reference, then life spans vary at least a million-fold among different species of "higher" plants and animals. The rates of senescence are difficult to define and compare across populations of different species, and short maximum life spans for a species do not rule out a slow mortality rate doubling time. Furthermore, life spans may vary at least several-fold among individual members of birth cohorts of the same species in the same locations, even when individuals are genetically identical. Leading causes of "natural" death (barring accidents or predation) differ even among class Mammalia: laboratory rats tend to die of renal failure; human beings tend to die of cardiovascular catastrophes; and both species get cancers. At present it is probably best to suppose that a representative value of r_{si} represents an aggregated parameter reflecting influences of the many relevant aspects (see Aspect Theories) of aging. Senescence is multicausal, and no single, unambiguous senescence process is likely ever to be found. However, for members of a given species it is still possible that a common, uniform senescence process with rate **r** is added to or modulated by independent, nonsenescence but deleterious processes that produce a composite or accelerated loss rate for that individual. Epigenetic influences from both internal and external environments can strongly affect life spans. [See MODELS OF AGING: VERTEBRATES.]

VIII. EVOLUTIONARY BIOLOGY OF AGING

A. What Senesces?

Obligatory, inevitable functional and structural losses over time, leading to increasing frailty, instability, and finally death seem not to be a property of prokaryotes, whether aerobic or anaerobic, and has not been unambiguously observed in single-celled eukaryotes. In contrast, the evolution of aerobic eukaryotes into both photosynthetic (algae, plants) and nonphotosynthetic organisms (animals, fungi, slime molds, protozoa) has revealed evidence of senescence in many of the noncolonial, multicellular organisms so far studied from that perspective. The total number of species of living organisms has been variously estimated to be between 8 and 30 million, and the carefully studied subset is small. The available evidence suggests that only organisms that have achieved some substantial level of complexity such as differentiated multicellularity do senesce, but admittedly, compared to physical objects such as subatomic particles, or atoms themselves, even the simplest living organism is astoundingly complex.

B. Complexity Threshold

Multicellular organisms that have differentiated parts and many pathways of communication and control have sufficient complexity to manifest senescence, and it is here postulated that they will inevitably do so. In recent years complexity has become a technical subject of great interest, but there is not a simple (!) descriptor or measure of it. Although complexity usually involves a high number of parts and interactions among them, there are striking mathematical models of simple structure that have complicated, if not complex dynamics, such as chaos.

C. Themes

Evolutionary biology provides a refreshingly different perspective on senescence compared to those arising from molecular or cellular biology or organismal physiology. A central theme is that the force of natural selection declines with the aging of a population. The contribution that each age-class makes to the genetic endowments of future generations decreases with age. Age-specific fecundity assumes great importance from this perspective. For some organisms it increases steadily from the onset of reproductive capability (as in the case of some trees), but for other organisms, as in the case of human beings, fecundity diminishes gradually (men) or abruptly (women) with advancing age.

The approach to senescence from evolutionary biology is founded upon population genetic hypotheses, in contrast to the medical model that collects data on pathologies of the individual.

Evolutionary theorists largely agree that whatever the proximate cause of senescence, the ultimate cause is the declining force of natural selection on an aging population.

The assumption that the force of natural selection declines with age would be bolstered if there were genes affecting specific age classes, rather than having a uniform genetic effect on survival and reproduction throughout the life span. Whether or not such genes exist in all species in which senescence is observed is an open question still.

In many species there is an antagonistic relationship between reproduction and survival: if *Drosophila melanogaster* males are allowed to mate, they usually die sooner than do males without such opportunities. Inadequate conditions for reproduction in laboratory studies can be a source of error in research on aging.

Available genetic evidence does not establish that aging is evolutionarily bound to fitness. Aging and fitness appear to be genetically distinct, but genetic independence does not necessarily imply evolutionary independence. Senescence is as physiologically diverse as other whole organism attributes, inasmuch as it is a residue of evolutionary forces that have acted upon the full range of genetic variability of each species.

No version of evolutionary theory of senescence entails any particular medical or pathological explanation of why individuals grow old and die, or, conversely, why we as a species live so long.

IX. SUMMARY

1. Prokaryotes apparently do not senesce; it is not yet clear that single-celled eukaryotes ever do. Probably all complex, multicellular eukaryotes senesce, including both photosynthetic organisms (algae, plants) and nonphotosynthetic organisms (animals, fungi). Multicellular colonies (e.g., sponges) present ambiguities.

2. Some structures and functions may remain unimpaired during long life spans.

3. Genomic mechanisms in senescence may be more complex and phyletically diverse than are the genetic mechanisms of development itself.

4. There is not likely to be a simple, unifying explanation based on a single mechanism to account for the manifest diversity of senescence. However, there may be a general principle based on the thermo-

dynamics of complex, open systems that gives a uniform account of senescence [*See* HOMEOSTASIS.]

BIBLIOGRAPHY

Birren, J. E., & Bengtson, V. L. (Eds.). (1988). *Emergent theories of aging*. New York: Springer.

Cutler, R. G. (1991). Human longevity and aging: Possible role of reactive oxygen species. In W. Pierpaoli & N. Fabris (Eds.), *Physiological senescence and its postponent* (Vol. 621, pp. 1–28). New York: New York Academy of Sciences.

Finch, C. E. (1990). *Longevity, senescence, and the genome*. Chicago: University of Chicago Press.

Gavrilov, L. A., & Gavrilova, N. S. (1991). *The biology of lifespan: A quantitative approach* J. Payne and L. Payne, Trans. New York: Harwood.

Rose, M. R. (1991). *Evolutionary biology of aging*. New York: Oxford University Press.

Sacher, G. A. (1980). Theory in gerontology. *Annual Review of Gerontology and Geriatrics, 1,* 3–25.

Sacher, G., & Duffy, P. H. (1979). Genetic relation of lifespan to metabolic rate for inbred mouse strains and their hybrids. *Fed. Proc., 38,* 184–189.

Yates, F. E., & Benton, L. A. (1995). Loss of integration and resiliency with age: A dissipative destruction. E. J. Masoro (Ed.), *Handbook of physiology. section 11: Aging.* (pp. 591–610). New York: Oxford University Press for the American Physiological Society.

Theories of Aging: Psychological

Johannes J. F. Schroots

University of Amsterdam

I. History
II. Concepts of Aging
III. Classical Theories
IV. Modern Theories
V. New Theories

Chaos Theory Fluctuations of far-from-equilibrium systems can create order out of chaos through a process of self-organization.

Gerodynamics Dynamic systems theory of aging, based on general systems theory and chaos theory.

Gerotranscendence Shift in metaperspective, from a materialistic and rational vision to a more cosmic and transcendent one.

Gompertz' Law Regular acceleration in the rate of death with age from about age 10 to the end of the usual life span.

Psychology of Age Study of age differences in behavior.

Psychology of Aging Study of behavioral patterns of change with age.

Psychology of the Aged Study of problematic and nonproblematic behavior in the elderly.

Research in the **PSYCHOLOGY OF AGING** has been guided by a diverse collection of theories. Historically, there are three approaches: the aged, age, and aging: (a) The psychology of the aged focuses on the behavior of older people. Grounded in a stages-of-life perspective, most studies of the aged demonstrate a thematic approach and little coherence (e.g., studies of Alzheimer's disease, retirement, widowhood, etc.). (b) The psychology of age studies age differences in behavior by comparing groups of people of different ages in cross-sectional research. Productive research focuses on identifying the causes and consequences of the processes responsible for age-related differences (e.g., processing speed, attentional capacity, etc.). (c) The psychology of aging studies behavioral patterns of change with age, integrating both the psychology of age and the aged in longitudinal research. In this article major but diverse psychological theories of aging will be presented chronologically, to begin with early nineteenth-century theorizing on processes of aging.

I. HISTORY

A. Early Roots

The roots of psychological theories of aging lie in the European soil of nineteenth-century science. The intellectual climate fostered a strong conviction that the scientific method could be applied to all natural phenomena and that all matters could be examined by research and reduced to lawful generalizations, including the subject matter of aging. In 1825 the English actuary Benjamin Gompertz published his classic paper on the force of mortality, which expresses a lawful relationship between death rates and age within a given population. He noted the regular acceleration in the rate of death with age from about age 10 to the end of the usual life span. The regularity of this observation has led to much research into the genetic and biological basis of aging and the causes of death.

Although scientific effort was devoted to identifying specific relationships like *Gompertz' law*, the Belgian mathematician and astronomer Quetelet attempted to demonstrate that all facets of the changes in human behavior across the life span were lawful. In 1835 he published his book on humans and the development of their faculties. In addition to information about differences in mortality rates, he included material about physical and behavioral characteristics of people according to age. As a mathematician, Quetelet emphasized observations of many individuals that would lead to the characterization of *"the average man"* around whom observations are distributed. His commitment to studying the lawfulness of the life span is seen in the following statement: "It will first be necessary to determine the period at which memory, imagination, and judgment commence, and the stages through which they necessarily pass in their progress to maturity: thus having established the maximum point, we may extend our inquiries to the law of their decline." Quetelet's thinking represented the breadth of nineteenth-century scientists, who aimed for theories encompassing the total organism.

B. Pioneers

Little systematic work was conducted on the processes of aging during the latter part of the nineteenth century and the beginning of the twentieth century, the years in which psychology became established as a separate discipline. In addition, the subdiscipline of developmental psychology turned out to be child psychology. However, a few early pioneers in the study of child development did turn their attention to the psychology of aging later in their careers. Among these were G. S. Hall, Charlotte Bühler, Carl Jung, and Walter Miles.

In 1922 G. S. Hall published his book *Senescence: The Second Half of Life*. He summarized what was known about aging in several scholarly fields but it can be looked upon as the beginning of a focus on the psychology of aging. *Senescence* was a broadly conceived book, and he reviewed the evidence about aging from all contemporary sciences and the general literature at the time (e.g., physiology, medicine, anatomy, philosophy) and something of the humanistic content about the psychology of the aging adult, in particular the psychological issues of death. For Hall, the experience of aging was a matter of walking up the hill of life toward maturity and then walking carefully down the other side toward old age.

Charlotte Bühler began publishing articles on child developmental psychology during the 1920s and pro-duced her original book on the course of human life in German in 1933. Relying upon diverse material (biological and psychological studies; production and performance records; biographical and autobiographical material), she laid the foundation of what later has been called life span developmental psychology. Although Bühler emphasized psychological processes of development and aging, she considered this in conjunction with the biological life cycle. The underlying biological structure of life provided a ground plan of growth, maintenance, and decline as the basis of psychological expansion (development) and restriction (aging).

From the beginning, psychoanalytic theory has been a developmental theory only of childhood and adolescence. Yet there has been an exception in the person of the Swiss clinician Carl G. Jung, who in 1933 described stages of development in adulthood, assuming maturational processes of the adult person to account for stage change. Jung's focus was on exploring the self over the life span. He noted a transformative shift from extraversion to introversion in middle and later life: the later years are not a simple addition to youth, but have their own purpose and significance. From this perspective, Jung accepted also older patients for psychotherapy.

The first laboratory of psychology devoted to the study of aging was founded in 1927 at Stanford University. At that time a good amount of research had already been completed on age differences in psychomotor skills and sensory capacities. By 1931 Walter Miles was able to publish a review on the psychology of aging, "Measures of Certain Human Abilities Throughout the Life Span," and in 1933 he followed it with a longer paper on life span changes. Miles directed most of his attention to psychomotor functions and was led to distinguish motility (i.e., the speed of motor movements) from the speed of simple reaction. For historical reasons, the research at Stanford was not continued when Miles left in 1933 for Yale University.

II. CONCEPTS OF AGING

A. Theory, Model, and Metaphor

Before reviewing specific psychological theories of aging following World War II, it is instructive to amplify on a few theoretical concepts. In this respect, one should recall the classic dictum that there is nothing so practical as a good theory. A theoretical framework helps the scientist to accumulate and integrate data into a body of knowledge, as well as to provide directions for new research. Recently, several researchers in gerontology came to the conclusion that the psychology of aging is data rich, but theory poor. This conclusion, of course, depends at least partially on their definition of the term *theory*.

Under the influence of logical positivism, it has been assumed that proper theory development is identical with theory formalization in terms of logically linked, mathematical propositions. From this view, attempts to develop formal (i.e., rigorous, precise, and at least potentially quantitative) theories in the psychology of aging have not been very successful. Almost imperceptibly, the attention of researchers was turned to the formalization of models, which—generally speaking—are regarded to be more simple and quantifiable than theories, but also focus on limited aspects of aging.

Formalization in terms of quantitative models (or theories, for that matter) ignores the constructivist view that in an essential way science is metaphorical or characteristically employs metaphors. In fact, models are extended and systematic metaphors. For instance, before World War II, most researchers in intellectual abilities adopted the model of decline with age, i.e., intellectual abilities declined just as functions of the physical body declined with increasing age. This model is based on the so-called hill metaphor as introduced by G. S. Hall in 1922, with development going uphill and aging going downhill.

The old hill metaphor is still alive to this day, and so are many other metaphors, hidden in the disguise of some model or theory. This explains why the terms *theory*, *model*, and *metaphor* are often used interchangebly in the literature. Briefly summarized, the relative significance of these terms can be phrased as follows: the metaphor drives the theory in the psychology of aging in the first place, and the model functions as a more general, extended, or systemetic kind of metaphor, which connects theory with empirical research. In the next section, the term *theory* should be understood in the broadest sense of the word.

B. Psychology of the Aged

Research in the psychology of aging has been guided—if at all—by a somewhat diverse collection of theories, models, and metaphors. Historically, there are three approaches in this field: the *aged*, *age*, and *aging*. The psychology of the aged focuses on *older people* and *later life*. Grounded in a stages-of-life perspective, most studies of the aged, whether the young-old or the old-old, demonstrate a thematic, descriptive approach and little coherence. In the research literature at least 70 different themes can be distinguished, varying from Alzheimer's disease (AD), life satisfaction, widowhood and retirement, to cognition, death and dying. Most research findings consist essentially of descriptive statements about the organization of behavior in the aged and their social-medical problems. Given the wide variety of themes and findings, the psychology of the aged may be broadly defined as the study of the problematic and nonproblematic elderly.

The lack of gerontological theory in psychological studies of the aged results from the traditional stability orientation to adulthood; i.e., ordered changes are restricted to childhood and adolescence, whereas further developments in adulthood are not assumed. It has been shown that the psychological study of the aged is heavily infested with biomedical conceptions of aging as a disease or a result of some deteriorative process. For instance, cognitive processes at older age are often described in terms of failure, loss, insufficiency, inadequacy, impoverishment, decrement, inefficiency, or impaired performance. These biomedical conceptions of aging reflect the dominant metaphor that aging is a biological or medical problem and that the elderly make up a problem group in society. The vast majority of older people, however, live independently and have the vitality and resilience to function at a satisfactory level.

C. Psychology of Age

The second approach in psychogerontology falls within the psychology of age, which focuses on *age differences*. Most research according to this approach has been cross-sectional, describing and comparing groups of people of different ages measured at the same time. The central research question concerns the relation between age as the primary independent variable and some other variable of interest as the primary dependent variable (e.g., mortality, morbidity, autonomy, quality of life, mental abilities, or productivity). The derived research question often concerns the extent to which intervening variables, such as sociodemographic, environmental, psychosocial, biophysiologic, or lifestyle factors, are related to the observed differences with age.

Cross-sectional age differences are frequently misinterpreted in terms of age changes, aging, or changes in behavior over time. Over the last three decades, however, researchers realized gradually that age differences do not equal age changes, or—to put it differently—that chronological age used as the independent variable does not help to explain, or at most partially, the aging process. In 1965, K. Warner Schaie was one of the first to realize that cohort and period may have more interesting explanatory properties than age, and accordingly he designed the age-period-cohort (APC) general developmental model. However, due to the dependency of these three time parameters upon calendar time (both dependent and independent variables are expressed in terms of the same calendar time), there is always the problem of time confounds, regardless of how data are collected or statistically analyzed. [See COHORT STUDIES; TIME: CONCEPTS AND PERCEPTIONS.]

Another point of view regarding the age variable is based on the conception of age as an index variable that is in need of further explanation in terms of aging processes. Most researchers use chronological age implicitly as a dummy variable that stands not for a single underlying aging process, but for a host of processes that independently and in concert bring about changes recognized as aging. From an experimental perspective this means that fruitful research will focus on identifying the causes and consequences of the processes responsible for age-related differences. Particularly in the field of cognitive aging this type of cross-sectional experiments can be found, though longitudinal information is needed to reach more definitive conclusions about the hypothesized aging processes.

D. Psychology of Aging

The third approach in psychogerontology concerns the psychology of aging, which studies (briefly summarized) the *regular changes in behavior* after young adulthood. In order to study changes over time, it is necessary to carry out longitudinal research, which essentially means that the performance of a group of subjects from a single cohort is compared with that group's own performance at other periods in time. In this context, the term *aging* is often used both as a label for an independent variable to explain other phenomena (e.g., mortality, productivity, health, competence) and as a dependent variable that is explained by other processes (e.g., wear-and-tear, genetics).

It should be noted in the above definition that the adjective *regular* in the phrase "regular changes in behavior" refers to the orderly or typical changes in behavior—or so-called behavioral patterns of change with age—as found in longitudinal research on aging. In the cognitive domain, for example, a general pattern of average declines with advancing age has been reliably established. Within this pattern, however, another classic pattern of cognitive aging can be distinguished, i.e., the relative increase of verbal information with age compared with decline in spatial-perceptual performance.

It is important to note also the implications of the phrase "after young adulthood" in the above definition. Thus defined, the psychology of aging is grounded in a two stages-of-life perspective, development and aging, which are usually described as two successive processes of change in time, with the transition point or apex at maturity. As noted before, the classic metaphor for the two stages of age-related change in life is the hill metaphor, which is based on biological conceptions of growth and decline, particularly, the so-called mortality curve: Mortality rates are high for infants, regularly decline to a minimum at about age 10, and then rise progressively throughout the remainder of the life span (Gompertz' law). Psychological processes of change, however, do not necessarily parallel biological changes along the life span. For example, fluid abilities like speed of information processing reflect genetic-biological determinants and tend to decline with age. Crystallized abilities, on the other hand, represent cultural-social influences (e.g., on general world knowledge) and may display some growth with age. This cognitive phenomenon raises the as yet unsolved problem of to what extent do psychological processes of development and aging differ from each other, as both processes alike refer to age-related changes.

III. CLASSICAL THEORIES

A. Developmental Tasks/Activity Theory

In 1948 Robert J. Havighurst published his many times reprinted book on the concept of developmental tasks in a life span perspective. A developmental task arises at or about a certain period in the life of the individual, successful achievement of which leads to his or her happiness and to success with later tasks, whereas failure leads to unhappiness in the individual, disapproval by the society, and difficulty with later tasks. All of these tasks have biological (physical maturation), psychological (aspirations or values), and cultural (expectations of society) bases. Havighurst has described the following six developmental stages or age periods, each with its own developmental tasks: infancy and early childhood, middle childhood, adolescence, early adulthood, middle age, and later maturity (beyond age 60). The developmental tasks of later maturity, for instance, can be summarized as follows: (a) coping with the physical changes of aging; (b) redirecting energy to new roles and activities such as grandparenting, retirement, and widowhood; (c) accepting one's own life; and (d) developing a point of view about death. Later on, the central organizing concept of age-related developmental tasks has been named *activity theory*, as opposed to disengagement theory.

B. Psychosocial Theory of Personality Development

With the publication of *Childhood and Society* in 1950, Erik Erikson made a major contribution to the understanding of personality development across the life span. Erikson formulated a psychosocial theory of eight stages of life, each with its own characteristic crisis that arises out of the conflict between two opposite tendencies. The developmental task of each age period is to resolve its conflict, which requires the integration of personal needs with the demands of society. The successful resolution of each conflict leads to developmental strength in terms of a new virtue. Failure, however, to deal adequately with a task during its period of ascendency is damaging to personality development. For example, the last stage of life, Old Age, refers to the opposite tendencies of "Integrity versus Despair." At this point an individual's life either makes sense because of some cross-cultural, human principles or is marked by a sense of despair, because it seems meaningless. The successful achievement of Integrity might lead, eventually, to the virtue of Wisdom.

Erikson's life stages and their respective age periods, opposing trends (crises), and potential virtues are as follows: (1) Infancy: 0–1 year, Basic trust vs. Basic mistrust/Hope; (2) Early Childhood: 1–6 years, Autonomy vs. Doubt and Shame/Will; (3) Play Age: 6–10 years, Initiative vs. Guilt/Purpose; (4) School Age: 10–14 years, Industry vs. Inferiority/Competence; (5) Adolescence: 14–20 years, Identity vs. Role confusion/Fidelity; (6) Young Adulthood: 20–35 years, Intimacy vs. Isolation/Love; (7) Maturity: 35–65 years, Generativity vs. Stagnation/Care; (8) Old Age: 65+ years, Integrity vs. Despair/Wisdom.

Erikson sees development as a function of both individual and cultural factors, hence the description of his theory as a psychosocial theory of personality development. In each stage of life, the social world widens, so that the infant whose society began with a dim image of the first caregiver at last becomes an elder whose view of the world encompasses humanity. It should be noted that—in spite of the seemingly accurate age division—Erikson's stages of life are not tied closely to specific age periods or age-related changes. The early stages are defined in much more detail than the later ones: postadolescence, for example, includes about three-quarters of the life span, but only three of the eight stages. This division reflects the increase in psychosocial variability with age: the developmental tasks of an infant are relatively universal, but the tasks in later life are dependent as much on personal experiences as on general principles.

C. Counterpart Theory

In 1960, James E. Birren, presented a general theory of aging as a counterpart of development. The use of the metaphor *counterpart* is meant to express the idea that there are latent structures of behavior (emotions, cognitions, and motivations) carried forward from earlier experience that interact with present situations. Aging is viewed as a transformation of the biological and behavioral development of the organism expressed in a counterpart manner in variable ecological contexts.

Observations of old persons suggested that there

is a pattern to the changes that occur in late life, which are not merely the consequences of happenstance or chance. In explanation of these late-life patterns of change, Birren noticed that natural selection as explanatory mechanism is not very obvious because some of the patterns or features in old persons (organisms) do not appear until long after the age of reproduction has passed. He concluded, therefore, that these regularly appearing features (including longevity) must be a consequence of traits that were selected for at the time of reproduction. Briefly summarized, Birren's counterpart theory states that any biologically based order in late-life characteristics must arise in association from counterpart characteristics of development that were subject to pressures of selection.

Birren has pointed out that behavioral factors can be involved in the counterpart process, that is, that patterning of late-life events could arise via natural selection of long-lived and intelligent persons. For example, although individual differences in longevity do not appear until long after reproduction has been completed, intelligent, long-lived parents are able to provide an environment in terms of food and protection favorable for their young to survive. In other words, counterpart theory advocates indirect selection for positive late-life characteristics that embrace a wide range of complex biological (e.g., potential for a long life) and behavioral (e.g., intelligence) characteristics. As such, counterpart theory expanded the classical hill metaphor of development and aging to include questions about their relationships and how behavior comes to be organized over the adult years of life, if not over the whole life span.

D. Disengagement/Activity Theory

The term *disengagement* refers to the withdrawal of people from previous roles or activities. Starting from the assumption that people turn inward from middle age and on, Cumming and Henry theorized in 1961 that this primary mental process produces (a) a natural and normal withdrawal from social roles and activities, and (b) an increasing preoccupation with self and decreasing emotional involvement with others. In positing the universality and normality of withdrawal, disengagement theory has been criticized for being neither natural nor inevitable. Although the theory professes to explain general psychological and social processes of aging, it has no more to offer than a one-

sided view of the aged, given the significant proportion of older people that do not lose interest in life and do not withdraw from society.

Disengagement theory encouraged the development of an opposing theory of the aged, activity theory, which is based on the concept of developmental tasks. According to its main proponent, Robert J. Havighurst, *activity theory* states that in order to maintain a positive sense of self, elderly persons must substitute new roles for those lost in old age. As such, activity theory presents a more realistic view of older people.

E. Personality Theory of Age and Aging

In 1968 Bernice L. Neugarten published her classic book of readings, *Middle Age and Aging* in a life cycle perspective. Starting from a series of studies begun in the 1950s, Neugarten and her associates described the life cycle in terms of two theoretical emphases. The first emphasis is on the study of timing of transitional events in the lives and roles of individuals. Life events, such as marriage, parenthood, occupational achievement, or retirement, are normatively scheduled; that is, they are expected to occur within certain ages and in a certain sequence. As such, they lead to changes in self-concept and identity. In metaphorical terms, individuals have internalized a *social clock*, and age norms act as prods and brakes upon behavior over the life span. However, unexpected events (such as automobile accidents) or age-normative events that occur off time (such as early widowhood) may have negative developmental consequences (e.g., life crises). [See LIFE EVENTS; TIME: CONCEPTS AND PERCEPTIONS.]

The second emphasis is on the study of personality type as a predictor for successful aging. Aging persons have differing capacities for coping with life stresses and for coming to terms with their changing life situations. Eight different patterns of aging have been distinguished, which Neugarten named the Reorganizers, the Focused, the Disengaged, the Holding-on, the Constricted, the Succorance-seeking, the Apathetic, and the Disorganized. Briefly summarized, aging is viewed as a process of adaptation in which personality is the key element. The aging individual not only plays an active role in adapting to the biological and social changes that occur with the passage of time but also in creating patterns of life that will give the greatest ego involvement and life satisfaction [*See* ADAPTATION.]

F. Cognitive Theory of Personality and Aging

In 1970 Hans Thomae described briefly a cognitive theory of the aging personality, one that is intended to integrate various biological, sociological, and interactionist perspectives while at the same time focusing upon the psychodynamics of aging. Central concepts in his theory are those of perception, perceived situation, and perceived self. Thomae postulates, for example, that perceived change rather than objective change is related to behavioral change; and that change is perceived and evaluated in terms of the aging person's dominant concerns and expectations. Successful adaptation to age-related changes, then, relates to the maintenance and restructuring of the balance between cognitive and motivational systems; (e.g., the balance between acceptance of oneself as old or rejection of this perception, which is one of the developmental tasks of aging persons).

IV. MODERN THEORIES

A. Life Span Development and Aging

Since the beginning of the 1980s, Paul B. Baltes and his associates have conducted a series of studies on psychological processes of development and aging from a life span perspective. In line with the tradition of life span developmental psychology, development and aging are conceived as synonyms for behavioral changes across the life span. Starting from these studies, Baltes has developed a theoretical framework of seven propositions about the nature of human aging from a psychological point of view: (a) there are major differences between normal, pathological, and optimal aging, the latter defined as aging under development-enhancing and age-friendly environmental conditions; (b) the course of aging shows much interindividual variability (heterogeneity); (c) there is much latent reserve capacity in old age; (d) there is aging loss in the range of reserve capacity or adaptivity; (e) individual and social knowledge (crystallized intelligence) enrich the mind and can compensate for age-related decline in fluid intelligence (aging losses); (f) with age the balance between gains and losses becomes increasingly negative; and finally (g) the self in old age remains a resilient system of coping and maintaining integrity.

Based on this framework of propositions, a psychological model of successful aging has been devised, named selective optimization with compensation. The central focus of this model is on the management of the dynamics between gains and losses, i.e., a general process of adaptation, consisting of three interacting elements. First, there is the element of selection, which refers to an increasing restriction of one's life world to fewer domains of functioning because of an aging loss in the range of adaptive potential. The second element, optimization, reflects the view that people engage in behaviors to enrich and augment their general reserves and to maximize their chosen life courses (and associated forms of behavior) with regard to quantity and quality. The third element, compensation, results also (like selection) from restrictions in the range of adaptive potential. It becomes operative when specific behavioral capacities are lost or are reduced below a standard required for adequate functioning.

The lifelong process of selective optimization with compensation allows people to age successfully, i.e., to engage in life tasks that are important to them despite a reduction in energy. For instance, the pianist Rubinstein remarked in a television interview that he conquers weaknesses of aging (adaptation) in his piano playing in the following manner: First, he reduces his repertoire and plays a smaller number of pieces (selection); second, he practices these more often (optimization); and third, he slows down his speed of playing prior to fast movements, thereby producing a contrast that enhances the impression of speed in the fast movements (compensation).

B. Reduced Processing Resources

For some time it has been generally accepted that there is an average age-related decline in cognitive performance. Researchers have advanced several explanations for this aging phenomenon, but so far only the resource-reduction view has found wide support. In this view, aging leads to a reduction in the quantity of one or more processing resources, such as attentional capacity, working-memory capacity, or speed of processing. According to Timothy A. Salthouse—a typical exponent of this view since the 1980s—

processing resources are characterized by three properties: (a) they are limited in quantity, with a measurable aspect such as quantity or effectiveness of allocation increasing up until maturity and then decreasing across the adult years; (b) they enable or enhance cognitive processing such that performance in many cognitive tasks is improved when greater amounts of the resources are available; and (c) they are not local or specific in the sense that they are restricted to a small number of highly similar cognitive tasks, but instead are relevant to a broad range of cognitive processes.

The three properties of processing resources have generated a number of specific theories. They can be classified into three categories, based on the dominant metaphor used in theorizing on resource-reduction, i.e., metaphors of space, energy, and/or time. That is, space limitations correspond to restrictions on the size of the computational or working-memory region available for processing; energy limitations correspond to attentional capacity restrictions; and time limitations refer to restrictions imposed by trade-offs between the rate at which information can be processed and the rate at which it becomes unavailable through decay, interference or some other mechanism. [See ATTENTION; MEMORY.]

In a series of experimental studies, Salthouse and his associates have focused on the time metaphor of processing speed as the explanatory construct of cognitive aging. Their findings indicate that processing speed is a fundamental construct in human cognition, linked to explicit changes in neural structure and functioning on the one hand and to higher order cognitive processes like reasoning and abstraction on the other. As such, Salthouse hypothesizes that processing speed may well provide the cornerstone for integrative theories of cognitive aging. It should be noted, however, that the resource-reduction view leaves unanswered the fundamental questions of why the reduction in resources occurs, and how that reduction results in lower levels of cognitive performance.

C. Personality and Aging

Studies of personality and aging reflect the concept of personality behind them, here defined as the set of characteristic dispositions that determine emotional, interpersonal, experiential, attitudinal, and motivational styles. Generally speaking, two theoretical traditions can be distinguished in this field, trait and developmental-stage models. In both traditions, the central issue concerns the extent and nature of personality stability and change over the life span; or, to put it differently, the extent to which aging processes per se are responsible for personality change.

Overall, longitudinal studies of personality traits have consistently found structural invariance of personality over time, i.e., a marked pattern of similarity in factor structure across instruments, cohorts, types, and times of measurement. According to Paul Costa and Robert McCrae—typical proponents of the trait model—the same five major factors (neuroticism, extraversion, openness to experience, agreeableness, and conscientiousness) have emerged from longitudinal studies using somewhat different approaches. In conclusion of the evidence, they state that people stay much the same in their basic dispositions and show a high degree of stability of personality, particularly during the latter half of their life course. [See PERSONALITY.]

More recent extensions of the trait model pertain to personality-linked constructs like locus-of-control and self-concept. Generalizations about stability and change are limited by the relatively small number of studies available, the large majority of which are cross-sectional in design. However, there is growing consensus that personality traits tend to be stable with age, whereas key aspects of self such as goals, values, coping styles, and control beliefs are more amenable to change. [See IDENTITY, PHYSICAL.]

Theoretical models of adult personality development represent the second tradition in the personality-and-aging field. Two theories—developed by Erik Erikson and Daniel Levinson, respectively—offer developmental stages beyond the period of early adulthood. As discussed before, Erikson's eight stages—extending from infancy to old age—were formulated more than 45 years ago. From this perspective, it is surprising that there has been collected only limited empirical evidence for the maturity and old-age stages, i.e., generativity vs. stagnation and integrity vs. despair. There are no longitudinal studies, for example, that ask whether the achievement of generativity in midlife is a necessary precursor for the achievement of integrity in the later years. As such, Erikson's theory deserves more critical attention from gerontologists.

In Levinson's theory of personality development (based on a series of in-depth interviews with 40 men), each man's life structure goes through an orderly sequence of periods that alternate between stable phases and transitional phases, which are generally crucial turning points in life. Beginning with a transition out of adolescence (17–22 years), there are three major periods: early adulthood (ages 17–45), middle adulthood (ages 40–65), and late adulthood (past age 60). The periods overlap because each is bridged by a 5-year transition that is part of both periods. The timing and length of each period and the development that takes place within it vary from man to man, depending on the biological, psychological, and social conditions of their life. Nevertheless, a close linkage of periods with age intervals is suggested. Levinson's theory can be severely criticized on many grounds, of which the impossibility of replicating the in-depth interviews, poses the most serious problem in aging research.

D. Behavioral Genetics and Aging

Behavioral geneticists of aging are concerned with the extent to which hereditary factors influence age-related changes over the life span of the individual. Here, heritability is defined as a descriptive statistic referring to the portion of observed, phenotypic variation in the population that can be accounted for by genetic differences among individuals; the rest of the variation, the nongenetic portion, is called environmental. Thus, change in heritability over the life span indicates that the relative roles of genetic and environmental influences can change with age in terms of their effects on biological and behavioral differences among individuals in the population. [*See* DNA AND GENE EXPRESSION.]

With regard to the issue of stability and change, Gerald E. McClearn, Nancy L. Pedersen and Robert Plomin—three leading researchers since the 1980s—make a distinction between phenotypic and structural stability. Phenotypic stability, as expressed in the familiar correlation between the same measures on successive occasions, refers to the stability of both genetic and environmental components. Structural stability, on the other hand, refers to either genetic or environmental invariance (stability) throughout the life span. Given this distinction, Pedersen states that theories of aging that rely on the demonstration of genetic variance only as support for claims of phenotypic stability need to be modified to incorporate findings of both genetic and environmental involvement in stability.

For example, early predictions of cognitive performance with age suggest that changes in phenotypic variance would reflect changes in environmental variance only, while assuming implicitly genetic stability. However, as the Swedish Adoption/Twin Study of Aging (SATSA) has shown, no simple explanation exists for changes in variance of cognitive performance with age: increases in phenotypic (total) variance resulted from increases in environmental experiences, whereas decreases in total variance were distributed equally among genetic and environmental components.

Theory formation in gerontological behavioral genetics is still in its infancy. On the basis of recent analyses, however Pedersen comes to the following tentative conclusions:

1. The relative importance of genetic and environmental effects on individual differences in the elderly is phenotype specific. Heritability is low to moderate for personality traits and measures of well-being, moderate for health-related phenotypes, and greater for cognitive abilities, whereas heritability for memory is lower than for verbal and spatial abilities or perceptual speed.

2. There are age differences in heritability, the pattern of which is phenotype dependent. For some measures, particularly health-related characteristics, the relative importance of genetic effects appears to decrease across age groups. For others, heritability is stable, increases, or reflects an inverted L-shaped function. Variance changes may reflect either an increase of environmental or genetic influences, depending on the phenotype. More often, environmental effects account for the increase in variability in health-related phenotypes.

3. Across short spans of time, genetic effects are more stable than environmental effects for personality and cognition. Environmental effects of importance for individual differences late in life are changing. Nevertheless, environmental influences are at least as important for phenotypic stability across short (3–6 year) spans of time.

V. NEW THEORIES

A. Gerotranscendence

In 1989 Lars Tornstam suggested that human aging, the very process of living into old age, encompasses a general potential towards gerotranscendence, i.e., a shift in metaperspective, from a materialistic and rational vision to a more cosmic and transcendent one, normally followed by an increase in life satisfaction. On the basis of qualitative and quantitative studies, Tornstam developed the theoretical concept of gerotranscendence at three levels of age-related, ontological change: (a) Cosmic level, for example, changes in the perception of time, space, and objects, increase of affinity with past and coming generations, changes in the perception of life, disappearing fear of death, acceptance of the mystery dimension in life, and increase of cosmic communion with the spirit of the universe; (b) Self, for example, discovery of hidden—both good and bad—aspects of the self, decrease of self-centeredness, self-transcendence from egoism to altruism, rediscovery of the child within, and ego integrity; (c) Social and individual relations, for example, less interest in superficial relations, increasing need for solitude, more understanding of the difference between self and role, decreasing interest in material things, and increase of reflection.

The new theory of gerotranscendence reminds one of the classical concepts of disengagement and integrity, but differs qualitatively in some opposite aspects. For example, gerotranscendence implies a redefinition of reality, whereas disengagement is restricted to turning inwards; also, gerotranscendence is connected with social activity and a need for solitary philosophizing at the same time, whereas disengagement encompasses social withdrawal only; next, gerotranscendence refers to offensive, multicoping strategies, whereas disengagement implies defensive coping strategies and social breakdown; finally, Erikson's integrity refers primarily to the integration of elements in life that have passed, whereas gerotranscendence implies more of a forward or outward direction, including the redefinition of reality. Summarizing, even though Tornstam's theory of gerotranscendence is based on limited empirical evidence, it nevertheless makes a promising attempt to integrate and further develop some classical and modern psychosocial theories of aging.

B. Branching Theory

In 1995 Johannes J. F. Schroots presented a brief outline of a dynamic systems theory of aging, called *gerodynamics*. This comprehensive theory *in statu nascendi* is based on general systems theory, notably the Second Law of Thermodynamics and dynamic systems theory (chaos theory). The Second Law states that there is an increase of entropy or disorder with age in living systems, resulting in the system's death. Chaos theory postulates that internal or external fluctuations of dynamic, far-from-equilibrium systems can pass a critical point—the transformation point—and create order out of disorder through a process of self-organization, that is, a process by which a structure or pattern of change emerges with the passage of time. From this metatheoretical viewpoint, the aging of living systems can be conceived as a nonlinear series of transformations into higher and/or lower order structures or processes, showing a progressive trend toward more disorder than order over the life span, and resulting in the system's death.

Gerodynamics lies at the root of a new aspect theory of aging, called *branching theory*. The basic principle of this theory is the bifurcation or branching behavior of the individual at the biological, psychological, or social level of functioning. Metaphorically speaking, bifurcation means that the fluctuating individual (organism) passes a critical point—the bifurcation, branching, or transformation point—and can branch off into higher and/or lower order structures or processes. Higher and lower order structures can be translated in terms of mortality (probability of dying, life expectancy), morbidity (disease, disorder, disability or dysfunction) and quality of life (well-being, life satisfaction). For example, traumatic life events and a healthy lifestyle may result in lower and higher order structures, respectively, and consequently in higher and lower probabilities of dying. It should be noted, however, that lower order bifurcations at the biological or psychological level of functioning (e.g., illness or divorce) do not always result in lower order branching behavior; i.e., some people are strengthened by illness, and divorce may have a positive rather than a negative effect on mental health in terms of life expectancy and quality of life.

Briefly summarized, branching theory studies the determinants and patterns of branching behavior across the life span. As yet, this innovative theory of aging is based on theoretical evidence. It remains to be seen how empirical research in progress lends support to its theoretical claims.

BIBLIOGRAPHY

Baltes, P. B., & Baltes, M. M. (1990). Psychological perspectives on successful aging: The model of selective optimization with compensation. In P. B. Baltes, & M. M. Baltes (Eds.), *Successful Aging*, (pp. 1–34). New York: Cambridge University Press.

Birren, J. E., & Bengtson, V. L. (Eds.). (1988). *Emergent theories of aging*. New York: Springer Publishing Company.

Birren, J. E., & Schaie, K. W. (Eds.). (1996). *Handbook of the psychology of aging* (4th ed.). San Diego: Academic Press.

Salthouse, T. A. (1991). *Theoretical perspectives on cognitive aging.* Hillsdale, NJ: Lawrence Erlbaum Associates.

Schroots, J. J. F. (1995). Psychological models of aging. *Canadian Journal on Aging, 14,* 44–66.

Schroots, J. J. F. (1995). Gerodynamics: Toward a branching theory of aging. *Canadian Journal on Aging, 14,* 74–81.

Tornstam, L. (1994). Gerotranscendence—A theoretical and empirical exploration. In L. E. Thomas, & S. A. Eisenhandler (Eds.), *Aging and the religious dimension.* Westport, CT: Greenwood Publishing Group.

Theories of Aging: Social

Victor W. Marshall

University of Toronto

I. Classifying Social Theories of Aging
II. The Legacy of Early Social Theorizing
III. Currently Dominant Theoretical Approaches
IV. Current Theoretical Challenges

Age-Stratification Perspective A theoretical approach that focuses on the progression of birth cohorts through the age strata of a society and, in addition, views the age-stratification system as changing in response to cohort characteristics and other social phenomena.

Disengagement Theory A theory that argues that successful aging involves a mutual withdrawal of the aging individual and society. This is seen as functional for society and beneficial, normal, typical, and ideally voluntary on the part of the individual.

Interpretive Theory Theory that assumes that individuals have significant freedom of action or choice, and that emphasizes that humans are capable of creating and using symbols.

Modernization Theory An argument that as societies modernize, industrialization, urbanization, new technology, improved health, and longevity contribute to a decline in the social status of the aged.

Political Economy Perspective A range of theoretical perspectives that emphasize the importance of power and economic forces in the structuring of society and the life chances of individuals.

Social gerontology for the most part draws on a broad array of social theories from several disciplines, but rarely has it developed its own multidisciplinary theories or theoretical perspectives. There are few attempts at formal statements of theory at a general level. Rather, most theorizing is directed to the articulation of theoretical perspectives and their applicability to further understand social processes of aging, the social status of the aged, and the ways in which social institutions are shaped by, adaptive, or reactive to changes in the age structure of societies. The first section of this article describes attempts to classify **SOCIAL THEORIES IN STUDIES OF AGING**. The second section gives a historical review of theoretical developments, focusing on enduring legacies. The third section describes current dominant theoretical perspectives. A final section considers current theoretical challenges.

I. CLASSIFYING SOCIAL THEORIES OF AGING

Although explicit discussions of theory have not been numerous in the field of aging, some classifications have been made. These have a strong sociological slant. Passuth and Bengtson described five major sociological theories, in which they list ten major theories of aging. The major sociological theories with the theories of aging (if differently named) in parentheses, are as follows: (a) structural functionalism (disengagement, modernization, age stratification, and life course); (b) exchange; (c) symbolic interactionism (activity, social breakdown and competence, and subculture); (d) Marxism (political economy of age); and (e) social phenomenology. More recently, research has presented a typology of eight theoretical approaches in social gerontology: (a) social constructivist theories; (b) social exchange theories; (c) the life-course perspective; (d) feminist theories; (e) social conflict theories; (f) age and society; (g) political economy; and (h) critical theory.

Marshall employs a typological approach that distinguishes social theories of aging along two dimensions and the cross-classification of these dimensions. The first is the micro–macro dimension, which describes whether the theoretical approach focuses on social psychological processes at the level of interaction, on social structural or large-scale social processes, or tries to link individual and small-scale social interaction in the context of social structure and macrolevel social processes. The second is the normative-interpretive dimension, which describes approaches that give little attention to human autonomy and the capacity for active meaning-construction on the one hand, or those that view the individual as a voluntaristic actor who at least attempts to exercise choice. Marshall classifies the theories noted in the work of Bengtson and colleagues, and additional theoretical approaches such as rational choice theory from sociology, or cultural anthropology, according to these dimensions.

Hendricks has classified sociological theories of aging in terms of three generations: (a) theories of the 1960s (disengagement, activity, subcultural, and continuity theories); (b) theories of the early 1970s (age stratification, modernization); and theories of the mid-1970s (political-economic theories, social psychological theories attuned to environmental and structural factors). These three generations of theories, Hendricks argues, successively emphasized functionalist and symbolic interactionist approaches that took social structure for granted; an antithesis that criticized the reductionism of the first generation and emphasized structure; and a synthesis of theories that postulate a more dynamic and more political view of aging. The specific theories that Hendricks discusses, when arrayed in Marshall's typology, illustrate that there has been a general development over this period from normative microtheories, to normative macrotheories, to interpretive theories that address both the macro- and microlevels as well as linking these levels.

II. THE LEGACY OF EARLY SOCIAL THEORIZING

Early social theorizing about aging, much of it directly traceable to the Committee on Social Adjustment of the Social Sciences Research Council chaired by Ernest W. Burgess, emphasized problems of adjustment of the older person to a changing society. A SSRC-initiated Committee on Socialization and Social Structure held a 1963 conference called Socialization Through the Life Cycle, which stimulated interest in lifelong socialization as a requirement for adjustment in later life. The view of socialization was structural-functional. Socialization into age-appropriate roles was seen as a key mechanism providing integration of the individual in society. This emphasis subsequently appeared in the theorizing of several key players of the time, including Matilda Riley, Bernice Neugarten, and Irving Rosow.

Integration of the individual into society through social roles provides a common ground linking activity theory and disengagement theory in this period, even though the two theoretical groups differed as to the relationship between role activity and social adjustment or life satisfaction. Work in this period addressed the problems of "normal aging," and the debate betweeen activity and disengagement theorists led to a recognition of diversity in the aging process as well as to recognition that aging is best viewed as a set of processes occurring at different levels, which mutually influence one another in complex, nonlinear ways. However, the first major attempt to construct a "grand theory" of aging, the disengagement theory, was largely discredited on both empirical and logical grounds.

In the early 1970s however, a "grand theory" of modernization and aging, and a "grand perspective" of age stratification came to prominence. Through Cowgill's efforts at formal theory construction, the theory of aging and modernization served as a useful reference point for researchers, leading to extensive qualification and substantial rejection of the theory. The age-stratification perspective provided a more loosely structured set of assumptions to guide research, and this looseness perhaps increased its survivability, because testing through falsification was never an issue. [See MODERNIZATION AND AGING.]

These two theoretical approaches emphasized the macrolevel of analysis and rested squarely on the normative perspective of structural functionalism. Theoretical evolution and reaction, the infusion of theoretical ideas from outside the aging field, and the interpretation of research data created the most recent theoretical activity in aging and the social sciences. Scholars working with both modernization theory and the age-stratification perspective came increasingly to recognize the importance of cultural diversity and a wide range of cultural adaptations to age and aging. The inclusion of historical, anthropological, and a broader range of psychological and social psychological theorizing in the age-stratification perspective contributed to its evolution into the life-course perspective, which is both less normative and less macro-oriented in practice than the age-stratification perspective. Reaction against the consensual assumptions of both the modernization theory and the age-stratification perspective stimulated the emergence of work in the political economy of aging; and an attempt to bring the human subject back into the analysis stimulated work from phenomenological, symbolic interactionist, critical, and feminist perspectives.

III. CURRENTLY DOMINANT THEORETICAL APPROACHES

The life-course perspective is currently the most broadly shared among social gerontologists. This is partly because the perspective is very abstractly defined. Variants of theorizing in this perspective draw heavily on several perspectives: (a) the structural functionalism of the stratification perspective and that of status attainment theory in the sociology of occupational mobility; (b) the interpretive or social constructionist perspective with its emphasis on the social construction of and cultural variation in age statuses; (c) theorizing about life transitions, social stress and health; (d) developmental theories of the life span (often with Freudian conceptual underpinnings); and (d) theorizing from the field of social ecology. What unifies life-course theorists despite these often contrasting theoretical perspectives is a small set of principles outlined by Matilda Riley in a number of her publications: aging is influenced by social processes and in turn influences these processes; aging is a lifelong process—to understand people at a given age one must understand where they have come from and where they are going; the age structure changes over time and is experienced differentially by different cohorts. Agreement on these principles leaves open, to some

extent, questions such as the degree to which social behavior is determined or free, or the degree to which society and social interaction are based on consensus or conflict. These questions are given specific answers in two other perspectives mentioned next. [See LIFE COURSE.]

A number of theorists are using, and elaborating, theory under the rubric of the political economy perspective to understand the social circumstances of the aged. This draws on European intellectual sources such as Weber and Marx and, in particular the Frankfurt School of social theorists. A Marxian emphasis on the important of social class and classlike differences between age groups that experience structurally different life chances is linked to an emphasis on the moral economy, which recognizes that social movements, the political process, and economic processes are shaped by cultural conceptions of legitimacy, equity or fairness, citizens' rights, and moral contracts between the generations. The link to processes of aging is made by viewing the life course as socially constructed in light of such economic and moral concerns. For example, political economists might view the category, "old age" as defined by retirement, and retirement as a humanly invented social institution reflecting trade-offs between different parties with at least potentially conflicting interests: workers seeking a citizens' wage, owners seeking ways to exercise more control over their workers, and the state seeking to provide for the welfare of its citizens. Much feminist theorizing in social gerontology draws heavily on the political economy approach, and some such theorists label themselves as "socialist feminists" or "Marxist feminists."

A number of researchers draw explicitly on strands of interpretive theory rooted in symbolic interactionist or phenomenological sociology and symbolic or cultural anthropology. These approaches emphasize that the human being is a symbol-creating and symbol-using creature who actively seeks meaning and to develop lines of action in order to realize individual interests or motivations. Human behavior, in this view, is seen as constrained, but not fully determined, by biological or social structural factors. This view, like the political economy perspective, is increasingly visible in contemporary social research in gerontology, although the premises are more often implicit than explicitly stated.

IV. CURRENT THEORETICAL CHALLENGES

The history of theory in social gerontology has seen specific theoretical approaches rise and fall. Disengagement theory and modernization theory have been largely eclipsed by age-stratification and life-course perspectives. The determinism implicit or often explicit in developmental theory has given way to the more voluntaristic approaches to interpretive theorizing. To this point, there has been little success in making explicit linkages between macrolevel social structures and processes and the lived experiences of aging individuals. In this sense, gerontology exemplifies the major problem of the social sciences from which it draws theoretical sustenance. Similarly, the postmodernist critique of the social sciences is now being voiced in the literature of gerontology. The extent to which this critique of the very purpose and nature of theorizing will lead gerontologists away from theory is impossible to fathom at this point. Social gerontology has always been heavily oriented to public policy issues, such as effective service delivery and the provision of adequate health care and income security. Because policy makers want specific answers, the importance of theory, which can be used to frame meaningful research questions to provide these answers, will no doubt always be high in gerontology.

BIBLIOGRAPHY

Climo, J. J. (1992). The role of anthropology in gerontology: Theory. *Journal of Aging Studies, 6*(1), 41–55.

Dannefer, D. (1992). Human action and its place in theories of aging. In J. F. Gubrium, & K. Charmaz (Eds.), *Aging, self, and community: A collection of readings* (pp. 35–54). Greenwich, CT: JAI Press.

Elder, G. H., Jr. (1995). The life course paradigm: Historical, comparative, and developmental perspectives. In P. Moen, G. H. Elder, Jr., & K. Luscher (Eds.), *Linking lives and contexts: Perspectives on the ecology of human development* (pp. 101–139). Washington, DC: American Psychological Association.

George, L. K. (1993). Sociological perspectives on life transition. *Annual Review of Sociology, 19*, 353–373.

Hendricks, J. (1992). Generations and the generation of theory in social gerontology. *International Journal of Aging and Human Development, 35*(1), 31–47.

Kohli, M. (1988). Ageing as a challenge for sociological theory. *Ageing and Society, 8*, 367–394.

Marshall, V. W. (1995). Social models of aging. *The Canadian Journal on Aging, 14*(1), 12–34.

Marshall, V. W. (1996). The state of theory in aging and the social sciences. In R. Binstock, & L. George (Eds.), *Handbook of aging and the social sciences* (4th ed. pp. 12–30). San Diego: Academic Press.

Passuth, P. M., & Bengtson, V. L. (1986). Sociological theories of aging: Current perspectives and future directions. In J. E. Birren, & V. L. Bengtson (Eds.), *Emergent theories of Aging* (pp. 335–355). New York: Springer.

Riley, M. W., Foner, A., & Waring, J. (1988). Sociology of age. In N. J. Smelser (Ed.), *Handbook of sociology* (pp. 243–290). Newbury Park, CA: Sage.

Thirst and Hydration

Margaret-Mary G. Wilson
St. Louis University Medical Center

John E. Morley
St. Louis VA Medical Center

I. Fluid Compartments
II. Fluid Homeostasis and Thirst
III. Dehydration
IV. Rehydration
V. Hypo-osmolality
VI. Prevention of Dehydration

Arginine Vasopressin (AVP) An antidiuretic hormone produced in the posterior pituitary gland, which facilitates renal tubular water reabsorption. This hormone plays a central role in the physiological regulation of fluid balance.

Atrial Natriuretic Peptide (ANP) A peptide located within atrial secretory granules and released in response to atrial distension. This peptide encourages renal excretion of sodium, abolishes thirst, and counteracts arginine vasopressin-induced water reabsorption.

Dipsogen A substance that stimulates thirst and voluntary fluid ingestion.

Homeostasis A state of physiological equilibrium achieved by maintenance of a balance of biological functions and biochemical reactions.

Hypodermoclysis The subcutaneous infusion of parenteral fluids.

Nocturia Increased frequency of nocturnal urination.

Syndrome of Inappropriate Antidiuretic Hormone Secretion (SIADH) The inappropriate secretion of arginine vasopressin leading to increased renal tubular reabsorption of water and dilutional hyponatremia.

Normal aging is associated with a decline in total body water. Advancing age is also associated with a decrease in **THIRST** perception and a reduction in voluntary fluid intake. Alterations in the secretion of arginine vasopressin (AVP) and atrial natriuretic peptide (ANP) with aging predispose the older person to mild dehydration. The maintenance of fluid balance is further compromised by the reduction in renal tubular function that occurs in many older people. This results in a decrease in free water clearance and may increase the predisposition toward hypo-osmolar states.

These age-related physiological changes provide a ready explanation for the proclivity with which the older person develops fluid imbalance and hypo- or hyperosmolality when water and electrolyte balance is further challenged by the development of disease or adverse effects of medication.

Dehydration is a common occurrence in older persons and is associated with a significant increase in mortality. Identification of risk factors, institution of appropriate preventive measures, and timely therapeutic intervention are crucial components of effective management.

I. FLUID COMPARTMENTS

Human longevity is dependent on the preservation of a *milieu interior* that is conducive to the sustenance of life. In humans the internal environment is predominantly fluid with water constituting the universal carriage medium for electrolytes and being the sole solvent in which all physiological and biochemical reactions occur. Total body water (TBW) constitutes about 60% of total body weight in the younger adult. In the older person, TBW comprises 52% and 46% of body weight in men and women, respectively. TBW exists within three physiological compartments, namely extracellular, intracellular, and plasma. In the younger adult these comprise 20, 75, and 5% respectively. The volumes of the intracellular and plasma compartments expressed as a percentage of total body weight show a progressive decrease with age. The effect of increasing age on the volume of the extracellular fluid (ECF) compartment is variable. ECF volume may remain unchanged or exhibit a slight increase or decrease in older persons. Compartmental transmigration of fluid occurs continuously and is determined mainly by osmolality and electrolyte content. Water and electrolyte homeostasis, which is ultimately dependent on renal and neuroendocrine function, ensures stability of the various fluid compartments. Thirst perception influences fluid intake and is vital to the maintenance of fluid balance. [*See* HOMEOSTASIS; ENDOCRINE FUNCTION AND DYSFUNCTION.]

In the older person, age-related changes in the renal and neurohypophyseal systems, decreased perception of thirst, superimposed disease states, and adverse effects of medication increase the risk of fluid and electrolyte disturbances. Thus, routine evaluation of the older person should include assessment of the hydration status and screening for relevant risk factors.

II. FLUID HOMEOSTASIS AND THIRST

The sensation of thirst, an awareness of a compelling desire to drink, is produced by a complex interplay between several hormones, peripheral sensors, and neurohypophyseal osmoreceptors. Aortic, carotid sinus, and atrial baroreceptors serve as peripheral sensors. The central osmoreceptors are in the supraoptic and paraventricular nuclei of the hypothalamus. The thirst center is located in the organum vasculosum of the anterior hypothalamus, in close proximity to the hypothalamic nuclei that subserve arginine vasopressin (AVP) secretion.

AVP is the principal hormone involved in the regulation of water balance. It is formed in the hypothala-

mus and transported in secretory granules to the posterior pituitary from where it is released into the circulation in response to plasma volume or osmolality changes. AVP acts via an increase in cyclic AMP (cAMP) concentrations to enhance permeability of the collecting tubules and the ascending limb of the loop of Henle thereby increasing water reabsorption. Studies have also shown that AVP increases hepatic production of urea, contributing to maintenance of medullary hypertonicity. This further encourages water reabsorption by increasing the efficiency of the countercurrent system.

An increase in the concentration of most extracellular solutes results in an increase in ECF osmolality. The central osmoreceptors are most sensitive to changes in sodium concentration, with glucose and urea evoking relatively weak responses. Stimulation of these osmoreceptors by changes in tonicity results in the release of AVP from the posterior pituitary gland. A simultaneous release of neuronal angiotensin 11 occurs, which stimulates the thirst center. Dehydration has also been shown to result in the release of endothelin 1 from the posterior pituitary. It is likely that this hormone may play a role in water conservation as studies have demonstrated an increase in AVP levels following administration of exogenous endothelin. However, the exact mechanism of action remains unclear.

Similar homeostatic changes result from baroreceptor stimulation in response to a reduction in circulating blood volume. High pressure receptors are located in the aortic arch, carotid sinus, and atria. These respond to a decrease in ECF volume by eliciting vagal stimulation of the hypothalamic nuclei via ascending noradrenergic pathways. The effect is an increase in AVP levels and relatively low atrial natriuretic peptide (ANP) levels. Volume-dependent stimuli are less effective than tonicity-induced stimuli in initiating homeostatic mechanisms. However, regardless of the nature of the initiating stimulus, fluid and electrolyte balance is restored by suppression of diuresis, induction of thirst, and the voluntary acquisition of fluid by drinking.

Drinking abolishes the sensation of thirst and leads to a simultaneous reduction in AVP levels. These changes are attributed to preabsorptive oropharyngeal reflexes, which are independent of gastrointestinal absorption or physiological restoration of fluid and electrolyte balance. The exact mechanism underlying these reflexes is yet to be determined. However, drinking, swallowing, and gastric distension are essential to initiation of this reflex. Following absorption of ingested water, correction of the fluid deficit and reduction in plasma osmolality result in the release of ANP from atrial secretory granules and central neural centers. This encourages natriuresis and further reinforces the abolition of thirst and suppression of AVP secretion. Finally, adequate fluid and electrolyte repletion results in the release of prostaglandin E2 from renal interstitial cells, which serves to inhibit the effect of AVP on the collecting ducts and discourage continued water reabsorption.

A. Thirst and Aging

Thirst perception and fluid ingestion are determined by a complex interplay between several factors, all of which may contribute to the onset of relative hypodipsia with advancing age. These include physiological, hormonal, and psychological factors. Age-related changes occur in each domain. Furthermore, in older persons, functional status, environmental, and social circumstances notably affect motivation to drink.

Several neurotransmitters, amines and peptides have been implicated in the physiology of thirst. These include angiotensin 11, endogenous opioid peptides, serotonin, histamine, neurotensin, neuropeptide Y, and prostaglandins that stimulate drinking. Alpha-adrenergic agonists, antihistamines, and substance P are antidipsogenic. Several studies have examined the role of the opioid system in fluid intake. It is recognized that advancing age is associated with reduced efficacy of the opioid system due to decreased production of neuropeptides and endogenous opioid peptides. A decrease in the number of opioid receptors also occurs in older persons. Current evidence indicates that the elevated thirst threshold and relative hypodipsia noted in healthy older persons is related to reduction in the opioid mu receptor-mediated drinking drive. [See NEUROTRANSMITTER AND NEUROTROPHIC FACTORS.]

With advancing age, there is a physiological decrease in food intake referred to as "the anorexia of aging." There is an obligatory fluid intake associated with food intake. Animal studies indicate that with aging there is a reduction in the volume of fluid voluntarily consumed with meals. It has been suggested that

this may be attributed to a decrease in the effectiveness of histamine-mediated signals that serve to prompt fluid ingestion. This reduction in fluid intake occurring in the setting of anorexia of aging further compromises adequate voluntary hydration in older persons.

Diseases that alter level of consciousness or cognitive function, such as dementia or delirium may also interfere with perception of thirst. Persons with Alzheimer's disease have been found to have blunted AVP responses to dehydration, which increases their tendency to fluid and electrolyte imbalance. [See DEMENTIA.]

Aging is associated with a reduction in the thirst response to both tonic and volume-dependent stimuli. Attenuation of cardiopulmonary baroreceptor sensitivity may explain blunting of the thirst response to volume mediated stimuli. It is likely that similar age related changes in osmoreceptor sensitivity may account for the decreased thirst response to hypertonic stimuli. Besides the elevated thirst threshold, fluid repletion in older persons is much slower further increasing the risk of inadequate voluntary fluid intake and dehydration.

B. Nocturia and Aging

With advancing age, there is a tendency toward an increase in the frequency of nocturnal micturition. Urinary incontinence during the night is not a rare occurrence in older persons. These changes are attributed to alterations in the circadian rhythm of AVP secretion. In younger persons, AVP levels increase at night resulting in increased urine absorption from the renal tubules and reduced bladder filling. With aging, there is loss of the circadian rhythm of AVP secretion resulting in failure to increase renal tubular fluid reabsorption during the night. The rate of nocturnal bladder filling remains unchanged, resulting in a relative increase in the frequency of nocturnal micturition. [See RENAL AND URINARY TRACT FUNCTION.]

C. Fluid Homeostasis and Aging

Advancing age is associated with compromised function of the hypothalamic-pituitary-renal system. In spite of these changes, the healthy older person retains sufficient functional reserve to allow for adequate fluid and electrolyte balance. However, during acute and chronic illnesses or under extreme physiological or environmental conditions the older person has an increased predisposition to fluid and electrolyte imbalance.

Age-related renal cortical sclerosis and hyalinosis result in a notable reduction in renal cortical perfusion and glomerular filtration rate. Compromised renal perfusion results in reduction of the ability to concentrate urine. Abnormal renal physiology in older persons manifests as an inability to handle water and sodium. This results in inappropriate sodium retention or natriuresis. Free water clearance is adversely affected, and the older person may be unable to conserve water during periods when fluid intake is restricted. This may be due, in part, to decreased responsiveness to AVP that occurs with aging. In older persons, inappropriate natriuresis may also result from the elevation in ANP levels that occurs with advancing age. ANP levels are even further elevated in older persons with heart failure.

The integrity of the renin angiotensin–aldosterone system is impaired by age. Decreased plasma rennin activity and aldosterone secretion have been noted. It is likely that this contributes to the age-related elevation of the thirst threshold and the suboptimal vasopressin release in response to volume-mediated stimuli. Paradoxically, older persons have been found to have an increased vasopressin response to osmotic-mediated stimuli.

III. DEHYDRATION

Dehydration occurs commonly in older persons and is the most common cause of fluid and electrolyte imbalance. Studies in hospital populations have found the incidence of dehydration in the older population to range from 0.3% in the United Kingdom to 6.7% in the United States. Approximately half the persons admitted with dehydration are dead within 1 year of admission. Even higher rates of dehydration are reported in nursing homes and in this setting dehydration has been associated with a significant increase in mortality. Several causes of dehydration are recognized (see Table I). The basic mechanisms underlying dehydration are inadequate fluid intake and excessive renal or extrarenal fluid loss. Dehydration frequently coexists with other illnesses and may be overlooked

Table I Causes of Dehydration in Older Persons

Extra renal fluid depletion
- Diarrhea
- Vomiting
- Intestinal obstruction
- Massive ascites
- Excessive diaphoresis

Renal losses
- Chronic renal failure
- Postobstructive diuresis
- Renal salt wasting disease

Endocrine/Metabolic
- Hyperglycemia
- Hypercalcemia
- Diabetes mellitus
- Diabetes insipidus
- Addison's disease
- Hypoaldosteronism

Drugs
- Diuretics
- Lithium
- Propoxyphene
- Demeclocycline
- Ethanol

in the presence of a blunted thirst response or altered level of consciousness. In the older person, early clinical recognition of dehydration is particularly important as diminished functional reserves may significantly hamper compensatory ability. Suboptimal hydration significantly increases morbidity and mortality in older persons. Thus, identification of risk factors for dehydration is a necessary component of effective geriatric evaluation (see Table II). The commonest cause of dehydration in older persons is infection. Infections may result in a decrease in voluntary fluid intake and an increase in insensible fluid loss. Diseases such as chronic renal failure, diabetes mellitus, or diabetes insipidus result in significant polyuria. A metabolic imbalance such as occurs in hypercalcemia, hyperglycemia, and uremia may lead to an obligate polyuria.

Acute pancreatitis and intestinal obstruction may be complicated by occult sequestration of large volumes of intraabdominal fluid. Congestive cardiac failure, liver cirrhosis, nephrotic syndrome, thoracic, and intraabdominal malignancies may result in the accumulation of large volumes of fluid within the third

Table II Risk Factors for Dehydration in Older Persons

Restricted mobility
Impaired functional status
Social isolation
Self-neglect
Reduced cognitive function
Depression
Anorexia
Acute infection
Delirium
Multiple chronic diseases
Chronic diuretic, laxative, or sedative usage
Enteral or parenteral nutritional supplementation
Previous episodes of dehydration

space. Significant intravascular volume depletion may result from these conditions.

Iatrogenic fluid imbalance is not infrequent. Persons on diuretics, chronic laxatives, fluid restriction regimens, or dialysis therapy are at risk. Cerebrovascular disease and Parkinson's disease complicated by dysphagia can significantly compromise fluid intake. The syndrome of primary adipsia is recognized as a long-term complication following cerebrovascular thromboembolic events in older persons. The absence of thirst in such patients is attributed to multiple cortical infarcts. Diseases that affect mood, behavior, or cognitive function such as dementia, delirium, and depression may further blunt the thirst response and result in inadequate voluntary fluid intake.

It may not be fallacious to state that many older persons live in a "water desert." Social isolation and reduced functional status are recognized factors that may prevent or discourage access to fluids. Adverse environmental conditions such as occur during heat waves predispose to excessive sweating. In the face of inadequate fluid replacement a significant fluid deficit may result. Restricted mobility, which may either be disease-related or iatrogenic as occurs when physical restraints are used may also result in a decrease in voluntary fluid intake. When physical restraints are used in younger persons for only 6 hours, there is a dramatic decrease in fluid intake.

Following review of the history for predisposing factors, a detailed history and clinical examination are essential to detect the presence of dehydration and to estimate the severity. Clinical indicators of dehydration may be unreliable in older persons, and frequently the classical signs of dehydration are absent. The physician should remain aware that self-reported perception of thirst is a notoriously unreliable index of dehydration in older persons. In mild dehydration, thirst may be a prominent symptom. However, as fluid depletion progresses alteration in the patient's level of consciousness may blunt the perception of thirst. Constipation is a common symptom of dehydration in older persons. Other recognized symptoms of dehydration include apathy, nausea, vomiting, anorexia, and dizzy spells. Frank syncope may result from symptomatic orthostasis. Dehydration in older people may also manifest with dysarthria, dysphasia, and delirium.

Skin and soft tissue changes may be helpful. The presence of a dry tongue and oral mucosa, decreased salivation, and increased furrowing of the tongue are highly indicative of dehydration. However, similar changes may be produced by mouth breathing, Sjögren's syndrome, and anticholinergic medication. Loss of skin turgor is often considered indicative of dehydration in the younger person. In the older person, this may simply be a reflection of the reduction in skin elasticity. Age-related dermatological changes are less pronounced over the anterior chest wall and forehead. Assessment of skin turgor over these sites may provide a more accurate reflection of the state of hydration. Sunken eyes and a reduction in intraocular pressure may result from significant dehydration. In the older person, the coexistence of glaucoma and the inaccuracy of the clinical assessment of intraocular pressure may render these indices unhelpful.

The most reliable index of dehydration is a sudden reduction in baseline body weight. This however mandates previous knowledge of the patient's weight and is therefore of greater practical value in serial monitoring. Daily body weight losses in excess of 300–500 g usually indicate free water loss. However, loss of lean body mass arising from hypercatabolism in acute illnesses may interfere with the predictive value of body weight in the diagnosis of dehydration. Hypercatabolic weight loss rarely exceeds 300–500 g. Thus, weight loss exceeding this can usually be considered secondary to fluid depletion.

Rapid changes in circulating volume and notable hemodynamic instability may result from sudden-onset severe dehydration. Tachycardia may occur with significant volume depletion, but in the setting of an acute illness, this is a nonspecific sign. The diagnostic value of tachycardia is further impaired by the fact that impaired autonomic reflexes in the older person may blunt the chronotropic response to dehydration. Furthermore, in profound volume depletion, with losses ranging from 15–25%, bradycardia and hypotension may supervene.

The presence of postural hypotension is the most sensitive index of significant intravascular volume depletion. In the dehydrated older person, the presence of impaired autonomic reflexes may exacerbate postural changes in blood pressure resulting in orthostasis with relatively mild dehydration. Profound dehydration may result in symptoms arising from hypovolemic shock and multiorgan hypoperfusion. Typical features include an altered sensorium, cold clammy skin, tachycardia, and hypotension. The resultant renal hypoperfusion results in oliguria with urine flow rates of less than 30 ml/hr.

A. Investigation and Management of Dehydration

The definitive management of dehydration is best preceded by the objective assessment of clinical severity and plasma osmolarity. A helpful classification of dehydration in older persons is based on serum sodium levels. Proportionate deficits of water and sodium result in isotonic dehydration, which is characterized by normal plasma osmolarity and serum sodium levels. An absolute water deficit leads to hypertonic dehydration that is typically associated with hypernatremia and elevated plasma osmolarity. In older persons this usually results from restricted access to fluid or a diminished thirst response. Typical clinical settings in which this may occur include acute illnesses, significant frailty, physical restraints, inappropriate environmental barriers, marked confusion or inappropriate sedation. Hypotonic dehydration results from a disproportionate loss of sodium leading to hyponatremia and low plasma osmolarity. The commonest cause in older persons is inappropriate use of diuretics.

The plasma osmolarity may be measured or calculated as follows (BUN—blood urea nitrogen).

$$\text{Serum osmolarity} = 2[\text{Na}] + \frac{[\text{glucose}]}{18} + \frac{[\text{BUN}]}{2.8}$$

Ideally, both values should be obtained as accumulation of a nonphysiological substance such as mannitol, sorbitol, or lactic acid may result in an osmolar gap.

Serum sodium, urea, and creatinine levels assist in the estimation of severity of dehydration and the adequacy of renal perfusion. An elevation of the BUN to creatinine ratio of greater than 10:1 indicates dehydration with coexisting prerenal failure. Hematological investigations may reveal an apparent polycythemia resulting from hemoconcentration due to contraction of the circulating blood volume. Dehydration in older patients is often associated with an occult infection. An attempt should be made to screen for urinary tract infections, bronchopneumonia, sinusitis, and diverticulitis, which are highly prevalent in the older population.

IV. REHYDRATION

Effective correction of dehydration mandates replacement of established fluid loss, continuing fluid loss and daily fluid requirements. In persons with predominantly free water loss, the net fluid deficit may be calculated using the following equation:

Body water deficit (liters) = Expected TBW − Current TBW
Current TBW (liters) = current body weight (kg) × 0.5*
Expected TBW = $\dfrac{\text{Measured serum Na (mEq/liter)} \times \text{current TBW}}{\text{Normal serum Na (mEq/liter)}}$

The formula for calculation of current TBW in older persons has been modified to reflect the increase in total body fat and reduction in lean body mass that occurs with aging. Use of this formula should be restricted to persons without grossly abnormal serum sodium levels.

Accurate assessment of continuing fluid loss is significantly enhanced by the maintenance of records to reflect fluid intake and output from all sources. In patients with urinary incontinence transient short-term external catheterization may be helpful. Daily sensible and insensible fluid losses must be estimated. Insensible fluid loss occurs mainly from the skin and lungs and is approximately 500–600 ml/m². Adjustments should be made for the ambient temperature. Twenty percent of the calculated fluid requirements should be added to the total daily requirements for each centigrade elevation in ambient temperature. A daily intake of 500 ml of fluid is required to replace sensible fluid loss for ambient temperatures above 28°C or body temperatures above 38°C. With higher temperatures or when the patient is experiencing overt perspiration the required replacement volume is 1000 ml/24 hr.

The rate of fluid replacement is dictated predominantly by hemodynamic parameters. The presence of features of circulatory collapse requires rapid replacement until hemodynamic stability is achieved. Subsequently the rate of infusion should be such that the estimated deficit is replaced gradually over 3–4 days. Acceptable therapeutic goals would be to replace half the estimated fluid volume over 24 hours and the other half over the next 2–3 days.

In patients with significant hypernatremia, extremely rapid reductions of serum osmolarity may precipitate central pontine myelinosis. The physician should aim to reduce serum osmolarity to 300 at a rate that should not exceed 1 mEq/liter. Subsequently, the electrolyte deficit should be corrected gradually over 48–72 hours. The ideal fluid for replacement therapy in hypernatremic dehydration is half normal saline. In patients with isotonic or mild hypertonic dehydration, isotonic fluids are best used. Most cases of hyponatremic dehydration are treated with normal saline.

The method of fluid replacement depends on the clinical state of the patient and the clinical setting. In patients who can drink, mild dehydration may be corrected using oral fluids. Hypodermoclysis refers to the subcutaneous infusion of parenteral fluids. This route of administration is minimally invasive and ideal for use in the nursing home setting. This route may also be utilized in patients with difficult intravenous access who require long-term parenteral fluids. Infused fluids should be isotonic to avoid undue soft tissue irritation. Subcutaneous areas with a relatively large surface area, such as the thigh and abdomen, are preferred for use as infusion sites to encourage speedy absorption. The addition of hyaluronidase to the infusion fluids may further facilitate systemic absorption. Intravenous fluid replacement in older persons is best utilized for short-term therapy in the acute-care setting. Central venous cannulation may be indicated in severe hypovolemic shock with circulatory collapse.

A. Complications of Fluid Replacement Therapy

Persons on fluid replacement therapy should be monitored serially to assess the efficacy of treatment. This should include serial assessments of hemodynamic parameters, urine output, daily weight, and blood biochemistry. Inappropriate replacement therapy may result in several recognized complications (see Table III). Age-related diastolic dysfunction renders the older patient particularly vulnerable to circulatory overload from aggressive fluid replacement. The infusion rate should be carefully monitored as rapid correction of the fluid deficit may lead to neurological impairment from cerebral edema. During dehydration the brain generates idiogenic osmoles to provide protection against neuronal dehydration. Rapid correction of serum hyperosmolarity may consequently generate an osmotic gradient resulting in rapid migration of free water into neurones. Such patients may manifest with delirium or significant alterations in the level of consciousness. Transient or permanent neurological deficits may also result.

Dilutional hyponatremia frequently complicates the administration of iso-osmolar electrolyte free solutions, such as 5% dextrose, in older persons. The resultant hyponatremia is often mild and does not require specific treatment. Five percent dextrose should be discontinued in such persons and substituted with a sodium-containing infusion. A less frequent complication of dextrose infusions is the precipitation of thiamine deficiency. Undernourished persons and chronic alcoholics with subclinical thiamine deficiency

Table III Complications of Fluid Replacement Therapy

- Circulatory overload
- Dilutional hyponatremia
- Electrolyte imbalance
- Syndrome of inappropriate antidiuretic hormone secretion
- Cerebral edema
- Thiamine deficiency
- Cannulation complications:
  Local sepsis
  Thrombophlebitis
  Peripheral thromboembolic disease
  Bacteremia or septicemia
  Air embolism

are at high risk for this complication. The administration of dextrose infusions to these patients should be accompanied by concurrent thiamine supplements.

V. HYPO-OSMOLALITY

Hyponatremia may occur with fluid overload, euvolemia, or hypovolemia. The prevalence of hyponatremia in institutionalized older persons ranges from 11.3 to 22.5%. Clinical features of hyponatremia include delirium, lethargy, muscle cramps, seizures, anorexia, hypothermia, and hyporeflexia.

Several causes of hyponatremia are recognized (see Table IV). However, the commonest cause of hyponatremia is diuretic usage, which may also be complicated by hypokalemic alkalosis. The syndrome of inappropriate antidiuretic hormone (SIADH) is not a rare occurrence in older persons. This frequently occurs as a complication of a wide variety of drugs. SIADH may also complicate neoplastic, neurological, or pulmonary disease (see Table V).

Other causes of hypo-osmolality include Addison's disease, hypothyroidism, renal salt wasting, and enteral tube feeding. Psychogenic polydipsia is uncommon in older persons.

VI. PREVENTION OF DEHYDRATION

Identification and correction of risk factors are a crucial aspect of management of dehydration in older

Table IV Causes of Hyponatremia

Sodium depletion
- Renal, gastric, or cutaneous sodium losses

Sodium and water overload
- Congestive cardiac failure
- Liver cirrhosis
- Nephrotic syndrome
- Hypoproteinemic states
- Hypotonic intravenous infusions

Pure water overload
- Syndrome of inappropriate antidiuretic hormone secretion
- Renal failure
- Psychogenic polydipsia

Miscellaneous
- Hypothyroidism
- Addison's disease
- Sick cell syndrome

Table V Causes of Inappropriate ADH (AVP) Secretion[a]

Pulmonary disease
- Pneumonia
- Chronic obstructive pulmonary disease
- Bronchial asthma
- Pulmonary tuberculosis
- Positive pressure mechanical ventilation

Neurological disease
- Head injury
- Cerebrovascular disease
- Meningitis/encephalitis
- Cerebral tumors/aneurysms

Drugs
- Chlorpropamide
- Opiate derivatives
- Carbamazepine
- Phenothiazines
- Butyrophenones
- Tricyclic antidepressants
- Selective serotonin release inhibitors
- Antineoplastic and immunosuppressive agents

[a]ADH, antidiuretic hormone; AVP, arginine vasopressin.

persons. Within the institutionalized and homebound population, environmental barriers are a frequent cause of suboptimal hydration. Access to water should be a prime consideration in adapting the immediate environment of persons with restricted mobility. Physical restraints should be completely avoided. The use of sedatives and psychotropic agents should be strictly regulated as these may contribute to decreased thirst perception, confusion, and an altered level of consciousness. Persons with decreased functional status or reduced manual dexterity may require assistance with drinking or adaptive appliances. Affective disorders, cognitive impairment, and behavioral disorders significantly compromise voluntary fluid intake. Such persons therefore require constant monitoring and frequent prompting to ensure adequate fluid intake. Persons who exhibit poor motivation or a reduced desire for fluids may benefit from a fluid prescription regime to ensure regular fluid intake at intervals throughout the day.

Dehydration in older persons contributes notably to an increase in morbidity and mortality. Physicians, other health personnel, and caregivers involved in the care of older persons must be aware of the relevant predisposing factors. Recognition of risk factors followed by the institution of appropriate preventive measures and early interventions are vital to effective management.

BIBLIOGRAPHY

Davis, K. M., & Minaker, K. L. (1994). Disorders of fluid balance: Dehydration and hyponatremia. In R. W. Hazzard, E. L. Bierman, J. P. Blass, W. H. Ettinger, J. B. Halter, R. Andres (Eds.), *Principles of geriatric medicine and gerontology.* New York: McGraw-Hill, Inc.

Hoffman, B. H. (1991). Dehydration in the elderly: Insidious and manageable. *Geriatrics, 46,* 35–38.

Methany, N. M. (1992). *Fluid and electrolyte balance* (2nd ed.). Philadelphia: J. B Lippincott.

Phillips, P. A., Johnston, C. I., & Gray, L. (1993). Distributed fluid and electrolyte homeostasis following dehydration in elderly people. *Age and Ageing, 22,* 26–33.

Phillips, P. A., Johnston, C. I., & Gray, L. (1991). Thirst and fluid intake in the elderly. In D. J. Ramsay & D. A. Booth (Eds.), *Thirst: Physiology and Psychology.* Berlin: Springer-Verlag.

Silver, J. A. (1990). Aging and risks for dehydration. *Cleveland Clinic Journal of Medicine, 57,* 341–344.

Silver, J. A., Flood, J. F., & Morley, J. E. (1991). Effect of aging on fluid ingestion in mice. *Journal of Gerontology, 46,* B117–B121.

Silver, A. J., & Morley, J. E. (1992). Role of the opioid system in the hypodipsia associated with aging. *Journal of the American Geriatric Society, 40,* 556–560.

Time: Concepts and Perceptions

Johannes J. F. Schroots

University of Amsterdam

I. Physical Time
II. Biological Time
III. Psychological Time
IV. Social Time
V. Intrinsic Time

Biological Clock Generic term for biological processes that show periodic behavior and are clocklike in their rhythmicity.

Biological Time A species-dependent unit of physical time required to complete a species-independent biological event or process.

Physical Time Generic term for solar, calendar, clock, objective, historical, dialectical, and social time.

Social Clock Metaphor for the timing of social events and age-appropriate behavior.

Time Confound Interdependency of seemingly independent time parameters.

Time Perception Generic term for the experience of time, subjective judgment and/or the amount of elapsed time.

Time Perspective The totality of the individual's views of his psychological future and his psychological past existing at a given time.

TIME is a symbol for a connection made by a group of beings with the capacity for memory and synthesis between two or more continua of changes, one of which is used by them as a frame of reference or standard for measuring the other or others. Relations of time are therefore connections between at least three continua: between people who bring about connections and two continua of changes, to one of which they give the function of standard continuum, a frame of reference for the other. In modern society, physical time—also called solar, calendar or clock time—plays the role of standard continuum, a frame of reference for other continua of changes such as biological, psychological, and intrinsic time. In this context, social time is conceived as a tautology for physical time. In this article, distinctions between major concepts of time will be presented, as well as their corresponding clocks and age scales, to begin with physical time in relation to calendar (days, months, years), clock (hours, minutes, seconds), and chronological age.

I. PHYSICAL TIME

A. History

In Western antiquity time was conceived in two ways, as a cycle and as a line. *Cyclic* time is the oldest concept, as the image of the cycle best applies to natural phenomena like the revolution of the planets, the succession of the seasons, night and day, sleeping and waking, growth and decay. *Linear* time, however, is not a product of observables, it is an abstraction, developed successively by the Greek philosophers Pythagoras (the nature of things is number), Plato (time equals the number of revolutions of the planets), and by his pupil Aristotle (384–322 B.C.), which defined time as "number of motion in respect of before and after." In brief, the classical concept of time is as an aspect of motion that makes possible the enumeration of successive states linearly by dividing up cycles (of planets) into units. This concept lasted in science for almost twenty centuries when, at the end of the seventeenth century, it was displaced by physicist Sir Isaac Newton (1642–1727).

Newton conceived of time as something *absolute*, an immaterial, fixed property of the universe by which motion or change can be measured. Thus, in classical physics, time is an absolute standard or measuring scale. In this view time is not only *linear*, but also *reversible*, for nothing changes when t is replaced by $-t$ in physical equations. Because the Newtonian concept of time is not a product of the perceiving subject, absolute time is often called objective time. This concept has become equated more and more with its measure, the mechanical clock. Consequently, time has become transformed and reified into *objective, mechanical, calendar,* or *clock* time. Objective time is basic to seemingly different time variables, such as period or historical time, chronological or calendar age, cohort or time of birth, calendar time, and clock time. They all can be reduced to the same, basic concept of classical-physical time.

B. Concept of Physical Time

Newton's physical time does not have intrinsic direction; there is no difference between its past orientation $(t-)$ and its future orientation $(t+)$. This concept of time violates generally accepted natural laws. Natural phenomena are described by the second law of thermodynamics, which states that chaos or disorder will increase irreversibly with energetic processes. Thus, the direction of physical time is defined by the irreversible destruction of macroscopic order, or the increase of *entropy*. In twentieth-century physics, time is no longer reversible but irreversible, at least at the macroscopic level.

It should be noted that the modern concept of *physical* time as *linear* and *irreversible* did not change the conception of chronological age as additive, that is, a quantity that can be added, subtracted, multiplied, and divided regardless of the age of the organism. The implication is that all possible calendar ages of the organism are equal. For instance, the first 20 years of life are equal to the middle or last 20 years of life. This, however, makes sense only from a purely clock or calendar time perspective.

II. BIOLOGICAL TIME

A. Biological Clocks

Many biological processes show periodic behavior and are clocklike in their rhythmicity, in particular biological processes on a 24-hour basis, the so called *circadian* rhythms. These rhythms, as well as the progressive reification of time in terms of mechanical clocks, encouraged the search for biological instead of mechanical clocks. The major anatomical clock for numerous physiological (blood pressure, hormones, body temperature) and behavioral (attention, reaction time) processes with circadian variation has been located in the *suprachiasmatic nucleus* at the base of the brain. The circadian rhythm of this clock differs slightly from the earth's rotation cycle of 24 hours, and from one individual to another (e.g., 24.5 or 25.5 hour periods instead of 24 hour). Because the internal period deviates somewhat from 24 hours, it has to be reset daily to retain synchrony with the external light–dark cycle. This process is called *entrainment* or synchronization. In brief, daily synchronization is reached under the external influence of physical and social timers like the light–dark cycle and the well-structured 8-hour working day.

Another major class of so-called *metabolic* clocks is based on *energy transformations* or metabolically related processes and functions in the organism. Metabolic clocks are inferred from the rhythmic activity of, for example, heart, lungs, and intestines, on the basis of the allometric power law $M^{0.25}$. This law says that the length of time between consecutive heart beats increases as a linear function of about the 0.25 power of body mass (M) in mammals. The *basal metabolic rate* (BMR), or the time needed to process one joule per gram, also increases with $M^{0.25}$. Corrected for weight, all mammals use an equivalent amount of joules per heart beat, per generation, or per life span. This suggests that metabolic clocks, as time measures of numerous periodic phenomena in the human organism, are closely associated with the *rate of living*. Also, positive or negative events influence biological-periodic phenomena, modulate metabolic clock rate, and thereby increase or decrease the rate of living within limits.

Using the clock metaphor, the human organism can be viewed as a clock shop with two master clocks—circadian and metabolic clocks—and many entrained slave clocks. Aging of the organism may involve *desynchronization* of the clock shop, in which the various master and slave clocks that are normally in synchrony are put out of phase; amplitude and period may be changed as well. There is more and more evidence for a strong relationship between the temporal organization of organisms with age and the occurrence of mortality and morbidity patterns (sleeping disorder, reduced thermoregulatory capacity, depression, and Alzheimer's disease). As such, measures of the degree of desynchronization in the elderly might function as predictors of nearness of death.

B. Concept of Biological Time

The individual human life might be viewed as governed by a single biological clock or individual life cycle with one period. The length of this period, that is, *length of life* or life span, reflects the rate of biological aging and is one of the most significant characteristics of biological time. Length-of-life as a variable, however, raises two serious problems. First, it is virtually impossible to construct a time scale for the measurement of biological time on the basis of a single clock with one period. To solve this problem, biologists have looked for an alternative length-of-life variable at the population level and have focused on the *probability of dying*. Second, biological time must be defined with reference to a specified biological process. The probability of dying is not a biological process but a statistical concept, and the length-of-life variable reflects at most an undetermined biological process.

Given the foregoing, biological time can be defined as a species-dependent unit of physical time required to complete a species-independent biological event or process. In other words, a biological timescale for a specified biological process can be constructed by transforming a chronological timescale so that the rate of change of the process becomes time-invariant in biological time. Recently, several physiologists have pointed out that the metabolism of the organism over the life span might be that biological process. It should be noted that *biological* time is not only *irreversible*, but also *nonlinearly* related to physical (objective) time or chronological (calendar, clock) time. Figure 1 shows how chronological and biological timescales might be related.

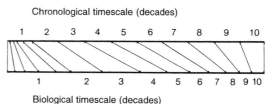

Figure I Schematic comparison of chronological and biological timescales. Much more biological activity (e.g., metabolic activity) can be packed into the first decades of biological time than into those of later life; hence the length of that part of the biological measuring rod appears to be longer in the early period of life than a comparable portion of the chronological measuring rod. At the other extreme of life the opposite relationship applies.

III. PSYCHOLOGICAL TIME

A. Time Perception

On a clock in Chester cathedral (U.K.) the following inscription can be read: "For when I was a babe and wept and slept, Time crept / When I was a boy and laughed and talked, Time walked / Then when the years saw me a man, Time ran / But as I older grew, Time flew." Put in this verse is the phenomenological view that time passes faster with age. This view refers to the perception, awareness and/or the experience of (the passage of) time. *Time perception* is used here as the generic term for the experience of time, subjective judgment and/or estimation of the duration of events or the amount of elapsed time. Since the publication of Paul Janet's study in 1877, several studies have sought to quantify the acceleration of time as a function of chronological age. Broadly speaking, three approaches can be distinguished.

First, classical psychophysical studies based on the metaphor of *temporal modality*. This metaphor implies a sensory receptor system for time, so that Weber's law can be put to the test for differences in duration between various time intervals. It has been suggested that subjective duration varies inversely with the square root of chronological age, but too many exceptions to the rule have been found in practice. In the final analysis, the psychophysical approach did not prove to be very productive.

Second, by analogy with biological clocks an *internal psychological clock* has been hypothesized. The slowing of this clock can occur with advanced age, decreased metabolic activity, lower body temperature, barbiturates, alcohol, and other drugs. External clock time by comparison seems to be going faster—time seems to fly like magic—and clock time will be underestimated. The reverse also holds: when a person's internal clock is going fast, then clock time by comparison seems to be going slow. This occurs when metabolic rate is increased, with higher body temperature (e.g., fever), and by the use of stimulants such as caffeine and psychedelic drugs. In general, the greater frequency of internal changes per unit of clock time makes clock time seem to be longer (and the other way around). The internal clock metaphor also explains to some degree why the days seem to pass slowly for children, but rush past faster and faster with increasing age: children have a slightly higher metabolic rate, and consequently a higher body temperature than the elderly.

Third, Ornstein introduced in 1969 the *temporal information-processing* approach in cognitive psychology, which relates the faster passage of time to the fact that with advancing age there are less novel events in life worthy of being stored in memory. For children, everything is new, whereas old age brings fewer surprises. The cognitive approach of time perception is a highly specialized area: models of time estimation are formulated in terms of event-related attributes rather than in terms of clocks, and the models used are only fit for the perception of brief durations in the 100 ms–10 s range.

Summarizing part of the results of both long-term and short-term memory research on the subjective experience of time, it might be said that unpleasant emotions are associated with a feeling of time urgency, making (external) clock time by comparison seem to pass slowly. During pleasant emotions, however, there is less time urgency and, therefore, clock time by comparison appears to go quickly.

B. Time Perspective

According to St. Augustine's *Confessions* (ca. 400) there are three times: a present of past things, a present of present things, and a present of future things. Together they form the basic elements of what has been called *time perspective*, which Kurt Lewin defined as the totality of the individual's views of his psychological future and his psychological past existing at a given time; in other words, the individual span of awareness extending into the past or future. This raises the question of the subjective duration of the present.

According to William James (1890), the *mental now*, classically known as the specious present, has a certain duration: It is no knife edge, but a saddle, with a certain breadth of its own on which one sits perched, and from which one looks in two directions into time. Some authors report 20–200 ms as minimum duration of the mental now, whereas others mention 4–7 s; the latter figures are more consistent with modern research data. Another characteristic of the individual present is its temporal *intentionality*; that is, the mental now is directed at the past, the private world of memories, as well as the future, with its individual expectations. How the past, present, and future temporal realms interrelate with one another can be stated as follows: Both past and future are hypothetical reconstructions interpreted from and bound together through the mental now. In other words, the psychological past and future are *constructions*, experienced as a series of presents.

In research on time perspective several dimensions of significance can be identified. The basic dimension of *time orientation* refers to the relative dominance of the past, present, and future in an individual's thinking. Most often dealt with is the dimension of *extension*, which is based on reported life events and their estimated ages of occurrence, which can be defined as the length of past, present, future, or total life time considered by the individual. In this context, the question arises whether the individual's future extension diminishes with advancing age. The answer on the basis of research evidence is that advancing age does not necessarily lead to a loss of futurity. The empirical studies of time perspective instead point to increasing individual differences with age as well as an increasing complexity of the individual's time perspective.

Finally, most research on time perspective is based on explicit reports or implicit expectations of (a) life events, and (b) their estimated ages of occurrence. This type of operationalization is notorious for methodological problems with the analysis, coding, and interpretation of the data, with the result that the outcomes of time perspective studies are difficult to replicate.

C. Concept of Psychological Time

Time perception and time perspective might be conceived as the two basic dimensions of psychological time, crossing each other in the mental now of the individual's temporal awareness. However, the concept of psychological time is extremely complex and embraces more than the temporal dimensions of perception and perspective. For example, *psychological time* might be simply defined—by analogy with biological time—as the unit of chronological time required to complete a psychological event. Next, this simple definition might be extended with the following characteristics or aspects: (a) psychological time may pass in a nonlinear fashion; (b) its flow may be perturbed by either internal or external influences; (c) it may become detached from the past, affirming persistence within the present; and (d) it may function in a manner unrelated to causality. To cut a long story short, a definition of psychological time can be given only in terms of temporal dimensions, characteristics, and/or aspects.

In the final analysis, however, the following conception of a psychological timescale comes closest to the ideal definition of psychological time, i.e., in which each psychological event has its own unique place on the absolute timescale of personal history and future, which defines a conscious present, a privileged now, but also beginnings and endings.

IV. SOCIAL TIME

A. Concept of Social Time

Concepts of physical, biological, and psychological time refer to corresponding timescales with specific features. It is difficult, perhaps even impossible, to delineate the features of a social timescale, which is identifiable with the concept of social time. Definitions, or even cues for possible definitions of social time, are not presented in the social sciences. At best, *social time* might be defined as the unit of chronological time required to complete a social event.

It should be noted that the term social time is used very frequently, but also improperly in social science.

What sociologists and other social scientists mean, if they refer to social time, is not essentially different from the calendar or clock time of social phenomena. In other words, the term social time, as well as the related term *dialectical time*, is simply another disguise of the basic concept of physical time.

B. Social Clocks

In the social sciences various age-related concepts have been introduced. Anthropologists were the first to introduce the concept of *age grading*. Age-graded systems are expressions of the fact that all societies divide time into socially relevant units, thus supposedly transforming calendar time into social time, although clustering rather than transforming calendar time into (chronological) age grades would be more to the point of the physical timescale used.

Another age-related concept is *age stratification*, i.e., chronological age strata function as an organizing principle in society. Because age-related roles may change under the influence of history-normative events, society will change as new birth cohorts replace older ones. The concept of age stratification emphasizes that there are significant variations in older people depending on the characteristics of their birth cohort. A second important feature of age stratification is the emphasis on the relations of cohorts within the age structure of society; this makes possible the analytical distinction between developmental age changes and cohort historical differences.

Age grading and age stratification lie at the root of the idea that every society has a system of *social expectations for age-appropriate behavior*, and that all members of that society internalize these expectations or so-called age norms as they grow up and move from one age stratum to the next. In brief, age norms constitute a script, timetable, calendar, or time schedule for the life course, and function therefore as social controls. In this context, social gerontologist Bernice Neugarten found widespread consensus regarding the timing of events, that is, the appropriate age when individuals are expected to go to school, to marry, to start a career, and so on. People know whether they are "on time" or "off time" as if they have a *social clock*; furthermore, they feel good about themselves when they are on time, but they feel bad if they have been either early or late.

The lack of fit between the individual timing of

events and social clocks is called desynchronization. In general, the greater the degree of individual temporal desynchronization, the greater will be the sense of stress. Recently, a *social entrainment model* has been developed, which emphasizes that various temporal rhythms underlie a wide range of social behavior and that synchronizations among them (or the lack of such synchronizations) have widespread and crucial implications for human cognition, social interaction, task performance, and role behavior, and therefore for human health and well-being. The basis for the model lies in the notion of *entrainment* as introduced in the section on biological clocks. Viewed from a social perspective, entraining cycles correspond with Neugarten's social clocks or prescriptive timetables, for example, but they may also refer to conversational behavior, group interaction, or task performance. Summarizing, the social entrainment model provides a framework for describing the operation of biological, psychological, and social clocks, their coupling to one another and potentially to outside pacers (signals), and the temporal patterns of behavior resulting from these clocks and rhythms of human behavior.

C. Time Confounds

The concepts of age grading, age norms, age strata, social clocks, and social time are all aspects of the same timescale, calendar time, or physical time, of which chronological age (or calendar age) is still the most popular, though much abused, index. Chronological age is usually introduced in developmental and aging research as an *independent* or *explanatory variable*. However, chronological age does not have much explanatory power by itself, which is not surprising after all, as both independent and dependent variables are expressed in terms of the same calendar time, the source of most time confounds. Precisely because of the problem of confounded time parameters, K. Warner Schaie proposed in 1965 a *general developmental model* with three interdependent, objective time parameters. This so-called *APC model* is based on the formula that Age = Period (or time-of-measurement) − Cohort (birth), and has served to separate statistically age, period, and cohort effects. However, regardless of how data are collected, there is a triple confound. In later studies it has been noted that the triangular confound is not unique to developmental or aging research, but even more important is the

observation that a strictly statistical solution to the APC problem, or any other triangular confound for that matter, is not possible.

A radical solution to the problem of time confounds is to get rid of time itself by redefining its meaning. In research practice, psychological and social phenomena are inferred from the calendar or clock. By identifying the meaning attributed to various time parameters, it should be possible to unlock some of the confounds. Recently, Schaie made an attempt to solve the APC problem by conceptually separating historical time (time-of-measurement or period) and cohort effects from calendar time. Essentially, he redefined cohort as a selection variable that characterizes the common point of entry for a group of individuals into a given environment. Period, on the other hand, is translated into a measure of event density. Thus Schaie is able to remove calendar age as a confound for cohort or period.

V. INTRINSIC TIME

A. Age Scales

James E. Birren has repeatedly observed that chronological age or the elapsed physical time in days, months, and years since birth is one of the most useful single items of information about an individual if not the most useful. Nevertheless, the useful, though rough index of *chronological age* is not very sensitive to individual differences. For that reason, Birren introduced three new age scales and contrasted them to chronological age. The first scale, *biological age*, can be defined as an estimate of the individual's present position with respect to his or her potential life span. Such a measure of biological age should be able to predict the residual life span of the individual with a smaller error than that based on chronological age alone. The second scale, *psychological age*, refers to the age-related adaptive capacities of the individual, such as perception, learning, and memory. Just as one may be older or younger than one's chronological age in a biological sense, one may also be older or younger psychologically. Presumably, a measure of psychological age would correlate highly with chronological age and also with environment. The third scale, *social age*, refers to acquired social habits and status, to the individual's filling the many social roles or expectancies of a person of his or her age in his or her culture and social group. An individual may be older or younger depending on the extent to which he or she shows the age-graded behavior expected by a particular society or culture. A measure of social age presumably would also be related to chronological age, somewhat to psychological age, and to a lesser degree to biological age.

Due to its popularity in industrial organizations, as well as its close affinity to biological, psychological, and social age scales, the functional age scale needs to be explained. *Functional age* can be defined as a dimension in which individuals could be younger or older than their chronological years in their ability to adapt to their environments. The individual's level of capacities for daily life functioning in society could be compared to other individuals of the same age by a series of measurements comprising operationalizations of biological, psychological, and social ages, respectively. Functional age scales have been severely critiqued for several reasons. First, there are different meanings of the terms *function* or *functional*, as they refer alternately to occupational functional age, biomedical functional age, or to the structural organization of human functioning. Second, functional age researchers vary to the extent that they hypothesize a unitary aging process on the one hand, or prefer to assume multiple aging processes and various combinations of variables, each of which may be optimally employed for different situations or against different criteria. Third, two criteria have been put forward: chronological age and length of life (residual life span). The most common approach is to employ multiple-regression techniques to predict chronological age or length of life. If the ultimate criterion is chronological age, then the functional age measure does not make much sense as chronological age can be assessed much easier (just ask for it). The second criterion, length of life, residual life span, or the person's time until death is more promising, although no conclusive studies have been conducted yet. For the time being, chronological age is the best general index to the residual life span of healthy individuals.

B. Concept of Intrinsic Time

In the foregoing discussion various concepts of time and age have been introduced from a physical, biological, psychological, and social perspective. The ques-

tion arises whether these different concepts can be integrated in a general concept of time and age, valid for all (levels of) living systems. A tentative answer has been given by theoretical biologist Robert Rosen who assumed that any given dynamics of any system will generate its own intrinsic time; that is, *intrinsic time* is created by physical, biological, psychological, or social processes as an emergent property of their *nonlinear dynamics* (energy transformations). In plain words, intrinsic time depends on the number of transformations or changes, intrinsic to the dynamics of the system. As such, intrinsic time is a *dependent variable*.

From the above it follows that intrinsic time is scaled by the system from which it emerges. As any dynamic process can serve as a clock, intrinsic time is measured by monitoring one of the state variables undergoing change. The dimensional unit of this intrinsic time is simply the unit of the state variable chosen for observation. For example, consider the primitive clock made by notching a candle at 1-inch intervals along its length. With a fresh candle as the initial condition, time is given as the length L of candle burned. The unit of time intrinsic to this particular dynamical system is inches. Mathematically this is expressed by $t = L$, where t is intrinsic time. This time is well defined and will serve for many purposes. However, it is particular and intrinsic—and thus is absolute. A metric is needed to calculate the relative relationship of the intrinsic times of two candles having different constitutive parameters. Such comparisons are made by the promotion of one time-keeping device to the status of the standard clock with clock time t.

Rosen has developed an *entropic time metric*, based on the second law of thermodynamics, which states that there is an increase of entropy in energetic systems (entropy is defined here as the degree to which relationships between the components of any system are mixed up, undifferentiated, or random). The entropic time metric scales the passage of intrinsic time to standard clock time. Given this metric, the *intrinsic age* of any system might be assessed. Intrinsic age as an intrinsic, directed measure of the state of a particular system should be distinguished from chronological age, which is extrinsic, universal, and reversible. For instance, two systems are in temporal corresponding states, that is, at the same intrinsic age, at equal instants of intrinsic time. However, although they are at the same intrinsic age, they may have traversed different periods of extrinsic clock time and are, then, of different chronological age.

C. Intrinsic Age Scales

Generally speaking, the transformation rules between intrinsic time and other times (biological, psychological, and social) are not known. However, in biological systems the entropic time metric is probably associated with the metabolism of the organism, which relates to entropy production. Given the known relationship between total rate of change of entropy or metabolic rate of an individual and his or her chronological age, it is feasible to define a metabolic or *intrinsic biological age* scale for human subjects. The definition of an intrinsic age scale at the psychological system level is less obvious, but nevertheless feasible. To start with, all psychological events should be formulated in entropic terms. Normally speaking, psychological events are formulated in informational terms. Given however the concept of *negentropy*, which is a measure of negative entropy or information, it should be possible to compute the *intrinsic psychological age* of individuals by feeding the external entropy flow rate, as calculated from informational data, into the entropy equation for living systems. Similarly, the *intrinsic social age* of social systems might be computed, based on Bailey's social entropy theory. By means of these three intrinsic age scales, it should no longer be difficult to develop an *intrinsic functional age* scale for human individuals, which is (a) a better predictor of length of life than chronological age, and (b) replaces chronological age as independent and dependent variable.

BIBLIOGRAPHY

Boxenbaum, H. (1986). Time concepts in physics, biology and pharmacokinetics. *Journal of Pharmaceutical Sciences, 75,* 1053–1062.

Fraser, J. T. (1987). *Time, the familiar stranger.* Amhurst: University of Massachusetts Press.

McGrath, J. E., & Kelly, J. R. (1986). *Time and human interaction: Toward a social psychology of time.* New York: Guilford.

Michon, J. A., & Jackson, J. L. (Eds.). (1985). *Time, mind and behavior.* Berlin: Springer Verlag.

Ornstein, R. E. (1969). *On the experience of time.* New York: Penguin.

Richardson, I. W., & Rosen, R. (1979). Aging and the metrics of time. *Journal of Theoretical Biology, 79,* 415–423.

Schroots, J. J. F., & Birren, J. E. (1990). Concepts of time and aging in science. In J. E. Birren & K. W. Schaie (Eds.), *Handbook of the psychology of aging* (3rd ed.) (pp. 45–64). San Diego: Academic Press.

Touch and Proprioception

Janet M. Weisenberger

Ohio State University

I. Touch
II. Proprioception
III. Summary

Cutaneous Term used in reference to receptors and stimulation that produce sensations of touch or pressure.

Glabrous Skin Hairless skin found on the palms of the hands and the soles of the feet.

Kinesthesia Term used to describe sense of movement of limbs.

Mechanoreceptor Cutaneous receptor that mediates aspects of touch or pressure sensations.

Nociceptor Cutaneous receptor that mediates pain sensitivity.

Proprioception Term used to describe sense of the position of limbs in space.

Somatosensory Term used to describe the receptors, afferent pathways, and cortical areas devoted to the senses of touch, temperature, and pain.

Thermoreceptor Cutaneous receptor that mediates temperature sensitivity.

The sense of **TOUCH** is the encompassing term for a complex variety of sensations, including pressure, arising from mechanical deformation of the skin surface; temperature, arising from thermal stimulation of the skin; and pain, arising from potentially damaging application of mechanical, thermal, chemical, or electrical stimulation. Considered by many researchers as a separate sense is **PROPRIOCEPTION**, the awareness of the position and movement of body and limbs in space. Both of these "senses" are mediated by a number of physiological receptive structures and central pathways, and both can be influenced by inputs from other sensory modalities, such as the visual and vestibular systems. And, like other sensory systems, the senses of touch and proprioception are vulnerable to the effects of aging. This chapter summarizes the state of knowledge in the psychophysics and physiology of touch and proprioception, together with research on how these senses change in aging individuals.

I. TOUCH

A. Physiology

The skin surface constitutes the largest sensory organ in the body, with a surface area of some 1.7 m^2 in the adult. The skin actually consists of numerous layers of tissue, which can be divided into two main sections, the epidermis, or outer layer, and the dermis, or inner layer. On the body surface are three kinds of skin: hairy skin, characterized by the presence of hair; glabrous skin, a hairless surface found on the palm and sole; and mucocutaneous skin, found at the entrance to various body cavities at the junction with mucous membrane. Although these skin types differ in the density and distribution of sensory receptors they contain, there are some general features that characterize most areas.

There are a number of structures believed to serve as receptors for transducing tactile stimulation. Variations in the density and distribution of receptors at different body sites influence responsiveness to a stimulus. For sensations of touch, pressure, and vibration,

Copyright © 1996 by Academic Press, Inc.
All rights of reproduction in any form reserved.

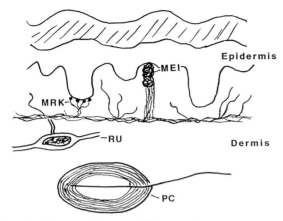

Figure 1 Schematic drawings of four mechanoreceptors. Shown are the Pacinian corpuscle (PC), Meissner corpuscle (MEI), Merkel disk (MRK), and Ruffini cylinder (RU).

four different structures have been investigated as putative mechanoreceptors. These include the Pacinian corpuscle (PC), Meissner corpuscle (MEI), Merkel disk (MRK), and Ruffini cylinder (RU), all shown in Figure 1. It should be noted that in many cases the structure of these receptors makes it difficult to record activity directly at the receptor; instead, the probable role of a mechanoreceptive structure is inferred from activity measured in primary afferent fibers innervating the structure. Recent studies have addressed the relationship between end receptor and primary afferent response via microneurography, a technique in which activity is recorded by percutaneous microelectrodes from primary afferent fibers in awake human subjects, who can report sensations based on stimuli delivered to the skin at the same time as afferent activity is measured. This technique permits some confidence in assigning mechanoreceptive roles to particular cutaneous end organs.

The primary afferent responses measured for mechanical indentation are of two types: (a) slowly adapting (SA), indicating a response at stimulus onset that continues for the duration of the stimulation; and (b) rapidly adapting (RA), indicating a vigorous onset response, and perhaps an offset response, but no sustained response to a prolonged stimulus. Each of these two types of afferent response can be subdivided, based on the size of the receptive field (skin surface area) that excites a particular afferent fiber. Thus, afferent responses fall into four categories: SA types I and II, and RA types I and II.

The relationship between afferent response and end organ is best understood for the PC. The PC is a relatively large receptor, which in the adult has numerous layers (lamellae) that produce an onion-like appearance. PCs are located rather deep in the dermis, as well as in joints. Each PC is innervated by a single afferent, and thus it is straightforward to assume that transduction for a fiber takes place at the PC at the fiber's termination. Based on this relationship, it has been determined that the PC is RA and has a large receptive field. The distribution and placement of MEI, located at the junction of epidermis and dermis in the dermal papillae, suggests that they serve as the other RA mechanoreceptor. MEI are surrounded by an elastic capsule that is attached to the epidermis above and to the dermis below, and are supplied by 2–6 afferent fibers. Receptive field size for the MEI is small, particularly in comparison to the large field of the PC. Identification of the mechanoreceptors for the two SA fiber types is even more tentative. However, likely candidates for these endings are the MRK for the small receptive-field SA I fibers, and the RU for the larger receptive field SA II fibers. The MRK is a disk-shaped terminal located on certain basal epidermal cells, and the RU is a spindle-shaped capsule-like structure found in the upper layers of the dermis, although in many cases it is considered too loosely organized to reflect true encapsulation. Although these pairings are presently rather speculative, advances in microrecording techniques should permit more certain identification in the future.

The situation for thermoreceptors is even less certain than that for mechanoreceptors. A variety of receptive structures at various levels in the skin show a response to thermal stimulation; however, many of these also respond to other kinds of stimulation, such as mechanical. For example, the response of the PC is quite affected by changes in skin temperature, but the PC is thought to be primarily mechanoreceptive in function, rather than thermoreceptive. Some researchers have suggested a role for the Krause end bulb, but others have been less willing to speculate about the identity of individual thermoreceptors. As for the mechanoreceptors, the main source of information about the system has been the response profiles of individual primary afferent fibers, which appear to change their firing rates in response to either temperature increases, or temperature decreases, but not both. Thus, one can speak of "cold" fibers and "warm" fibers. Some mechanoreceptors, as mentioned, modulate their response behavior in the face of temperature changes, but are not primarily considered to be thermoreceptors.

For sensations of pain, there appear to be several classes of receptors responding to excessive heat, excessive cold, or extreme mechanical deformation. Some also respond in the presence of chemical irritation. The fibers delivering information about noxious stimulation appear to terminate in free nerve endings scattered throughout the epidermis and dermis. A common feature of the pain receptors, or nociceptors, is their high thresholds for stimulation. In the case of pressure, the threshold for a pain receptor may be as much as 1000 times the displacement needed to detect pressure for a low-threshold mechanoreceptor. Similarly, thermal nociceptors may have thresholds of 45°C or higher for heat, or 15°C or lower for cold. Overall, it appears that the stimulus for these nociceptors must be intense enough to cause actual or potential damage to skin tissues. [See PAIN AND PRESBYALGOS.]

All of these receptors, whether mechanical, thermal, or pain, pass information via primary afferent fibers from the periphery to more central structures via the spinal cord. Cell bodies for these afferents are located in the dorsal root ganglia. Within the spinal cord, a functional division of fibers takes place, with larger-diameter fibers (carrying mainly mechanoreceptive information) forming the lemniscal bundle, and smaller-diameter fibers (carrying mainly thermoreceptive and nociceptive information) forming the spinothalamic bundle. The lemniscal fibers ascend to the medulla, where they cross to the contralateral side before continuing on to the ventral posterolateral nucleus of the thalamus. Projection from the thalamus terminates in the somatosensory cortex, located in the parietal lobe of the brain on the postcentral gyrus. Representation of different areas of the body in somatosensory cortex is *somatotopic*, that is, different parts of cortex are devoted to inputs from particular areas of the body. It is important to note that sensations of touch or pressure are mediated by cortical areas on the side of the brain opposite to the side of the body on which they occur, in contrast to projections from the visual and auditory systems, which are both ipsilateral and contralateral. In the spinothalamic pathway, neurons actually cross contralaterally while still in the spinal cord, synapsing in the dorsal horn, and ascend to the ventrobasal portions of the thalamus, from which they project to somatosensory cortex. The cortex itself is organized into two general areas, SI and SII, both of which may contain complete representations of all body areas.

B. Psychophysics

In characterizing the response of the tactile system to input stimuli, it is important to understand the impact of changes in various parameters of the physical stimulus, specifically, changes in spatial, intensive, and temporal aspects. In this section research into these stimulus aspects is summarized.

Spatial sensitivity in touch has been studied rather extensively, primarily using techniques such as two-point discrimination (in which the observer determines whether one or two points have touched the skin, at different point separations) and error of localization (in which the observer indicates the place where the skin was touched). More recently, tactile acuity for grating stimuli with varying separations impressed onto the skin has been measured. These measurements indicate that spatial acuity for tactile stimuli varies substantially across body sites. Areas such as the fingertips, tongue, and lips show excellent spatial sensitivity, whereas areas such as the abdomen and back are far less acute. At the fingertip, stimuli separated by as little as 0.5 mm can be discriminated, whereas on the abdomen, resolution is closer to 40 mm. Recent research has pointed to the MRK as the primary receptor for spatial sensitivity, based on its distribution across body sites. The MRK is most numerous at sites having the greatest spatial acuity. A secondary role in spatial sensitivity may be played by the MEI, which is also relatively dense in highly sensitive areas. Both of these receptors evidence small receptive fields, making them good candidates for spatial acuity mediation.

For the slowly-adapting mechanoreceptive channels, SA I and SA II, punctate indentation is an adequate stimulus for excitation. However, to obtain consistent responding from the PC and RA channels, simple pressure is not sufficient. For these channels, it is necessary to provide a stimulus that has repeated onsets and offsets; vibration has proved to be an ideal stimulus for this purpose. The tactile response to vibration has been extensively investigated, and it has been determined that response to vibration in different

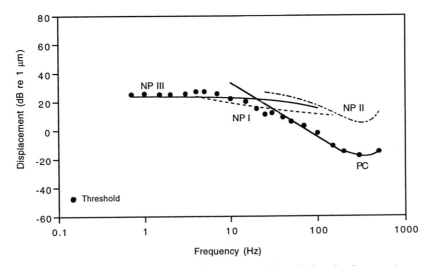

Figure 2 Threshold for detection of a vibratory stimulus applied to the thenar eminence (palm), for different frequencies of vibration. PC, Pacinian corpuscle; NP, non-Pacinian. (From Bolanowski, S. J., Gescheider, G. A., Verrillo, R. T., and Checkosky, C. M., 1988. Four channels mediate the mechanical aspects of touch. *Journal of the Acoustical Society of America, 84,* 1680–1694.)

frequency ranges is most likely mediated by different mechanoreceptors. Figure 2 shows tactile sensitivity to vibration, as a function of vibration frequency. Current models of vibrotactile response postulate that the PC is responsible for the U-shaped portion of this curve, covering frequencies above about 40 Hz. Maximum sensitivity to vibration is seen at around 250 Hz. Threshold measures in the middle-frequency range (from about 10–40 Hz) are thought to be mediated by the MEI (labeled NP I, or non-Pacinian I on the figure). The lowest frequency portion, labeled NP III, is assumed to be the MRK, and the high-frequency, high-amplitude curve labeled NP II may be the RU, serving the SA II afferent fibers.

Measures of intensity response indicate that the tactile system has a dynamic range, or range between threshold and uncomfortable stimulation, of 40–50 dB. Current physiological studies suggest that firing rate in the primary afferents may be the primary code for intensity perception. Temporal sensitivity measures produce varied results, depending on the task employed. In the best case, temporal resolution on the order of 3–5 ms has been observed.

In response to thermal stimulation, the tactile system again shows variation in sensitivity depending on the area and location stimulated. In measuring

temperature sensitivity, the typical task involves detecting a change in the temperature of an area of skin from its previous temperature. Under the best circumstances, changes in skin temperature of as little as 0.003°C have been measured. The detection of a temperature change, however, depends on the initial temperature of the skin. Over a range of temperatures, between approximately 28 and 37°C, the body adapts to the skin's temperature, such that it is perceived to be neutral. This neutrality is referred to as "physiological zero." Thus, detection of temperature changes from an initial neutral point may vary considerably, depending on the neutral temperature.

Measurement of pain responsiveness is much more complex. Individuals vary widely in their sensitivity to pain, as well as in their willingness to report it. In addition, pain produced by stimulation in the laboratory ("laboratory pain") evokes a very different response from pain produced by disease or injury ("clinical pain"). Furthermore, long-term or chronic pain may be perceived very differently from short-term or acute pain. The additional factors involved may be psychological, in that pain has emotional or affective components of anxiety, unpleasantness, or depression. Furthermore, if the pain results from a serious illness or injury that debilitates physical condition, the response to it may be different from short-term pain experienced by a healthy individual. One current theory of pain perception posits three aspects of pain: sensory or discriminative, motivational or affective, and cognitive or evaluative. As a result, the measurement of pain requires considerable resourcefulness on the part of the researcher. One technique that has yielded promising results in the evaluation of pain perception is signal-detection analysis, in which it is possible to separate sensitivity effects from response bias effects. Other approaches often focus on adjectival scales and questionnaires to get information about pain perception beyond simple detection. These scales involve sets of adjectives that fall into sensory, affective, and evaluative categories.

C. Changes in Tactile Response over the Life Span

The most comprehensive study of the effects of aging on peripheral receptor anatomy was that of Cauna in 1965, who examined changes across the entire life span in a group of some 200 persons ranging in age from birth to 95 years. He reported observations for PC, MEI, MRK, and free nerve endings.

PCs, according to this report, begin development in the fourth fetal month, and are fully formed before birth. In infants, PCs are numerous and oval in shape, with a length of 500–700 μm. During the course of life, the number of PCs decreases steadily, and the receptors themselves change in size and appearance. Increases in size with age are accompanied by the addition of lamellae, or layers, that give the corpuscle an irregular shape and an onion-like appearance. The spaces between lamellae contain collagen, free cells, and blood vessels. The result of these added lamellae is the extension of the axon's myelin sheath inside the cell. The receptor segment of the nerve fiber also increases in length. By late in life, there are far fewer PCs than were present in the infant or even the young adult, and those that remain are large and irregular in shape.

The MEIs, which are found in the dermal papillae, have a spherical shape in the infant, and are some 25 μm in diameter. In young children they are relatively numerous, with a density of up to 70 per mm^2, and begin to assume a cylindrical shape, with a firm attachment to the epidermis. At this point in life, the nerve endings are neurofibrillar networks. In young adults

who do not engage in heavy manual work, these networks are maintained. However, in individuals with a history of manual labor, the nerve endings develop into long, winding terminals of much larger diameter. With aging, the epidermal attachment is reduced, and the corpuscles take on a radically different appearance. Continued longitudinal growth over the life span results in a coiling of the receptor and a disarrangement of the nerve endings. Taking all coils into account, an individual MEI can reach a length of up to 1 mm. These changes are easily observable by middle age. With advanced age, some corpuscles undergo atrophy and are lost, with density reports as low as 4 per mm^2. Up to 90% of MEI receptors can be lost in very old individuals. The remaining corpuscles show terminal nerve fibers that branch repeatedly, producing long, winding filaments with an irregular organization. It is possible that this ramification of nerve fibers is the result of inactivity in old age.

MRKs are also very numerous during late fetal life and can cover almost the entire epidermal undersurface. In infants, they become restricted to the undersurface of the intermediate ridge of glabrous skin. MRKs undergo relatively little change in structure over the course of life, remaining relatively densely distributed even in old age. However, some disks can enlarge in an uneven fashion, resulting in an altered appearance compared to the circular disk shape of infancy and young adulthood.

The free nerve endings, arising from medium-size myelinated fibers, undergo the least change over the life span. In elderly individuals, their appearance, number, and distribution are very similar to that of younger persons. However, changes in psychophysical measures thought to be mediated by free nerve endings do show some changes with aging, so the lack of obvious difference in appearance may not indicate functional changes in the activity of free nerve endings with age.

Psychophysical studies of tactile response as a function of age have not been pursued as actively as might be desired; thus, there is still a considerable amount of research needed to specify in detail the changes in tactile function with aging. Early reports indicated a decrease in sensitivity to light touch with increasing age. More recently, a series of studies has focused on changes in vibrotactile sensitivity across the life span. Measurements of vibratory threshold indicate a systematic decrease in sensitivity with age, starting quite

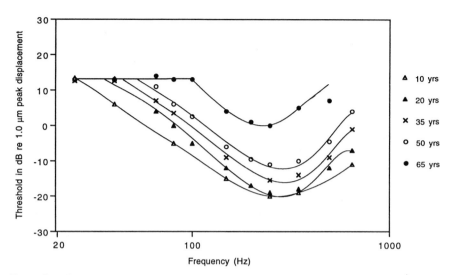

Figure 3 Changes in threshold detection of vibration, across age groups. (From Verrillo, R. T., 1979. Change in vibrotactile thresholds as a function of age. *Sensory Processes, 3,* 49–59.)

early in life. Elevations in threshold have been observed even between 10- and 20-year olds, in both longitudinal and cross-sectional studies. By the age of 65, thresholds at 250 Hz, the frequency at which the tactile system is most sensitive, can change by as much as 20–25 dB. Figure 3 shows the systematic change in vibrotactile thresholds by decade. As can be seen, the greatest loss of sensitivity occurs for higher frequencies, which are thought to be mediated by the PC. As mentioned, PCs decrease substantially in number in aging individuals, and those remaining assume a large and irregular shape. The loss of PCs most likely underlies the changes in vibrotactile sensitivity that are observed for frequencies above 40 Hz. At first it was believed that there was not a similar elevation in threshold with age in the lower frequency range, but recent results suggest that sensitivity also declines for these frequencies, just not as dramatically as for the higher frequencies. An additional consideration here is the fact that PCs have been shown to modify their response when skin temperature is altered. PCs show maximum sensitivity at fairly warm temperatures and have elevated detection thresholds when skin is cooled. Many aging individuals have lower body temperatures, and it is possible that this could affect the response of the remaining PC population. The MEI corpuscle does not show great sensitivity to temperature variation, however.

A number of hypotheses have been proposed to account for decreased sensitivity to vibration with aging. In addition to changes in the number of receptors, as mentioned above, other possibilities include altered receptor morphology, decreases in the number of spinal root fibers, dietary deficiencies in older persons, decreases in circulation, decreases in nerve conduction velocity, and general changes in the aging nervous system.

Magnitude estimation of the perceived loudness of suprathreshold vibratory stimuli indicates that older individuals have simply shifted their entire dynamic range (i.e., both threshold and suprathreshold stimuli are perceived less acutely). Although results are mixed, it is generally believed that most individuals do not exhibit a phenomenon similar to that of auditory "recruitment," in which the dynamic range of the system is much smaller than would be predicted based on the threshold elevation.

Temporal resolution is also affected by aging. Measures of persistence, which is the duration over which a stimulus has an effect on perception, are longer in older persons. This result has been interpreted as indicating that the activity of aging neurons to a stimulus lasts longer than for neurons in younger persons. This result is supported by data from studies of temporal masking, a paradigm in which a previously presented stimulus interferes with the detection of another, target stimulus (forward masking), or in which a stimulus presented after the target interferes with target detection (backward masking). Both kinds of temporal masking are greater in older persons, again suggesting greater persistence of neural activity in response to both the target and masking stimuli. This effect, like those of detection, is more pronounced at high frequencies.

Far less is known about changes in sensitivity to temperature with aging. Some studies have shown changes in the ability to detect a thermal stimulus, but others have not. One report indicates a decrease in the ability to distinguish between two temperatures in older persons, but overall, results are inconclusive. It is possible that differences in stimulus delivery methods, or in subject criterion, may have great effects on the obtained measures. For example, one study reported that older subjects were poorer at detecting a radiant-heat stimulus than younger subjects. The radiant stimulus does not actually touch the skin surface, eliminating mechanoreceptive cues that might be used by older persons to supplement thermal perception per se. Criterion effects are a consideration in all studies of older persons. Results from a variety of studies indicate that old persons tend to set a very conservative response criterion, and are reluctant to report the presence of a stimulus until they are very sure that it is there. This tendency could lead to the assumption that older persons simply have reduced sensitivity to the stimulus.

In measurements of pain sensitivity, two types of tasks have been evaluated: detection of onset of a painful stimulus, and the tolerance limit for pain. In older subjects, threshold for detecting the onset of a painful stimulus is not particularly affected by age, but mixed results are obtained in studies of tolerance limits for pain. In fact, some studies show that older persons are more tolerant of pain, and others show that older persons are less tolerant of pain. Furthermore, there are some indications that the effectiveness of analgesic drugs is greater in older persons. As mentioned, pain sensitivity is postulated to be controlled by free nerve endings, which do not show great changes in either number or morphology with age. Thus, the lack of difference in the detection of pain onset between older and younger persons is not surprising. The mixed findings regarding tolerance for pain are most likely affected by the same emotional and cognitive considerations as are inherent in any pain research, and at present no definitive statement about pain sensitivity and aging can be made.

II. PROPRIOCEPTION

A. Physiology

Sensations generated by the body that give rise to a knowledge of the location and movement of limbs in space are the province of proprioception. Technically, the appropriate term for the sensation of movement is *kinesthesia*, whereas proprioception is reserved for the knowledge of static limb position. In practice, however, researchers use the two terms interchangeably. Sensations of body location and movement are mediated by specialized sensory receptors, that convey information about joint angles, muscle length, muscle tension, and the rate at which each of these changes during movement. Historically, the physiologist Sherrington referred to proprioception as "muscle sense."

Over the years, researchers in kinesthesis have ascribed to differing notions of which receptors actually provide the necessary information. At various times, the field has held that the crucial receptors are in the muscles, or in the joints, or both, or neither. The current position is that the most important receptors are indeed located in the muscles, with joint receptors playing a minor part.

In considering the information that is provided to the central nervous system from the receptors, two classes of input would be required for accurate sensing. First, information about the position of limbs, or their displacement, could be coded in joint angle. Second, movement cues could be coded in transient responses signaling rate or acceleration.

Possible receptors that have been examined as participants in the coding of kinesthetic or proprioceptive information have included mechanoreceptors in the skin, receptors in the ligaments or capsules of the joints, and receptors in muscle. In skin, the RU, which has been implicated in the SA II mechanoreceptive response, seems to respond also to skin stretch, and to change its discharge rate in response to changes in joint position. However, RU density in most areas of skin is not great enough to provide detailed information about position, and activation of RUs in isolation does not produce any conscious sensation of position or movement. It is possible that they do contribute to position sense, but perhaps only in conjunction with other receptors. Furthermore, they may play a more important role at body sites that have a high density of RU innervation, such as the tongue or fingers. Studies where topical anesthetic has inactivated mechanoreceptor response in the fingers indicate that movement of the affected areas is also inhibited. This result suggests that the mechanoreceptors may contribute to kinesthetic sensibility, but only at certain body sites, since in some areas (e.g., the knee), topical anesthesia does not inhibit movement or kinesthetic awareness. An additional consideration is that tactile input from pressure mechanoreceptors, such as the MRK, can enhance the sense of position of a body part. For example, placing the fingertips on a table improves the salience of perceived location of the fingertips.

In the joints, ligament and capsule structures are well innervated with SA mechanoreceptors that show responses to stretch of the joint or to stretching or bending of the capsule. In ligaments, Golgi-type endings, which have a dense branching of nerve terminals, show a strong response to stretch when stimulated in isolation. However, in the intact preparation, these endings tend to fire only at the extremes of movement, rather than to any movement. This tendency has led researchers to postulate that the Golgi joint receptors may serve a protective function, to indicate when a limb has been moved too far. In the capsule, SA responses from Ruffini receptors occur to stretching or bending, and could signal some aspects of joint position. It should be noted that local anesthesia of joint receptors, delivered by injection, does not impair the performance of motor tasks.

In muscles, there are two candidate receptors for proprioceptive sensation. First, the Golgi tendon organ, which is a thinly encapsulated bundle of fascicles with a spindle-like shape, may signal information about muscle tension. This receptor is shown in Figure 4. Because the Golgi tendon has low compliance, it could in fact respond to muscle tension. It is clear that this information is of great importance for regulating muscle contraction, but not as clear that it signals position per se. However, it is possible that muscle tension information is fed to other receptors, to correct their position judgments.

The most likely candidate receptor for mediation of kinesthetic and proprioceptive sensation is the muscle spindle receptor, also shown in Figure 4. Muscle spindles consist of a bundle of 2–12 intrafusal muscle fibers in a fluid-filled capsule. These spindles receive both sensory and motor innervation, and in fact a substantial amount of motor control outflow from

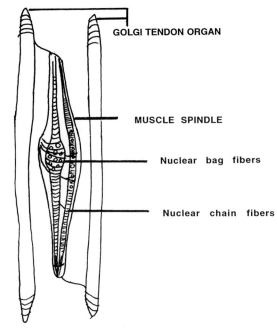

Figure 4 Schematic drawings of muscle receptors involved in proprioception, the Golgi tendon organ and the muscle spindle.

the CNS is directed to the muscle spindles, for regulation of muscle contraction. The number of spindles found in a muscle varies greatly, depending on the size of the muscle, from 4 or 5 spindles to over 500. Smaller muscles show a greater density of spindles. These spindles lie parallel to the main, or extrafusal, fibers. There are two kinds of intrafusal spindle fibers: the nuclear bag and nuclear chain fibers, distinguished by the arrangement of cellular nuclei. Sensory innervation of these spindles terminates in the center region, and stretch here activates potentials in the receptor endings. Contraction of the end regions of the muscle spindles changes the sensory function of the fiber but does not appear to add to overall muscle tension. Instead, these changes are used to signal length and rate of change of length information to the CNS. Two different kinds of spindle endings have been discriminated. These include primary endings, located at the middle of the spindle, and secondary endings, located just off the middle. The primary endings show strong responses to velocity of movement, as well as to muscle length, suggesting that they can signal both position and movement. Secondary endings, on the other hand, provide primarily length responses. For both, the optimal stimulus falls between 0.1 and 2 Hz; it is important to note that few voluntary movements occur at rates higher than this. The fact that primary fibers show a temperature dependence in their responses but the secondary fibers do not, and that the secondary fiber firing rate is dependent on spontaneous rate but the primary fiber rate is not, suggest that the two kinds of fibers employ different encoding mechanisms. To some degree, differences in the contractile properties of the nuclear bag and nuclear chain fibers can account for observed response patterns in the muscle spindle afferents. In any case, it has been demonstrated that impulses from muscle spindles reach both sensory and motor cortex areas, reinforcing the notion that they may be the primary encoders for proprioceptive information.

Studies in which passive movement of joints is performed and the output of muscle spindles recorded indicate that muscle receptors signal movement over virtually the entire range of a joint's movement. The range appears to be about equally divided between the agonist and antagonist muscles governing the movement. Vibration of muscle tendons, which would activate spindle receptors, gives rise to a sensation that the joint is being moved, and further reinforces the notion that these receptors play a major role in kinesthesia.

Yet another putative source of information about joint and limb position and movement could be provided by motor commands that control voluntary movement. These commands, called corollary discharges, could provide information about the planned position of joints and limbs after the movement occurs. It is assumed that such corollary discharges, if present, arise at high levels in the CNS, at least above the cerebellum, which controls involuntary movements. There is some disagreement regarding the exact location of corollary discharges, but it is agreed that such discharges may be particularly important in the sense of effort that accompanies voluntary movement. [See MOTOR CONTROL.]

At the CNS, a number of different possible codes have been considered as the primary input for proprioceptive sensibility. Rate-dependent discharges in the peripheral afferents, including differences in primary and secondary receptor activity, could signal directional information. It has been observed that primary receptors have a greater firing rate during muscle lengthening, whereas secondary fibers show a greater response to shortening. Although it is generally agreed that kinesthetic information is coded in firing rate, some difficulties have not yet been resolved, such as the fact that firing rate will increase with movement rate as well as direction and extent. [See NEUROMUSCULAR SYSTEM.]

B. Psychophysics

In measuring the behavioral response of an observer to static position or movement, several kinds of information can be obtained. These include movement rate, direction, and extent, as well as the awareness of static limb position, the perceived amount of weight supported by a limb, the force produced by muscular contraction, and the sense of effort necessary to contract a muscle. Much of this work has focused on nonvoluntary movements and placements of limbs. For example, in studies of passive limb extension, subjects can typically sense that movement has occurred before they can determine the direction of the movement. The dependent variable in such studies is often the displacement of the limb required for reliable detection of movement, at a particular movement velocity. Velocity is an important control, in that subjects tend to perceive very fast movements as having larger displacements than they do. However, errors are also more prevalent in very slow movements, and subjects show the greatest sensitivity to movement when velocity approximates the range in which most voluntary movements occur (in the vicinity of 5 m/sec, for the hand). Accuracy is also dependent on the starting and ending position of the limb, and for different limbs, sensitivity may be better for movement in one direction than in another.

In general, proximal joints, those closer to the body, have greater sensitivity to movement than more distal ones, those at the extremities. This may be because in real movement, operation of the lever principle means that proximal joints move less than do distal ones. The poorest sensitivity to movement is seen for the finger, if displacement is the value measured. However, if responses are evaluated in terms of muscle stretch, different joints appear more similar in response, suggesting that the CNS may monitor muscle stretch rather than displacement per se.

Another measure of perceived movement is obtained via joint rotation. Minimum values for detection of passive joint rotation range from 0.2° for the hip to 0.7° for the first metatarsal phalange (big toe). These values, obtained from young adults, generally are higher by .1 to .2° in older persons. However, joint rotation detection is also rate dependent, and the range of movement necessary for detection of movement may be as high as 6°, depending on rate.

It is also possible to measure a more purely proprioceptive sensation, that of judged limb position, rather than movement. This measurement is more complex, of course, because responses to limb movement necessary to change limb position could influence responding. Thus, rather than asking whether the limb has changed position following passive movement by the experimenter, some studies have employed a technique in which the subject is instructed to move the limb to a particular position, or to point to a position after a limb has been passively moved there. Results of such studies indicate that errors are greatest when the limb is passively moved and held there by the experimenter, and lowest when the subject actively moves the limb and actively maintains its position. Variability in positioning accuracy increases as the distance to be moved increases, and in general, subjects tend to overestimate short movement distances and underestimate long ones.

A major consideration in measuring proprioceptive sensation is the necessity of eliminating additional sources of information that might be used to signal limb position or movement. Two important sources of such information are visual and cutaneous inputs. Studies suggest that when vision is permitted, it dominates kinesthesis, even when the visual information is misleading, as when a distorted visual image is provided. In this case, position errors are made consistently, even though the kinesthetic information is maintained. At first, when vision and kinesthesis are decoupled in such a manner, they feel separated, but subjects quickly adapt to the changed visual environment, and the two modalities again feel congruent. In any event, measurement of proprioceptive feedback requires the elimination of visual cues, typically accomplished by blindfolding the subject. Elimination of cutaneous feedback from mechanoreceptors in response to passive movement of limbs has been approached in a number of creative ways. The most successful involve the use of air-bladder splints, which produce minimal cutaneous sensation, and topical ischemia, or reduction of circulation to a particular limb, which eliminates cutaneous sensations and in-

duces a feeling of numbness in the limb after about 20 min. The need to eliminate these cues suggests that in normal activity, their inputs contribute to position sense.

Other studies have found that human subjects are surprisingly good at remembering previous limb positions, over remarkable periods of time. Up to 24 hours later, subjects can indicate the position in which a limb was previously placed. This aspect of kinesthetic memory is of considerable interest, particularly given that most subjects are poor at verbal encoding of movement and position, and given the notion that verbal encoding of stimuli permits them to be retained in longer term memory.

Furthermore, it appears that individuals are better at judgments involving *relative* limb position (i.e., how one position is different from another) than those involving absolute limb position. This may be related to phenomena of "postural persistence," the persistence of sensations related to a particular limb position. In any case, results indicate that judgments of the current position of a limb are influenced by its prior position, particularly if that prior position has been held for some period of time.

Researchers have also investigated the perceptual aspects of the sense of effort, or force, required to perform particular activities. There are two possible mechanisms for estimating effort: monitoring sensory inputs from Golgi tendon organ receptors in muscles; or monitoring motor command signals generated in the CNS (the "corollary discharges" discussed above). However, judgments of the heaviness of weights, for example, depend not only on the actual weight of the object, but also on the condition of the muscles involved in lifting it. Intervening muscle exertion that induces fatigue will make a lifted object seem heavier than before the exertion. Interestingly, the same phenomenon occurs for the perceived weakness of muscles following stroke, when peripheral muscle processes may in fact be unaffected. This result suggests that there is a central component in the estimation of weight, such that CNS signals generated during voluntary movement are also input to sensory areas, where they can influence perception. In addition, adaptation of heaviness occurs, for example, in situations in which light weights seem even lighter after heavier weights are lifted. And as for other proprioceptive functions, in the fingers cutaneous receptors may play a role; results indicate that anesthesia of cutaneous mechanoreceptors in the fingers also affects perceived heaviness.

Involved in the perception of effort is the sensation of muscle tension. Vibrating a muscle that facilitates or opposes the lifting of a weight will influence the perceived heaviness and thus the perceived effort of lifting. However, subjects do appear to be able to distinguish muscle tension from overall effort. If subjects are instructed to keep effort constant, the exerted force of muscle will vary with the object to be lifted. However, if subjects are instructed to keep tension constant, the exerted muscle force does not change. Weakening of muscles with injected curare will cause an increase in perceived effort.

In summary, humans seem to have good ability to sense limb position and limb movement, as well as judge the degree of effort required in task completion. Under normal circumstances, these sensations are influenced by visual and/or cutaneous inputs, at least at some body sites. In measuring the integrity of kinesthetic sensibility after injury or disease, a number of tasks have been employed. Some of these are also used in assessing the effects of aging on proprioceptive sensation, and will be discussed in the next section.

C. Effects of Aging on Proprioception

It has been well documented that motor performance becomes slower and less accurate with age. However, opinion is divided on why this occurs. One hypothesis is that a decline in the quality of sensory input associated with movement results in a deterioration of motor performance. Thus, researchers have taken an active interest in changes in proprioceptive and kinesthetic sensation associated with aging.

Studies of the effects of aging on kinesthesis indicate that passive movement thresholds for the knee, hip, and ankle were as much as twice as high for older subjects (over 50 years) as those for younger subjects (under 40 years). However, little difference in sensitivity was observed for upper extremities (hands, fingers). These differences between upper and lower extremities may be partially attributable to the fact that the ankle and knee are weight-bearing joints that may be more susceptible to aging effects. Other results indicate that older subjects have higher thresholds for detection of joint movements when movement rate is slow. For higher rates of movement, differences due to age are less apparent. In examining the tasks used in such stud-

ies, it can be noted that some tasks are more memory intensive than others. Specific evaluation of the effects of memory load on kinesthetic perception shows that when the memory demands are low, differences between older and younger subjects are minimal, but when memory load is increased, elderly subjects exhibit worse performance. [See MEMORY.]

Nonetheless, even relatively simple tasks, such as reproducing a passive movement, were found in some studies to be more difficult for older subjects. The problem with movement reproduction studies is that the subject must store the proprioceptive input from the first movement in order to complete the matching movement. Some researchers have argued that immediate reproduction of a movement of one limb with the opposite limb reduces the memory requirements of the task.

One study investigated differences in performance of younger and older subjects on two different tasks, one involving "constrained" movement and one involving "preselected" movement. In the constrained movement condition, subjects were instructed to match a passive movement controlled by the experimenter, and in the preselected movement condition, subjects could select a movement that they wished to match. Results indicated that older subjects were much worse than younger ones in the constrained movement condition, showing many errors in matching experimenter-controlled passive movement. In the preselected movement condition, however, older and younger subjects performed similarly. Interpretation of these data was based on the notion that preselected movements can benefit from the corollary discharges that accompany voluntary movements, but passive movements cannot. If the older subjects' proprioceptive sensibility were reduced, performance in the constrained movement condition would be impaired, but the ability to use corollary discharge information in the preselected movement condition could compensate for any decreases in proprioceptive afferent function, such that performance would not necessarily suffer. In younger subjects, such corollary discharge facilitation is not needed, because proprioceptive input is sufficient for performance.

Many studies of aging and proprioception have focused on changes in the ability to maintain balance, or postural control. Numerous experiments have demonstrated that older subjects exhibit increased postural sway, and increased tendency to lose balance when stress is placed on the system, due to a slower initiation of balance control movements. One difficulty with such studies is the need to separate the effects of aging per se from the effects of decondition of muscles associated with reduced activity and possible subclinical pathologies in elderly individuals.

Postural control, under normal circumstances, involves the coordination of inputs from several systems, both motor and sensory. The strength and condition of effector muscles involved in balance, as well as the range of motion of knee, hip, and ankle joints will affect postural control. In addition, sensory inputs from kinesthetic, visual, cutaneous, and vestibular systems may play a role in the maintenance of balance. A number of studies have investigated the interactions of visual and vestibular factors in postural control, by selectively eliminating factors in tasks where balance is challenged by perturbation of a platform on which subjects stood. In general, it appears that in the average adult, the influence of visual cues was most evident at low perturbation frequencies, less than 0.1 Hz. Vestibular function is divided in its effects: the otolith organs respond maximally below 0.1 Hz for postural sway, but the semicircular canals, which mediate angular acceleration, are most responsive above that range. Cutaneous inputs could respond well above 1 Hz.

Results for younger adults indicate that postural sway increases by about 50% when the eyes are closed, as compared to open. Postural sway is also increased when the head is placed in an odd orientation, affecting vestibular inputs. Lower extremity ischemia, induced by applying a blood pressure cuff at the ankle, eliminated cutaneous sensation, and also resulted in increased postural sway. These data indicate that all of these systems could contribute to postural control. However, researchers argue that if any two of the systems are intact in the young adult, balance can be maintained. Reflexive responses appear not to be affected by these other modality inputs, but instead seem to be organized in advance based on past experience, and are not flexible in implementation. A more continuous monitoring mode seems to be more dependent on visual, vestibular, and proprioceptive input for the ongoing maintenance of balance.

Studies comparing performance of younger and older subjects in postural control tasks show that older subjects can maintain balance as well as younger ones when conditions were not stressful, but that un-der stressful conditions, such as a greater degree of platform perturbation, older subjects were more likely to lose balance. In addition, although all subjects showed some deficits when inputs from other sensory modalities were limited, older subjects showed greater impairment of balance control. Modifications of vestibular or cutaneous inputs via the methods described above were very disturbing to older subjects. Both younger and older subjects were most affected by elimination of visual inputs. Furthermore, when two sensory input sources were disturbed simultaneously, older subjects showed severe deterioration of postural control, far greater than was seen for younger subjects. The implications of these results are that older individuals rely more heavily on input from additional sources, such as visual and vestibular modalities, to maintain balance, in the face of decreased proprioceptive sensibility. When these additional sources are eliminated, balance fails. [*See* BALANCE, POSTURE, AND GAIT.]

Interestingly, attempts to correlate decreases in proprioceptive, visual, cutaneous, and vestibular function with postural sway measures have not indicated strong relationships. For example, visual acuity was not associated with degree of postural sway, except to the degree that both show decreases with age. Vibration detection by cutaneous receptors was related to postural sway, but did not correlate with proprioceptive measures. Finally, vestibular functioning was only weakly related to postural sway. The lack of strong correlations here should not be misinterpreted, however. It is possible that the detection measures used here would not show deficits correlated to postural sway, but this does not mean that declines in sensory ability at suprathreshold levels might not contribute to increases in postural sway. Furthermore, some investigators believe that decreases in postural control with aging are mediated more centrally, at some point where peripheral inputs are integrated. This notion is reinforced by the finding that in many cases, the longer-latency, voluntary corrections to balance are more affected in older persons than are short-term, monosynaptic reflex corrections.

III. SUMMARY

Overall, results indicate that both touch and proprioception are susceptible to the effects of aging, and that declines in function can be observed for many tasks. For touch, sensitivity to vibration shows a systematic decline with age, and the perceived intensity of vibratory stimuli is also reduced at suprathreshold levels. Some reports also indicate reduced sensitivity to thermal stimulation, together with a general decrease in body temperature in older persons. In addition, pain sensitivity in older persons also appears to differ from that of younger persons, although differences in response criterion may underlie some of this difference. In many cases, these psychophysical changes are accompanied by decreases in number and density, and changes in morphology, of cutaneous receptors, particularly the PC and MEI.

Proprioceptive and kinesthetic function also appears to decline in older persons, although care must be taken to rule out declines in muscle condition due to inactivity. Threshold for detection of limb movement and the ability to reproduce changes in limb position seem to be worse for older persons, particularly in situations in which proprioceptive memory load is high. Postural control, an important consequence of proprioceptive sensibility, is also impaired in older persons, especially when balance is challenged. It appears that older individuals maintain postural control by relying more heavily on inputs from multiple sensory modalities, including visual, vestibu-lar, and cutaneous sensations, to compensate for reductions in proprioceptive input, and that when these sensations are eliminated, postural control is more strongly affected than in younger persons.

There is a pressing need for further research into the physiological mechanisms and behavioral function of the senses of touch and proprioception, both in younger adults and in older adults. A better understanding of how these modalities are affected by age could lead to strategies to remediate or avoid these deficits, improving quality of life for older persons.

BIBLIOGRAPHY

Cauna, N. (1965). Effects of aging on the receptor organs of the human dermis. In W. Montaga, (Ed.), *Advances in biology of skin-aging VI* (pp. 63–96). New York: Pergamon Press.

Clark, F. J., & Horch, K. W. (1986). Kinesthesia. In K. Boff, L. Kaufman, & J. Thomas (Eds.), *Handbook of perception and human performance* (Vol. 1) New York: Wiley.

Sherrick, C. E., & Cholewiak, R. W. (1986). Cutaneous sensitivity. In K. Boff, L. Kaufman, & J. Thomas (Eds.), *Handbook of perception and human performance* (Vol. 1) New York: Wiley.

Stelmach, G., & Sirica, A. (1986). Aging and proprioception. *Age 9*, 99–103.

Verrillo, R. T. (1993). Effects of aging on the sense of touch. In *Sensory research: Multimodal Perspectives* (pp. 285–298). Hillsdale, NJ: Erlbaum.

Vision

Charles T. Scialfa and Donald W. Kline

University of Calgary

I. The Aging Visual System
II. Light and Visual Functioning
III. The Perception of Detail and Location
IV. The Perception of Visual Events over Time
V. Attention and Visual Search
VI. Visual Disorders
VII. Effects of Visual Aging on Real-World Tasks

Acuity   Ability to resolve fine detail, usually in stationary, high-contrast targets.

Age-Related Maculopathy   (ARM): Also known as age-related macular degeneration, a visual disorder involving atrophy of the photoreceptors and neurons within the central retina.

Contrast Sensitivity   Ability to detect luminance differences, usually between spatially contiguous surfaces.

Dark Adaptation   Increase in the visual system's light sensitivity in low illumination.

Glaucoma   An age-related visual disorder involving the loss of peripheral vision due to excessive pressure within the eye.

Optic Media   Transparent anterior components of the eye responsible for focusing images on the retina.

Presbyopia   Age-related loss of the ability to alter the refractive power of the lens to focus objects at varying distances.

Retina   Sensorineural structure in the posterior of the eye that contains the photoreceptors (rods and cones) and neural elements that transform retinal images into neural code.

Saccades   High-velocity, largely ballistic eye movements used to fixate different objects in visual scenes.

Useful Field of View   Visual area over which targets can be recognized and localized without eye or head movements.

Good **VISION** is important in almost all daily activities and may explain why severe loss of vision is one of the most feared consequences of aging. Although severe losses are not common among the elderly, and are often treatable, their prevalence does increase markedly with aging. For most people, loss in visual functioning occurs gradually, and is moderate in degree. Although both optical and sensorineural factors contribute to age-related change, the former normally precede the latter. Both, however, can adversely affect an older person's ability to carry out everyday tasks.

I. THE AGING VISUAL SYSTEM

The transformation of light into recognizable visual scenes and objects is carried out in three types of sequentially organized structures. First, the optic media, consisting of transparent structures in the anterior part of the eye, must form a clear image on the retina (see Figure 1). Next, photosensitive elements in the retina, the photoreceptors (i.e., the rods and cones), transform light into a neural signals. Neural structures compose the final element in the visual system. Beginning in the retina, they conduct information to various cortical and subcortical areas, as well as transform it into neural codes that mediate our perception of brightness, color, form, motion, and depth.

Encyclopedia of Gerontology
Volume 2

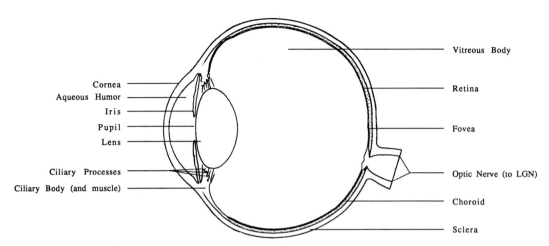

Figure I   Cross-sectional diagram of the structures of the human eye.

A. Image Formation

The cornea, the first optic structure through which light must pass, is the primary refractive body in the eye. Although it yellows and becomes somewhat thicker with aging, the perceptual effects of these changes are usually negligible. Posterior to the cornea, the anterior chamber of the eye contains a fluid called aqueous humor responsible for the metabolic needs of the cornea and lens. The production and drainage of aqueous humor both decline with age. The latter can lead to an increase in the eye's internal pressure, contributing to the development of a visual dysfunction known as glaucoma (see section VI on Visual Disorders).

Light passes from the anterior to posterior chamber of the eye through the pupil and lens. Changes in pupil size, made by the iris, influence image quality by affecting depth of focus and optical aberration, and by moderating the amount of light reaching the retina. Resting pupil size declines with adult aging (senile miosis), reducing retinal illuminance proportionately.

The shape of lens is controlled by the ciliary muscles to focus images on the retina, a process termed accommodation. The lens is made more spherical for near objects, and less spherical for far objects. Age-related reductions in the strength of the ciliary muscles, along with increases in the thickness and hardness (sclerosis) of the lens diminish its accommodative amplitude (presbyopia). By age 60, the accommodative loss is virtually complete, and often necessitates the use of corrective lenses (e.g, reading or bifocal lenses) for near tasks such as reading. Along with the loss in amplitude, the speed of accommodation declines, particularly under degraded viewing conditions. The lens also yellows and becomes more opaque, changes that are hastened by exposure to sunlight.

Due to changes in the optic media, light reaching the senescent retina is attenuated, scattered, and altered spectrally. From early adulthood to age 60, retinal illuminance is reduced by about two-thirds, primarily due to the changes in the lens and pupil. Light scatter is also increased in the older eye, reducing contrast independently of refractive state and pupil size. Yellowing of the lens increases its absorption of short-wavelength light (blues and greens), which in turn reduces the ability to discriminate colors in the blue end of the spectrum. Change in retinal illuminance most adversely effects the visual performance of older observers under low illumination conditions.

B. Photosensitive Response

The photoreceptors responsible for generating the eye's initial response to light are of two types: cones and rods. The cones operate at higher light (i.e., photopic) levels and are responsible for acuity and color vision. They are most densely concentrated in the central 5° to 7° of the retina; the fovea, the most central 1°, contains mostly cones. Rods, which are more plentiful outside the fovea, are responsible for low-illumination (i.e., scotopic) sensitivity.

There appears to be minimal age-related loss of foveal cones, but some decline has been noted more peripherally. There is a pronounced decline in rod density near the central retina. Due to an increase in their size, however, the remaining rods appeared to maintain a fairly constant ability to capture light. Retinal pigment epithelium cells that provide for the metabolic needs of photoreceptors appear to decline in parallel with them, suggesting a possible causal link.

C. Neural Changes

The signal generated by photoreceptors is transformed and conducted to various parts of the brain by a complex series of neural structures that begins in the retina. Electroretinographic (ERG) data derived from the electrical responses of the retina to various types of stimuli suggest that there are age-related declines in the functioning of the rods and cones as well as in the neural bipolar cells, Mueller cells, and retinal ganglion cells that receive cone inputs. Little is known about the impact of aging on the functioning of rod-fed ganglion cells. There is anatomical evidence of a decline in the number of axons in retinal ganglion cells, the neurons that form the optic nerve leading from the retina to the lateral geniculate nucleus (LGN), the principal visual relay station in the *thalamus* of the brain.

Two major visual pathways through which retinal signals are communicated to the visual cortex have been identified, based on the thalamic areas to which they project. About 90% of ganglion cells lead to the color-sensitive parvocellular pathway responsible for detailed pattern perception; the balance contributes to the contrast-sensitive magnocellular pathway that is most responsive to stimulus change. There are some data to suggest age-related declines in cell counts in both pathways, but differential age effects on their functioning have not been established.

From the LGN, visual information is conducted primarily to the visual (striate) cortex in the occipital area of the brain. Recent studies indicate that there is little decline with age in the density of neurons in the human or monkey striate cortex. However, some evidence of degeneration of dendrites in the striate cortex of the monkey has been reported. Most studies of cortical visually evoked potentials (VEPs) indicate an increase with age in the latency with which visual information arrives at the brain. Many, but not all studies also report a reduction in the amplitude of the VEP that is most pronounced at high spatial frequencies and low temporal frequencies. This suggests that the parvocellular pathway may be more greatly affected by aging.

Relatively little is known about how aging affects visual neural processes beyong the primary visual cortex. One way to examine such age difference is to use positron emission tomography (PET) scans to determine cerebral blood flow to different cortical areas as tasks mediated by those areas are carried out. A study that did so found that blood flow increases for two different visual tasks were less site-specific among older participants, suggesting reduced effectiveness of the cortical areas primarily responsible for each task. There is also some evidence that cortical integration of information received from the right and left eyes is less effective in old age.

D. Eye Movements

Eye movements, which can be categorized as reflexive or voluntary, are controlled by three pairs of extraocular muscles that attach each eye to its orbit. Reflexive eye movements are important for image stabilization and play a critical role in postural stability. They occur when large areas of the visual world move relative to the observer. Voluntary eye movements enable one to direct his or her gaze to objects whether still or moving.

Two types of reflexive eye movements are the vestibulo-ocular reflex (VOR) and the optokinetic response (OKR). The VOR, in which both eyes move in a direction opposite to the head, occurs in response to large changes in head position. The OKR refers to eye movements in the same direction as a large moving field, such as when a bus slowly pulls up next to one at a stoplight. Both VOR and OKR show age-related slowing and loss in coordination with the retinal signal, which is consistent with vestibular aging, as well as age-related declines in postural stability.

There are three major types of voluntary eye movements, vergence, pursuit, and saccadic. Vergence movements occur when one converges or diverges the eyes to focus on objects at different viewing distances. Although there are changes in some components of vergence (e.g., the diminished influence of accommodation), the overall vergence response remains relatively stable across the life span. Pursuit eye movements (PEMs) are translations of the eyes that allow us to maintain fixation on continuously moving objects, and saccadic eye movements (SEMs) are high-velocity, largely ballistic eye movements that are used to redirect gaze to different parts of the visual scene. Because one does not always track objects with perfect accuracy, PEMs are frequently interspersed with SEMs. Changes in either type of eye movement can affect the ability to perform dynamic tasks and search the visual environment.

PEMs are less adequate among older observers, especially for rapidly moving targets. They are also more likely to be interrupted when older adults are performing a concurrent cognitive task. In consequence, a larger number of SEMs often are required for elderly observers to image a target on the fovea. But the speed and accuracy of SEMs also decrease with aging. This, combined with deficits in peripheral processing, means that elderly observers are likely to make more time-consuming eye movements when inspecting a scene.

For some tasks, it is important to be able to maintain gaze steadily on a particular location. This ability seems to be relatively unchanged with age, at least among healthy observers who are viewing isolated objects.

II. LIGHT AND VISUAL FUNCTIONING

With its photopic and scotopic systems, the human eye is capable of effective functioning over a very wide range of light levels. The ability of the senescent visual system to function in different lighting conditions is reduced because less light reaches the retina, light is scattered by the optic media, and lastly, the older eye needs more light to produce the same response. This has been seen in studies of dark adaptation, glare effects, and color perception.

A. Sensitivity to Light

Dark adaptation, the process by which the visual system increases its sensitivity in response to reduced light levels, occurs in two distinct stages. The first is a relatively brief (8–10 min) cone-based process, and the second, a more protracted rod-adaptation period (30–40 min). Although the rate of adaptation appears

to be invariant with age, maximum light sensitivity that is reached is reduced among older persons. Such age differences in dark adaptation are due in large measure to a decline in retinal illumination, with the balance attributable to deficits in retinal metabolism and/or the neural pathways.

Aging is also associated with increased susceptibility to glare. The ability to discern detail in the presence of glare is more adversely affected among old than young observers, an effect that may be explained at least in part by increased light scatter in the senescent eye. The time to regain sensitivity after exposure to an intense glare is also considerably more extended in old age, an effect that likely reflects changes in recovery of the photoreceptors or retinal pigment epithelium or both.

B. Color Vision

With aging there is a small decline in color discrimination that is more pronounced for shorter wavelengths and increases as illumination is reduced. The illumination effect is consistent with the involvement of reduced retinal illumination, but could also include declines in foveal cone pigment density or generalized cone loss or both. The interaction of age and wavelength may reflect both differential spectral absorption by the senescent optic media and atrophy of short-wavelength-sensitive cones.

III. THE PERCEPTION OF DETAIL AND LOCATION

A. Static Acuity

The most common measure of the ability to see spatial details is static visual acuity (SVA), the finest detail that can be discriminated in stationary high-contrast stimuli. Although an age-related loss of SVA is greater among observers not optically corrected for the viewing distance, or who are in poor visual health, a decline is seen even in those who are using their best correction and have been screened for visual pathology. Although reduced retinal illuminance and increased ocular light scatter contribute to this decline, sensorineural factors also appear to be involved. Acuity is reduced in older observers whose lenses have been replaced with an intraocular implant, and when the effects of optical media changes are bypassed.

B. Static Spatial Contrast Sensitivity

Contrast sensitivity refers to the ability to detect luminance differences. Most commonly this is tested using stationary gratings, bar-like stimuli in which luminance varies in periodic sinusoidal fashion. The sensitivity for gratings of varied coarseness (i.e., spatial frequency) is represented by the contrast sensitivity function (CSF). Because it measures the ability to see objects that vary widely in size, it provides a more comprehensive assessment of an individual's spatial vision than does acuity.

Older observers exhibit reliable declines on the CSF at intermediate and higher spatial frequencies. Because spatial frequencies in this range are affected by retinal illumination, these declines may be offset partially by increases in ambient light. Several studies suggest that age-related changes in neural factors also contribute to the decline in the detection of contrast at threshold levels. They also indicate that any age differences in contrast discrimination at suprathreshold levels can be accounted for by the elevation in threshold detection.

C. Dynamic Acuity and Contrast Sensitivity

On many tasks it is important to discern detail in objects that are in motion relative to the observer. Rapid motion makes the resolution of small features more difficult, especially among older people. For example, age deficits on dynamic visual acuity (DVA), the ability to resolve details in moving acuity targets, are exacerbated at higher velocities. Similarly, age differences in contrast sensitivity are magnified by movement of gratings of higher spatial frequency. At least two factors appear to contribute to this relationship. The first is that static acuity, which sets the upper limit on dynamic resolution, falls with age. In addition, the inadequate PEMs of older adults increase slippage of the image on the retina. The resulting blur reduces image contrast, making resolution more difficult.

D. Peripheral Vision

Although the visual system has evolved to provide human observers with impressive spatial and color vision in the fovea, a great deal of important environmental information comes to us from outside of central vision. Processing of such peripheral information guides our eyes and directs attention to critical stimuli. Information from the visual periphery is also important for postural stability and the perception of motion.

The most common measure of the spatial extent of vision is the visual field test in which the observer is required to detect a luminance target presented at varying radial distances from fixation. Studies using this measure have found that binocular visual fields decline with age, from an average of 180° in young adults to 140° by age 70.

Age-related declines in acuity for peripheral targets have also been shown to be greater than for central targets. Optical lenses, more frequently worn by the elderly, exhibit off-axis image distortion, and lenses are prescribed to provide the best correction centrally, leaving the lens wearer less well corrected in the periphery. Both factors may contribute to age-related declines in peripheral visual function.

Recent studies of the useful field of view (UFOV) embody a new and more realistic approach to the study of age differences in peripheral processing. The UFOV is defined as the area within which targets can be recognized and localized without eye and head movements. Because the size of the UFOV changes with various stimulus and task characteristics, it can be used to estimate performance in settings where standard perimetry is inadequate.

The UFOV is more restricted among older observers, and although practice allows its expansion, older adults do not benefit more than young adults. The reduced UFOV may be caused by the optic and neural factors that have been described earlier, but may also reflect a shrinkage in the size of the "attentional spotlight," the dimensions of which appear to vary with task complexity. There is growing evidence that UFOV restrictions can contribute to age deficits in other visual-cognitive tasks, including visual search and driving.

E. Depth and Distance

Humans use a variety of monocular and binocular cues to gauge absolute (i.e., self-centered) and relative (i.e., object-centered) distance of objects. Despite its importance in daily life, other than a few studies of *stereopsis*, the depth information available from the different perspectives of the right and left eyes, age differences in depth perception have not been well studied. Studies of stereoptic thresholds show relatively little age-related decline; however, the number of individuals who fail the test completely does increase in older groups.

F. Discrimination of Position

When the spatial layout of stimuli permits it, human observers can discriminate shape and position differences of only a few seconds of arc, a level considerably finer than the diameter of a foveal cone. This ability depends on the integration of spatial information over a fairly large area of the retina, and is the basis for its somewhat misleading hyperacuity label. Only a few studies have examined age differences on hyperacuity. Most of them have used a static vernier task to determine the minimal detectable misalignment of two or more features (as when reading a thermometer or aligning a ruler). These studies find that static vernier acuity and thus, the neural processes that mediate it, is unaffected by age. In contrast, hyperacuity tasks using temporally modulated targets show pronounced age deficits, indicative of a neurally based decline in temporal resolution.

IV. THE PERCEPTION OF VISUAL EVENTS OVER TIME

A. Detecting Change

Temporal resolution refers to the ability to see as separate, events that occur closely in time. Age differences in temporal resolution and motion perception are often considered together because they appear to be served by some common neural mechanisms (i.e., the magnocellular pathway).

Most studies indicate that the older visual system has a reduced ability to resolve quickly changing stimuli. Critical flicker frequency (CFF), the threshold for detecting temporal discontinuity in a rapidly flashing light, falls with age. More recently, age differences in temporal resolution have been studied employing a more comprehensive measure, the *temporal contrast sensitivity function* (TCSF). The TCSF determines the contrast an observer needs to detect sinusoidal luminance changes of varied frequency. The TCSF may be valuable for separating aging effects from those due to visual disease. For example, it has been shown that sensitivity to flicker modulation can discriminate healthy eyes from those with exudative age-related maculopathy (ARM).

The spatial characteristics of the stimulus also appear to be a determinant of age differences in temporal resolution. At low rates of temporal change, age differences in sensitivity are limited to intermediate and high spatial frequencies. As the flicker rate is increased, age differences in sensitivity emerge at progressively lower spatial frequencies.

B. Seeing Motion

By most measures, the perception of motion is more difficult for older observers. For example, for target oscillation to be detected by the elderly, it must occur over greater spatial excursions. Most studies also find that coherence thresholds, the proportion of elements in a random array that must move in a common direction to produce a perception of global motion, are also higher in the elderly.

The movement of images across the retina also occurs when observers move through static environments. Visual guidance of self-motion is dependent on the ability to make effective use of the optical flow information that results. Compared to the young, older observers are less accurate in judging motion direction from several types of flow field. They also appear to be more dependent than the young on visual information for maintaining postural stability. Together, these findings may help explain why older people are more likely than their younger counterparts to be victims of falls.

V. ATTENTION AND VISUAL SEARCH

A. Visual Search

On most visual tasks one must selectively attend to and process task-relevant stimuli, while ignoring distracting information. Older adults appear to have more difficulty doing this, presumably because of declines in both active attention and inhibition. Age deficits increase with both the number of items in a display and target-distractor similarity. Conversely, age differences in search are slight when targets are featurally distinct from distractors. This effect may be related to increased internal "noise," slower feature extraction, slower featural comparisons, or a reduced UFOV. [See ATTENTION.]

Search becomes largely an effortless (i.e., automatic) process if people are given sufficient practice with the same target object. Such automaticity results, in part, because targets gain and distractors lose the ability to attract attention. Once it develops, automaticity appears to be maintained in adult life. However, the development of automaticity for new tasks is more difficult for older persons, perhaps due to a failure to inhibit processing of distractors.

Often one is able to rapidly detect a sought-after object on the basis of expectancy and other environmental cues. The costs and benefits of such advance cuing provide additional measures of attentional selectivity. There are only small age differences in the magnitude and time course of attentional allocation. In fact, older adults frequently show greater benefit from advance information. However, they also take more time to reject a distractor and reallocate attention that has been inaccurately directed.

B. Vigilance

Sustained attention, such as that involved in driving or industrial inspection, is examined in vigilance tasks, where observers must detect an infrequent target over prolonged periods. Unless the stimuli to be detected are degraded, there is little evidence that aging is associated poorer vigilance performance.

VI. VISUAL DISORDERS

As with most biological systems, the risk of visual pathology increases with aging. Almost half of those who are legally blind, and about two-thirds of those with severe visual impairment (inability to read newspaper print with best correction) are 65 years of age or older. Such losses are considerably more common among institutionalized than community-resident elderly. Cataract, glaucoma, age-related maculopathy (ARM), and diabetic retinopathy are the most common causes of severe visual dysfunction in the elderly.

A. Cataract

A cataract is an opacity in one of the refracting elements of the eye, usually the lens. Cataracts diminish absolute sensitivity to light and increase light scatter, but their greatest effect is to increase image blur. In the absence of neural damage, good vision can usually be restored by replacement of the lens with an artificial intraocular lens (IOL) implant. The relative ease, great benefit, and low cost of this procedure explain why it is quite common in those over 65 years of age.

B. Glaucoma

Glaucoma refers to a small group of pathologies that are associated with elevated intraocular pressure. If left untreated, it causes atrophic changes in the optic nerve and retinal components that mediate peripheral sensitivity, in turn producing tunnel vision. Because it often goes unnoticed until the damage is irreparable, regular measurement of intraocular pressure is recommended beginning in the fourth or fifth decade.

C. Age-Related Maculopathy

ARM, also called *age-related macular degeneration* (AMD), is a term applied to the as-yet-unexplained atrophy of sensory receptors and higher order neurons within the central retina (i.e., macula). In serious cases, due to rapid growth of new blood vessels, there is fluid leakage into the macula. This can cause the destruction of cones, producing serious reductions in acuity. Laser photocoagulation techniques can be used in the early stages of such cases to reduce leakage and slow the progression of the disease. The use of magnifying lenses and practiced reliance on peripheral vision can ameliorate the effects of impairment in its early stages.

D. Diabetic Retinopathy

One of the serious complications of long-term diabetes, the prevalence of which increases with age, is the changes that it induces in the structure and function of blood vessels. In diabetic retinopathy, the swelling of blood vessels, and if it progresses, the growth of abnormal new blood vessels and fibrous tissue, can damage neural and photoreceptor cells. The rate of such atrophic changes can be slowed through proper maintenance of blood sugar levels. Laser photocoagulation techniques can be used to slow such neovascularization, and more broadly, to reduce the metabolic demands of the retina.

VII. EFFECTS OF VISUAL AGING ON REAL-WORLD TASKS

Normal age-related visual changes are often sufficient to adversely affect the older person's ability to carry out important daily tasks. Such changes are most likely to occur when lighting is poor, and when stimuli are small, too close, of low contrast, change or move quickly, appear in the periphery, involve the discrimination of short-wavelength hues, or are presented against spatially complex backgrounds.

A. Driving

Most of the information used in driving is visual and, not surprisingly, older drivers are less likely to drive in adverse visual conditions, such as occur at night or in poor weather. Severe visual problems frequently contribute to the cessation of driving altogether. The performance of older drivers appears to be particularly impaired by reductions in binocular visual fields, the UFOV, contrast sensitivity, and divided visual attention. They also report increased difficulty on several driving-related visual tasks, including seeing dim instrument panels, seeing through windshield glare and haze, judging vehicle speed, being surprised by vehicles in the periphery, and reading signs in time to respond to them.

B. Other Everyday Tasks

Age-related reductions in spatial vision can make it more difficult to read, identify objects, judge distance, maintain mobility, or engage in work tasks, especially if the stimuli involved are low in contrast or poorly illuminated. Studies have shown that older observers need higher levels of contrast to identify faces, highway signs, and common objects. Relatedly, performance on such tasks is often better predicted by con-trast-sensitivity measures than acuity. Consistent with objectively determined aging effects, when older persons are asked about the visual problems they encounter in everyday life, they indicate an increased degree or frequency of difficulty on tasks involving rapid visual processing, dynamic vision, visual search, near vision, and dim illumination. Research has shown that many of these problems can be reduced by increasing stimulus contrast, elevating luminance, and optimizing the spatial format of the displays to which older persons must respond.

ACKNOWLEDGMENT

The writing of this article was supported in part through research funding to each of the authors from the Natural Science and Engineering Research Council of Canada. The authors extend their great appreciation to Ms. Lisa Lynk for creating the diagram of the structure of the eye.

BIBLIOGRAPHY

Bagnoli, P., & Hodos, W. (Eds.) (1991). *The changing visual system: Maturation and aging in the central nervous system.* New York: Plenum Press.

Garzia, R. P., & Trick, L. R. (1992). Vision in the 90's: The aging eye. *Journal of Optometric Vision Development, 23*, 4–41.

Kline, D. W. (1991). Light, ageing and visual performance. In J. Marshall & J. R. Cronly-Dillon (Eds.), *Vision and visual dysfunction: Vol. 16. The susceptible visual apparatus* (pp. 150–161). London: MacMillan.

Kline, D. W., & Scialfa, C. T. (in press). Sensory and perceptual functioning: Basic research and human factors implications. In A. D. Fisk & W. A. Rogers (Eds.), *Handbook of human factors and the older adult.* San Diego: Academic Press.

Kline, D. W., & Scialfa, C. T. (1996). Visual and auditory aging. In J. E. Birren & K. W. Schaie (Eds.), *Handbook of the psychology of aging* (4th ed., pp. 181–203). San Diego: Academic Press.

Owsley, C., & Sloane, M. E. (1990). Vision and aging. In F. Boller & J. Grafman (Eds.), *Handbook of the neuropsychology* (Vol. 4, pp. 229–249). Amsterdam: Elsevier.

Schieber, F. (1992). Aging and the senses. In J. E. Birren, R. B. Sloan, & G. D. Cohen (Eds.), *Handbook of mental health and aging* (2nd ed., pp. 251–306). San Diego: Academic Press.

Spear, P. D. (1993). Neural bases of visual deficits during aging. *Vision Research, 33*, 2589–2609.

Volunteer Activity by Older Adults

Robert A. Harootyan

American Association of Retired Persons*

I. Trends in the Prevalence of Volunteering
II. Factors Related to the Likelihood of Volunteering
III. Trends in Volunteerism in the Older Population
IV. Implications for Future Volunteerism by Older Americans

Formal Volunteering Any activity intended to help others that is freely provided through a charitable, religious, civic or similar organization and for which no pay or other type of material compensation is received.

Independent Sector A nonprofit coalition of over 800 foundation, corporate, and voluntary organization members with interests in philanthropy and voluntary action.

Informal Volunteering Any activity intended to help others that is freely provided on an ad hoc basis by an individual and for which no pay or other material reward is received.

Intensity of Volunteering Hours spent per week or per month in either formal or informal volunteer activity.

Volunteer Participation Rate Incidence of volunteer activity within a specified population or group.

VOLUNTEER ACTIVITY is generally defined as any activity intended to help others that is provided without obligation and for which the volunteer does not receive pay or other material compensation. Volunteers usually provide such assistance through a religious, charitable, or civic organization, but their assistance also can be given on an ad hoc or nonorganizational basis. This article uses the broader definition of volunteer activity that includes assistance to others (except immediate family members or relatives), which is either organized and formal or episodic and informal in nature. Because there is no standard definition of what constitutes volunteer activity, it is somewhat difficult to provide a precise picture of trends in volunteerism in the United States. I use data from national surveys as well as information from studies on various aspects of volunteering to provide some general trends and findings about volunteerism and the older population in recent decades. The article concludes by looking to prospects for expanded volunteerism among older Americans in the future.

I. TRENDS IN THE PREVALENCE OF VOLUNTEERING

Although they use somewhat different definitions of volunteering, national surveys conducted during the last two decades in the United States indicate that the prevalence of volunteering increased steadily during the late 1970s and throughout the 1980s, but declined slightly since 1990. At the same time, the composition of the volunteer population has changed—a reflection of wider trends in society as a whole. One of the more noteworthy trends is a recent increase in the incidence of volunteering among older Americans.

---

* Any views expressed in this article are those of the author and do not necessarily represent formal policies of the American Association of Retired Persons.

Table I Volunteer Participation Rates by Annual Income, Employment Status, and Educational Attainment (%): United States 1974–1993[a]

	1993–1994	1991–1992	1989–1990	1987–1988	1973–1974
Total	48%	51%	54%	45%	24%
Household income:					
Under $10,000	34	32	30	23	17
$10,000–$19,999	37	38	42	40	29
$20,000–$29,999	53	51	56	50	—
$20,000 and over	—	—	—	—	37
$30,000–$39,999	56	56	64	51	—
$40,000–$49,999	55	67	67	44	—
$50,000–$74,999	61	61	63	57	—
$75,000–$99,999	58	63	62	50	—
$100,000 and over	68	74	74	62	—
Employment:					
Employed	52	59	60	49	25
Unemployed	41	43	45	38	17
Retired	41	34	39	35	22
Education:					
High school or less	37	38	42	34	19
Some college	53	62	66	56	32
College grad or more	67	77	74	64	43

[a]Sources: For 1987–1994: Hodgkinson, V. A., and Weitzman, M. S. *Giving and Volunteering in the United States.* 1994 edition. Washington, DC: Independent Sector (1994); for 1973–1974: ACTION (1975). *Americans Volunteer: 1974.* U.S. Bureau of the Census, Washington, DC.

A series of national surveys conducted in 1988, 1990, 1992, and 1994 by Independent Sector (IS) provides the most consistent set of data measuring volunteer activity among adult (aged 18 and over) Americans. The IS biennial surveys explicitly define volunteer activity as "not just belonging to a service organization, but actually working in some way to help others for no monetary pay." This definition, which includes both formal and informal volunteering, is the most common way that volunteerism is measured and discussed.

As shown in Table I, the prevalence of volunteer activity increased during the 1980s, reaching a peak of 54% in 1989–1990. Since then, however, overall rates of volunteerism decreased to 48% in 1993–1994. (The IS surveys, conducted in March, ask about volunteer work "during the previous 12 months"; resulting in data covering most of the previous year and the first-quarter of the year in which the survey was taken.)

Also shown in Table I are volunteerism data for 1973–1974, based on a national survey conducted by the Census Bureau for ACTION, the federal agency for volunteer service. It is important to note, however,

that the ACTION survey restricted its data only to "unpaid volunteer work for a group ... or ... any other type of organization" that regularly uses volunteers—a distinctly more restricted definition than in the IS surveys. Although Table I includes these earlier data, the rates are not directly comparable to those for the later years. I include them because they indicate the prevalence of *formal* volunteering in 1973–1974. An analysis by Susan Chambre of the recent IS survey data showed that less than 10% of the respondents who say they volunteered did so solely on an informal basis. Applying this difference to the 1973–1974 survey results would adjust upward the rates of overall volunteerism at that time. But even after this adjustment, it appears that volunteerism—both formal and informal—was less prevalent before the 1980s.

II. FACTORS RELATED TO THE LIKELIHOOD OF VOLUNTEERING

Definitive explanations for these changing rates of volunteerism are elusive. There are few in-depth national studies on the complex aspects of volunteering.

Most studies are descriptive in nature and confined to small populations of specific programs, making it difficult to generalize about volunteerism in the United States during the past three decades. Although there is no clear "model" that consistently predicts rates of volunteering, who volunteers, or what motivates volunteer activity, enough information is available from both national surveys and case studies to indicate which factors are most commonly associated with volunteerism.

Some researchers believe that volunteer activity increases during periods when the economy is growing or steady, but decreases during periods of economic sluggishness or recessions. This theory is based on the assumption that people are more likely to seek out opportunities to help others when they themselves feel economically and emotionally secure. The IS survey data in Table I provide limited support for this thesis. The incidence of volunteer activity in the United States increased from 45% to 54% of all adults during the last half of the 1980s—a period of steady economic growth—and began declining during the recessionary period of 1991–1992 (51%). But the most recent survey indicates further declines in these rates (down to 48% in 1993–1994) even though the economy was growing once again.

This anomaly may be related to the type of volunteering that has declined. Although not shown in Table I, the latest decline in the proportion who volunteer is largely due to lower incidence of *informal* volunteering. The proportion of respondents who gave assistance to individuals or organizations on an ad hoc or informal basis declined from 23% in 1991–1992 to 17% in 1993–1994. In contrast, rates of formal volunteerism remained steady during the same period. The surveys also indicate that those who are members of various organizations—religious, civic, charitable, educational—are significantly more likely to do formal volunteering than those who do not belong to such organizations.

Organizational membership is the bedrock of volunteering, providing a relatively steady stream of formal volunteers. In contrast, informal volunteering is less consistent and more prone to variation over time. This type of volunteer work is more sensitive to economic conditions or, more precisely, people's *perceptions* of their economic well-being. National opinion polls in recent years indicate that a large proportion of Americans feel insecure about their economic well-being and uncertain of their future security, despite the relative health of the economy. Those perceptions may reflect economic realities that are not evident in standard macroeconomic measures. Recent studies indicate that during the 1990s real wages and income were stagnant for most middle-income Americans, declined for those in the lowest income quintile, and increased for those in the highest income quintile. These economic trends and a growing sense of insecurity among many Americans coincide with the recent downturns in volunteerism. [*See* ECONOMICS: INDIVIDUAL; ECONOMICS: SOCIETY.]

The link between volunteerism and economic factors is supported in many studies indicating that income and education are strongly related to likelihood of volunteering. Table I shows that the highest rates of volunteering are among those who are better educated, wealthier, and employed. These persons are also most likely to be members of communal organizations through which most formal volunteering occurs. Multivariate analysis by Robert Harootyan and Robert Vorek of national survey data on volunteerism found that education and income are the two strongest predictors of volunteering. Their model also shows that—all else being equal—volunteerism is determined by (in descending order of influence) altruistic attitudes (e.g., belief in sharing one's benefits with those who are less fortunate), having positive perceptions of the contributions that others make to society, being aged 35–44, being satisfied with one's quality of life, having a larger household, and being married (the latter is reflected in Table II).

Their findings stress the simultaneous influence of socioeconomic and attitudinal factors on volunteerism. In addition, being married, having a large household, and/or being in a child-rearing age group suggests that the presence of a spouse, children, or other family member increases the likelihood of volunteer activity. These characteristics are likely to generate greater awareness and more opportunities for volunteering, especially through educational, religious, and civic or charitable organizations. Such opportunities may be due to a family member's awareness of or involvement in community-based organizations. A child's school-related activities or participation in extracurricular or recreational programs often leads to parental involvement as volunteers, which may be truly voluntary or the result of implicit expectations or explicit requests for volunteer assistance.

The relevance of household size is also related to

Table II Volunteer Participation Rates by Gender and Marital Status (%) and Average Hours per Week in Vounteer Activity: United States 1974–1993[a]

	1993–1994	1991–1992	1989–1990	1987–1988	1973–1974
Total	48%	51%	54%	45%	24%
Gender					
Male	44	49	52	44	20
Female	51	53	56	47	26
Marital status					
Married	52	56	59	50	27
Single	41	48	44	40	20
Divorced, separated, or widowed	40	36	47	34	15
Hours spent in volunteer work per week	4.2	4.2	4.0	4.7	9.0

[a]Source: See Table I.

findings from the IS and other surveys, which indicate that simply being asked to volunteer greatly increases the likelihood that persons will do so. This is especially true when persons are asked by relatives, close friends, or co-workers. Being a member of a large household naturally increases the chance that individuals will not only hear about volunteer opportunities but be asked to do volunteer work. The IS studies indicate that more than four out of five persons (82%) who are asked to volunteer do so. In contrast, only one out of five persons (21%) who are not asked to volunteer actually do so.

Not only is volunteerism induced by family circumstances and employment, it is also strongly related to involvement in educational and religious organizations. By far the most frequently mentioned vehicle for volunteer activity is a religious organization. Most studies show that 45–50% of all volunteers donate some or all of their time through a synagogue or church. The second most prevalent vehicle for volunteerism is educational organizations, which are mentioned by one-fourth to one-third of all volunteers. Other types of organizations—hospitals, civic groups, and charitable organizations—are less common avenues for volunteerism. [*See* RELIGION AND SPIRITUALITY.]

To summarize, volunteers are most likely to be better educated, financially comfortable, employed, satisfied with their quality of life, concerned about the welfare of others, younger adults, married, and living in relatively large households (probably comprising two or three generations). These findings indicate the complex manner by which socioeconomic,

attitudinal, and structural factors influence volunteerism in contemporary American society. Those who are most integrated into the social fabric and the economic structure of society are most likely to be volunteers.

III. TRENDS IN VOLUNTEERISM IN THE OLDER POPULATION

The findings about volunteerism in general also help to describe and explain age-specific and age-related trends in volunteer behavior. Elderly persons (aged 65–74 and 75+) and those who are retired are less likely than nonelderly persons and those who are employed to be volunteers (see Table III). The data are consistent with the general thesis associating volunteerism with socioeconomic status, household size, and degree of involvement in communal life. Until recently, aging and old age were often viewed negatively and characterized by the loss of important roles such as parent and paid worker. Old age usually brings lower income upon retirement. Households headed by older persons tend to be small. The older population's average level of educational attainment has been significantly lower than for persons under age 65. For many older persons mobility becomes restricted and community activities decrease. [*See* RETIREMENT.]

We are not surprised, then, that elderly persons are less likely to volunteer than nonelderly persons. Yet some observers have suggested that old age should be a time of increased volunteer activity precisely *be-*

Table III Volunteer Participation Rates by Age (%): United States 1974–1993[a]

	1993–1994	1991–1992	1989–1990	1987–1988	1973–1974
Total	48%	51%	54%	45%	24%
Age group:					
18–24	45	48	43	42	18
25–34	46	53	62	45	—
35–44	55	61	64	54	—
25–44	—	—	—	—	30
45–54	54	56	56	48	25
55–64	47	49	51	47	21
65–74	43	42	47	40	—
75 and over	36	27	32	29	—
65 and over	—	—	—	—	14

[a]Source: See Table I.

cause of the role losses that occur. This perspective assumes that volunteer activity is a key way for older persons to fill an assumed void in their lives. But numerous studies indicate that role loss is unlikely to induce volunteerism among the elderly. In a comprehensive examination of the potential for "unpaid productive roles" (i.e., volunteerism) by older Americans in the future, the Committee for an Aging Society concluded in 1986 that unpaid work does *not* appear to be a substitute for paid work. The report emphasized that societal values and the meanings attached to paid and unpaid work are notably different. One does not take the place of the other. The committee's conclusions are consistent with the findings that volunteerism is strongly associated with being employed rather than unemployed or retired. Chambre's thorough analysis of volunteerism and the elderly reached the same conclusion. Volunteer activity is supplemental to and intrinsically different from paid work.

Moreover, the IS surveys and a 1991 national survey on senior volunteerism sponsored by Marriott Senior Living Services indicate that neither loneliness, lack of activity, extra time, nor desire for socialization is a strong motivator for volunteerism. Rather, the desire to help others—altruism—and to make a real difference in the well-being of the community—a sense of accomplishment or self-fulfillment—are significant determinants (along with income and education) of who volunteers. In addition, positive perceptions of the importance of charitable and civic organizations, as well as active involvement in religious institutions are highly likely to influence who volunteers, whether old, middle-aged, or young.

For older persons, however, volunteerism can be restricted by social and physical barriers. Poor health is most often cited by older persons as the reason for not volunteering. Health problems, combined with limited economic resources (lack of reimbursement for costs associated with volunteering affects lower income persons the most), lower educational levels, and transportation difficulties all serve as barriers to volunteering by older persons. The Committee on an Aging Society also stressed that biases against older people, especially when combined with negative orientations toward some types of volunteer work, serve to thwart elder volunteerism.

Finally, a life-course perspective is necessary to fully understand the relationship between age and volunteerism. People do not suddenly become "old" at age 65 or 70. Nor do values, attitudes, ethical standards, political philosophies, and general personality traits change significantly with age. Similarly, people who have not been active volunteers during most of their lives or those who have not had positive role models of volunteer behavior in their youth are unlikely to become volunteers when their parental responsibilities end, when they retire, or when they reach age 65. As with other characteristics, volunteerism tends to be a lifelong activity that begins in youth and continues in old age.

Viewed from the life-course perspective, volunteerism among younger age groups in earlier decades becomes important for understanding volunteerism among today's older population. The attitudes, experiences, and behaviors of specific birth cohorts provide clues to volunteerism in the future. Although the data are limited, most surveys show that volunteerism in general was less prevalent before the 1980s, regardless of educational level, income, marital status, or age (see Tables I, II, and III). Thus, the lower incidence of volunteering among those who were aged 35–54 in the 1970s is reflected in the lower proportions of volunteers among those aged 55–64 and 65 and over today. The life-course perspective, when combined with knowledge of the key predictors of volunteerism, provides a basis for projecting changes in the volunteer activity of older Americans. [See LIFE COURSE.]

IV. IMPLICATIONS FOR FUTURE VOLUNTEERISM BY OLDER AMERICANS

Will significant age differences in volunteer activity persist in the future? I think not. As discussed above, birth cohort differences help explain the lower rates of volunteerism among retirees and persons aged 65 and over through the early 1990s. But differences by age and employment status in volunteer participation rates appear to be lessening. As seen in Table I, between 1987 and 1992 the difference between the volunteer participation rates of employed and retired persons increased from 14 percentage points to 25 percentage points. By 1993–1994, however, the difference declined to its lowest level—11 percentage points—during the years covered by the IS surveys.

More significantly, the direction of the changes within these groups has reversed. Since 1991–1992, the volunteer participation rate among employed persons declined from 59 to 52% in 1993–1994. For retired persons, however, the participation rate during this time *increased* from a low of 34% to a high of 41%. It is premature to suggest that this short-term change will continue as a long-term trend, but the degree of change in the rates of volunteering among retired Americans is very large. And because this change occurred in just 2 years, the possible influence of the trend toward lower average retirement age is not a factor, as shown by the age-specific data for those years.

The same pattern emerges in the age-specific rates of volunteerism. Since 1991–1992, the proportion of volunteers decreased in each age group *under* 65, while the incidence of volunteering among those aged 65–74 increased one percentage point, reaching 43% in 1993–94. More dramatic was the increase from 27 to 36% for those aged 75 and over—the highest rate recorded for this age group in any national survey (the Marriott survey recorded 39% among those aged 75–79 and 27% among those aged 80 and over).

Although the volunteer participation rate of Americans aged 65–74 is still lower than for some younger age groups, it now approaches the rates of those aged 18–24 and 25–34. These trends cannot be explained simply by the aging of the U.S. population. More complex processes influence the growing involvement of older persons in volunteering—processes that exemplify the "coming of age" of today's older population and those who will soon reach their 65th birthday. This emerging trend reflects the changing characteristics of older Americans—characteristics that tend to make them more similar than dissimilar to the rest of the population.

I have emphasized that retirement does not induce volunteering and that employment is a predictor of it. It seems ironic, then, that the increasing labor force participation rates of women have constrained their level of volunteerism. The IS surveys indicate that, as with other population subgroups, volunteer participation rates have declined since 1990 for both women and married persons. Also, the number of hours that can be devoted to volunteer work has been constricted for those who traditionally have been the most active volunteers—women aged 35–64, especially married women. Among all women, the labor force participation rate surpassed 57% in 1993, compared to less than 50% in 1970. Most significant are the changes since 1970 in the employment rates for married women in this age range. Among those aged 35–44, the rate increased from 47% in 1970 to 75% in 1993. For married women aged 45–64, labor force participation grew from 44 to 60% during this period. These employment trends have reduced the incidence of volunteerism and the amount of time spent by those who do volunteer (especially for informal volunteering), *except* among those aged 65 and over. [See WORK AND EMPLOYMENT.]

Indeed, older Americans are in part making up for the reduced incidence and "intensity" (hours spent per week or month) of volunteering by young-adult and middle-aged persons in recent years. The two trends may be serendipitous and not causally related, but the pattern is clear.

Other forces also have influenced the growing incidence of volunteerism by older persons. Significant changes in birth cohort characteristics that span less than two decades are the most likely reasons for the increasing rates of elder volunteerism in the 1990s. Amendments to the Social Security Act that introduced automatic annual cost-of-living adjustments for retiree benefits in 1975 have reduced the poverty rate among the elderly. Also, more than 40% receive some type of private or public pension payment. Similarly, the 30-year-old Medicare program has helped reduce a major fear of older persons—the potentially high burden of health-care costs. Thus, older Americans in general feel more economically secure today than in previous decades. But it is unclear if this sense of security will last. Older Americans now pay a higher proportion of their average income out-of-pocket for their health-care expenses than 30 years ago (22 versus 15%, respectively). Congressional proposals to dramatically reduce federal spending on Medicare are raising concerns among many elders.

As discussed in section II concerning Americans in general, perceptions of economic well-being and a sense of security allow persons to look beyond themselves and reach out to help others. Older Americans are no different in that regard. Altruism and a sense of accomplishment are important inducements to volunteering among all age groups. So, too, are socioeconomic characteristics other than income or perceived economic security. Among older persons themselves, those who are employed (whether full-time or part-time), married, and better educated are more likely to volunteer than are other older persons. Labor force participation rates have declined steadily for males and risen only slightly for females aged 55 and older during the last 20 years. The overall effect is to reduce their likelihood of volunteering. In contrast, a slightly higher proportion of older Americans are married than in previous decades, which increases their likelihood of volunteerism.

But the most significant and rapid change in birth cohort characteristics of older Americans has been educational attainment, which is the *most* influential predictor of volunteerism in the regression and discriminant analyses by Harootyan and Vorek. As recently as 1980, 43% of all persons aged 65 and over had less than 8 years of schooling, compared to 24% in 1993. Less than one-fourth (24%) had completed high school in 1980, but by 1993 more than one-third (34%) had done so. And in 1980, 17% had some college education or beyond, rising to 26% in 1993. This minor "revolution" in the educational attainment of older Americans in less than 15 years promises to continue as new co-

horts with higher average years of schooling reach age 65 during ensuing decades. Current projections indicate that the difference in median years of schooling between those aged 65 and over and all other adults will almost disappear by 2005.

The implications of this upward trend in educational attainment are highly significant for future volunteerism by older Americans. As the most influential predictor of volunteerism, educational attainment will foster new levels of volunteerism among older persons. Multivariate analysis indicates that after controlling for other factors, older persons with at least some college education are almost three times more likely to volunteer than those with a high school education or less. The educational trend also bodes well for increased volunteer activity by older persons that focuses on young people. Harootyan and Vorek found that disproportionately high percentages of elders with college degrees (37%) and education beyond college (28%) volunteer in programs benefiting youth, compared to 22% with a high school degree and 8% of elders with less than a high school education. An additional benefit from higher educational attainment among older Americans is its positive relationship to health status. New cohorts of older Americans who are both better educated and healthier than their predecessors will "double" the likelihood of increased volunteerism.

Another factor is especially important regarding future prospects of elder volunteerism—the influence of religious organizations. Studies such as the IS surveys consistently point to religious affiliation and activity as important determinants of volunteerism. Harootyan and Vorek showed that volunteer activity through a religious organization increases with age, rising from 38% among those aged 18–34 to 54% among those aged 65 and over. As the average age of religious congregations continues to rise, so too will the concentration of older volunteers.

It is also possible that new cohorts of older Americans will not only be members of religious organizations but also more likely than their current age peers to be members of secular organizations. For reasons that are not clear, the typical older American today is less likely to be a member of secular organizations in the community. But middle-aged Americans have relatively high incidence of such memberships, which are expected to be maintained over their life courses. Should this pattern continue, the likelihood of increased formal volunteering by elders in the future is quite strong.

A "hidden" indicator of the potential impact of more older volunteers is the multiplier effect of the time they devote to such activity (the intensity of volunteer time). The data from various national surveys during the last decade indicate that the average volunteer gives about 4 hours per week. The Harootyan and Vorek survey showed wide variation by age in average hours volunteered per month. The monthly average for all volunteers is 17 hours, compared to 26 hours for those aged 65–74. Even the oldest volunteers—those aged 75 and over—average 14 hours per month, the same amount as volunteers agd 35–44. Although elder volunteer participation rates are lower than most other age groups, the intensity of their volunteer time is the highest.

Past attempts to increase the number and proportion of older volunteers also may prove beneficial in the future. The federal government has administered a number of voluntary action programs to foster the availability of older Americans as a community resource. They are currently administered under the umbrella of the National Senior Volunteer Corps. Some of these programs have a second purpose—to provide a modest stipend for low-income older persons who would otherwise be unable or unlikely to volunteer. They also focus the volunteer effort on populations with special needs. The Foster Grandparent Program is targeted to children with special needs, whereas the Senior Companion Program promotes volunteer activity that assists elders who are isolated. The largest federal elder volunteer program is the Retired and Senior Volunteer Program, which accounts for almost 500,000 volunteers aged 55 and over who serve all age groups in communities throughout the nation.

Taken together, however, these government efforts provide only a fraction of the potential volunteer force within the older population. And cutbacks in federal spending are likely to constrict the growth of these programs. Helping to fill the void are new nationally oriented volunteer service programs. Most notable among them is the National Retiree Volunteer Center, which fosters the development of corporate and educational retiree programs that have the potential to recruit hundreds of thousands of new volunteers among the retired.

The effects of private nonprofit initiatives, whether in a local community or on a national scale, can be profound. The potential resource they can tap within the older population is greater than most realize. Already, the American Red Cross notes that more than half of its volunteers are aged 55 and over. The Committee on an Aging Society reported that for every five older volunteers, there are another two older Americans who are willing to volunteer but do not. National surveys, such as the 1991 Marriott study, since then support that estimate.

The barriers to elder volunteerism discussed above provide some of the reasons why those elders are not volunteers. Embedded in one of those barriers—ageism—is a key element to promoting more volunteerism by older Americans. I already alluded to this simple yet historically overlooked factor: people are far more likely to volunteer if they are asked (e.g., being in a larger household). Ageism, perhaps abetted by negative self-images, has kept many older persons who might otherwise volunteer from doing so. However, the changing socioeconomic characteristics of older Americans will increase their propensity to volunteer. Tapping that propensity may be no more difficult than simply *asking them to help*.

BIBLIOGRAPHY

American Association of Retired Persons. (1991). *Resourceful aging: Today and tomorrow. Volume II: Volunteerism.* Washington, DC: AARP.

Chambre, S. M. (1987). *Good deeds in old age: Volunteering by the new leisure class.* Lexington, MA: Lexington Books.

Committee on an Aging Society, Institute of Medicine and National Research Council. (1986). *America's aging: Productive roles in an older society.* Washington, DC: National Academy Press.

Fischer, L. C., & Schaffer, K. B. (1993). *Older volunteers: A guide to research and practice.* Newbury Park, CA: Sage Publications.

Harootyan, R. A., & Vorek, R. E. (1994). Volunteering, helping, and gift giving in families and communities. In V. L. Bengtson & R. A. Harootyan (Eds.), *Intergenerational linkages: Hidden connections in American society.* New York: Springer Publishing Company.

Herzog, A. R., & Morgan, J. N. (1993). Formal volunteer work among older Americans. In S. Bass, F. Caro, & Y. P. Chen (Eds.), *Achieving a productive aging society,* Boston: Auburn House.

Hodgkinson, V. A. and Weitzman, M. S. (1994). *Giving and Volunteering in the United States,* 1994 Edition. Washington, DC: Independent Sector.

Marriott Seniors Volunteerism Study (1991). Commissioned by Marriott Senior Living Services and the U.S. Administration on Aging, Washington, DC.

Widowhood and Widowerhood

Anne Martin-Matthews

University of Guelph

I. Demographic Realities
II. Widowhood as a Relative Life Event
III. Social Supports
IV. Comparisons and Contrasts in the Experience of Widowhood
V. Limitations of Research

Anticipatory Socialization In the process of anticipatory socialization to the role of widowed person, individuals who are not yet widowed engage in behaviors or have experiences typical of widowhood. The extent to which this occurs varies with age and the expectedness of widowhood, the duration of the spouse's final illness, and the forewarning of death.
Grief Work The actual process of bereavement and mourning. Although some argue that bereavement cannot be assigned a specific amount of time, clinicians and researchers generally suggest that the process can take a full 2 years; some suggest even longer.
Social Support That set of personal contacts through which the individual maintains social identity and lifestyle. Supports may be economic, tangible, or emotional in nature.

WIDOWHOOD OR WIDOWERHOOD is both a status and a process. The status of widowhood refers to the situation of an individual who has not remarried following the death of their spouse. Widowhood is also a process of transition, progressing from the illness of the spouse (which may vary from lengthy to very short term); through the death of the spouse and related events involving burial and mourning, grieving, and reconstruction of one's social world.

Women who have experienced the death of their husbands are referred to as widows, and men who have been widowed are referred to as widowers. The experience of widowhood varies considerably from one society to another, and within societies, as a function of social and cultural norms surrounding death, mourning, and remarriage; the age, gender, socioeconomic status, and resources of the widowed person and the deceased spouse, the nature of the marital relationship prior to bereavement, and the status of women in the society.

I. DEMOGRAPHIC REALITIES

In many countries, the proportion of the population aged 15 and over who are widowed is approximately 6%. Two factors typically characterize the incidence of widowhood in the population: its sex-selectivity and its age-related nature. In the United States and Canada, widows outnumber widowers nearly five to one. It is estimated that half of all marriages end with the death of the husband, and only one-fifth with the death of the wife. Among women aged 65 and over, almost 70% are widowed; the comparable figure among men is 22%. Because of this demographic reality, discussions of widowhood generally focus on women. [*See* DEMOGRAPHY.]

Several factors account for why most widowed persons are women. These include the differential life expectancy of males and females; the mating gradient, meaning that husbands are generally 2 or 3 years older than their wives; and differences in the rates of remarriage for widows and widowers. Not only are men far less likely than women are to become widowed, they are also less likely than women are to remain widowed. It is estimated that less than 1 in 5 widowers and 1 in 10 widows do eventually remarry. However, even amongst the elderly, widowed men have remarriage rates over eight times those of elderly women.

In recent decades the average age at widowhood has steadily increased. Thus widowhood is associated not only with women but now also with the elderly. On the average, women become widowed at age 66 in the United States (age 69 in Canada) and men at age 69 in the United States (age 73 in Canada). Almost three-quarters of widows in North America are over the age of 65. The average age of the widowed population is 75 years for both men and women.

Two final features characterize the demography of widowhood: the expectability of widowhood as a life event, and the relative duration of widowhood in the lives of the elderly. Because most individuals in society marry, the experience of widowhood has been an "expectable" life event of later life for most people; however, there is some evidence that this pattern is changing. Recent trends in North American and Europe indicate that growing proportions of older populations are married, declining proportions are widowed, and the percentage of older people who are divorced or separated is small but rising precipitiously. Because of increases in the proportions of the population who are entering old age outside of a marriage (because of having remained single or through separation and divorce without remarriage), the likelihood of being widowed in later life is in decline. Indeed, there is some suggestion that widowhood will become an increasingly nonnormative life event among future cohorts of women.

Because of the mating gradient referred to earlier, and the longer life expectancy of women, the average length of widowhood for women is considerably longer than for men. In the United States, the average duration of widowhood is 6 years for men and approximately 15 years for women. There are indications that differences in life expectancy between men and women are increasing. Because of this, and because of the anticipated increases in the absolute numbers of widowed persons in the population, the careful attention of policy makers will need to be directed to the needs of widows in particular.

II. WIDOWHOOD AS A RELATIVE LIFE EVENT

As a relative life event, widowhood is considered among the most stressful of role transitions. Although research findings are somewhat equivocal, there is evidence that the timing of widowhood in the life course and the duration of the spouse's final illness contribute significantly to the experience of bereavement. The experience of widowhood as "on time" or "off time" affects individuals in terms of their psychological preparedness, their opportunities for anticipatory socialization, and the societal resources and supports available to them. The age at which a person experiences the death of the spouse is a very important feature of the experience of widowhood because of the way in which his or her life is embedded in other social roles at that point in time. Similarly, the duration of the spouse's final illness also influences opportunities for anticipatory socialization to the role of widowed person. However, this relationship appears to be stronger in the case of early, off-time widowhood than for widowhood in later life.

Estimates of the duration of time for the completion of grief work among the bereaved suggest a period of 2 to 4 years for adjustment to the loss of the spouse. Although the early bereavement period is typically associated with profound psychological disorganization and feelings of status loss, widowhood also provides opportunities for personal growth and independence, and, for some, release from an unhappy union.

Research on the relationship between widowhood and morbidity and mortality is fraught with contradictory findings. Although there is evidence of short-term decreases in health status and perceived health following widowhood, long-term health appears largely unaffected. Despite early research findings of high mortality rates among widowers, more current epidemiological studies have found no significant relationship between bereavement and mortality. Findings of the long-term impact of widowhood on mental health are similarly equivocal, although the early bereavement period is generally associated with depression, mood alterations, disrupted sleep patterns, obsessive thoughts of the deceased, and disorientation. Nevertheless, the degree of disorganization produced by widowhood is influenced by many factors, especially by the degree of dependence upon a social network associated with the role of husband or wife and upon the level of commitment to that role. [*See* BEREAVEMENT AND LOSS.]

Despite the view of widowhood as a particularly stressful life event, most individuals adapt well over time, although the process of reconstruction of a new life and social world is for some a long and painful one. Many women, in particular, fare well in widowhood and underscore the point that widowhood is not necessarily a state of deprivation or deficit. For many people, widowhood represents a crisis not in the sense of a threat of catastrophe but rather a turning point, a crucial period of increased vulnerability and heightened potential. Many realize that potential, although as they advance in age and grow increasingly frail, the threat of becoming dependent looms large in their lives. [*See* LIFE COURSE; LIFE EVENTS.]

III. SOCIAL SUPPORTS

The role, function, and meaning of social support has been extensively examined in the gerontological literature. There is strong empirical evidence of a positive relationship between social support and health. The need for support in widowhood is by no means fixed. Thus the types and sources of support beneficial at one point in the process of widowhood may not necessarily be appropriate at a later point in the transition. Researchers have also questioned the assumption of the inherent value of social support. Loose, low-density networks, rather than tightly bound, all embracing networks, may be most appropriate in enabling widowed men and women to develop new social roles consistent with their new status.

Research findings indicate the predominant role of the family in the informal helping network following widowhood. However, it should be noted that fully one in five widowed persons report not having a single living relative to whom they feel particularly close. Clearly, there are many sources of variability in the experience of widowhood, all of which will influence the patterns of access to available social supports and their perceived benefit.

Adult children provide much of the assistance received by older widowed parents. But patterns of contact between widowed individuals and their adult children are not necessarily uniform, either across children or in terms of the duration of widowhood. Most contact is with daughters, and although the support of adult children is crucial during acute grief, it may become less salient over time as friends increase in importance.

Sibling relations hold a unique place in the support network in terms of their longer duration in comparison with other family ties and their essentially egalitarian nature. The research literature shows generally strong patterns of emotional support between widowed persons and their siblings, especially sisters, although frequency of contact and exchange of aid may be comparatively low. Other extended-family members, such as nieces and nephews, also act as viable members of the support networks of the widowed, especially in terms of emotional support. Research has also found that the memory of a deceased spouse can provide a form of support in widowhood.

Friendship relations change substantially with widowhood. Not distinguished by the feelings of obligation that characterize family relations, friendships—especially those with members of a married couple—may not survive widowhood. The ability to make new friendships may indeed be an important indicator of how an individual is coping with the loss of the spouse. Self-help and mutual support groups represent particular kinds of peer relationships. Although typically utilized by only a minority of the widowed, such groups have been demonstrated to effectively reduce the distress of the widowed in intervention groups. Formal organizational supports are consistently underutilized by the widowed.

In relation to all these sources of support, the redefined personal resources of the widowed person strongly influence the utilization of potential social supports. In any study of changes in patterns of social support in widowhood, the possibility of change in the widowed themselves as an influencing factor must be considered. [*See* SOCIAL NETWORKS, SUPPORT, AND INTEGRATION.]

IV. COMPARISONS AND CONTRASTS IN THE EXPERIENCE OF WIDOWHOOD

Many factors distinguish the experience of widowhood for men and for women. The greater expectability of widowhood as a life-course event for women frequently leads to a mental rehearsal or anticipation of circumstances associated with being "unattached" in later life. Although considerable research has debated whether the loss of the spouse is more difficult for men than for women, the meaning and consequences of death and widowhood for men and women under varying sets of circumstances remain little understood. The challenge of analyzing the effects of gender is complicated by the demography of widowhood, such that studies of widowed persons often result in samples wherein only about 13% are men.

Despite these research difficulties, studies have identified overall differences between widows and widowers in attitudes towards remarriage and in the issues that are most problematic to them in widowhood. Loneliness is a major problem for both men and women; financial resources are much more typically a concern for widows. Widows are far more likely than are widowers to be poor in old age. Feelings of competency in the completion of household tasks and issues involving sexuality are more often reported as major areas of concern for widowers, although this may reflect cohort effects for older men in genereral. [See ECONOMICS: INDIVIDUAL; LONELINESS.]

There are also points of contrast between widows and widowers on measures of social support. Overall, widowers report smaller support networks and less involvement with friends and family than do widows. In negotiating their social worlds, widowers rely almost exclusively on themselves or their children. Many widows, by contrast, have much more extensive and diverse social networks. Overall, then, widowers appear comparatively disadvantaged in their ties to family and in their domestic skills, but both these patterns may be cohort-specific.

An increasing number of widowed persons live alone, many of them residing in the same community and the same housing unit for many years. Although home ownership may be an important source of economic security for the widowed person, high housing-related costs may seriously undermine the financial benefits of ownership. In addition, long residential tenure, often for reasons of sentimental attachment to home as well as inertia at the prospect of relocation, may confine widowed men and women to homes whose physical characteristics are no longer appropriate to their needs and to a neighborhood no longer able to provide a supportive environment.

Widowed persons living in rural areas have marginally stronger supportive relationships with family and friends, but often lack the economic resources and access to transportation available to the urban widowed. When relocation finally comes for those widowed in later life, it is often into an institutional setting. Although comparatively few elderly people are institutionalized, the widowed are proportionally overrepresented among those who seek institutional care in later life.

Other factors that contribute to the variability of widowhood include whether or not widowed persons have living children and their ethnic identification and culture. Childlessness does not appear to exacerbate the transition to widowhood. There also appears to be little empirical support for the popular assumption of more extended networks and more involvement in those networks by widows and widowers with strong ethnic group identification. However, there is very limited research on sociocultural influences on the experience of widowhood. Except for the well-known traditional Indian practice of suttee (the expectation that widows would immolate themselves on their husband's funeral pyre) and more recent accounts of the crippling poverty and destitution of Indian widows without sons, comparatively little is known of how societal norms and expectations of bereavement and widowhood shape the experience in non-Western societies.

Competing demands associated with the performance of other roles or the experience of simultaneous transitions may also have an impact on the experience of widowhood in later life. Although the experience of retirement from the paid labor force is rarely coincident with widowhood, the loss of ongoing contact with work associates exacerbates the loneliness of widowhood for some individuals. Responsibilities involving providing care to dependent adult children or disabled parents may also complicate the transition to widowhood.

V. LIMITATIONS OF RESEARCH

Although the aging of the population is well documented and widely acknowledged, the implications of old age for the experience of widowhood is, surprisingly, not well recognized. Although widowhood is age-related and is a characteristic feature of later life, particularly of late old age and especially so for women, most studies have focused on younger populations. Relatively few studies extensively examine issues specific to elderly widowed persons.

Most studies of widowhood do not include comparison groups of those who have not experienced the loss of the spouse, or of those who have experienced other kinds of losses. As a result, conclusions that any observed patterns are, in fact, due exclusively to widowhood may be questionable.

Although in some countries (such as Canada) social policies have been developed to address issues of particular concern to the widowed (such as income supplementation), few such policies exist worldwide. Where they are present, social programs will need to be as flexible as possible. Today's widowed elderly have characteristics—in terms of social roles and expectations, availability of family members, labor force history, education, and financial resources—which are quite different from the attributes of the widowed elderly of tomorrow.

BIBLIOGRAPHY

Bankoff, E. A. (1983). Social support and adaptation to widowhood. *Journal of Marriage and the Family* 45(4), 826–839.

Lopata, H. Z. (1987a). *Widows. Vol. 1, The Middle East, Asia, and the Pacific.* Durham, NC: Duke University Press.

Lopata, H. Z. (1987b). *Widows. Vol. 2, North America.* Durham, NC: Duke University Press.

Lopata, H. Z. (1995). Feminist perspectives on social gerontology. In R. Blieszner & V. Hilkevitch Bedford (Eds.), *Handbook of aging and the family* (pp. 114–131). Westport, CT: Greenwood Press.

Lopata, H. Z. (1996). *Current widowhood: Myths and realities.* Newbury Park, CA: Sage.

Lund, D. A. (1989). *Older bereaved spouses: Research with practical implications.* New York: Hemisphere Publishing.

Martin-Matthews, A. (1991). *Widowhood in later life.* Toronto: Butterworths/Harcourt Brace.

O'Bryant, S. L. (1990/91). Forewarning of husband's death: Does it make a difference for older widows? *Omega: The Journal of Death and Dying* 22(3): 227–239.

O'Bryant, S. L., & Hansson, R. O. (1995). Widowhood. In R. Blieszner & V. H. Bedford (Eds.), *Handbook of aging and the family* (pp. 440–458). Westport, CT: Greenwood Publishing.

Work and Employment

Jeanette N. Cleveland

Colorado State University

Lynn M. Shore

Georgia State University

I. Conceptions of Age
II. Entry into Employment
III. Experiences in Organizations
IV. Upward Mobility in Organizations
V. Exiting the Organization
VI. Future Research Issues Concerning Older
   Workers
VII. Conclusions

Age Discrimination in Employment Act (ADEA)
Congressional legislation passed in 1967 and amended in 1978 and 1986 that protects workers age 40 years and older from unfair discrimination at work.
Age Stereotypes Generalized beliefs about the characteristics of older people.
Downsizing The systematic reduction of employees and possibly occupational areas within an organization.
Equal Employment Opportunity Commission (EEOC) A regulatory agency with the responsibility of enforcing discrimination laws concerning the workplace.
Functional Age Performance-based measures of age that are based on the premise that there is great individual variability in abilities and functioning at all ages.
Psychosocial Age Measures of age based on social perceptions of the individual including perceptions of the characteristics of the individual and self-perceptions of age.

The **WORKFORCE PARTICIPATION** of older adults has changed significantly in the past 30 years.

In 1950, 87% of males and 27% of females between 55–64 years were in the workforce. For adults over 65, 46% of males and 10% of females were still working. In 1990, 65% of males and 42% of females between 55 to 64 were in the workforce. For people over 65, 14% of males and 7% of the females were still working. Older workers both male and female continue to be an important segment of the workforce.

Researchers increasingly have investigated the relationships among worker age and important work processes and outcomes, including unemployment, hiring, performance appraisal, work attitudes, career characteristics, turnover, absence and terminations, and discrimination. In this article we examine issues concerning older workers as they seek employment, secure employment within the organization, work within the organization, and when they exit the paid employment domain. Before these employment issues are explored, however, a brief discussion is presented on the meaning and measurement of age in work-related research, and the many definitions of the "older worker." This discussion is important because the information accumulated on older workers is based on research using chronological age. However, chronological age may not be the best assessment of how "old" a person is.

I. CONCEPTIONS OF AGE

The study of aging and work, specifically, industrial gerontology, examines issues concerning the employment and retirement of middle-aged and older workers. A continuing problem in the field of industrial gerontology is the lack of an agreed upon definition for mature and older workers. One reason for the difficulty in securing an adequate definition is that aging is a multidimensional process that is difficult to embrace in a single definition or measure. In the present section, we will discuss five approaches to defining the older worker's age: (a) chronological or legal, (b) functional, (c) psychosocial, (d) organizational, and (e) life span. It is important to keep in mind however, that each of these five approaches to defining age can be categorized into two general groups: person-based measures and context-based measures of age. Person-based measures focus chiefly on the age characteristics of the individual, whereas context-based measures incorporate aspects of the work situation and often reflect comparisons among persons in the situation.

A. Chronological or Legal Age

Chronological or legal age is the most widely used person-based measure in research on older workers. The Age Discrimination in Employment Act (ADEA) of 1967 and amended in 1978 and 1986 protects workers over the age of 40, reflecting the fact that job openings may be disproportionately barred to applicants 40–45 years and more so for applicants over 55 years. The Job Training Partnership Act and Older Americans Act serves as another reference for recognizing individuals over 55 years as older workers. Although legally convenient, chronological age provides a narrow view of the role of aging at work; that is, it is often used as a proxy for the meaning that an individual attributes or ascribes to age or for functional or biological age. For example, an individual's interpretation of his or her age may reflect perceptions of health, appearance, energy, and so forth. Two individuals with the same chronological age may vary in terms of the subjective meaning that age has for them.

B. Functional Age

Another largely person-based age measure is functional age. Functional age is a performance-based definition of age and is based on the premise that there is great individual variation in abilities and functioning at all ages. As chronological age increases,

individuals change both biologically and psychologically, including declines in abilities as well as increases in experience and judgment. The concept of functional age has been criticized on a number of grounds including definitional, research design, and statistical points of view. The major limitations are the use of a single index and the assumption of decline with increasing chronological years. More recent alternative approaches draw from industrial and organizational psychology emphasizing appropriate assessment strategies and measures that assess attributes directly related to job performance. Even where there are measured age-related functional changes, these changes may not translate to performance decrements in any particular job.

C. Psychosocial and Organizational

Psychosocial definitions of older workers are based on social perceptions of the individual, including stereotypic perceptions of older workers and self-perceptions of age. These perceptions may depend in part on the age-type of the job that one holds or the age composition of the work group. The organizational view of older workers recognizes that age and tenure or seniority are related and may often be confounded. Furthermore, the organization itself may be perceived as old depending upon the average age of its employees. Both of these approaches are discussed together because both include largely context-based definitions of age; they vary perhaps in terms of unit of focus (i.e., psychosocial is a more individual unit of analysis, whereas organizational may use the group or organization as unit of analysis).

Industrial gerontologists have suggested that the older worker should be examined in relation to the work context, which includes characteristics of the group or setting in which a person works including his or her own self-perceptions of age, perceptions of one's own and other's age compared to work group members, perceptions of one's own and other's age compared to one's supervisor, and perceptions of self and others in relation to typical age within a given occupation or career path.

There is evidence that context-bound measures of age can predict such work outcomes as self- and manager-rated performance, manager-rated promotability, perceptions of organizational support, and self- and manager-rated on-the-job training. Furthermore, differences in the ages of supervisors and subordinates have been used to predict work outcomes. The similarity–attraction model has been used to conceptualize the impact of differences in age between the supervisor and subordinate. Proponents of this model have proposed that similarity of supervisor–subordinate dyads in terms of age contributes to a high level of attraction, which in turn leads to better work outcomes (e.g., higher performance and lower turnover). Empirical studies provide little support for this paradigm; similarity of supervisor and subordinate age had no effect on performance ratings, manager's liking of the subordinate, employee attitudes, or propensity to quit. Others have argued that age differences between the supervisor and subordinate are most important when they defy social norms (e.g., the subordinate is older than the manager). It also appears that a person's perceived age or chronological age interacts with the age type of the job or of the tasks performed at work to influence promotability ratings. Furthermore, support for age as defined by the specific organizational context has been found from research on age norms. For example, performance ratings are higher for managers who are perceived as younger than the perceived typical ages of individuals at that career stage and lower for managers who are perceived as older than the "norm" for that career stage. In general, men who are "behind schedule" (older than the norm) with respect to schooling, marriage, and job entry are more likely to have lower overall career earnings than men who are on schedule (or similar to the normative age group).

D. Life Span Approach

Another approach to defining the meaning of age in a work context focuses on behavior changes over the life span. Three sets of factors are seen as stimulating these behavioral changes during the life cycle: (a) normative, age-graded biological and/or environmental determinants; (b) normative, history-graded influences that affect most members of a cohort in a similar way (i.e., the Oklahoma City bombing of the Federal building); and (c) nonnormative factors including unique career and life change and individual health and stress-inducing events. Although some career development and management research has used this approach, the longitudinal approach has not yet been widely applied in ad-

dressing aging and work processes and outcomes. [*See* LIFE SPAN THEORY.]

The key factor to keep in mind when defining older workers is that we often are referring to people who are substantially younger than the subjects in more typical gerontological research. Typically, older workers include individuals who are 45, 50, 60, 65, or perhaps 70 years old. In gerontological research, "older" populations might be 80–100 years old, and are likely to have been out of the workforce for several decades. Therefore, in the discussion of age and work outcomes, employees that might be considered older can range from 40 to over 75 years old.

II. ENTRY INTO EMPLOYMENT

A. Job Search and Unemployment

In 1991, the unemployment rate for workers 45 and older was 4.3%, which was lower than the general unemployment rate of 6.7%. Nonetheless, older workers stayed unemployed longer than younger workers. Very little research has been done on job search behaviors of older workers. It is generally assumed that older workers are less likely than younger workers to search for alternative employment if they are presently employed. This is consistent with research showing lower turnover intentions for older workers. Age is viewed as one factor affecting marketability, which influences a candidate's likelihood of seeking jobs. Interestingly, recent research on employed managers showed that age had little impact on job search behavior, whereas job satisfaction, compensation, and perceptions of organizational success were negatively related to job search behavior. This suggests that it is working conditions, not age, that influence job search behavior. Furthermore, research suggests that age does not influence the type of recruiting sources used. Both young and old people are most likely to use newspaper ads. However, school referrals are more likely to be used by younger people when seeking employment.

B. Hiring Practices

Research investigating the impact of age on hiring decisions has chiefly focused on issues pertaining to discrimination. Of particular interest is when and if older workers are discriminated against in hiring. Research findings have been quite varied, perhaps due in part to the nature of the samples employed. Some studies ask undergraduates to simulate hiring decisions, and other studies are based on participants who are employed. The latter group includes both simulation studies and studies of actual hiring decisions. We discuss the literature by first examining studies using students as subjects, then simulation studies using workers, and finally studies of workers making actual hiring decisions.

Several studies based on student samples found evidence of age bias in favor of the young, with younger applicants receiving higher ratings on future potential, overall interview performance, and hiring recommendations. In contrast, starting salary recommendations were found to be higher for older than for younger applicants. Other studies found that such factors as competence and work experience had a greater impact on hiring recommendations than age. Interestingly, one study showed that students viewed young and old applicants to be equally appropriate for a low-status position, but view the older applicant as more appropriate than the young applicant for a high-status position.

Simulation studies using actual workers has also produced varied results. One study showed that young applicants were recommended for hire more often than old applicants. Other studies suggest that factors such as competence and job status moderated age effects; qualified older applicants fare well in high-status jobs.

Studies of actual hire decisions have also shown inconsistent results. One study showed that older applicants received lower hiring recommendations, and were rated lower in intelligence than younger applicants. A second study showed that age correlate positively with interview scores, suggesting that older applicants were preferred over younger applicants. However, the latter sample was fairly young (most applicants ranged from 21–30 years old), raising questions of generalizability. A final study examined similarity in age between the interviewer and applicant, and found that age similarity had no impact on the interview outcome.

All three types of subject samples reviewed showed mixed results in terms of age bias in hiring decisions. A number of possibilities emerge to explain the mixed findings. First, student subjects and working subjects react somewhat differently to older and younger applicants, particularly in relation to jobs of varying status. This may be due to the differences in the ages of subjects, or difference in work experience. Second, several studies showing age bias had subjects compare old and young applicants with identical qualifications. The design of these studies may actually contribute to age bias effects because subjects may assume that a young person with equal qualifications to an older person is more competent, having reached the same skill level at a younger age. A third possibility is that characteristics of the job in terms of age stereotyping may be at work. A number of studies suggest that jobs are typed in terms of whether they are appropriate for young, middle-aged, and older workers. This age-typing in turn affects treatment of older workers. However, this issue has not been systematically investigated in prior studies of hiring. Finally, the age composition of the applicant pool appears to have an impact on the hiring process, such that older workers are more likely to be hired when other older workers are already in the applicant pool.

III. EXPERIENCES IN ORGANIZATIONS

A. Stereotypes of Older Workers

The negative stereotypes of older workers have been documented in the industrial gerontology and industrial and organizational psychology literatures. Older workers are perceived as less efficient, less creative, less promotable, more resistant to change, slower, disinterested in training or retraining, incapable of adapting to change, undependable, costly, unable to meet the physical and mental demands of work, more rigid, and prone to illnesses and accidents. Furthermore, older workers are viewed as more passive, reserved, obsolete, and inflexible than younger workers. Some human resource managers believe that older workers have different work styles, which clash with the work style of younger workers. However, as people age, some positive characteristics are ascribed to them. For example, older people have also been described as more reliable, loyal, careful, and conscientious than their younger counterparts. Older workers are perceived to take longer and take fewer risks in decision making than younger managers. However, when risks must be taken and decisions made quickly to avoid missing an opportunity, these characteristics may be viewed as a potential negative. Although attitudes toward older workers are generally more negative than attitudes toward younger workers, the magnitude of the difference decreases as the age of the perceiver (the rater) increases. Furthermore, negative perceptions of older workers may play a greater role in some occupations than in others. Older employees in jobs typically occupied by younger persons or requiring skills associated with younger incumbents may be perceived most negatively, whereas older employees in positions occupied by or associated with older individuals may be perceived positively and in nonstereotypic terms. [See AGEISM AND DISCRIMINATION.]

B. Age and Job Performance

Considerable research in both lab and field settings indicates that job performance does not decline with age. However, there are a number of issues to consider in this research. The first is the definition of the domain of performance. Performance measures used in this research include supervisory ratings, productivity indices and other objective measures (e.g., sales volume), turnover, and absenteeism (discussed later). There is some indication that the age–performance relationship varies with the type of performance measure used. Supervisory ratings reflect a slight decline with age, whereas more objective production data (i.e., sales) may not. For nonprofessional occupations, the relationship is more positive but still weak; for professional occupations, age showed a slight negative relationship with performance. Apparently the largest moderator of the relationship between age and performance is the age range of the sample. For younger samples with ages in the twenties, the age–performance relationship is modest; for samples with older ages, the relationship is near zero. That is, age appears to be more predictive of performance for younger workers than for older workers.

Physical capacity, which refers to outcomes of coordinated activity among major components of the motor system involved in carrying out work, begins to show a decline in middle age. Declines are most noticeable in tasks involving perceptual or psychomotor speed. However, each individual will experience performance declines at different ages. Declines in physical capacity should be examined on an individual

basis, because they may not translate into any perceptible interference with the essential activities of the job. [See MOTOR CONTROL; PERCEPTION.]

Research on the effects of aging on managerial performance have produced mixed results. There is evidence of modest performance decrements on some managerial tests. Older managers make slower decisions but consider a greater number of facts related to a problem. In one study, older managers asked for less additional information, showed less breadth to the overview of the task, used fewer approaches to promote changes, and engaged in planning that was less effective and optimal (i.e., less complex).

Any modest relationship found between age and performance may be better understood as a relationship between job knowledge and job performance. Some industrial and organizational psychologists have suggested that job incumbents acquire most of the job knowledge needed for successful performance during the first several years on the job. Individual differences in job experience may be associated with significant differences in job performance, especially during the first few years. After a while however, job experience makes diminishing contributions to job knowledge and thus job performance. Small differences in job experience among younger workers may translate into large differences in job knowledge and job performance. Therefore, among younger workers, age differences will be related to differences in job performance; but as additional job experience contributes little incremental job knowledge, amount of new job knowledge gained each year becomes less and less such that, overall, age has a weak relationship with job knowledge and little or no relationship with job performance.

Laboratory studies of task performance and age have shown age-related sensory deficits across a wide range of psychological functions, including peripheral and motor mechanisms, memory, and information processing. Especially with complex or demanding tasks, such as in multisource monitoring, older people tend to be particularly disadvantaged. Although one would expect that older individuals would perform less well on more complicated real-world tasks, the assessment of age effects in occupational settings involves considerable methodological problems. These methodological deficiencies include a lack of reliability and comparability of performance measures across age groups, selective attrition of subjects with healthier ones surviving, and selection biases. [*See* ATTENTION; MEMORY.]

1. Performance: Production Records

Research both in Britain and the United States indicates that the productivity of workers in their fifties exceeds that of workers in their teens or twenties. Peak productivity occurred in the forties and in their fifties, and then worker productivity declined between 2 and 16% thereafter. In the United States, productivity peaked during the mid-thirties and early forties, and then gradually declined reaching only 17% below peak in employees aged 65 and older.

2. Accidents

Although research results are mixed, the most common finding is that accident rates are lower among older workers compared to workers age 24 and younger and equivalent to rates among workers of 25 to 44 years. However, research has also found a positive age–accident relationship as well as an inverted-U, U-shaped or nonsignificant age–accident relationship. Moderators of this relationship include sex and type of occupation. Accident rates are generally lower among women and higher for blue-collar work (blue-collar jobs account for 70% of all injuries and are eight times riskier than white-collar occupations). Older employees who occupy jobs normally held by younger workers incurred more accidents than their younger counterparts. [*See* ACCIDENTS: FALLS.]

Although older workers may experience lower rates of injury, they generally lose more time per injury than do younger workers. The severity of injury may increase with age and require a longer time to recover. An injury is also more likely to result in a permanent disability for older employees. Deaths due to accidents also increase with age.

C. Absenteeism and Turnover

Absenteeism and turnover reflect two forms of withdrawal behavior, which can be costly both to the organization and to individuals. Several reviews suggest that age is negatively related to turnover. However, a recent metaanalysis showed that age provides little useful information about whether an employee will voluntarily leave an organization. However, given the measurement problems associated with the turnover variable (i.e., wide variety of measures used),

the relationship between age and turnover may be underestimated. Intentions to quit and propensity to leave have been found to be the best predictors of voluntary turnover. Older workers consistently show lower turnover intention.

Metaanalyses of the relationship between age and absenteeism showed significant results that depended upon the type of absence measure used. Absence frequency is a measure of avoidable absence, whereas absence duration is a measure of unavoidable absence. Absence frequency (avoidable) is negatively related to employee age; for unavoidable absences, research findings are mixed. Recent research suggests that employee age interacts with employee sex for both avoidable and unavoidable absenteeism behavior. Females show a stronger negative relationship between age and time lost than males, whereas males show a negative relationship between age and frequency of absences, and females show a positive relationship. Older female employees are more likely to have frequent absences, but are less likely to have a number of consecutive days absent from the workplace compared to male employees. Although multifactor models have been proposed and tested for understanding absenteeism, age itself is thought to be a weak predictor of attendance. Furthermore, with increasing numbers of women in the workforce, career, dual-career, and family issues need to be considered and incorporated into these models.

D. Age and Training

As the average age of workers increases, the issue of training older workers becomes more important. Research suggests that the relationship between age and success in training depends on both the context of training and the specific criteria used to define "success." Age has the greatest influence when the content is novel (e.g., computer use) and the criterion for success is speed in completing training.

Several decades of research on the effectiveness of training interventions with workers of various ages has been carried out. Older workers learn less quickly than their younger counterparts. However, if work procedures remain unchanged for long periods of time, the age difference in mastery time becomes trivial. In rapidly changing occupations that require frequent training in new work methods, older workers may be more costly to the employer and less productive than younger workers. [*See* LEARNING.]

Laboratory samples showed consistently larger age differences in training performance than field samples. There are two methodological issues that may exaggerate the actual age differences in training. First, designs typically employed in age training research are extreme group designs. The performance of a younger group of employees (i.e., 23 years old) is compared with a significantly older group (i.e., 55 or 60 years old). Although designs of this kind may accurately assess the difference between the groups, it may exaggerate the degree of the relationship between age (as a continuous variable) and training performance. Second, there may be a bias in the selection of tasks in the lab so as to maximize the possibility of finding large age differences. In the field with real-world tasks, there is more variation in tasks as well as the possibility that practice and experience can counter age-related decrements.

E. Age and Work Attitudes

An extensive review of the work attitude literature indicates that consistent age-related differences exist in a number of attitudes. Overall job satisfaction has consistently been shown to be positively (but weakly) related to age. This relationship may be moderated by occupation. Human services and white-collar jobs had the strongest relationships between age and job satisfaction, whereas in factory, clerical, and teaching jobs, there appears to be no relationship between age and job satisfaction. In addition, other research suggests that tenure (which is typically strongly associated with age) is a more consistent predictor than age of job satisfaction. Research on facet satisfaction shows that there is, in general, a positive relationship between age and satisfaction with the work itself, whereas studies of satisfaction with pay have produced mixed results. Furthermore, satisfaction with promotion, the supervisor, and co-workers appears to be unrelated to age. This pattern of relationships is consistent with research suggesting that job characteristics may explain the age–job satisfaction relationship, in that older employees appear to obtain more intrinsic rewards (but not necessarily extrinsic rewards) out of work than younger employees.

Studies of work values suggest that there may be a positive relationship with age. Although age typically is positively related to job involvement, a number of studies suggest that age may be less important than job and organizational characteristics, as well as individual differences in determining level of job involvement. A recent metaanalysis showed moderately positive relationships between age and both Protestant work ethic and prestige (the effect a job has on a person's social standing). However, age was not found to be related to Maslow's concept of growth need strength or autonomy.

A number of theoretical models have included age as an antecedent of organizational commitment. Two forms of commitment have been extensively investigated in the literature, including affective commitment and continuance commitment. For affective commitment, it is assumed that as employees age, they become increasingly attached to the organization, and their identification with the employer increases. In contrast, for continuance commitment, age is viewed as a factor that constrains future employment options due to nonportable investments in the organization. This makes leaving more costly, leading to higher levels of continuance commitment. A recent metaanalysis suggested that age is more strongly associated with affective commitment than with continuance commitment, but that age is not strongly related to either form of commitment.

In conclusion, although age does appear to be fairly consistently associated with overall job satisfaction and some types of work values, there is less evidence to support links between age and other attitudinal variables. In addition, there is fairly compelling evidence that even when age is associated with work attitudes, that other variables, such as job and work conditions, may in fact account for these associations.

F. Age and Alternative Work Options and Schedules

Both older employees and management can mutually benefit from a choice of work arrangements other than the standard 40-hour schedule. Six different job arrangements have been identified in industrial gerontology that can be used effectively to accommodate the work needs of older workers and their employers. These work arrangements can be categorized into two groups: part-time work schedules and job modifications. Increasingly, organizations are experimenting with various forms of part-time employment for older personnel including job sharing and phased retirement programs. Part-time reemployment of retirees is also an option. Job sharing usually involves two part-time employees sharing one full-time position. Work time is reduced. Yet an older individual's expertise and experience, as well as the opportunity to mentor, continue to be available to the organization.

Phased retirement is one option for full-time employees who are 2–3 years away from retirement. Here employees are allowed to reduce their weekly work hours from 40 to 30 hours and then later to 20 hours until retirement. An individual can literally phase into retirement. This slow reduction of hours allows the organization the time to train and replace workers. Reemployment of retired workers on a part-time basis has become common in fast-food industries, banks, and insurance companies. The retiree is retained as a consultant or is rehired on a temporary basis. In a random sample of over 400 organizations, approximately 25% had job sharing and another 25% had phased retirement programs. Nearly 50% were reemploying their retirees. These part-time work options appear to be reasonably popular methods for utilizing older personnel.

In contrast, a smaller number of organizations make changes in the actual work performed by older workers. Job modifications may be found within the manufacturing industry. Three kinds of modifications are typically used with older employees: job redesign, job transfer, and job retraining. Job redesign involves either restructuring the work to be performed or reshaping the physical environment of the worker. This can include special chairs, magnifying glasses, and so forth. A number of these accommodations may fall under the 1991 American with Disabilities Act. Job transfer involves moving an older employee to a less physically or mentally demanding job. Finally, job retraining involves the updating of older experience worker skills to keep pace with changing technology in their field. This occurs often in engineering-related fields.

IV. UPWARD MOBILITY IN ORGANIZATIONS

A. Age Structures of Occupations and Experiences of Older Workers

Among industrialized countries, older workers are concentrated in a narrow range of occupations. The concentration or age grading becomes more pronounced as age increases. In the United States, older men are found in disproportionate numbers in the retail trade, in miscellaneous services (including many unskilled service jobs), and in declining industries such as mining, textiles, and railways. Workers age 65 and over are concentrated in more marginal occupations that are defined in terms of job security, number of weeks worked per year, rate of occupational growth or decline, and social status. Among professional workers, older individuals occupy jobs with little opportunity for growth or are disproportionately self-employed. Self-employment often involves longer hours and lower earnings.

The reasons that older workers are concentrated in a narrow range of occupations is attributable to economic, social, and cultural factors. Economic and technological changes have necessitated higher education and vocational skill levels. Older workers tend to have less education and vocational skill training than younger workers. Furthermore, older workers may be increasingly unable to cope with job demands among a variety of jobs. Age structures of jobs may result from task requirements that present problems for older workers, including requirements for heavy perceptual demands, speed, or physical labor.

Finally, perceptions and attitudes towards older workers vary by occupation, especially by blue-collar, white-collar, and managerial, professional, and technical occupations. More blue-collar respondents embraced the following negative statements, followed by white-collar, and then managerial, professional, and technical: older workers compared to younger workers (a) tend to be less flexible and more resistant to change, (b) tend to be less productive, (c) tend to be less creative, (d) are less likely to keep up with new developments in their fields, and (e) take longer to train. Generally, more unfavorable comparisons between older and younger workers are made for jobs that (a) require physical strength or exertion; (b) are largely routine and tedious; (c) require little or no training; (d) have lesser educational requirements; and (e) involve lesser responsibility.

Occupational segregation of the older workers may greatly limit their career mobility. Nevertheless, there are many older workers in jobs and occupations where opportunities for promotion still exist, and these workers may face special career challenges including fewer promotions and challenging assignments which can lead to career plateauing.

B. Promotions, Challenging Assignments, and Career Plateauing

Most career theories include stages in which before retirement, individuals become "obsolete" or "deadwood" in preparation for leaving their employer. This commonly accepted view is inconsistent with the evidence that adults make many career transitions throughout their life span. Furthermore, many individuals in their sixties, seventies, and eighties continue to work and seek ways to expand their careers. Nonetheless, many organizations have strongly held belief systems about the age-related nature of careers, so that promotion and development systems are oftentimes designed for younger workers.

One factor that may contribute to lack of career development opportunities for older workers is the negative ways in which these individuals are often viewed. These negative features are often times viewed as essential to good performance, and organizations are likely to seek leaders with these types of attributes. Older workers are rated high in attendance, solid performance record, and punctuality. These attributes are likely to be associated with reliable and dependable employees but those who may be viewed as unlikely to advance. These studies also suggest that younger workers may be seen as more appropriate for the types of challenging jobs that many employees are currently faced with in times of downsizing, mergers, and acquisitions. Longitudinal research further indicates that challenging assignments early in one's career are highly predictive of upward career mobility.

Age stereotypes may contribute to less development of older than of younger workers. Older workers are viewed as resistant to change and are given less feedback and fewer opportunities to improve their performance. Furthermore, research suggests that the age composition of the work group may affect the degree to which older workers receive developmental opportunities. Older workers who work with other older employees are least likely to receive career counseling. In contrast, older workers are most likely to receive on-the-job training when they work with younger people. Nonetheless, older workers are much less likely than either younger or middle-age workers to receive career counseling and on-the-job training. This shows that although age context affects the degree to which older workers receive developmental opportunities, older workers are still the least likely to receive those opportunities.

Again, age stereotypes may underlie differential performance attributions made about younger and older workers, limiting the upward mobility of older employees. Poor performance by older workers is attributed to more stable factors, such as ability, than similar performance by younger workers. In addition, job simplification is viewed as more appropriate and training (for more demanding tasks) as less appropriate for poorly performing older workers. Older employees are also viewed as causing their own career problems due to loss of motivation or complacency. Thus, differential performance attributions may also explain why older workers receive fewer developmental opportunities than younger workers.

Research on promotability suggests that age context plays an important role. Although middle-age and older workers are viewed as most promotable when they work with people who are younger than they are, younger workers are seen as most promotable when they work with people who are older than they are. Similar findings have been shown in the performance appraisal area. Managers who are younger than most other managers at their organizational level receive higher performance ratings than those who are older than most others at their organizational level. Because performance ratings are often used in making promotions decisions, this suggests that being younger than the norm may have some distinct career advantages in terms of promotion opportunities.

The pattern of results for studies of developmental opportunities, promotability, and performance suggest that age stereotypes may adversely limit older workers' career opportunities. Age stereotypes regarding older workers' capabilities, willingness to change, and technical obsolescence surely lead to career plateauing and stagnation. Promotion denials for older employees may be more common than outright dismissals and are a frequently cited basis for a lawsuit under ADEA. However, denial of promotion based on age is more difficult to prove than an illegal dismissal.

Future research is needed which addresses methods for overcoming stereotypes that limit opportunities for older workers.

V. EXITING THE ORGANIZATION

A. Economics of Age

Many employers seem to believe that older workers are more costly (relative to their productive value) than younger workers. There is evidence that there are age-specific costs for benefit pension plans and health insurance for active workers. In a defined benefit (DB) plan, there is a positive relationship between age and cost of benefits. At ages 50–54, the compensation package is worth between 101% and 107% of the value of the benefits offered between the age of 45–49, from 101–116% at ages 55–59 years, and about 105–135% at ages 60–64. Retiree health insurance plans provide a strong disincentive to hiring older workers not yet eligible for Medicare. Wages and salaries tend to increase up until age 50 or so and then level off (e.g., older workers typically earn more than younger workers). During layoffs, downsizing, and mergers, the financial savings by reducing the number of more highly paid older workers may be an attractive method for organizations in the short run. Health costs and other compensation costs are greater for older workers despite the finding that most older workers are healthy enough to keep working longer than they do. [See PENSIONS]

Proponents of reducing the number of older workers may overlook costs associated with recruiting and training new employees. Further costs are incurred in relocating new workers, assisting spouses in finding work, and the learning curve associated with new workers adjusting to the new work environment. Considerations such as turnover may actually counterbalance the cost of benefits. As mentioned previously, older workers tend to have lower voluntary turnover rates than younger workers. Greater stability of an older workforce may offset disadvantages associated with high fringe benefit costs.

B. Age and Job Terminations

The percentage of the labor force that consists of older men has decreased substantially since 1975. Men in the 55–65-year-old age group decreased by 8%, and men in the 65 and older group decreased by 5% between 1975 and 1990. For older women, a somewhat smaller increase occurred in the 55–64-year-old age group (4%), and a negligible increase occurred in the 65 and over group (less than 1%). It is not clear whether this trend for older men is due chiefly to voluntary departure from the workforce, or whether substantial number of older workers are being forced out of the workplace.

Downsizing is an increasingly popular organizational strategy for reducing costs. Downsizing methods include voluntary severance programs, voluntary early-retirement programs, attrition, relocation, pay and hiring freezes, and outright firing. Information is not available on the extent to which older workers are affected by downsizing relative to other age groups. However, voluntary early-retirement programs, which have been a very popular downsizing method, are clearly targeted toward older groups. Many of those who take early retirement do so voluntarily, partially due to dissatisfaction with the job, supervisor, and company. Some also recognize the lack of promotion opportunities available to them, and opt for retirement. However, others are forced to take early retirement, or face the prospect of termination. Of particular concern are organizations that change performance appraisal systems or ratings to justify the desire to rid themselves of older workers. Abrupt changes in the performance appraisal system are likely to create mistrust, not only among those who are retiring, but also possibly for those who remain with the organization.

In addition, formal age discrimination complaints are on the rise. Since the ADEA was passed in 1967, charges filed with the EEOC rose from 1,000 in 1969 to over 5,000 in 1976 to approximately 11,000 in 1982 to more than 17,000 in 1986. Perceived unlawful discharge or termination was mentioned in 58 percent of the age charges filed at the EEOC in 1985. When older workers are stereotyped as less aggressive, less ambitious, and less concerned with work achievement, organizations may look to this group as one to layoff when reducing the workforce. However, terminations of older workers are resulting in lawsuits. One reason for this is inadequate evidence of poor performance; another is the existence of employer discrimination against older workers. Although older workers may be terminated more often in mergers and downsizing efforts, the basis for such termination may be only indirectly age based. As mentioned previously, employers frequently perceive older workers to be more costly than younger workers; so terminations may be made on largely an economic basis. Research is needed which focuses on the effects of downsizing on older workers. Of particular value would be research on the impact of early retirement programs on worker attitudes.

C. Age Discrimination

Although many charges are terminated by the Equal Employment Opportunity Commission (EEOC) due to lack of evidence, some cases do make it to court. The overwhelming percent of plaintiffs in age-discrimination suits are men, especially senior white male professionals and managers. The greatest number of cases concern wrongful termination. Employees tended to lose their cases in court. It may be that in strong cases (for the plaintiff), organizations settled out of court, and employers would carry through only on cases they felt sure of winning. Women were more likely than men to win their cases (64 vs. 29%), although these comparisons should be made cautiously due to the small number of women filing age-discrimination claims. Regardless, there are some organizational practices that may be indicative of age discrimination including older workers being passed over in favor of younger workers with similar credentials, being told no openings exist when they do, being discouraged from jobs where interviews use "too much experience" as a proxy for age, being replaced by younger workers with the same or fewer skills, being denied opportunities to participate in training programs, being considered not promotable, being laid off before younger workers, being paid less for the same work, being demoted without just cause, and having challenging assignments transferred to other younger workers.

D. Retirement

A great deal of research has focused on factors that predict retirement. These factors can be divided into three major categories, including personal variables, work-related factors, and environmental factors. In terms of personal factors, the date people choose to retire is influenced by eligibility for a pension plan, and their anticipated financial situation at retirement. Health is another personal variable that is related to when people retire. It has also been found that people who anticipate adjusting well to retirement are more likely to plan an early retirement. For work-related factors, a number of studies suggest that work satisfaction may influence when people retire. Organizational commitment is another attitude that may influence when workers retire. However, the evidence for work attitudes is not overly compelling. For environmental factors, these can include family and marital situations (being widowed or still have children in college), as well as leisure activities. Individuals with strong interests outside of work may well opt to retire early in order to pursue those interests.

It is not entirely clear what the impact of retirement is on employers. Large numbers of retirements may provide more career opportunities for young people, and allow organizations to hire people with up-to-date skills. On the other hand, organizations may lose critical knowledge or skill areas that older, more tenured workers provide. One study found that an early-retirement program did not have a substantial effect on the firm's management talent, nor was there any indication that the most capable managers were the most likely to retire early. Moreover, it appeared that the more highly motivated managers with more positive attitudes toward their work and toward the company were less likely to retire. However, additional research is clearly needed in this area to determine if these results generalize to other organizations. [See RETIREMENT.]

VI. FUTURE RESEARCH ISSUES CONCERNING OLDER WORKERS

A. Older Women

Workforce participation rates for women have increased dramatically during the last four decades. For women from 55–64 years, participation rates rose from the early 1940s and peaked during the late 1960s. In the past two decades participation rates have leveled off at approximately 41.7 women in the labor force for every 100 men. In 1987, 56% of women were working and on average, the woman was married, a mother, and had a high school education. Participation rates of women age 65 and over reached their record highs between the mid-1950s and 1960s when they ranged between 10.2 to 10.9 for every 100 women in the population. By the mid-1980s, the participation rates drifted downward to 7.5. Furthermore, the proportion of older women who work continues to be substantially lower than the proportion of older men; the proportion who retire early is somewhat higher than for men.

The typical female employee does not resemble the typical male employee. Furthermore, middle-aged and older women are a heterogeneous group in terms of skills, work-life expectations, centrality and necessity of work, child-care responsibilities, and elder-care responsibilities. Some researchers have speculated that different standards of aging exist for men and women. Because women are more likely to be judged on their physical appearance than men, women are viewed more negatively as they age. In contrast, as men age, their prestige may be enhanced by increased money and power, and they are judged less on their physical appearance. Some authors have argued that these different standards for judging men and women affect women in the workplace, such that women may be devalued at work at an earlier age than men. Perhaps some of the "glass ceiling" effects that women experience are partially due to the devaluation of women that occurs as they age. Women may have fewer career opportunities not just because of their lower status in the workplace, but also because of the way in which society views older women. Clearly, future rsearch needs to examine the interactive effects of age and gender to determine whether men and women are treated differently as they age.

B. Age and Minority Status

In 1980, about 17% of ethnic minorities in the United States were over 65 years. This proportion of the population is growing more rapidly than is the white population. Very little research that we are aware of to date has been conducted in this area. Generally, however, older minority males and females tend to be worse off economically and in terms of employment than nonminority counterparts. With significantly increasing diversity, there is a great need for the existing and future research in this area to be highlighted and mainstreamed in major gerontological and work employment research and practitioner journals. If minorities are concentrated in occupations

that require physical labor, speed, and routinization of tasks, minority employees may be at greater risk for potential negative experiences resulting from age bias. Furthermore, because lower-level employees are in the most financial need of work, once retired they are often forced (due to their age) to accept lower-paying jobs if they can find them. Women, blacks, and Hispanics experience severe hardships because they often lack financial reserves, pension plans, and find it harder to gain reemployment at an adequate wage. [*See* RACIAL AND ETHNIC DIVERSITY.]

C. Current Organizational Issues

1. Working in Teams

In some types of work groups, there may be a generational problem for older workers. Younger groups may be better able to draw on the performance of the best individuals (e.g., most knowledgeable), and to identify and use their members' resources. In older groups, members may be more concerned with establishing and preserving status, leadership, and avoiding looking bad to peers. Research suggests that younger people may have more experience in group-process work and group decision making than do older workers, have less concern with status and control, have less competition in a group, and are more focused on securing optimal results on the task. This suggests that older workers who are expected to operate in and contribute to group activities may need to be trained or counseled in how to be effective group members. Studies of older managers suggest that they are less often in teams (except in competitive situations); believed informal teams were viewed as cliques and were to be avoided; did not know much about working cooperatively; had been raised in autocratic modes of management and saw asking for or accepting help as a sign of weakness; relied on "experts"; and even when committed to teamwork, lacked skills to make it work. Given the trends toward approaching work using teams of people, these findings suggest a number of training and other human resource interventions for both younger and older employees.

2. Older Workers and Technology

High technology, including computer-integrated manufacturing and robotics, frees many workers from hard physical labor and increases the need for workers with a wide range of technical and problem-solving approaches. Jobs created by robotic technology will often require at least 2 years of college education as well as additional training and retraining. Technology has influenced work site location. Certain regions of the country have attracted a significant proportion of information-processing and smaller high-tech companies. The computer has played a large role in the development of telework and telecommuting, specifically working from one's home or neighborhood satellite offices. These and other technological changes will affect the increasingly diverse workforce. Older workers will not fare well if speed is a characteristic of working with technology. On the other hand, work that is not contingent on physical labor and that requires alternative methods of problem solving may be a positive source of employment for the older employee. More research is needed to determine how people's perceptions of older workers influence their judgments about their employability in such occupations.

3. Older Workers and Customer Service Orientation

Most of the new job opportunities between now and the early 2000s will be in the service sector. Older workers may be appropriate for these jobs, which are assumed not to be physically demanding. However, thorough job analysis of these jobs is necessary because many service jobs are stressful and demanding (e.g., nursing, food-counter work). For some service positions, task-related experience may be an important requirement. The majority of the occupations with the largest project job growth are female dominated, including retail sales, nurses, secretaries, receptionists, food preparation, and teachers (secondary school and kindergarten). Women should end up with about 65% of the new jobs by the year 2000 and hopefully a proportionate number will go to older

women, especially because this is a rapidly expanding group in the workforce.

VII. CONCLUSIONS

Research on age and employment shows that age affects many work processes. Yet many studies of the same work process (e.g., hiring, performance evaluation) show inconsistent results. This may be largely due to the influence of the work context and age stereotypes. Contextual variables such as age composition of departments or applicant pools, occupations, and jobs all appear to influence decisions about older workers. Furthermore, age stereotypes of workers and of tasks may serve to limit older workers' career opportunities, and may encourage early-retirement programs and other forms of downsizing that can adversely affect older workers. More systematic research is needed to better understand how the work context and age stereotypes affect older workers. More theory development pertaining to older working adults is needed. Given the aging of the workforce, research and theory focused on the role of aging at work is particularly timely.

BIBLIOGRAPHY

Dennis, H. (Ed.) (1988). *Fourteen steps in managing an aging work force.* Lexington, MA: Lexington Books.

Doering, M., Rhodes, S. R., & Schuster, M. (1983). *The aging worker: Research and recommendations.* Beverly Hills, CA: Sage Publications.

Rix, S. E. (1990). *Older workers.* Santa Barbara, CA: ABC-CLIO.

Sterns, H. L., & Miklos, S. M. (1995). The aging worker in a changing environment: Organizational and individual issues. *Journal of Vocational Behavior, 47,* 248–268.

Warr, P. (1994). Age and employment. In H. C. Triandis, M. D. Dunnette, & L. M. Hough (Eds.), *Handbook of industrial and organizational psychology* (vol. 4, pp. 485–551). Palo Alto, CA: Consulting Psychologists Press, Inc.

Contributors

William H. Adler
Immune System
    Clinical Immunology Section
    National Institute on Aging
    National Institutes of Health
    Baltimore, Maryland 21224

Hiroko Akiyama
Social Networks, Support, and Integration
    Institute for Social Research
    University of Michigan
    Ann Arbor, Michigan 48106

Philip A. Allen
Attention
    Department of Psychology
    Cleveland State University
    Cleveland, Ohio 44115

M. D. Altose
Respiratory System
    School of Medicine
    Case Western Reserve University
    Cleveland, Ohio 44106

Truman O. Anderson
Allergic Reactivity in the Elderly
    Department of Medicine
    College of Medicine
    University of Illinois
    Chicago, Illinois 60612

Toni C. Antonucci
Social Networks, Support, and Integration
    Institute for Social Research
    University of Michigan
    Ann Arbor, Michigan 48106

Sara Arber
Gender Roles
    Department of Sociology
    University of Surrey
    Guildford, Surrey GU2 5XH, United Kingdom

William J. Aronson
Prostate
    Division of Urology
    University of California School of Medicine
    Los Angeles, California 90095

Robert C. Atchley
Retirement
    Scripps Gerontology Center
    Miami University
    Oxford, Ohio 45056

Elizabeth S. Badley
Arthritis
> Arthritis Community Research and Evaluation
> Unit
> Wellesley Hospital Research Institute
> Toronto, Ontario M4Y 1J3, Canada

Arthur K. Balin
Oxidative Damage
> Department of Pathology
> Medical College of Pennsylvania and
> Hahnemann University
> Philadelphia, Pennsylvania 19104

Richard L. Bauer
Bone and Osteoporosis
> Department of Medicine
> University of Texas Health Science Center
> San Antonio, Texas 78284

Vern L. Bengtson
Self-Esteem
> Andrus Gerontology Center
> University of Southern California
> Los Angeles, California 90089

Carolyn D. Berdanier
Metabolism: Carbohydrate, Lipid, and Protein
> Department of Food Service and Nutrition
> University of Georgia
> Athens, Georgia 30609

C. S. Bergeman
Behavioral Genetics
> University of Notre Dame
> Notre Dame, Indiana 46556

Claudio Bilato
Atherosclerosis
> National Institute on Aging
> National Institutes of Health
> Bethesda, Maryland 21224

James E. Birren
History of Gerontology
> Center on Aging
> University of California
> Los Angeles, California 90024

Anders Bjelle
Rheumatic Diseases
> Department of Rheumatology
> Gothenburg University
> Gothenburg 41310, Sweden

Fredda Blanchard-Fields
Decision Making and Everyday Problem Solving
> Department of Psychology
> Georgia Institute of Technology
> Atlanta, Georgia 30332

Dan G. Blazer, II
Depression
Suicide
> Departments of Psychiatry and Behavioral
> Sciences
> Duke University School of Medicine
> Durham, North Carolina 27710

Kaj Blennow
Dementia
> Institute of Clinical Neuroscience
> Section of Neurochemistry
> Mölndal Hospital, Sweden

William Bondareff
Brain and Central Nervous System
> Department of Psychiatry and the Behavioral
> Sciences
> Division of Geriatric Psychiatry
> University of Southern California
> Los Angeles, California 90033

Stephen Borst
Autonomic Nervous System
> Geriatric Research Education and Clinical Center
> Veterans Administration Medical Center
> Gainesville, Florida 32608

Herman Bouma
Gerontechnology
> Eindhoven University of Technology
> Eindhoven, The Netherlands

Lawrence J. Brandt
Gastrointestinal System: Function and Dysfunction
> Division of Gastroenterology
> Montefiore Medical Center
> Bronx, New York 10467

Marjolein Broese van Groenou
Network Analysis
> Department of Sociology and Social Gerontology
> Free University
> Amsterdam 1075-AZ, The Netherlands

Susan Brownlee
Self-Regulation, Health, and Behavior
Department of Psychology
Rutgers University
New Brunswick, New Jersey 08903

Irene M. Burnside
Reminiscence
Department of Nursing
San Diego State University
San Diego, California 92115

Robert N. Butler
Life Review
International Longevity Center
Mount Sinai School of Medicine
New York, New York 10024

Erin L. Cassidy
Adaptation
Department of Psychology
University of Massachusetts
Amherst, Massachusetts 01003

Nadine M. Castellano
Consumer Behavior
Department of Marketing
University of Iowa
Iowa City, Iowa 52242

Anthony Cerami
Glycation
The Picower Institute for Medical Research
Manhasset, New York 11030

Yung-Ping Chen
Economics: Society
Gerontology Institute
University of Massachusetts
Boston, Massachusetts 02125

N. S. Cherniack
Respiratory System
School of Medicine
Case Western Reserve University
Cleveland, Ohio 44106

Jeanette N. Cleveland
Work and Employment
Department of Psychology
Colorado State University
Fort Collins, Colorado 80523

Catherine A. Cole
Consumer Behavior
Department of Marketing
University of Iowa
Iowa City, Iowa 52242

Timothy J. Collier
Neurotransmitters and Neurotrophic Factors
Department of Neurological Sciences
Rush-Presbyterian Medical Center
Chicago, Illinois 60612

Linda M. Collins
Research Design and Methods
The Methodology Center and
Department of Human Development and Family
  Studies
The Pennsylvania State University
University Park, Pennsylvania 16802

Robert H. Cox
Cholesterol and Cell Plasma Membranes
Bockus Research Institute
Graduate Hospital
Philadelphia, Pennsylvania 19146

Vincent J. Cristofalo
Growth Factors and Cellular Senescence
Center for Gerontological Research
Medical College of Pennsylvania and
  Hahnemann University
Philadelphia, Pennsylvania 19128

Michael T. Crow
Atherosclerosis
National Institute on Aging
National Institutes of Health
Bethesda, Maryland 21224

Neal E. Cutler
Pensions
Boettner Center of Financial Gerontology
University of Pennsylvania
Philadelphia, Pennsylvania 19104

Jean B. deKernion
Prostate
Division of Urology
University of California School of Medicine
Los Angeles, California 90095

Judith de Luce
Mythology
　Department of Classics
　Miami University
　Oxford, Ohio 45054

Helen M. DeVries
Cognitive–Behavioral Interventions
　Department of Psychology
　Wheaton College
　Wheaton, Illinois 60187

Adam Drewnowski
Diet and Nutrition
　Program in Human Nutrition
　University of Michigan
　Ann Arbor, Michigan 48109

Sherry L. Dupuis
Life Satisfaction
　Department of Family Studies
　University of Guelph
　Guelph, Ontario N1G 2W1, Canada

Richard M. Eastman
Literary Representations of Aging
　Department of English
　North Central College
　Naperville, Illinois 60566

Mitchell L. Eggers
Demography
　Populations Activities Unit
　United Nations Economic Commission for
　　Europe
　Geneva, Ch-1211, Switzerland

Dariush Elahi
Body: Composition, Weight, Height, and Build
　Department of Medicine
　University of Maryland
　Baltimore, Maryland 21201

R. Darin Ellis
Human Factors and Ergonomics
　Wayne State University
　Detroit, Michigan 48202

William Edwin Fann
Pharmacology
　Department of Pharmacology
　Baylor College of Medicine
　Houston, Texas 77030

Mike Featherstone
Images of Aging
　Nottingham Trent University
　Nottingham, NG1 4BU
　United Kingdom

Geoff R. Fernie
Accidents: Falls
　Centre for Studies in Aging
　Sunnybrook Health Sciences Centre
　University of Toronto
　Toronto, Ontario M4N 3M5, Canada

Edith Elisabeth Flynn
Crime and Age
　College of Criminal Justice
　Northeastern University
　Boston, Massachusetts 02115

Lauren S. Fox
Mental Health
　Department of Psychology
　University of Southern California
　Los Angeles, California 90089

James L. Fozard
Gerontechnology
　Eindhoven University of Technology
　Eindhoven, The Netherlands, and
　National Institute on Aging
　National Institutes of Health
　Baltimore, Maryland

Michael L. Freedman
Cancer and the Elderly
　School of Medicine
　New York University
　New York, New York 10016

Joel S. Freund
Learning
　Department of Psychology
　University of Arkansas
　Fayetteville, Arkansas 72701

Bruce Friedman
Health Care and Services
　Institute for Health Services Research
　University of Minnesota School of Public Health
　Minneapolis, Minnesota 55455

Christine L. Fry
Comparative and Cross-Cultural Studies
Department of Sociology and Anthropology
Loyola University Lake Shore Campus
Chicago, Illinois 60626

Roseann Giarrusso
Self-Esteem
Andrus Gerontology Center
University of Southern California
Los Angeles, California 90089

Grover C. Gilmore
Perception
Department of Psychology
Case Western Reserve University
Cleveland, Ohio 44106

Joseph H. Goldberg
Human Factors and Ergonomics
The Pennsylvania State University
University Park, Pennsylvania 16802

Sandra Gordon-Salant
Hearing
Department of Hearing and Speech Sciences
University of Maryland
College Park, Maryland 20742

Philip B. Gorelick
Stroke
Department of Neurological Sciences
Rush Medical Center
Chicago, Illinois 60612

Jan A. M. Graafmans
Gerontechnology
Eindhoven University of Technology
Eindhoven, The Netherlands

David A. Greenwald
Gastrointestinal System: Function and Dysfunction
Division of Gastroenterology
Montefiore Medical Center
Bronx, New York 10467

Tamara K. Hareven
Life Course
Department of Family Studies and History
University of Delaware
Newark, Delaware 19716

S. W. Harkins
Pain and Presbyalgos
Department of Gerontology
Virginia Commonwealth University
Richmond, Virginia 29298

Calvin B. Harley
Telomeres
Department of Research
Geron Corporation
Menlo Park, California 94025

Robert A. Harootyan
Volunteer Activity by Older Adults
American Association of Retired Persons
Washington, District of Columbia 20049

S. D. R. Harridge
Neuromuscular System
Copenhagen Muscle Research Center
Rigs Hospitalet 7652
2200 Copenhagen North, Denmark

Bert Hayslip, Jr.
Hospice
Department of Psychology
University of North Texas
Denton, Texas 76203

Franz Hefti
Neurotransmitters and Neurotrophic Factors
Andrus Gerontology Center
University of Southern California
Los Angeles, California 90089

Mike Hepworth
Images of Aging
Department of Sociology
University of Aberdeen
Aberdeen, Aberdeenshire AB9 2TY, United
Kingdom

William J. Hoyer
Life Span Theory
Department of Psychology
Syracuse University
Syracuse, New York 13244

S. Michal Jazwinski
*Models of Aging: Invertebrates, Filamentous Fungi,
and Yeasts*
Department of Biochemistry
Louisiana State University Medical Center
New Orleans, Louisiana 70112

Nancy S. Jecker
Ethics and Euthanasia
Department of Medical History and Ethics
University of Washington School of Medicine
Seattle, Washington 98195

Thomas E. Johnson
Genetics
University of Colorado
Boulder, Colorado 80309

Donald A. Jurivich
Physiological Stress
Department of Medicine and
Buehler Center on Aging
Northwestern University Medical School
Chicago, Illinois 60611

Dike N. Kalu
Bone and Osteoporosis
Department of Physiology
University of Texas Health Science Center
San Antonio, Texas 78284

Robert L. Kane
Health Care and Services
Institute for Health Services Research
University of Minnesota School of Public Health
Minneapolis, Minnesota 55455

Robert Kastenbaum
Death and Dying
Department of Communication
Arizona State University
Tempe, Arizona 85287

John R. Kelly
Activities
Leisure
Department of Leisure Studies
University of Illinois
Champaign, Illinois 61820

Joseph W. Kemnitz
Bioenergetics
Primate Center
University of Wisconsin
Madison, Wisconsin 53715

Bryan Kemp
Rehabilitation
Gerontology Service
Rancho Los Amigos Medical Center
Downey, California 90242

Hal Kendig
Housing
La Trobe University
Bundoora, Australia

Gary M. Kenyon
Philosophy
Department of Gerontology
St. Thomas University
Frederiction, New Brunswick E3B 5G3, Canada

Jennifer M. Kinney
Home Care and Caregiving
Gerontology Program
College of Health and Human Services
Bowling Green State University
Bowling Green, Ohio 43403

Helen Q. Kivnick
Grandparenthood
School of Social Work
University of Minnesota
St. Paul, Minnesota 55108

Donald W. Kline
Vision
University of Calgary
Calgary, Alberta T2N 1N4, Canada

Bob Knight
Mental Health
Andrus Gerontology Center
University of Southern California
Los Angeles, California 90089

Harold G. Koenig
Depression
Suicide
Departments of Psychiatry, Behavioral Sciences,
and Internal Medicine
Duke University School of Medicine
Durham, North Carolina 27710

Edward G. Lakatta
Atherosclerosis
National Institute on Aging
National Institutes of Health
Bethesda, Maryland 21224

David Lapotofsky
Cholesterol and Cell Plasma Membranes
Department of Physiology
Medical College of Pennsylvania
Philadelphia, Pennsylvania 19129

Jacqueline Leavitt
Modernization and Aging
    Department of Urban Planning and
    School of Public Policy and Social Research
    University of California
    Los Angeles, California 90095

Annette T. Lee
Glycation
    The Picower Institute for Medical Research
    Manhasset, New York 11030

Elaine A. Leventhal
Self-Regulation, Health, and Behavior
    Department of Medicine
    Robert Wood Johnson School of Medicine
    University of Medicine and Dentistry of New
        Jersey
    New Brunswick, New Jersey 08903

Howard Leventhal
Self-Regulation, Health, and Behavior
    Institute for Health, Health Care Policy and
        Aging Research
    Rutgers University
    New Brunswick, New Jersey 08903

Phoebe S. Liebig
Organizations on Aging
    Program in Policy and Services
    University of Southern California
    Los Angeles, California 90089

Robert D. Lindeman
Renal and Urinary Tract Function
    Department of Medicine
    School of Medicine
    University of New Mexico
    Albuquerque, New Mexico 87131

Edith S. Lisansky Gomberg
Alcohol and Drugs
    Department of Psychiatry
    University of Michigan
    Ann Arbor, Michigan 48109

Gordon J. Lithgow
Genetics
    University of Colorado
    Boulder, Colorado 80309

Richard Lockshin
Cell Death
    Department of Biological Sciences
    St. Johns University
    Jamaica, New York 11439

Charles F. Longino, Jr.
Migration
    Department of Sociology
    Wake Forest University
    Winston-Salem, North Carolina 27109

Dale A. Lund
Bereavement and Loss
    Gerontology Center
    University of Utah
    Salt Lake City, Utah 84112

David J. Madden
Attention
    Center for the Study of Aging and Human
        Development
    Duke University Medical Center
    Durham, North Carolina 27710

Brian E. Maki
Accidents: Falls
    Centre for Studies in Aging
    Sunnybrook Health Science Centre
    University of Toronto
    Toronto, Ontario M4N 3M5, Canada

Ronald J. Manheimer
Adult Education
Humor
    North Carolina Center for Creative Retirement
    University of North Carolina
    Asheville, North Carolina 28804

Roger C. Mannell
Life Satisfaction
    Department of Recreation and Leisure Studies
    University of Waterloo
    Waterloo, Ontario N2L 3G1, Canada

Kenneth G. Manton
Epidemiology
Longevity and Long-Lived Populations
    Department of Demographic Studies
    Duke University
    Durham, North Carolina 27708

Jan Marcusson
Dementia
    Department of Geriatric Medicine
    University Hospital
    Linkoping, Sweden

Kyriakos S. Markides
Racial and Ethnic Diversity
Department of Preventive Medicine and
Community Health
University of Texas, Medical Branch
Galveston, Texas 77555

Victor W. Marshall
Theories of Aging: Social
Centre for Studies of Aging
University of Toronto
Toronto, Ontario M5T 3J1, Canada

Anne Martin-Matthews
Widowhood and Widowerhood
Gerontology Research Center
Guelph, Ontario N1G 2W1, Canada

R. Preston Mason
Cholesterol and Cell Plasma Membranes
Neurosciences Research Center
Allegheny General Hospital
Pittsburgh, Pennsylvania 15212

Edward J. Masoro
Models of Aging: Vertebrates
Aging Research and Education Center
University of Texas Health Science Center
San Antonio, Texas 78284

Gerald E. McClearn
Markers of Aging
Center for Developmental and Health Genetics
The Pennsylvania State University
University Park, Pennsylvania 16802

Lynn McDonald
Abuse and Neglect of Elders
Faculty of Social Work
University of Toronto
Toronto, Ontario M5S 1A1, Canada

Joan M. McDowd
Inhibition
Occupational Therapy Education
University of Kansas Medical Center
Kansas City, Kansas 66160

Susan H. McFadden
Religion and Spirituality
Department of Psychology
University of Wisconsin
Oshkosh, Wisconsin 54901

Thomas G. McGowan
Ageism and Discrimination
Departments of Anthropology and Sociology
Rhodes College
Memphis, Tennessee 38112

Jane D. McLeod
Life Events
Department of Sociology
University of Minnesota
Minneapolis, Minnesota 55455

Thomas H. McNeil
Neurotransmitters and Neurotrophic Factors
Andrus Gerontology Center
University of Southern California
Los Angeles, California 90089

Arshag D. Mooradian
Endocrine Function and Dysfunction
Department of Internal Medicine
St. Louis University
St. Louis, Missouri 63104

John E. Morley
Thirst and Hydration
Geriatric Research Education and Clinical Center
St. Louis Veterans Administration Medical
Center
St. Louis, Missouri 63104

Larry C. Mullins
Loneliness
Department of Sociology
Auburn University
Montgomery, Alabama 36117

Shin Murakami
Genetics
University of Colorado
Boulder, Colorado 80309

George C. Myers
Demography
Center for Demographic Studies
Duke University
Durham, North Carolina 27708

James E. Nagel
Immune System
Inhibition
Clinical Immunology Section
National Institute on Aging
National Institutes of Health
Baltimore, Maryland 21224

Linda S. Noelker
Caregiving and Caring
  Margaret Blenker Research Center
  Benjamin Rose Institute
  Cleveland, Ohio 44115

Felicia V. Nowak
Endocrine Function and Dysfunction
  Department of Internal Medicine
  St. Louis University
  St. Louis, Missouri 63104

Loraine K. Obler
*Language and Communication in Aging and
  Dementia*
  City University of New York
  New York, New York 10036

Aurora K. Pajeau
Stroke
  Department of Neurology
  Mount Sinai Medical Center
  Chicago, Illinois 60608

Sharon M. Papciak
Immune System
  Clinical Immunology Section
  National Institute on Aging
  National Institues of Health
  Baltimore, Maryland 21224

Robert Plomin
Behavioral Genetics
  Institute of Psychiatry
  University of London
  Denmark Hill, London SE5 8AF, United
    Kingdom

Richard L. Port
Conditioning
  Department of Psychology
  Slippery Rock College
  Slippery Rock, Pennsylvania 16057

Lisa A. Primus
Identity, Physical
  Department of Psychology
  University of Massachusetts
  Amherst, Massachusetts 01003

Jon Pynoos
Housing
  Program in Policy and Services
  University of Southern California
  Los Angeles, California 90089

Jon J. Ramsey
Bioenergetics
  Primate Center
  University of Wisconsin
  Madison, Wisconsin 53715

Karen M. Reiser
Extracellular Matrix
  Department of Internal Medicine
  School of Medicine
  University of California
  Davis, California 95616

Jan Rietsema
Gerontechnology
  Eindhoven University of Technology
  Eindhoven, The Netherlands

Matilda White Riley
Age Stratification
Cohort Studies
  National Institute on Aging
  National Institutes of Health
  Bethesda, Maryland 20892

Barbara J. Rolls
Diet and Nutrition
  Department of Nutrition
  The Pennsylvania State University
  University Park, Pennsylvania 16801

Michael R. Rose
Evolution and Comparative Biology
  Department of Ecology and Evolutionary
    Biology
  University of California
  Irvine, California 92717

Linda M. Rothman
Arthritis
  Arthritis Community Research and Evaluation
    Unit
  Wellesley Hospital Research Institute
  Toronto, Ontario M4Y 1J3, Canada

Laurence Z. Rubenstein
Geriatric Assessment: Physical
  Geriatric Research Education and Clinical Center
  Sepulveda Veterans Administration Medical
    Center, and University of California School of
    Medicine
  Los Angeles, California 91343

Laura Rudkin
Racial and Ethnic Diversity
 Department of Preventive Medicine and
  Community Health
 University of Texas, Medical Branch
 Galveston, Texas 77555

Jan-Erik Ruth
Personality
 Kunto Kallio Center for Gerontology Research
 01100 Ostersundom, Finland

Alice S. Ryan
Body: Composition, Weight, Height, and Build
 Department of Medicine
 University of Maryland
 Baltimore, Maryland 21201

John M. Rybash
Life Span Theory
 Department of Psychology
 Hamilton College
 Clinton, New Jersey 13323

Carol D. Ryff
Psychological Well-Being
 Department of Psychology
 University of Wisconsin
 Madison, Wisconsin 53706

Timothy A. Salthouse
Reaction Time
 School of Psychology
 Georgia Institute of Technology
 Atlanta, Georgia 30332

B. Saltin
Neuromuscular System
 Copenhagen Muscle Research Center
 Rigs Hospitalet 7652
 2200 Copenhagen North, Denmark

K. Warner Schaie
Generational Differences
 Department of Human Development and Family
  Studies
 The Pennsylvania State University
 University Park, Pennsylvania 16802

Susan S. Schiffman
Smell and Taste
 Department of Psychiatry
 Duke University Medical Center
 Durham, North Carolina 27710

Johannes J. F. Schroots
Theories of Aging: Psychological
Time: Concepts and Perceptions
 Department of Psychology
 European Research Institute on Health and
  Aging
 Amsterdam 1018WB, The Netherlands

Charles T. Scialfa
Vision
 University of Calgary
 Calgary, Alberta T2N 1N4, Canada

Robert B. Scott
Pain and Presbyalgos
 Departments of Internal Medicine and Geriatric
  Medicine
 Virginia Commonwealth University
 Richmond, Virginia 23298

Rachael Seidler
Motor Control
 Motor Control Laboratory
 Arizona State University
 Tempe, Arizona 85287

Christian Sell
Growth Factors and Cellular Senescence
 Center for Gerontological Research
 Medical College of Pennsylvania and
  Hahnemann University
 Philadelphia, Pennsylvania 19128

Vijay Shanmugam
Stroke
 Department of Neurological Sciences
 Rush Medical Center
 Chicago, Illinois 60612

Aurora M. Sherman
Social Networks, Support, and Integration
 Institute for Social Research
 University of Michigan
 Ann Arbor, Michigan 48106

David R. Shook
Genetics
 University of Colorado
 Boulder, Colorado 80309

Lynn M. Shore
Work and Employment
 Georgia State University
 University Plaza
 Atlanta, Georgia 30303

David P. Shuldiner
Folklore
   School of Family Studies
   University of Connecticut
   Storrs, Connecticut 06269

Dean Keith Simonton
Achievement
Creativity
   Department of Psychology
   University of California
   Davis, California 95616

Heather M. Sinclair
Grandparenthood
   School of Social Work
   University of Minnesota
   Minneapolis, Minnesota 55455

Ingmar Skoog
Dementia
   Department of Psychiatry
   Sahlgrenska Hospital
   S 413-45 Goteborg, Sweden

Timothy M. Smeeding
Economics: Individual
   Center for Advanced Study in the Behavioral
      Sciences
   Stanford, California 94305

Anderson D. Smith
Memory
   School of Psychology
   Georgia Institute of Technology
   Atlanta, Georgia 30332

Lijun Song
Immune System
   Department of Medicine
   Johns Hopkins University School of Medicine
   Baltimore, Maryland 21224

Janie S. Steckenrider
Political Attitudes and Behavior
   Department of Political Science
   Loyola Marymount University
   Los Angeles, California 90045

George Stelmach
Motor Control
   Exercise Science Department
   Arizona State University
   Tempe, Arizona 85287

David L. Strayer
Skill Aquisition
   Department of Psychology
   University of Utah
   Salt Lake City, Utah 84112

Judith A. Sugar
Memory Strategies
   Graduate School
   University of Nevada
   Reno, Nevada 89557

Alvar Svanborg
Cardiovascular System
Postponement of Aging
   Department of Geriatric Medicine
   University of Illinois
   Chicago, Illinois 80812

Thomas N. Tulenko
Cholesterol and Cell Plasma Membranes
   Department of Physiology, Biochemistry, and
      Surgery
   Medical College of Pennsylvania
   Philadelphia, Pennsylvania 19129

Mitchell S. Turker
Premature Aging
   Department of Pathology
   Markey Cancer Center
   University of Kentucky
   Lexington, Kentucky 40536

Peter Uhlenberg
Cohort Studies
   Department of Sociology
   University of North Carolina
   Chapel Hill, North Carolina 27599

Theo van Tilburg
Network Analysis
   Department of Sociology and Social Gerontology
   Free University
   Amsterdam 1075-AZ, The Netherlands

Max J. Vercruyssen
Gerontechnology
   Eindhoven University of Technology
   Eindhoven, The Netherlands,
   University of Hawaii
   Honolulu, Hawaii 96816, and
   University of Minnesota
   Minneapolis, Minnesota 55455

Jan Vijg
DNA and Gene Expression
   Beth Israel Hospital
   Gerontology Division, Department of Medicine
   Harvard Medical School
   Boston, Massachusetts 02115

Michael M. Vilenchik
Oxidative Damage
   Department of Biophysics
   Longevity Achievement Foundation
   Chester, Pennsylvania 19013

Patricia F. Waller
Accidents: Traffic
   Transportation Research Institute
   University of Michigan
   Ann Arbor, Michigan 48109

Ruth B. Weg
Sexuality, Sensuality, and Intimacy
   Andrus Gerontology Center
   University of Southern California
   Los Angeles, California 90089

Janet M. Weisenberger
Touch and Proprioception
   Department of Speech and Hearing
   Ohio State University
   Columbus, Ohio 43210

Joseph F. Welk
Physiological Stress
   Department of Medicine and
   Buehler Center on Aging
   Northwestern University Medical School
   Chicago, Illinois 60611

Susan Krauss Whitbourne
Adaptation
Identity, Physical
   Department of Psychology
   University of Massachusetts
   Amherst, Massachusetts 01003

Carol J. Whitlatch
Caregiving and Caring
   Margaret Blenker Research Center
   Benjamin Rose Institute
   Cleveland, Ohio 44115

Margaret-Mary G. Wilson
Thirst and Hydration
   Department of Geriatrics
   St. Louis University Medical Center
   St. Louis, Missouri 63104

Diana S. Woodruff-Pak
Conditioning
   Department of Psychology
   Temple University
   Philadelphia, Pennsylvania 19122

Marjorie H. Woollacott
Balance, Posture, and Gait
   Department of Exercise and Movement Science
   University of Oregon
   Eugene, Oregon 97403

F. Eugene Yates
Homeostasis
Theories of Aging: Biological
   Departments of Medicine and Geriatrics
   University of California
   Los Angeles, California 90025

Zahra Zakeri
Cell Death
   Department of Biology
   Queens College and Graduate Center of the
   City University of New York
   Flushing, New York 11367

Subject Index

*Volume numbers are boldfaced, separated from the first page reference with a colon.
Subsequent references to the same volume are separated by commas.*

A

Absenteeism, pattern analysis, **2:**632
Absorptiometry, body composition measurement, **1:**197
Abuse, *see* Domestic violence; Elder abuse
Accidents, *see* Falls; Traffic accidents
Accumulative advantage, creativity measurement, **1:**349
Acetylcholine, autonomic nervous system stimulation,
    1:143
Achalasia
    esophageal dysfunction, **1:**547
    parasympathetic response reduction, **1:**145
Achievement, **1:**27–36
    creativity, **1:**31–32
    entertainers, **1:**32–34
        athletes, **1:**32–33
        chess masters, **1:**33
        movie stars, **1:**33–34
    leaders, **1:**28–31
        entrepreneurs, **1:**30
        military commanders, **1:**29–30
        politicians, **1:**28–29, 35–36
        religious leaders, **1:**30–31
    overview, **1:**27–28
    theoretical explanations, **1:**34–36
        biological processes, **1:**34–35
        psychological processes, **1:**35
        sociological processes, **1:**35–36

Acid balance
    citric acid cycle, **2:**135
    kidney excretion rate changes, **2:**411
    uric acid, gout attacks, **1:**115
Acid reflux, esophageal dysfunction, **1:**547–548
Acquired immunodeficiency syndrome
    cancer risk, **1:**227
    family stress, **1:**696
    sexual response changes, **2:**487
Actin, definition, **2:**211
Active life expectancy, *see* Longevity
Activities, *see also* Leisure
    achievement, *see* Achievement
    bereavement adjustments, **1:**181–182
    contexts, **1:**42–45
        home activities, **1:**42–43
        market sector, **1:**44–45
        organized recreation, **1:**43–44
        social character, **1:**45
    dementia treatment, **1:**400–401
    explanatory theory, **1:**47–49
    flow, **2:**22
    implications, **1:**49
    importance
        activity types, **1:**41–42
        health, **1:**40–41
        life satisfaction, **1:**40; **2:**63
        stress reduction, **1:**52–53

Activities (*continued*)
  later-life course
    age-related change, **2**:23
    constriction patterns, **2**:23–24
    continuity patterns, **2**:24–25
    issues, **2**:25–26
  life satisfaction, **1**:40; **2**:63
  meaning
    dialectics, **1**:45–46
    domains, **1**:47
  memory enhancement, **2**:122
  overview, **1**:37–40
  participation patterns, **1**:38–40
Activities of daily living, *see also* Instrumental activities
  of daily living
  acute rehabilitation, **2**:383–385
  bereavement adjustments, **1**:180–181
  comprehensive geriatric assessment, **1**:590
  definition, **1**:667; **2**:381
  disability effects
    arthritis, **1**:118–119
    dementia, **1**:385–386
  epidemiological studies, **1**:496
  ergonomics
    assistive devices, **1**:602, 719
    importance, **1**:718
    interventions, **1**:719
    physical activities, **1**:718–719
  ethnic differences, **2**:373–374
  everyday problem solving
    contextual perspective, **1**:375
    developmental differences
      age differences, **1**:376–378
      efficacy criteria, **1**:376
      process, **1**:375–376
    differential task structures, **1**:374–375
    ecological validity, **1**:374
    mediating factors
      emotional salience, **1**:379–380
      individual differences, **1**:380
      personal relevance, **1**:379
      problem appraisal, **1**:378–379
    traditional approaches, **1**:373–374
  in-home caregiving, **1**:673
  later-life family challenges, **1**:668–669
  motor control, *see* Motor control
Activity theory, *see also* Disengagement theory;
  Gerotranscendence theory; Leisure
  ageism, **1**:75–76
  consumer behavior, **1**:331
  historical perspective, **2**:570
  psychological aging, **2**:561–562

Adaptation
  balance control, **1**:159–160
  cognitive–behavioral interventions, **1**:290–292
  cognitive change, **1**:54
  definition, **2**:135
  environment
    competence adaptation model, **1**:51, 54
    fall prevention, **1**:16–17, 154
  identity
    ego integrity, **1**:58–59
    life cycle role changes, **1**:56–58
  muscle adaptability
    capillary number, **2**:219
    fiber number, **2**:218
    fiber types, **2**:218–219
    membrane-bound regulatory proteins, **2**:219
    mitochondrial enzymes, **2**:219
    strength, **2**:217–218
  overview, **1**:51–52
  physical changes, **1**:54
  psychological aging, **2**:562–563
  social roles, **1**:54–56
  stress, **1**:52–53
Adolescence, grandparent influence, **1**:620–621
Adrenal gland
  adrenal medulla, **1**:485
  α-adrenergic response, sympathetic nervous system
    changes, **1**:144–145
  β-adrenergic response
    sodium balance control, **2**:412
    sympathetic nervous system changes, **1**:144–145
  function, **1**:478–479
  physiology, **1**:483–485
  structure, **1**:482
Adrenocorticotropic hormone
  adrenal function, **1**:483–485
  pituitary function, **1**:478–479
Adult children
  caregiver ties, **1**:258–259
  protection legislation, **1**:7–8
  social role adaptation, **1**:55
Adult development theory, retirement, **2**:445–446
Adult education, *see* Learning
Advanced glycation end products
  atherosclerosis pathogenesis, **1**:128
  definition, **1**:123, 605
  pharmacological intervention, **1**:609
Advance directive
  definition, **1**:361
  end-of-life issues, **1**:371–372
Advertising, *see* Marketing

Advocacy, *see also* Hospice; Public policy; Social
  networks
  elder abuse protection, **1:**10
  organizations
    current status, **2:**231
    future trends, **2:**231–232
    historical perspective, **2:**230–231
    interest group theory, **2:**229–230
    social movement, **2:**229–230
Age Discrimination, *see* Ageism; Elder abuse
Ageism, *see also* Elder abuse
  activity theory, **1:**75–76
  age strata differences, **1:**86
  cognitive–behavioral therapy, **1:**293
  conceptualization, **1:**76–78
  definition, **1:**71, 743
  disengagement theory, **1:**75–76
  geriatric rehabilitation, **2:**383
  gerontology development, **1:**75
  historical emergence, **1:**71–73
    cultural factors, **1:**72–73
    industrialization, **1:**71–72
  humor, **1:**728–729
  identity role, **1:**741–742
  marketing fraud, **1:**330–331
  media
    contemporary humor, **1:**729
    literary representations, **2:**73–75
    multicultural awareness, **1:**749–750
    overview, **1:**743–744
    social role, **1:**744–749
  social dislocation
    minority group theory, **1:**74–75
    status loss, **1:**73–74
  societal attitudes toward death, **1:**364–367
  theoretical considerations, **1:**78–80
  traditional practices, **1:**535
  workplace discrimination
    Age Discrimination and Employment Act, **1:**74;
      2:627–628
    career development, **2:**635
    hiring practices, **2:**629–630
    organizational experiences, **2:**630–631, 637
    retirement rationale, **2:**439, 444, 447–448
Age-period-cohort model
  psychological aging, **2:**560
  time confounds, **2:**588
Age scales
  biomarkers, **2:**103–104
  intrinsic time, **2:**588–590
Age stratification, *see also* Cohorts
  bereavement, **1:**179

dynamics, **1:**90–92
  alterability, **1:**91–92
  role imbalances, **1:**90–91
overview, **1:**81–84
  class, **1:**83
  conceptual framework, **1:**82–83
  ideology, **1:**83
  pervasive themes, **1:**84
population composition, **1:**84–86
relationships, **1:**87
social clocks, **2:**587–588
social roles, **1:**87–90
Aggression
  drug treatment, **1:**402
  testosterone link, **1:**355
Aging, *see* Aging theories; Models of aging; Premature
  aging; Senescence
Aging postponement, *see also* Premature aging
  caloric restriction
    definition, **1:**185
    delayed physiological aging, **1:**186, 190–191
    DNA aberrations, **2:**137–138
    exercise effects, **1:**190–192
    extracellular matrix modulation, **1:**528
    senescence rate, **2:**548–549
  exogenous factors
    clinical medicine, **2:**338–339
    cognition, **2:**335
    health, **2:**334–335
    joints, **2:**336
    osteoarthritis, **2:**336–337
    osteoporosis, **2:**337
    sensory deprivation, **2:**335
    social contacts, **2:**338–339
    striated muscles, **2:**336
    urinary incontinence, **2:**337–338
  extracellular matrix modulation, **1:**528
  historical perspective, **2:**333–334
Aging theories, *see also* Time
  biological aging
    creativity, **1:**348
    primary aging, **2:**66–67
    senescence
      aspect theories, **2:**547–550
      definition, **2:**546
      entropic processes, **2:**550–553
      evolutionary biology, **2:**553–554
      negentropic processes, **2:**550–553
      rate determinants, **2:**553
      time effects, **2:**546
      views, **2:**547
  epistemology, **2:**311–313

Aging theories (*continued*)
  psychological aging
    achievement characteristics, **1**:35
    branching theory, **2**:566
    classical theories, **2**:561–563
    concepts, **2**:558–560
    creativity, **1**:350
    definition, **2**:557
    gerotranscendence theory, **2**:565–566
    historical perspective, **2**:557–558
    modern theories, **2**:563–565
  social aging
    challenges, **2**:572
    classification, **2**:569–570
    creativity, **1**:349
    current theory, **2**:571
    early theory, **2**:570–571
    self-esteem, **2**:461–462
AIDS, *see* Acquired immunodeficiency syndrome
Aids, mechanical, *see* Gerontechnology
Alcohol
  abuse
    blood alcohol concentration, **1**:19, 22–23
    bone loss, **1**:211
    cancer risk, **1**:226, 229
    chronic suicide, **2**:530
    cognitive impairment, **1**:97–98
    cognitive–behavioral therapy, **1**:295
    cohort differences, **1**:23, 97
    depression, **1**:423
    ethnic differences, **1**:98–99
    grandparent caregivers, **1**:617
    prevention, **1**:99–100
    stroke risk, **2**:519
    traffic accident risk, **1**:22–23
    treatment, **1**:99–100
  drug interactions, **2**:305
  use, **1**:96–97
Aldose reductase inhibitors, aging postponement, **1**:528
Aldosterone
  potassium balance control, **2**:412–413
  secretion, mineralocorticoid role, **1**:485
Allergies, *see also* Immune system
  allergens, **1**:106–107
  hypersensitivity states
    involution, **1**:108–110
    manifestations, **1**:107–108
  immunologic response, **1**:104–106
  overview, **1**:103–104
  sensitization, **1**:106–107
Allopurinol, rheumatic disease treatment, **2**:455
Allosterism, definition, **2**:135

Alzheimer's disease
  aging studies
    genetics, **1**:579
    premature aging, **2**:351
  apolipoprotein E role, **1**:391–392
  chronic pain, **2**:255, 258
  clinical characteristics, **1**:387–389
  cognitive–behavioral interventions, **1**:294
  definition, **1**:383
  effects, **1**:386–387
  euthanasia, **1**:506
  eyeblink conditioning studies, **1**:323–325
  heterogeneity, **1**:393
  language difficulties, **2**:4–6
  membrane cholesterol analysis, **1**:285–286
  memory strategies, **2**:119, 124
  neuropathology, **1**:220–221, 389–391
  neurotransmitter disturbances, **1**:392–393; **2**:222, 225–226
  neurotrophic factor effects, **2**:226–227
  nonenzymatic glycation effects, **1**:608
  pharmacological treatment, **1**:401–402
  postmitotic cell death, **1**:276
  protein oxidation role, **2**:242
  reminiscence therapy, **2**:403–404
  spatial contrast sensitivity, **2**:272–273, 277–278
Amadori products
  diabetes, **2**:352–353
  glycation chemistry, **1**:605–607
Amateurism, activity engagement, **1**:41
American Association of Retired Persons, historical perspective, **2**:230
American Urological Association Symptom Score
  benign prostatic hyperplasia diagnosis, **2**:359
  prostate cancer diagnosis, **2**:362
Amyloids, deposition, Alzheimer's disease neuropathology, **1**:389–390
Amyotrophic lateral sclerosis, premature aging studies, **2**:351
Anabolism, definition, **2**:135
Androgens
  definition, **1**:477
  secretion, **1**:484–485
Animals, *see* Models of aging; *specific species*
Ankylosing spondylitis, *see also* Rheumatic diseases
  symptoms, **2**:455
Anorexia nervosa
  definition, **1**:429
  food intake regulation, **1**:433, 438–439
Antagonistic pleiotropy
  definition, **1**:509
  population genetics, **1**:511, 513–514
  senescence theory, **2**:549

Antechinus, premature aging model, 2:344
Anthropology
    ageism, 1:78–80
    grandparenthood, 1:611–612
Anthropometry
    body composition measurement, 1:196, 198–199
    definition, 1:715
    ergonomic designs, 1:716
Antibiotics, allergic response, 1:107–108
Antibodies, *see* Immune system
Antioxidants, *see also* Oxidative damage
    definition, 2:83, 233
    extracellular matrix modulation, aging postponement, 1:528
    oxidative damage defense mechanisms, 2:236–237
Anxiety
    cognitive–behavioral therapy, 1:295
    death anxiety, 1:367–369
    health care services, 2:126
    pharmacological treatment, 1:402
Aphasia, communication difficulties, 2:3–4, 6
Apolipoprotein E, Alzheimer's disease role, 1:391–392
Apoptosis, *see also* Senescence
    carcinogenesis, 1:227, 230
    cell shrinkage, 1:274
    definition, 1:223, 269, 753
    in vivo characteristics, 1:271–272
    lymphocyte differentiation, 1:759
    nucleus degradation, 1:273–274
    oxidative injury-dependent pathway, 2:242–243
    phagocytosis, 1:274
Appearance, physical identity, 1:735–736
Appropriate death, hospice role, 1:694–695
Arginine vasopressin
    definition, 2:573
    dehydration susceptibility, 2:413
    nocturia, 2:575
    thirst role, 2:573
    water metabolism, 1:490–491; 2:574–576
Arrhythmia, neuroconductive system dysfunction, 1:249
Art
    age representations, 2:76
    contemporary humor, 1:729
    folk art, 1:538–539
    multicultural awareness, 1:749–750
    overview, 1:743–744
    social role, 1:744–749
Arthritis, *see also* Bones; Rheumatic diseases
    aging postponement, 2:336–337
    fall risk, 1:15
    impact, 1:118–119
    management, 1:119–121
    overview, 1:111–112

types
    calcium phyrophosphate deposition arthropathy, 1:115–116
    crystal-induced arthritis, 1:115; 2:455–456
    gout, 1:115
    osteoarthritis
        aging postponement, 2:336–337
        cartilage changes, 2:452
        definition, 2:333
        disease course, 1:112–115
        symptoms, 2:457
    polymyalgia rheumatica, 1:117–118
    rheumatoid arthritis, 1:116–117; 2:455
Asbestos, cancer risk, 1:233
Assisted living
    definition, 1:703
    government programs, 1:710–711
    housing continuum, 1:707–708
    prevalence, 1:257
    technology needs, 1:598
Assisted suicide
    definition, 1:505; 2:529
    ethical arguments, 2:537–538
    hospice care, 1:691–692
    societal attitudes, 1:364, 371
    voluntary practice, 2:530–531
Assistive listening devices, hearing loss remediation, 1:601, 652, 717–718
Asthma, immune response, 1:105
Astroglia
    definition, 1:217
    neuronal microenvironment changes, 1:219–220
Atherogenesis, definition, 1:493
Atherosclerosis, 1:123–128
    epidemiological studies, 1:495
    membrane cholesterol analysis, 1:286–287
    overview, 1:123–124
    pathogenesis, 1:126–127
    risk factors, 1:124–126
        cholesterol, 1:125–126
        hypertension, 1:125
        multiple factors, 1:124–125
        smoking, 1:126
    stroke
        pathophysiology, 2:520–521
        risk, 2:520
    vessel biology, 1:127–128
Athletes
    achievement characteristics, 1:32–33
    muscle composition, 2:213, 218–219
Atonement, *see* Life review
ATP
    age-related metabolic change, 2:139
    definition, 2:135

Atrial natriuretic peptide
   definition, **2**:573
   sodium balance control, **2**:412
   thirst role, **2**:573
   water metabolism, **1**:490–491
Atrophy
   muscle mass, **2**:213–215, 219–220
   nucleus basalis of Meynert, **1**:218
Attention, *see also* Perception
   balance control, **1**:155–156
   capacity differences, **1**:132–137
      effort, **1**:132–135
      internal representation quality, **1**:136
      neurophysiological measurement, **1**:136–137
      speed, **1**:135–137
   categories, **1**:131–132
   inhibition
      behavioral indices, **1**:762–763
      orienting response index, **1**:762
   reduced processing resources, **2**:563–564
   selectivity differences
      attention allocation, **1**:138–139
      behavioral indices, **1**:762–763
      definition, **1**:131, 761
      inhibitory processing, **1**:139
      relevant information selection, **1**:137–138
   skill acquisition, speed–accuracy trade-off functions,
      2:492
   vigilance differences, **1**:139–140
   visual search, **2**:610–611
Auditory system
   age-related performance changes
      behavioral measures
         auditory thresholds, **1**:646–648
         speech recognition, **1**:648
      electrophysiologic measures
         acoustic reflexes, **1**:648–649
         auditory evoked potentials, **1**:649–650
         otoacoustic emissions, **1**:650–651
      hearing loss
         impact, **1**:651–652; **2**:3
         postponement, **2**:335
         prevalence, **1**:643
         prevention, **1**:652–653
         remediation, **1**:601, 652, 717–718
   pain, **2**:249–250
   perceptual noise, **2**:276
   physiologic changes
      central auditory nervous system, **1**:646
      inner ear, **1**:644–646
      middle ear, **1**:643–644
      outer ear, **1**:643–644

Autobiography, *see also* Life review; Reminiscence
   definition, **2**:53
   epistemology, **2**:312–313
   life review, **2**:57
   spiritual development, **2**:396
Autocrine pathway, definition, **2**:355
Automobiles
   ergonomics, **1**:719–720
   leisure activity constriction, **2**:24
   motion perception deficit effects, **2**:278
   traffic accidents
      alcohol use, **1**:22–23
      alternative transportation, **1**:24–25
      cohort differences, **1**:23
      commercial drivers, **1**:23–24
      driving performance, **1**:20–21
      medical impairments, **1**:23
      pedestrian casualties, **1**:24
      risk, **1**:21–22
      technology, **1**:24
   vision effects, **2**:612
Autonomic nervous system, *see also* Central nervous
   system
   age changes, **1**:143–144
   cardiovascular responses
      blood pressure control, **1**:145–146
      exercise performance, **1**:146
   chronic pain, **2**:256–257
   definition, **1**:141–142
   description
      anatomy, **1**:142–143
      pharmacology, **1**:143
      predominant tone principle, **1**:143
   disease, **1**:146
   drug responses, **1**:146–147
   functional changes
      adrenergic responses, **1**:144–145
      circulating catecholamines, **1**:144
      parasympathetic nervous system, **1**:145
      sympathetic nervous system, **1**:144–145
   gastrointestinal motility, **1**:546
   Parkinson's disease, **1**:146; **2**:222
Autonomy
   control beliefs, **2**:285
   definition, **2**:365
   ethical issues, **2**:313–315
   euthanasia, **1**:505–507
   self-regulation
      intervention models
         action plans, **2**:471–472
         age impact, **2**:474–476
         chronological approach, **2**:473–474
         disease threat representation, **2**:470

life span context, **2**:472–473
prevention, **2**:469–470
issues, **2**:468–469
overview, **2**:467

B

Baby boom generation
  crime rates, **1**:358–359
  definition, **1**:329
Balance
  control
    anticipatory postural adjustments, **1**:154–155
    cognitive systems, **1**:155–156
    early studies, **1**:151–152
    proprioception changes, **2**:601–602
    retraining research, **1**:156–157
    systems approach studies
      adaptation, **1**:154
      musculoskeletal system, **1**:152
      neuromuscular response patterns, **1**:152–153
      sensory contributions, **1**:153–154
  ergonomic designs, **1**:716–717
  fall biomechanics, **1**:13–14
  walking characteristics, **1**:157–160
    adaptive control, **1**:159–160
    gait, **1**:150–151, 160
    kinematic analysis, **1**:158–159
    kinetic analysis, **1**:159
    neuromuscular analysis, **1**:159
    stride length, **1**:158
    velocity changes, **1**:158
BALBc cells, definition, **1**:625
Baroreceptor reflex, definition, **1**:141
Basal metabolic rate
  bioenergetics, **1**:186, 189–190
  biological clock, **2**:584
  definition, **1**:185
  exercise effects, **1**:190–192
  thyroid hormone economy, **1**:480–481
bcl-2 Gene, definition, **1**:269
Behavior
  achievement, *see* Achievement
  cognitive–behavioral therapy, **1**:289–296
    adaptations
      age differences, **1**:291
      heterogenous populations, **1**:291
      slower pace, **1**:291–292
      socialization, **1**:292
      therapist role changes, **1**:291
    definition, **1**:289

effectiveness, **1**:295–296
theoretical assumptions
  problem causes, **1**:289–290
  strategies, **1**:290
treatment approaches
  ageism, **1**:293
  alcohol abuse, **1**:295
  anxiety, **1**:295
  bereavement, **1**:292
  chronic illness, **1**:292–293
  depression, **1**:293–294, 424
  disabilities, **1**:292–293
  drug abuse, **1**:295
  self-esteem, **1**:293
  social change, **1**:293
use rationale
  format, **1**:291
  normal problems, **1**:290–291
conditioning
  classical, **1**:319–325
  classical eyeblink conditioning
    animals, **1**:320–321
    brain substrates, **1**:321–325
    humans, **1**:321
  instrumental, **1**:325–327
    acquisition, **1**:325–326
    extinction, **1**:325–326
    reinforcement schedule, **1**:326
    retention, **1**:326–327
consumer behavior, *see* Consumer behavior
creativity, *see* Creativity
genetics, *see* Behavior genetics
grandparenthood roles, **1**:613–615
psychological aging, **2**:560, 562
self-regulation
  intervention models
    action plans, **2**:471–472
    age impact, **2**:474–476
    chronological approach, **2**:473–474
    disease threat representation, **2**:470
    life span context, **2**:472–473
    prevention, **2**:469–470
  issues, **2**:468–469
  overview, **2**:467
suicide, *see* Suicide
Behavior genetics
  aging differences, **1**:163–166
    developmental genetics, **1**:165–166
    environmental influence, **1**:164–165
    genetic influence, **1**:164–165
    theory, **1**:163–164; **2**:342
  biodemography, **1**:413
  definition, **1**:163

Behavior genetics (*continued*)
  epidemiological studies, 1:497
  future research directions, 1:171–172
  late-life developments
    cognitive functioning, 1:168–169
    dementia, 1:170
    depression, 1:170
    family environment, 1:170–171
    health, 1:167–168
    life events, 1:170–171
    longevity, 1:167–168
    personality, 1:169
    social support, 1:170–171
  psychological aging, 2:565
  studies, 1:166–167
Beliefs, *see* Folklore; Religion
Benign prostatic hyperplasia
  diagnosis, 2:358–360
  etiology, 2:358
  incidence, 2:357–358
  medical treatment, 2:360
  physiology, 2:358
  surgical treatment, 2:360–361
Bereavement
  adjustment course, 1:176–182
    age-stratification theory, 1:179
    continuity theory, 1:179
    coping theories, 1:177–178
    engagement theory, 1:179
    family theories, 1:178
    predictors, 1:181–182
    psychoanalytic theories, 1:177
    research, 1:179–181
    stage models, 1:178
    stress, 1:177–178
    symbolic interaction theory, 1:179
    system theories, 1:178
    task models, 1:178
  cognitive–behavioral therapy, 1:292
  definition, 1:173
  depression, 1:422–423
  experience variety, 1:173–174
  hospice care, 1:699–701
  interventions, 1:182–183
  knowledge sources, 1:175–176
  life-support ambiguity, 1:363
  loneliness, 2:80
  multidimensional nature, 1:174–175
  nutrient intake changes, 1:438
  social network role, 1:178; 2:199
  suicide loss, 2:536
Bile, digestive function, 1:544

Biodemography, 1:412–413
Bioelectrical impedance, body composition measurement, 1:196–197
Bioenergetics, *see also* Metabolism
  body composition, 1:188–189
  energy expenditure, 1:189–190
  energy intake, 1:187–188, 190–192
  exercise, 1:190–192
  nutrient metabolism, 1:188–189
  overview, 1:185–187
Biography, *see* Autobiography; Life review
Biological clock
  characteristics, 2:584–585
  definition, 2:583
  social entrainment model, 2:584, 588
Biological processes, *see specific type*
Biomarkers
  animal models, 2:100
  cancer diagnosis, 1:232
  changing systems, 2:102–103
  chronological age limitations, 2:98–99
  complex systems, 2:101–102
  definition, 2:97, 545
  longevity-associated markers, 1:579
  marker diversity, 2:98
  nuclear DNA, 2:136–138
  reliability, 2:100–101
  scale, 2:103–104
  validity, 2:99–100
Bipolar disorder, epidemiology, 1:417
Bird, aging model, 2:167
Birth cohort, *see* Cohorts
Bisphosphonates, osteoporosis treatment, 1:214
Bladder cancer, 1:237–238
Bladder control
  aging postponement, 2:337–338
  lower urinary tract dysfunction, 2:416–417
α1 Blockers, benign prostatic hyperplasia treatment, 2:360
Blood alcohol concentration
  accident risk, 1:22–23
  definition, 1:19
Blood pH, kidney excretion rate changes, 2:411
Blood pressure
  age-related change, 1:250–251
  atherosclerosis risk, 1:125
  control, 1:145–146
  hearing loss prevention, 1:653
  stroke risk, 2:518–519
Bloom's syndrome
  oxidative damage role, 2:245
  premature aging studies, 2:349

B lymphocytes
  definition, **1:**753
  immune system, **1:**756
Body composition
  age-related changes, **1:**199–200
  body weight, **1:**193–195
  disease relationship, **1:**200–201
  measurement
    regional assessment
      anthropometrics, **1:**198–199
      computerized tomography, **1:**198
      magnetic resonance imaging, **1:**198
      sonography, **1:**198
    total body composition
      anthropometry, **1:**196
      bioelectrical impedance, **1:**196–197
      dual-photon absorptiometry, **1:**197
      electrical conductivity, **1:**196–197
      hydrodensitometry, **1:**195–196
      isotope dilution, **1:**196
      neutron activation analysis, **1:**197–198
      potassium, **1:**196
      urinary excretions, **1:**197
  nutrient metabolism, **1:**188–189
Body image, *see* Images of aging
Body weight
  body composition, **1:**193–195
  body mass index
    definition, **1:**193, 429
    nutritional statistics, **1:**431
  food intake regulation, **1:**438–439
  lean body mass
    basal metabolic rate changes, **1:**188
    dietary restriction, **1:**191
    nutrient metabolism, **1:**188
Bones
  age-related changes, **1:**199–200, 210–211; **2:**452
  bone cells, **1:**205–206
  composition, **1:**204–205
    measurement
      density, **1:**212
      dual-photon absorptiometry, **1:**197
  density
    measurement, **1:**212
    peak density achievement, **1:**210
  disorders, *see specific disorders*
  fall injuries, **1:**11–12
  function, **1:**203–204
  growth, **1:**206–209
    cytokine role, **1:**208–209
    growth factor role, **1:**208–209
  immune function, **1:**754–755
  metabolism, **1:**487–488

organization, **1:**204
remodeling, **1:**206–208
Brain, *see also* Central nervous system
  anatomy, **1:**217–218
  aphasia, **2:**3–4, 6
  creativity theories, **1:**348
  event-related potential, **1:**131
  eyeblink conditioning substrates, **1:**321–325
    cerebellum, **1:**322
    hippocampus, **1:**322–324
  functional decline, *see* Dementia
  neuropathology
    microenvironmental changes, **1:**219–220
    neuronal plasticity, **1:**220
    neurotransmitters
      age changes, **1:**218; **2:**223–225
      brain function, **2:**221–222
  stroke
    consequences, **2:**526–527
    diagnostic studies, **2:**522
    epidemiology, **2:**517–520
      prevalence, **2:**518
      risk factors, **2:**518–520
    overview, **2:**517
    pathophysiology, **2:**520–522
    prevention, **2:**525–526
    treatment, **2:**522–525
Brain death, definition, **1:**361
Branching theory, psychological aging, **2:**566
Breast cancer
  mastectomy, sexual response changes, **2:**487
  overview, **1:**234–235
Breathing, *see* Respiratory system
Brush border, definition, **1:**541

C

Caenorhabditis elegans
  aging models
    human applications, **2:**160–161
    mutational analysis, **2:**157–158
    quantitative genetics, **1:**582; **2:**156
    study rationale, **2:**151–153
  mortality trajectories, **2:**89
  programmed cell death studies, **1:**272–273
Calcitonin
  bone growth role, **1:**207–208
  osteoporosis treatment, **1:**214
Calcium
  absorption, **1:**545

Calcium (*continued*)
  body composition
    bones, 1:204–205
    measurement, 1:197–198
  bone metabolism, 1:487–488
  calcium phyrophosphate deposition arthropathy,
      1:115–116
  osteoporosis treatment, 1:213
Calcium-ion release channels, neuronal microenvironment
    changes, 1:219
Caloric restriction
  aging postponement
    delayed physiological aging, 1:186, 190–191
    extracellular matrix modulation, 1:528
    senescence rate, 2:548–549
  definition, 1:185
  DNA aberrations, 2:137–138
  exercise effects, 1:190–192
Calorimetry, definition, 1:185
Cancer
  biology
    apoptosis, 1:230
    carcinogenesis, 1:227–228, 493; 2:240–242
    cell cycle, 1:230–232
    chromosome abnormalities, 1:232
    classification, 1:223–224
    cytokines, 1:232
    definition, 1:223
    epidemiology, 1:224–225, 495–496
    gene regulation, 1:229
    growth factors, 1:232
    immune response, 1:758–759
    malignancy
      cancer classification, 1:224
      cell death mechanisms, 1:275
    metastases, 1:230
    molecular markers, 1:232
    occurrence patterns, 1:225
    oncogenes, 1:229–230
    oxidative damage, 2:240–242
    telomerase reactivation, 2:541–543
  emotional reactions, 2:472
  possible causes, 1:226–227
  prevention, 1:228–229
  quality of life, 1:242–243
  screening, 1:239
  support care, 1:242–243
  therapy, 1:239–242
    chemotherapy, 1:241
    gene therapy, 1:241–242
    hormonal therapy, 1:229, 241; 2:363
    immunotherapy, 1:241
    pain management, 2:253–254
    progesterone replacement, 1:213

  radiation, 1:240–241
  surgery, 1:240
  types
    benign prostatic hyperplasia
      diagnosis, 2:358–360
      etiology, 2:358
      incidence, 2:357–358
      medical treatment, 2:360
      physiology, 2:358
      surgical treatment, 2:360–361
    bladder cancer, 1:237–238
    breast cancer, 1:234–235
    colorectal cancer, 1:233–234, 550–551
    esophageal tumors, 1:547–548
    gallbladder cancer, 1:552
    kidney cancer, 1:238
    lung cancer, 1:232–233
    ovarian cancer, 1:238–239
    pancreas cancer, 1:552
    prostate cancer, 1:236–237
    stomach cancer, 1:548–549
    uterus cancer, 1:239
Capital punishment, societal attitudes, 1:364
Carbohydrates
  absorption, 1:545
  glycation
    age-related metabolic change, 2:140
    biological consequences
      extracellular proteins, 1:607–608
      intracellular proteins, 1:607
      nucleic acids, 1:608–609
      pathologic consequences, 1:608
    chemistry, 1:605–607
    definition, 1:605
    immunofluorescence detection method, 1:526–527
    pharmacological intervention, 1:609
    sugar-derived collagen cross-links, 1:525–526
    theory, 1:185
    thyroid hormone economy, 1:480–481
  metabolism, 1:189, 489–490
Carcinogenesis, *see* Cancer
Cardiovascular system
  atherosclerosis, 1:123–128
    overview, 1:123–124
    pathogenesis, 1:126–127
    risk factors, 1:124–126
      cholesterol, 1:125–126, 201
      hypertension, 1:125
      multiple factors, 1:124–125
      smoking, 1:126
    stroke
      pathophysiology, 2:520–521
      risk, 2:520
    vessel biology, 1:127–128

drug distribution, 2:298–299
epidemiological studies, 1:495
estrogen replacement therapy effects, 1:213
exercise effects
    oxygen consumption, 2:433–434
    performance response, 1:146
geriatric rehabilitation, 2:383
hypertension
    age-related blood pressure change, 1:250–251
    atherosclerosis risk, 1:125
    blood pressure control, 1:145–146
    hearing loss prevention, 1:653
    stroke risk, 2:518–519
morphological alterations, 1:247–248
muscle capillary changes, 2:219
myocardial function, 1:248–249
neuroconductive system, 1:249
overview, 1:246–247
pain presentation, 2:254
physical health identity, 1:737–738
pulmonary vascular bed, 1:250
stroke
    consequences, 2:526–527
    diagnostic studies, 2:522
    epidemiology, 2:517–520
        prevalence, 2:518
        risk factors, 2:518–520
    overview, 2:517
    pathophysiology, 2:520–522
    prevention, 2:525–526
    treatment, 2:522–525
systemic veins, 1:250
vascular system characteristics, 1:249–250
Career age
    age conceptions, 2:627–629
    creativity measurement, 1:345–346
    definition, 1:341
Careers, *see* Employment
Caregivers, *see also* Health care services
    alcohol abuse, 1:617
    caregiver heterogeneity, 1:259–260
    definition, 1:1
    demographics, 1:253–254, 257
    elder abuse
        perpetrator characteristics, 1:3–6
        prevalence, 1:2–3
            domestic settings, 1:2
            institutions, 1:2–3
        social isolation, 1:6–7
        stress, 1:6, 675
    grandparents, 1:616–618
    home caregiver characteristics, 1:671–673
        appraisal importance, 1:672

        coping, 1:672–673
        life orientation, 1:672–673
        motivation, 1:671–672
    primary versus secondary caregivers, 1:255–256
    racial differences, 1:260
    stress, 1:6, 256, 264–267, 675, 694
Caregiving, *see also* Health care services
    cancer patients, 1:242–243
    cultural differences, 1:260
    definition, 1:253
    dementing patients, 2:126
    drug use, 1:94
    feminist theories, 1:262
    formal care, 1:256–259
    gender differences, 1:259, 561
    gerontechnology, 1:602
    hospice care, *see* Hospice
    informal care, 1:254–256
    in-home care, *see* Home care
    prevalence, 1:253–254, 257
    reciprocity, 2:505, 510–513
    theory
        current theory integration, 1:265–268
        family functioning, 1:262–264
        individual functioning, 1:264–265
        social functioning, 1:260–262
Cat, aging model, 2:168
Cataracts, characteristics, 2:611
Catastrophe theory, homeostasis, 1:684
Catecholamines, *see specific types*
Cell culture, *in vitro* life spans, 1:270–271
Cell cycle
    cancer biology, 1:230–232
    definition, 1:625
Cell death
    age-related cell death
        gradual cell loss, 1:275–276
        immune self-destruction, 1:276
        malignancy, 1:275
        postmitotic cell loss, 1:276
    apoptosis
        carcinogenesis, 1:227, 230
        cell shrinkage, 1:274
        definition, 1:223, 269, 753
        in vivo characteristics, 1:271–272
        lymphocyte differentiation, 1:759
        nucleus degradation, 1:273–274
        oxidative injury-dependent pathway, 2:242–243
        phagocytosis, 1:274
    cellular senescence
        definition, 1:625
        human fibroblast cells
            cell requirements, 1:626–627

Cell death (*continued*)
    endogenous production, **1:**629–630
    gene expression, **1:**631–632
    growth factor receptors, **1:**628–629
    growth factor stimulation, **1:**627–628
    insulin-like growth factor binding protein,
      1:630–632
    insulin-like growth factor-1 response, **1:**629
    temporal requirements, **1:**627
  defense mechanisms, **1:**448–449
  definition, **1:**269–270
  heat shock gene expression, **2:**320–323
  in vitro studies, **1:**270–271
  in vivo studies, **1:**271–272
  mechanisms, **1:**274–275
  programmed cell death
    definition, **1:**269
    in vivo characteristics, **1:**271
    overview, **1:**272–273
    oxidative injury-dependent pathway, **2:**242–243
  protein turnover rates, **2:**140
  telomere genetics, **1:**446–447; **2:**539–540
Cellular stress response
  age-dependent changes, **2:**320–323
  gene expression, **2:**317–320
Central nervous system, *see also* Autonomic nervous
    system; Brain
  attention capacity slowing, **1:**136–137
  auditory nerves, **1:**646, 648–650
  degenerative dementia classification, **1:**386–387
  lipophilic drug effects, **2:**299
  neuropathology
    microenvironmental changes, **1:**219–220
    neural noise, **1:**136
    neurotransmitters
      age changes, **1:**218
      brain function, **2:**221–222
      neurotrophic factor role, **2:**222–223
  postmitotic cell death, **1:**276
  reaction time response initiation, **2:**178–180
Cerebellum
  eyeblink conditioning substrate, **1:**322
  stroke pathophysiology, **2:**521
Cerebrospinal fluid, dementia diagnosis, **1:**399–400
Change, *see* Adaptation; Social change
Chaos theory
  definition, **2:**557
  homeostasis, **1:**684–685
  psychological aging, **2:**566
Chautauquas, adult education, **1:**61
Chemical senses, *see* Smell; Taste
Chemotherapy, cancer treatment, **1:**241

Chess masters, achievement characteristics, **1:**33
Children, *see* Adolescence; Adult children
Chlorine, total body composition measurement,
    1:197–198
Cholecystokinin
  digestive function, **1:**544
  food intake regulation, **1:**433
Cholelithiasis, gallbladder dysfunction, **1:**552
Cholesterol
  atherosclerosis risk, **1:**125–126, 201
  epidemiological studies, **1:**495
  neuronal microenvironment changes, **1:**219
  oxidative damage, **2:**241–242
  plasma membrane, **1:**279–282
    fluidity changes, **2:**138–140
    isolation, **1:**282–283
    lipid composition, **1:**280–281
    membrane cholesterol alterations, **1:**283–287
      Alzheimer's disease-related alterations, **1:**285–286
      atherosclerosis-related alterations, **1:**286–287
      compensatory alterations, **1:**283–285
    membrane structure, **1:**279–280
    physical characteristics, **1:**280–281
    regulation, **1:**281–282
Chromatin, definition, **1:**441
Chromosomes
  cancer biology, **1:**232; **2:**541–543
  telomere genetics
    age-related loss, **2:**541–543
    cancer-induced telomerase reactivation, **2:**541–543
    end-replication problems, **2:**540–541
    implications, **2:**543
    somatic replicative senescence, **2:**539–540
Chronic stress, *see* Stress
Chronological age, *see* Aging theories; Time
Chylomicron, definition, **1:**541
Cigarettes, *see* Smoking
Circadian rhythms
  biological clock, **2:**584–585, 588
  senescence theory, desynchronosis, **2:**549
Circumplex model, family caregiving theory, **1:**263
Cirrhosis
  definition, **1:**541
  liver dysfunction, **1:**551
Citric acid cycle, definition, **2:**135
Class, *see* Socioeconomic status
Classical conditioning, *see* Conditioning, classical
Climacteric, *see also* Menopause
  age changes, **2:**483–484
Cocaine, use, **1:**96
Cockayne's syndrome, premature aging studies,
    2:349–350

Cognition, *see also* Learning; Memory
  adaptative change, 1:54
  adjustment theory, 2:292
  aging postponement, 2:335
  balance control, 1:155–156
  consumer decision making, 1:336–337
  definition, 2:377
  ergonomic designs, 1:718
  generational differences, 1:571–572
  genetic influences, 1:168–169
  impairment, alcohol use, 1:97–98
  individual differences, 2:115–116
  learning capacity, 2:8
  moderating variables, 2:114–115
  neuroscience, 2:116
  personality changes, 2:563–564
  reaction time importance, 2:379–380
  resource theory, 2:113–114
  skill acquisition
    components
      automatic, 2:492–494
      strategic, 2:490–492
    definition, 2:489–490
    strategies, 2:494–495
  speech recognition, 1:648
  task performance, attention, *see* Attention
Cognitive–behavioral therapy, 1:289–296
  adaptations
    age differences, 1:291
    heterogenous populations, 1:291
    slower pace, 1:291–292
    therapist role changes, 1:291
    therapy socialization, 1:292
  definition, 1:289
  effectiveness, 1:295–296
  theoretical assumptions
    problem causes, 1:289–290
    strategies, 1:290
  treatment approaches
    ageism, 1:293
    alcohol abuse, 1:295
    anxiety, 1:295
    bereavement, 1:292
    chronic illness, 1:292–293
    depression, 1:293–294, 424
    disabilities, 1:292–293
    drug abuse, 1:295
    self-esteem, 1:293
    social change, 1:293
  use rationale
    format, 1:291
    normal problems, 1:290–291

Cohorts
  across cohort connections, 1:306–307
  active life expectancy, 1:302–303
  age-period-cohort model, 2:560, 588
  age stratification, 1:81–92
    dynamics, 1:90–92
      alterability, 1:91–92
      role imbalances, 1:90–91
    overview, 1:81–84
      class, 1:83
      conceptual framework, 1:82–83
      ideology, 1:83
      pervasive themes, 1:84
    population composition, 1:84–86
    relationships, 1:87
    social roles, 1:87–90
  aging process, 1:300–301; 2:66–67
  alcohol use, 1:23, 97
  consumer decision making, 1:333–337
  death anxiety, 1:368
  definition, 1:81, 353; 2:333, 459
  driving experience, 1:23
  epidemiological studies, 1:497–500
  gender roles, 1:563
  generational differences
    cognitive–behavioral interventions, 1:293
    findings
      cognitive abilities, 1:571–572
      demographic characteristics, 1:572–574
      family environment perceptions, 1:574–575
    generation verses cohort, 1:568
    historical perspective, 1:567–568
    literary representations, 2:75
    methodological issues, 1:568–570
    political attitudes, 2:327–329, 331–332
    sources, 1:300–301
  home ownership, 1:706
  intracohort variation, 1:304–306
  life course paradigm, 2:32–33
  mortality, 1:301–302; 2:89–93
  pensions, 1:303–304
  political behaviors, 1:36; 2:325–326
  research methods, 2:422–423
  retirement, 1:303
  self-esteem differences, 2:462
  size effects, 1:308
  social interplay, 1:307–308
  status transitions, 1:303–305
  subcohort impact, 1:305–306
  suicide rates, 2:532
Colitis, large intestine dysfunction, 1:550

Collagen
definition, **1**:519
extracellular matrix
age-associated changes, **1**:527–529
assessment methods
collagen content, **1**:522–523
collagen synthesis, **1**:523–524
elastin content, **1**:523
electron microscopy, **1**:522
enzymatically-mediated cross-links, **1**:524–525
histochemistry, **1**:520–521
immunofluorescence, **1**:526–527
mechanical properties, **1**:521–522
solubility, **1**:522
sugar-derived cross-links, **1**:525–526
overview, **1**:519–520
nonenzymatic glycation effects, **1**:607–608
oxidative damage, **2**:243–244
Colon
anatomy, **1**:542–543
colitis, **1**:550
colorectal cancer, **1**:233–234
Colony-stimulating factors, definition, **1**:203
Comedy, *see* Humor
Commanders, military, achievement characteristics, **1**:29–30
Communication
aphasia, **2**:3–4, 6
dementia, **2**:4–5
ergonomic designs, **1**:720
normal aging
comprehension, **2**:2
nonlanguage interaction abilities, **2**:3
societal factors, **2**:3
syntax, **2**:2
social inhibition, **1**:763–764
Community college, *see also* Learning
adult education, **1**:66
job training, **2**:632–633
Comparative biology
aging models, *Drosophila,* **2**:159
evolutionary studies, **1**:514–516
Comparison load effect, attention capacity measurement, **1**:132–135
Competence, *see also* Skill acquisition
environmental adaptation model, **1**:51, 54
falls, **1**:737; **2**:215
physical identity, **1**:736–737
Social Competence and Breakdown Theory, **1**:260–261
Comprehensive geriatric assessment, *see* Geriatric assessment

Computers
computerized tomography, body composition measurement, **1**:198
motor-skill learning, **2**:11–12
work environment, ergonomic designs, **1**:723–724; **2**:639
Conditioning
classical
eyeblink conditioning, **1**:319–325
animals, **1**:320–321
brain substrates, **1**:321–325
humans, **1**:321
learning, **2**:9
instrumental
extinction, **1**:325–326
learning, **2**:10
reinforcement schedule, **1**:326
retention, **1**:326–327
simple acquisition, **1**:325–326
operant, learning, **2**:9–10
physical, *see* Exercise
Conflict resolution, *see* Life review
Congregate Housing Services Program, **1**:711
Constipation, large intestine dysfunction, **1**:550
Consumer behavior
decision making
age differences, **1**:333–337, 378
alternative evaluation, **1**:336–337
information gathering, **1**:334–336
improved consumers, **1**:337–339
advertising, **1**:338
decision aids, **1**:337–338
training, **1**:338
model, **1**:332–333
definition, **1**:329
economic well-being, **1**:475–476
future research directions, **1**:339–340
study motivation, **1**:329–332
business interest, **1**:330
public policy, **1**:330–331
theoretical models, **1**:331–332
Continuity theory
activity engagement, **1**:48–49
bereavement, **1**:179
definition, **1**:37
Contractile proteins, function, **2**:213
Control, *see* Autonomy; Balance; Homeostasis; Motor control
Controlled substances, *see* Pharmacology; Substance abuse
Control theory
definition, **1**:679
homeostasis, **1**:682–683

Coping, *see also* Stress
  adaptation
    cognitive change, **1**:54
    environment
      competence adaptation model, **1**:54
      fall prevention, **1**:16–17
    identity, **1**:56–59
      ego integrity, **1**:58–59
      life cycle role changes, **1**:56–58
    overview, **1**:51–52
    physical change, **1**:54
    social roles, **1**:54–56
    stress, **1**:52–53
  bereavement, **1**:177–178, 181–182
  definition, **1**:51
  home caregiving, **1**:672–673
  life satisfaction, **2**:61
  one-to-one reminiscence, **2**:402–403
  personality types, **2**:290–291
  physical identity, **1**:739–741
  suicide, *see* Suicide
  well-being modification, **2**:48
Core activities, definition, **1**:37
Corticotropin-releasing hormone, adrenal function,
    1:483–484
Counterpart theory
  psychological aging, **2**:561–562
  senescence, **2**:550
Creatinine
  age-related clearance changes, **2**:409–410
  definition, **2**:407
  total body composition measurement, **1**:197
Creativity
  achievement characteristics, **1**:31–32
  epigenetic stage theory, **2**:287
  humor role, **1**:731
  interpretation
    economic theories, **1**:349–350
    psychobiological theories, **1**:348–349
    psychological theories, **1**:350
    sociological theories, **1**:349
  literary representations, **2**:75–76
  overview, **1**:341–342
  productivity measurements, **1**:343–348
    age decrement magnitude, **1**:344
    career versus chronological age, **1**:345–346
    creative domains, **1**:344–345
    equal-odds rule, **1**:346–347
    lifetime output differences, **1**:345
    productivity influences, **1**:346
    qualitative transformations, **1**:347–348
  psychometric assessments, **1**:342–343

Crime
  age relationship, **1**:354–355, 358–359
  capital punishment, societal attitudes, **1**:364
  career offenders, **1**:357–358
  criminology, **1**:353
  etiology, **1**:355–357
    abuse, **1**:356
    family dysfunction, **1**:356
    neighborhood, **1**:357
    peer groups, **1**:356–357
    school performance, **1**:357
Critical flicker fusion, **2**:273
Crohn's disease, large intestine dysfunction, **1**:550–551
Cryotherapy, prostate cancer therapy, **2**:363
Crystal arthropathies, *see also* Rheumatic diseases
  symptoms, **1**:115–116; **2**:455–456
Crystallized intelligence, achievement characteristics, **1**:35
Culture, *see also* Race
  ageism emergence, **1**:72–73
  aging images, **1**:749–750
  comparative studies
    caregiving, **1**:260
    definitions, **1**:316
    demographics, **1**:313
    design, **1**:312–313
    future research directions, **1**:316–317
    health, **1**:314–315
    importance, **1**:311–312
    kinship, **1**:315–316
    life course, **1**:316–317
    security, **1**:315
    social support, **1**:315–316
    well-being, **1**:314; **2**:368
  cross-cultural grandparents, **1**:621–622
  folklore, *see* Folklore
  gender roles, **1**:556
  modernization effects
    architecture, **2**:174–175
    definition, **2**:171
    demographics, **2**:172–173
    life quality, **2**:174
    old-age experience, **2**:171–172
    planning innovations, **2**:174–175
    social network erosion, **2**:174
  mythology, *see* Mythology
  social network differences, **2**:512–513
Cumulative advantage, definition, **1**:341
Cumulative trauma disorder
  definition, **1**:715
  ergonomic designs, **1**:721–722
Cybernetics, homeostasis model, **1**:682
Cytokine receptors, immune system role, **1**:757–758

Cytokines
  bone growth role, **1:**208–209
  cancer biology, **1:**232
  immune system role, **1:**757–758

D

Daily life, *see* Activities of daily living
Death, *see also* Cell death; Mortality; Senescence
  anxiety, **1:**367–369
  appropriate death, **1:**694–695
  bereavement
    adjustment course, **1:**176–182
      age-stratification theory, **1:**179
      continuity theory, **1:**179
      coping theories, **1:**177–178
      engagement theory, **1:**179
      family theories, **1:**178
      predictors, **1:**181–182
      psychoanalytic theories, **1:**177
      research, **1:**179–181
      stage models, **1:**178
      stress, **1:**177–178
      symbolic interaction theory, **1:**179
      system theories, **1:**178
      task models, **1:**178
    definition, **1:**173
    experience variety, **1:**173–174
    interventions, **1:**182–183
    knowledge sources, **1:**175–176
    multidimensional nature, **1:**174–175
  definition, **1:**361
  ego integrity, **1:**58–59
  end-of-life issues, **1:**370–372
  hospice care, *see* Hospice
  immune response, **1:**104
  individual orientations
    death anxiety, **1:**367–369
    living through dying, **1:**369–370
  life-support technology, **1:**362–363
  new questions, **1:**362–363
  societal attitudes
    consequences, **1:**364–367
    death system, **1:**363–364
  suicide, *see* Suicide
  widowhood, *see* Widowhood
Decision making
  consumer behavior
    age differences, **1:**333–337
      alternative evaluation, **1:**336–337
      information gathering, **1:**334–336

    improved consumers, **1:**337–339
      advertising, **1:**338
      decision aids, **1:**337–338
      training, **1:**338
    model, **1:**332–333
  everyday problem solving
    contextual perspective, **1:**375
    developmental differences
      age differences, **1:**376–378
      efficacy criteria, **1:**376
      process, **1:**375–376
    differential task structures, **1:**374–375
    ecological validity, **1:**374
    mediating factors
      emotional salience, **1:**379–380
      individual differences, **1:**380
      personal relevance, **1:**379
      problem appraisal, **1:**378–379
    traditional approaches, **1:**373–374
Dehydration
  causes, **2:**576–577
  investigation, **2:**578
  management, **2:**578
  prevention, **2:**580–581
  rehydration, **2:**578–580
  susceptibility, **2:**413
Dehydroepiandrosterone
  adrenal androgen secretion, **1:**484–485
  senescence theory, **2:**550
Delinquency, *see* Crime
Delusion
  definition, **1:**415
  symptoms, **1:**422
Dementia
  aging-related genetic studies, **1:**579
  Alzheimer's disease, *see* Alzheimer's disease
  care
    activity training, **1:**400–401
    pharmacological treatment, **1:**401–402
    services, **2:**126
  caregiver abuse, **1:**4, 6
  causes, **1,** 386–387; **2:**501
  chemosensory loss, **2:**501
  cognitive–behavioral interventions, **1:**294
  communication difficulties, **2:**4–5
  definition, **2:**1
  depression, **1:**385, 423–424
  diagnosis, **1:**397–400
  epidemiology, **1:**387
  euthanasia, **1:**506
  eyeblink conditioning studies, **1:**323–325
  fall risk, **1:**15
  frontal lobe dementia, **1:**396–397

genetic influences, 1:170
literary representations, 2:75
membrane cholesterol analysis, 1:285–286
mixed dementias, 1:395
neuropathology, 1:220–221
nonenzymatic glycation effects, 1:608
overview
    background, 1:383–384
    definition, 1:384–385
    severity, 1:385–386
pain, 2:255
postmitotic cell death, 1:276
premature aging studies, 2:351
reminiscence therapy, 2:403–404
spatial contrast sensitivity, 2:272–273, 277–278
stroke consequences, 2:526–527
thirst perception, 2:575
traffic accident risk, 1:23
vascular dementia
    hemodynamic dementia, 1:394
    multi-infarct dementia, 1:394
    overview, 1:393–394
    white matter lesions, 1:394–395
Demographics
aged populations, 1:409–410, 598
age strata, 1:84–86
caregiving, 1:253–254, 257
cross-cultural studies, 1:313
dependency, 1:470–471
ethnic diversity, 2:371
future research directions
    biodemography, 1:412–413
    family demography, 1:410
    family dynamics, 1:411–412
    household structures, 1:411
    kinship structures, 1:410–411
gender roles, 1:557–558
generational differences, 1:572–574
intergenerational relations, 1:612
modernization, 2:172–173
population aging, 1:405–409
    historical development, 1:406
    policy implications, 1:409
    population dynamics models, 1:406–407
    trends, 1:408–409
suicide rates, 2:531–532
traffic accidents, 1:19–20
volunteerism, 2:613–614, 616–617
widowhood, 1:174, 558–559; 2:621–622
workforce participation, 2:627, 637–638
Dependency
costs, 1:473–474
death anxiety, 1:367–369

demographics, 1:470–471
elder abuse, 1:6
Depression
acute mental illness, 2:126
appetite loss, 1:187
bipolar disorders, 1:417
clinical presentation, 1:421–423
    grief, 1:422–423
    major depression, 1:421–422
    minor depression, 1:422
    mood disorders, 1:423
definition, 1:415
dementia related, 1:385, 423–424
diagnostic classification, 1:416
differential diagnosis, 1:423–424
epidemiology, 1:416–417
ethnic differences, 2:374–375
future outlook beliefs, 2:285
future research directions, 1:426–427
genetic influences, 1:170
hearing loss related, 1:652
humor therapy, 1:729
importance, 1:416
institutionalization, 1:417
life event consequences, 2:46
management
    cognitive–behavioral therapy, 1:293–294, 424
    electroconvulsive therapy, 1:426
    psychopharmacology, 1:425–426
    psychotherapy, 1:424
pharmacological treatment, 1:401–402
prognosis, 1:426
risk factors, 1:418–421
selective information processing, 1:764
suicide, *see* Suicide
therapy, reminiscence, 2:401–402
Desynchronosis, senescence theory, 2:549
Developmental models, *see also* Life course
personality
    conceptualizations, 2:285–286
    environmental verses genetic aging influences,
        1:165–166
    epigenetic stage theory, 2:287–288
    gero-transcendence, 2:288–289
    period model, 2:286–287
    theory, 2:282–283
    well-being, 2:288
Developmental tasks, psychological aging, 2:561
Dexamethasone, human fibroblast cell senescence,
    1:626–628
Diabetes
definition, 1:605
extracellular matrix modulation, 1:528

Diabetes (*continued*)
  glucose metabolism
    bioenergetics, 1:189, 489–490
    biological consequences
      extracellular proteins, 1:607–608
      intracellular proteins, 1:607
      nucleic acids, 1:608–609
      pathologic consequences, 1:608
    chemistry, 1:605–607
    sugar-derived collagen cross-links, 1:525–526
    thyroid hormone economy, 1:480–481
  immunofluorescence detection method, 1:526–527
  pharmacological intervention, 1:609
  premature aging studies, 1:528; 2:352–353
  stroke risk, 2:519
  theory, 1:185
  weight relationship, 1:201
Diabetic retinopathy, characteristics, 2:611–612
Diarrhea, characteristics, 1:549–550
Dicoumarol, drug interactions, 2:305
Diet, *see* Nutrition
Dietary restriction
  aging postponement
    delayed physiological aging, 1:186, 190–191
    extracellular matrix modulation, 1:528
    senescence rate, 2:548–549
  definition, 1:185
  DNA aberrations, 2:137–138
  exercise effects, 1:190–192
Dietary supplements
  cancer prevention, 1:228–229
  malnutrition intervention strategies, 1:439–440
  vitamin C, oxidative stress measurement, 2:237–238
  vitamin D
    bone metabolism, 1:487–488
    calcium absorption, 1:545
    osteoporosis treatment, 1:210, 213–214
  vitamin E
    epidemiological studies, 1:500–503
    extracellular matrix modulation, 1:528
Digestion
  gastrointestinal function, 1:542–543
  glucose metabolism, *see* Glycation
  small intestine dysfunction, 1:549
Dipsogen, definition, 2:573
Disabilities, *see also specific types*
  arthritis impact, 1:118–119
  cognitive–behavioral therapy, 1:292–293
  definition, 2:382
  gender inequality, 1:560
  geriatric assessment
    benefits, 1:591
    components, 1:589–590

    definition, 1:587
    future research directions, 1:592
    historical perspective, 1:588–589
    objectives, 1:587–588
    program models, 1:590–591
  gerontechnology, 1:602
  mortality trajectories, 2:93
  rehabilitation
    acute rehabilitation, 2:383–385
    definition, 2:381
    emerging issues, 2:385
    relevance, 2:381–383
    unique geriatric aspects, 2:383
Discrimination, *see* Ageism; Race; Sexism
Disease, *see also* Epidemiology; Immune system; *specific types*
  autonomic nervous system dysfunction, 1:146
  body composition relationship, 1:200–201
  chronic illness, cognitive–behavioral therapy, 1:292–293
  fall risk, 1:15–16
  human age-related genetic studies, 1:579
  self-regulation model, 2:470
Disengagement theory, *see also* Activity theory; Gerotranscendence theory
  activity meaning, 1:45–46
  adaptation, 1:51
  ageism, 1:75–76
  consumer behavior, 1:331
  definition, 2:569
  historical perspective, 2:570
  leisure activity, 2:21
  psychological aging, 2:561–562
Diversity, social stratification, 1:84
Diverticula, large intestine dysfunction, 1:550
Divorce, grandparent–family relationships, 1:618
DNA, *see also* Gene expression
  age changes
    cellular defense mechanisms, 1:448–449
    damage, 1:443–444
    epigenetic changes, 1:447–448
    mutational hotspot regions, 1:446–447
    sequence changes, 1:444–446
  cell death
    nucleus degradation, 1:273–274
    premature aging, 2:342
    in vitro, 1:270–271
  definition, 1:605; 2:151
  evolutionary theory, 1:442–443
  metabolic regulation, 2:136–138
  nonenzymatic glycation effects, 1:608–609
  oxidative damage, *see* Oxidative damage
  senescence theory, repair failure, 2:549

somatic mutation, **1:**585
telomere genetics
  age-related loss, **2:**541–543
  cancer-induced telomerase reactivation, **2:**541–543
  end-replication problems, **2:**540–541
  implications, **2:**543
  somatic replicative senescence, **2:**539–540
Dog, aging model, **2:**168
Domestic violence
  feminist models, **1:**4–5
  intergenerational transmission, **1:**6
  legislative programs, **1:**9–10
Dopamine, brain aging effects, **2:**223–225
Double ABCX model, family caregiving theory, **1:**263
Doubly labeled water method, definition, **1:**185
Downsizing, *see* Employment
Down's syndrome
  oxidative damage role, **2:**244–245
  premature aging studies, **2:**350–351
Drinking, *see* Alcohol
Driving
  accidents
    alcohol use, **1:**22–23
    alternative transportation, **1:**24–25
    cohort differences, **1:**23
    commercial drivers, **1:**23–24
    damage, **1:**20
    demographics, **1:**19–20
    driving performance, **1:**20–21
    injuries, **1:**20
    medical impairments, **1:**23
    pedestrian casualties, **1:**24
    risk, **1:**21–22
    technology, **1:**24
    vision effects, **2:**612
  ergonomics, **1:**719–720
  leisure activity constriction, **2:**24
  motion perception deficit effects, **2:**278
Drosophila
  aging models
    comparative biology, **2:**159
    evolutionary biology, **2:**158–159
    gene enhancer traps, **2:**160
    human applications, **2:**160–161
    mitochondrial biochemistry, **2:**160
    study rationale, **2:**151–153
    transgenic approach, **2:**159–160
  evolutionary aging studies, **1:**512–514
  genetic aging studies, **1:**581–582
  premature aging model, **2:**345–346
Drugs, *see* Pharmacology; *specific types*
Dual-photon absorptiometry, body composition
  measurement, **1:**197

Dual-task assessments, attention capacity measurement, **1:**133–135
Dying, *see* Death

E

Ecological validity
  definition, **1:**373
  everyday problem solving, **1:**374
Economics, *see also* Employment; Socioeconomic status
  ageism, **1:**79
  class stratification, **1:**83
  consumer behavior, **1:**329–340
    decision making
      age differences, **1:**333–337
      improved consumers, **1:**337–339
      model, **1:**332–333
    definition, **1:**329
    future research directions, **1:**339–340
    study motivation, **1:**329–332
      business interest, **1:**330
      public policy, **1:**330–331
      theoretical models, **1:**331–332
  creativity theories, **1:**349–350
  future economic status, **1:**465
  future research directions, **1:**465–466
  human needs, **1:**460–461
  income
    changes, **1:**457–458
    gender inequality, **1:**559–560
  individual economics overview, **1:**455–457
  international comparisons, **1:**461–463
  market activities, **1:**44–45
  migration impact, **2:**149
  pensions, *see* Pensions
  population aging, implications, **1:**409
  poverty, **1:**459–461
  retirement policy, *see* Retirement
  social role adaptation, **1:**54–55
  societal economics
    dependency costs, **1:**473–474
    depression relief, **1:**421
    entitlement programs, **1:**471–472
    fiscal capacity, **1:**470–471
    overview, **1:**469–470
    social policy, **1:**472–473
    supply-and-demand view, **1:**474–476
  volunteer activity effects, **2:**615, 618–619
  wealth, **1:**463–464
  well-being variation, **1:**458–459
Economic status, *see* Socioeconomic status

Education, *see* Learning
Effort, attention capacity, **1:**132–135
Ego integrity, adaptation, **1:**51, 58–59
Elastin
  definition, **1:**519
  extracellular matrix
    age-associated changes, **1:**527–529
    assessment methods
      collagen content, **1:**522–523
      collagen synthesis, **1:**523–524
      elastin content, **1:**523
      electron microscopy, **1:**522
      enzymatically-mediated cross-links, **1:**524–525
      histochemistry, **1:**520–521
      immunofluorescence, **1:**526–527
      mechanical properties, **1:**521–522
      solubility, **1:**522
      sugar-derived cross-links, **1:**525–526
    overview, **1:**519–520
Elder abuse, *see also* Ageism
  definition, **1:**1–2
  literary representations, **2:**75
  perpetrator characteristics, **1:**3–4
  prevalence, **1:**2–3
    domestic settings, **1:**2
    institutions, **1:**2–3
  risk factors
    abuser traits, **1:**5–6
    dependency, **1:**6
    intergenerational violence transmission, **1:**6
    social isolation, **1:**6–7
    stress, **1:**6
    structural factors, **1:**7
  social responses, **1:**7–10
    adult protection legislation, **1:**7–8
      child welfare model, **1:**7–8
      mandatory reporting, **1:**8
    programs, **1:**8–10
      adult protection, **1:**8–9
      advocacy, **1:**10
      domestic violence, **1:**9–10
      integrated model, **1:**10
    services, **1:**10
  societal attitudes toward death, **1:**364–367
  theoretical explanations, **1:**4–5
    feminist models, **1:**4–5
    situational model, **1:**4
    social exchange theory, **1:**4
    symbolic interaction approach, **1:**4–5
  victim characteristics, **1:**3–4
Elderhostel, adult education, **1:**66–67
Elderly
  driver demographics, **1:**20

representations, *see* Folklore; Literature; Mythology
Electrical conductivity, body composition measurement, **1:**196–197
Electroconvulsive therapy, depression management, **1:**426
Electroencephalography, dementia diagnosis, **1:**397, 399
Electrolytes, homeostasis changes, **2:**412
Electron microscopy, extracellular matrix assessment, **1:**522
Emotion, *see also* Mental health
  bereavement, **1:**173, 180
  coping, *see* Cognitive–behavioral therapy
  coping strategies, **1:**52
  everyday problem solving, **1:**379–380
  loneliness
    bereavement adjustments, **1:**180
    definition, **2:**79
    emotional isolation, **2:**80
    research findings, **2:**80–81
    social isolation, **2:**79
    theory, **2:**79
  pain role, **2:**249
  salience, **1:**373
  self-regulation, **2:**472–473
  socioemotional selectivity theory, **2:**293
  spiritual meaning, **2:**390–391
Employee Retirement Income Security Act, pension protection, **2:**521–522, 526–527
Employment, *see also* Economics; Retirement
  absenteeism, **2:**632
  accumulative advantage, **1:**349
  achievement, **1:**27–36
    creativity, **1:**31–32
    entertainers, **1:**32–34
      athletes, **1:**32–33
      chess masters, **1:**33
      movie stars, **1:**33–34
    leaders, **1:**28–31
      entrepreneurs, **1:**30
      military commanders, **1:**29–30
      politicians, **1:**28–29, 35–36
      religious leaders, **1:**30–31
    overview, **1:**27–28
    theoretical explanations, **1:**34–36
      biological processes, **1:**34–35
      psychological processes, **1:**35
      sociological processes, **1:**35–36
  age conceptions, **1:**345–346; **2:**627–629
  ageism, **1:**71–74
  alternative work options, **2:**633–634
  creativity measurement, **1:**345–346
  current trends, **1:**457; **2:**638–639
  entry, **2:**629–630

ergonomic designs
    computer jobs, 1:723–724
    fatigue, 1:723
    information-processing jobs, 1:722
    lifting, 1:721
    repetitive motion jobs, 1:721–722
    shiftwork, 1:723
    strength-related jobs, 1:721
    sustained monitoring jobs, 1:722
    visual inspection jobs, 1:722–723
    workforce aging, 1:721
exiting, 2:636–637
future research directions
    minority status, 2:638
    older women, 2:637–638
    organizational issues, 2:638–639
income
    changes, 1:457–458
    gender inequality, 1:559–560
    housing tenure, 1:705–706
    international comparisons, 1:461–463
    joint distribution, 1:464
    leisure activity constriction, 2:24, 28
    life satisfaction, 2:61
job performance, 2:631–632
occupational status, life satisfaction, 2:61–62
occupational therapy
    acute rehabilitation, 2:384
    arthritis management, 1:120
organizational employment
    current issues, 2:638–639
    exiting, 2:636–637
    upward mobility, 2:634–635
participation, 2:627
social role adaptation, 1:55
stereotypes, 2:630–631
training, 2:632–633
turnover, 2:632
volunteer participation, 2:618
work attitudes, 2:633
Empty-nest syndrome, *see* Later-life families
Endocrine system
    adrenal gland
        adrenal medulla, 1:485
        physiology, 1:483–485
        structure, 1:482
    age-related metabolic change, 2:139–140
    calcium metabolism, 1:487–489
    carbohydrate metabolism, 1:489–490
    digestive function, 1:543–545
    epidemiological studies, 1:503
    female reproductive system, 1:486–487
    fluid homeostasis, 2:574–576

food intake changes, 1:187
    hormonal changes, 1:477–478
    male reproductive system, 1:485–486
    muscle growth, 2:216–217
    nutrient metabolism, 1:188–189
    osteopenia, 1:488–489
    pituitary gland
        dynamic testing, 1:479
        functional changes, 1:478–479
    prostate
        anatomy, 2:355
        benign prostatic hyperplasia
            diagnosis, 2:358–360
            etiology, 2:358
            incidence, 2:357–358
            medical treatment, 2:360
            physiology, 2:358
            surgical treatment, 2:360–361
        male reproductive system changes, 1:486
        physiology, 2:355–356
        prostate cancer, 2:361–364
        prostatitis, 2:356–357
    renal dysfunction, 2:416
    senescence theory
        hormonal deficiency, 2:549
        hysteretic disinhibition, 2:549
    thyroid gland
        dysfunction, 1:481–482
        structure, 1:479–480
        thyroid hormone economy, 1:480–481
    water metabolism, 1:490–491
Energy metabolism, *see* Metabolism
Engagement theory, bereavement, 1:179
Entertainers, achievement characteristics, 1:32–34
    athletes, 1:32–33
    chess masters, 1:33
    movie stars, 1:33–34
Entertainment, *see* Leisure
Entitlement, *see specific program*
Entrepreneurs, achievement characteristics, 1:30
Entropy
    homeostasis, 1:685
    intrinsic time measurement, 2:589–590
Environment
    aging differences
        cognitive function, 1:168–169
        dementia, 1:170
        depression, 1:170
        family environment, 1:170–171
        health, 1:167–168
        heritability, 1:164–165
        life events, 1:170–171
        longevity, 1:167–168

Environment (*continued*)
  personality, **1:**169
  social support, **1:**170–171
 aids, *see* Gerontechnology
 cancer risk, **1:**226–227
 competence adaptation model, **1:**51, 54
 fall prevention, **1:**16–17
Epidemiology
 bipolar disorder, **1:**417
 cancer occurrence, **1:**224–225
 conceptual frameworks, **1:**497–500
 definition, **1:**493
 dementia prevalence, **1:**387
 ethnic differences, **2:**373
 late life suicides, **2:**531–533
 osteoporosis, **1:**209–210
 overview, **1:**493–497
 rheumatic diseases, **2:**454
 stroke, **2:**517–520
  prevalence, **2:**518
  risk factors, **2:**518–520
 study designs, **1:**500–503
Epidermal growth factor, human fibroblast cell
  senescence, **1:**626–629
Epigenetic stage theory, personality development,
  2:287–288
Epinephrine, sympathetic nervous system changes, **1:**144
Epistasis, definition, **2:**151
Epistemology
 definition, **2:**307
 philosophical perspective, **2:**311–313
Epstein–Barr virus, cancer risk, **1:**227
Equal-odds rule
 creative achievement, **1:**31–32, 346–347
 definition, **1:**27, 341
Equity theory, definition, **2:**505
Ergonomics
 auditory aids, **1:**601, 717–718
 conceptual approaches, **1:**599–600
 daily living
  activities
   assistive devices, **1:**719
   communication, **1:**720
   driving, **1:**719–720
   importance, **1:**718
   instrumental activities, **1:**719
   interventions, **1:**719
   physical activities, **1:**718–719
  concerns
   anthropometry, **1:**716
   balance, **1:**716–717
   cognition, **1:**718

   health, **1:**718
   hearing, **1:**717–718
   motor skills, **1:**716–717
   strength, **1:**716–717
   vision, **1:**717
 definition, **1:**593
 future research directions, **1:**724–725
 historical perspective, **1:**595–596
 motivation, **1:**715–716
 systems approach, **1:**597
 working life
  computer jobs, **1:**723–724
  fatigue, **1:**723
  information-processing jobs, **1:**722
  lifting, **1:**721
  repetitive motion jobs, **1:**721–722
  shiftwork, **1:**723
  strength-related jobs, **1:**721
  sustained monitoring jobs, **1:**722
  visual inspection jobs, **1:**722–723
  workforce aging, **1:**721
Escherichia coli, bacterial prostatitis, **2:**356
Esophagus
 anatomy, **1:**542–543
 dysfunction, **1:**547–548
Estrogen
 definition, **2:**333
 female reproductive system changes, **1:**486–487
 replacement therapy
  cancer prevention, **1:**229
  life expectancy changes, **2:**93–94
  osteoporosis treatment, **1:**212–213
Ethics
 definition, **2:**307
 philosophical perspective, **2:**313–316
Ethnicity, *see* Culture; Race
Euthanasia
 definition, **1:**505, 687; **2:**529
 ethical arguments
  hospice care, **1:**691–692
  opposition, **1:**506–507; **2:**536–538
  supportive, **1:**505–506; **2:**536–538
 persistent vegetative state, **1:**361
 societal attitudes, **1:**364, 371
 voluntary practice, **1:**507–508; **2:**530–531
Event-related brain potential, definition, **1:**131
Evolutionary biology
 comparative studies, **1:**514–516
 experimental studies
  laboratory evolution, **1:**512–513
  population genetics, **1:**513–514
 historical gerontology, **1:**660–662

models, *Drosophila,* 2:158–159
premature aging, 2:342
senescence, 2:553–554
theory
  definition, 1:509
  early theories, 1:509–510
  gene expression, 1:442–443
  mathematical theories, 1:510–511
  population genetic hypotheses, 1:511–512
Exchange theory
  definition, 2:505
  retirement, 2:444
  social exchange, 2:510–511
  social network differences, 2:512–513
Exercise
  balance control, 1:156–157
  basal metabolic rate changes, 1:190–192
  cardiovascular response, 1:146
  food intake
    change, 1:188
    restricted energy intake, 1:191–192
  geriatric rehabilitation, 2:383
  gerontechnology, 1:601
  health effects, 1:40–41
  life expectancy changes, 2:93
  muscle adaptability, 2:217–220
  respiratory response, lung function, 2:433
Existentialism
  definition, 2:307
  ontology, 2:310
Experiential–contextual model, personality development, 2:283
Extended family, *see* Family; Social networks
Extracellular matrix
  age-associated changes, 1:527–528
  aging postponement, 1:528
  assessment methods
    biochemical studies
      collagen content, 1:522–523
      collagen synthesis, 1:523–524
      elastin content, 1:523
      enzymatically-mediated cross-links, 1:524–525
      sugar-derived cross-links, 1:525–526
    electron microscopy, 1:522
    histochemistry, 1:520–521
    immunofluorescence, 1:526–527
    mechanical properties, 1:521–522
    solubility, 1:522
  atherosclerosis pathogenesis, 1:126–127
  overview, 1:519–520
Eyeblink conditioning
  animal models, 1:320–321
  brain substrates, 1:321–325
    Alzheimer's disease treatment, 1:323–325
    cerebellum, 1:322
    hippocampus, 1:322–324
    humans, 1:321
Eyes, *see* Vision

F

Fainting, blood pressure control, autonomic nervous system changes, 1:145–146
Falls
  balance control
    anticipatory postural adjustments, 1:154–155
    cognitive systems, 1:155–156
    early studies, 1:151–152
    retraining research, 1:156–157
    systems approach studies
      adaptation, 1:154
      musculoskeletal system, 1:152
      neuromuscular response patterns, 1:152–153
      sensory contributions, 1:153–154
  biomechanics, 1:12–14
  causal factors, 1:13–16
    cognitive factors, 1:15
    environmental factors, 1:16
    gait control, 1:14–15
    medical risk factors, 1:15–16
    multifactorial nature, 1:13–14
    postural balance control, 1:14
    volitional movement, 1:14–15
  fainting, postural hypotension, 1:145–146
  fear of falling, 1:12, 156, 160
  hip fractures
    definition, 1:11
    fall biomechanics, 1:13
    incidence, 1:12
    osteoporosis related, 1:209–211
  incidence, 1:11, 13
  job-related accidents, 2:632
  medical consequences, 1:12
  motion vision perception, 2:610
  physical competence, 1:737; 2:215
  post fall syndrome, 1:11
  postfall syndrome, 1:11–12
  prevention, 1:16–17, 602
  psychosocial consequences, 1:12
  resulting injuries, 1:11–12
Family
  attitudes toward death, 1:363–364
  bereavement, 1:178; 2:199

Family (*continued*)
  bonding, intergenerational bonds, cohort differences,
    1:306
  caregiver ties, 1:258–259, 674
  caregiving theory
    boundary ambiguity, 1:263–264
    circumplex model, 1:263
    double ABCX model, 1:263
    dyads, 1:262–263
  criminal behavior, 1:356
  cross-cultural studies, 1:315–316
  definition, 1:611
  demographics, 1:410–412
  generational perception differences, 1:574–575
  grandparenthood, *see* Grandparenthood
  hospice care, *see* Hospice
  in-home caregiving, *see* Home care
  life course paradigm, *see* Life course
  literary representations, 2:75
  modernization effects, 2:174
  stress reduction, 1:53, 58
  support roles, 2:509–510, 513–514
  widowhood, *see* Widowhood
Fanconi's anemia
  oxidative damage role, 2:245
  premature aging studies, 2:348–349
Fas ligand
  apoptosis induction, 1:274
  definition, 1:269
Fat
  absorption, 1:545
  age-related changes, 1:199–200
  bioenergetics, 1:186, 189
  body weight, 1:193–195
  cancer prevention, 1:228
  disease relationship, 1:200–201
  food selection, 1:436–437
  measurement
    regional assessment
      anthropometrics, 1:198–199
      computerized tomography, 1:198
      magnetic resonance imaging, 1:198
      sonography, 1:198
    total body composition
      anthropometry, 1:196
      bioelectrical impedance, 1:196–197
      dual-photon absorptiometry, 1:197
      hydrodensitometry, 1:195–196
      isotope dilution, 1:196
      total body electrical conductivity, 1:196–197
Father–offspring bonds, cohort differences, 1:306
Fatigue, *see also* Stress
  work environment, ergonomic designs, 1:723

Fatty streak, definition, 1:123
Fear, *see* Phobias
Female reproductive system
  endocrine function, 1:486–487
  estrogen replacement therapy
    cancer prevention, 1:229
    definition, 2:333
    life expectancy changes, 2:93–94
    osteoporosis treatment, 1:212–213
  hysterectomy, sexual response changes, 2:484–485,
    487
  menopause
    bone loss role, 1:210–211
    definition, 2:479
    female reproductive system changes, 1:486–487
    progesterone replacement therapy, 1:213
    sexual expression changes, 2:483–484
  physical health identity, 1:738–739
Feminist theories
  caregiving, 1:262
  elder abuse, 1:4–5
  gender role demographics, 1:557–558
  social aging theory, 2:571
Fetal development, life-course consequences, 1:306
F_1 hybrid, definition, 2:163
Fiber, cancer prevention, 1:228
Fibroatheroma, definition, 1:123
Fibroblasts, *see* Human fibroblast cells
Field research, *see* Research methods
Fish, aging model, 2:166–167
Fitness, *see* Evolutionary biology
Flow, activity immersion, 2:22
Fluctuation theory, senescence, 2:550
Fluid intake, *see* Thirst
Fluid intelligence, achievement characteristics, 1:35
Fluoride, osteoporosis treatment, 1:214
Folklore, *see also* Literature
  application, 1:539–540
  art, 1:538–539
  definition, 1:531
  medicine, 1:536–538
  myth, 2:188
  narratives, 1:533–534
  oral tradition, 1:534–535
  overview, 1:531–532
  practices, 1:535–536
  rituals, 1:535–536
  spiritual development, 2:396
  traditional beliefs, 1:532–533
  wisdom, 1:534–535
Follicle-stimulating hormone
  male reproductive system changes, 1:486
  pituitary function, 1:478–479

Food intake, *see* Nutrition
Food restriction, *see* Caloric restriction
Fractures
    definition, **1:**11
    fall biomechanics, **1:**13
    incidence, **1:**12
    osteoporosis related, **1:**209–211, 496
Fraternal organizations, organized activity, **1:**44
Free radicals, *see also* Oxidative damage
    definition, **1:**185; **2:**233
    dietary restriction, **1:**191
    measurement, **2:**237–239
    mitochondrial DNA aberrations, **2:**138, 140
    senescence theory, **2:**549
Friendship
    gender patterns, **1:**562–563
    loneliness, **2:**80, 510
    networks, *see* Social networks
    support roles, **2:**509–510, 513–514
Frontal lobe dementia
    characteristics, **1:**396–397
    definition, **1:**383
Functional theory
    employment, **2:**628
    intrinsic time, **2:**589
    retirement, **2:**444
Funerals, *see also* Bereavement
    societal attitudes, **1:**366
Fungi, aging models
    filamentous fungi, **2:**153–154
    human applications, **2:**160–161
    premature aging, **2:**343–344
    study rationale, **2:**151–153
    yeast, **2:**154–156

G

Gait, *see also* Motor control
    balance variability, **1:**150–151
    control, **1:**14–15, 159–160
    ergonomic designs, **1:**716–717
    posture control, **1:**149–151
    proprioception changes, **2:**601–602
    walking characteristics, **1:**157–160
        adaptive control, **1:**159–160
        change factors, **1:**160
        kinematic analysis, **1:**158–159
        kinetic analysis, **1:**159
        neuromuscular analysis, **1:**159
        stride length, **1:**158
        velocity changes, **1:**158
Gallbladder, dysfunction, **1:**552

Gastrin, digestive function, **1:**544
Gastroesophageal reflux disease, esophageal dysfunction,
    1:547–548
Gastrointestinal system
    drug absorption, **2:**297–298
    dysfunction
        esophagus, **1:**547–548
        gallbladder, **1:**552
        large intestine, **1:**549–551
        liver, **1:**551–552
        oral cavity, **1:**546
        pancreas, **1:**552
        parasympathetic input reduction, **1:**145
        small intestine, **1:**549
        stomach, **1:**548–549
    food intake regulation, **1:**433
    function
        absorption, **1:**545
        anatomy, **1:**541–543
        digestion, **1:**543–545
        motility, **1:**545–546
        nutrition, **1:**545
        secretion, **1:**543–545
    health identity, **1:**738
Gender roles, *see also* Identity; Social roles
    achievement characteristics, movie stars, **1:**33–34
    caregiver differences, **1:**259, 561
    caregiving theory, **1:**262
    cohort differences, **1:**563
    definition, **1:**555
    feminization, **1:**557–558
    friendship patterns, **1:**562–563
    income inequality, **1:**559–560
    life satisfaction, **2:**62–63
    literary representations, **2:**75
    living arrangements, **1:**558–559
    loneliness, **2:**80
    marital roles, **1:**558–559, 561–562
    overview
        gender relations, **1:**557
        ideologies, **1:**556–557
        sex verses gender, **1:**555–556
        societal differences, **1:**556
    personality development, **2:**286
    religious differences, **2:**392
    social network differences, **2:**511–512, 514
    suicide rates, **2:**532
    third age, **1:**563–564
    well-being variation, **2:**367–368
Gene expression, *see also* DNA; Genetics
    age changes
        consistent changes, **1:**451
        genome organization, **1:**451–452

Gene expression (*continued*)
    nonconsistent changes, 1:450–451
    overview, 1:449–450
    cancer-induced telomerase reactivation, 2:541–543
    cell death
        premature aging, 2:342
        in vitro studies, 1:270–271
    cellular stress response, 2:317–320
    enhancer traps, 2:160
    epistasis, 2:151
    growth factor response, cellular senescence
        G_1 genes, 1:631–632
        late G_1 genes, 1:632
        response alterations, 1:631
    senescence regulation, 1:585–586
General estimates system, definition, 1:19
Generational differences, *see* Cohorts
Gene therapy, cancer treatment, 1:241–242
Genetic markers
    animal models, 2:100
    cancer diagnosis, 1:232
    changing systems, 2:102–103
    chronological age limitations, 2:98–99
    complex systems, 2:101–102
    definition, 2:97, 545
    longevity-associated markers, 1:579
    marker diversity, 2:98
    nuclear DNA, 2:136–138
    reliability, 2:100–101
    scale, 2:103–104
    validity, 2:99–100
Genetics, *see also* Gene expression
    behavior genetics
        aging differences, 1:163–166
            developmental genetics, 1:165–166
            environmental influence, 1:164–165
            genetic influence, 1:164–165
            genetic theory, 1:163–164
        definition, 1:163
        future research directions, 1:171–172
        late life developments
            cognitive functioning, 1:168–169
            dementia, 1:170
            depression, 1:170
            family environment, 1:170–171
            health, 1:167–168
            life events, 1:170–171
            longevity, 1:167–168
            personality, 1:169
            social support, 1:170–171
    cancer biology, 1:229
    cancer risk, 1:227
    definition, 1:577

evolutionary biology
    comparative studies, 1:514–516
    experimental studies
        laboratory evolution, 1:512–513
        population genetics, 1:513–514
    theory
        definition, 1:509
        early theories, 1:509–510
        mathematical theories, 1:510–511
        population genetic hypotheses, 1:511–512
future research directions, 1:586
human studies, 1:577–580
    aging heritability, 1:579–580
    cellular senescence, 1:578
    disease association, 1:579
    longevity markers, 1:579
    segmental progeroid mutations, 1:578–579
model systems
    Caenorhabditis elegans
        mutational analysis, 2:157–158
        polygenic approaches, 1:582
        quantitative genetics, 2:156
    Drosophila
        comparative biology, 2:159
        evolutionary biology, 2:158–159
        gene enhancer traps, 2:160
        mitochondrial biochemistry, 2:160
        polygenic approaches, 1:581–582
        transgenic approach, 2:159–160
    filamentous fungi, 2:153–154
    mouse, polygenic approaches, 1:580–581
    mutational analysis, 1:582–584
    study rationale, 1:580
    transgenic studies, 1:584; 2:159–160
    yeast, 2:154–156
molecular studies, 1:585–586
Geniculate nucleus, stimulus persistence, 2:273–274
Genograms
    definition, 2:399
    reminiscence therapy, 2:405
Genotype, definition, 2:163
Geriatric assessment
    benefits, 1:591
    components, 1:589–590
    definition, 1:587
    future research directions, 1:592
    historical perspective, 1:588–589
    objectives, 1:587–588; 2:126
    pain, 2:257–258
    program models, 1:590–591
Geriatrics
    definition, 1:593
    public policy, 1:640

Gerodynamics
  definition, 2:557
  psychological aging, 2:566
Gerontechnology
  arthritis management, 1:120
  cross-cultural studies, 1:315
  definition, 1:594
  ergonomics
    daily living
      activity importance, 1:718
      anthropometry, 1:716
      assistive devices, 1:719; 2:174
      balance, 1:716–717
      cognition, 1:718
      communication, 1:720
      driving, 1:719–720
      health, 1:718
      hearing, 1:601, 652, 717–718
      instrumental activities, 1:719
      interventions, 1:719
      motor skills, 1:716–717
      physical activities, 1:718–719
      strength, 1:716–717
      vision, 1:717
    future research directions, 1:724–725
    motivation, 1:715–716
    working life
      computer jobs, 1:723–724; 2:639
      fatigue, 1:723
      information-processing jobs, 1:722
      lifting, 1:721
      repetitive motion jobs, 1:721–722
      shiftwork, 1:723
      strength-related jobs, 1:721
      sustained monitoring jobs, 1:722
      technology impact, 2:638–639
      visual inspection jobs, 1:722–723
      workforce aging, 1:721
  fall prevention, 1:16–17
  fundamental principles, 1:596–603
    application modalities, 1:602–603
    approaches, 1:599–600
    concepts, 1:598–599
    demographic changes, 1:598
    objectives, 1:600–602
    systems approach, 1:597
    target population, 1:598
    technology gap, 1:597–598
  historical perspective, 1:595–596
  Intelligent Transportation Systems, 1:19, 24
  life-support technology, 1:362–363
  memory aids, 2:120
  overview, 1:594–595

Gerontology
  definition, 1:655
  historical perspective
    ageism role, 1:75
    contemporary gerontology, 1:663–664
    Greco-Roman philosophers, 1:657–659
    modern period, 1:662–663
    mythic period, 1:656–657
    overview, 1:655–656
    renaissance, 1:659–660
    scientific era, 1:660–662
  literary representations, 2:73–74, 76–77
Gerotranscendence theory, see also Activity theory;
    Disengagement theory
  definition, 2:557
  developmental model, 2:288–289
  psychological aging, 2:565–566
Glaucoma
  characteristics, 2:611
  definition, 2:605
Glomerular disease, pathology, 2:414–415
Glomerular filtration rate
  age-related changes, 2:409–410
  definition, 2:407
Glucocorticoids
  adrenal function, 1:483–484
  definition, 1:477
  rheumatic disease treatment, 2:455
Gluconeogenesis, definition, 2:135
Glucose, see Diabetes; Glycation
Glycation, see also Diabetes
  advanced glycation end products
    atherosclerosis pathogenesis, 1:128
    definition, 1:123, 605
    pharmacological intervention, 1:609
  age-related metabolic change, 2:140
  biological consequences
    extracellular proteins, 1:607–608
    intracellular proteins, 1:607
    nucleic acids, 1:608–609
    pathologic consequences, 1:608
  chemistry, 1:605–607
  definition, 1:605
  extracellular matrix modulation, aging postponement,
    1:528
  immunofluorescence detection method, 1:526–527
  pharmacological intervention, 1:609
  sugar-derived collagen cross-links, 1:525–526
  theory, 1:185
  thyroid hormone economy, 1:480–481
Gompertz' law
  definition, 2:557
  mortality model, 2:86–88
  psychological aging, 2:557–558, 560

Gonadotropin-releasing hormone, reproductive system
    changes, **1:**486–487
Gout, **1:**115
Government, *see* Politics; Public policy
Grandparenthood
    background
        anthropological context, **1:**611–612
        intergenerational demographic changes, **1:**612
        research, **1:**613
        socioeconomic changes, **1:**612–613
    cross-cultural grandparents, **1:**621–622
    definition, **1:**611
    future outlook
        practice, **1:**623
        research, **1:**622
    influence
        adolescent grandchildren, **1:**620–621
        child development, **1:**620
        elusive influence, **1:**619
        symbolic influence, **1:**619–620
    roles
        ambiguity, **1:**615–616
        behavior, **1:**613–615
        instrumentality
            caretaking, **1:**616–618
            divorce, **1:**618
            reciprocal caregiving, **1:**618
        meaning, **1:**615
        satisfaction, **1:**618–619
        timing, **1:**616
Greek mythology, *see* Mythology
Grief, *see* Bereavement
Gross domestic product, entitlement spending,
    1:471–472
Growth factors
    bone remodeling, **1:**208–209
    cancer biology, **1:**232
    cellular senescence
        endogenous production, **1:**629–630
        gene expression
            G$_1$ genes, **1:**631–632
            late G$_1$ genes, **1:**632
            response alterations, **1:**631
        human fibroblast cell requirements, **1:**626–627
        insulin-like growth factor binding protein
            in vivo studies, **1:**630–632
            production, **1:**630
        insulin-like growth factor-1 response, **1:**629
        receptors, **1:**628–629
        stimulation, **1:**627–628
        temporal requirements, **1:**627
    definition, **1:**203, 625

Growth hormone
    bone metabolism, **1:**488
    muscle growth, **2:**216–217
    pituitary function, **1:**478–479
Guanethidine, drug interactions, **2:**305
Guided autobiography, *see also* Autobiography; Life
    review; Reminiscence
    life review, **2:**57

H

Hamster, aging model, **2:**167–168
Handicap, *see* Disabilities
Handwriting, motor control alterations, **2:**183
Happiness, *see* Life satisfaction; Well-being
Hayflick limit, definition, **2:**539
Health
    activity role, **1:**40–41
    aging postponement, **2:**334–335
    coping strategies, **1:**52–53
    cross-cultural studies, **1:**314–315
    ethnic differences, **2:**373–374
    gender inequality, **1:**560
    genetic influences, **1:**167–168
    leisure activity constriction, **2:**24
    life satisfaction, **2:**61
    physical identity, **1:**737–739
    public policy, **1:**330–331
    self-regulation
        intervention models
            action plans, **2:**471–472
            age impact, **2:**474–476
            chronological approach, **2:**473–474
            disease threat representation, **2:**470
            life span context, **2:**472–473
            prevention, **2:**469–470
        issues, **2:**468–469
        overview, **2:**467
Health care services, *see also* Caregivers; Caregiving
    costs, **1:**460, 472–473, 476, 640
    entitlement budgets, **1:**471–472
    ethical issues, **2:**313–316
    folk medicine, **1:**536–538
    geriatric assessment
        benefits, **1:**591
        components, **1:**589–590
        definition, **1:**587
        future research directions, **1:**592
        historical perspective, **1:**588–589
        objectives, **1:**587–588
        program models, **1:**590–591

hospice care, *see* Hospice
hospital care
    acute rehabilitation, **2:**384–385
    geriatric assessment, **1:**587–592
    mental health care services, **2:**129
    Prospective Payment System, **1:**638
    utilization rates, **1:**637
managed care, **1:**638–640; **2:**133
Medicaid, *see* Medicaid
Medicare, *see* Medicare
mental health services
    care provision models
        care delivery problems, **2:**131
        community-based care, **2:**130–131
        long-term care, **2:**129–130
        program principles, **2:**131–132
    payment system impact, **2:**132–133
    populations
        acutely distressed older adults, **2:**126
        dementia, **2:**126
        medically ill, **2:**126–127
        severely mentally ill, **2:**125–126
        sexual disorders, **2:**127
        substance abuse, **2:**127–128
    services, **2:**128–129
policy issues
    chronic links, **1:**640–641
    costs, **1:**640
    demographic pressures, **1:**640–641
    geriatrics, **1:**640
rheumatic disorders, **2:**454
service use, **1:**637–638
Health maintenance organizations
    health care coverage, **1:**638–640
    rehabilitation costs, **2:**385
    service payment impact, **2:**133
Hearing, *see* Auditory system
Heat shock
    age-dependent changes, **2:**320–323
    Caenorhabditis elegans models, **2:**157–158
    definition, **2:**317
    stress response, **2:**317–320
Hemodynamic dementia, characteristics, **1:**394
Hepatitis, liver dysfunction, **1:**551
Hepatitis B virus, cancer risk, **1:**227
Heritability, *see* Genetics
Heroin, use, **1:**96
Herpes zoster, chronic pain, **2:**255
Hip fractures
    definition, **1:**11
    fall biomechanics, **1:**13
    incidence, **1:**12
    osteoporosis related, **1:**209–211, 496

Hippocampus
    definition, **1:**217
    eyeblink conditioning substrate, **1:**322–324
Histochemistry, extracellular matrix assessment,
    1:520–521
Historical perspective, ageism role, **1:**75
Historical perspectives
    contemporary gerontology, **1:**663–664
    Greco-Roman philosophers, **1:**657–659
    modern period, **1:**662–663
    mythic period, **1:**656–657
    ontology, **2:**308–310
    overview, **1:**655–656
    renaissance, **1:**659–660
    scientific era, **1:**660–662
    sexual myths, **2:**480–482
Holocultural
    definition, **1:**311
    research design, **1:**313
Home care
    future generations, **1:**677
    gerontechnology, **1:**602
    institutional care comparison, **1:**256
    later-life families
        challenges, **1:**668–669
        configuration, **1:**667–668
        normative life event, **1:**669–670
    primary versus secondary caregivers, **1:**255–256
    process
        caregiver characteristics, **1:**671–673
            appraisal importance, **1:**672
            coping, **1:**672–673
            life orientation, **1:**672–673
            motivation, **1:**671–672
        consequences, **1:**675
        contextual variables, **1:**673–675
            competing responsibilities, **1:**674–675
            kinship ties, **1:**674
            preprocess relationship quality, **1:**674
        impairment characteristics, **1:**673
        transactional models, **1:**670–671
    services
        availability, **1:**675–676
        intervention assistance efficacy, **1:**677
        utilization, **1:**676–677
Home equity conversion mortgages, government backing,
    1:711
Homeostasis
    biomarkers, **2:**102–103
    catastrophe theory, **1:**684
    chaos, **1:**684
    classical themes, **1:**682
    control theory, **1:**682–683

Homeostasis (*continued*)
  cybernetics, **1:**682
  definition, **1:**680; **2:**83, 135–136, 573
  historical perspective, **1:**680–681
  homeodynamics, **1:**684–685
  homeorhesis, **1:**679, 683–684
  homeostatic index, **1:**681–682
  longevity relation, **2:**84
  physiological variables, **1:**685
  prehomeostatic models, **1:**681
  resiliency senescence, **1:**685
  water metabolism, **1:**490–491; **2:**574–576
Home remedies, use, **1:**96
Homosexuality
  definition, **2:**479
  old age, **2:**486
Hormonal therapy
  cancer therapy, **1:**229, 241; **2:**363
  estrogen replacement
    cancer prevention, **1:**229
    life expectancy changes, **2:**93–94
    osteoporosis treatment, **1:**212–213
  progesterone replacement, cancer risk, **1:**213
  prostate cancer therapy, **2:**363
Hospice
  alternative care, **1:**369
  bereavement process
    principles, **1:**699–700
    services, **1:**700–701
  community context
    family education, **1:**697–698
    professional education, **1:**697
    public education, **1:**699
    volunteer training, **1:**698–699
  concepts
    models, **1:**688
    philosophy, **1:**687–688
  definition, **1:**361, 687
  economics, **1:**367
  elderly care, **1:**364
  future directions, **1:**700–701
  interdisciplinary approach
    attrition, **1:**694
    burnout, **1:**694
    team member roles, **1:**693–694
    team philosophy, **1:**692–693
  life review therapy, **2:**55
  operation
    appropriate death, **1:**694–695
    patient-family dynamics, **1:**695–697
  United States hospice development
    care delivery, **1:**689–690
    death attitudes, **1:**688–689

  ethical aspects, **1:**691–692
  historical perspective, **1:**689
  legal aspects, **1:**691–692
  patient reimbursement mechanisms, **1:**690–691
Hospitals
  acute rehabilitation, **2:**384–385
  geriatric assessment
    benefits, **1:**591
    components, **1:**589–590
    definition, **1:**587
    future research directions, **1:**592
    historical perspective, **1:**588–589
    objectives, **1:**587–588
    program models, **1:**590–591
  mental health care services, **2:**129
  Prospective Payment System, **1:**638
  utilization rates, **1:**637
Housing
  elder abuse, prevalence, **1:**2–3
    domestic settings, **1:**2
    institutions, **1:**2–3
  future research directions, **1:**712–713
  gender differences, **1:**558–559, 561
  household structures, **1:**411
  income, **1:**705–706
  living arrangements, **1:**705
  location, **1:**708–709
  modernization effects, **2:**174–175
  overview, **1:**703–705
  policy, **1:**709–712
  problems, **1:**706–708
  relocation rates, **2:**50
  retirement migration, *see* Migration
  segregation
    life satisfaction, **1:**77
    social dislocation, **1:**73–74, 77–78
  tenure, **1:**705–706
  types, **1:**706–708
Human factors, *see* Ergonomics
Human fibroblast cells, cellular senescence
  endogenous production, **1:**629–630
  gene expression
    G_1 genes, **1:**631–632
    late G_1 genes, **1:**632
    response alterations, **1:**631
  growth factors
    receptors, **1:**628–629
    stimulation, **1:**627–628
  human fibroblast cell requirements, **1:**626–627
  insulin-like growth factor binding protein
    in vivo studies, **1:**630–632
    production, **1:**630

insulin-like growth factor-1 response, 1:629
   temporal requirements, 1:627
Human immunodeficiency virus
   cancer risk, 1:227
   deliberate cell death, 1:276
   family stress, 1:696
   sexual response changes, 2:487
Human leukocyte antigen, diabetes role, 2:352
Humor
   concepts
      Aristotle's comedy, 1:727–728
      definition, 1:727
   contemporary humor, 1:729–731
   creativity, 1:731
   elderly humor, 1:728–729
   humor therapy, 1:729
   wisdom relationship, 1:731
Huntington's disease
   aging-related genetic studies, 1:579
   protein oxidation role, 2:242
Hutchinson–Gilford syndrome
   oxidative damage role, 2:244–245
   premature aging studies, 2:347
   segmental progeroid mutations, 1:578–579
Hydration, see Hydrotherapy; Thirst
Hydrodensitometry, body composition measurement,
   1:195–196
Hydrotherapy
   arthritis management, 1:120
   fluid homeostasis, 2:574–576
   fluid intake requirements, 1:432
   rehydration, 2:578–580
Hydroxyproline, collagen synthesis marker, 1:523–524
Hyperlipidemia, stroke risk, 2:519–520
Hypernatremia, see Thirst
Hypersensitivity
   allergen response mechanisms, 1:106–107
   involution, 1:108–110
   manifestations, 1:107–108
Hypertension
   age-related blood pressure change, 1:250–251
   atherosclerosis risk, 1:125
   blood pressure control, 1:145–146
   hearing loss prevention, 1:653
   stroke risk, 2:518–519
Hypertrophy, see Cardiovascular system
Hypochondriasis, symptoms, 1:423
Hyponatremia, causes, 2:580
Hypothyroidism, clinical aspects, 1:481–482
Hypoxanthine phosphoribosyl transferase, DNA
   sequence change detection, 1:445–446
Hysterectomy, sexual response changes, 2:484–485, 487

I

Iconic memory, perceptual span, 2:274–276
Identity, see also Gender roles
   activity participation patterns, 1:38–40
   change adaptation, 1:54, 56–59
   cognitive–behavioral interventions, 1:293
   death anxiety, 1:368
   definition, 1:51, 733–734
   identity-relevant life events, 2:43
   life events measurement, 2:44–45
   multiple threshold model, 1:734–735
   personality traits, 2:291
   physical identity
      appearance, 1:735–736
      competence, 1:736–737
      coping, 1:739–741
      health, 1:737–739
      principles, 1:734
   psychological aging, 2:564
   stereotypes, 1:741–742
   well-being modification, 2:48
Ideology
   gender roles, 1:556–557
   social stratification, 1:83
I-dopa, autonomic nervous system dysfunction, 1:146
Illness, see Disease; specific types
Images of aging
   ageism, 1:73
   age representations, 2:76
   contemporary humor, 1:729
   folk art, 1:538–539
   multicultural awareness, 1:749–750
   overview, 1:743–744
   social role, 1:744–749
Immune system
   allergic reactivity, 1:103–110
      allergens, 1:106–107
      hypersensitivity states
         involution, 1:108–110
         manifestations, 1:107–108
      immunologic response, 1:104–106
      overview, 1:103–104
      sensitization, 1:106–107
   antibody immune response, 1:105
   B lymphocytes, 1:753, 756
   cell death, life spans, in vitro, 1:270–271
   chemosensory loss, 2:500, 503
   clinical significance, 1:758–759
   cytokine receptors, 1:757–758
   cytokines, 1:757–758
   definition, 1:753

Immune system (*continued*)
  deliberate cell death, **1:**276
  future research directions, **1:**759
  lymphoid tissue, **1:**754–755
  overview, **1:**753–754
  physical health identity, **1:**740
  respiratory defense system, **2:**435–436
  rheumatoid factor test, **2:**453
  stress response, **1:**52
  T lymphocytes, **1:**753, 755–756
Immunocompetent cells, definition, **1:**269
Immunofluorescence, extracellular matrix assessment,
    1:526–527
Immunoglobulins, definition, **1:**103
Immunotherapy, cancer therapy, **1:**241
Impedance, bioelectrical, body composition measurement,
    1:196–197
Income, *see also* Employment; Pensions
  changes, **1:**457–458
  gender inequality, **1:**559–560
  housing tenure, **1:**705–706
  international comparisons, **1:**461–463
  joint distribution, **1:**464
  leisure activity constriction, **2:**24, 28
  life satisfaction, **2:**61
Incontinence
  postponement, **2:**337–338
  urinary tract dysfunction, **2:**416–417
Independence, *see* Autonomy; Gerontechnology
Industrialization
  ageism emergence, **1:**71–73
  employment experiences
    absenteeism, **2:**632
    alternative work options, **2:**633–634
    current issues, **2:**638–639
    exiting, **2:**636–637
    job performance, **2:**631–632
    stereotypes, **2:**630–631
    training, **2:**632–633
    turnover, **2:**632
    upward mobility, **2:**634–635
    work attitudes, **2:**633
Information processing, inhibition, **1:**761, 764
Inhibition
  behavioral indices, **1:**762–763
  definition, **1:**761
  information processing, **1:**761, 764
  learning process, **2:**8–9
  mental health, **1:**764
  orienting response, **1:**762
  physiological indices, **1:**762
  process, **1:**761
  selective attention, **1:**762–763
  verbal communication, **1:**763–764

working memory, **1:**763; **2:**114
Institutionalization, *see also* Health care
  depression, **1:**417
  elder abuse, **1:**2–3
  malnutrition, **1:**431
  prevalence, **1:**257
  sexual expression, **2:**482
Instrumental activities of daily living, *see also* Activities
    of daily living
  acute rehabilitation, **2:**383–385
  arthritis impact, **1:**118–119
  comprehensive geriatric assessment, **1:**590
  definition, **2:**381
  ergonomics, **1:**719
  functional health, ethnic differences, **2:**373–374
  in-home caregiving, **1:**673
  later-life family challenges, **1:**668–669
Instrumental conditioning, *see* Conditioning, instrumental
Insulin
  carbohydrate metabolism, **1:**189, 489–490
  human fibroblast cell senescence, **1:**626
Insulin-like growth factor-1, human fibroblast cell
    senescence
  endogenous production, **1:**629–630
  gene expression, **1:**631–632
  growth factors
    receptors, **1:**628–629
    stimulation, **1:**627–628
  human fibroblast cell requirements, **1:**626–627
  insulin-like growth factor binding protein, **1:**630–632
  response characteristics, **1:**629
  temporal requirements, **1:**627
Insurance, *see specific types*
Intelligence, *see also* Knowledge; Learning; Memory;
    Wisdom
  achievement characteristics, **1:**35
  acuity deficit effects, **2:**276–278
  crystallized verses fluid intelligence, creativity theory,
    1:348
  global decline, *see* Dementia
  learning capacity, **1:**63–64
  semantic memory, **2:**112–113
Intelligent Transportation Systems
  definition, **1:**19
  potential use, **1:**24
Interest group theory, **2:**229–230
Interferon-γ, immune function, **1:**758
Interiority, personality development, **2:**286
Interleukins
  bone growth role, **1:**208–209
  definition, **1:**103
  hypersensitivity reactions, **1:**109–110
  immune function, **1:**755–758
Interpretive theory, definition, **2:**569

Intestinal system, *see* Gastrointestinal system
Intima, definition, 1:123
Intimacy, 2:482–483
Inulin
  age-related clearance changes, 2:409–410
  definition, 2:407
Invertebrate aging models, *see specific species*
Ischemia
  oxidative damage role, 2:245–246
  small intestine dysfunction, 1:549
  stroke
    risk, 2:520
    treatment, 2:522–523
Isolation, elder abuse, 1:6–7
Isotope dilution, body composition measurement, 1:196
Isotype switch
  definition, 1:103
  immune response, 1:105

J

Jaundice, definition, 1:541
Jobs, *see* Employment
Jokes, *see* Humor

K

Kidney cancer, overview, 1:238
Kidney function, *see* Renal Function
Kinesthesia
  aging effects, 2:601–603
  gait characteristics, 1:158–159
  physiology, 2:597–599
  psychophysics, 2:599–601
Kinetic analysis, gait characteristics, 1:159
Kinship, *see* Family
Knowledge, *see also* Intelligence; Learning; Wisdom
  consumer decision making, 1:332–333
  epistemology, 2:311–313
Krebs cycle, definition, 2:135

L

Language
  acute rehabilitation, 2:384
  aphasia, 2:3–4, 6
  dementia, 2:4–5
  normal aging
    comprehension, 2:2

  language production, 2:1–2
  neurological changes, 2:3
  nonlanguage interactions, 2:3
  recognition, age-related hearing loss, 1:648
  verbal-task learning
    paired-associate learning, 2:12–14
    transfer effects, 2:14–15
Large intestine
  anatomy, 1:542–543
  dysfunction, 1:549–551
Last-works effects
  creative achievement, 1:32
  definition, 1:27
Lateral geniculate nucleus, stimulus persistence, 2:273–274
Later-life families, *see also* Life course
  definition, 1:667
  home care
    challenges, 1:668–669
    configuration, 1:667–668
    normative life event, 1:669–670
  timing
    family transition synchronization, 2:34–35
    historical changes, 2:35–36
    individual life transitions, 2:33–34
Laughter, *see* Humor
Leadership, achievement characteristics, 1:28–31
  entrepreneurs, 1:30
  military commanders, 1:29–30
  politicians, 1:28–29, 35–36
  religious leaders, 1:30–31
Lean body mass
  basal metabolic rate changes, 1:188
  body mass index
    definition, 1:193, 429
    nutritional statistics, 1:431
  dietary restriction, 1:191
  nutrient metabolism, 1:188
Learning, *see also* Cognition; Memory
  adult education, 1:61–69
    curricula, 1:66–68
    future trends, 1:68–69
    historical perspectives, 1:61–63
    learning capacity, 1:63–64
    motivation, 1:64–65
    participation rates, 1:68–69
    program models, 1:66–68
    public policy, 1:65–66
  conditioning
    classical eyeblink conditioning, 1:319–325
      animals, 1:320–321
      brain substrates, 1:321–325
      humans, 1:321
    instrumental, 1:325–327

Learning (*continued*)
    extinction, 1:325–326
    reinforcement schedule, 1:326
    retention, 1:326–327
    simple acquisition, 1:325–326
  food intake habits, 1:437–439
  job training, 2:632–633
  life satisfaction, 2:61–62
  loneliness, 2:80
  nonverbal tasks
    classical conditioning, 2:9
    instrumental learning, 2:10
    motor skills, 2:11–12
    operant conditioning, 2:9–10
  overview, 2:7
  school performance, delinquency correlation, 1:357
  skill acquisition
    components
      automatic skills, 2:492–494
      strategic skills, 2:490–492
    definition, 2:489–490
    strategies, 2:494–495
  theory, 2:8–9
  verbal tasks
    paired-associate learning, 2:12–14
    transfer, 2:14–15
Learning in Retirement Institutes, adult education, 1:67
Leber's hereditary optic neuropathy, premature aging
    studies, 2:352
Legend, *see* Folklore; Mythology
Legislation, *see* Public policy
Leisure, *see also* Activities
  community context, 2:26–27
  functional challenges
    deprivation factors, 2:28–29
    stereotypes, 2:27–28
  gerontechnology, 1:601
  home activities, 1:42–43
  later-life course
    activity, 2:23
    constriction patterns, 2:23–24
    continuity patterns, 2:24–25
    issues, 2:25–26
  life satisfaction, 2:63
  meaning, 2:21–23
  organized recreation, 1:43–44
  participation patterns, 1:38–40
  physical identity, 1:734–735
  resource policies, 2:29–30
  theory, 2:19–21
    definition, 2:20–21
    later-life changes, 2:21
  volunteerism, 2:26, 613–614
Leukocyte antigen, diabetes role, 2:352

Leutinizing hormone, prostate cancer therapy, 2:363
Life course
  cohort patterns, 1:307
  cross-cultural studies, 1:316–317
  cumulative life event impact, 2:36–37
  fetal development consequences, 1:306
  gender roles, 1:556
  grandparenthood
    background
      anthropological context, 1:611–612
      intergenerational demographic changes, 1:612
      research, 1:613
      socioeconomic changes, 1:612–613
    cross-cultural grandparents, 1:621–622
    definition, 1:611
    future outlook
      practice, 1:623
      research, 1:622
    influence
      adolescent grandchildren, 1:620–621
      child development, 1:620
      elusive influence, 1:619
      symbolic influence, 1:619–620
    roles
      ambiguity, 1:615–616
      behavior, 1:613–615
      instrumentality, 1:616–618
      meaning, 1:615
      satisfaction, 1:618–619
      timing, 1:616
  leisure activity
    age-related change, 2:23
    constriction patterns, 2:23–24
    continuity patterns, 2:24–25
    issues, 2:25–26
    retirement, 2:439
  life span theory
    characteristics, 2:67–69
    definition, 2:65–66
    emergence, 2:66
    implications, 2:70
    primary aging, 2:66–67
    study methods, 2:69
  marital roles, 1:561–562
  migration motivation, 2:146
  network building, 2:199
  normative transitions, 2:37–39
  paradigm, 2:31–33, 39
  self-esteem changes, 2:459–460, 462
  social aging theory, 2:571
  subjective perspective, 2:37–39
  timing
    family transition synchronization, 2:34–35
    historical changes, 2:35–36
    individual life transitions, 2:33–34

turning points, 2:37–39
volunteer participation, 2:617–618
well-being variation, 2:367
widowhood, *see* Widowhood
Life events
  consequences
    age-related differences, 2:49
    number differences, 2:49–50
    sociodemographic pattern prediction, 2:50
    study design, 2:45–46
    type differences, 2:49–50
    well-being modifiers, 2:47–48, 368–369
  cumulative impact, 2:36–37
  definition, 2:41
  future research directions, 2:50–51
  genetic influences, 1:170–171
  normative transitions, 2:37–39
  personality theory, 2:290–291, 562–563
  research methods
    measurement, 2:44–45
    report reliability, 2:45
    social readjustment rating scale, 2:43–44
  retirement, *see* Retirement
  theoretical background, 2:41–43
  turning points, 2:37–39
  widowhood, *see* Widowhood
Life expectancy, *see* Longevity
Life review, *see also* Meaning
  autobiography, 2:57
  definition, 2:53
  memory, 2:54–55
  new directions, 2:57–58
  ontological image, 2:310–311
  oral histories, 2:57
  psychotherapeutic value, 2:55–56
  reminiscence
    benefits, 2:405
    definition, 2:53
    historical perspective, 2:400–401
    overview, 2:399–400
    past experience importance, 2:405–406
    techniques, 2:404–405
    therapy
      dementia patience, 2:403–404
      group reminiscence, 2:403
      one-to-one-interaction, 2:402–403
    typologies, 2:401–402
  theoretical concept, 2:53–54
  validity, 2:56–57
Life satisfaction
  activity engagement, 1:40–42, 47–49
  constructs, 2:60–61
  correlates
    activity, 2:63

age, 2:62
    education, 2:61–62
    gender, 2:62
    health status, 2:61
    income, 2:61
    marital status, 2:62
    occupational status, 2:61–62, 633
    race, 2:62
    role loss, 2:63
    social interaction, 2:63
  definition, 2:365
  historical perspective, 2:366
  measurement, 2:60–61
  modernization effects, 2:174
  personality types, 2:289–290
  prospects, 2:63–64
  research focus, 2:59–60
  segregated housing, 1:77–78
Life span theory, *see also* Longevity
  characteristics, 2:67–69
  definition, 2:65–66, 84, 505
  developmental tasks, 2:561
  emergence, 2:66
  employment context, 2:629
  gerontechnology role, 1:603
  implications, 2:70
  oxidative damage role, 2:243–244
  personality development
    conceptualizations, 2:285–286
    epigenetic stage theory, 2:287–288
    experiential-contextual model, 2:283
  primary aging, 2:66–67
  psychological aging, 2:563
  self-regulation
    intervention models
      action plans, 2:471–472
      age impact, 2:474–476
      chronological approach, 2:473–474
      disease threat representation, 2:470
      life span context, 2:472–473
      prevention, 2:469–470
    issues, 2:468–469
    overview, 2:467
  social network role, 2:507
  study methods, 2:69
Life-support technology, dying ambiguity, 1:362–363
Life table
  data availability, 2:164
  definition, 2:163
Light microscopy, extracellular matrix assessment,
    1:520–521
Light sensitivity, *see* Vision
Light therapy, depression relief, 1:422

Lipid peroxidation, *see* Free radicals
Lipids, oxidative damage, 2:241–242
Lipogenesis, definition, 2:136
Lipophilic drugs
  distribution, 2:299
  metabolism, 2:300
Lipoproteins, *see specific types*
Literature, *see also* Folklore; Images of aging; Mythology
  aging representations
    art verses gerontological evidence, 2:76
    concerns, 2:74–76
    gerontological applications, 2:76–77
    historical perspective, 2:74
    importance, 2:73–74
    life review, 2:54
    new directions, 2:77
    well-being, 2:366
  entertainment value, 1:42
Liver
  digestive function, 1:544
  drug metabolism, 2:300–301
  dysfunction, 1:551–552
Living wills, ethical aspects, 1:691–692
Locus ceruleus, definition, 1:217
Loneliness
  bereavement adjustments, 1:180
  definition, 2:79
  emotional isolation, 2:80
  friendship, 2:510
  research findings, 2:80–81
  social isolation, 2:79
  social network role, 2:198
  theory, 2:79
Longevity, *see also* Life span theory
  active life expectancy, 1:302–303, 493
  aging postponement
    exogenous factors
      clinical medicine, 2:338–339
      cognition, 2:335
      health, 2:334–335
      joints, 2:336
      osteoarthritis, 2:336–337
      osteoporosis, 2:337
      sensory deprivation, 2:335
      social contacts, 2:338–339
      striated muscles, 2:336
      urinary incontinence, 2:337–338
    historical perspective, 2:333–334
  animal models, 2:164
  apologism, 1:655
  cohort differences, 1:301–302
  concepts, 2:83–86
  construct model
    definition, 1:51

  identity role, 1:56–59
  counterpart theory, 2:561–562
  definition, 1:361; 2:83
  end-of-life issues, 1:370–372
  epidemiology, 1:494, 497–500
  ethnic differences, 2:372–373
  extracellular matrix role, 1:521–522
  future research directions, 2:95
  grandparenthood, 1:612
  heritability, 1:167–168, 579–580; 2:151
  later-life families
    definition, 1:667
    home care
      challenges, 1:668–669
      configuration, 1:667–668
      normative life event, 1:669–670
  life expectancy changes, 2:93–95
  modernization effects, 2:172–173
  mortality models, *see* Mortality
  mythical perspective, 1:656–657
  self-esteem theory, 2:461
Longevity-assurance gene, definition, 2:151
Long-term health care
  epidemiological studies, 1:501–502
  mental health services, provision models, 2:129–130
  pain management, 2:258
  social policy, 1:256–257
Loss, *see* Bereavement
Lou Gehrig's disease, premature aging studies, 2:351
Lumbar puncture, dementia diagnosis, 1:399–400
Lung cancer, overview, 1:232–233
Lungs, *see* Respiratory system
Luteinizing hormone
  female reproductive system changes, 1:486–487
  male reproductive system changes, 1:485–486
  pituitary function, 1:478–479
Lymphocytes
  B lymphocytes, 1:753, 756
  definition, 1:103
  T lymphocytes, 1:753, 755–756
Lymphoid tissue, immune function, 1:754–755

M

Mackworth Clock Test, vigilance measurement, 1:140
Maculopathy, characteristics, 2:611
Magnesium, total body composition measurement, 1:197–198
Magnetic resonance imaging
  Alzheimer's disease diagnosis, 1:388–389
  body composition measurement, 1:198
  dementia diagnosis, 1:398

Major histocompatability complex, allergen response
    mechanisms, **1:**107
Maladaptive schemas, *see* Cognitive–behavioral therapy
Male reproductive system
    endocrine function, **1:**485–486
    physical health identity, **1:**738–739
    prostate
        anatomy, **2:**355
        benign prostatic hyperplasia
            diagnosis, **2:**358–360
            etiology, **2:**358
            incidence, **2:**357–358
            medical treatment, **2:**360
            physiology, **2:**358
            surgical treatment, **2:**360–361
        cancer, **1:**236–237; **2:**361–364
        changes, **1:**486
        physiology, **2:**355–356
        prostatitis, **2:**356–357
        sexual dysfunction, **2:**487
    testosterone
        age-related production decrease, **1:**485–486
        aggression link, **1:**355
        benign prostatic hyperplasia etiology, **2:**358
        libido enhancement, **2:**479, 484
        replacement therapy, **1:**229
Malignancy
    cancer classification, **1:**224
    cell death mechanisms, **1:**275
    definition, **1:**223
Malthusian parameter
    definition, **1:**509
    mathematical evolutionary theory, **1:**510–511
Maltreatment, *see* Elder abuse
Managed care
    definition, **1:**635
    health care coverage, **1:**638–640
    rehabilitation costs, **2:**385
    service payment impact, **2:**133
Mania, definition, **1:**415
Marital status
    divorce, grandparent–family relationships, **1:**618
    first marriage age, **1:**572–573
    gender roles
        demographics, **1:**558–559
        life course, **1:**561–562
    life satisfaction, **2:**62
    sexual expression, **2:**481–482
Markers of aging, *see* Biomarkers
Marketing, consumer behavior, **1:**329–340
    decision making
        age differences, **1:**333–337

improved consumers, **1:**337–339
    model, **1:**332–333
    future research directions, **1:**339–340
    study motivation, **1:**329–332
        business interest, **1:**330
        public policy, **1:**330–331
        theoretical models, **1:**331–332
Marxism, social aging theory, **2:**571
Mass action law, homeostasis model, **1:**681
Mastectomy, sexual response changes, **2:**487
Matrix, *see* Extracellular matrix
Meaning, *see also* Life review
    activity role, **1:**45–47
    grandparenthood, **1:**615
    leisure, **2:**21–23
    ontology
        contemporary views, **2:**309–310
        definition, **2:**307
        life story, **2:**310–311
        traditional perspectives, **2:**308–309
Mechanical aids, *see* Gerontechnology
Media, *see* Images of aging
Medicaid
    costs, **1:**257, 460
    definition, **1:**635
    fiscal budget, **1:**472
    future status, **1:**465
    health care coverage, **1:**636
Medical care, *see* Health care services
Medical insurance, *see specific types*
Medicare
    costs, **1:**460, 638–640
    definition, **1:**635
    epidemiological studies, **1:**500–501
    fiscal budget, **1:**472
    future status, **1:**465
    health care coverage, **1:**635–637
    health maintenance organizations, **1:**638–640
    historical perspective, **2:**230
    hospice care provisions, **1:**690–691
    political attitudes, **2:**326
    Prospective Payment System, **1:**638
    public resource transfer, cohort differences, **1:**307
    service payment impact, **2:**132–133
Medications
    allergic response, **1:**107–108
    chemosensory effects, **2:**497–500, 502
    over-the-counter drugs, **1:**95–96
        abuse, **2:**127–128
        use, **1:**95–96
    overview, **1:**93–94
    pharmacology
        drug interactions, **2:**304–306
        drug side effects, **2:**304–306

Medications (*continued*)
  overview, **2:**295–296
  pharmacodynamics, **2:**304
  pharmacokinetics, **2:**296–304
    absorption, **2:**297–298
    distribution, **2:**298–299
    excretion, **2:**301–304
    metabolism, **2:**299–301
  psychotropic drugs, **2:**128
Medigap insurance, health care coverage, **1:**636
Meissner corpuscle
  tactile response changes, **2:**595–597
  touch physiology, **2:**592–594
Membrane, *see* Plasma membrane
Membrane-bound regulatory proteins, exercise-induced
  change, **2:**219
Memories, *see* Reminiscence
Memory, *see also* Cognition; Learning; Perception
  cognitive capacity, **2:**8
  cognitive interface, **2:**115–116
  communication, **2:**1–2
  function, **2:**54–55
  genetic influences, **1:**169
  global decline, *see* Dementia
  iconic memory, perceptual span, **2:**274–276
  kinesthetic perception, **2:**601
  memory strategies
    age differences, **2:**122–123
    instruction programs, **2:**123–124
    rationale, **2:**119–120
    types, **2:**120–122
  moderating variables, **2:**114–115
  theoretical perspectives
    procedural memory, **2:**113
    resource theory, **2:**113–114
    semantic memory, **2:**112–113
    stage theory, **2:**107–109
    system theory
      long-term memory, **2:**110–112
      sensory-perceptual memory, **2:**109–110
      short-term memory, **2:**110
  working memory
    definition, **1:**329; **2:**107
    reduced processing resources, **2:**563–564
    selective attention inhibition, **1:**763
Menopause
  bone loss role, **1:**210–211
  definition, **2:**479
  estrogen replacement therapy, **1:**212–213
  female reproductive system changes, **1:**486–487
  progesterone replacement therapy, **1:**213
  sexual expression changes, **2:**483–484

Mental health
  care provision models
    care delivery problems, **2:**131
    community-based care, **2:**130–131
    long-term care, **2:**129–130
    program principles, **2:**131–132
  depression risk, **1:**420
  emotional stress, *see* Emotion
  ethnic differences, **2:**374–375
  information processing, inhibition, **1:**764
  loneliness, **2:**80
  neuroticism, **2:**281
  payment system impact
    managed care, **2:**133
    Medicare reimbursement, **2:**132–133
  populations
    acutely distressed older adults, **2:**126
    dementia, **2:**126
    medically ill, **2:**126–127
    severely mentally ill, **2:**125–126
    sexual disorders, **2:**127
    substance abuse, **2:**127–128
  religion role, **2:**394–395
  service efficacy, **2:**129
  services, **2:**128–129
  suicide, *see* Suicide
Mental illness, *see specific types*
Messenger RNA, gene expression changes, **1:**451
Metabolism, *see also* Endocrine system
  bioenergetics, **1:**185–192
    body composition, **1:**188–189
    energy expenditure, **1:**189–190
    energy intake, **1:**187–188, 190–192
    exercise, **1:**190–192
    nutrient metabolism, **1:**188–189
    overview, **1:**185–187
  biological clock, **2:**584–585
  calcium, **1:**487–488
  carbohydrates, **1:**489–490
  drugs, **2:**299–301
  food intake regulation, **1:**433
  fuel fluxes, **2:**141–143
  glucose, *see* Glycation
  intracellular communication, **2:**140
  membrane role, **2:**138–140
  mitochondrial DNA role, **2:**138
  nuclear DNA role, **2:**136–138
  osteopenia, **1:**488–489
  respiration, *see* Respiratory system
  skeletal muscle endurance, **2:**216
  water, **1:**490–491
Metaphysics, *see* Ontology
Metastases, cancer biology, **1:**230

Metatheory
  definition, 2:65
  life span approach, 2:67
Methicillin, acute renal failure, 2:414
3-Methlyhistidine, total body composition measurement,
  1:197
Micronutrients, cancer prevention, 1:228–229
Microscopy, *see specific types*
Migration, *see also* Retirement
  cohort changes, 1:305
  conceptual issues, 2:145–146
  definition, 2:145
  impact, 2:149
  metropolitan migration, 2:148–149
  nonmetropolitan migration, 2:148–149
  patterns, 2:146–148
  return migration, 2:149
  seasonal migration, 2:148
  selectivity, 2:148
Military commanders, achievement characteristics,
  1:29–30
Mineralocorticoids
  adrenal function, 1:484–485
  definition, 1:477
Mini-Mental State Examination, dementia diagnosis,
  1:398
Minorities, *see* Race
Mistreatment, *see* Elder abuse
Mitochondria
  aging models, biochemical analysis, 2:160
  definition, 2:136
  diseases, premature aging studies, 2:352
  DNA
    aberrations, 2:138
    mutations, 1:447
    oxidative damage, 1:444; 2:243–244
  exercise-induced change, 2:219
Mitogens, definition, 1:753
Mnemonics, memory strategy, 2:120–121
Model-fitting techniques, environmental verses genetic
  aging influences, 1:164–165
Models of aging
  fungi
    filamentous fungi, 2:153–154
    human applications, 2:160–161
    senescence, premature aging, 2:344–345
    study rationale
      genetics, 2:152–153
      physiology, 2:153
      simplicity, 2:151–152
    yeast, 2:154–156
  historical gerontology, 1:663–664

invertebrates
  Caenorhabditis elegans
    mutational analysis, 2:157–158
    programmed cell death, 1:272–273
    quantitative genetics, 2:156
  Drosophila
    comparative biology, 2:159
    evolutionary biology, 2:158–159
    gene enhancer traps, 2:160
    mitochondrial biochemistry, 2:160
    senescence, 2:345–346
    transgenic approach, 2:159–160
  evolutionary biology, 1:515
  human applications, 2:160–161
  sexual metazoa aging, 1:515
  study rationale
    genetics, 2:152–153
    physiology, 2:153
    simplicity, 2:151–152
  markers, *see* Biomarkers
  semelparous species, premature aging, 2:343–344
  vertebrates
    biodemography, 1:413
    biomarkers, 2:100
    current use status, 2:169–170
    husbandry issues, 2:165–166
    Mus musculus, premature aging, 2:346
    research role, 2:163–164
    selection criteria, 2:164–165
    species used, 2:166–168
Modernization
  architecture, 2:174–175
  cross-cultural societal transformations, 1:317
  definition, 2:171, 569
  demographics, 2:172–173
  historical perspective, 2:570–571
  life quality, 2:174
  old-age experience, 2:171–172
  planning innovations, 2:174–175
  retirement, 2:440–441
  social dislocation, 1:73–75
  social network erosion, 2:174
Monoamine oxidase, depression relief, 1:422, 425–426
Mood disorder, symptoms, 1:423
Morale, *see* Life satisfaction
Moral economy theory, retirement, 2:445
Moral strength, mythological representations, 2:191–192
Morbidity, *see* Death; Disease; Epidemiology; Mortality
Mortality, *see also* Death; Epidemiology
  body composition relationship, 1:200–201
  cancer occurrence, 1:224–225
  cohort differences, 1:301–302, 304
  definition, 2:545

Mortality (*continued*)
  epidemiological studies, **1**:494
  ethnic differences
    functional health, **2**:373–374
    life expectancy, **2**:372–373
  hip fracture effects, **1**:209
  population dynamic models, **1**:406–407; **2**:86–88
  stroke deaths, **2**:518
  trajectories, **2**:89–93
  world population trends, **1**:408
Mortgage, home equity conversion, **1**:711
Motion, perception sensitivity, **2**:274, 278
Motivation
  adult education, **1**:64–65
  instrumental–expressive continuum, **1**:64–65
  personality traits, **2**:284–285
  retirement migration, **2**:145–146
Motor control, *see also* Activities of daily living; Gait
  decline
    explanations, **2**:183–184
    transitory nature, **2**:184–185
  definition, **2**:177
  ergonomic designs, **1**:716–717
  handwriting control alterations, **2**:183
  job performance, **2**:631
  learning, **2**:11–12
  movement slowing, **2**:180–182
  neuromuscular properties, **2**:215–216
  overview, **2**:177–178
  proprioception
    aging effects, **2**:601–603
    physiology, **2**:597–599
    psychophysics, **2**:599–601
  reach-to-grasp movements, **2**:182–183
  reaction time
    attention capacity measurement, **1**:132–137
    definition, **1**:131; **2**:377
    historical perspective, **2**:377
    importance, **2**:377–380
      age-relate robustness, **2**:378–379
      cognition, **2**:379–380
      neurological status indicator, **2**:378
    negative priming, **1**:762–763
    postural balance control
      anticipatory adjustments, **1**:155
      fall factors, **1**:14
    response initiation time determinants, **2**:178–180
    selective attention allocation, **1**:138–139
    skill acquisition, speed–accuracy trade-off functions, **2**:490–492
    slowing, **2**:178
    transitory nature, **2**:184
  rheumatic disease effects, **2**:453
Mourning, *see* Bereavement
Mouse, genetic aging studies, **1**:580–581; **2**:167, 346

Movies, aging images
  contemporary humor, **1**:729
  multicultural awareness, **1**:749–750
  overview, **1**:743–744
  social role, **1**:744–749
Movie stars, achievement characteristics, **1**:33–34
Multi-infarct dementia
  characteristics, **1**:394
  definition, **1**:383
  language difficulties, **2**:5–6
Multiple threshold model, physical identity, **1**:734–735
Muscles
  aging postponement, **2**:336
  balance control, **1**:152
    anticipatory postural adjustments, **1**:154–155
    response patterns, **1**:152–153
  disorders, *see* Rheumatic diseases; *specific disorders*
  gait analysis, **1**:159
  mass measurement, regional assessment
    computerized tomography, **1**:198
    magnetic resonance imaging, **1**:198
  muscle adaptability
    capillary number, **2**:219
    fiber number, **2**:218
    fiber types, **2**:218–219
    membrane-bound regulatory proteins, **2**:219
    mitochondrial enzymes, **2**:219
    strength, **2**:217–218
  physical competence, **1**:737
  proprioception physiology, **2**:597–599
  skeletal muscle properties
    aging mechanisms, **2**:216–217
    contractile characteristics, **2**:215
    contractile proteins, **2**:213
    diversity, **2**:212–213
    force production, **2**:213–215
    function, **2**:213
    mass, **2**:213–215
    metabolism, **2**:216
    motor unit properties, **2**:215–216
    muscle contraction types, **2**:211–212
    structure, **2**:212–213
Myocardial function, *see* Cardiovascular system
Mythology
  divine old age, **2**:189–190
  historical gerontology, **1**:656–657
  human old age
    elder action, **2**:192–193
    elder advisers, **2**:192
    general view, **2**:190–191
    moral strength, **2**:191–192
    old age view, **2**:194–195
    parent–child relations, **2**:193–194
    physical frailty, **2**:191
  overview, **2**:187–189

N

Name generator, social network delineation, **2:**200–203
Narrative Rating Method, life events measurement, **2:**45
National Education Association, adult education, **1:**62
National Housing Act, **1:**710
National Long Term Care Survey, epidemiological
  studies, **1:**501–502
Nationwide Personal Transportation Survey
  definition, **1:**19
  driver licensure, **1:**20
Naturally Occurring Retirement Communities
  definition, **1:**703
  housing location, **1:**709
Necrosis, definition, **1:**269
Nefiracetam, Alzheimer's disease treatment, **1:**325
Negative priming, selective attention inhibition, **1:**139,
  762–763
Negentropic processes
  definition, **2:**546
  senescence, **2:**550–553
Neglect, *see* Elder abuse
Nematodes, *see Caenorhabditis elegans*
Neomycin, drug interactions, **2:**305
Neoplasm
  cancer classification, **1:**224
  definition, **1:**223
Nephrotic syndrome, pathology, **2:**414–415
Nereis diversicolor, premature aging model, **2:**343–344
Nerve growth factor
  brain aging effects, **2:**225
  neuronal plasticity, **1:**220
Nervous system, *see* Autonomic nervous system; Central
  nervous system
Networks, *see* Social networks
Neurofibrillary tangles
  aging neuropathology, **1:**220–221
  Alzheimer's disease neuropathology, **1:**390–391
Neuromuscular system
  balance control, response patterns, **1:**152–153
  cardiovascular neuroconductivity, **1:**249
  disorders, *see* Rheumatic diseases
  gait analysis, **1:**159
  muscle adaptability
    capillary number, **2:**219
    fiber number, **2:**218
    fiber types, **2:**218–219
    membrane-bound regulatory proteins, **2:**219
    mitochondrial enzymes, **2:**219
    strength, **2:**217–218
  nutrient metabolism, **1:**188–189
  physical competence, **1:**737
  proprioception physiology, **2:**597–599

reaction time
  attention capacity measurement, **1:**132–137
  definition, **1:**131; **2:**377
  historical perspective, **2:**377
  importance, **2:**377–380
    age-relate robustness, **2:**378–379
    cognition, **2:**379–380
    neurological status indicator, **2:**378
  postural balance control
    anticipatory adjustments, **1:**155
    fall factors, **1:**14
  response initiation, **2:**178–180
  selective attention allocation, **1:**138–139
skeletal muscle properties
  aging mechanisms, **2:**216–217
  contractile characteristics, **2:**215
  contractile proteins, **2:**213
  diversity, **2:**212–213
  force production, **2:**213–215
  function, **2:**213
  mass, **2:**213–215
  metabolism, **2:**216
  motor unit properties, **2:**215–216
  muscle contraction types, **2:**211–212
  structure, **2:**212–213
vision system organization, **2:**605–608
  eye movements, **2:**607–608
  image formation, **2:**606
  neural changes, **2:**3, 607
  photosensitive response, **2:**606–607
Neurons
  aging models, posture and gait control, **1:**149–150
  density loss, **1:**143–144
  extracellular microenvironment changes, **1:**219–220
  injury, **1:**218
  loss, **1:**218
  plasticity changes, **1:**220
  synaptic nerve degeneration, **1:**391
  taste, **2:**501–502
Neurospora, aging model, **2:**153–154, 343–344
Neuroticism, *see also* Mental health
  definition, **2:**281
Neurotransmitters, *see also specific type*
  age-related changes, **1:**218
  Alzheimer's disease role, **1:**392–393
  autonomic nervous system stimulation, **1:**142–143
  brain aging, **2:**223–225
  brain function, **2:**221–222
  definition, **2:**221
  depression risk factor, **1:**418
  fluid homeostasis, **2:**575
  neurodegenerative disease, **2:**225–227
  pituitary function, **1:**478–479

Neurotrophic factors
   brain aging, 2:223–225
   definition, 2:221
   nervous system function, 2:222–223
   neurodegenerative disease, 2:225–227
Neutron activation analysis, body composition
      measurement, 1:197–198
Nicotine, *see* Tobacco
Nitrogen, total body composition measurement,
      1:197–198
Nocturia
   arginine vasopressin role, 2:575
   definition, 2:573
Noise, *see* Auditory system
Nonenzymatic glycation, *see* Glycation
Nonsteroidal anti-inflammatory drugs
   acute renal failure, 2:414–415
   definition, 1:111
   heat shock stress reduction, 2:323
   peptic ulcers, 1:548
   rheumatic disease treatment, 2:455
   use, 1:95
Norepinephrine
   autonomic nervous system stimulation, 1:142–143
   secretion, adrenal medulla function, 1:485
   sympathetic nervous system changes, 1:144
NSAIDs, *see* Nonsteroidal anti-inflammatory drugs
Nuclear factor-κB, definition, 1:123
Nuclear family, *see* Family
Nucleic acids, nonenzymatic glycation effects, 1:608–609
Nucleosomes, definition, 1:269
Nucleus basalis of Meynert
   definition, 1:217
   neuronal atrophy, 1:218
Nurses, hospice role, 1:693
Nutrition
   bioenergetics, 1:185–192
      body composition, 1:188–189
      energy expenditure, 1:189–190
      energy intake, 1:187–188, 190–192
      exercise, 1:190–192
      nutrient metabolism, 1:188–189
      overview, 1:185–187
   caloric restriction
      definition, 1:185
      delayed physiological aging, 1:186, 190–191
      DNA aberrations, 2:137–138
      exercise effects, 1:190–192
      extracellular matrix modulation, 1:528
      senescence rate, 2:548–549
   cancer implications
      prevention, 1:228–229
      risk, 1:227
   dietary variety, 1:436–437
      food intake regulation, 1:432–433
      gastrointestinal function, 1:542–543
      intervention strategies, 1:439–440
      life expectancy changes, 2:93
      overview, 1:429–430
      prostate cancer inhibition, 2:361
      risks, 1:430–432
      smell deficits, *see* Smell
      socioeconomic issues, 1:437–439
      taste deficits, *see* Taste
      water regulation, *see* Thirst

O

Obesity, *see also* Fat
   aging postponement, 2:337
   body weight, 1:193–195
   bone fracture risk, 1:210
   disease relationship, 1:200–201
Obsessive-compulsive disorder, selective information
      processing, 1:764
Occupational status, life satisfaction, 2:61–62
Occupational therapy, acute rehabilitation, 2:384
Occupations, *see* Employment
Octopus cyanea, premature aging model, 2:343
Older Adult Service and Information System, adult
      education programs, 1:68–69
Older Americans Act, adult education, 1:65
Olfaction, *see* Smell
Oncogenes
   cancer biology, 1:229–230
   cell death mechanisms, 1:275
   definition, 1:223, 269
Ontogeny
   definition, 2:65
   life span approach, 2:69
Ontology
   contemporary views, 2:309–310
   definition, 2:307
   life story, 2:310–311
   traditional perspectives, 2:308–309
Oral cavity, dysfunction, 1:546
Oral history, *see also* Life review; Reminiscence
   definition, 2:53
   folk wisdom, 1:534–535
   life review, 2:57
   spiritual development, 2:396
Organ donation, ambiguity, 1:362–363
Organic mood disorder, symptoms, 1:423
Organizations, *see also specific organizations*
   current status, 2:231
   future trends, 2:231–232

historical perspective, 2:230–231
interest group theory, 2:229–230
social movement, 2:229–230
Orienting response, inhibition index, 1:762
Osteoarthritis, *see also* Rheumatic diseases
aging postponement, 2:336–337
cartilage changes, 2:452
definition, 2:333
disease course, 1:112–115
symptoms, 2:457
Osteoblasts, composition, 1:205
Osteoclasts, composition, 1:205–206
Osteopenia
bone metabolism, 1:488–489
definition, 1:477
Osteoporosis, *see also* Bones; Rheumatic diseases
bone changes, 2:452
clinical evaluation
bone density measurement, 1:212
risk factors, 1:211
secondary osteoporosis, 1:211–212
definition, 1:493; 2:333
epidemiology, 1:496
fracture risk
age-related bone loss, 1:210–211, 488–489
epidemiology, 1:209–210
falls, 1:12, 15, 211
peak bone density achievement, 1:210
postponement, 2:337
symptoms, 2:458
treatment strategies
bisphosphonates, 1:214
calcitonin, 1:214
calcium, 1:213
estrogen replacement, 1:212–213
fluoride, 1:214
vitamin D, 1:213–214
Otologic disorders, hearing loss, 1:648
Ovarian cancer, overview, 1:238–239
Over-the-counter drugs, *see* Medications
Oxidative damage
antioxidants
definition, 2:83, 233
function, 2:236–237
biochemical aspects
damage sources, 2:235–236
defense mechanisms, 2:236–237
measurement, 2:237–239
mediators, 2:235–236
definition, 2:233
extracellular matrix modulation, aging postponement,
1:528
free radicals
definition, 1:185; 2:233

dietary restriction, 1:191
measurement, 2:237–239
mitochondrial DNA aberrations, 2:138, 140
senescence theory, 2:549
historical perspective, 2:234–235
methodology, 2:234–235
molecular physiology, 2:239–240
pathophysiology
carcinogenesis, 2:240–242
connective tissue, 2:243–244
degenerative diseases, 2:241–242
diabetes, 2:244
DNA damage
mitochondrial DNA, 1:444; 2:243–244
nuclear DNA, 2:240–241
hereditary diseases, 2:244–245
ischemia, 2:245–246
life span limitation, 2:243–244
lipid damage, 2:241–242
premature aging, 2:244–245
programmed cell death, 2:242–243
protein damage, 2:241–242
skin aging, 2:243–244
Oxidative phosphorylation
definition, 2:136
mitochondrial diseases, 2:352

P

p53 Gene, cancer biology, 1:230
Pacinian corpuscle
tactile response changes, 2:595–597
touch physiology, 2:592
Pain
assessment, 2:257–258
cancer therapy, 1:242
definition, 2:247–249
depression risk, 1:420
nonsteroidal anti-inflammatory drug use, 1:95, 114
overview, 2:247–250
rheumatic disease effects, 2:453
tactile response changes, 2:597
touch physiology, 2:593–595
types
acute procedural pain, 2:251–253
arthritis pain, 1:114
atypical pain presentation, 2:254
cancer pain, 2:253–254
chronic pain, 2:254–257
experimental pain, 2:250–251
postsurgical pain, 2:253
recurrent pain, 2:254–257

Paired-associate learning, verbal tasks, 2:12–14

Pancreas
anatomy, 1:542–543
dysfunction, 1:552

Para-aminohippuric acid
age-related clearance changes, 2:410
definition, 2:407

Parasympathetic nervous system
age changes, 1:145
anatomy, 1:143

Parathyroid hormone
bone growth role, 1:207
bone metabolism, 1:487–488

Parents, mythological representations, 2:193–194

Parkinson's disease
autonomic nervous system dysfunction, 1:146; 2:222
chronic pain, 2:255, 257
neurotransmitter effects, 2:225–226
protein oxidation role, 2:242

Part-task training
definition, 2:489
skill acquisition, 2:494

Patient Self-Determination Act, end-of-life issues, 1:372

Penicillin, acute renal failure, 2:414

Pensions
cohort differences, 1:303–304
concepts, 2:523–525
coverage, 2:524
participation, 2:524–525
vesting, 2:525
defined benefit versus defined contribution, 2:521–522,
527–529
employment exiting, 2:636
funding, 2:525–527
future status, 1:465
gender inequality, 1:560
overview, 2:521–522
retirement resource allocations, 1:458; 2:437–442,
522–523

Pentose phosphate shunt, definition, 2:136

Peptic ulcers, stomach dysfunction, 1:548

Perception, see also Attention
acuity, 2:272, 276–277, 608–610
definition, 2:271
light sensitivity, 2:271–272, 608
motion perception, 2:278
motor discrimination, 2:274
perceptual noise, 2:276
perceptual span, 2:274–276
resource theory, 2:114
selective attention, 1:137–138
spatial contrast sensitivity, 2:272–273, 277–278
stimulus persistence, 2:273–274
visual search, 2:610–611

Perceptual-motor learning, see Motor control

Performance Operating Characteristic, attention capacity
measurement, 1:134

Peristalsis, definition, 1:541

Persistent vegetative state, see also Euthanasia
definition, 1:361

Personality
definition, 2:281
genetic influences, 1:169
psychological aging, 2:562–565
psychosocial development theory, 2:561
research findings
cognitive theory of adjustment, 2:292
control beliefs, 2:285
coping, 2:290–291
developmental conceptualizations, 2:285–286
developmental periods model, 2:287
developmental trajectories, 2:289–290
epigenetic stage theory, 2:287–288
future outlook beliefs, 2:285
motives, 2:284–285
personality types, 2:289–290
selective theories, 2:292–294
self-management, 2:291–292
synthesized developmental models, 2:288–289
traits, 2:283–284
self-esteem theory, 2:460–461
theoretical approaches, 2:281–283
developmental model, 2:282–283
experiential-contextual model, 2:283
trait model, 2:282

Personal network, see Social networks

Personhood, ageism, anthropological dimension, 1:78–80

pH
drug distribution, 2:298–299
drug excretion, 2:302
kidney excretion rate changes, 2:411

Phagocytosis
apoptosis induction, 1:274
definition, 1:269

Pharmacology
advanced glycation end product intervention, 1:609
adverse reactions, 1:94; 2:304–306
alcohol, see Alcohol
Alzheimer's disease treatment, 1:324–325
autonomic responses, 1:146–147
cancer therapy, 1:241
depression management, 1:425–426
drug abuse
cognitive–behavioral therapy, 1:295
grandparent caregivers, 1:617
health care services, 2:127–128
folk medicine, 1:536–538
illegal substances, 1:96

medications
    chemosensory effects, 2:497–500, 502
    drug interactions, 2:304–306
    over-the-counter drugs, 1:95–96
    use, 1:94–95
nicotine
    atherosclerosis risk, 1:126
    cancer risk, 1:226, 229, 233
    stroke risk, 2:519
    use, 1:96
    overview, 1:93–94; 2:295–296
    pharmacodynamics, 2:304
    pharmacokinetics, 2:296–304
        absorption, 2:297–298
        distribution, 2:298–299
        excretion, 2:301–304
        metabolism, 2:299–301
    psychotropic drugs, 1:94–95, 425–426; 2:128
    sexual dysfunction, 2:487
    side effects, 1:94; 2:304–306
Phenomenology, definition, 2:281
Philosophy
    epistemology, 2:311–313
    ethics, 2:313–316
    historical gerontology
        Greco-Roman philosophers, 1:657–659
        renaissance, 1:659–660
        scientific era, 1:660–662
    ontology
        contemporary views, 2:309–310
        life story, 2:310–311
        traditional perspectives, 2:308–309
    overview, 2:307–308
Phobias
    falling, 1:12, 156, 160
    health care services, 2:126
    personality traits, 2:284
Phospholipids
    membrane fluidity changes, 2:138–140
    plasma membrane composition, 1:280–281
Photographs, aging images
    contemporary humor, 1:729
    multicultural awareness, 1:749–750
    overview, 1:743–744
    social role, 1:744–749
Photon absorptiometry, body composition measurement, 1:197
Physical abuse, *see* Domestic violence; Elder abuse
Physical environment, *see* Environment
Physical fitness, *see also* Activities of daily living
    competence, 1:736–737
    ergonomics, 1:718–719
    exercise
        balance control, 1:156–157

    basal metabolic rate changes, 1:190–192
    cardiovascular response, 1:146
    food intake changes, 1:188
    geriatric rehabilitation, 2:383
    gerontechnology, 1:601
    health effects, 1:40–41
    life expectancy changes, 2:93
    muscle adaptability, 2:217–220
    respiratory response, lung function, 2:433
    restricted energy intake, 1:191–192
geriatric assessment
    benefits, 1:591
    components, 1:589–590
    definition, 1:587
    future research directions, 1:592
    historical perspective, 1:588–589
    objectives, 1:587–588
    program models, 1:590–591
mythological representations, 2:191
Physical therapy
    acute rehabilitation, 2:384
    arthritis management, 1:120
Physician-assisted suicide
    definition, 1:505; 2:529
    ethical arguments, 2:537–538
    hospice care, 1:691–692
    persistent vegetative state, 1:361
    societal attitudes, 1:364, 371
    voluntary practice, 2:530–531
Physicians, hospice role, 1:693
Physiological stress, *see* Stress
Pick's disease
    characteristics, 1:396–397
    language difficulties, 2:5–6
Pitressin, urine concentration study, 2:411
Pituitary gland, endocrine function
    dynamic testing, 1:479
    functional changes, 1:478–479
Plasma membrane
    cholesterol analysis, 1:279–287
        membrane cholesterol alterations, 1:283–287
            Alzheimer's disease-related alterations, 1:285–286
            atherosclerosis-related alterations, 1:286–287
            compensatory alterations, 1:283–285
        membrane isolation, 1:282–283
        overview, 1:279–282
            cholesterol regulation, 1:281–282
            lipid composition, 1:280–281
            membrane structure, 1:279–280
            physical characteristics, 1:280–281
    exercise-induced regulatory protein change, 2:219
    lipid fluidity, 2:138–140
    osmolarity
        dehydration management, 2:578
        hypo-osmolality, 2:580

Platelet-derived growth factor, human fibroblast cell
    senescence, 1:626–628
Play, *see* Leisure
Podospora anserina, aging model, 2:153–154, 343–344
Policy, *see* Politics; Public policy
Political economy theory, retirement, 2:444–445
Politics, *see also* Public policy
    attitudes
        misconceptions, 2:326
        overview, 2:325–326
        seniors
            group benefit trend, 2:327–329
            ideology, 2:326–327
            low-stimulus elections, 2:330–331
            party identification, 2:331–332
            voter registration, 2:329
            voter turnout, 2:329–330
        trends, 2:326
    interest group theory, 2:229–230
    political action committees, 2:231
    politician achievement characteristics, 1:28–29, 35–36
Pollution, cancer risk, 1:226
Polymerase chain reaction, DNA sequence change
    detection, 1:445–446
Polymyalgia rheumatica, 1:117–118
Population aging
    age stratification, 1:84–86
    definition, 1:405
    demographics
        aged populations, 1:409–410
        dynamic models, 1:406–407
        future research directions
            biodemography, 1:412–413
            family demography, 1:410
            family dynamics, 1:411–412
            household structures, 1:411
            kinship structures, 1:410–411
        historical development, 1:406
        policy implications, 1:409
        trends, 1:408–409
    genetics
        experimental studies, 1:512–514
        hypotheses, 1:511–512
        mathematical evolutionary theory, 1:510–511
    sampling methods, 2:420, 464
    volunteerism, 2:616–618
Positron emission tomography
    Alzheimer's disease diagnosis, 1:388–389
    attention capacity measurement, 1:136–137
    body composition measurement, 1:198
    definition, 1:131
    dementia diagnosis, 1:398–399
    memory analysis, 2:109
    visual neural changes, 2:607

Postfall syndrome
    consequences, 1:12
    definition, 1:11
Postural hypotension, control, autonomic nervous system
    changes, 1:145–146
Posture
    anticipatory adjustments, 1:154–155
    ergonomic designs, 1:716–717
    gait control, 1:149–151
    proprioception changes, 2:601–602
    vision decline role, 1:153
Potassium
    body composition measurement, 1:196
    homeostasis changes, 2:412–413
    neutron activation analysis, 1:197–198
Poverty
    gender inequality, 1:559–560
    individual economics, 1:459–461
    international comparisons, 1:461–463
Predominant tone principle, autonomic response, 1:143
Premature aging, *see also* Aging postponement
    human studies
        Alzheimer's disease, 2:351
        amyotrophic lateral sclerosis, 2:351
        Cockayne's syndrome, 2:349–350
        diabetes, 1:528; 2:352–353
        Down's syndrome, 2:350–351
        Hutchinson–Gilford syndrome, 2:347
        mitochondrial diseases, 2:352
        Werner syndrome, 2:347–349
        xeroderma pigmentosum, 2:349–350
    models
        Drosophila melanogaster senescence, 2:345–346
        fungi senescence, 2:344–345
        Mus musculus, 2:346
        semelparous species, 2:343–344
    overview, 2:341–342
    oxidative stress, 2:244–245
Presbyalgos, *see* Pain
Presbycusis, *see* Auditory system
Presbyopia, *see* Vision
Prescription drugs, *see* Medications
Press-competence model, selective coping, 2:293–294
Primary care, *see* Caregiving
Primates, aging model, 2:168
Probenecid, drug interactions, 2:305
Problem solving, everyday problems
    contextual perspective, 1:375
    developmental differences
        age differences, 1:376–378
        efficacy criteria, 1:376
        process, 1:375–376
    differential task structures, 1:374–375
    ecological validity, 1:374

mediating factors
  emotional salience, **1:**379–380
  individual differences, **1:**380
  personal relevance, **1:**379
  problem appraisal, **1:**378–379
  traditional approaches, **1:**373–374
Productivity, creativity measurements, **1:**343–348
  age decrement magnitude, **1:**344
  career versus chronological age, **1:**345–346
  creative domains, **1:**344–345
  equal-odds rule, **1:**346–347
  lifetime output differences, **1:**345
  productivity influences, **1:**346
  qualitative transformations, **1:**347–348
Progeria, *see* Hutchinson–Gilford syndrome
Progesterone replacement therapy, cancer risk, **1:**213
Progestin, definition, **2:**333
Programmed cell death
  definition, **1:**269
  in vivo characteristics, **1:**271
  overview, **1:**272–273
  oxidative injury-dependent pathway, **2:**242–243
Prolactin, pituitary function, **1:**478–479
Proprioception
  aging effects, **2:**601–603
  physiology, **2:**597–599
  psychophysics, **2:**599–601
Prospective Payment System, hospital discharge policy, **1:**638
Prostate
  anatomy, **2:**355
  benign prostatic hyperplasia
    diagnosis, **2:**358–360
    etiology, **2:**358
    incidence, **2:**357–358
    medical treatment, **2:**360
    physiology, **2:**358
    surgical treatment, **2:**360–361
  cancer, **1:**236–237; **2:**361–364
  male reproductive system changes, **1:**486
  physiology, **2:**355–356
  prostatitis, **2:**356–357
  sexual dysfunction, **2:**487
Prostate-specific antigen
  age-specific ranges, **2:**363–364
  prostate cancer diagnosis, **2:**361–362
Protein, *see also specific types*
  age-related metabolic change, **2:**140
  contractile proteins function, **2:**213
  membrane-bound regulatory proteins, exercise-induced change, **2:**219
  metabolism, **1:**188
  nonenzymatic glycation effects, **1:**607–608
  oxidative damage, **2:**241–242
Proteoglycans, definition, **1:**519; **2:**333

Psychoanalytic theories, bereavement, **1:**177
Psychological aging, *see* Aging theories, psychological aging
Psychological well-being, *see* Well-being
Psychologists
  historical gerontology, **1:**662
  hospice role, **1:**694
  services, **2:**128
Psychopharmacology
  definition, **1:**415
  depression management, **1:**425–426
  psychotropic drugs, **1:**94–95; **2:**128
Psychotherapy
  definition, **1:**415
  depression management, **1:**424
  life review
    autobiography, **2:**57
    definition, **2:**53
    memory, **2:**54–55
    new directions, **2:**57–58
    oral histories, **2:**57
    theoretical concept, **2:**53–54
    validity, **2:**56–57
    value, **2:**55–56
  services provided, **2:**128
Public policy, *see also* Politics
  activity programming, **1:**49
  adult education programs, **1:**65–66
  career criminals, **1:**357–358
  comprehensive geriatric assessment, **1:**588–589
  consumer behavior, **1:**330–331
  euthanasia, **1:**508
  gerontechnology, **1:**716
  health care coverage, **1:**256–257, 640–641
  housing programs, **1:**709–712
  legislation
    domestic violence programs, **1:**9–10
    elder abuse protection
      advocacy programs, **1:**10
      child welfare model, **1:**7–8
      mandatory reporting, **1:**8
      programs, **1:**8–9
  leisure activity, **2:**29–30
  Patient Self-Determination Act, **1:**372
  physician-assisted suicide, **2:**537–538
  population aging, **1:**409
  retirement, **2:**447–448
  societal economics
    dependency costs, **1:**473–474
    entitlement programs, **1:**471–472
    fiscal capacity, **1:**470–471
    overview, **1:**469–470
    policy role, **1:**472–473
    supply-and-demand view, **1:**474–476
Pyelonephritis, **2:**414

R

Rabbit, eyeblink conditioning, 1:320–321
Race, *see also* Culture
  alcohol use, 1:98–99
  cancer occurrence, 1:225
  caregiving differences, 1:260
  cross-cultural grandparents, 1:621–622
  ethnic diversity, 2:371–376
    demographics, 2:371
    economic status, 2:375
    future research directions, 2:376
    mental health, 2:374–375
    physical health
      functional health, 2:372–373
      life expectancy, 2:372–373
      mortality, 2:372–374
    social relationships, 2:375
    study methods, 2:372
  fracture risk, 1:210
  leisure deprivation, 2:29
  life satisfaction, 2:62
  literary representations, 2:75
  loneliness, 2:80
  minority group theory, ageism, 1:74–75
  poverty rates, 1:459
  prostate cancer incidence, 2:361
  religious differences, 2:392–393
  social stratification, 1:83
  stroke incidence, 2:518
  wealth distribution, 1:464
  workforce participation, 2:638
Radiation
  cancer therapy, 1:240–241; 2:363
  ultraviolet radiation
    aging models
      enhancer traps, 2:160
      yeast, 2:155
    cancer risk, 1:226
    oxidative damage, 2:244–245
    xeroderma pigmentosum, 2:349–350
Rat, aging model, 2:167
Reaction time
  attention
    capacity measurement, 1:132–137
    selective allocation, 1:138–139
  definition, 1:131; 2:177, 377
  historical perspective, 2:377
  importance, 2:377–380
    age-relate robustness, 2:378–379
    cognition, 2:379–380
    neurological status indicator, 2:378

  negative priming, 1:762–763
  postural balance control
    anticipatory adjustments, 1:155
    fall factors, 1:14
  response initiation, 2:178–180
  skill acquisition, speed–accuracy trade-off functions, 2:490–492
  transitory nature, 2:184
Reactive oxygen species, *see* Oxidative damage
Reading, *see also* Literature
  entertainment value, 1:42
Reasoning, generational differences, 1:571–572
Reciprocity
  definition, 2:505
  retirement, 2:444
  social exchange, 2:510–511
  social network differences, 2:512–513
Reconciliation, *see* Life review
Recreation, *see* Activities; Leisure
Rehabilitation
  acute rehabilitation, 2:383–385
  definition, 2:381
  emerging issues, 2:385
  relevance, 2:381–383
  unique geriatric aspects, 2:383
Releasing hormones, definition, 1:477
Religion, *see also* Folklore
  bereavement process, 1:175
  biblical humor, 1:731
  coping strategies, 1:53
  depression relief, 1:420–421
  early studies, 2:387–388
  elder participation, 2:390–394
    ethnicity, 2:392–393
    gender, 2:392
    pluralism, 2:393–394
  historical gerontology, 1:657–660
  hospice role, 1:693–694
  ontology, 2:310
  organized activity, 1:43
  religious gerontology, 2:388–389
  religious leaders, achievement characteristics, 1:30–31
  skill acquisition, 2:493
  spirituality
    definition, 2:387
    development, 2:395–396
    study, 2:390–391
  study, 2:389–390, 395–396
  verbal tasks, 2:12–14
  volunteer participation, 2:616, 619
  well-being, 2:394–395
Reminiscence
  benefits, 2:405

definition, **2:**53
historical perspective, **2:**400–401
life review
   autobiography, **2:**57
   definition, **2:**53
   memory, **2:**54–55
   new directions, **2:**57–58
   oral histories, **2:**57
   psychotherapeutic value, **2:**55–56
   theoretical concept, **2:**53–54
   validity, **2:**56–57
overview, **2:**399–400
past experience importance, **2:**405–406
techniques, **2:**404–405
therapy
   dementia patience, **2:**403–404
   group reminiscence, **2:**403
   one-to-one-interaction, **2:**402–403
typologies, **2:**401–402
Renal function
  body composition measurement, **1:**197
  drug excretion, **2:**301–304
  electrolyte homeostasis, **2:**412–413
  fluid control changes, **2:**412–413
  kidney cancer, **1:**238
  kidney function changes
    acid excretion, **2:**411
    glomerular filtration rate, **2:**409–410
    maximum tubular transport capacity, **2:**410–411
    plasma flow, **2:**410
    renal decrease pathophysiology, **2:**411–412
    renal morphology, **2:**408–409
  kidney–urinary tract disease, **2:**414–416
  nocturia, **2:**575
  overview, **2:**407–408
  physical health identity, **1:**738
  prostate
    anatomy, **2:**355
    benign prostatic hyperplasia
      diagnosis, **2:**358–360
      etiology, **2:**358
      incidence, **2:**357–358
      medical treatment, **2:**360
      physiology, **2:**358
      surgical treatment, **2:**360–361
    male reproductive system changes, **1:**486
    physiology, **2:**355–356
    prostate cancer, **2:**361–364
    prostatitis, **2:**356–357
  urinary incontinence
    aging postponement, **2:**337–338
    lower urinary tract dysfunction, **2:**416–417
Renin-angiotensin system, definition, **1:**141

Repetitive motion, ergonomic designs, **1:**721–722
Reproductive system, *see* Female reproductive system;
  Male reproductive system
Research methods, *see also* Models of aging
  cohort studies, *see* Cohorts
  cross-cultural studies, **1:**311–317
    definitions, **1:**316
    demographics, **1:**313
    design, **1:**312–313
    future research directions, **1:**316–317
    health, **1:**314–315
    importance, **1:**311–312
    kinship, **1:**315–316
    life course, **1:**316–317
    security, **1:**315
    social support, **1:**315–316
    well-being, **1:**314
  fundamentals
    causation concept, **2:**419–420
    controls, **2:**421
    external validity, **2:**423–424
    field research, **2:**421–422
    internal validity, **2:**423
    laboratory experiments, **2:**421
    operational definitions, **2:**421
    quasi-experiments, **2:**421–422
    subject sampling, **2:**420
    temporal studies, **2:**422–423
    theory role, **2:**419
    variables, **2:**420
  generational differences, **1:**568–570
  life span study, **2:**69
  measurement
    behavioral observation, **2:**429
    precision, **2:**427–429
    validity, **2:**426–427
  self-esteem studies
    design, **2:**463
    measurement, **2:**462–463
    population sampling, **2:**464
    statistical analysis, **2:**463–464
  statistical analysis
    descriptive statistics, **2:**424
    inference, **2:**424–425
    procedures, **2:**425–426
    self-esteem studies, **2:**463–464
Reserve capacity
  definition, **2:**65
  life span theory, **2:**68
Resilience, life span theory, **2:**68
Respiratory system
  aging effects
    defense system, **2:**435–436

Respiratory system (*continued*)
    lung function, 2:432–433
      muscle function, 2:433
      respiration regulation, 2:433–434
    lung cancer, 1:232–233
    normal operation, 2:431–432
    pulmonary vascular bed, 1:250
    sleep breathing, 2:434–435
Respite care, home care services
    availability, 1:675–676
    intervention assistance efficacy, 1:677
    utilization, 1:676–677
Restricted energy intake, *see* Dietary restriction
Retinopathy, characteristics, 2:611–612
Retirement, *see also* Employment
    adult education
      certificate programs, 1:67
      community college, 1:66
      Elderhostel, 1:66–67
      Learning in Retirement Institutes, 1:67
      senior centers, 1:67–68
      The Third Age, 1:62–63
    cohort differences, 1:303–304
    concepts, 2:438–440
    current trends, 1:457; 2:441–442
    definition, 2:437
    Employee Retirement Income Security Act, 2:521–522
    employment exiting, 2:636–637
    explanations, 2:443–447
    future directions, 2:447–448
    historical perspective, 2:230, 440–441
    home ownership, 1:706
    household effects, 2:442–443
    income, *see* Pensions
    income loss, 2:50
    individual effects, 2:442–443
    leisure issues, 2:25–26
    migration patterns, *see* Migration
    Naturally Occurring Retirement Communities, 1:703, 709
    pensions, *see* Pensions
    phased retirement, 2:634
    political behavior, 2:326
    public resource transfer, cohort differences, 1:307
    retirement communities
      activity engagement, 1:44–45
      alcohol use, 1:99
    social roles
      adaptation, 1:55–56
      age stratification, 1:89–90
      importance, 2:437–438
    volunteer participation, 2:616, 618–619
Reverse mortgages, home equity conversion, 1:711

Rheumatic diseases, *see also specific diseases*
    definition, 2:451
    disease symptoms, 2:455–458
    epidemiology, 2:454
    health care, 2:454
    immune system, 2:453
    locomotor function, 2:453
    musculoskeletal tissues, 2:451–453
    pain, 2:453
    therapy, 2:454–455
Rheumatoid arthritis, *see also* Rheumatic diseases
    symptoms, 1:116–117; 2:455
Risk behaviors
    atherosclerosis, 1:124–126
    bone fractures, 1:13–15, 210–211
    cancer, 1:226–227, 229, 233
    driving, 1:21–23
    smoking, 1:126, 226, 229, 233
    stroke, 2:518–519
Rituals, *see also* Religion
    traditional practices, 1:535–536
Roles, *see* Gender roles; Grandparenthood, roles; Social roles
Ruffini cylinder
    proprioception physiology, 2:597–599
    touch physiology, 2:592–594

S

Sarcopenia
    definition, 2:211
    muscle atrophy, 2:213
Satisfaction, *see* Life satisfaction
Schiff base
    diabetes role, 2:352–353
    glycation chemistry, 1:605–607
Schizophrenia
    depression, 1:424
    selective information processing, 1:764
    services, 2:125–126
Secondary care, *see* Caregiving
Security, *see also* Well-being
    cross-cultural studies, 1:315
    pension protection, 2:521–522, 526–527
    wealth, 1:474–475
Segmental progeroid diseases
    definition, 1:577
    human genetics studies, 1:578–579
Selective attention
    age differences, 1:137–139
      attention allocation, 1:138–139

inhibitory processing, **1**:139
relevant information selection, **1**:137–138
behavioral indices, **1**:762–763
definition, **1**:131, 761
Selective serotonin reuptake inhibitors, dementia
treatment, **1**:401–402
Selectivity theory
definition, **2**:506
personality traits, **2**:293
support relationships, **2**:510
Self-efficacy, *see* Autonomy
Self-esteem, *see also* Well-being
bereavement adjustments, **1**:181–182
change adaptation, **1**:54
cognitive–behavioral therapy, **1**:293
definition, **2**:459
empirical studies, **2**:464
future research directions, **2**:464–466
group reminiscence, **2**:403
identity, *see also* Gender roles
activity participation patterns, **1**:38–40
change adaptation, **1**:54, 56–59
cognitive–behavioral interventions, **1**:293
death anxiety, **1**:368
definition, **1**:51, 733–734
multiple threshold model, **1**:734–735
physical identity
appearance, **1**:735–736
competence, **1**:736–737
coping, **1**:739–741
health, **1**:737–739
principles, **1**:734
stereotypes, **1**:741–742
life course changes, **2**:459–460
life review therapy, **2**:55–56
personality traits, **2**:291–292
social dislocation, **1**:73–74
study methodology, **2**:462–464
theory
life-course perspectives, **2**:462
life span developmental theories, **2**:461
personality trait theories, **2**:460–461
role theories, **2**:461–462
Self-perception, *see* Identity
Self-regulation
control beliefs, **2**:285
definition, **2**:365
ethical issues, **2**:313–315
euthanasia, **1**:505–507
intervention models
action plans, **2**:471–472
age impact, **2**:474–476

chronological approach, **2**:473–474
disease threat representation, **2**:470
life span context, **2**:472–473
prevention, **2**:469–470
issues, **2**:468–469
overview, **2**:467
Semelparity, premature aging models, **2**:343–344
Senescence, *see also* Apoptosis; Cell death
aspect theories, **2**:547–550
definition, **1**:577, 655; **2**:65, 546
entropic processes, **1**:685; **2**:550–553
evolutionary biology, **2**:553–554
gene expression regulation, **1**:585–586
heat shock gene expression, **2**:320–323
homeodynamic resiliency, **1**:685
human genetics studies, **1**:578
life span theory, **2**:67
longevity relation, **2**:84–86
negentropic processes, **2**:550–553
psychological aging, **2**:558
rate determinants, **2**:553
skill acquisition, age-related changes, **2**:493
telomere genetics, **2**:539–540
time effects, **2**:546
views, **2**:547
Senile dementia, *see* Alzheimer's disease
Senile plaques
aging neuropathology, **1**:220–221
Alzheimer's disease neuropathology, **1**:389–390
Senior centers
adult education programs, **1**:67–68
organized recreation, **1**:43
SENIORNET, adult education programs, **1**:68–69
Sensory systems, *see specific types*
Sensuality, *see* Sexuality
Serotonin, selective reuptake inhibitors, dementia
treatment, **1**:401–402
Sexism, older sexual partners, **2**:484–485
Sexual abuse, *see also* Elder abuse
delinquency correlation, **1**:356
Sexuality
achievement characteristics, **1**:34–35
age changes, **2**:483–486
dysfunction, **2**:127, 486–488
intimacy, **2**:482–483
overview, **2**:479–480
physical health identity, **1**:738–739
research, **2**:480–482
social role adaptation, **1**:55
stereotypes, **2**:480
Shepherd's Centers, adult education programs, **1**:68–69
Shy–Drager syndrome, autonomic nervous system
dysfunction, **1**:146

Simvastasin, cholesterol lowering effects, **1**:126
Situational theory, elder abuse, **1**:4
Skeletal system, *see* Arthritis; Bones; Osteoporosis
Skill acquisition, *see also* Competence
   components
      automatic, **2**:492–494
      strategic, **2**:490–492
   definition, **2**:489–490
   strategies, **2**:494–495
Skin
   epidermal growth factor, **1**:626–629
   oxidative damage, **2**:243–244
Sleep
   disorders
      health care services, **2**:126
      pharmacological treatment, **1**:402
   patterns
      breathing, **2**:434–435
      physical health identity, **1**:738
Small intestine
   anatomy, **1**:542–543
   digestive function, **1**:544, 546
   dysfunction, **1**:549
Smart highways
   definition, **1**:19
   potential use, **1**:24
Smell
   compensation, **1**:433–436; **2**:503
   drug effects, **2**:497–500, 502
   flavor enhancement, **2**:500, 503
   overview, **2**:497
   perception loss, **2**:502–503
   physiology, **2**:500–502
Smoking
   atherosclerosis risk, **1**:126
   cancer risk, **1**:226, 229, 233
   death rates, **1**:96
   stroke risk, **2**:519
Social activity, *see also* Social networks
   health effects, **1**:40–41
   leisure, **2**:26
   life satisfaction, **1**:40; **2**:63
   relationships, **1**:45–46
   role changes, **1**:88–89
   verbal communication inhibition, **1**:763–764; **2**:3, 6
Social attitudes, *see also* Social policy
   cohort interplay, **1**:308
   death, **1**:364–367
Social change
   cognitive–behavioral therapy, **1**:293
   modernization
      architecture, **2**:174–175
      definition, **2**:171

      demographics, **2**:172–173
      life quality, **2**:174
      old-age experience, **2**:171–172
      planning innovations, **2**:174–175
      social network erosion, **2**:174
Social Competence and Breakdown Theory, caregiving,
   1:260–261
Social dislocation
   disengagement theory, **1**:75–76
   elder abuse, **1**:6–7
   minority group theory, **1**:74–75
   status loss, **1**:73–74
Social entrainment model, biological clocks, **2**:584, 588
Social environment, *see* Environment
Social exchange theory, elder abuse, **1**:4
Social interaction, *see* Social activity; Social networks
Social justice theory, retirement, **2**:445
Social movement, organizations, **2**:229–230
Social networks
   aging postponement, **2**:338–339
   analysis
      advantages, **2**:207–208
      age strata relationships, **1**:87
      aging impact, **2**:199–200
      delineation
         methods, **2**:200–203, 208–210
         research choices, **2**:203–204
      determinants, **2**:199
      features
         content, **2**:206–207
         network structure, **2**:204–206
      overview, **2**:197–199
   bereavement adjustments, **1**:181–182
   cancer patient care, **1**:242–243
   coping, **2**:291
   cross-cultural studies, **1**:315–316
   cultural differences, **2**:512–513
   data sources, **2**:508
   definition, **2**:505
   delinquent peer groups, **1**:356–357
   depression relief, **1**:420
   ethnic differences, **2**:375
   family, **2**:507–510
   friendship relationships, **1**:562–563; **2**:509–510
   gender differences, **2**:511–512
   genetic influences, **1**:170–171
   grandparent–family relationships, **1**:618
   health continuum, **2**:508–509
   life course paradigm, **2**:32
   life satisfaction, **2**:61, 63
   loneliness effects
      bereavement adjustments, **1**:180
      emotional isolation, **2**:80

friendship, **2:**510
   research findings, **2:**80–81
   social isolation, **2:**79
   social network role, **2:**198
   theory, **2:**79
measurement, **2:**507–508
modernization effects, **2:**174
physical identity, **1:**734–735
reciprocity, **2:**207–208, 510–511
social activity
   health effects, **1:**40–41
   leisure, **2:**26
   life satisfaction, **1:**40; **2:**63
   relationships, **1:**45–46
   role changes, **1:**88–89
   verbal communication inhibition, **1:**763–764; **2:**3, 6
theory, **2:**506–507
well-being modification, **2:**47–48, 513–514
widowhood, **2:**623
Social policy, *see also* Politics
   activity programming, **1:**49
   adult education programs, **1:**65–66
   career criminals, **1:**357–358
   comprehensive geriatric assessment, **1:**588–589
   consumer behavior, **1:**330–331
   euthanasia, **1:**508
   gerontechnology, **1:**716
   health care coverage, **1:**256–257, 640–641
   housing programs, **1:**709–712
   leisure activity, **2:**29–30
   Patient Self-Determination Act, **1:**372
   physician-assisted suicide, **2:**537–538
   population aging, **1:**409
   retirement, **2:**447–448
   societal economics
      dependency costs, **1:**473–474
      entitlement programs, **1:**471–472
      fiscal capacity, **1:**470–471
      overview, **1:**469–470
      policy role, **1:**472–473
      supply-and-demand view, **1:**474–476
Social Readjustment Rating Scale, life events
   measurement, **2:**43–44
Social roles
   age strata relationships, **1:**87–90
   change adaptation, **1:**54–56, 88–89
   loss, life satisfaction, **2:**63
   self-esteem theory, **2:**461–462
Social Security
   benefits, **1:**457–458; **2:**446–448
   dependency ratios, **1:**473–474
   fiscal budget, **1:**472
   future status, **1:**465

historical perspective, **2:**230
life event consequences, **2:**51
political attitudes, **2:**326, 328
public resource transfer, cohort differences, **1:**307
retirement resource allocations, **1:**460–461; **2:**437–438, 441–442
Socioeconomic status, *see also* Economics
   cancer occurrence, **1:**225
   ethnic differences, **2:**375
   food intake habits, **1:**437–439
   grandparenthood, **1:**612–613
   life satisfaction, **2:**61–62
   retirement resource allocations, **2:**442
   stress recovery, **2:**50
   well-being variations, **1:**458–459; **2:**47–48, 368
Socioemotional selectivity theory
   definition, **2:**506
   personality traits, **2:**293
   support relationships, **2:**510
Sociological processes, achievement characteristics, **1:**35–36
Sodium
   homeostasis changes, **2:**412
   total body composition measurement, neutron activation analysis, **1:**197–198
Sonography, body composition measurement, **1:**198
Sound, *see* Auditory system
Speech, *see* Language
Spirituality, *see* Religion
Spleen, immune function, **1:**754–755
Sports, *see also* Exercise
   athletes
      achievement characteristics, **1:**32–33
      muscle composition, **2:**213, 218–219
   health effects, **1:**40–41
   organized recreation, **1:**43–44
Spouse abuse, *see* Domestic violence
Stability, *see* Balance; Homeostasis; Well-being
Stage theory
   bereavement, **1:**178
   death anxiety, **1:**370
   memory, **2:**107–109
Starvation, chronic suicide, **2:**530
Statistical analysis
   definition, **2:**419
   descriptive statistics, **2:**424
   inference, **2:**424–425
   measurement
      behavioral observation, **2:**429
      precision, **2:**427–429
      validity, **2:**426–427
   procedures, **2:**425–426
   self-esteem studies, **2:**463–464

Stereotyping
  ageism emergence, **1:**73
  aging images
    contemporary humor, **1:**729
    multicultural awareness, **1:**749–750
    overview, **1:**743–744
    social role, **1:**744–749
  communication skills, **2:**3
  definition, **1:**71, 743
  identity role, **1:**741–742
  leisure activity, **2:**21, 27–28
  sexual expression, **2:**479–482
Stimulus–response learning, *see* Cognitive–behavioral
    therapy
Stomach
  anatomy, **1:**542–543
  dysfunction, **1:**548–549
Stress
  acquired immunodeficiency syndrome, family stress,
    1:696
  adrenal function, **1:**484
  aging models
    Caenorhabditis elegans, **2:**157–158
    enhancer traps, **2:**160
    human applications, **2:**160–161
    yeast, **2:**155–156
  bereavement, **1:**177–178
  caregiver stress, elder abuse, **1:**6
  caregiving, **1:**256, 264–267, 675, 694
  definition, **2:**41, 317
  drinking onset, **1:**98
  emotional stress, *see* Emotion
  hospice caregiver burnout, **1:**694
  life events
    consequences
      age-related differences, **2:**49
      number differences, **2:**49–50
      sociodemographic pattern prediction, **2:**50
      study design, **2:**45–46
      type differences, **2:**49–50
      well-being modifiers, **2:**47–48
    definition, **2:**41
    future research directions, **2:**50–51
    research methods
      measurement, **2:**44–45
      report reliability, **2:**45
      social readjustment rating scale, **2:**43–44
    theoretical background, **2:**41–43
  physiology
    age-dependent changes, **2:**320–323
    immune response, **1:**52
    molecular responses, **2:**317–320

  oxidative stress
    measurement, **2:**237–238
    premature aging, **2:**244–245
  reduction
    activity importance, **1:**52–53
    adaptation, **1:**52–53
    coping strategies, *see* Cognitive–behavioral therapy;
        Coping
    family life, **1:**53, 58, 696
    one-to-one reminiscence, **2:**402–403
  suicide, *see* Suicide
Stroke
  consequences, **2:**526–527
  diagnostic studies, **2:**522
  epidemiology, **2:**517–520
    prevalence, **2:**518
    risk factors, **2:**518–520
  overview, **2:**517
  pathophysiology, **2:**520–522
  prevention, **2:**525–526
  treatment, **2:**522–525
Structural lag, age stratification, **1:**81, 90–92
Structured Events Probe, life events measurement, **2:**45
Substance abuse, *see also* Pharmacology
  alcohol
    chronic suicide, **2:**530
    cognitive impairment, **1:**97–98
    cognitive–behavioral therapy, **1:**295
    depression, **1:**423
    grandparent caregivers, **1:**617
    traffic accident risk, **1:**22–23
  cognitive–behavioral therapy, **1:**295
  grandparent caregivers, **1:**617
  health care services, **2:**127–128
  illegal substances, **1:**96
  tobacco
    atherosclerosis risk, **1:**126
    cancer risk, **1:**226, 229, 233
    stroke risk, **2:**519
    use, **1:**96
Successful aging, *see* Well-being
Suicide
  assisted suicide
    definition, **1:**505; **2:**529
    ethical arguments, **2:**537–538
      hospice care, **1:**691–692
    societal attitudes, **1:**364, 371
    voluntary practice, **2:**530–531
  epidemiology, **2:**531–533
  ethical issues, **2:**536–538
  gender differences, **1:**94
  intervention, **2:**535–536
  legal issues, **2:**536–538

older adult suicide evaluation, 2:533–535
overview
late life association, 2:529–530
scope, 2:530–531
Suicide nuclease, programmed cell death, 2:242–243
Sunbelt, migration patterns, 2:146–147
Superoxide dismutase, premature aging role, 2:350–351
Support networks, *see* Social networks
Suprachiasmatic nucleus, biological clock, 2:584
Surgery
cancer therapy, 1:240
postsurgical pain, 2:253
Survival, *see* Longevity
Sustained attention, *see* Vigilance
Swan-song phenomenon
creativity measurement, 1:348
definition, 1:341
Symbolic interaction theory
bereavement, 1:179
caregiving, 1:260–261
elder abuse, 1:4–5
Sympathetic nervous system, functional changes
adrenergic responses, 1:144–145
circulating catecholamines, 1:144
Syndrome of inappropriate antidiuretic hormone
secretion
definition, 2:573
hypo-osmolality, 2:580
Systemic lupus erythematosus, *see also* Rheumatic
diseases
symptoms, 2:455
System theory, bereavement, 1:178

T

Tactile system, *see* Touch
Task models
bereavement, 1:178
caregiving theory, 1:261
Task performance, *see* Attention
Taste
compensation, 1:433–436; 2:503
drug effects, 2:497–500, 502
flavor enhancement, 2:500, 503
overview, 2:497
perception loss, 2:502–503
physiology, 2:500–502
Technology, *see* Gerontechnology
Telemarketing, public policy, 1:330–331
Television
ageism, 1:73

aging images
contemporary humor, 1:729
multicultural awareness, 1:749–750
overview, 1:743–744
social role, 1:744–749
entertainment value, 1:42
leisure activity, 2:28
Telomeres
age-related loss, 2:541–543
cancer-induced telomerase reactivation, 2:541–543
end-replication problems, 2:540–541
implications, 2:543
longevity relation, 2:85–86
mutational hotspots, 1:446–447
senescence theory, 2:549
somatic replicative senescence, 2:539–540
Temporal organization, *see* Time
Terminal decline, *see* Senescence
Terminal illness, *see* Bereavement; Death; Hospice
Terminal restriction fragment, definition, 2:539
Testosterone
age-related production decrease, 1:485–486
aggression link, 1:355
benign prostatic hyperplasia etiology, 2:358
libido enhancement, 2:479, 484
replacement therapy, 1:229
Theories of aging, *see* Aging theories
Thermoreceptors
pain tolerance, 2:250–252
tactile response changes, 2:597
touch physiology, 2:592–593
Thermoregulation
basal metabolic rate changes, 1:190
definition, 1:185
setpoint control, 1:683
Third Age
adult education, 1:62–63
gender roles, 1:563–564
Thirst
definition, 2:573
dehydration
causes, 2:576–577
investigation, 2:578
management, 2:578
prevention, 2:580–581
susceptibility, 2:413
fluid compartments, 2:573–574
fluid homeostasis, 2:574–576
fluid intake requirements, 1:432
hypo-osmolality, 2:580
rehydration, 2:578–580
water metabolism, 1:490–491
Thymus, immune function, 1:754

Thyroid gland, endocrine function
    dysfunction, 1:481–482
    structure, 1:479–480
    thyroid hormone economy, 1:480–481
Thyroid-stimulating hormone
    hypothyroidism, 1:481–482
    pituitary function, 1:478–479
    thyroid hormone economy, 1:480–481
Time, *see also* Aging theories
    biological time, 2:584–585
    definition, 2:583
    intrinsic time, 2:588–590
    physical time, 2:583–584
    psychological time, 2:585–587
    social time, 2:562, 587–588
Tip-of-the-tongue state, 2:109
T lymphocytes
    definition, 1:753
    immune system, 1:755–756
Tobacco
    atherosclerosis risk, 1:126
    cancer risk, 1:226, 229, 233
    stroke risk, 2:519
    use, 1:96
Tomography, *see* Positron emission tomography
Touch
    aging effects, 2:602–603
    overview, 2:591
    pain perception, 2:248
    physiology, 2:591–593
    proprioception
        aging effects, 2:601–603
        physiology, 2:597–599
        psychophysics, 2:599–601
    psychophysics, 2:593–595, 599–601
    tactile response changes, 2:595–597
Traditions, *see* Folklore
Traffic accidents
    alcohol use, 1:22–23
    alternative transportation, 1:24–25
    cohort differences, 1:23
    commercial drivers, 1:23–24
    damage, 1:20
    demographics, 1:19–20
    driving performance, 1:20–21
    injuries, 1:20
    medical impairments, 1:23
    pedestrian casualties, 1:24
    risk, 1:21–22
    technology, 1:24
Traits, *see* Personality
Transcription, *see also* Gene expression
    age-related changes, 1:449–450

Transcription factors
    oxidative damage role, 2:235, 239–240
    programmed cell death, 2:242
Transfer paradigms, paired-associate learning, 2:14–15
Transgenics
    definition, 1:441
    DNA sequence change, 1:445
    model systems, 1:584; 2:159–160
Transient ischemic attack, *see* Ischemia
Transportation, *see* Automobiles
Travel
    life satisfaction, 1:41
    marketing, 1:44
Triiodothyronine, thyroid hormone economy, 1:480–481
Trophic hormones, definition, 1:477
Tuberculin, *see* Hypersensitivity
Tumor necrosis factor, immune function, 1:758
Tumor-suppression genes, cancer biology, 1:230
Tunica intima, definition, 1:123

U

Ulcerative colitis, large intestine dysfunction, 1:550
Ultraviolet radiation
    aging models
        enhancer traps, 2:160
        yeast, 2:155
    cancer risk, 1:226
    oxidative damage, 2:244–245
    xeroderma pigmentosum, 2:349–350
Ureogenesis, definition, 2:136
Uric acid, gout attacks, 1:115
Urinary system, *see* Renal function
Uterus cancer, overview, 1:239

V

Vagal tone, parasympathetic input, 1:145
Variable-priority training
    definition, 2:489
    skill acquisition, 2:494
Vascular dementia
    definition, 1:383
    effects, 1:386–387
    hemodynamic dementia, 1:394
    multi-infarct dementia, 1:394
    overview, 1:393–394
    pharmacological treatment, 1:401
    white matter lesions, 1:394–395
Vascular smooth muscle cells
    atherosclerosis pathogenesis, 1:127–128
    compensatory membrane cholesterol alterations,
        1:283–285

Vascular system, *see* Cardiovascular system
Vasculitis, *see also* Rheumatic diseases
    dementia role, 1:396
    symptoms, 2:456–457
Veins, vascular function, 1:250
Vertebrate aging models, *see specific species*
Vestibular nerve, balance control, 1:153–154
Veteran's Administration, hospital-based care, 2:132
Vigilance
    attention differences, 1:139–140
    definition, 1:131
Violence, *see* Domestic violence; Elder abuse
Viruses, cancer risk, 1:226–227
Vision
    age-related changes, posture control, 1:153
    attention, 2:610–611
    disorders, 2:611–612
    ergonomic designs, 1:717
    fall incidence, 1:15
    motor control declines, 2:184
    pain, 2:249–250
    perception
        data limitations, 2:271–276
            acuity, 2:272
            light sensitivity, 2:271–272
            motor discrimination, 2:274
            perceptual span, 2:274–276
            spatial contrast sensitivity, 2:272–273
            stimulus persistence, 2:273–274
        deficit impact
            acuity, 2:276–277
            motion perception, 2:278
            spatial contrast sensitivity, 2:277–278
        definition, 2:271
        detail, 2:608–610
        light, 2:608
        visual search, 2:610–611
    real-world tasks, 2:612
    sensory deprivation, aging postponement, 2:335
    system organization, 2:605–608
        eye movements, 2:607–608
        image formation, 2:606
        neural changes, 2:607
        photosensitive response, 2:606–607
    time events, 2:610
    traffic accident risk, 1:23
    visual inspection jobs, ergonomic designs, 1:722–723
Visual representation, *see* Images of aging
Visual search
    attention capacity measurement, 1:132–133, 138
    definition, 1:131, 761
Vitamin C, oxidative stress measurement, 2:237–238
Vitamin D
    bone metabolism, 1:487–488

calcium absorption, 1:545
    osteoporosis treatment, 1:210, 213–214
Vitamin E
    epidemiological studies, 1:497–500
    extracellular matrix modulation, aging postponement, 1:528
Volunteerism
    future implications, 2:618–620
    hospice training, 1:698–699
    leisure activity, 2:26
    likelihood factors, 2:614–616
    older population trends, 2:616–618
    prevalence, 2:613–614
Voting
    low-stimulus elections, 2:330–331
    party identification, 2:331–332
    presidential election turnout, 2:329–330
    registration, 2:329

W

Waist-hip circumference ratio, definition, 1:193
Walking
    gait characteristics, 1:157–160
        adaptive control, 1:159–160
        change factors, 1:160
        kinematic analysis, 1:158–159
        kinetic analysis, 1:159
        neuromuscular analysis, 1:159
        stride length, 1:158
        velocity changes, 1:158
    health effects, 1:41
    mode of travel, 1:20–21
    pedestrian casualties, 1:24
Warfarin, stroke prevention, 2:523–525
Water, *see also* Thirst
    doubly labeled water method, 1:185
    metabolism, 1:490–491; 2:574–576
Wealth
    economic security, 1:474–475
    importance, 1:463–464
    joint distribution, 1:464
Weight, *see* Body weight
Well-being, *see also* Self-esteem; Stress
    activity engagement, 1:40
    age patterns, 2:367
    class differences, 2:368
    cross-cultural studies, 1:314
    definition, 2:41
    developmental model, 2:288
    economic security, 1:474–476
    ethnic differences, 2:368, 374–375
    future research directions, 2:369

Well-being (*continued*)
  gender differences, 2:367–368
  historical perspective, 2:366
  life event consequences, 2:46–48
  life experience, 2:368–369
  life satisfaction
    activity, 2:63
    age, 2:62
    constructs, 2:60–61
    definition, 2:365
    education, 2:61–62
    gender, 2:62
    grandparenthood, 1:618–619
    health status, 2:61
    income, 1:458–459; 2:61
    marital status, 2:62
    measurement, 2:60–61
    occupational status, 2:61–62
    prospects, 2:63–64
    race, 2:62
    research focus, 2:59–60
    role loss, 2:63
    social interaction, 2:63
  multidimensional model, 2:366–367
  positive functioning, 2:365–366
  post fall syndrome, 1:11
  postfall syndrome, 1:11–12
  religion role, 2:394–395
  retirement rationale, 2:445–446
  social network role, 2:513–514
Werner's syndrome
  oxidative damage role, 2:244–245
  premature aging studies, 2:347–349
  segmental progeroid mutations, 1:578–579
White matter lesions
  definition, 1:383
  dementia role, 1:394–395
WI-38 cells, *see* Human fibroblast cells
Widowhood, *see also* Bereavement
  consequences, 2:49
  definition, 2:621
  demographics, 1:174, 558–559; 2:621–622
  experience, 2:623–624
  friendship patterns, 1:562–563
  income loss, 2:50
  life event, 2:622–623
  research limitations, 2:624–625
  social supports, 2:206, 623
Wife abuse, *see* Domestic violence
Windkessel phenomenon
  definition, 1:245
  vascular restriction, 1:249–250
Wisdom, *see also* Intelligence; Knowledge; Learning
  epigenetic stage theory, 2:287–288

epistemology, 2:312
  folklore
    oral tradition, 1:534–535
    traditional beliefs, 1:532–533
  humor role, 1:731
  uniqueness, 1:63–64
Women, *see also* Gender roles
  abuse, *see* Domestic violence
  age strata composition, 1:84
  alcohol use, 1:97–98
  driver demographics, 1:20
  health inequality, 1:560
  income inequality, 1:559–560
  leisure deprivation, 2:28
  physical identity, 1:736
  reproductive system, *see* Female reproductive system
  retirement patterns, 1:303
  sexuality changes, 2:484–485
  traditional beliefs, 1:532–534
  widowhood, *see* Widowhood
  workforce participation, 2:637–638
Work, *see* Employment
Working memory
  definition, 1:329; 2:107
  measurement, 2:110
  reduced processing resources, 2:563–564
  resource theory, 2:113–114
  selective attention inhibition, 1:763

X

Xeroderma pigmentosum, premature aging studies, 2:349–350
Xerostomia, parasympathetic input reduction, 1:145
X-linked genes
  epigenetic changes, 1:448
  gene expression changes, 1:451
X-ray absorptometry, body composition measurement, 1:197
X rays
  cancer risk, 1:226
  cardiovascular system alterations, 1:247

Y

Yeast, aging model, 2:154–156

Z

Zinc, prostate antibacterial factor, 2:356

ISBN 0-12-226862-8

90018